FIFTH EDITION

Theories of Counseling and Psychotherapy
Systems, Strategies, and Skills

Victoria E. Kress
Professor, Youngstown State University

Linda Seligman
Late Professor Emeritus, George Mason University

Lourie W. Reichenberg
Licensed Professional Counselor, Falls Church, Virginia

Please contact https://support.pearson.com/getsupport/s/contactsupport with any queries on this content

Copyright © 2021, 2014, 2010 by Pearson Education, Inc. 221 River Street, Hoboken, NJ 07030. All Rights Reserved. Manufactured in the United States of America. This publication is protected by copyright, and permission should be obtained from the publisher prior to any prohibited reproduction, storage in a retrieval system, or transmission in any form or by any means, electronic, mechanical, photocopying, recording, or otherwise. For information regarding permissions, request forms, and the appropriate contacts within the Pearson Education Global Rights and Permissions department, please visit www.pearsoned.com/permissions/.

Acknowledgments of third-party content appear on the appropriate page within the text

PEARSON, ALWAYS LEARNING, and MYLAB are exclusive trademarks owned by Pearson Education, Inc. or its affiliates in the U.S. and/or other countries.

Unless otherwise indicated herein, any third-party trademarks, logos, or icons that may appear in this work are the property of their respective owners, and any references to third-party trademarks, logos, icons, or other trade dress are for demonstrative or descriptive purposes only. Such references are not intended to imply any sponsorship, endorsement, authorization, or promotion of Pearson's products by the owners of such marks, or any relationship between the owner and Pearson Education, Inc., or its affiliates, authors, licensees, or distributors.

Library of Congress Cataloging-in-Publication Data
Names: Seligman, Linda, author. | Kress, Victoria E., author. | Reichenberg, Lourie W., author.
Title: Theories of counseling and psychotherapy : systems, strategies, and
  skills / Victoria E. Kress, Professor, Youngstown State University,
  Linda Seligman, Late Professor Emeritus, George Mason University, Lourie
  W. Reichenberg, Licensed Professional Counselor, Falls Church, Virginia.
Description: Fifth edition. | Hoboken, NJ : Pearson, [2021] | Includes
  bibliographical references and index.
Identifiers: LCCN 2019055833 (print) | LCCN 2019055834 (ebook) | ISBN
  9780134460864 (paperback) | ISBN 9780134450223 (access card)
Subjects: LCSH: Counseling--Textbooks. | Psychotherapy--Textbooks.
Classification: LCC BF637.C6 S445 2021 (print) | LCC BF637.C6 (ebook) |
  DDC 616.89/14--dc23
LC record available at https://lccn.loc.gov/2019055833
LC ebook record available at https://lccn.loc.gov/2019055834

1 2020

ISBN 10:   0-13-446086-3
ISBN 13: 978-0-13-446086-4

*This work is dedicated to the world's helpers and healers:
You leave something of yourself in every interaction you have
with another person. Never underestimate the power of human
connection and the positive impact you can, do, and will have
on others. You are important not just to your clients but also
to the people around them who benefit from their growth
and development—their children, family, partners, friends,
and community. One warm connection at a time,
you are making the world a better place.*

~ Victoria Kress

PREFACE

I want to thank Linda Seligman (deceased) and Lourie Reichenberg for constructing and developing the earlier versions of this text. It was an honor to have the opportunity to be involved in the new edition of this book, and I am grateful to Pearson for this opportunity, and to Linda and Lourie for the work they invested in previous editions of this text.

This text was first published in 2001, and since that time it has been used by tens of thousands of students. Many changes to the text have been made based on developments in the helping professions; feedback and reviews received from students and faculty who have used this text in their courses; and feedback received from practitioners and instructors about what students and new professionals most need to know relative to counseling theories.

The basic structure of the text has been maintained, but extensive changes were made to this version. The BETA (**B**ackground, **E**motions, **T**houghts, and **A**ctions) format used in the previous text was removed to reflect the organic evolution of the theories, and to allow more space to thoroughly address the theories presented. In addition, the discussions of relevant research, documenting the validity of each approach, have been expanded. Updated information is provided on all approaches presented in the text, with considerably expanded information on many (see the "New to This Edition" section later in this Preface). Descriptions of important theories, skill development sections, case studies, and reflect and respond activities (formerly referred to as exercises) were retained.

ORGANIZATION OF THIS TEXT

This text organizes the major theories of counseling and psychotherapy in a unified format. Each chapter that presents a theory follows the same organizational format to facilitate comparison and ease of use, beginning with a brief overview of the approach and a biographical sketch of its developer, and then moving on to the theory's key concepts, therapeutic process (including therapeutic goals, the therapist's function and role, and the role of the relationship between the therapist and client), therapeutic techniques and procedures, application and current use, and strengths and limitations. Particular attention is given to the application of each theory to people from diverse backgrounds. Finally, at the end of each chapter, skill development and personal development activities allow students to apply the knowledge they have gained around each theory. These activities are as follows:

- *Skill development section:* This section teaches one or more key skills associated with the treatment system under review.
- *Case illustration with the Diaz family:* Edie, her husband Roberto, and their daughter Ava appear throughout the text to illustrate how treatment approaches can be used and applied.
- *Reflect and Respond:* These activities will help readers develop self-awareness and solidify learning.

Although this text focuses primarily on counseling theories that are designed for use with individuals, an overview of family systems theory is included in Chapter 14. Chapter 15 discusses the nature, strengths, and shortcomings of integrated and eclectic counseling approaches, and provides summary tables and overviews of all the major theories discussed in this text.

NEW TO THIS EDITION

Based on reviewers' comments and the feedback received from various sources, significant changes have been made to this fifth edition. It was my intent to make the text practical and functional for both students and instructors.

Changes to the Text

- The theories discussed in this text have some foundational common threads, yet they are unique. The BETA model was removed from the text to create more space to engage with the richness and complexity of the theories. As such, the four overview chapters that applied the BETA model were removed.
- Three new chapters were added: Contemporary Cognitive Behavioral Therapies (Chapter 8; e.g., acceptance and commitment therapy, dialectical behavior therapy, schema therapy, and mindfulness-based cognitive therapy), Feminist Therapy (Chapter 12), and Postmodern Therapy (Chapter 13; e.g., solution-focused brief therapy and narrative therapy). The contemporary cognitive behavioral theories have a solid research base which supports their use, and the feminist and post modern therapies play an increasingly important role in our diverse, rapidly evolving society. This edition addresses these theories more explicitly and systematically.
- The individual application activities at the end of each chapter—intended to help students apply aspects of the theories to their own experience—were expanded and additional activities were included. This section was previously referred to as "Exercises" and it is now called "Reflect and Respond."
- The fifth edition of this text brings a stronger multicultural focus. In each theoretical chapter in the text, a revised multicultural section intended to draw attention to cultural considerations was provided.
- To permit more space in the text to expand on important theoretical concepts, the large- and small-group activities that had been in each chapter were moved to the instructor's manual. Instructors are encouraged to use these activities in class so that students have an opportunity to apply what they are learning.
- A glossary was added to the text. In the eText version of this book, readers can click on the highlighted terms and be digitally linked the corresponding definition.
- Each chapter has been updated to include an overview of the latest research available on each theory.
- The common factors approach and support for the importance of an effective and sustained therapeutic alliance have been the focus of much newly published research. This information is integrated where relevant (usually in the discussion of the therapeutic alliance) throughout the text. Chapter 1, Foundations of Effective Counseling, includes an extended discussion of this topic, as does the chapter on theoretical integration.
- Changes were also made to the writing style of the text to help improve the flow and readability, and thus enhance the reader experience.
- Additional content was added to all of the chapters, as were updated resources and references.
- This version of the text has MyLab Counseling™.

Also Available with Mylab Counseling

This title is also available with MyLab Counseling, an online homework, tutorial, and assessment program designed to work with the text to engage students and improve results. Within its structured environment, students see key concepts demonstrated through video clips, practice what they learn, test their understanding, and receive feedback to guide their learning and ensure they master key learning outcomes.

LEARNING OUTCOMES AND STANDARDS MEASURE STUDENT RESULTS   My Lab Counseling organizes all assignments around essential learning outcomes and national standards for counselors.

VIDEO- AND CASE-BASED EXERCISES DEVELOP DECISION-MAKING SKILLS   Video- and Case-based Exercises introduce students to a broader range of clients, and therefore a broader range of presenting problems, than they will encounter in their own pre-professional clinical experiences. Students watch videos of actual client–therapist sessions or high-quality role-play scenarios featuring expert counselors. They are then guided in their analysis of the videos through a series of short-answer questions. These exercises help students develop the techniques and decision-making skills they need to be effective counselors before they are in a critical situation with a real client.

LICENSURE QUIZZES HELP STUDENTS PREPARE FOR CERTIFICATION   Automatically graded, multiplechoice Licensure Quizzes help students prepare for their certification examinations, master foundational course content, and improve their performance in the course.

VIDEO LIBRARY OFFERS A WEALTH OF OBSERVATION OPPORTUNITIES   The Video Library provides more than 400 video clips of actual client–therapist sessions and high-quality role-plays in a database organized by topic and searchable by keyword. The Video Library includes every video clip from the MyLab Counseling courses plus additional videos from Pearson's extensive library of footage. Instructors can create additional assignments around the videos or use them for inclass activities. Students can expand their observation experiences to include other course areas and increase the amount of time they spend watching expert counselors in action.

EFFECTIVE WAYS TO USE THIS TEXT

This text has been designed for flexibility and ease of use. Although each college and university has its own curriculum and required courses, this text can be adapted to almost any curriculum in counseling, psychology, social work (or any other helping professions) and also can be used for training and staff development. Here are a few suggestions for using the text:

1. Most schools offer a counseling theories course in only one term, and the entire text could be covered in a one-semester course.

2. The text is also ideally suited for use in a two-semester or two-quarter course on theories and techniques of counseling and psychotherapy. The first part of the text could be covered in the first semester, with the remaining sections covered in the second semester to provide students with an in-depth and comprehensive understanding of the counseling theories.

3. The Skill Development sections are designed to accompany the theories taught in that particular chapter. However, these sections can be used independently of the theoretical portions, perhaps taught in a subsequent semester following a course on theories of counseling and psychotherapy or used as part of a practicum or internship to facilitate skill development.

4. Like the Skill Development sections, the Reflect and Respond activities are intended to accompany review of the theory in each chapter. However, they are designed to be used flexibly. These activities offer people the opportunity to work alone and apply their learning to themselves.

The large-group and small-group exercises have been moved to the Instructor's manual and are appropriate for encouraging classroom discussion. Small-group exercises allow clusters of a few learners to practice and improve their clinical skills with the benefit of peer feedback and support. Faculty members, of course, can choose to use any or all of the activities that accompany each chapter. Ideally, time should be allocated, either during or outside class, for at least some of the activities in each chapter. However, if time is limited, the individual activities enable students to continue their learning and skill development outside class. Although instructors may decide to review students' journals at the end of a course to determine whether they have completed the individual activities, I encourage them not to grade or evaluate these journals so that students feel free to express themselves, try out new skills, and gain learning and self-awareness. Students should be told at the beginning of the course whether they will be required to share their journals in any way so that they can determine how much they share.

ACKNOWLEDGMENTS

A big thank you goes out to my publishing team at Pearson. Kevin Davis taught me so much over the past 5 years; his wisdom, support, and patience have been priceless, and I will miss working with him as he moves into retirement. Rebecca Fox Gieg's never-ending warmth and support provided me with the confidence I needed to get creative in developing this text. Thank you to both Kevin and Rebecca for believing in me! Because of their unconditional support, I have been able to reach my potential as an author.

Sometimes the universe gives you a gift when you most need it. With regard to this text, my gift came in the form of one Christine A. McAllister. It is impossible to communicate in words how grateful I was to have Christy assist me in developing this text. Christy is wise and gifted beyond her years. Her insights and opinions greatly informed the development of this text. She is a wonderful writer and editor. I could not have made my tight deadlines were it not for her support.

Thank you to Linda Seligman and Lourie Reichenberg, who constructed the original version of this text. I dramatically changed the structure and content of the text, but underneath those changes are the words and ideas they constructed. This text would not be what it is were it not for them.

Stephanie Sedall was very helpful in the earlier stages of the text's development. Her conscientiousness and warm way were much needed at that time.

Matt Paylo, thank you for your assistance in thinking through the restructuring of the text. You were missed more than you could know on this one!

Thank you to Dr. Robert Wubbolding, who graciously took time away from his busy schedule to read and provide very thoughtful feedback on the reality therapy chapter. It was a true honor to have an original theorist share his wisdom, experience, and insights.

I would also like to thank the following people who offered useful suggestions that helped in developing this text: Eric Baltrinic, you are always exceptionally thoughtful, and I appreciate your insights around what constitutes a "good" theories text; Richard Watts, thank you for sharing Adlerian resources; Dana Unger, thanks for taking time to talk with me about what you look for in a theories text; and David Johnson, you are a deep thinker, and I so appreciate your assistance in thinking through the presentation of the forces that have influenced the development or waves of counseling theories.

Thank you, Amy Williams, for reviewing the systems chapter and sharing your thoughts.

Thank you, too, to the Pearson book reviewers: Ellyn Herb, San Jose State University; James Overholser, Case Western Reserve University; Joya A. Crear, George Mason University;

Dr. Chuck Barké, University of Texas at Tyler; and R. J. Davis, Lamar University, who provided invaluable feedback that served to make this text better.

The editorial staff at SPi Global were amazing during the production stages of this text. Thank you to Janelle Criner, my content producer, and Joanne Boehme my copy editor, for being so thorough.

Last, but not least, writing a book necessarily requires sacrifice not only from the authors but also from the people who surround them. My profound thanks go out to my husband, Rob, and my children, Ava and Isaac, for their patience during this text's development. Thank you to my Department Chair, Jake Protivnak, for your flexibility and the support you regularly offered.

ABOUT THE AUTHORS

Victoria E. Kress, PhD/LPCC-S (OH), NCC, CCMHC, is a professor, counseling clinic director, and the director of the clinical mental health and addictions counseling programs at Youngstown State University. She previously worked as the director of advocacy for the National Board of Certified Counselors. She has over 25 years of clinical experience working with youth and adults in various settings, which include community mental health centers, hospitals, residential treatment facilities, private practices, and college counseling centers. She has published over 130 refereed articles and book chapters, and she has coauthored 5 books on counseling youth and adults. She was identified as the top producer/publisher in counseling journals between the years 2000 and 2017. She previously served as the associate editor of the Theory and Practice Sections of the *Journal of Mental Health Counseling*, and as an editorial board member for the *Journal of Counseling and Development* and other counseling journals. Dr. Kress has lectured throughout the United States, as well as internationally, on various topics related to counselor practice. Dr. Kress served two terms as a governor-appointed member of the Ohio Counselor, Social Worker, and Marriage and Family Therapist Board, and served as the chair of the Counselor Professional Standards Committee. She also served as the ethics liaison for Ohio's state regulatory board and presently serves as a consultant/expert witness for counselor ethics cases. She has been the recipient of over 40 professional and community service awards, most of which were for her advocacy, leadership, scholarship, community service, and mentorship initiatives. She has also received awards for her work with people who have intellectual disabilities, for empowering girls in her community, for her sexual assault prevention efforts, and for her child abuse advocacy work. The Council for Accreditation of Counseling and Related Educational Programs (CACREP) honored her with the Martin Ritchie Award for Excellence in Advocacy. She also received the following American Counseling Association (ACA) Awards: the ACA Fellow Award, the Gilbert and Kathleen Wrenn Award for a Humanitarian and Caring Person, the Distinguished Mentor Award, the Counselor Educator Advocacy Award, and the Government Relations Award. She has been the recipient of the following Association for Counselor Education and Supervision (ACES) Awards: the Counseling Vision and Innovation Award, the Outstanding Mentor Award, the Robert Stripling Award for Excellence in Standards, and the Leadership Award. She has also received a number of Youngstown State University awards (e.g., the Giant Award, Distinguished Scholar, Distinguished Public Servant) as well as various Ohio Counseling Association awards, including the Counselor of the Year Award, the Research and Writing Award, the Legislative Advocacy Award, and the Leadership Award. She is a past president of Chi Sigma Iota International and the Ohio Counseling Association; she is a past ACA region chair; and she is the president of the Association for Humanistic Counseling. She has also worked and volunteered in Malawi, Zambia, Tanzania, and Rwanda, promoting mental health awareness and training, as well as the professionalization of counseling.

Linda Seligman, PhD, received her doctorate in counseling psychology from Columbia University. Her primary research interests included diagnosis and treatment planning as well as counseling people with chronic and life-threatening illnesses. Dr. Seligman was a professor at George Mason University for 25 years. She served as codirector of the doctoral program in education, coordinator of the Counseling Development Program, associate chair of the School of Education, and head of the Community Agency Counseling Program. She was later named professor emerita. Dr. Seligman also served as associate at Johns Hopkins University and as a faculty member in counseling psychology at Walden University.

During her lifetime, Dr. Seligman authored 15 texts, including *Selecting Effective Treatments, Diagnosis and Treatment Planning in Counseling, Developmental Career Counseling and Assessment,* and *Promoting a Fighting Spirit: Psychotherapy for Cancer Patients, Survivors, and Their Families*. She also wrote more than 80 professional articles and text chapters. She lectured throughout the United States, as well as internationally, on diagnosis and treatment planning and was recognized for her expertise on that subject. In 1990, the American Mental Health Counselors Association (AMHCA) designated Dr. Seligman as Researcher of the Year. In 2007, AMHCA honored her with the title of Counselor Educator of the Year.

Lourie W. Reichenberg, MA, LPC is a licensed professional counselor in private practice in Falls Church, Virginia. She also provides clinical supervision for therapists and interns at The Women's Center in Vienna, Virginia. She earned her master's degree in counseling psychology from Marymount University. She has taught crisis counseling, abnormal psychology, and counseling theories to graduate and undergraduate students.

She is currently on the executive committee of the Virginia Association of Clinical Counselors and serves on the board of directors for the Northern Virginia Licensed Professional Counselors.

Reichenberg is a member of the CrisisLink LOSS team, which provides assistance in the community after a suicide has occurred. She served on the CrisisLink Board of Directors from 2003 to 2006 and is on the organization's Advisory Council. She is a past editor of the Northern Virginia Licensed Professional Counselors and was the editor of the *Journal of the College and University Personnel Association* from 1988 to 1993. She coauthored *Selecting Effective Treatments* (2007, 2012) with Dr. Seligman and has published many professional articles, including a chapter on grief and loss in *Crisis Assessment, Intervention and Prevention* (Jackson-Cherry & Erford, 2010, 2013). She has edited more than 30 texts and monographs. Her primary interests include crisis counseling; grief and loss; and helping individuals, couples, and families cope with life transitions. She approaches her work as a therapist, educator, and community volunteer from a humanistic, person-centered, and emotionally focused perspective, and incorporates mindfulness into her practice.

ABOUT THE CONTRIBUTORS

Katherine A. Feather, PhD, is a licensed professional counselor and an assistant clinical professor in the Department of Educational Psychology at Northern Arizona University. Katherine has an extensive clinical background working with persons with disabilities—specifically, children diagnosed with autism spectrum disorder (ASD) and adults adjusting to their visual disability. She has published and presented on these topics at the regional, national, and international level. Her research interests include ASD and establishing competencies for the counseling profession, counselors' preparedness to work with persons with disabilities, school-to-career transition of students with disabilities, and psychosocial adjustment and family adaptation to a disability.

Jessica A. Headley, PhD, is an assistant professor in the Counseling and Art Therapy Department, as well as codirector of the Women's Center, at Ursuline College. She is also a licensed professional clinical counselor in private practice, specializing in women and gender issues. She has additional clinical experience working in community mental health, college counseling, and hospital settings. Her research interests include women and gender issues, feminist therapy and supervision, and the use of relational-cultural theory and creativity in counseling. She has published and presented in these areas and has experience serving as an assistant editor for feminist academic journals, including *Psychology of Women Quarterly* and *Sex Roles*.

Christine A. McAllister, MAEd., is a licensed professional counselor. She has conducted research and presented on topics such as mood-related disorders, best practices for clients who are suicidal, counseling clients who have sexual abuse histories, and counseling individuals with intellectual disabilities. Her clinical and research interests include trauma, suicide, chronic illness, and LGBTQ+ issues. She was a 2019 National Board for Certified Counselors (NBCC) Minority Fellow and is passionate about serving diverse populations, specifically people who identify within the gender and sexual/affectional minority spectrum. She is active in the profession and engages in professional service work with the American Counseling Association, Chi Sigma Iota, the American Mental Health Counseling Association, the Eastern Ohio Counseling Association/Ohio Counseling Association, the Association of Counselor Education and Supervision, and the Association for Humanistic Counseling.

BRIEF CONTENTS

PART ONE **Foundations of Effective Counseling** 1

    Chapter 1   Foundations of Effective Counseling 1

PART TWO **The First Force in Psychotherapy: Psychoanalysis and Psychoanalytic Theories** 51

    Chapter 2   Freud and Classic Psychoanalysis 51
    Chapter 3   Adlerian Therapy 77
    Chapter 4   Post- and Neo-Freudian Psychoanalytic Therapies 108

PART THREE **The Second Force in Psychotherapy: Behavioral and Cognitive Behavioral Theories** 149

    Chapter 5   Behavior Therapy 149
    Chapter 6   Cognitive Behavioral Therapies 179
    Chapter 7   Reality Therapy 224
    Chapter 8   Contemporary Cognitive Behavioral Therapies 246

PART FOUR **The Third Force in Psychotherapy: Humanistic-Existential Theories** 278

    Chapter 9   Existential Therapy 278
    Chapter 10   Person-Centered Therapy 307
    Chapter 11   Gestalt Therapy 334

PART FIVE **The Fourth Force in Psychotherapy: Culture, Context, and Constructivism** 361

    Chapter 12   Feminist Therapy 361
    Chapter 13   Postmodern Therapy 392
    Chapter 14   Family Systems Therapies 425

PART SIX **Pulling it All Together** 467

    Chapter 15   Developing Your Theoretical Orientation 467

Glossary 509
Reference 528
Name Index 567
Subject Index 576

CONTENTS

Part One   Foundations of Effective Counseling   1

Chapter 1   Foundations of Effective Counseling   1
Development of Counseling Theories   2
Understanding Counseling Theories   4
    Counseling Is Effective   5
    Common Factors   6
Characteristics of Successful Clients   7
    Client Motivation   7
    Client Expectations   7
    Client Engagement   8
The Therapeutic Alliance   8
    Empathy   9
    Unconditional Positive Regard   9
    Congruence   9
Characteristics of Effective Therapists   10
    Effective Therapist Personal Qualities   10
    Effective Therapist Professional Qualities   11
Developmental Considerations   13
Culture and Diversity   15
    Therapist Awareness   16
    Understanding Clients' Worldviews   16
    Culturally Appropriate Interventions   17
A Strengths-Based Perspective   20
Counseling Theories and Setting   22
Ethical and Legal Considerations   28
    Informed Consent/Assent   30
    Competence   31
    Assessment and Diagnosis   31
    Evidence-Based Practices   33
    Multiple Relationships and the Therapeutic–Fiduciary Relationship Tension   34
    Ethical Decision Making: Practical Suggestions   35
Skill Development: Questioning and Interviewing   39
    Asking Helpful Questions   39
    Conducting an Intake Interview and Assessment   42

Example of an Intake Interview   43
Reflect and Respond   48
> Summary   49   •   Recommended Readings   50

Part Two   The First Force in Psychotherapy: Psychoanalysis and Psychoanalytic Theories   51

Chapter 2   Freud and Classic Psychoanalysis   51

The First Force in Psychotherapy: Psychoanalysis and Psychodynamic Theories   51
Introduction/Development of Psychoanalysis   55
Key Concepts   57
- Biological Processes: Attachment and Development   57
- Personality Structure   57
- Life and Death Instincts   59
- Stages of Development   59
- Levels of Consciousness   61
- Defense Mechanisms   61

The Therapeutic Process   63
- Therapeutic Goals   63
- Therapist's Function and Role   64
- Relationship Between Therapist and Client   64

Therapeutic Techniques and Procedures   65
- Free Association   65
- Analysis and Interpretation   66
- Dream Analysis   67
- Abreaction   67
- Dealing with Resistance   68

Application and Current Use of Psychoanalysis   68
- Counseling Applications   69
- Application to Multicultural Groups   69

Evaluation of Freudian Psychoanalysis   70
- Limitations   70
- Strengths and Contributions   71

Skill Development: Interpretation   72
Case Application   72
Reflect and Respond   75
> Summary   75   •   Recommended Readings   76

Chapter 3   Adlerian Therapy   77
    Introduction/Development of Adlerian Therapy   78
    Key Concepts   79
        Patterns of Human Personality   80
        Family Constellation and Birth Order   84
        Social Interest and Community Feeling   86
    The Therapeutic Process   87
        Therapeutic Goals   87
        Therapist's Function and Role   87
        Relationship Between Therapist and Client   88
    Therapeutic Techniques and Procedures   89
        Phases of Adlerian Therapy   89
        Phase 1: Establishing a Relationship   89
        Phase 2: Assessing Clients' Psychological Dynamics   90
        Phase 3: Encouraging Insight and Self-Understanding   93
        Phase 4: Putting Insights into Practice   97
    Application and Current Use of Adlerian Therapy   98
        Counseling Applications   98
        Application to Multicultural Groups   101
    Evaluation of Adlerian Therapy   102
        Limitations   102
        Strengths and Contributions   103
    Skill Development: Analyzing Earliest Recollections   104
    Case Application   105
    Reflect and Respond   106
        Summary   106   •   Recommended Readings   107

Chapter 4   Post- and Neo-Freudian Psychoanalytic Therapies   108
    Introduction/Development of Analytical Psychology   110
    Key Concepts   110
        The Components of the Psyche   110
        Individuation   112
        Balance and Polarities   113
        Dimensions of Personality: Functions and Attitudes   113
    The Therapeutic Process   114
    Therapeutic Techniques and Procedures   115
        Use of Symbols   115

        Dream Interpretation   115
        Word Association Tests   116
        Rituals   116
   Application and Current Use of Jungian Analytical Psychology   116
   Introduction/Development of Ego Psychology   117
   Key Concepts: Karen Horney's Ego Psychology   119
        Self-Realization   119
        Neurosis and Basic Anxiety   119
        Selves and Self-Image   120
        Female Development and Culture   121
   The Therapeutic Process   121
   Therapeutic Techniques and Procedures   121
   Key Concepts: Anna Freud's Ego Psychology   122
        Child Development   122
        Ego Defenses   123
   The Therapeutic Process   123
   Therapeutic Techniques and Procedures   123
        Developmental Assessment   123
        Child Psychoanalysis   123
        Enhancing Social Supports   124
   Application and Current Use of Ego Psychology   124
   Introduction/Development of Object Relations Theory   125
   Key Concepts   126
        Attachment Theory Across the Lifespan   126
        Objects   127
        Separation-Individuation Theory   127
        The Fundamental Positions   128
   The Therapeutic Process   128
   Therapeutic Techniques and Procedures   128
        Projective Identification   129
        Resistance   129
        Countertransference   129
        Interpretation   129
   Application and Current Use of Object Relations Theory   129
   Introduction/Development of Self Psychology   131
   Key Concepts   131
        The Self   131

Positive Potentials: A Responsive Environment   132
Narcissism   132
The Therapeutic Process   132
Therapeutic Techniques and Procedures   133
Interpretation   133
Vicarious Introspection   133
Transference   133
Application and Current Use of Self Psychology   134
Introduction/Development of Brief Psychodynamic Therapy   134
Key Concepts   135
Therapy Is Brief   135
Ego Strengthening   135
The Triads   136
The Therapeutic Process   136
Therapeutic Techniques and Procedures   138
Supportive Techniques   138
Expressive Techniques   138
Countertransference   139
Application and Current Use of Brief Psychodynamic Therapy   140
Application and Current Use of Post- and Neo-Freudian Psychoanalytic Therapies   141
Counseling Applications   141
Application to Multicultural Groups   141
Evaluation of Post- and Neo-Freudian Psychoanalytic Therapies   142
Limitations   142
Strengths and Contributions   142
Skill Development: Identifying a Focal Concern   143
Case Application   144
Reflect and Respond   146
Summary   146   •   Recommended Readings   147

Part Three   The Second Force in Psychotherapy: Behavioral and Cognitive Behavioral Theories   149

Chapter 5   Behavior Therapy   149
Introduction to the Second Force in Counseling and Psychotherapy: Behavior and Cognitive Behavioral Therapies   149
Focus on Behaviors and Behavioral Change   151

Measurement, Evaluation, and Research 151
Behavior Therapy: The Three Waves 151
Introduction/Development of Behavior Therapy 154
Key Concepts 155
- Classical Conditioning 156
- Operant Conditioning 156
- Social Learning Theory 157

The Therapeutic Process 158
- Therapeutic Goals 159
- Therapist's Function and Role 160
- Relationship Between Therapist and Client 160

Therapeutic Techniques and Procedures 161
- Assessment 161
- Operant Conditioning Techniques 162
- Classical Conditioning Techniques 169
- Skills Training 172

Application and Current Use of Behavior Therapy 173
- Counseling Applications 173
- Application to Multicultural Groups 174

Evaluation of Behavior Therapy 174
- Limitations 174
- Strengths and Contributions 175

Skill Development: Progressive Muscle Relaxation 175
Case Application 176
Reflect and Respond 178
Summary 178 • Recommended Readings 178

Chapter 6 Cognitive Behavioral Therapies 179

Development and Key Concepts of Cognitive Behavioral Therapies 179
- Development of Cognitive Behavioral Therapy 179
- Key Concepts of Cognitive Behavioral Therapy 181

Introduction/Development of Rational Emotive Behavior Therapy 183
Key Concepts 184
- Irrational Beliefs as the Cause of Struggle 184
- A-B-C–D-E-F Model 186

The Therapeutic Process 188
- Therapeutic Goals 189
- Therapist's Function and Role 190
- Relationship Between Therapist and Client 191

Therapeutic Techniques and Procedures 191
   A-B-C–D-E-F Technique 191
   Approaches to Disputing Irrational Beliefs 192
Introduction/Development of Cognitive Therapy 196
Key Concepts 197
   The Cognitive Model 197
   Cognitive Restructuring 197
The Therapeutic Process 199
   Therapeutic Goals 199
   Therapist's Function and Role 200
   Relationship Between Therapist and Client 201
Therapeutic Techniques and Procedures 201
   Case Formulation 202
   Assessment 202
   Dysfunctional Thought Record 203
   Determining the Validity of Cognitions 204
   Labeling Cognitive Distortions 206
   Strategies for Modifying Cognitions 207
   Termination and Relapse Prevention 209
Application and Current Use of Cognitive Behavioral Therapies 209
   Counseling Applications 209
   Application to Multicultural Groups 213
Evaluation of Cognitive Behavioral Therapies 214
   Limitations 214
   Strengths and Contributions 215
Skill Development: Exposure-Based CBT for Hoarding 216
Case Application 219
Reflect and Respond 221
   Summary 221 • Recommended Readings 222

Chapter 7 Reality Therapy 224

Introduction/Development of Reality Therapy 226
Key Concepts 227
   The Five Basic Human Needs 228
   Concept of Mental Illness and Mental Health 228
   Total Behavior and Motivation 229
   Quality Worlds 230
   Axioms of Choice Theory 231
   WDEP System 231
The Therapeutic Process 234

Therapeutic Goals   234
Therapist's Function and Role   234
Relationship Between Therapist and Client   235
Therapeutic Techniques and Procedures   236
  Metaphors   236
  Relationships   236
  Questions   237
  WDEP and SAMI^{2}C^3 237
  Positive Addictions   237
  Using Verbs and "ing" Words   238
  Reasonable Consequences   238
  Paradoxical Interventions   238
  Development of Skills   238
Application and Current Use of Reality Therapy   239
  Counseling Applications   239
  Application to Multicultural Groups   240
Evaluation of Reality Therapy   241
  Limitations   241
  Strengths and Contributions   242
Skill Development: Caring Confrontation   242
Case Application   243
Reflect and Respond   245
  Summary   245   •   Recommended Readings   245

Chapter 8   Contemporary Cognitive Behavioral Therapies   246

The Third Generation of Behavior Therapy   246
Introduction/Development of DBT   247
Key Concepts   248
  Dialectics   248
  Emotion Regulation   248
The Therapeutic Process   249
Therapeutic Techniques and Procedures   250
  Emotion Regulation Skills   250
  Mindfulness   251
  Distress Tolerance   252
  Interpersonal Effectiveness   253
Application and Current Use of DBT   254

Introduction/Development of ACT   255
Key Concepts   255
   Experiential Avoidance   255
   Relational Frame Theory   256
The Therapeutic Process   256
Therapeutic Techniques and Procedures   257
   The Hexaflex Model   257
   Awareness and Acceptance   257
Application and Current Use of ACT   258
Introduction/Development of MBCT   258
Key Concepts   258
   Acceptance   258
   The Being Mode   259
   Tenets of Mindfulness   259
The Therapeutic Process   260
Therapeutic Techniques and Procedures   260
   Conscious Thought Processing   260
   Mindfulness   261
   Decentering   261
Application and Current Use of MBCT   263
Introduction/Development of Schema Therapy   264
Key Concepts   264
   Early Maladaptive Schemas   264
   Schema Domains   264
The Therapeutic Process   268
Therapeutic Techniques and Interventions   268
   Limited Reparenting and Empathic Confrontation   268
   Cognitive Interventions   269
   Schema Flash Cards   269
Application and Current Use of Schema Therapy   269
Evaluation of Third-Wave CBT   270
   Limitations   270
   Strengths and Contributions   270
Skill Development: Mindfulness   273
Case Application   274
Reflect and Respond   276
   Summary   276   •   Recommended Readings   277

Part Four The Third Force in Psychotherapy: Humanistic-Existential Theories 278

Chapter 9 Existential Therapy 278

Introduction to the Third Force in Counseling and Psychotherapy: Humanistic-Existential Theories 278
- Self-Actualizing Tendency 280
- Phenomenological Perspective 280
- Experiential Awareness 281

Introduction/Development of Existential Therapy 283
- Philosophical Foundations of Existential Therapy 283
- Existential Thought Compared to Other Theories 285

Key Concepts 286
- The Human Condition: Ultimate Concerns 286
- Existential and Neurotic Anxiety 287
- Dasein 288
- The Human Condition: Potentials 289

The Therapeutic Process 292
- Therapeutic Goals 293
- Therapist's Function and Role 293
- Relationship Between Therapist and Client 294

Therapeutic Techniques and Procedures 294
- Symbolic Growth Experience 294
- Frankl's Logotherapy 295
- Paradoxical Intention 295
- Dereflection 295
- Addressing the Four Dimensions of the Human Condition 296

Applicaton and Current Use of Existential Therapy 296
- Counseling Applications 296
- Application to Multicultural Groups 298

Evaluation of Existential Therapy 298
- Limitations 299
- Strengths and Contributions 299

Skill Development: Values Clarification 300

Case Application 302

Reflect and Respond 304

Summary 305 • Recommended Readings 306

Chapter 10 Person-Centered Therapy   307

Introduction/Development of Person-Centered Therapy   308
Key Concepts   309
   Human Potential and Actualization   310
   Conditions of Worth   310
   Organismic Valuing Process   311
   The Fully Functioning Person   311
The Therapeutic Process   312
   Therapeutic Goals   312
   Therapist's Function and Role   313
   Relationship Between Therapist and Client   313
Therapeutic Techniques and Procedures   314
   Facilitative Conditions   314
   Nondirectiveness   318
Application and Current Use of Person-Centered Therapy   318
   Counseling Applications   318
   Application to Multicultural Groups   325
Evaluation of Person-Centered Therapy   326
   Limitations   326
   Strengths and Contributions   326
Skill Development: Empathic Responding   327
Case Application   329
Reflect and Respond   330
     Summary 332 • Recommended Readings 332

Chapter 11 Gestalt Therapy   334

Introduction/Development of Gestalt Therapy   335
Key Concepts   336
   Wholeness, Integration, and Balance   337
   Awareness   341
The Therapeutic Process   344
   Therapeutic Goals   344
   Therapist's Function and Role   345
   Relationship Between Therapist and Client   346
Therapeutic Techniques and Procedures   347
   Exercises, Experiments, and Enactments   347
   Use of Language   347

Dreams 348
Fantasy 349
Role Play Using Empty Chair Methods 349
The Body as a Vehicle of Communication 351
Group Gestalt Therapy 351
Application and Current Use of Gestalt Therapy 352
Counseling Applications 352
Application to Multicultural Groups 353
Evaluation of Gestalt Therapy 354
Limitations 354
Strengths and Contributions 354
Skill Development: Gestalt Chair Work 355
Case Application 357
Reflect and Respond 358
Summary 359 • Recommended Readings 360

Part Five   The Fourth Force in Psychotherapy: Culture, Context, and Constructivism 361

Chapter 12   Feminist Therapy 361

Introduction to the Fourth Force in Counseling and Psychotherapy: Culture, Context, and Constructivism 361
Introduction/Development of Feminist Therapy 363
Key Concepts 367
The Personal Is Political 367
Women's Experiences Are Honored 368
Reframing Mental Health and Disorders 368
The Primacy of the Egalitarian Relationship 369
The Role of Social Locations and Multidimensional Identities 369
The Therapeutic Process 370
Therapeutic Goals 370
Therapist's Function and Role 371
Relationship Between Therapist and Client 371
Therapeutic Techniques and Procedures 374
Gender-Role Analysis 374
Power Analysis 376
Assertiveness Training 377
Reframing and Relabeling 378
Therapy-Demystifying Strategies 379
Consciousness-Raising 379

        Social Activism   380
    Application and Current Use of Feminist Therapy   380
        Counseling Applications   380
        Application to Multicultural Groups   382
    Feminist Therapy Spotlight   383
    Evaluation of Feminist Therapy   385
        Limitations   385
        Strengths and Contributions   386
    Skill Development: Self-Disclosure   386
    Case Application   388
    Reflect and Respond   389
            Summary   390   •   Recommended Readings   391

Chapter 13 Postmodern Therapy   392

    Development of Postmodern Theories   392
    Introduction/Development of Narrative Therapy   395
    Key Concepts   397
        Stories   397
        Listening with an Open Mind   398
    The Therapeutic Process   398
        Stages of Narrative Therapy   398
        Therapeutic Goals   399
        Therapist's Function and Role   400
        Relationship Between Therapist and Client   400
    Therapeutic Techniques and Procedures   401
        Mapping   401
        Externalizing   401
        Therapeutic Documents   402
    Application and Current Use of Narrative Therapy   403
        Counseling Applications   403
        Application to Family Interventions and Involvement   404
        Application to Multicultural Groups   405
    Evaluation of Narrative Therapy   405
        Limitations   405
        Strengths and Contributions   405
    Introduction/Development of Solution-Focused Brief Therapy   406
    Key Concepts   407
        A Future-Oriented Focus   407
        Strength-Based Orientation   408

　　　　　A Focus on Solutions   408
　　　The Therapeutic Process   409
　　　　　Therapeutic Goals   411
　　　　　Therapist's Function and Role   411
　　　　　Relationship Between Therapist and Client   412
　　　Therapeutic Techniques and Procedures   413
　　　　　Pre-Therapy Changes   413
　　　　　Formula First Session Tasks   413
　　　　　Miracle Question   413
　　　　　Exception Questions   414
　　　　　Scaling Questions   415
　　　　　Solution Talk   416
　　　　　Preferred Future   416
　　　　　Therapist Feedback to Client   417
　　　　　Solution Prescriptions   417
　　　Application and Current Use of Solution-Focused Brief Therapy   417
　　　　　Counseling Applications   418
　　　　　Application to Multicultural Groups   418
　　　Evaluation of Solution-Focused Brief Therapy   419
　　　　　Limitations   419
　　　　　Strengths and Contributions   419
　　　Skill Development: Mapping   419
　　　Case Application   421
　　　Reflect and Respond   423
　　　　　Summary   423   •   Recommended Readings   424

Chapter 14   Family Systems Therapies   425
　　　Introduction/Development of Family Therapy   426
　　　Key Concepts   427
　　　　　Behavioral Functions Within Family Systems   428
　　　　　Reciprocal Influence   428
　　　　　Enhancing Communication   429
　　　Introduction/Development of Bowenian Family Therapy   431
　　　Key Concepts   432
　　　　　Differentiation of Self   432
　　　　　Triangulation   432
　　　　　Nuclear Family Emotional System   433
　　　　　Family Projection Process   433
　　　　　Emotional Cutoff   433

- Multigenerational Transmission Process 433
- Sibling Position 434
- Societal Regression 434

Relationship Between Therapist and Client 434

The Therapeutic Process 434

Therapeutic Techniques and Procedures 435
- Genograms 435
- Detriangulation 436

Application and Current Use of Bowenian Family Therapy 437

Introduction/Development of Experiential and Humanistic Family Therapy 438

Key Concepts 438
- Humanistic 438
- Process/Experiential 438
- Communication 438

Relationship Between Therapist and Client 439

The Therapeutic Process 440

Therapeutic Techniques and Procedures 440
- Family Sculpting 441
- Choreography 441

Application and Current Use of Experiential and Humanistic Family Therapy 441

Introduction/Development of Structural Family Therapy 441

Key Concepts 442
- Subsystems 442
- Boundaries Between Systems 442
- Family Hierarchy 443

The Therapeutic Process 444

Therapeutic Techniques and Procedures 444
- Joining 444
- Reframing 444
- Enactment 445
- Family Maps 445

Application and Current Use of Structural Family Therapy 445

Introduction/Development of Strategic Family Therapy 445

Key Concepts 446
- Problem-Centered 446
- Nature of Symptoms 446

Relationship Between Therapist and Client 446

The Therapeutic Process   446
Therapeutic Techniques and Procedures   447
  Ordeals   447
  Paradoxical Interventions   447
  Circular Questioning   448
Application and Current Use of Strategic Family Therapy   448
Introduction/Development of Emotionally Focused Couple Therapy   449
Key Concepts   450
  Systemic   450
  Humanistic-Experiential   450
  Attachment   450
  Emotion   450
Relationship Between Therapist and Client   450
The Therapeutic Process   451
Therapeutic Techniques and Procedures   451
Application and Current Use of Emotionally Focused Couple Therapy   452
Individual Therapy Theories Applied to Family Therapy   452
  Psychoanalysis   452
  Adlerian Therapy   453
  Behavior Therapy   453
  Cognitive Behavioral Therapy   453
  Reality Therapy   454
  Existential Therapy   454
  Person-Centered Therapy   454
  Gestalt Therapy   455
  Feminist Therapy   455
  Postmodern Therapy   455
Application and Current Use of Family Therapy   455
  Counseling Applications   455
  Application to Multicultural Groups   456
Evaluation of Family Therapy   457
  Limitations   457
  Strengths and Contributions   457
Skill Development: Genograms   457
  Gathering Information   458
  Drawing a Genogram   458
  Sample Genogram   459

Case Application 460
Reflect and Respond 461
  Summary 462 • Recommended Readings 466

Part Six Pulling it All Together 467

Chapter 15 Developing Your Theoretical Orientation 467

Integrative Therapies 467
  The Growth of Eclectic and Integrated Approaches 468
  The Challenges of Eclectic and Integrated Approaches 469
  The Benefits of Eclectic and Integrated Approaches 470
  The Nature of Eclectic and Integrated Approaches 470
  Examples of Eclectic and Integrated Approaches 470
  Characteristics of Sound Eclectic and Integrated Approaches 471
  Formulating an Integrative Theory 472
  Examples of Integrative Theories 472
Finding Your Counseling Theory 482
  Determinants of Theoretical Orientation 483
  Counseling Theory and Therapist Personality 484
  Theoretical Orientation Reflection Questions 485
Overview of Counseling Theories 485
  Basic Philosophy/Key Concepts 485
  Therapy Goals 489
  Relationship Between Therapist and Client 491
  Counseling Techniques and Applications 493
  Multicultural Counseling 497
  Strengths and Limitations of Theories 501
Future Directions In Counseling and Psychotherapy 505
Reflect and Respond 506
  Summary 507 • Recommended Readings 507
Glossary 509
References 528
Name Index 567
Subject Index 576

CHAPTER 1
Foundations of Effective Counseling

Learning Outcomes

When you have finished this chapter, you should be able to:
- Explain the development and commonalities of Counseling Theories.
- Identify the characteristics of successful clients and of successful counselors.
- Describe why clients' developmental levels are important in the context of counseling and counseling theory selection.
- Describe how culture/diversity issues and legal/ethics issues are important in the context of counseling theories.
- Explain the value of a strengths-based perspective in counseling.

Before considering specific theories of counseling and psychotherapy, it is important to pave the way by providing some information on the history and development of these approaches. This chapter focuses on some of the foundational elements that relate to effective counseling (e.g., the counseling relationship) and considerations that influence the counseling theories used (e.g., the counseling setting, a client's developmental level). The chapter addresses the following topics:

- Characteristics of clients who benefit from counseling
- The therapeutic alliance
- Helpful personal and professional characteristics of the counselor
- Client developmental considerations
- Culturally competent counseling
- The importance of a strengths-based perspective
- Counseling settings and how this relates to counseling theories used
- Ethical and legal guidelines and standards that relate to counseling theories.

Later in this chapter, the Diaz family—Roberto, Edie, and Ava—make their first appearance. The Skill Development section focuses on a review of effective questioning and interviewing techniques that lead to productive intake assessments. The Reflect and Respond section includes activities that reinforce those skills. The use of minimal encouragers and the Reflect and Respond section center on questioning and interviewing for a productive intake/initial assessment.

DEVELOPMENT OF COUNSELING THEORIES

Prior to the late 19th century, people understood little about mental and emotional difficulties and approaches that could be used to help individuals change. Many people with severe mental health symptoms were forcibly confined in institutions and exposed to largely ineffective therapies, while those with mild or moderate difficulties typically received no professional help.

The development of psychodynamic approaches to psychotherapy, spearheaded by the work of Sigmund Freud, led to the emergence of what has been called the first force of psychotherapy. Viewing past experiences as the source of people's present emotional difficulties and emphasizing unconscious processes and long-term therapy, psychodynamic approaches provided a solid foundation for the field of psychotherapy, but that approach had clear limitations.

The research and practice of B. F. Skinner, as well as more modern theorists such as Albert Ellis, Aaron Beck, William Glasser, and Donald Meichenbaum, led to the emergence of the second force of psychotherapy: behavioral and cognitive theories and interventions. Behavioral approaches, which originated in the 1950s, have been integrated with cognitive approaches, developed primarily in the 1980s, leading to the cognitive behavioral approaches that received considerable attention and empirical support in the 1990s. Cognitive and behavioral approaches emphasize the interaction between thoughts, feelings, and behaviors. They use interventions that generally focus on the present and seek to minimize dysfunctional cognitions and behaviors while replacing them with more helpful and positive thoughts and actions.

Carl Rogers' innovative work emerged in the 1960s and led to the development of the third force of psychotherapy: existential-humanistic psychotherapy. The work of Fritz Perls, Viktor Frankl, and others contributed to this force, which emphasizes the importance of emotions and sensations and of people taking charge of and creating meaning in their own lives. These approaches also drew attention to the importance of the therapeutic alliance.

During the later part of the 20th century and the front end of the 21st century, therapists have entered the era of the fourth force of psychotherapy: therapies that focus on Contextual/Systemic approaches (e.g., feminist, family systems, postmodern, multicultural). Contextual/Systemic therapists concentrate on individual identity (e.g., gender, culture, age, race, and sexual orientation) and consider context and culture as they impact clients' experiences and their change processes. Becoming culturally competent, being an ally with clients, and remaining open to their multiple perspectives of themselves and their world are essential for today's therapists. Networking and collaboration with other mental health professionals, providers of community resources, and important people in clients' lives are now viewed as integral to successful counseling. Theories of counseling and psychotherapy, as well as their implementation, have changed in response to the fourth force.

More than 400 counseling theories have been identified and described in the literature (Zarbo, Tasca, Cattafi, & Compare, 2015). Of course, all these theories cannot be reviewed in this text. Therefore, the following criteria were used to select the theories covered in this text:

1. The theories are clear, coherent, and easily communicated.
2. They are compatible with or can be adapted to include the therapeutic commonalities.
3. They encompass a concept of positive emotional development and health that can be used in setting goals and assessing progress.
4. They help therapists organize and make sense of information.

5. They are comprehensive, explaining and addressing a broad range of concerns and disorders.
6. They give therapists direction, steps, and guidelines for facilitating positive change.
7. They encompass strategies and interventions that grow out of and are consistent with the underlying theory.
8. They provide therapists with a common language that facilitates counseling and collaboration.
9. They are widely used in practice and generate research. Even if these approaches have not been conclusively validated by empirical research, the research is promising and their widespread use or growing popularity suggests that therapists find these approaches beneficial to their clients.
10. They focus on individual counseling and psychotherapy. (This book primarily addresses counseling with individuals, with the exception of one chapter that summarizes the major family therapy theories.)

Whether therapists describe themselves as integrative or eclectic (incorporating a variety of themes and techniques into their work), or affiliated with a particular theoretical model, counseling theories all shed light on people's challenges and change processes and provide skills that promote emotional health. It is difficult to determine the most popular theoretical orientations of various mental health providers. Little research on this topic exists, and when practitioners are asked about their theory preferences, only a small number of theories are presented to them as options, thus limiting the findings. With that said, Table 1.1 presents an overview of the theoretical orientation of choice of U.S. counselors, clinical psychologists, counseling psychologists, and social workers.

TABLE 1.1 Theoretical Orientations of Mental Health Providers in the United States

Orientation	Clinical Psychologists (%)	Counseling Psychologists (%)	Social Workers (%)	Counselors (%)
Behavioral	15	2	11	8
Cognitive	31	19	19	29
Constructivist	1	1	2	2
Existential/Humanistic	1	7	4	5
Gestalt/Experiential	1	1	1	2
Integrative/Eclectic	22	31	26	23
Interpersonal	4	8	3	3
Multicultural	1	2	1	1
Psychoanalytic	3	1	5	2
Psychodynamic	15	9	9	5
Rogerian/Person-Centered	2	3	1	10
Systems	2	4	14	7
Other	2	12	4	3

Source: Data from Bechtoldt, H., Norcross, J. C., Wyckoff, L., Pokrywa, M. L., & Campbell, L. F. (2001). Theoretical orientations and employment settings of clinical and counseling psychologists: A comparative study. *The Clinical Psychologist, 54*(1), 3–6; Bike, D. H., Norcross, J. C., & Schatz, D. M. (2009). Processes and outcomes of psychotherapists' personal therapy: Replication and extension 20 years later. *Psychotherapy, 46*(1), 19–31; Goodyear, R. Lichtenberg, J., Hutman, H., Overland, E., Bedi, R., Christiani, K., . . . Young, C. (2016). A global portrait of counselling psychologists' characteristics, perspectives, and professional behaviors. *Counselling Psychology Quarterly, 29*, 115–138. doi: 10.1080/09515070.2015.1128396; Norcross, J. C., & Karpiak, C. P. (2012). Clinical psychologists in the 2010s: Fifty years of the APA Division of Clinical Psychology. *Clinical Psychology: Science and Practice, 19*, 1–12.

UNDERSTANDING COUNSELING THEORIES

Counseling, at its most basic level, is about helping people grow and change. When clients present for counseling, it can be difficult to know what information needs to be gathered and how to proceed in best helping clients make the changes they seek. Therapists use theories to organize and simplify the vast amount of information that clients present. Therapists' theories serve as the roadmap for determining the best way to help clients change. Theories assist counselors in organizing information about clients and in determining how to use such information to support clients.

Available resources on various techniques and interventions to facilitate client change are abundant. A quick Internet search reveals millions of counseling techniques and interventions. As an example, the Jongsma (e.g., Jongsma, Peterson, & Bruce, 2014) series includes numerous treatment planning books, which provide examples of short-term objectives, long-term goals, and therapeutic interventions for helping clients achieve their goals. There has also been a recent trend toward the use of computer software systems that generate predetermined counseling goals, objectives, and interventions based on clients' presenting concerns.

These resources can be very helpful tools, but counselors must pull on a counseling theory that can guide their conceptualization of their clients' situations and help them identify what interventions might be most useful (Kress & Paylo, 2019). Counselors who rely on a hodgepodge of techniques or interventions that are not thoughtfully linked to theory run the risk of harming their clients. Clients deserve to have counselors who thoughtfully conceptualize their situations and select counseling techniques grounded in both theory and science (Kress & Paylo, 2019). Anyone can apply counseling interventions and techniques, but skilled therapists will apply a theory and use this theory to guide and focus counseling and to determine when and how to apply specific interventions; the application of theory is what makes us unique and what separates us from the proverbial "armchair psychologists" of the world.

At the most basic level, theories are important because they help counselors to do the following:

- Weed through a vast amount of presenting information and understand and recognize what client information needs to be identified, gathered, and organized
- Conceptualize clients' situations and identify what is supporting their problems in living
- Identify ways of approaching clients that can help them make changes.

Theories of counseling and psychotherapy have been referred to as counseling or therapy approaches, treatment systems, treatment approaches, and theories of change, along with other terms. In this text, the terms therapy and counseling will primarily be used to refer to an integrated set of concepts that provides explanations for and descriptions of the following:

- Stages, patterns, and important factors in people's emotional development
- Healthy emotional development, as well as problematic or abnormal emotional development
- How to help people develop in positive ways and reduce symptoms that are distressing and/or cause impairment in functioning
- The role of therapists and how that role contributes to counseling
- Strategies for putting the theory into practice (e.g., identifying and modifying cognitive distortions, reflecting feelings, developing a clear plan for behavioral change)
- Specific skills or interventions that can enhance implementation of the counseling approach (e.g., use of earliest recollections, analysis of dreams, diaphragmatic breathing)
- Information on people who are likely to benefit from this counseling approach; this information might include people's age, cultural background, strengths, presenting issues, counseling settings, and other factors.

An effective theory is easily understood and comprehensive, provides explanations for a wide variety of presenting issues, and generates research. Effective counseling theories are also encouraging and instills in clients the confidence required to make positive changes; therefore, effective counseling theories integrate encouragement to some extent (Wong, 2015). Effective theories are grounded in an understanding of human development. They offer a framework for gathering and organizing information and exploring personality. They present a theory of development and change that helps us understand people and their concerns. They supply steps and interventions that encourage learning and growth and that allow for evaluation of progress and modification of treatment/counseling plans if needed. They provide reassurance and direction. They lend themselves to development of testable hypotheses that can be investigated to determine the validity and usefulness of the approach, and they promote further study and improvement of the counseling process. Counseling approaches that have proven their value over time are also reasonably well validated.

Readers of this text come from diverse backgrounds, including professional counseling, psychology, marriage and family therapy, social work, art therapy, and other professions. A number of terms can be used to describe those who help people make changes. People's professional background, the setting in which they work, and their formal job title are just a few of the factors that determine whether they refer to themselves as clinical mental health counselors, school counselors, psychologists, therapists, psychotherapists, and so on. To accommodate the broad array of backgrounds of readers, in this text, the generic terms *counselor* and *therapist* will generally be used to describe those who help people change.

Counseling Is Effective

Before proceeding, it is important to ask ourselves if counseling and therapy are effective. In fact, research consistently suggests the effectiveness of counseling (Leichsenring, 2009; Levy, Ablon, & Kachele, 2012). Approximately 75% to 80% of clients benefit significantly from counseling (Clement, 2013). This improvement rate is comparable to the improvements perceived by those receiving various medical procedures (Maltzman, 2016). Counseling outcomes do not differ based on the education or on the degree or license of the person providing services (Norcross & Lambert, 2011). The positive effect of counseling and therapy is achieved in the first 10 to 20 sessions. Studies also indicate that positive effects of therapy last long after counseling has ended (Bolier et al., 2013).

What makes therapy effective? Common factors—that is, factors common to all therapeutic approaches—such as the therapeutic alliance, counselors' demonstration of empathy, clients' and counselors' expectations for change, and the hope that clients experience improvement secondary to meeting with a counselor, may be what makes counseling effective (Ardito & Rabellino, 2011; Wampold, 2015). We should feel good about the fact that what we do as counselors matters and that our efforts are effective.

Although differences in outcome among various forms of therapy are not strong, this does not detract from the importance of effectively using various approaches and strategies and tailoring them to the individual's unique needs. Therapists and researchers no longer ask whether counseling is effective; that has been conclusively demonstrated. Nor do they ask which counseling modality works best. Now we know that most therapies work.

Even though we know counseling is effective, many important questions need to be asked: What are the key ingredients of a successful therapeutic relationship? When is counseling most likely to be effective? What characteristics set apart the successful therapist? What client traits, attitudes, and behaviors enhance counseling, and how can these features be fostered? What counseling approaches and strategies are most effective for specific problems? Which theories can be integrated to produce even greater effectiveness? What are some common factors inherent in all counseling approaches? These are only a few of the important questions that today's therapists are asking and that will be addressed in this text.

Current research suggests that specific counseling approaches and interventions are just one factor in producing change. Research indicates that clients attribute 40% of the change they experience in counseling to *extratherapeutic factors* (including the internal resources and events that occur in their lives), 30% to the *therapist–client relationship*, 15% to particular *techniques and interventions*, and 15% to their *hope and expectation of positive change* (Duncan, Miller, Wampold, & Hubble, 2010).

Several important points emerge from this finding. First, therapists may not be as powerful as they might think; in fact, clients' life experiences and circumstances and their inner resources seem to be the most powerful factor in change. Consequently, therapists must take the time to know and understand their clients, to grasp their perspectives on the world, to hear their stories, and to learn about their lives so that therapists can help their clients to make the most of those extratherapeutic factors. Second, the therapeutic alliance is of great importance. Promoting a positive relationship characterized by conditions and interactions that encourage desired changes can make a significant difference in the success of counseling. Observing that interventions represent only 15% of the factors contributing to change, readers may be tempted to ask, "Why, then, pay so much attention to learning specific counseling theories?" In reality, 60% or more of client change can be attributed to the theories used, because in addition to the techniques and interventions used (15%), the skills and strategies of the therapist are largely responsible for the development of the therapeutic alliance (30% of the source of change) and for engendering hope and positive expectations in clients (15% of the source of change). Furthermore, counseling can also make a difference in people's ability to make positive use of extratherapeutic factors such as support systems, community resources, and educational programs. Thus, techniques and interventions associated with various theoretical approaches are important not only for their direct impact on symptoms and problems, but also for their indirect impact on the therapeutic alliance as well as on client attitudes and behaviors associated with successful counseling.

Common Factors

Common factors, or a common set of variables, are at play in the different forms of therapy, and these common factors make all therapies effective. What follows is a summary of what we believe makes therapy effective:

- A **therapeutic relationship** characterized by collaboration, trust, mutual investment in the therapy process, shared respect, genuineness, and positive emotional feelings
- A safe, supportive, and healing context
- Goals and a sense of direction as to where counseling is headed
- A shared understanding between therapists and clients about the nature of the problems and concerns to be addressed in treatment and the change processes that will be used to resolve problems
- A credible approach to addressing the client's presenting problems
- Therapeutic learning, which typically includes feedback and corrective experiences
- The encouragement of client self-efficacy and problem-solving abilities
- Improvement in clients' ability to identify, express constructively, and modify their emotions
- Improvement in clients' ability to identify, assess the validity of, and modify their thoughts
- Improvement in clients' ability to assess and change dysfunctional behaviors as well as acquire new and more effective behaviors that promote coping, impulse control, sound relationships, and good emotional and physical health.

Later in this chapter, the therapeutic relationship, the working alliance, and the ingredients that contribute to successful counseling will be discussed in greater depth.

CHARACTERISTICS OF SUCCESSFUL CLIENTS

Both the personal qualities and the backgrounds of clients help determine the success of counseling (Bohart & Tallman, 2010). Therapists can maximize the positive influence of client characteristics by adopting a strength-based perspective (Duncan et al., 2010; discussed later in this chapter); by believing that clients are motivated and capable of change and using that belief to instill hope and optimism during the counseling process; and by promoting an environment where clients feel safe discussing their struggles and trying out new ways of being.

Both pretherapy characteristics—or characteristics that clients bring to counseling—and those qualities that clients manifest in counseling can have an impact on therapy outcome. For example, some research has found that client intelligence, education, and socioeconomic level all play a role in positive counseling outcomes (Leibert & Dunne-Bryant, 2015). The following behaviors and attitudes that clients demonstrate during counseling play an important part in the counseling process.

Client Motivation

The term **motivation** is a broad one that therapists use to describe a range of client behaviors associated with readiness for change and an ability to engage productively in that process. Particularly important aspects of client motivation include engagement in and cooperation with counseling and a willingness to self-disclose, confront problems, put forth effort to change, and, if necessary, experience some temporary anxiety and discomfort in the hope of eventual benefit. Other signs of strong client motivation include low levels of defensiveness and a belief that counseling is necessary and important. Not surprisingly, self-referred clients are less likely to terminate counseling prematurely than are clients referred by others.

Clients often struggle to make behavior changes; part of them wants to change, but part of them does not want to change. It may be that change is frightening, or that the behaviors to be changed may be working for clients in some way, or it may be that clients feel, in some ways, comfortable with things the way they are. Motivational interviewing (Miller & Rollnick, 2012), discussed later in this text, can encourage a client's readiness for change. Motivational interviewing is a directive, client-centered counseling approach that is focused on encouraging clients' behavior change by helping them to explore and resolve their ambivalence toward making changes. Motivational interviewing techniques can be particularly helpful with clients who have substance use disorders, eating disorders, and other behavior problems, as they help these clients prepare for, and make the most of, counseling.

Client Expectations

Hope or *optimism* is another essential element of counseling. Therapy is hard work for both clients and therapists. For people to persist in that process and tolerate the increased anxiety it often causes, as well as the commitment of time and resources, they must believe that counseling has something positive to offer and that, at the end of the process, they will be better off than they were before counseling.

People who have a clear and accurate understanding of counseling and its strengths and limitations are more likely to have successful therapy outcomes. Pretherapy preparation of clients via role induction can make a considerable difference in people's expectations for counseling and correspondingly in their commitment to counseling, willingness to self-disclose, and alliance with the therapist (Shaw & Murray, 2014; Patterson, Anderson, & Wei, 2014). Similarly, effective engagement of the client in the very first session has been shown to make a positive contribution to successful therapy (Shaw & Murray, 2014).

In general, clients who are informed of what to expect—or understand their role as a client—have a better grasp of counseling and their role in the process, seem more optimistic about making positive changes, and demonstrate greater willingness to self-disclose and talk about their concerns. **Role induction** is the process of orienting clients to counseling so they are more likely to become successful clients who comprehend and can make good use of the therapeutic process. Role induction can help both the client and the therapist engage productively in a common endeavor and can contribute greatly to the efficiency and success of therapy.

Role induction occurs during the first counseling session as part of the intake and assessment process.

Role induction typically entails discussing the following topics with clients early in the therapeutic relationship and ensuring that clients understand and are comfortable with the information that has been discussed:

- The nature of the counseling process
- How counseling promotes positive change
- The kinds of issues and concerns that usually respond well to counseling
- The collaborative nature of the client–counselor relationship
- The roles and responsibilities of the counselor
- The roles and responsibilities of the client
- How clients can get the most out of counseling
- The importance of honesty and self-disclosure on the part of the client
- The kinds of changes people can realistically expect from counseling.

Client Engagement

Counseling is not something that is *done* to clients; rather, clients and their families are active participants in the counseling process (Kress & Paylo, 2019). Clients who succeed in counseling freely present their concerns, collaborate with the therapist in a mutual endeavor, and take steps to improve their lives. They develop a problem-solving attitude and maintain positive expectations of change (Patterson et al., 2014). They recognize that at least some of their difficulties come from within themselves and believe they have the power to improve their situation. They view the need for personal change as significant and can identify a specific problem they want to address. Clients who do better in counseling and maintain gains believe that the changes made in therapy were primarily a result of their own efforts (Scholl, Ray, & Brady-Amoon, 2014). These people probably feel empowered as a result of their counseling successes and are optimistic that they can continue to make positive changes and choices, even after counseling has ended.

THE THERAPEUTIC ALLIANCE

Fifty years of research indicates, with increasing clarity, that the strength of the therapeutic alliance is one of the most powerful predictors of client outcome regardless of the therapist's theoretical orientation (Norcross, 2010). Therefore, it is imperative that therapists acquire a sound understanding of the elements of a positive therapeutic alliance, develop the skills and strategies they need to create successful working relationships with their clients, and be able to adapt their therapy style to individual clients to help them participate in and appreciate the value of the therapeutic alliance. They must also learn to attend to the alliance, to monitor the relationship, and to mend any ruptures as they occur.

Carl Rogers's person-centered counseling, discussed in greater detail later in this book, emphasizes the importance of essential therapist characteristics that he believed would promote client self-esteem and self-efficacy. Rogers referred to these traits—empathy, unconditional positive regard, and congruence (or being genuine with a client)—as the necessary conditions in which change could occur.

It seems intuitive: A therapist should be competent, caring, warm, and trustworthy and should have strong interpersonal skills. Empirical research continues to point to "the relationship" as the most important ingredient of change. This comes as no surprise, and we all intuitively know that the comfort of a warm relationship and human interaction is what makes counseling work (Norcross, 2010). Although other variables are also at play, including specific interventions, the presence of the following essential conditions of the therapeutic relationship makes it likely that those interventions will succeed.

Empathy

Empathy is the therapist's ability to see the world through the client's eyes and to communicate that understanding so that the client feels heard and validated. Therapists' empathy helps clients feel that their therapists can relate to their experiences and are connecting with them emotionally. Therapist empathy is strongly associated with positive change in clients and may be an even better predictor of counseling outcome than are specific interventions. Indeed, therapist empathy accounts for 9% of the variance in counseling outcomes (Elliott, Bohart, Watson, & Greenberg, 2011).

Unconditional Positive Regard

Unconditional positive regard is transmitted through emotional warmth, appropriate reassurance, the communication of confidence and interest in the client, and the use of therapeutic interventions that empower the client. It gives clients the message that they matter. Good therapists are nonjudgmental and perceive it a privilege to witness the client's experience, and they recognize that the client's experience always trumps the therapist's expertise (Norcross, 2010). Therapists who are warm and caring have a higher likelihood of a positive therapy outcome than do those who are aggressive and confrontational (Bucci, Seymour-Hyde, Harris, & Berry, 2016).

Congruence

Being genuine with a client, or **congruence**, also contributes to the establishment of a positive therapeutic relationship. Therapists who are genuine with clients give them clear, accurate, unambiguous, and honest, yet sensitive, messages. The therapist does not merely verbalize concern while counting the minutes until lunch. If therapists believe clients are making harmful or self-destructive choices, they provide feedback and clarification and show clients possible alternatives, but they never coerce, attack, or humiliate clients.

As with other essential conditions of counseling, therapists must be careful not to move beyond encouraging positive change into an authoritarian role in which they tell clients how they should be and make value judgments about the clients' thoughts, feelings, and actions. Occasionally, clients present a danger to themselves or others, and therapists must intervene forcefully to prevent harm. However, under most circumstances, therapists must honor their clients' right to decide what is best for them.

The essential conditions of counseling are intertwined and build on each other. Consequently, empathy, unconditional positive regard, and congruence all facilitate the development of hope in clients, as do support, encouragement, and affirmation (Wampold, 2015). In addition, the therapist's communication of direction and optimism, emphasis on the client's strengths, ability to address problematic client behaviors and attitudes, and building of a collaborative client–therapist relationship all can foster the client's positive expectation of change (Duncan et al., 2010).

Having a shared vision of the counseling process and the goals of counseling is another important element in the therapeutic alliance (Hill, 2009). If client and therapist view themselves as engaged in an important shared endeavor that is likely to be successful, have clear and mutually established goals in mind, and agree on the tasks and procedures used to achieve those goals, their collaboration is likely to be smooth and efficient.

The counseling theories discussed throughout this book provide therapists with many skills and strategies for developing and enhancing the all-important client–therapist relationship and thereby maximizing the likelihood of a successful therapy outcome. Although the client–therapist relationship evolves over time and can improve throughout the counseling process, a positive therapeutic alliance must develop by the fifth session if counseling is to be successful (Sperry, 2010).

CHARACTERISTICS OF EFFECTIVE THERAPISTS

As previously discussed, research suggests that the facilitative interpersonal skills of the therapist account for much of the variability in counseling outcomes. Also, establishing a collaborative, client-centered relationship and the ability to address and repair any ruptures that occur in that relationship are the essential facilitative skills for a therapist. New therapists must aim to develop these skills.

Research has not clearly demonstrated that a particular age, gender, professional orientation, or background of a therapist is associated with successful counseling outcomes. However, clients often express strong preferences for therapists in a certain age group, of one gender or the other, or with a particular cultural or religious affiliation. For example, most women prefer a female therapist (Landes, Burton, King, & Sullivan, 2013). When clients have the type of therapist they prefer, they may have more confidence that counseling will help them, which may enhance the therapeutic alliance. Recent research has found improved outcomes or effectiveness when female clients and therapists are matched by gender (Lambert, 2016). However, some research also suggests that the quality of counseling is the same and long-term outcomes are no different based solely on gender (Kuusisto & Artkoski, 2013). Therefore, more research is needed in the area of matching clients and therapists based on certain characteristics.

Effective Therapist Personal Qualities

The literature also suggests personal and professional qualities in therapists that contribute to counseling effectiveness. Many are the same qualities that most of us value in friends and colleagues. The profile of the effective therapist is, in many respects, comparable to that of an emotionally healthy individual. In terms of personal characteristics, effective therapists are typically:

- Interpersonally skilled; possessing good skills that include patience, warmth, caring, a sense of humor, and friendliness
- Genuine, sincere, and authentic; able to make appropriate self-disclosures, provide useful feedback, and acknowledge their mistakes and limitations
- Emotionally stable, mature, and responsible
- Well-adjusted and fulfilled, self-aware, with positive and realistic self-esteem, good relationships, a sense of direction, and a rewarding lifestyle
- Able to acknowledge their mistakes and limitations
- Capable of high levels of thinking and conceptualizing
- In possession of good insight into themselves and others
- Aware of, sensitive to, and respectful of cultural characteristics and differences
- Engaged in and appreciative of the value of personal and professional growth and learning
- Ethical, objective, and fair
- Flexible and open to change and new experiences, willing to take reasonable risks
- Affirming and encouraging of others
- Clear and effective in both oral and written communications

Effective therapists are likely to manifest emotional health and well-being as well as the ability to put their own needs aside at least temporarily so they can understand, support, and help others. Having past personal difficulties does not prohibit people from becoming emotionally healthy and effective therapists. In fact, the process of honestly looking at and bravely tackling their own issues and concerns may enable people to develop the positive traits often found in successful therapists. Not surprisingly, the majority of mental health professionals (more than 75%) have participated in their own therapy (Wilson, Weatherhead, & Davies, 2015).

Effective Therapist Professional Qualities

We know that the quality of the counseling relationship is the single most important aspect of the individual counseling process, and certain therapist behaviors facilitate strong counseling relationships (Norcross & Lambert, 2011; Norcross & Wampold, 2011; Wampold, 2010). Empathy, unconditional positive regard, and congruence have already been discussed as essential features of a strong therapeutic relationship.

Relationship factors are characteristics of the therapeutic interaction between the client and the therapist; these include active listening, unconditional acceptance, and the insight and awareness of current issues. Therapists should be attuned to their clients' verbal and nonverbal messages, regularly ask them for feedback and their reactions to counseling, and directly address any barriers to the establishment of a positive alliance. What follows is a brief overview—based on 50+ years of research—of the therapist qualities and behaviors that predict successful counseling outcomes (i.e., client satisfaction with counseling, clients reaching their goals) regardless of factors such as age or presenting issues (Norcross & Wampold, 2011; Wampold, 2010):

- Effective therapists have advanced ***interpersonal skills***, an ability to convey warmth and empathy, and a capacity to understand and focus on what is important to clients. These interpersonal skills facilitate a warm connection and a positive therapeutic relationship. A positive therapeutic relationship helps clients to feel understood, it invites trust, and clients come to believe that their therapist can help facilitate change.
- Effective therapists are able to form a ***working alliance*** with a diverse array of clients. The working alliance involves the previously mentioned therapeutic relationship but also includes an agreement on the goals of counseling and how those goals will be achieved (the tasks of counseling). A strong working alliance suggests that the counselor and client are both working in a deliberate, focused, agreed-upon manner toward mutually agreed-upon counseling goals. When working with youth, therapists must take care to ensure they have a strong working alliance with both the young client and the family. Effective therapists also understand that they need to constantly assess and monitor these working alliances for changes or alliance disruptions or ruptures. Demonstrations of alliance ruptures include clients questioning the usefulness of counseling, clients disengaging from counseling, or clients shifting away from counseling and avoiding important topics.
- Effective therapists provide an ***explanation for clients' problems*** or struggles that is acceptable (i.e., the explanation fits within the clients' comfort level based on their socioeconomic status, culture, self-perceptions); adaptive (i.e., the explanation suggests that a means of overcoming the struggle in a productive manner is possible); and culturally sensitive (i.e., the explanation fits with the clients' attitudes, values, culture, and worldview). Effective therapists are exquisitely sensitive to clients' worldviews, perceptions, and explanations of the problem and consider these before sharing an explanation for the clients' struggles. These explanations are cohesive with the clients' understanding of the problem.
- Effective therapists develop a ***counseling or treatment plan that is consistent with the explanation for the problem*** that was provided to—or co-constructed with—the clients. If the

explanation of the problem and the plan to address the struggles is mutually agreed upon, clients will be more compliant and remain engaged in counseling. It is critical that clients understand how counseling will be helpful, know what the goals and objectives are, and believe in the plan. An effective therapist must be persuasive and facilitate client "buy in" with regard to the counseling plan. If clients believe in their counseling plan, they will be hopeful, have expectations for success, and will feel motivated to action.

- Effective therapists *monitor clients' progress*. Monitoring does not necessarily need to include the use of assessment instruments. It might simply involve checking in with clients on their progress and their reactions to the counseling experience. It is important for therapists to communicate that they authentically care about clients and their progress and that they genuinely value clients' input. Monitoring helps therapists to identify potential problems before they arise, and it serves as an excellent tool to help process clients' reactions to specific counseling interventions and to counseling in general.
- Effective therapists are *flexible*, and they adjust their approach if clients are not responding and/or not motivated to change. They adjust their methods as needed, and when required, they use a different theoretical approach, refer to another provider, and integrate adjunctive services (e.g., psychiatric referrals, family therapy).
- Effective therapists are able to *address difficult counseling material* and topics. They know when to approach and avoid such material, and they are comfortable and skilled enough to directly address such material. Sometimes the difficulties may relate to clients' experiences (e.g., a fear of approaching painful material), or they may relate to aspects of the relationship between the client and the therapist (e.g., client dissatisfaction with counseling). When the difficult material involves the relationship between the therapist and the client, an effective therapist is able to address the situation in a productive, therapeutic way.
- Effective therapists *communicate hope, enthusiasm, and optimism*. This communication is not unrealistic or flippant optimism, but rather an authentic and genuine expression that hurdles can be overcome and solutions found. Related to this, effective therapists are able to recognize clients' strengths, capacities, and resources and to communicate these and the role they can play in helping clients master their problems.
- Effective therapists *display sensitivity to clients' personal characteristics* (e.g., culture, race, ethnicity, spirituality, sexual orientation, age, physical health, motivation for change) and clients' context (e.g., socioeconomic status, family and support networks, community resources and services). Sensitivity to these factors helps therapists to coordinate client care with other psychiatric, physical, psychological, or social service providers. Effective therapists are also aware of their own personal characteristics (e.g., culture, gender, personality, background, lived experiences) and they understand how clients perceive these characteristics and interact with them.
- Effective therapists are *self-aware* of their own psychological processes and dynamics, and they keep these out of the counseling process unless it is therapeutic to include them. Effective therapists reflect on their own reactions to clients (i.e., countertransference) and monitors these reactions.
- Effective therapists seek to *continually improve*. They recognize that the development of a skill requires intensive training and practice as well as consultation and supervision. They seek supervision and continuing education and aim to continually grow and enhance their skills.
- Effective therapists are *aware of the research* related to clients' presenting issues, and they pull from this literature base in selecting theories and counseling approaches. They use **evidence-based approaches**, which are therapies that have been tested and proven to be effective through procedures and research.

In Table 1.2, readers will find an overview of the foundational counseling skills that help facilitate good counseling.

TABLE 1.2 Summary of the Foundational Skills That Effective Therapists Possess

- Practice appropriate and helpful interpersonal skills.
- Form a working alliance with a diverse array of clients.
- Provide an explanation for clients' problems or struggles that is acceptable, adaptive, and culturally sensitive.
- Provide a counseling or treatment plan that is consistent with the explanation for the problem that was provided to clients.
- Monitor clients' progress.
- Adjust their approaches as needed and remain flexible.
- Address difficult counseling material and topics.
- Communicate hope, enthusiasm, and optimism.
- Display sensitivity to clients' personal characteristics.
- Self-monitor and become increasingly self-aware.
- Seek to continually improve as therapists.
- Maintain knowledge and stay aware of the research and evidence-based approaches.

DEVELOPMENTAL CONSIDERATIONS

Clients' developmental needs must be considered when selecting counseling theories and interventions. **Development** is a process of growth that involves cognitive, physical, social, personal, and emotional maturity (Broderick & Blewitt, 2015). Developmental changes occur across the lifespan; however, growth and change are especially dramatic in the earlier years of development. When working with clients, counselors' conceptualizations, theories, and interventions must be grounded in a firm understanding of human development. In fact, the American Counseling Association's (2014) *Code of Ethics* states that professional counselors should encourage the growth and development of their clients (Standard A.1b) and provide interventions that are effective and appropriate to clients' developmental levels.

People develop at different rates, and they may experience different rates of development, depending on their life experiences and physical characteristics. For example, a 10-year-old girl who was abused, traumatized, and abandoned by her parents as a child may not experience the same developmental milestones as her peers because she has not been able to move out of earlier developmental stages (Zilberstein, 2014). Examples like this one highlight the impossibility of understanding clients' developmental struggles without understanding their lived experiences and contexts.

Counselors value a developmental focus, and we believe that many of our clients' problems in living are rooted in disruptions in typical developmental processes, the unblocking of which can foster healthy transitions and change (Vereen, Hill, Sosa, & Kress, 2014). In other words, normal developmental struggles provide opportunities for growth. For example, a 22-year-old woman whose parents were just divorced might struggle with feelings of sadness and loss secondary to this transition. If we consider this woman's situation from a developmental perspective, loss and sadness would be a normal reaction, and the resolution of this struggle would provide an opportunity for her to build her sense of resilience. Problems in living can also arise in response to normal developmental transitions (e.g., puberty, transitioning out of one's family home, getting married, having children).

In applying counseling theories and techniques, counselors must be sensitive to their clients' developmental levels. Counselors who are able to put themselves in their clients' shoes, at their clients' developmental level, will be better able to help their clients make changes (Kress et al., 2019). As an example, it is important for counselors to maintain awareness of the developmental distinctions between children and adolescents. Adolescents, more so than younger children, tend to be better aware of the counseling process, skeptical of its ability to be helpful, and less trusting of authority figures; thus, these factors will influence how a counselor responds to clients (Whitmarsh & Mullette, 2009). Even a year's difference in age (say, for example, the difference between an 8- and a 9-year-old) can make a significant difference in how clients respond to different counseling approaches (Kress et al., 2019). Being sensitive to developmental matters and recalling our own childhood experiences can help in building a therapeutic, trusting relationship, and in selecting appropriate theories and interventions (Kress et al., 2019).

A developmental focus depicts people as dynamic, rather than static, organisms, and it highlights their natural inclinations toward growth and health. Developmental perspectives offer hope because client problems or positions are not permanent; instead, they are constantly changing and growing. Inherent in a developmental perspective is the understanding that clients have the capacity to move forward, to change, to adapt, to heal, and to attain optimal mental health.

Clients are developing and constantly changing, yet they grow and change at different rates. Many factors, including the safety of one's community, nutrition, environmental stimulation, and trauma and abuse experiences, can have an impact on the rate at which people meet developmental milestones. Even as people meet developmental milestones, individual variability in their capabilities can be noted. Counselors must consider each client's developmental level and the client's unique capacities and how this could relate to the theories and interventions used with the client. Just a few of the developmental factors that influence a client include the following:

- Attachment—Attachment has to do with the bonds that youth develop with their caregivers and their subsequent ability to trust and develop emotional connections with others. Disrupted attachments can have a serious impact on clients' development throughout their lives, and any associated struggles will need to be considered in terms of how the therapeutic relationship is approached and what theories are used (e.g., a client who has not been able to develop healthy attachments to caregivers may act out in counseling sessions and test the counselor; counselors thus will need to be patient and allow time for the relationship to develop before pushing forward with more active, directive interventions).
- Social and emotional development—People have different capacities for social and emotional functioning, and they can always grow in this regard. Social skills, self-awareness, and the ability to self-regulate behaviors and emotions are several capacities that relate to social and emotional development and should be considered (e.g., when using a feeling chart as a tool in counseling, a 5-year-old will need a more basic feeling chart that demonstrates, say, 5 emotions, whereas some adults could benefit from a feeling chart with 50 emotions).
- Moral development—Morality relates to an individual's connection with concepts like justice and equality. An understanding of a client's stage of moral development and capacity for moral decision making can help inform counselors' thinking (e.g., when providing cognitive behavioral sex offender treatment to a 10-year-old boy, a counselor will need to consider the boy's moral development, as this will affect how the counselor helps the boy develop victim empathy).
- Educational development—Clients have different degrees of, and capacities for, education. For example, clients' ability to read and write may differ, and their general knowledge of the world and its complexities is diverse. Counselors should take these factors into account (e.g., when counseling an adult client who cannot read or write, a counselor must ensure that homework assignments do not focus on reading and writing).
- Physical development/biological and genetic factors (e.g., physical health and growth)—Clients have a unique genetic and biological blueprint. Genetics, biochemical considerations,

and various factors such as innate intelligence or physical abilities influence clients and must be considered when treatment planning (e.g., an 8-year-old will struggle to understand the systems-level thinking associated with feminist therapy; thus, some of the associated techniques [e.g., a gender role analysis] may not be useful with younger children).

- Cognition or thinking (e.g., egocentrism, perspective taking, information processing)—Clients have unique mental processes, which include learning, memory, language, problem solving, reasoning, attention, and decision making. While this factor is linked to developmental level, variability exists in terms of how capable clients are of engaging in these mental processes. Thus, some clients have a significant capacity to engage in metacognitive thinking (i.e., thinking about their thinking), while others struggle with this (e.g., a cognitive behavioral therapy approach may not be a good fit for a client who has a moderate intellectual disability and thus a limited capacity to understand complex concepts).

CULTURE AND DIVERSITY

Culture is a set of beliefs, attitudes, and value systems that we learn early in life through enculturation, and culture permeates how we think and behave (Schnyder, 2009). Since we live in an increasingly diverse society, therapists must be sensitive and attuned to the ways culture impacts clients. Counseling has optimal effectiveness when culture is factored in (Schnyder). In fact, clients' culture may influence the counseling theories that clients connect with. For example, a client from a culture that values a direct approach to communication, and devalues a focus on introspection, emotions, and feelings, may find the less directive, introspective approach taken by person-centered therapists to be unnerving. Overall, culture influences clients in multiple ways, including their experience of problems, their internal sense of distress, their interpretation of problems, and their presentation of complaints (Eriksen & Kress, 2005).

Wide variations exist among people from different cultures in terms of their perspectives of appropriate or "normal" behavior. For instance, children's parents often bring them to counseling because of perceived misbehavior. Expectations of appropriate child behavior and how to manage misbehavior are largely based on cultural norms and expectations (Kress, Paylo, & Stargell, 2019). Culture may influence what behaviors are acceptable and how children—and parents—are permitted to express frustration and suffering, and manage distress. Culture also determines how one's friends, family, and community respond to distress or problematic behaviors, and it dictates the type and severity of the problem that must be evident before counseling intervention is deemed necessary. Culture also determines acceptable help-seeking behaviors and interventions, and who may—and may not—intervene to address clients' problems.

The American Counseling Association's (ACA) *Multicultural Counseling Competencies* (2015) suggest that therapists should acquire culturally appropriate skills and practical strategies for addressing multiculturalism. Culturally competent practice involves the application of psychological skills that integrate a focus on clients based on their cultural context. For example, when working with a 67-year-old Hispanic woman who lives with her daughter and was recently diagnosed with stage 4 ovarian cancer, a therapist making a culturally competent assessment would consider a number of factors including racism, fluency in English, changes in social status, spiritual or religious tradition, mobility, acculturation, generational history, family support, and community resources as they relate to the presenting problem. Diversity comes in many forms, and guidelines that provide a frame of reference for working with clients from diverse sexual and gender orientations are available (e.g., see the ALGBTIC Competencies for Counseling LGBQIQA Individuals, 2013).

Culture is a dynamic concept that changes across generations as a result of the changing environment. Culture, then, is specific to the individual, and to be truly culturally competent, therapists must take into account any culturally relevant components that impact a client's life. This includes not only those components that relate to the presenting problem, but also taking a culturally relevant history; learning how culture affects the client's meaning-making abilities, attitudes toward seeking help, and expectations about counseling; and then tailoring counseling to the client's individual needs.

Asian Americans, for example, are a widely diverse group, counting as many as 30 different cultural backgrounds in their ranks. This population is highly educated: 50% of Asian Americans have at least a bachelor's degree, compared with 30% of the total U.S. population. They embrace many different religions, including Christianity, Islam, Buddhism, Taoism, and Confucianism. Many are first-generation Americans, some are recent arrivals to this country, and still others come from families who have lived in the United States for generations. Like other groups, Asian Americans are very diverse.

It is not enough for therapists to understand their Asian clients' social locations; they must also understand Asian cultural values, such as emotional self-control, collectivism, conformity, achievement, humility, and respect for elders (Sue et al., 2019). In Asian culture, social roles are important, as are academic and career success and putting the family's needs above those of the individual. Enculturation, or adherence to one's culture of origin, is also important. Some elements of culture, such as food preferences or native language, may diminish over time or over generations, but values may remain (e.g., filial piety, emotional self-control).

Cultural identity and level of acculturation are important in developing an effective therapeutic alliance (Lee, 2013; Ratts, Singh, Nassar-McMillan, Butler, & McCullough, 2016). Three important aspects of cultural competence are (Sue et al., 2019) as follows:

1. Therapists being aware of their own cultural values and biases
2. Understanding the worldview of culturally diverse clients
3. Developing culturally appropriate interventions.

Therapist Awareness

Therapists must not only be culturally aware but they should also consider their own biases, experiences, and lack of expertise. Therapists must also recognize that culture impacts their perceptions of clients' problems, their style of interviewing, and their choice of theoretical perspectives and counseling approaches. Rather than taking the perspective that some implied "norm" exists and that some people differ from that norm, it is more helpful for therapists to recognize their own multiple social locations and consider them in relation to their clients' multiple social locations. Even people who are similar in age, gender, and cultural background can have very dissimilar worldviews and may respond best to very different counseling approaches.

Culturally sensitive therapists:

- Value and respect differences
- Are aware of their own cultural heritage
- Feel comfortable with the differences among people
- Become aware of circumstances that may require referral to another professional
- Acknowledge their own gender, racial, ethnic, or sexual biases.

Understanding Clients' Worldviews

Therapists place a premium on understanding culture and its impacts on clients' reality; it is impossible to understand clients and how to best help them if cultural considerations are not made. More specifically, therapists should consider cultural explanations of problems in living, cultural experiences and help-seeking behaviors, the cultural framework of clients' identities, cultural meanings of healthy functioning, and cultural aspects that relate to the therapist–client relationship (Eriksen & Kress, 2005).

Therapists must be open to the worldview or social location of others. This does not mean that therapists must adopt their clients' worldviews but, rather, that the therapist is nonjudgmental, open, and willing to learn. Allowing clients to tell their stories without fear of being judged or challenged is encouraging to clients. To do this, therapists must have knowledge beyond their own cultures, be aware of culture-bound syndromes, and understand that an individual's beliefs, values, and practices should be understood based on that individual's own culture, rather than be judged against the criteria of another (Sue et al., 2019).

Socioeconomic status and social position also influence how clients manifest and respond to their perceived problems both within and across cultures. Therapists must consider the complex relationship and interaction of culture, race, ethnicity, gender, and socioeconomic status with experiences of oppression and social position (Kress, Dixon, & Shannonhouse, 2018). Culturally sensitive therapists are also aware that those with less power in society experience a greater quantity of life's difficulties and are more likely to be vulnerable to mental health struggles, economic difficulties, and problems in living than are those from the dominant race, ethnicity, age, sexual orientation, or gender (Kress et al., 2019). They also realize that those from nondominant cultural groups garner fewer of society's resources, and thus often acquire interventions and supports later in their problem cycles; because those with less power are less likely to seek help, they may come to the attention of therapists only when the problems have reached a greater intensity. All these factors will impact the theories with which therapists identify as well as the theories that may best fit clients' needs.

Culturally Appropriate Interventions

No one style of counseling or type of intervention is appropriate for all populations. To be most effective, counseling must be respectful of the individual's values, religious beliefs, worldviews, goals, and preferences.

When shaping interventions, it is important for therapists to consider their clients' historical, cultural, and environmental experiences. The use of a holistic approach, learning a variety of theories and techniques, and examining the traditional helping skills of various cultures may facilitate culturally sensitive practices (Sue et al., 2019). Therapists should also consider that it might not be enough to offer interventions on the individual level; it may become necessary to take action to effect systemic change at the organizational or institutional level, if programs, policies, and practices used by the organizations are oppressive to their clients.

Therapists must have awareness of how their clients' worldview (gender, age, culture, ethnicity, socioeconomic status, religion, and family background) has shaped their experience of personal problems and their views of counseling as a way to address those problems. Therapists must also be culturally competent and able to respond appropriately to people whose cultural backgrounds differ from their own. To help people understand themselves and others in all their "social locations" that are constructed in the context of social, interpersonal, and relational realities, the acronym ADDRESSING can be used (Hays, 2008):

    A = age

    D = disability (acquired)

    D = disability (developmental)

    R = religion and spirituality

    E = ethnicity

    S = socioeconomic status

S = sexual orientation

I = indigenous heritage

N = national origin

G = gender/sex

The ADDRESSING acronym is a foundation on which to build, and not an all-inclusive model (Hays, 2008). Every individual will have diverse experiences across all of the dimensions (Brown, 2008). Clearly, therapists have much to consider when meeting any new client. Knowing the history of an individual's culture is critical (Hays, 2009). Not only is the cultural background or cultural history important, but also the level of acculturation or identity development with which the client currently identifies.

An understanding of cultural factors may point to a theory that is more or less well suited for given clients. One resource that therapists can use in conducting a contextual assessment on clients is the Cultural Formulation Interview (CFI; this measure can be found in the *Diagnostic and Statistical Manual of Mental Disorders (DSM-5)*; APA, 2013). The CFI is a standardized, 16-question interview tool. The CFI can be used to enhance therapists' understanding of information that relates to a clients' culture. This systematic interview is intended for use in initial counseling sessions, and it involves four lines of inquiry (APA, 2013):

1. *Cultural definition of the problem* (e.g., the client's definition of the presenting problem; defining the problem through the perspective of the client's family, friends, or relevant community members)
2. *Cultural perceptions of cause, context, and support* (e.g., personal perceptions of the causes of the problem; causes of the problem that family, friends, or relevant community members might suggest; supports and stressors; components of client's background/identity, or cultural identity)
3. *Cultural factors affecting self-coping and past help seeking* (e.g., coping skills; past advisement, help, and treatment; barriers to past attempts at help seeking)
4. *Cultural factors affecting current help seeking* (e.g., preferences of counseling style and approach; concerns about the present counseling relationship).

Armed with a solid understanding of a client's individual, family, community, and cultural context, the therapist is ready to explore the more formal components of the assessment process. Table 1.3 provides questions therapists can ask to assess culture and cultural understanding of problems.

TABLE 1.3 Interview Questions that Can be Used To Assess Clients' Cultural Context

The following are questions that can be asked of clients and/or families to assess their culture and the cultural understanding of the problems they bring to counseling. When asking any questions, the counselor should take into account developmental considerations.

ASSESSING THE CLIENT'S CULTURAL BACKGROUND

How do you identify yourself (i.e., age, race, ethnicity, culture, socioeconomic status (SES), sexual orientation, gender, disability/ability)?

What is your country of origin?

Where were your parents born? Where were your children born?

Where do you call home?

Have you always lived in the United States? If not, when did you come to the United States?

What was life like before you came to the United States?

TABLE 1.3 (*Continued*)

What was it like when you first came to the United States? How is it now?

Why did you leave your country of origin?

What languages do you speak? What languages do you prefer to speak? What language is spoken at home/with your family members/in your community?

How would you describe your culture, ethnicity? What are your foundational values and beliefs?

How would you describe your family? Who are the members of your family?

Who raised you?

Do you want your extended family or other important people in your life included in counseling? Would you like me to talk with any of them?

In what ways does your family impact and support you?

How would you describe your community? Do you belong to any groups or organizations?

What do you view as important sources of support?

What activities are you associated with or participate in?

Are religion and/or spirituality important to you?

Are you comfortable talking about values, beliefs, and spirituality with me?

Is religion or spirituality an important aspect of treatment you wish to address?

Is there a religious, spiritual, or healing person who should be part of counseling?

Do you feel that others have discriminated against you because of your culture? Have you seen this at work/school/in the community/in relationships/in other settings?

Have you ever felt that people discriminated against you or judged you because of your religious, spiritual, political, or ethnic worldview?

Have you ever been discriminated against due to your race, social-economic class, sexual orientation, gender, disability, or for any other reason that you would like to talk about and make me aware of?

What is your sexual orientation?

How would you describe your gender identity?

How would you define your social-economic status?

Do you have any customs or practices that you would like me to know about or pull into counseling?

UNDERSTANDING THE PROBLEM

How would you/the family describe what is going on with you? How would you/the family define the problem?

How might your other family members, friends, or others within your community define the problem?

What is the most troubling part of the problem?

What would you like to be doing that you are not able to do?

Have you/the family sought help for this problem in the past? If so, from whom? What parts of reaching out to others were helpful? What parts were not?

Have you ever had times when you thought you would have the problem, but did not?

How would you name or label what is happening (i.e., the presenting problem)?

Are there any beliefs or cultural considerations that you would like to discuss concerning the problem?

Is there anything you are afraid of, or fear related to the problem?

Do your family members, friends, or others within your community support your decision to seek help?

What do you/the family think caused or is causing this problem?

What would your family members, friends, or others within your community say is causing your problem?

Is there any kind or type of support that makes the problem better?

(*Continued*)

TABLE 1.3 (*Continued*)

Do you/the family feel supported by family members, friends, and others within the community?

What seems to make the problem worse? What stressors make the problem more difficult to deal with or tolerate?

How have you/the family dealt with the problem in the past?

How are you/the family currently coping with this problem?

BARRIERS TO COUNSELING/INTERVENTION

Has anything ever gotten in your way of seeking help for this problem?

What barriers have prevented you from seeking help in the past?

Do you perceive the services here will help you and your family?

Do you see any potential challenges in your receiving counseling?

Considering what you know about counseling, is there anything you feel uncomfortable about?

POSSIBLE SOLUTIONS

How have you dealt with the problem in the past?

Has anything been helpful?

How are you currently coping with this problem?

COUNSELING AND COUNSELING RELATIONSHIP PREFERENCES

What kind or type of help is most useful to you/the family?

What kinds of help would your family members, friends, or others within your community deem as most useful?

What would you/the family like from me in this relationship?

What expectations do you have for me in this relationship?

What expectations do you have for yourself in this relationship?

What expectations do you have for your child/the family in this relationship?

How do you see counseling progressing?

What type of pace is ideal?

How often would you like to attend sessions?

What would indicate to you that counseling or this counseling relationship is not working?

Do you have any reservation that I will not understand your situation, your culture, or your lived experience? If so, what do you think I need to know?

Is there anything I have failed to ask you that would be helpful in facilitating counseling and making you feel safe here?

Source: Kress, V. E., Paylo, M., & Stargell, N. A. (2019). *Counseling children and adolescents*. 1st Ed., ©2019. Reprinted and Electronically reproduced by permission of Pearson Education, Inc., New York, NY.

A STRENGTHS-BASED PERSPECTIVE

It is important that therapists understand mental health and wellness (Myers & Sweeney, 2005), apart from mental illness. Clients typically present to counseling with problems and it is easy to center only on these struggles; however, all clients also have strengths, resources, and capacities. A focus on client strengths, or a **strengths-based approach**, has increasingly become a part of the landscape in counseling settings, with many agency accreditors and some third-party payers requiring the integration of client strengths into the therapy process (Kress & Paylo, 2019). In fact, many agencies and third-party payers now require that providers explicitly address client strengths and integrate these strengths into their counseling approach and clients' treatment plans (Kress & Paylo, 2019).

A strengths-based approach holds to the assumption that therapists not only should explore client struggles but should also invest equal time and energy in exploring a client's assets and strengths, providing a more holistic and balanced approach to counseling each individual. Working from this type of clinical perspective, therapists can instill hope through the building of personal competencies, and they can enhance growth through building upon strengths, all while concurrently addressing aspects of the individual that may be perceived as deficits of well-being (Smith, 2006).

All counseling, regardless of theoretical orientation, is based, in part, on the idea that clients can understand their problems and that they have access to solutions to their problems. Some theories (e.g., person-centered therapy, feminist therapy) are more explicit in their assumption that clients are resourceful and forward moving, but even theories that are more deterministic (e.g., psychoanalytic approaches) assume that clients have a capacity for awareness, growth, and change.

A strengths-based approach is grounded in the assumption that the development and amplification of strengths and assets within and around the individual provides clients with a greater sense of resilience against problems in living and/or mental illness. Therapists who work from a strengths-based perspective actively focus on enhancing, developing, and highlighting clients' resources, strengths, times of resilience, and ability to cope and persevere (Smith, 2006). A strength-based focus is empowering and thus enhances clients' sense of esteem by increasing their sense of self-determination, sense of mastery of life, and ability to endure and persevere.

To be more concrete, therapists can work from a strengths-based perspective by identifying the unique strengths that a client has or has access to, and amplifying those strengths. Therapists might also promote client virtues and character strengths that are known to promote resilience, and these include responsibility, gratitude, nurturance, altruism, civility, moderation, tolerance, and a solid work ethic (Seligman, 2012). Resilience, or the ability to resist against difficulties, is an essential consideration when working from a strengths-based approach. Therapists can attempt to foster resilience in their clients by enhancing their individual competencies within the following areas (Benard, 2004): (1) social competence, (2) problem solving, (3) autonomy, and (4) sense of purpose. Therapists should not just highlight these strengths but should also seek to amplify these strengths throughout the counseling process, in an attempt to build a client's resilience against illness and future difficulties. Table 1.4 provides examples of specific character strengths and resiliencies that can be identified and integrated into counseling.

TABLE 1.4 Examples of Client Strengths and Resiliencies

• Accepting	• Gentle	• Playful
• Adventurous	• Graceful	• Positive
• Affectionate	• Grateful	• Powerful
• Alert	• Hard-working	• Practical
• Altruistic	• Helpful	• Problem solver
• Ambitious	• Honest	• Prudent
• Appreciative	• Hopeful	• Punctual
• Aspiring	• Humble	• Purposeful
• Aware	• Humorous	• Rational
• Brave	• Hygienic	• Regulated
• Calm	• Imaginative	• Relaxed
• Capable	• Independent	• Reliable
• Caring	• Industrious	• Religious

(Continued)

TABLE 1.4 (Continued)

• Cheerful	• Innovative	• Resilient
• Committed	• Insightful	• Respectful
• Compassionate	• Inspirational	• Responsible
• Confident	• Intelligent	• Restrained
• Conscientious	• Interested	• Self-confident
• Considerate	• Intuitive	• Self-esteemed
• Cooperative	• Knowledgeable	• Self-regulated
• Courageous	• Leadership	• Selfless
• Creative	• Logical	• Sensitive
• Curious	• Loving	• Sincere
• Determined	• Loyal	• Skilled
• Disciplined	• Mastery	• Social
• Educated	• Modest	• Spiritual
• Empathetic	• Motivated	• Spontaneous
• Empowering	• Moral	• Strong-willed
• Encouraging	• Nonviolent	• Successful
• Energetic	• Nurturing	• Supportive
• Engaged	• Observant	• Sympathetic
• Enthusiastic	• Open-minded	• Tactful
• Ethical	• Optimistic	• Talented
• Expressive	• Organized	• Tenacious
• Fair	• Patient	• Thoughtful
• Fitness	• Peaceful	• Thrifty
• Flexible	• Persistent	• Tolerant
• Focused	• Personable	• Trusting
• Forgiving	• Persuasive	• Trustworthy
• Friendly	• Physically fit	• Work-oriented
• Generous		

Source: Kress, V. E., Paylo, M., & Stargell, N. A. (2019). *Counseling children and adolescents.* 1st Ed., ©2019. Reprinted and Electronically reproduced by permission of Pearson Education, Inc., New York, NY.

To help therapists identify clients' strengths, detailed interview questions for assessing clients' and families' strengths and capacities are provided in Table 1.5. As part of a strengths-based approach, therapists should address barriers to healthy development and intervene with their clients to harness as many internal and external assets as possible, and pull these into counseling. A strengths-based focus can be integrated with all of the counseling therapies discussed in this text. Many of the theories we will explore have a strengths-based philosophy at their core (e.g., person-centered therapy, feminist therapy).

COUNSELING THEORIES AND SETTING

The setting in which counseling occurs is another important factor, and the setting will influence the counseling theory a therapist uses. School counselors, for example, may have as little as 10 minutes to assess a student's situation and figure out what a student needs; thus, only certain theories will be

TABLE 1.5 Interview Questions to Assess Clients' Strengths, Capacities, and Resources

Family of Origin Strengths

- Who are you most similar to in your family?
- When you grow up, who in your family do you want to be like?
- Who is the kindest person in your family?
- Who is the smartest person in your family?
- Tell me about your grandparents.
- Which family members are you closest to?
- How often do you share quality time with your family?
- Tell me about your family values.
- Who are the most special people in your life?
- What is one good thing about each of your family members?
- What makes your family unique?
- In what ways do your family members support you and your life?
- What lessons have you learned from your family?
- Which family member would you ask for help in school?
- Which family member would you ask for help with friends?
- What special traditions does your family share?
- Which family member do you trust the most?
- On a scale of 1 (very little) and 5 (very much), how well do you fit in with your family?
- How does your family deal with problems or disagreements?
- When was the last time you and your family worked on a project together?
- What is one way your family could be more helpful in your life?
- What was the biggest challenge your family has overcome?
- What do you contribute or add to your family?
- How have you made your family proud?
- Which family members are you proud of?
- What activities do you do for fun with your family?

Community/Cultural Strengths

- What roles do you play in the community?
- How does your culture fit into the culture of the whole community?
- What are the best parts of your community?
- What are some unique aspects of your culture?
- What are your favorite parts of your culture?
- What are your favorite parts of your community?
- How do you help other people in your community?
- In your community, who do you admire the most?
- What community resources can you use to achieve your goals?
- How have people in your community helped you to learn and grow?
- How can you connect with more people in the community?
- Can you think of any ways that you can use your talents, abilities, or traits to help others in the community?

(Continued)

TABLE 1.5 (*Continued*)

- What is your age, race, ethnicity, culture, SES, sexual orientation?
- What gendered pronoun (e.g., him, her, they) do you prefer?
- Where were your parents born? Where were you born?
- Where is your home?
- What languages do you speak at home?
- What do you miss most about your last home?
- What are the key parts of your cultural identity?
- How would you describe your community? Do you belong to any groups or organizations?
- Have you ever been discriminated against because of your culture? Where/how did it occur?
- Have you ever been discriminated against due to your race, gender, or sexuality?

Spiritual Strengths

- Is religion or spirituality important to you?
- How do you make meaning of your life?
- What does religion mean to you?
- What are your religious or spiritual values?
- What does it mean for you to live your life to the fullest?
- In what ways do religion or spirituality comfort you in times of difficulty?
- How can spirituality or religion help you to achieve your goals?
- Is there anyone in your religious community you feel can help support or guide you in times of need?
- How have members of your religious community helped you or your family in the past?
- How are your spiritual/religious beliefs unique?
- How are your spiritual/religious beliefs similar to your peers' or family's?
- Do you ever meditate or pray? When do you most often do so?
- How do your religious or spiritual values affect your schooling or peer relationships?
- How do your beliefs impact your interactions with others?

Individual Strengths

- How do you go about making friends?
- With whom do you usually share problems?
- How did you usually go about solving problems (e.g., physical, emotional, educational, occupational)?
- Talk about a situation in which you took a risk.
- Tell me something that you are proud of.
- Have you ever won any awards or received any honors? How did this make you feel about yourself?
- When you're faced with a challenging situation, what helps you to maintain perspective?
- When confronted with a frustrating or disappointing situation, how do you tend to respond?
- What enables you to maintain an inner equilibrium when you're faced with difficult circumstances?
- Do you have any skills/talents?

TABLE 1.5 (*Continued*)

- What are the most rewarding activities in your life? What other activities do you most enjoy?
- Whom do you most admire? What is it that you most admire about that person?
- What are your short-term goals? How can you use your abilities to achieve them? Who can help you?
- What are your long-term goals? How can you use your strengths to achieve them? Who can help you?
- Talk about your plans around how you can reach your goals.
- How do you work well with others?
- How do you participate as a part of a team?
- Have you ever been a leader?
- What are your best traits and abilities?
- Talk about your sense of humor.
- Do people seek you out for help with tasks or problems?
- Do you have any hobbies?
- Can you think of a time when you were able to use your abilities to help others?
- What academic classes or job activities are you most interested in?
- If you could improve an area of your life that you have control over, what would it be?
- Are you able to apologize when you have hurt another person?
- Are you able to forgive others who have hurt you?
- Do you accept responsibility for your actions?
- When are you the most relaxed/happy/satisfied?
- Do you complete your work on time?
- Do you do well on assignments and exams?
- Do you try to the best of your abilities in your work/school?
- Do you treat others with respect and fairness?
- Are you genuine and honest?
- What are some of your favorite memories? What made them so special?
- Are you supportive of others (i.e., family members, friends, significant other)?
- Do you have any special responsibilities (e.g., chores, taking care of sibling/pet)?
- What makes you feel good about yourself?
- When do you feel the most confident?
- What are some things that you are good at?
- What makes you special/sets you apart from others?
- Do you know how to interact well with others at social events?
- Have you ever helped another person who didn't fit in?
- Have you ever included a person who was being left out?
- Do you enjoy close relationships with others? If so, tell me about those relationships.
- Are you creative?
- Are you accepting of life's uncertainties?
- How do you manage stress?
- What do you find fascinating?

(*Continued*)

TABLE 1.5 (*Continued*)

- What do you enjoy learning about?
- Do you find it easy to make decisions? Have you ever helped anybody else make a decision?
- How do you solve problems?
- Do you finish tasks that you start?
- Are you persistent in working toward your goals even when you meet challenges?
- What areas interest you?
- How do you spend your free time?
- If you could spend your free time doing anything you wanted, what would it be?
- Have you ever stood up for your beliefs?
- Have you ever confronted somebody who you felt was bullying you/somebody else?
- Do you ever do favors for others without expecting anything in return?
- Do you do any volunteer work?
- Do you have any special cause that you identify with?
- If you could go back and start your life from the beginning, what would you keep the same?
- Have you ever been responsible for the welfare of another (e.g., a pet, a person)?
- Are you able to become comfortable in situations where the places, people, and occasions are unfamiliar?
- Have you ever been supportive or encouraging to another person?
- Talk about how you engage in self-discipline.
- Talk about how you control your emotions in stressful situations.
- Has there ever been a time when you have treated someone kindly who has not been kind to you?
- What are some things for which you are grateful?
- What positive things do you expect to happen in the future?
- What are your dreams for the future?
- Do you thank others when they have helped you?
- Do you have relationships that bring meaning to your life?
- Do you feel that your life has purpose/purposes?
- Do you seek to find meaning and purpose in life?
- Can you view challenges as an opportunity to learn and grow?
- Do you try new activities, even if they frighten you a bit?
- Do you seek opportunities to learn and enhance yourself?
- Do you consider other people's feelings when interacting or before making decisions?
- Do you notice others' emotions?
- What conditions of your life are you the most satisfied with?
- What are some things in your life that you wanted and were able to obtain?
- Can you think of a situation when you were a good friend to somebody?

Source: Kress, V. E., Paylo, M., & Stargell, N. A. (2019). *Counseling children and adolescents.* 1st Ed., ©2019. Reprinted and Electronically reproduced by permission of Pearson Education, Inc., New York, NY.

useful to them in this setting. Therapists working in clinical settings generally have about 1 hour to assess a client, and by their second session they are required to develop a treatment plan in which a counseling theory is applied. It is important that therapists have theories and models they can use to efficiently direct their thinking, as failure to be thorough and thoughtful could result in harm to the client (Kress & Paylo, 2019).

The setting and services offered typically limit the range of clients and problems addressed. In addition, the setting may set guidelines and dictate the number and frequency of sessions and even determine the counseling approach used. Counseling in a high school, for example, will differ greatly from counseling offered in a private practice that specializes in treating those who have posttraumatic stress disorder (PTSD), or in an inpatient program for people who are at risk for suicide or homicide.

Therapists must be aware of the guidelines and requirements of the setting in which they practice and also be knowledgeable about the typical clients seen for counseling in that setting. Of course, the therapist's primary goal is to provide people with the help they need. However, sometimes a referral is indicated to a counseling program that is more appropriate for a client's needs.

Counseling settings also have a strong impact on client expectations. The individual seeking help from a career counseling center will almost always have different expectations and concerns than an individual contacting a community mental health center.

A client's **level of care** refers to the setting and intensity of services that clients require to be safe and successful in meeting their counseling goals. The setting and the level of care will impact the counseling theories therapists use. Ideally, clients will be placed in the least restrictive level of care they require. In terms of level of care decisions, therapists must consider differing therapy settings (i.e., residential treatment hospitalization, outpatient treatment), modalities of therapy (i.e., individual, group, family), and the pacing of therapy (i.e., daily, weekly, monthly). All these considerations will affect which theory the therapist uses with clients.

As an example, consider a 14-year-old who is experiencing severe depression, sleeps all day, and just made a suicide attempt. She was admitted into a hospital for 24-hour observation to stabilize her mood and keep her safe from further suicide attempts. While there, her therapist developed a treatment plan that had the goal of zero additional suicide attempts. The therapist focused on behavior therapy principles (e.g., waking up in the morning and engaging in a routine; talking to staff members when she had urges to harm herself). The next day she is released into a partial hospitalization group therapy, day treatment program. Here the theory used with her is cognitive behavioral therapy aimed at changing thinking patterns that contribute to depression and suicidal thinking.

A continuum of care refers to the idea that clients enter therapy at a level of care appropriate to their needs and they then step up to more intense levels or they step down to less intense treatment as needed. The trend in community mental health is toward close collaboration across providers and agencies, and the merging of agencies and services to be able to provide a greater number of services to clients in one place and with the greatest ease. As an example, many schools are hiring mental health providers to offer services, and many agencies are providing their services within the school setting.

Some issues that therapists should consider when determining appropriate therapy settings, theories to be applied, and frequency of sessions include:

- The severity of the client's mental health symptoms
- Any mental health diagnoses (i.e., mental disorders) and their associated prognoses

- Physical limitations or medical conditions
- Suicidal ideation (i.e., threat to self) and homicidal ideation (i.e., harm to others), or a client's ability to be safe in the community and/or not harm others
- Ability to care for one's self (i.e., activities of daily living [ADL] like showering, eating, using the toilet, dressing)
- Past therapy settings and responsiveness to those settings
- Aims and goals of therapy
- Social and community support systems and resources
- The desired level of care from the client's/family's perspective.

Therapists take into consideration the client's diagnosis, specific needs, the severity of the symptoms, any situation-specific matters, and client characteristics when matching clients with the appropriate level of care. Residential treatment, inpatient hospitalization, day treatment/partial hospitalization, in-home family services, and outpatient treatment are the most common settings or levels of care (see Table 1.6 for an overview of these levels of care).

ETHICAL AND LEGAL CONSIDERATIONS

Therapists face legal and ethical considerations in nearly every encounter they have with clients; ethics considerations should always be at the forefront of therapists' thinking. There is no way I can do justice to this important topic in this chapter, but this section does discuss several considerations that relate to the use of counseling theories and methods and to ethical and legal issues. I present an overview of several important theories/techniques–related ethical issues, along with practical suggestions for tackling ethical dilemmas.

Ethics, in the context of counseling, involves therapists' behaving in moral, virtuous, or principled ways and taking professional actions that support clients' well-being. Guidelines regarding the ethical behaviors that should direct our decision making are outlined in our professions' various codes of ethics. The code of ethics mental health professionals use will depend on their professional background and training, and license/certification, and these codes of ethics may include those of the National Board of Certified Counselors (2012), American School Counselor Association (2016), American Association for Marriage and Family Therapy (2012), American Counseling Association (2014), American Psychological Association (2016), National Association of Social Workers (2017), American Art Therapy Association (2013), American Association of Christian Counselors (2014), and others. The ethical standards of the various mental health professions have far more similarities than differences.

Legal issues are different from ethics issues in that legal issues relate to laws and are created by the legislature (elected officials), enforced by law enforcement officers, and interpreted by officials within the legal system, and not necessarily members or associations of one's profession. Laws indicate the minimum standards of behavior that society will tolerate before legal involvement will be required. The violation of laws can result in civil (i.e., the system of law concerned with private relations between members of a community) or criminal (i.e., system of law concerned with the punishment of those who commit crimes) penalties. Licensure boards are government agencies charged with enforcing the laws that govern a given profession's practice. Licensure board members make judgments regarding mental health professionals' violations of laws.

TABLE 1.6 Level of Care Continuum

Service Restrictiveness: More ←——→ Less

Aspects of Service	Inpatient Hospitalization	Residential Treatment	Partial Hospitalization/ Day Treatment	In-Home Therapy Programs	Community Intervention
Level of Restriction	• Most restrictive and highly structured environment • Involves staying at a facility under 24-hour supervision	• Highly structured 24-hour or intermittent supervision • Involves temporarily living in a facility	• Permitted to live in the community, but highly structured environment • Involves attending an office-based program during the day	• In-home counseling • Manualized and highly structured treatment model	• Least restrictive and structured • Outpatient and/or college/school-based counseling
Primary Foci	• Safety of client and others • Symptom stabilization (e.g., reduce suicidal behavior; psychosis) • Medication titration • Discharge to less restrictive level of care once stable	• Reduce symptom severity and improve functioning • Prepare client/families for a less restrictive level of care and continued engagement in treatment	• Continue to reduce symptom severity, develop skills, and restore adaptive functioning • Prevent hospitalization and/or deterioration • Facilitate aftercare through case management	• Prevent inpatient and/or higher levels of care • Address other psychosocial/environmental concerns (e.g., school, needs) • Link clients to community resources and services	• Eliminate or reduce symptom severity to a level of minimal distress • Enhance wellness (e.g., leisure activities; friendships)
Intensity of Services	• Intensive psychiatric evaluation (i.e., risk assessment, mental status exam, medication management) • Intensive brief counseling	• Ongoing evaluation and medication management • Individual, group, and/or family counseling • Educational services provided	• Between 2 and 5 days per week at a minimum of 3 hours per day • Individual, group, family, and/or rehabilitative therapies (e.g., daily living and social skills)	• In-home visits one to three times per week • Typically 4–6 direct hours per week • Indirect hours commonly needed to collaborate with or obtain other services	• Dependent on clinical necessity • Weekly, biweekly, or monthly sessions • Individual, group, and/or family counseling • Advocacy as needed
Duration of Services	• Overnight stay to less than 1 month • Shorter periods than residential treatment	• Extended period of stay • Duration not typically prescribed in advance	• Timely discharge intended • Typically 2–6 weeks, with some programs lasting up to 6 months	• Extended period of services • Duration typically 60–120 days but can extend longer	• Time-limited service • Discharge after achievement of goals or effective functioning

Source: Kress, V. E., Paylo, M., & Stargell, N. A. (2019). *Counseling children and adolescents.* 1st Ed., ©2019. Reprinted and Electronically reproduced by permission of Pearson Education, Inc., New York, NY.

The ethical and legal considerations that pertain to therapist practice relative to theories and techniques are endless. Consider the following examples, which highlight considerations therapists regularly navigate:

- You are a college counselor and a client who has a severe eating disorder presents for counseling. You determine the client requires an intensive, structured eating disorder treatment program. However, the client refuses to tell her family about the eating disorder and insists she will only receive counseling services, with you, at the college counseling center. Does the therapist work with the client and what theory or approach should she use with this client, since the client will not receive the level of care or the type of therapy you believe she requires?
- You are a therapist who works for your local Child Protective Service's board. Using the evidence-based Systemic Training for Effective Parenting (STEP) model, you provide counseling and parenting skills training to parents who have abused their children. You are responsible for graduating the parents and attesting that they have successfully completed their skills training course. At the end of your time together, your client tells you that in her culture, parents hit their children and that she does not plan to change her approach to discipline. How do you manage this? Do you tell the courts that the parent has successfully completed the training?
- A therapist's 17-year-old client mentions she has been engaging in nonsuicidal self-injury, and her parents do not know this. She reports she has no intention of stopping the behavior. Does the therapist need to tell her parents? Should a counseling goal be the cessation of the self-injury if that is not what the client wants?
- A therapist has been working with a 44-year-old client for 5 months on a specific phobia using cognitive behavioral approaches. The client reports she is not making progress in overcoming the phobia. Should the therapist refer the client? How does a therapist know when to refer a client? What if there are no other providers in the community to refer to?

Informed Consent/Assent

It is also ethically and legally necessary for counselors to identify a theory and to communicate this theory to clients. Many state regulatory/licensing boards even require that licensed mental health providers share information with their clients about their practices so that clients can provide informed consent. Therefore, therapists are required to ensure that clients understand the nature of counseling. Clients have a basic right to understand the limitations and advantages of counseling, and how the counseling process will unfold (Remley & Herlihy, 2016). Therapists should explain the theory and counseling methods they use, and if they are learning a new theory or using an experimental approach with clients, clients should be made aware of these methods and consent to the use of these methods. The formal action of consenting to counseling—with a full awareness of all that is involved—is referred to as **informed consent**, and this consent serves as an agreement between all parties involved that they understand what will happen as the counseling experience moves forward (Remley & Herlihy, 2016).

As noted above, clients have a right to fully understand a therapist's theory and methods, as a part of informed consent. The benefits and risks of therapy procedures should be discussed with clients *prior* to their consenting to participate in the procedures. Therapists may find themselves challenged by the task of realistically portraying the therapy process without unnecessarily deterring clients from pursuing needed help, but clients do have a right to this information.

Informed consent procedures should be thorough. Clients are generally required to sign informed consent paperwork, but they typically have a limited understanding of the information on the documents. As such, clients should be engaged in a discussion of informed consent–related considerations. Ethics codes also suggest the importance of young clients playing a role in **assent**—or generally agreeing to—counseling, even though they may not be able to legally consent to participate in counseling.

Counseling informed consent generally addresses certain elements, and these include, but are not limited to:

- Limits of confidentiality (e.g., a therapist needs to call the police to have a client who is suicidal taken to the emergency room for an evaluation)
- The therapist's theoretical approach and commonly used techniques and methods as well as strengths and limitations of these techniques
- Information about the therapist's license and credentials and the government agency or organization that oversees these (e.g., a state licensing board)
- Mandated reporting requirements (e.g., child abuse reporting)
- Notice of privacy practices and clients' rights
- Procedures related to emergency situations
- Procedures related to missed appointments
- Procedures related to payments and missed payments
- Procedures related to referral if the client wants a new provider or if the therapist believes he or she is not helping the client.

When counseling youth, at the onset of counseling, therapists should clarify the relationship they will have with the youth and each person involved in counseling. Therapists should also review how they will share information, and all parties involved should understand what information will be shared with whom and under what circumstances.

Issues of consent can become especially complicated when working with a child whose parents are divorced. Some suggest that ideally, in a divorce situation, both parents should provide consent to counsel the child (Welfel, 2015). Therapists should also be aware of the rights of noncustodial parents as they generally have a right to be involved in counseling and to review their child's records (Welfel).

Competence

Competence involves possessing the knowledge, skills, and diligence required to effectively function and meet professional expectations and standards (Remley & Herlihy, 2016). Competence is not something an individual has and retains; rather, it is part of an on-going process and therapists must commit to being lifelong learners (Corey et al., 2015). The primary reason for having ethical and legal standards related to competence is to ensure the safety and welfare of clients. Therapists must possess adequate professional education, training, and supervised practice in the theories and methods they use. Over their career, therapists will learn many new theories and techniques. It is important that they receive supervised practice in using these techniques so they can build their competencies. Especially when trying new techniques, therapists should be cautious, receive supervision, and provide informed consent to clients regarding the fact that they are still learning the techniques they are using.

Assessment and Diagnosis

For most therapists, assessment and diagnosis play important roles in their day-to-day practice. Therapists use the assessment process to arrive at a diagnosis, and assessment is an on-going part of the counseling process. Assessment and diagnosis help to guide and direct counseling and often dictate the approach, the level of care, and the theories and interventions a therapist uses with a given client. For example, a school counselor may assess a student to identify why he is having a difficult time in school. If the counselor finds the student is lacking in study, time management, and test-taking skills, the counselor may apply behavioral therapy principles and teach the child strategies he can use to be successful. If the counselor suspects the student may have a more serious issue (e.g., attention-deficit hyperactivity disorder [ADHD]), the counselor may talk with the student's parents and refer them to a mental health counselor for an evaluation. The theories discussed in this text vary in terms of their emphasis on assessment as a precursor to the counseling process.

In the United States, the manual typically used to categorize diagnoses is the *Diagnostic and Statistical Manual of Mental Disorders* (*DSM-5*; American Psychological Association [APA], 2013). Mental health professionals (i.e., those in community mental health settings, hospitals, private practices) typically receive third-party payments and, to be reimbursed, are generally required to apply a *DSM-5* diagnosis to a client.

The American Counseling Association's (ACA) Code of Ethics (2014) states, "Counselors take special care to provide proper diagnosis. . ." (E.5.a.). Research suggests, however, that mental health providers frequently engage in the practice of giving a client a more severe diagnosis than symptoms warrant, and this practice is referred to as upcoding. As an example, a therapist may elect to "upcode" a child from the unreimbursable "parent–child relational problem" to a potentially reimbursable diagnosis such as oppositional defiant disorder (Kress & Paylo, 2019). At other times, therapists may engage in downcoding, or giving a client a less significant diagnosis than is warranted. In these cases, therapists may choose inaccurate diagnoses as a means of protecting clients from the stigma of certain diagnoses. Some research (e.g., Danzinger & Welfel, 2001) suggests that nearly half of therapists indicate they have changed or would change a client's diagnosis to receive additional managed care reimbursement. When therapists provide an inaccurate diagnosis, they misrepresent their work to third parties (Danzinger & Welfel).

An important concern related to diagnosis is its validity and reliability and the imperfections inherent in the diagnostic process (Eriksen & Kress, 2005; Welfel, 2015). Research suggests that the DSM system is used in an uneven fashion, and that the categories are inconsistent, overlap in terms of symptoms, and are vulnerable to social class, gender, and racial biases (Eriksen & Kress).

Risks are associated with the anticipated, unanticipated, and inadvertent release of diagnoses and diagnostic information, and clients have a right to be made aware of these risks. The risks attached to receiving a diagnosis have been well documented (see Eriksen & Kress, 2005, for a thorough discussion of this topic). They include, but are not limited to:

- Self-stigmatization, with clients coming to think of themselves as flawed or damaged
- Diagnoses used as evidence against clients during legal proceedings (e.g., custody hearings)
- Information being released to third-party payers
- Clients who receive diagnoses having difficulty obtaining their own health or life insurance due to documented pre-existing mental health issues.

With that said, receiving a diagnosis has many benefits. *DSM* diagnoses offer opportunities for clients to receive needed services via billing third-party payers, which is particularly important given the high costs of mental health treatment. In organizations that obtain government or grant funding to treat those who have a specific diagnosis (e.g., opioid addictions), only clients diagnosed with those problems may receive services from those organizations. It is important to note that many clients also find a sense of relief and validation when they have a label that can be used to describe the experiences with which they have struggled (Goodwin, 2009). Another benefit of diagnosis is that, when working from a medical model, a diagnosis can help therapists select a theory and interventions.

Because assessment and diagnosis are so central to therapists' work and associated with the application of counseling theories and methods, it is important for therapists to understand the ethical complexities associated with diagnosing. For a more thorough discussion of the ethical issues associated with the ascription of diagnoses, see Kress and Paylo (2019).

Evidence-Based Practices

Daily, mental health professionals select interventions to use with their clients. Historically, therapists have used their theory of choice to guide decision making. More recently, a shift has occurred toward using evidence-based practices (APA Presidential Task Force on Evidence Based Practice, 2006). Expressed simplistically, **evidence-based practices** (EBPs) are research-based treatments and interventions used in addressing and treating those who have various mental disorders or specific presenting problems. EPBs have been supported as effective by the gold standard for clinical health care research: randomized controlled trials (RCTs). RCTs are scientific experiments that are controlled (i.e., meaning they have a control group or a nontreatment group that the treatment group is compared to) and are randomized (i.e., meaning that a participant has an equal or random chance of being assigned to any of the treatment groups or the control group). It is a time-consuming and resource-intensive undertaking to conduct an RCT, and because of this we know little about effectively addressing many disorders.

Mental health professionals can face ethical challenges as they apply EBPs. As previously discussed, many aspects of counseling impact therapy outcomes. The therapy relationship, therapist and client characteristics, and clients' resources are just a few of the qualities that affect therapy outcomes. EBPs are unidimensional in that they do not take other factors besides research into account, and they focus only on the best *available* research. EBPs are typically detailed in treatment manuals that prescribe how many sessions will be needed to reach certain outcomes. A session-by-session cookbook approach is applied and each session has a set curriculum that is addressed.

While it is difficult to deny that research and evidence are important and should guide therapists' decision making, the use of EBPs has limitations. The most obvious one is that the reliability and validity of EBPs can be questioned. All research is flawed and limited. Even the questions asked can skew the results that are found. Another issue is that many clients have co-occurring disorders (i.e., more than one mental health diagnosis), so choosing an evidence-based approach can be difficult. Typically, to minimize the influence of extraneous variables, established evidence-based approaches have been tested on participants possessing only one mental disorder. It is known only that the treatment for the disorder worked for people who had just the one disorder. But would that same treatment work with people who have more than one disorder? And what treatment is used if someone has more than one disorder? For example, when working with a client who has borderline personality disorder and a substance use disorder, it may be difficult to know how and when to begin applying the most effective evidence-based treatments that pertain to each disorder.

Another limitation of EBPs is that this approach does not take into account relational aspects of counseling and their value. It is also reductionist, prescriptive, and mechanistic; thus, individual factors that may be critical will be lost in conceptualizing the client's situation. As an example, a number of EBPs and manualized treatments for addressing posttraumatic stress disorder (PTSD) are available, yet if a woman who has PTSD is living in an abusive relationship and has a hard time leaving, this treatment will likely be of little value to her, as she is still unsafe. Counseling that focuses on facilitating the client's safety, and exploring the factors keeping her in the relationship and how these might be altered, would likely be a better course of action in this scenario. Also, not all clients come to counseling because they want to address a disorder. Consider, for example, a man who comes to counseling seeking support in navigating a divorce. The man may meet the criteria for generalized anxiety disorder, but the issues he wants to address relate to his divorce. While there will surely be some overlap between his anxiety and divorce struggles, a manualized treatment approach would likely miss the life adjustment issues he is navigating.

EBPs may be especially useful for therapists who specialize in working with certain populations or with those who have certain disorders. Consider, for instance, eating disorders. Those who have eating disorders have the highest mortality rate of any mental disorder, and those who work with people who have eating disorders must be aware of a myriad of important, life-threatening clinical issues. The eating disorder itself must be targeted, and it will be difficult to make any progress in therapy around any other issues until the client's health and weight have stabilized (Kress & Paylo, 2019). Because of such factors, those who work with this population often use EBPs and manualized treatments.

The rising cost of health care and increasingly limited resources across all settings (e.g., schools, colleges, hospitals) means that a focus on therapist accountability is here to stay (Norcross, Hogan, & Koocher, 2008). All mental health providers need to do their best to ensure that their services are effective and efficient, and they should strive to demonstrate this success to clients and others. If we do not show success with those we serve, we run the risk of others dictating our counseling methods.

Multiple Relationships and the Therapeutic–Fiduciary Relationship Tension

The American Mental Health Counselors Association (AMHCA) Codes of Ethics (2015) states: "a) Mental health counselors make every effort to avoid dual/multiple relationships with clients that could impair professional judgment or increase the risk of harm. Examples of such relationships may include, but are not limited to: familial, social, financial, business, or close personal relationships with the clients."

Mental health providers generally receive reimbursement from the client or a third party for their services. Thus, they are, by definition, engaged in a dual or multiple relationship with clients. The purpose of a counseling relationship is to meet clients' needs, and when a therapist enters into a multiple relationship with the client, conflicts may arise. Therapists stand to benefit from this fiduciary relationship, and this may place clients at risk (Kress & Paylo, 2019). When therapists ask for and take money from third parties (e.g., grant sponsors, government payer sources, insurance companies, employers) they may relinquish control over therapeutic decisions to these third parties. For example, consider a client who has a severe alcohol abuse disorder and could benefit from a hospital detoxification, but the insurance company will only pay for an Intensive Outpatient Program (IOP). This lower level of care may not be in the client's best interest.

While some therapists receive a set salary, many therapists' paychecks depend on clients coming in to meet with them. Therapists often only get paid if they see their clients. Additionally, many therapists are experiencing rising productivity quotas from their employers and pressure to maintain billable hours. Therapists' judgment could be influenced by these pressures. Consider this actual situation: a therapist is in private practice. She charges her clients $120 an hour (cash) for each counseling session. Over the years, the therapist's caseload becomes filled with wealthy clients who have personality disorders and who use counseling, year after year, as their space to vent. Clients make minimal changes, and the therapist never suggests termination to any of her clients.

This situation raises many important questions: How do we, as helpers, ensure that we do not take advantage of our clients financially? How do we manage the complex boundaries inherent in financial transactions with clients? How can we ensure that we use our counseling theories in such a way that we help, not harm, clients? How can we encourage clients' independence and self-sufficiency?

Therapists must consider ways they can manage the therapeutic–fiduciary relationship. Therapists might consider discussing the potential risks associated with this multiple/dual relationships with clients at the onset of counseling. Honest conversations about these issues may increase clients' abilities to make informed decisions about their therapy experience.

Ethical Decision Making: Practical Suggestions

While ethical and legal considerations can feel intimidating to new therapists, they can make use of many resources to support their decision making. This section provides concrete suggestions for how therapists can handle ethics issues. Therapists are advised to do the following (Corey et al., 2015; Herlihy & Corey, 2015; Kress et al., 2019; Remley & Herlihy, 2016; Welfel, 2015):

BE THOROUGH AND THOUGHTFUL

Carefully consider and define the potential ethics problem. Determine if the matter involves ethics, legal, or clinical issues (Remley & Herlihy, 2016). Ask yourself, is this a matter that requires you to gather factual information? If you need legal information, consult with an attorney or someone at your licensing or credentialing board who specializes in ethics and gather the factual information you need to make a decision. If the matter relates to clinical decision making, consult with a supervisor or colleague. If the matter involves ethics, you will likely need to gather information and supports from multiple sources, as ethics matters are typically complex. It is important to be patient, consider the problem from multiple perspectives, and avoid settling on overly simplistic solutions (Remley & Herlihy, 2016). Understand that just because you responded a certain way in one situation previously, each new situation has a unique context and considerations.

Consider ethical principles and virtues. Determine how moral principles (e.g., nonmaleficence, fidelity, beneficence, autonomy, veracity, justice) apply to the problem, and identify the ways these principles may connect or conflict with each other. Also consider how bigger picture ethics might apply to the situation, and instead of focusing on what you need to *do* in the situation, ask yourself who you want to *be* and how your actions might impact or reflect on your sense of self (Remley & Herlihy, 2016).

Identify the desired outcome(s) and consider all possible ways these outcomes can be achieved. In any given ethical dilemma, multiple optimal outcomes are usually possible. Therapists can brainstorm all ideal outcomes and all actions that can achieve these outcomes. Therapists might list desired outcomes on one side of a page and on the other side list all actions that might facilitate the achievement of each outcome (Remley & Herlihy, 2016). Consider the implications and consequences of each option not just for the client, but also for others who will be affected, including the therapist (Remley & Herlihy, 2016).

Document communications. Maintain thorough records of counseling matters as well as any consultations and document these.

BE SELF- AND OTHER-AWARE AND SENSITIVE

Be aware of your personal attitudes, values, and beliefs. When necessary, refer when your personal characteristics may hinder your ability to help clients. In particular, be comfortable with the ambiguity associated with ethical matters, as it is rare that any ethics situation is black and white. Therapists should avoid quickly foreclosing and making snap decisions because of their discomfort with the uncertain. Instead, make decisions on ethical matters only after examining all sides of the situation. Become comfortable with the idea that ethics matters do not typically progress in a linear way, and, in fact, as you gain more context and information, your decision making will shift.

Pay attention to your feelings. When considering an ethics situation, consider your emotional reactions to the situation as well as your emotional reactions to the various ways you might respond to the situation. Poor ethical decision making is often rooted in situations in which prejudices, emotional needs, or values impact the ability to see a situation objectively (Corey et al., 2015). Consider the ways you are being influenced by fear, hurt, self-doubt, insecurity, and/or a sense of personal responsibility (Remley & Herlihy, 2016).

Work to understand clients' context and their diverse cultural backgrounds. Understand that any ethical dilemma will be colored by your worldview and cultural context. Develop an awareness of how your own worldview and cultural factors, and those of your clients, influence your values and beliefs and how they relate to a given dilemma. Consider clients' context and how a given course of action might impact not just the clients but also their family and community.

Make decisions that are in the best interests of your clients. Make decisions that are in good faith and have no malicious intent. Be sure to check yourself and your intentions. Ask yourself if a certain course of action will be in your clients' best interest, or yours.

Practice within your personal scope of practice. Everyone has a unique scope of practice. Be aware of what you are and are not competent to manage as a therapist. Practice only within the boundaries of your personal competence. Understand your professional limitations and be aware of the populations or presenting issues you may need to refer to other providers. Ask yourself if you have the education, training, and supervised experience required to work with a client around a particular issue or in a given situation.

BE TRANSPARENT AND COMMUNICATIVE

Inform clients of the limitations of counseling. Communicate an accurate portrayal of what counseling can and cannot do. Make clients aware of any potentially negative repercussions of the counseling experience prior to starting counseling.

Develop a well-articulated explanation of what you do as a therapist. Be confident in your methods and counseling practices. Know who you are and what you believe to be true as a professional, and know how this information may conflict with alternative ideas and practices. Be able to articulate the methods you use to help clients change. Be sure you have a theoretical rationale that guides your counseling approach.

Involve your clients in the decision-making process. All clients (and their guardians, if applicable) should be involved in decisions that affect their care. Demystifying the process along with asking for client input is important to facilitating good communication.

Provide thorough informed consent. At the onset of counseling, be sure to outline all possible matters that clients may need awareness of relative to your approaches and the limits of the practice or setting in which you work. Obtain all consent matters in writing. Ensure that all informed consent information has been communicated in a developmentally appropriate way and that all parties have an opportunity to ask clarifying questions. Be especially clear about how confidentiality will be handled. Understand that consent is not a one-time event, but rather an ongoing process.

BE EDUCATED

Engage with professional counseling associations. Attend conferences, seek continuing education opportunities, and read association publications to ensure you understand contemporary ethical and legal developments.

Be aware of and practice to the ethical standards of your profession. These ethics are outlined in the various codes of ethics and in the professional literature.

Be aware of the laws in the state in which you practice. Stay on top of current court rulings within your state. Each state may have unique laws related to different issues (e.g., bartering may be acceptable in one state but illegal in another).

BE SUPPORT SEEKING

Ensure you have a group of people with whom you can consult. Difficult ethics situations will emerge, and you need to have reliable, thoughtful colleagues with whom you can consult. Decisions made in isolation are rarely as good as decisions made in consultation with others (Remley & Herlihy, 2016). Your support group might include former or current supervisors, colleagues, former professors, a professional association ethics committee, or a representative at your state licensing board. In legal or court-related contexts, consultation and documentation of such consultation can also support your decision-making processes.

Maintain professional liability insurance and consult with an attorney. Access to an attorney is a resource provided through your liability insurance, so be sure to maintain liability insurance. Keep in mind that most people who have complaints filed against them with licensing boards are not charged. Also, no one is exempt from having charges filed against him or her—not even those who engage in ethical practices. In questionable cases, seek legal advice prior to initiating action. The time invested in sorting through complex issues in *advance* of action is time well spent.

Engage in self-support and self-care. Navigating ethical decisions can be stressful for counselors, and it can even contribute to counselor burn out. Education and consultation are helpful in preventing burnout (Remley & Herlihy, 2016), but counselor self-care is also important.

Throughout their careers, counselors must continually grow and evolve as ethical practitioners. What follows is an introduction to the Diaz family, who will be with us throughout the course of this book. Following this introduction, a skill development review on questioning and interviewing and a sample intake assessment complete this chapter.

INTRODUCTION TO THE DIAZ FAMILY

Because this text promotes both theoretical understanding and skill development, extensive clinical examples are provided. The clients who will become most familiar to readers are the Diaz family, introduced here. This three-person family is used to illustrate counseling approaches so that readers can become familiar with the application of interventions to both genders, to adults and children, and to people of different cultural groups. This family includes Edie Diaz; her husband, Roberto; and their daughter, Ava. Family members present a range of concerns. However, many avenues are available to help them improve their lives, as the case examples at the end of each chapter will illustrate. By studying these examples, readers will learn to apply the systems, strategies, and skills presented in the chapters.

Edie Diaz

Edie Diaz initiated the family's request for counseling. Now age 38, she is a White, Jewish woman. She was born in Brooklyn, New York, and spent her early years living with her biological parents and older sister. Her father was an accountant, and initially her mother stayed at home with the children. When Edie was 4 years old, her mother discovered that Edie's father was having an extramarital affair and insisted on a divorce. At that point, the father, who had been very close to Edie, withdrew from the family.

After her parents separated, Edie's mother found employment as a sales clerk in a department store to support her family and, with her two daughters, moved in with her parents. Edie's maternal grandparents cared for the children while their mother worked. The grandmother resented her caretaker role and was very critical of the children, especially Edie. The grandfather abused both Edie and her sister. Both grandparents are now deceased, but Edie has clear memories of the mistreatment she received and continues to experience strong resentment toward her grandparents.

When Edie was 10 years old, she was diagnosed with cancer. She had to undergo chemotherapy, which caused her to lose her hair and gain weight. Teasing from her classmates contributed to her already low self-esteem. However, a positive aspect of her illness was her increased involvement with her father. He visited her regularly in the hospital, brought her gifts, and gave her a sense of family once again. Edie and her father have continued to have contact and they currently see each other at least once a month.

Although Edie's prognosis for recovery from cancer was poor, she has been in good health since her treatment. However, her treatment raised questions about whether she could ever become pregnant and created a sense of anxiety and foreboding that never left her.

When Edie was 14, her mother remarried. Edie described her stepfather as physically and emotionally abusive. He yelled at the children, told them they were worthless, and frequently hit them. Edie dealt with this by avoiding her stepfather as much as possible. She was afraid to complain to her mother about the stepfather's behavior, thinking that her mother would become angry and punish her.

Edie continued to live with her mother and stepfather until she was 18. She had always been a good student and was able to earn a college scholarship. After college, she received a master's degree in library science and worked as a librarian until Ava's birth.

Edie had not dated much before she met Roberto. He had installed a computer system in the library where she worked and then asked Edie out for lunch. After dating for 6 months, Roberto proposed marriage, and Edie accepted. They were married when Edie was 24 and Roberto 28. Although their relationship was initially very close, with many shared interests and activities, their lengthy efforts to conceive a child had an adverse effect on the marriage. Finally, after a year of infertility treatments, Edie became pregnant and then gave birth to Ava. Despite subsequent fertility treatments, she has not been able to become pregnant a second time, a source of great sadness to her.

Edie reported marital and emotional difficulties since her initial efforts to become pregnant. When Ava was born, Edie left her job to care for her child. She missed her rewarding and successful career, but felt that she had to do everything in her power to safeguard her only child. Edie reported long-standing and increasing symptoms of sadness, loneliness, and discouragement. Since her marriage, she has gained more than 50 pounds and finds little joy or intimacy in her relationship with Roberto. Finally, last year when Ava was 9, Edie resumed work as a librarian. However, she is now experiencing strong feelings of self-doubt, guilt, and worry about Ava.

Edie has maintained contact with her mother and sister, as well as with her father. Her mother is still married to the stepfather who mistreated Edie. She finds it painful to be in his presence and never lets Ava spend time alone with him. Edie and her sister communicate frequently by e-mail but see little of each other because of geographic distance. Her sister has had a series of unrewarding relationships with men and now has an intimate relationship with a woman—her best relationship so far.

Roberto Diaz

Roberto's background is very different from Edie's. Roberto's grandparents and parents came to the United States from Puerto Rico. Roberto was born in New York City, the fifth of eight children. Although he always had frequent contact with both his mother and father, his parents separated when he was young. Nevertheless, he describes his family as warm and loving, always ready to help.

Roberto's neighborhood was rough, and he became involved with street gangs at an early age. His father taught him to defend himself with both fists and weapons. Because he was tall and stocky and had few fears, Roberto became a leader among his peers.

Roberto had little interest in school, preferring to teach himself. When he was 17, he left school to learn about computers. He received a GED as well as some specialized training in computers and now has a job he enjoys, installing Internet systems. He takes great pride in his abilities and his success in earning a good income for his family.

Roberto had two brief marriages and many relationships before he met Edie. He was impressed by her intelligence, stability, and caring and hoped that by marrying her he would find the committed and loving relationship he was seeking. He stated that, although he was very attached to his family, he was disheartened by Edie's long period of unhappiness. He reported that they were rarely intimate and no longer had a rewarding relationship. He told the therapist that he was "almost at the end of his rope" and that Edie had better make some changes fast if this marriage were to continue. At age 42, he was eager to get his life back on track.

Ava Diaz

Ava, age 10, is a tall girl who resembles her father both physically and temperamentally. She has recently been misbehaving at school, and her teacher describes her as a bully. A good student, Ava has excelled in English and history but seems to be losing interest in school. She has one close friend in the neighborhood but otherwise socializes with a wide variety of children.

Throughout this book, you will learn more about the Diaz family and their strengths and difficulties. You will also learn effective ways to help Edie, Roberto, and Ava, as well as your own clients.

SKILL DEVELOPMENT: QUESTIONING AND INTERVIEWING

This chapter reviews two important skills: asking questions and conducting an intake interview. Regardless of their theoretical orientations, all therapists use questions. They do so throughout counseling to elicit information and to promote client self-exploration, self-awareness, and self-expression.

Questions are especially important in eliciting background information and are the primary intervention used in conducting an intake interview. Many mental health agencies use a structured intake interview as a way to systematically gather information on clients. This helps therapists to be consistent and thorough in the information they seek and increases the likelihood of obtaining information that is essential to understanding each client. Although counselors in schools, private practices, and career counseling settings may not conduct formal intake interviews, those therapists, too, can benefit from bearing in mind the topics that are usually covered in these interviews, although they might elicit that information from their clients in less structured ways.

Asking Helpful Questions

Questions are a powerful intervention. They can focus counseling on core issues and provide enough information to deepen the therapist's awareness and understanding. Questions can also exaggerate the power imbalance between therapist and client; lead people to feel judged, attacked, and demeaned; and turn a counseling session into an inquisition. Consider the following example of a client statement followed by four questions posed by therapists:

CLIENT: I got a speeding ticket on my way to our session today.
INTERVENTION 1: What happened?
INTERVENTION 2: How did you feel about that?
INTERVENTION 3: Why did you do *that*?
INTERVENTION 4: How fast were you going?

Each of the four therapist interventions moves the session in a different direction, some more positive than others. The first two responses are likely to be helpful. Intervention 1 gives the client an opportunity to describe and process the incident, perhaps leading to recognition of difficulties with behavior and impulse control; intervention 2 encourages exploration of feelings, perhaps leading to a discussion of emotions related to the client's counseling. Neither intervention is judgmental, and both give the client many possible ways in which to respond. Interventions 3 and 4, however, are unlikely to have a positive impact on the therapeutic process. The third question may be interpreted by the client as suggesting that he made poor choices and perhaps deserves punishment. The fourth question focuses on a specific piece of information. Although this information may be relevant to the discussion, asking immediately for the speed may suggest that it is the most important aspect of the incident. If, indeed, the individual was going at a high speed, having to disclose that information to the therapist may be embarrassing and may even lead the client to withhold accurate information. Clearly, the nature and timing of a question are instrumental in both building rapport and achieving counseling goals.

PURPOSEFUL QUESTIONING When therapists make an intervention or respond to a client, they consider the direction in which they want to move the session and the impact they want their words to have on the client. To beginning therapists, having such a high level of awareness and direction may seem almost impossible. However, with training and experience, that sort of clinical thinking becomes rapid and almost automatic. Even new therapists should be able to look at a transcript of a counseling session and discuss the probable intention and impact of an intervention.

When formulating questions, therapists should consider:

- What information they want to elicit
- How that information will advance the therapeutic process
- What they want to focus on or emphasize with their question
- What tone they want to establish in the session.

OPEN AND CLOSED QUESTIONS Questions can be open or closed. An open question is usually designed to elicit narration, perhaps about clients' feelings, thoughts, behaviors, or experiences. Open questions encourage people to talk at greater length or depth than do closed questions and generally are more powerful and productive. Open questions are broad and give clients responsibility and flexibility in how they might respond. Open questions often begin with "how," "could," "what," and "why" but may have other openers. Interventions 1, 2, and 3 in the previous example are open questions, encouraging the individual to respond with at least a few sentences. Therapists rely much more on open rather than closed questions because they are more likely to promote client self-awareness and exploration.

Closed questions ask for a specific piece of information, often a fact, and invite a limited response of only a few words. Closed questions often begin with "who," "when," "where," "are," "do," and "is." Closed questions can make people feel as though they are on the spot. Intervention 4 in the previous example is a closed question.

However, closed questions do have a place in counseling. Questions such as "Do you have siblings?" "Would you like to schedule an appointment for next week?" and "Where were you born?" yield important information. In addition, closed questions can help narrow the focus of a session that is drifting or can help confused or highly emotional clients present clearer information. For example, the therapist might say, "It sounds like your experience of being robbed was terrifying and overwhelming. I'd like to get a better idea of what happened. When did you first realize you were being followed? . . . What did the thief say to you? . . . When did you decide to give him your money? . . . Who was the first person you told about the robbery?" Although focusing on emotions is generally helpful to clients, closed questions can help people who are overwhelmed and distraught to ground themselves in the facts before focusing on feelings.

PHRASING QUESTIONS As with most interventions, questions should be phrased so that they are clear, concise, and easily understood. They should encourage and empower, moving counseling toward its goals. In general, questions that begin with "what" and "how" promote exploration and are well received by clients, whereas questions that begin with "why" can sound negative and accusatory (as in intervention 3 on page 39).

Questions may end in a question mark or may be a statement that suggests a question, such as "Tell me more about the robbery." These implied or indirect questions should follow the same guidelines as direct questions.

PACING OF QUESTIONS An uninterrupted series of questions can have a negative impact on the counseling process. Like questions beginning with "why," this pattern can increase an individual's defensiveness and exaggerate the therapist's power. Even in an initial or intake session, therapists should not deliver a barrage of questions. Instead, other interventions, such as reflections of feeling and meaning (discussed later in this book), should be interspersed among or combined with the questions so that the session has the flow of a dialogue, preserving the collaborative nature of counseling. The following example demonstrates how a series of questions can be softened by varying the nature of the questions and including other interventions:

CLIENT: Yesterday, I got so anxious, I thought I would pass out.

THERAPIST: That must have been frightening to you. What seemed to trigger your anxiety?

CLIENT: I guess it was a telephone call I received.

THERAPIST: Telephone call?

CLIENT: Yes, from my brother. We've been out of touch for years. And then he suddenly calls to invite me to his daughter's wedding.

THERAPIST: That must have brought up all sorts of feelings.

CLIENT: You're right. I felt shocked and angry, but also relieved to hear from him. I hadn't even known if he was still alive.

THERAPIST: A mix of positive and negative emotions! What thoughts did you have about the call?

SUBJECT MATTER OF QUESTIONS Of course, just as the format and the pacing of questions have an impact on the development of the therapeutic relationship, so does the content of the questions. Although no topics are unacceptable in counseling, therapists should introduce topics when they believe a client will be fairly comfortable discussing them. For example, initiating discussion of a client's history of abuse during the first 10 minutes of an initial session usually is unwise; discussing that information with the client after some rapport has developed, however, is probably essential to effective counseling.

Questions usually should be presented so that they do not cause great discomfort. Asking questions about areas that the client is reluctant to discuss, as well as about painful memories or other highly charged subjects, should be done with extreme caution.

Questions generally yield more useful information when they focus on the client rather than on people who are not involved in the counseling. For example, asking "What thoughts did you have when your mother left your father?" is likely to be more productive than "What was your mother's reason for leaving your father?" The first question keeps the focus on the client and encourages self-exploration, whereas the second shifts the focus away from the client and asks for mind reading. Exercises at the end of this chapter are designed to improve your questioning skills and give you an opportunity to apply some of the concepts covered in this section.

Conducting an Intake Interview and Assessment

An intake interview may be a formal process that precedes the referral of a client to another therapist, a structured interview that occurs during the first session or two of counseling, or simply the informal get-acquainted process that occurs during the early sessions of counseling. Intake or initial interviews differ greatly, depending on client, therapist, and context. For example, school counselors rarely conduct structured intake interviews but, rather, gradually acquire information about their students over many brief meetings. Intake interviewers in hospital emergency rooms generally focus on the present, assessing the urgency and dangerousness of a client's symptoms. In community mental health centers, structured and comprehensive intake interviews are the norm.

The primary purpose of a comprehensive intake interview is for therapists to obtain enough information on clients' history, current situation, presenting concerns, and characteristics to conduct an assessment and formulate an accurate diagnosis and develop a treatment plan that is likely to succeed. Therapists also need to assess whether clients are at risk of harming themselves or others. Because the intake interview occurs during the first session, therapists must also orient clients to counseling (which is accomplished through role induction, discussed earlier) and must promote rapport and a collaborative therapeutic alliance.

Although clients may complete forms to provide some information, the intake process is primarily a dialogue between client and therapist. Questions are the major vehicle for eliciting information; as was discussed, however, a barrage of questions is unlikely to be productive either in eliciting important personal material or developing rapport. Therapists should follow the guidelines for formulating questions (presented in the previous section) when conducting an intake interview.

CONTENT OF THE INTAKE INTERVIEW A comprehensive intake interview and assessment generally covers the following topics, with questions, sequence of subjects, and depth of interview adapted to the client's age, concerns, motivation for help, and level of self-disclosure, as well as to the setting and the theoretical orientation of the therapist (Kress & Paylo, 2019):

- Demographic and identifying information, including age, relationship status, and living situation
- Presenting problems, including reasons for seeking help now, symptoms, onset and duration of difficulties, the impact of concerns on the individual's lifestyle, and previous efforts to obtain help
- Prior and additional emotional difficulties
- Current life situation, including important relationships, occupational and educational activities, social and leisure activities, stressors, and sources of gratification
- Ethnic, cultural, religious, and socioeconomic information
- Family background, including information on the composition of family of origin and current families, relationships within the families, parenting styles, parental role models and messages, family values, family strengths and difficulties
- Developmental history
- Career and educational history
- Medical history, including significant past and current illnesses, medical treatments, and medications
- Health-related behaviors, including use of drugs and alcohol, exercise, diet, and overall self-care.

In addition, clients should have the opportunity to provide information that was not covered in the intake interview but that they view as important.

EXAMPLE OF AN INTAKE INTERVIEW

The following intake interview is with Edie Diaz. Edie sought counseling from a community mental health center. Her therapist is a woman, about 10 years older than Edie. Assume that Edie has already been provided with information about the nature of counseling and her role as a client.

When reading this transcript, pay particular attention to how questions are used in the interview. Look at whether they are open or closed and how they are integrated with other kinds of interventions. Think about what the therapist's intent might have been in asking each question. Also, compare the content of this interview with the list of topics usually covered in an intake interview. An initial interview may not cover all topics. Are important aspects of this client's life ignored? Should these areas have been discussed in this session, or are they better left for exploration after Edie and her therapist build some rapport? Consider whether some topics or questions were particularly fruitful, and whether others had a negative impact on the session. How would you have improved this intake interview?

THERAPIST: Edie, we've gone over the informed consent forms and talked about the counseling process. Do you have any further questions about that information?

EDIE: No, it all seems pretty clear.

THERAPIST: Well, feel free to ask any questions that come up during our work together.

EDIE: Thank you. I will.

THERAPIST: I can see from the forms you completed that you are 38 years old and live with your husband, Roberto, and your daughter, Ava.

EDIE: Yes, that's right.

THERAPIST: What prompted you to seek some help at this time?

EDIE: A lot of things. It's hard to know where to begin.

THERAPIST: We can start almost anywhere, and probably one issue will lead us to talk about another. But often people have a specific concern in mind when they actually pick up the phone to make an appointment. I wonder if that happened for you?

EDIE: Well, yes, I guess it did. Ava will be 10 in a few weeks, and she and I were planning her birthday party. After she went to bed, I started to think about when I was ten. That was such a hard time for me.

THERAPIST: I can see even thinking about it brings up strong feelings. What made that such a hard time for you?

EDIE: I was diagnosed with cancer when I was 10. It was awful. I had chemotherapy, lost all my hair, even my eyebrows, and gained lots of weight. Can you imagine what that's like for a child? I felt like such a freak. And everybody was acting like I was going to die. *Almost* everybody. . . .

THERAPIST: That must have been a terrible experience for you. Very frightening.

EDIE: Yes, it was. And I'm so afraid it's going to happen to Ava. She means the world to me. I couldn't stand it if she had to go through what I went through. And I still worry about my health, too. The doctors told me years ago that I was cured, but it's hard for me to believe that.

THERAPIST: So not only are you worrying about Ava, who means so much to you, but also about yourself. . . . When you were talking about having had cancer, it sounded like someone came into your mind who had been optimistic about your prognosis.

EDIE: Yes, my father.

THERAPIST: How did that affect your experience with cancer?

EDIE: It made an enormous difference. It was the one good thing that came out of that whole mess. You see, my parents divorced when I was about 4. My mother told me my father had been involved with another woman, so she divorced him and tried to keep me and my sister away from him. I didn't see much of him for about 6 years. Then, when I was diagnosed with cancer, he insisted on seeing me. We formed a relationship for the first time. He would take me out for ice cream and talk with me about what was happening to me. No one else would. He was there for me. And we've been close ever since.

THERAPIST: Sounds like you really value your relationship with him.

EDIE: I do. I wish Roberto and Ava could have that kind of bond.

THERAPIST: We'll certainly talk more about your experience with cancer, but maybe this is a good time to talk about your family. How do you perceive the relationship between Roberto and Ava?

EDIE: It's interesting because they look alike, both tall and big boned. They even have similar personalities, but they often conflict. Both of them are pretty headstrong. Roberto is really a workaholic. If he's not actually at work, he's glued to the computer, trying out some new piece of software or surfing the Net. He's good at his work and thrives on new challenges, but he almost feels like a visitor in our home.

THERAPIST: How does that affect you?

EDIE: I feel a real sense of loss. Roberto and I were so happy when we married. It felt like we couldn't be together enough. We would take walks and go dancing and go to the beach. Anything we did together was wonderful. And then gradually things changed.

THERAPIST: Changed?

EDIE: Yes, I guess it started when we decided to have a baby. That cursed cancer came into the picture again. The doctors told me that I probably couldn't become pregnant because of all the medical treatments I had. But I was determined. We saw every specialist I could find, and after many months of trying I did become pregnant with Ava. But all that took a toll on our marriage. Even sex went on a time schedule, trying to do everything we could to conceive. It was worth it to have Ava, but things have been difficult ever since.

THERAPIST: So, having Ava was a great joy for you, but it sounds like you had to pay quite a price.

EDIE: Yes, and then when we tried to have a second child, things got even worse. Years of trying. I guess we have given up on that now. Ava is wonderful, but I still wish I had a second child.

THERAPIST: I hear your sadness and longing.

EDIE: Yes.

THERAPIST: We'll want to talk more about those feelings, too. But I'd like to broaden the picture and talk about other parts of your life. What would a typical day be like for you?

EDIE: Not very exciting. I get up early, get dressed, wake Ava and Roberto, make breakfast, and help Ava get ready for school. After they both leave, if I don't have to go to work, I might clean the house, do some shopping, plan dinner, and then I make sure to be home when Ava gets back from school. If I have any extra time, I read or watch television. Last year I went back to work part-time. I'm employed as a librarian, working two days a week.

THERAPIST: How do you feel about the way you spend your time?

EDIE: It's all right. We have a beautiful home, and I want to be there for Ava. Lately I've started to think about working more hours, though. I loved being home with Ava, but I missed having a job and being in more contact with the world. I was out of work so long that I worried about learning the new library computer systems, but I've managed so far.

THERAPIST: So for now, your time is focused on caring for your family and working part-time. Let's look at some other aspects of your current life. In addition to your father, what contact do you have with other family members?

EDIE: I see my mother fairly often. She comes over at least once a week, usually after Ava comes home from school, so they can have some time together.

THERAPIST: What is your time with your mother like?

EDIE: We get along all right most of the time.

THERAPIST: I hear some mixed feelings there.

EDIE: I just can't respect the choices my mother made, and it makes me angry. My mother remarried when I was about 14. I don't like to say this about anyone, but I really hate my stepfather. I lived with him and my mother for 4 years, and I don't think he ever said a kind word to me. Any little thing I did wrong, like leave my schoolbooks on the table, he would yell at me and hit me. And he treated my mother that way too. Still does. I don't know why she stays with him.

THERAPIST: Sounds like you have a lot of anger at your stepfather. How do you handle those feelings?

EDIE: I try not to think about him much. I rarely see him and, of course, I won't let Ava be alone with him. But things still happen that make me angry. Last week, my mother was visiting, and we were going to take Ava shopping for a dress for her party. We were heading out the door when he calls, saying he doesn't have to work late after all, and my mother should come home and make dinner. And off she goes without a second thought.

THERAPIST: So you had some bad feelings about your relationship with your mother as well as anger at your stepfather. How do those feelings affect your relationship with your mother?

EDIE: I used to tell her how I felt. And when I was a teenager, I sure let her know how unhappy I was. But it didn't seem to make any difference to her, so I just gave up. She knows how I feel, but she won't change. It's a barrier between us.

THERAPIST: It sounds like you've found a way to maintain a relationship with your mother but you wish it could be better.

EDIE: Yes, I do.

THERAPIST: That might be another aspect of your life that we could work on.

EDIE: Yes, I'd like that.

THERAPIST: Besides your mother and father, I know you have an older sister. What is your relationship with her like?

EDIE: That's another relationship that has had problems over the years. We used to be very close when we were children. She's 4 years older than I am, and she would try to protect me from . . . things.

THERAPIST: Protect you?

EDIE: We had some problems with my grandparents, but I don't want to talk about that.

THERAPIST: That's up to you. Perhaps as we continue to work together, you will want to talk about that, but that's your decision. How do you and your sister get along now?

EDIE: We don't see each other much. She lives in Las Vegas, likes the fast track. Beth's had lots of problems with men, drugs, and gambling. I try to talk to her and have helped her out with money a couple of times. Actually, she has settled down some lately. She's living with a woman. . . . I guess she's a lesbian. At first I was real uncomfortable with that, but whenever I call her, she seems okay. This sounds like her best relationship yet.

THERAPIST: So there has been a sort of reversal in your relationship with your sister. When you were younger, she tried to protect you from some difficult situations, but as adults, you have tried to protect her.

EDIE: True, but neither of us was really able to protect the other one.

THERAPIST: You wish it had been different?

EDIE: Yes, I do. But Beth *is* doing better.

THERAPIST: And that must be a relief for you. I wonder what your own use of drugs and alcohol is like?

EDIE: No problems there for me. I had all the drugs I wanted when I had cancer. I never drank much, but I had to stop drinking for so long when I was trying to become pregnant that I just never started again.

THERAPIST: You've told me about your history of cancer, but what is your current medical condition like?

EDIE: The doctors say I'm doing well, though they think I might go into menopause early because of the chemotherapy. I have gained a lot of weight though, nearly 50 pounds since before I was pregnant. I feel tired a lot . . . maybe because of the extra weight.

THERAPIST: Tell me about your sleeping and eating.

EDIE: I have trouble falling asleep most nights, and then I'm tired for the rest of the day because I get up early. My eating isn't very good, either. I try to make nutritious meals for my family, but I snack during the day . . . peanut butter, cookies, whatever is around. I know I should do something about my weight and get some exercise, but I've been saying that for years and haven't done anything. Maybe you can help me with that, too.

THERAPIST: We can certainly talk about ways to address those concerns. There are a few more areas I want to cover before we finish our session today. I know you are employed as a librarian, but I'd like to hear more about your education and work.

EDIE: I was always a good student and enjoyed school. I guess it was an escape for me from all the problems at home. The only time when school got bad was during my cancer treatments; all the kids would tease me, and I hated to go to school. I was never very social or popular, and I guess I withdrew even more after that. But I still got good grades. My goal was to get a scholarship so I could go away to college. And I did! So I left home when I finished high school and went to the state university, majored in English. I like to read, so that major made sense to me. But after I graduated, I really didn't know what to do. I worked in sales for a while, but that was definitely not right for me. After a year or so, I decided to get my master's in library science. I borrowed some money from my dad and went to graduate school. I got a good job with the New York Public Library right after I got my degree, paid my father back for the loan, and was moving up in the system when Roberto and I got married. I guess my priorities shifted then. I focused more on my marriage and trying to become pregnant, but work was still rewarding for me. I felt like I had found my niche there.

THERAPIST: So your academic work and your job as a librarian have been great sources of success and pride to you.

EDIE: Well, you're putting it more strongly than I would, but I guess you're right. In some ways, I feel more content in the library than anywhere else I've ever been.

THERAPIST: So it also is a source of comfort for you. There is almost a spiritual quality to your talk about the library, and that makes me wonder about the place of religion and spirituality in your life.

EDIE: Formal religion doesn't mean much to me anymore. Both of my parents are Jewish, but we hardly ever went to synagogue, just on the holidays. I never had any religious education either. I still put down Jewish on forms that ask for your religion, but I don't practice the religion. And Roberto isn't Jewish. His family is Catholic. They used to go to church, but he hasn't gone in years. I worry about Ava's lack of religious education, but she doesn't seem to miss it. I do talk to her about God, though. I think believing in God comforted me as a child, and I want her to have that feeling too. When she was little, I taught her prayers to say at bedtime, but I don't think she prays anymore. I gave you a long answer to your question, but I guess this is a part of my life that confuses me. I have always felt a connection to God, to a spiritual side of myself, but then I wonder if I'm being a hypocrite because I don't follow any organized religion. Maybe that's something we can talk about, too, but it's pretty far down on the list.

THERAPIST: Yes, we can get back to that. I'd like to hear some more about your childhood years. We've talked about your parents' divorce, your relationships with your sister and your parents, your stepfather, your treatment for cancer, and your enjoyment of most of your school years. What else stands out as important during those years?

EDIE: Not too much. My mother says I was precocious as a baby, walking and talking early. I had a few friends in the neighborhood, but I've always been kind of shy and was never very popular. I only dated three or four guys very briefly before I met Roberto. I guess I haven't told you about my grandparents, my mother's parents.

THERAPIST: What do you want to tell me about them?

EDIE: They took care of us when my mother went back to work after the divorce. I don't want to talk about them any more right now.

THERAPIST: All right. Let's put that topic on the shelf until you want to take it down. What other parts of your life might be important to talk about?

EDIE: I do want to mention my friend, Sandi. She lived near me and had her first child when I was pregnant with Ava. Our children played together, and we became good friends. Three years ago she moved to California. I really miss her, but we're still in touch by e-mail.

THERAPIST: So Sandi is another important person in your life, but here's another relationship that has involved loss. What else do you want to be sure to mention before we finish our session?

EDIE: I think that's about it. I didn't think I would have so much to say!

THERAPIST: Yes, you did cover a lot of ground. I can see that trying to get some help through counseling is really important to you and that you are already involved in that process. We'll get back to most of these topics again and probably also find some important areas we overlooked, but it's time to stop for today. How did you feel about our first session?

EDIE: I liked talking to you; I wasn't sure I would. Where do we go from here?

THERAPIST: Let's schedule another appointment and try to think of some goals.

REFLECT AND RESPOND

1. In this chapter, three essential characteristics of an effective therapeutic relationship were identified: empathy, unconditional positive regard, and congruence or genuineness. Therapists also instill hope in their clients. List each of these characteristics on a piece of paper. Then select at least one (but no more than three) that you believe is already a strength for you. For each, write out your rationale for believing you would be successful in transmitting that quality to a client. For example, you might perceive yourself as very empathic because you can easily engage people in conversations and are a good listener who is not judgmental. For each of the items you did not select, write down one change you might make to maximize your ability to transmit that characteristic to clients. For example, you might try to communicate more unconditional positive regard to others by deliberately acknowledging positive statements they have made about themselves. To improve your ability to communicate hope, you might focus on making fewer judgmental statements and instead look for new possibilities.
2. List some of the important perspectives or viewpoints you would bring with you if you were a client. Write briefly about how you would like a therapist to adapt counseling to meet your needs. What can you learn from this about your own work as a therapist?
3. Using your journal, write a letter to yourself as a future therapist. Imagine that you can see all your strengths as a professional and reflect on those strengths. How do you see yourself as an effective therapist? Much like setting a goal for yourself, this exercise may help you become more self-aware of what you strive to be and may help you apply those desires to your future work as a therapist. What can you take away from this exercise? How can this help you become an effective therapist?

4. Self-care is not practiced as often as it should be practiced. Therapists are encouraged to practice self-care as frequently as they can to avoid burnout. Using your journal, create a section dedicated to a self-care challenge. For 1 week, your challenge is to take care of yourself by dedicating time each day to practice self-care. Pick seven challenges that you can do each day (i.e., one challenge per day) and write about each one in your journal. Some examples may be to cook a healthy meal, read for 1 hour, go for a walk, or grab a cup of coffee. After you picked seven challenges, start the 7-day challenge and document feelings and thoughts about each day. After the 7-day challenge, reflect on what changed in your routine, how you've felt all week, and how you would like to continue the practice of self-care.

Summary

This chapter introduced the foundations of theories of counseling, the elements of a useful theory, the common factors of therapeutic approaches that make counseling effective, and the foundational counseling ingredients that facilitate positive change. The nature of a positive therapeutic alliance, therapist and client characteristics, the importance of cultural competence, and relevant ethical and legal considerations were also discussed.

The chapter started out by explaining the development of counseling theories, which gives readers a basis for understanding the context of this book. Common factors such as interpersonal skills and a strong therapeutic relationship were then discussed to help readers understand basic, yet important, counseling characteristics. Qualities of effective therapists, including authenticity, flexibility, and sensitivity to cultural differences, were also discussed. For the counseling process to be beneficial, it is important to understand not only the therapist's role but also the characteristics of the client. For example, successful clients tend to be motivated and active in their counseling process.

Therapists also value a developmental focus and believe that normal development struggles provide opportunities for growth. It is important for therapists to be sensitive and aware of their clients' developmental levels. The developmental perspective offers hope to clients because their problems are not permanent; instead, clients are inclined toward growth and health.

Therapists need to be aware of how to respond appropriately to clients whose cultural backgrounds may differ from their own. An easy-to-remember acronym, ADDRESSING, was discussed. Therapists must understand their clients' worldviews and use culturally appropriate interventions. Therapists may also refer to The American Counseling Association (ACA) *Multicultural and Social Justice Counseling Competencies* for further guidance on practical strategies on addressing multiculturalism. It is important to be mindful of our own worldviews and beliefs and how they intersect with clients' cultural experiences. If we are not aware, we can harm clients. In view of this, the chapter discussed the importance of therapist awareness, which can be used as a therapeutic tool.

Taking a strengths-based perspective has merit, and in fact, many professions strongly value this approach (e.g., professional counselors, social workers). When using a strengths-based approach, therapists pay special attention to clients' resources, strengths, and capacities. This approach facilitates a more holistic, balanced, and optimistic approach to counseling. Interview questions about clients' strengths and a focus on strengths throughout the counseling process allow clients to build on their resources, provide their own solutions, and overcome their problems.

Counseling setting is also an important consideration. Where counseling takes place, such as in a school or clinical setting, may influence the frequency, duration, and approach to counseling. The setting may also influence guidelines and requirements that therapists must be aware of. A client's level of care is particularly important for determining which setting is required, and therapists aim to provide the care most appropriate for the client's needs.

This chapter also discussed ethical and legal considerations. Ethics involves therapists behaving in moral, virtuous, or principled ways to support clients' well-being and keep their best interest in mind.

At the same time, legal issues involve following laws that represent the minimum standards of behavior that society will tolerate. Ethical and legal considerations related to the use of counseling theories and techniques include, but are not limited to, informed consent/assent, competence, assessment and diagnosis, evidence-based practices, and multiple relationships.

In the next section, the Diaz family was introduced. A Skill Development section followed. Because questioning and interviewing skills are so central to the counseling process, these skills were described and applied to a case scenario. Finally, Reflect and Respond questions were provided. Readers can use these activities to help deepen their understanding of concepts discussed in the chapter.

Recommended Readings

Duncan, B. L., Miller, S. D., Wampold, B. E., & Hubble, M. A. (Eds.). (2010). *Heart and soul of change in psychotherapy* (2nd ed.). Washington, DC: American Psychological Association.

Kress, V. E., & Paylo, M. J. (2019). *Treating those with mental disorders* (2nd ed.). Upper Saddle River, NJ: Pearson.

Remley, T. P., & Herlihy, B. (2016). *Ethical, legal, and professional issues in counseling* (5th ed.). Upper Saddle River, NJ: Pearson.

MyLab Counseling

In the Topic 11 Assignments: Multicultural, try Application Exercise 11.2: Assumptions of MCT.

Then try Application Exercise 11.3: Developing a Personal Theory with MCT and Licensure Quiz 11.3: Developing a Personal Theory.

CHAPTER 2

Freud and Classic Psychoanalysis

Learning Outcomes

When you have finished this chapter, you should be able to:
- Understand the context and development of Psychoanalysis.
- Communicate the key concepts associated with Psychoanalysis and understand how they relate to therapeutic processes.
- Describe the therapeutic goals of Psychoanalysis.
- Identify the common techniques used in Psychoanalysis.
- Understand how Psychoanalysis relates to counseling diverse populations.
- Identify the limitations and strengths of Psychoanalysis.

THE FIRST FORCE IN PSYCHOTHERAPY: PSYCHOANALYSIS AND PSYCHODYNAMIC THEORIES

The first force in psychotherapy began in the late 19th century and early 20th century with Freud's theory of psychoanalysis. Freud's theory laid the foundation for modern psychotherapy practices. Freud is considered one of the most influential theorists in psychology and psychotherapy, as he was the first to create a talk therapy. Freud's theory influenced and led to the development of many other psychodynamic theories, and all subsequent forces in counseling evolved from—and were informed by—Freud's work. Carl Jung, Alfred Adler, Karen Horney, and Erik Erikson are just some of the many theorists who used Freud's work as a foundation but headed in different directions.

Many influences contributed to the development of the first force in psychotherapy. During this period, philosophy began to address the concept of the unconscious, and this idea became popular among various professions and the general public (Schultz & Schultz, 2011). The unconscious was viewed as having a dominating influence over people without their full awareness. Within philosophy the iceberg theory, which holds that most of the mind is unconscious, or under the water, became popular. Philosophy-based theories of the unconscious, such as the iceberg theory, contributed to Freud's theory of the unconscious.

The early forms of treatment for psychopathology also influenced the development of the first force in psychotherapy (Schultz & Schultz, 2011). In ancient times, the Babylonians, Ancient Hebrew cultures, and Christianity held that mental illness was caused by evil spirits and sin; thus, magic and prayer were the main treatments for mental illness. People who had mental illness were sometimes tortured, put to death, or forced to live in jail-like institutions. Historically, the rotating chair, draining blood from or pumping blood into people, and the sedating technique were all used as a way to help people with mental illness. Around Freud's time, people became increasingly interested in finding more humane treatments for mental illness due to a growing idea that people with mental illness were sick rather than possessed by demons, and these ideas influenced Freud's thinking, which focused on people's struggles as being psychologically-based.

The Emmanuel Movement also grew in the early 1900s (Caplan, 1998; Gifford, 1997). The Emmanuel Movement was a movement that encouraged talk, individually or in small groups, as a vehicle for treating mental illness. Religious leaders facilitated this early version of therapy. The general public and medical professionals became increasingly aware of the influence of psychological factors in the development of psychopathology. Mental illness received more humane treatment, and this focus on psychology as the root of struggle and on talk as an effective way to create change influenced the development of the first force in psychotherapy tremendously.

Hypnosis and mesmerism also led to the development of the first force in psychotherapy. Mesmerism, which was later known as neurohypnology, was used to restore equilibrium in magnetic forces that were believed to reside in the body. The magnetic forces were natural sources of energy in the body that were used as a vehicle for hypnosis. These types of techniques became popular in physics and came to influence the belief that mental illness results from emotional rather than physical disturbances.

Evolutionary theory, developed by Charles Darwin, also contributed to the development of the first force in counseling and psychotherapy (Ritvo, 1990). Both share common themes, such as a focus on the influence of biological factors, a recognition of the importance of development, and an emphasis on the functions of behaviors.

In the late 19th century, sex and sexuality became a topic of interest (Makari, 2008). Scientific literature, conversation, and scientific study in both Europe and the United States increasingly began to address a topic that had been taboo. Research on sexual impulses, sexual pathology, and sexual perversions increased. Childhood sexuality also became a more popular topic. Freud's focus on sex and society's newfound interest in the topic helped Freud's theory to become popular and receive attention.

Psychodynamic theories are based on the assumption that the psyche (the mind) is active and dynamic. According to Freud, all people have unconscious motives and much of the psyche is in the unconscious, out of awareness. The most important motives for behavior are instincts, and, in particular, the sexual instinct. Psychodynamic theories also rely on the assumption that people go through stages of development. For Freud, the stages were based on types of gratification and ways to achieve the gratification.

Psychodynamic theorists also believe that the roots of current problems lie in the past and that exploration and interpretation of past experiences are essential to alleviating current concerns. Repetitive patterns and possible precipitants of current and future difficulties can be identified. For example, a therapist can better understand an adolescent who is disrespectful to his teacher by knowing whether the boy has long-standing difficulty with authority figures or whether this is an isolated and uncharacteristic incident.

Psychodynamic theory focuses heavily on past life experiences and how those influence personality and behaviors. These experiences shape people's deepest understanding of themselves and their external world. This approach places a premium on the idea that early relationships have long-term impacts on development and thus these relationships affect all aspects of an individual's life. This theory places a premium on early caretaker attachments; if clients are able to have healthy, trusting attachments with caretakers early on, they are better able to explore their world with self-confidence and less apprehension and fear. An emphasis on early life experiences is especially relevant when counseling clients. Psychodynamic theory also emphasizes defense mechanisms, and it holds that people experience internal, often unconscious conflicts. Interpersonal experiences, especially those with parents, can heavily influence a client's internal conflicts and defense mechanisms, and these then affect all future relationships. The therapist's role is to facilitate insight into an individual's inner world and to help unconscious conflicts become conscious.

According to the psychodynamic theorists, people's presenting problems are not always their most significant concerns. Embarrassment, guilt, shame, distorted perceptions, limited self-awareness, or other factors can lead clients to focus initially on minor concerns while withholding information on more significant issues. An example is a young woman who sought help in dealing with the end of a recent relationship. An overview of her history during the intake and assessment process revealed a background of abuse by her father and brother, as well as a series of subsequent self-destructive relationships.

Sigmund Freud (1856–1939) is considered the founder of psychodynamic theory, and Anna Freud, Melanie Klein, and Erik Erikson are among those who substantiated that the psychodynamic approach could directly and effectively be used with children and adolescents (Kegerreis & Midgley, 2014). While these historical giants diverged on different aspects of their theories, they all contributed in unique ways to the theory's development, and they all held in common a value of enhancing people's insight into their inner world and using a therapeutic relationship to enhance people's growth (Kegerreis & Midgley, 2015).

Therapists who use a psychodynamic approach attempt to enhance people's understanding of what influences, motivates, and impacts their behaviors, thoughts, and feelings. Psychodynamic counseling processes intend to reveal behavior patterns and generate insight into defenses and responses to internal conflicts that are held in the unconscious of clients. The major assumption in psychodynamic counseling is that symptomology or problematic experiences diminish as clients become more aware of their internal conflicts, and as these conflicts move from the unconscious to conscious.

Psychodynamic theories are diverse and their applications vary. Before we take a look at the evolution of psychodynamic psychotherapy from Freud's initial psychoanalysis, we must keep in mind that all of the approaches under the psychodynamic umbrella share the following basic assumptions (Fonagy & Target, 2009):

1. *Psychology Causation Underlies Behavior.* The psychodynamic approaches assume that conscious or unconscious thoughts, feelings, and beliefs lie at the root of psychological problems and disorders. Thoughts, motives, emotional responses and behaviors are not random but are the product of biological and psychological processes.
2. *The Unconscious Influences Us.* Not all thoughts, feelings, and actions are conscious. An active unconscious mind exists in each of us, which we might be completely unaware of. Internalized unconscious conflicts (e.g., anger, anxiety, depression) are present. The goal of psychodynamic therapy is to bring awareness to these unconscious thoughts that motivate behavior so that the individual can act in a more conscious manner. The central role is bringing the unconscious into the conscious.
3. *Interpersonal Relationships Are Internalized.* Interpersonal relationships, especially early attachment figures, are internalized and contribute to expectations about relationships and views of the self. They also help shape the organization of personality.
4. *Psychological Conflict Is Inevitable.* Thoughts, feelings, and desires cause internal conflict and have the potential to undermine healthy development.
5. *Everyone Develops Defense Mechanisms.* Defense mechanisms exist to protect the ego and help reduce anxiety.
6. *Complex Meanings Underlie Behaviors.* Complex meanings are at the root of symptomatic behaviors. (e.g., behavior can be seen as problem solving and attempts to cope). For example, an inability to be around people may reflect inner feelings of shame. These feelings may be unconscious.
7. *The Therapeutic Relationship Is Powerful.* It is a generally accepted (and empirically validated) assumption that the therapeutic relationship is one of the most important and helpful ingredients of good counseling. The development of a strong therapeutic alliance and counseling as a means of providing corrective experiences is important. In particular, transference-based thoughts, emotions, and behaviors are essential to facilitating counseling.

8. *A Developmental Perspective Is Assumed.* Psychodynamic psychotherapists work from a developmental perspective. The background is important to understanding how and why problems have developed. Strong importance is placed on early life experiences.

Although each of the different psychodynamic theories provides a comprehensive working model based on the assumptions listed earlier, no one theory provides an approach that suits everybody. Just as we grow and our lives change to meet new circumstances, counseling theories evolve and grow to meet the ever-changing (and challenging) needs of clients as well. Following is a brief introduction to the historical psychodynamic theories that will be the focus of Part 2 of this text. All have evolved during the past century since Sigmund Freud first laid the foundation.

Psychoanalysis is the term used to describe traditional psychotherapy developed by Sigmund Freud more than 100 years ago. His theory focused on biological, sexual, and aggressive instincts as the primary motivators for behavior. Alfred Adler and Carl Jung both created their own theories, as they disagreed with Freud's thinking, and these will be discussed in more depth later in this section of the text.

Ego psychology was then introduced, primarily by Anna Freud, Karen Horney, and Harry Stack Sullivan. This theory expanded on Freud's theory and relies on the assumption of ego functions as inborn and independent of biological drives. Ego psychology had a greater emphasis on ego functioning and ego defenses. Object relations theory was then introduced, primarily by Melanie Klein and John Bowlby. This theory asserts that early attachments, the internalized self-representation, and the internalized caretaker representations influence individuals as they go through their life. Instead of drive being the primary motivator for behavior, the crave for connection is what influences behavior. Based on object relations and attachment theory, relational therapy was developed; this therapy focuses on the relationships people have with others and the relationship between the therapist and the client. Self psychology, developed by Heinz Kohut, is based on the assumption that self-cohesiveness and self-esteem are the most important influencers of behavior. The development of healthy narcissism is the focus of self-psychology, rather than drives, the ego, or object relations. In this chapter, Freud's theory will be discussed, and the Neo- and Post-Freudian psychodynamic theories will be discussed in the following two chapters of this text.

CLASSIC PSYCHOANALYSIS: SIGMUND FREUD

SIGMUND FREUD (1856–1939)

Sigmund Freud, the developer of psychoanalysis, was born in Freiberg, Moravia, on May 6, 1856. Freud was the first child, born 2 years after his parents' marriage. As the firstborn and reportedly his mother's favorite (Jones, 1953), Freud had a special place in his family, although his mother gave birth to seven more children in the next 10 years. When Freud was a young boy, his 8-month-old brother Julius died. Freud recalled early feelings of jealousy and resentment toward his brother and later reproached himself when his brother died. Memories such as these probably contributed to Freud's emphasis on the formative power of early childhood experiences.

Freud's family was Jewish, and this cultural and religious background affected him throughout his life. His Jewish heritage, with its emphasis on learning and family, contributed to Freud's appreciation for study, family history, and in-depth analysis. It also influenced his place of residence, his career choice, the reception his work received, and eventually led him to flee from Austria when Hitler came into power.

When Freud was a child, the ill treatment of Jews in many parts of Europe prompted his family to move to Vienna, Austria (at that time a relatively safe place for Jews), where he spent most of his life. Freud was a diligent student, studying at the University of Vienna between 1873 and 1881, when he completed medical school. Career choices open to Jews in Vienna at that time included business, law, and medicine (Jones, 1953). Although Freud felt drawn to politics or social work, he chose medicine as the best available option. He was interested in learning about the mind and did his residency in neurology, beginning his medical career in theoretical medical work.

Freud began developing his theory of psychoanalysis in the 1880s. Growing international recognition of Freud's work led to Freud's first visit to the United States in 1909, where he lectured at Clark University at the invitation of its president, Stanley Hall. Hall was a pioneer in experimental psychology and viewed Freud's work as a major contribution. *Five Lectures on Psycho-Analysis* was eventually published. These lectures were widely read and broadened awareness of Freud's work. Freud authored many other important books, including *The Interpretation of Dreams* (1900), *Three Essays on the Theory of Sexuality* (1905), and *Introduction to Psychoanalysis* (1917). Freud is also credited with the founding of the Vienna Psychoanalytic Society, which later became known as the International Psychoanalytic Association. Freud is known as one of the most influential psychologists.

Love had an important influence on Freud's career. He became engaged to Martha Bernays, daughter of the chief rabbi of Hamburg, in 1882. To earn enough money to marry and support a family, Freud took a position at a psychiatric clinic. Over their 4-year engagement, Freud wrote more than 900 letters to his wife-to-be, providing her with the details of his daily life.

Freud married Martha Bernays in 1886 and, around the same time, opened a private practice in neuropathology in Vienna. Growing up in a large family likely influenced him to have a large family himself and to value and feel comfortable with family around him. The couple had six children during the first 10 years of their marriage.

Freud's work and his family were the most important parts of his life. Freud and Martha aimed to raise their children in an atmosphere that would minimize anxiety, limitations, and criticism, and allow personalities to develop freely. Although he often saw 10 patients a day, Freud found time for his hobbies, especially collecting antiquities, reading biographies and other literature, studying mushrooms and rare wildflowers, and traveling. He was much affected by family joys and sorrows; his letters reflect the profound impact of the military involvement of his three sons, the capture of one during World War I, the death of his daughter Sophie in 1920, and the death of a grandson in 1923.

In that same year, Freud was diagnosed with cancer, probably related to the many cigars he smoked each day. During his remaining years, he had 33 operations on his jaw and palate, which prolonged his life but caused him considerable pain. Despite this, Freud continued to see patients and to write until the year of his death. Freud's writings fill 24 volumes.

Despite additional surgery in England, Freud's cancer was deemed incurable. Because he wanted to continue writing and seeing patients as long as possible, he put off taking the painkillers that might cloud his mind until 4 months before his death. He died on September 23, 1939, leaving a legacy that many of his followers have shaped into psychodynamic psychotherapy.

INTRODUCTION/DEVELOPMENT OF PSYCHOANALYSIS

Freud's early work focused on the study of neurology. His research on the brain and spinal cord was his first notable contribution to the field. During the 1880s, he became interested in the work of Josef Breuer, a well-known physician in Vienna. Breuer used hypnosis and verbal expression to treat emotional disorders. His famous case of Anna O., a woman who experienced conversion symptoms (paralysis of limbs and disturbances of sight, eating, and speech) and dissociative symptoms in relation to the death of her father, captured Freud's attention. Freud became increasingly interested in psychological disorders and their treatment (Freud, 1938). He studied hypnosis with Jean-Martin Charcot and investigated the use of electrotherapy, baths, and massage treatments for people with emotional difficulties. Although Freud sometimes used hypnosis, none of these other strategies seemed effective to him. Experimentation led him to initiate what he called the **concentration technique**, in which patients lay down with their eyes closed while Freud placed his hand on their foreheads and urged them to say whatever thoughts arose. This process of saying whatever thoughts arise is now called free association. He used questions to elicit material and promote self-exploration. This was an early version of modern psychotherapy. Although Freud later stopped touching his patients in this way because of its erotic possibilities, he continued to emphasize the importance of patient self-expression and free association.

Freud first used the term **psychoanalysis** in an 1896 paper. His writings during the 1890s reflected growing awareness of the importance of sexuality in people's lives. He initially believed that symptoms of hysteria and neurosis were due to childhood sexual experiences, perhaps traumatic sexual abuse, such as seduction of the child by the father. A combination of difficulty in substantiating this idea and the negative reactions it elicited led Freud to change his ideas. He subsequently focused more on infantile sexuality and fantasies rather than actual sexual experiences as instrumental in determining emotional difficulties. In retrospect, Freud probably was wiser than he even knew. More than 100 years later, therapists are now well aware of the high incidence of child sexual abuse. It is likely that many, if not most, of his patients who described early sexual experiences did indeed have those experiences.

The combination of Freud's interest in understanding the human psyche and an effort to address difficulties he experienced in his own life led him to explore the meaning of his dreams and fantasies, as well as his childhood sexual feelings toward his mother and anger toward his father. His major work, *Interpretation of Dreams* (Freud, 1938), was completed in 1899 and advanced the powerful concepts that dreams reflect repressed wishes and that mental and physical processes are intertwined. Freud's ideas were largely ignored or rejected when the book was published. However, again he expressed ideas that ultimately gained widespread acceptance: the close connection between the mind and the body.

Despite the mixed reactions to his work, Freud moved forward to collaborate with colleagues who shared his viewpoints. In 1902, Freud suggested to Alfred Adler (discussed in the next chapter) and several others that they meet to discuss Freud's work. This meeting evolved into the Vienna Psycho-Analytical Society, which met weekly at Freud's home. In 1910, Freud designated Carl Jung as president of the International Psychoanalytical Association. Adler and Jung eventually separated from the psychoanalytical association and went on to make their own important contributions to psychotherapy.

By this time, Freud had replaced hypnosis with free association in his work and encouraged analysts to experience their own analysis, a requirement still maintained by programs that train psychoanalysts. He also believed that patients needed to lie on a couch during therapy, with the therapist out of view, to relax them, facilitate self-expression, allow transference reactions to develop, and enable analysts to think freely without worrying about their nonverbal messages. Patients were told never to withhold any thoughts so that Freud could understand the unconscious, often reflected in sexually related fantasies stemming from early childhood experiences, that had produced symptoms.

Freud's interests broadened during the war years. He became interested in what was then called shell shock or traumatic neurosis, symptoms that developed after exposure to war experiences. The primary treatment for this disorder had been electrical stimulation of the skin and muscles. According to Freud, psychoanalysis, not electricity, was the proper treatment for this disorder, which he believed reflected an emotional conflict between the desire to escape and the need to honor one's sense of duty. Freud's thinking paved the way for our modern understanding of post-traumatic stress disorder.

Freud also became interested in understanding sexual orientation, writing, "homosexuality is assuredly no advantage, but it is nothing to be ashamed of, no vice, no degradation, it cannot be classified as an illness" (Jones, 1957, p. 195). Here, too, Freud's ideas were very advanced—not until the 1970s did the American Psychiatric Association and the American Psychological Association officially declare that same sex attraction was not a mental disorder. Freud was less insightful in his understanding of women, a controversial aspect of his theory. This is discussed more later in this chapter.

KEY CONCEPTS

Freud began his work as a theoretician, a person who forms or develops a theory, and it is through his comprehensive theory of personality that he has made his major contributions. This section reviews the most important aspects of his theory, including his concepts of human nature, the three structures of the personality, life and death instincts, how personality develops, levels of consciousness, dreams and the unconscious, and defense mechanisms.

Biological Processes: Attachment and Development

Freud placed great emphasis on the influence of biology and of early childhood experiences. He believed that, because of their biology, people go through predictable stages of psychosocial development and must struggle to find a balance between their strong sexual drives and their need to behave in socially acceptable ways. According to Freud, biological processes are mediated by early patterns of attachment, as well as by how people negotiate the stages of development.

Freud also recognized the importance of context. For example, he viewed people as seeking to win love and approval by acting in ways that reflected the dictates of their families and societies. This perspective is compatible with current thinking on diversity and multiculturalism.

Freud has been criticized for taking a deterministic stance, emphasizing irrational and instinctual forces in shaping people. Certainly, he viewed those forces as important, but perhaps the essential message in his work is that people need not be the victims of biology. Rather, they can use psychotherapy and other sources of help and personal growth to gain insight, lessen the power of the unconscious, and free themselves to make conscious and healthy choices. Understanding early development, as well as the pressures of the libido and the superego, and strengthening our egos can enable people to lead the sorts of lives and have the types of relationships that they desire. Freud himself achieved much both personally and professionally, apparently reflecting his own success in balancing the competing pressures inside him.

Personality Structure

According to Freud, the personality comprises three systems: the id, the superego, and the ego. These structures often overlap and intertwine and are not discrete entities, although each has distinctive properties. Keep in mind that Freud's concept of the id (the biological component), the ego (the psychological component), and the superego (the social component) is simply a sort of map designed to clarify the nature of the personality. Just as states and countries are separated by artificial boundaries, so are these structures of the personality separated into artificial constructs. In reality, they operate together as the internal forces that form our personalities. However, using this theoretical structure can facilitate understanding of strengths and areas of difficulties in a personality.

THE ID The **id** is the first system of the personality. Present at birth, it encompasses all of the inherited systems, including the instincts, and is largely unconscious. The id derives its energy from bodily processes and is in close touch with the needs and messages of the body, seeking to satisfy them when possible. The id is subjective and emotional and, in its pure form, is not moderated by the external world. Simply put, the id wants what it wants when it wants it. The id, like the infant in which it originates, is intolerant of tension, pain, and discomfort and seeks to avoid them through **the pleasure principle** (pursuing pleasure and gratification). It is demanding and its needs, rather than logic, morality, or the constraints of society, determine the direction of its wants. The pleasure principle leads people to engage in **object cathexis**, which is the investment of psychic energy or libido in objects outside the self. The id also contributes to **intrapsychic processes**, which are impulses, ideas, conflicts, or other psychological phenomena that occur within the mind.

THE SUPEREGO The **superego** can be thought of as the opposite of the id. The superego is a sort of rigid conscience that internalizes the rules and guidelines of an individual's world. Messages from parents, teachers, and society, as well as racial, cultural, and national traditions, are important contributors to the development of the superego. On the one hand, when an individual follows the idealistic dictates of the superego, the individual typically feels proud and righteous but may sacrifice pleasure and gratification. On the other hand, when the individual ignores the superego, shame, guilt, and anxiety may result. The superego serves an essential function in curtailing the drives of the id; but like the id, the superego is too controlling and extreme in its directives.

THE EGO The **ego**, like the superego, becomes differentiated from the id as the child develops, although energy from the id provides the power for both the ego and the superego. The ego is not present at birth but evolves as the baby realizes its separateness from the mother.

The ego is aware of both the pressures of the id and the constraints of the superego and seeks to moderate both while still meeting their needs. The ego is a mediator and organizer. The ego can have control over the id to keep id impulses out of consciousness, which is called **anticathexes**. The **reality principle**, which allows gratification so that environmental demands can be met, guides the ego and has considerable power; it can effect changes in the environment, postpone or suppress instinctual demands, and encourage sound moral judgment and flexibility. In Table 2.1, a brief summary of the structural model of personality is provided.

TABLE 2.1 Summary of the Structural Model of Personality

Aspects of the Personality	Overview	Definition
Id	"Instincts"	The id, which is present from birth, comprises the basic instincts and drives of the human being. These basic instincts are often irrational and impulsive and are firmly rooted in the unconscious. Ruled by the pleasure principles, the id seeks immediate gratification.
Ego	"Executive Mediating"	The executor of the mind, the ego is the only part of the personality that is in direct contact with reality. The ego functions as a means of mediating the impulses of the id and the inhibitions of the superego. The ego resides in the conscious mind and can be thought of as the logical mind; it works to appease the id in a socially acceptable way.
Superego	"Conscience"	The judge of the mind, the superego is the part of the personality that internalizes values and houses the moral code. In young children, the superego has not totally formed, but in older children and adolescents, it is firmly at work judging and pushing against id impulses.

Life and Death Instincts

Freud believed that people have both life instincts and death or destructive **instincts**. Life instincts, reflecting the needs of the id, lead us to pursue pleasure and avoid pain. The **libido**, present at birth, is an important aspect of the life instinct. This was originally defined by Freud as sexual desire, but its meaning has been broadened over the years to refer to energy and vitality, a zest for life. A desire for sexual fulfillment is only one facet of the life instinct, but it is an essential one because it leads people to procreate and continue the human race. The life instinct (*eros*) and the death instinct (*thanatos*) are in opposition to each other, much like good and evil. According to Freud, the death instinct has its origins in aggression and other destructive forces. Freud's concept of a death instinct, or a "death drive," was a longing to return to the state of nonexistence that we experienced before we were born (Higdon, 2012). The idea was controversial in his time and has not received much support over the years. Even so, self-defeating behaviors, repeating painful patterns, self-inflicted wounds, and death wishes are all internalized aggression, which indicates masochism and self-loathing. If the energy created by the death instinct is directed outward, it results in violence and aggression. Based on Freud's definition of a death instinct, it appears that at least for some people, a drive toward self-destruction does exist.

In *Civilization and Its Discontents* (1930), Freud explains the dualistic model in terms of civilization. The life instinct strives to unite people, families, and nations, whereas the death instinct results in an opposite pull of destruction. Freud believed that human aggression is innate, but it can be channeled into nondestructive activities (e.g., sports, power, positive energy). The death instinct is Freud's attempt to explain the human tendency toward destruction that overrides the pleasure principle. Recognizing the possible presence of this force can help us to understand human behavior, particularly the compulsion to repeat, which results in the development of patterns of behavior.

Stages of Development

Freud believed that people develop according to predictable stages, referred to as **psychosexual stages of development**, with those occurring during the first 5 years of life being the most important. The importance of inborn **drives** (physiological state of tension that motivates an individual) during those early years is a major factor in determining later personality development. Understanding the relationships between children's bodily functions and the subsequent personality development of children can help define healthy parenting as well as provide insight into emotional difficulties that may stem from early developmental problems.

THE ORAL STAGE The **oral stage** makes up the first year or so of a child's life. The mouth is the most important zone of the body for the infant, with sucking and eating providing the nurturance that will sustain the child's life during the oral-incorporative phase. Biting is a way for the child to express aggression during the subsequent oral-aggressive period. The mouth also becomes the child's first erotic zone. Freud believed that developmental problems at this point could later manifest themselves in symbolic and sublimated forms through symptoms such as gullibility (swallowing anything), overeating, and argumentativeness (oral aggressiveness).

THE ANAL STAGE Freud termed the second stage of development, between the ages of 18 and 36 months, the **anal stage** because of the importance of toilet training and the process of elimination during those years. In this second stage, the focus of gratification shifts from oral functions to the social pleasure of impressing the parents and the physical pleasure of emptying the bowels. According to psychoanalytic theory, **fixation** (being "stuck" in any stage of psychosocial development) can lead to different personalities. Parents who use punitive and restrictive means to develop children's bowel and bladder control are likely to promote stingy, compulsive, controlling, and withholding characteristics in their children. This is called anal retentive (i.e., one who hates mess and is obsessively tidy, punctual, and respectful of authority). Parents who reward and praise their children lavishly for appropriate elimination are likely to foster creativity and an anal explosive personality (i.e., one who is messy, disorganized, and rebellious). Feelings about the body and its functions are also shaped during these years.

THE PHALLIC STAGE The third stage, between ages 3 and 6, is known as the **phallic stage**. According to Freud, this complex stage is strongly related to our adult sexual relationships. During these years, feelings of pleasure become associated with the genitals, and masturbation and sexual fantasies develop.

Freud believed that at this age, children harbor unconscious sexual desires for the parent of the other gender, along with an unconscious wish to eliminate the parent of the same gender, perceived as standing in the way of the child's desires. In boys, this is termed the **Oedipus complex**, referring to a man who, according to the literature of ancient Greece, unknowingly married his mother. According to Freud, fear of retribution from the father causes boys to develop **castration anxiety** (the fear of losing or having one's penis damaged), which, in turn, allows them to repress their desire for their mother and resolve their feelings appropriately through identification with the father.

In girls, the parallel situation is referred to as the **Electra complex**, named after a woman in Greek literature who had strong feelings of love and devotion toward her father. Freud hypothesized that the female equivalent of castration anxiety is **penis envy**, in which girls become jealous and resentful because of their lack of a penis. He believed that girls, like boys, typically resolve this phase by identifying with their same-sex parent.

Contemporary psychoanalysts acknowledge the possibility that a girl may experience penis envy but also believe that a boy may have womb or breast envy. However, they downplay the importance of both patterns, viewing them as only one of many internal and external experiences that may be important in children's development. In addition, although Freud saw many parallels between the ways in which both boys and girls passed through this stage, many modern theorists now emphasize that, for both genders, the mother is typically the first love and source of nurturance. Mothers are, of course, the same gender as their daughters but not as their sons. Most girls, then, must shift the primary source of their attachment from women to men, while most boys do not make this shift, probably an important difference in their development of love and attachments.

Many aspects of emotional development evolve during the phallic years, including self-esteem and self-image, sexuality, need for love and approval, feelings toward authority figures, and sense of initiative.

THE LATENCY STAGE Freud viewed the time between ages 6 and puberty as a relatively quiet period in a child's sexual development; therefore, he called these years the **latency stage**. Sexual drives become less important, while social interests increase. Children turn outward, form relationships, progress through school, and develop rewarding hobbies and activities. Emotional development focuses on their ability to take on and succeed in new challenges and endeavors and to set and achieve realistic goals. Children who successfully navigate this stage typically develop feelings of empowerment and have initiative, whereas those who cannot deal with the demands of this stage may experience low self-esteem.

THE GENITAL STAGE The final stage in Freud's model is the **genital stage**, which follows the latency stage and continues throughout the lifespan. During this stage, adolescents and adults solidify their personal identities, develop caring and altruistic feelings toward others, establish positive loving and sexual relationships, and progress in successful careers. In this stage, puberty takes place and the sexual instinct is directed toward romantic relationships. Each stage builds on and integrates the growth and learning of the previous stage and ideally results in the development of an emotionally healthy adult. See Table 2.2 for an overview of each of Freud's psychosexual stages of development.

Levels of Consciousness

Most people have few, if any, memories of times before the age of 3 or 4. In addition, we all have had experiences we either cannot recall at all or that only come into awareness when something reminds us of them, triggering their recall. What has happened to those memories?

According to Freud, we have three levels of consciousness: the conscious, the preconscious, and the unconscious. The **conscious** is material in awareness, always available to us. The **preconscious** holds information that may not be part of current awareness but that can be readily accessed. This material may be benign, such as the memory of an individual we knew years ago but do not think of until we see her again in the grocery store; or it may be aversive, such as the memory of a car accident that returns to us each time we hear the screech of car brakes applied in a hurry. The **unconscious** holds memories that are highly charged, including repressed drives and impulses (such as a child's sexual feelings toward a parent) and recollections of experiences that may be too painful or unacceptable to be allowed into the conscious or preconscious. Freud believed that the unconscious held many more memories than were in the preconscious or the conscious. Psychoanalysis can bring memories from the unconscious into the conscious. However, without benefit of therapy, those memories may either remain in the unconscious or emerge into consciousness in symbolic or distorted ways, perhaps via dreams or symptoms.

For Freud, errors, omissions, slips, and poorly performed tasks also had latent meaning, and the term **Freudian slip** has come to mean a misstatement that reveals an unconscious wish or feeling. For example, a man who was attracted to his next-door neighbor, a woman called Lou, left her a note about a package that had been delivered to him by mistake. However, he addressed the note to "Dear Love" rather than "Dear Lou."

Defense Mechanisms

Many of us have experienced frequent and painful episodes of anxiety. According to Freud, people have an innate drive toward reduction of tension and anxiety. Freud was particularly interested in what he labeled **signal anxiety**, the anxiety that results from a conflict between internal wishes or

TABLE 2.2 Freud's Psychosexual Stages of Development

Stage	Timeframe	Description
Oral stage	Birth to 18 months	Pleasure is associated with the mouth (e.g., sucking, biting, breastfeeding).
Anal stage	18 months to 3 years	Pleasure is associated with the anus (e.g., defecating). Youth become better aware of their individuality and their ability to self-control.
Phallic stage	3 to 6 years	Pleasure is concentrated on genitals (e.g., rubbing and/or masturbation) and the increased awareness of sex differences can create internal conflict such as jealousy, rivalry, and/or fear (e.g., Oedipus complex or Electra complex).
Latency stage	6 to puberty	The libido becomes dormant or even hidden during this time, and youth focus on acquisition of skills, hobbies/play, and new areas of knowledge.
Genital stage	Puberty through adulthood	This stage encompasses the process of sexual experimentation and successful establishment of a loving, monogamous relationship.

drives and constraints that come from either internalized prohibitions or external reality. He believed that signal anxiety would automatically trigger defense mechanisms, usually learned during early childhood and developed as a way of dealing with inner conflict, anxiety, pain, shame, sorrow, and other negative emotions. **Defense mechanisms** are ways of thinking or behaving that protect us from conflict or anxiety, and they help the ego fight off instinctual outbursts of the id or warnings that come from the superego.

Everyone has defenses. Some are healthy, mature defenses that promote adjustment and enable people to transform undesirable wishes into ones that can be fulfilled. For example, **sublimation** is a defense mechanism that can change a self-destructive sexual desire into the drive to create a work of art. In contrast, some defenses distort reality and interfere with efforts to build relationships. An example is **splitting**, in which people view themselves and others as being either all good or all bad and vacillate from idealization to devaluation of themselves and others. The defense mechanism people use at a particular time depends on their level of development and the degree of anxiety they are experiencing.

The literature identifies and describes more than 40 defense mechanisms. See Table 2.3 for an overview of common defense mechanisms.

TABLE 2.3 Common Defense Mechanisms

Healthy, Adaptive Defense Mechanisms	
Defense Mechanism	**Definition**
Affiliation	Turning to others for help and support, but retaining responsibility for one's own difficulties
Altruism	Deriving satisfaction from investing heavily in helping others
Anticipation	Reducing anxiety by considering the probable consequences of future events and finding ways to address them effectively
Humor	Focusing on the amusing aspects of situations
Sublimation	Redirecting potentially harmful emotions or impulses into socially acceptable ones
Conscious Suppression	Intentionally avoiding paying attention to nonproductive and troubling issues, experiences, and emotions
Unhealthy, Maladaptive Defense Mechanisms	
Acting Out	Exhibiting negative behaviors rather than using thoughts, words, or emotions to deal with a situation
Avoidance	Refusing to deal with troubling situations or experiences
Denial	Refusing to acknowledge an aspect of reality that is evident to others
Displacement	Transferring strong feelings from the situation in which they originated to a less threatening situation
Dissociation	Temporarily disconnecting from a situation via memory loss or loss of awareness
Idealization	Exaggerating the positive and ignoring the negative aspects of a person or situation
Identification	Modeling oneself after another person to gain approval
Intellectualization	Avoiding emotions by focusing on thoughts and abstractions
Passive aggressive	Expressing anger and hostility in indirect ways (e.g., "accidentally" breaking a person's heirloom vase)
Projection	Attributing one's own unacceptable thoughts, emotions, or actions to another

TABLE 2.3 (Continued)

	Unhealthy, Maladaptive Defense Mechanisms
Defense Mechanism	**Definition**
Rationalization	Justifying one's choices in self-serving but invalid ways
Reaction Formation	Replacing unacceptable thoughts and emotions with their opposite to overcompensate
Regression	Reverting to a lower developmental level in thoughts, emotions, and behavior
Repression	Relegating disturbing thoughts and feelings to the unconscious rather than dealing with them effectively
Resistance	Blocking memories, insights, or avenues to positive change
Somatization	Channeling conflicts into physical symptoms
Splitting	Perceiving the self and others as either all good or all bad

The study of people's use of defense mechanisms is a fruitful line of inquiry today and provides insight into ways in which therapists can help people cope with anxiety and other emotional difficulties.

THE THERAPEUTIC PROCESS

Psychoanalysis, as performed by Freud as well as by contemporary therapists, is usually a long-term, intensive process. People are typically seen for counseling from two to five times a week for 3 to 5 years. During Freud's time, most clients who sought analysis were women. They would lie on a couch with Freud seated on a chair at the head of the couch outside the client's field of vision. Through the use of free association and transference feelings toward the therapist, the client would do the work of psychoanalysis, to make the unconscious conscious (Freud, 1957).

Psychoanalysis is a fluid process of discovery (Luborsky, O'Reilly-Landry, & Arlow, 2008). Clients may also experience **catharsis**, which is when previously repressed feelings are expressed. Therapists must utilize assessment, establish a therapeutic alliance, deal with resistance, understand transference and countertransference, and be well versed in psychoanalytic counseling interventions to aid clients in meeting their therapeutic goals.

Therapeutic Goals

The overall goal of psychoanalysis is to achieve equilibrium between the id and the superego. The ego must be strong enough to handle the demands of living and not be overwhelmed by feelings of guilt, shame, or anxiety (Austad, 2009). It is through the process of **working through**—exploration of the unconscious and of defense mechanisms—that the ego is transformed. Strengthening the ego encourages behavior that is realistic rather than behaviour derived from cravings and urges. Another main goal of psychoanalysis is to bring the unconscious into the conscious. Other important goals are to improve overall functioning, decrease symptoms, and reduce conflict. Working through childhood experiences in particular is important. Specifically, childhood experiences are discussed, interpreted, analyzed, connected to present moment concerns, and reconstructed. Instead of solely a reduction in symptoms or a change in behavior, psychoanalysis aims to change the clients' character by delving into the past. A greater understanding and new feelings resulting from these new understandings is the aim of psychoanalysis. Specific counseling objectives include the following:

- Improving the ego's control over irrational and harmful impulses and instincts
- Enriching the nature and variety of the ego defense mechanisms so that they are more effective, mature, and adaptable
- Encouraging development of perspectives that are grounded in an accurate and clear assessment of reality and that promote adjustment
- Developing a capacity for healthy and rewarding intimate relationships along with the ability to express oneself in rewarding ways
- Reducing the perfectionism, rigidity, and punitiveness of the superego.

Therapist's Function and Role

Therapists typically adopt a **"blank-screen" approach**, which is an anonymous stance to facilitate transference, which allows clients to project feelings for another person onto the therapist, thereby helping them to work through unresolved feelings.

Therapists encourage clients to share openly and freely their thoughts, feelings, experiences, and history. Although clients do most of the talking in psychoanalysis, therapists actively guide the sessions in meaningful directions and promote the uncovering of repressed material. They can be described as listening with a third ear attuned to underlying meanings, symbols, contradictions, and important omissions that may point the way to unlocking the unconscious. Questions, interpretations, and free association are common interventions that psychoanalysts use in their work.

Therapists are continuously using analysis to help clients gain freedom to love, work, and play. Through interpretation, establishing a strong therapeutic alliance, and listening empathically, therapists can help clients to gain self-awareness, manage anxiety in healthy ways, and acquire control of unhealthy behaviors. Therapists are also responsible for paying attention to and dealing effectively with resistance.

Relationship Between Therapist and Client

Transference and countertransference are important aspects of the therapeutic relationship. In **transference**, clients project onto the therapist the characteristics of another individual, usually a parent, and react to the therapist as though the therapist really does possess those characteristics. Transference involves a distortion or misperception of the therapist and is not a direct response to the way the therapist actually is. The unobserved and neutral psychoanalyst is more likely to elicit transference reactions than is a therapist who engaged in self-disclosure and interacts more actively with clients.

Transference can be positive, negative, or mixed. For example, clients may project onto the therapist the seductive but loving traits of their mother (mixed), the angry and rejecting attitude of their father (negative), or the warm and nurturing characteristics of their grandmother (positive). Freud saw the establishment of transference as a key component of successful counseling. Processing clients' working through of the transference is an important source of personal growth.

Three stages are involved in the lengthy process of working through a transference. Once the transference develops, it is further established and explored to elicit repressed material. Gradually, the original dysfunctional pattern re-emerges, now in terms of the transference to the therapist. Finally, the origins of the transference are understood and resolved, strengthening the ego and freeing the client to relate to others in healthier ways.

In classic psychoanalysis, **countertransference**, the therapist's feelings about the client, were to be avoided. Clearly, therapists were instructed not to respond to a client's transferential feelings of love, as in the case of Anna O., a client who developed an erotic transference to Freud's colleague, Breuer (Freud, 1915). Freud wrote that therapists should recognize the distinction between the client's transference and their own reactions to the client, which spring from the therapist's unresolved issues. Therapists should not assume that they are too skilled or insightful to develop countertransference reactions, but should carefully monitor any strong emotional reactions they have to clients for the possibility of countertransference. The importance of therapists having an awareness of their reactions is one of the primary reasons personal analysis is a required part of training in psychoanalysis.

A major change has occurred in how psychodynamic therapists think about the role of the therapist. No longer is the analyst aloof and anonymous, providing a blank slate for the client's projections. Rather, contemporary psychoanalysis assumes that therapists and clients each view the world through their own cultural lens, backgrounds, and biases. As a result, the therapist cannot be objective and neutral. Together, they collaborate in determining whether and what kind of therapy is appropriate and how it will be structured.

THERAPEUTIC TECHNIQUES AND PROCEDURES

Extensive supervision and training are required to master the rich array of counseling strategies associated with classic psychoanalysis. This text presents an overview of these strategies, but readers should bear in mind that additional training is needed before they can be used skillfully.

Free Association

Freud used many approaches to access repressed material, including analysis of dreams, transference, and free association. The process of **free association** reflects the most important rule of psychoanalysis: People should say whatever comes into their minds without censoring or judging. Free association is the automatic linking of one thought to another, which we all experience. We may hear a song that reminds us of the dance we attended when we first heard it, reminding us of our date for the dance, reminding us of the rage a parent expressed when we returned home after curfew, reminding us of the beatings we received from that parent, reminding us of our repressed impulse to attack the parent. A song, then, through a chain of association, can bring up strong feelings of anxiety because of its link to emotions that we have been unable to accept and process successfully. Freud encouraged free association in his patients to facilitate their recall of past material and release intense feelings. Blocks in the chain of association are another source of information about repressed material.

During free association, therapists look for continuity of emotions, thoughts, and behaviors, which can be displayed in the clients' interactions, play, resistance to the counseling process, as well as in the client–counselor relationship (i.e., transference). Therapists should attempt to look beyond the surface level of the client's behaviors and verbalizations to examine the underlying connectedness of the client's mental processes (e.g., emotions, thoughts). Therapists can use three pragmatic ways to further assess and explore these underlying processes, which include looking for discrepancies, omissions, and excesses (Shapiro, 2015):

- **Discrepancies** are the observed disagreement between things that are said and/or done. For example, a child might state she does not care about a fight she had with her best friend in school, yet she appears to perseverate over it all night and even become emotionally reactive when an adult brings the situation up in conversation.
- **Omissions** are things that were not said, done, or felt, but likely should have been said, done, or felt, given the situation. An example is a child who experiences violence and trauma within his home yet says everything at home is "great." The child may refuse to talk about these situations and displays avoidance behavior to avoid the expressions of anxiety, sadness, or anger.

- **Excesses** are overreactions, overdramatic emotions, or extreme behaviors related to benign events that do not justify such behavior. Clients may find their overreactions to these events difficult and/or threatening to discuss. For example, a child has a tantrum and yells at the therapist, "I hate you, I hate you" after the therapist asks the child "to please return all of her play toys" to the assigned places at the end of a session.

From a drive theory perspective, therapists are continually exploring and assessing these emerging patterns within clients' emotions, thoughts, and/or behaviors (e.g., clinical symptomology and presentation) and attempting to understand and explain the clients' difficulties or concerns as an internal conflict of personality structures (e.g., id, ego, superego), thus moving the unconscious into the conscious by increasing insight.

Analysis and Interpretation

The most fundamental techniques in Freudian psychotherapy are analysis and interpretation, designed to promote awareness and insight. Whether his focus was on dreams, slips, transference, free association, or symptoms, the tools of analysis and interpretation enabled Freud to bring unconscious material into consciousness. Once this had occurred, people could gain insight into and work through previously repressed material and make connections between that material and their present difficulties, resulting in positive change.

Psychoanalysis is the process of thoroughly exploring and understanding the unconscious representations in the material people present in counseling. Analysis also involves understanding resistance, transference, and dreams. For example, in analyzing a dream, Freud would explore with the client the meaning of each item in the dream. The individual would be encouraged to free-associate to the dream, to talk about both the emotions reflected in the dream and those experienced upon awakening and recalling the dream, and to discuss events in the recent past that might have triggered the dream. Emphasis would center on the wish fulfillment represented by the dream and on suggestions of repressed, unacceptable sexual or other urges.

Interpretation is the process of elucidating the unconscious meaning of the symbols in material that clients present and of linking those new insights to their present concerns and blocks. Cognitively and emotionally working through material previously housed in the unconscious enables people to understand the influence the past has had on them and to use the mature defenses and strategies of the ego to make choices that are wiser and freer of the negative impact of unconscious material.

Within the psychodynamic approach, a major catalyst for change is insight that increases a client's self-understanding. Inherent in this approach to counseling, insight is a significant enough catalyst to increase self-understanding, thereby resolving symptomology (e.g., anxiety, disruptive behaviors). Therapists aim to increase an individual's self-understanding or insight through accurate interpretations. An interpretation is a comment or statement that brings an unconscious process to the individual's attention. More than paraphrasing or a reflection of feeling, interpretation is helping a client to understand something that he or she did not know or was not aware of previously.

Interpretations link the behaviors, thoughts, and feelings within a client's awareness and the client's unconscious: (1) defenses, (2) wishes, (3) past experiences, and/or (4) dreams (Kernberg et al., 2012). Interpretations can be shared in a number of ways, including through (Kernberg et al., 2012):

- *Direct observation*—"You look irritated today."
- *Indirect presentation*—During imaginary play with the therapist, the therapist says, "Sophia, the lion, seems to be really sad because no one asks her to play today. What should Sophia do next?"

- *Using the client–therapist relationship*—"I wonder if you are thinking of me as a strict teacher or a parent who only asks you all the questions?"
- *Revealing the therapists' perspective*—In a game in which the client is cheating, the therapist can say, "If I was a kid playing this game, I wouldn't want to play anymore because I'm feeling angry." Thus, the client may realize that others may avoid playing with him because of these antagonistic behaviors.

When presenting interpretations or even confronting defense mechanisms, a therapist should consider working within the client's perception of reality, demonstrating the defense mechanism while interacting with the client, or posing a question rather than being direct.

Insight becomes the catalyst for change especially when clients are armed with why they feel the way they do, or why they do what they do. These insights often help clients feel less confused, irritated, and out of control. From a psychodynamic perspective, once clients are able to think consciously about a previous unconscious process, they are able to utilize a more mature ego to deal with the now known internal conflict. Expressed simply, insight is not compatible with defenses, because as insight increases, defenses decrease (Lacewing, 2014). Therefore, the therapist's interpretation can be the catalyst for clients' increase in self-understanding and movement toward change. Clients can then apply their more developed, rational, and adaptive thinking to the long-buried conflict.

Dream Analysis

According to Freud, there is no more direct path to the unconscious mind and its content than through the path of dreams (Freud, 1910). Therefore, dream analysis has historically been an essential part of Freud's drive theory. In **dream analysis**, clients recount the latent and manifest content of the dream. Manifest content is the actual content of the dream, such as a fox walking through the woods or a bearded lady playing a steel drum. Conversely, the latent content is the underlying pattern and meanings of the content interpreted from the manifest content. For example, consider that a female adolescent expresses that she dreamed she was in jail, her mother was the warden, and her cell smelled of jasmine. The manifest content is the jail and the smell of jasmine, yet the latent content behind those representations may be her desire to be free from her mother, who she feels is holding her captive with all of her rules and expectations. In addition to dreams, the daydreams of clients are ripe with manifest and latent content (Freud, 1946). Therefore, Anna Freud (1946) contended that therapists should conduct dream and daydream analysis when working with younger people. While traditional psychoanalysis focused considerable time in session on the interpretative meaning (i.e., latent content) of dreams, contemporary psychodynamic counseling focuses as much on the actual content of the dream (i.e., manifest content) as connected with the client's self-concept, internal conflicts, ego defense mechanisms, and transference reactions (Lane, 1997).

Abreaction

Although Freud placed primary emphasis on uncovering repressed material, he also recognized the importance of affect and emotions. He believed that affect needs to accompany the recall of past material for people to successfully understand and work through the importance that material has for them. To facilitate this link between emotions and the recall of repressed information, Freud often encouraged abreaction in his patients. **Abreaction** entails recalling a painful experience that had been repressed and working through that painful experience and the conflicts it created by reliving in memory the experience and its associated emotions. Analyzing that experience and achieving an emotional release at the peak of that process are also important. This technique is used today not only in psychoanalytic counseling but also in other counseling approaches that help people cope with strong emotional reactions to past events.

Dealing with Resistance

Counseling sessions are not just an opportunity for people to talk about their concerns and difficulties; they also serve as a place where difficulties, emotions, interactions, and behaviors can manifest. **Resistance** is the blocking of counseling progress and involves clients ceasing to discuss, address, think about, or accept an interpretation from a therapist. From a psychodynamic perspective, resistance is an unconscious defense used in the context of counseling to thwart progress (Cramer, 2006).

As an example, avoiding discussion of painful events, wasting time within sessions, not attending sessions on time, or being unprepared for sessions can all be considered ways clients resist counseling. Some possible examples of how clients may display resistance in counseling sessions include:

- Irrelevant or off-topic discussions
- Silence or minimal responsiveness
- Insulting and disrupting comments and/or disposition
- Perseverating on an object, toy, or game
- Preoccupation with someone else (e.g., parent, peer, counselor)
- Ignoring or not attending to the counselor
- Excessive wordiness or verbosity that is lacking in content.

While these behaviors can be frustrating to therapists, using these obstacles as an opportunity to learn about the internal dynamics of clients and to help bring these unconscious obstacles closer toward the conscious is the essence of a psychodynamic approach. In these situations, therapists need to reframe resistance not as an obstacle to overcome but as an authentic means of exploring and addressing how clients are attempting to defend their ego in real life. In addition, therapists need to consider that resistance has little to do with them and more to do with the clients' frustrations, defenses, pain, and lived experiences. In dealing with resistant clients, therapists should attempt to continually respect the clients; express honest, authentic curiosity about the resistance; slow down the pace of the session and explore the details (e.g., meaning of behaviors, feelings, pain); and honor the resistance by making it the focus (e.g., use immediacy to talk about it in the present; Elliott, 2015; Wagner, 2008).

APPLICATION AND CURRENT USE OF PSYCHOANALYSIS

Freud himself recognized that his approach was only suitable for a limited group of people. In light of the length and depth of the psychoanalytic process, readers might be tempted to conclude that it is designed for only those people with severe mental disorders. In fact, the opposite is true.

Traditional psychoanalysis seems best suited to those who have at least moderate ego strength and have already achieved some success and satisfaction in life via relationships and occupational and leisure activities. Such people are in reasonable contact with reality and, on the surface, may seem to lead normal lives and to be fairly functional. In fact, however, these people are significantly impaired by long-standing symptoms such as depression, anxiety, and sexual or physical symptoms without any identified medical cause. Their lives may be constricted, they may have repeated failures in relationships or work that are caused by their own self-destructive behaviors, they may have pervasive and harmful personality patterns, and they may not have succeeded in ameliorating their difficulties.

Because it is resource intensive, the number of people participating in traditional psychoanalysis is limited. Despite the limited application of traditional psychoanalysis, schools to train analysts flourish in New York City, Washington, DC, and other large cities (Norcross & Karpiak, 2012). Not only do people seek training in this approach, but clients seek psychoanalysis from these training facilities and also from psychoanalysts in independent practice. In addition, in a survey of members of the American Psychological Association, 27% identified their theoretical orientation as psychodynamic, the most popular orientation after eclectic (Norcross & Rogan, 2013). Few psychoanalysts today, however, draw exclusively on the ideas of Freud. Rather, they use his ideas as the basis for their work but incorporate those of his contemporaries.

Counseling Applications

Quantitative research exploring the effectiveness of the psychodynamic approach is limited (Wagner, 2008), yet a significant amount of qualitative, practice-based psychodynamic research does exist (Kegerreis & Midgley, 2015). This practice-based research covers a variety of ages (e.g., 3–18), emotional and behavioral disorders (e.g., anxiety, depression, eating disorders), and settings (e.g., outpatient, residential, school based), thus suggesting the clinical potential and relevance of psychodynamic approaches in counseling clients (Kegerreis & Midgley, 2015).

During Freud's time, mental disorders were categorized into two broad groups: psychoses and neuroses. **Psychoses** involve a loss of contact with reality, a significant disturbance in people's ability to accurately perceive and interpret both internal and external experiences. Because they are likely to be experiencing delusions, hallucinations, and other perceptual distortions, people with psychoses and severe mental illnesses cannot engage in the sort of self-examination required in psychoanalysis. This population is unlikely to benefit from this mode of counseling.

People with **neuroses**, in contrast, experience disorders of thoughts, emotions, and behaviors that interfere with their capacity for healthy functioning. Although their defenses and difficulties may lead to some confusion and misunderstanding about the meaning of their experiences, they have a capacity to form relationships, can engage in productive analysis, and can distinguish dreams and fantasies from reality.

Long-term psychodynamic psychotherapies have demonstrated effectiveness in the treatment of borderline personality disorder (Levy, Wasserman, Scott, & Yeomans, 2012) and panic disorder (Levy, Ablon, & Kachele, 2012). Empirical evidence is available to support the efficacy of contemporary psychodynamic approaches based on psychoanalytic concepts (Shedler, 2010, 2012). These newer approaches are of shorter duration and require fewer sessions than classic psychoanalysis. More will be said about contemporary psychodynamic theories in the following chapters.

Application to Multicultural Groups

Many reasons exist for questioning the appropriateness of using traditional psychoanalysis with clients from a collectivist background. Psychoanalysis encourages anonymity in the therapist, and it seems to view the importance of self-satisfaction and individual development as greater than that of social and family involvement and dedication. With its emphasis on talk, analysis, and uncovering, psychoanalysis is a Western or Eurocentric approach. A classic psychoanalytic approach may not feel comfortable to people from diverse backgrounds and cultures and may not be well accepted by people with strong spiritual or religious beliefs or by those from a collectivist societal context in which interdependence and group cohesion are valued. However, contemporary psychoanalysis, as influenced by relational psychoanalysis, indicates a shift toward a social constructivist understanding of human relationships, which allows for more open dialogues about the spiritual lives of clients.

In recent years, spirituality and religion as part of identity formation from a contemporary psychoanalytic perspective have been explored, since both psychoanalysis and spirituality share the goal of a search for particular aspects of people's identity (Tummala-Narra, 2009). In addition, psychodynamic therapists can convey a cultural openness with their clients (Kakar, 2006). Being aware of assumptions underlying the culture into which clients were born and the culture in which the therapist has been professionally trained can increase multicultural sensitivity. Practitioners of contemporary psychoanalysis recognize that people are a product of their life experiences and that the cultural background of clients and of the therapist must be taken into consideration.

EVALUATION OF FREUDIAN PSYCHOANALYSIS

The continued attention to Freud's ideas reflects the important and enduring contributions of his work. Freud provided a solid foundation for future theorists, who elaborated and expanded on his theories. Their contributions will be discussed in the remaining chapters in Part 2 of this text.

Limitations

Despite the broad applicability of Freudian psychoanalysis, some constraints limit the use and appropriateness of this approach. Psychoanalysis has a lengthy and costly format. Few people have the time, financial resources, and inclination to engage in such intensive therapy. In addition, the approach is not designed to help people with urgent concerns, may not pay adequate attention to multicultural dimensions, and says little about developing healthy adult lifestyles.

The slowly paced nature of the process; the relatively passive role of the client on the couch; and the emphasis on sexuality, early childhood, and the unconscious make the approach a poor choice for many people. Those in crisis, those who want to play a more active and equal role in counseling, and those who are uncomfortable with or do not believe in Freud's focus on infantile sexuality are unlikely to respond well to psychoanalysis.

Unfortunately, despite his admission that his understanding of women was limited, Freud advanced some erroneous and harmful ideas about women. Because they typically are children's primary caregivers, he blamed mothers, and largely exonerated fathers, for their children's emotional distress (Enns, 1993). He distinguished between vaginal orgasm (experienced during intercourse) and clitoral orgasm and stated that vaginal orgasms reflected sexual maturity in women, an idea that we now know to be untrue (Matlin, 1996). He suggested that women experience penis envy that can be at least partially resolved by giving birth. Freud seemed to view men as emotionally healthier than women (Bradley, 2007), whom he viewed as suffering from greater narcissism, masochism, shame, and envy. Even in the 1920s, opposition erupted in response to Freud's explanation of female sexuality (Mitchell & Black, 1995). Freud's theory of female sexuality considers women to be "essentially castrated men" (Moore, 2007, p. 321). Freud's ideas of penis envy, castration anxiety, and the Oedipus complex suggested that the penis is the core of masculine identity (Bradley, 2007).

Dispelling these mistaken beliefs took many years and likely did harm to women. We now know that taking a holistic and family systems approach is essential in understanding the causes of children's distress; that only one type of orgasm exists, no matter how it is achieved; that any envy that girls and women experience toward males can stem from many factors, including preferential treatment they perceive males as receiving; and that men are not healthier overall than women. Karen Horney (1950), one of the first female psychoanalysts, was also the first woman to challenge Freud's views publicly. She dismissed the Oedipal conflict and suggested instead that it was perhaps young boys who were jealous of women's ability to give birth.

Reading about Freud's misconceptions about women may bring up feelings of anger, and some may tend to dismiss his entire theory. However, keep in mind that these misconceptions represent only a small fraction of Freud's ideas and that Freud lived in an era when women and their roles were very different from those of today. Freud always valued women, including his wife; his daughter Anna, who will be discussed later in this book; and his female patients, colleagues, and supporters. His later work advanced a more contemporary view of women, perceiving them as more personal and emotional in their decisions than men are and as having a more flexible superego.

Research substantiating the value of classic psychoanalysis is limited, partly because the lengthy and intense nature of the approach means that each analyst works with only a small number of people and that each client's counseling process is unique. Some contend that psychoanalysis can never demonstrate its value because it does not lend itself to empirical research. However, there is a growing body of evidence for the effectiveness of long-term approaches in general and psychodynamic approaches in particular. Findings have demonstrated that clients who participated in long-term psychotherapy (50 to 150 sessions) not only improved but also continued to improve over time (Shedler, 2010).

Strengths and Contributions

Freud's most important contribution is the profound impact his thinking had on our understanding of personality development. Most of us acknowledge the importance of childhood experiences, understand the major role that sexuality plays in development, recognize the powerful influence of parent figures in our lives, assume that dreams and slips are often meaningful, and acknowledge that internal conflicts commonly occur within the three structures of our personalities. We also recognize the healing power of the therapeutic relationship, believe that talk therapy can be a powerful vehicle for promoting positive change, and are optimistic that counseling can help most people to lead more productive and rewarding lives.

We also accept the existence of the unconscious. We can observe consistency between Freud's model of the unconscious and newer neurobiological research indicating that the conscious mind is just the tip of the iceberg and that most thoughts, feelings, and experiences are unconscious and out of awareness (Fonagy & Target, 2009). Human consciousness does not understand or even know the underlying causes of maladaptive behavior. A developmental perspective of psychopathology appears to be correct, and we are increasingly understanding the role of early adverse childhood experiences and trauma and their long-term impacts on development.

In 2006, on the 150th anniversary of Sigmund Freud's birth, the cover of *Newsweek* proclaimed "Freud Is Not Dead." The question of whether psychoanalysis, reflecting the ideas of Sigmund Freud, is outdated has often been explored. However, even the frequent revisiting of this question testifies to the strength and influence of Freud's ideas. The American Psychological Association (2006) devoted a special edition of the journal *Psychoanalytic Psychology* to "The Relevance of Sigmund Freud for the 21st Century." Freud established the foundation for today's counseling and psychotherapy; he succeeded in bringing our knowledge of personality, human development, and psychological symptoms into everyday knowledge. Many of Freud's concepts, including the unconscious, the ego, and defense mechanisms, have become so widely accepted that we sometimes forget they began with Freud.

Freud's efforts required great courage; he disagreed radically with the thinking of his peers, withstood years of verbal and written attacks, and worked impressively to advance his ideas. Freud's contributions can be seen in all areas of psychological inquiry today. Transgenerational, biological, and evolutionary psychology all have their roots in Freud's original scientific theories. Even though some of Freud's theories are no longer accepted, his legacy has laid the groundwork for current theories of counseling.

Although many theories of human development and psychotherapy have been advanced since Freud's time, he is generally regarded as the father of psychotherapy. His ideas and strategies continue to inform and contribute to counseling in the 21st century. Whether or not we agree with his ideas, Freud's profound contributions to our understanding of psychological development and knowledge of psychotherapy are undeniable. Although few readers will go on to become psychoanalysts, all will find that their conceptions of mental health and mental illness and their approaches to counseling are colored by their knowledge of Freudian psychoanalysis.

SKILL DEVELOPMENT: INTERPRETATION

Interpretation is one of the fundamental skills of psychoanalysis and is used by all of the Post- and Neo-Freudian theorists, as well. Interpretations provide people with an alternative frame of reference for viewing a problem or situation. Interpretations can link a current reaction that may appear unimportant to a past experience that has considerable depth and significance, thereby providing clients new understanding and routes to change.

Interpretations often reflect insights that therapists have into clients' motives and behaviors that may not yet be in clients' awareness. For that reason, practitioners must deliver interpretations with great care. Ideally, questioning and information giving can be used to help clients make their own interpretations. Timing is another critical variable in effective interpretations; they should be presented when people are ready to accept and understand them. Therapists also should be clear about what they hope to accomplish in making an interpretation. Although it may enhance therapists' self-esteem to realize they are insightful and have drawn important connections between pieces of information that clients have presented, interpretations, of course, should never be self-serving or primarily for the purpose of demonstrating the therapists' skills. Rather, they should be used to move clients forward in positive ways such as helping them gain insights that will enhance their self-esteem, empower them, help them make better choices, facilitate their efforts to manage and change their emotions, and improve their interpersonal and other behaviors. Finally, presentation of interpretations should never create an adversarial situation in which therapists and clients are in conflict or engaged in a debate about who is right. Generally, interpretations are most successful if they are presented tentatively as information for clients to think about and discuss. If interpretations are not meaningful to clients, they should have the right to reject them without being made to feel as though they are cowardly, unintelligent, or fearful of change. Using language carefully and thoughtfully can contribute to the successful delivery of interpretations.

CASE APPLICATION

Read the following excerpt from a session between Edie and her therapist. Think about the therapeutic relationship and the concept of countertransference. Today, with the onset of more relational therapies, and the growing amount of research on both attachment and the therapeutic process, most psychodynamic psychotherapists use a broader definition of countertransference that includes the "normal" or expected responses of the therapist to the client. Countertransference is a clinically meaningful experience that can provide the therapist with insight into the client's interpersonal dynamics and the reactions that others have to the client. Psychodynamic psychotherapists who monitor their own countertransference feelings can often use this information in the service of the therapy, because it provides a rich source of clinical information about the client. The exercises following the dialogue will give you the opportunity to discuss your observations.

EDIE: I'm sorry I was late. I might have to leave early, also.

THERAPIST: Is there a problem?

EDIE: No, I just have a lot of things going on.

THERAPIST: Okay. Well, let's get started then.

EDIE: Things are so busy right now. Roberto and I are just like two ships passing. We really don't talk much anymore, and when we do it's about Ava. You know, arranging who's picking her up after school, or making sure she's eaten lunch, that type of thing.

THERAPIST: So you feel like you and Roberto are drifting apart?

EDIE: I don't know if we were ever close to begin with. He's always on the computer. I told you he's a workaholic. I almost feel like he's abandoning me for his computer.

THERAPIST: Abandoning is a strong word.

EDIE: What would you call it? I'm married, but I'm home alone every night. I mean, he's there, but he's in the basement on his computer. I feel like he's left me for another woman, except his "woman" is his computer.

THERAPIST: You sound pretty upset. Can you think of any other times when you've felt this way?

EDIE: (thinks for a minute) Umm . . . right after my parents separated. They'd been arguing a lot and I was only 5 when my dad finally left, but I remember feeling so abandoned (starts to tear up). He just left me. How could he do that? He just walked out of my life one day and I didn't see him for 6 years. Every birthday, every holiday, I would get all hopeful the night before, anticipating that he would call the next day. But nothing. As the years went by, I just got used to it. Looking back now, at myself as a little girl, I think about Ava at that age. It was so devastating to me. To not be wanted by my father . . . I know how much I went through to have Ava, and leaving her is something I would never consider doing. I just don't know how my father could do that to me.

THERAPIST: What were you feeling?

EDIE: Alone . . . abandoned . . . angry.

THERAPIST: Like you feel now, when Roberto goes down to the computer room?

EDIE: Wow, yeah. That's exactly how I feel. Like he's leaving me. I get so angry at him.

THERAPIST: But he's downstairs.

EDIE: Yeah . . . (thinking).

THERAPIST: I wonder if the strong reaction you have when Roberto "abandons" you to the computer is related to the feelings you had as a little girl when your father left.

EDIE: Yeah, like I'm that little girl sitting on the sofa just waiting for him to come back.

THERAPIST: Your father? Or Roberto?

EDIE: (gives a little laugh). Either. Both. I guess it's the same reaction, but I just realized that at least Roberto's working. It's not like he's out with another woman or anything. He's actually working to make more money at his job, so he can provide more for us.

THERAPIST: It doesn't sound like he's abandoning you.

EDIE: No. No, he's really not. I never thought of it that way before. He's really just trying to get ahead financially. Do you think this could be because of my dad walking out when I was 5 that I just think everyone is going to abandon me?

THERAPIST: I'd be curious to know if there are other times you've felt that way.

EDIE: Well (smiling sheepishly). Actually, today before I came here. I wasn't really too busy this morning. I was late because I couldn't decide if I wanted to come here today. I didn't know if I could trust you to tell my story to. I was afraid you'd be like that other therapist who canceled on me. That's why I said I might have to leave early. But I don't want to leave. I just realized something about myself. I guess I get really mad at people when I feel like they're abandoning me.

THERAPIST: And what does your anger do?

EDIE: What do you mean?

THERAPIST: When you get angry, how do people react? Do they get closer to you, or further apart.

EDIE: Oh, further apart. Nobody wants to be around me when I'm angry.

THERAPIST: So your anger serves a purpose.

EDIE: I guess so. I guess it keeps people away from me.

THERAPIST: And then you don't have to get close to them.

EDIE: Or feel vulnerable. It's kind of a vicious circle, isn't it? I want to be closer to Roberto, but when he gets on the computer at night to do work, I feel abandoned, so I get angry at him. Then he doesn't want to be around me, so he comes to bed late, and we don't talk.

THERAPIST: There is a lot here to think about this week.

In psychodynamic therapy, the "work" of the session is in helping the individual work through childhood issues and feelings that might have been adaptive at that time (i.e., Edie getting angry at her father protected her from becoming depressed and overly sad) but that are not working now or are not truly applicable to the current situation. For instance, Roberto's workaholism, while distressing to Edie, is not a sign that he is abandoning her. Quite the contrary, he is working harder to support her and Ava. But Edie is reacting as if she were still 4 years old. The therapist gently suggests an interpretation, and because Edie was open to it, this allowed a dialogue that provided insight into how her past relationships were affecting her current relationship, including the here and now of her feelings toward the therapist.

CONSIDERATIONS

1. Discuss the dialogue you just read. Consider the following dimensions of this therapist's intervention: timing, purpose, content, impact on the client–therapist relationship, overall effectiveness. What would you have done differently to improve this intervention? Now imagine what the effect on Edie would have been if the therapist had not used her countertransferential feelings. Would Edie have benefited? Why or why not? How might it have impacted the therapeutic relationship if the therapist had remained silent? How would Edie have changed in her relationship with Roberto?
2. Sometimes the use of countertransference may be almost inseparable from the therapist's work as a therapist. In the above scenario, the therapist was actively working to help Edie recognize the differences between her childhood feelings and those she had as an adult. What if Edie's relationship with Roberto had been harmful? Would the therapist still have proceeded? How directive should the therapist be?

REFLECT AND RESPOND

1. Now that you have an understanding of the three structures of the personality—the id, the superego, and the ego—you can be more aware of the dynamics of some of your inner conflicts. Write briefly about a time when you experienced a conflict between your id and your superego and how you resolved that conflict.
2. We all make mistakes, make slips, and forget commitments. Try to be more conscious of these processes in your own life for the next week. Each time you notice one of these errors, think about whether it is a random occurrence or whether it might reflect a wish or another psychological process.
3. Using an iceberg analogy, create an iceberg metaphor for a client. Choose any diagnosis you want and create an iceberg scenario using the concepts of the conscious, unconscious, and subconscious. The tip of the iceberg will be conscious thoughts or behaviors that you may see with your client. Then, under the water line, list conflicts that your client may battle. For example, a client with an eating disorder may consciously have body image concerns or obsessions about food, but underneath this client may battle with low self-worth, trauma, or family conflict. After you create the iceberg, reflect on how you may go about addressing your client's underlying battles.
4. As mentioned in the text, defense mechanisms serve as a way of dealing with inner conflict, anxiety, pain, and other negative emotions. People use defense mechanisms to cope with situations. In your journal, write down a client scenario for each defense mechanism and reflect on how you may help the client cope with that situation in a healthier way.

Summary

The chapter reviewed psychoanalysis, which is considered the first form of psychotherapy and was developed by Sigmund Freud. Freud's theory is based on instincts; all instincts are either life or death drives—eros, thanatos, and libido. Freud's theory also emphasizes the three structures of the personality (i.e., the id, superego, and ego). The id is the animalistic and largely unconscious component. The superego is the perfectionistic part, characterized by a rigid conscience. The ego is the mediator between the id and the superego to meet the needs of both. The five stages of psychosexual development (i.e., oral, anal, phallic, latency, and genital), defense mechanisms, and levels of consciousness (unconscious, preconscious, and conscious) are also important in Freud's theory.

The primary goals of psychoanalysis are to bring the unconscious into the conscious and to strengthen the ego through achieving equilibrium between the id and the superego. In classic psychoanalysis, therapists acted as a blank slate on which clients projected their transference feelings. In Freudian times, countertransference, which is the therapist's feelings about the client, was to be avoided. Free association, which allows clients to say whatever comes to mind without filter, is an important aspect of this approach. The therapist is responsible for analyzing and interpreting what clients say. Dream analysis, abreaction, and dealing with resistance are also important psychoanalytic techniques.

During Freud's time, psychoses and neuroses were separated into two categories of mental disorders. Psychoses involve a loss of contact with reality, and neuroses involve disorders of thoughts, emotions, and behaviors that affect the capacity for healthy functioning. Many psychoanalysts view nonpsychotic disorders as most treatable by psychoanalysis. Classic psychoanalysis is primarily a Eurocentric or Western approach and may not be applicable for diverse clients. However, spirituality has been explored more and can be incorporated into psychodynamic approaches, which may be suitable for some cultures. Psychoanalysis has been criticized for being too lengthy, too expensive, and passive. Freud also had some ideas that were harmful about women. Freud has contributed greatly to the counseling field because he created the first form of talk therapy, influenced our views on personality development, and recognized the importance of understanding the history and background of clients.

Recommended Readings

Freud, S. (1955). *The basic writings of Sigmund Freud* (A. A. Brill, Trans.). New York, NY: Modern Library.

Higdon, J. (2012). *Psychodynamic theory for therapeutic practice* (2nd ed.) New York, NY: Palgrave Macmillan.

Jones, E. (1953, 1955, 1957). *The life and works of Sigmund Freud* (3 vols.). New York, NY: Basic Books.

Roth, M. S. (Ed.) (1998). *Freud: Conflict and culture: Essays on his life, work, and legacy.* New York, NY: Alfred A. Knopf.

Stafford-Clark, D. (1965). *What Freud really said.* New York, NY: Schocken.

MyLab Counseling

Try the Topic 16 Assignments: Psychoanalytic Therapy.

CHAPTER

3 Adlerian Therapy

> **Learning Outcomes**
>
> **When you have finished this chapter, you should be able to:**
> - Understand the context and development of Adlerian Therapy.
> - Communicate the key concepts associated with Adlerian Therapy and understand how they relate to therapeutic processes.
> - Describe the therapeutic goals of Adlerian Therapy.
> - Identify the common techniques used in Adlerian Therapy.
> - Understand how Adlerian Therapy relates to counseling diverse populations.
> - Identify the limitations and strengths of Adlerian Therapy.

ALFRED ADLER (1870–1937)

Alfred Adler was born in Vienna, Austria, the third of six children. Adler had a difficult childhood. When he was 3 years old, his brother died in the bed they shared, and Adler himself was prone to accidents and illnesses. Twice he was run over in the streets; he had pneumonia, suffered from rickets and poor eyesight, and was frequently ill. Because of his medical problems, Adler was pampered, especially by his mother. However, when his younger brother was born, Adler felt dethroned as his mother shifted her attention from him to her new baby. This led Adler to transfer his attention to his father and to his peers. Adler's subsequent interest in birth order, inferiority, and parental overprotectiveness may have originated in his own childhood experiences.

Everett Collection Historical/Alamy Stock Photo

Adler was initially not a good student; a teacher suggested that Adler's father should encourage him to be an apprentice to a shoemaker rather than encourage his academic pursuits. However, Adler subsequently became a strong student, demonstrating in his own life that people can change their goals and their lives. From childhood on, Adler was interested in psychology and social issues. Even in his first professional position (as an eye specialist) after he completed medical school, Adler was interested in the total person; he sought to understand the connection between mental and physical processes and their impact on people's work and social lives. Adler found his next position as a general physician more rewarding because it meshed with his beliefs. However, he was troubled by feelings of helplessness when counseling people with terminal illnesses. This led Adler to another career change; he entered the field of neurology while continuing to study psychology and social science in an effort to understand people more fully.

Adler's insights into personality development brought him recognition in his field and likely helped capture Freud's attention. In 1902, Freud wrote to Adler and several other leaders in the fields of neurology and psychology, suggesting they meet to discuss his work. This led to Adler's involvement in the Vienna Psycho-Analytical Society.

Adler was displeased with Freud's belief that sexual impulses are basic determinants of psychological development. This rift finally led Adler to separate himself from the Psycho-Analytical Society, where he had achieved power and leadership, to form the Society for Individual Psychology. Alfred Adler moved away from Freud's sphere of influence to focus on psychosocial rather than psychosexual underpinnings of human behavior. His work for the rest of his life had the goals of deepening his understanding of people and finding better ways to help them.

Adler, who was Jewish, experienced anti-Semitism and the atrocities of World War I. These associated experiences contributed to his emphasis on humanism and his belief that people can effectively and collaboratively work together. These experiences also made him aware of the importance of context and culture and how this influences human personality.

Adler cared deeply about the common person and he desired to take his ideas and apply them to improving peoples' day-to-day lives. He wrote and spoke in non-technical ways that were easy to understand. He spoke out about issues such as child-rearing practices, prejudice, and school reforms. He advocated for children who were at risk, women's rights, and the importance of community mental health (Watts, 2012). His efforts contributed to the development of 32 child guidance clinics in the Vienna public schools. Using live demonstrations and writing books for the general public, he made his ideas and techniques accessible to a wide audience. His wife, Raissa, described as a strong feminist and political activist, was an ardent supporter of Adler's social activism (Sherman & Nwaorgu, 2002).

Beginning in the 1920s, Adler traveled frequently to the United States, where he generated considerable interest in his ideas. Adler's book *Understanding Human Nature* (1927/1959) was the first psychology book to sell hundreds of thousands of copies in the United States. His tireless involvement in his work continued until his death. In 1937, while preparing for a lecture in Scotland, he died of a heart attack.

INTRODUCTION/DEVELOPMENT OF ADLERIAN THERAPY

Adler called his theory of human development **Individual Psychology**, to reflect the unique beliefs and skills that people develop from early childhood and that serve as a reference for their attitudes, behaviors, and private view of self, others, and society. According to Adler, mental health difficulties are not rooted in developmental deficits; instead, mental health problems are simply an extension or exaggeration of typical, normal developmental processes, and people have the resources they need to reach their potential. Individual Psychology also holds that people have a basic human need to be accepted by others and to contribute positively to society. Individual Psychology is a strength-based approach that promotes the idea that people constantly strive to become better versions of themselves, and that they do their best to improve themselves and the world with the resources to which they have access. Adlerian therapists work to harness client resources and help clients access these resources. In Adlerian therapy, the positive traits, characteristics, and inherent drives of every individual are identified and enhanced to effectively overcome any undesirable drives or motivations.

Alfred Adler (1958) was a humanistic theorist who developed Individual Psychology as an alternative to psychoanalytic explanations of mental health. Although the term Individual Psychology might seem to suggest the isolation of the client from others, Adlerian concepts actually highlight the unique experience individuals have in relation to their social context (e.g., society, family, peers, society). In fact, Adlerian theory is one of the most comprehensive counseling theories, as it highlights the way that biological, psychological, and genetic factors interact with environmental and social influences in explaining human behavior and in helping people change. Adler promoted a holistic model for viewing the individual in context, noting that both nature and nurture give rise to human development. That is, every child is born with an inherent personality, and external factors determine the expression of the personality over time.

Adler's ideas are compatible with contemporary thinking about mental health. Adlerian therapy pays considerable attention to social context, family dynamics, and child rearing. This approach is phenomenological, empowering, and oriented toward the past, present, and future. As a result, experts currently view Adler's ideas as an important approach to therapy, especially for therapists working with children and their families.

Adler's professional development falls roughly into four time periods. The first phase of his career followed his completion of medical school. Neither his early work as a physician nor his subsequent work in neurological research was fully satisfying to him, although he made contributions in both areas. His great interest lay in the mind rather than the body.

In 1902, Alfred Adler and Freud were charter members of the Wednesday afternoon psychoanalytic meetings that later became known as the Vienna Psycho-Analytical Society. When he joined forces with Freud to further the field of psychoanalysis, Adler entered the second phase of his career and seemed, at least temporarily, to have found his place professionally; he was finally focusing on promoting healthy emotional development. However, before long, he felt stifled by the apparent rigidity of some of Freud's beliefs and his limited interest in considering people through a more holistic lens. As Adler's thinking evolved, he came to disagree with the emphasis Freud placed on biological and physiological determinants of psychological development. Adler believed that early childhood experiences played an integral part in future development, but he viewed Freud's concepts as too deterministic and limited.

Adler's disengagement from Freud signaled the third period in his professional development. This separation freed Adler to move forward with working out his own ideas. Adler developed a practical, teleological approach that replaced Freud's theory of sexual drives and libido with his belief in the goal-striving nature of people. People are not viewed as the victims of their biology or circumstances but can choose to change both their goals and their behaviors. Adler replaced biological and objective causal explanations of behavior with psychological and subjective causal explanations (Ansbacher & Ansbacher, 1956). He replaced the concept of the sexual drive and the libido with the drive to gain power, achieve superiority, and become a fully functioning adult. The goal of Adler's Individual Psychology was to understand and help the unique individual, a departure from what he perceived as Freud's overgeneralized ideas.

The final stage in Adler's career came after his service as a psychiatrist in World War I. Seeing the bonds among soldiers during their war experiences convinced him that the drive toward social interest was even stronger than the drive for superiority and power. He proposed that people's basic motivation is for social interest and that this motivation is innate in all humans (Grey, 1998). He viewed people as driven primarily by needs for significance, self-worth, and social involvement. Adler's thinking moved in directions compatible with what many now view as the fundamental purpose of therapy: to help people feel empowered and self-actualized and build rewarding social involvement and relationships.

KEY CONCEPTS

Adler's theory, like Freud's, has considerable depth and richness. Adler's concepts emphasize the unity and uniqueness of each individual. He believed that to truly understand and help people, their family constellations, private logic, social contexts, and styles of life must be assessed. According to

Adler, people are not victims of biology or circumstance, and they can choose to change both their goals and their behaviors. Adler shared Freud's belief that much of what determines the direction of people's lives is unconscious and needs to be brought into conscious awareness.

Adler, like Freud, acknowledged the importance of the first 5 years of life in influencing people's future development; however, Adler's view was less deterministic. He believed that biological and physiological factors provided probabilities for future growth, but that the self is the most important variable that determines success (Ansbacher & Ansbacher, 1956).

For Adler, those characteristics of the individual that were determined by heredity and early upbringing had less importance than what the individual chose to do with life experiences. He believed that behavior is purposeful and goal directed, and that people can channel their behavior in ways that promote growth. Adler believed that what matters to people are developing and working to achieve meaningful and rewarding goals, along with a lifestyle that leads to a positive sense of themselves, connectedness to other people and their communities, and satisfying work (Adler, 1963a).

For Adler, the internal and subjective were more important than the external and objective. We can think of his theory as **phenomenological**, meaning that he focused on a person's inner reality, that is, the way that person perceived the world. Adler saw each person as a unique individual and believed that we can only really make sense of and know that person by understanding that person's perceptions of the world, private logic, lifestyle, and goals; in this way, phenomenology is central to Adler's theory.

Patterns of Human Personality

Adler had a holistic and unified view of personality in that he believed it important to understand the whole person and how each part of a person is connected. In fact, Adler selected the name of his theory, Individual Psychology, because he wanted to avoid developing reductionistic categories for understanding human behavior (e.g., breaking human personality into categories, as Freud did with the concept of the id, ego, and superego). According to the holistic view, people cannot be understood in parts; people can only be understood in relation to others and in the broader context of their lives, such as their culture, school, and work. Adler believed that we are creative, social, and forward moving and that we cannot be fully known outside the context of our life and what has meaning for us (Sherman & Dinkmeyer, 1987). People are unified through striving to achieve their life goals. The concepts of inferiority/superiority and lifestyle are discussed next because they constitute an important aspect of Adler's thinking around the human personality.

INFERIORITY AND SUPERIORITY Striving to achieve superiority is an important concept in Adlerian theory. **Superiority** is the drive that allows individuals to become skilled, competent, and creative. In contrast, **inferiority** is the feeling of inadequacy and incompetency that develops during infancy and serves as the basis to strive for superiority to overcome feelings of inferiority. Not to be superior over others, but to achieve mastery in one's own life and to overcome feelings of inferiority, becomes a goal as strong as Freud's drive theory and Carl Rogers' theory of self-actualization. Adler (1963b) believed that feelings of inferiority during the early childhood years have a great impact on development. Nearly all children experience these feelings, perceiving themselves as small and powerless in relation to their parents and older siblings. How young children are treated and how they deal with their feelings of inferiority are important in shaping their personality and way of being in the world. By mastering an issue, and thereby attaining a sense of superiority, people achieve a sense of accomplishment. Human beings create their own internalized goals and then strive to meet them. Through effort, improvement, success, and completion, they live up to their own high standards.

All individuals have an internalized ideal self they are trying to live up to. People can develop what Adler referred to as a **superiority complex**, in which they mask feelings of inferiority by displaying boastful, self-centered, or arrogant superiority to overcome feelings of inferiority. Individuals may also develop an **inferiority complex**, or a strong and pervasive belief that they are not as good as other people. An inferiority complex may be caused by issues like a perceived physical inferiority (e.g., deficiencies in the body such as a chronic illness, physical or learning disabilities, or various mental disorders such as attention-deficit hyperactivity disorder [ADHD]) (Schultz & Schultz, 2013). When parents are underattentive, this may suggest to children that they are unlovable and may also lead to an inferiority complex (Schultz & Schultz). Parents who are overattentive may also thwart children's efforts to become independent and feel a sense of mastery in the world (Schultz & Schultz).

Adler's thoughts around the inferiority/superiority concept developed secondary to his own struggle to overcome multiple childhood illnesses. He believed children who succeed in reducing their feelings of difference and inferiority by building their strengths and abilities, making wise and creative choices, and striving in healthy ways toward growth and power are likely to experience healthy development. In contrast, children who are pampered or neglected and whose efforts toward empowerment are thwarted are far less likely to experience positive growth and development. Adler believed that pampered children often grow up expecting others to take care of them and so they do not develop their own resources, while neglected children may become discouraged and hopeless when their efforts to overcome an inferior role are ignored or rejected.

Individual efforts to overcome inferiority can have an impact on overall lifestyle. For instance, a child who cannot compete in sports with his older brother, who is physically stronger and more mature, may choose instead to stay home and study, ultimately surpassing his brother in academic ability. As another example, a middle child who cannot keep up with her popular and successful older sister may elect instead to drop out of school and underachieve. Through the attainment of superiority, regardless of venue, an individual achieves mastery, achievement, and life satisfaction.

Adler's theory also highlights the key human struggle of not feeling valued and/or feeling incompetent, inadequate, or generally less acceptable than others. This feeling of inadequacy is referred to as a **felt minus** in Adlerian theory (Schultz & Schultz, 2013). Youth often interpret the fact that they are smaller and less capable than older individuals as an inherent inferiority, although this is simply a reflection of the developmental human process. Regardless, though, Adler (1963a) believed that all humans are born with a felt minus because they are fully dependent upon caregivers until significant developmental milestones are reached. The felt minus functions as a motivator for youth to strive and achieve throughout life. Humans are inherently **social beings** who need connection with others and generally wish to contribute in positive ways to society (Sweeney, 2009). Children often gauge their worth by comparing themselves to others. Children who have especially discouraging social interactions or who experience difficulty finding their own unique strengths will experience a felt minus in their particular areas of struggle. Although the initial felt minus is a universal experience caused by helplessness at birth, the felt minus can fade away in early childhood, or it can linger (and even grow) throughout early development, and in reaction to lived experiences (Adler, 1963a).

To overcome a felt minus or an inferiority complex, individuals work to find certain behaviors at which they feel especially successful or talented. The areas in which people excel contribute to a **perceived plus**, or the subjective perception that they have achieved an area of mastery above peers. Often, individuals pursue a perceived plus in an area that compensates for their sense of a felt minus. For example, an individual who was sick throughout childhood might feel physically inferior to others and focus on sports to gain a sense of a perceived plus. Some individuals develop unhealthy behaviors to compensate for a felt minus. For example, a neglected child might feel unlovable and engage in early sexual behaviors to experience a perceived plus.

Although some individuals use unhelpful behaviors to achieve a perceived plus, Adler (1958) proposed that all humans are inherently on a path of **forward motion and creativity**. As a result of the felt minus, people are constantly growing and reinventing themselves to create a life progressively more similar to their perceived plus. Viewed as creative and responsible, people are in a trajectory of growth and development toward their healthiest and happiest capabilities (Watts, 2013). Essentially, all individuals do the best they can to achieve social significance and contribute positively to society.

People's behaviors gradually direct a move toward an idealized version of the self. Individuals often create a mental schema of the perfect self, known as the **fictional final goal**. The fictional final goal is developed early in life as the result of individual qualities, social interactions (especially with caregivers and peers), and environmental influences and popular culture. These life goals are unique for every individual, and they are created to overcome perceived inferiorities or deficiencies in:

- Intellectual ability
- Physical appearance
- Personal level of ambition
- Level of cooperation or opposition from others
- Degree of independence/dependence with others (Kelly & Lee, 2007).

All individuals develop a fictional final goal to find ways to feel good about themselves and experience the social validation they crave. An individual's **lifestyle**, or way of being, is fundamentally informed by his or her fictional final goals.

LIFESTYLE The composition and interactions of families exert the major influence on the development of people's lifestyle, another important concept in Adler's theory. Lifestyle is one of the most fundamental of Adler's concepts because it is a sum of people's aspirations that drives them to accomplish their goals (Grey, 1998).

Similar to the personality or the self, lifestyle encompasses four ingredients: (1) the person's subjective worldview, including beliefs about the self and others, values, inner narratives, expectations, and attitudes; (2) the person's goals; (3) behavioral strategies that the person uses to achieve goals and negotiate the life journey; and (4) the outcomes or consequences of those behaviors. Lifestyle can be assessed informally via exploration of these four areas or it can be explored using a formal inventory.

Lifestyle, then, is the unique way in which each individual seeks to find a place in the world, to overcome feelings of inferiority, and to achieve goals. These goals nearly always involve attainment of significance, superiority, competence, and mastery. Each person has an image, usually unconscious, of what life will be like when those goals have been reached. Adler called this **fictional finalism**, and he believed that these images were firmly established between the ages of 6 and 8 and remained constant throughout a person's life.

Adler (1958) posited that people adopt one of four typical lifestyle patterns. These patterns of interacting with the world are used to overcome difficulties and achieve a perceived plus. The four general lifestyles include:

- Dominant lifestyle—individuals work to assert control over others.
- Getting lifestyle—individuals receive personal satisfaction from the way others treat them.
- Avoiding lifestyle—individuals avoid acknowledging social difficulties and/or uncomfortable feelings.
- Socially useful lifestyle—individuals perform behaviors that promote the well-being of the self and society (Schultz & Schultz, 2013).

The getting lifestyle is most commonly used by individuals, but the socially useful lifestyle is most beneficial to society (Schultz & Schultz, 2013). The socially useful lifestyle also proves the most effective in facilitating and supporting mental health because individuals are able to achieve a perceived plus in ways that benefit themselves and others simultaneously. Helping others further contributes to a sense of perceived plus, and helpful and productive behaviors are cyclically reinforced. As such, Adlerian therapists strive toward supporting the development of a socially useful lifestyle.

Basic mistakes are self-defeating aspects of individuals' lifestyle that may affect their later behavior. Adler believed that people tend to upset themselves by the way they think. Basic mistakes represent irrational ways of thinking, which can be disputed and changed. These often reflect avoidance of others, seeking power, a desperate need for security, or faulty values. Five of the most common basic mistakes include (Mosak, 2013):

1. *Overgeneralizations.* "Everyone hates me."
2. *False or impossible goals.* "I must be the best for everyone to love me."
3. *Misperceptions of life and life's demands.* "Life is too difficult for me to handle."
4. *Denial of one's basic worth.* "I am ugly and stupid, so why would anyone want to be with me?"
5. *Faulty values.* "I must be the best before someone else beats me to it."

Adler also held that individuals sometimes have mistaken goals they use to achieve a perceived plus. Table 3.1 identifies examples of common mistaken goals. Individuals often use unhelpful behaviors to achieve these goals, and achievement of the mistaken goals provides clients with a perceived plus.

TABLE 3.1 Adlerian Therapy: Examples of Common Mistaken Goals

Mistaken Goal	Faulty Logic Examples	Relevant Behaviors	Therapeutic Goal
Seeking attention	To feel valued, I need others to pay attention to me.	People might exaggerate and engage in unhealthy or unproductive behaviors to get attention, and/or struggle when they are not the focus of attention.	• Identify and reframe faulty logic. • Help clients garner attention through healthy behaviors (e.g., hobbies). • Implement coping skills that make alone time enjoyable and satisfying.
Seeking power	I am only important when I have control of a situation.	People might intimidate others and attempt to exert control over them.	• Identify and reframe irrational beliefs. • Provide clients with healthy opportunities to assert personal preferences and control.
Seeking revenge	I want you to feel bad when I feel bad.	People might become physically violent or emotionally volatile. People might spread rumors or lies about someone to prevent them from having opportunities or to hurt them emotionally.	• Identify and reframe irrational beliefs. • Help clients identify and express their feelings.
Feelings of inadequacy	I am going to fail, so you shouldn't ask me to try.	People might avoid difficult tasks. People might purposely perform poorly so no one asks them to do a task again. People may also isolate themselves or deny themselves opportunities for success.	• Identify and reframe irrational beliefs. • Praise clients for trying new things (regardless of the level of success). • Encourage clients to complete difficult tasks to encourage a sense of mastery.

Source: Based on Sweeney, T. J. (2009). *Adlerian counseling and psychotherapy: A practitioner's approach* (5th ed.). New York, NY: Routledge.

Therapists should work with clients to create insight around mistaken goals and develop healthier methods for achieving a perceived plus in a socially useful manner (e.g., by helping others who have been wronged).

Family Constellation and Birth Order

Adler paid considerable attention to other early influences on development, including family constellations and birth order. He believed that, through an examination of the family constellation, we can understand people's lifestyles. Conversely, by understanding their outlooks on life, we can understand the roles people have in their families (Dreikurs, 1973).

A person's **family constellation** includes the composition of the family, each person's roles, and the reciprocal transactions that a person has with siblings and parents during the early formative years. Children are not passive recipients of these transactions; rather, children influence how parents and siblings respond to them. Each child plays a role in the family that is determined by the interactions and transactions within that family (Adler, 1963b).

Children are affected by both their similarities to and differences from their family members. According to Adler, siblings who are most different from us influence us the most. That difference gives us the opportunity to compare and contrast ourselves with others, see new possibilities, and rethink the choices and roles we have taken on in our own lives.

Birth order is another aspect of families that, according to Adler (1963b), has a profound impact on development. According to his theory, the order of birth (e.g., first born, second born, third born) can influence later personality and future relationship patterns and functioning. Five psychological positions in the family, described by Adler, and characteristics commonly believed to be associated with each position are as follows:

1. *Oldest children* tend to be the most intelligent and achieving of the five groups. Their verbal skills are especially strong. Firstborns, who initially grow up in a family of adults, tend to be dependable, well organized, and responsible. They generally are well behaved and cooperative, conforming to societal expectations and being fairly traditional. Their many strengths often help them attain positions of leadership.

At the time firstborns are the only child in the family, they tend to be the center of attention; however, when siblings are born, oldest children tend to feel dethroned and may feel threatened, angry, fearful, and jealous in response to losing their special role as an only child. Dealing successfully with the birth of a sibling can help firstborns to become more affiliative and self-confident.

2. *Second children* feel pressure to catch up and compete with the oldest child. Because second-born children usually realize they cannot outdo the successes the firstborn has already achieved, they gravitate toward endeavors in which the older sibling is either unskilled or uninterested. A common pattern is for a firstborn to excel in a traditional area, such as English or mathematics, and for the second-born to seek success in a more creative and less conventional area, such as singing or drawing, and to emphasize social rather than academic success. The more successful the firstborn, the more likely the second-born will move in directions opposite to those of the typically well-behaved and achievement-oriented firstborn. Second-born children never have the opportunity to be the only child. As a result, second-born children are never fully the center of attention, but they also do not have the experience of losing such power (as the first child has experienced). Second-born children often receive less attention and fewer rules than the first child did at the same age. Second-born children tend to be more caring, friendly, and expressive than their older siblings.

3. *Middle children* are often the second child and are likely to manifest many strengths of the second-born. However, some middle children feel squeezed between older children who have already found their place and younger children who seem to receive more love and attention. Middle children sometimes have difficulty finding a way to become special and can become discouraged, viewing themselves as unloved and neglected. This pattern is usually less evident in large families in which two or more children share the role of middle child, but is particularly likely in families with only three children. With encouragement and positive parenting, however, middle children often become well-adjusted, friendly, creative, and ambitious, prizing their individual strengths.

4. *Youngest children* encounter three common pitfalls: They may be pampered and spoiled by the rest of the family, they may feel a need to go at top speed at all times to keep up with their older siblings, and they may become discouraged about competing with their siblings. Decisions may be made for them, and they may not need to take on much responsibility for themselves or others. Adler expressed concern that these children would experience strong feelings of inferiority. However, last-born children can also acquire considerable power in the family and thrive on the special attention they receive. As a result of their freedom, youngest children might be highly self-sufficient and successful. They often become adventurous, easygoing, empathic, sociable, and innovative. They typically pursue interests that are their own to avoid competition with siblings. However, youngest children who are spoiled might become just the opposite: highly dependent and lacking motivation.

5. *Only children* have much in common with both firstborn and last-born children. They seek achievement like firstborns and usually enjoy being the center of attention like the youngest. They may become pampered and spoiled, focusing only on their own needs, but also may integrate the achievement orientation of the firstborn with the creativity of later-born children. Because other family members are all adults, these children typically mature early and learn to cooperate and deal well with adults. However, if their parents are insecure, only children may adopt parental worries and insecurities.

Birth spacing, or the years between the birth of the children within a family, may also have an impact on the dynamics of birth order. A gap of 5 or more years between children may cause the child to be treated as an only child or as a firstborn. If large gaps exist between groups of children in a large family, each subgroup may be treated as a separate unit and have unique birth order experiences (Carlson & Englar-Carlson, 2017). For example, if child 1 and child 2 are 3 years apart, and there is a gap of 7 years before child 3 is born, and child 4 and child 5 follow in 2-year intervals, then child 1 and child 2 form a birth order grouping of firstborn and second, and child 3 and child 4 may form another grouping of firstborn and second. Similarly, large families may operate as though they have more than one group of children, with each group having a child who functions as the oldest, one who functions as the youngest, and children in the middle. This is especially likely in families in which many years separate groups of children.

Gender may also play a role in how children experience and are treated relative to their birth order. Regardless of where in the sibling order the child falls, the firstborn of either gender will often be treated as a firstborn. As an example, if a family has two sons and then has two daughters, the first daughter and the first son will both be treated as firstborns. The son is the true firstborn, but the first daughter is the first female child in the household.

In addition, if a family has three daughters and only one son, the son will often be treated as a firstborn no matter where in the birth order he is born. The fact that he is the only one of his sex allows him to take on the characteristics of a firstborn and be treated as such. This dynamic can also apply if the family consists of one daughter in a household of sons.

Research has validated many of Adler's assumptions about the impact of birth order on personality, but some discrepant results suggest that caution should be used when drawing conclusions about the connections between personality and birth order (Bleske-Rechek & Kelley, 2014; Hotz & Pantano, 2015; Rohrer, Egloff, & Schmukle, 2015). Variables within families can have a complex impact on these patterns. For example, when twins are born, families tend to treat one child as older than the other, artificially determining their birth order. When a firstborn is a girl or is impaired in some way, families may inadvertently promote the second child into the position of firstborn. High expectations will be held for that child, while the firstborn will be treated like a second-born. In addition, the way in which children respond to their positions will have an impact on their personalities and behaviors.

Therapists should not stereotype people according to birth order. At the same time, exploring birth order and the influence it has on the development of an individual's personality can help with understanding an individual. Inventories such as the White-Campbell Psychological Birth Order Inventory (White, Campbell, & Steward, 1995) can facilitate accurate assessment of the unique impact birth order has had on a client's development.

Birth order occurs within a complex, multifaceted family constellation. Younger siblings, for instance, may crave stimulation and may be used to having things done for them. They are also constantly playing "catch-up" to the oldest children. Middle children are often diplomats and people pleasers who dislike conflict; they often feel "left out" due to the privileges of the oldest born and the pampering of the youngest born. Firstborns are often used to being number one, tend to be very detailed and analytical, and have the highest rate of academic success (Carlson & Englar-Carlson, 2017). Researchers have also found that career choice and lifestyle themes correlate with birth order (Carlson & Englar-Carlson). While more research needs to be done, some evidence suggests that people are influenced, in some ways, by their birth order.

Social Interest and Community Feeling

Adler had strong ideas on what constitutes emotional health. He distinguished between well-adjusted and maladjusted people on the basis of their goals and their lifestyles. People who are well-adjusted have a private logic that reflects common sense as well as social interest; they perceive themselves as part of a community and appreciate individual differences. Those who are maladjusted focus only on their own needs and fail to recognize the importance of their social context and the needs of others. Therefore, two of Adler's most important concepts are social interest and community feeling.

He believed that people are, by nature, social beings interested in belonging to a group and desiring to solve the problems of their society. Consequently, people want to feel connected to others and when they accomplish this, they experience a **community feeling**, which is the sense that they belong to and are connected to all of humanity and committed to making the world a better place.

Social interest involves being as concerned about others as one is about oneself. People's social interest is best reflected in their accomplishment of what Adler viewed as the three life tasks: work, love, and social interest (Adler, 1938). Social interest can be assessed by how successfully people negotiate relationships, the degree of closeness they maintain in those relationships, and their connectedness and contributions to society. Although Freud acknowledged the importance of love and work, Adler (1938) added social interest, which refers to people's awareness of belonging in the community and the extent of their sense of being a fellow human. Although Adler viewed early childhood experiences as important in determining the nature of our social interest, he believed that social interest could be taught and developed; thus, he conveyed optimism not only for the individual but also for our society.

Through awareness that we are part of the human community, as well as through the development of social interest, our feelings of inferiority, alienation, and anxiety diminish, and we develop feelings of belonging and happiness. We no longer view ourselves as alone, seeking to diminish others to advance ourselves. Instead, we recognize that the goods and ills in our society all have an impact on us and that we can best achieve our own goals of significance and competence by contributing to the greater good. Adler's emphasis on social connectedness is very timely and congruent, given the importance of therapists to develop multicultural competence and appreciate diversity.

THE THERAPEUTIC PROCESS

Adler's theory is optimistic, growth-oriented, and educational. Adler believed that people could change their goals and lifestyles to achieve happier and more fulfilling lives. In this section, we address the phases of Adlerian therapy, along with the therapeutic goals, function and role of the therapist, and a discussion of the therapeutic relationship in Adlerian therapy.

Therapeutic Goals

Adler viewed healthy, well-functioning adults as individuals who are independent, emotionally and physically self-reliant, useful and productive, and able to cooperate with others for both personal and social benefit. The main goal of Adlerian therapy is to help clients increase their sense of belonging and to increase behaviors that are more centered on social interest and community feeling. This is accomplished through assisting clients in developing insight and self-awareness, and helping them to modify their lifestyles so that they are more adaptive and useful. Adler sought to help people realize that feelings of pain and inadequacy are caused not by others but by their own faulty logic and the behaviors and attitudes that stem from that logic. Therapists often help clients through education, providing information, teaching, and, most importantly, offering encouragement. By enabling people to become aware of their faulty logic; to establish healthy, realistic, and rewarding goals; and to align their lifestyles, their thinking, and their behavior with those goals, therapists can help people overcome their feelings of inferiority, dependency, and excessive fears of failure. Therefore, another goal of Adlerian therapy is to replace feelings of inferiority and discouragement with self-confidence and courage. When people develop self-confidence, courage, and social interest, they are more likely to achieve a healthier adjustment and a more rewarding lifestyle.

These concepts can be applied to Edie Diaz, the woman discussed throughout this book. Edie developed a guiding self-ideal, early in life, of being a wife and mother in a caring and supportive family. Her short- and long-range goals all focused on that ideal, as did many elements of her lifestyle. However, the abuse and neglect she experienced during childhood have made it difficult for her to overcome her feelings of inferiority; she does not know how to realize her goals, to become part of a family and community, and to appreciate herself. She is working, in counseling, to develop an effective private logic and lifestyle and to align her lifestyle with her self-ideal. Overall, the main goals of Adlerian therapy include the following:

- Increase clients' sense of belonging through social interest and community feeling.
- Replace clients' feelings of discouragement and inferiority with self-confidence and courage.
- Alter clients' lifestyles through modification of goals and perspectives.
- Encourage clients to view others as equals.
- Help clients to actively contribute to society.

Therapist's Function and Role

Therapists using Adlerian therapy take on many roles. One of the most important tasks therapists have is to assess their clients accurately. Therapists rely on the lifestyle assessment, family constellation, early recollections, and dreams. These tools are believed to be the best ways to gather information about clients and their level of functioning. By assessing accurately, therapists can learn about their client's failures and successes, their stories, and the relationships they have with their family members. In addition, therapists learn about how their clients think, behave, and feel in both adaptive and maladaptive ways.

Therapists also do not label, diagnose, or pathologize their clients. Instead, they aim to understand their clients fully. By doing so, they can help their clients gain more awareness, challenge themselves, and modify their life stories. The goal is to help clients see how their current life stories are limiting them and how to change them to more fulfilling and preferable alternatives.

Therapists aim to understand clients' private logic. **Private logic**, our beliefs about ourselves and our place in the world, is subjective and based on lifestyle. Adler believed that every situation depends on the view taken of it. Thus, private logic, no matter how faulty, provides a life pattern or "law of movement" that begins in childhood and offers a compass by which to live. If the idea proves wrong, it will eventually be confronted by reality. The need (for superiority, for power, or to be aversive) does not change; rather, our worldview or personal logic will contrive to drive our thinking and behavior (Adler, 1998). Private logic has been described as the inner rationale we use for justifying our lifestyle and the way to achieve our goals (Dreikurs, 1973).

Because we are part of a larger social system and must learn to interact with that system, we develop our own set of rules to help us to overcome our feelings of inferiority and achieve our goals. Consider, for example, a 4-year-old boy who does not want to put on his shoes, despite his mother's request to do so. The child evaluates the situation and knows he must cooperate with his mother and put on the shoes. But how can he do this without caving in to his mother's wishes and feeling inferior? Using his private logic, he comes up with a solution and tells his mother to close her eyes. His private logic is telling him that if she closes her eyes and does not see him putting on the shoes, she will not have gained the upper hand, and he will not feel inferior for having lost the battle.

Private logic is unique to each person—and is not always logical! Fear of inferiority or feelings of superiority are meaningful only to the individual. The individual who lacks social interest can become disconnected from society, experience anxiety about group interactions, and fear rejection. These feelings of inferiority can cause a self-focus that leads to neurosis, psychosis, addictions, and an inability to cope in the world. In the case of the psychopath, the result of erroneous private logic manifests as uncooperativeness, social isolation or withdrawal, and the development of an antisocial personality.

One of the goals in Adlerian therapy is to understand people's private logic to help them better understand where their beliefs get in the way of daily functioning, to lessen the faulty thinking of private logic, and to help people change this framework and see things in a healthier way. People are responsible for how they achieve the three tasks of life (work, love, and social interest; discussed below), and social interest is the key component of developing a healthy lifestyle (Manaster, 2009).

Just as therapists pay particular attention to private logic, they also pay attention to other thoughts, behaviors, and background experiences that have an impact on and are important to the client. Therapists aim to learn about their clients' private logic, lifestyle, and the guiding self-ideal, which all stem from heredity and early experiences. Therapists pay attention to their clients' basic mistakes, faulty thinking, and useless or selfish goals. Some of the most common faulty thinking involves mistrust, selfishness, unrealistic aspirations, and lack of confidence. By pointing faulty thinking out to their clients, therapists can help them understand these constructs and thereby enable them to challenge and modify their beliefs and to develop new and more rewarding goals, a modified lifestyle, and constructive and positive social interest and behaviors.

Relationship Between Therapist and Client

Adler was ahead of his time in emphasizing the importance of a positive therapeutic relationship. He advocated for the use of many of the techniques—later described by Carl Rogers—in building the therapeutic relationship. Adler believed in the importance of true caring and involvement, the use of empathy, and solid listening skills, and he believed that these are what help clients overcome the feelings of inferiority and fear that they often bring into counseling. Initial questions explore clients' expectations for counseling, their views of their problems, how they have tried to improve their lives, and what has led them to seek counseling at the present time.

Adler emphasized the importance of a cooperative interaction that involves establishment of shared goals as well as mutual trust and respect. The therapeutic relationship in Adlerian counseling is egalitarian, in which the client is as much an expert as the therapist. The therapist and client work together to map the client's lifestyle, create insight, and foster change. This view is consistent with the aims of his approach; he sought to foster responsibility and social interest and saw the establishment of a therapeutic relationship in which client and therapist collaborated to achieve goals they had formulated together as important in promoting client growth.

Therapists following Adler's approach have a complex role that calls for the application of a broad range of skills. These therapists are educators, fostering social interest and teaching people ways to modify their lifestyles, behaviors, and goals. They are analysts who identify faulty logic and assumptions. They explore and interpret the meaning and impact of clients' birth order, dreams, early recollections, and drives. They act as role models, demonstrating ways to think clearly, search for meaning, collaborate with others, and establish and reach meaningful goals. Particularly valuable is the modeling of good communication skills and acting honestly and fairly. They are also supportive and encouraging, urging clients to take risks and helping them accept their own mistakes and imperfections. Therapists also encourage clients to explore their lifestyles, gain insight into aspects of incongruity or inaccuracy, and take action to correct any existing difficulties.

THERAPEUTIC TECHNIQUES AND PROCEDURES

Adlerian therapists use a wide variety of techniques and interventions. In this section, the phases of Adlerian therapy and commonly used Adlerian counseling techniques will be discussed.

Phases of Adlerian Therapy

Although they often merge and overlap, four counseling phases can be identified in Adler's model: (1) establishing a collaborative therapeutic relationship and a shared view of the counseling goals; (2) assessment, analysis, and understanding of the person and the problem; (3) encouraging clients' self-understanding and insight; and (4) reorientation by turning insight into action and focusing on **assets** (strengths) rather than weaknesses (Carlson, Watts, & Maniacci, 2006; Day, 2008). These phases do not necessarily progress in a linear fashion, and clients may move back and forth between phases.

Phase 1: Establishing a Relationship

As previously mentioned, Adlerian therapists place a premium on the therapeutic relationship, and it is the starting place for therapeutic change. In fact, Adlerian therapists make it a point to focus on the person first, then the problem. To establish the relationship, Adlerian therapists listen, understand, care for, believe in, respect, and support their clients. Providing support is also important because clients tend to feel discouraged and lack self-worth. Client **encouragement** helps to build relationships with clients and prevent discouragement, and it is important in all phases of counseling. When therapists encourage clients, they support their beliefs and behaviors to foster change. Therefore, focusing on strengths and skills clients have, rather than on their weaknesses, is essential. Suggestions for how counselors can effectively encourage clients are provided in Table 3.2.

TABLE 3.2 Counselor Strategies for Effective Encouragement

- Focus on what people are doing rather than evaluating their performance. Asking "What did you do to pass all of your courses?" is more encouraging than "Did you get the best grades in your class?"
- Focus on the present as opposed to the past or the future.
- Focus on the client's behavior rather than the person. "Your careful driving really helped you deal with the sudden snowstorm" is more encouraging than "You're a great driver."
- Focus on the effort rather than the outcome. "Sounds like you really feel good about developing your skating skills" is more encouraging than "Sounds like your skills are almost good enough to make the team."
- Focus on motivation from within (intrinsic) rather than from the outside (extrinsic). "You must have felt a great sense of satisfaction, knowing that all your studying resulted in success on the bar exam" is more encouraging than "You finally passed the bar. Now you'll get that raise."
- Focus on what is being learned rather than the lack of learning. "What did you learn from this challenging relationship?" is more encouraging than "You really need to make better choices in your friends."
- Focus on what is positive rather than what is negative. "So, the odds are on your side" is more encouraging than "So the physician said there is a 40% chance that your disease will recur."

Source: Based on Sweeney, T. J. (2009). *Adlerian counseling and psychotherapy: A practitioner's approach* (5th ed.). New York, NY: Routledge.

As the client and therapist build a collaborative, democratic, and trusting relationship, they can work together to formulate a clear statement of the problem, as well as meaningful and realistic goals. They can also discuss and negotiate agreement on the structure of counseling and the guidelines and procedures for their work.

One way to establish collaborative goals is by developing a contract at the beginning of therapy. While this is not a requirement for Adlerian therapy, it can be helpful for focusing the sessions and establishing an egalitarian relationship. The contract, or plan, can include various aspects, such as what changes clients desire to make, what steps they will take to get there, what may get in the way of clients achieving their goals, how they can change their behavior into more adaptive ways, and how they can use their skills to achieve their goals. This contract can help develop the therapeutic alliance in that it promotes a collaborative relationship and encourages clients to take responsibility for their change process.

Phase 2: Assessing Clients' Psychological Dynamics

A distinctive feature of Adlerian therapy is the focus on in-depth assessment. The importance of the family constellation in the individual's functioning, birth order, and earliest childhood recollections are all considered. Both the initial interview and the Lifestyle Interview provide detailed information about clients' current level of functioning and background leading up to the current distress (Carlson et al., 2006). In the initial interview, the therapist conducts a general assessment of six key domains (Adler, 1956): identifying information, background, current level of functioning, presenting problem, expectations for counseling, and the summary. The goals of this phase of counseling are understanding clients' family background, lifestyles, private logic, and goals, and identifying self-destructive behaviors and faulty logic.

LIFESTYLE ASSESSMENT The lifestyle assessment, which is completed during Phase 2 of counseling, is one of the characteristic features of Adlerian theory and practice. The Lifestyle Interview (see Figure 3.1) is a semistructured process that takes place over three consecutive sessions and consists of 10 sections (Carlson et al., 2006). The first 9 sections are referred to as the family constellation interview, which solicits information from early childhood through adolescence.

Following is an abbreviated list of the types of information that might be asked by an Adlerian therapist in a Lifestyle Interview to elicit background information and developmental influences affecting the **style of life**—a way of seeking to fulfill particular goals that individuals set in their lives (Carlson et al., 2006).

I. *Sibling Relationships/Birth Order.* Names and ages of siblings (in order of birth); relationship (as a child) with siblings; sibling behavior toward client; current relationship.

II. *Physical Development.* Health; childhood growth; physical characteristics. Development delays can lead to a felt minus and/or inferiority complex. Appropriate or above-average physical development can contribute to a perceived plus and/or superiority complex.

III. *School Experience.* Grades; relationship with teachers; attitudes toward school.

IV. *Meanings Given to Life.* Religious beliefs; childhood fears, dreams, ambitions. If you could have changed anything from childhood, what would you have changed?

V. *Sexual Development.* Attitudes toward sexuality, masturbation; questions of sexual abuse or sex play. Healthy sexual development can lead to a perceived plus and difficulty with sexual development can lead to a felt minus.

VI. *Social Development.* Friendships (depth and breadth).

VII. *Parental Influences.* Childhood relationship with each parent described individually; how each handled conflict; showed affection; any preferential treatment.

VIII. *Influence of Neighborhood and Community During Early Development/Cultural values.* Socioeconomic; cultural factors; role of family in the community; values held within the family, neighborhood, community, and society.

IX. *Other Influences and Role Models/Hero Identification.* Any other role models or significant relationships in the child's life; person idolized by individuals who embody their fictional goal. The behaviors and qualities of heroes will likely be replicated to strive toward a perceived plus.

X. *Collection of Early Recollections/Strange Early Memories.* Early memories, before age 10. Individuals may also remember a key event from their early years in a highly distorted way and these memories highlight the individual's key fears and struggles.

XI. *Childhood Attributes.* All individuals have biological and genetic factors that make them organically unique. These attributes, combined with their own unique, subjective life experiences, form the individual's personality.

XII. *Personal Strengths.* Individuals can use the things at which they are inherently talented (e.g., sports, academics) to contribute meaningfully to society and experience a perceived plus.

XIII. *Gender Guidelines.* The messages individuals receive about their genders are key contributors to personality development. When an individual's thoughts, feelings, and behaviors align with gender guidelines from family, friends, or society, a perceived plus is experienced; if significantly different from the messages about gender, felt minus can occur.

XIV. *Dream Analysis.* Dreams can be used to highlight key feelings about current and relevant problems the individual is facing. Events in the dream can be interpreted to identify solutions to problems.

XV. *Three Wishes.* Asking individuals to identify three wishes that they hope will come true in the future is one way to identify areas of felt minus or perceived plus.

FIGURE 3.1 Sample Outline of the Lifestyle Interview.

Source: Adapted from Schultz, D. P., & Schultz, E. S. (2013). *Theories of personality* (11th ed). Boston, MA: Cengage; Sweeney, T. J. (2009). *Adlerian counseling: A practitioner's approach* (5th ed.). New York, NY: Routledge.

The final section gathers early childhood recollections. Focusing primarily on how people have addressed the tasks of love, work, and friendship, therapists seek a holistic understanding of their clients and comprehension of their goals and private logic.

Particularly important are assessing people's levels of satisfaction with themselves, their relationships, and their lives, and looking for examples of faulty logic. Structured guidelines are available to help therapists conduct comprehensive and informative lifestyle assessments. Among these are *Understanding Life-Style: The Psycho-Clarity Process* (Powers & Griffith, 1987), the *Individual Psychology Client Workbook* (Powers & Griffith, 2012), the *BASIS-A Interpretive Manual* (Kern, Wheeler, & Curlette, 1997), and the *Manual for Life Style Assessment* (Shulman & Mosak, 2015). The lifestyle assessment has become a popular tool for therapists in many areas of counseling. Adler's complete assessment for children can be found in *Social Interest: A Challenge to Mankind* (Adler, 1938, pp. 218–225). Furthermore, therapists use the lifestyle assessment to understand the following aspects:

- Social relationships
- Thoughts, feelings, behavior
- Overarching goals
- Internal/external factors
- Felt minus
- Fictional final goal.

The three most important parts of the lifestyle assessment—family constellation and birth order, dreams, and earliest recollections—will be discussed below. Clients' priorities and ways of being, and how these relate to the lifestyle assessment, will also be discussed.

FAMILY CONSTELLATION AND BIRTH ORDER The family constellation is the most complex and dynamic aspect of an Adlerian lifestyle assessment. An understanding of the impact of the family constellation on a person comes from both objective and subjective sources. Objective information includes people's birth order, the number of children in the family, the gender of each child, the number of years between the births of each child, and any special circumstances such as the death of a child or the presence of a physical or intellectual disability in any of the children. Subjective information includes people's perceptions of themselves as children, how their parents felt about and treated each child, clients' relationships with their parents and siblings, ways in which they resembled and differed from their siblings, and patterns of rivalry and cooperation within the family. Additional information on birth order was presented earlier in this chapter.

DREAMS Adler used dreams as a vehicle for promoting self-awareness. De-emphasizing symbolism, Adler viewed dreams as providing important information on lifestyle and current concerns. He believed that both past and current dreams were useful sources of information, with recurrent dreams and recurrent themes within dreams of particular importance. The key to understanding dreams, according to Adler, is the emotion they create and their usefulness in solving current life problems.

EARLIEST RECOLLECTIONS Adler viewed people's earliest recollections as important sources of information on their current lifestyles. According to Adler (1931), whether memories are recalled accurately is unimportant. Rather, he believed that people only retained early memories that were consistent with their views of themselves. Consequently, what mattered were people's reports of their memories, not the accuracy of the memory.

Adlerian therapists usually elicit at least three early memories so that they can identify recurrent themes and patterns. Once the memories have been elicited and written down, each memory is explored with the client. The therapist usually asks about the age when the person believes the recalled events occurred and the thoughts and emotions associated with the recollections. The client's role in the memories is explored, because his or her relationships and interactions with other people in the memories are believed to reflect the person's lifestyle. More information on analyzing earliest recollections is provided in the Skill Development section of this chapter.

PRIORITIES AND WAYS OF BEHAVING People's behaviors also provide a rich and endless source of information about their lifestyles. Inquiring in detail about a person's behavior over a period of time or looking at a series of choices and actions can reveal consistent and repetitive behavioral patterns that reflect lifestyle. The following lifestyles are common reflections of how people orient themselves toward the world (Adler, 1956; Mosak, 2013):

- Ruling and dominating others
- Avoiding challenges (e.g., interpersonal challenges)
- Pleasing and seeking approval from others
- Controlling and managing
- Depending on others and needing to be cared for
- Pursuing superiority and perfection
- Seeking achievement
- Being a martyr or victim
- Seeking comfort
- Promoting social welfare and progress.

After an extensive process of exploration, assessment, and analysis, therapists formulate hypotheses about the nature of clients' lifestyles as well as the faulty assumptions and self-destructive thoughts and behaviors that interfere with their efforts to achieve their goals. This information is presented to clients for discussion and revision, paving the way for the third phase of counseling.

Phase 3: Encouraging Insight and Self-Understanding

Phase 3 can be especially difficult for therapists because they need to be both encouraging and challenging. While remaining supportive, they use **confrontation**, which is facing the conflict head on, and **interpretation**, which is expressing insights to their clients that relate to the client's goals. Confrontation and interpretation are used to help people gain awareness of their lifestyles, recognize the covert reasons behind their behaviors, appreciate the negative consequences of those behaviors, and move toward positive change. Several strategies can help therapists remain caring through this phase of counseling:

- They can focus on the present rather than the past.
- They can be more concerned with consequences than with unconscious motivation.
- They can present their interpretations in ways that are likely to be accepted by clients.

Rather than being dogmatic or authoritarian, therapists state interpretations as guesses or hunches. They might say, "I have a hunch that you threw your brother's hat in the sewer because you wanted more attention from your parents" or "I wonder if you have refused to set a more realistic sale price for your house because the house represents part of your ideal self." With gentle interpretations such as these, therapists seek to educate clients and to promote self-awareness, insight, and discussion rather than to persuade clients to agree with them.

Therapists continue to play an active role during this phase of counseling, presenting alternate possibilities, providing information, and helping people weigh their options and make decisions.

The counselor should emphasize beliefs, attitudes, and perceptions because, according to Adler (1998), only by cognitive means and social interest will behavioral change occur.

Adlerian therapy offers a cohesive, unified theoretical approach that is technically eclectic in the sense that it pulls on a diverse array of techniques (Watts, 2013). Adlerian therapists are multimodal in that they use techniques associated with a variety of theoretical approaches, selecting techniques that will best help clients reach their goals (Watts). More than with many other therapy approaches, Adlerian therapists pull on a variety of dynamic, creative counseling techniques. Adlerians have created their own unique techniques, and many more modern theories use variations of Adlerian techniques (Watts). Table 3.3 provides an overview of commonly used Adlerian therapy

TABLE 3.3 Adlerian Therapy Techniques

Technique	Description	Example
"The question"	This technique allows clients to create goals and to start thinking about possible solutions for their problem. Therapists ask clients, "How would your life be different if you no longer had this problem?" Therapists can also ask, "What if you had a magic wand," or "Let's say you woke up and suddenly didn't have this problem anymore. What would you notice?"	A client who is experiencing depression may answer that the first thing he would notice is waking up in the morning feeling rested and motivated for the day. This might suggest that the client's goal is to have more energy and interest in his day, and the client and therapist can work toward understanding what will help him connect with a greater sense of motivation.
Catching oneself	Therapists can enhance clients' awareness and self-control by helping them to catch themselves when they slip into old, unproductive behaviors. Therapists help clients to identify warning signs or triggers that a negative experience is about to occur. Once clients are aware of their warning signs, therapists encourage them to view the warning signs as stop signs that remind them to pause and redirect themselves. This approach helps clients develop self-awareness and monitor themselves without being self-critical.	A man who often lost his temper and became inappropriately angry recognized that his whole body became tense before he exploded. He was taught to identify signs of physical tension, view them as stop signs, and use deep breathing as a quick and effective way to diffuse his anger.
Pushing the button	Using this technique, therapists help clients become better aware of the control they can have over their emotions, as opposed to allowing their emotions to control them. Therapists encourage clients to alternately imagine pleasant and unpleasant experiences, observe the emotions that accompany each image, and recognize that they can determine which button to push (the pleasant or the unpleasant button).	A young woman who frequently consumed too much alcohol at social events imagined the pride she took in remaining sober (pleasant experience) as well as the embarrassment and physical discomfort she felt after becoming intoxicated (unpleasant experience). Vivid images of these two contrasting experiences helped her abstain from alcohol (push the healthy button).

TABLE 3.3 (*Continued*)

Technique	Description	Example
Spitting in the client's soup	When clients evade or avoid the responsibilities associated with basic life tasks, this confrontive technique may be helpful. Therapists use this technique to increase client awareness and prevent clients from engaging in the maladaptive behaviors in the future. Therapists identify the underlying motivations behind clients' self-defeating behaviors or experiences and then spoil their imagined payoff by making it unappealing.	An aging woman avoids going out in public for fear of how her appearance will be judged. The therapist might point out that this assumes others care about her appearance. The client connects that caring what others think is a sign of vanity and this minimizes the reward she gets from the behavior.
Immediacy	Immediacy involves therapists addressing an interaction between the client and the therapist and/or their experiences with the client in the present moment. Often these experiences mirror the client's interactions outside the session.	A client accused a therapist of disliking him when the therapist provided information on parenting that differed from the client's style of parenting. The therapist used immediacy, and this helped the client see that when people disagree with him, he views it as evidence that they dislike him.
Prescribing the symptom/ Paradoxical intention	Adler was one of the first theorists to discuss the use of paradox in therapy. Therapists invite clients to engage in the problem behavior. The goal of prescribing the symptom is to help clients realize the problem behavior, become aware of the consequences to the behavior, and recognize that it is within their control to change it. Often, the exaggeration seems silly or humorous. Clearly, this intervention should not be used if the symptom poses a danger to the client, such as self-harming behaviors, substance use, or suicide.	A therapist might invite a person who is struggling with often being late to try to be late. Doing so may enhance the client's awareness and increase the client's sense of control over the behavior.
Confrontation	Therapists point out discrepancies or incongruencies in the material that clients present.	A therapist might say, "Talk to me about your decision to spend two thousand dollars on a necklace. You told me that you're concerned about being able to make the down payment on the house you want to buy. Tell me about that discrepancy."

(*Continued*)

TABLE 3.3 (*Continued*)

Technique	Description	Example
Task assignments	Therapists assign a task for clients to complete between sessions. The clients and therapist agree that the clients will engage in a planned activity that will help them reach their goal. Not only do the specific tasks advance counseling, but the process of coming to an agreement on tasks, making a commitment to complete them, and planning and executing the tasks can promote feelings of competence and responsibility.	A client who is frequently angry may be asked to observe and list times when she feels angry in order to gain awareness and identify triggers. Another example may be asking a client to exercise three times a week.
Acting "as if"	This technique serves as a beneficial way for the therapist to change the way clients approach their situations and to promote feelings of confidence and motivation. This technique involves the therapist asking clients to engage in the behaviors or actions they may require for success. The therapist asks clients to act "as if" they were already the person they would like to be, or "as if" their situation was what they wanted.	A single female client comes to counseling reporting that she would like to have a partner; she is lonely and wants companionship. During the lifestyle assessment, it is discovered that she perceives men as untrustworthy. Because of this belief, she is afraid of men, pushes them away, and avoids relationships. Using the "as if" technique, the therapist and client might agree that for 1 week the client will act "as if" men are trustworthy. The assumption of this approach is that when the client can pretend she is able to trust men, new attitudes will begin to develop, and positive changes will occur.
Reflecting "as if"	This is similar to acting "as if"; however, clients are asked to take a step back and reflect on how they would theoretically act. The therapist might ask clients how they would act if they were acting like the person they would like to be. The therapist and client then formulate a list of "as if" behaviors, ranking the behaviors from least difficult to most difficult. Clients begin to enact the least difficult behaviors, gain self-efficacy through success, and then move on to the more difficult behaviors.	A client has social anxiety and fear related to going out in public and meeting new people. The "as if" behavior would be to go out in public with no fear and speak to others. The least difficult "as if" behavior may be to go to the store without talking to anyone. The most difficult "as if" behavior may be public speaking. The client would start with the least difficult behavior and work her way up to the most difficult behavior to assist with overcoming her social anxiety.
An Aha response	The development of a sudden insight into a solution to a problem is an aha response. Clients become aware of their own beliefs and behaviors and suddenly develop understanding. The therapist's role is to notice this awareness and use encouragement and reinforcement to help clients explore their own strengths and encourage aha moments.	A client is struggling with arriving to work on time in the morning, especially due to fatigue. An aha response would be when the client realizes his tardiness to work occurs because he frequently stays up late at night watching TV, which prevents him from waking up on time. He realizes that going to bed earlier will help him wake up on time in order to arrive at work without being late.

TABLE 3.3 (*Continued*)

Technique	Description	Example
Avoiding the tar-baby	A tar-baby is a reference from a 19th-century story. The story tells of a doll made of tar and turpentine, and the more the character in the story tries to pull away from the tar-baby, the more stuck he becomes. Thus, this reference refers to a problem situation that is only aggravated by additional involvement with it. This technique can help the therapist to stay out of the client's faulty assumptions. The tar-baby refers to the perceptions of life that the client carries into counseling and in which therapists sometimes get stuck. "Avoiding the tar" is a way of saying, "not getting stuck or caught up in the client's perceptions." Therapists need to stay in the role of a guider and be nonbiased.	A client may view the world as unsafe and think that people do not have his best interest in mind. The client places this belief onto the therapist and sees her as untrustworthy and pushes her away. The therapist stays neutral and unbiased to avoid the false perception, and also to avoid falling into the trap of not being supportive secondary to being pushed away by the client.

techniques. Therapists can use these during any phase of counseling. Note that for any of these techniques to be effective, a solid therapeutic relationship is required.

Phase 4: Putting Insights into Practice

Once clients have gained some insight and modified their distorted beliefs, they are ready to reorient their lives and initiate new ideas and patterns of behaviors. **Reorientation** involves clients changing their lifestyles by altering their rules of interaction and their behaviors. Clients now view their lives from different perspectives and can make more rewarding choices. Therapists foster this outcome by helping people become full participants in their social system, shift their roles and interactions, and take positive actions to achieve their revised goals. Specifically, therapists help their clients enhance their sense of belonging, take an interest in others, increase their courage and humor, and accept their imperfections. Throughout this phase, therapists model and nurture optimism and flexibility; they support clients in developing the courage to be imperfect and take on rewarding challenges.

The reorientation and change phase can be divided into four parts (Sweeney, 2009):

1. Clients clarify their goals and determine whether they are realistic.
2. Common sense and clear thinking are applied to clients' feelings, beliefs, and goals. Although clients are reminded that their choices are their own, therapists help them use common sense to evaluate and, if necessary, modify their thinking.
3. New learning is applied to the clients' lives.
4. Any barriers to progress are addressed and removed.

This final phase of counseling enables people to solidify the gains they have made and move forward with their lives in healthier and more fulfilling ways. Therapists continue to provide education, teach skills, and make interpretations. However, their primary role is reinforcing positive changes. It is particularly important for clients to continue to make changes outside therapy. Applying what they learned in therapy in their daily life helps solidify the progress they have already made. Clients and therapists collaborate in evaluating progress, strengthening social interest and healthy and rewarding beliefs, and planning future steps toward goal attainment. Together, they determine when the client is ready to complete counseling and agree on follow-up procedures to ensure that clients stay on track and continue their positive growth and forward movement.

APPLICATION AND CURRENT USE OF ADLERIAN THERAPY

Adler's model of Individual Psychology can be applied to a broad range of situations and clients. It can be used when counseling children, individuals, couples, families, and groups, and it also is used in career development, education, training, supervision, consultation, and organizational development.

Counseling Applications

Adler was a theorist ahead of his time in that he called on helpers to become social activists and to address the prevention and remediation of social conditions that were harmful to human development. His focus on prevention and early intervention was also pioneering. He frequently advocated for the integration of his theory into school, mental health, and family settings.

Adler's theory is based on a growth model and does not have a focus on psychopathology or problems in living. As such, it has broad application to a variety of settings. In addition to individual counseling with youth and adults, his theory has been used effectively in family therapy, in group counseling, in parenting training, in many diverse mental health settings, in school counseling and school psychology, and even in addressing cultural conflicts. His ideas have even been used in dealing with various social problems (e.g., poverty), in business settings, and they have been applied in a number of diverse countries around the world. Adlerian therapy also lends itself to integration with other types of therapies (Carlson & Robey, 2011) and can be adapted as a resilience-focused brief family therapy (Nicoll, 2007).

Most of the common problems seen in counseling and psychotherapy are amenable to counseling via Adlerian therapy (Noronha, 2014; Paige, DeVore, Chang, & Whisenhunt, 2017). The research literature provides many examples, techniques, and descriptions of the use of Adlerian therapy, and it has been researched and applied to different populations. As an example, this approach is useful with people who are experiencing dysfunctional responses to traumatic experiences (Morrison, 2009; Paige et al.). Adlerian therapy may also be helpful for people who are struggling with grief and loss (Noronha, 2014). People experiencing self-esteem struggles and social and relationship concerns also seem likely to benefit from Adlerian therapy. Children with behavioral problems and those who have been traumatized are well suited to counseling with Adlerian play therapy (Morrison, 2009; Meany-Walen, Kottman, Bullis, & Taylor, 2015). Adlerian therapy can also be effective with children who have ADHD, oppositional youth, and at-risk youth (Day, 2008; Sapp, 2006). Adlerian theory is compatible with Alcoholics Anonymous and other 12-step programs, and it can help empower people who are struggling with addictions (Stone, Contech, & Francis, 2017).

Individual Psychology has applications for school counseling and school psychology. School-based interventions can be used to closely attend to a specific student's mistaken goals. Therapists can help teachers understand a youth's mistaken goal (e.g., seeking attention) and find ways to preemptively meet the youth's needs in the classroom. For example, a teacher might report that a youth is often out of his seat and joking with peers. Therapists can find socially useful ways for the youth to get positive attention, such as being a hallway monitor or having a special job in the classroom. Therapists can even implement behavioral interventions (e.g., token reward system) in conjunction with Adlerian theory to shape desirable behaviors that meet the youth's underlying social needs while being more helpful in the classroom.

APPLICATION TO GROUP COUNSELING Adlerian concepts have been used in group counseling. Because Adlerian theory views problems as primarily of a social nature, group counseling is particularly beneficial because group members have the opportunity to develop social interest, community, and belonging. Adlerian group counseling focuses heavily on early recollections. Through sharing early recollections, group members can gain a better understanding of their basic mistakes, attitudes and beliefs, and goals for future behavior. Adlerian group therapists are also recognized for their use in implementing action and modifying goals for a more active change process. For example, group members are often asked to use the technique **acting as if**, to demonstrate the person they desire to be, and catching themselves, to challenge their beliefs and behaviors. Group members are encouraged to utilize what they learned in group in their everyday life and to take active steps for finding solutions.

APPLICATION TO FAMILY THERAPY AND PARENTING Alfred Adler was the first psychoanalyst to adopt a holistic view that considered the importance of family relationships in the creation of the individual. By 1922, Adler was involving the entire family in the counseling process. In later years, he helped to create child guidance clinics where teachers, parents, and schools worked together to help children develop better self-esteem, overcome feelings of inferiority, and create more positive child development processes.

Adlerian constructs such as birth order, sibling rivalry, inferiority, and social interest implied that the individual could only be understood in relation to the whole. Adler's holistic approach introduced the following concepts to psychotherapy, which had, until that time, been largely influenced by Freud's theories of drives:

- The effect of the family constellation—the overall structure of the family—on individual and family functioning
- The idea that people must be viewed in their family, social, and cultural contexts
- The importance of establishing a collaborative therapeutic alliance
- A positive focus that emphasizes strengths, encouragement, empowerment, and support
- A focus away from pathology (i.e., problems are a normal part of life that provide opportunities for growth)
- Psychoeducation as part of the therapeutic process.

Family therapists can implement proven systems for family therapy that were derived from Adlerian theory. Specifically, *Active Parenting Today* is a family-based intervention for children that is included in the Substance Abuse and Mental Health Services Administration's (SAMHSA's) National Registry of Evidence-Based Programs and Practices (Active Parenting, 2016). *Active Parenting for Teens* is an evidence-based method for implementing Adlerian-based principles in family therapy with adolescent clients who have mental health and behavioral difficulties. In addition, Systematic Training for Effective Parenting (STEP) evolved from Adlerian theory and is one of the leading parent education programs in the United States (Dinkmeyer & McKay, 1997).

When using family-based interventions, parents are invited to evaluate the ways in which they might be contributing to a youth's feelings of inadequacy and ways in which their children can be encouraged to get their needs met in more helpful ways. Parents are also taught how to be more empathetic, understanding, and supportive of their child. Some helpful techniques for creating insight and supporting behavioral change include Socratic questioning, creative activities that highlight social connections, role plays, and systematically reframing thoughts to produce healthier feelings and behaviors. Therapists pay special attention to harnessing resources that meet children's needs in healthy ways, such as membership in an after-school program or increased quality time with parents. When possible, therapists teach parents and stakeholders to encourage desirable traits in youth, and therapists praise positive youth behaviors in session as well.

The **CARE acronym** has been proposed as one way therapists can help parents interact with youth from an Adlerian perspective (Sweeney, 2009). First, parents should *Catch* themselves and avoid acting impulsively and emotionally in difficult situations, as doing so can lead to unhelpful interactions with children. Next, instead of reacting out of frustration or anger, parents should *Assess* the goals of a child's behaviors. That is, therapists should help parents understand the child's social needs, their experience of the felt minus, mistaken goals, and fictional final goals. Therapists can educate parents about the ways that these factors, compounded by various other lifestyle factors, lead youth toward unhelpful behaviors. Parents who are able to understand the underlying motivations of youth behaviors are able to avoid taking such behaviors personally and are better able to *Respond* in empathic, encouraging ways. Finally, parent responses must be *Executed* consistently.

Therapists can teach parents to respond to youth in ways that effectively allow the youth to grow and develop. As previously mentioned, encouragement is a key method for helping youth find healthy ways to meet their needs. Whenever possible, parents should be encouraged to highlight the youth's positive intention behind an unhelpful behavior and provide a more helpful alternative. For example, consider a youth who steals a sibling's toy to get his attention. A parent could respond in this way: "Johnny, it is so good that you want to make a connection with your brother. Could you please ask him to play with you instead of stealing his toy?"

Adler's ideas, especially as interpreted by Dreikurs, Dinkmeyer, and others, can provide a solid foundation for teaching parenting skills, improving family functioning, and helping parents to raise healthy children. Dreikurs had a vision of families that emphasized communication, respect, encouragement, teaching, the use of natural and **logical consequences**, and the expectation that children should assume age-appropriate responsibilities. He also recognized the importance of families having fun together, an aspect of family life often forgotten in our busy society. Dreikurs advocated the use of a family council in which all family members convene at the same time each week to talk about their family and address any concerns or difficulties. Even young children should be involved in these meetings and should have the opportunity to express themselves. This fosters a sense of belonging, responsibility, cooperation, and participation. It also teaches children to solve problems in relation to the whole family and not just the individual, which is consistent with the Adlerian focus on social interest (Shifron, 2010). For a child, improving the family connection and feelings of belonging can also reduce feelings of inferiority.

Adlerian concepts have also been applied in working with couples. An understanding of each partner's lifestyle and the interaction between the lifestyles, especially the compatibility, is essential. The goal of Adlerian couples counseling is to assess the beliefs and behaviors of the couple and to develop ways to effectively meet their relationship goals. Couples counseling using Adlerian concepts is usually brief and involves understanding the couple's early recollections of their relationship, including social relationships, occupations, spirituality, and self-worth (Hawes, 1993). Therapists strive to increase social interest, decrease feelings of inferiority, and modify goals to become more realistic (Carlson, Watts, & Maniacci, 2006). Counseling emphasizes choices, resources, and skill building to help the couple achieve satisfaction in their relationship. In addition, couples are taught how to communicate more effectively by using skills like listening, paraphrasing, and understanding expectations.

APPLICATION TO CHILDREN Adlerian therapy is well suited for use with children and has been adopted by many school counselors and therapists who treat children. Adler's approach offers therapists a flexible yet structured approach that lends itself well to addressing both immediate and long-standing concerns of young people. His emphasis on cooperation, character building, and development of self-esteem is compatible with current emphases in counseling children and adolescents.

Adlerian therapy principles applied in the schools often involve a focus on:

- Increasing awareness and appreciation of individual differences
- Teaching about the range of human emotions, promoting awareness of our own feelings, clarifying the impact our actions have on other people's feelings, and encouraging the development of empathy
- Fostering good communication skills
- Promoting cooperation and collaboration skills
- Encouraging responsibility and using natural consequences.

Rudolf Dreikurs, a therapist and writer, spread awareness of Adler's ideas among educators and parents. Dreikurs drew on Adler's ideas in his writings on effective parenting. *Children: The Challenge* (Dreikurs & Soltz, 1991) and *Discipline Without Tears* (Dreikurs, Cassell, & Ferguson, 2004), originally published in 1972, have become classics and are still used in parenting classes. Dreikurs suggested that children's misbehavior reflects their goals and lifestyle. All behavior has a purpose, and he identified four possible motives behind childhood misbehavior, which include attention getting, power, revenge, and withdrawal (displays of inadequacy) (Dreikurs et al., 2004):

> Teachers and parents typically have negative responses to these behaviors. However, their automatic reactions often reinforce an undesirable behavior. For example, they may engage in a power struggle with the child who wants to be in charge or may reprimand an attention-seeking child, inadvertently providing the desired attention. By understanding the goal of a child's misbehavior, people can address it more successfully. For example, teachers and parents should attend to and reinforce only the positive behaviors of attention-seeking children and acknowledge the power of children who want to be in charge, encouraging cooperation and responsibility as part of their leadership role.

Adlerian play therapy is yet another extension of Adler's work. Its purpose is to build relationships with children that (1) enhance their social interest; (2) overcome or reduce their feelings of inferiority; and (3) make changes in their life goals and mistaken beliefs about self, others, and the world (Menassa, 2009).

Application to Multicultural Groups

Adlerian therapy not only has much that would appeal to a diverse and multicultural population, but it also actively seeks to address problems of discrimination and disenfranchisement. Adlerians believe that social discrimination based on ethnicity, gender, poverty, religion, and education level matters and that counseling addresses these issues (Carlson & Robey, 2011). Adler's approach focuses on a constructivist model that works flexibly and collaboratively with individuals and their families.

Therapists who use an Adlerian approach are familiar with the dichotomy of inferiority and superiority. Acknowledging, understanding, and actively challenging feelings of inferiority or stigmatization with clients who feel disenfranchised may be particularly helpful. The emphasis on culture (broadly defined to include age, developmental or acquired disability, ethnicity, religion or spirituality, socioeconomic status, sexual orientation, indigenous heritage, national origin, and gender), social interest, and the family constellation, as well as the importance of collaboration, has wide appeal. According to Adler, prejudice, racism, and gender discrimination grow out of misguided efforts to gain superiority by degrading others. True self-esteem comes not from oppressing others but from working cooperatively to contribute to the common good, empowering ourselves as well as others, and facing life's challenges together.

Adler's focus on community and social interest is consistent with the values of clients who come from more collectivist societies, such as the Middle East, Asian countries, and Latin America. Religion and spirituality are also consistent with Adlerian theory, which considers religion to be a part of social interest (Carlson & Englar-Carlson, 2012).

Adler's approach has particular relevance to people with disabilities. He wrote of the feelings of discouragement and inferiority and the efforts toward compensation that often emerge in people with developmental or acquired disabilities. His understanding of this dynamic, as well as his emphasis on understanding maladjustment and promoting healthy empowerment, responsibility, and realistic self-esteem, should be helpful in counseling people who have difficulty coping with physical and mental challenges (Carlson & Englar-Carlson, 2017). Of course, therapists should be cautious not to overgeneralize and assume that all people with disabilities experience feelings of inferiority.

Adler's insights into people who live with disabilities have a logical extension to those who experience other potential challenges in their lives, such as recent immigrants, people who have experienced adverse childhood events, those who experience poverty or abuse, and those who feel disenfranchised for any reason. Therapists should be aware of social exclusions of groups of people, whether ethnic and racial groups, sexual minorities, women, people who have disabilities, or others. Adler's understanding of the connection between early experiences and the development of lifestyles and goals provides insight into ways in which people with difficult backgrounds cope with their lives, as well as ways to help and empower them.

Although Adler's theories seem compatible with multicultural competence, therapists must still exercise caution when using this approach. Adler's approach in its traditional form involves an extensive gathering of history and background information that may be seen as intrusive by people from some cultures, who may prefer to proceed slowly and establish trust before revealing too much information. The in-depth, lengthy information-gathering process might also not be well suited to people in crisis, who are focused on more immediate concerns, and those who have little interest in lengthy self-analysis. His emphasis on individual responsibility and power, as well as his exploration of early recollections, also may be incompatible with the thinking of some people from non-Western cultures. Consequently, the approach may need to be adapted to such clients.

EVALUATION OF ADLERIAN THERAPY

The strengths in Adler's approach far outnumber its shortcomings and weaknesses. Although developed nearly a century ago, his ideas seem remarkably timely and relevant today. His ideas have endured because they draw on the important concepts of Freudian psychoanalysis; incorporate many elements of modern cognitive, behavioral, and humanistic counseling approaches; and add their own valuable and useful ideas. They also appeal to common sense.

Limitations

Like other approaches that focus on a person's background experiences, Adlerian therapy suffers from a lack of empirical research; however, the research literature in general supports the foundational constructs of Adler's theory (Carlson et al., 2006). Many of Adler's concepts, such as fictional finalism and superiority, are not well defined, risk oversimplification, and are based too heavily on common sense, and this makes it difficult to apply them and measure their validity and effectiveness. Adlerian therapy understands and gives credence to underlying psychological and societal impacts on pathology but fails to account for biological or genetic influences. We now know the impact of genetics on many issues with which clients present (e.g., anxiety and depressive/bipolar disorders, schizophrenia) and reco,gnize that biopsychosocial factors interact in the development of many conditions. Some argue, too, that Adler may have been overly optimistic in his belief that social interest is innate (Bitter, 2011; Stoykova, 2013).

Strengths and Contributions

Adler's contributions, not only to the current practice of psychotherapy but also to the thinking of some of the other leaders in our field, is enormous. Rollo May, Viktor Frankl, Carl Rogers, and Abraham Maslow all acknowledged their debt to Adler, leading Albert Ellis to predict that even more than Freud, Adler is likely the true father of modern psychotherapy (Watts, 2003). The development of cognitive therapy, reality therapy, person-centered counseling, Gestalt, existentialist, and constructivist approaches to counseling have been influenced by Adler's ideas (Rule & Bishop, 2005). Whether or not therapists describe themselves as followers of Adler's approach, nearly all counseling and psychotherapy now reflects some of his concepts, including:

- The impact of early experiences and family constellation on current functioning
- The importance of taking a holistic approach that considers mind, body, and spirit
- The need to view people in their family, social, and cultural contexts
- The recognition that thinking influences emotions and behavior
- The emphasis on strengths, optimism, encouragement, empowerment, and support
- The relevance of lifestyle and goals
- The need to identify, understand the purpose of, and modify repetitive self-defeating behaviors
- The importance of a collaborative therapeutic alliance
- The benefits of having a therapist and client with realistic and mutually agreed-on goals
- The recognition that having problems and differences is a normal part of life and that these can be viewed as opportunities for growth rather than as pathology
- The view of therapy as an educational and growth-promoting process as well as a remedial one.

Adler's theory can easily and effectively be combined with many contemporary counseling approaches. Its emphasis on beliefs and behavior is compatible with cognitive-behavioral therapy, rational emotive behavior therapy, and reality therapy. Adlerian lifestyle assessment has much in common with narrative therapy's emphasis on stories that provide the structure of life. Of course, the attention to early memories and childhood experiences is psychoanalytic in origin, whereas the emphasis on the therapeutic alliance reflects elements of humanistic approaches.

Many of Adler's ideas have become more important than ever in light of some of the pervasive problems in our society today. Our growing awareness of the enduring harm that can result from childhood trauma has focused attention on the significance of how early childhood experiences and memories can impact one's development. Adler's call for social equality of women, respect for cultural and religious diversity, and an end to marginalization of minority groups still needs attention in our society (Sharf, 2016). His emphasis on responsibility, resilience, character building, and social interest seems especially relevant in light of the many acts of bullying, torture, and violence in our society. The importance of fathers and of sibling relationships is another area of current attention. Probably of greatest importance are Adler's emphasis on respect for individual differences and the importance of each of us becoming a contributing part of a larger social system.

SKILL DEVELOPMENT: ANALYZING EARLIEST RECOLLECTIONS

Eliciting and analyzing people's earliest recollections can provide understanding of their lifestyles and how they view the world. The following four-step procedure, followed by examples, will help you learn to use **early recollections** (memories of actual incidents that clients recall from their childhood) in counseling. Exercises later in this chapter give you the opportunity to practice these skills.

1. *Eliciting the recollections.* Begin by inviting people to think back to their childhood, as early as they can remember, and describe at least three incidents they recall. They should come up with experiences that included them and that they remember clearly rather than family stories or pictures they have seen. The therapist should write down each recollection as it is described.
2. *Processing each memory.* Ask about the person's feelings during the memory; discuss any actions or movements in the memory, especially transactions between the client and others; ask what part of the memory seems most vivid or important; and ask what meaning the memory has for the teller.
3. *Analyzing the memories.* Looking particularly for commonalities among the three or more recollections, consider the role of the client in the memories, the emotions associated with the memories, who else is present and how they are interacting with the client, the nature of the situations recalled, and the way in which the client responded to the events and interactions in the memories.
4. *Interpretation and application.* Develop a hypothesis or hunch, based on the common themes and patterns in the recollections, as to what these memories disclose about the person's goals and lifestyle. Present this hypothesis to the client for discussion and clarification.

Consider the following three recollections provided by a 27-year-old single woman:

Recollection 1: I remember being in my bed. It was very dark and I felt afraid. I was crying. Then my father came into the room. He picked me up and held me. He said something like, "What's the matter? Everything is all right now."

Recollection 2: I was in a department store. Somehow I got separated from my mother. I looked around, and I couldn't see her. I didn't know what to do, and I started to scream. This man came over, a salesperson or a manager in the store. He took me into a little room—an office, I guess—and he said he would help me find my mommy. He asked my name and then I heard something about a lost child over the loudspeaker. The man gave me some candy and kept talking to me. It seemed like a long time, but finally my mother came. She was crying, too. I was so happy to see her.

Recollection 3: I was riding a tricycle, and I fell down. Nobody was around to help me. My knee was bleeding. I was crying and hurt, but nobody came. Finally, a neighbor heard me. He came out to see what the problem was, and then he called my mother. I felt better as soon as there was somebody to help me.

Analysis: In all three recollections, the woman is scared and perceives herself as needing help. Through crying, she is able to let others know that she needs help but is not able to otherwise help herself. In all three instances, caring men rescue her. They reassure her and provide the help she needs. Although her mother subsequently provides help in two of the memories, the men are the ones there when the child really needs help. Discussion revealed that this woman often felt fearful and doubted her own ability to move ahead in her career and cope with her life. She had been engaged twice and was eager to marry, but both times her fiancés had broken the engagement, telling her that she was too needy and dependent. The woman became aware that, although she was a successful teacher, she expected to get into trouble in some way and was hoping to be rescued from the demands of her career by marriage. At the same time, she indicated that she didn't trust people very much, especially women, and that she often felt overwhelmed by the day-to-day demands of her life. By assuming a needy and helpless role, she was actually undermining her relationships but believed that the way to find a man to rescue her was to become as needy as possible: the child crying loudly for help. This information played an important part in her counseling.

CASE APPLICATION

Ava, age 10, is Edie and Roberto's daughter. The family's therapist decided to have some individual sessions with Ava to get to know her and her role in the family and to develop a positive relationship with her. In addition, both Edie and Roberto expressed concerns about Ava's behavior. They described her as always being willful and independent, with these problems worsening in recent months. They reported that Ava is disobedient, both at home and at school, and that her teacher told them that some of the children do not want to play with her because she is "bossy." In addition, Ava's grades have been declining.

Ava was willing to meet with the therapist for an individual session. Ava was quite open and started off the session by describing how much she liked the new Spider-Man movie she had seen the night before. She expressed her enjoyment at how Spider-Man "got the bad guys" and "saved the day." Ava talked about some of her concerns related to her family. She described her mother as "crying a lot and moping around," while her father worked long hours and "just yells about everything." She also reported a dream that she compared to *Alice's Adventures in Wonderland*, in which her mother was getting smaller while Ava was getting larger. As Ava talked, the therapist began to formulate hypotheses about Ava's lifestyle, her goals, and the reasons for her misbehavior.

Toward the end of the session, the therapist asked Ava to describe three early recollections:

Recollection 1: Ava recalled that when she was about 4 years old she became afraid of spiders. Once, while taking a walk with her father, she noticed a spider on her shoe and became upset. Her father brushed the spider off and squashed it. Ava was so impressed by his act that she began squashing every bug she saw until her mother discouraged this.

Recollection 2: Another memory from a year or so later involved an incident when the mother of her friend Lori took Ava and Lori swimming. When Ava got out of the car, she swung her car door into another car and chipped the paint. The person sitting in the car complained to Lori's mother, but she just told him "not to make a big deal out of nothing" and took the children into the pool.

Recollection 3: The last memory involved a fight between her parents when Ava was in kindergarten. Her mother had burned the lasagna that was to be served for dinner. When Roberto arrived home, he yelled at Edie for being careless. Edie began to cry, but Roberto just went into the other room and ordered pizza. Ava remembered thinking that the pizza was much better than the lasagna would have been.

In all three memories, Ava's initial role is that of observer. Although her own behavior is a factor in the first two memories, what she recalled most sharply were the actions of the adults who used strength and anger to gain power and control. In the last two memories, other people's feelings are disregarded. Roberto and the friend's mother seem admirable to Ava, while she views her own mother as weak.

These memories confirmed many of the therapist's hypotheses. Ava's misbehavior seemed to be a misguided attempt to gain power. She wanted to be in charge and wanted other people to stop controlling her. Her recollections suggest that she believes the way to obtain power is to become dominating, telling other people what to do, a behavior she has observed in her father and others. Her mother, who has a very different style, is devalued in Ava's mind because she seems to lack power. This has carried over to Ava's loss of interest in school, which her mother highly values. Ava's behavior is harming her relationships with both her peers and her parents.

Future sessions will involve both play therapy and talking to help Ava recognize her self-destructive efforts to obtain power and to change both her private logic and her repertoire of behaviors so that she finds more rewarding ways to gain power. Discussion would include exploration of Ava's roles and relationships with family members, basic messages and coping behaviors she learned as a child, her current lifestyle, and whether her beliefs and behavior are helping her to achieve the central goals of her life. This information also will be used in sessions with Roberto and Edie to help them parent Ava more effectively.

REFLECT AND RESPOND

1. List at least three of your earliest memories. Process and analyze them according to the guidelines in the Skill Development section. What patterns emerge? What sorts of goals and lifestyle do they suggest? How does this information relate to your image of yourself? Write your memories and responses to these questions in your journal.
2. Identify a challenge you are facing that you are not sure you can handle successfully. Imagine yourself capable of dealing with that challenge. Be sure the image of yourself is clear and vivid in your mind. Now think about how the person reflected by this image of yourself would handle the challenge. As you address this issue in your life, act as if you are that image of yourself and keep reminding yourself that you can handle the situation. After you have made some progress, monitor your success. Think about how well this technique is working and how you might improve on this intervention. Write a summary of this experience in your journal.
3. For one week, keep a dream journal. Set a goal each night to get about 7 hours of sleep. Before you go to bed, take a few seconds to write about your day. Then, when you wake up each morning, grab your journal and write about your dream using the following prompts:
   - Provide as much detail as you can, and include names, colors, textures, visions, and smells.
   - Share your emotional responses to your dream.
   - What dream symbols or metaphors did you identify?
   - Provide a brief evaluation of this process.

Summary

This chapter focused on the development of Adlerian therapy. Adlerian therapy made an important contribution to our understanding of therapy and continues to be widely practiced. One of the most important strengths of Individual Psychology is its flexibility (Watts, 2000). As one of the oldest approaches to psychotherapy, Adler's model is useful with a broad range of people and difficulties. His emphasis on encouragement and logic rather than pathology, power and importance rather than sexuality, and family and society rather than the unconscious are appealing to many therapists and contribute to client empowerment. Many of Adler's concepts, including goals, private logic, priorities, and lifestyle, provide a useful framework for understanding people. In addition, the interventions and tools that have grown out of his model help therapists use his ideas to assess, educate, and encourage change in their clients.

The basic goal of Adler's approach is to help clients identify and adjust their cognitions and beliefs about the self, others, and life. This chapter discussed family constellations and birth order, explaining the significance of birth order on personality and development. Adler believed that many things, such as social interest, private logic, basic mistakes, and lifestyle, have a huge impact on emotional and mental health. In this chapter, the typical phases of Adlerian counseling and associated counseling techniques were discussed.

Recommended Readings

Adler, A. (2011). *Social interest: A challenge to mankind.* Eastford, CT: Martino Fine Books.

Adler, A. (2011). *The practice and theory of individual psychology.* Eastford, CT: Martino Fine Books.

Carlson, J., & Maniacci, M. P. (2011). *Alfred Adler revisited.* New York, NY: Routledge.

Dreikurs, R., & Soltz, V. (1991). *Children: The challenge: The classic work on improving parent-child relations—intelligent, humane & eminently practical.* New York, NY: Plume.

Grey, L. (1998). *Alfred Adler, the forgotten prophet: A vision for the 21st century.* Westport, CT: Praeger.

Hoffman, E. (1994). *The drive for self: Alfred Adler and the founding of individual psychology.* Reading, MA: Addison-Wesley.

Stein, H. T. (2007). Adler's legacy: Past, present and future. *Journal of Individual Psychology, 63,* 205–213.

Sweeney, T. J. (2009). *Adlerian counseling: A practitioner's approach,* (5th ed.). Philadelphia, PA: Taylor & Francis.

MyLab Counseling

Try the Topic 1 Assignments: Adlerian Therapy.

CHAPTER 4

Post- and Neo-Freudian Psychoanalytic Therapies

Learning Outcomes

When you have finished this chapter, you should be able to:
- Understand the context and development of Neo-Freudian Psychoanalytic Therapies.
- Communicate the key concepts associated with Neo-Freudian Psychoanalytic Therapies and understand how they relate to therapeutic processes.
- Describe the therapeutic goals of Neo-Freudian Psychoanalytic Therapies.
- Identify the common techniques used in Neo-Freudian Psychoanalytic Therapies.
- Understand how Neo-Freudian Psychoanalytic Therapies relates to counseling diverse populations.
- Identify the limitations and strengths of Neo-Freudian Psychoanalytic Therapies.

One of Freud's greatest contributions was his ability to attract people to his ideas who were themselves brilliant and innovative thinkers with a deep interest in human development and psychology. Carl Jung, like Alfred Adler, was a close colleague of Freud and was strongly influenced by his concepts. Jung, however, disagreed with Freud on several major theoretical concepts and went on to develop his own innovative ideas. Jung and Adler were not the only analysts to develop alternatives to strict psychoanalytic orthodoxy. Anna Freud, the youngest daughter of Sigmund Freud who became "the spokesperson for psychoanalysis" after her father died, and a pioneer in child psychology, extended his theories into child analysis, education, and parenting (Hergenhahn, 2009, p. 565). At the same time, Melanie Klein began developing her own views on analysis with children, and Karen Horney, another follower of psychoanalysis, disagreed with Freud's theory that anatomy is destiny and suggested instead that men envy womens' capacity for motherhood. Within Horney's work are the first seeds of feminist theory.

Each of these important people were among the first to propose alternatives to psychoanalytic orthodoxy. These Freudian revisionists, men and women who initially accepted the tenets of Freudian psychoanalysis, were followed by Harry Stack Sullivan, John Bowlby, Heinz Kohut, and others who moved forward to develop their own influential ideas. These post-Freudians can be loosely categorized into the following four groups:

- *Analytical psychologists*—Carl Jung
- *Ego psychologists*—Karen Horney, Harry Stack Sullivan, and Anna Freud
- *Object relations theorists*—Melanie Klein, John Bowlby, Harry Stack Sullivan, Margaret Mahler, and others
- *Self psychologists*—Heinz Kohut and others.

Although some therapists still practice classic psychoanalysis, most of those who embrace the basic tenets of Freud's work have gravitated toward different theoretical models of psychodynamic psychotherapy. The difference between the approaches lies in their choice of which aspect of childhood development to emphasize (Sharf, 2016). We turn now to a brief look at each of these theorists. Due to space limitations, we can only briefly review these theories, but readers are encouraged to explore in greater depth the theories that most interest them.

ANALYTICAL PSYCHOLOGY: BRINGING THE CONSCIOUS AND UNCONSCIOUS TOGETHER TO HELP PEOPLE FEEL BALANCED AND WHOLE

CARL JUNG (1875–1961)

Carl Gustav Jung was born on July 26, 1875, in Kesswil, Switzerland. His father was a minister descended from a long line of clergy associated with the Swiss Reformed Church. Jung was apparently a lonely and introverted child who began experiencing terrifying dreams at an early age (Ewen, 1993; Jung, 1963).

Jung's impressions of his parents had a great impact on his thinking, as his work reflects. His father disappointed Jung because of the father's inability to fully experience his faith; Jung placed great emphasis on the experience of spirituality and viewed that as an important part of our inner world (Schwartz, 1995). Just as his father seemed paradoxical (the minister who was a disbeliever), so did his mother, a woman who followed socially accepted norms and often repressive standards in her outward behavior, but had a different and almost clairvoyant inner self.

From adolescence, Jung was an avid reader who studied philosophy, anthropology, the occult, and parapsychology on his own. Jung attended medical school at the University of Basel, where he initially specialized in internal medicine but subsequently shifted his focus to psychiatry.

An important turning point occurred for Jung in 1907, when he defended Freud against an attack by a professor at the University of Heidelberg (Kelly, 1990). This led Freud to welcome Jung as his disciple and eventually as his successor, not recognizing the important differences in their ideas (Jones, 1955). The two worked closely for 6 years. During that time, Jung accompanied Freud to lecture at Clark University in the United States. However, in 1913, Jung resigned as both president and member of the International Psychoanalytical Association because of his conviction that delusions and hallucinations frequently reflected universal archetypes rather than repressed memories.

Jung was a prolific theorist and writer throughout his life, with his work filling 18 volumes. Nevertheless, throughout his career, he had many periods in which he questioned himself and sought to resolve his doubts by immersing himself in his unconscious, using vehicles such as sand play, dialogues with figures in his dreams, and art to develop his understanding of the unconscious. Jung worked productively in his later years (Ewen, 1993). His work reflects his belief that the years from midlife on are the time when creativity and personality integration are at their height. Jung not only continued his writing but also maintained a psychotherapy practice and lectured throughout the world. He received many honors and considerable professional recognition. His work continues on at the International Association for Analytical Psychology, founded in Zurich in 1966 as a training and accreditation center for Jungian analysts. Jung died on June 6, 1961, at the age of 85, having lived long enough to witness the considerable impact of his work.

INTRODUCTION/DEVELOPMENT OF ANALYTICAL PSYCHOLOGY

Carl Jung was once a close colleague of Freud. However, Jung's ideas, like those of many important theoreticians, went through several phases during the 60 years of his professional life and evolved into an individual theory of his own.

Early in his career, Jung became popular because of his writings on mental disorders (Jung, 1907/1960). During the early years of his collaboration with Freud, Jung's writings focused primarily on his experimental studies of word association, memory, and physiological responses to emotional changes. The publication of *Symbols of Transformation* (Jung, 1912/1956) led to the end of his association with Freud and marked a shift in his writings.

During the subsequent 20 years, Jung's work continued to address many of the concepts that had grown out of psychoanalysis, notably analytical psychology, the ego, the conscious, and the unconscious. However, his view of these concepts was quite different from Freud's. Jung also wrote about art, literature, and culture during these years.

The focus of his writing shifted again during the last 25 years of his life. His work became increasingly spiritual, and he developed many of the constructs that make his work unique, including archetypes, the collective unconscious, anima and animus, and the shadow, which will be discussed later in the chapter.

KEY CONCEPTS

Jung's theory, known as analytical psychology, rests on his concept of the psyche. His concept of psychotherapy, in turn, focuses on helping people integrate and make conscious aspects of the psyche or personality with the aim of helping them to feel balanced and whole.

The Components of the Psyche

Jung's concept of the **psyche** is much more complex than that of Freud's. Figure 4.1 offers a simplified picture of Jung's conception of the psyche. According to Jung, psychic functioning includes three levels: the conscious mind, the collective unconscious, and the personal unconscious. Jung believed, as did Freud, that the conscious mind was only a small fraction of the psyche, including the ego, the persona, two attitudes, and four functions. The collective unconscious and the personal unconscious make up the unconscious mind, each containing their own and shared components.

Conscious Mind

Ego

Persona

Two Attitudes (Extraversion and Introversion)

Four Functions (Thinking, Feeling, Sensation, Intuition)

Unconscious Mind

Collective Unconscious	Personal Unconscious
Archetypes	Repressed or Forgotten Memories
Self	Complexes
Anima/Animus	Archetypes
Shadow	Shadow
Other Images, Myths, Symbols	

FIGURE 4.1 Jung's Conception of the Psyche.

THE CONSCIOUS MIND The **ego** is the center of the conscious mind. The ego gives us our sense of the world and our reality. It therefore exerts considerable influence over our transactions with our environment. It is formed of perceptions, memories, thoughts, and feelings that are within our awareness and give us a sense of identity. The development of the ego, along with our bodily sensations, allows us to differentiate ourselves from others. Although the ego is relatively weak in relation to other parts of the psyche, it can protect itself by delivering threatening material to the personal unconscious through the process of repression. In this way, it connects and integrates the conscious and unconscious levels of personality.

The **persona** is the idealized side of ourselves that we show to the outside world, the face of the collective psyche. This mask or protective facade conceals our problems and sorrows but enables us to function well in society, deal with other people, and pursue our daily needs and activities. Our persona may change in an effort to adapt to social situations and is affected by the group or person we are with at a particular time. The persona is a sort of compromise. It is inauthentic in that it usually does not reflect our true thoughts and emotions, which might not be socially acceptable. At the same time, it usually captures enough of who we are and what we need to make us comfortable with it.

The conscious mind also includes the two attitudes and the four functions. The two **attitudes**, which is the way the psyche interacts with the world, are **extraversion** and **introversion**. The four **functions** include thinking and its opposite, feeling; **sensation** and its opposite, **intuition**. People tend to respond to the world through one of the four functions, termed their primary or **superior function**. Its opposite function is the least developed and the most problematic, which is known as the **inferior function**. For example, if an individual's superior function were thinking, this would guide most of the individual's decisions. Its opposite, feeling, would probably not be well developed and the individual would have difficulty giving emotions much weight in decisions. Opposites in the personality provide **psychic energy**—that is, the energy of the psyche that develops from desire, motivation, thinking, and looking, which, in the well-functioning individual, are in balance.

THE UNCONSCIOUS MIND Freud and Jung agreed on the nature of the unconscious up to a point. Both believed that it was a large and powerful part of the psyche and contained repressed material. However, Jung presented a more complex and potentially positive view of the unconscious, viewing it as a source of creativity, spirituality, and emotional growth, as well as of confusion and symptoms. The unconscious includes fantasies, knowledge and learning, memories of experiences and relationships, and subjective reactions to events and people (Sedgwick, 2001). According to Jung, these are housed in the personal unconscious and the collective unconscious, the two levels of the unconscious mind.

The **collective unconscious** has been described as the storehouse of latent memory traces inherited from the past that predispose people to react to the world in certain ways. The collective unconscious transcends individual experience and reflects "the cumulative experiences of humans throughout their entire evolutionary past" (Hergenhahn, 2009, p. 556). Fear of the dark and fear of snakes are examples of reactions that Jung believed originated in the collective unconscious, reflecting fears that have been passed down. The collective unconscious includes archetypes, the self, the anima/animus, and the shadow.

The collective unconscious includes a wealth of myths, images, and symbols of which archetypes are especially important examples. **Archetypes** are unconscious universal energies that result from repeated human experience and predispose people to view the world and organize their perceptions in particular ways. Archetypes are innate and have been transmitted through cultures and generations. Archetypes appear in dreams and fantasies, often through symbols, and influence how people think, feel, and behave throughout their lives. Jung wrote extensively about certain well-developed archetypes.

The Self, a central archetype, is the regulating center of the personality, integrating and balancing the needs and messages of the conscious, the personal unconscious, and the collective unconscious. Primarily located in the collective unconscious, the Self can emerge through dreams, symbols, perceptions, and images. It rarely emerges before the second half of our lives and is reflected in our spiritual and philosophical attitudes. The Self gives the personality unity, equilibrium, and stability (Jung, 1953, 1960). It is the goal of personality development, approached but rarely reached.

The **anima** is the psychological feminine component in a man, whereas the **animus** is the psychological masculine component in a woman (Schwartz, 1995). The anima and animus are archetypes that have evolved from generations of experience. They have two functions: They are a part of the Self and are also projected onto others. These archetypes influence how we feel about and present the masculine and feminine sides of ourselves. The anima and animus also shape our relationships, especially with the other gender.

The **shadow** originates in ancestral archetypes but can be manifested in both the collective and the personal unconscious. It is our dark side that we do not wish to acknowledge, so we attempt to hide it from ourselves and others. The shadow includes morally objectionable traits and instincts and has the potential to create thoughts, feelings, and actions that are socially unacceptable, shameful, and evil. At the same time, the shadow's unrestrained and primitive nature is a wellspring of energy, creativity, and vitality. The shadow is, in a sense, the opposite of the persona. The persona seeks social acceptance and approval, while the shadow embraces the socially undesirable.

The **personal unconscious** is the second part of the unconscious, which is unique to each individual and forms over that person's lifetime. The personal unconscious reflects the history of the individual, while the collective unconscious "pertains to world history . . . to the evolutionary history" of the human mind (Sedgwick, 2001, p. 32). It includes memories of thoughts, feelings, and experiences that were forgotten or repressed; have lost their intensity and importance over time; or never had enough energetic charge to enter consciousness. It also includes complexes, archetypes, and shadow.

Daily stimuli can trigger images from the personal unconscious. For example, a view of a child riding on a pony can bring back a long-forgotten image of oneself as a young child being led around a ring on a pony. Memories that have merely been forgotten or deposited in the personal unconscious because of their lack of importance may be recalled clearly or in fragments when something triggers their entry into consciousness. Repressed material, however, will generally emerge from the personal unconscious in incomplete or disguised forms, via dreams or symbols.

Complexes are dynamic structures of the personality, located in the personal unconscious. They have an archetype at their core that has attracted a related and emotionally charged collection of feelings, thoughts, perceptions, and memories. Complexes have an impact on our daily lives but, because they are located in the unconscious, are generally out of our awareness. The most well-known complexes are the Oedipus complex and the Electra complex.

Individuation

Jung envisioned people's lives as divided into two periods. During the first half of life, we find our place and accomplish the basic tasks of developing values and interests, finding a partner, and making career choices. During the second half of life, with our foundation in place, we progress toward individuation. The search for **individuation** is a lifelong process in which a person becomes a psychological individual and develops a whole personality (Jung, 1953). We gain greater access to the unconscious and our latent potentials; we move toward a state of greater balance, harmony, and equilibrium; and we clarify who we are in relation to others. We become more of our own person and less a reflection of the ways in which we have been programmed throughout our lives. During the second half of life, the Self evolves, the persona is weakened, the shadow is better integrated and understood, and archetypes emerge that empower us. Our values shift from materialism, sexuality, and procreation to spiritual, social, and cultural values. Our visions of our purpose and the meaning of our lives become clearer.

Jung's theory of development is an optimistic one, emphasizing growth that can accelerate throughout the lifespan. Part of the appeal of his ideas rests on his positive view of human development in the second half of life.

Balance and Polarities

To Jung, life consists of opposites—polarities—with their balance determining the psychological health and development of the individual. He viewed extremes as harmful because they prevent the opposite construct from being realized and gaining satisfactory expression. A consequence of imbalance is the tendency of any extreme emotion to turn into its opposite over time. For example, idealizing, unrealistic love can be transformed into hatred if the love object fails to live up to the ideal image.

We have inborn self-regulating systems that govern energy flow and help maintain balance. These include the principle of equivalence, which states that energy lost in one system will reappear in another system, with the sum total of energy remaining constant; and the principle of entropy, in which the libido (defined broadly by Jung as total psychic energy) tends to flow from a more intense to a less intense component to prevent the overload of energy in any one area. Self-regulation is also facilitated by transcendent functions, which allow us to make the transition from one dimension of our personalities to another (Kelly, 1990).

Dimensions of Personality: Functions and Attitudes

Jung attributed individual differences in personality to two dimensions: (1) the typical ways in which people take in and understand internal and external stimuli (the four functions) and (2) the characteristic directions of their libidos (the two attitudes; Jung, 1921/1971).

The four functions determine how people process internal and external stimuli:

1. *Thinking*. People with a dominant thinking function react cognitively and intellectually, seeking to interpret and understand a stimulus.
2. *Feeling*. The feeling function is the opposite of the thinking function. People with a primary feeling function react emotionally, focusing on pleasure, dislike, anger, and other emotions raised by a stimulus.
3. *Sensation*. Sensation involves receiving and identifying physical stimuli through the senses and relaying them to consciousness. People who have sensation as their dominant function look at the facts and the substance of a stimulus, seeking concrete evidence of its meaning and value.
4. *Intuition*. Intuition is the opposite of sensation. People with a dominant intuition function rely on hunches about where a stimulus has come from, where it is going, and what the possibilities are to determine their reactions and decisions related to the stimulus.

One role of the unconscious is to compensate for the dominance of the superior function by encouraging the opposite tendencies. A personality that remains overly one sided despite efforts of the unconscious benefits from psychotherapy to restore balance.

The second determinant of personality is the libido's (or energy's) direction of movement. For each individual, energy moves primarily in one of the two following ways:

1. *Extraversion.* People with this attitude as dominant direct their energy toward the outside world; they tend to be outgoing and adapt easily to external change. They are energized by social and interpersonal situations rather than by solitude.
2. *Introversion.* This is the opposite of extraversion. People with introversion as dominant are most comfortable channeling their libido inward. Although they may have good social skills, they tend to be introspective and replenish their energy by being alone. Crowds of people exhaust them.

Each of the four functions of the first dimension can be paired with each of the two attitudes of the second dimension, making eight possible personality types (e.g., thinking and introversion, thinking and extraversion, feeling and extraversion, etc.). The functions and attitudes may sound familiar because they form the basis for the Myers-Briggs Type Indicator, a popular test that assesses personality characteristics (note that variations of this text can be taken online).

THE THERAPEUTIC PROCESS

Like Freudian psychoanalysts, Jungian analysts view counseling as a lengthy and intensive process. Ideally, people are seen at least twice a week, usually with client and therapist facing one another (Schwartz, 1995).

Jungian counseling typically has four stages (Ewen, 1993):

1. *Catharsis and emotional cleansing.* Strong emotions are discharged while the therapeutic alliance forms. People begin to understand their pasts but do not need to relive them; Jung saw the reliving of past traumas as undesirable. Rather, catharsis and an understanding of both past and present allow people to ameliorate their present difficulties without increasing their pain.

2. *Elucidation.* The meaning of symptoms, the anima and animus, the shadow, and the person's current life situation and difficulties are clarified. In addition, people work through the childhood origins of their emotional difficulties, as well as their immature and unrealistic thoughts and fantasies. Transference and countertransference are explored and analyzed; Jung believed that both can inform and guide counseling.

3. *Education.* Education can help remedy any gaps in development or maturation that have resulted from maladjustment or imbalances. During this stage, the therapist is supportive and encouraging, helping people take risks to improve their lives. Many people stop counseling at this point, but some continue on to the fourth stage.

4. *Transformation.* This occurs when people have achieved an in-depth access to the collective unconscious and the archetypes. Transformation facilitates an ego–Self dialogue, leading to further emergence of the Self and greater balance. This in turn promotes individuation and self-realization (Dehing, 1992).

Jungian analysis is deep and intensive, encouraging the emergence and understanding of material from both the personal and the collective unconscious. Regression facilitates access to the unconscious and is followed by progression, as the painful and unacceptable elements of the unconscious are made conscious, acceptable, and meaningful. This ultimately leads to resolution of inner conflicts, greater balance and integration in the person, individuation, growth in creativity and energy, and the expansion of spiritual feelings. Jung does not seek to bring people happiness but, rather, to enable them to cope with the inevitable pain and suffering of life and to find a balance between joy and sorrow.

Jungian analysts take an active part in the counseling process. They are not only analysts but also educators and collaborators in the therapeutic endeavor. Through therapeutic techniques (discussed in the next section), therapists promote awareness and analysis of the unconscious, usually beginning with the recognition of the anima and the animus as well as the personal unconscious and the shadow. With awareness, these elements of the personality can become integrated and their impact on the individual better understood and modified, leading to greater social awareness and personal transformation.

Jung placed great emphasis on the person of the therapist, not only as a transference object but as an individual. He believed that both client and therapist have an unconscious influence on each other that can facilitate counseling. Therapy, for Jung, was a reciprocal process in which both client and therapist experienced healing and growth, with each participant benefiting from the positive changes in the other. To ensure the emotional growth of the therapist did not create a barrier to counseling, Jung insisted that every therapist undergo personal analysis.

Jung also emphasized the special atmosphere of the psychotherapy process. Viewing it as a sort of sacred place, he thought of psychotherapy itself as archetypal, providing healing, comfort, and guidance (Sedgwick, 2001). Jung moved psychotherapy away from the Freudian theory of drives and toward a more relational view (Colman, 2011).

THERAPEUTIC TECHNIQUES AND PROCEDURES

Other than the following interventions and an exploration of the individual's personality in terms of the four functions and two attitudes, Jung's theory does not devote much attention to techniques. In this approach, the material for analysis (dreams, visions, fantasies, and perceptions) provides the broad focus, rather than the tools used to explore the material.

Use of Symbols

Jung's model of the psyche rests on his concepts of the Self and the archetypes (Goodman, 2010). Therefore, Jungian work stresses the capacity to think symbolically and see the underlying dynamics and patterns driving clients' thoughts, feelings, and actions. These patterns may appear in symbolic and indirect forms in people's dreams, symptoms, fantasies, and other material. Therapists' ability to understand this psychological subtext can be enhanced by knowledge of the wide range of **symbols**—the content, representations, and expressions of archetypes—found in myths, fairy tales, art, literature, and religions, which are our cultural storehouses. Even the therapeutic frame can become a space for symbolic meaning (Colman, 2011).

Dream Interpretation

Jung (1964) saw dreams as providing the easiest access to the unconscious and viewed them as reflecting people's inner lives as well as their unconscious responses. Jung took a broader view of dreams than did Freud; Jung believed they represented not only wishes and fears but also fantasies, memories, experiences, visions, truths, and more. Jungian dream interpretation involves retelling the recalled dream; describing its impact on consciousness; exploring events that may have triggered the dream; investigating the dream's objective and subjective content for archetypal images and symbols of the unconscious; and assimilating the dream into consciousness, having made sense of it.

Word Association Tests

In **word association tests**, the therapist reads single words one at a time and the client replies with the first word that comes to mind. Unusual responses, repeated responses, hesitations, and physiological changes such as flushing and visible tension all provide clues to the presence of complexes and other unconscious material. Associations are also used to explore the meaning of dreams.

Rituals

Jung recognized the importance of religious and secular rituals such as confirmations, weddings, and retirement celebrations in facilitating people's growth and passage from one phase of life to another, although he was skeptical about the value of rigid and entrenched rituals (Al-Krenawi, 1999). Jung sometimes incorporated rites and rituals into therapy, and some modern Jungian analysts have embraced this intervention. Incorporating rich and meaningful interventions into Jungian analysis can enhance that process and increase its individual and cultural relevance and impact.

APPLICATION AND CURRENT USE OF JUNGIAN ANALYTICAL PSYCHOLOGY

Jung conceptualized his work as having broad application. However, in determining the application of Jungian analysis, several factors must be considered, including typical populations with whom Jung worked, Jung's writings on the application of his theory, and how his approach is used today. Jung's typical patients were sophisticated and relatively well-functioning people who sought greater self-awareness and self-realization. Most were in midlife or older and craved a deeper meaning in their lives. People who experienced Jung's approach enhanced their spiritual meaning, sometimes went through direct transpersonal experience, and viewed it as encouraging (Sedgwick, 2001).

Evaluating Jungian analytical psychology is difficult for several reasons. Jung's concepts are complex, ill defined, and sometimes seem contradictory. His counseling approach entails few specific interventions and is presented in broad and global terms. Similarly, the outcomes that Jung views as desirable involve such elusive constructs as self-realization and balance and rarely address amelioration of specific symptoms. In many ways, Jung's ideas fail to meet the criteria for a sound and testable theory. Consequently, any discussion of limitations, strengths, and contributions must have a backdrop of the serious shortcomings of Jung's theory.

Despite growing attention to his ideas, Jung's work has not been empirically validated (Hill, Schottenbauer, Lui, Spangler, & Sim, 2008). His counseling approach is a lengthy one that pays little attention to immediate crises. Jung does not offer much in the way of readily accessible tools and techniques, and the practice of Jungian analysis requires extensive training and supervision. Although proponents of this approach attest to its positive impact, the literature provides little in the way of either empirical research or case studies that offer clear and replicable steps and procedures. These shortcomings suggest that therapists drawn to Jungian analysis should be cautious in how they use this theory.

Despite the esoteric nature of his theory, Jung's work has contributed to the thinking of the existentialists, the humanists, the Gestalt therapists, and others and can be integrated with these and many other approaches. His belief in **synchronicity**, the idea that nothing happens without having meaning and purpose, is reflected in the thinking of many transpersonal therapists (Colman, 2011). Jung's awareness that people have a strong need for meaning in their lives and his emphasis on spirituality and the universality of people's images and experiences are very much in keeping with current psychological thought.

Current practice reflects several applications of Jung's work. The Myers-Briggs Type Indicator, a widely used and popular personality inventory, is based on Jung's ideas. His concept of the collective unconscious places our lives in a broad context and further contributes to the meaning and historical continuity of our lives. His belief in spirituality as part of a healthy lifestyle found a home in the early creation of Alcoholics Anonymous. Jung's indirect influence on the creation of Alcoholics Anonymous, through its founder Bill Wilson, has been illuminated in numerous books and articles (Finlay, 2000; Forcehimes, 2004; Schoen, 2009).

Several writers and theorists have drawn on Jung's ideas in their work. Joseph Campbell, an author and mythologist best known for *The Power of Myth* and *The Hero with a Thousand Faces,* was influenced by Jung's work, particularly his writings on archetypes. Campbell focused his attention on myths, stating that myths embody the eternal essence of life and are about identity and the unrealized parts of the self (Ellwood, 1999). The influence of Campbell's writings about the mythological hero are reportedly evident in the *Star Wars* films. Another important and timely concept advanced by Campbell is the spiritual unity of culture and myths.

Although Jung has a relatively small group of devoted followers, his work has not been embraced by most therapists except in their use of the Myers-Briggs Type Indicator. However, many people have manifested interest in his concepts of symbols, archetypes, and synchronicity as people increasingly recognize the importance of spirituality in their lives. The publication of *Liber Novus: The "Red Book" of C. G. Jung* (Shamdasani, 2009) 50 years after Jung's death invigorated analytical and depth psychologists, if not all of psychotherapy (Stein, 2010). The "Red Book" is Jung's diary and sketchbook account of his life from 1913 to 1930, a period when he refined his theories of archetypes and the collective unconscious. The thought-provoking nature of his work and the originality and depth of his concepts continue to lead people to become Jungian analysts and to read Jung's works.

Despite its long-term in-depth orientation, Jungian analysis continues to have a loyal following among therapists. A re-energized interest in spirituality in recent years has fueled renewed interest in Jungian analysis. An interest in the melding of spirituality, religion, psychology, and philosophy has resulted in a wealth of books on topics such as tracking the sacred, the metaphysical and transpersonal, the shadow self, dream analysis, synchronicity, the nature of the psyche in a connected universe, and archetypes of good and evil (Cambray, 2009; Dourley, 2008; Haule, 2010; Schoen, 2009; Stein, 2010; Tacey, 2009.) Recent advances in neuroscience, which seem to indicate that the quest for spirituality or religious experience may have a biological basis (Saroglou, 2012), have also contributed to a renewed interest in Jung's ideas. Jungian analysis continues to increase in popularity.

The growth-promoting aspects of this approach are particularly compelling. Jungian analytical psychology is most appropriately thought of as a method for achieving personal growth and self-awareness for people who feel unfulfilled. This approach, then, seems best suited for people who are already fairly healthy but who believe that greater access to their spiritual dimension as well as greater understanding of their unconscious can bring them more integrated, balanced, and fulfilling lives.

EGO PSYCHOLOGY: THE EGO AS MORE IMPORTANT THAN THE ID

INTRODUCTION/DEVELOPMENT OF EGO PSYCHOLOGY

Ego psychologists moved away from Freud's emphasis on the drives and the id to a focus on the development of the ego. Most of the ego psychology theorists took a broader perspective than did Freud, concentrating on development over the lifespan and emphasizing the importance of both the self-image and relationships. Beyond that, these theorists differed considerably, and those differences sometimes led to rifts in the profession.

Karen Horney, Erik Erikson, Anna Freud, and others built on Freud's personality structure (id, ego, superego) and focused on faulty ego development, rather than libidinal or sexual drives, as the cause of pathology. Thus, they were referred to as "ego psychologists." Karen Horney was the first to challenge Freud's Oedipus complex from a woman's perspective. Horney and Helene Deutsch proposed drives inherent in females, such as the drive toward motherhood and security. Horney emphasized the role of culture and environment in the developmental process, and how people often fall victim to what she referred to as the **"tyranny of the shoulds"**—the expectations that people put on themselves.

Erikson, who was a student of Horney, was concerned with the interplay of superego (societal norms) and biological drives in the development of identity across the lifespan. Erikson divided the life cycle into eight psychosocial stages of development, with each stage having its own important life task to be mastered. He contributed to our understanding of human development through his theory of psychosocial life stages (e.g., infancy: trust versus mistrust; adolescence: identity versus role confusion), a theory that readers will learn more about in their human development course(s). Erikson believed that as they go through life, people master these life stages, and if they do not, it creates difficulty as they face new life stages. For example, if an infant does not achieve a sense of trust, he or she will struggle with trust issues at all other stages of development. Erikson also developed several innovative approaches to play therapy, and is known for his work applying psychoanalytic practices to therapy with children and adolescents. In his 1980s, he started work on the ninth and final stage in his book, *The Life Cycle Completed* (Erikson, 1982), which was published posthumously.

Harry Stack Sullivan is another important ego psychologist and is considered one of the most influential figures in psychoanalysis. He was the first to emphasize the importance of interpersonal relationships in the development of personality, and he identified the important role anxiety plays in motivating human behavior. He made an important contribution to the development of future generations of interpersonal and relational therapy, which has become popular in recent years, that should not be overlooked.

KAREN HORNEY (1885–1952)

Karen Horney was born in Hamburg, Germany, on September 16, 1885. She always planned to be a doctor, even at a time when no German universities were admitting women to medical school (Eckardt, 2005). She received her medical degree from the University of Berlin, trained as a psychoanalyst, and began a practice in 1919. Her own analysis was with Karl Abraham and Hans Sachs, leaders in their field.

Karen Horney initially believed in the ideas of Freud. However, as her clinical experience grew, she developed her own ideas, which laid the groundwork for important concepts of human development and psychotherapy. Karen Horney broke ground for women in psychoanalysis. She was a founding member and the first woman teacher at the Berlin Psychoanalytic Institute (Day, 2008). Between 1923 and 1935, she wrote a series of papers that critically examined the relevance of Freud's theories to women, challenging biological determinism and considering a more holistic approach that included cultural, social, and interpersonal factors in the formation of personality. During the 1960s, these papers were embraced by proponents of the feminist movement because of their enlightened view of women (Gilman, 2001).

In 1932, Horney moved to the United States to become the assistant director of the newly established Chicago Institute for Psychoanalysis and subsequently became involved with the New York Psychoanalytic Institute. A complicated person who elicited strong and often conflicting reactions from others, Horney directly challenged Freud's work in her book *New Ways in Psychoanalysis* (1939), which apparently led to her disqualification as instructor and analyst at the New York Psychoanalytic Institute (Day, 2008). In response, she resigned from the institute and formed the American Institute for Psychoanalysis. Horney served as dean of this organization, which is still in existence.

Karen Horney died of cancer on December 4, 1952, shortly after her return from a trip to Japan, where she had studied Zen Buddhism. She left a substantial body of work reflecting her broad and timely interests in topics such as women's development, parental and societal influences on children, and the causes of anxiety.

KEY CONCEPTS: KAREN HORNEY'S EGO PSYCHOLOGY

Horney's early works presented an analysis of Freud's theories with her own revisions. This ultimately evolved into her theory, which explored human nature and development in both men and women and paid particular attention to culture.

Self-Realization

Horney's view of human nature is positive and optimistic, more consistent with humanistic theorists than with Freud's ideas. She suggested that the purpose of life was actualization of the real self, the repository of the healthy conscience and values that promoted the best interests of all humanity (Paris, 1994). **Self-realization** involves developing one's innate capacities, emotions, and interests. Horney believed that people who achieve self-realization are self-aware, responsible, and able to make sound judgments. They seek healthy relationships and care about the welfare of others while maintaining their own integrity.

According to Horney, our potential for growth and self-actualization is present at birth and extends across the lifespan (Danielian, 2010). Children whose environments are nurturing and harmonious, promoting their healthy development, move toward self-realization. However, children raised in aversive environments, especially those that do not provide security, are likely to develop in unhealthy directions. They may develop unrealistic and idealized self-images rather than fulfilling their inherent potential.

Neurosis and Basic Anxiety

The drive for security, according to Horney, is a more powerful force than either the sexual or the aggressive drive. She believed that hostile, threatening, and unfriendly environments compound children's natural insecurity and lead them to develop a basic anxiety, including feelings of helplessness, isolation, and anger. This, in turn, leads to neurotic conflicts involving a repressed and apparently insoluble dilemma (Horney, 1945). For example, an individual might want close relationships yet believe that people are untrustworthy. Neurotic conflicts are expressed indirectly through characteristics such as inconsistency, indecisiveness, fear of change, shyness, sadistic and vindictive behavior, and unexplained fatigue.

Horney (1945) believed that, in an effort to cope with their conflicts, people gravitate toward one of three styles of relating to others:

1. *Moving toward people* involves seeking safety through the protection of others, becoming compliant and self-effacing to please others, blaming ourselves for our interpersonal difficulties, and suppressing our own needs.
2. *Moving against people* is characterized by seeking mastery and domination over others, externalizing blame, being arrogant and vindictive, caring only about ourselves, exploiting and manipulating others, and feeling superior.
3. *Moving away from people* is reflected by avoidance of interpersonal contact, withdrawal and detachment, feelings of differentness, pursuit of self-sufficiency, numbing of emotions, and disregard of rules and restrictions.

Extreme versions of these styles are maladaptive because they restrict growth, lead to poor interpersonal relationships, and may increase the risk of physical illness (Horney, 1945). Emotionally healthy people do not need to use exaggerated and inflexible styles of relating to others but deal with the world in balanced and integrated ways that promote positive self-esteem, rewarding relationships, and personal development.

Selves and Self-Image

Horney believed that people have four competing selves (Paris, 1994):

1. The real self, which has potential for growth
2. The idealized self, which is an image of what we should be to be accepted
3. The despised self, which results from recognizing that we fall short of the idealized self
4. The actual self, which is all we are at a given time.

The more self-actualizing we are, the more congruent are the real self, the idealized self, and the actual self.

For people without good self-esteem and a sense of wholeness, the idealized image typically dominates. Designed to enhance feelings of worth and provide a sense of identity, the idealized self-image may form the basis for intense striving or actually lead people to feelings of self-contempt because of their failure to live up to this image.

Although efforts to achieve the idealized self-image inevitably fail, people develop strong guidelines about what they must do in their efforts to reach this goal. Horney spoke of the "tyranny of the shoulds" (Hergenhahn & Olson, 2007; Horney, 1950), designed to make us into our idealized selves. Horney (1950) described four patterns of "shoulds":

- Self-effacing people believe they should be grateful, humble, trusting, and giving.
- Arrogant-vindictive people believe they should be in charge and independent, attack before being attacked, and distrust others.
- Narcissistic people think they should be supremely competent, admired by all, and accept no limitations.
- Detached people believe they should not need other people or expect anything out of life.

Female Development and Culture

Horney also emphasized the role of culture and environment in shaping personality, as well as the importance of understanding people in context. As such, Horney paid considerable attention to the development of girls and women. She could not understand Freud's focus on penis envy and believed it to be more of a metaphor for power. Women do not have penis envy; instead, they envy the freedom and power that men have. Horney believed it was equally possible that men experienced womb envy, since the goal of life is self-actualization and productivity, which women achieve naturally through giving birth. Men, she believed, compensate for their inability to give birth by directing their energy and productivity into work and careers (Horney, 1939).

Horney also spoke out against Freud's male bias. She proposed instead that the causes of anxiety and neurosis were the same for women as they are for men and that change could be effected by empowering women and modifying their social roles.

She believed that people's innate characteristics were not fixed but were possibilities shaped through reciprocal interaction with their environments. Horney saw anxiety less as a result of sexual conflict and more as a result of conflicts in American society, such as competition versus love of humankind and autonomy versus rules and laws. Horney wrote, "The most important neurotic conflict is between a compulsive and indiscriminate desire to be the first under all circumstances and the simultaneous need to be loved by everybody" (Horney, 1937, p. 258). Mental health, then, is defined not as adaptation, but as a centering experience between these dualities.

THE THERAPEUTIC PROCESS

Horney's system of psychotherapy is an optimistic one. She believed that through counseling, people can resolve deeply repressed inner conflicts and free their innate constructive forces to grow and develop. She suggested that, with help, people could give up their idealized images and find satisfaction in seeking actualization of their real selves (Hergenhahn & Olson, 2007). Horney viewed the therapist's role as helping people become aware of their conflicts without being overwhelmed by them (Rossano, 1996), facilitating both emotional and intellectual insight, and reawakening the capacity for self-realization and joy. To accomplish this, the therapist works collaboratively with the client. Techniques of free association, analysis of dreams, countertransference and transference, empathy, and education are important in both recovering the past and unraveling the personality structure. Emotional awareness and psychological growth are a two-way process, impacting both the therapist and client. Horney's approach also pays considerable attention to exploring the cultural, social, family context, and life situation of the client.

THERAPEUTIC TECHNIQUES AND PROCEDURES

Horney used techniques similar to those of classic psychoanalysis, such as free association, interpretation, and dream analysis. However, her use of analysis was slightly different than Freud's. Horney primarily relied on analysis to help her clients. Horney saw analysis as a cooperative undertaking. It is especially important for therapists to provide a trusting and safe atmosphere that will allow clients to feel more comfortable to share their thoughts and feelings. Free association and sharing of dreams were the two main ways clients expressed themselves, and it was the responsibility of the therapist to analyze what clients were saying. One way therapists used analysis was by understanding their own emotions. Therapists must listen to clients with reason and with intuition and emotion. Particularly important when listening to clients was understanding their defenses. Therapists aimed to analyze the purposes and consequences of the clients' defenses to lessen the clients' anxiety and enable them to function in a healthier manner.

ANNA FREUD (1895–1982)

Anna Freud was born on December 3, 1895, the youngest of Sigmund Freud's six children and the only one to become a psychoanalyst. She first worked as a teacher but quickly shifted her interest to psychoanalysis. In 1922, she qualified to become a psychoanalyst. Current ethical standards were not in place when Anna Freud began to practice. She was psychoanalyzed by her father for 4 years, and she treated the children of family friends (Young-Bruehl, 2008).

Anna Freud was her father's colleague, travel companion, secretary, and later his caregiver (Coles, 1992). However, Anna Freud's theory differed from her father's theory in various ways. Whereas Sigmund Freud focused on inborn drives as determinants of personality development, Anna Freud focused more on the ego's needs to adapt to the environment developmentally. She took a structured, developmental approach to her work. Anna Freud was the first to identify a developmental aspect to anxiety. She was also an innovative theorist and therapist who focused on child development, analysis, and the ego defense mechanisms. Her study of the impact of trauma on children is particularly relevant today.

Initially, Anna Freud focused her practice on adults. However, her involvement in teaching, rescue work with children and families during World War I, and care of her nephew after her sister's death led her to focus on treating children and adolescents. Anna Freud believed in direct observation and assessment of children, the need to understand child development, and the importance of social interest, as well as the necessity of working with both healthy and troubled children. She combined these interests when she established an experimental nursery designed to serve Vienna's poorest families and provide a vehicle for study of the second year of life and the initial separation of the child from the mother (Sayers, 1991). Freud continued her work in London, where she opened a nursery for children who had been orphaned or separated from their families during World War II. Subsequently, she developed the Hampstead Child Therapy Clinic (now the Anna Freud Centre) for both research and treatment.

Freud wrote numerous books on subjects such as family law and the impact of war on children. Her most important book may be *The Ego and the Mechanisms of Defense* (Freud, 1946), an 80th birthday present for her father. During her long life, Anna Freud witnessed the growing influence and importance of her own work as well as her father's. She died in London on October 9, 1982.

KEY CONCEPTS: ANNA FREUD'S EGO PSYCHOLOGY

Anna Freud's areas of specialization were child development and the ego defenses. Because she did not believe that traditional analysis was effective with young children, she emphasized a supportive and educational approach rather than an analytical one.

Child Development

Developmental thinking was fundamental to Freud's work. She believed that children mature along a basic trajectory—from the infant's dependency on the mother to the adult's emotional self-reliance. Periods of imbalance or regression can signal problems in maturation, although Freud saw adolescent turmoil as normal, usually requiring time rather than psychotherapy.

The strengthening of the ego so that it gradually gains control over the id allows children to mature from primary process, instinctual, id-governed behavior to the secondary process, ego-driven behaviors and experiences of adults. Freud believed that the role of the mother, especially during the second half of the child's first year of life, is critical in ego development. She asserted that the presence of a constant maternal object and a reciprocal mother–infant relationship were essential for development of the child's healthy capacity for attachment. Thus, Freud suggested that orphaned or displaced children should reside with relatives or foster families rather than in institutions and that hospitalized children should be allowed to have a parent stay with them.

Ego Defenses

One of Freud's major contributions was her comprehensive description of ego defense mechanisms (Sandler & Freud, 1985). She believed that people used defense mechanisms to cope with anxiety stimulated by either unacceptable drives from the id or harmful threats and commands from the superego. Freud shifted the emphasis of her approach from the drives to the ego defenses.

THE THERAPEUTIC PROCESS

Anna Freud's counseling process was optimistic and holistic and focused on the therapeutic alliance. The primary goal of Anna Freud's work was to help clients adapt to their environment better and to replace their defenses with healthier forms of coping. Although Freud's work has particular relevance when counseling young people, she believed that psychoanalysis of adults could be enhanced by understanding and reconstructing childhood developmental issues (Coles, 1992). She emphasized the importance of therapist flexibility, letting counseling follow the needs of the child.

THERAPEUTIC TECHNIQUES AND PROCEDURES

Developmental Assessment

Freud believed strongly in the assessment of both emotionally healthy and troubled children as a way of identifying the hallmarks of age-appropriate development. She maintained a flexible concept of healthy development, recognizing that individual variations and fluctuations in development were often normal. She sought to obtain a balanced picture of children's development, focusing on areas of positive growth and adjustment as well as areas of impairment. To enhance her work, Freud developed several tools and assessment procedures, including the Diagnostic or Metapsychological Profile and the Hampstead Psychoanalytic Index, which systematized the process of gathering information on children's development (Sandler, 1996).

Child Psychoanalysis

Freud conceived of child psychoanalysis as a method of understanding and asking questions, leading to the emergence of the child's inner experiences and internal world (Mayes & Cohen, 1996). She recognized that children rarely have an active wish to engage in counseling. Rather, they cooperate with therapists primarily for three reasons (Freud, 1965):

1. They trust and believe in an adult whom they perceive as helpful and interested.
2. They wish to please the therapist.
3. They view the therapist as a sort of understanding and safe parent.

These attitudes need to be nurtured to address children's reluctance to engage in counseling. Freud viewed child analysis as different from adult analysis in important respects. She believed that children often cannot benefit from direct interpretation but can gain more from the use of stories about toys or other children. She recognized that behavior that appears maladaptive might reflect children's best effort to cope with environmental stressors. In addition, what might be resistance in adults may be a developmentally appropriate response in children. The therapist has to take an active role to facilitate children's self-expression and to clarify the connection between their symptoms and the content of sessions. Freud's approach with children usually focused on current life events rather than transference and repressed material.

Enhancing Social Supports

Anna Freud believed that therapists must pay attention to children's environments and context. She emphasized the need to establish a therapeutic alliance with the child's parents and to understand the child's social and family situation.

She believed that analysis should be used primarily to treat internal conflicts, not problems due essentially to external causes (Mayes & Cohen, 1996; Sayers, 1991). Anna Freud saw the impact of environmental factors on children who had been separated from their parents during World War II. She had great compassion for these children and sought to help them, but did not view analysis as the best approach for such externally caused difficulties. According to Anna Freud, efforts to change the environment, as well as supportive interventions, were often more appropriate to facilitate development and address the aftereffects of external events such as inadequate parenting and environmental traumas.

APPLICATION AND CURRENT USE OF EGO PSYCHOLOGY

Horney's belief that neglectful parenting results in the creation of children with emotional problems and that parents should be educated in how to raise children with genuine love and affection have been borne out by the research. This emphasis on early healthy relationships with parents helped set the stage for the relational model of psychoanalysis.

Sullivan's work has had an impact on ego psychology, self psychology, phenomenological approaches, interpersonal and relational psychotherapy, family systems therapy, and other methods. He maintained a deep respect for the uniqueness and power of the individual and for the limitations of psychotherapy. De-emphasizing the importance of dreams, free association, the libido, and transference in counseling, he focused instead on real-life interactions, behaviors, and interpersonal relationships, all of which are important in counseling today.

Anna Freud's moderate and realistic stance led to her great influence in the field of child analysis; even today, her methods are widely used in the Western world and continue to be consistent with current thinking about childhood development, assessment, and treatment (Lerner, 2008).

Anna Freud has left a legacy of childhood developmental analysis, expanded ego defense mechanisms, and recommendations on child care policy. She was among the first to view childhood pathology in terms of developmental evolution (Lerner, 2008). The implications are important for therapists who should focus not only on etiology and development of symptoms but also on providing developmentally appropriate help to get the child back on the course of normal development (Freud, 1965).

Anna Freud's ideas and writings have left their mark. Her writings on child rearing include *Beyond the Best Interests of the Child* (Goldstein, Freud, & Solnit, 1979) and *Before the Best Interests of the Child* (Goldstein, Freud, & Solnit, 1979); those on the impact of war on children include *War and Children* (Freud & Burlingham, 1943) and *Infants Without Families* (Freud & Burlingham, 1944). Also important are her pioneering works on child and adolescent analysis and development; her emphasis on health and on the ego and its defenses; her belief that all people dealing with children must have practical as well as theoretical training; and her appreciation of the importance of the therapeutic alliance, healthy early attachment, the family system, and context.

Anna Freud's ideas also paved the way for other theorists and therapists to focus on the bond between the child and the parent. Particularly important is research on attachment theory, increasingly acknowledged as a key variable in human development. The object relations theorists, including John Bowlby and Melanie Klein and their important work on attachment theory (Bowlby, 1978; Greenberg & Mitchell, 1983), are discussed next.

OBJECT RELATIONS THEORY: EARLY RELATIONSHIPS ARE CRITICALLY IMPORTANT

INTRODUCTION/DEVELOPMENT OF OBJECT RELATIONS THEORY

Many theorists are associated with the development of object relations theory. For the purposes of this chapter, Melanie Klein and John Bowlby will be featured. Others who contributed to the development of object relations theory include W. R. D. Fairbairn, D. W. Winnicott, Otto Kernberg, Margaret Mahler, and Ivan Boszormenyi-Nagy.

In the 1980s and 1990s, the psychodynamic tide shifted away from instinctual drive theory to a more developmental, relation-centered perspective that focused on the now classic research of John Bowlby and Mary Ainsworth, which related to early childhood attachment and the concept of the secure base (Ainsworth, Blehar, Waters, & Walls, 1978; Bowlby, 1978).

The central concept of object relations theory is that adult personality characteristics depend on the nature of the individual's early relationships, particularly that which the child has with the mother or primary caregiver. According to this theory, the infant is driven to attach to an **object**, defined not as another person but as the internal mental structure that the infant forms of that person through introjection. **Introjection** is a defense mechanism that involves the individual internalizing attitudes, behaviors, emotions, and perceptions of others, usually influential or authoritative people in one's life, such as parents. This internal mental structure or representation is based on both actual and fantasized experiences that involve an investment of emotions and energy. The first primary caregiver is often the first internal object, but others evolve over time.

As the infant forms these introjections, feelings will inevitably arise that the infant cannot tolerate. Anger toward the mother is one of these feelings. Because experiencing these feelings might jeopardize the child's emotional gratification and safety, the child splits off and represses these unacceptable emotions. These are dealt with via **projective identification**, in which the split-off parts of the self are projected onto another person with whom the self can then identify.

In healthy infant development, in which consistent and nurturing parenting has been provided throughout the child's life, the infant becomes able to reclaim the unacceptable feelings at about 8 months of age as the infant begins to individuate and separate from the caregiver. The infant then can accept the notion that the self and the caregiver each have both positive and negative emotions. Object relations theory sees the early mother (or primary caretaker) and child experience as the template for relationship patterns that follow. For these theorists, then, the critical events that shape people's lives occur not at 5 or 6 years, but at 5 or 6 months.

Freudian psychoanalysis forms the backdrop for object relations therapists. Many of their approaches stem from Freud's school of thought, and their work typically entails long-term and intensive analysis. However, changes in emphasis, application, and technique distinguish object relations therapists from classic Freudian analysts.

Melanie Klein is regarded as the mother of object relations theory (Cashdan, 1988). Her work as an analyst grew out of her fascination with Sigmund Freud's work and her own experience in analysis. Like Anna Freud, Klein focused on treating children.

John Bowlby is currently one of the best known object relations theorists because of his popular theory, attachment theory. Bowlby hypothesized the existence of a universal human need to form close emotional bonds (Fonagy & Target, 2009). He believed that a strong causal relationship existed between children's attachment to their parents and their later capacity to form affectional bonds and experience positive emotional development (Bowlby, 1988). The main variable in this connection is the extent to which children's parents provide them with a secure base that allows for growth and exploration.

KEY CONCEPTS

Attachment Theory Across the Lifespan

Attachment theory, developed by Bowlby, is based on the idea that the style of attachment experienced between youth and their parents predicts peoples' personal characteristics and patterns of relating to others (Ainsworth & Bell, 1970). Attachment theory is at the core of object relations. Object relations theorists focus more on the attachment between the early "objects" (or caregivers) and the young child. Early childhood attachment, they believe, is the foundation on which personality and future relationships are formed.

Bowlby indicated that the attachment system remains active across the lifespan. Since the 1980s, many assessment tools, including individual and family questionnaires and structured interviews, have been developed to assess the type and quality of adult attachment (Bartholomew & Horowitz, 1991; George et al., 1996).

Attachment style and patterns in current relationships are correlated (Hazan & Shaver, 1987). For example, children with a history of secure attachment are more likely than those without this type of attachment to manifest many positive personal characteristics, including resilience, self-reliance, empathy, social interest, and ability to form close intimate relationships. Securely attached adults exhibit more energy, friendliness, and emotional stability (Conradi & de Jonge, 2009; Surcinelli, Rossi, Montebarocci, & Baldaro, 2010).

Mary Ainsworth (Ainsworth, Blehar, Waters, & Walls, 1978) conducted what is probably the most important and best known research based on Bowlby's concepts. Ainsworth and her colleagues created what they termed the "strange situation" in which infants were observed before, during, and after a brief period of time in which they were separated from their caregivers and left with a stranger in an unfamiliar environment. The infants' responses were classified into the following four categories:

1. *Secure.* Children demonstrated curiosity and comfort in the presence of their caregiver, became anxious and distressed in the presence of the stranger, and sought and accepted comfort when the caregiver returned, soon resuming exploration.
2. *Anxious/avoidant.* These children were less anxious with the stranger, did not seek comfort from the caregiver, and did not seem to prefer the caregiver over the stranger. These children probably had experiences in which the caregiver did not help them regulate their emotions; consequently, they over-regulate emotions and avoid troubling situations.
3. *Anxious/resistant.* Children in this group engaged in little exploration, were highly distressed during the separation, but had difficulty accepting comfort from the caregiver and continued to manifest anxiety or anger.
4. *Disorganized/disoriented.* Children in this group manifested confusing and undirected behavior, such as head banging and a wish to escape, even after the caregiver had returned. Ainsworth suggested that the caregivers of these children had evoked both fear and comfort. A history of neglect or abuse often is associated with this pattern.

According to attachment theory, these attachment styles establish an important relational foundation and go on to inform all future relationships.

Bowlby's clinical approach reflected his emphasis on attachment. He believed that, like a good parent, therapists need to respect and encourage clients' desire to explore the world and make their own decisions. Therapists applying attachment theory provide the following conditions (Bowlby, 1988):

- A secure base from which people can explore painful and unhappy aspects of their lives
- Help and encouragement with this exploratory process, facilitating people's efforts to understand the connections between patterns in their current relationships and those in unconscious and internalized images
- Encouragement for people to consider whether and how their current perceptions, expectations, emotions, and actions may be the products of childhood experiences and messages, especially those connected to their parents
- A therapeutic alliance that can be analyzed and understood in light of clients' new insights and information
- Help in assessing the appropriateness, accuracy, and helpfulness of people's models of themselves and others.

Objects

There are two main types of objects in object relations theory: external objects and internal objects. External objects are things and people in the environment. **Internal objects** are the more important objects, consisting of the psychological structures people internalize from their interactions with others. They include an image of the self, an image of the other person, and associated emotions (Cashdan, 1988). Internal objects are at the core of influencing how people will function and how their relationships will be. These internal representations affect people's later sense of themselves as well as their perceptions of and capacity for forming external relationships. Object relations theorists believe that symptoms such as anxiety, depression, and impaired relationships reflect the nature of people's problems with object relations and corresponding threats to their sense of self. For example, if an individual had a healthy attachment to the caregiver, that individual is more likely to have healthy attachments in adult life.

Separation-Individuation Theory

Mahler's theory of separation-individuation is an example of an object relations theory that concentrates on intrapersonal processes (Mahler, Pine, & Bergman, 1975). Mahler focused on young children's ability to establish a sense of separateness in relation to others, especially in relation to their primary **love object**, who most often is their mother but possibly another primary caregiver (Mahler et al., 1975). Mahler's theory centers on how children develop a sense of themselves as separate and unique from others. Children's task is to separate from their mothers and eventually become independent. Mahler believed that disruptions in the fundamental process of separation-individuation during the first 3 years of life could result in disturbances in the ability to maintain a reliable sense of individual identity later in life. Children whose needs are not met do not develop the healthy sense of security needed to appropriately separate and individuate from their caretakers. As such, they struggle to develop a healthy sense of themselves as unique, autonomous individuals.

Mahler contended this process reverberates throughout the lifespan of the individual and is constantly being reinforced; as people go through their lives, they often play out their separation and individuation processes in new relationships which can reinforce their attachment patterns (Mahler et al., 1975).

The Fundamental Positions

Building on Freud's drive theory, Klein believed that all of life is a movement between the forces of the life instinct (*eros*) and the opposite death instinct (*thanatos*). As a result, Klein postulated that people have two fundamental positions: paranoid-schizoid, which arises from thanatos, and depressive, which is related to the eros position. The **paranoid-schizoid position** stems from infants' natural fearfulness or paranoia. In an attempt to ward off danger, infants separate good objects and feelings from bad objects and feelings. Klein termed this pattern **splitting**, referring to splits in the ego as well as in the conceptual and emotional organization of the self. In the paranoid-schizoid position, people's emotional focus is on aggression and other-directed destructiveness, manifested through envy and grandiosity, and characterized by defenses such as splitting and projective identification. Splitting is conceptualized as a defense, common among people with borderline personality disorders, in which they view themselves, others, and their life experience in extremes—as either all good or all bad.

The **depressive position** reflects people's concern that images of and connections with the internalized objects are threatened by internal conflicts. The depressive position is characterized by the defense of regression; people in this position focus on emotions such as love, understanding, empathy, and reparation of the internalized object.

How these positions are manifested varies throughout people's lives. Mature people primarily manifest the depressive position, which is never fully overcome (Lubbe, 2011; Scharff & Scharff, 2005). Less healthy people are likely to turn their aggression against themselves through the use of self-harming behaviors, eating disorders, addictions, and suicide (Sweet, 2010; Waska, 2010).

THE THERAPEUTIC PROCESS

Establishing a warm, supportive therapeutic alliance is much more important to object relations theorists than it was to classic psychoanalysts. Just as an important element in the mother's role is to provide nurture and care, so is that element perceived as significant in the therapeutic process. According to object relations theory, therapists should deliberately introduce this and other elements into therapy to facilitate transference and projective identification. In a sense, therapists become good-enough mothers, providing a holding environment for people who may never have had adequate parenting. Affective exchanges between therapists and clients bring the internal object relationships into the here and now, allows clients to re-experience those relationships, and promotes insight and change.

The therapist, in collaboration with the client, assesses the client's development; unconscious patterns; internalized object relationships; and underlying anxieties, defenses, and projective identifications. A thorough assessment is necessary to pave the way for well-timed and accurate interpretations that will make a difference.

The goal of object relations theory is to develop healthy object relations, which will in turn allow clients to assume a cohesive sense of self. Bowlby in particular believed that the essence of counseling was to help people understand the nature and development of representational models of attachment figures that were governing their perceptions, expectations, and actions and, if indicated, to help them modify those in light of more recent experiences (Bowlby, 1978).

THERAPEUTIC TECHNIQUES AND PROCEDURES

While most of these techniques are similar to classic psychoanalysis techniques, object relations theory uses the techniques in slightly different ways.

Projective Identification

All of the Neo-Freudian theorists viewed the process of projective identification, along with its exploration and analysis, as an essential counseling ingredient. Projective identification should be distinguished from transference. In transference, the therapist is viewed inaccurately as having characteristics of significant people in the client's early life; for example, the therapist may be seen as an angry and judgmental parent. In projective identification, a part of the internalized object or the self is projected onto the therapist. The internal object relationship is then re-created in the client–therapist relationship, where it can be reworked to allow modification of the internalized object (Scharff & Scharff, 2005). Being receptive to a client's projective identification is the first step in being able to uncover overwhelming feelings of rage and despair and, ultimately, contain them (Sweet, 2010).

Resistance

Resistance in clients is viewed as reflecting a rigid transference, growing out of the strong need for a particular type of object relationship. Resistance leads to clients' inability to relate to the therapist in ways that are flexible and reflective of present relationships. Resistance provides a way for people to keep painful emotions and fantasies buried in the unconscious to protect the self from the threat these pose. Therapists can reduce resistance by acknowledging and accepting clients' internal worlds and by being patient, consistent, safe, and available.

Countertransference

Understanding countertransference and transference is important in object relations theory. Countertransference is viewed as inevitable in the interaction between the client and the therapist and is a source of important clues regarding the nature of the transference relationship (Greenberg & Mitchell, 1983). In understanding and dealing with their countertransference reactions, therapists should be clear about whether those reactions stem largely from interactions with a client or from the therapists' own issues and experiences.

Interpretation

Interpretation is a primary route to change in all psychodynamic approaches. Through analysis and interpretation of transference, projective identification and countertransference, past and present experiences, and the manifestations of the unconscious, people work through their internalized and unconscious emotions and relationships. **Working through** is the process of obtaining clarification and resolution of projective identification patterns by experiencing them over and over at progressively higher levels of development, which constitutes the main work of therapy (Kaner & Prelinger, 2005). Rather than a linear process, it is more like a dance between therapist and client. This enables people to develop the capacity to transcend old patterns and have genuine emotional contact with others. When old patterns are transcended, when people can have loving relationships, cooperate with and perceive others accurately, have empathy and concern for others, and manage their own stress, they are ready for their analysis to terminate.

APPLICATION AND CURRENT USE OF OBJECT RELATIONS THEORY

Object relations theory has become the dominant theoretical perspective within psychodynamic psychotherapy today and continues to evolve. The idea that attachment plays an important role in human development, and thus in counseling, is important and supported by research. Empirical studies of adult attachment have found distributions roughly equivalent to attachment patterns in infants: 55% securely attached, 25% avoidant, and 20% anxious (Levy, Ellison, Scott, & Bernecker, 2011). Early attachment-related trauma increases the risk for anxiety disorders not only in childhood but also in adolescence and into adulthood (Bateman & Fonagy, 2012; Green et al., 2010). Contemporary neuroscience is just beginning to understand the intergenerational transmission of anxiety as well as the protection (or risk) that early attachment relationships offer against the development of psychopathology across the lifespan (Fonagy & Luyten, 2009; Nolte, Guiney, Fonagy, Mayes, & Luyten, 2011).

With the findings of Ainsworth and her colleagues as a basis, researchers have developed the Adult Attachment Interview, a structured clinical instrument designed to elicit narratives of childhood attachment relationships. Scoring classifies respondents as secure/autonomous, insecure/dismissing, insecure/preoccupied, or unresolved in terms of their attachments as adults (George, Kaplan, & Main, 1996).

Bowlby's ideas have provided the basis for many articles and research studies supporting and extending his concept of attachment to include experiences across the lifespan. For example, research suggests attachment style is related to interactional patterns in romantic relationships, parenting, and friendships (Simpson & Rholes, 2017). Research showed that children with a history of secure attachment are more likely than those without this sort of attachment to manifest many positive personal characteristics, including resilience, self-reliance, empathy, social interest, and ability to form close intimate relationships (Panfile & Laible, 2012). In general, secure attachment in adulthood is characterized by better mental health, whereas insecure attachment is associated with negative thinking and a corresponding increase in depression and anxiety (Surcinelli et al., 2010). Adults who have an anxious or avoidant attachment style are more prone to depressive symptomology, and those who feel insecurely attached and have negative thinking are more vulnerable to developing psychopathology (Owens, Held, Hamrick, & Keller, 2018).

Object relations theories have made many important contributions to counseling and psychotherapy and remain important to these professions. Research by Bowlby (1978, 1988) and others has affirmed object relations theorists' emphasis on children's attachment to the caregiver. Many believe that attachment problems in Western society are becoming more prevalent because of the high divorce rate, high stress in our daily lives, and demanding and busy schedules that may make parents less able to meet children's attachment needs. This, in turn, has been implicated as a factor in the growing rates of youth violence and family instability. Cult and gang membership can be understood from an object relations perspective as a way of exploiting the universal need for attachment and belonging (Salande & Perkins, 2011).

Other contributions of object relations theory to contemporary counseling and psychotherapy include:

- The link it established between developmental theory and psychoanalytic practice
- The emphasis it placed on ensuring that the therapeutic situation is a safe place, a holding environment, and a place of containment that enables people to meet the challenges of emotional growth without being engulfed by troubling emotions
- The recognition of the importance of both countertransference and transference, the person of the therapist, the therapeutic alliance, and attention to the here-and-now clinical situation.

Similarly building on attachment theory, Greenberg and Johnson (1988; Johnson & Whiffen, 2005) integrated Bowlby's attachment theory with humanistic person-centered therapy in the creation of emotion-focused therapy. Their approach, which provides a structure and process for understanding the importance of relationships and the connection between people, is particularly effective in work with people who have difficulty with emotion regulation, and as a theoretical orientation for work with couples (Johnson, 2004; Greenberg & Goldman, 2008). We will say more about Susan Johnson's emotion-focused couple's therapy in the family therapy chapter.

Object relations theory also contributed greatly to the development of relational theory. Relational theorists attend not only to the relationship between the client and others, but more specifically on the interrelationship between the client and therapist. Based on the work of Harry Stack Sullivan, an interpersonal relational framework arose in psychoanalysis. Stephen A. Mitchell (1988) was a leading proponent and author of relational psychoanalysis theory. The relational model also incorporates Bowlby's earlier work with attachment, the importance of subjective experience over objective knowledge, the relationship-seeking tendency of human nature, and the latest developmental and neurological evidence of the protective effect of positive relationships on the development of good mental health. Today, many psychodynamic psychotherapists follow the interpersonal relational model.

SELF PSYCHOLOGY: A FOCUS ON THE SELF AND EMPATHY

INTRODUCTION/DEVELOPMENT OF SELF PSYCHOLOGY

Unlike object relations, in which the internalized relationships are at the center of development, self psychology places the self at the center of development. Beginning with publication of *The Analysis of the Self* in 1971, Heinz Kohut developed a theory of self psychology. Kohut was a classic Freudian psychoanalyst who believed the sense of self was deeply influenced by early caregivers. Children who do not receive adequate nurturing develop an impaired sense of self, which becomes the basis of much pathology. However, as did others before him, Kohut rejected Freud's drive theory, replacing it instead with an emphasis on the subjective experiences of the individual.

Self psychology is developmental, beginning with the first needs of infants; and relational, recognizing the importance of social interactions. These experiences with others provide the opportunity for growth across the lifespan. Self psychology uses concepts such as selfobject experiences, which nurture the self and help to develop self-esteem; vicarious introspection, in which the therapist empathizes with and validates clients; and healthy narcissism, which helps clients to recognize and value their true self.

KEY CONCEPTS

The self is considered the nucleus of the individual that regulates self-esteem, organizes experiences, and gives meaning to life (Strozier, 2001).

The Self

Kohut emphasized the importance of establishing meaningful goals and of the attachment of young children to their parents. He conceived of the self as evolving out of this relationship. The observable self was the focus of analysis rather than Freud's ego, id, and superego (Cocks, 1994). Kohut believed that a strong self allows people to tolerate and successfully handle successes and failures, while a deficient self is developmentally frozen and prone to fragmentation (Gabbard, 2005; Kohut & Wolf, 1978). He described the self structure, which begins at 18 months of age, as having three self object needs (Goldstein, 2001):

1. The need for confirmation, validation, and mirroring responses from others
2. The need to internalize an idealized *selfobject*, which provides nurturing and helps the child learn to self-soothe
3. The need for a twin or alter ego, which seeks mutuality and equality in relationships with others as well as sharing of values and preferences.

Kohut's concept of the **selfobject** is broader than the internalized object discussed by the object relations theorists. Object relations theorists referred primarily to children's internalization of their image of the mother, whereas Kohut used *selfobject* as a generic term for our intrapsychic experiences of others, our mental representations of them experienced as part of the self or in service of the self. Selfobjects are needed throughout our lives. These internalized images constantly change and mature to provide us with a sense of ourselves, self-esteem, soothing, and validation, and to meet our needs for mirroring, idealizing, and twinship (Goldstein, 2001). These three concepts make up the empathic relationship between parents and children. **Mirroring** involves parental approval and admiration; idealizing involves parents allowing children to see them as perfect; and twinship occurs when people feel as though they belong because they are similar to another person. At times, parents do not meet these three needs for their children. This results in **optimal frustration**, which is a mild disruption in empathy that pushes people to take steps to form a cohesive self. Maturation and emotional health are reflected by the ability to use more appropriate and growth-promoting selfobjects.

Positive Potentials: A Responsive Environment

Self psychology is based not on efforts to contain the drives but on understanding and promoting people's development in the context of a responsive environment so that they can achieve their positive potentials (Lachmann & Beebe, 1995). For Kohut, feelings of sexuality and aggression, appropriately moderated, are part of our normal development and integral parts of ourselves, not the primary source of our difficulties.

According to Kohut (1982), traditional psychoanalysis views a person with emotional difficulties as the "guilty man"—a person trapped in a conflict between the drives of the id and the constraints of the superego. Instead, Kohut speaks of the "tragic man," which results when an individual's failures overshadow their successes (Kohut, 1982). Kohut viewed the tragic man as typically the product of an unempathic mother and an absent father. A representation of both men and women with emotional difficulties, the tragic man has the potential for growth, joy, adjustment, and fulfillment but consistently fails to reach that potential (Cocks, 1994).

Empathy, providing affirmation and mirroring, is essential to development of the healthy self. Initially, children need empathy from their parents to promote the development of children's psychological strengths (Lerner, 2008); however, as people develop, they come to seek empathy in other relationships.

Narcissism

Kohut perceived narcissism, one of the central concepts of his later work, as existing on a continuum. Healthy narcissism allows people to value themselves and their needs and to have self-confidence. Pathological narcissism often results when healthy development of a cohesive self is blocked. Unhealthy narcissism involves an unstable self-concept, grandiose fantasies of self-importance, a sense of entitlement, and an inability to think of others as anything but need-gratifying objects. Pathological narcissism can be reflected in a broad range of symptoms, including depression, anxiety, hypochondriasis, misuse of drugs, acting out, and dysfunctional sexual experiences, as well as fragmentation of the self and lack of a zest for life (Wolf, 1994). Kohut believed that this sort of narcissism was at the root of many people's emotional difficulties and that it could be modified through counseling.

THE THERAPEUTIC PROCESS

In self psychology, counseling focuses on a client's subjective experiences and meanings, enabling the therapist to enter the client's world. From that vantage point, therapists address the condition of the self, including symptoms, developmental deficits, intrapsychic conflicts, and relational and behavioral difficulties. The ultimate goal of self psychology is the development of a healthy and cohesive self.

Because Kohut believed in the need for empathy for the development of a healthy self, empathy is an essential ingredient of the therapeutic relationship. This thinking reflects Kohut's emphasis on the present—what he called the **experience near** (as distinguished from the experience far, which refers to the id, ego, and superego and to early childhood experiences). Kohut believed that, although past experiences have a profound impact on our development, it is the present or here-and-now experiences that lead to their resolution. **Intersubjectivity**, based on **intersubjectivity theory**, is also important in the therapeutic relationship. This is the process through which the therapist and client influence each other in therapy.

THERAPEUTIC TECHNIQUES AND PROCEDURES

Interpretation

The most important technique in self psychology is interpretation. For interpretation to be effective, understanding and explanation must first occur. Through understanding, therapists can provide empathy by validating the needs and feelings of the clients, but also be careful to not satisfy those needs. Through interpretation, therapists can help their clients to understand their internalized self structure and to establish a new, healthier self-structure.

Vicarious Introspection

Kohut viewed empathy (which he labeled **vicarious introspection**) as essential to effective counseling. Self psychology theorists believe that therapists should take a nurturing role; emphasize active and open listening; and provide acceptance, understanding, and explanations or interpretations to facilitate the unfolding of the client's subjective world. Therapists constantly reflect the essence of what clients have said, and clients' confirmation or rejection of these reflections allows therapists to truly understand clients' inner reality.

Therapists practicing self psychology avoid judging and view even narcissistic needs as developmentally understandable rather than immature and self-centered. Resistance and symptoms are viewed as efforts to protect the vulnerable self and maintain some internal cohesion. Therapists' obvious interest in clients and their valuing of clients' words increase client investment in counseling and encourage disclosure of painful and unacceptable material.

Transference

Therapists' empathy for clients is used as a way to facilitate the development of transference. In an idealizing selfobject transference, vulnerable clients perceive the therapist as a source of strength and safety who is able to respond to unmet developmental needs, including mirroring, idealizing, and twinship (Lerner, 2008). Clients' needs reflect those that were frustrated in the course of development, and the transference is viewed as a reactivation of the selfobject experience. Empathy allows therapists to contain and rebuild the early selfobject reflected in the transference relationship. Optimal frustration and **optimal responsiveness** (the response from the therapist that is most relevant for the client) allow clients to change their internalizations, incorporating the skills provided by the therapist, so that clients develop an inner sense of self-competence that allows them to deal successfully with frustrations and nurture themselves. Kohut discusses this process in his books, *The Restoration of the Self* (1977) and *How Does Analysis Cure?* (1984).

APPLICATION AND CURRENT USE OF SELF PSYCHOLOGY

Kohut's emphasis on the importance of the client–therapist collaboration, his understanding of narcissism and the role it often plays in emotional disorders, and his phenomenological perspective, emphasizing people's subjective reality, are important contributions to the practice of depth psychotherapy and also to the development of humanistic approaches to counseling and psychotherapy. Kohut's work has also contributed greatly to our understanding of self, especially in the areas of personality disorders, narcissism, and the transferential relationship. Kohut provides a way of understanding and helping people that is analytical in nature but at the same time consistent with the current clinical emphasis on early attachments; subjective reality; and the importance of promoting resilience, optimism, and empowerment in clients. Kohut's view of the tragic man captures the pitfalls of our ambitious and hurried society and enhances the timeliness of his theory. In addition, Kohut's emphasis on empathy, self-image, current experience, and the importance of taking a holistic view of people, as well as his groundbreaking work on narcissism, made essential contributions to counseling and psychotherapy.

BRIEF PSYCHODYNAMIC THERAPY

The final theory to be discussed in this chapter is brief psychodynamic therapy (BPT). Like all of the theories reviewed in this section of the text, BPT is anchored in Freudian psychoanalysis. In fact, Freud himself often provided therapy for 1 year or less. BPT also has been influenced by Anna Freud's ego psychology, developmental psychology, object relations theories, Kohut's self psychology, Sullivan's interpersonal theories, and family systems concepts (Strupp, 1992).

INTRODUCTION/DEVELOPMENT OF BRIEF PSYCHODYNAMIC THERAPY

Several names are associated with the early development of BPT, including Sándor Ferenczi and Franz Alexander. Ferenczi, from Budapest, was one of Freud's followers. However, Ferenczi objected to the passive stance assumed by traditional psychoanalysts and sought a more active, efficient approach to counseling. He encouraged clients to face their fears, advocated a narrower focus of clinical attention, and believed that therapists should assume an active role in the counseling process.

Alexander, practicing at the Chicago Institute of Psychoanalysis in the 1940s, viewed therapy as providing a corrective emotional experience designed to promote new learning in which people could relive an old conflict. He also believed that because the therapist's attitude is different than the parental or interpersonal response, clients could intellectually understand and experientially feel the irrationality underlying the emotional reaction (Alexander & French, 1946). Clients could relive old conflict but with a new ending. Alexander stated that this correction of a neurotic pattern is what forms the basis of therapeutic change. Rather than seeking to elicit transference, he suggested that therapists behave in ways opposite to those likely to provoke transference. This could provide people with an experience designed to heal rather than reopen old wounds. Alexander later wrote of the need for flexibility in counseling, of choosing the best techniques suited to the situation, and of the therapist taking a more directive stance. He experimented with short-term counseling that focused on current life problems and believed that counseling should enable people to apply what they learned to their lives outside therapy.

A particular model of BPT, time-limited dynamic psychotherapy, was developed by Hans Strupp, working with his colleagues at Vanderbilt University, who drew heavily on both object relations theory and the work of Harry Stack Sullivan. Hanna Levenson expanded on and clarified the nature of time-limited dynamic psychotherapy. Time-limited dynamic psychotherapy was developed as an interpersonal, flexible, and time-sensitive approach and can be used with people who have chronic and dysfunctional ways of relating to others, such as those who have personality disorders, reflecting patterns of dependency, negativism, or externalization of blame, along with long-standing interpersonal difficulties (Levenson, 2003). Integrative, attachment-based, and experiential, time-limited dynamic psychotherapy focuses on resilience, not pathology.

The many models of BPT are too numerous to discuss in detail in this text. Time-limited dynamic psychotherapy will be described in this section of the chapter. The following are recognized as popular examples of brief dynamic psychotherapies (Demos & Prout, 1993; Summers & Barber, 2009):

- Tavistock system of short-term dynamic psychotherapy (David Malan)
- Time-limited dynamic supportive-expressive psychotherapy (Lester Luborsky; Luborsky, 1984; Messer & Warren, 1995)
- Time-limited psychotherapy (James Mann)
- Time-limited dynamic psychotherapy (Hans Strupp and Hanna Levenson)
- Sifneos' short-term anxiety-provoking therapy (Sifneos, 1979b, 1984)
- Davanloo's intensive short-term dynamic psychotherapy (Davanloo, 1979, 1980).

The names of these approaches in themselves reflect their nature. They are brief, intensive, and active, and they all pay considerable attention to feelings and relationships.

KEY CONCEPTS

Therapy Is Brief

Although BPT is similar to classic psychoanalysis, it differs from psychoanalysis in some important ways:

- Specific client features are believed to have a positive effect on counseling outcomes.
- BPT is relatively brief, having a time limit or a specific termination date, or having the number of sessions fixed at the start of therapy. Therapy is rarely longer than 1 year and is typically 12 to 20 sessions in duration (Presbury, Echterling, & McKee, 2008).
- The focus is on specific intrapsychic conflicts identified early in counseling.
- Goals are established to clarify priorities.
- The therapist is active and sometimes challenging, using interpretation but discouraging regression. Client and therapist sit face to face to promote interaction in a reality-based relationship that de-emphasizes transference but promotes a corrective emotional experience.
- Termination, with its issues of loss, separation, and ending, receives considerable attention.

Ego Strengthening

According to BPT, emotional difficulties often result from people's inability to deal successfully with unacceptable feelings or impulses. When their ego defenses fail to mediate between their drives and the demands of external reality to suppress or modify unacceptable feelings, problematic anxiety arises. Therapists using BPT believe that early interactions and intrapsychic experiences form enduring patterns in the mind and that these patterns show up in current difficulties, which typically reflect a repetition of early childhood issues (Alexander & French, 1946).

For example, a woman might find herself frequently attracted to married men who either reject her or take advantage of her. This may re-create her early relationship with her father, who was both seductive and rejecting, and her own inability to move beyond that relationship. Her ego defenses have been unsuccessful in mediating between her drive toward an intimate relationship with her father and the social unacceptability of such a relationship. Because these feelings have not been suppressed or modified in positive ways, the woman is caught in a conflict. She sabotages her efforts to find a rewarding relationship and is unhappy and frustrated about this pattern, but she is unable to alter her impulses so that she can establish a healthy relationship with an appropriate partner.

According to most BPT approaches, by strengthening the ego so that it can control self-destructive impulses, helping people gain insight and resolve conflicts, and using the therapeutic relationship to teach effective ways of relating to others, therapists can help clients break out of their repetitive dysfunctional patterns and grow in healthy ways. Important ingredients for change include emotional release, a corrective emotional experience with the therapist, and acquisition of greater insight. As people succeed in connecting with their therapists, expressing their emotions, and understanding themselves better, energy that has been bound up in defensive and self-protective maneuvers is now freed to enable them to move forward.

The Triads

Triads are important areas of focus in BPT (Messer & Warren, 1995). One type of triad, the **triangle of insights**, includes interpretations from the therapist that connect emotional past relationships, emotional current relationships, and the relationship with the therapist. The therapist pays particular attention to clients' defense mechanisms within relationships. In a counseling session, the therapist might point out consistencies of past relationships or defenses with current relationships or defenses. For example, the therapist might interpret a client's guarded and vague answers as similar to how she dealt with conflict with her parents as a child. The purpose of the triangle of insight is for clients to gain awareness of how they are using the same defense mechanisms currently that they developed in childhood. Another type of triad, the **triangle of conflict**, includes the defense mechanisms people use to protect themselves from feeling anxious or uncomfortable in regard to relationships (e.g., past relationships, current relationships, relationship with therapist). For instance, the therapist might point out that a client uses intellectualization as a defense mechanism when she feels angry. The triangle of conflict is typically related to the presenting problem of clients, and it is the therapist's responsibility to understand and point out any connections. Exploration of these triads, leading to insight into their nature, can promote new learning and positive changes in people's lives.

THE THERAPEUTIC PROCESS

The people probably best suited to brief psychodynamic psychotherapy include those who have healthy object relations (i.e., the presence of at least one good relationship in the past or present); realistic expectations; presentation of a circumscribed chief complaint understandable through BPT; motivation toward change and growth, not just motivation toward symptom relief (Leichsenring, 2009).

Compared to traditional psychoanalysis, BPT is much more compatible with today's clinical emphasis on the establishment of specific goals, efficiency of counseling, and an interactive and often reparative client–therapist relationship. Although brief therapy is not always brief, it is time limited, taking place in 6 to 50 sessions. BPT focuses on a specific crisis or problem, establishes circumscribed goals, and uses a broad and flexible array of interventions. What makes this approach psychodynamic is the assumption that a person's focal problem reflects or repeats earlier issues in that person's family of origin. Therapists who practice BPT believe that, by addressing both the current focal conflict and its origins, the client's presenting concerns can be resolved, and the client's ability to deal with similar issues in the future can improve.

Typically, most models of BPT have five phases (Sifneos, 1979a):

1. *Client–therapist encounter.* Client and therapist develop rapport and build a therapeutic alliance. They identify a feasible and mutually agreeable focus of counseling, an emotional problem that is related to the client's core difficulties. The therapist begins to develop a psychodynamic formulation to explain the difficulty, generally reflected in repetitive dysfunctional relational patterns stemming from childhood. Client and therapist might prepare a written statement of goals and probable therapy accomplishments.
2. *Early treatment.* This phase emphasizes the importance of reality in BPT. Clients' positive transference reactions are confronted to curtail regression, while clients are encouraged to distinguish magical and wishful thinking from reality.
3. *Height of treatment.* The primary thrust of this phase is to link present problems to the past. Although the past is explored in BPT, it is examined only in relation to the current focal problem. Anger toward and anxiety about the therapist are common during this phase, leading to manifestations of resistance. Transference may be explored, when resistance is evident, to facilitate understanding of clients' discomfort and reduce their resistance. More commonly, the therapeutic relationship will be a source of information on dysfunctional relational patterns and a venue for trying out new ways of interaction. Clients are encouraged to make increasing use of new ways to solve problems.
4. *Evidence of change.* Clients become able to generalize and apply what they have learned through therapy. Positive changes may be noted, including symptom reduction, improved problem solving, and enhanced interpersonal skills and relationships.
5. *Termination.* Initial goals have been sufficiently met for client and therapist to determine that therapy should end. Efforts are not made to expand goals or to effect significant personality change; therapists remain aware of the limitations of therapy. Attention is paid to addressing issues of loss and separation as therapy ends. Clients are congratulated on their efforts and accomplishments, and therapy is brought to a close with clients' awareness of work they can continue on their own.

BPT seeks to resolve presenting problems and promote overall growth. Another primary goal of BPT is some character change. Specific goals typically target the resolution of a focal conflict, such as independence versus dependence, activity versus passivity, positive versus diminished self-esteem, and resolved versus unresolved grief. Growth-related goals include promoting understanding and change in people's inner experiences, increasing positive feelings toward the self, and facilitating application of learning so people can live their lives more successfully (Strupp, 1992). In addition, therapists strive to give people the insight and tools they need to continue exploring their conflicts and their interpersonal contexts in order to address them more effectively.

The primary goal of time-limited dynamic psychotherapy, in particular, is to change patterns of interpersonal interactions that probably stem from childhood relationships with caregivers. The therapeutic relationship is the primary vehicle for change. According to time-limited dynamic psychotherapy, clients interact with their therapists in the same ways they have interacted with others throughout their lives. By identifying these persistent and problematic ways of relating and by helping clients develop both understanding and new ways of interacting through the corrective emotional experience of the therapeutic alliance, therapists help people improve their relationships (Najavits & Strupp, 1994; Strupp, 1992).

The role of the therapist is exploratory and positive. The quality of the therapeutic alliance in this approach is strongly related to outcome; therapists who are perceived as warm, affirming, and protective of their clients have more positive outcomes. Assessment must be rapid and interventions prompt; verbal contracts are sometimes set that delineate the length, breadth, and scope of therapy. Success outcomes may be spelled out with emphasis on strengths and resilience. Cognitive behavioral and other intervention strategies may also be integrated into the time-limited dynamic psychotherapy therapist's work (Levenson, 2010).

Formation of a positive relationship with the therapist can help people to re-experience and handle experiences successfully they did not handle well in the past, thereby enabling them to change maladaptive patterns. The corrective experience of the therapeutic alliance can enable them to compensate for deficits in their early childhood relationships and form healthier relationships in the present. In addition, internalization of the therapists' attitudes, behaviors, and values that were introjected can help clients treat themselves more positively (Strupp, 1992). A great deal of responsibility rests on the therapist in this model; consequently, personal therapy is recommended for those who practice BPT.

Although BPT acknowledges that therapy may need to address transference and countertransference responses, traditional interpretations of transference, focused on childhood attachment issues, are used sparingly. When transference and countertransference do occur, these theorists generally think of those processes in new ways. The goal of exploring transference is not gaining insight into early childhood attachment experiences, but, rather, providing a corrective emotional experience. Rather than encouraging transference responses, therapists actively use client behaviors and reactions to the therapist as a way to increase clients' awareness of their habitual dysfunctional relationship patterns and promote more effective relationship skills.

THERAPEUTIC TECHNIQUES AND PROCEDURES

Brief psychodynamic therapy is not associated with a broad range of distinctive techniques; rather, it is an attitude the therapist embraces. It draws heavily on analysis, interpretation, and other strategies associated with classic psychoanalysis. Practitioners of BPT also make extensive use of strategies associated with other theories, such as narrative therapy, cognitive therapy, emotion-focused therapy, and motivational interviewing (Presbury et al., 2008). However, some generalizations can be made about approaches associated with BPT. BPT uses techniques such as supportive techniques, expressive techniques, and countertransference. In time-limited dynamic psychotherapy, therapists use countertransference with a particular goal in mind, as discussed below.

Supportive Techniques

Supportive techniques are those that help clients feel safe in the therapeutic setting. It can be uncomfortable for clients to experience their unconscious moving into their conscious; therefore, it is pertinent they feel supported by their therapist. In addition, clients will have great difficulty expressing themselves if they do not feel safe. Supportive techniques involve establishing boundaries with clients, using empathic statements, and maintaining vital defenses. Supportive techniques also involve utilizing selfobject transferences and setting limits, which includes encouraging clients to reduce unhealthy behavior. Therapists can also successfully use supportive techniques by acknowledging the progress clients make, showing genuine interest and concern for their clients, and staying in the present moment perspective.

Expressive Techniques

The use of expressive techniques encourages clients to experience and express their previously repressed thoughts, feelings, and urges. Clients are encouraged to allow their unconscious to come to the surface and to express their true thoughts and feelings in the context of the safe therapeutic relationship. Therapists must apply supportive techniques before initiating expressive techniques so that clients feel safe enough to express their repressed material. Empathic comments by the therapist can validate clients and help them explore their repressed material even further. Another expressive technique, clarification, can elucidate vague or blurred material, which clients often use as a defense mechanism. Clients also use confrontation, which is not argumentative, but rather helps them see matters from a different perspective and confront a reality of which they are unaware. Interpretation is yet another expressive technique; this involves the therapist pointing out consistencies with past relationships and how they are affecting current relationships. Interpretation also helps clients work through and resolve previously repressed material.

Countertransference

Countertransference is viewed as a "form of interpersonal empathy" (Levenson, 2010, p. 25) during which therapists use themselves to re-create the faulty dynamics of the individuals needing therapy. Using metacommunication, therapists help clients recognize their patterns of relationship behavior, acknowledge the role they play in the relationship problem, and how they can change. Initially, therapy concentrates on present relationship patterns, but it shifts to exploring early origins of difficulties once current patterns have been identified and understood. Once these have been clarified, therapists help their clients to understand that, although their patterns of relating may have been adaptive at one time, they are no longer helpful. This paves the way for revision in interpersonal patterns, as well as the development of new skills.

Most Post-Freudian therapists make use of their countertransference feelings. During Freudian times, a therapist's reactions toward clients were viewed as something to be avoided at all costs. The current view is that these feelings are a normal part of interpersonal relationships and can be used to enhance the relationship and deepen therapy. Mutuality of the therapeutic process is important, and both clients and therapists are believed to influence each other. Therapists who are in tune with their countertransference feelings can use those feelings in the service of therapy, helping clients to better understand themselves and their relationships.

From a psychodynamic perspective, therapists' emotional response to clients is one of the most important tools for therapeutic work. Attitudes about disclosing those feelings to clients have also changed over the years. During Freud's time, it would have been considered a technical error to share personal reactions. Contemporary psychodynamic theory takes a different approach and tends to address countertransference when issues arise. However, knowing what to disclose and when to disclose it is vital. Therapists must share their perceptions of clients in an appropriate manner, because such disclosure can have a positive or negative effect on the therapy (Maroda, 2010). The following overall guidelines are provided:

- Disclosure always relates to the material at hand.
- It is an immediate and emotional reaction to the client.
- It is only done in the best interest of the client.
- Therapists do not share material from their own lives.
- The disclosure is not made to further a therapist's personal agenda.
- It is never seductive.

Today, many psychoanalytic and other theoretical orientations pay attention to countertransference as a therapist's natural response to clients. Countertransference is used to help the therapist understand clients and help provide a corrective emotional experience. In all forms of therapy, the therapist must be aware of countertransferential feelings toward clients and avoid inappropriate reactions. Therapists learn to seek consultation, supervision, or personal psychotherapy if necessary, as part of a lifelong process of screening their own countertransferential feelings. When therapists provide feedback in a judicious manner, the therapeutic alliance is strengthened, clients' self-esteem is increased, and clients are more likely to use the newfound knowledge outside the session in their own relationships. This reparative learning has been termed a corrective emotional experience.

APPLICATION AND CURRENT USE OF BRIEF PSYCHODYNAMIC THERAPY

BPT is an important, widely used counseling approach. In addition, extensive research supports the value of BPT in treating a broad range of people and mental disorders. All therapists do some form of therapy that is brief, whether planned or not (Levenson, 2010). Empirical research indicates that most significant changes occur in the first eight sessions (Patterson, Anderson, & Wei, 2014).

We cannot doubt that all types of psychodynamic psychotherapies are effective in reducing symptoms, healing interpersonal relationships, and improving mental health. Empirical evidence supports the general effectiveness of these approaches (Lazar, 2010; Norcross, 2011; Shedler, 2012).

Of course, this approach is not appropriate for all people or problems, and many practitioners of brief psychodynamic therapy carefully assess people to determine their suitability for counseling using a BPT approach. However, because BPT is a flexible approach that focuses on improving relationships, BPT can help in addressing a variety of issues.

Research on the use of time-limited dynamic psychotherapy to treat people diagnosed with personality disorders indicated that 60% achieved positive outcomes after an average of 14 sessions (Levenson, 2010). Time-limited dynamic psychotherapy is not appropriate, however, for people who have cognitive processing problems; those with psychosis, neurological issues, or substance abuse; or those whose behavior requires constant case management or support (Levenson, 2010).

Therapists should keep in mind the selection criteria listed previously in this chapter when deciding whether to use BPT with a client. Particularly suitable for BPT are people who are intelligent, insightful, interested in increasing their self-awareness, and open to change. Good candidates for BPT also have mature defenses, a focal complaint that is central to their concerns, and a history of at least one close, positive relationship (Horowitz et al., 2001). In other words, people who are relatively healthy and well functioning seem to respond particularly well to this approach.

Some concerns and criticisms have also been voiced about BPT. BPT's sometimes confrontational and authoritarian nature and its emphasis on early childhood issues can elicit anger, dependency, and even regression. Its short-term nature can result in a superficial sort of therapy that ameliorates symptoms but does not sufficiently address underlying personality patterns that adversely affect interpersonal functioning (Binder, 2004).

Risks are inherent in the process of interpretation as used in BPT. It is difficult to make accurate interpretations, and interpretations that are off can damage the therapeutic relationship; thus, therapists must use judgment and skill in applying this technique (Hoglend, Daul, Hersoug, Lorentzen, & Perry, 2011).

The theorists who developed BPT have made an important contribution through their efforts to build on the strengths of Freudian psychoanalysis and enhance that model through approaches that make it more efficient, more acceptable to many people, and more compatible with today's emphasis on brief therapy and on relationships.

One of the greatest contributions of BPT is the strong commitment of its proponents to research in order to improve and determine the value of this approach. Recent evidence indicates that a substantial research base supports the efficacy of a brief psychodynamic approach. Psychodynamic approaches have an effect size similar to that reported for cognitive behavioral therapy, and therapeutic gains are maintained and even increase after therapy has ended (Fonagy, 2015). In addition, brief therapy saves time and money; is suitable for people in crisis as well as for people with interpersonal problems, career concerns, or difficult decisions to make; and alleviates depression and anxiety.

As the name implies, brief psychodynamic psychotherapy offers a time-limited, focused approach that respects the psychodynamic frame but may incorporate other cognitive, experiential, and behavioral interventions. At a time when managed care, insurance requirements, and other financial considerations require therapy to be focused, efficient, and effective, most psychodynamic psychotherapies practiced today fall under the brief model.

The development of BPT continues. Integration of BPT with other modalities is being pursued. The approach is being refined to treat specific groups of disorders. Tailoring the application of this rich and flexible approach should enhance its value and application even further over time. As we have seen, the research evidence indicates that many people benefit from brief psychodynamic therapy, and BPT is a popular therapy approach (Fonagy, 2015; Goldstone, 2017).

GENERAL ASSESSMENT OF POST- AND NEO-FREUDIAN PSYCHOANALYTIC THERAPIES

APPLICATION AND CURRENT USE OF POST- AND NEO-FREUDIAN PSYCHOANALYTIC THERAPIES

Counseling Applications

The Post- and Neo-Freudian theories can apply to a wide variety of populations and presenting concerns. In particular, BPT is a sound treatment approach for many people who have mental disorders. BPT has shown positive effects for personality and somatic disorders (Town & Driessen, 2013). Research has substantiated BPT's value in treating posttraumatic stress disorder (PTSD) and other trauma-related disorders, grief, substance use disorders, physical complaints of psychological origin, bulimia, childhood psychosis, obsessive-compulsive disorder, all types of mood disorders, and borderline personality disorder (Fonagy, 2015; Woon, Kanapathy, Zakaria, & Alfonso, 2017). Of course, not all approaches to BPT are effective in treating all of these disorders. Matching of clients to type of BPT should increase the likelihood of effective treatments. Time-limited dynamic psychotherapy, for example, is directed particularly at people with chronic and pervasive interpersonal difficulties, whereas interpersonal psychotherapy is especially effective in treating depression.

Object relations theory also has clinical applications. Research has verified Bowlby's belief that the therapist and the therapeutic relationship can provide a secure base from which clients can explore new experiences (Bowlby, 1988; Farber & Metzger, 2009; Goodman, 2010; Levy et al., 2011). In other words, the therapist can become a healing attachment figure, and through this relationship clients can explore their worlds and grow.

Kohut's concepts also have clinical significance. For example, his concepts have been expanded on and substantiated through empirical research on infant development (Lachmann & Beebe, 1995). In addition, his work has also gained importance as it has been increasingly applied to understanding and treating those who have personality disorders (Kress & Paylo, 2019).

Application to Multicultural Groups

Jung's concepts offer an alternative to conventional therapy that may be compatible with the spiritual and cultural beliefs and behaviors of many diverse clients. Jung's attention to spirituality and universal symbols is likely to have relevance to people from a broad range of cultures. The flexible use of rituals is another element of Jungian analysis that gives this approach multicultural relevance

(Al-Krenawi, 1999). The use of rituals casts the therapist in a role resembling that of the traditional healer and this, too, may promote acceptance of this approach. Its emphasis on social context and its view of dreams and archetypes from cultural perspectives are other ingredients that enhance the multicultural relevance of Jungian analysis.

Horney's (1950) emphasis on unpacking cultural and interpersonal factors, what she referred to as "deep culture," and the development of nonlinear systemic connections that are inconsistent with the unconscious assumptions of mainstream Western scientific thought confounded many of her colleagues, but seem to be consistent with today's postmodern, constructivist belief in the fluidity of subjective and objective reality (Bertolino, 2010; Danielian, 2010). In addition, many of her concepts, such as the tyranny of the shoulds, self-actualization, the idealized self-image, basic anxiety, and neurotic styles of relating to the world, influenced the development of humanistic psychology and continue to facilitate our understanding of people.

BPT is currently being used with people of all ages. The literature has described its use with children, adolescents, older people, and other adults (Hinrichsen & Clougherty, 2006). Some research suggests its effectiveness with people across cultures (Abbass, Rabung, Leichsenring, Refseth, & Midgley, 2013; Kim, Chen, Kools, & Wiess, 2016). However, given that BPT is an explicitly time-limited and focused therapy, it would seem difficult to fully comprehend the cultural context of clients, which includes daily life, myths, folklore, literature, language, and family interactions. Getting to this level of understanding of the background of clients is time intensive and, therefore, may not be congruent with the time-sensitive nature of BPT. In addition, techniques such as exploration of childhood experiences, probing, confrontation of maladaptive patterns, and interpretation may be uncomfortable for people from some cultures. One approach that may provide therapists with an emotional understanding of clients from their cultural context is to have clients express their feelings about an experience initially in their primary language and then translate those feelings into English (Kakar, 2006). This often reveals feelings, memories, symbols, and variations in affect expressed through associational links, reducing the impersonal tone that often results from reporting significant experiences, and allowing for a more accurate interpretation for the therapist and better understanding of clients.

EVALUATION OF POST- AND NEO-FREUDIAN PSYCHOANALYTIC THERAPIES

Limitations

Post- and Neo-Freudian theories tend to pull on complicated concepts, making them difficult to understand and apply. These theories also define terms in complex ways instead of using simple language; the language tends to be abstract. In addition, some of the theories are applied to specific client problems (e.g., narcissism), making it difficult to broaden the use of the approaches to all populations. In addition, Neo-Freudian theories are diverse, yet they are similar to each other in many ways. These similarities makes it challenging to understand the differences between the theories.

Strengths and Contributions

Post- and Neo-Freudian theories have made an important contribution to therapy landscape. Human behavior is complex, and these theories attempt to address the important role that early life experiences play in shaping all future relationships. These theories address severe distress, specifically personality disorders, and these theories were the first to address the treatment of personality disorders. Therefore, clients with more severe psychopathology may benefit from these approaches. Another strength of Post and Neo-Freudian approaches is that they de-emphasized the importance of sexuality. While many of the Neo-Freudians used Freud's psychoanalysis as a foundation, each theorist emphasized various aspects of Freud's theory to describe human behavior. The Neo-Freudians were also the first to consider how children should be counseled, and the first to develop approaches specific to working with youth.

SKILL DEVELOPMENT: IDENTIFYING A FOCAL CONCERN

Identifying a focal concern is important in brief psychodynamic therapy (BPT). This strategy can improve effectiveness and clarify the direction of other approaches to counseling. The focal issue in BPT usually reflects dysfunctional interpersonal interactions and patterns that occur repeatedly in an individual's life. These patterns are often linked to early childhood experiences, especially formative aspects of people's lives such as their early childhood attachment to and separation from their primary caregivers.

Whether or not therapists seek an early childhood origin for focal concerns, analysis of present interactions can provide understanding of the dysfunctional patterns these concerns perpetuate. The core conflictual relationship theme (CCRT), which is a version of the focal concern, can be identified by listening for patterns in three key areas: "the patient's wishes from the other person, the other person's actual or expected responses, and how the patient responds" (Luborsky & Mark, 1991, p. 119). By eliciting examples of relationship difficulties and examining these three areas for similarities, therapists can make a tentative formulation about the nature of people's focal interpersonal concerns. This can be shared with clients, modified if necessary, and written down as a statement of the focus of counseling.

The following example illustrates the identification of a focal concern or CCRT for Julie, a divorced woman with a 5-year-old son named Jacob. Julie sought counseling for interpersonal problems, especially in relationships with her parents, her ex-husband, and her boyfriend. Julie complained that these people did not really seem to care about her and treated her unfairly. When she was asked for examples of her relationship difficulties, Julie produced the following, with accompanying analysis according to the three key areas (Luborsky & Mark, 1991):

1. *Example 1: Asking my parents for financial help.*
   - *What I wish for from the other person:* I had worked up a detailed budget of my monthly expenses. It took me a long time to do that. It clearly showed that I needed at least $1,000 more a month. I wanted my parents to provide that.
   - *The actual or expected response:* Although I thought my parents would make up the difference between what I got from my ex and what my expenses were, instead they said I should get a part-time job. All they agreed to do is pay for after-school child care and gas for my car until I found a job.
   - *My reaction:* I feel really hurt and angry. I don't know if I can manage a job and a child. My parents don't understand how hard it is to be a single parent, and they don't seem to care. They had it easy. They always had each other and never had to struggle like this. If I didn't need them to baby-sit so I could take a break every once in a while, I wouldn't even let them see Jacob. Then they would feel sorry.

2. *Example 2: Telling Jacob to clean up his room before bedtime.*
   - *What I wish for from the other person:* I think he should just do it. You know that T-shirt that says, "Because I'm the mom." Well, that's what I want. I tell him to clean up his room, and he should do it.
   - *The actual or expected response:* Oh no, not Jacob; he always has to give me a hard time. I think he's putting things away; and then as soon as I leave his room to make a phone call or something, he's playing with his toys.
   - *My reaction:* Who does he think I am? His maid? I've sacrificed a lot for that kid, and the least he can do is obey me. So I yelled at him and gave him a time-out.

3. ***Example 3: Learning that before the divorce, my husband loaned his brother some money without discussing it with me.***
   - **What I wish for from the other person:** I said to my husband, "Where are your priorities? Your own family needs money, and you lend it to your brother so he can start another business that will fail." I wanted him to see he had made a mistake and that he should try to get the money back.
   - **The actual or expected response:** Well, I didn't know if he would really ask for the money back, but at the very least I thought he would see he was wrong and promise not to do it again. No way! He just said, "I didn't tell you because I knew what you would say, and I really wanted to help my brother."
   - **My reaction:** I knew what really happened. He wanted his parents to think he was so great. He was more concerned with pleasing them than with helping us. I was really mad, so I took some money out of the checking account and bought an expensive dress. Then when he asked me about it, I said, "You think you can do whatever you want with our money. Well, so can I."

Although more information should be obtained to conclusively establish the presence of patterns, these three examples provide enough information to allow the development of a hypothesis about Julie's focal conflict or CCRT. These examples suggest that, on one level, Julie views herself as special and deserving of counseling that reflects her specialness. When people do not treat her as special, particularly when she asks for something and is refused, she becomes angry and even punitive. Conflict arises because, under the surface, she seems to have considerable self-doubt. She questions her ability to be both a parent and an employee, perceives her husband as valuing his parents' opinions more than hers, and even feels powerless in her role as mother. Behind her unrealistic demands and expectations is a woman who needs others to reassure her of her importance. Not surprisingly, as a young child, Julie apparently received little affirmation and affection from her parents. The primary way in which she got attention was by throwing a temper tantrum, paralleling her current behavior. In addition, Julie's transference relationship with her therapist reflected her need for special treatment to counteract her doubts. She requested telephone conversations between sessions as well as reduced fees.

Analysis of Julie's CCRT and the similarities in the triad of her current relationships, her past relationships, and her transference to the therapist all shed light on patterns related to her focal relationship concern. Once these patterns have been understood and worked through, Julie might be able to make changes that will improve her relationships and help her feel better about herself.

CASE APPLICATION

Consider the following dialogue between Roberto and his therapist. The dialogue demonstrates the use of interpretation. Think about the strengths and weaknesses in the dialogue and what you can learn from it about the use of interpretations. Notice the therapist's efforts to deliver interpretations in ways that are meaningful and acceptable to Roberto.

> ROBERTO: I just don't understand what's wrong with Edie. She has a wonderful daughter and husband. Why can't she be happy with what she has?
>
> THERAPIST: I wonder how Edie's role compares with the one your mother took when she had young children.

ROBERTO: Oh, my mother was very different from Edie. She devoted her whole life to her children. Me especially. I think I'm her favorite. She was so happy with her family. I don't understand why Edie doesn't feel that way.

THERAPIST: So the nurturing you received from your own mother and the joy she took in her role as mother make it especially hard for you to understand Edie.

ROBERTO: Yes, I guess that's true. But Edie loves Ava, and she's so sad that we can't have more children. Shouldn't she feel happy that she has a home and family?

THERAPIST: I can understand that this would puzzle you and maybe even make you angry sometimes because Edie doesn't seem to be the kind of mother you think she should be.

ROBERTO: Yes, I guess I don't want to admit that to Edie, but I suppose she senses my anger. I'm trying to help her find herself, and I realize that not all women can be like my mother, but it still bothers me sometimes. I want Ava to have the best possible mother . . . like I did.

THERAPIST: I can hear you really struggling with a conflict inside yourself. On the one hand, you want to help Edie figure out what would make her happy; and on the other hand, you are concerned that it might keep Ava from having the good mothering you had.

ROBERTO: Yes, that's really it.

THERAPIST: Could it also be that sometimes you feel angry and almost deprived because Edie is not giving you the caring that your mother taught you to expect from a woman?

ROBERTO: Well . . . I don't know. . . . I mean, I'm a grown man; I don't need anybody to mother me anymore. I can take care of myself.

THERAPIST: You have become very self-sufficient. Yet sometimes most of us still feel that little child inside us who wants a loving mother to ease our fears and tell us how special we are.

ROBERTO: Isn't there something wrong with a grown man having those feelings?

THERAPIST: I don't think so, especially if we can recognize those feelings and use them in ways that help us.

ROBERTO: Well, I guess I do feel that way sometimes. Every once in a while I get this feeling like I'm a scared kid, like I just skinned my knee, and I want somebody to tell me it's all right. But that's a fantasy; there's nobody to wipe my eyes and wash my knee and make everything all right. And my problems now go way beyond a skinned knee.

THERAPIST: It sounds like it's hard for you to let yourself talk about those feelings and even to have those feelings. But from what you're saying, they are there sometimes, and maybe they have an impact on your relationship with Edie and your expectations of her.

ROBERTO: You may have something there. I never thought about any connection between my feelings toward Edie and the kind of mother I have. What can I do about that?

REFLECT AND RESPOND

1. Think about your relationships with your parents. What kind of parents do you think they were when you were very young? Write a paragraph in your journal in which you discuss ways in which the parenting you received as a young child might be affecting your current expectations and behaviors in relationships.
2. Consider Jung's theory of the unconscious mind. The persona is the representation of ourselves that we are most likely to present to other people. It seeks social acceptance and approval. In contrast, the shadow is the least acceptable part of ourselves; it generally reflects negative qualities and a dark side that we hide from ourselves and others due to its unacceptable nature. Think about the persona you project. What image of yourself do you present to other people? Then think about your shadow. Determining the nature of the shadow can be difficult, especially for ourselves. However, we have several places to look for information on our shadows. Because the characteristics of our shadows are so unacceptable to us, they are the characteristics we are most likely to find unpleasant in others and even to project onto people who do not possess them. Our own areas of moral weakness, difficulties in adaptation, and socially unacceptable behavior provide other clues to the nature of our shadows. Comprehending our shadows takes effort, but the reward can be the ability to channel the obsessive and powerful attributes of the shadow into expanded energy and creativity. Take a look at your shadow side. Write about your observations about your persona and your experiences of finding your shadow in your journal.
3. Using Horney's four selves, write about each self as it pertains to you. In your journal, write about your perceptions of your "real" self, "idealized" self, "despised" self, and "actual" self. Pay attention to which self dominates the others and write about why that may be. Also notice the comparison and the differences between all the selves and write about that. Write about your observations of this activity and how this can be helpful to a future client. What were the challenges of this activity and how may this activity be challenging to a client?
4. Brief, time-limited therapy has elicited much debate among mental health professionals. If you were to enter counseling, would you prefer an open-ended, extended approach or brief, time-limited therapy? Write about what you think your experience would be like in each case, highlighting benefits and limitations you would expect with each type.

Summary

This chapter reviewed four schools of psychoanalytic thought that evolved after Freud: analytical psychology, ego psychology, object relations theory, and self psychology. All of the theorists discussed in this chapter initially embraced the ideas of Sigmund Freud but later developed their own ideas. Carl Jung called attention to the innate patterns and images that influence psychological development, the importance of spirituality in our lives, our need for wholeness and balance, and the levels of the unconscious. As a therapist and educator, Jung sought to help people find knowledge, meaning, and fulfillment, as well as individuation and self-realization, by developing and accessing awareness of their psyches. Other theorists de-emphasized the role of drives in human development and placed considerable emphasis on other aspects. Ego psychology emphasized the ego; self psychology, the self; and object relations theory, early parent–child relationships and attachment. Most believed that children internalize images of their parents and that those images have a significant impact on the children's sense of themselves and their subsequent relationships. Although most of these theorists continued to view the transference relationship as important, they also believed in the collaboration of therapist and client and advocated for the use of empathy, acceptance, and other affective and humanistic interventions to enhance counseling. The work of nearly all these theorists continues to be read and studied. Their influence has been great, not only on psychoanalysis but also on other theories that will be discussed in this book.

Also discussed was brief psychodynamic therapy, which derived from traditional Freudian psychoanalysis and grew out of the work of Alexander, Ferenczi, and others, who found that length and depth of analysis were not clearly correlated with amount and stability of gains (Horowitz et al., 2001). Known as one of the oldest of the modern approaches to therapy, brief psychodynamic psychotherapy has evolved from psychoanalytic theory and has been clinically applied to working with people who have a wide range of psychological disorders. The time period for BPT is typically much shorter than that for traditional analysis. It often has a fixed time limit and centers on a focal concern or core relationship pattern that is linked to the individual's symptoms. Although therapists practicing BPT assume that early childhood experiences, especially attachment to and separation from caregivers, are related to current relationship issues and do pay attention to transference, their primary focus is on the therapeutic alliance, present relationships, and ways to help people lead more rewarding lives. The central focus is developed during the initial evaluation process, occurring during the first session or two, as this focus must be agreed on by the client and therapist (Steinert, Munder, Rabung, Hoyer, & Leichsenring, 2017). The central focus singles out the most important issues and thus creates a structure and identifies a goal for the treatment, as the therapist addresses only the circumscribed problem area.

Goals are clear and circumscribed; therapists are active and flexible; and strategies are designed not only to promote insight but also to elicit feelings, promote new learning, and change behavior. Research supports the value of this approach in treating a broad range of mild to moderately severe difficulties, notably depression (Steinert et al., 2017).

Recommended Readings

Carl Jung
Galanter, M., & Kaskutas, L. A. (Eds.). (2008). *Recent developments in alcoholism, Vol. 18: Research on Alcoholics Anonymous and spirituality in addiction recovery*. Totowa, NJ: Humana Press.

Journal of Analytical Psychology.
Jung, C. G. (1963). *Memories, dreams, reflections*. New York, NY: Pantheon.
Jung, C. G. (1971). *Man and his symbols*. Garden City, NY: Doubleday.
Shamdasani, S. (2011). *C.G. Jung: A biography in books*. New York, NY: W. W. Norton.

Karen Horney
Paris, B. J. (1996). *Karen Horney: A psychoanalyst's search for self understanding*. New Haven, CT: Yale University Press.

Harry Stack Sullivan
Chapman, A. H. (1978). *The treatment techniques of Harry Stack Sullivan*. New York, NY: Brunner/Mazel.
Grey, A. L. (1988). Sullivan's contributions to psychoanalysis: An overview. *Contemporary Psychoanalysis, 24*, 548–576.

Anna Freud
Sandler, A. (1996). The psychoanalytic legacy of Anna Freud. *Psychoanalytic Study of the Child, 51*, 270–284.

Young-Bruehl, E. (2008). *Anna Freud: A biography*. New Haven, CT: Yale University Press.

Object Relations Theorists
Cashdan, S. (1988). *Object relations therapy: Using the relationship*. New York, NY: Norton.
Celani, D. P. (2010). *Fairbairn's object relations theory in the clinical setting*. New York, NY: Columbia University Press.
Lubbe, T. (2011). *Object relations in depression: A return to theory*. New York, NY: Routledge.
Mitchell, S. A., & Black, M. J. (2016). *Freud and beyond: A history of modern psychoanalytic thought*. New York, NY: Basic Books.
Scharff, J. S., & Scharff, D. E. (2005). *The primer of object relations* (2nd ed.). Northvale, NJ: Aronson.
Strozier, C. B. (2004). *The making of a psychoanalyst*. New York, NY: Farrar, Strauss and Giroux.

Heinz Kohut and Self Psychology
Lachmann, F. M. (1993). Self psychology: Origins and overview. *British Journal of Psychotherapy, 10*, 226–231.
Livingston, M., & Livingston, L. (2000). Sustained empathic focus and the clinical application of self-psychological theory in group psychotherapy. *International Journal of Group Psychotherapy, 56*, 67–85.

Brief Psychodynamic Therapy

Berzoff, J., Flanagan, L. M., & Hertz, P. (2016). *Inside out and outside in: Psychodynamic clinical theory and psychopathology in contemporary multicultural contexts* (4th ed.). Lanham, MD: Rowman & Littlefield.

Goldfried, M. R. (2004). Integrating integratively-oriented brief psychotherapy. *Journal of Psychotherapy Integration, 14,* 93–105.

Messer, S. B., & Warren, S. (1995). *Models of brief psychodynamic therapy: A comparative approach.* New York, NY: Guilford.

Presbury, J. H., Echterling, L. G., & McKee, J. E. (2008). *Beyond brief counseling and therapy: An integrative approach* (2nd ed.). Upper Saddle River, NJ: Pearson.

Teyber, E., & Teyber, F. H. (2017). *Interpersonal process in therapy: An integrative model* (7th ed.). Belmont, CA: Thomson/Brooks Cole.

Weissman, M. M., Markowitz, J., & Klerman, G. L. (2007). *Clinician's quick guide to interpersonal therapy.* New York, NY: Oxford.

MyLab Counseling

Try the Topic 14 Assignments: Neoanalytic Therapy.

CHAPTER 5

Behavior Therapy

Learning Outcomes

When you have finished this chapter, you should be able to:
- Understand the context and development of Behavior Therapy.
- Communicate the key concepts associated with Behavior Therapy and understand how they relate to therapeutic processes.
- Describe the therapeutic goals of Behavior Therapy.
- Identify the common techniques used in Behavior Therapy.
- Understand how Behavior Therapy relates to counseling diverse populations.
- Identify the limitations and strengths of Behavior Therapy.

We are the only ones who can be aware of our feelings and thoughts; they can be kept private, and any given thought or emotion will not have an impact on our lives if we choose not to act on them. That is not the case with behaviors. Once we take action—choose which road to travel—we make an irreversible move in a certain direction. In addition, the potentially public and observable nature of behaviors intensifies their impact. The actions we take are most likely to determine the direction of our lives as well as our relationships with others and their perceptions of us. Even a small act such as leaving for work early has a profound impact if it enables us to avoid a car accident, make a new friend at the coffee shop, or make a positive impression on a supervisor.

Sometimes people feel overwhelmed and immobilized when they consider the possible impact of their behaviors, so they avoid making choices and taking action. However, inaction is an action in itself and does have consequences. Behaviors and behavior therapy will be the focus of this chapter.

We will start off with a discussion of the second force in theories of counseling and psychotherapy, theories that focus on client behaviors and cognitions. The rest of the chapter will then discuss behavior therapy, or theories that target client behavior change.

INTRODUCTION TO THE SECOND FORCE IN COUNSELING AND PSYCHOTHERAPY: BEHAVIOR AND COGNITIVE BEHAVIORAL THERAPIES

The second force of counseling began with behaviorism, and many factors influenced the development of this force. During the early 1900s, interest in animal intelligence was growing, and this interest led people to study learning principles and how animals, and then humans, learn (Schultz &

Schultz, 2011). As an example, Clever Hans, a horse who displayed intelligence by answering questions accurately with the tapping of his hoof and the nodding of his head, was of interest to many. There was growing fascination with Clever Hans and his supposed intelligence, but his supposed intelligence also had some detractors. People discovered that Clever Hans was conditioned to tap his foot the correct number of times when people knew the right answer because they would unknowingly make a movement signifying that he was right. This was a process of operant conditioning, an important concept in behavior therapy, in which Hans was reinforced for answering correctly. These types of popular examples intrigued many and led to further examination of learning principles and their applications. Animal psychology linked humans and animals together in such a way to show that they share similar processes.

Another influencer on the development of the second force in psychotherapy was the increased focus on functionalism, William James' ideas; instead of relying on mental processes, people were increasingly concerned with observable and objective ways to describe behavior (James, 1890). People like William James began to use more objective measures to assess behavior, such as various recording devices, as well as examinations of specific behaviors and of anatomy and physiology.

The development of cognitive theory also influenced the development of the second force in counseling. Three main influencers account for the development of cognitive theory: the detractors of behaviorism, the growing popularity of the modern computer, and an increased interest in cognitive neuroscience. The significant role of mental processes in cognitive theory brought back the importance of thoughts and the consciousness. In the early 20th century, concepts in physics began to reflect the idea that subjectivity cannot be neglected and that mechanistic and deterministic views are not the only ways to describe events. Specifically, the observations people make are subjective and likely to influence their perception of the experience; different people can experience the same thing differently (Matson, 1964). The inclusion of subjectivity and consciousness in physics led to the development of cognitive therapy. In addition, some people did not agree with behaviorism and its assumption that human behavior can be explained through reflexes. Instead, people became increasingly concerned with the processes of the mind and how they influence behavior.

The development of the modern computer was another important contributor to the second force in psychotherapy, in particular, cognitive therapy (Crowther-Heyck, 1999). Cognitive theory focuses on the belief that people are similar to computers, which are "information-processing" machines. Information-processing systems gather information from the environment; organize the information through stages, each of which is influenced by the previous stage; and yield a conclusion based on the original information. Humans gather information from the environment, process through the information in stages, and then come to a conclusion that results in a behavior and/or thought. Cognitive theory views behavior as the result of cognition, or information processing. People make decisions and behave in ways based on the information they process through. To put it simply, the modern computer was an example of human cognition and artificial intelligence.

Cognitive neuroscience also played a role in the development of cognitive theory (Sarter, Bernston, & Cacioppo, 1996). Cognitive neuroscience aimed to understand the parts of the brain responsible for cognitive functioning. The correlation between the structure of the brain and mental processes was of particular interest. This movement provided support for the idea that people can control their thoughts and the objects in their environment, which overlaps with the view of cognitive therapy that changing cognitions can lead to better mental health.

All of the previously mentioned historical factors came together to influence the development of the second force in counseling. Now we look at some of the core concepts associated with the second-force counseling theories.

Focus on Behaviors and Behavioral Change

Clients' presenting problems often focus on behaviors. People rarely seek treatment because they worry they have dysfunctional thoughts, although they do frequently seek help for negative emotions such as depression and anxiety. Often, though, what leads clients to seek help is an upsetting behavior, either their own or someone else's. Common behavioral concerns include overeating, unhealthy drug or alcohol use, poor impulse control, difficulty finding a rewarding job, problems managing school expectations, and challenges in developing rewarding relationships. Because behaviors often prompt people to seek counseling, people are more likely to feel heard and to believe that therapy will be helpful if, at least initially, it addresses those expressed concerns.

Many times, too, clients are forced to seek help for their behavior. For example, people who are fulfilling court-mandated treatment requirements, those who have been encouraged to meet with an employee-assistance counselor at work, or those who have been brought for help by a concerned parent or dissatisfied partner are usually in counseling because their behaviors have violated the law or have been unsatisfactory or troubling to others.

Discussion of behaviors is likely to be less threatening to clients than discussion of their early childhood experiences or their troubling emotions and somewhat less uncomfortable than discussion of their cognitions. People are accustomed to talking about their activities with others but are less likely to talk about their thoughts and emotions. Therefore, behavioral approaches may feel more comfortable to people from certain demographics or cultures who experience discomfort with discussions of feelings.

Many clients may be better able to present accurate information about their behaviors than about their emotions or even their cognitions. Having clear and valid information, especially at the beginning of counseling, can help direct the focus of counseling.

Measurement, Evaluation, and Research

All behavior and cognitive behavioral therapy theories have some focus on measurement and evaluation of client thoughts and/or behaviors. These approaches all center on developing measurable counseling goals that target changing specific behaviors and replacing them with more adaptive behaviors. Because behavior can be readily measured, clients can determine the baseline frequency or occurrence of a behavior and then assess change in such variables as how many beers they drink each day, how often they exercise, how many hours they devote to work, and how much time they spend with friends. Because even small changes can readily be identified, clients trying to modify their actions often have rapid evidence of improvement. This can be empowering and promote motivation, optimism, and further change. Similarly, if a client is struggling to make behavior changes being targeted in counseling, it can indicate to the therapist that a revised counseling approach is needed.

Not surprisingly, these approaches also all lend themselves well to research and external validation of their effectiveness. An extensive body of literature describes and affirms the effectiveness of behavior and cognitive behavioral therapy in addressing a variety of client-presented struggles (e.g., depression, anxiety, youth behavior problems). These approaches have generally received more research support than other approaches, not necessarily because behavior and cognitive behavioral therapies are superior, but because of the extensive research conducted on these approaches. Those who practice from these theoretical approaches place a premium on the use of counseling techniques that are based on research-demonstrated effectiveness.

Behavior Therapy: The Three Waves

Behavior therapy is generally presented as occurring in three waves:
- First-wave behaviorism (i.e., behavior therapy), which focused on the use of traditional behaviorism principles in helping people change

- Second-wave behaviorism (i.e., cognitive behavior therapy, reality therapy), which focused on integrating cognitive principles with behavior therapy principles into therapy
- Third-wave behavior therapy (e.g., dialectical behavior therapy), which focused on integrating mindfulness-based concepts with the more traditional behavior and cognitive therapy principles.

The first wave of behaviorism that arose in the 1950s and 1960s throughout the United States, South Africa, and Great Britain was developed, in large part, as a response to psychoanalysis. At that time, behavior therapy was intended to show that behavioral techniques were effective and could be used instead of psychoanalysis. In the 1970s, behavior therapy principles increasingly had a significant impact on education, psychology, counseling, psychiatry, social work, businesses, and child-rearing problems. Techniques that evolved from behavior therapy were considered the treatment of choice at the time.

In the 1980s, emotions and biological factors were increasingly taken into consideration, and this influenced the second wave of behaviorism, cognitive behavioral therapy (CBT). Bandura's research and the development of social learning theory, which will be discussed later in the chapter, demonstrated that cognition is an important focus for behavior therapy and his views contributed to the development of CBT. During this time, CBT emerged and behavioral techniques were increasingly applied to physical health and mental health problems.

The third-wave CBTs arose in the early 2000s. Research and practice grew to incorporate mindfulness and acceptance of the individual's thoughts, concepts central to many third-wave CBT theories. Due to the increasing prominence of these third-wave approaches, they will be discussed in Chapter 8.

Table 5.1 provides an overview of the first, second, and third "waves" or generations of behavior therapy from which CBT approaches evolved (Hayes, 2004).

In most real-world practice and application, approaches and techniques associated with the second-force counseling theories focus on both thoughts and behaviors; they are believed to be inseparable. The second-force counseling theories, including all three waves of behavior therapy, have become some of the most dominant theories in modern counseling practice. In this chapter, we will discuss the first wave of behaviorism, behavior therapy.

The first wave of behaviorism provided a basis on which behavioral counseling theories were built. Behavior therapy will be discussed in depth in the remainder of this chapter.

Chapter 6 will address the second wave of behaviorism, which focused on the integration of thoughts into behavioral approaches (i.e., CBT approaches). Because of their significance and popularity, Ellis' rational emotive behavior therapy and Beck's cognitive therapy are the two CBT approaches that will be discussed in Chapter 6. In CBT, clients learn, through the process of cognitive restructuring, to replace their faulty thinking with healthy, positive, and constructive thoughts that help them to also change their behavior. In Chapter 6, many useful strategies will be discussed.

In Chapter 7, reality therapy will be discussed, which is a type of cognitive behavior therapy. Because of its applications to school counseling and school psychology, and because it has a number of theoretical tenets that make it stand apart from some of the other CBT approaches, reality therapy has its own chapter.

Finally, the third wave of behavior therapies, which include the more modern approaches which incorporate mindfulness and acceptance, will be discussed in Chapter 8. These third-wave CBT approaches are, at present, very popular. A quick search of continuing education programs for mental health professionals highlights the popularity of these third-wave counseling approaches. Their focus on the complexities of human behavior and the change process, their emphasis on a variety of dynamic interventions and techniques, and the integration of evidence-based, mindfulness principles make them attractive to many helpers.

TABLE 5.1 Development and Progression of the Three Generations of Behavior Therapy

	Theories and Principles	Core Characteristics	Counseling Applications
First generation: Radical behaviorism, 1950s–1960s	• Scientific method • Learning theory • Classical conditioning • Operant conditioning • Social cognitive theory	• Experimental • Observable behavior change • Environmental determinants • Stimulus-response • Reinforcement • Modeling	• Behavior therapy • Systematic desensitization • Progressive muscle relaxation (PMR) • In vivo exposure • Applied behavior analysis (ABA) • Social skills training
Second generation: Cognitive and CBT approaches, 1960s–1990s	• Cognitive theories (e.g., Beck's model) • Integration of cognitive and behavioral change strategies	• Irrational beliefs and cognitive distortions • Cognitive, affective, and behavioral relationship • Cognitive change strategies • Problem solving • Coping skills	• Rational emotive behavior therapy • Cognitive therapy • Cognitive behavior modification • CBT–play therapy • Self-management programs
Third generation: Mindfulness-based therapies, 1990s–present	• Buddhism • Mindfulness • Acceptance • Metacognition • Behavioral and cognitive change strategies	• Meditation • Awareness of the present experience • Nonjudgment • Emotion regulation • Distress tolerance • Interpersonal effectiveness	• Dialectical behavior therapy • Acceptance and commitment therapy • Mindfulness-based cognitive therapy • Mindfulness-based stress reduction

Readers should keep in mind that the differences among the various behavioral and cognitive behavioral counseling approaches are primarily those of emphasis. To greater or lesser extents, the theories focus on changing thoughts and/or behaviors.

ALBERT BANDURA (b. 1925)

One of the most influential social learning theorists, Albert Bandura was born in Canada and received his PhD from the University of Iowa. He later moved to Stanford University, where he is now a distinguished professor emeritus. Bandura applied the principles of both classical and operant conditioning to social learning (1969, 1977, 1986). Bandura (1973) has written extensively on aggression, violence, and adolescence and has testified repeatedly before Congress about the causes and possible solutions to aggressive behavior. One of Bandura's most well-known experiments is the Bobo doll experiment, which demonstrated observational learning. As a result of his theories, most behavior therapies

(including exposure therapy and social skills training) now include a modeling component (Antony & Roemer, 2011). Albert Bandura has been honored by the American Psychological Association with a lifetime achievement award. He has written seven books and published innumerable articles in scholarly journals. Now in his 80s, he continues to conduct research and teach at Stanford University, where he has worked since 1953.

B. F. SKINNER (1904–1990)

B. F. Skinner was born in Pennsylvania in 1904. Skinner received a PhD from Harvard in 1931 and stayed there as a researcher for several years. Skinner taught at University of Minnesota and then became chair of the psychology department at Indiana University. In 1948, he returned to Harvard as a tenured professor and stayed there until his death. Skinner was a strict behaviorist who believed that the only scientific approach to psychology was one that studied behaviors, not internal (subjective) mental processes. Building on the work of Ivan Pavlov and John W. Watson, B. F. Skinner developed a theory of behavior, operant conditioning, that has become the foundation on which behavior modification is based (Martin & Pear, 2007). He believed that who we are and everything we do is shaped by our experiences of punishment and reward. The results of Skinner's early studies in operant conditioning were published in his first book, *The Behavior of Organisms* (1938).

The best summary of his theories is contained in his book *About Behaviorism* (1974). Skinner continued to write (*Walden II,* 1948/2005; *Beyond Freedom and Dignity,* 1971; and a three-part autobiography), lecture, and receive numerous awards for his contributions to psychology until his death from leukemia in 1990. His principles are still incorporated into treatments of phobias and addictive behaviors, and are used to enhance classroom performance (as well as computer-based self-instruction).

INTRODUCTION/DEVELOPMENT OF BEHAVIOR THERAPY

Behavior therapy, which developed during the 1950s and 1960s, presented a powerful challenge to the principles of psychoanalysis. Behavior therapy's focus on observable behaviors rather than the unconscious; on the present rather than the past; and on short-term treatment, clear goals, and rapid change had considerable appeal.

As its name implies, behavior therapy centers on specific behaviors, with the goal of changing or modifying that behavior. Behaviorism conceptualizes people's problems as occurring secondary to maladaptive learning. From a behaviorist's perspective, children are essentially born a blank slate, neither good nor bad; they are simply the products of their environment. As people go through their lives, they have experiences that shape and mold their reactions, feelings, thoughts, and behaviors. The premise is that all behavior is learned; faulty learning (i.e., conditioning) is the cause of problems. Since behaviorists believe that everything people struggle with is a result of learning, then learning new behaviors is how people make meaningful changes. Therefore, therapy concentrates on learning new behaviors. An important feature of behavior therapy is its focus on current problems, not the past, and on attempts to remove behaviors the client finds to be a challenge. Behavior therapies, sometimes referred to as behavior modification, are based on the theories of classical and operant conditioning, which will be further discussed later in this chapter.

In recent years, health-related behaviors such as opioid abuse, smoking, obesity, and a sedentary lifestyle have received increased attention in the United States because these unhealthy behaviors have been linked to illness and preventable deaths. Similarly, childhood behaviors such as bullying, tantrums, or academic difficulties may be effectively targeted by behavior therapy. Moreover, behavior therapy can address commonly presented counseling issues like anxiety, depression, and phobias. In fact, behavior therapy can work with almost any human behavior.

Many people have contributed to the evolution of this approach. Some, like B. F. Skinner and Ivan Pavlov, used principles of behavior change to shape the actions and reactions of animals. Others, including Hans Eysenck, Arnold Lazarus, Joseph Wolpe, and Albert Bandura, applied behavior therapy and learning theory to people.

Behavior therapy sometimes has a reputation for being mechanical and rigid, but it should be noted that over the past few decades the application of behavior therapy has broadened and it has become increasingly flexible and sensitive to individual needs. A positive and collaborative therapeutic alliance is now considered an essential element of behavior therapy, and the incorporation of mindfulness and other concepts has provided this approach with an entirely new focus. Therapists who use behavior therapy principles are likely to integrate other evidence-based interventions and place some emphasis on factors beyond just learning principles.

KEY CONCEPTS

Behavior therapy sees people as both producers and products of their environments. Therefore, clients are taught the skills they can use to best meet their goals. When people overcome their difficulties, they have more options to choose from, such as how they will respond to their environment. Behavior therapy upholds the scientific view of behavior and is a structured, systematic approach. All behavior therapies generally subscribe to the following ideas (Antony & Roemer, 2011):

- Although genetics plays a role, individual differences are derived primarily from different experiences.
- Behavior is learned and acquired largely through modeling, conditioning, and reinforcement.
- All behavior has a purpose or function (e.g., nail biting causes one to feel more relaxed).
- Therapy should focus on understanding and changing behavior.
- Therapy should be based on the scientific method and be systematic, empirical, and experimental.
- Therapy goals should be stated in behavioral, specific, and measurable terms, with regular assessment of progress toward goal attainment.
- Counseling should generally focus on the present. Even if behaviors are long-standing, they are maintained by factors in the current environment.
- Behaviors must be viewed and understood in the context in which they occur.
- A client's environment can be manipulated to increase appropriate behaviors and decrease harmful behaviors (e.g., reinforcing a child for positive, prosocial behaviors will decrease temper tantrums).
- Education and teaching, or promoting new learning and the transfer of learning, is an important aspect of therapy.
- Clients need to take an active role in their counseling experience to successfully change their behaviors. Clients have the primary responsibility for defining their goals and completing homework tasks. The treatment plan is formulated collaboratively, with both the client and therapist participating actively in that process.

In the following sections, classical conditioning, operant conditioning, and social learning—concepts foundational to understanding behavior therapy—will be discussed. Because understanding these concepts can present a challenge, a short case application of some of these concepts appears in Table 5.2 at the end of this section. Readers are encouraged to be patient as they learn these concepts. While behavior therapy can be difficult to understand and technical, the concepts are valuable, have broad applicability, and should not be dismissed.

Classical Conditioning

In the early 1900s, Ivan Pavlov (1927), a Russian physiologist, identified and described a type of learning that is now known as **classical conditioning**. Classical conditioning involves the repeated presentation of a certain stimulus that, over time, causes a given response when paired with something else. This is referred to as stimulus-response pairing. Thus, the stimulus and response become associated with one another, or paired, and every time the stimulus is presented, the associated response occurs. Pavlov's classic study of conditioning responses of dogs demonstrated that, by simultaneously presenting an unconditioned stimulus (food) and a conditioned stimulus (the sound of a bell), researchers could elicit the dogs' salivation using only the conditioned stimulus (the sound) because the dogs learned to associate the sound with the food.

Extinction is another important behavior therapy concept. Extinction involves the conditioned response decreasing over time after the presentation of the conditioned stimulus is removed. Using the Pavlov's dogs example, for a while, the dogs salivated to the sound of the bell, even when the sound was no longer accompanied by the food. However, over time, the salivating response diminished and eventually disappeared in response to the bell alone.

John Watson, an American psychologist, used Pavlov's principles of classical conditioning, concepts of learning theory (discussed in the next section), and **stimulus generalization** (responding the same way to similar stimuli) to change human behavior. When people learn to respond in a particular way to one stimulus, they often behave or respond in that same way when presented with similar cues or similar stimuli. As an example of stimulus generalization, an unconditioned stimulus (a loud bell), paired with a conditioned stimulus (a white rat), could lead a child to emit a conditioned response (startle) in reaction not only to a white rat but also to white cotton, Watson's white hair, and other similar stimuli. **Behaviorism** is the theory that behavior can be explained by conditioning, without emphasis on thoughts or feelings, and that behavioral problems are best addressed and altered by changing behavior (Watson, 1925).

Joseph Wolpe (1969) described a similar process, **reciprocal inhibition**, in which eliciting a novel response brings about a decrease in the strength of a concurrent habitual response. A parent who makes a silly face to cheer up a child who is crying after a minor fall is a simple example; the silly face elicits amusement, which automatically reduces the sad emotions associated with the fall. These concepts led to the development of **systematic desensitization**, a powerful therapy technique that pairs relaxation with controlled exposure to a feared stimulus, such as heights or dogs. This technique is widely used, especially in the treatment of phobias.

Wolpe's work reflects the concept of stimulus generalization. For example, a child who is taught to be respectful of teachers is likely to behave respectfully toward other authority figures. Sometimes behavior is overgeneralized and becomes inappropriate or unhealthy. Because of this, people then need to learn **stimulus discrimination**—the ability to distinguish among similar cues. For example, most people have learned to confide in a small number of close friends but recognize that it is inappropriate to share many details of their personal lives at work (stimulus discrimination). However, some people share intimate details of their lives not only with close friends but also with casual associates, perhaps reflecting inappropriate stimulus generalization.

Operant Conditioning

Operant conditioning is also applicable to counseling clients, as many behavioral treatment interventions pull on operant conditioning principles. Operant conditioning is a type of learning based on consequences, in which behavior is influenced by the positive or negative association of the consequence that follows a behavior. Therapists frequently use behavior modification interventions such as **positive reinforcement**, **negative reinforcement**, **punishment**, and **extinction** techniques to increase the frequency of client's positive behavior, and decrease or eliminate undesired behaviors. These terms will be discussed further in the techniques section of this chapter.

The more frequently a stimulus and a response coincide, with the response being rewarded, the stronger is the tendency to emit the response when that stimulus occurs, leading to the development of a habit or habitual response. This is the essence of the **stimulus-response (S-R)** concept, which, according to behavior theorists, determines the behaviors that people learn.

For example, Jamila was the third child in a family of seven children. Both parents worked outside the home and had little time for positive interactions with their children. Whenever one of the children was sick, however, the parents gave them extra time and attention. Jamila learned that illness was the best way to elicit her parents' attention and so exaggerated even minor physical symptoms for the nurturance that she would receive. She continued this behavior into adulthood, even though it had a harmful effect on her relationships, her employment, and eventually on her marriage.

John Dollard and Neal Miller found that **counterconditioning** could reverse habits. This involves pairing the behavior with a strong incompatible response to the same cue to change the behavior. For example, Jamila's behavior gradually changed as her employer, friends, and partner became annoyed with her frequent complaints of physical discomfort and withdrew from her when she reported feeling ill.

Social Learning Theory

While not an approach to therapy, social learning theory principles are, like operant and classical conditioning, foundational to behavior therapy. Social learning theory (Bandura, 1986) differs slightly from the aforementioned classical and operant conditioning methods that solely focus on behavior and the environment. It differs by including an additional focus on people's worldview, beliefs, perspectives, and other cognitive processes, as internal appraisals or interpretations of events are assumed to significantly influence one's behavior. **Social learning theory** emphasizes how individuals learn by observing and **modeling** others (Bandura, 2006). Modeling has to do with learning by imitating others' behavior. Bandura found that in addition to direct experience, learning and subsequent behavior change could occur vicariously through observation of other people's behavior.

Modeling can elicit both positive and negative behaviors. On the one hand, modeling often has a beneficial impact, as when a parent models appropriate behavior. On the other hand, as Bandura's famous Bobo doll experiments suggests, children who observed an adult acting aggressively and hitting the Bobo doll were more likely to manifest aggressive behavior than children who had not been exposed to the aggressive behavior. Thus, modeling can also elicit negative behavior.

Modeling has more than just an impact on behavior (Bandura, 1969). Modeling can actually change our cognitions about our abilities and improve our **self-efficacy**. Self-efficacy is our belief in our ability to accomplish something and thus be efficacious. Observing someone we admire undertake a challenging task can reduce our fears and facilitate our own belief in our efforts to perform the task. People with strong beliefs in their own efficacy are more likely to face problems as challenges to be reckoned with rather than threats to be avoided. Bandura found that self-efficacy impacts how people think, feel, motivate themselves, and behave.

Self-efficacy theory posits that people will be able to perform a certain task based on their beliefs about how well they will perform (their competencies), as well as the consequences that come from doing it (environmental reinforcement). Over time, people develop a sense of their own competency at a given task. This sense of competency shapes their future attempts (Bandura, 1977). Many behavioral approaches, such as behavior activation therapy and exposure-based therapies, are based on the premise that self-efficacy increases as people spend more time on behaviors at which

TABLE 5.2 Case Application of Basic Behavior Therapy Concepts

Following is a review of important terms, illustrated by the experiences of Theresa, a 33-year-old woman receiving chemotherapy for breast cancer.

Theresa presented many issues and struggles related to her diagnosis of cancer. She had always been fearful of injections and found blood tests and intravenous chemotherapy difficult. She had anticipatory nausea associated with her chemotherapy, becoming queasy when driving into the parking lot of the clinic where she received treatment, whether or not she was scheduled for chemotherapy. In addition, although her prognosis was encouraging, Theresa constantly ruminated about the likelihood of her death.

Theresa's anticipatory nausea can be explained by **classical conditioning**. The **unconditioned stimulus**, the chemotherapy, elicited the response of nausea. Because that stimulus was paired with the **conditioned stimulus** of driving to the clinic, entering the parking lot became a stimulus that also elicited the response of nausea whether or not the chemotherapy was also present.

Theresa, like all of us, had an innate drive to avoid pain. When she received vaccinations as a child, her parents reinforced her fears by paying special attention to her when she became fearful. As a result of this **operant conditioning**, her fear of injections became habitual and evolved into a phobia. In fact, through the process of **stimulus generalization**, Theresa experienced a great deal of anxiety in reaction to any medical appointment, whether or not it necessitated an injection. Her learned behavior reflected a **stimulus-response** pairing process; because her fearful behavior was rewarded in childhood, Theresa demonstrated fear and avoidance in response to the stimulus of any medical visit.

Her therapist used several behavioral approaches to modify Theresa's responses. **Systematic desensitization** was used in the hope of **extinguishing** Theresa's excessive fear of medical visits and vaccinations. An **anxiety hierarchy** was created, listing her fears in ascending order from the mildest fear (a visit to a dermatologist that would not involve any physical discomfort) to the most frightening (a visit to the oncologist for chemotherapy). Beginning with the mildest fear, the therapist helped Theresa to relax and feel empowered while visualizing the frightening stimulus. This process of **reciprocal inhibition** paired relaxation and positive feelings with an **aversive stimulus** (a frightening image) to decrease the strength of the fear response. Theresa also learned to use both relaxation and **stimulus discrimination** to reduce her fears; she learned to relax when approaching medical visits and driving into the parking lot at the oncology clinic and reminded herself that not all medical appointments involved discomfort.

Counterconditioning was used to help Theresa further reduce her fears; when she began to ruminate or felt anxious, she visualized herself triumphantly completing her chemotherapy and setting off on a trip to Bali that she was planning. The feelings of pride and optimism elicited by that image counteracted and reduced her apprehension. To make sure she could readily access this positive image, the therapist led Theresa through a process of **covert modeling** in which she mentally rehearsed dealing effectively with her fears about chemotherapy. Joining a support group of other women diagnosed with breast cancer also provided Theresa with an experience in **social learning** and **positive reinforcement** and gave her an opportunity to model herself after others.

they feel competent. Social learning theory expands on behavior theory and cognitive behavioral theory by recognizing that not only reinforced behaviors or faulty thoughts are responsible for human behavior, but also a complicated cognitive mediational process that includes cognitive, affective, and motivational processes.

THE THERAPEUTIC PROCESS

The therapeutic process of behavior therapy emphasizes:

- The individual assessment and evaluation of objective, operationally defined behaviors
- Identification of specific **target behaviors**, or those behaviors most significantly interfering with the current daily functioning of clients (i.e., those that are often the initial focus of counseling)

- Identification of the functions of behaviors, or why they occur; the consequences that follow specific behavior; and how clients respond to these consequences
- Selection of interventions aimed at systematically extinguishing undesirable behaviors while reinforcing desired behaviors, and teaching clients to implement interventions independently
- Ongoing assessment and monitoring of behavior to determine the effectiveness of interventions, and modifying treatment plans and interventions as needed throughout the counseling process
- Conducting follow-up assessments after the completion of counseling goals to determine the overall effectiveness of counseling, as evidenced by the maintenance of adaptive behaviors and the elimination of maladaptive behaviors.

Because of the deliberate, targeted, and methodical nature of behavior therapy, counseling processes are highly structured, active, and, most notably, learning oriented. In the broadest sense, behavior therapy is essentially a process of unlearning maladaptive behaviors and replacing them with new, relearned behaviors or skills that enhance adaptive functioning (Spiegler & Guevremont, 2016). As an example, consider a 4-year-old boy whose father brings him to counseling for hitting his younger brother and children at his daycare. A counselor working from a behavior therapy perspective would focus on carefully defining the problematic behavior (e.g., the boy hits children at school), teaching the boy how to respond when angry or frustrated (e.g., the use of a relaxation exercise such as imagining he has a balloon in his belly that he blows up when he inhales, and then a candle he blows out upon the exhale) while removing the behavioral reinforcers by teaching the adults around him to respond in a manner that will extinguish the negative behaviors (e.g., placing the boy in a time-out when he hits and not reinforcing the behavior with adult contact).

Therapeutic Goals

Behavior therapy, as its name implies, seeks to extinguish maladaptive behaviors and help people learn new, more adaptive behaviors. The overriding goal of behavior therapy is to help clients become more flexible and sensitive in their reactions to changes in their environment and to establish tools that are effective in helping them meet their needs (Antony & Roemer, 2011). Counseling goals must be clear, specific, measurable, and agreed upon. The following are examples of issues behavior therapy techniques can address:

- Reduction in use of, or abstinence from, drugs and alcohol
- Reduction of undesirable habits, such as nail biting or pulling out one's own hair
- Improvement in social skills, such as assertiveness and conversation
- Reduction of fears and phobias, such as fear of flying, apprehension about public speaking, and excessive fear of snakes
- Improvement in concentration and organization
- Reduction in undesirable behaviors in children, such as tantrums, disobedience, acting out, aggressiveness, and difficulty going to bed
- Improvement in health and fitness habits, such as more nutritious eating, increased exercise, and more regular sleep patterns.

In addition to specific goals like these, behavior therapists also have the general goal of teaching people skills that will help them improve their lives. Skills such as decision making, problem analysis and resolution, time management, assertiveness, and relaxation are often incorporated into behavior therapy.

It is important to note, however, that enhancing insight, exploring underlying internal conflicts, or demonstrating unconditional positive regard to foster self-actualization is not of interest to behaviorists. Behavior therapy focuses on action; clients are expected to practice and use the new skills and strategies they have learned in counseling to assist them with changing their behavior and achieving their counseling goals (Wagner, 2008).

Therapist's Function and Role

Therapists who use a behavioral approach with clients serve as consultants, teachers, architects, and/or problem solvers. Behavior therapists conduct sessions in a directive, planned, and instructional manner, and they value the systematic, objective, observable, and rigorous elements of research-based therapeutic procedures and practices (Miltenberger, 2012; Spiegler & Guevremont, 2016).

Despite this linear, scientific approach, behavior therapists believe that relational factors can influence counseling processes, and therapists who practice contemporary behavior therapy recognize the importance of establishing a strong therapeutic alliance when working with clients. Because learned behaviors can be difficult to change, the process of behavioral change can present challenges. As such, behavior therapists understand that they must assign the same degree of time and effort to the therapeutic relationship as they do to assessment, evaluation, and implementation of behavioral interventions if they are to effectively promote change and help clients achieve their goals.

Behaviorists believe that all behavior is learned, and thus problem behaviors can be unlearned and replaced with more desirable ones. Through this lens, the etiology of maladaptive behavior is not attributed to the individual or considered to be a personally held disturbance or impairment. In this way, a behavior therapist assumes an inherently empowering stance.

Following the completion of assessment processes, therapists analyze obtained data and shift their role toward:

- Developing *initial* individualized counseling goals and objectives that target specific, observable behaviors
- Identifying evidence-based behavioral interventions, and teaching clients how they can be utilized, generalized across settings, and independently maintained
- Continually monitoring behavior, assessing the effectiveness of interventions, and modifying counseling goals and objectives as needed throughout counseling
- Completing follow-up assessments to determine counseling effectiveness and the maintenance of positive behavioral change.

Therapists also strive to establish a clear agreement with the client about the goals of counseling and the roles of both participants. A **contingency contract**, a type of behavior contract between the therapist and the client that specifies the behaviors to be addressed in counseling, is often developed.

Relationship Between Therapist and Client

Behavior therapists are more directive and focused than the therapists who use the other approaches discussed in this book. Behavior therapists are likely to develop and concentrate on formalized treatment plans, set goals and objectives, and monitor homework assignments in their efforts to help clients effect behavioral change. Behavior therapists recognize the importance of a collaborative and positive therapeutic relationship and the communication of encouragement as vital in promoting learning and motivation. Therapists can foster a positive therapeutic relationship by learning about the strengths, interests, and unique personal qualities of clients and integrate such themes into their individually tailored interventions. They tend to take a holistic approach—interpreting behavior broadly as anything an organism does, including thinking and feeling—and are interested in the total person. Although objectivity and the scientific method are valued, behavior therapists also recognize the importance of understanding and respecting individual differences.

Behavior therapy inherently emphasizes individualized counseling practices that consider specific settings, environmental circumstances, people, and other factors associated with a client's behavior. Therapists aim to individually tailor assessment processes and intervention techniques in a manner that is developmentally, intellectually, and contextually sensitive to the needs of each client.

THERAPEUTIC TECHNIQUES AND PROCEDURES

Behavior therapists emphasize that counselors should individually tailor assessment processes and intervention techniques in a manner that is developmentally, intellectually, and contextually sensitive to the needs of each client. For example, counselors working with children can design treatment plans that look similar to coloring books or children's stories, create rating scales with smiley faces as opposed to numbers to track self-report data, or use role playing as a creative avenue for children to verbally express the new competencies they have learned throughout counseling or to demonstrate before and after examples of the behavioral changes they have made.

Behavior therapists pull on a variety of interventions and techniques to help clients make changes. Some of the more commonly used behavior therapy interventions follow, but many more are available that could not be included in this text due to space limitations.

Assessment

Behavioral counselors gather initial information related to a client's presenting concerns through a variety of different assessment approaches (Flynn & Lo, 2016). To understand a client's behavior, a counselor might ask the client to thoroughly explain a typical instance of the problem behavior. It is important for the client to offer detailed accounts, as it is within these details that the counselor can identify what may be maintaining the problem.

Generally speaking, counselors working from a behavioral approach are interested in three questions:

1. What does the problem look like in concrete, specific, behavioral terms?
2. What happens before the problem occurs?
3. What happens after the problem occurs?

These three questions provide answers to behavioral change.

Understanding and gaining awareness of reasons for certain behaviors and ways to change behavior are important. **Functional behavior assessments (FBAs)** involve identifying a specific target behavior, the purpose of the behavior, and what factors maintain the behavior. Even maladaptive behaviors serve a purpose; therefore, it is helpful to understand the dynamics that go into creating and sustaining the behaviors. The function of maladaptive behaviors can be met through more adaptive and beneficial ways of behaving. In addition, understanding what happens before the behavior (the antecedents or triggers) and what happens after the behavior occurs (the consequences) gives a better picture of the relationships between the stimuli and responses.

FBAs have become one of the most frequently used assessment methods among behavioral counselors. FBAs are intended to objectively identify clients' problem behaviors, and determine the individual and environmental determinants that trigger and maintain behavior (Leaf et al., 2016; Oliver, Pratt, & Normand, 2015). The systematic procedures of FBAs are recognized as a particularly advantageous behavioral assessment, as they enable helping professionals to obtain a comprehensive and precise understanding of the *cause-effect correlations* between specific behaviors and environmental circumstances that help determine the underlying function of clients' behavior (Shriver et al., 2001). That is, by making connections between the behavior and factors that include the setting, time, around whom, and what happens before and after, FBAs allow counselors to identify what purpose behaviors serve and what clients are getting from engaging in a certain behavior.

FBAs are conducted using the **Antecedent-Behavior-Consequence (ABC) Model**, in which counselors observe and gather data on **A**ntecedents, observed **B**ehaviors, and the **C**onsequences of behavior. Counselors first seek to identify the *antecedent* events or cues that occur before a certain behavior is displayed or, in other words, identify what factors or aspects of a client's environment are responsible for eliciting the behavioral response. These responses in turn serve as the target *behaviors* counselors focus on. For example, while observing a child in the classroom to determine antecedents of target behaviors, counselors aim to answer questions about target behaviors similar to the following: In what setting do they occur? What are the physical characteristics of the setting, or how is the setting uniquely arranged? What time of day do behaviors occur? What is typically occurring in the environment before behaviors are displayed? Is the child experiencing academic difficulties? Who is around? Are there peer influences? Antecedents provide counselors with an understanding of the beforehand factors that prompt youth to demonstrate a certain behavioral response. Other people's responses or events that follow a behavior are known as *consequences*; and not only do they keep clients' behaviors maintained, but they also explain the function of behavior.

Once antecedents, behaviors, and consequences have been identified, counselors form hypotheses about the function of behavior based on their conceptualization of how environmental determinants are influencing the expression and maintenance of target behaviors. Counselors then test their hypotheses by staging brief experiments in which clients are systematically presented with a series of events or situations that are expected to elicit target behavior responses. That is, counselors intentionally introduce previously identified antecedents to determine if clients exhibit target behaviors. Alternatively, counselors may also stage different events specifically related to certain functional behavior domains and track which set of circumstances most frequently elicit target behavior responses. Maladaptive functional relationships—those in which environmental determinants lead to a client's engagement in undesired target behaviors—serve as a foundation to establish treatment goals and objectives aimed to extinguish such relationships, and assist clients in developing more adaptive behaviors.

While functional behavior assessments take some effort to complete, they are very pragmatic and hold great utility for counselors, especially counselors working with children or those who have autism spectrum disorders or intellectual disabilities (Kress et al., 2019). As functional behavior assessments reduce complex behaviors into isolated components or smaller parts, counselors can provide clients with concrete, logical interpretations of problems. Reducing behaviors into smaller specific components can help in formulating realistic and attainable goals. Such behavioral approaches are particularly applicable in the school environment, as many youth who experience behavioral problems in the classroom also encounter academic difficulties. Establishing small goals that clients are able to accomplish in a prompt time period can engender an advantageous sense of success and self-efficacy. Fostering clients' personal agency can increase therapeutic momentum, as goal achievement naturally serves as reinforcement.

Operant Conditioning Techniques

As previously mentioned, operant conditioning is a type of learning based on consequences and reinforcement, in which behavior is influenced by the positive or negative association of the consequence that follows a behavior (Miltenberger, 2012). Subsequent to the completion of an individualized functional behavior assessment and the establishment of clear, measurable, and observable goals, counselors identify empirically validated interventions that support the desired counseling outcomes.

TABLE 5.3 Operant Conditioning Interventions

Intervention	Application	Example
Positive reinforcement	• The addition of a positive stimulus as a consequence of behavior. • Behavior is increased.	• A teacher gives his student a sticker for following directions. • A mother praises her son for receiving good grades.
Negative reinforcement	• The removal of an aversive stimulus as a consequence of behavior. • Behavior is increased.	• A student can leave detention after completing a late assignment. • A child shares a toy to stop her younger sister's nagging.
Punishment	• Positive punishment is the addition of an aversive stimulus as a consequence of behavior. • Negative punishment, or response cost, is the removal of a reinforcing stimulus as a consequence of behavior. • Behavior is decreased.	• A father puts his son in time-out for hitting his younger brother (positive punishment). • Parents take the car keys of an adolescent for staying out past curfew (negative punishment).
Extinction	• Behavior stops or extinguishes due to a lack of reinforcement. • Behavior is decreased.	• A teacher ignores a child's tantrum. • A father refrains from giving candy to his son each time he cries.
Prompting	• A verbal, visual, or physical cue is used to cause a behavior. • Behavior is likely to occur and, with reinforcement, will increase.	• A teacher raises her hand to remind students who are speaking out to settle down. • An adolescent points at his teacher to redirect a friend who is talking in class.
Shaping	• Reinforcing successive approximations, or displayed behaviors that are similar to the target behavior until it occurs. • Gradually increasing similar behaviors until the target behavior is learned.	• Praising a shy adolescent for progressively moving toward talking to other students. • Providing a child with a reward for completing small sections of her homework until the entire assignment is complete.
Chaining	• Reinforcing step-by-step, or "chained" behaviors that lead to the learning of a complex behavior. • Gradually increasing each step-by-step behavior until the more complex behavior is achieved.	• A child receives a gold star for each letter of the alphabet that is learned. • A child is praised for mastering each step required to tie her shoes.

A number of behavior therapy techniques and interventions are based on operant conditioning principles (Table 5.3). Some of the foundations and principles that support operant conditioning techniques will be discussed in the following sections.

The use of the words "positive" and "negative" can be confusing at first. For example, negative reinforcement is often mistaken for punishment, when in fact the two are separate, and important, concepts in behavioral theory. Negative does not necessarily mean "bad"; it means removing something from the environment. The opposite of negative is positive, which means adding something to the environment, which does not necessarily mean "good," as we will see when we discuss positive punishment. Punishment intends to decrease undesirable behavior, and reinforcement intends to increase desirable behavior. These terms combined make up the four contingencies of operant conditioning: positive reinforcement, negative reinforcement, positive punishment, and negative punishment, which will be discussed below.

REINFORCEMENT Reinforcements and rewards encourage behavior change, enhance learning, and solidify gains. Reinforcements are used to increase desirable behavior. Reinforcements should be carefully selected and planned; should be meaningful and worthwhile to the individual so that they are motivating; and should be realistic and reasonable. For example, giving a child a video game for cleaning his room once is not realistic, but setting aside $3 toward the purchase of a video game each week the child cleans his room 5 out of 7 days probably is. Reinforcement is of two types:

- **Positive reinforcement:** A behavior followed by a positive reinforcement has an increased probability of being repeated. Positive reinforcement involves providing a "reward" to a client upon completion of a desired behavior (at the schedule of reinforcement that has been determined). Positive reinforcement encourages a behavior to be repeated, much as a parent's smiles and excitement reinforce a baby to smile.
- **Negative reinforcement:** The removal of an already active aversive stimulus (e.g., turning off the electricity when the mouse stands on its hind legs will result in the mouse standing more) is known as negative reinforcement. Therefore, behavior followed by the removal of an aversive stimulus results in an increased probability of that behavior occurring in the future.

Adults can create their own reinforcement plans. One woman who had difficulty paying bills on time set aside 1 hour twice a week for organizing her finances. Each time she completed the hour of financial planning, she rewarded herself by going to the bookstore to buy a new mystery and spending the rest of the evening reading her book.

Rewards do not need to be material. Social reinforcement, such as parental approval, a positive rating at work, and admiration from friends, can be as powerful or even more powerful. In addition, clients can reward themselves through positive affirmations and reminders of their success, such as the declining balance on their credit card bill and their improved grades. Reinforcements usually are most powerful if they are provided shortly after the success and are clearly linked to the accomplishment. Such reinforcers are particularly likely to solidify the desired change in behavior and contribute to either further change or maintenance of goal achievement.

PUNISHMENT The opposite of reinforcement is punishment, or reasonable consequences, which are the logical, and usually unpleasant, outcomes of undesirable behavior. Punishment is used to decrease undesirable behavior. Getting fired for repeatedly coming to work late is an example of such a consequence. Punishment consists of two main types:

- **Positive punishment:** A behavior followed by positive punishment has a decreased probability of being repeated. **Positive punishment** involves adding something aversive to the environment upon completion of an undesirable behavior. For example, the child who does not pick up her toys before dinner must clean her room after dinner instead of watching her favorite television program.
- **Negative punishment:** The removal of an already active favorable stimulus (e.g., toys) is known as **negative punishment** or **response cost**. Therefore, behavior followed by the removal of a favorable stimulus results in a decreased probability of that behavior occurring in the future. An example of negative punishment is giving children a time-out or taking away their toy after they misbehave.

Although reasonable consequences can be viewed as punishment, they are preferable to arbitrary and contrived punishments because they have a logical connection to the undesirable behavior and give people a strong message about the implications of their behavior. Reasonable (or natural) consequences avoid some of the potentially harmful consequences of other types of punishment while still giving a powerful message. Reasonable consequences are designed to grow logically out of an undesirable behavior; for example, a boy who neglects his homework is required to keep a notebook in which his teachers write down daily homework assignments for parent follow-up. The girl who uses six towels each time she bathes is made responsible for doing the laundry.

Although penalties or punishments are sometimes used instead of rewards to shape behavior, rewards are generally more effective. They make the process of change a positive and empowering experience and promote motivation. In addition, if other people are giving the consequences, those people are likely to be perceived positively if they are giving rewards but viewed negatively if they are providing punishments. However, punishments can provide a powerful and immediate message and do have a place in behavior change. Arrest of people guilty of domestic abuse, for example, can break through their denial, leading them to enter counseling and make positive changes.

Despite the fact that punishment is not generally an effective strategy for modifying behavior, people from the United States generally approve of using corporal punishment (e.g., washing children's mouths out with soap, spanking or hitting children with some type of an instrument; Aronson-Fontes, 2005), and counselors in all settings will frequently find themselves needing to advise adults on effective discipline strategies. Many mental health associations have made public statements condemning the use of spanking and corporal punishment, and research demonstrates that it is not an effective way to modify children's behavior. In fact, the more children are spanked, the more likely they are to defy their parents, experience increased aggressive behavior, and struggle with mental health problems (Gershoff & Grogan-Kaylor, 2016). Armed with research and knowledge on effective and ineffective discipline and parenting strategies, therapists can play an important role in applying behavior principles and assisting parents to help their children.

EXTINCTION Extinction involves withdrawing the payoff or reinforcement of an undesirable behavior in hopes of reducing or eliminating it. For example, parents who give their children extra attention whenever they misbehave may be inadvertently reinforcing the undesirable behavior. Coaching the parents to pay attention to positive behavior and ignore misbehavior as much as possible is likely to reduce undesirable behavior.

SHAPING Skinner first introduced **shaping**, which refers to the process of gradually reinforcing particular target behaviors to approximate the desired behavior. In other words, this technique is used to effect a gradual change in behaviors. Shaping can help people make **successive approximations** of desired behaviors, eventually leading to new patterns of behavior. Drawing on the principles of operant conditioning in one of his studies, Skinner was able to reinforce a pigeon to turn in a circle and peck at a red disk by reinforcing small successive approximations of the desired behavior until the pigeon was able to complete an entire turn with only one reinforcement. Shaping can also reinforce undesirable behavior. For example, children's behavior can be shaped through parental reinforcement; parents who give attention primarily to children's misbehavior inadvertently reinforce that behavior. Another example of shaping is the way children learn to talk—they are rewarded for making a sound that is similar to a word until they can say the word. The following steps might help people with social anxiety improve their interactions with others:

- Spend 5 to 10 minutes at a social gathering. Do not initiate any conversations.
- Spend 5 to 10 minutes at a social gathering and greet at least two people.

- Spend 15 to 20 minutes at a social gathering, greet at least two people, introduce yourself to at least one person, and ask a question of one other person.
- Follow the previous step and, in addition, have a brief conversation about the weather and compliment the host on the food.

CONTINGENCY MANAGEMENT AND TOKEN ECONOMIES **Contingency management** is the theoretical foundation of **token economies**. Contingency management is based on the behavioral principle that if a behavior is reinforced or rewarded, it is more likely to occur in the future. In more formal terms, contingency management is the systematic delivery of reinforcing or punishing consequences contingent on the occurrence of a target response, and the withholding of those consequences in the absence of a target response. As an example, a client receiving methadone treatment for heroin addiction is provided with take-home methadone privileges for maintaining a long period of abstinence. The client is reinforced for positive behavior by not having to come into a clinic to dose each morning.

Token economy systems, an applied form of contingency management, are operant reinforcement programs that are particularly useful in group settings such as schools, day treatment programs, hospitals, prisons, and within families. Token economies effectively and efficiently change a broad range of behaviors in a group of people. As with all behavioral counseling processes, a target behavior or set of behaviors must initially be identified and defined. Behavioral rules, guidelines, or goals must first be established and then understood and learned by all participants in the token economy system. These guidelines are generally written out and posted to maintain awareness. Clients earn something that is reinforcing for them based on their age, developmental level, and current needs (e.g., tokens, points, tickets) for demonstrating desired target behaviors. Tokens are provided *each time* the behavior occurs. With children, it can be helpful to store the tokens in a visible jar or container as a reminder of success. Once a predetermined number of tokens are earned, they can be traded in for a reward. The rewards should be clear, realistic, and meaningful to the participants and be given in ways that are fair and consistent. For example, consider a child who is staying in a residential treatment facility: 2 points might be exchanged for television time, 5 points might merit a trip to the movies, and 15 points might be exchanged for a telephone call to a friend. To provide reinforcement, opportunities should be offered for frequent redemption of rewards. In addition, social reinforcement (praise, appropriate physical affection) should be paired with the material rewards to develop intrinsic motivation and internalization of the desired behaviors. **Generalization** of the behaviors outside the therapeutic setting promotes their establishment.

Behavior contracts can document the terms or conditions of the token economy system, including specific behavioral expectations and schedules of reinforcement. Then a system of rapidly identifying and recording each individual's performance of the desired behaviors is developed. Creating behavior contracts and using other visual aids help to make token economies more concrete and understandable when working with children or people who have developmental or intellectual delays.

APPLICATION OF OPERANT CONDITIONING PRINCIPLES: APPLIED BEHAVIOR ANLAYSIS One of the most powerful applications of behavior therapy principles in recent years has been the development of **applied behavior analysis** (ABA), a gold standard treatment for those who have autism spectrum disorder (Boutot & Hume, 2012; Matson et al., 2012). ABA is often delivered one-on-one in a school, home, or clinical setting. ABA can also be delivered in social skills group settings that sometimes incorporate siblings or peers who do not have autism to serve as models for appropriate behavior and social communication. ABA uses Skinner's behavioral principles of operant conditioning to elicit positive behavior change. ABA can be used to teach age-appropriate communication skills, social skills, adaptive behavior skills, and academic content to adults and children with autism, while simultaneously decreasing negative behaviors such as tantrums and outbursts. ABA also involves functional behavior assessment procedures or a functional assessment. Counselors use functional behavior assessment to systematically identify the contributing and maintaining factors of problem behaviors, and the function or purpose these behaviors serve (Harvey, Luiselli, & Wong, 2009). Following the completion of assessment processes, counselors analyze obtained data and shift their role toward (1) developing *initial* individualized treatment goals and objectives that target specific, observable behaviors; (2) identifying evidence-based behavioral interventions and teaching youth how they can be utilized, generalized across settings, and independently maintained; (3) continually monitoring behavior, assessing the effectiveness of interventions, and modifying treatment goals and objectives as needed throughout counseling; and (4) completing follow-up assessments to determine treatment effectiveness and the maintenance of positive behavioral change. To bring to life some of the behavior therapy concepts we have been discussing, a summary of several ABA techniques, with examples of their application, is provided in Table 5.4.

TABLE 5.4 Applied Behavior Analysis (ABA): An Application of Operant Conditioning Techniques

ABA Techniques	Brief Summary	Example
Discrete Trial Training	A discrete trial training (DTT) attempts to decrease problematic behaviors and increase more adaptive functioning behaviors. DTT involves: (a) identifying and presenting a behavior; (b) providing a prompt; (c) allowing the client to respond to the prompt; (d) providing a consequence; and (e) after a pause beginning another trial.	A counselor presents a behavior (e.g., to pick up the hair brush), a prompt (e.g., please pick up the hair brush), the client responds (e.g., either by picking up the brush or not), a consequence follows (i.e., either reinforcement or a correction), and after a short pause (i.e., inter-trial interval) another trial can begin. Once this behavior is mastered (e.g., pick up the hair brush), the counselor can introduce another associated behavior (e.g., using brush to brush hair) following the same process.
Modeling	Demonstrating a behavior that the counselor wants the client to engage in. Anyone can model these adaptive behaviors (e.g., the counselor, peers, parents, siblings).	A counselor demonstrates a behavior (e.g., asking for a toy and waiting patiently) to teach a client a predetermined skill. It is essential to the learning process that the client be engaged in the observation. A counselor may create and videotape a play interaction between two toy figures (e.g., Jake and Captain Hook) which involves an adaptive skill such as sharing. The counselor can then have the client watch this taped video play interaction. Finally, the child can be invited to recreate this play interaction—including verbal dialogue and actions—with the provided toys.

(Continued)

TABLE 5.4 (*Continued*)

ABA Techniques	Brief Summary	Example
Naturalistic Teaching Strategies	Engaging a client in his or her natural environment to teach functional skills. Working within a client's environment, the counselor can utilize the environment or objects in it to engage the client and increase his or her adaptive functioning.	A counselor can use a ball in the client's play area. The counselor uses language to describe it (this is a ball; it is round), show the action of it (the ball can roll back and forth). After a brief pause, the counselor can ask the client to repeat these actions. The counselor can provide running comments on what is happening (you ask for the ball so nicely; you are doing a great job rolling the ball back and forth; I love to see you play like this).
Peer Training	Since clients with autism often spend less time interacting with others, spending time with accessible and competent models of social interactions in intentional ways can impact their ability to initiate and interact socially.	Counselors can utilize a group setting, peer networks, and peer-mediated social interactions to increase awareness and utilization of social skills. Counselors need to thoughtfully plan these interactions by training peers how to get the attention of the client, facilitate sharing, model appropriate play, and help to organize activities. A counselor may decide to integrate others without social skills deficits into a group setting to aid those with deficits by demonstrating the target behaviors within the context of the group.
Schedules	Following a task list (picture or words) through a series of steps to complete an activity.	A counselor can use a group of sequential pictures depicting each step needed for a client to complete the process of preparing for bedtime (e.g., changing of clothes, brushing teeth, washing face).
Self-Management	Helping a client regulate his or her reactions or behaviors through the recording of the target behavior.	A counselor can aid a client in recording the occurrence of a desired behavior in some concrete, meaningful way (e.g., behavioral chart placed in a prominent place). The client can place a star on the behavioral chart for each day he completes his chores which may include cleaning his room and helping with dinner clean up.
Story Based Interventions	Reading stories that present situations with the specific, target behaviors.	A counselor can use a visual, narrative depiction of a target behavior (e.g., introducing one's self to a new person; keeping hands to one's self). These stories can deconstruct the complicated behaviors into small tasks; thus, teaching the client who, when, why, and how social interactions can be strengthened within a narrative/story context.

Source: National Autism Center. (2009). *National standards report* (phase 1). Retrieved from http://www.nationalautismcenter.org/reports/; Kress, V. E., Paylo, M., & Stargell, N. A. (2019). *Counseling children and adolescents.* Upper Saddle River, NJ: Pearson.

Classical Conditioning Techniques

Interventions founded on the principles of classical conditioning are most applicable to clients who experience distress related to anxiety, panic, fear, or trauma—all of which share common features of heightened body responses, such as increased heart rate, rapid breathing, or shaking, along with upsetting thoughts about the feared object, event, or situation. Accordingly, classical conditioning interventions not only use behavioral learning principles to target the physiological responses characteristic of stress-related presenting concerns (e.g., separation anxiety, specific phobia disorder, social anxiety disorder, agoraphobia, panic disorder, posttraumatic stress disorder [PTSD]) but also include supplemental cognitive-oriented exercises to address thought-based symptoms (e.g., worrying about getting lost; being embarrassed in front of others; anticipation that harm, injury, or death will occur). Interventions including progressive muscle relaxation, systematic desensitization, and exposure-based strategies are all commonly used with clients and are all backed by empirical evidence.

EXPOSURE-BASED INTERVENTIONS Exposure is one of the most important components of behavior therapy for anxiety disorders. Through the use of **exposure**, people learn to identify their fear responses; recognize maladaptive cognitions; confront or "sit with" the uncomfortable feelings without avoiding, running away, or otherwise modifying the experience; and achieve a certain amount of self-efficacy or control over the feelings of distress. As a result, people learn new methods of coping and handling emotions, rather than giving in to fear (Bandura, 1977). Research has found that repeated contact with a feared or avoided stimulus will result in adaptation. In other words, the more exposure individuals have to a feared object (e.g., a snake, tarantula, or tall building), the less fear they will experience. In contrast, avoidance of the feared object reinforces the fear and actually increases the resulting anxiety. Most exposure-based therapies and interventions also include a cognitive component, usually cognitive restructuring, to help increase the client's positive coping statements and reduce thought distortions, self-blame, and anxiety.

Virtual reality therapy uses technology to provide another delivery method for exposure-based therapies. By creating a human–computer interaction that imitates *in vivo exposure,* virtual reality can be particularly helpful for anxiety disorders, including social anxiety, phobias, obsessive-compulsive disorder [OCD], PTSD, and the fear of public speaking (Powers & Emmelkamp, 2008; Wallach, Safir, & Bar-Zvi, 2009). Interactions can occur via video or three-dimensional (3D) technology and may include use of a joystick, glove, or similar device to provide interactive feedback between the individual and the computer. A distinct advantage of virtual reality over other approaches is the ability to adjust the level of stimuli the individual receives. Virtual reality therapy has also helped individuals who have snake phobias or fear of heights (Klinger et al., 2005). Sensitivity and clinical judgement must be used when incorporating virtual reality into counseling, and the technique should never be used as a substitute for therapy (Rothbaum, 2005).

Pacing is another important consideration in exposure-based therapies. Some therapies are designed to take place within one session. Flooding, for example, usually provides intensive exposure over 30 minutes to 8 hours to the individual's most feared stimulus (see below). Because of the intense emotions, flooding can be overwhelming and is not appropriate for treating phobias for which it might pose danger, such as phobias of driving over bridges or on highways. **Implosion** is another type of prolonged, intense exposure therapy in which the client imagines anxiety-producing situations or events in order to develop a more appropriate response for the future.

Graduated exposure involves having the individual confront the fear for a short period, and then gradually increasing the length of exposure with each session. Systematic desensitization is a type of graduated exposure. An example of graduated exposure for an elevator phobia would involve taking the elevator to more floors with each successive therapy session. Flooding, systematic desensitization, and interoceptive exposure are the most common exposure-based therapies and are discussed below.

Flooding involves exposing an individual to high doses of a feared stimulus, with the expectation that this will desensitize them to the feared stimulus. The person must remain in the feared situation long enough for the fear to peak and then diminish. If the person leaves the situation prematurely, the fear may worsen and the person may learn to fear those who staged the flooding. In addition, the fear may lead the person to act in unsafe ways. Flooding is a high-risk intervention that must be used with caution, and only by therapists who are well versed in its appropriate use.

Some people believe that pushing a child into a swimming pool is a way to cure a fear of water. This misguided belief can endanger the child's life, create a traumatic experience, and impair the child's trust in others. Flooding should rarely be used, and then only after the client is fully informed about the risks associated with the procedure and consents to participate in the procedure.

Systematic desensitization, as created by Wolpe, is a powerful exposure intervention for reducing fears, phobias, obsessions, compulsions, and anxiety. Initial fears are generally worsened when the individual avoids the feared stimulus and the avoidance is reinforced by the relief that follows. Systematic desensitization is designed to reverse this process by gradually exposing an individual to the disturbing stimulus in ways that reduce rather than increase fear.

Counselors who use systematic desensitization generally begin counseling with one or two sessions focused on relaxation techniques, followed by the creation of an anxiety hierarchy. The least frightening presentation of the feared object (a picture of a spider, for example) is shown as clients engage in relaxation techniques. As clients become more comfortable with the spider picture, they might be shown a picture of multiple spiders, gradually moving up the hierarchy to watching a video of spiders, watching a spider in a terrarium, and eventually handling a spider. Systematic desensitization can be conducted in the imagination (imaginal), **in vivo** (in real life contexts), or as a combination of both.

Another type of exposure, **interoceptive exposure**, is a structured approach that encourages people to experience feared bodily sensations (such as shortness of breath or heart flutters) in the safe environment of a therapy session without engaging in avoidance or escape strategies. Counseling continues until adaptation occurs and the feelings are no longer frightening. An example of interoceptive exposure is spinning in a chair to achieve dizziness. Interoceptive exposure is used most frequently in the treatment of panic disorder (Forsyth, Fuse, & Acheson, 2009).

Other elements that add to the effectiveness of exposure-based therapies include behavioral strategies such as relaxation training, deep-breathing instruction, paradoxical intention, rehearsal, hypnosis, role playing, and modeling. Many different types of exposure-based therapies are available, and they can be individualized for each client's needs. Box 5.1, Prolonged Exposure Therapy, discusses an exposure-based behavioral treatment approach.

RELAXATION TECHNIQUES Relaxation is often combined with other techniques such as systematic desensitization, abdominal breathing, hypnosis, and visual imagery. Teaching relaxation strategies in a counseling session and encouraging practice between sessions can facilitate people's efforts to reduce stress and anxiety and make behavioral changes. Several well-established relaxation strategies are available, including progressive muscle relaxation (sequentially tensing and relaxing each muscle group in the body); a body scan (each part of the body is systematically assessed and relaxed); and simple exercises such as head rolls, shoulder shrugs, and shaking one's body until it feels loose and relaxed.

Progressive Muscle Relaxation. Anxiety or other stress-related presenting concerns involve a wide variety of physical symptoms, including muscle tension, heart palpitations, dizziness, fatigue, or sleep disturbance. Progressive muscle relaxation (Jacobson, 1938; Lopata, 2003) is one intervention

> **Box 5.1 Prolonged Exposure Therapy: An Application of Behavior Therapy Exposure Techniques**
>
> Building on the exposure therapy techniques historically used to treat anxiety disorders, prolonged exposure therapy (PET) was specifically designed to treat PTSD (Foa & Yadin, 2011). The purpose of PET is to help clients recall trauma and associated fears, develop new information about the trauma and their responses, and learn new ways of reframing and coping with pathological fear associated with the trauma. Among people who have experienced recent traumatic events, exposure therapy has contributed to decreased PTSD symptoms, when compared to cognitive interventions. In fact, exposure therapy is recommended as an early intervention for people who experience a traumatic event and who are thus at high risk of developing subsequent PTSD (Bryant et al., 2008). Furthermore, exposure therapy has been well studied and empirically supported as a treatment for PTSD and has emerged as the most effective approach for addressing trauma (Foa et al., 2009; Foa & Yadin, 2011).
>
> PET is typically offered over 8 to 15 sessions, each session lasting between 60 and 90 minutes. Different formats may be used, such as meeting once or twice per week, using guided imagery, incorporating in vivo exposure, or using recordings. The most effective method is combining imaginal exposure of the trauma memory with in vivo exposure to people, places, and situations associated with the trauma that do not pose a realistic risk of harm (Foa et al., 2009).
>
> Regardless of variations in how this approach is conducted, the critical aspect is facilitating client exposure to the part of a specific traumatic event that elicits the greatest fear in order to gradually reduce the fear and anxiety. Using visual imagery, virtual reality, or a combination, clients emotionally engage with the recollection. In doing so, they confront the feared event, identify and acknowledge their fears, and learn that expected disasters do not occur when they encounter the feared stimuli.
>
> Revisiting trauma as part of therapy helps clients organize their memories of the traumatic event(s); re-evaluate negative cognitions about their involvement with the trauma; develop new perceptions about themselves and others; differentiate between recalling the trauma and re-experiencing the trauma; develop skills that will allow them to recall the trauma without experiencing undue anxiety; and understand that memories of the trauma will not harm them (Foa & Yadin, 2011).

behavior therapists use to assist clients with calming their bodies and relaxing when they are feeling anxious or worried. Clients are encouraged to breathe deeply as they find a comfortable seated or lying position with their eyes closed. Therapists systematically guide clients to tense the muscles of a certain body area for approximately 5 seconds, release or let go of the muscle tension, and notice the state of relaxation that ensues. A progression through the major muscle area of the body from head to toe is typically done. The most critical component of progressive muscle relaxation involves clients' discrimination between sensations of tension and relaxation. Clients begin to recognize how their bodies respond to anxiety, and with continued practice, they learn to relax their muscles on cue when presented with an anxiety-provoking stimulus. However, as with all conditioning interventions, repetition is imperative to yield the desired effect. Later in this chapter, the Skill Development section provides an example of how progressive muscle relaxation can be applied.

Breathing Techniques. Breathing techniques are typically used to help manage stress, anxiety, sleep problems, and anger. One type of breathing technique is **diaphragmatic breathing**, which involves taking slow, deep breaths and focusing on the breath. People breathe in through the nose, expand the diaphragm, and then expel the air through the mouth. This sort of breathing supplies the body with more oxygen, focuses concentration, and has been associated with increased self-control and mindfulness. Breath focus can also be used, which involves picturing a calming image in the mind and repeating a word or phrase. It is especially helpful to imagine breathing in peace and calmness and breathing out stress and anxiety. People can also breathe in and breathe out for equal periods of time and eventually increase the length of breathing in and out.

Biofeedback. **Biofeedback** involves the use of instruments that monitor bodily functions such as heart rate, sweat gland activity, skin temperature, and pulse rate and give people feedback on those functions via a tone or light. Biofeedback can promote reductions in tension and anxiety and increased relaxation. It also can have physical and medical benefits, such as lowering blood pressure and improving pain control. It has been used to treat brain injuries, sleep disorders, attention-deficit hyperactivity disorder (ADHD), and depression (Myers & Young, 2012). **Neurofeedback**, a subset of biofeedback, allows people to monitor and regulate brain wave patterns and change behavior as a result.

Skills Training

An important component of promoting positive change is teaching people the skills they need to effect that change. Skills training can be used in individual counseling or in group counseling. For example, social skills training can work well in a group setting. Therapists can teach clients both general skills (e.g., assertiveness training, decision making, problem solving, communication skills) and those serving the needs of particular individuals (e.g., interviewing, anger management, work-related skills). **Assertiveness training** is often used to teach clients to empower themselves and effectively express positive and negative feelings to others. Parents often benefit from learning these skills to use behavior change strategies with their children. **Bibliotherapy**, or relevant readings, can supplement therapists' efforts to teach new skills. Many books are available, for example, on assertiveness, time management, parenting, and other positive behaviors.

Modeling is a type of **observational learning** in which people are influenced by observing the behaviors of another. Modeling can figure importantly in skills training and development, and it is an adjunct to approaches such as assertiveness training; relationship training; social skills for children, adolescents, or adults; or any other situations in which people would like to develop certain behaviors. People are most likely influenced by models who are similar to them in terms of gender, age, race, and beliefs; perceived as attractive and admirable in realistic ways; and viewed as competent and warm (Bandura, 1969). Modeling can occur in different ways:

1. Therapists can serve as models, demonstrating target behaviors, including social skills training or negotiation skills.
2. Clients can observe others engaged in behaviors or activities they would like to emulate, such as public speaking, conversing at social gatherings, or offering suggestions at a meeting with their clients.
3. Covert or imaginal modeling involves the therapist describing a situation for the client to visualize. An example of covert modeling would be asking a 14-year-old boy to imagine saying "no" to a friend who was trying to get him to drink a beer.
4. Symbolic modeling via movies or books is a common approach to teaching children and young adults appropriate behavior.
5. Self-modeling is also an option. Clients can serve as their own models by making audio or video recordings of themselves engaged in positive and desired behaviors (Bandura, 1969).

Related to modeling, **behavioral rehearsal**, or practicing a behavior clients wish to develop, gives them an opportunity to practice new behaviors they have perhaps witnessed or want to engage in. The rehearsal might involve a role play with the therapist or a practice session with a friend.

Video-recording the rehearsal or observing themselves in the mirror while practicing the desired behavior offers opportunities for feedback and improvement.

Behavioral rehearsal can be used for a wide variety of experiences. Making or refusing requests to promote assertiveness and sharing positive and negative feelings with others lend themselves particularly well to behavioral rehearsal. Behavioral rehearsal also can help people improve their social skills—for example, by practicing ways to initiate and maintain conversations or invite other people to join them in social activities.

APPLICATION AND CURRENT USE OF BEHAVIOR THERAPY

Behavior therapies have a broad range of applications. Used either alone or in combination with other approaches, their principles and strategies can be applied in almost any setting and with almost any client or problem. Behavior therapy has more applications than could ever be addressed in this text.

Counseling Applications

Many empirical studies support the use of behavior therapy with populations and presenting issues. Behavior therapy is helpful in treating people who have autism spectrum disorder, depressive/bipolar disorders, anxiety and traumatic stress disorders, some personality disorders, eating disorders, and substance use disorders.

Behavior therapy is particularly effective with those who are struggling with depression. Behavior change strategies such as activity scheduling and systematic decision making can reduce the severity of depression, counteract the inertia and confusion often associated with depression, and promote feelings of mastery and competence (Kress & Paylo, 2019).

Exposure-based therapies have shown value in addressing a wide range of anxiety disorders, including specific phobias (e.g., animals, thunderstorms, public speaking, and flying), PTSD and trauma, and panic disorder. Behavior therapy can also be adapted for use with children to help them overcome a variety of fears (e.g., fear of the dark or other frightening situations; Kress, Paylo, & Stargell, 2019).

People who have a social phobia (i.e., a fear of social situations) often benefit from behavioral techniques such as training in social skills involving instruction in assertiveness and communication, modeling, roleplaying, and practice (Beidel et al., 2014). Substitution of positive activities for negative ones and distraction can help people cope with obsessive-compulsive disorder (Olatunji, Davis, Powers, & Smits, 2013).

Behavioral interventions, including **contingency management**, shaping, stimulus fading, and exposure, have shown effectiveness in addressing selective mutism (i.e., a childhood anxiety disorder in which a child does not speak; Busse & Downey, 2011; Hung et al., 2012; Zakszeski & DuPaul, 2017). Meta-analyses have reported that behavior therapy (i.e., habit reversal training) has demonstrated efficacy in treating trichotillomania (i.e., hair pulling; McGuire et al., 2014; Slikboer, Nedeljkovic, Bowe, & Moulding, 2015).

Behavior therapy has been used successfully when working with children and adolescents diagnosed with oppositional defiant disorder, conduct disorder, and ADHD (Miller et al., 2014). Relaxation, activity scheduling, and time management can be helpful when working with people who have ADHD. Behavior therapy has demonstrated effectiveness in helping people diagnosed with intellectual disabilities, impulse-control disorders, sexual dysfunctions, sleep disorders, paraphilias (i.e., sexual disorders), and aggressive behavior (Hofmann, 2012; Lanza et al., 2002).

The use of behavior therapy extends far beyond work with people who struggle with various mental disorders. Relaxation, hypnosis, and visual imagery have been used in behavioral medicine to reduce pain and help people cope with cancer, heart disease, and other chronic and life-threatening illnesses. Schools and correctional institutions, as well as day treatment and inpatient treatment programs, rely heavily on behavior therapy to teach and establish positive behaviors.

Family and group counseling can use behavior therapy, as well. Parents can benefit from learning behavior change strategies and using those to shape their children's behavior. Such common parental interventions as time-out, rewards, consequences, and limit setting reflect behavior therapy.

Application to Multicultural Groups

Behavior therapy has wide appeal and is easily integrated into counseling with people from a variety of backgrounds and situations. These approaches are easily understood and logical, respect individual differences, and offer a large repertoire of interventions to address almost any concern. Behavior therapy encourages people to play an active and informed role in their counseling process, promotes learning and competence, and can produce rapid and positive results that are reinforcing.

The focus on behaviors rather than feelings may fit well with certain cultures. Behavior therapy does not typically emphasize catharsis or expression of emotion. Of particular importance, a focus on behavior can make the counseling process more acceptable to people who are not used to sharing their emotions, including some men, many older people, and some people from Asian and other cultural backgrounds who may view expression of emotions to a stranger as inappropriate, weak, or in conflict with their upbringing and self-images (Sue, Sue, Neville, & Smith, 2019). The specificity, objectivity, present-focus, and problem-solving components are possible strengths of behavior therapy for certain cultures. Clients who are seeking action and specific plans will likely benefit from this approach.

Therapy that is active, directive, and short term is compatible with many people's cultural expectations regarding therapy (Sue et al., 2019). People who are highly motivated, fairly resilient, pragmatic, logical, and tough minded are most likely to enjoy this energetic and interactive approach and appreciate the directness of the behavior therapist. However, just as therapists vary in their comfort with the active and directive stance of behavior therapy, clients vary in their reactions to this approach. Of course, behavior therapists must use culturally competent skills and communication styles, and not make assumptions about what is in the individual's best interest.

EVALUATION OF BEHAVIOR THERAPY

Limitations

Behavior therapy, like many other therapies, has drawn several criticisms. For example, behavior therapy has been criticized for changing behavior but failing to change feelings. Behavior therapy may not spend enough time focusing on feelings or allowing clients to experience their feelings. In addition, some believe that to change behavior, emotions must be changed first. Another criticism is that behavior therapy does not help clients acquire insight. Some believe that insight and awareness about problems and how change is occurring are necessary components for change and growth. However, a change in behavior may lead to gaining insight. Therefore, instead of focusing on insight first, behavior therapy may initially concentrate on changing behavior, which will then help clients reach an understanding of their problems and how change occurred. It may be helpful to create open communication with clients regarding any insights they may have noticed after making the behavior change. A further criticism is that behavior therapy strategies are superficial and likely to worsen or shift symptoms from one problem area to another (symptom substitution). Therefore, symptoms may change, but underlying causes stay the same, which prevents true change from occurring. Finally, some therapists believe that the role of the behavior therapist is controlling and has too much social influence. However, behavior therapists aim to include clients in the counseling process, to be explicit about the roles of both therapists and clients, and to take more of a psychoeducational approach. That said, the following three criticisms of behavior therapy are the most common:

1. The possibility exists that therapy will accomplish only superficial and temporary gains.
2. Emotions and insight may not receive the attention they merit.
3. Therapists may focus too quickly on behaviors, without sufficiently exploring their underlying antecedents and dynamics. For example, a therapist may emphasize development of social skills in a woman who is fearful of dating and neglect her history of abuse.

Strengths and Contributions

Most of us use behavior change strategies in our everyday lives. When we reward ourselves with a snack after finishing a difficult chore, give a chronically late friend a message by deciding not to wait more than 15 minutes, or embark on a plan to improve our diet and exercise, we are using behavior change strategies. These approaches have been around for decades, and have a great deal to offer. They are also easily integrated with a broad range of other approaches, including psychodynamic therapy, Gestalt therapy, and person-centered counseling. Such combinations can deepen the impact of counseling and ensure that resulting changes are meaningful and enduring.

Behavior therapy has made important contributions to counseling and psychotherapy. It has emphasized the importance of research on counseling effectiveness. The emphasis on goal setting, accountability, and outcome is very much in keeping with the requirements of managed care for treatment plans and progress reports, as well as clients' demands for efficient and effective counseling. Behavior therapy has also provided a foundation for the development of numerous other approaches—for example, reality therapy and multimodal therapy.

Behavior therapy is specific and concrete, which helps clients move from unclear goals toward plans and action. Behavior therapy emphasizes doing rather than insight gathering, so clients and therapists collaborate on a plan to enhance change. While behavior therapists instruct clients on how to change behavior, clients choose what behaviors they want to change, which follows the ethical principle of autonomy. A wide variety of behavioral strategies are also available, which helps therapists choose the strategies most beneficial for their clients.

Today, therapists practicing behavior therapy recognize that problems must be viewed in context. Therapists explore the historical roots and antecedents of people's concerns, are sensitive to individual differences, develop positive and collaborative therapeutic alliances, and seek to know and understand their clients as individuals. Therapists help to empower clients so that they not only can deal with immediate presenting concerns but also can develop skills and strategies to use in the future for healthier and more rewarding lives.

The positive outcomes of behavior therapy tend to be enduring. Rather than leading to symptom substitution, these approaches often lead to a generalization of positive change in which people spontaneously apply the skills they have learned to many areas of concern.

SKILL DEVELOPMENT: PROGRESSIVE MUSCLE RELAXATION

As previously discussed, progressive muscle relaxation is a technique that can be used with almost all clients. What follows is a relaxation script for teaching children how to use progressive muscle relaxation as a way to relax and manage anxiety.

"Today we are going to do an exercise to help you see how good it feels to be relaxed, and to teach you how you can help your body become more relaxed. We are going to focus on different parts of the body, and when I tell you, you are going to tense that body part as much as you can. If you feel like you're ready and comfortable, please close your eyes and listen to the sound of my voice. We will start at the top, so let's start with your face. Pretend you just ate something really sour—like a piece of lemon. Scrunch your eyes and lips as much as you can because that lemon was SOUR! Now relax your lips and eyes. Relax your lips so much that your mouth may even open a bit.

Now scrunch your nose and your forehead. See how tense you can make them. Picture your eyebrows getting so high that they almost touch your hair. Now relax the muscles in your forehead, letting your muscles slide back into place. Doesn't it feel good to relax your face?

Next we will move to relaxing the lower part of your face. Pretend you have a big jawbreaker candy in your mouth and the jawbreaker has a piece of bubble gum in its center. You really want to get to that bubble gum, but you are going to have to bite down hard to break it open. Now gently bite down and try to crack the jawbreaker open. It is really tough! Take a break and let your muscles relax. Give me one more good bite and the jawbreaker will break. Ready? Go! Fantastic! You did it! Now relax your neck and jaw muscles, letting your chin roll down to your chest. Maybe even let your mouth hang open a little bit. It sure feels good to relax after biting down so hard, doesn't it?

Next, bring your attention to your neck and shoulders. You already used your neck muscles a little bit to break the jawbreaker, and we are going to use them again. Tense your back and shoulders up so much that your shoulders are close to your ears. Maybe try to make your shoulders like earrings. Squeeze your muscles and make them as tight as you can. See if you can get your shoulders just a little bit higher. Tuck your chin to your chest and keep pushing your shoulders higher. Now let go. Pay attention to how good it feels to let your muscles relax and go back to their natural places. Doesn't it feel much better to relax?

Let's move to your belly. Pretend you are trying to suck your belly button in so hard that it is going to touch your back. Good. Now hold it in even tighter, like you are going to squeeze sideways through a tiny door. Make yourself as tiny as you can be. Now let your muscles relax, and take a deep breath to fill up your tummy. That feels good, doesn't it?

Bring your attention to your legs and feet. Stand up, and pretend you are on a sandy beach and you are pushing your feet into wet sand. Spread your toes down into the sand as the waves from the ocean are rolling by your waist. The waves are big and you need to really make your legs strong and spread your toes into the sand so you don't get swept onto shore. You have to stand really strong. Flex your leg muscles as strongly as you can, a really big wave is coming! You don't want to get washed ashore! Good job. Now relax your muscles again.

Think of how good it feels to relax your muscles after they have been tightened up. It feels much better to relax than to be tense, doesn't it? You can practice this exercise anytime to help you relax. Maybe you would like to practice this at bedtime to help you to relax before sleep. You can do these exercises anywhere, anytime you feel stressed or your muscles feel tense. You did a great job today! Keep practicing, and you will be an expert relaxer!"

This script can be modified to fit the client's developmental level. For example, when working with an adolescent or an adult the counselor might be more literal and talk about scrunching the mouth instead of suggesting the client imagine tasting a sour lemon.

CASE APPLICATION

Roberto has recently been isolating after having arguments with Edie. This is disrupting his connections with Ava, Edie, and his friends. His isolating behavior is leading to feelings of depression, as well. Using functional behavior assessment, the therapist works with Roberto to identify causes of isolating, consequences of isolating, and the function the behavior serves.

THERAPIST: Roberto, how have things been going for you lately?

ROBERTO: Well, Edie and I are still arguing pretty frequently. She thinks I don't spend enough time with her or Ava.

THERAPIST:	So it sounds like there have been some misunderstandings lately. Walk me through what normally happens while you and Edie argue.
ROBERTO:	We both tend to hold things in until we explode. She seems to get mad at me all of a sudden and it makes me get defensive.
THERAPIST:	Okay. How do you normally respond to Edie?
ROBERTO:	I get upset that she thinks I don't spend enough time with her or Ava. I normally try to end the argument as soon as possible. I start ignoring her.
THERAPIST:	So what do you normally do after you argue?
ROBERTO:	I isolate myself. I don't want to talk to anyone. Edie, Ava, my friends, no one.
THERAPIST:	You tend to withdraw from people after arguments with Edie. What else is going through your mind before you withdraw?
ROBERTO:	I'm stressed with work. I can't seem to get a break.
THERAPIST:	So work is another stressor that may lead to some isolation. When you isolate, what is that experience like for you?
ROBERTO:	My anxiety decreases. I get time to myself. I don't really have to worry about anything. It's my escape.
THERAPIST:	I'm noticing that after arguments you isolate yourself, which makes you worry less. How else does isolating affect you?
ROBERTO:	Well sometimes I feel sad if I isolate too long. Edie gets even more mad at me because I spend less time with her and Ava. My social life gets worse and my friends stop inviting me to things because I always say no.
THERAPIST:	So on one hand, isolating initially helps you feel better in the moment. On the other hand, it is also causing some problems in your relationship and your social life. It also seems to be contributing to feelings of depression.
ROBERTO:	I'd say so, yeah.
THERAPIST:	Is there anything other than isolating that makes you feel better?
ROBERTO:	I like reading and going for walks. Those things tend to calm me down a bit, too.
THERAPIST:	Okay, great. So it sounds like doing things you enjoy also seems to help. Anything else?
ROBERTO:	I don't know. I typically choose isolating over anything. I'm just not sure how to stop.
THERAPIST:	How often would you say you isolate after arguments?
ROBERTO:	Almost every time. But it never actually makes me feel better. In the moment it helps but it makes things worse overall.
THERAPIST:	I'm sensing a desire to change the isolating behavior. Maybe we can start with implementing some coping skills like the relaxation techniques we've talked about.
ROBERTO:	Yes. That is a good idea.

This case analysis shows that the problem behavior is isolating. The common antecedents (causes) of isolating are arguments with Edie and stress related to work. The function the behavior serves is an immediate reduction of anxiety; however, increased depression and increased fights occur due to isolating, which are the consequences.

REFLECT AND RESPOND

1. Identify a fear or source of apprehension in your life. Develop a plan to use exposure therapy to help yourself reduce this fear. Write down the plan in your journal and then try to implement it.
2. Consider a behavior that you would like to increase, decrease, or change. Develop a written plan to help yourself make that change. The plan should include, but not necessarily be limited to, determining how to establish a baseline, setting specific goals, identifying counseling strategies, establishing rewards or reinforcements, and specifying ways to track progress. Continue your learning by actually implementing the plan you have developed. Write in your journal about the successes and challenges you experience as you try to implement this plan.

Summary

Behavior therapy evolved during the 20th century from the research of B. F. Skinner, Ivan Pavlov, John W. Watson, Joseph Wolpe, Albert Bandura, and others. This counseling approach takes the stance that behavior is learned and consequently can be unlearned. Behavior therapists are concerned about results; so they take the time to establish a baseline, develop interventions that facilitate behavioral change, use reinforcements to solidify gains, carefully plan implementation, and monitor progress.

Behavior therapy uses the key principles of classical conditioning, operant conditioning, and social learning theory. Classical conditioning is a type of learning that involves a stimulus-response pairing process. Behavioral interventions such as systematic desensitization and progressive muscle relaxation developed from classical conditioning. Operant conditioning involves learning in which a behavior is either increased through reinforcement or decreased through punishment. The goal is for desirable behavior to increase and undesirable behavior to decrease or stop entirely. Operant conditioning techniques include token economies and shaping. Social learning theory involves learning through observing and modeling others.

Behavior therapy is present focused, active, and educational. The main goal of behavior therapy is to extinguish maladaptive behaviors and help people learn new adaptive ones. Goals specific to each client are also important to consider. Behavior therapists are directive and serve as consultants, teachers, and problem solvers. Behavior therapists implement a wide variety of techniques such as exposure, **exposure and response prevention**, and habit reversal training.

Behavior therapy is applicable to a wide variety of populations with a wide variety of presenting concerns. People with mood disorders and anxiety disorders may particularly benefit from behavior therapy. People with OCD, conduct disorders, and issues with substance use may also benefit. Certain diverse groups may particularly enjoy behavior therapy due to its focus on the present, its objectivity, and its concentration on behavior rather than emotions. Behavior therapy has many strengths and contributions as well, such as the development of behavioral parent training.

Recommended Readings

Martin, G., & Pear, J. (2007). *Behavior modification: What it is and how to do it* (8th ed.). Upper Saddle River, NJ: Pearson/Prentice Hall.

Spiegler, M. D., & Guevremont, D. C. (2010). *Contemporary behavior therapy* (5th ed.). Belmont, CA: Wadsworth.

Numerous journals focus on CBT and behavior therapy, including *Behavior Therapy, Cognitive and Behavioral Practice, Advances in Behaviour Research and Therapy, Child and Family Behavior Therapy, Cognitive Therapy and Research,* and *Journal of Behavior Therapy and Experimental Psychiatry.*

MyLab Counseling

In the Topic 3 Assignments: Cognitive-Behavioral Therapy, Application Exercise 3.2: Behavioral Techniques and Licensure Quiz 3.2: Behavioral Techniques.

CHAPTER 6

Cognitive Behavioral Therapies

Learning Outcomes

When you have finished this chapter, you should be able to:
- Understand the context and development of Cognitive Behavioral Therapies.
- Communicate the key concepts associated with Cognitive Behavioral Therapies and understand how they relate to therapeutic processes.
- Describe the therapeutic goals of Cognitive Behavioral Therapies.
- Identify the common techniques used in Cognitive Behavioral Therapies.
- Understand how Cognitive Behavioral Therapies relates to counseling diverse populations.
- Identify the limitations and strengths of Cognitive Behavioral Therapies.

DEVELOPMENT AND KEY CONCEPTS OF COGNITIVE BEHAVIORAL THERAPIES

Development of Cognitive Behavioral Therapy

Behavior therapy has evolved and broadened into cognitive behavioral therapy (CBT), the second wave of behavior therapy (Parker, Roy, & Eyers, 2003). CBT developed out of a concern that something was missing in behavior therapy, which therapists believed was a focus on clients' thoughts and their thought change processes. CBT therapists were also dissatisfied with traditional behavior therapy, which de-emphasized the therapeutic alliance, viewed the therapist as the authority, and sometimes seemed dehumanizing. CBT incorporates behavior therapy principles but centers on thought processes and changing thoughts. CBT shares the same principles and methods discussed in the behavior therapy chapter; however, CBT also integrates a focus on cognitions. CBT assumes that changes in thought processes will lead to changes in behavior.

Cognitive behavioral therapies emerged in the 1960s, largely as a result of the work of two very different and distinctive individuals—Albert Ellis and Aaron Beck—who will be the featured theorists in this chapter. However, it is important to note that many important theorists have contributed to the development of CBT. Donald Meichenbaum is just one of many theorists who have contributed to the growth of CBT. Textbox 6.1 provides information about Donald Meichenbaum and several important CBT techniques he developed.

Textbox 6.1 CBT Spotlight: Donald Meichenbaum

DONALD MEICHENBAUM (b. 1940)

Donald Meichenbaum, a founder of CBT, is a distinguished professor emeritus at the University of Waterloo, Ontario, Canada. Meichenbaum was raised in New York City before moving to the Midwest to get his PhD. He then moved to the University of Waterloo, where he worked for more than 30 years. Since his retirement in 1998, he has served as the research director of the Melissa Institute—an institute that focuses on preventing violence and promoting safer communities through education and application of research-based knowledge. Meichenbaum has been named one of the 10 most influential psychotherapists of the century. He has written numerous books and articles, including *Stress Inoculation Training* (1985). His book
Cognitive–Behavior Modification (1977) is considered a classic in the field. He continues to lecture, write, and present on topics from spirituality in psychology to posttraumatic stress disorder (PTSD), the educational potential of children, and inner dialogue. Through his doctoral dissertation research, Meichenbaum (1969) found that people with schizophrenia who were taught healthy self-talk responded better on a variety of other measures and were less distracted. This led him to conduct additional research on the role of cognitive factors in behavior modification (1974, 1977).

Influenced by Vygotsky (1967) and the recognition that behavioral control comes about first through external regulation (by parents or significant others) and later through self-regulation (via internalized self-instruction), Meichenbaum created a **self-instructional training** program for impulsive children (Dobson & Dozois, 2010). His method of self-instruction teaches people to respond with positive self-talk in the face of stressors or negative thinking. Meichenbaum's theory combines cognitive strategies designed to modify maladaptive self-talk with knowledge of the developmental manner in which children learn by modeling behavior.

Meichenbaum also developed one of the earliest, most useful, and most effective CBT techniques: **stress inoculation training** (SIT). People typically experience stress because they perceive that their life circumstances exceed their capacity to cope. Stress inoculation training is an approach to reduce stress. It assumes that if people can successfully cope with relatively mild stressors, they will be able to tolerate and successfully cope with more severe ones. In other words, as its name implies, stress inoculation training seeks to immunize people against the adverse impact of stress by helping them successfully handle increasing levels of stress. Stress inoculation training has three phases (Meichenbaum, 1985). The first phase, conceptualization, involves the development of a collaborative relationship and an educational component of stress. The second phase, skills acquisition and rehearsal phase, teaches clients to cope effectively with mild stressors by gathering information, using coping self-statements, learning relaxation strategies, changing their behaviors, or using other strategies to reduce those fears. In addition, people learn to apply problem solving to their fears. In phase 3, application and follow-through, people implement their plans to solve problems and reduce stress. Stress inoculation uses a **subjective units of distress scale (SUDS)** to help clients rate their stressors in hierarchical order on a scale from 0 to 100.

SIT is a self-management tool that provides a way for people to overcome negative self-talk, encourage themselves with more positive words, and teach themselves how to effectively cope in situations that had previously been difficult for them. In general, the therapist models behavior and the client practices the behavior by repeating it back. SIT can be used with all ages, and for many behaviors (e.g., anger, overeating, substance use) as well as specific disorders (e.g., depression, anxiety, phobia).

Meichenbaum (1993) also developed cognitive behavior modification in an effort to integrate psychodynamic and cognitive approaches with the "technology of behavior therapists" (p. 202). He believed that neither approach alone was sufficient to explain psychopathology and promote behavior change but that the combination could accomplish both goals.

Three assumptions of cognitive behavior modification clarify how Meichenbaum (1993) integrates cognitive and behavior theory:

1. *Constructive narrative.* People actively construct their own reality; "reality is a product of personal meanings" (p. 203).
2. *Information processing.* An activating event taps into people's core cognitions, leading to an unhelpful, inaccurate, and distorted thought. People experience negative emotions and engage in unwise and harmful behaviors because they distort reality as a result of cognitive errors and misperceptions.
3. *Conditioning.* Cognitions are viewed as **covert behaviors** (behaviors that others cannot directly perceive or see) that have been conditioned. Correspondingly, they can undergo deconditioning and modification through both external and internal contingencies (rewards or punishments), thereby strengthening new and healthier cognitions. Modeling, mental rehearsal, and other strategies figure importantly into effecting cognitive change.

Albert Ellis, a native of New York City who received a PhD from Columbia University, trained as a psychoanalyst, and Aaron Beck, a Yale-educated physician trained in psychoanalysis, worked at the University of Pennsylvania. Although they did not know each other at that point, both became disillusioned with psychoanalysis, the leading theoretical orientation at that time. Ellis preferred to be more directive in helping people with their problems, so he developed rational emotive therapy, later changed to rational emotive behavior therapy (REBT). REBT uses persuasion, teaching, and evidence gathering to help people dispute and modify their irrational beliefs and learn to accept themselves as they are.

Meanwhile, in Pennsylvania, Beck was conducting research on the efficacy of psychoanalysis for depression and became disillusioned with the results. Beck had concluded that the most important element in the therapeutic recovery of people was the way they think, the thoughts they tell themselves, and the manner in which they react. He developed a theory of his own that he called cognitive therapy, but it is a CBT approach. Now we will look in more detail at the dimensions that cut across the range of cognitive behavioral therapies, the ideas and concepts that these theorists all value.

Key Concepts of Cognitive Behavioral Therapy

From a CBT approach, the etiology of clients' presenting distress or behavior problems is not attributed to external environmental factors or unique life circumstances but rather to the influence of the clients' internal cognitive processes. CBT holds that dysfunctional thinking (which influences clients' mood and behavior) is common to all psychological disturbances, and when clients learn to evaluate their thinking in a more realistic and adaptive way, they experience improvement in their emotional state and behavior (Beck, 2011). Therefore, the situation does not cause people's distress; rather, their perception or unhelpful thinking about the situation does so. The purpose of CBT is to teach people to identify, evaluate, and modify their own dysfunctional thoughts and beliefs. This approach also emphasizes behavior change and problem solving.

Merging the rigor, objectivity, and systematic approach of behaviorism, CBT approaches concentrate on the importance of changing beliefs, perceptions, and thinking patterns to produce positive affective and behavioral changes. Although the cognitive behavioral theories have theoretical differences, they are all based on the idea that an interactive relationship exists between cognitions, emotions, and behaviors, in which changing any of these aspects will significantly influence the other aspects. It is important to note, however, that most CBT approaches emphasize the role of cognitions, as they are assumed to be the primary vehicle for change, and those most readily controlled by clients.

CBT's broad focus on altering faulty thinking patterns, developing coping skills, and enhancing problem-solving abilities and positive decision-making promote a variety of competencies that correspond to clients' natural developmental growth and learning processes. As such, CBT approaches can serve an important function in helping clients grow in ways that prevent future problems from developing. For example, consider a client who participates in a CBT group to learn skills for being more assertive. These skills will be useful in many situations, such as in family relationships, in friendships, and with a significant other. These skills will also help her in other situations for many years to come and prevent future problems from emerging.

The following are common elements of all CBT approaches (Beck, 1995, 2011; Beck, Davis, & Freeman, 2015):

- Careful assessment is important, and CBT therapists generally appreciate a more medical model approach to helping—one in which a case conceptualization is constructed, the client or the problem is defined and diagnosed, and a treatment plan is developed. CBT therapists are sensitive to the fact that their clients' situations are constantly evolving and thus they must adapt their methods.
- A sound therapeutic alliance is necessary for successful therapy outcomes. Therapists must be empathetic, supportive, and warm.
- Therapists expect clients to be active in therapy and take responsibility for the effort they make. Clients and therapists collaborate on counseling goals and homework assignments.
- CBT is goal-oriented, problem focused, present focused, and short term.
- CBT is psychoeducational. Clients can utilize what they learn in therapy in their everyday lives and are taught how to be their own therapists. It promotes emotional health and prevents relapse by teaching people to identify, evaluate, and modify their own cognitions.
- Counseling sessions are structured and agendas are discussed in the beginning of therapy.
- Clients learn how to identify, evaluate, and modify their dysfunctional thoughts and behaviors to feel and behave in healthier ways.
- CBT uses a broad range of strategies and interventions to help people evaluate and change their cognitions. Inductive reasoning (providing evidence for and against the thought) and Socratic questioning (questions used to elicit and change thoughts) are particularly important strategies.
- Task assignments, client follow-up, and client and therapist feedback are important in ensuring the success of this approach.
- Homework is an essential component of CBT. Clients complete homework assignments outside of session based on their goals. Self-monitoring and implementation of skills learned are common homework assignments.

As the behavioral health care industry has moved toward evidence-based practice, CBT has become even more popular. Its focus on outcomes and its strong evidence base with a variety of presenting issues make it attractive to third-party payers. Moving forward, we will look at rational emotive behavior therapy in more detail.

RATIONAL EMOTIVE BEHAVIOR THERAPY

ALBERT ELLIS (1913–2007)

Albert Ellis, the originator of REBT, was born in 1913 in Pittsburgh, Pennsylvania. He moved to New York as a young child and lived there for most of his life. Ellis' family of origin included an independent mother, a father who cared about the family but was often absent, and a younger brother and sister (Bernard, 2011). Ellis got along well with the others in his family, although in many ways he had a difficult childhood. At an early age, he perceived his family as "pretty crazy" and stated that he basically raised himself from the age of 7 (Ellis, 2009). In addition, Ellis was sickly as a child and was often hospitalized, usually for nephritis. Ellis noticed that he frequently worked himself into a miserable state, and it was then that he decided not to be miserable about his circumstances and maintained strong positive thoughts about his competence and worth (Ellis, 1997, 2009). Thus, at an early age he learned that the way people think can enable them to overcome adversity.

In the 1940s, Ellis received MA and PhD degrees in clinical psychology from Columbia University and began practicing as a marriage, family, and sex therapist. Seeking to help people achieve profound change, he obtained training as a psychoanalyst with an emphasis on the work of Karen Horney (Ellis & Dryden, 2007). However, his dissatisfaction with the inefficiency of psychoanalysis as well as his readings in Greek and Asian philosophy led him to develop a way of helping people that focused on changing their thoughts.

Ellis began practicing what he initially called rational therapy in 1955, founded the still-active Institute for Rational Emotive Therapy (now the Albert Ellis Institute) in 1959 to offer both counseling and training in this approach, and published the first of his many works on REBT in 1962. A prolific writer, Ellis authored more than 800 academic papers and 80 books and monographs. Ellis' final book, titled *Rational Emotive Behavior Therapy*, was published after his death (Ellis & Ellis, 2011). He received many awards over the course of his career, including the Distinguished Professional Psychologist Award in 1974 and the Distinguished Professional Contributions Award in 1985, both from the American Psychological Association.

Ellis was open about his personal life and often used himself as a role model in his work. A classic story he told about himself was that, as a young man, he was apprehensive about asking women on dates. To overcome his fears, he forced himself to approach 100 women and invite them out. Although all refused, this experience of forcing himself to do repeatedly what he feared most enabled him to overcome his anxieties.

Ellis continued to be the primary advocate and spokesperson for this approach until his death in 2007 at the age of 93. In his obituary, the *New York Times* (Kaufman, 2007) referred to Ellis as irreverent and charismatic. Indeed, his creativity, humor, and crackly personality made him a dynamic speaker and trainer.

INTRODUCTION/DEVELOPMENT OF RATIONAL EMOTIVE BEHAVIOR THERAPY

Developed in the 1950s, rational emotive behavior therapy (REBT) has evolved considerably, although its basic premise—that emotions and behavior can best be modified by changing thinking—has not changed. Early influences on REBT include the writings of the philosopher Epictetus, Buddhist and

Taoist philosophy, and writings on happiness, secular humanism, and behaviorism. The Greek Stoic philosopher Epictetus influenced the development of REBT from his writings, stating that "People are disturbed not by events, but by the views which they take of them" (as cited in Ellis, 2001, p. 16). This is in line with Ellis' view that people cause their own disturbances. In addition, Karen Horney's concepts, especially those about the power of "shoulds" in our lives, are evident in REBT.

Ellis changed the name of his theory twice. In 1961, rational therapy became rational *emotive* therapy (RET), reflecting the attention this approach paid to feelings. This modification may, at least in part, have been a response to the popularity of Carl Rogers' ideas, which emphasized the importance of emotions. RET became rational emotive *behavior* therapy in 1993, reflecting its increased emphasis on behavior (Ellis, 1995). The inclusion of *behavior* in the name of the approach highlighted Ellis' evolving belief that the integration of behavioral techniques and the understanding that thoughts and emotions influence behavior, and vice versa, was important. As practiced today, REBT emphasizes thoughts but views emotions, behaviors, and thoughts as intertwined and inseparable; to maximize success, counseling must attend to all three.

Since its initial development, the theories, structure, and strategies of REBT have become less absolute and more compatible with postmodern counseling approaches, including narrative therapy, constructivist therapy, and existential therapy (Ellis & MacLaren, 2005). Over the years, interventions used in REBT have become more varied and eclectic. In addition, REBT now pays greater attention to understanding the background and viewpoints of clients and is more accepting of people's religious and other beliefs, as long as they are not rigid and harmful. Rational emotive behavior therapy was the first well-developed CBT (Ellis, 1957).

KEY CONCEPTS

As with all CBTs, REBT focuses on helping people identify, evaluate, and modify dysfunctional cognitions. Despite its recognition of the impact of biological, social, and other forces on human development, REBT maintains an optimistic view of human nature. It emphasizes will and choice and perceives people as having inborn drives toward actualization, happiness, self-preservation, and growth (Ellis & MacLaren, 2005; Ellis, 2001). REBT perceives people as able to exercise choice, to see that their thoughts are responsible for disturbing them, and to actively and continually work toward positive change and fulfillment (Ellis & MacLaren, 2005). In addition, this theory holds that all individuals are born with the innate capacity to think both rationally and irrationally.

Irrational Beliefs as the Cause of Struggle

According to REBT, the psychological distress and problem behaviors people experience stem from inflexible, extreme, or self-defeating beliefs, misinterpreted events, and poor emotional reactions learned over time. People's emotions are primarily influenced by their beliefs, and thus people are considered the source of their own distress. In particular, REBT most strongly emphasizes the role of blame, as well as absolute should, must, ought, always, never demands or statements that people desire for themselves, from others, or in the world around them. Demands of personal success, love and acceptance from others, and favorable life circumstances or experiences are the three primary irrational beliefs that occur most frequently and, although highly desirable, are not necessary according to Ellis. When people's musts, oughts, and shoulds are not fulfilled as expected, they develop and internalize rigid irrational beliefs.

REBT suggests that, because irrational thinking is so widespread, people must have a strong innate tendency to think dysfunctionally and believe that life should go their way. People tend to react to situations in particular patterns regardless of the environment playing a role in their experience.

However, people do vary in their inclination to think irrationally. REBT recognizes that childhood difficulties and traumas may contribute to the tendency to think and act in unhealthy ways. Emotional disturbance, then, results from a combination of an innate predisposition toward irrational thinking and life experiences.

According to REBT, change only occurs when people recognize and accept that they are largely responsible for creating their own emotional problems because of their thought processes (Ellis, 1988). Regardless of when and how the problems began, REBT maintains that emotional and behavioral problems stem primarily from **irrational beliefs**, which are absurd views or feelings that are not rational or logical. Rational emotive behavior therapists have found that, through hard work and practice, people can change their absolute and irrational beliefs and correspondingly alleviate their emotional difficulties. In particular, through the A-B-C–D-E-F model, clients learn how to identify their irrational beliefs, change their beliefs to more accurate and helpful beliefs, and behave and feel in healthier ways. More will be said about the A-B-C–D-E-F model later in the chapter.

Rational beliefs are logical, pragmatic, and based in reality. They are flexible and not extreme (Dryden, DiGiuseppe, & Neenan, 2010). In addition, a rational belief is a cognition that is effective or helpful, as well as empirically or logically valid (Ellis, 1995). In contrast, irrational beliefs usually are characterized by at least one of the following themes: awfulizing; self-deprecation, including global evaluations of human worth and self-criticism; and frustration intolerance (Ellis, 2001). Irrational beliefs often include words such as *should, ought,* and *must* and may incorporate immediate demands about the self, others, and the world. Several examples of these beliefs follow (Ellis, 1984, p. x; 2003, pp. 236–237):

1. I must act perfectly and be achieving and lovable at all times. If I do not, I am incompetent and worthless. (This belief usually leads to feelings of anxiety, depression, and low self-esteem.)
2. Other people must always treat me kindly and fairly or I can't stand it and they are terrible, evil people who should be punished for mistreating me. (This belief typically leads to rage and vindictiveness.)
3. Life must go the way I want it to go and must never be too difficult or frustrating. Otherwise, life is terrible and I cannot bear it. (This belief often results in inaction, **low frustration tolerance**, self-pity, anger, and depression.)

Irrational beliefs are typically absolutes about oneself, other people, or one's circumstances. Albert Ellis used the phrase **musterbation** to explain the behavior of clients who are inflexible and absolutistic in their thinking, and who set absolute and unrealistic demands on themselves. Irrational beliefs also tend to be evaluative and judgmental, viewing life in extremes. They are illogical, inconsistent with reality, and prevent people from attaining their goals (Dryden et al., 2010).

Common types of irrational beliefs identified by therapists practicing REBT are similar to Beck's cognitive distortions, described later in the chapter (Ellis & Dryden, 2007). Examples of irrational beliefs include thoughts such as these:

VINCE: If I don't have a date for New Year's Eve by tomorrow, I will be the laughingstock of my fraternity.

MARTIN: My supervisor should praise me and is a jerk for not seeing how hard I work.

NATASHA: I ought to spend every evening with my family. I am a terrible mother if I don't do that.

Here are rational versions of the same beliefs:

VINCE: I would like to have a date for New Year's Eve so that I can join my friends in that celebration.

MARTIN: I believe that my supervisor is not really familiar with my work and so is not giving me the praise I would like.

NATASHA: My family and I enjoy spending time together and I believe that is helpful to my children, but I can take some time for myself and still be a good mother.

The preceding irrational beliefs are extreme statements that promote negative emotions and difficulties in relationships. They do not facilitate problem solving or constructive action because they view success or failure in extreme terms, are demanding and inflexible, and blame people rather than assess a situation clearly. The rational beliefs, however, reflect preferences, hopes, and wishes. They do not judge but instead look at possibilities. Problem solving and constructive action are facilitated because, without extremist thinking, many options and solutions are available. Vince can take steps to find a last-minute date but still may be able to celebrate the holiday with his friends even if he doesn't have a date. Martin can plan to acquaint his supervisor with the quality of his work. Natasha can build in more time with her family while not demanding perfection from herself.

Insight matters to REBT therapists only if it has to do with better understanding thought processes and making behavior changes. In other words, insight and awareness of thought processes are important, whereas helping people gain insight into the origins of their problems and emotional disturbances is not an essential part of REBT. Not only is insight viewed as insufficient for change, but it is also seen as potentially harmful, leading to self-blame and immobilization. However, gaining insight into the principles of REBT is important. Insight consists of three levels, which are viewed as necessary for people to make positive changes (Ellis, 1988):

1. The insight to see that we choose to upset ourselves
2. The insight to see that we acquire our irrational beliefs and to see how we continue to maintain them
3. The insight to see that we need to work hard to change.

Ellis (1986) distinguished between inappropriate/self-destructive emotions and appropriate/nondefeating emotions. **Self-destructive emotions** are enduring, immobilizing, and nonproductive; reflect overreactions to stimuli; and lead to negative self-images and actions. There are eight emotional problems: guilt, shame, jealousy, hurt, anxiety, depression, envy, and unhealthy anger (Dryden, 2011). In contrast, **appropriate emotions** are transient, manageable, in proportion to the stimulus, and enhancing of self-acceptance. They include both positive emotions such as joy, satisfaction, and peacefulness and negative emotions such as annoyance, regret, and sadness. Of course, we all have negative reactions when we experience losses and disappointments. However, our thoughts about those disappointments determine whether we develop emotions that are inappropriate and self-destructive or appropriate and nondefeating.

Like emotions, behaviors are a secondary focus of counseling. They provide a measure of progress, are used to modify and reinforce thoughts, and are a prime target of homework assignments. Although REBT views behaviors, emotions, and thoughts as having a reciprocal relationship, thoughts are the primary route to change. Changing thoughts and the accompanying self-statements leads to changes in both actions and emotions.

A-B-C–D-E-F Model

REBT uses a structured format for identifying, assessing, disputing, and modifying beliefs—a plan represented by the letters A-B-C–D-E-F (Ellis & Ellis, 2011). Originally conceived as the **A-B-C Model**, over the years, this model has evolved to include new components. The A-B-C model originally included activating events, consequences, and beliefs. Therapists used these three components for psychoeducational purposes and to conceptualize and identify clients' problems. The D (disputing) and E (new rational effects or beliefs) components were then added for use as therapeutic interventions to assist clients with changing their thoughts. Finally, F (feeling and behaving in new ways) was added to illustrate that once clients' change their beliefs, they are more likely to feel and behave in healthier and happier ways. F demonstrates the important role of emotions in people's lives. To illustrate the **A-B-C–D-E-F model**, we consider Martin's beliefs about his supervisor (presented earlier in this chapter).

A, the first step, is identification and description of the *activating event*. This is the external and objective source of discomfort, the experience that initiates the process of irrational thinking and precipitates the negative thoughts, emotions, and behaviors.

> *Martin A:* "My supervisor gave me an average rating on my evaluation."

B is the *belief* about the activating event, evaluating that stimulus as positive, negative, or neutral. The belief may be rational or irrational. REBT holds that people may not have a choice about experiences or activating events but do have a choice about their beliefs related to those activating events.

> *Martin B:* "My supervisor should praise me more and is a jerk for not seeing how hard I work. It is awful that I work so hard and am not valued as I ought to be."

C stands for the *consequences* of the belief. Of course, the activating event itself can produce negative consequences; but according to REBT, beliefs mediate between events and consequences, with beliefs being a major determinant of most consequences. By assessing the nature and consequences of a belief, therapists can determine whether the belief is irrational and harmful to the client or rational and either neutral or helpful. If the belief is irrational, consequences are likely to be unhealthy and harmful and might include inappropriate and self-destructive emotions (e.g., rage, anxiety, depression) and inappropriate and self-destructive behaviors (e.g., excessive use of alcohol, blaming self and others, withdrawal). Rational beliefs usually lead to healthier and more constructive consequences such as appropriate emotions (e.g., disappointment, annoyance) and appropriate behaviors (e.g., taking effective steps to change the situation or distracting oneself with exercise or a creative pursuit).

Initial consequences of an irrational belief can lead to subsequent reinforcing consequences that create more problems for a person. For example, if Martin expressed his anger toward his supervisor in loud and attacking ways and the supervisor reacted with further disapproval, Martin's irrational beliefs and negative emotions would likely be reinforced; he would continue to have unproductive thoughts toward his supervisor, and may become even more entrenched in his irrational beliefs.

> *Martin C:* Martin experienced anger, shame, and anxiety about the possibility of losing his job. His behavior included berating his supervisor.

D, dispute (also referred to as debate), is the next step in the process. Exploration of beliefs and their consequences determines whether they are rational or irrational. In general, therapists begin by focusing on irrational beliefs about immediate situations and then move to more generalized and abstract irrational beliefs.

Later in the chapter, we will talk more about the many strategies available to help people contest their irrational beliefs. Some are similar to strategies discussed in this section. However, in REBT, therapists rely more on persuasion, teaching, and techniques that elicit strong emotions than do other cognitive therapists, who rely more on logic.

> *Martin D:* Strategies to dispute irrational beliefs include cognitive, behavioral, and emotional approaches to change. For Martin, all three are relevant. Cognitive approaches might

involve examining the logic of his belief, including the adequacy of the supervisor's information on Martin's performance and whether receiving an average evaluation was truly awful or simply undesirable. Ellis would probably have used emotional methods, pointing out Martin's awfulizing, his tendency to **catastrophize** (exaggerating the consequences of an event), and his perfectionistic need to have his life be exactly as he wishes. Martin may be encouraged to feel appropriate and nondestructive emotions such as annoyance and disappointment, which contribute to rational thinking, rather than shame and anger, which are self-destructive and inappropriate emotions. Martin might also benefit from behavioral strategies, such as meeting with his supervisor, providing her additional information about his work, and planning an outing or creative project to help him focus on rewarding aspects of his life.

E stands for *new rational effects or beliefs,* describing the desired outcome of the disputation. The outcome of REBT is likely to include both effective rational beliefs and an effective new philosophy. Out of this philosophy flow new feelings and behaviors and greater, long-lasting happiness (Bernard et al., 2010).

Martin E: After disputing his beliefs, Martin developed more rational beliefs such as: "Although I am disappointed that my evaluation was average, it is not the end of the world. I will take steps to familiarize my supervisor with my work and obtain a more positive evaluation next time."

F, the last step, stands for *feeling and behaving in new ways*. When clients think more effectively, their thinking influences the emotions and behaviors (consequences) they experience in response to activating events. Clients are more likely to experience more appropriate and healthy feelings.

Martin F: After Martin has more rational beliefs, he is more likely to feel less angry and shameful. He is also less likely to create confrontation with his supervisor. Instead, Martin may feel slight annoyance or feel more positive about the situation and may even re-evaluate his work experiences to take positive steps forward.

THE THERAPEUTIC PROCESS

Therapists who practice REBT foster the therapeutic alliance and use a wide range of strategies, particularly the **A-B-C–D-E-F model**, to help clients modify their irrational beliefs. Examples of irrational beliefs are found later in the chapter. Sessions in REBT tend to follow a relatively predictable pattern. A typical session includes the following 10 steps (Walen, DiGiuseppe, & Dryden, 1992, p. 65):

1. Review old business from the previous session.
2. Check up on mood, behavior, thoughts, symptoms, and medication.
3. Elicit new business, especially any major life changes.
4. Follow up on homework.
5. Establish the agenda for the sessions.
6. Do the work according to the A-B-C–D-E-F format.
7. Summarize the work that has been done.
8. Assign new homework.
9. Obtain feedback on the session.
10. Close the session.

Therapists typically begin by explaining the theory of REBT and familiarizing clients with its procedures and with what is expected from them as clients. Although therapists who practice REBT are less likely to use a formal assessment process and incorporate inventories than are some other CBT therapists, they, too, engage in assessment during the first few sessions of counseling, exploring clients' history and background, thoughts, emotions, behaviors, and symptoms. Once that has been accomplished, the focus shifts to helping clients recognize that they largely create their own disturbance; understand that psychological difficulties typically stem from irrational beliefs; and see that they can change their beliefs and alleviate their difficulties.

Homework assignments form an important part of the counseling process and help to reinforce lessons learned. Even if the client has not completed the previous week's homework, the lesson should be reviewed (Neenan & Dryden, 2011).

By the end of counseling, clients should have learned to evaluate and dispute their own beliefs using a variety of strategies, and be prepared to continue that process throughout their lives. Follow-up sessions facilitate people's efforts to continue REBT on their own. Relapse prevention is especially important for people who have made significant philosophical changes and helps with maintaining those changes.

Although REBT is often a relatively brief process, therapists generally do not predetermine the number of sessions. Rather, counseling lasts as long as necessary to help people accomplish their goals. Efficiency rather than brevity is valued.

Therapeutic Goals

REBT is a goal-oriented approach that focuses on outcomes such as changes in beliefs and reduction in symptoms. Although REBT enables people to become more aware of their thoughts, emotions, and behaviors, this approach is primarily concerned with helping people to learn cognitive skills that promote rational thinking and lead to greater happiness and self-acceptance (Ellis & Ellis, 2011). REBT also aims to help clients lessen emotional disturbance and decrease self-defeating behaviors. Improving the **rationality** of clients is also important; therefore, therapists teach clients skills on how to think, feel, and behave in a more healthy and effective way to achieve their goals.

According to REBT, through counseling, therapists facilitate clients' psychological health, which involves helping them to (Ellis & Dryden, 2007, pp. 18–19):

- Increase their awareness, acceptance, and appreciation of self and others
- Increase their social interest; recognizing that contributing to the world enhances their own happiness
- Increase their self-direction and personally meaningful goals
- Increase their involvement in long-range, absorbing creative pursuits; commitment to something outside the self
- Become present, yet also able to defer immediate gratification and seek pleasure in the future
- Accept uncertainty and ambiguity
- Be flexible and able to adapt to change
- Tolerate frustration and not be devastated by disappointments
- Think in a clear, logical, scientific, and rational way
- Take sensible risks, experiment, and be reasonably adventurous
- Recognize that they cannot always be totally happy and that life will not always go exactly as hoped
- Accept responsibility for their own emotional difficulties.

REBT therapists help clients deal more effectively with negative feelings, such as sadness, frustration, anxiety, and regret. Not only is changing irrational thoughts to rational thoughts important, but also a philosophical change of beliefs that will benefit clients in the long run is particularly vital. REBT also aims to provide people the skills they need to become their own therapists—to enable them to use the methods of REBT throughout their lives to identify and change their self-destructive thoughts.

Self-acceptance is also an important goal in REBT. This approach suggests that emotional difficulties are often found in people with conditional self-acceptance; they value themselves because of their accomplishments rather than because of their basic worth as a person. When they experience failures or disappointments, they tend to rate themselves harshly and their self-esteem decreases as a result (Bernard, Froh, DiGiuseppe, Joyce, & Dryden, 2010). Ellis believed that people should have a realistic sense of their strengths and weaknesses and take pride in their achievements. At the same time, they will feel happier and more stable if they accept, value, and believe in themselves even when they are disappointed in their behaviors or experiences. REBT teaches people to assess their thoughts and behaviors, not themselves.

Therapist's Function and Role

Therapists practicing REBT assume many roles. They are teachers, coaches, role models, confidence builders, cheerleaders, and motivators. They strive to communicate acceptance and caring to their clients, helping them to overcome problems and lead happier lives.

REBT therapists are responsible for explaining REBT theory to clients, and then teaching them how to apply related strategies in their daily lives to experience greater self-acceptance, acceptance of others, and, ultimately, an increased degree of happiness. That is, therapists teach clients the manner in which maladaptive beliefs, appraisals, and attitudes can influence emotions and behaviors, and assist them with identifying examples related to their presenting distresses. Therapists assist clients with identifying and minimizing irrational beliefs by disputing and replacing them with more logical, accurate, and affirming thoughts and attitudes. Therapists also **challenge absolutes** by paying particular attention to statements that are usually exaggerations (i.e., never, no one, always) so that clients become more aware of their thinking and replace their thoughts.

In addition, REBT therapists assign homework exercises to help their clients build insight into their unhelpful thought patterns and examine how their new thought patterns are affecting their emotions, behaviors, and associated consequences. Homework assignments can be cognitive, behavioral, or emotive in nature.

Overall, therapists teach clients about rational and irrational thinking; help them identify, dispute, and modify their irrational beliefs; and facilitate their efforts to develop a more rational philosophy of life. Although problem solving is part of counseling, REBT therapists go beyond this and help people to establish more balanced, logical, and rewarding lives.

REBT therapists encourage clients to stay focused on present rather than past events. Although therapists recognize the significance of the past, their role is to discourage lengthy, in-depth exploration of people's backgrounds and the origins of their thoughts. Instead, they believe that a present-oriented focus is more meaningful to people, more likely to enhance rapport, and in keeping with the idea that people's current thoughts and behaviors maintain their self-defeating thoughts, despite the origins of those thoughts.

Believing that irrational thoughts underlie all psychological problems, therapists use forceful and creative strategies to help people identify and dispute their irrational beliefs; REBT asserts that positive results are obtained when people gain awareness of their irrational beliefs and take effective action to change them (Dryden & Branch, 2008).

Relationship Between Therapist and Client

Clients and therapists have a collaborative relationship in REBT. Clients assume some responsibility for planning and implementing their counseling experience, just as they are encouraged to take considerable responsibility for their difficulties. Rapport and empathy are essential to building a therapeutic alliance. These traits also align with an active and directive counseling approach like REBT. Creating a positive therapeutic alliance and adapting REBT to the needs of individual clients are essential to effective counseling. Using clients' words and incorporating language that is meaningful to clients can help improve rapport (Dryden, 2011).

Rational emotive behavior therapists are highly involved in the counseling process, often using their influence on clients to effect change. Ellis had a directive, sometimes abrupt, therapeutic style. He was genuine and authentic, and recognized that flexibility is important (Dryden & Branch, 2008). Most therapists practicing REBT do not seem to emulate Ellis; they have their own flavor of counseling. REBT therapists do not hesitate to use persuasion, praise, exaggeration, instruction, humorous songs, and anecdotes from their own lives to help people think more rationally and make positive changes. Therapists should not be blank screens; they should be highly active, genuine, and directive, revealing their own thoughts and experiences, but always maintaining a professional relationship with clients (Ellis, 1992). Of course, Ellis recognized that the degree to which therapists are active and directive is a personal choice (Dryden & Ellis, 2001).

It is suggested that therapists practicing REBT be (Ellis & Dryden, 2007, p. 29):

- Structured but flexible
- Intellectually, cognitively, and philosophically inclined
- Active and directive in their style
- Comfortable using behavioral instruction and teaching
- Untroubled by fear of failure and willing to take thoughtful risks
- Emotionally healthy, accepting of themselves and others as fallible
- Practical and scientific rather than mystical and magical
- Comfortable with a variety of interventions.

THERAPEUTIC TECHNIQUES AND PROCEDURES

Ellis believed that experiential techniques that are active, directive, and vigorous lead to more rapid change. Strategies commonly used by therapists practicing REBT are cognitive, behavioral, or emotive (Ellis, 1996; Ellis & Dryden, 2007). Following are some strategies for modifying thoughts and solidifying behavioral change.

A-B-C–D-E-F Technique

As previously discussed, REBT uses a structured format for identifying, assessing, disputing, and modifying beliefs—a plan represented by the letters A-B-C–D-E-F (Ellis & Ellis, 2011). Figure 6.1 provides an overview of the A-B-C–D-E-F model. Although the A-B-C–D-E-F process may seem simple and straightforward, changing irrational beliefs to rational ones is a challenging and complex process. It requires effort and practice on the part of clients, as well as well-chosen and skillfully used interventions on the part of therapists. The process can be complicated by the tendency of many people to have second-order disturbances: to feel bad about feeling bad. This creates several layers of irrational beliefs that need attention. In addition, people sometimes prefer their familiar

A: Activating event	An event, environment, person, interaction, or any source that causes client stress.
B: Beliefs	The client's beliefs about the activating event or the thoughts that come to mind in response to the event.
C: Consequences	The consequences of beliefs, or the emotional or behavioral responses that the client experiences due to beliefs about the activating event.
D: Disputing irrational beliefs	The intervention component of the A-B-C model; therapists challenge and debate the client's unrealistic beliefs in an effort to assist the client with thinking in more accurate, rational, and positive ways.
E: Effective new thinking	Disputing causes the client to develop the ability to replace irrational beliefs with more realistic and self-affirming thoughts. Over time, the client learns to monitor, dispute, and replace faulty thinking independently.
F: Feeling and behaving in new ways	The client's application of effective new thinking influences the emotions and behaviors (consequences) the client experiences in response to activating events.

FIGURE 6.1 Rational Emotive Behavior Therapy's A-B-C–D-E-F Model.

discomfort to risking the unknown discomfort of change (Ellis & Dryden, 2007). They may also value the sympathy, attention, and other secondary gains they receive as a result of their problems.

Approaches to Disputing Irrational Beliefs

Even if people can intellectually grasp the *A-B-C–D-E-F* model and the message that our beliefs, rather than activating events, are the primary source of our disturbance, people often have difficulty modifying their thoughts. It takes effort to address these entrenched beliefs. Using a combination of cognitive, emotive, and behavioral interventions in a forceful and persistent way, REBT therapists actively work with clients to identify their irrational beliefs, dispute them, and replace absolutist and irrational beliefs with flexible preferences.

The four *strategies of disputation* include (Beal, Kopec, & DiGiuseppe, 1996):

1. *Logical disputes* identify magical thinking and leaps in logic. Example: "Just because your sister seemed quiet and distracted when she visited you on her birthday, it doesn't logically follow that she is rejecting a close relationship with you."
2. *Empirical disputes* focus on an accumulation of evidence. Example: "You told me that after her visit, your sister called to tell you what a good time she had and suggested you visit her soon. You also told me that your sister is a quiet person. When we examine this evidence, there is little reason to believe that your sister is withdrawing from you. In fact, the evidence suggests just the opposite."
3. *Functional disputing strategies* focus on the practical consequences of people's beliefs, looking at whether their beliefs get them what they want. Example: "Believing that your sister is withdrawing leads you to withdraw from her and brings up memories of past wrongs you believe she has done to you. This belief isn't helping you rebuild your relationship with your sister, as you want to do."
4. *Rational alternative beliefs* offer a viable alternative belief. Example: "I know your sister is going through a difficult divorce. I wonder if another possible explanation for her quietness could be that she felt sad because she wasn't with her husband on her birthday."

The *four disputing styles* include (Beal et al., 1996):

1. A *didactic style* is explanatory, educational, and efficient but involves giving information rather than using dialogue. Example: "Marnie, I think you may be jumping to unwarranted conclusions about the significance of your sister's behavior. Keep in mind that she is still recovering from her divorce and that may be affecting her mood."

2. A *Socratic style* involves using questions to promote client reasoning. The dialogue between individuals (i.e., therapist and client) that is based on asking and answering questions to stimulate and challenge ideas and thoughts is known as **Socratic questioning**. This is the most common REBT technique and is helpful for rapport building and allowing clients to come to their own conclusions. Example: "What do you make of your sister's call and invitation to visit? Do those behaviors suggest she is withdrawing from your relationship?"
3. A *metaphorical style* uses analogies, especially from the client's own experience, to dispute beliefs. Example: "Your reaction to your sister's visit reminds me of the time you believed your supervisor was dissatisfied with your work because she did not offer you a ride to a conference. Then later you learned that she had to leave the meeting early because of a medical appointment and so could not give you a ride. I think that was the same month you received a top evaluation from your supervisor."
4. A *humorous style* disputes the belief in a lighthearted way. Therapists should be sure never to make fun of people, only of their thoughts and behaviors. Example: "So let's see. . . . It sounds like you are equating the number of words a person speaks to you with how much they like you. How about for the next day you count how many words each person you encounter says to you. Then we can determine which one likes you best."

The therapist can combine the strategies of disputation and disputing styles to form different ways to approach the process of disputing beliefs. This great variety of strategies allows the therapist to adapt approaches according to the needs of a particular client as well as to the therapist's own personality. Following is a discussion of how the therapist can use cognitive and Socratic questioning strategies, behavioral strategies, and emotive strategies to dispute irrational beliefs.

COGNITIVE AND SOCRATIC QUESTIONING STRATEGIES

- **Cost-benefit analysis** may help with making decisions. By gaining awareness about the advantages and disadvantages of a decision or a behavior, clients will have a better understanding of which direction to take. In addition, clients can identify the advantages and disadvantages of particular thoughts, actions, and feelings.
- Journaling can be helpful for identifying, expressing, and exploring thoughts, feelings, and behaviors. In addition, clients have the opportunity to use a rating scale for experiences on a continuum to counteract awfulizing. Clients can also rate the degree of conviction in beliefs and then re-rate after engaging in thought changing strategies. Writing can help in planning for the future. For example, therapists can use **decatastrophizing** by asking clients "what if" scenarios. Clients can then list ways to cope with the worst that might happen. In addition, to solidify rational thought and rational coping statements, clients can formulate, write down, and repeat their rational coping statements.

BEHAVIORAL STRATEGIES

- **Shame-attacking exercises** are potentially embarrassing experiences such as singing loudly on a bus to protect oneself against feelings of shame. Another example may be initiating conversation with strangers. These exercises can help clients decrease **ego anxiety**, which is when their sense of self-worth is threatened and they feel they must perform well. These exercises assist clients in confronting their fears of what people may think of them and in coping better with disapproval from others. The exercises are continued until clients no longer feel shame or fear.
- **Role playing** can also promote change. For example, clients can use two chairs to represent a rational and an irrational belief; clients enact a dialogue between the two beliefs, moving

from one chair to another. Reversing roles can be used when the therapist takes on the clients' irrational beliefs and the clients talk the therapist out of those beliefs. Clients can also act as if they were someone else, stepping out of character.

EMOTIVE STRATEGIES

- **Rational emotive imagery (REI)** is a technique used to help clients change their self-defeating emotions into more adaptive emotions. REI can reinforce positive change after people have learned to identify irrational beliefs. First, the therapist asks clients to imagine the situation and experience the negative emotions that come with it. Then, the clients continue to imagine the situation but take on more appropriate emotions. In this way, clients learn the difference between inappropriate and appropriate emotions, which can help reduce the severity of negative emotions.
- **Forceful self-statements and forceful self-dialogue** are typically used to combat musturbating beliefs in a strong and forceful manner. Self-statements involve a single thought being replaced, and self-dialogue involves a conversation with oneself. The vigorous and powerful disputing of thoughts can lead to greater success in replacing thoughts and a strong change in emotion.

Strategies such as these may be incorporated into homework or used within sessions. As in cognitive therapy, task assignments are viewed as an essential part of counseling and are planned collaboratively. This promotes client responsibility, builds optimism, and facilitates progress. Table 6.1 provides an overview of REBT cognitive, behavioral, and emotive strategies that can be used with clients.

TABLE 6.1 Cognitive, Behavioral, and Emotive-Based REBT Therapy Techniques

Cognitive
- Clients can learn to detect, evaluate, dispute, and modify irrational cognitions.
- Clients can use writing to express and explore thoughts and feelings.
- Clients can learn the difference between rational and irrational beliefs.
- Clients can learn to confront irrational beliefs.
- Clients can learn to identify disadvantages of particular thoughts, actions, and feelings.
- Clients can learn to reduce thinking to the point of absurdity, to highlight irrational thoughts.
- Clients can learn to identify and change self-talk.
- Clients can learn to reframe a situation by changing labels and language.
- Clients can list ways to cope with the worst that might happen.
- Clients can rate experiences on a continuum to counteract awfulizing.
- Clients can learn to distract themselves as appropriate.
- Clients can rate their degree of conviction in beliefs and then re-rate after they have applied thought change strategies.
- Clients can learn to formulate, write down, and repeat rational coping statements.
- Clients can learn how to promote a focus on happiness.
- Clients can exercise and practice frustration tolerance.

Behavioral
- Clients can learn relaxation strategies that help them manage upsetting thoughts.
- Clients can learn shame-attacking exercises.

TABLE 6.1 *(Continued)*

- Clients can create challenging situations in their heads and then identify how they can cope with them.
- Clients can engage in role-playing exercises.
- In reversing roles, therapist takes on client's irrational beliefs, and client talks therapist out of those beliefs.
- Using two chairs to represent a rational and an irrational belief, clients enact a dialogue between the two beliefs, moving from one chair to another.
- Clients can read self-help books and listen to their own or others' recordings (e.g., podcasts) intended to effect change.
- Clients can get training in skills such as assertiveness and effective communication.
- Clients can engage in planning pleasurable activities and involvement in an absorbing interest or a long-range pursuit.
- Clients can learn to use visualization and imagery techniques to help them manage their thoughts, behaviors, and emotions.

Emotive

- Clients can imagine the worst that might happen if a thought came true.
- Therapists can provide emotionally powerful stories, metaphors, and parables to solidify ways clients can apply REBT principles.
- Clients can use emotionally charged language and then challenge it.
- Clients can elicit upsetting emotions via imagery and then practice changing them.
- Clients can learn to use humor as a coping skill.
- Therapists can encourage willpower and determination to change.
- Therapists can promote unconditional therapist acceptance and self-acceptance.

COGNITIVE THERAPY

AARON BECK (b. 1921)

Aaron T. Beck, known for the development of cognitive therapy, was born in New England in 1921. He was the fifth and youngest child of Harry Beck and Elizabeth Temkin Beck, Russian Jewish immigrants to the United States (Weishaar, 1993). Two of the five children born to this family died in infancy, apparently contributing to emotional problems in Beck's mother. He perceived her as depressed, unpredictable, and overprotective—very different from his calm father.

Leif Skoogfors/Corbis Historical/Getty Images

Beck himself had many difficulties during childhood. He was often ill, missing many days of school. As a result, he had to repeat a grade, leading him to develop negative views of his intellectual abilities. In addition, his illnesses left him with many apprehensions, including a blood/injury phobia, a fear of public speaking, and a fear of suffocation. Beck successfully used reasoning to alleviate his anxieties as he studied surgery as part of his medical training and gave many presentations throughout his life. A connection seems probable between his early experiences with anxiety and depression and his subsequent work, which focused on treating those symptoms.

Beck graduated from Brown University and Yale Medical School, where he studied psychiatry. Although he was trained in psychoanalysis, he had little faith in that approach, even early in his career. At the University of Pennsylvania Medical School, Beck, an assistant professor of psychiatry, engaged in research designed to prove psychoanalytic principles. Instead, his work led him to develop cognitive therapy, which has since been the focus of his teaching, research, writing, and clinical work. He has spent most of his professional career at the University of Pennsylvania, where he established the Beck Institute for Cognitive Therapy and Research.

Beck has acknowledged a strong debt to Albert Ellis' work (Weishaar, 1993). At the same time, Beck's personal style, as well as the development of his theory, differs from Ellis'. Beck enhanced the importance of his system of cognitive therapy through research, clinical application, and writing. In demonstrations and videotapes, he appears reserved and thoughtful, a researcher at least as much as a therapist.

Beck created a methodology that is easily replicated and lends itself to clinical trials. He developed a model of therapy that works for depression and anxiety and is also testable. Beck published his first outcome study in 1977. Since that time, he has published more than 500 articles, authored or coauthored 25 books, and lectured throughout the world. His books, articles, and inventories, including recent titles such as *Cognitive Therapy of Anxiety Disorders* (Clark & Beck, 2011), *Schizophrenia: Cognitive Theory, Research and Therapy* (Beck, Rector, Stolar, & Grant, 2008), and "The Empirical Status of Cognitive–Behavioral Therapy: A Review of Meta-Analyses" (Butler, Chapman, Forman, & Beck, 2006), continue to expand the application of cognitive therapy and validate its effectiveness.

INTRODUCTION/DEVELOPMENT OF COGNITIVE THERAPY

Beck's cognitive therapy, a type of CBT, and Ellis' rational emotive behavior therapy evolved around the same time. Cognitive therapy had its beginnings in the 1960s and has grown in importance in the past 60 years to become one of the leading approaches to counseling and psychotherapy used today. Aaron Beck's carefully designed research and professional writing led to the current widespread use of cognitive therapy. Cognitive therapy was initially created by Aaron Beck to provide a structured treatment of depression.

Both Beck's and Ellis' theories have in common a belief that cognitions are at the root of clients' suffering and thus the therapist's job is to help clients modify their ways of thinking. The two theories have several important differences as well. Beck was critical of Ellis' use of the term irrational, suggesting that unhelpful thoughts are not irrational but are inaccurate and too broad; thus, he preferred to use the term maladaptive to describe unhelpful thoughts (Beck, 1976).

According to Judith Beck (2011), like Ellis, the roots of her father's cognitive therapy lie in the ideas of the Stoic philosophers of ancient Greece and Rome, and their thinking that people are disturbed not by things but by the view they take of them is particularly relevant. George Kelly's (1955) personal constructs psychology is a modern precursor of cognitive therapy. Kelly was one of the first theorists to recognize the role of beliefs in controlling and changing thoughts, emotions, and actions. He suggested that people each have a set of personal constructs that enables them to make sense of and categorize people and experiences. These constructs operate like scientific hypotheses, paving the way for people to make predictions about reality. When their predictions are not borne out or when they recognize that their personal constructs are harmful, they may seek alternative constructs (Hergenhahn & Olson, 2007).

Working at the University of Pennsylvania in the 1960s, Beck and his colleagues initially sought to develop a structured, short-term, present-oriented, problem-solving approach to the treatment of depression (Beck, 1995). The book *Cognitive Therapy of Depression* (Beck, Rush, Shaw, & Emery, 1979) described the results of this work, which had a powerful impact on the field of psychotherapy. It offered a clear and structured approach to the treatment of depression, the symptom therapists most often see in both inpatient and outpatient mental health settings. Beck and his colleagues provided evidence that cognitive therapy was more effective in treating depression than the antidepressant medications of that time.

Many others deserve mention for their contributions to cognitive therapy. Aaron Beck's daughter, Judith S. Beck, has been collaborating with him for many years. Now director of the Beck Institute for Cognitive Therapy and Research and professor at the University of Pennsylvania, she continues the development of cognitive therapy, most recently with the publication of the second edition of her book *Cognitive Behavior Therapy: The Basics and Beyond* (2011). In addition, other therapists such as Donald Meichenbaum (1994), who was among the first to combine cognitive therapy with behavioral interventions, Beck's colleagues (Beck, Davis, & Freeman, 2015; Scott & Freeman, 2010), and others have expanded the model of cognitive therapy over the decades. Cognitive therapy is a well-organized, powerful, usually short-term approach that has proven its effectiveness.

KEY CONCEPTS

The Cognitive Model

Cognitive therapists believe that many factors contribute to the development of dysfunctional cognitions and psychological disorders, including people's biology and genetic predispositions, life experiences, and their accumulation of knowledge and learning. However, regardless of the cause of the psychological disorder, cognitive distortions play a huge role. Beck's cognitive therapy is based on the **cognitive model**, which holds that the way that individuals perceive a situation is more closely connected to their reaction than the situation itself. Distorted cognitions begin to take shape in childhood and are reflected in people's fundamental beliefs, which makes people more susceptible to problems. In considering a **stress-vulnerability model**, as more stress occurs, the more people's automatic thoughts are at the mercy of underlying dysfunctional beliefs and schemas. Because the processing of thoughts is already biased, distorted cognitions result (Scott & Freeman, 2010).

According to cognitive therapy, psychologically healthy people are aware of their cognitions. They can systematically test their own hypotheses, and if they find they have dysfunctional and unwarranted assumptions, they can replace them with healthier, more accurate, and more helpful beliefs that lead to more positive emotions and behaviors.

Cognitive Restructuring

Cognitions can be categorized according to four levels: automatic thoughts, intermediate beliefs, core beliefs, and schemas (Beck, Davis, & Freeman, 2015). In cognitive therapy, therapy typically begins with a focus on automatic thoughts and then proceeds to identification, evaluation, and modification of intermediate and core beliefs and finally to revision of schemas, a process called **cognitive restructuring**.

Automatic thoughts are the stream of cognitions that constantly flow through our minds. As we go through our day, situation-specific thoughts spontaneously arise in reaction to our experiences: "I don't think I'll ever be able to get all that work done," "I think I'll eat a healthy lunch today," "I don't think I should call my father yet," "I'm going to help Bill with his homework tonight," "That man makes me think of my brother," and on and on. Automatic thoughts are internal conversations or self-talk and are completely normal to experience. However, they are often biased, faulty, or extreme. When we pay attention to our thoughts, they become more accessible and we can articulate and evaluate them.

Automatic thoughts mediate between a situation and an emotion. Consider the following example:

Situation: Michael learns that his sister has been in town but did not call him.
Michael's automatic thought: She finds me unlikable and doesn't want to be with me.
Michael's emotion: Sadness.

What caused the sad emotion was not the situation itself but Michael's automatic thought, reflecting the meaning he made of the situation. Understanding people's automatic thoughts is important in helping them change their emotions.

Intermediate beliefs are underlying attitudes, perspectives, assumptions, standards, or rules for living that guide behavior and influence automatic thinking and appraisal processes. Intermediate beliefs connect core beliefs to automatic thoughts and often reflect extreme and absolute rules and attitudes. In the previous example, Michael's intermediate beliefs might include "A sister should call her family when she is in town" and "Being ignored by your sister is a terrible thing."

Core beliefs are central ideas about ourselves, other people, the world, and the future that underlie many of our automatic thoughts and are often reflected in our intermediate beliefs. Core beliefs are often global, rigid, and overgeneralized (Beck, 2011). They typically stem from childhood experiences, are not necessarily true, and can be identified and modified. Most negative core beliefs can be categorized as *helpless core beliefs*, such as "I am weak" and "I am a failure," or as *unlovable core beliefs*, such as "I am not good enough" and "I am bound to be abandoned" (Beck, 2011, p. 233). In our example, Michael seems to have core beliefs related to being unlovable.

Schemas, also known as **cognitive schemas**, have been defined as a mental structure that organizes information around core beliefs (Beck, 2011, p. 33). Schemas are overarching systems or information-processing filters that function to interpret, integrate, organize, store, and ascribe meaning to lived experiences. They go beyond core beliefs, in breadth and depth, and include cognitive, affective, behavioral, physiological, and motivational schemas. Schemas have content as well as structural qualities such as breadth, flexibility, and prominence.

Beck viewed schemas as rules that govern our information processing and thus behavior (Beck, Davis, & Freeman, 2015). Schemas lead us to have expectations about experiences, events, and roles and to amplify these with information contained in our schemas. Schemas can act as mental filters, affecting the way we perceive reality. Schemas are distinctive and habitual ways of viewing ourselves, the world, and the future. They can be personal, familial, cultural, religious, gender related, or occupational in origin and application (Beck, Davis, & Freeman, 2015).

When a schema has been activated, it readily incorporates any confirming information and tends to neglect contradictory information. For example, when people view themselves as incompetent, they accept negative information they receive about themselves and overlook or dispute anything positive. Schemas tend to influence retention and distortion of memories (Tuckey & Brewer, 2003). We are more likely to recall observations that are consistent or inconsistent with our schemas, compared to observations that are irrelevant to our schemas. Inaccuracies in recollections are particularly likely to be schema consistent, as our memories tend to confirm our schemas, which may not necessarily be true. Schemas become amenable to analysis and modification after we have experienced some change as a result of assessing and altering our automatic thoughts, intermediate beliefs, and core beliefs.

The distinctions among automatic thoughts, intermediate beliefs, core beliefs, and schemas can be confusing. Consider the following example, illustrating each of these. After several disappointing relationships, Joshua has developed a rewarding relationship with Mia. After living together for 2 years, Mia suggests marriage and Joshua agrees. He has the following thoughts:

- *Automatic thoughts:* I can't be the sort of husband Mia wants and our marriage will end.
- *Intermediate beliefs:* A good husband must be willing to sacrifice his own needs for those of his wife and children. Marriage is a difficult endeavor at which few succeed.

- *Core belief:* I am not able to love another person and have little to offer in my relationships.
- *Schema:* I am inadequate and am destined to fail, no matter how hard I try. This makes me feel discouraged about my upcoming marriage; I feel disaster and shame hanging over my head. What's the point of trying if I know I will fail at whatever I do.

Because of this maladaptive schema, Joshua will probably focus on information that confirms his beliefs and ignore or explain away disconfirming information. He will enter marriage with a negative attitude, accompanied by ineffective behaviors that will contribute to the destruction of his marriage and the substantiation of his beliefs.

Cognitive therapy operates at several levels, seeking to elicit and change people's symptoms as well as their automatic thoughts, intermediate beliefs, core cognitions, and underlying schemas. Once healthy thinking has been restored, therapists help people to develop skills needed to monitor, assess, and respond to their own cognitions as well as lead their lives more successfully.

THE THERAPEUTIC PROCESS

Although cognitive therapists focus primarily on thoughts, they take a holistic view of people and believe that learning about and understanding their feelings and behaviors is also important. Particularly important—and related to positive outcome—is understanding the emotional responses people have to their faulty cognitions and the impact of those cognitions on mood (Leahy, Tirch, & Napolitano, 2011). Having a comprehensive understanding of people especially helps therapists develop interventions that target all three areas of functioning: thinking, feeling, and behaving.

The following five steps provide an overview of a typical CBT counseling session (Wright, Basco, & Thase, 2006):

1. Structure the session and set an agenda with clients.
2. Review previously learned content and skills, and process weekly homework assignments. Therapists may wish to bridge these discussions to the counseling goals of clients, or even establish goals for the session.
3. Introduce new material, psychoeducation, and the practicing of techniques or skills.
4. Collaborative processing and feedback of the session provided by both therapists and clients.
5. Assign homework based on session content and new skills for clients to complete over the course of the week.

Cognitive therapists make sure to explain to clients the nature and purpose of the sessions' structure. Clients generally find that structure reassuring. They know what to expect and are optimistic that this plan will help them as it has helped others. Of course, an agenda may require modification if needed, perhaps if a crisis has occurred, but any changes are planned when the agenda is determined at the beginning of each session.

Therapeutic Goals

Cognitive therapists carefully specify goals for their counseling, and they draw on a rich array of interventions to achieve them. The overall goal of cognitive therapy is to help people recognize and correct errors in their information-processing systems. Put simply, the goal of cognitive therapy is to teach people how to recognize, identify, and respond to dysfunctional thoughts, emotions, and behaviors. Throughout counseling, people learn to use this process and to develop the skills and attitudes needed to think more realistically and lead more rewarding lives. Once clients are able to identify and modify their automatic thoughts, more attention is paid to identifying and modifying schemas. By working with schemas, which are often the underlying causes of automatic thoughts, clients are more likely to view the world, themselves, and others in more positive ways. Other goals of cognitive therapy include assisting clients with identifying automatic thoughts; exploring for evidence to support or negate cognitions; challenging maladaptive thoughts with evidence and positive self-talk; and developing more plausible, affirming, and self-enhancing ways of thinking, feeling, and behaving. In a nutshell, the goal of CBT is to help clients recognize and respond adaptively to difficult thoughts and feelings and to engage in healthy, functional, and adaptive behaviors.

In addition to focusing on cognitive change, behavioral interventions are also applied to encourage the development of new skills and behavioral strategies that can help people effectively get their needs met. For example, if a child thinks, "My parents won't love me as much after my baby brother is born," she may experience feelings of inadequacy or low self-worth, which may lead to an increase in unhealthy behaviors intended to grab the parents' attention. In this situation, cognitive behavioral therapists would assist the child with identifying her thoughts, recognizing any thought patterns that contribute to the bad feelings, developing more realistic ways of thinking, and learning to earn attention from her parents in a positive manner. Cognitive behavioral therapies essentially use changes in thinking to bring about changes in clients' doing and feeling. In CBT, cognitive goals and behavioral goals are usually complementary and often intertwined. Therapists and clients collaborate on determining specific goals based on the clients' presenting concerns and what they would like to work on. Once identified, goals are written down, with copies made for both clients and therapists. Goals are referred to regularly to assess progress, make modifications, and develop plans. Having clear, specific, and measurable goals is an important component of cognitive therapy and increases the likelihood that clients and therapists will collaborate to achieve a shared objective. In addition, having concrete goals helps therapists choose what interventions to implement that best fit the needs of their clients.

Therapist's Function and Role

The most significant role of therapists, regardless of the theoretical approach, pertains to the cultivation of a warm, accepting therapeutic relationship and a safe, affirming counseling atmosphere. Establishing and maintaining a trusting therapeutic alliance is particularly important for therapists who use CBT, as the counseling process may involve a degree of confrontation and challenging clients' thoughts may feel threatening if a relationship is not established. If clients are not well informed about the purpose or function of the interventions, they may feel invalidated or question the therapist's intent or disposition. As such, to ensure clients' understanding of how interventions are designed to help them achieve their desired goals, it may be necessary for therapists to allocate time to discussing psychoeducational content. Not only do comprehensive psychoeducation practices promote clients' initial comprehension and eventual mastery of intervention strategies, but they also provide clients with an additional sense of predictability with regard to the direction or aim of in-session activities and exercises.

Therapists who use cognitive therapy take a collaborative approach and explore the thoughts of clients through a process based on **guided discovery**; they collaboratively assess the validity of clients' thoughts by searching for evidence or practical examples, typically through the use of questions. Therapists' degree of guidance throughout cognitive exploration processes should be individually adapted as well to the unique needs of the clients. Therapists adopt a not-knowing stance and curiously pose questions that guide clients in a direction enabling them to arrive at their own conclusions. Guided discovery processes inherently minimize power differentials that exist within the counseling relationship due to the nondirective and explorative nature of the techniques. Through guided discovery, therapists help people identify both their immediate (automatic) and their underlying (intermediate, core, schema) thoughts and beliefs, as well as associated emotions and behaviors; evaluate the validity of these thoughts and beliefs; and modify them if indicated.

The four stages of guided discovery are:

1. Socratic questioning to elicit the client's concerns
2. Active listening for clarification, inconsistencies, and emotional reactions
3. Summarization to provide feedback and enhance clarification
4. Synthesis or analytical questions that pull all of the information together, along with the client's original concern, and pose an analytical question (Scott & Freeman, 2010).

Cognitive therapists are also responsible for implementing a variety of techniques. Cognitive therapists use inventories, assessments, suggested tasks or homework, and other techniques and strategies to advance treatment goals.

Relationship Between Therapist and Client

A sound therapeutic alliance is essential for cognitive therapy (Beck, 2011). Cognitive therapists are active, collaborative, goal oriented, and problem focused. Even though cognitive therapists are directive in their approach, they still must focus on the common factors of a collaborative therapeutic relationship: a supportive and healing environment characterized by respect, genuineness, and unconditional positive regard; a holistic understanding of clients and their backgrounds; a sense of direction or goals; a shared understanding about the nature of the problems to be addressed in treatment; and the use of a valid treatment approach to address clients' symptoms. Cognitive therapists strive to be nonjudgmental and help clients develop skills needed to make their own judgments and choices.

Therapists are ultimately responsible for expertise of thoughts, feelings, and behaviors in guiding their clients. While therapists tend to be active and directive, clients are also responsible for their progress. For example, clients may be asked to complete homework assignments between counseling sessions and to participate in the cognitive restructuring process. It is essential for therapists and clients to collaborate, and therapists must ensure that clients feel comfortable with homework assignments and the counseling process by conveying warmth and understanding. Therapists typically encourage clients to try out new behaviors, complete tasks between sessions, provide feedback to the therapists, and **self-monitor** (keep records of events, feelings, and/or thoughts).

The therapeutic relationship is crucial to the success of this approach, and cognitive therapists maintain a great deal of role flexibility. Problems that arise within the therapeutic relationship need to be explored. Asking clients for feedback at the end of the session or anytime a client's affect appears to become negative during the session is helpful (Beck, 2011). Especially when working with difficult clients, therapists need to identify when such problems occur, conceptualize the reason they occurred, and work toward correcting the problems to prevent a rupture in the therapeutic alliance.

THERAPEUTIC TECHNIQUES AND PROCEDURES

Because cognitive therapy is based on research and clients' practical experience of what works best to fit their needs at a particular time, the approach is constantly evolving. The main techniques of cognitive therapy involve focusing on clients' cognitions; however, many techniques are borrowed from behavior therapy and integrated into cognitive therapy to provide more of a hybrid of behavior management and action.

Case Formulation

Before cognitive therapists move forward with interventions designed to modify cognitions, they take the time to develop a case formulation, reflecting in-depth understanding of the client. A complete case formulation includes six elements (Persons, 1989):

1. Generating a list of the client's problems and concerns
2. Hypothesizing about the underlying mechanism (core belief or schema)
3. Understanding the relationship of the belief to current problems
4. Identifying the precipitants of current problems
5. Understanding background relevant to development of underlying beliefs
6. Anticipating obstacles to counseling.

A thorough case formulation enables therapists to develop a counseling plan that is likely to be successful. Cognitive therapists identify the best points for initial intervention, counseling strategies likely to be helpful, and ways to reduce anxiety and other obstacles to progress. Counseling usually focuses first on overt automatic thoughts related to clients' presenting problems and, as progress is made, shifts to identification and assessment of underlying core beliefs and schemas.

Assessment

Cognitive therapists value the importance of making an accurate diagnosis. An extensive intake interview gives therapists a good understanding of their clients' history, development, and background. Cognitive theory suggests that each mental disorder is characterized by relatively predictable types of underlying **cognitive distortions**, that is, ways that people's minds convinces them that something is true when it is not, which reinforce negative thinking, emotions, and behavior. For example, feelings of depression typically stem from thoughts of loss. An accurate diagnosis can therefore facilitate identification of those distortions and ways to change them. It also can guide therapists' information gathering so that they can better understand their clients. For example, discussion of childhood experiences probably is important when counseling people with personality disorders, whereas discussion of traumatic experiences is essential for people diagnosed with posttraumatic stress disorder (PTSD). However, discussion of past experiences is less likely to be important in the treatment of people with disorders that are mild, brief, transient, and recent, such as adjustment disorders.

Assessing mood is also an important part of cognitive therapy for many reasons. Upsetting emotions are likely to be close to the surface and presented early in counseling. Those feelings can point the way to distorted cognitions. In addition, monitoring the nature and intensity ratings of people's emotions can provide evidence of progress, while improvement in mood can enhance clients' motivation and optimism. Cognitive therapists use structured approaches to assess emotions, as they do to assess thoughts. One of Beck's major contributions to psychotherapy is the development of brief, concise inventories that provide a quick measure of the nature and intensity of emotions that are most likely to be troubling to people, such as the Beck Depression Inventory (BDI), the Beck Anxiety Inventory (BAI), the Beck Hopelessness Inventory, and the Beck Scale for Suicidal Ideation.

Cognitive therapists can also use the cognitive triad to assist with assessment, as the negative thinking patterns clients disclose about themselves, their environment, and the future can provide insight into their deeply held beliefs and schemas. Beck referred to the aforementioned domains in which negative thoughts occur (i.e., views about one's self, the world or environment, or the future) as the **cognitive triad.** For example, a client with depression may report the following automatic thoughts: "I hate myself" (self belief); "I let everyone down" (environmental belief); and "I'll never succeed" (future belief). Such automatic thoughts may reflect the client's intermediate beliefs about

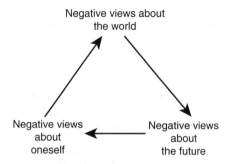

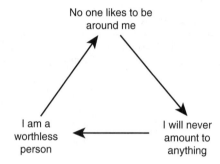

FIGURE 6.2 Beck's Cognitive Triad.

not meeting some type of self, other, or societal standard; a core belief of "I'm a failure" that is based on prior life experiences; and a cognitive schema oriented toward ascribing negative meanings to neutral experiences or filtering information, interactions, situations, or events in a pessimistic fashion. This type of cognitive schema may be associated with additional symptoms of depression experienced by adolescents, including feelings of shame, guilt, or despair (emotional schema); social withdrawal (behavioral schema); anhedonia (motivational schema); and increased sleeping patterns (physiological). Refer to Figure 6.2 for an example of Beck's *cognitive triad.*

Dysfunctional Thought Record

One way to elicit an individual's thoughts is by using a basic question: "What was going through your mind just then?" (Beck, 2011, p. 83). Once one thought is presented, it often leads to production of other thoughts. Especially important are thoughts that appear repeatedly in conjunction with a variety of experiences and have a negative impact on the individual. Self-monitoring is also often used to assess a client's thoughts, emotions, or behaviors outside of therapy by the client keeping track of events, feelings, and/or thoughts. This self-monitoring—and in particular, **thought sampling**—is helpful for gaining more awareness of one's own thoughts in everyday life. A **dysfunctional thought record** to facilitate identification and modification of such thoughts can be used (Beck, 2011, p. 95). This record may include the following items:

1. The situation that elicited the thoughts and its accompanying physical responses
2. Date and time of the situation
3. Automatic thoughts and extent of belief in those thoughts rated on a 0% to 100% scale
4. Emotions and their intensity, rated on a 0% to 100% scale

5. Nature of distortion and ways of modifying the thoughts
6. Outcome, including revised beliefs, ratings of automatic and revised thoughts, current emotions and intensity ratings, and new actions.

See Table 6.2 for an example of a dysfunctional thought record.

Determining the Validity of Cognitions

Once the cognitions have been elicited and placed in context, people can assess their validity. Especially important is therapists' use of guided discovery (also called Socratic dialogue) via skillful questioning and experiments to help people test the reality of their thoughts. These are powerful

TABLE 6.2 Dysfunctional Thought Record Example

Date/Time	Situation	Automatic Thoughts	Emotions	Alternative Response	Outcome
	1. What event led to the unpleasant emotions? 2. What (if any) physical responses did you experience?	1. What thoughts and/or images went through your mind? 2. How much did you believe them?	1. What emotions did you have? 2. What was the intensity of the emotion(s)?	1. What cognitive distortions did you have? 2. What ways can you modify your thoughts? 3. What new thoughts do you have?	1. How much do you believe the automatic thoughts? 2. What emotions do you have now and what are the intensity? 3. What actions did you or will you take?
Monday morning at 8:30 a.m.	The school called to tell me that my son had been seen breaking into the school over the weekend. He was accused of vandalizing the computer room. I felt a knot in my stomach; I felt light-headed and tense all over.	I am a failure as a parent: 95%. My son is a hopeless criminal and it's my fault: 90%.	Anxious: 95% Sad: 85%	Mislabeling, personalization, and all-or-nothing thinking I can remind myself that my son has not done anything like this before and there is hope. I can think about times when I have been a good parent and how I have influenced positive behavior. My new thought is "While I am upset with my son, I know that I am a good parent and he can overcome this."	Automatic thoughts rating: 50% New emotions: Anxious (60%) Sad (50%) I will be there for my son and talk with him.

techniques that must be used with care. Therapists should never act as though they know better than clients, should not debate or argue with clients, and should remain neutral on whether a thought is distorted. The role of therapists is to help clients find the truth.

The following dialogue illustrates the use of questioning to help the client in the previous example (the dysfunctional thought record) assess the logic and validity of her thoughts:

THERAPIST: One thought you had was that your son was a hopeless criminal. What led you to have that thought?

CLIENT: Well, it sounds like he committed a crime.

THERAPIST: Yes, he may have. Does he have a history of criminal behavior?

CLIENT: No, not at all. He's always been very well behaved.

THERAPIST: So this is the first time he has been suspected of breaking the law?

CLIENT: Yes.

THERAPIST: And what is your definition of a hopeless criminal?

CLIENT: I guess it's someone who repeatedly breaks the law, who can't be rehabilitated.

THERAPIST: And does that sound like your son?

CLIENT: No. I guess I overreacted when I said he was a hopeless criminal.

THERAPIST: And what about your thought that you are to blame for his behavior. What led you to think that?

CLIENT: I'm his parent. Aren't I the biggest influence in his life?

THERAPIST: Yes, your role is certainly an important one. How might you have encouraged him to become a criminal?

CLIENT: I don't know what you mean.

THERAPIST: I wonder if you have engaged in criminal behavior yourself.

CLIENT: No, of course not.

THERAPIST: Perhaps you condoned criminal behavior or didn't try to teach him the difference between right and wrong?

CLIENT: No, just the opposite. I have very strong values, and I always tried to transmit them to my son. When he misbehaved, I would talk to him about what was wrong with his behavior and teach him how to act differently.

THERAPIST: I'm confused then, about how you might have caused his criminal behavior.

CLIENT: I guess I was just feeling bad and wanted to find an explanation. But I can see that I certainly never taught him to break the law.

Experiments designed to test hypotheses stemming from faulty thinking are another important approach that can help people evaluate the reality of their cognitions. In the previous example, the client might use her statements "My son is a hopeless criminal" and "I am to blame for my son's criminal behavior" as hypotheses. The therapist and client then develop experiments or ways to test these hypotheses. The client might talk with her son about the reasons for his behavior, confer with school personnel about this incident as well as about her son's usual behavior at school, and read about criminal behavior.

A third approach is to use the three-question technique, a form of the Socratic method that helps the client to revise negative thinking. The therapist asks the client the following: (1) What evidence is there for the belief? (2) How else could the situation be interpreted? (3) If it is true, what would the implications be? Each of the three questions helps the client to delve deeper into the distorted belief, recognize the distortion, and adopt more objective thinking.

In our example, the boy might have been falsely accused of breaking into the school. Even if he had committed the crime, mitigating factors might have played a part, such as being forced or coerced to engage in the break-in.

Following are additional approaches that cognitive therapists use to help people evaluate the validity of their cognitions:

- Asking clients how another individual whom they respect would view the situation
- Asking them what they would say if their child or friend had the thoughts they have
- Using humor or exaggeration to take an idea to its extreme
- Helping people recognize their tendency to think negatively
- Encouraging people to imagine "what if" their worst fears came true and then think of ways to deal with them so the fears have less power over them
- Suggesting alternative explanations for a situation
- Helping people find a middle ground to counteract extreme ways of thinking using **scaling**
- Redefining or reconceptualizing a problem so that it is more amenable to change
- Decentering, or helping people see they are not the cause of the problem or the center of attention.

Labeling Cognitive Distortions

Categorizing and **labeling** distorted cognitions can facilitate evaluation of these distortions. This helps people see more clearly the nature of their unrealistic thinking, reminds them that other people have had similar distorted cognitions, and gives them a tool for assessing subsequent thoughts. Many lists of cognitive distortions have been published (Beck, 1976; Burns, 1999). These categories are illustrated with statements made by the previous client:

- *All-or-nothing thinking or polarized thinking (dichotomous thinking, black-and-white):* Viewing a situation in terms of extremes rather than on a continuum, such as all positive or all negative. "Either my son is innocent, or he is a hopeless criminal."
- *Overgeneralization:* Drawing sweeping conclusions that are not justified by the evidence; making conclusions based on a single situation and associating them broadly or to dissimilar situations. "I am a failure as a parent because my son was arrested."
- *Mental filter (selective abstraction):* Focusing selectively on negative details and failing to see the broad picture. "I know my son has been a good student and has not caused any problems in the past, but all I can think about is that he broke the law."
- *Disqualifying the positive:* Paying attention only to negative information. "What good are all my efforts to be a good mother if this is the result?"
- *Jumping to conclusions (arbitrary inferences):* Drawing hasty and unwarranted conclusions without facts or evidence to support beliefs. "My son must be guilty. Someone saw him hanging around the school late that night."
- *Mind reading:* Attributing negative thoughts and reactions to others without confirming they are present; knowing what others are thinking. "My husband will never forgive Kevin for this. He'll disown him."
- *Fortune telling:* Predicting that something bad is going to happen, but without any evidence to support this. "Kevin is going to continue going down the wrong path and will never want a relationship with me."
- *Magnification/minimization:* Making too much of the negative or blowing things out of proportion; devaluing positive information. "My son stole a candy bar from another child when he was four. He was destined to become a criminal."

- *Emotional reasoning:* Believing that something is true because it feels that way; paying no attention to contradictory evidence. "I just feel like this is my fault, and no one can convince me it isn't."
- *"Should" and "must" statements:* Having definite and inflexible ideas about how we and others should behave and how life should be. "I should never have let Kevin get his driver's license. I should have made sure I met all his friends. I should have been a better mother to him."
- *Labeling and mislabeling:* Attaching an extreme, broad, and unjustified label to oneself or someone else; defining the identity of oneself or others based on imperfections or on past behavior or mistakes. "Kevin is a hopeless criminal."
- *Personalization:* Assuming excessive responsibility for events or others' behaviors without any plausible reason to do so. "My son and I had an argument about his curfew 3 days before the school break-in. If I hadn't yelled at him, this probably never would have happened."
- *Catastrophizing:* Predicting a negative outcome without considering other possibilities. "I just know Kevin will be sent to prison for this."
- *Tunnel vision:* Focusing only on the negative aspects of a situation. "I can't do anything right as a parent. There I was, eating dinner, while my son was breaking into the school. How could I not have known what was going on?"

Becoming familiar with these categories of cognitive distortions can help people identify, understand, and dispute their own cognitive distortions. In addition, reviewing this list can reassure clients that having cognitive distortions is common and that dysfunctional thinking can be changed. This reassurance can reduce self-blame and facilitate efforts to formulate healthier and more valid cognitions.

Strategies for Modifying Cognitions

Cognitive therapists draw on a wealth of strategies to accomplish cognitive restructuring. What follows are some of the strategies that enhance the work of cognitive therapists:

- *Reattributing blame.* Clients often turn internally and blame themselves whenever something goes wrong in their lives. This false attribution of blame can start a cascade of negative emotions and behaviors. Through the use of Socratic dialogue and asking questions that get to the heart of the problem, therapists can help clients look at the situation more clearly. This process, known as **reattribution**, is illustrated in this brief dialogue:

    CLIENT: A pipe burst at my parent's house while they were on vacation and now the whole condo is flooded. It's all my fault.

    THERAPIST: Were you watching your parent's house while they were gone?

    CLIENT: No, I haven't been there in years. They live in Florida, but I should have had the water turned off before they left.

    THERAPIST: Did they ask you to turn the water off?

    CLIENT: No.

- *Cognitive rehearsal* is a strategy in which people mentally rehearse a new behavior and then create a cognitive model of themselves successfully performing that behavior. Some athletes use this technique to improve their skills in their sport. A woman married to a verbally abusive husband used this approach to rehearse asserting herself to her husband, making it easier for her to stand up to him when he spoke to her in a demeaning way. A variation is for people to

imagine themselves as someone they admire and then tackle a challenging situation as if they were that individual.
- *Diversions* or *distractions* can also help people reduce their negative thinking. As an example, a woman who was diagnosed with a life-threatening illness had a good prognosis but still experienced constant thoughts of death. To distract herself from these troubling thoughts, she mentally categorized each item in her extensive wardrobe, beginning the mental list anew each time the negative thoughts returned.
- *Self-talk* is a technique in which people repeat positive and encouraging phrases that they have identified as helpful to themselves many times throughout the day. As an example, people who experience anxiety may say to themselves, "Don't let fear control you. You can do it." In essence, they are giving themselves a pep talk.
- *Affirmations* are closely related to self-talk. An affirmation is a slogan that is positive and reinforcing. People can post these in prominent places, such as the refrigerator, or keep them in a binder of index cards, where they can review them frequently and be reminded to shift their thinking. An adolescent girl chose as her affirmation, "Someday you will realize your great potential." Keeping those words in mind helped her deal effectively with challenges. In addition, many phone applications have positive affirmations and inspiring quotes that can remind people of positivity and improve their self-worth.
- *Letter writing* provides another avenue for exploring and expressing thoughts and feelings. The woman whose son was accused of breaking into his school (discussed previously) might benefit from drafting a letter to her son expressing her reactions to his behavior. The letter need not be mailed but can be used as the focus of a session.
- *Systematic assessment of alternatives* (cost-benefit analysis) is an approach that can help people make wise decisions. They first list their options, along with the pros and cons of each one. Then they assign numbers on a scale of 1 to 10, showing the importance of each advantage and disadvantage. Finally, they total the numbers assigned to the pros and cons of each option. A man considering a career change used this approach to help him decide whether to remain in his secure, well-paying position in computer technology or pursue his lifelong goal of becoming a counselor; the numerical totals strongly reflected a preference for becoming a counselor, whereas the list of cons pointed out obstacles to this goal.
- *Role playing* can enable people to actualize some of the new thoughts they have about themselves. For example, a man who had developed a more positive view of his abilities role-played sharing his accomplishments with his friends, asking his supervisor for a raise, and inviting a colleague to join him for lunch. Role playing can also be done via a dialogue between old and new thoughts, in which clients can use two chairs to represent both their old and their new thoughts. Moving from one chair to another, they engage in a dialogue between the two groups of thoughts. This can help people clarify changes in their thinking and solidify their rational thoughts.
- *Distancing* involves looking into the future to put a problem in perspective and diminish its importance. A woman who was discouraged about getting a *B* in a college course realized that this would mean little to her in 10 years and would likely not have an impact on her future.
- *Bibliotherapy,* or the use of books in the counseling process, can help people modify their thinking. Clients can read books about other people who have coped well with experiences similar to their problems and can also read educational books about various topics such as time management, stress management, and relationship satisfaction. Other types of bibliotherapy include interactive bibliotherapy in which a workbook is used to help the client address the ongoing issue. Bibliotherapy can be cathartic, provide emotional release, show new ways of thinking and interacting, and help clients to solve problems. The following recommendations are best when using bibliotherapy (Erford et al., 2010): (1) Therapists should only use books they have

read; (2) the client's specific reality should be kept in mind during the process; (3) reading level and interest should be taken into account; and (4) not all clients will enjoy reading or have the time to complete the book. Movies and videos can also be used as a form of bibliotherapy.

One example of bibliotherapy involves counseling with a 12-year-old boy who had lost his mother. The boy was sad, especially when he came home from school and she was not there. In therapy, after the therapist conducted an assessment and recognized the client's need for catharsis, she gave him a copy of *Tear Soup,* a picture book about grief and loss in which a woman is cooking soup (tear soup) that helps her express her underlying feelings of grief. The boy began to identify with the person who was making the soup and gained the recognition that it was acceptable to grieve.

- *Graded task assignments* are activities that clients complete between sessions. Starting with easy assignments that guarantee success, therapists gradually increase the difficulty of the tasks, so that people continue to learn from them and feel a sense of mastery and accomplishment.

Termination and Relapse Prevention

Like the other phases of cognitive therapy, the concluding phase is carefully planned and structured to help people successfully apply what they have learned in counseling. Sessions are scheduled less frequently, typically shifting to every other week, then to once a month, then to every 3 months for at least a year (Beck, 2011). This gives people the opportunity to test their skills and cope with any setbacks while maintaining contact with their therapists.

Normalizing setbacks and stressing the importance of ongoing learning can enable people to cope with future disappointments successfully. Life skills such as assertiveness, decision making, coping strategies, and communication skills, which are often taught throughout the counseling process, are reviewed and solidified. Therapists also review progress, with every effort made to help clients accept credit for and take pride in their accomplishments. Therapists address any concerns that clients have about termination and elicit feedback about the counseling process. Finally, clients and therapists collaborate in developing goals and plans for clients to continue their progress on their own.

GENERAL ASSESSMENT OF COGNITIVE BEHAVIORAL THERAPIES

APPLICATION AND CURRENT USE OF COGNITIVE BEHAVIORAL THERAPIES

Cognitive behavioral therapies are well-established and widely used approaches to counseling. It is appropriate for a broad range of people, problems, and settings. CBT is effective with a variety of populations and has an ever-expanding range of applications.

CBT therapists, especially Aaron Beck and his colleagues, have encouraged and engaged in extensive research on the impact of this approach; its effectiveness has been more clearly demonstrated in thousands of outcome studies (Beck, 2011). CBT approaches have increasingly been combined with other approaches to create powerful integrated counseling approaches.

Counseling Applications

Whether used in individual or group counseling, CBT is helpful in addressing a variety of presenting issues and problems. Possibly more than any other theories discussed in this text, CBT has demonstrated its effectiveness in addressing a number of mental disorders. Specifically, CBT approaches can be helpful when counseling those who have depressive disorders, anxiety disorders, and adjustment disorders (Dobson, 2010; Iftene, Predes, Stefan, & David, 2015; Turner, & Marker, 2013).

CBTs are among the most popular and effective therapeutic approaches for treating youth and adults who have depression in either individual or group counseling formats (Dunn et al., 2012; Hofmann, Asnaani, Vonk, Sawyer, & Fang, 2012; Kress & Paylo, 2019; Lam, Kennedy, McIntyre, & Khuller, 2014). CBT interventions can modify dysfunctional thoughts that maintain hopelessness and low self-esteem, as well as specific symptoms associated with depression. Evidence suggests that those who have depression and a comorbid personality disorder may respond better to CBT because of their lower levels of insight into interpersonal problems, and because of CBT's directive and structured nature (Carter et al., 2011). CBT may also prevent the relapse of depression symptoms (Segal et al., 2019).

CBT is also effective in treating many types of anxiety disorders (Clark & Beck, 2011). As applied to treating those with panic disorder, CBT aims to address distorted and dysfunctional thoughts related to panic attacks by identifying, challenging, and modifying these ideas (Beck & Emery, 2005; Craske & Barlow, 2014; Koemer, Vorstenbosch, & Antony, 2012). When therapists use evidence-based approaches such as CBT, the prognosis for people with panic disorder is excellent (Barlow et al., 2015). When counselors incorporate client education about anxiety and panic symptoms, cognitive therapy, some blending of exposure therapy, and coping skill development, clients' symptomology is significantly reduced (i.e., often with panic-free rates in 70% to 80% of those with panic disorder; 50–70% for those with panic disorder with mild agoraphobia), and results are often maintained (e.g., at 2-year follow-ups; Craske & Barlow, 2014). CBT is also helpful in treating clients who have agoraphobia due to panic attacks (Barlow et al., 2015).

CBT approaches for treating social anxiety disorder aim to address clients' anxiety-provoking thoughts related to social and performance situations (Beck et al., 2005; Gregory & Peters, 2017). Studies have suggested that a combination of CBT and relaxation exercises appear to be the most promising treatment for generalized anxiety disorder (Barlow et al., 2015; Ouimet, Covin, & Dozois, 2012).

Variations of CBT have long been considered the most efficacious treatment for obsessive-compulsive disorder (OCD), and randomized controlled studies have consistently supported their use. A recent meta-analysis of 16 randomized controlled studies using CBT to treat OCD revealed that clients completing CBT outperformed those assigned to control groups in posttreatment symptom reduction (Olatunji, Davis, Powers, & Smits, 2013; McKay et al., 2015). CBT is also effective in treating OCD in children and adolescents (Williams et al., 2010; McGuire et al., 2015). CBT uses techniques aimed at modifying cognitive (e.g., intrusive thoughts) and behavioral (e.g., compulsive behaviors) components to produce changes in the overall condition.

In addition, presenting issues that often respond well to CBT include anger and aggression, obsessiveness, sexual difficulties, low frustration tolerance, a lack of assertiveness, low self-esteem (Obiageli, 2015; Roghanchi, Mohamad, Mey, Momeni, & Golmohamadian, 2013), and hopelessness (Jeffrin, Margreat, & Rohini, 2014).

CBT can also be effective when counseling those who have substance abuse problems (Penn, Brooke, Brooks, Gallagher, & Barnard, 2016). SMART Recovery, the self-help group for people with substance use problems, is an outgrowth of REBT. An alternative to Alcoholics Anonymous (AA) and other 12-step programs, SMART Recovery diverges from AA in its controversial belief that people are not always in the process of recovering but can actually recover from drug and alcohol problems. In addition, unlike AA, which emphasizes the importance of a higher power, SMART Recovery focuses on personal responsibility for effecting change.

Trauma-based disorders such as PTSD also respond well to CBT approaches (Hofmann, 2012). Strategies such as education about PTSD, cognitive restructuring, breathing retraining, imaginal desensitization, and confrontation of feared situations have been shown to give people a greater sense of control and alleviate symptoms. Cognitive processing therapy is also helpful in addressing PTSD and substance use, especially when these disorders co-occur (Kaysen, Schumm, Pederson, Seim, Bedard-Gilligan, & Chard, 2014; Peck, Coffey, McGuire, Voluse, & Connolly, 2018). Textbox 6.2 provides an overview of trauma-focused cognitive behavioral therapy, an evidence-based approach to treating young people who have been abused or otherwise traumatized.

CBT Spotlight: Trauma-Focused Cognitive Behavioral Therapy (TF-CBT)

An example of an evidence-based CBT approach that can be used with abused or traumatized children is trauma-focused cognitive behavioral therapy (TF-CBT; Cohen et al., 2006). TF-CBT is a conjoint child and caregiver psychotherapy approach used with children and adolescents who are experiencing significant emotional and behavioral difficulties secondary to traumatic life events. This model integrates trauma-sensitive interventions with cognitive behavioral techniques, humanistic principles, and family involvement. Through TF-CBT, children and caregivers learn new skills to help them process thoughts and feelings related to traumatic life events; manage and resolve distressing feelings, thoughts, and behaviors that are related to the traumatic life event(s); and develop an enhanced sense of safety, personal growth, parenting skills, and improved family communication (Cohen et al., 2006).

More specifically, TF-CBT involves young people discussing their trauma narratives while utilizing anxiety reduction techniques to regulate their physical, emotional, cognitive, and biological responses to the memory of the trauma (Underwood & Dailey, 2017). What follows is an overview of essential components of TF-CBT. As can be seen, this approach incorporates a focus on thoughts, behaviors, psychoeducation, and the other CBT components we have discussed in this chapter.

Essential Components of Trauma-Focused-Cognitive Behavioral Therapy and Associated Counseling Tasks

	Essential Components	Associated Tasks
P	Psychoeducation and parenting skills	• Increase knowledge of common reactions to trauma (e.g., physical, emotional, cognitions). • Identify trauma triggers and reminders. • Connect behaviors and reactions with trauma experiences. • Instill hope for recovery. • Increase parenting skills (e.g., praise, attention, use of reinforcements).
R	Relaxation skills	• Learn and implement focused breathing. • Learn and implement progressive muscle relaxation. • Increase ability to relax/relaxation skills (e.g., blowing bubbles). • Increase mindfulness (when appropriate for development and spirituality).
A	Affective modulation skills	• Increase affective identification and expression. • Increase problem-solving skills. • Learn and implement anger management skills.

(Continued)

Essential Components		Associated Tasks
C	Cognitive coping skills	• Increase awareness of connection between thoughts, feelings, and behaviors. • Learn and implement cognitive restructuring (e.g., replacing unhelpful/inaccurate thoughts with more helpful/accurate ones).
T	Trauma narrative and processing	• Develop a detailed trauma narrative. • Process the narrative and events involved in the youth's narrative. • Utilize cognitive processing and coping skills (e.g., relaxation and affective modulation).
I	In vivo mastery	• Develop a fear/anxiety hierarchy.
C	Conjoint sessions	• Implement family safety plans. • Share child's trauma narrative. • Enhance family communication. • Increase healthy family interactions and relationships (e.g., reactions to family stress; family activities).
E	Enhancing safety	• Develop and implement safety plans. • Learn and implement social skills. • Develop a discharge plan.

Source: Adapted from Kress, V. E., Haiyasoso, M., Zoldan, C. A., Headley, J. A. and Trepal, H. (2018), The Use of Relational-Cultural Theory in Counseling Clients Who Have Traumatic Stress Disorders. *Journal of Counseling & Development*, 96: 106–114.

Recent research indicates that CBT approaches are also effective in the treatment of borderline and other personality disorders, for pain management, and in the treatment of sexual disorders (Hofmann, 2012). CBT has been used successfully to treat insomnia (Lee, Ree, & Wong, 2018), to alleviate stress and worry, and to reduce suicidal thoughts (Dobson, 2010; Hofmann, 2012).

CBT has also shown effectiveness in treating eating disorders. Systematic reviews have highlighted the efficacy of CBT in treating clients who have anorexia nervosa (Galsworthy-Francis & Allan, 2014). These results indicated that CBT treatment led to improvement in eating disorder symptoms and increased body mass. To date, CBT has the strongest empirical support for the treatment of bulimia nervosa, with studies suggesting that approximately 50% of clients diagnosed with bulimia nervosa recover when CBT treatment is used (Fairburn et al., 2015; Hay, 2013).

Neurobiology and psychology have also been combined to show how a cognitive approach can be used to understand and treat schizophrenia (Beck et al., 2008; Lanfredi et al., 2017). Growing research in the area of severe mental disorders, such as bipolar disorder and schizophrenia, has found CBT to be an effective adjunct to medication in addressing delusions and hallucinations (Beck et al., 2008). Interventions include helping clients to recognize nonpsychotic misinterpretations and challenge their upsetting interpretations; behavioral experiments to help clients test delusional misinterpretations; and treatment to reduce symptoms of depression and anxiety and reduce suicidal risk. CBT approaches have become so popular, and their effectiveness so widespread, that treatment manuals and workbooks that address most mental disorders or common presenting issues have been developed.

CBT can be helpful in group counseling. The reinforcement and modeling provided by the other group members make the group setting especially well suited for CBT. Cognitive behavioral group counseling enables people to learn and experiment with new behaviors, while receiving information and feedback from multiple sources. Hearing other people's thoughts also can help people to broaden their perspectives, identify and modify their own dysfunctional thoughts, and reinforce their valid and reasonable thoughts and feelings.

CBT is an effective counseling approach for people of all ages. CBT can be adapted to work with older adults to accommodate age-related cognitive decline (Gallagher-Thompson, Steffen, & Thompson, 2008). It has been used successfully with young children and may improve self-esteem (Seiler, 2008), and it has been used to address childhood attention-deficit hyperactivity disorder (ADHD; Gharebaghy, Rassafiani, & Cameron, 2015), conduct disorder, oppositional defiant disorder (Battagliese et al., 2015), adolescent depression and anxiety, eating disorders, and childhood trauma (Hoch, 2009).

CBT approaches can also prove helpful when working with families and couples. For example, REBT couples therapy focuses on common irrational beliefs about relationships, such as "My partner should know intuitively what I want" and "Romantic love will always endure." Counseling goals include modifying cognitions, resolving disturbances, and increasing relationship satisfaction. REBT can help family members realize they have little power to change others and thus they need to take responsibility for changing themselves. As an example, REBT might be used with family members who have a severely disturbed family member; counseling encourages the family to accept that person as a fallible human being, and one whom they cannot control, and enables them to increase happiness in the family.

Application to Multicultural Groups

CBT can be used with a diverse group of people. The value of using CBT approaches with people from diverse cultures has been supported by research (Pantalone et al., 2010). CBT is culturally sensitive in that it explores the worldviews and core beliefs of clients and takes these into consideration during the counseling process. Assessment is important throughout counseling, which is helpful in identifying and evaluating clients' belief systems relative to their culture. In addition, the collaborative approach of CBT allows for clients to be active while receiving guidance from therapists, which may be well suited for diverse clients who prefer structure and problem solving. CBT is considered inherently multicultural due to the focus on tailoring the therapeutic style to meet the needs of all clients, empowering clients by introducing skills, exploring the role culture plays in people's lives, and focusing on clients' inner strengths and resources.

Beck's cognitive therapy in particular is respectful, addresses present concerns, and does not require disclosure of emotions and experiences that may feel very personal; thus, this approach appeals to people from a wide variety of ages and backgrounds. It is especially useful for people who are more comfortable with, and accepting of, sharing thoughts instead of sharing emotions. The emphasis on thoughts and actions inherent in this approach may be well suited for people from Asian backgrounds, who are often reluctant to share deeply personal experiences and emotions with people who are not close family or friends.

Cognitive therapy is also being used as a culturally sensitive method to help people with trauma. For example, cognitive therapy has been adapted to help traumatized refugees and immigrants (Hinton et al., 2012).

Ellis noted that REBT practitioners are almost "intrinsically multicultural" (Ellis, 2001, p. 196). Through the use of **unconditional other acceptance-multicultural (UOA-M)** REBT therapists accept people from other cultures "as they exist," with no judgment (Ellis, 2001, p. 196).

Therapists should exercise care in using REBT with people from non-Western backgrounds, especially those whose cultures stress interdependence, privacy, and respect; those who may not have the background needed to appreciate the linguistic subtleties of REBT; and those whose strong or mystical spiritual beliefs may conflict with REBT's pragmatic stance. In addition, therapists should not attack beliefs that are strongly anchored in people's ethnic, religious, and cultural backgrounds unless they are clearly self-defeating (Nielsen & Ellis, 1994).

Ellis (2002) suggested that therapists are not a very diverse group themselves. Ellis believed that most therapists are politically liberal and may be prejudiced against more conservative points of view. Therapists, like other people, need to guard against being narrow minded and intolerant. By practicing **unconditional other acceptance (UOA)**, they can be good role models (Ellis, 2007).

CBT, along with medication, has been found to reduce depression in low-income young African American and Latina women, especially when enhanced with encouragement, intensive outreach, and direct services such as child care and transportation (Miranda et al., 2003). CBT may be well suited to Latino clients, given its transparency, its consistency with the culture's traditional directness, and its problem-solving approach (Reyes-Rodriguez, Bulik, Hamer, & Baucom, 2013).

REBT emphasizes the use of humor. Because humor is so culturally dependent, therapists should be cautious in using humor with people from diverse backgrounds.

EVALUATION OF COGNITIVE BEHAVIORAL THERAPIES

Perhaps more than any other counseling approach, CBT has been the focus of extensive research. The literature suggests that counseling focused on cognitions and behavior can be very powerful and effective. Of course, it also has limitations.

Limitations

Despite, or perhaps because of, the evidence-based approach of CBT, criticisms still arise. For example, therapists may become so caught up in the need to follow protocol for evidence-based practice that they fail to address real-time changes occurring in clients' lives. As a result, clients may feel unheard and powerless rather than experience the growth in self-efficacy and competence that should result from counseling.

In many ways, CBT is based on a medical model approach to helping that relies on the accurate diagnosis of clients' problems and mental disorders (as applicable). Comorbidity—or co-occurring issues or diagnoses experienced by clients—can complicate counselors' use of CBT or any other evidence-based approaches. Most people do not fit neatly into one category of diagnosis but overlap (e.g., as when people experience both anxiety and depression; Emmelkamp, Ehring, & Powers, 2010). CBT treatment manuals that focus on one diagnosis or the other will not do justice to the totality of the problem when people have complicated presenting issues.

Counseling limited to CBT is not the ideal approach for all clients; some may not benefit or be successfully helped using CBT. It is a structured approach that requires people to assume an active and collaborative role in their counseling and to complete suggested tasks between sessions. Many clients struggle to just get through their days, and the energy required to actively change thoughts and behaviors may be difficult for many clients.

In addition, CBT's focus on present-oriented, relatively brief counseling may not fit for all clients' needs. Some clients may prefer less structured, more insight- or relationship-oriented counseling approaches. In addition, people who are reluctant to participate fully in their own counseling, are intellectually limited, or are unmotivated to make changes may not be good candidates. Careful screening of clients as well as discussion about the nature of CBT can help therapists determine if a client is an appropriate candidate for counseling.

In addition, although CBT can help people with psychotic and other severe disorders, medication and other interventions (e.g., case management services) are also needed. CBT is useful with almost all clients but often must be combined with other approaches to maximize their effectiveness.

CBT is also not a good fit for all therapists. Therapists must be organized, comfortable with structure, and willing to use inventories and forms to elicit and assess clients' concerns and progress. They must be knowledgeable about learning theory, behavior therapy, and diagnosis, as well as able to skillfully use a broad range of interventions. Planning and effort are integral to the success of cognitive therapy. In addition, therapists are required to learn the cognitive formulation for each mental disorder and the accompanying techniques. Both clients and therapists should be aware of the commitment required by this approach. Extensive training and learning are required to use CBT effectively.

Therapists should also exercise caution in how they use and apply CBT. At its starting point, some therapists mistakenly view CBT as a rapid solution to immediate concerns; they may neglect to develop a strong therapeutic alliance, downplay the importance of empathy, and even become critical and judgmental of what they perceive as people's dysfunctional thoughts. These views reflect a misunderstanding of CBT. Cognitive therapy has also been criticized for focusing too much on positive thinking, being overly simplistic, relying too much on techniques, and not paying enough attention to feelings. Readers should keep in mind that cognitive therapy has more depth and complexity than may be evident initially, and care should be taken to fully understand this powerful approach.

More empirical research on the effectiveness of REBT, in particular, is needed. The use of REBT with people who have specific mental disorders and with people from diverse cultural, religious, and ethnic backgrounds needs more study. REBT has been criticized for sometimes paying too little attention to clients' histories and moving too rapidly toward promoting change. Therapists should ensure adequate time to assess and understand people before moving forward.

REBT has also been criticized for its confrontational nature, especially if a strong therapeutic alliance is not in place. Clients may find this confrontation offensive and invalidating, and they may become withdrawn or lose motivation for counseling. It is important for therapists who use this approach to establish their own style that fits with their personality and to not overlook the importance of developing rapport. In addition, therapists may impose their own ideas of irrational thinking rather than eliciting their clients' thoughts and opinions about what constitutes irrational thoughts.

Despite its broad application, REBT, with its forceful and directive nature and its emphasis on client responsibility, should be avoided or used with extreme care when counseling those who have certain mental disorders. REBT may not be appropriate for people with psychotic disorders, dangerous impulse control disorders, other severe mental disorders, or for people who are highly suicidal or very fragile. In addition, REBT should be used with great caution, if at all, with those who have had traumatic childhood experiences. Misapplication of REBT may lead inexperienced therapists to ask those who have survived traumas whether their experiences were "really so awful" or whether they "really can't stand the feelings and flashbacks." Questions such as these may retraumatize or otherwise harm clients who have been victimized.

Strengths and Contributions

CBT has many strengths. Perhaps the most basic, but important, contribution of cognitive therapy is the message that analysis and modification of distorted cognitions are important ways to help people change. REBT in particular demonstrates that the response to situations matters, rather than the situations themselves, and that people's unhealthy thoughts are what causes disturbances in people's lives.

Cognitive behavioral therapies provide a choice of empirically supported treatments, they lend themselves well to the development of guidelines that can be followed by other mental health professions based on what works, and they offer a straightforward approach to counseling that has both face and empirical validity. These approaches emphasize goal setting, accountability, and results. They are respectful and collaborative, encouraging people to take responsibility for themselves.

Although improved behaviors and thinking are the targets, counseling also seeks to improve emotional health. Manualized treatments are also easy to disseminate and transport to community and academic settings for training (Emmelkamp et al., 2010).

Because this approach is effective at addressing some of the most common counseling concerns—depression and anxiety—it has great value. It is well received by most people because it is clear and logical and is not intrusive. Cognitive therapy does not require people to share intimate details of their past or focus extensively on their emotions. It is an empowering and nonthreatening approach. As we have seen, cognitive therapy draws on a broad array of interventions and can be integrated with many other counseling approaches.

The clear and carefully planned structure of CBT facilitates both teaching of, and research on, this counseling approach. Its time-limited nature makes it efficient and appealing, while its use of long-term follow-up provides a safeguard against relapse. Its emphasis on building a collaborative client–therapist alliance, providing assignments between sessions, giving the client credit for progress, reinforcing positive changes, and teaching skills is empowering. Through these interventions, clients remain active and can put insight into action to create positive change. This approach is designed not just to resolve immediate problems but to enable people to manage their lives successfully.

The focus on psychoeducation and teaching clients how to be their own therapists is an important strength of CBT. Clients are taught skills, behaviors, and cognitive restructuring, all of which can be used outside of therapy and generalized to many problems of life. In addition, clients have the skills they need to prevent future problems from occurring. The psychoeducational approaches of bibliotherapy, self-monitoring, and homework assignments are particularly valuable.

Although mastery of CBT is not as simple as it seems, with training and experience most therapists can easily learn and use it effectively. All therapists should be familiar with CBT concepts, as they will, at times, likely need to use this approach with some clients. In addition, CBT has shown efficacy for a wide variety of populations and presenting problems and can be easily integrated with other approaches.

CBT has made important contributions to counseling and psychotherapy. Aaron Beck's work, in particular, has emphasized the importance of research and evidence of effectiveness. Beck's cognitive therapy focuses on case formulations and treatment planning, which help therapists understand their clients holistically and can guide treatment. This focus is compatible with today's emphasis on goal setting and accountability in counseling and has established a standard that many clinical therapists are expected to follow.

SKILL DEVELOPMENT: EXPOSURE-BASED CBT FOR HOARDING

CBT is one of the most supported evidence-based approaches for treating anxiety disorders. CBT is particularly effective in the treatment of OCD, phobias, and excessive fears of certain situations, such as socializing, flying, and public speaking. It is also useful in addressing other apprehensions and anxieties. Exposure-based CBT can be particularly helpful. Exposure therapies were discussed in the behavior therapy chapter, but in recent years they have been integrated with cognitive restructuring to create a powerful CBT intervention for managing anxiety, referred to as exposure-based CBT. Exposure-based CBT can help to reduce stress and anxiety in people who have problems with hoarding, which involves having a difficult time parting with objects or throwing things away, even when failure to do so results in clutter to such an extent that it ultimately results in the inability to use a room for its intended purpose. For example, the kitchen becomes so cluttered the homeowner cannot cook in it anymore; or boxes and papers are piled so high in the bedroom that the door cannot be opened. Strong negative emotions (feelings of loss, grief, or depression) occur when people who have this disorder think about giving away their possessions. Conversely, positive emotions are likely to result when acquiring and saving items. As a result, people begin a cycle of behavior in which cleaning or sorting clutter makes them feel bad, so they avoid those negative feelings that accompany their thoughts, and instead seek to shop or acquire more to make themselves feel better.

Recent research indicates that excessive acquisition and difficulty discarding items to the extent that results in hoarding may stem from information-processing deficits, problematic beliefs and behaviors, and emotional distress and avoidance (Steketee, Frost, Tolin, Rasmussen, & Brown, 2010). Counseling, therefore, must address the faulty cognitions. A combined CBT approach that uses habituation (exposure to the avoided situation to reduce anxiety), direct exposure to sorting, and cognitive strategies to challenge errors in thinking and beliefs that contribute to hoarding behavior has been recommended (Steketee et al., 2010).

Relaxation and fear are incompatible responses. As a result, fear of a stimulus typically diminishes if relaxation can be achieved and maintained during exposure to that stimulus. However, this counseling approach can have a reverse effect if not well planned; premature, or too intense, exposure (in this case to overwhelming and uncomfortable feelings of letting go of objects) can result in the client quitting counseling or refusing to participate. Consequently, careful pacing is essential to successful counseling using exposure-based therapies.

The therapist can work with clients on location, or in the counseling session with the use of guided imagery, to help them re-create the distressful feelings that occur when they attempt to dispose of objects. Clients are asked to describe and rate their feelings or thoughts on a hierarchy of discomfort every 5 to 10 minutes as they imagine removing their objects. A simple 0 to 10 scale can be used to rate global feelings of anxiety or discomfort.

After developing the therapeutic alliance, exploring the antecedents and symptoms of the fear, and discussing the individual's history and present life situation so that the symptoms can be viewed in context, exposure-based therapy can then be used, which typically follows a series of steps. These steps are illustrated with the case of Jennifer, a 48-year-old woman who could not part with things and as a result has developed a hoarding problem that prevents her from inviting people over to her house because of the shame and embarrassment she feels. It is also beginning to cause tension at home with her husband.

1. *Teach an effective relaxation strategy.* Jennifer was taught to relax by shifting her breathing to a pattern of slow diaphragmatic breaths while focusing on her breathing. She also was taught to relax her body using progressive muscle relaxation, by gradually moving her attention down from her head to her toes until her entire body felt relaxed.
2. *Help the client identify cognitive distortions that reinforce the hoarding behaviors.* Cognitive restructuring is an important element of counseling for hoarding. Following several sessions with Jennifer, her therapist was able to identify the following distortions underpinning Jennifer's hoarding behavior:
    - *All-or-nothing thinking:* "If I give the blender away, even though I haven't used it in years, I won't be able to make margaritas" (even though Jennifer never invites anyone to her house).
    - *Moral reasoning:* This type of reasoning is seen in "should" statements: "I should be able to clean up this room. What is wrong with me?"
    - *Emotional reasoning:* "I can't give away that vase. It was a wedding present from my Aunt Jayne."
    - *Discounting the positive:* "Even if I clean off the bed so I can sleep in it, the rest of the room is still a mess."

    Thoughts that lead to hoarding behavior are different for everyone (Steketee et al., 2010). What is difficult for some people may be easy for others. When working with people who cannot get rid of clutter, some of the most difficult feelings relate to perfectionism ("I can't do it perfectly, so why even bother?"), money ("It might be valuable some day"), or personal identity ("My vase is a part of who I am").

The next step in cognitive restructuring is for the therapist to help Jennifer create a list of statements to refute her beliefs, such as:

- "I'm giving away the clothes that don't fit. If I lose weight, I'll treat myself and buy some new ones!"
- "I can do this. I will feel the anxiety and do it anyway."

3. *Establish an anxiety hierarchy.* Jennifer was asked to create a list of anxiety-provoking stimuli ranked according to the amount of anxiety or fear each elicits. She was requested to rate her anxiety on a scale of 1 to 10, with 10 being the strongest negative emotion. Jennifer decided that a 10 rating would be the overwhelming process of cleaning out the storage unit she rents, which initiates panic whenever she thinks about it. Jennifer gave a rating of 5 to going through her clothes closet and donating items to charity. A much easier task, rated a 1 on Jennifer's hierarchy scale, is sorting through the mail that had piled up and throwing out unnecessary items.

4. *Provide controlled exposure.* Jennifer's therapist used in vivo desensitization and went on location to Jennifer's house for the first few sessions to help her confront her avoidance. The more people avoid something associated with negative feelings, the more the feelings are reinforced. Multiple types of avoidance responses have been identified in association with hoarding behavior—for example, not having people over to the house because of the clutter, or starting to sort through a box of clutter, feeling anxious, then becoming overwhelmed and quitting. Strong negative feelings trigger the urge to avoid the feelings, and set the stage for the development of anxiety problems.

After helping Jennifer relax as fully as possible, the therapist asked Jennifer to complete the least stressful task on her list—sort through the box of mail that had accumulated. Jennifer went through the mail without too much anxiety until she came upon some birthday cards from friends that she could not bring herself to throw away. The therapist encouraged Jennifer to hold the cards and think about the people who had sent them. After a few minutes, Jennifer relaxed and smiled. She was able to think of the people without needing to hold on to the cards. The therapist suggested Jennifer take a picture of her cards with her iPhone so she could look at them again whenever she wanted to. But Jennifer decided she was still having problems throwing the cards away.

Using Socratic questioning to ask deeper levels of questions can help the therapist get clients to see the absurdity of their thinking (Steketee et al., 2010). If Jennifer had wanted to keep the birthday cards, the therapist might have asked:

THERAPIST: "Talk about their importance to you?"

JENNIFER: "They were the only birthday cards I got this year."

THERAPIST: "What does that signify to you?"

JENNIFER: "These are my friends. They are the only people who love me."

THERAPIST: "What would happen if you threw the cards away?"

JENNIFER: "Well, they would still love me!"

After this discussion, she could let them go. During the next session at Jennifer's house, the therapist helped her create a three-pile sorting system in which she would sort items for trash or donation, items she wanted to keep, and those she would box up and decide what to do with later. Helping clients to develop a list of guidelines beforehand helps the process run more smoothly and confronts avoidance. Jennifer decided to endorse the following: "I will donate clothing that isn't flattering" and "I will give away any books that I have two copies of."

Jennifer began to categorize, sort, remove, and repeat. Her discomfort was then rated every 5 to 10 minutes, so the therapist could control the level of exposure to ensure Jennifer would not become overwhelmed and quit. Habituation helped Jennifer recognize the anxious feelings, but continue sorting and cleaning anyway, recognizing that although her anxiety and emotional thinking made her uncomfortable, those feelings would not hurt her.

After Jennifer had successfully decluttered an area, the therapist helped her to create a new set of rules related to acquisition, so that the problem would not occur again. Acquisition rules might include "I won't buy any more books unless I pay cash" or "Even if it's on sale, I won't buy anything that won't be used in the next 30 days."

Continuing the desensitization between sessions, with the help of a friend or a family member who has been coached by the therapist, is one option that can also accelerate progress, as long as the person is never exposed to more than she had successfully handled in her counseling sessions. In Jennifer's case, after multiple sessions on location, she was able to continue the process in the therapist's office. She took a picture of the closet she needed to clean and brought it in to the session. After five more sessions, she brought in another picture that showed the progress she had made.

Although Jennifer was able to deal with some of the items on her list, she continues to have intense feelings of being overwhelmed whenever she thinks about the storage unit. However, she has made much progress inside her house, enough so that she was able to celebrate her success by inviting friends over for dinner.

The exposure and desensitization process must be carefully planned so that it does not raise anxiety but instead promotes feelings of self-confidence, optimism, and control. Eventually, Jennifer learned to tolerate some discomfort and develop new skills for discarding items and experiencing the anxiety as it arises. As we have seen, combining cognitive methods with behavioral exposure is more effective than either technique alone for reducing hoarding behavior (Steketee et al., 2010).

CASE APPLICATION

In this case illustration, the therapist uses the *A-B-C–D-E-F* model with Ava, who expresses upsetting feelings about an interaction she recently had with her parents.

THERAPIST: Ava, tell me about the situation or activating event [A] that upset you.

AVA: This awful thing happened to me at school. I was in gym class, and I was in such a hurry to get dressed and catch the bus that I forgot to zip up my skirt. I went out in the hall like that! Some kids were looking at me, but I did not know what was wrong. One boy started whispering and the kids were staring at me and then I got it. I was so embarrassed. All I wanted to do was go home and tell my mother. But when I got home, she was on the phone with my grandmother and couldn't be bothered with me. "I'm busy now," she said. "Go out and play with your friends." That was the last thing I wanted to do. So I took the dog and went up to my room. I wanted to die so that I wouldn't ever have to go back to school.

THERAPIST: Tell me some more about the feelings [emotional consequences/C] you had when all this happened.

AVA: Well, I told you I felt embarrassed, like I was the big joke of the school. I bet all the kids will be talking about me tomorrow. It was so awful! And then when I got home, even my mother didn't care. I felt horrible, like nobody loved me, like I was just a hot mess.

THERAPIST: You had some strong negative emotions, feeling embarrassed and rejected and unlovable, that were really disturbing you. Ava, remember we talked about irrational beliefs last week. Let's take out that list I showed you of common irrational beliefs [B] and figure out if any of them reflect the thoughts you had in reaction to this incident.

AVA: I certainly had this thought: "I am a bad or worthless person when I act weakly or stupidly." And then when my mom was too busy to talk to me, I thought this one: "I need to be loved by someone who matters to me a lot," and this one: "I am a bad, unlovable person if I get rejected." I thought this one too: "It's awful or horrible when major things don't go my way." I also thought, "My mom doesn't really love or care about me."

THERAPIST: Many of the thoughts on the list really hit home for you. It seems like you had two groups of thoughts: one about not being loved by your mother and another about feeling worthless and devastated when the kids teased you.

AVA: Yes, that's right.

THERAPIST: Let's start with the first group, thoughts about your mom not loving you and your feeling unlovable. Have there been other times when you needed to talk to your mom and she *was* there for you?

AVA: Yes, I guess most of the time.

THERAPIST: Then just because your mom was in a phone conversation and couldn't talk to you this one time, does it logically follow that she doesn't love you [logical dispute]?

AVA: She should have known I really needed to talk to her!

THERAPIST: Talk about how she should have known that [empirical dispute]?

AVA: I don't know. I guess I didn't really tell her that.

THERAPIST: Then does it logically follow that if she didn't want to talk to you at that time, that she doesn't love you?

AVA: No, I know she loves me. I was just disappointed that she wasn't there for me. It made me *feel* like she didn't love me.

THERAPIST: Does the thought that she doesn't love you help you or hurt you [functional dispute]?

AVA: Well, it's making me feel pretty bad, and it kept me from talking to her when she finally got off the phone, so I guess it's hurting me.

THERAPIST: Could there be other explanations for her not wanting to talk to you at that time [rational alternative]?

AVA: Yes, she was on the phone with her mother. It sounded like Grandma's husband had wrecked her car. I guess my mom needed to help her.

THERAPIST: So can you tell me a thought that seems to be a more accurate reflection of your interaction with your mother?

AVA: Yes. My mom loves me, but I can't expect her to read my mind or be there for me every minute. She does her best to help me when I'm upset, but Grandma

	needed her then [effective rational belief].
THERAPIST:	And how are you feeling now?
AVA:	I still feel disappointed that my mom was on the phone when I needed to talk to her. I felt so hurt that I never did tell her what happened.
THERAPIST:	What can you do about that now?
AVA:	I guess I could go home and tell her about it. I think that would help me to feel better [new feelings and behaviors].

This process helped Ava alter her beliefs about the activating events, resulting in changes in her feelings and behaviors. Her level of disturbance and the absolute nature of her thoughts both have changed, and she is no longer devastated by her interaction with her mother. This allows her to take constructive action to communicate her concerns to her mother.

REFLECT AND RESPOND

1. Select a recent experience that elicited strong emotions for you. Identify at least two thoughts, three emotions, and one action that accompanied the experience. Try to identify at least one cognitive distortion that you had in relation to the experience. Write down the distortion in your journal. Then, in writing, go through the steps of rating, assessing, classifying, disputing, replacing, and re-rating your cognition(s). What new emotions and actions now seem available to you?
2. We all have thoughts, emotions, and actions. Observe yourself as you go through the day. Which of these categories is most accessible to you? Are you most likely to discuss thoughts, feelings, or actions with other people? Which of the three is most likely to worry you and stay with you? Write your answers in your journal. Give examples of the category you chose. For example, if emotions are most accessible to you, what kind of emotions did you have? What themes did you notice?
3. Write briefly in your journal about a time during the past week when you felt very upset or disturbed. Identify and dispute your irrational thoughts using the *A-B-C–D-E-F* format. Write your responses to each step in the process.

Summary

CBT, promoted by Albert Ellis, Aaron Beck, Donald Meichenbaum, and others, expanded the application of cognitive and behavioral strategies and created a powerful counseling approach. CBT has demonstrated strong effectiveness with a wide range of people and problems. Although practitioners of CBT focus on improving thoughts and behaviors, they also pay attention to the whole person; recognize the importance of history, background, and context; explore emotions; and take steps to develop a positive and collaborative therapeutic alliance.

REBT was the first prominent form of CBT. REBT, developed by Albert Ellis, takes the position that people disturb themselves by their irrational beliefs and that changing those beliefs to rational ones will reduce people's levels of disturbance and lead to positive changes in emotions and behaviors. Therefore, a focus on insight is not necessary; present thoughts are the main concern, and emotions and behaviors are secondary concerns. Self-acceptance is important in REBT because having a rational sense of one's strengths and weaknesses and taking pride in one's accomplishments will lead to a more stable self-worth. REBT also emphasizes problem solving.

Therapists using REBT make use of a broad range of strategies to effect rapid change. Sessions typically focus on a process to modify cognitions by using the *A-B-C–D-E-F* model: identifying the activating event (*A*), identifying irrational beliefs (*B*), looking at the negative consequences of those beliefs (*C*), disputing the beliefs (*D*), and replacing them with effective rational beliefs (*E*) that lead to changes in feelings and behaviors (*F*). Other intervention strategies such as Socratic questioning, behavioral strategies such as shame-attacking exercises, and emotive strategies such as rational emotive imagery are used.

Cognitive therapy, developed by Aaron Beck and his associates, is another form of CBT. Cognitive therapy is a relatively brief, structured approach that offers specific plans for change, gives people clear explanations of all steps in the counseling process, and teaches skills that empower people and promote their emotional well-being. Cognitive therapy typically focuses on the present, and careful assessment, diagnosis, and treatment planning are essential.

Cognitions consist of four main levels: automatic thoughts, intermediate beliefs, core beliefs, and schemas. Although cognitive therapists focus primarily on thoughts, they take a holistic view of people and believe that learning about and understanding their feelings and behaviors are also important. Particularly important—and related to positive outcome—is comprehending the emotional responses people have to their faulty cognitions and the impact of those cognitions on mood.

Therapists draw on an extensive array of creative interventions to promote and reinforce positive change. For example, therapists challenge absolutes; reattribute blame; and help clients elicit, rate, and determine the validity of their cognitions. Therapists also educate their clients about common cognitive distortions, such as all-or-nothing thinking, jumping to conclusions, and personalization, which helps clients label their cognitions. Task assignments and inventories are also used and contribute to the clarity and impact of cognitive therapy.

The main goal of CBT is to teach people how to recognize, identify, and modify dysfunctional thoughts, which will in turn lead to healthier feelings and behavior. Therapists and clients together determine specific goals to best fit the needs of individual clients. The therapeutic relationship is essential to positive outcomes, and therapists aim to be active, directive, warm, and nonjudgmental. Clients and therapists work collaboratively through a process called guided discovery. Therapists use Socratic questioning to help clients provide evidence for and against their dysfunctional thoughts and then modify their thoughts when necessary.

CBT has demonstrated effectiveness when working with a wide variety of populations. It is especially effective in treating depression and anxiety. REBT can also be appropriate for a range of presenting concerns, such as depression, anxiety, and low self-esteem, and for many types of populations, such as children, adolescents, adults, and older adults. In addition, REBT can be used in groups, family therapy, and couples therapy. CBT has been criticized for paying too little attention to clients' pasts and moving too rapidly toward change. However, CBT is easily integrated with other approaches, teaches clients how to help themselves outside of therapy, and can lead to a rapid reduction in symptoms.

Recommended Readings

Beck, A. T., Davis, D. D., & Freeman, A. (2015). *Cognitive therapy of personality disorders* (3rd ed.). New York, NY: Guilford.

Beck, J. S. (2005). *Cognitive therapy for challenging problems: What to do when the basics don't work.* New York, NY: Guilford.

Beck, J. S. (2011). *Cognitive behavior therapy: Basics and beyond* (2nd ed.). New York, NY: Guilford.

Clark, D. A., & Beck, A. T. (2010). *Cognitive therapy of anxiety disorders.* New York, NY: Guilford.

Cohen, J. A., Mannarino, A. P., & Deblinger, E. (2012). *Trauma-focused CBT for children and adolescents: Treatment applications.* New York, NY: Guilford.

Ellis, A. (2001). *Overcoming destructive beliefs, feelings, and behaviors: New directions for rational emotive behavior therapy.* Amherst, NY: Prometheus Books.

Ellis, A., & Dryden, W. (2007). *The practice of rational emotive behavior therapy* (2nd ed.). New York, NY: Springer.

Ellis, A., & MacLaren, C. (2005). *Rational emotive behavior therapy: A therapist's guide* (2nd ed.). Atascadero, CA: Impact Publishers.

Hofmann, S. G. (2012). *An introduction to modern CBT: Psychological solutions to mental health problems.* New York, NY: Wiley.

Meichenbaum, D. H. (2007). Stress inoculation training: A preventative and treatment approach. In P. M. Lehrer, R. L. Woolfolk, & W. E. Sime (Eds.), *Principles and practice of stress management* (3rd ed., pp. 497–516). New York, NY: Guilford.

MyLab Counseling

Start with the Topic 2 Assignments: Cognitive Therapy.

Then, in the Topic 3 Assignments: Cognitive-Behavioral Therapy, try :

- Application Exercise 3.1(a), Application Exercise 3.1(b), and Licensure Quiz 3.1
- Application Exercise 3.3 and Licensure Quiz 3.3
- Application Exercise 3.4 and Licensure Quiz 3.4
- Application Exercise 3.5 and Licensure Quiz 3.5

Finish with the Topic 18 Assignments: REBT.

CHAPTER 7

Reality Therapy

Learning Outcomes

When you have finished this chapter, you should be able to:
- Understand the context and development of Reality Therapy.
- Communicate the key concepts associated with Reality Therapy and understand how they relate to therapeutic processes.
- Describe the therapeutic goals of Reality Therapy.
- Identify the common techniques used in Reality Therapy.
- Understand how Reality Therapy relates to counseling diverse populations.
- Identify the limitations and strengths of Reality Therapy.

WILLIAM GLASSER (1925–2013)

William Glasser was born in 1925 and grew up in Ohio. His early years were difficult. Glasser (1998a) reported that his father was occasionally violent and that his mother was controlling. Even as a child, he recognized the challenges evident in his family. This history is telling in light of Glasser's later emphasis on personal responsibility, not harming others, and the importance of the marital or partner relationship.

Glasser became a chemical engineer but later changed his career goals and entered medical school. He received his medical degree from Case Western Reserve University in 1953 and then became a psychiatrist.

Between 1956 and 1967, Glasser was a psychiatrist for the Ventura School for Girls, a prison school operated by the California Youth Authority, housing 400 adolescents. This experience had a profound impact on Glasser's views of mental health and psychotherapy. He concluded that traditional psychoanalysis offered little to help the young women at the Ventura School, and thus he began to develop what would later become reality therapy.

Glasser concluded that many difficulties the adolescents experienced at the Ventura School stemmed from their failure to take responsibility for themselves and their lives and to act in ways that truly met their needs. Although they might have believed they were seeking to meet their needs, the result—their involuntary stay at the Ventura School—was not their desired outcome. By guiding the girls to think more clearly about their present needs, holding them responsible for their behavior, and playing an active and involved role in therapy, Glasser perceived he was better able to help them. It was suggested that implementation of his ideas for change resulted in an 80% success rate for the adolescents at the school.

Glasser began to present on "reality psychiatry," but few psychiatrists took an interest in his approach. Instead, educators, counselors, social workers, and corrections workers came to hear his ideas, thus prompting him to change the name of his system to reality therapy.

Reality therapy holds that we are all responsible for our choices. We are internally motivated by universal needs and wants, and we can control our behaviors and choices.

Glasser's first book, *Mental Health or Mental Illness?* (1961), laid the groundwork for reality therapy. His book *Reality Therapy* (1975) spelled out the principles that continue to be fundamental to this approach: that people who take **responsibility** for themselves and their behaviors and are aware of and able to meet their basic needs without harming others are likely to lead happy and fulfilling lives. In 1968 he wrote the book *Schools Without Failure*, which had a significant impact on the ways school administrators and teachers approached children and learning. In his book he advocated that schools help children achieve a *success identity* as opposed to a *failure identity*. Glasser's work emphasizes the importance of relationships as well as personal responsibility. He believed that a warm, accepting therapeutic relationship is essential to the success of counseling, just as he believed that close and positive relationships are essential to mental health and happiness.

Relationships were important in Glasser's own life. His first wife, Naomi Glasser, contributed to the development of reality therapy. That marriage ended after 46 years, with his wife's death from cancer. Glasser said he married his present wife, Carleen, after they checked their needs to ensure they were compatible. Together they wrote several books on relationships (1999, 2001, 2007). Glasser's three children also played a significant role in his life.

Over his career, Glasser developed and expanded the scope of reality therapy. Focusing his writings and lectures on the application of reality therapy in counseling as well as its use in school and business settings, he has succeeded in establishing its importance. Glasser continued to play an active role in the development of reality therapy until his death in 2013.

ROBERT WUBBOLDING (b. 1936)

Robert Wubbolding was born and raised in Cincinnati, Ohio. Wubbolding has played an important role in developing and promoting reality therapy and has lectured and taught reality therapy on five continents. He has written more than 17 books and more than 150 articles, essays, and chapters in textbooks, and prepared more than 20 recordings of his work and the application of reality therapy.

Wubbolding serves as the director of the Center for Reality Therapy in Cincinnati, Ohio; he was a faculty associate at John Hopkins University; was the training director at the William Glasser Institute (1988–2011); and is a professor emeritus of counseling at Xavier University in Cincinnati.

Wubbolding extended the theory and practice of reality therapy with his work involving the **WDEP system**. His writings facilitate implementation of reality therapy through case studies, exercises, and treatment protocols. He has also played an important role in adapting choice theory and reality therapy to various cultural and ethnic groups.

INTRODUCTION/DEVELOPMENT OF REALITY THERAPY

Reality therapy, initially developed by William Glasser (1986, 1975, 2001) in the 1960s, is solidly grounded in cognitive and behavior therapy principles. **Reality therapy** is a didactic, collaborative, and action-oriented therapeutic modality. It is based on **choice theory** and aims to assist clients with changing their maladaptive behaviors so they can more effectively meet their individual needs, and experience more satisfying relationships. To use a metaphor, choice theory is the train track that provides direction, and reality therapy is the train which delivers the product. Like other cognitive behavioral approaches, reality therapy focuses on the present and helps people change their thoughts and actions so they can lead more rewarding lives.

Reality therapy, however, is more philosophical than other cognitive behavioral approaches and emphasizes self-determination. This approach encourages people to take responsibility for both their difficulties and their joys. Reality therapists do not allow clients to make excuses when they are not successful; instead, these therapists work with clients to overcome barriers and reach their goals. While acknowledging that environment, heredity, and culture play a role in development, reality therapy holds that people always have at least some ability to make choices in their behavior. People do not need to be a victim or feel trapped by circumstance (Wubbolding, 2011)—"We choose *everything* we do, including the misery we feel" (Glasser, 1998a, p. 3). Wubbolding has tempered this absolute statement and expresses it as choosing much of what we do (personal communication). Helping people make choices that increase their happiness and meet their needs without harming others is the essence of reality therapy. Drawing heavily on cognitive and behavioral strategies, reality therapists guide people through a process of change that helps them become aware of their needs, recognize the ingredients of a rewarding life, and establish goals and procedures to improve their lives. Through this process, people gain more control over their lives and assume responsible and rewarding roles in society.

The central foci of reality therapy are choice and behavior: What are clients doing, and is what they are doing getting them what they want? Are their behaviors working to meet their needs, and are these behaviors helping them in ways that matter to them? How can clients choose to behave in ways that best help them satisfy their wants? Reality therapy emphasizes the importance of the following: counselors and clients being present focused; a strong therapeutic alliance; a concentration on satisfying clients' basic needs through the use of adaptive behavioral choices; personal responsibility for choices; and **self-evaluation** (Wubbolding, 2000, 2011).

Reality therapy has been used in many settings. Schools and substance abuse treatment programs are particularly well suited to this approach. According to Glasser, almost everyone, regardless of the presenting issue or background (1998a), can benefit from reality therapy.

Early writings identified eight steps for therapists to follow in using reality therapy (Evans, 1982): (1) Build rapport with clients; (2) ask "What are *you* doing?"; (3) collaborate with clients in evaluating their behavior; (4) help people make a plan to do better; (5) help clients commit to the plan; (6) do not accept excuses; (7) do not interfere with reasonable consequences; and (8) do not give up! Wubbolding, (2000, 2011, 2017) has updated and extended these principles with the WDEP formulation (wants, doing, self-evaluation, and planning), discussed later in this chapter.

With the publication of his book *Warning: Psychiatry Can Be Hazardous to Your Mental Health* (2003), Glasser raised concerns about the psychiatric profession's dependence on psychotropic drugs for the management of mental health. He developed a format for choice theory that uses groups to help people with conditions that are traditionally treated with medication (e.g., fibromyalgia, severe mental illness), and as a preventive measure for symptoms of mental disorders.

In the 1970s, Glasser discovered the writings of Powers (1973) and others on **control theory** or control system theory and used control theory as the theoretical basis for reality therapy. He conceptualized people as driven by inner control systems that guide behaviors and emotions and are instrumental in moving people in directions that seem likely to fulfill their needs (Glasser, 1984). Unfortunately, people's control systems sometimes cause difficulties by misdirecting their efforts and leading them to try to control others.

For Glasser, awareness and assessment are the keys to modifying our control systems and improving our lives. He believed that the first step in improving our lives is to be cognizant of the pictures in our heads that reflect our needs and wants. We then can become aware of what we are doing to reach our goals. By assessing the impact and success of our behaviors, we can determine whether change is warranted and, if so, use creative strategies to modify our thoughts, emotions, and behaviors. Although Glasser (1984) recognized that immediate, intense, short-term feelings can emerge spontaneously at times of frustration or satisfaction, he was convinced that we can ultimately choose and control our long-term feelings.

For many years, this approach was known as reality therapy or control theory. However, in 1996, Glasser determined that underlying reality therapy was personal choice, and he moved away from using the term control theory, and instead used *choice theory*. Choice theory postulates that people's choices of thoughts, feelings, and actions largely determine the quality of their lives. Choice theory, underpinning reality therapy, is important in helping people improve their lives, and is the current theory base that informs reality therapy (Glasser, 1998a).

KEY CONCEPTS

Reality therapy has evolved considerably over the years and has expanded its applications. At present, it is a well-developed counseling approach used successfully in a broad range of settings.

According to Glasser (1998a), problems originate during early childhood when we encounter people who believe they know what is right for us. Because of our youth, inexperience, and self-doubt, we accept this external control and come to believe that others make us feel or act as we do. However, Glasser believed that this sense that others control us and how we feel harms everyone, both the controllers and the controlled.

Instead, according to reality therapy, the way to rear emotionally healthy children is to surround them with loving and supportive people who enable them to experience freedom, power, and fun in responsible ways. Children's self-efficacy as well as their ability to identify and meet their needs in positive ways should be fostered, instilling attitudes and behaviors that will serve them well as they mature.

Despite this emphasis on childhood development, reality therapy views people as basically self-determining and able to overcome their early difficulties. Glasser suggested that people do not have to choose to be victims of what happened to them in the past. However, if people have not learned to satisfy their needs during the early years, they may require help in developing new ways of feeling, thinking, and behaving, thus taking control of their reactions and emotional experiences.

Reality therapists pay attention to the past, only in their emphasis that past issues are expressed in present unsatisfying relationships and behaviors. Counseling is most likely to succeed by focusing on those present manifestations. Wubbolding (1991, 2017) suggested that childhood conflicts, unconscious motivations, and external pressures do not cause present behavior. Instead, a motivation to fulfill internal needs directs our choices and behavior.

The Five Basic Human Needs

Human **needs** are at the core of human existence and dictate all choices made (Wubbolding & Brickell, 2008). Reality therapy holds that all people are born with the following five basic needs that are fixed at birth (Glasser, 1998a). The relative strengths of these five needs determines people's unique personalities (Wubbolding, 1991):

1. *Belonging:* Loving and being loved; having contact, connections, interactions, and relationships with people
2. *Power/achievement:* Feelings of accomplishment and competence, self-esteem, success, and control over one's own life; power described by Wubbolding (2017) as inner control
3. *Fun/enjoyment:* Pleasure; the ability to laugh, play, and appreciate being human
4. *Freedom/independence:* The ability to make choices; to live without excessive and unnecessary limits or constraints
5. *Survival/self-preservation:* The essentials of life, including good health, food, air, shelter, safety, security, and physical comfort.

Because these needs overlap, fulfillment of one need may increase fulfillment of others. For example, people with positive relationships probably have greater enjoyment of life. However, these needs can also cause people to feel conflicted. For example, people who channel too much effort into achieving power or independence may have difficulty forming rewarding relationships.

Although all five basic needs are presumed to be universal, the degree of satisfaction and intensity of each need varies by the moment and depends on our unique life circumstances and perceptions of reality. Glasser (1998a, 2001, 2005) believed that our need for belonging and love, both given and received, is the most essential of all the basic needs; however, because this need requires the cooperation of others, and because our needs can often conflict with those of others, it is also the most difficult one to satisfy.

Reality therapy takes the position that all human behavior is purposeful and directed at meeting one or more of the fundamental needs (Wubbolding, 2011). Although the five needs are universal, the specific wants that people pursue in an effort to meet their needs are unique to the individual. For example, having a family may be a want that satisfies one individual's need for belonging, whereas another individual may satisfy that need with an involvement in team sports. People are motivated to bridge the gaps between what they have and what they want to meet their needs. However, feelings such as loneliness and deprivation can limit people's motivation. Reality therapists seek to change those feelings, not by directly addressing emotions, but by changing thoughts about wants and needs, especially as related to enhancing purposeful behaviors.

When peoples' basic needs are unfulfilled, they experience unhappiness, pain, or loneliness (Wubbolding, 2000). In an effort to mitigate such distress, individuals choose behaviors that are sometimes maladaptive to satisfy their unmet needs. All behavior, even maladaptive behavior, is considered a reflection of individuals' current degree of knowledge and ability to best fulfill their needs.

Concept of Mental Illness and Mental Health

Although trained as a physician and psychiatrist, Glasser did not ascribe to the disease model of mental illness. He accepted that people have symptoms, but he did not believe there is anything wrong with people's brains that cannot be altered through supportive relationships and behavioral changes. Glasser believed that choice theory is superior to medication, even in the treatment of severe mental disorders.

Wubbolding (2018) states, though, that the use of medication, as prescribed by a medical professional, for some clients is standard practice regardless of the personal and private opinions of the counselor.

Mental illness, according to reality therapy, is actually people's failure to meet their five needs in responsible and effective ways—overemphasizing some needs while neglecting others. According to Glasser (1998a), people engaged in antisocial behavior, for example, generally focus on their needs for power and freedom and do not satisfactorily address their needs for love and enjoyment. Glasser believed that even people with psychotic disorders and depression choose their symptoms. Symptoms are chosen because people have little control over the real world and thus decide to use "crazy creativity" (Glasser, 1984) in the form of hallucinations and delusions over which they do have control. Conventional diagnostic terminology is often necessary in the practice of counseling, but not central to the process and use of reality therapy principles; instead, mental illness is conceptualized as problems in choices, need satisfaction, and responsibility. Common symptoms of emotional difficulties include loneliness (rather than belonging); loss of inner control (rather than empowerment); boredom and depression (rather than fun); frustration, inhibition, or rebelliousness (rather than freedom); and illness or deprivation (rather than safety and security). Glasser (2003) suggested that severe unhappiness could lead to the development of bipolar disorder, schizophrenia, and chronic, unexplained pain. Instead of treating these disorders exclusively with medication, Glasser believed that using reality therapy to help people choose to connect with others in their quality world could relieve their symptoms and help people overcome their unhappiness (Glasser, 2003).

Reality therapy has a clear vision of emotionally healthy people: Those who achieve success in meeting their five basic needs are emotionally healthy. Such people choose thoughts, feelings, and behaviors wisely and responsibly. Their choices help them meet their needs while respecting the rights of other people to fulfill their own needs. Reality therapists do not view setbacks and suffering as inevitable parts of life, but rather as early warning signs that people need to look at their behavior and relationships and make better choices. Furthermore, emotionally healthy people not only seek to improve their own lives, but also take steps to help others and make the world a better place (Wubbolding, 1991). Such people have a success identity rather than a failure identity. They have a clear and positive sense of themselves that reflects their own internal frames of reference; they do not derive their sense of themselves from the perceptions of others.

Total Behavior and Motivation

As Glasser (1985, 1998a) observed, all people can do at birth is behave. All aspects of functioning are linked to behavior. Glasser called people's overall functioning **total behavior**, which is composed of four inseparable components:

- *Acting*
- *Thinking*
- *Feeling*
- *Physiology.*

Reality therapists believe that most behavior is chosen, that an individual can directly control the acting and thinking components and thereby gain indirect control over feelings and physiology. Glasser compared the four elements in total behavior to the four wheels of a car, with acting and thinking represented by the front wheels. When the car moves, all four wheels move. The direction of the car cannot be changed by the movement of only one wheel. Neither can an individual's actions be separated from the other components of thinking, emotion, and physiology. When an individual swings a golf club, the action cannot be separated from the total behavior. Similarly, when an individual chooses to depress, the entire being is involved.

As in Adlerian therapy, reality therapists believe all behavior is intentional and has a purpose. To continue the car metaphor, change may occur in overall direction, in specific actions (the two front wheels), or by altering the individual's wants (Wubbolding, 2011, 2017). Regardless of the specific concern, reality therapy believes in changing actions first; changes in thoughts or self-talk will follow. Eventually, changes in feelings and physiology will happen as well, just as the back wheels of the car must follow the direction of the front wheels. Of course, the individual must drive the vehicle with intentionality; otherwise, erratic driving (behavior) will result.

When people want to change behavior, it is best to start with the most easily altered component—actions. People have more direct control over actions and thinking than over emotions and physiology. As in the car analogy, the front wheels move first, and steer where the vehicle goes, while the rear wheels follow. By changing the action or behavior, the total behavior is changed. As in other cognitive therapies, feelings and emotions are secondary. Feelings are considered but are seen as analogous to the lights on the dashboard of the car. In other words, people's emotions provide clues that they are heading in either a healthy or an unhealthy life direction (Wubbolding & Brickell, 2008). This emphasis on thoughts and behaviors is what makes reality therapy a cognitive behavioral counseling approach. Figure 7.1 provides a visual depiction of the total behavior car metaphor.

Quality Worlds

Choice theory suggests that we do not satisfy our needs directly (Wubbolding, 2000). Rather, beginning at birth, our brains begin to store information about what feels or is perceived to be good for us, thus developing what Glasser referred to as our **quality world.** Unlike the five basic needs universal to all humans, the quality world is unique to each of us and contains a **picture album** of personal wants, or subjective perceptions of our ideal reality (Glasser, 2001). The quality world picture album is an accumulation of specific mental images of people, events, life circumstances, and possessions that represent our very own personal utopia, or most preferred life experience. These pictures guide our efforts to satisfy needs and are linked to the success reached in meeting those needs. For example,

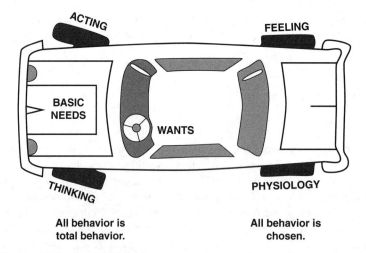

FIGURE 7.1 The Total Behavior Car Metaphor.

if a woman with good work skills puts a promotion into her quality world, representing a way for her to meet her need for achievement, she has made responsible picture choices, and her related behaviors will probably be successful. However, if her way to satisfy her need for love is represented in her quality world by a picture of her best friend's husband, she is not making responsible choices and is unlikely to meet her needs.

Reality therapists believe that people can choose the pictures they put in their quality worlds. If they choose pictures that are unattainable or unlikely to satisfy their needs, they probably will experience frustration and disappointment. By gaining awareness of their needs, as well as the pictures in their quality world, people can make better, wiser, and more realistic choices, have greater control over their lives, and fulfill their needs.

Wants are associated with the five basic needs and serve as inner forces that motivate behavior. Counselors and other helping professionals can engage in collaborative exploration processes with clients; these processes aim to identify the behavioral choices clients make in an effort to fulfill their basic needs and achieve the wants of their quality world (Wubbolding, 2000, 2011, 2017).

Axioms of Choice Theory

Glasser (1998) set forth 10 essential axioms, or principles, that serve as a foundation for choice theory. The following 10 axioms provide an overview of choice theory's conceptualization of human nature and inform the practice of reality therapy:

> **The 10 Axioms of Choice Theory:**
> 1. The only person whose behavior we can control is our own.
> 2. The best a counselor or another person can do is to give information to a client.
> 3. All long-lasting psychological disturbances are rooted in relationship problems.
> 4. People's problematic relationships are always part of their present life.
> 5. Although the past may affect who we are today, we can only satisfy our basic needs in the present and plan to continue satisfying them in the future.
> 6. We can only satisfy our needs by satisfying the pictures in our quality world.
> 7. All we do can best be described as behaving.
> 8. All behavior is total behavior and is made up of four components: acting, thinking, feeling, and physiology.
> 9. All total behavior is chosen, but we only have direct control over the acting and thinking components. We control our feelings and physiology indirectly through how we choose to act and think.
> 10. All total behavior is named by verbs and named by the most recognizable part.

WDEP System

The procedures involved in reality therapy are represented by the acronym WDEP, which includes four main elements: **W**ants, **D**irection and **D**oing, **E**valuation, and **P**lanning (Wubbolding, 1995, 2011, 2017). These can be applied in whatever order seems most helpful.

W: WANTS Reality therapists explore clients' wants and the pictures in their quality world, focusing on what they want that they *are* getting, what they want that they *are not* getting, and what they are getting that they *do not want* (Wubbolding, 2011, 2017). Keeping in mind that wants are linked to needs, therapists also encourage clients to look at that connection by asking questions such as "How do you perceive your want to drop out of high school as meeting your needs?" Reality therapists help the client to recognize that some wants are better off being delayed. Helping people to realize that some wants are unrealistic or unreasonable, while others can be helpful to the establishment of interpersonal relationships, and the recovery process, is an important role of reality therapists (Wubbolding, 2011, 2017).

Reality therapy, a **phenomenological** approach, recognizes the role of perceptions in behavior. This therapy helps people become aware of their perceptions so that they can modify them if appropriate. According to Wubbolding (1991, 1995), perceptions pass through two filters. The lower-level filter, called the **total knowledge filter**, recognizes and labels perceptions; the upper-level filter, the **valuing filter**, evaluates perceptions. Reality therapists facilitate this evaluation by suggesting that people distinguish among positive or need-satisfying perceptions, negative perceptions, and neutral perceptions. For example, "That is an attractive piece of jewelry" is a neutral perception. "I deserve that diamond more than she does" is a negative perception that can lead to relationship difficulties, whereas "I share my friend's happiness about receiving a beautiful engagement ring" is a positive perception because it enhances feelings of love and belonging. Becoming aware of and evaluating their perceptions can help people meet their needs. Wubbolding (2000, 2017) has added a third filter and placed it between the total knowledge filter and the valuing filter. Through this **relationship filter**, humans perceive relationships or functions. For instance, perceiving an object and labeling it a chair and then labeling the chair as comfortable illustrates the first two filters (the total knowledge filter and the valuing filter). Logically, a middle level filter (the relationship filter) exists whereby we see a relationship between the object and its function. A chair is for sitting. It is not a table, a hammer, or a computer. A piece of jewelry is an object and is beautiful. But it is also something to be worn and enhances one's appearance.

An aspect of the *W* in WDEP is helping people choose to make positive changes. Wubbolding (2016, p. 303) identified five levels of client **commitment** to change:

1. I don't want to be here.
2. I want the outcome, but not the effort.
3. I'll try; I might.
4. I will do my best.
5. I will do whatever it takes.

If people begin counseling at the first or second level, an important goal of counseling is to help them see how they can benefit from changing their choices so that they can move on to higher levels of commitment.

D: DIRECTION AND DOING Reality therapists devote considerable attention to exploring people's total behavior, including actions, thoughts, emotions, and physiology. Helping people describe their total behavior as specifically as possible, as well as the goals and impact of those behaviors, is integral to counseling. Reality therapy centers on what people are doing, not on why they are acting in certain ways.

E: EVALUATION Therapists encourage clients to evaluate their goals, their actions, their perceptions, and the consequences of all these. Evaluation does not involve a judgment about the goodness or badness of these dimensions. Instead, evaluation is based on whether behaviors and perceptions are realistic and helpful to clients as well as to others. Therapists might facilitate the process by asking thought-provoking questions such as "How realistic is it to expect that your daughter will never misbehave?" and "What success have you had in using drugs to build relationships?"

Both the discussion of doing and the evaluation process focus primarily on the present and emphasize positive and successful aspects of people's lives. The past is discussed only in terms of its impact on the present. Helping clients conduct evaluations is the main focus of the WDEP process (Wubbolding, 2011).

P: PLANNING Reality therapists view planning as essential and encourage people to have long-range plans and goals that are subdivided into a series of short-term, realistic plans. "To fail to plan is to plan to fail" (Wubbolding, 1991, p. 95). Plans should evolve from self-evaluation and reflect desired changes in wants and total behavior. What follows are eight qualities of viable plans, represented by the acronym SAMI^{2}C^3 (Wubbolding, 2007b). Plans should be:

- *Simple*, clear, and understandable
- *Attainable*, able to be accomplished by the client
- *Measurable* via inventories, diaries, and other methods of recording progress
- *Immediate*, implementation can start right away
- *Involving* the therapist in appropriate ways, such as giving feedback, serving as a sounding board
- *Controlled* by the client rather than someone else
- In keeping with the client's *commitment* to change and recognition that this change is important
- Reflecting *consistent* and repeated changes in behavior.

Usually, planning focuses on modifying and improving actions because that is the aspect of total behavior over which people have the greatest control. However, centering on thoughts may provide a point of entry, enabling people to believe that choosing different actions will be beneficial. According to reality therapy, feelings do not need to be addressed directly, although they can be important sources of information on wants and perceptions; if actions change, emotions will correspondingly change.

Planning and choice go hand in hand. The primary goals of planning are to help people make better choices and take more control of their lives. According to Glasser (1998a), if people can make bad choices, they can also make better choices. This planning component of reality therapy fits with the written treatment plans often required by third-party insurance payers (Wubbolding, Casstevens, & Fulkerson, 2017).

Unlike some other approaches to cognitive and behavior therapy, reality therapy focuses more on process than outcome, more on the behaviors used to achieve desired results than on the actual achievement of the results. This perspective offers two advantages: It encourages people to develop behaviors they can generalize to other situations and reduces the risk that people will view themselves as failures if they make better choices in their behaviors but do not immediately obtain their desired outcomes. Table 7.1 provides an overview of the WDEP system.

TABLE 7.1 WDEP System

	Questions	Objectives
W	What do you want?	Explore **W**ants, needs, and perceptions
D	What are you doing?	**D**irection and **D**oing (total behavior)
E	Is what you are doing helping you?	Self-**E**valuation
P	What is your plan?	**P**lan to replace ineffective behaviors

THE THERAPEUTIC PROCESS

Therapeutic Goals

As a cognitive behavioral approach, reality therapy uses many of the same strategies that have been discussed in this section of this book. However, reality therapy also has its own set of goals, relationships, and strategies.

The fundamental goal of reality therapy is to enable people to have greater control over their lives by making better choices. Wise choices are perceived as those that meet the following three criteria:

1. They help people meet their innate needs and their specific wants, reflected by the pictures in their quality world.
2. The choices are responsible; they not only help the individuals making the choices but also respect the rights of other people and contribute to their efforts to make wise choices.
3. The choices are realistic and are likely to be attained through sound planning.

The following goals are also important:

- People form and sustain positive, mutually rewarding, respectful relationships.
- They develop a success identity rather than a failure identity.
- They have a consistent repertoire of healthy actions that enhances their total behavior by helping them think clearly, experience happiness and other positive emotions, and take steps to maintain their physical health.

Therapist's Function and Role

Reality therapists always function within the boundaries of professional ethics as expressed by professional organizations and state licensing boards. Clients and therapists form a collaborative team to help clients explore, evaluate, and revise their choices. Therapists do not assume responsibility for telling clients what choices to make or for evaluating clients' behaviors. However, they do take considerable responsibility for the direction and success of counseling. They promote motivation and commitment, provide support and encouragement, guide the WDEP process, teach planning and other skills, and use creativity, imagination, and humor to motivate clients and provide new perspectives.

Therapists help people formulate realistic and viable plans. As part of this process, they negotiate clear commitments and contracts with their clients. They avoid wasting time on excuses and strive to move forward rather than backward. Reality therapists are firm and determined to help people. They do not give up.

Language is important in this approach. Reality therapists consciously establish a positive environment free from criticism, fault finding, or blaming. Problems are referred to in the past tense and solutions in the present or future tense. Therapists ask about wants and needs and reduce the time clients spend "venting" or complaining. Feelings must be attached to actions (Wubbolding, 2011, 2017). Reality therapists make extensive use of the first-person pronouns *I* and *we* to emphasize the collaborative nature of the counseling process. They ask *what* rather than *why* questions.

Therapists use compassionate **confrontations**, when necessary, to highlight a discrepancy in the client's thoughts or actions. Confrontations are handled sensitively and nonjudgmentally, using questions that invite exploration and feedback. Enhanced client awareness is the ultimate goal of these compassionate confrontations (Bratter, Esparat, Kaufman, & Sinsheimer, 2008). Confrontations also represent the voice of society, reminding the client of the reality of moral, legal, and ethical standards. The Skill Development section provided later in this chapter addresses caring confrontations in more depth.

The ABCDEFG approach can guide reality therapists' interactions with clients, and should be used when applying confrontations (Wubbolding, 2016):

- **AB: Always Be...**
- **Courteous**
- **Determined**
- **Enthusiastic**
- **Firm**
- **Genuine.**

Reality therapy holds that the majority of long-term problems result from unsatisfying relationships. Thus, for counselors to effectively assist clients with changing their behaviors to better fulfill unmet needs, clients must first perceive their relationships with counselors as satisfying. A variety of interventions can promote change-facilitating environments and relationships, and these can be found in Table 7.2.

Relationship Between Therapist and Client

Reality therapists view a positive client–therapist relationship as essential to counseling (Glasser, 1975). Reality therapists are very much human beings in the counseling process. They share their perceptions and experiences and frequently ask for feedback. They pay little attention to transference

TABLE 7.2 Interventions That Promote Change-Facilitating Environments and Relationships

Suspend judgment	Monitor your judgments, and convey this suspended judgment to clients.
Do the unexpected	Reframe undesirable client behaviors to identify and emphasize strengths (e.g., tantrum behaviors = emotionally expressive).
Use humor	Be fun and laugh with clients while maintaining boundaries.
Set boundaries	Set clear and concrete limits with clients.
Self-disclose	Foster trust with appropriate sharing of your experiences.
Listen for metaphors	Metaphors offer additional insight into clients' needs and wants.
Listen for inner control talk	Identify and celebrate clients' acceptance of responsibility and control over their behavioral choices.
Listen for themes	Emphasize themes related to wants, needs, and choices.
Summarize and focus	Let clients know they are being heard and keep the focus on clients rather than external forces they cannot control.
Allow or impose consequences	Consequences need to be within reason and should emphasize responsibility rather than punishment.
Silence	Allow clients time to process and self-evaluate.
Create anticipation and communicate hope	Be curious and optimistic for adaptive behavioral changes and create a sense of imminent success.

Source: Adapted from Wubbolding, 2000, 2011.

and countertransference. Instead, they present themselves as people with skills and information they can use responsibly to help others. They are warm, caring, respectful, optimistic, attentive, and authentic with clients, and they demonstrate a demeanor of **friendly involvement**. Although reality therapists maintain ethical and professional behavior, they may talk about a sports event or give clients advice about what to wear to a meeting if such interactions promote rapport and help people achieve their goals.

THERAPEUTIC TECHNIQUES AND PROCEDURES

Reality therapists value creativity, as well as understanding, appreciating, and motivating all clients. As a result, they draw on a broad range of interventions to promote clients' involvement in counseling and bring energy and interest to the sessions. A wide variety of cognitive and behavioral interventions make up the repertoire of reality therapists.

Client progress in therapy is rarely smooth; occasional lapses or backsliding are the norm. When this occurs in reality therapy, therapists use renegotiation to help people do something different. When renegotiating, the emphasis is on developing new or revised plans with a high likelihood of success and identifying and rehearsing ways to cope with temptations to diverge from agreed-on plans and goals.

Metaphors

Reality therapists use metaphors, similes, images, analogies, and anecdotes to give clients a powerful message in a creative way (Wubbolding, 2011, 2017). Therapists also listen for and use metaphors and themes that clients present. For example, a therapist told a client whose hobby was fishing that his efforts to meet his goals seemed like fishing without bait in a lake with few fish.

Relationships

Since its inception, reality therapy has viewed relationships as key to both the development of difficulties and the achievement of a more rewarding life. People who lack close relationships are almost always lonely and feel bad (Glasser, 1998a). Reality therapists encourage clients to form relationships and coach them on ways to make these relationships rewarding. The foundation of a strong relationship includes the following characteristics (Wubbolding, 1991): Effort is put into the relationship; the relationship is valued by each person; it is enjoyable; it focuses on the positive; it is noncritical and nonargumentative; it is regular and repetitive, but time limited; and it promotes awareness of each other.

Glasser (1998a, 2000) was particularly interested in partner relationships and suggested that the best marriages are between people with similar personalities. In addition, he believed that marriages are most likely to succeed if both people are low in power and freedom needs and high in their needs for fun, love, and belonging.

In terms of parenting, Glasser advocated loving children no matter what, but suggested that parents may dislike how children behave and they can let them know that some behaviors are frustrating. He cautioned parents to avoid being punitive and judgmental, although he believed they do need to establish guidelines, rules, and limits for their children. Encouragement and acceptance are seen as far more helpful than disapproval or criticism. Like Adlerian therapists, reality therapists maintain that an essential element in good parenting is helping children learn from their mistakes, thereby turning disappointments into successes rather than promoting feelings of failure.

Glasser (1992, 2000) posited seven deadly habits and seven caring habits to explain the interaction between behavioral choices and interpersonal relationships. The seven deadly habits include criticizing, blaming, complaining, nagging, threatening, punishing, and bribing or controlling with rewards. As choice theory postulates that the vast majority of problems and unhappiness stem from unsatisfying relationship dynamics and experiences, clients are encouraged to replace deadly habits with caring habits, which are caring, listening, supporting, contributing, encouraging, trusting, and negotiating differences. For example, rather than complaining about others, counselors can encourage clients to identify ways they can fix their relationship problems by being flexible and compromising.

Questions

Although reality therapists advocate evaluation of total behavior, they want that assessment to come from the clients. Reality therapists avoid telling people what is not working for them or how they should change. Rather, they use carefully structured questions to help people take a closer look at their lives and determine what does and does not need to change (Wubbolding, 2011). Examples of such questions include "What did you do yesterday to satisfy your need for belonging?" "Is what you are doing helping you?" "Is the plan you have made the most effective plan you are capable of formulating?" Reality therapy can be easily adapted, via language and word change, for people from different cultures. For example, people from Japan may be put off by a direct question such as "What do you want?" but may be more comfortable being asked, "What are you looking for?" or "What are you seeking?" (Wubbolding, 2011, p. 113).

WDEP and SAMI^{2}C^3

As was previously discussed, the concepts represented by these acronyms play an important part in keeping both clients and counselors focused and productive. WDEP reflects the process of moving toward change by *evaluating wants* and *direction* and formulating *plans*. **SAMI^{2}C^3** represents the elements that maximize the success of plans: simple, attainable, measurable, immediate, involving, controlled, consistent, and committed.

Positive Addictions

According to Glasser (1976), negative addictions or repetitive self-destructive behaviors, such as misuse of substances, acting out, and depressing oneself, reflect giving up. Such behaviors characterize people who either have never learned to meet their needs in effective and responsible ways or have lost that ability.

Glasser suggested that people can reduce negative behaviors by developing **positive addictions**, which are behaviors that provide mental strength and alertness, creativity, energy, confidence, and focus but do not dominate or control people's lives. Examples include regular exercise, journal writing, playing music, yoga, and meditation. Acquiring a positive addiction generally takes 6 months to 2 years of regular practice, usually 45 to 60 minutes at a time. Glasser (1976) suggested the following guidelines for choosing and nurturing positive behavioral patterns:

- The behavior should be noncompetitive and capable of being done alone.
- The behavior can be accomplished without too much mental or physical effort.
- The behavior should have value to you.
- The behavior should be one that you believe will lead you to improve in some way if you persist in it.
- The behavior should be one that you can perform without criticizing yourself.

Using Verbs and "ing" Words

Because reality therapists want people to realize they have considerable control over their lives and can choose their total behavior, therapists deliberately make extensive use of active verbs and "ing" words. Rather than describing people as *angry, depressed, phobic,* or *anxious,* they describe them as *angering, depressing, phobicking,* or *anxietying.* This implies that these emotions are not fixed states but instead are actions that can be changed. Counselors can demonstrate this notion by asking clients to safely act out different **paining behaviors**: "Show me what *depressing* looks like" or "Act out *angering* for me." Following enactments, counselors can process how clients actively chose to perform the behavior as an example in session, and how they hold control over their behavioral choices during all other lived experiences, as well. This conception may seem harsh to some clients—that they are being told they are choosing to experience distress, misery, or suffering—but counselors can teach clients that paining behaviors like depressing, anxietying, or angering make up only two components of their total behavior (i.e., acting and thinking), and associated experiences of distress or misery are indirect manifestations of the other two components of their total behavior (i.e., feeling and physiology) that are not chosen (Kress et al., 2018). Consistent with cognitive behavioral explanations of behavior, if people choose to alter their actions, other elements of their total behavior—thinking, feeling, and physiology—will also begin to change.

Reasonable Consequences

Reality therapists believe that people should be responsible and therefore should experience the consequences of their behaviors. For example, the adolescent who returns home after curfew may have to be grounded for the next weekend, and the woman who is never ready when her carpool arrives may need to be dropped from the carpool. Reality therapists do not advocate making excuses or special exceptions. At the same time, they are not punitive; rather than focusing on what people did wrong, they focus on what people can choose to do differently so that they do not suffer the negative consequences of irresponsible and unrealistic behaviors.

Paradoxical Interventions

Reality therapists use paradoxical interventions, initially discussed and elaborated on by Viktor Frankl, an existential therapist. These creative interventions encourage people to assume responsibility for themselves. Paradoxical interventions typically take two forms (Wubbolding, 1988):

1. They *relabel* or *reframe* to promote choice and control. People might be viewed as lacking in skills rather than as psychotic. Disappointments might be referred to as learning experiences rather than failures.
2. They involve *paradoxical prescriptions.* Reality therapists might encourage people to imagine the worst that could happen and find ways to cope with that, to choose their symptoms rather than fight them, to do the opposite of what is not working, or to schedule a relapse. Of course, suggestions always reflect accepted ethical standards.

Development of Skills

Education is an important aspect of reality therapy. Therapists help people develop skills for fulfilling their needs and wants in responsible ways. Reality therapists might teach people assertiveness, rational thinking, development of positive addictions, planning, and other skills that promote growth and responsibility.

APPLICATION AND CURRENT USE OF REALITY THERAPY

Reality therapy is a flexible approach used for individual, group, and family therapy, and found to help a variety of people who experience diverse problems. It is widely used in schools, correctional institutions, both inpatient and outpatient mental health settings, and rehabilitation programs, and it is a popular approach to addressing problems associated with drug and alcohol use.

Counseling Applications

Reality therapy continues to have a strong following among mental health professionals. In addition to its well-established use in schools and substance use treatment programs, reality therapy works in a broad range of other settings. Particularly important are efforts to combine and integrate reality therapy with other approaches (Schoo, 2008).

Reality therapists view their approach as useful with almost all people, regardless of the nature of their backgrounds, problems, or mental health. Although this perspective is questionable, assessing the effectiveness of reality therapy for those who have different mental disorders is difficult, since reality therapists avoid using common diagnostic nomenclature and view the concept of mental illness as invalid and harmful. As a result of this stance, few empirical studies describe the use of reality therapy with people diagnosed with specific mental disorders. Glasser (1998a), Wubbolding (2000, 2017), and others do offer case studies of people presenting concerns that suggest the presence of mental disorders. For example, Wubbolding described the successful use of reality therapy with adults and adolescents who are incarcerated, with people who misuse substances, and with those experiencing depression and low self-esteem. He also provided examples of the effective use of reality therapy with people who experience bullying, domestic violence, and family conflict.

Therefore, when working with people who have severe disorders such as bipolar and psychotic disorders, as well as those with long-standing conditions such as personality disorders, reality therapy should be used with caution, if at all, and will probably need to be combined with other counseling approaches. Some research indicates reality therapy also shows effectiveness in treating children who have been sexually abused (Ellsworth, 2007) and those who have Internet addictions (Kim, 2007).

Reality therapy principles are often used in school environments and replace the punitive and judgmental atmosphere of many schools with an environment that is encouraging and reinforcing (Wubbolding 2007a, 2011).

Glasser suggested several approaches to effecting positive change in schools, and these have received some research support:

- *Learning teams.* Groups of two to five students of varying ability levels study and learn cooperatively, motivated by feelings of belonging in the group. Their goals include both learning new material and convincing their teachers that they have mastered the material. Teams are changed regularly to promote interaction.
- *Quality School Model.* This model reconceptualizes the school environment to eliminate coercion and promote cooperation, safety, and consideration (Glasser, 1998b). Teachers strive to make course work useful and meaningful and to teach in a way that meets students' basic needs and contributes to their sense of fulfillment. Features of this model include year-round education to promote continuity, parent action teams to increase involvement, teachers and students sharing lunch and other activities, partnerships with businesses, elimination of bells to signal times, elimination of grading, peer tutoring in multi-age learning groups, open classrooms, computer-aided learning, student portfolios, student-led conferences and businesses, and daily self-evaluations for staff and students. The model recognizes the importance of both psychological and academic growth and emphasizes a win–win perspective.

In addition, the WDEP model can be used to create a classroom environment in which students' basic five needs are met and teachers are content. By minimizing fear and coercion, and focusing instead on the need for freedom, power, love and belonging, survival, and fun, students learn to develop an internal locus of control rather than seeking external sources of rewards. The teacher uses the principles of choice theory to develop a customized classroom environment in which students learn to monitor and motivate themselves. The focus is always on behavior and choice.

Application to Multicultural Groups

Reality therapy is well suited to diverse and multicultural populations. Reality therapy is phenomenological and is interested in getting to know people and understanding their worldviews and quality world. It helps people identify their wants, evaluate them, and develop responsible plans to achieve them. It is a respectful and humanistic approach in that it focuses on what clients want and assumes clients are motivated and capable of making changes. Counselors demonstrate respect for clients' culture by having them determine their reactions to their behaviors. The plans clients develop to address their behaviors are based on their worldviews, not others' worldviews. Reality therapy advocates treating people as individuals, recognizes the importance of relationships, and encourages people to help each other. Although reality therapy promotes self-evaluation, therapists do not make judgments or impose their values on others. While all people have the same basic needs (i.e., survival, love and belonging, power, freedom, and fun), counselors should be aware that the client's cultural context largely shapes the way these needs are expressed. Therapists must be flexible and cognizant that clients will meet different needs in diverse ways. In addition, Reality therapists' focus on thinking and action may feel more comfortable to some clients. As such, some populations may display less resistance to the counseling process.

Over the past two decades, the reality therapy literature, particularly the *International Journal of Choice Theory and Reality Therapy*, has focused heavily on the use of this approach with diverse client populations. The principles underlying choice theory are universal, thus making choice theory applicable to all populations (Wubbolding, 2011). All people have needs, all make choices, and all attempt to influence the world around them. Wubbolding, who has taught reality therapy in Asia, Australia, Europe, North Africa, and the Middle East, has described ways to adapt this approach to other cultures. For example, he emphasizes the importance of looking at the particular balance of basic needs in each culture. He also stresses that reality therapy's procedures should be modified based on the psychological needs and developmental levels of individuals from different cultures. For example, when working with Japanese clients, he suggests that modifications to practice might involve the following: softening direct questions and confrontations being aware that some commonly used reality therapy words (e.g., plan, accountability) are not recognized in Japanese culture, and so language shifts may be needed; and being sensitive to the fact that in Japanese culture, a client saying "I'll try"—language that is generally not accepted by reality therapists—likely means the client is committed and plans to make the change discussed. These are just several examples of the ways reality therapy might be adapted when working with those from different cultures.

Some have raised concerns about the application of reality therapy to certain cultural groups (Sanchez & Garriga, 1996). They point out, for example, that fatalism (the idea that some things are meant to happen regardless of what people do) is an important belief in Hispanic culture. Therapists should exercise particular caution and sensitivity when using reality therapy with people whose belief system emphasizes a higher power, predestination and predetermination, and the value of an external locus of control. Sharing action and responsibility with a higher power but still striving for an improved quality world and better need satisfaction may be helpful ways to approach this issue.

Those who use reality therapy must take into account that many clients experience very real cultural and environmental factors that impact their day-to-day lives, and this can make choice difficult. Reality therapy does not directly address environmental and social problems such as racism, sexism, heterosexism, homophobia, ageism, and ableism and these forces can severely limit the ability to choose different paths. Therapists must be sensitive to the fact that clients do not choose to be victims of oppression and that people may face many barriers to living their ideal lives. In other words, a danger exists that reality therapists could overemphasize clients' ability to take control of their lives, thereby overlooking systemic factors that affect clients' ability to make deliberate choices.

EVALUATION OF REALITY THERAPY

Like the other cognitive behavioral approaches to counseling, reality therapy has a great deal to offer clients and therapists. However, it also has limitations.

Limitations

Reality therapy has some important shortcomings that therapists should bear in mind. It pays only limited attention to helping people understand and deal with their environments and minimizes the importance of the past in people's development and difficulties. As a result, reality therapists may overlook some of the barriers and experiences that limit people's choices, and they may focus too much on symptoms.

In addition, reality therapists' disregard of the importance of diagnosis is inconsistent with current professional guidelines. Equating mental illness with lack of knowledge about responsible ways to meet one's needs is highly questionable and may neglect important areas of concern. Many therapists also disagree with Glasser's (1998a) doubts about the existence of repressed memories and the diagnosis of posttraumatic stress disorder.

In addition, reality therapy minimizes the value of psychotropic medication (Glasser 1998a, 2003). Glasser wrote: "Good psychotherapy precludes the need for [brain] drugs" (1998a, p. 88). Glasser believed that medication is dangerous to people's health and undermines their ability to help themselves (Lennon, 2003). In contrast, Wubbolding (2018) has attempted to ensure that reality therapy is a mainstream system and insists that medication is now accepted by professionals as a legitimate treatment intervention and is compatible with the ethical practice of reality therapy.

The John Dewey Academy (JDA) in Great Barrington, Massachusetts, uses a learning-centered variation of reality-based therapy with angry adolescents, many of whom have previously been hospitalized for psychiatric disorders such as attention-deficit hyperactivity disorder (ADHD), conduct disorder, and self-destructive behavior (Bratter, 2010). No psychotropic medications are allowed, only education and compassionate, caring confrontation in a residential treatment setting. The study's authors write: "Personality and affective disorders are rarely cured by medicinal approaches. There is no pill that teaches self-respect and cures noxious narcissism, dishonesty and anti-social attitudes. Therefore we eschew the use of psychotropic medications at JDA and view drug-free as a viable treatment goal" (Bratter et al., 2008, p. 22). The study cites a 28% graduation rate, with 100% of those students going on to higher education. More research is needed to substantiate the effectiveness of this nontraditional approach for dually diagnosed and self-destructive adolescents.

Although effectiveness research on choice theory has yet to support Glasser's claims, changes in our understanding of the dynamics of the brain have been in line with some of Glasser's beliefs. Specifically, neurological research during the past 20 years has revealed the neuroplasticity of the brain. That is, the brain is capable of changing across the lifespan and some portions can be regenerated. Social interactions and learning have been shown to contribute to those changes at a cellular level. Barber (2008) wrote, "Neuroplasticity supports the efficacy of old-fashioned psychotherapy.... Who would have thought neuroscience would show that psychotherapy is a robust treatment capable of working at a biological level?" (p. 198). In fact, those changes are not additive, but synergistic, with the interactions changing brain function, which in turn improves interactions (Barber, 2008; Kandel, 2008). No doubt the additional positive impacts of psychotherapy will continue to be documented as neurobiological research continues to evolve.

Strengths and Contributions

Despite some limitations, reality therapy has many strengths. It is a clear, positive, straightforward approach to counseling that makes sense to most people. It is respectful, empowering, and encouraging and addresses fundamental issues in people's lives, such as motivation, need satisfaction, and control. Reality therapists become involved with their clients in appropriate professional ways. Reality therapy's emphasis on the importance of both relationships and responsibility in people's lives is relevant and timely in light of prevalent problems of violence and family disruption. Also relevant is its emphasis on choice at a time when many people feel overcommitted and overprogrammed. In addition, reality therapy has a strong preventive component and offers sound and hopeful ideas for changes in schools and other institutions.

Research documents positive outcomes for reality therapy, particularly in schools and therapeutic communities (Wubbolding, 2007a). In addition, many published case studies describe the successful use of reality therapy with a variety of clients (Wubbolding, 2000, 2017). However, continued research on the application of reality therapy to specific client groups is needed so that therapists have a clearer idea of its appropriate use.

Reality therapy has made important contributions to counseling and psychotherapy. It provides a clear and structured approach to therapy that is widely used in schools and rehabilitation programs. It emphasizes the importance of values in counseling and reminds therapists not to neglect relationships and responsibility. Its appreciation and description of the collaborative therapeutic relationship have broadened the appropriate role of the therapist. It can be easily integrated with other counseling approaches, such as Gendlin's focusing technique, to create a powerful tool (Burdenski & Wubbolding, 2011) and play therapy (Stutey & Wubbolding, 2018). Finally, it centers attention on the need to help people engage in honest self-evaluation and make wise and responsible choices and plans.

Wubbolding (2011, 2017) noted that Glasser's greatest contribution may be in developing a system (reality therapy) of mental health rather than a system to treat mental dysfunction.

SKILL DEVELOPMENT: CARING CONFRONTATION

Confrontation is a highly charged word that may seem incompatible with the supportive and encouraging role of the therapist. However, when done with care and sensitivity, confrontations—or what some refer to as "carefrontations"—can help people more honestly and accurately evaluate their behaviors, acquire a better grasp of reality, and act in more responsible ways.

Confrontation can be defined as the process of noting discrepancies, usually in an individual's words and behaviors, and reflecting those discrepancies back to the individual. Confrontation should never involve shaming, belittling, or attacking, and should not precipitate a debate between client and therapist about who is right.

A confrontation typically has three parts:

1. An introduction, which identifies the client statements, actions, or thoughts that prompted the intervention.
2. The body of the confrontation, which points out the issues or discrepancies. In keeping with reality therapy, this statement should be tentative, gentle, and respectful.

3. An invitation for the client to respond. Questions such as "What do you make of that?" and "Would you be willing to explore that with me?" typically are used. They prompt the client to reflect and self-evaluate and are unlikely to lead the client to feel judged. Questions also offer the client the opportunity to choose not to discuss the confrontation or to disagree with the therapist. These responses suggest that the therapist probably should not pursue the topic at present. However, it has been mentioned and is likely to arise again.

Consider the following example of a caring confrontation:

THERAPIST: Ronnie, several weeks ago, you told me that you and your fiancé are on a limited budget and are saving to buy a house. Today, you told me that you are buying a wedding gown that costs five thousand dollars. I wonder if buying the wedding gown will help you meet your need for your own home. Would you be willing to take a look at that with me?

The therapist has identified a discrepancy in the information that Ronnie has presented. This is reflected back to her in an unemotional and nonjudgmental way, with an invitation for Ronnie to explore this discrepancy.

Ronnie may respond in a variety of ways. She may have information that resolves the discrepancy: "I didn't tell you that my aunt gave me five thousand dollars specifically to buy a wedding dress." She may open the door to further clarification of her values and choices: "This is the most important event in my life, and I want it to be as special as possible." Or she may reflect on her choices and make a self-evaluation: "I never put those two pieces together. Maybe it isn't a good idea for me to spend so much on a dress that's only important for one day, but the house will mean something to us for years." Whether or not Ronnie sees the situation as her therapist does is not important; what does matter is that she has an opportunity to reflect on, clarify, evaluate, and possibly change her choices so that they better meet her needs. The exercises later in this chapter will provide an opportunity to develop some caring confrontations.

CASE APPLICATION

Roberto consulted his therapist a few weeks before Thanksgiving because of family difficulties during the previous year's Thanksgiving holiday. His therapist applied the WDEP and $SAMI^2C^3$ formats in the context of reality therapy to help Roberto plan to make the holiday more rewarding this year.

ROBERTO: Thanksgiving last year was a disaster. I don't want a repeat of that.

THERAPIST: What did you do?

ROBERTO: Well, I came home early on the day before Thanksgiving to have some extra time with Edie and Ava. I did have to bring some work home, and I wanted to get that done first, so I just said hello and headed over to the room where we have the computer. Before I know it, Edie flings the door open and is in my face about how I never help and am not really part of the family. I could not calm her down, so I just picked up my stuff and went back to the office. Who needs that! Of course, this spoiled Thanksgiving Day; Edie and I just glared at each other for most of the day.

THERAPIST: So even though you came home early and were thinking of your family, somehow your actions backfired and you wound up not meeting either your needs or your family's. When you think about the five basic needs that we have discussed, how do you evaluate your efforts?

ROBERTO: You know, I can see that my thoughts and actions were at cross-purposes. In coming home early, I was focused on my needs for love and fun; I really wanted to have a close, enjoyable time with my family. But I did not give them that message. When I went right to the computer, all Edie saw was me trying to meet my need for achievement. She didn't know I just had a little work to do and then was going to spend time with the family. I guess I really didn't try to see things from her perspective.

THERAPIST: So you have some new thoughts about what happened last year. What are the needs you want to focus on this Thanksgiving?

ROBERTO: Definitely fun and love and belonging.

THERAPIST: And what pictures do you have in your head about what that would look like?

ROBERTO: We would all get along. We'd all pitch in to cook dinner. We'd have some good food and good conversation. I'd make a fire in the fireplace. Then maybe we could do something fun like taking a walk or going to a movie.

THERAPIST: Let's develop a plan to help you make those pictures real. We've reviewed the eight steps in the $SAMI^2C^3$ model for making successful plans: simple, attainable, measurable, immediate, involving, controlled, consistent, and committed. What plan comes into your mind?

ROBERTO: I could come home early again on the day before Thanksgiving but not bring any work home. I could ask Edie if she needs any help. And I could suggest something fun to do after Thanksgiving dinner.

THERAPIST: How does that plan fit the criteria?

ROBERTO: It seems simple and attainable. I guess it's measurable; I can tell if I'm doing what I planned or not. I'm certainly committed to changing our holiday experience. But I'm not sure the plan is immediate; and I don't know how I could make it more involving, controlled by me, or consistent.

THERAPIST: So you've made a start at planning, but how could you modify the plan so that it meets more of the criteria?

ROBERTO: I could make it immediate by starting right now. I'll write down the plan and tell Edie about it when I get home. I could even ask her now if there are ways I could help, like shopping or cleaning the house. If I offer specific ways to help, I have more control over the plan, and I'm taking more initiative. Edie complains that I leave everything at home up to her, so taking the initiative seems like a good idea.

THERAPIST: So you see ways to make the plan more immediate and consistent as well as more under your control. Are there ways I could be involved in helping you?

ROBERTO: Maybe you could touch base with me sometime during the week to help me stay on track. I really want to, but sometimes I get so caught up with work. . . .

THERAPIST: How about if I telephone you on Tuesday to see how things are going?

ROBERTO: That would be great.

THERAPIST: Now let's look at the plan again to evaluate how well it promises to fulfill your needs and wants in realistic and responsible ways. Then you can write down the specifics.

REFLECT AND RESPOND

1. Identify a positive addiction that you would like to make part of your life. Write out a plan, following the SAMI^{2}C^3 format, to establish that positive behavior in your life.
2. Reality therapy stresses the key role that relationships play in both people's happiness and their misery. Write one or two pages in your journal about ways in which relationships have had an impact on your feelings of well-being. Then identify two small and specific changes you would like to make in the way you relate to others. Write them down and consider making a commitment to implementing those changes.
3. Draw a picture of the images in your quality world. Write a paragraph about what your drawing represents and means to you.

Summary

Reality therapy, developed by William Glasser in the 1960s and developed primarily by Glasser and Robert Wubbolding, is an optimistic and encouraging counseling approach. It focuses on present thoughts and behaviors and helps people meet their basic needs more successfully by making better choices. Responsibility is key to this approach, as are positive relationships. Therapists play an active and involved role, and function as teachers, mentors, and models, confronting clients so that they can determine if what they are doing is helping clients to fulfill basic needs without harming themselves or others. Glasser (2003) summed up the essence of reality therapy when he stated that accepting that everything we do is a choice is essential to good mental health.

Reality therapy has broad applicability to a variety of presenting concerns (e.g., ADHD, communication problems). Many clients appreciate the concrete nature of reality therapy. This active and directive counseling approach can also demystify the counseling process and facilitate client understanding, autonomy, and "buy-in" of counseling, and may also allow clients to perceive behavioral change as a nonthreatening, realistic, and achievable task. This action-oriented approach is highly culturally appropriate, as clients from many cultures prefer this clear, directive approach to counseling.

Recommended Readings

Ellsworth, L. (2007). *Choosing to heal: Using reality therapy in treatment with sexually abused children*. New York, NY: Routledge.

Erwin, J. C. (2004). *The classroom of choice: Giving students what they need and getting what you want*. Alexandria, VA: Association for Supervision and Curriculum Development.

Glasser, W. (1975). *Reality therapy*. New York, NY: Harper & Row.

Glasser, W. (1986). *Control theory in the classroom*. New York, NY: Harper & Row.

Glasser, W. (2001). *Counseling with choice theory*. New York, NY: HarperCollins.

Glasser, W., & Glasser, C. (2009). *Eight lessons for a happier marriage*. New York, NY: HarperCollins.

Wubbolding, R. (1991). *Understanding reality therapy*. New York, NY: HarperCollins.

Wubbolding, R. (2015). *Reality therapy training manual* (16th rev.). Cincinnati, OH: Center for Reality Therapy.

Wubbolding, R. (2017). *Reality therapy and self-evaluation: The key to client change*. Hoboken, NJ: Wiley.

MyLab Counseling

Try the Topic 17 Assignments: Reality Therapy.

CHAPTER 8

Contemporary Cognitive Behavioral Therapies

With Christine A. McAllister

Learning Outcomes

When you have finished this chapter, you should be able to:
- Understand the context and development of Contemporary Cognitive Behavioral Therapies.
- Communicate the key concepts associated with Contemporary Cognitive Behavioral Therapies and understand how they relate to therapeutic processes.
- Describe the therapeutic goals of Contemporary Cognitive Behavioral Therapies.
- Identify the common techniques used in Contemporary Cognitive Behavioral Therapies.
- Understand how Contemporary Cognitive Behavioral Therapies relates to counseling diverse populations.
- Identify the limitations and strengths of Contemporary Cognitive Behavioral Therapies.

THE THIRD GENERATION OF BEHAVIOR THERAPY

The third generation of cognitive behavioral therapies (CBT) refers to the development and introduction of acceptance-based therapies, such as dialectical behavior therapy (DBT), acceptance and commitment therapy (ACT), mindfulness-based cognitive therapy (MBCT), and schema therapy (Dobson & Dozois, 2010; Herbert & Forman, 2011). The third-wave CBT approaches, or the more contemporary CBT approaches, make up a group of psychological therapies that target the process of thoughts or thinking (rather than their content, as in traditional CBT) to help people become aware of their thoughts and accept them in a nonjudgmental way. Instead of problem solving and reducing symptoms quickly, these therapies focus on the processes of developing skills to navigate the world more effectively. Both second- and third-wave CBT approaches are goal oriented, but second-wave therapies focus more on presenting symptoms, whereas third-wave therapies center more on working toward broader life goals. These approaches share important traits with other CBT approaches; specifically, their ultimate goal is to change thinking and behavior (Dobson & Dozois, 2010). However, unlike the second-wave CBT approaches, the third-wave ones focus more on finding peace and ease within the self and the world, as well as shifting perspective. Instead of pushing away troublesome feelings, thoughts, and situations, the goal is to be mindful and accept them, which will help facilitate behavior change. In addition, practitioners of these approaches prefer to focus on wellness over dysfunction, a holistic perspective over concentration on isolated aspects of functioning, and understanding the larger context fully as opposed to identifying specific problems in living.

These approaches combine experiential and mindfulness techniques with cognitive and behavioral approaches. Mindfulness-based interventions have become extremely popular, are empirically supported, and are easily integrated into treatment for all sorts of medical and psychiatric conditions, including pain management, heart conditions, head injuries, and nearly all behavioral disorders (Crane, Kuyken, Hastings, Rothwell, & Williams, 2010). Most of these approaches incorporate similar actions: acceptance of what is happening, nonjudgment of thoughts, and present-moment awareness. The most common third-wave approaches—dialectical behavior therapy, acceptance and commitment therapy, mindfulness-based cognitive therapy, and schema therapy—will primarily be discussed. As readers will learn, the third-wave approaches are very different from the traditional CBT approaches discussed so far. At the end of this chapter, three other popular third-wave CBT theories—behavior activation therapy, compassion-focused therapy, and metacognitive therapy—will be discussed briefly in Textbox 8.1 (behavior activation therapy) and Textbox 8.2 (compassion-focused therapy and metacognitive therapy).

DIALECTICAL BEHAVIOR THERAPY

MARSHA M. LINEHAN (b. 1943)

Marsha M. Linehan, the developer of DBT, was born in Tulsa, Oklahoma, in 1943. Her own diagnosis of borderline personality disorder and her experiences managing this disorder led to the development of DBT, a theory that focuses on emotion regulation and mindfulness. DBT has a special focus on addressing suicidal behavior. Linehan earned her PhD in social and experimental personality psychology from Loyola University Chicago. Linehan has founded many organizations, including The Linehan Institute, Behavioral Research and Therapy Clinics (University of Washington), Behavioral Tech Research, and the DBT-Linehan Board of Certification. The goal of these organizations is to provide effective services for a wide variety of complex mental health issues, especially borderline personality disorder. She is currently a professor at the University of Washington and the director of the Behavioral Research and Therapy Clinics. Linehan has conducted research, provided supervision, and conducted trainings throughout the world. She has authored many books, including *Cognitive-Behavioral Treatment for Borderline Personality Disorder* and the *Skills Training Manual for Treating Borderline Personality Disorder*. Many awards have come her way, including a Career/Lifetime Achievement award by the Association for Behavioral and Cognitive Therapies and the Distinguished Research in Suicide Award.

INTRODUCTION/DEVELOPMENT OF DBT

Dialectical behavioral therapy (DBT) is a type of cognitive behavioral therapy that was developed in the 1980s. Marsha Linehan (1993) and her colleagues initially developed DBT to treat people with borderline personality disorder (BPD) who were chronically suicidal, but over the years it has been applied to work with people who have a wide variety of presenting issues (e.g., depression, complex trauma). Borderline personality disorder involves difficulty in regulating strong feelings and controlling behavior, especially in the context of relationships. Linehan's research indicated that clients treated with DBT were less likely to drop out of counseling, had fewer hospitalizations, and experienced better overall counseling outcomes (Linehan, 1993). DBT relies on the assumption that a balance exists between acceptance and change, which helps clients create a meaningful, satisfying life. Based on its initial success, DBT has since been adapted for use with couples, children and adolescents, and as a tool for anyone needing help with emotion regulation. Since emotion regulation is something that many people struggle with on some level, this theory has wide applicability. DBT is a structured, technique-heavy counseling theory that may appeal to therapists who value a more concrete, well-defined counseling approach.

KEY CONCEPTS

Dialectical behavioral therapy is based on a dialectical philosophy, a biopsychosocial view of problems, and the integration of behavior therapy with the Eastern beliefs and attitudes of mindfulness, acceptance, and compassion. The development of emotion regulation is a foundation of DBT.

Dialectics

The philosophy of dialectics is a way of looking at reality (Linehan, 1993). Within every person's story lies "an alternative story (a dialectic pole). A person who tells us how she has failed in life can tell a success story, too" (Almagor, 2011, p. 33). In other words, **dialectics** is defined as the art of investigating the relative truth of principles, opinions, and guidelines, and DBT involves arriving at the truth by examining the argument and resolving the two into a rational synthesis (Linehan et al., 2006). Dialectics involves the belief that two things that appear opposing or contradicting can actually work together.

The use of dialectics helps clients to (Almagor, 2011):

1. Develop a broader perspective of their problem
2. Learn to look for the dialectic pole
3. Consider more options and possibilities
4. Get "unstuck" and develop a sense of efficacy and competence.

For example, a common dialectic between married couples revolves around the use of free time. Frequently, one person wants to spend more time with the partner, while the other is comfortable with the current situation. The issue is one of independence and dependence. When couples begin to realize the dialectic pole between the two ideals, they begin to understand the other person's perspective. The husband might think, "Erin is at work all day, and just wants to relax when she comes home," and Erin might think, "Even though I sometimes feel pressured by my husband to spend time together, it's really a *good* thing that he wants to spend more time with me."

When the couple can consider the problem from a different angle, more creative and egalitarian solutions become available to them. In dialectics, therapists help clients to see the dialectic pole inherent in the problem, consider all the options, and then make a choice that leads toward change.

An underlying assumption in DBT is that clients are experiencing a dialectical conflict between themselves and their environment. From a dialectical perspective, everyone is right. All behavior is functional and serves a purpose. DBT therapists work hard to understand the worldview of clients, to validate their feelings, and then to help them consider alternative possibilities.

Emotion Regulation

Borderline personality disorder is considered to have both biological and environmental causes (Linehan, McDavid, Brown, Sayrs, & Gallop, 2008). Emotion dysregulation may be the result of attachment wounds, traumatic experiences, loss, the competition between wants and needs, or genetic or other causes (Marra, 2005). DBT assumes that strong, painful emotions and difficulty regulating these emotions cause psychopathology and problems in living (Marra, 2005). According to DBT, emotions precede the development of thoughts. Once the neural networks associated with emotions begin to fire, they light up other neural networks and incite even stronger emotions. Once a pattern has been established, similar events may set off "triggers" that result in repeated incidents of intense emotion, feelings of abandonment, or a need to take action to stop the unpleasant emotions. Linehan believes borderline personality disorder results from the combination of emotional vulnerability and an invalidating environment. As such, emotion regulation is central to DBT.

Emotion regulation is the ability to respond to emotions in healthy ways. The demands and hardships of life are likely to disrupt emotions. For some people, these demands can feel out of control or too overwhelming to manage. However, when people learn to regulate their emotions, they can live healthier and more fulfilling lives. Emotion regulation often involves reducing the intensity of negative emotions. For example, a man who is sad may intentionally watch something funny to decrease his sadness. Emotion regulation involves having control over emotions so as to avoid emotional extremes.

Emotion regulation skills are essential and critical to healthy functioning, and for those who have borderline personality disorder, they are especially important, as this population frequently engages in unsafe behaviors (e.g., suicide attempts, self-injury) secondary to difficulties with emotion regulation. Emotion regulation allows people to manage and respond to emotions in a way that allows them to cope effectively. When people respond to emotions in healthy ways, this increases their likelihood of understanding and processing through their emotions more fully.

THE THERAPEUTIC PROCESS

The goal of DBT is to develop dialectical thinking and practice skills that result in emotion regulation, reduced suffering, and improved relationships. DBT helps clients to recognize how their attempts to deny, avoid, and escape strong emotions paradoxically make those emotions more intense. By helping clients to accept their feelings, providing tools for emotion recognition and regulation, and decreasing emotional avoidance (through psychoeducation and exposure to upsetting situations and triggers), DBT empowers clients to increase their tolerance of distress and use coping skills such as meditation and mindfulness to regulate their emotions. DBT therapists focus on the following therapy goals:

- *Teaching clients new skills:* A core component of therapy is to help clients to develop new strengths and skills so they can successfully interact in the world.
- *Understanding and Increasing client motivation:* Therapists in DBT are trained to understand and recognize clients' capacity for change and motivation to change. DBT attempts to keep the clients' motivation high through the use of therapeutic techniques and through the involvement of family members and peers. Therapists are trained to work at individual clients' levels while helping them to develop their motivation and capacity for change.
- *Helping clients accept what cannot be changed:* Despite all of the therapeutic techniques available in DBT, there are always things that will upset clients; things they cannot change. Helping clients accept what they cannot change and helping them adjust to this is an important part of DBT.
- *Real-world applications and functionality:* Therapists ensure that the new skills learned in therapy can be applied in the real world by the client.

The role of therapists is an important factor in the success of DBT, which considers the relationship between clients and therapists to be reciprocal. Both clients and therapists are changed from the therapeutic relationship. DBT is also collaborative in that it requires constant attention to the therapeutic relationship; a collaborative therapeutic relationship is essential if clients are to trust the therapist and engage in the work of treatment. DBT is an active therapy, with therapists participating in the dialectical

TABLE 8.1 Stages and Goals of Dialectical Behavior Therapy

Stage	Targets or Goals
Stage 1: *"Moving from being out of control of one's behavior to being in control"*	**Reduce and then eliminate:** • Behaviors that are life threatening • Behaviors that serve as barriers to counseling • Behaviors that reduce one's quality of life • Stage 1 also focuses on developing emotion regulation skills to promote the above targets.
Stage 2: *"Moving from being emotionally shut down to experiencing emotions fully"*	**Experience emotions:** • Without allowing them to take over • Without experiencing symptoms associated with posttraumatic stress disorder (e.g., dissociation or derealization) • Without avoiding them or shutting down.
Stage 3: *"Building an ordinary life, solving ordinary problems"*	**Work to accomplish goals surrounding:** • Ordinary problems of living (e.g., problems at school or in the home, with peers, teachers, and family members) • Continued use and engagement in treatment services.
Stage 4: *"Moving from incompleteness to completeness and connection"*	**Discover and engage in ways to feel complete:** • Meaningful interests and/or activities • Meaningful groups that share interests • Relationships with others.

process as well as providing psychoeducation, skills training, coaching, and group work. It requires clients to complete homework assignments, role-play, practice new ways of interacting with others in individual sessions and groups, and practice using a variety of skills such as self-soothing and distress tolerance when upset.

DBT, if applied in a pure way, is an intensive therapy model, with clients receiving at least 1 year of 1-hour weekly individual therapy sessions and 2-hour weekly group therapy, emphasizing skills training and problem solving. Table 8.1 presents the stages and goals of DBT.

THERAPEUTIC TECHNIQUES AND PROCEDURES

Emotion Regulation Skills

Although mindfulness practices are at the core of DBT's underlying philosophy, facilitating clients' development of emotion regulation skills is the first and most critical task of therapists. Emotion regulation skills aim to promote clients' ability to effectively understand and identify distressing emotions. This is especially important when working with clients who have BPD or are otherwise at risk for self-harm, as emotion regulation skills can help prevent life-threatening behaviors, such as suicidal behaviors or self-injury. When focusing on reducing clients' life-threatening behaviors, it is important for therapists to implement not only affect-oriented interventions but also those that address the cognitive, physiological, and behavioral aspects of distress. It is imperative for clients to develop awareness of the manner in which their thoughts and physical body sensations are associated with their self-destructive behaviors, and the ways in which such behavior engagement can function to prevent them from experiencing a higher quality of life. Thus, emotion regulation interventions may emphasize identifying, processing, and ultimately reducing clients' vulnerability to the following aspects associated with distress: negative perceptions or automatic thinking patterns; communication styles that lead to highly reactive emotional responses; how the body feels when strong emotions are experienced; and behaviors that serve to contribute to, rather than prevent, life-threatening behaviors, such as poor sleeping or eating patterns, alcohol or drug use, or lack of exercise. Maintaining a dialectical framework, the aforementioned targets associated with clients' identification of distress-related treatment factors are paradoxically met with emotion regulation targets oriented toward engaging in pleasant activities and using effective problem-solving skills, as well as increasing positive emotions. Once clients are feeling stable and life-threatening behaviors are no longer an imminent concern, they can begin to learn and use mindfulness practices in ways that will enhance their emotion regulation even further. That is, clients' subsequent development of mindful attending and observing skills will enable them to better sense, identify, and more fully understand a broader range of ways in which they experience distress. Ideally, over the course of counseling, clients will develop their emotion regulation skills. Therapists may find it helpful to use worksheets or other visual means to assist clients with identifying and understanding their cognitive, affective, physiological, and behavioral manifestations of distress, how they interact and influence one another, and pre-existing strategies they have effectively utilized to cope with distress in the past.

Mindfulness

Mindfulness not only is a fundamental component of the client's emotion regulation skills training, but, in fact, mindfulness components are also integrated into DBT treatment modules intended to promote distress tolerance and interpersonal effectiveness. Because of DBT's dialectical underpinnings, however, mindfulness practices are implemented into counseling and conceptualized through a slightly different lens than other third-generation modalities. The concept of the **wise mind** essentially represents the DBT treatment approach as a whole, integrating philosophical foundations of dialectics, CBT, and mindfulness through three different mind states that are used to explain behavior based on cognitive, affective, and balanced ways of responding to distress (Linehan, 2015):

- *Rational mind:* The rational mind pertains to logic, reason, planning, and clients' ability to use information and skills to effectively problem solve and manage distressing situations in a safe, calm, and appropriate manner. The rational mind becomes difficult to use without adequate and healthy quantities of sleep, food, and exercise, or when clients are engaging in substance use or abuse.
- *Emotional mind:* The emotional mind is associated with mood and sensations, impulsivity, reactivity, and feelings of high intensity and passion. When a distressing event occurs, the emotional mind can take over and distort the thinking of clients or make them feel out of control. Such experiences prevent clients from using aspects of the rational mind when faced with distress.
- *Wise mind:* The wise mind is the integration of the rational and emotional minds. When clients are living balanced and mindful lives, they can effectively respond to distress in intuitive ways, or ways that they both know and feel are right.

Because the wise mind represents the fusion of dialectically opposing rational and emotional forces, therapists can use a Venn diagram to easily explain the wise mind to clients, or to explore the ways in which clients have responded to situations using aspects of their rational, emotional,

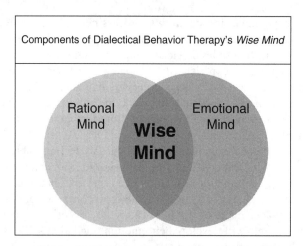

FIGURE 8.1 Components of Dialectical Behavior Therapy's Wise Mind concept.

and wise minds. For example, therapists can ask clients to label such experiences in the respective mind-domain of a Venn diagram (see Figure 8.1) and subsequently process behaviors that were logical but still did not feel right (i.e., excess use of rational mind), times when behaviors felt right but weren't rational (i.e., excess use of emotional mind), or when they responded intuitively, knowing and feeling as though they made the best decision.

Therapists who use DBT aim to cultivate people's wise minds through the implementation of core mindfulness practices, such as deep breathing, attending to the present moment, observing inner experiences, letting go of distress, and **radical acceptance** (i.e., complete and total acceptance of something or some situation). Mindfulness practices are intended to function as an independent means to promote the distress tolerance of clients, and serve to enhance their awareness of when additional strategies may be necessary.

Distress Tolerance

Most broadly, DBT **distress tolerance** skills can be categorized into two primary domains: (1) self-soothing skills and (2) distraction skills. Self-soothing skills are intended to combat intense emotions and physiological sensations, and assist clients with letting go of distress. DBT integrates cognitive behavioral distraction-based techniques that can be implemented by clients when they are unable to practice radical acceptance (i.e., accept something or a situation as it is) or when letting go of intense emotions does not seem possible. Essentially, distraction strategies are quick, easy to use, and useful in preventing crisis situations or in high-risk behaviors. Therapists can cultivate mindfulness and introduce both self-soothing and distraction oriented distress tolerance interventions to clients through the use of scripts or acronyms. Clients can repeat scripts, mantras, slogans, positive affirmations, or other preferred statements to assist them with tolerating distress, or to remind themselves of additional coping strategies. For example, therapists can teach clients to use **The Wise Mind ACCEPTS** acronym as a script to help them work through distressing situations effectively (Linehan, 2015), and this acronym follows:

When experiencing distress, the Wise Mind ACCEPTS:

- **A**ctivities: Engage in pleasurable self-soothing and distracting activities, such as listening to music, going for a walk, exercising, painting, drawing, coloring, writing, reading, talking to a friend, or watching a positive movie or television show.

- **C**ontributing: Enhance feelings of generosity and find ways to contribute to your school, neighborhood, community, the environment, or the well-being of others. Write a friend a gratitude letter to make that friend smile, clean up a dirty sidewalk, or volunteer at a local pet rescue shelter.
- **C**omparisons: Do not forget about the positives! Compare your current situation to all of the positive aspects of your life that you enjoy and are going well.
- **E**motions: Remember that your current emotions are not permanent—they will pass! Accept the present moment as only the present moment. Let go of distressing emotions, and do things to replace them with positive or calming feelings.
- **P**ushing away: If you are unable to accept or let go, it's okay—intentionally push away your current distress and solve the problem when you're feeling better.
- **T**houghts: Ask yourself the following questions: Are my thoughts controlling me or am I controlling my thoughts? Am I using my wise mind—a balanced integration of emotional *and rational* minds? Do not forget to use logical thinking and problem solving when responding effectively to distress.
- **S**ensations: Do something to cool down, self-soothe, or relax. Have a glass of juice, eat a cookie.

Therapists can also use the acronym **IMPROVE** to provide clients with a foundation of distress tolerance skills that can be practiced and developed over the course of counseling (Linehan, 2015). IMPROVE your current experience with:

- **I**magery: Imagine your happy place, or relaxing nature scenes such as a beach, mountains, a meadow, or field of flowers.
- **M**eaning: Identify all the meaningful things in your life. Thinking dialectically, what meaning might this difficult experience bring, or how might it cause you to grow in meaningful ways?
- **P**rayer: Engage in prayer, meditation, contemplation, introspection, or other spiritual practices to help ease emotional pain or uncertainty.
- **R**elaxation: Engage in activities that are relaxing, such as taking a warm bath, yoga, stretching, lying down, deep breathing, or brushing your hair.
- **O**ne thing at a time: Focus your attention on the present moment, simply observe, and practice nonjudgment, radical acceptance, and loving kindness.
- **V**acation: Take a break from the stresses of daily life and disconnect from social media, e-mail, texting, or electronics for a day, take a nap, or reconnect with an old friend for a special event at the park or your favorite restaurant.
- **E**ncouragement: Use positive affirmations or scripts to encourage yourself and foster self-compassion.

Interpersonal Effectiveness

The final skills-building training module of DBT targets interpersonal effectiveness, as some clients—especially those presenting with features of borderline personality disorder or other severe mental health distresses—experience difficulties with maintaining stable relationships with others. Moreover, some clients experience chronic exposure to invalidating and/or traumatic experiences throughout development, and they may need to learn assertiveness skills and the ability to set age-appropriate and healthy relational boundaries. Many people struggle with interpersonal boundaries; thus, these skills are very important for clients, especially as they navigate through the complexities of relationships. When applying DBT, therapists use interpersonal effectiveness interventions to promote clients' skills building in three core domains: (a) objective effectiveness; (b) relationship effectiveness; and (c) self-respect effectiveness. In summary, **interpersonal effectiveness** interventions aim to provide clients with the skills necessary to help them appropriately make requests or convey their wants to others, manage and resolve conflicts, establish and maintain positive relationships with others, and maintain and enhance self-respect when interacting with others. Although DBT's interpersonal effectiveness targets are indeed comprehensive and require clients to learn and practice a variety of nuanced social skills, therapists can simplify such processes with the acronyms such as **DEAR MAN GIVE FAST** (Linehan, 2015):

- **D**escribe: Describe what you want by stating information or facts.
- **E**xpress: Express your feelings and explain why you want what you are requesting.
- **A**ssert: Be assertive and specifically ask for exactly what you want. When others say "no," use skills to help you effectively cope with feelings and maintain self-respect.
- **R**einforce: Provide evidence of past experiences that further support your request.

- **M**indful: Remain focused on what you want and don't allow small details to distract you.
- **A**ppear confident: Look at others and convey your message in a clear and direct manner.
- **N**egotiate: Remain willing to discuss alternative options or compromise to get what you want.

- **G**entle: Maintain a nonjudgmental stance and do not make threats or attack others for having their own opinions.
- **I**nterested: Be open when listening to others and take their perspective into account.
- **V**alidate: Validate others by reflecting their feelings and/or statements to let them know you are listening.
- **E**asy manner: Convey kindness, smile, keep the conversation light-hearted, be friendly, and use appropriate humor.

- **F**air: Work to maintain fairness for yourself and others throughout the discussion.
- **A**pology free: Do not apologize for asking for what you want.
- **S**tick to your values: Remember your values and maintain integrity when compromising or negotiating.
- **T**ruthfulness: Be honest and refrain from exaggerating the truth to get what you want.

APPLICATION AND CURRENT USE OF DBT

Initial empirical research on DBT has yielded positive results. People treated with at least 1 year of DBT achieved considerable reductions in suicidal ideation, hospitalization, anxiety, and anger and increases in occupational and social adjustment (Linehan & Kehrer, 1993). Randomized controlled trials suggest that DBT is effective in reducing the symptoms of BPD, especially the associated self-injurious and suicidal symptoms, and it decreases emotionality and increases distress tolerance (McMain et al., 2009; Linehan et al., 2006; Linehan, 2015). Those participating in DBT also tend to stay in therapy longer than those in control groups and require fewer hospitalizations. These and other studies indicated that common symptoms accompanying borderline personality disorder, including substance misuse and dysfunctional eating, were also alleviated.

Since its initial development, the dialectical perspective and DBT techniques have been applied to other disorders, including substance use disorders, impulse control disorders, anxiety and depressive/bipolar disorders, trauma disorders, and other personality disorders (Goldstein et al., 2015; Marra, 2005; Van Dijk, Jeffrey, & Katz, 2013). DBT is appropriate for any clients who experience intense emotions, especially those who attempt to escape from such emotions through dissociation, distraction, and participation in harmful behaviors such as substance use, self-injury, eating disorders, and other impulse control disorders.

ACCEPTANCE AND COMMITMENT THERAPY

STEVEN C. HAYES (b. 1948)

Steven Hayes created relational frame theory, which later impacted his development of acceptance and commitment therapy (ACT). Hayes earned his PhD in clinical psychology from West Virginia University. He has specialized in the treatment of anxiety disorders; however, his research and clinical interests extend far beyond anxiety. Hayes has worked to develop contextual behavioral science. Hayes is currently working in the behavioral analysis program at the University of Nevada, Reno, as a foundation professor. Hayes has published many research articles and has presented at numerous training workshops and conferences. He has also authored many books, such as *Acceptance and Commitment Therapy: The Process and Practice of Mindful Change* (Hayes, Strosahl, & Wilson, 2012), *Mindfulness and Acceptance for Addictive Behaviors* (Hayes & Levin, 2012), and *Acceptance and Commitment Therapy* (Hayes & Lillis, 2012). Hayes has received many awards, such as the Lifetime Achievement Award from the Association for Behavioral and Cognitive Therapy.

INTRODUCTION/DEVELOPMENT OF ACT

Steven Hayes is the name most widely associated with the development of acceptance and commitment therapy (ACT). ACT shares common philosophical roots with constructivism, narrative, and feminist psychology. ACT has much in common with dialectical behavior therapy in that it is considered a behavior therapy, attends to cognitions, focuses on acceptance of one's thoughts, and helps clients learn that they do not have to act on their thoughts or emotions. ACT assumes that avoidance of negative emotions and thoughts worsens the problem; therefore, full experiencing and acceptance of present-moment thoughts and emotions is how positive change occurs.

KEY CONCEPTS

Experiential Avoidance

Acceptance and commitment therapy does not support the use of cognitive-change techniques or clients' avoidance of distressing thoughts, emotions, interactions, or events. Although these interventions may indeed help people cope with difficult experiences, they are ultimately escape oriented, and hold limited clinical utility because they provide clients with only temporary alleviation from distress. In fact, from an ACT perspective, the etiology of suffering and maladjustment is attributed to **experiential avoidance**, as such avoidance allows clients' current sources of distress to continue to serve as barriers throughout development. When clients embrace acceptance of all their experiences, however, distress becomes less prominent, and clients are enabled to pursue and engage in meaningful life activities.

Clients' nonavoidance of distressing thoughts and emotions can help them to adapt to the experiences, thus diminishing their negative impact, similar to the concept of repeated exposure in exposure-based therapies. In other words, as clients repeatedly observe and process distressing thoughts and experiences without attempting to change or control these inner experiences, their distress becomes desensitized, making it easier for them to practice acceptance.

Relational Frame Theory

Acceptance and commitment therapy is based on **relational frame theory**, a behavioral theory of human language and cognition that helps people recognize how they become entangled in thoughts and words and how those entanglements result in internal struggles against themselves. Hayes believes that people's fusion with their thoughts can lead to suffering; thus, he recommends **defusion** (i.e., the ability to "step back" and separate from thoughts and language) whenever clients become "mindy" or perseverate (Hayes et al., 2012, p. 243). Relational frame theory asserts that language and verbal communication can support clients' maladaptive thinking in that the mind generates thoughts based on past experiences rather than the present situation. As a result, thoughts are often out of context with a current situation and they do not necessarily have the same meaning as an old context or hold valid truth. This process of thoughts from old contexts being placed on new contexts is problematic because individuals tend to avoid distressing thoughts and emotions even if they are out of context, which subsequently leads to the avoidance of events associated with the uncomfortable experiences (Hayes, 2004). Thus, mindfully attending to thoughts and feelings, verbally processing, and accepting distressing thoughts and feelings removes their power to prevent clients from engaging in meaningful events. Once clients develop the psychological flexibility to recognize and accept their private events as out of their control, counseling processes then shift toward the values and **committed action** of clients. That is, therapists collaboratively assist clients with exploring and committing to valued, enriched ways of living. Due to the complexity of ACT's underlying theoretical bases and its abstract nature of acceptance, it is important for therapists to select psychoeducational content based on the developmental and intellectual functioning of clients, and convey such material in an easily comprehensible manner.

THE THERAPEUTIC PROCESS

The major goals of acceptance and commitment therapy are to help clients accept cognitions and emotions that are outside of their control and to encourage clients to make a commitment to creating a life they value. Mindfulness practices, including present-moment awareness, staying centered in the body, and acceptance, are also used, especially to enhance clients' understanding of what they find meaningful and important. Acceptance of thoughts and feelings is an alternative to avoidance (Hayes, 2004). Acceptance is voluntary, open and receptive, and it involves a willingness to interact with the feared object or feelings (Hayes). Acceptance can sometimes have a negative connotation, as in giving up or defeat; however, in the context of ACT, acceptance is a positive emotional response. The acronym ACT captures the core concepts of acceptance and commitment therapy quite well, and these concepts follow:

> A = Accept and embrace thoughts and feelings, especially difficult feelings such as anxiety or pain.
>
> C = Choose a direction in life that reflects who the client truly is.
>
> T = Take steps toward action.

In ACT, the therapeutic alliance is "strong, open, accepting, responsible, and loving" (Morris & Oliver, 2012, p. 71). As is true with DBT, the relationship is also bidirectional, with therapists impacting clients and clients impacting therapists. Therapists are more experiential than cognitive, providing empathic encouragement, compassion, and reassurance. ACT therapists are also respectful of cultural differences, honor diversity and community, and are generally open to clients' spirituality.

ACT therapists initially focus on cultivating clients' acceptance of distress through the use of psychoeducation and creative metaphors pertaining to the mindfulness practices of openly observing one's inner experiences; remaining in the present moment without judgment; and engaging in cognitive defusion, or the distancing of the self from "private events" (e.g., thoughts, evaluations, emotions, mental images, memories, sensations) without reactivity. Additionally, therapists promote clients' development of acceptance by facilitating exercises in which clients are prompted to mindfully attend to their distressing private events or inner experiences, and verbally process them without avoidance. Finally, counseling ends with a review of counseling gains and a plan for relapse and maintenance.

THERAPEUTIC TECHNIQUES AND PROCEDURES

Through the use of metaphor, paradox, and experiential exercises, clients learn how to break up fused thoughts and make healthy contact with their cognitions, feelings, memories, and physical sensations. Rather than challenging their thoughts, as in traditional cognitive therapy, clients gain the skills necessary to accept their thoughts, develop greater clarity about personal values, and commit to needed behavioral change.

The Hexaflex Model

Counseling involves changing clients' responses to the thoughts and feelings associated with their concerns. This can be done through addressing the different components of the "hexaflex" model, which proposes that six processes contribute to healthy, flexible living: (1) attention to the present moment; (2) acceptance; (3) defusion; (4) self-as-context (i.e., people's realization that they are not their thoughts, feelings, and memories; although these aspects are a part of people, they are not the essence of who people are); (5) values (i.e., what people find meaningful in life); and (6) committed action (i.e., setting goals according to values and carrying them out in responsible ways). When one or more of these aspects of the hexaflex model are absent, people risk psychological rigidity. The premise of ACT is that psychological pain is a natural consequence of living; however, psychological rigidity is the cause of unnecessary suffering and maladaptive functioning.

One example of how to use defusion is by repeating a thought over and over again until it loses its meaning. For example, a client may have the thought "I am a bad person." Repeating this thought over and over again, rather than changing the thought, allows for clients to take a step back from their distressing thoughts by allowing these thoughts to lose their meaning. Another example of defusion is instructing clients to thank their mind for the thought or noting the thought as interesting, rather than trying to push the thought away.

Awareness and Acceptance

One example of an ACT intervention is encouraging clients to begin participating in the activities they once enjoyed but withdrew from as a result of their concerns. Instead of rejecting and avoiding feelings, thoughts, and urges, clients are taught through ACT interventions to be aware and accepting instead. ACT also encourages clients to refrain from activities that bring temporary pleasure (e.g., scrolling through their social media feeds) but impair progression toward goals that are important to the clients (e.g., spending time with others). As time spent engaging in positive activities increases, time spent engaging in the undesirable behavior will decrease. As clients' avoidance decreases, they are able to move toward their valued goals with less obstruction. A nonjudgmental awareness may also reduce the negative emotions that clients attach to their concerns.

APPLICATION AND CURRENT USE OF ACT

In keeping with behavioral therapies, ACT is committed to empirical research and can be applied to a wide range of problems and disorders, with change strategies being tailored to meet the needs of clients. ACT is an emerging cognitive behavioral therapy for those who have anxiety, especially those with social anxiety disorder (Brady & Whitman, 2012; Hayes et al., 2012; Smout, Hayes, Atkins, Klausen, & Duguid, 2012). Phobias, posttraumatic stress disorder (PTSD), panic, and other types of anxieties that are reinforced by avoidance also tend to respond well to the experiential exercises of ACT, such as externalization, exposure to the avoided feelings, and acceptance (Hayes et al., 2012). Because those with generalized anxiety have a tendency to restrict their engagement in meaningful activities to avoid negative internal experiences, ACT draws on various metaphors and mindfulness exercises to change clients' relationship with their internal experiences (Avdagic, Morrissey, & Boschen, 2014; Hayes et al., 2012). A recent meta-analysis determined that ACT was an efficacious therapy for obsessive-compulsive disorder (OCD) and reduced symptomology related to comorbid diagnoses (Bluett et al., 2014).

Randomized controlled studies have shown the effectiveness of ACT in treating depression, psychosis, heroin addiction, substance abuse, chronic pain, and borderline personality disorder (Hayes et al., 2012; Morris & Oliver, 2012). Meta-analytic reviews supporting ACT and the publication of treatment manuals and practitioner's guides have helped ACT wind its way into mainstream practice (Hayes, Luoma, Bond, Masuda, & Lillis, 2006; Ost, 2008; Powers, Zum Vorde Sive Vording, & Emmelkamp, 2009).

MINDFULNESS-BASED COGNITIVE THERAPY

JON KABAT-ZINN (b. 1944)

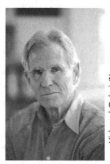

Jon Kabat-Zinn is known for the development of mindfulness-based stress reduction (MBSR; Kabat-Zinn, 1990). Kabat-Zinn studied meditation with several Buddhist teachers, and much of his time was spent at the Insight Meditation Society, where he later taught. He focused on mindfulness and stress reduction and placed MBSR in a scientific context rather than linking it to the Buddhist framework. Kabat-Zinn has published many books, such as *Full Catastrophe Living: Using the Wisdom of Your Body and Mind to Face Stress, Pain, and Illness* (1991) and *Wherever You Go, There You Are.*

INTRODUCTION/DEVELOPMENT OF MBCT

MBSR captured the attention of three cognitive scientists in the United Kingdom and Canada—Zindel Segal, Mark Williams, and John Teasdale—who were conducting research on the cognitive processes that trigger and maintain depression (Crane, 2012). In conjunction with Kabat-Zinn, the trio developed a manualized version of therapy, mindfulness-based cognitive therapy (MBCT), that is closely aligned with MBSR but emphasizes cognitive processes, as well (Segal, Williams, & Teasdale, 2002).

KEY CONCEPTS

Acceptance

Like ACT and DBT, MBCT holds that when people experience acceptance, the need to escape, avoid, or experience severe emotional reactivity to a triggering event is reduced and positive change occurs. The construct of **acceptance** can be understood as a willingness to experience psychological events (i.e., thoughts, feelings, memories) without having to avoid them or let them unduly influence behavior (Butler & Ciarrochi, 2007). The concept of acceptance is generally discussed in the context of clients' distressing or unpleasant feelings. However, acceptance pertains to accepting and being aware of enjoyable or pleasurable experiences, as well; the prolonged holding on to, or excessive prizing of, positive experiences without letting go also has the potential to result in distressing thoughts, feelings, or maladaptive behaviors, as people try to hold on to things they crave or desire, yet these things are often fleeting. MBCT and ACT are two approaches that place a heavy emphasis on the concept of acceptance.

The Being Mode

Mindfulness-based cognitive therapy helps to explain the ways that depression is activated and reactivated. Human brains are hard wired to react to threat, and once those neural pathways have been developed, they are more likely to be activated by another event that the brain perceives as threatening. MBCT reduces the threat by helping to break the cycle in which ruminative thoughts erupt, in an effort to problem solve a given situation deemed unacceptable by the person. Through mindfulness meditation and the practice of acceptance, the aversive or avoidant feelings that keep the negative thoughts in the mind are eliminated (Hayes et al., 1999). A fallacy arises in the brain that instinctively wants to be "doing" something to solve the problem, return to equilibrium, and make the negative feelings go away, but the more an individual tries to analyze, ruminate, and problem solve, the more the individual is triggering the very cycle from which that individual is trying to escape (Williams, 2010).

The alternative response to "doing" is "being," a paradigm shift that is referred to as the "doing and being mode of mind" (Crane et al., 2010). The doing mode, as previously mentioned, is what the brain does; it creates thoughts. The being mode is in touch with direct experience, moment by moment, recognizing bodily sensations as they arise, without agendas or judgments, and letting go of thoughts. The result is an openness to new experience, rather than ruminating on how to achieve an objective or solve a problem. In mindfulness meditation, all thoughts that arise are acceptable, but the person does not have to follow the story line associated with the unwanted thoughts.

Tenets of Mindfulness

Specific components of mindfulness are believed to lead to positive change. It is very difficult to learn and successfully apply mindfulness techniques. Success with this approach demands constant effort directed toward regular practice and application. Throughout life, mindfulness practices must be applied and honed, but with practice, they become easier to use. The five commonly held tenants of mindfulness that are believed to help people decrease distress and feel better include (Baer, Smith, Hopkins, Krietemeyer, & Toney, 2006):

1. *Observing inner experiences:* Attending to one's inner experience, or observing internal and external sensations, cognitions, emotions, and perceptions
2. *Acting with awareness:* Paying attention to the present moment and one's behavior
3. *Nonjudgment of inner experience:* Remaining nonjudgmental of one's inner experience
4. *Describing or labeling inner experience:* Using words to express oneself, or describe inner experiences, sensations, cognitions, emotions, and perceptions
5. *Nonreactivity:* Remaining nonreactive to inner experiences, or noticing distressing cognitions, emotions, or sensations without reacting.

Some research suggests that the following components of mindfulness meditation are what creates a process of self-regulation: (1) attention regulation, (2) body awareness, (3) emotion regulation, and (4) change in perspective of self (Holzel et al., 2011). Attention regulation involves staying in the present moment and focusing attention on something in particular. Body awareness is the ability to be aware of and attend to bodily sensations. This is important to achieve a holistic mindfulness experience. Mindfulness also helps people regulate their emotions by responding to intense emotions in healthy ways, which is known as emotion regulation. Finally, a change in perspective of the self involves viewing the self in a more positive and mindful way, which allows people to live in the present moment.

THE THERAPEUTIC PROCESS

Mindfulness-based cognitive therapy is intended to prevent depression relapse. The goal of this approach is to assist clients in moving away from obsessing and perseverating on thoughts and feelings of their concern and, instead, teach them to be more present in the here and now. By focusing on the present moment and gaining awareness of their thoughts and feelings, clients are less likely to relapse. Therapists working from a MBCT approach help clients shift away from their negative thoughts and moods toward a place of personal acceptance. Therapists using this approach are empathic, warm, and caring. Therapists stay mindful of the therapeutic relationship, which is pertinent to therapeutic outcomes. Therapists listen deeply and stay in the present moment.

As mentioned, MBCT is manualized and thus highly structured. Generally, MBCT is conducted in eight group sessions of 2 to 2.5 hours in length and one all-day session. Follow-up sessions may be scheduled randomly in the following year to reinforce practice. Group size is usually limited to 10 or 12 participants, and each person is interviewed in advance to determine their readiness for counseling. The treatment protocol is similar to the following (Crane, 2012):

Weeks 1–4: Developing skills, mindfulness meditation training, present-moment awareness, recognition of thoughts, emotions, bodily sensations, and behaviors

Weeks 5–8: Shifting toward recognition of more challenging thoughts and feelings, working on acceptance.

Breath meditation, yoga, and body scans are the most commonly used techniques for the MCBT program. The delivery modality is predominantly verbal communication and experiential activities.

THERAPEUTIC TECHNIQUES AND PROCEDURES

Mindfulness-based cognitive therapy combines both mindfulness and cognitive techniques to help clients gain a better understanding of their feelings. These techniques also help clients manage their thoughts and feelings to alleviate distress. The techniques reviewed in this section include conscious thought processing, mindfulness, and decentering.

Conscious Thought Processing

Instead of allowing thoughts and feelings to direct an individual's behaviors or reactions, in this approach, clients are instructed to acknowledge that these thoughts or feelings exist, but alternatively allow them to pass over them and not control them. This approach aids clients in moving away from a place in which unconscious automatic thought patterns rule their behaviors, and toward more conscious thought processing. This conscious thought processing significantly disrupts and disables their traditional, destructive thought patterns. MBCT seeks to help the client to observe intrusive thought patterns without judgment. Techniques of this approach involve clients being mindful of patterns of thoughts, feelings, and bodily sensations.

Mindfulness

Mindfulness can be classified most broadly into two categorical domains of practice: (a) *focused attention*, or concentrative practices; and (b) open monitoring, or *bare attention* practices (Ainsworth, Eddershaw, Meron, Baldwin, & Garner, 2013). Focused attention involves focusing on one thing at a time, and open monitoring involves gaining awareness of one's thoughts, feelings, and sensations. Both concentrative and bare attention mindfulness practices are used as intervention strategies to promote mindfulness; however, it is imperative to note that mindfulness is not something to be achieved or an end goal of therapy. Rather, it is the application of mindfulness that enhances inner awareness, builds nonjudgmental acceptance of both pleasure and distress, and ultimately cultivates an enriched experience of living and well-being. MBCT helps one to recognize these experiences while promoting relaxation and calming the mind and body.

People who practice mindfulness meditation are expected to set aside a certain amount of time daily for practice. They learn to conduct a body scan, to pay attention to their breathing, how to meditate, and how to bring their mind back to the present moment when it wanders. Instruction on mindful movement and walking meditation are also taught as part of the repertoire of skills. Therapists who use this approach should embody the spirit of mindfulness, as this helps them to be authentic in helping clients develop their mindfulness practices (Crane, 2012).

Decentering

Using mindfulness, people learn to stay in the moment using a decentering approach that reduces "black and white" (i.e., either/or thinking) and encourages an accepting attitude. As people focus on their breath, thoughts become like clouds floating through their mind, without judgment and without getting stuck. **Decentering**, also known as **diffusion**, is the process of maintaining a degree of separation from inner experiences, such as thoughts, feelings, or perceptions, and recognizing such experiences as mental processes rather than facts or truth. That is, decentering and diffusion essentially mirror the mindfulness tenet of observing inner experiences, which enables clients to simply notice their thoughts, allow these thoughts to pass without believing they must reveal truth about themselves or their environment, and respond to distress in a desirable, adaptive manner. Decentering is described as being similar to the process of distancing in CBT, in which clients gain objectivity over thoughts (Hofmann et al., 2010). However, instead of changing troublesome thoughts, or avoiding them, a decentered attitude is one of accepting things exactly as they are, in the moment.

Breathing exercises, meditation, body scanning techniques, and yoga are commonly part of MBCT. This approach also encourages self-acceptance in clients and assists them in releasing feelings of guilt and embarrassment associated with their concerns.

To gain optimal benefits, individuals must regularly practice mindfulness techniques. In this way, therapists can help clients to cultivate enhanced awareness, acceptance, nonjudgment, self-compassion, and loving kindness through the use of mindfulness-based assignments both in and between sessions. Table 8.2 provides examples of activities that therapists can use with both youth and adults to help them cultivate mindfulness.

TABLE 8.2 Mindfulness Exercises

Title	Description
My five senses	This activity can be used with clients to help promote relaxation and awareness of all five senses. With the list below, therapists may help guide the clients' awareness of using all five senses: Have clients notice five things they can see (e.g., small tear or mark on the table, a shadow on the wall). Have clients notice four things they can feel (e.g., cool breeze against their face, the sweater they are wearing). Have clients notice three things they can hear (e.g., chirping of a bird, sound of cars in the background). Have clients notice two things they can smell (e.g., smell of fresh cut grass, smell of perfume). Have clients notice one things they can taste (e.g., a piece of gum, aftertaste of food that was just eaten). This exercise can help bring awareness to each of the five senses and can be used anywhere to help promote calmness and relaxation. Remember to remind clients that it is okay if they do not find the specified number for each sense. The purpose of the activity is to feel more grounded.
Connecting the smell	This activity involves clients using their sense of smell and different scents to promote awareness and relaxation. Therapists use calming scents and/ or scent-related objects, such as an orange peel, a flower, a bar of lavender soap, a chamomile tea bag, or any other pleasant smells. Clients are instructed to close their eyes and touch and smell each object as a way to connect with the fragrances. They are then asked to share what they smelled, how it smelled, and what it was like to focus their attention on the different scents of the objects. Ways they can use their sense of smell and scents to deepen their mindfulness practices can be discussed.
My colorful emotions	In this exercise, clients are first guided into a state of relaxation. They are then instructed to think about where they feel a certain uncomfortable emotion (e.g., anger) and visually imagine that area on their bodies (e.g., jaw). Therapists ask clients to think about what color they imagine the area to be. Is the color warm or cold? How big is the area when they feel the emotion, and what shape does it take? Therapists ask clients to then visualize a magic color that has the power to change the color and size of the emotion (e.g., cold blue to warm yellow). Direct the clients to visualize that area with the new color for a minute and invite them to reflect on how that feels. As the exercise continues, the goal is for clients to gain control of their feelings and to understand that, through using awareness and visual imagery, they have the power to control how they manage pain and emotion.
Self-compassion	This activity can be used to help promote self-awareness of emotions and an ability to stay in the present moment. Therapists invite clients to think about what self-compassion means them. Therapists may ask: What does self-compassion look like to you? Whom do you feel compassion for? How does that influence your self-compassion? What feelings are you feeling right now? Clients are instructed to write a paragraph on what self-compassion means to them and what feelings they are currently feeling. Clients are then invited to sit and pause, noticing their emotions (i.e., positive or negative) and thoughts. They are invited to do this without judgment, to simply observe. Creating this space gives clients an opportunity to reflect on their immediate emotions and the experiences they have when they consider self-compassion.

APPLICATION AND CURRENT USE OF MBCT

Meditation has been shown to change the way the brain functions (Young et al., 2018). It reduces emotions, improves rational decision making, and prevents relapse in depression by reducing or altering the brain's neural response to sad mood. This neural response can trigger a flood of ruminative and avoidant behavior in people with a prior history of depression (Coelho, Canter, & Ernst, 2007; Farber & Metzger, 2009; Kirk, Downar, & Montague, 2011). Research using functional magnetic resonance imaging (MRI) scans has shown that the mechanism by which mindfulness and acceptance strategies are effective is that of exposure and response prevention (Holzel et al., 2011). The use of MBCT to prevent relapse of major depressive disorder has been well documented in the literature. Two randomized controlled trials have since provided the evidence base to support MBCT's effectiveness (Ma & Teasdale, 2004; Teasdale et al., 2000).

Studies indicate that MBCT is effective in treating a variety of different psychiatric conditions, including depression relapse prevention, acute depression, residual depression, bipolar disorder, generalized anxiety disorder, panic disorder, and adjustment disorders (Deckersbach, Hölzel, Eisner, Lazar, & Nierenberg, 2014; Sundquist et al., 2015). A recent meta-analysis of randomized controlled trials reported that mindfulness-based interventions were associated with improvements in anxiety, depression, stress, and overall quality of life among individuals with chronic medical conditions, those with mental health disorders, and those in good mental and physical health (Gotink et al., 2015).

The literature suggests that mindfulness may help clients with obsessive-compulsive disorder to regain a sense of control and break the link between automatic thought patterns and subsequent compulsive behaviors (Key, Rowa, Bieling, McCabe, & Pawluk, 2017). Research supports that MBCT helps clients with obsessive-compulsive disorder to better regulate negative emotions and reduce symptoms (Hertenstein et al., 2012; Key et al., 2017).

Mindfulness shows effectiveness in working with a myriad of client presenting concerns. This approach is helpful in preventing relapse for drug and alcohol addiction, in reducing gambling, and in treating children with attention-deficit hyperactivity disorder (ADHD) and emotion dysregulation (Vallejo & Amaro, 2009). It may also have implications for couples counseling, suicide prevention, and as an adjunct to medication management in the treatment of bipolar disorder (Miklowitz, 2010; Williams et al., 2008).

Research is ongoing to differentiate between the various aspects of mindfulness to determine what exactly produces the changed effect. Aspects of mindfulness such as body scan, focus on breathing, acceptance of thoughts, and present-moment awareness may be at work individually or may be found to work together to generate a synergistic effect (Vallejo & Amaro, 2009).

Some authors (e.g., Harrington & Pickles, 2009) have questioned whether counseling approaches that include mindfulness should be classified as cognitive therapy, since the focus of mindfulness techniques varies from the cognitive goal of identifying and changing dysfunctional thoughts to instead recognizing and accepting thoughts and then letting them pass without judgment or action.

SCHEMA THERAPY

JEFFREY E. YOUNG (b. 1950)

Jeffrey Young, the developer of Schema Therapy, has specializations in personality disorders, self-esteem, and relationship issues. He obtained his undergraduate degree from Yale University and his PhD from the University of Pennsylvania. He then worked with Aaron Beck during his postdoctoral internship at the Center for Cognitive Therapy at the University of Pennsylvania.

He also served as the Director of Research and Training at the University of Pennsylvania. Young is the founder of the Schema Therapy Institute and has conducted many trainings, workshops, and lectures throughout the world. Young also founded the Cognitive Therapy Centers of New York and Connecticut and serves as director at the Cognitive Therapy Center of New York. In addition, Young has been a professor in the Department of Psychiatry at Columbia University. He has authored many research articles and books, including *Schema Therapy: A Practitioner's Guide (2003)* and *Reinventing Your Life (1993)*.

INTRODUCTION/DEVELOPMENT OF SCHEMA THERAPY

Schema therapy, developed by Jeffrey Young (1990/1999), goes beyond Beck's cognitive therapy and integrates psychodynamic, interpersonal, attachment, and experiential techniques to achieve change at an emotional level. Schema therapy was originally developed to work with clients who have personality disorders and those with chronic problems for whom focused interventions were not working. The approach goes deeper than most cognitive therapies, to recognize that core schemas have developed in childhood that can have lifelong implications. The approach offers a bridge between regular CBT or brief forms of counseling and longer interventions that attempt to get at the root of more ingrained problems.

KEY CONCEPTS

Early Maladaptive Schemas

By looking at early childhood adaptive patterns, schema therapy helps clients understand how actions in the present trigger **early maladaptive schemas**, or self-defeating emotional patterns from childhood. **Early maladaptive schemas** are existing schemas that individuals assume to be true about themselves and their world that develop early on in life, develop in response to family environments, and tend to be chronic (Young, Klosko, & Weishaar, 2003).

Maladaptive schemas from childhood can be thought of as occurring when a child's needs (e.g., safety, acceptance, respect, nurturance, approval) are unmet. If unmet, these needs can transform into personality disorders or patterns of interacting with the world in adulthood. People who have personality disorders often have maladaptive coping strategies that are overcompensating, surrendering, or avoidant in nature. For example, people who develop borderline personality disorder often experience their families as demeaning, unstable, unsafe, neglectful, or punitive. Over time and with repeated exposure, these experiences develop into schemas that become core aspects of the personality structure. The modes involved with borderline personality disorder are (1) the abandoned and abused child; (2) the angry and impulsive child; (3) the detached protector; (4) the punitive parent; and (5) the healthy adult (Kellogg & Young, 2006). Those with borderline personality disorder will respond to their relationships in accordance with these schemas, often rapidly flipping between different modes. For example, when facing the withdrawal of affection from a partner, a client with borderline personality disorder may enter the abandoned child mode, then move into the angry and impulsive child mode and act out, and then move into the punitive parent mode in which the client blames herself for being "bad" and causing the withdrawal of affection. Clients all have unique schemas that are related to their past experiences.

Schema Domains

Schema therapy helps clients to recognize their maladaptive patterns, which fall within five schema domains:

1. *Disconnection and rejection:* Abandonment, defectiveness/shame, social isolation, emotional deprivation, mistrust/abuse

2. *Impaired autonomy and performance:*
   a. Dependence/incompetence
   b. Vulnerability (to harm or illness)
   c. Enmeshment (codependency)
   d. Failure
3. *Impaired limits:* Entitlement/grandiosity, lacking self-control or discipline
4. *Other directedness:* Approval- or recognition-seeking, subjugation, self-sacrificing
5. *Overvigilance and inhibition:* Negativity, emotional inhibition, punitiveness, unrelenting standards/criticalness.

Table 8.3 includes common early maladaptive schemas.

TABLE 8.3 Schema Therapy: Early Maladaptive Schemas

Abandonment/ instability (AB)	The perceived instability or unreliability of those available for support and connection. Involves the sense that significant others will not be able to continue providing emotional support, connection, strength, or practical protection because they are emotionally unstable and unpredictable (e.g., angry outbursts), unreliable, or erratically present; because they will die imminently; or because they will abandon the individual in favor of someone better.
Mistrust/ abuse (MA)	The expectation that others will hurt, abuse, humiliate, cheat, lie, manipulate, or take advantage. Usually involves the perception that the harm is intentional or the result of unjustified and extreme negligence. May include the sense that one always ends up being cheated relative to others or "getting the short end of the stick."
Emotional deprivation (ED)	Expectation that one's desire for a normal degree of emotional support will not be adequately met by others. The three major forms of deprivation are: A. Deprivation of nurturance: absence of attention, affection, warmth, or companionship B. Deprivation of empathy: absence of understanding, listening, self-disclosure, or mutual sharing of feelings from others C. Deprivation of protection: absence of strength, direction, or guidance from others.
Defectiveness/ shame (DS)	The feeling that one is defective, bad, unwanted, inferior, or invalid in important respects; or that one would be unlovable to significant others if exposed. May involve hypersensitivity to criticism, rejection, and blame; self-consciousness, comparisons, and insecurity around others; or a sense of shame regarding one's perceived flaws. These flaws may be private (e.g., selfishness, angry impulses, unacceptable sexual desires) or public (e.g., undesirable physical appearance, social awkwardness).
Social isolation/ alienation (SI)	The feeling that one is isolated from the rest of the world, different from other people, and/or not part of any group or community.
Dependence/ incompetence (D)	Belief that one is unable to handle one's everyday responsibilities in a competent manner, without considerable help from others (e.g., take care of oneself, solve daily problems, exercise good judgment, tackle new tasks, make good decisions). Often presents as helplessness.
Vulnerability to harm or illness (VH)	Exaggerated fear that imminent catastrophe will strike at any time and that one will be unable to prevent it. Fears focus on one or more of the following: (A) medical catastrophes: e.g., heart attacks, AIDS; (B) emotional catastrophes: e.g., going crazy; (C): external catastrophes: e.g., elevators collapsing, victimized by criminals, airplane crashes, earthquakes.

(Continued)

TABLE 8.3 (*Continued*)

Enmeshment/ undeveloped self (EM)	Excessive emotional involvement and closeness with one or more significant others (often parents), at the expense of full individuation or normal social development. Often involves the belief that at least one of the enmeshed individuals cannot survive or be happy without the constant support of the other. May also include feelings of being smothered by, or fused with, others; OR insufficient individual identity. Often experienced as a feeling of emptiness and floundering; having no direction; or, in extreme cases, questioning one's existence.
Failure to achieve (FA)	The belief that one has failed, will inevitably fail, or is fundamentally inadequate relative to one's peers, in areas of achievement (school, career, sports, etc.). Often involves beliefs that one is stupid, inept, untalented, ignorant, lower in status, less successful than others, etc.
Entitlement/ grandiosity (ET)	The belief that one is superior to other people; entitled to special rights and privileges; or not bound by the rules of reciprocity that guide normal social interaction. Often involves insistence that one should be able to do or have whatever one wants, regardless of what is realistic, what others consider reasonable, or the cost to others; OR an exaggerated focus on superiority (e.g., being among the most successful, famous, wealthy)—to achieve power or control (not primarily for attention or approval). Sometimes includes excessive competitiveness toward, or domination of, others: asserting one's power, forcing one's point of view, or controlling the behavior of others in line with one's own desires, without empathy or concern for others' needs or feelings.
Insufficient self-control/self-discipline (IS)	Pervasive difficulty or refusal to exercise sufficient self-control and frustration tolerance to achieve personal goals, or to restrain the excessive expression of emotions and impulses. In its milder form, the individual presents with an exaggerated emphasis on discomfort-avoidance: avoiding pain, conflict, confrontation, responsibility, or overexertion, at the expense of personal fulfillment, commitment, or integrity.
Subjugation (SB)	Excessive surrendering of control to others because one feels coerced—usually to avoid anger, retaliation, or abandonment. The two major forms of subjugation are: A. Subjugation of needs: suppression of one's preferences, decisions, and desires B. Subjugation of emotions: suppression of emotional expression, especially anger. Usually involves the perception that one's own desires, opinions, and feelings are not valid or important to others. Frequently presents as excessive compliance, combined with hypersensitivity to feeling trapped. Generally leads to a buildup of anger, manifested in maladaptive symptoms (e.g., passive-aggressive behavior, uncontrolled outbursts of temper, psychosomatic symptoms, withdrawal of affection, "acting out," substance abuse).
Self-sacrifice (SS)	Excessive focus on voluntarily meeting the needs of others in daily situations, at the expense of one's own gratification. The most common reasons are to prevent causing pain to others; to avoid guilt from feeling selfish; or to maintain the connection with others perceived as needy. Often results from an acute sensitivity to the pain of others. Sometimes leads to a sense that one's own needs are not being adequately met and to resentment of those who are taken care of. (Overlaps with concept of codependency.)

Approval-seeking/ recognition-seeking (AS)	Excessive emphasis on gaining approval, recognition, or attention from other people, or fitting in, at the expense of developing a secure and true sense of self. One's sense of esteem is dependent primarily on the reactions of others rather than on one's own natural inclinations. Sometimes includes an overemphasis on status, appearance, social acceptance, money, or achievement as a means of gaining approval, admiration, or attention (not primarily for power or control). Frequently results in major life decisions that are inauthentic or unsatisfying; or in hypersensitivity to rejection.
Negativity/ pessimism (NP)	A pervasive, lifelong focus on the negative aspects of life (pain, death, loss, disappointment, conflict, guilt, resentment, unsolved problems, potential mistakes, betrayal, things that could go wrong, etc.) while minimizing or neglecting the positive or optimistic aspects. Usually includes an exaggerated expectation—in a wide range of work, financial, or interpersonal situations—that things will eventually go seriously wrong, or that aspects of one's life that seem to be going well will ultimately fall apart. Usually involves an inordinate fear of making mistakes that might lead to financial collapse, loss, humiliation, or being trapped in a bad situation. Because potential negative outcomes are exaggerated, these individuals are frequently characterized by chronic worry, vigilance, complaining, or indecision.
Emotional inhibition (EI)	The excessive inhibition of spontaneous action, feeling, or communication—usually to avoid disapproval by others, feelings of shame, or losing control of one's impulses. The most common areas of inhibition involve: (1) inhibition of anger and aggression; (2) inhibition of positive impulses (e.g., joy, affection, sexual excitement, play); (3) difficulty expressing vulnerability or communicating freely about one's feelings, needs, etc.; or (4) excessive emphasis on rationality while disregarding emotions.
Unrelenting standards/ hypercriticalness (US)	The underlying belief that one must strive to meet very high internalized standards of behavior and performance, usually to avoid criticism. Typically results in feelings of pressure or difficulty slowing down; and in hypercriticalness toward oneself and others. Must involve significant impairment in: pleasure, relaxation, health, self-esteem, sense of accomplishment, or satisfying relationships. Unrelenting standards typically present as: (1) perfectionism, inordinate attention to detail, or an underestimate of how good one's own performance is relative to the norm; (2) rigid rules and "shoulds" in many areas of life, including unrealistically high moral, ethical, cultural, or religious precepts; or (3) preoccupation with time and efficiency, so that more can be accomplished.
Punitiveness (PU)	The belief that people should be harshly punished for making mistakes. Involves the tendency to be angry, intolerant, punitive, and impatient with those people (including oneself) who do not meet one's expectations or standards. Usually includes difficulty forgiving mistakes in oneself or others, because of a reluctance to consider extenuating circumstances, allow for human imperfection, or empathize with feelings.

Source: Rafaeli, E., Bernstein, D. P., & Young, J. (2011). *Schema therapy: The CBT distinctive features series.* New York, NY: Routledge.

When a schema is activated, we respond in one of three ways: (1) overcompensation, (2) avoidance, or (3) surrender to the schema as if it were true (Ohanian & Rashed, 2012). All three of these responses could lead to problems in coping with life and relationships. For example, Suzanne is a divorced woman who has an attachment schema that causes her to fear abandonment. Her attachment schema is activated one Friday night when a man she has been seeing for 3 weeks does not show up at the restaurant at the agreed-upon time. When activated, Suzanne responds with emotions: anger that he does not respect her enough to be on time, sadness that he might not be the right man for her, and fear that she will always be alone. She responds by leaving the restaurant with a temper, avoiding his calls, and not responding to his text messages. Suzanne's method of coping (avoidance) was learned in childhood, when she would avoid her mother's anger and wrath by leaving the house and going to the neighbor's house. However, the childhood method of coping does not work so well now that Suzanne is an adult. In this case, by actively avoiding the man's attempts to reach her, she prevented him from explaining that he had been in a car accident and was unable to keep the date. By resorting to her childhood pattern of avoidance, Suzanne unconsciously contributed to the creation of the very situation that she feared most—an end of the relationship and the result that she is alone once again. We all carry around internalized schemas based upon past experiences that impact how we interact with others.

THE THERAPEUTIC PROCESS

The goal of schema therapy is to help people achieve and maintain a healthy adult mode of functioning (Ohanian & Rashed, 2012). Another goal is to help clients develop and sustain a healthy adult schema and stop engaging in maladaptive coping styles so they have greater amounts of flexibility and freedom and, ultimately, are happier. This is accomplished by aiding clients in getting their needs met (within and outside the therapeutic relationship), resisting previously controlling schemas and modes, and constructing healthier (more adaptive) schemas and modes. According to schema therapy, avoidance strategies are believed to stem from unmet needs, such as a need for approval, self-expression, acceptance, and attention. Therefore, counseling aims to make clients aware of these strategies, connect present behaviors with childhood events, and replace them with more adaptive strategies.

Schema therapy can be brief, but is generally longer in duration, depending on the client's needs. Ideally, this approach involves clients participating in two individual counseling sessions per week over an average of 3 years (Arntz et al., 2009). The assessment phase may include the use of experiential exercises and schema inventories, such as the *Young Schema Questionnaire* (Young, 2005), the *Young Compensation Inventory* (Young, 2003a), the *Young Parenting Inventory* (Sheffield et al., 2006; Young, 2003b), and the *Schema Mode Inventory* (Young et al., 2007).

The empathic therapeutic relationship is considered foundational to schema therapy (Kellogg & Young, 2006). Therapists' own responses to clients also provide valuable information. Therapists who use schema therapy are openly warm, caring, and flexible. Therapists must also understand their own emotional needs through schema development and awareness of early experiences.

People have a variety of schemas they use in different situations, including emotional, decisional, relational, and physical schemas (Beck et al., 2015). Recent neurobiological research reinforces that a great deal of mental processing occurs at the unconscious or implicit level (Uhlmann, Pizarro, & Bloom, 2008). Temperament, biological predisposition, and life experience contribute to the development of coping styles. When working with schemas, the therapist must take care to balance empathic attunement with caring confrontation.

THERAPEUTIC TECHNIQUES AND INTERVENTIONS

Interventions in schema therapy include the use of cognitive, experiential, and emotion-focused techniques to help clients recognize and change self-defeating patterns (Kellogg & Young, 2008). Experiential and gestalt techniques used involve imagery work related to early dysfunctional relationships as well as dialogues between the different schema modes.

Limited Reparenting and Empathic Confrontation

Using the power of the therapeutic alliance as an intervention is known as **limited reparenting** (Rafaeli et al., 2011). Limited reparenting takes a variety of forms, depending on the clients' needs and may involve connection, warmth, and nurturance. This process encourages dependency of clients on the therapists by regulating emotions. Once this healthy dependency is created, clients can then learn new ways of developing autonomy. Clients learn to develop trust because their needs have been met. By recognizing that people develop maladaptive schemas because core needs were not met in childhood, the therapist works to create a therapeutic environment in which clients' needs can be met. Therapists also use empathic confrontation to challenge clients' maladaptive schemas in a warm and respectful manner (Edwards & Arntz, 2012).

Cognitive Interventions

Cognitive behavioral interventions include the use of homework exercises, challenging beliefs, and the modification of maladaptive behaviors.

Cognitive techniques in schema therapy include (Young, Klosko, & Weishaar, 2003):

1. Testing the validity of the schema
2. Reframing evidence that supports the schema
3. Evaluating the advantages and disadvantages of the client's coping styles
4. Facilitating dialogues between the "schema side" and the "healthy side"
5. Constructing schema flash cards
6. Filling out schema diary forms.

Schema Flash Cards

After the schema restructuring process is complete, clients are invited to develop schema flash cards. The flash cards are examples of healthy ways clients can respond to activating schema triggers. Clients can carry the flash cards with them and reference them whenever they have a schema that is activated. The flash cards provide clients with the most powerful evidence against the schema, and ideally it helps them change their thinking (Young et al., 2003). The schema flash cards are used, as needed, before and during a triggering event. The therapist plays a very active role in helping clients develop the flash card, as the clients' healthy side is not yet developed enough to provide a strong opposing rationale (Young et al., 2003).

After clients have become skilled at developing and using schema flash cards, therapists can introduce the concept of a schema diary (Young et al., 2003). Using a schema diary, clients construct healthy responses to their schema that they can use in their day-to-day life. Clients are directed to carry copies of schema diary forms with them, and when they are triggered, they complete the form so that they can handle the situation in an adaptive way. The schema diary involves clients identifying triggering events, thoughts, emotions, schemas, behaviors, healthy views, overreactions, realistic concerns, and healthy behaviors (Young et al., 2003).

APPLICATION AND CURRENT USE OF SCHEMA THERAPY

Schema therapy is effective in treating people with borderline personality disorder (Farrell, Shaw, & Webber, 2009; Giesen-Bloo et al., 2006; Nadort et al., 2009), people with relational problems (Rafaeli et al., 2011), and people who are dually diagnosed with a co-occurring personality disorder and another mental disorder. Schema therapy is also a promising treatment for avoidant personality disorder (Weinbrecht et al., 2016). Schema therapy can be seamlessly integrated with CBT approaches to address personality disorders, substance abuse, depressive and anxiety disorders, or eating disorders (Rafaeli, Bernstein, & Young, 2011). Research indicates schema therapy has also shown effectiveness in treating pain management and sexual disorders (Hofmann, 2012).

GENERAL ASSESSMENT OF THIRD-WAVE CBT

EVALUATION OF THIRD-WAVE CBT

Limitations

While third-wave approaches have received a lot of support, some limitations can be noted. For example, concern has been raised over the spiritual aspects of mindfulness-based approaches, as spirituality-related concepts may *not* resonate with some clients (Fruzzetti & Erikson, 2010).

DBT has also been criticized for being too narrow due to its primary focus on individuals with BPD. It can also be seen as negative because it is a theory of dysfunction, as opposed to health. However, DBT can be modified to meet the needs of clients not diagnosed with BPD, and research has shown its effectiveness with many populations and presenting concerns. It is important to use DBT carefully when working with clients who do not meet the criteria for which DBT was originally created (Bedics, Korslund, Sayrs, & McFarr, 2013).

DBT tends to be demanding of therapists, and extensive training is required to effectively implement the techniques. The application of DBT in its pure form is also resource intensive, requiring clients engage in intensive therapy over an extended period. DBT is also not for everyone; this therapy can demand much from clients and requires them to be active participants in counseling.

ACT has also received some criticism because of the complexity of its theoretical base, relational frame theory. A misunderstanding of relational frame theory may lead to misuse of the approach.

Strengths and Contributions

The third-wave approaches may be well suited to meet the needs of culturally diverse clients. For example, many of these approaches emphasize clients' values; thus, therapists are encouraged to respect the worldviews of their clients. In addition, context is important in the third-wave approaches, and a focus on context is inherently culturally sensitive.

Mindfulness is an intervention that has demonstrated success in addressing a variety of issues. For example, practicing mindfulness can help people become aware of and understand their feelings; recognize their vulnerabilities and the triggers that may lead to problems; and become better aware of the connections between their thoughts and feelings. Mindfulness meditation can also be part of a spiritual practice, or it can be part of behavioral or psychological practice. The third-wave approaches can readily be integrated with other counseling approaches or used as stand-alone approaches.

ACT is a promising new approach that adds an element of experiential theory to the traditional cognitive and behavioral milieu. ACT's focus on experiencing and accepting emotions and thoughts may fit well with people who have a difficult time letting go.

Schema therapy's major contribution is the understanding that early maladaptive schemas play a role in adult development and mental health. For some people, cognitive work solely for automatic thoughts may not be helpful. Instead, exploring ingrained problems and core schemas that have emerged from earlier life experiences is necessary for change to occur.

DBT can be a demanding, resource-intensive approach, yet its power is well demonstrated via research. Changes that take place as the result of dialectic shifts have been shown to be long lasting (Samai & Algamor, 2011).

In addition, the third-wave approaches are manualized; therefore, therapists can use techniques in a structured format. The collaborative nature of these approaches, as well as their clear rationale and use of structure and achievable goals, also enhances its effect in addressing a variety of presenting concerns. They have all been adapted for use with children and adolescents, especially in the area of emotion regulation. They can also work well with adolescents, adults, and older adults.

Behavior activation therapy, compassion-focused therapy, and metacognitive therapy are three other popular third-wave CBT theories that have received attention and are demonstrated to be effective in addressing a variety of client presenting issues. Textbox 8.1 addresses behavior activation therapy and Textbox 8.2 addresses compassion-focused therapy and metacognitive therapy.

Textbox 8.1 Third-Wave CBT Spotlight: Behavioral Activation Therapy: Overview and Application

Behavior activation therapy (BAT) is commonly considered a third-wave CBT approach. BAT is highly effective when working with clients who are experiencing severe depression (Tindall et al., 2017). While BAT does not explicitly use acceptance and mindfulness procedures, it is considered a third-wave approach because BAT encourages clients' commitment to following a plan and enhances clients' understanding of their experiences rather than focusing on changing their thoughts. In addition, BAT concentrates more on processes than on content and enables people to live more long-term satisfying and fuller lives, which is consistent with the third-wave approaches. **Behavioral activation** involves increasing pleasurable activities on a daily basis to help motivate people with depression who may experience low energy and who may have withdrawn from life. Behavioral activation is usually started in the beginning of counseling for depression for people who are not capable of participating in cognitive therapy, do not have enough energy to recognize or discuss cognitive distortions, or cannot seem to overcome what may be keeping them stuck in their depression. Behavioral activation is used to help people increase their activity levels, improve their mood, and provide a source of pleasure on which they can build. By scheduling pleasant activities throughout the day, and creating regular times for sleeping and eating, clients can keep track of their initial activity levels and chart their progress.

The most frequently used strategies in behavioral activation include establishing a list of pleasant activities; scheduling, monitoring, and charting activities; relaxation and skills training; recognizing aversive and avoidant behaviors; and confronting cognitive distortions. The pleasurable activities in behavioral activation are considered sources of positive reinforcement and seem to work best if they are pleasant, stable, repeatable, and diverse (Curran, Ekers, McMillan, & Houghton, 2012; Kanter, Busch, & Rusch, 2009).

Behavioral activation has been around since Skinner first created behavior modification and has recently been expanded into a stand-alone therapy program that is easily administered and generally well received by clients; its efficacy is similar to that of cognitive therapies (Hayes, Strosahl, & Wilson, 2012).

Behavioral activation is a popular technique often used to help those struggling with depression. This therapy is particularly helpful for clients who are lacking motivation and isolating themselves. When people are depressed, their everyday activities may be impeded and they may have trouble even getting out of bed. Therefore, they engage in negative avoidance behaviors, such as isolation, sleeping through the day, and not seeing their friends or family. Using behavioral activation, clients begin to expand their daily activities little by little to increase motivation and energy. Clients begin to experience more positive reinforcement from the pleasurable activities they are engaging in and they break the cycle of isolation and depression.

Consider Sarah, who is experiencing depression and having trouble engaging in her everyday activities. The therapist would begin by educating Sarah about the theory behind behavioral activation, how it is used, and why it works. Education is important because the goals of behavioral activation may be unclear, and it is important for the client to perceive that the techniques will be helpful. While behavioral activation is helpful in the long run, it can be challenging for the client to

(Continued)

get the motivation needed to actually apply it due to the influence of the depression. Although isolation behaviors are reinforcing in the moment, they actually tend to worsen depression. The therapist must listen to the client and then explain how the avoidant behaviors are causing more stress and depression. The therapist may even draw a diagram to visually depict how behavioral activation may be helpful.

As an example, Sarah explains that she has been sleeping in and lying in bed each day until 1 p.m. The immediate consequences include missing breakfast and lunch and not making it to her classes. The immediate consequences lead to her feeling more stressed about school, more depressed for not completing her responsibilities, and lethargic due to her unhealthy diet and oversleeping. The increased depression and stress then contribute to the continuation of sleeping in and missing more classes.

The next step would be for Sarah to keep track of her current activities throughout the week, using a schedule. This is important to ensure that clients choose activities that are reasonable and that they are likely to succeed with. When clients keep track of their current activities, they can also keep track of their mood during those times. It is likely that their mood will be low when they are engaging in avoidant and isolating behaviors. Later on, it could be helpful for clients to assess their mood while engaging in the pleasurable activities and compare it to their mood prior to the new activities. This may increase awareness that their mood is better when engaging in pleasurable activities, which may increase their motivation to continue with their behavioral activation plan.

Once clients are educated about behavioral activation and an accurate assessment of current activities is obtained, the next step is developing positive behaviors to replace the current avoidant behaviors. It is extremely important to ensure that the activities selected are easy to do and rewarding. For example, Sarah has been having a hard time getting out of bed for class. It is unlikely that Sarah would be successful with waking up at 5 a.m., completing all of her homework assignments, and working out at the gym. Starting off slowly in easy manageable steps is necessary for success. Once clients accomplish a small goal, they are more likely to build self-efficacy, notice changes in their mood, and then implement more advanced positive behaviors. During this step of developing pleasurable behaviors, it may be helpful to provide worksheets for clients to write down activity ideas and rank them from 1 to 10 for ease of activity and reward. Therapists can also give clients a list of pleasurable activities that clients can choose from. Sarah has expressed that she enjoyed running, reading, and spending time with friends in the past. Therefore, Sarah might consider going for a walk, reading a couple pages of a book, or calling a friend on the phone to catch up.

After Sarah develops a list of activities, the therapist will work with her to implement the behavioral activation plan. The therapist and client will collaborate on when and how she will implement her plan. It is important to be specific when scheduling activities throughout the week. Sarah may want to call a friend on Wednesday, but it would be best to schedule a specific time on Wednesday, as specificity will help her with follow-through. Discussing how she will remember to call a friend, what obstacles she may face, and how to overcome those obstacles is helpful. A complete schedule for the week with times and specific activities may also aid clients with remembering and following through with their plan. Therapists may also consider helping clients use social support by telling a loved one about their plan, which may help them feel more accountable while also enhancing connections with others and eliciting support.

Once clients implement their plan, it is important for therapists to follow up at the beginning of each session. When clients are successful, therapists should respond with praise. When clients are unsuccessful, problem solving may be helpful. Common reasons for unsuccessful attempts are forgetting to do the activity and choosing activities that are too challenging. Assessing the clients' mood before, during, and after the activity is also important. Once clients accomplish their goals, they can continue to increase their pleasurable activities and break the cycle of depression and isolation.

> **Textbox 8.2 Third-Wave CBT Spotlight: Compassion-Focused Therapy and Metacognitive Therapy**
>
> Compassion-focused therapy (CFT), developed by Paul Raymond Gilbert, is a third-wave CBT approach that helps clients learn how to be more compassionate and kind to themselves (Gilbert, 2010). The world can feel overwhelming, so CFT aims to help clients feel safer and more capable. This approach is particularly useful for clients who experience shame and self-criticism. Specifically, clients who have experienced trauma may benefit from this approach because it provides not only cognitive resources but emotional resources, as well. Clients with eating disorders, self-esteem issues, anxiety, depression, and an inability to trust may also benefit from this approach. CFT pulls from a wide variety of sources, such as psychology, neuroscience, Buddhism, and evolutionary theory, making it an integrative approach. While most theoretical approaches involve compassion, CFT is different because compassion and being kinder to oneself is the ultimate focus. Generating new thoughts and new emotions that are positive and revolve around kindness is one of the main goals in this approach. Compassionate attention, compassionate behavior, and compassionate imagery are all used to increase people's compassion and kindness toward themselves and others. Therapists who use CFT are warm, supportive, and compassionate in creating a safe environment where clients can learn to be kind to themselves. It may take time to learn these skills, so clients are encouraged to be patient and gentle with themselves, as this is also a form of self-compassion.
>
> Metacognitive therapy, developed by Adrian Wells, is a cognitive approach that assumes that clients lose control over their thoughts and behaviors, which worsens emotional suffering (Wells, 2009). Metacognition controls mental processes and thinking. There is both conscious experience and unconscious experience of metacognition. Most of metacognition experience is in the unconscious. Metacognition can explain the "tip-of the tongue-effect," in which people cannot recall information but it is stored in their memory. The purpose of metacognition is to retrieve this information to help people experience it in consciousness. The pattern of rumination of thoughts is recognized and helped through the process of metacognitive therapy. Clients are taught how to modify metacognitive thoughts and relate to their thoughts in new ways. This approach can be used with a wide variety of populations, such as those with those who experience PTSD, anxiety, depression, and OCD.

SKILL DEVELOPMENT: MINDFULNESS

Mindfulness is a core component in many of the third-wave approaches and is useful for treating anxiety, depression, and more. Mindfulness teaches clients how to become aware of what's happening in the present moment, including their own thoughts, feelings, and sensations, and accepting the present moment without judgment.

Consider Becca, who has been experiencing anxiety. After establishing a therapeutic relationship with Becca, the therapist would introduce mindfulness and use a psychoeducational approach, sharing information on how mindfulness works and why it is effective. The therapist would invite Becca to share her own experiences with mindfulness, if any, to build on those. Explaining what mindfulness is would be the first step: a nonjudgmental awareness and acceptance of the present moment. The explanation of the benefits of mindfulness and why it is used is particularly important in order to include Becca in the therapeutic process. Some potential benefits of mindfulness that may relate to Becca are reduced symptoms of anxiety, greater satisfaction within relationships, reduced rumination of a thought or problem, and an improved ability to manage negative emotions and stressful situations.

Education about the nature of mindfulness is helpful. For example, mindfulness does not mean getting rid of thoughts, it means noticing those thoughts with curiosity and nonjudgment. It is only natural for people's thoughts to wander as they are practicing mindfulness. Noticing those thoughts and then bringing the attention back to the present moment comes with practice. Utilizing self-compassion and patience may help clients feel more motivated to continue the practice of mindfulness.

When introducing mindfulness, it is important to meet clients where they are in the therapeutic process. If Becca has no previous experience with mindfulness, introducing deep breathing in session may be the first step. In fact, it would be helpful to teach the client the basic skill of deep breathing and awareness of the breathing in session and have her practice it in session. Clients can then build on these skills and use more in-depth mindfulness exercises.

If Becca has had some experience with mindfulness, introducing more complex mindfulness exercises may be helpful. One example of a mindfulness exercise is a body scan, which involves paying attention to the sensations in one's body for each body part. Becca would be instructed to start from her feet and then work her way up the body, just noticing what she is feeling in each part of her body and paying attention to the thoughts and feelings she is experiencing. Another mindfulness meditation is the mindfulness walk. Becca may be instructed to practice mindfulness as she walks, noticing how her body moves and how she feels each step of the way. Becca can also become aware of her surroundings and what she hears, feels, and smells. These mindfulness techniques can be used throughout the day and in other activities as well. Many types of mindfulness exercises are available, and it is important to tailor the exercise to the client's needs. Becca may find that she prefers the walking meditation over the body scan and the therapist should build on that.

It is also important to take into consideration individual differences. For example, someone who experiences chronic pain may benefit from a mindfulness meditation that takes the focus off of the body and the areas of pain and puts the focus on something outside the body or on deep breathing. Clients with chronic pain may also benefit from a body scan that focuses on the areas without pain, to facilitate with relaxation.

Some clients may be hesitant to start mindfulness practices. For example, they may feel as though they have no time to practice mindfulness, they do not feel motivated to start, or they do not believe it will help them. It is important to be compassionate with clients and start slowly with mindfulness techniques. Even if clients practice mindfulness for 5 minutes a day, that is a good beginning. When they start noticing changes, they will be more likely to continue mindfulness. Continued assessment and discussion of mindfulness throughout sessions can help facilitate the process.

CASE APPLICATION

Ava is having trouble getting along with her friends. Her therapist uses the Wise Mind ACCEPTS technique to encourage the development of distress tolerance skills.

> THERAPIST: Ava, your mom mentioned you have been having some troubles with your friends the past couple weeks and you've been having a hard time sleeping.
>
> AVA: Yes, I'm upset with my friends. We haven't been getting along lately. I just get mad at them and then I lay in bed thinking about it all.
>
> THERAPIST: So there has been some tension with you and your friends lately and it's been impacting your sleep. Tell me a little bit more about what's been going on.
>
> AVA: We can never agree on what to do. I want to go to the park but they always want to do something else like go to the mall or the movies. I like being outdoors and I'm upset that no one wants to do anything I want to do.

THERAPIST: I can imagine that is really frustrating. You're arguing with your friends and you're wanting to be outside more, but that just isn't happening.

AVA: Yes, and it just makes me not want to even hang out with them anymore.

THERAPIST: You feel hurt and frustrated and you are wondering if you even want to be around your friends. Ava, remember how we talked about distress tolerance a few weeks ago? I'm wondering about applying that skill to this situation. We could try applying the Wise Mind ACCEPTS tool to this situation. I wonder if you think that might be helpful, or not? What are your thoughts on trying this?

AVA: Okay. That sounds like a good idea.

THERAPIST: A stands for activities, so your hobbies. What kind of hobbies do you have? It sounds like being outside is one.

AVA: Yes, I like walking in the park and playing soccer outside. No one wants to do that with me.

THERAPIST: I wonder if you can think of anyone that may want to spend time outside with you?

AVA: Well my cousin has been wanting to spend more time with me. Maybe we can plan a day to go to the park.

THERAPIST: What a great idea! Anything else you can think of?

AVA: I guess I can always go for a walk around my neighborhood by myself.

THERAPIST: Okay, great. The C stands for Contributing, so thinking of others. How can you apply this when things get hard?

AVA: Maybe I can remember that when we do things my friends want to do like go to the movies, it makes them happy. And I do enjoy going to the movies sometimes, too.

THERAPIST: That makes a lot of sense. Caring about your friends and also doing things you enjoy is a good balance. The C stands for comparisons, which involves comparing yourself to others who are coping with something worse. What do you think would be helpful for this?

AVA: Hmm . . . I am always seeing terrible things on the news. I guess the arguments I have with my friends aren't nearly as bad as having like cancer or something.

THERAPIST: Your feelings and experiences are valid and it's normal that you get upset with your friends at times. Having empathy for the people on the news is also a great perspective to take! The E stands for emotions, so creating more positive emotions when you're upset. I wonder what ways you can create new emotions?

AVA: I love watching funny YouTube videos! They are really funny.

THERAPIST: That's awesome. So maybe when you're upset with your friends you can take a step back and watch something funny. The P stands for pushing away, so leaving the situation for a little while. What can you do for this?

AVA: Maybe tell my friends that I am going to go for a walk and then come back when I feel better.

THERAPIST: Yes, that sounds like a great idea! Giving yourself a break is helpful. The T stands for thoughts, so distracting your mind by doing things like counting to 10 or doing puzzles. Do either of these sound helpful to you?

AVA: I love puzzles! My mom, dad, and I sometimes do puzzles together.

THERAPIST: Great. The last letter, S, stands for sensations, so doing something that will stimulate the sensations in your body. What can you do for sensations?

AVA: I really like taking baths. Maybe that will help. And I can also pet my dog. She is soft and fluffy.

THERAPIST: Great ideas! So whenever you are upset with your friends or anything else, remember the ACCEPTS acronym and try to do some of the things we talked about.

AVA: That sounds good. Maybe I can go home and call my cousin and ask if her if she wants to go to the park.

REFLECT AND RESPOND

1. Mindfulness-based stress reduction often begins with a body scan to help focus breathing and present-moment awareness. When you are alone, stretch out into a comfortable position, and take several deep, cleansing breaths. Begin by focusing your attention on the toes of your right foot. Notice how your toes feel; they might be tingling, or you might not notice any sensation at all, in which case just notice a lack of sensation. Continue focusing on the various parts of your body, slowly working your way from your toes to the top of your head. If your mind wanders (which it will) just gently bring it back to focus on your body, without criticism or judgment. When you have finished, write about your experience in your journal. Was it easy to focus your awareness on your body, or was it difficult? If thoughts or restlessness prevented you from completing the body scan, you might want to try a mindfulness exercise that is more active, such as a walking meditation.

2. Using your journal, write down a negative thought, negative experience, or negative emotion that you want to let go of. Keep focus on that thought and then close your eyes. Think of a round circle to place that thought in and then incorporate your answers to these questions:

   - What color is the circle?
   - How big is the circle?
   - Is the circle transparent?

After you think about the details of the circle, move on to this next segment. As your thought, experience, or emotion is placed in this circle, think about it floating away. Where is it floating to? Visualize the landscape, beach, or sky that the circle is floating away into and watch it float on by until all you can see is the image (i.e., sky, beach). Then, with your eyes closed, think of the sounds you hear and the smells you smell until you feel calm. Bring your awareness back toward your breath, and process the guided meditation following its completion.

Summary

The third wave CBT approaches that were discussed in this chapter were dialectical behavior therapy, acceptance and commitment therapy, mindfulness-based cognitive therapy, and schema therapy. The third-wave approaches target the process of thoughts (i.e., how they are constructed and how clients experience their thoughts) rather than the content of thoughts to help people become aware of their thoughts and accept them in a nonjudgmental way. Mindfulness, acceptance, and holism are key concepts with all of the third-wave approaches.

Marsha Linehan developed DBT as a treatment for borderline personality disorder and chronic suicidal ideation, but it has been expanded and applied for work with a variety of populations. DBT relies on the assumption that a balance exists between acceptance of situations and experiences and change. The primary goal of DBT is to develop skills and develop dialectical thinking that promotes healthy adaptability. Emotion regulation, mindfulness, distress tolerance, and interpersonal effectiveness are the primary techniques used in DBT to help clients develop skills and tolerate and effectively manage their emotions.

ACT, developed by Steven Hayes, assumes that avoidance of emotions or attempts to control thinking and emotions worsen the problem. Full experiencing and acceptance of present-moment thoughts and emotions are the goals of ACT. Clients are also encouraged to create a life that is meaningful to them. The hexaflex model is used to guide therapeutic techniques, which include attention to the present moment, acceptance, defusion, self-as-context, values, and committed action. ACT has been effectively used with a wide variety of populations, especially those who have anxiety disorders.

Jon Kabat-Zinn is known for the development of mindfulness-based stress reduction (MSBR), which later led to the development of mindfulness-based cognitive therapy (MBCT), with the help of Zindel Segal, Mark Williams, and John Teasdale. An important concept of MBCT, the being mode, involves being in touch with experience in the present moment and letting go of thoughts without judgment. The goal of MBCT is to move away from obsessing over thoughts and feelings to being present in the here and now. Cognitive thought processing, mindfulness, and decentering are essential techniques in MBCT. This approach is primarily used to help people who experience depression and anxiety.

Schema therapy was developed by Jeffrey E. Young and focuses on core schemas developed in childhood. Techniques are used to get at the root of ingrained thought patterns to achieve change at the emotional level. One of the main goals of schema therapy is to help clients develop a healthy adult schema and to stop engaging in unhealthy coping skills so that they might experience healthier and happier lives. Techniques include the use of limited reparenting, empathic confrontation, cognitive interventions, and schema flash cards. Schema therapy can work with a wide variety of people, but it is often used to help those who have personality disorders, disorders that are especially difficult to change.

Recommended Readings

Baer, R. A. (Ed.). (2006). *Mindfulness-based treatment approaches: Clinicians guide to evidence base and applications.* Burlington, MA: Elsevier.

Crane, R. (2017). *Mindfulness-based cognitive therapy: Distinctive Features.* New York, NY: Routledge.

Dimeff, L. A., & Koerner, K. (Eds.). (2008). *Dialectical behavior therapy in clinical practice: Applications across disorders and settings.* New York, NY: Guilford.

Hayes, S. C., Strosahl, K. D., & Wilson, K. G. (2012). *Acceptance and commitment therapy: The process and practice of mindful change* (2nd ed.). New York, NY: Guilford.

Hick, S. F., & Bien, T. (Eds.). (2008). *Mindfulness and the therapeutic relationship.* New York, NY: Guilford.

Kabat-Zinn, J. (1990). *Full catastrophe living: Using the wisdom of your body and mind to face stress, pain, and illness.* New York, NY: Delacorte.

Linehan, M. (1993). *Cognitive-behavioral treatment of borderline personality disorder.* New York, NY: Guilford.

Linehan, M. (1993). *Skills training manual for treating borderline personality disorder.* New York, NY: Guilford.

Linehan, M. (2015). *DBT skills training manual* (2nd ed.). New York, NY: Guilford.

Rafaeli, E., Bernstein, D. P., & Young, J. (2011). *Schema therapy: The CBT distinctive features series.* New York, NY: Routledge.

MyLab Counseling

Try the Topic 10 Assignments: Mind-Body.

CHAPTER 9

Existential Therapy

Learning Outcomes

When you have finished this chapter, you should be able to:
- Understand the context and development of Existential Therapy.
- Communicate the key concepts associated with Existential Therapy and understand how they relate to therapeutic processes.
- Describe the therapeutic goals of Existential Therapy.
- Identify the common techniques used in Existential Therapy.
- Understand how Existential Therapy relates to counseling diverse populations.
- Identify the limitations and strengths of Existential Therapy.

This section of the text focuses on the third force in counseling and psychotherapy, humanistic-existential counseling theories. These include, but are not limited to, existential therapy, person-centered therapy, and gestalt therapy, each of which will be discussed over the next three chapters.

INTRODUCTION TO THE THIRD FORCE IN COUNSELING AND PSYCHOTHERAPY: HUMANISTIC-EXISTENTIAL THEORIES

The development of the third force in counseling, which grew around the mid-20th century was, in part, a response against the mechanistic foundations of behaviorism and psychoanalysis. The third force, the humanistic-existential theories, focused more on people's strengths, optimism, and free will. During the 1960s, resistance to mainstream cultural values (e.g., traditions that were racist/patriarchal, materialism) grew. Groups that were counterculture arose (e.g., beatniks, bohemians, "flower children"), and in many ways their values reflected and influenced numerous ideas that are apparent in the humanistic theories. For example, common beliefs and values around this time included a focus on self-expression, questioning authority as all knowing, personal fulfillment, focusing on the here and now, and the importance of emotions and relationships.

Around this time period, philosophy showed an increased concentration on phenomenology, which involves experiencing events as they occur in the immediate moment. Instead of reducing one's experiences into components, understanding one's unique experience was believed to provide a richer, less biased understanding.

Changing ideas in physics also influenced the development of the third force in counseling. For example, physicists at this time increasingly focused on wholeness and perception as important, both of which are essential in Gestalt therapy. Instead of concentrating on atoms or smaller parts, physicists began considering the fields, which are larger and more whole. Elements became less important as wholes became more important. At this time, psychologists increasingly made an effort to use science as their base; therefore, Gestalt ideas reflected the new ideas in physics and vice versa.

The phi phenomenon, developed by Max Wertheimer, a psychologist, also influenced the development of the third force in counseling, Gestalt therapy in particular. This phenomenon involves a sensation and perception experience of perceiving movement when no movement is actually taking place. This goes against the previous belief that analyzing sensory elements could lead to a better understanding of conscious experience. The phi phenomenon suggests that one's individual perception is what matters and cannot be simplified and focuses on the whole as more important than the parts which is a Gestalt belief.

The growing popularity of encounter groups also led to the development of the third force in counseling (Elkins, 2009). Encounter groups (also referred to as T- or training groups, or sensitivity training groups) were groups of people that formed to achieve personal growth and to learn about sensitivity training and interpersonal skills. These groups were popular in the 1960s and 1970s. Some people at the time were craving closer connections to other people and valued expression of emotions. The relationships between people were viewed as important, and encounter groups gave people an opportunity to achieve greater self-acceptance and self-awareness. During this time in history, many people valued social connections and the opportunity to be themselves completely. Encounter groups both influenced the development of humanism and continued to thrive in popularity throughout the humanistic movement. While encounter groups had their detractors, people like Carl Rogers enhanced their significance at the time.

Humanistic-existential therapies changed the way psychotherapy had been conducted. Up until that time, psychoanalysis, with its emphasis on the unconscious, and behavior therapy, which focused on stimulus and response, were the only methods in widespread practice. In both approaches, the therapist was traditionally seen as the expert. Carl Rogers, who will be discussed in the following chapter, revolutionized psychology and proclaimed clients as the experts of their own lives and experiences. Rogers (1995b) wrote: "It is the client who knows what hurts, what directions to go, what problems are crucial, what experiences have been deeply buried" (pp. 11–12). Humanistic approaches take away the emphasis off the therapist as knowing what is best and trusts that clients can understand themselves, their experiences, and how to make progress.

The humanistic-existential theorists presented in this section of the text view what people have observed, encountered, and experienced as important. Humanistic approaches are based on **phenomenology**, or phenomenological principles that place importance on how people view and experience themselves and their world. Specifically, all clients have unique experiences, and they must use their own perceptions rather than those of others in deciding how to move forward. Therapists must understand clients' unique perspectives. Humanistic theories share the following common beliefs:

- The individual should be viewed holistically.
- Each individual has an innate self-actualization tendency.
- Humans have free will and are able to make choices.
- Because humans have free will and choice, they also have responsibility for those choices.

Humanistic-existential theories emphasize the positive nature of human beings, which humanists believe overshadows any emphasis on dysfunction or psychopathology. Humanistic thinking has impacted more recent approaches to counseling as well. For example, **positive psychology**, a modern approach that emphasizes clients' strengths and resources as opposed to their problems has been influenced by humanistic thinking. Eastern-influenced therapies and **transpersonal therapy**, an approach that focuses on a person's spirituality, also center on optimal functioning.

Compared to Freud's complicated theory of drives and the unconscious, humanistic theories seem rather simple with regard to what motives human behavior; humanists generally assume only one drive—the innate need to self-actualize. However, the humanistic theorists consider the whole person, to account for the complexity of people. Just as the mind cannot be contemplated without the brain, neither can the person be helped without considering cognitive, emotional, physical, and spiritual issues. Gestalt therapy and focusing techniques are centered on bodily sensations to address the physical aspect and to bring awareness to the mind, body, and spirit connection (Gendlin, 1996). Humanistic theorists value experiential reactions over thought processes.

A common misconception is that humanistic therapists are passive, when in fact they are quite active. Humanistic-existential therapists take an active interest in their clients. They are responsive, authentic, and real, engaging with the client and being affected by the truths of the client's story. Gestalt is the most active of the humanistic therapies, and Rogers' client-centered therapy is the least directive of the humanistic approaches. Now we look at some of the core concepts of humanistic-existential therapy in more detail.

Self-Actualizing Tendency

Implicit in all humanistic theories is a strong belief in the dignity and worth of individuals. Practitioners believe that people must be appreciated and accepted for themselves, not shaped to fit a mold. Humanists maintain that people have a right to their own thoughts and opinions, should be free to construct their own lives, and are fundamentally good and trustworthy. Humanists believe in the human potential—in the inherent tendency of people to develop in positive ways that enhance and maintain themselves as well as humanity (Cain, 2012). In other words, self-actualization is a calling to be, or to become, the best person possible and reaching one's full potential.

Phenomenological Perspective

Humanistic therapies share a phenomenological way of viewing the world. Objective reality does not exist; rather, all people have their unique perception of the world. That perception determines people's beliefs, behaviors, emotions, and relationships. The experiences clients have, such as thoughts, feelings, and behaviors, is what truly matters. Individual experience is valuable and is ultimately the main focus of humanistic therapies. To put it simply, clients' reality is their reality, and that must be believed and embraced for therapy to be effective. Humanistic psychotherapies allow clients to explore various aspects of their lives without the fear of judgment from the therapist. By understanding clients' perspectives, therapists enable clients to feel heard and seen for who they are (De Saeger, Bartak, Eder, & Kamphuis, 2016). Furthermore, validating clients' lived experiences through empathic responding allows them to gain new insights and dig deeper for understanding themselves better. Through the phenomenological perspective, clients feel empowered and understood, which can allow them to make changes to grow.

In addition, humanistic theorists believe in basic equality in the client–therapist relationship. The person coming in for counseling is never referred to as a "patient," a medical term historically used in psychoanalysis. Instead, they are client and therapist, a team, working together to help clients grow, not seeking a cure.

Only by understanding people's perceptions of reality can we fully appreciate them and the ways in which they direct and organize their lives. For example, assume that a group of people in an office hears a loud noise. Timi, who delights in social gatherings, believes the noise is a balloon bursting at a nearby party and wishes she were there. Kane attributes the noise to a car backfiring and is reminded that his own car needs repair. Tom, who experienced combat in the military, thinks the noise might be gunfire and feels apprehensive, while Alice is so immersed in her work that she does not even hear the noise. This example illustrates how people can distort, interpret, and organize objective information based on their perceptions of the world, with those perceptions leading to thoughts ("I really should get my car repaired"), behaviors ("I'm going to check out that party"), and emotions ("I feel afraid").

Experiential Awareness

Humanistic approaches consider experiential awareness to be crucial to understanding the self. Increased awareness can help clients become more proficient at accessing, identifying, understanding, and regulating their emotions and experiences so they can live more fully. Awareness is facilitated in the safe environment of the therapy session. In therapy, awareness helps clients to become cognizant of and understand their emotional experiences, thus creating new self-narratives and meanings that incorporate a more resilient, self-actualized, and authentic sense of self (Pos, Greenberg, & Elliott, 2008).

VIKTOR FRANKL (1905–1997)

Viktor Frankl was born in 1905 in Vienna, Austria, and received both MD and PhD degrees from the University of Vienna. Before the Second World War, he was a practicing physician. Between 1942 and 1945, however, he was a prisoner in the Nazi concentration camps in Dachau and Auschwitz. His mother and father, his brother, his first wife, and their children all perished in the camps. Of course, these experiences had a profound impact on Frankl's thinking. Although his interest in existential thought began before his imprisonment, his difficult years in the concentration camps led him to conclude that the will to create meaning and purpose is the prime human motivator (Frankl, 2014). For Frankl, his purpose became surviving his imprisonment so that he could tell others about those experiences and the terrible impact of war and hatred. His book, *Man's Search for Meaning* (Frankl, 2014), is a powerful description of his experiences, his existential struggles, and what he learned from them. In that book, which the Library of Congress has listed as one of the 10 most influential books, Frankl quotes Nietzsche: "He who has a why to live for can bear with almost any how" (p. 121) and "That which does not kill me, makes me stronger" (p. 130). These quotations reflect Frankl's own triumph over tragedy, his ability to make the terrible losses and experiences he endured meaningful.

Frankl called his counseling approach logotherapy—therapy through meaning. According to Frankl, every single situation, even the most extraordinary, has meaning and people have the ability to make choices to find meaning in all situations and in their lives (Frankl, 2000). He suggested that to be fully alive, humans must integrate body, mind, and spirit (Frankl, 1965).

Frankl's writings as well as his lectures throughout the world certainly made his life a meaningful one. In addition, he married again in the late 1940s and reportedly found personal as well as professional success. Frankl lived until 1997, continuing to write throughout his life about the most important aspects of all our lives, including meaning, love, work, and society (Frankl, 1978, 1987, 1992, 2000).

ROLLO MAY (1909–1994)

Rollo May was born in 1909 into a family of six children and spent his childhood in Ohio and Michigan, where he graduated from Michigan State University. He originally trained as a Lutheran minister and later became a psychoanalyst. He studied with Alfred Adler in Vienna and was influenced by Adler and European existential thought. In addition, May's own difficult life, including an unhappy childhood, two unsuccessful marriages, and two years in a sanitarium with tuberculosis, contributed to the development of his ideas.

In the 1950s, Rollo May wrote a comprehensive introduction on the beginnings of existential psychology, of which the following provides a brief synopsis and introduction to existential concepts that will be expanded on in this chapter. Rollo May has been credited with bringing existentialism to the United States with the publication of *Existence: A New Dimension in Psychiatry and Psychology* (May, Angel, & Ellenberger, 1958). He is also credited with applying key concepts of existential thought to psychotherapeutic practices. His writings were instrumental in elucidating the similarities between existential philosophy and psychology. Both were concerned with the same issues and could be used together to promote better understanding.

His work initially focused on the anxiety he believed all people experience as they struggle with the difficulties of growth and change, their aloneness in the world, their apprehensions about death, and the courage required to pursue goals of independence and growth (May, 1950). Also important to him were people's roles and relationships with their society, reflecting Adler's emphasis on social responsibility. May believed that people often avoid difficult conflicts and confrontations, such as those that involve culture and destiny (including death), leading us to neglect the potentials for meaning in our lives. Many of May's landmark writings and studies addressed fundamental human experiences such as love, will, intentionality, isolation, loneliness, evil, and the daimonic. May thought that existentialism should not be considered a school of therapy but instead an attitude toward all people (May, 1990a). Furthermore, May believed that a constant struggle goes on within us because while we want to strive for growth, it is a painful process.

Like Frankl, Rollo May lived a long and productive life, dying in 1994 at the age of 85.

IRVIN YALOM (b. 1931)

Born in 1931 in Washington, DC, Irvin Yalom grew up in a small apartment over his parents' grocery store. His escape from the poverty and danger of his inner-city neighborhood was the library, where he developed an enduring love of reading. Yalom was trained as a psychiatrist, and after some years in the army he became a professor of psychiatry at Stanford University School of Medicine. Yalom and his wife Marilyn, a scholar of women's studies and French literature, have four children and many grandchildren.

Yalom is a prolific writer on both existentialism and group psychotherapy (Yalom & Leszcz, 2005). His ideas have been influenced by both European and American existential thought. His 1980 book *Existential Psychotherapy* contributed greatly to the understanding of this approach, particularly in the United States. "There is a basic aloneness to existence that must be faced," he wrote. "In existential therapy the goal is to help clients be authentic and face their limitations and challenges with courage" (Yalom & Leszcz, 2005, p. 102). Yalom's existential clinical approach can be found in his book *The Gift of Therapy* (2017), among others. Yalom also has written books for the general reader, describing his therapy with people coping with existential issues. In *Love's Executioner and Other Tales of Psychotherapy* (2012), Yalom discussed the four ultimate concerns of the human condition: the inevitability of death, freedom and responsibility to make choices, isolation and aloneness, and meaninglessness in life. However, he believed that when we recognize these concerns, we gain knowledge and redemption (Yalom, 1989).

In clarifying the nature of existentialism, Yalom (1980) identified the basic difference between his concept of existentialism and Freudian psychoanalysis. Freud viewed people as struggling with a conflict between the instinctual strivings of the id and the socialized forces of the ego and superego, whereas Yalom saw our conflicts as stemming from a search for meaning in life when life has no inherent meaning (Yalom, 1980). "It's not easy to live every moment wholly aware of death. It's like trying to stare the sun in the face: you can stand only so much of it. Because we cannot live frozen in fear, we generate methods to soften death's terror. We project ourselves into the future through our children; we grow rich, famous, ever larger; we develop compulsive protective rituals; or we embrace an impregnable belief in an ultimate rescuer" (Yalom, 2008, p. 5). Yalom and other existential therapists believe that confronting the fear of death will allow us to live life in a richer, fuller, more compassionate, and meaningful way. Irvin Yalom continues to lecture and write about his ideas as well as his psychotherapy practices.

INTRODUCTION/DEVELOPMENT OF EXISTENTIAL THERAPY

To focus on life's purpose, meaning, and our death; to be free of life's trivial matters, and to live fully and authentically; to live a life that balances freedom of choice with responsibility toward our fellow citizens of the world; to construct a full life and work toward a purpose and a goal—what could be more meaningful or important than these pursuits? All of us, therapists and clients alike, grapple with these issues on and off and at various points over the course of our lives. Existential psychotherapy, one of the most widely used forms of therapy, provides a philosophical approach with which to address these ultimate concerns.

Events such as terrorist attacks, rapidly changing political landscapes, environmental degradation, natural disasters, and financial uncertainty contribute to a climate of heightened anxiety, fear of death, and a sharpened sense of loneliness and isolation. In modern society, people often turn to religious and spiritual leaders and sometimes therapists to help them cope with tragedies, adjust to change, and attempt to find some meaning in their suffering. Existential therapy is well suited to addressing these concerns.

Existentialism focuses on the belief that humans have freedom and choice, and thus they are responsible for their lives. This theory stands in contrast to the more deterministic view of human nature held by other theories, such as behavior therapy or some psychoanalytic approaches. Existentialists hold that while people cannot control the events that happen to them, they can control how they respond to them. Believing that people determine their own lives, therapists encourage clients to accept responsibility, make choices to strategically shape their lives, and take personal responsibility for their experiences.

Philosophical Foundations of Existential Therapy

The roots of existential thought can be traced back to the philosophical writings of Aristotle, Socrates, the ancient Greek and Asian thinkers, and others who addressed issues of personal meaning. The philosophical movement we now call existential philosophy came in two waves. The first wave took place in late 19th-century Europe with the writings of the Danish philosopher and Christian theologian, Søren Kierkegaard, who is known as the father of **existentialism**. Friedrich Nietzsche and Edmund Husserl also contributed to the first wave of existentialism. The second wave occurred in Europe during the 1940s and 1950s. Social, political, and scientific events during those years contributed to the development of this approach. The deaths of tens of millions of people beginning with World War I and ending with World War II led to a pervasive sense of alienation and meaninglessness. Growing industrialization and urbanization of society, as well as scientific advances, added to this dehumanization. Even psychology, dominated at that time by psychoanalysis and behaviorism, conceptualized people as consisting of separate parts that could be controlled and changed by external forces (Bauman & Waldo, 1998). People needed a force that would restore their sense of humanness and also help them cope with their concerns about the meaning of life in the face of devastation, isolation, and death. Existentialism, which both flows from and contributes to humanistic psychology, evolved in response to those needs.

Kierkegaard (1944), who actually coined the term "existentialism," wrote about anxiety and dread, also known as angst, as constant companions to the human condition. He described anxiety as the struggle between the living being and the nonbeing—the existential crisis of life against death. Anxiety lies in the middle between the two opposing forces. This anxiety occurs when we are not being ourselves and, while unpleasant, it is necessary for becoming who we create ourselves to be. This universal truth that every human being must struggle is the focus of existential psychology.

In addition to Kierkegaard's (1941) work on angst, he and William James, an American psychologist and philosopher, wrote about free will. Humans are free to make choices in life. Within the constrictions of what life hands us, we have the ability to rise above it and to make life meaningful. Existential issues are at the core of human existence and repeatedly come back to challenge us. Jean-Paul Sartre (1956) wrote, "We are our choices," and May (1960) added, "within the limits of our given world" (p. 13). Freedom then, involves transcendence, or pushing ourselves beyond our normal limits of being and experience. Acknowledging this freedom of choice produces anxiety, largely as a result of what we give up when we choose.

German philosopher and mathematician Edmund Husserl (1859–1938) was instrumental in the development of phenomenology. Later, his student Martin Heidegger (1962), helped turn attention to the universal experience of one's need to make sense of it all, of what it means to exist. Heidegger wrote about **Dasein** (being-in-the-world). Specifically, Heidegger focused on living with awareness to become who we want to be and looking forward to authentic future experiences (but not taking them for granted, as we do not live forever). Heidegger also suggested that to avoid other people's expectations, it is best to minimize superficial conversation or small talk and to minimize everyday routine by being more spontaneous. Heidegger suggested that people forget to be free and live for themselves, instead interacting in a superficial mode of being he called "they-selves" as opposed to "our-selves." We are quick to be swept up in others' stories and expectations and in the media that bombard us. Heidegger suggested that only when we realize that other people cannot save us from our eventual nonbeing are we likely to stop concentrating on them, to stop worrying so much about what others think, and to stop focusing our lives and energies on people who never really had our interest in mind in the first place.

Later, Sartre (1956), who studied under Husserl and Heidegger, expanded on their ideas and discussed how human beings are constantly changing, and no system, whether scientific or otherwise, can adequately explain the ability of humans to transcend experience. This idea that people have the ability to shape themselves and their lives through choices and the chances provided to them is essential to existential thought (Sartre, 1956; Tillich, 1952).

What unites existential ideas into a movement is the sense that the prevailing worldview—science, religion, and, to a certain extent, politics—had dehumanized what it meant to be human. By reducing the lived experience of the person into a series of "universal truths" that applied to everyone, modern thought had negated the uniqueness of the individual and the fact that every person has free will. Nietzsche, in particular, spoke out against the idea that human beings are merely fulfilling some grand design set in motion by some unknown entity. In particular, Nietzsche focused on the subjectivity that comes from values within each individual's "will to power," which is where creativity and originality come from (Sharp & Bugental, 2001).

In addition to the European existentialists such as Friedrich Nietzsche, Paul Tillich, and Martin Buber, writers, including Albert Camus, Jean-Paul Sartre, and Franz Kafka, helped to shape European existentialism. Swiss psychiatrists Medard Boss and Ludwig Binswanger created *Daseinsanalysis* (Binswanger, 1963, Boss, 1963), one of the first schools of existential psychology. They drew on Heidegger's notion of being-in-the-world and South Asian spiritual traditions as a way to help clients understand their own internal experiences through psychotherapy (Cooper, 2008). Around 1929, Viennese psychiatrist Viktor Frankl developed **logotherapy**, a form of existential psychotherapy that helps people discover purpose and meaning in their lives. More will be said about these approaches and ideas later in this chapter.

Existential Thought Compared to Other Theories

When the ship of existential thought landed on American shores in the middle of the last century, it found a welcome home. Existential psychology is not so much a comprehensive theory of counseling as it is an attitude toward living. By accepting that people are much more than drives, instincts, or behaviors that can be measured and predicted, the therapist works from an existential perspective.

Freudian psychodynamic therapy had become the main system of psychotherapy in the United States, and while Freud advanced our knowledge about people in their environments (what existentialists refer to as *Umwelt*), Freud's theory was not an entire theory of the human experience. Existentialists found Freudian theory similar to scientific attempts that explain living phenomena—it provided some information but missed the mark. It was missing a soul.

Existentialism, therefore, found a partner with the American humanists, including Carl Rogers and other theorists who valued experience, the organismic valuing process, self-actualization, freedom and responsibility, and the importance of the relationship between client and therapist.

Humanists reject scientific and linear explanations about reality and view the universe as constantly changing. This state of flux is considered the norm. Rather than an aberration or a problem requiring correction, change is viewed as a natural and innate tendency of all things.

If existence precedes, or comes before, and is more important than essence or one's nature, as existentialists believed, then any theory that seeks to explain human behavior must first take a **phenomenological** perspective, which holds that no such thing as truth or reality exists, apart from how people participate in, are conscious of, or have some relationship to their reality (May, 1969a). In this way, human beings cannot be understood in terms of drives or the behavioral models applied to them. It is more complicated than that. The totality of human existence can only be lived and experienced. As we saw, Freud explained the human experience in relation to nature (*Umwelt*); what was missing was people in relation to other people (*Mitwelt*), and to the self (*Eigenwelt*).

The works of Frankl and May were widely read in the United States during the 1950s and 1960s, became popular, and increased general awareness of existential concepts. Attention to the approach seemed to decline after the 1960s, partially as a result of the growing emphasis on accountability in therapy and the corresponding increase in the use of more structured, easily measured, and empirically validated approaches, such as cognitive and behavior therapy. Interest in existential therapy has been kept alive by the writings of Yalom, Bugental, Vontress, and others. With the growing recognition that the therapeutic relationship is an empirically supported intervention in and of itself, and that factors common to most theories are responsible for counseling effectiveness, an increasing number of therapists are returning to the philosophical and holistic underpinnings of existentialism.

Of course, the individual does not exist in a vacuum, and events in the world such as terrorist attacks, political upheavals, wars, mass shootings, and a growing dependency on gadgets and technology that tends to isolate rather than connect people have contributed to the creation of a culture in which people are once again searching for meaning, connection, and some type of guiding principle that explains individual existence in the vastness of the universe.

In recent years, the popularity of existential therapy has experienced a resurgence, as evidenced by the publication of existential therapy and psychology textbooks (Craig, Vos, Cooper, & Correia, 2015; Shapiro, 2015; Van Deurzen & Adams, 2016), writings that incorporate existential and Eastern spiritual traditions into Western psychology (Stratton, 2015), and integration of an existential perspective into other theoretical approaches, including art and other expressive therapies (Adibah & Zakaria, 2015).

Existentialism continues to exert an influence today, particularly on our conception of the therapist's role and the realization that, for many people, counseling and psychotherapy are not just tools for solving problems but ways to give meaning to individuals' lives that seem to lack purpose and fulfillment.

KEY CONCEPTS

Existential therapy focuses on exploring the universal issues that people face and ways for people to address them that are life enhancing and actualizing. Through their understanding of these issues, therapists can connect with people on a deep and personal level and help them change their lives so that they have more meaning and fulfillment.

The Human Condition: Ultimate Concerns

For the existentialists, life has no inherent meaning and is replete with challenges. Unless people meet these challenges with awareness, openness, and courage, their emotional development can become blocked or delayed. Existentialist theory suggests four ultimate concerns of the human condition. Table 9.1 provides an overview of these ultimate concerns.

The *inevitability of death* is the ultimate concern we experience. From childhood, we realize that our death is inevitable, as are the deaths of our loved ones. No matter how gifted we are, no matter how special our lives are, death is the outcome for everyone. The fear of our ultimate nonbeing can cast a shadow over our lives and make them seem pointless.

Isolation is another ultimate concern all of us face. Although we may surround ourselves with colleagues, friends, and family, we are ultimately alone. No one can truly understand us or sense our thoughts and feelings as we do. No one can rescue us from the inevitability of death and other losses we will experience in our lives. Some of us seek to fuse with and become dependent on others in an effort to counteract the sense of alienation and loneliness, but those efforts inevitably fail because they detract even further from our sense of ourselves and the purpose of our lives. In fact, loneliness can be most acute when we are with others and are aware of our lack of a true connection with them.

TABLE 9.1 Ultimate Concerns of the Human Condition

Death: Humans are unique in that we have an awareness we will eventually die. Such an awareness can cause us pain, suffering, and lead to the development of pathology. It is important that we respond to this reality in a positive, adaptive way, and live our lives in such a way that when we die, we are satisfied with how we lived.

Isolation: We come into this world and leave this world alone; ultimately, we are all always alone. We can use language to communicate our experiences to others as best as we can, but no one will ever fully understand our individual experience. This awareness can either lead us to cut off relations with others or develop unrealistically close, codependent relationships. Developing a healthy acceptance of our isolation can facilitate healthy relationships.

Meaninglessness: The only meaning in the universe is the meaning we create. The meanings that we create (i.e., our understanding of the world and ourselves, our values, our spiritual beliefs, our goals) become part of our individual identities. To resolve the existential concern of meaninglessness, we must develop a healthy identity in the context of the greater world, identify a will and purpose, and construct meaning where possible.

Freedom: As humans, we are all capable of a broad range of behaviors, and experiencing this level of freedom, with the responsibility involved, is an uncomfortable reality. Will, intentionality, and creating a worthwhile existence for ourselves in the limited time we have on Earth are critical.

Meaninglessness is another ultimate concern of the human condition. The only certainties in our lives are birth and death. Beyond that, life seems to be a random process and inherently meaningless. The lack of meaning in life can lead to hopelessness, discouragement, and a sense of emptiness, called the **existential vacuum**, which involves experiencing a lack of meaning in life that can lead to hopelessness, discouragement, and a sense of emptiness.

All of us at one point or another ask ourselves, "What *is* the meaning of life?" Viktor Frankl believed that instead of us asking life this question, we should ask ourselves this question; thus, it is our responsibility to determine the meaning of our lives (Frankl, 2000). The only way to answer questions about the meaning of life is to take responsibility for our lives and understand that we have the freedom to make choices about how we live. Early on, Frankl determined that we find meaning in life through:

- A good deed or work we do
- Experiences, interactions with others, and love
- A positive attitude toward an unchangeable fate (e.g., an incurable disease).

Just as Viktor Frankl found meaning in his efforts to survive the concentration camp so that he could share his ideas with the world, all people are unique and must discover their own meaning. In addition, part of what makes humans amazing is that they have the ability to turn suffering into celebration. For example, many believe that suffering is an experience that helps people achieve a higher meaning of life—it inspires us to grow spiritually and become more compassionate.

The final ultimate concern of life relates to *freedom and responsibility*. Modern society presents us with an overwhelming and constantly increasing array of choices: choices of lifestyles, choices of experiences, choices of acquisitions, and others. We have both the freedom and the responsibility to make choices that create a worthwhile existence for ourselves in the limited time we have on Earth. That is a weighty responsibility, and a daunting prospect for most of us, especially those of us who face adverse life experiences and challenges (e.g., poverty, violence). **Will** is an action we take that we have envisioned, and apathy (or unhealthy will) often precedes mental distress (May, 1969b). In other words, will is our conscious capacity to move toward our self-selected goals, and it is an important aspect of good mental health. **Intentionality** is the ability to have a conscious and/or unconscious sense of purpose and to behave with purpose (May, 1969b).

Existential and Neurotic Anxiety

All people experience the four ultimate concerns of the human condition, and according to existentialist theory, these concerns create feelings of anxiety in everyone. However, the theory distinguishes between existential (normal) anxiety and neurotic anxiety. **Existential anxiety** is viewed as an inevitable part of the human condition. It is deeper than anxiety about career or health. Rather, it is a pervasive feeling of unease that arises from an awareness that existence is finite, people are mortal, and no purpose exists beyond what people create for themselves. Those who experience existential anxiety are living authentic lives in which they are aware of their self-and-world construct, strive to make wise choices, and take responsibility for their decisions. **Neurotic anxiety**, in contrast, is anxiety that is out of proportion to a particular event. It is often an indication that individuals are not living authentically and are not making choices and assuming responsibility. To decipher, neurotic anxiety is more of a pathological state and existential anxiety is a standard part of the human experience. While existentialism does not emphasize early childhood relationships, Frankl did believe that so-called neurotic difficulties often stem from an upbringing in which parents were punitive and deprived children of personal freedoms (Barton, 1992).

Existential guilt—guilt that results from the impossibility of fulfilling all of our innate potentials—and neurotic anxiety result when we lack awareness of our physical world, our relationships, and our psychological world; fail to take responsibility for making our lives meaningful and worthwhile; and realize that we have not become what we could have. It reflects our awareness that we have not fully realized ourselves as human beings and have allowed our lives to be controlled by chance and circumstance. We may not understand or be able to articulate the reasons for our feelings of guilt but, for many, an underlying sense of deep guilt and regret pervades our lives.

Depression is often the result of efforts to defend against existential guilt and anxiety and avoid the task of making our lives meaningful. As an example, Yalom (1980) suggests that among people nearing death, depression was greatest in those who had not created meaningful lives, whereas those who felt satisfied with the lives they had created for themselves were better able to accept death.

Dasein

Existentialists speak of *Dasein*—translated from the German as being present, being-in-the-world. *Dasein* relates to the idea that all people have consciousness, exist in the world, and have responsibility for themselves and their lives (Bauman & Waldo, 1998). Unlike other living things, human beings have consciousness. They are aware of their existence and participation in the world around them, and they are aware of this awareness. The phenomenological experience or ways of being-in-the-world include (Binswanger, 1963):

Umwelt—Refers to how we connect with the physical world around us. On a broad scale, this refers to the earth, biology, and the laws of nature. On a more personal level, *Umwelt* can be our personal space, living arrangements, or work environment. We interact with and are affected by our physical surroundings.

Mitwelt—Refers to being-in-the-world with other people, to relationships, interactions, and concepts we introject about society, race, gender, and religion. *Mitwelt* is subjective, based on personal experience.

Eigenwelt—Refers to our sense of our subjective world. This construct relates to our world of thoughts, feelings, and desires; the interrelationship of mind, body, and spirit. It is our beliefs about ourselves—awareness, identity, personal meaning, and our perceptions of ourselves. *Eigenwelt* encompasses our perceptions of ourselves along dimensions, such as interests,

Being-In-The-World (Dasein)

Umwelt Self in relation to world of nature and natural laws (time and space)	Eigenwelt Self in relation to self (thoughts, feelings, desires)
Uberwelt Self in relation to spirituality (how we construct meaning in our lives)	Mitwelt Self in relation to others (people)

(Dasein at center)

values, intelligence, motivation, and character. These self-perceptions impact how we live in the world and interact with other people.

Uberwelt—Refers to the spiritual or metaphysical dimension (van Deurzen, 2002). *Uberwelt* is the domain of experience where we create meaning for ourselves and organize and make sense of our worlds (van Deurzen, 2002).

These four ways of being-in-the-world are subjective, personal, and necessary for a complete understanding of the self, its experiences, and perceptions of the world. Being in a disconnected state in any of these four areas can result in purposelessness, alienation, and angst.

Dasein, being-in-the-world, is an interactive process. We are always of the world, but at the same time creating our world. We interact in the world, and the world impacts us. Things are always in a state of flux. Unlike other living things, we are also aware of the temporary nature of our lives. We are able to contemplate our not being-in-the-world (van Deurzen, 2010).

The concept of *Dasein* is complex and elusive but reflects people's ability to simultaneously live in the present, be conscious, and take responsibility for making their lives meaningful, while realizing fully that death will inevitably end their efforts. It reflects a dynamic process of potential and becoming rather than a fixed state.

Mental health involves being in balance and living in harmony with our inner self; with our family, friends, and colleagues; with our physical environment; and with our spirituality (Epp, 1998). In other words, mental health exists when all four aspects of *Dasein* (*Umwelt, Mitwelt, Eigenwelt*, and *Uberwelt*) are in harmony. Existential therapists emphasize the importance of experiencing the unity of self and world. Those of us who are not simply passive victims of circumstances but become the architects of our own lives provide good examples of emotional health. Whatever difficulties we encounter in our lives, we always have choices. As an example of this, Edith Eva Eger (2017), an Auschwitz concentration camp survivor, discussed how, while in captivity, carefully selecting the best blades of grass to eat reinforced her sense of control, gave her hope for the future, and helped her to believe she would survive the concentration camp. Eger believes that the more choices we have, the fewer choices we *think* we have; thus it is important to stay connected with our options and our power to choose. Eger suggests there are no problems in life, only challenges, and she believes strongly in taking personal responsibility for our destiny and being deliberate in choosing and living. Eger suggests that all of us are capable of doing good or bad, and that it is up to each of us to decide who we want to be.

Existential therapists think of the concept of unconscious in ways that reflect the tenets of existentialism. They concentrate on the unconscious conflict between people's wish to escape the ultimate concerns of the human condition and lose themselves in lethargy and denial, and their wish to achieve fulfillment despite the challenges and responsibilities that achievement entails. For the existentialists, emotional difficulties stem from people's failure to deal successfully with the inevitabilities of the human condition, by not transcending them to create a meaningful and authentic life for themselves.

The Human Condition: Potentials

Existential therapy is often misunderstood. For some, the inevitable concerns of the human condition, discussed previously, might present a bleak picture of life. However, existential therapy is actually an optimistic and hopeful approach to therapy that seeks to integrate the physical, psychological, and spiritual dimensions of humankind and focuses on people's capacity for growth (Xu, 2010). Existential therapy supports the idea that the human spirit has a healthy core, and that all people have a capacity for existential awareness and are thus able to face their existential fears (Moodley, 2010). It takes courage to live and to transcend psychological and environmental constraints, yet people still accomplish this daily. Existential therapy recognizes people's many strengths, and some of these strengths are discussed in the following section.

AWARENESS People have the capacity for awareness of both themselves and the world. The greater their awareness, the more possibilities are open to them and the more successfully they can address their fears and anxieties. The decision to increase self-awareness is pertinent to self-growth because it is at the heart of most human capacities. Although awareness will not always bring pleasure or peace, it allows people to recognize the limitations and challenges of their lives and make wise choices that can make their lives worthwhile.

One important example of self-awareness is the realization that everyone dies. Years ago, people were often not told when they had a terminal illness because of the belief that they were better off not knowing about their condition. However, that decision deprived them of the capacity to make meaningful choices about how they would live out their lives and encouraged inauthenticity and deceptive relationships. Now people are told the truth about their medical conditions so they can make choices such as whether or not to take medication that may hasten their deaths or relieve their pain. Other examples of self-awareness are the realizations that people have limited time in their lives, people have choices and responsibility, people can make meaning, and people are alone but can still connect with others (Schneider, 2008). Enhanced self-awareness through therapy is one of the goals of existential therapy. Therapists can focus on working with clients to increase their awareness of the following: how people's expectations impact them; ways that people focus on the past and how that impacts them; how people choose to respond to external events; how preoccupations with death distracts from an appreciation for life; how people are worthy as they are; and how people can live in the present moment.

AUTHENTICITY **Authenticity** involves people choosing the life they want to live based on their own values and decisions. Authentic people are genuine, real, and aware of their being. Those who are authentic consider and navigate the meaning of life, moral choices, and their innate humanness (Hergenhahn, 2009). Three essential features of authenticity include (Bugental, 1965):

1. People being aware of themselves and their relationships with the world
2. People making choices, knowing that decisions are the inevitable consequences of responsibility
3. People taking responsibility for their choices, recognizing that awareness is imperfect and sometimes leads to unanticipated results.

Taking responsibility for making choices based on awareness reflects authenticity and allows people to live more fully in the present and be themselves in their relationships. People whose decisions are based on denial, the wishes of others, or dependence are not truly living in the present. They may be driven by past losses or acting out of a hope for future gains. In addition, they are wearing a mask of inauthenticity that prevents others from really knowing who they are (Frank, 2007). Emotions and guilt often influence choice and people's way of being with others in the world (Boss, 1963). Each choice people make involves loss of many other alternatives. This ultimately shapes their lives and who they are in the process of becoming.

FREEDOM AND RESPONSIBILITY Freedom is a central concept in existential therapy, and it includes four aspects: awareness, choice, action, and change. Once people accept that they have freedom, no matter what their circumstances, they have the responsibility:

- To be aware of their past history, their current options, and their future potential
- To make choices that give meaning to their lives
- To exercise courage and thought in taking action toward life-enhancing change.

Once we see that we have choice, we can no longer view our decisions and behaviors as purposeless and accidental, make excuses for ourselves, or blame others for our unhappiness. We must assume responsibility and recognize that, ultimately, we alone are in charge of our lives. The enormity of that realization can be frightening but also empowering, as long as we can use our freedom in positive and growth-enhancing ways. The choices available to us may not be limitless, but we must recognize that even declining to make a decision is making a decision.

It is important for the therapist to take cultural differences into consideration while working with clients regarding the concept of choice. For example, if a client comes from a collectivist background and wants to make a decision that her family may not agree with, the therapist is responsible for helping the client assess the values she has for herself and her family. The therapist can assist the client in finding a balance that fits for her.

Furthermore, people from different cultures experience varied levels of oppression. Oppression can severely limit choices and options. Existentialism holds that while people cannot control what happens to them, they can control how they respond, perceive, and change the situation.

SELF-ACTUALIZATION Self-actualization, or reaching one's full potential, is an important concept for existential therapists, as it is for person-centered therapists. Abraham Maslow probably best described the nature of self-actualization (Maslow, 1954, 1968). He advanced the idea that each person has an essential nature, part of which is universal and part of which is unique to that individual. The will toward self-actualization is an innate and natural process that leads a person toward realization of that person's potential and toward growth and fulfillment.

Self-actualization can be blocked by many factors, including a cultural or family background that inhibits creativity, a repressive environment, and overwhelming fear and guilt. People who fail to move toward self-actualization typically experience confusion, agony, shame, defeat, anxiety, and a perception of life as meaningless (Vontress, 2008a; Yalom, 1980).

MAKING MEANING Existential therapists believe that life has the potential to be meaningful if we use our capacities to bring purpose and worth into our lives. One way to find meaning is through our will to love and to live (May, 1969b). Our awareness, our recognition that we have freedom, our authenticity, and our will toward self-actualization all enable us to know and confront disturbing aspects of ourselves and our world, such as the inevitability of death and our ultimate aloneness, and to transcend them by creating meaning in our lives.

Meaning is the purpose and logic of people's lives and is often reflected in choices people make. Dreams, visions, and fantasies also provide clues to meaning. Some people have social goals, such as Carl Rogers' efforts to increase world peace; others have competitive goals, such as breaking a world record, or creative goals, such as writing a novel. But most people find meaning in daily activities, such as raising healthy children; taking care of their homes; helping their friends, family, or community; or establishing a rewarding career.

People can also discover meaning by exploring values. However, clients often discard old values without replacing them with new ones or truly challenging their old beliefs. Therapists must help clients discover values that are consistent with who they are. Therapists trust that their clients will create their own value system.

Existential therapists pay attention to development throughout the lifespan and do not limit their focus to early childhood. They view life as a process of creating our own histories, with each choice and phase shaping and contributing to the next. Because life itself is a process, we are in a constant state of emerging and evolving, becoming more fully ourselves, and making meaning of each day as well as of the entirety of our lives. According to the existentialists, it is this journey that makes us human.

STRIVING FOR IDENTITY AND RELATIONSHIP TO OTHERS We all have a natural tendency to discover our true selves. Because we are social creatures and want to feel connected to others, we often change who we are to meet other people's expectations. It is challenging to discover who we are, and it takes courage to go through this process (May, 1975; Tillich, 1952).

Aloneness is part of the human condition, and people have to realize that they cannot rely on anyone else. They must rely on themselves, create their own meaning, and decide how to live. It is important to learn how to be alone before being with others. Therapists often guide clients in understanding their current relationships and deciphering between neurotically dependent attachment and life-affirming relationships. In other words, relationships can be sought either to fill a void or to fulfill and enhance life. Before establishing and maintaining healthy relationships, it is best to feel comfortable being alone.

Furthermore, many people get caught up in doing instead of being. They go through their day in ritualistic ways to confirm the identity that other people may have given them. Existential therapists challenge clients to explore ways they may have disconnected from their identity and how others have contributed to that. This exploration and realization that they must take back their freedom can be scary for clients. Clients generally do have fears, and therapists have the responsibility to help clients explore their fears and give them opportunities to face their fears with courage.

THE THERAPEUTIC PROCESS

Existential therapy is a process in which two people, client and therapist, embark on a journey to help the client cope more effectively with the inevitable conditions of life and make better use of the potentials of humankind. This approach makes minimal use of techniques but relies heavily on the therapist to effect change.

In existential therapy, clients are encouraged to take responsibility for making the changes that will enrich their lives. Awareness is not enough; clients must take action and move toward making the changes they desire.

Because existential therapy is not problem or crisis focused and involves the establishment of a deep relationship between client and therapist, it is almost never time limited or rushed. Typically, existential therapy has no clear stages or transitions.

However, the process generally begins by therapists developing an understanding of their clients and the clients' awareness of themselves and their world. Clients are encouraged to describe their values, beliefs, and assumptions, their histories and backgrounds, the choices they have made, and the choices they believe they cannot make. Therapists listen closely so they can comprehend their clients' views of the world and gradually help them express their deepest fears and take greater responsibility for their lives.

The middle phase of counseling enables people to use the information they have shared to find purpose, meaning, and value. During this phase, therapists start using various interventions, such as Symbolic Growth Experience, paradoxical intention, and addressing the ultimate concerns of the human condition. Therapists encourage client authenticity and awareness during this process.

Counseling moves toward a close when people can implement their awareness of themselves and go forward to establish more meaningful lives. They have learned that they cannot eliminate anxiety completely but have found ways to live full lives despite anxiety about the inevitabilities of the human condition. In addition, when clients are progressing along a path that seems natural and right for them and it is helping them become actualized, they may be ready to terminate counseling.

An important and challenging aspect of concluding counseling is the client's separation from the therapist. This can be a reminder of the inescapable endings in life and is often difficult for the client and maybe even the therapist. However, if both the therapist and client can be present in the moment, authentic, and aware of their reactions to the end of counseling, the separation process itself can foster growth, enabling the client to face and cope effectively with fears.

Therapeutic Goals

The fundamental goal of existential therapy is to help people find value, meaning, and purpose in their lives. Counseling does not specifically seek to alleviate symptoms or to "cure" clients of their perceived problems. Instead, the purpose of therapy is to help them gain more awareness and take control of their lives rather than playing the victim role (May, 1981).

To reach this goal, existential therapists help people confront their deepest fears and anxieties about the inevitable challenges of life, including death, isolation, and meaninglessness. Reviewing and reflecting on clients' histories can facilitate this process, especially if it helps clients identify barriers that impede their movement toward an authentic and personally meaningful life. In addition, counseling helps people become aware of the freedom they do have, recognize their options, and make choices that help them become more actualized and able to lead a life that reflects their values and priorities. Not only does therapy aim to help clients live more authentically, it also aims to help clients be fully present in their daily lives (Schneider & Krug, 2010). This is done through discovering behaviors that inhibit the clients' full presence, helping clients assume greater responsibility for being in the present moment, and encouraging clients to choose more extensive ways of being in their lives.

Therapist's Function and Role

As the primary vehicle for facilitating change, therapists who practice existential therapy have considerable responsibility. Their own values are very much a part of the counseling process. Therapists advocate for freedom and authenticity, encourage people to confront their fears, and promote their efforts to make meaningful choices (Hergenhahn & Olson, 2007). In keeping with the emphasis on personal freedom, existential therapists do not hold back their views. They express their values and beliefs, use humor, and make suggestions and interpretations, but always allow clients the freedom to determine how they will use this input.

Existential therapists are companions and co-explorers with their clients. Available and empathic, these therapists experience clients' pain without losing their sense of themselves. To understand their clients' deepest thoughts and feelings about issues such as death, isolation, and guilt, existential therapists need to be with their clients as fully as possible and to listen with both eyes and ears. Therapists should ask their clients about their deepest beliefs and thoughts, such as their worldviews, their hopes, goals, and dreams, and their interests (Yalom, 1980). They communicate respect, support, encouragement, and concern and are genuine, open, and caring. They have no expectations for outcome and no mandates for client behavior. They simply join people in their quest to use their freedom to craft a meaningful and rewarding life. To emphasize clients' personal responsibility, therapists often ask how they contributed to different situations in order to take the focus off blaming others. Therapists using this approach focus on process, rather than on content.

Many clients experience **restricted existence**, which is the lack of awareness of oneself and one's problems; therefore, a main task of therapists is to help their clients gain awareness (Bugental, 1997). By doing so, feelings of being trapped and helpless will decrease, clients will see what they are doing to contribute to a lack of awareness, and they will discover new ways to gain awareness to change their lives.

Maintaining relationships of this magnitude and intensity can be very demanding of therapists. Being an existential therapist requires openness to perpetual learning and the ability to maintain an intense level of involvement with a client through some of the client's most difficult experiences. Therapists who have not come to terms with their own fears about death and dying may be more likely to avoid or selectively inattend to such material presented by the client (Yalom, 1998). Remaining authentic as a therapist can also be challenging. Existential therapists remain true to their own beliefs while also recognizing and appreciating individual differences. The therapeutic relationship that develops between the client and therapist is always, by necessity, co-constructed (Richert, 2010).

That is, the bond created between therapist and client reflects the depth to which each person is willing to go to understand and to be understood.

The experience clients have in therapy is also unique. Because therapy is challenging, clients are encouraged to acknowledge the progress they have already made just by coming to therapy (May, 1981). Not only are clients expected to be active during their therapy sessions, they are also meant to experiment outside of session by engaging in new ways of being. Clients do not solve their problems or provide solutions during counseling; rather, they gain insight, create meaningful lives, and assume responsibility.

Relationship Between Therapist and Client

In existential therapy, the relationship is everything. The idea that the therapeutic relationship is an **I-Thou** (You) relationship is central to existential therapy. The I-Thou relationship refers to moments when people come together in an authentic and meaningful way, thus enriching each other's lives (Buber, 1970). In the I-Thou relationship, there is a realization of the other person as distinct from oneself and yet wholly valued as a human being. It is in these relationships that therapists are able to effectively enter their clients' worlds and assist them in improving their experiencing of that world. When communicating in an I-Thou fashion, therapists advance beyond stereotypes, putting clients in boxes, and prescribed social roles, and they can see the uniqueness of each individual. When this happens, therapists are able to move their clients into safe, meaningful interpersonal encounters in which thoughts and feelings can be freely expressed (Bugental, 1978). Therefore, existential therapists expand on Rogers' concepts of empathy and positive regard and focus even more on the therapeutic relationship as an expression of intimacy, openness, and real human exchange.

THERAPEUTIC TECHNIQUES AND PROCEDURES

The primary intervention in existential therapy—use of the person of the therapist–has already been discussed. Existential therapists do not rely on specific techniques and interventions. Instead, these therapists rely on philosophical views to understand their client's subjective reality. The approach also uses some other interventions, which are presented below.

Symbolic Growth Experience

Existentialists believe that learning and growth come from intense experiences (Frankl, 1963; Maslow, 1968). Building on the ideas of Frankl and Maslow, Willard Frick described a model, the Symbolic Growth Experience, to explain the relationship between experience and the discovery of meaning. The **Symbolic Growth Experience** is the intentional interpretation of an immediate experience to discover the symbolism and meaning behind it, in order to develop awareness, personal worth, and meaning (Frick, 1987). The exploration of a Symbolic Growth Experience has four steps:

1. People are educated about the concept of the Symbolic Growth Experience.
2. They select a salient past experience and explore its importance and symbolism in their lives.
3. They are helped to understand the meaning embedded in the experience.
4. They have a clearer sense of the meaning of their selected experience and use these strategies to grasp the significance of other experiences.

Symbolic Growth Experience is explored in more detail in the case application later in this chapter.

Frankl's Logotherapy

Viktor Frankl (1978) termed his version of existential therapy logotherapy, or therapy through meaning. He believed that even well-functioning people sometimes perceive life as meaningless and experience a sense of emptiness. Through counseling, he helped people recognize the depth of their need for meaning, reassured them that all people can create meaning in their lives, and supported them in their efforts to find purpose and meaning. The tasks of therapists using logotherapy are to help people:

- Discover and notice where they possess freedom and the potential for meaning
- Actualize those potentials to transform and make meaning of their lives
- Honor meanings realized in the past (Lantz, 2000).

For Frankl, as is true for all existentialist therapists, the central ingredient in counseling is the use of the therapeutic relationship to accomplish these goals.

Paradoxical Intention

Frankl described a cycle in which fears evoke symptoms that in turn increase the fears. For example, a person who fears heights avoids them. Because of the avoidance, anticipatory anxiety develops, the heights become increasingly frightening in the person's mind, and both the avoidance and the fear increase. Frankl (1978) suggested that the fear of fear increases fear.

To break this pattern, he recommended a technique called **paradoxical intention**, in which therapists encourage clients to do or wish for the very thing they fear most. For example, a woman was afraid to leave her house for fear of fainting. Frankl instructed her to go outside and try her best to faint. Not surprisingly, she was unable to faint. His intervention succeeded in both reducing her fear and strengthening her courage by changing the meaning of her fear. She could now accept her fear, as well as the slight possibility that she might faint.

Yalom (1980) believed that this paradoxical principle extended to people's search for meaning: The more people purposefully search for meaning, the less likely they are to find it. Instead, people who engage with their values fully are more likely to experience meaning naturally from their work, love, and creation. Finding meaning is a lifelong process of facing our fears, developing awareness, and making choices.

Dereflection

One type of paradoxical intervention is **dereflection**, which is based on **self-transcendence** and self-detachment, two necessary characteristics for human existence (Frankl, 1969). Unlike hyper-reflection, in which individuals become self-absorbed in their thoughts, dereflection takes the focus away from the individuals and helps them concentrate less on themselves and more on other people or goals they find meaningful. Dereflection is intended to reduce compulsive self-observation and redirect clients' attention in a more positive manner, helping them discover meaning in situations in the present moment, rather than becoming trapped in obsessive worry (Frankl, 1969).

Dereflection was originally formulated to treat couples with sexual dysfunction. By focusing away from one's own performance anxiety and instead pleasuring one's partner, the end result is less anxiety and less attention being paid to oneself (Schulenberg, Schnetzer, Winters, & Hutzell, 2010).

Dereflection can also be useful in group therapy. Rather than focusing on problems, the group's attention is turned to the present moment. Group members are not allowed to complain about fate, feeling victimized, or other negative emotions, but rather must focus on worthwhile, attainable goals. Dereflection is a positive, meaningful, and useful tool.

Addressing the Four Dimensions of the Human Condition

Earlier in this chapter, the four dimensions of the human condition that typically underlie emotional difficulties were presented: death, isolation, meaninglessness, and freedom. Theorists have suggested responses to concerns about these four conditions, such as the following (Bauman & Waldo, 1998):

- Faith in our own existence in the present can reduce fears of death.
- Love is the authentic response to isolation.
- Drawing on our inner creativity to find ways to realize our potential can counteract the inherent meaninglessness of life.
- Responsibility, commitment, making choices, and staying with them help us cope with our overabundance of freedom.

Addressing the four dimensions of the human condition can be effective in working cross-culturally. It is important for therapists to understand the human condition of all people before understanding the client's culture because there are more similarities between people than there are differences (Vontress, 2008a). Therapists who are attuned to universal issues of love, meaning, fear of death, and freedom have a greater likelihood of success.

APPLICATON AND CURRENT USE OF EXISTENTIAL THERAPY

Just as existential psychology swept the United States in the 1950s, today, Eastern traditions of Taoism, Confucianism, and Buddhism are beginning to influence the practice of existential psychology (Stratton, 2015). Both Eastern and Western traditions concern themselves with the essential elements of the human condition: awareness, impermanence, and the phenomenological experience of aloneness, which have prompted the basic questions that human beings have been asking themselves since the beginning of time. As this trans-theoretical dialogue continues, the universal concerns with living—both individually and collectively—will likely be integrated into the heart of psychotherapy (Hoffman, Yang, Kaklauskas, & Chan, 2009). Existential therapy is a useful approach for many types of problems and people.

Existential therapy's themes of meaningfulness, authenticity, freedom, and responsibility continue to have great relevance and broad application. The more our lives seem to be out of our control, the more we hear about terrorism, school violence, and bullying, and the more we are troubled by our own overcommitted lifestyles, the more many of us search for meaning and purpose in what we do and struggle to maintain a sense of freedom and authenticity.

In recent years, spirituality has emerged as an acceptable and important topic in counseling and psychotherapy. This emphasis on spirituality is consistent with an existential viewpoint. Although existentialism does not advocate any specific religious beliefs, it reminds us of the importance of having a sense of meaning that transcends our immediate and finite lives. Whether that meaning comes from traditional religion, the spirituality of nature, watching a child grow, or another source, it can help us cope with the challenges of the 21st century. We can find many similarities between existential therapy and Buddhist mindfulness practice. Both focus on accepting the finality of life, transcendence of self, and staying grounded in the here-and-now. These concepts are essential to self-acceptance and finding contentment in life (Claessens, 2009; Xu, 2010).

Counseling Applications

Because of its lack of specific interventions, its focus on philosophical issues rather than on concrete problems, its emphasis on the client–therapist relationship, and its use of thoughtful and open dialogue, existential therapy is appropriate for various types of people. For example, existential therapy is particularly helpful for people with long-standing, pervasive anxiety or depression and those who are coping with life-and-death matters such as grief and loss, diagnosis of a terminal illness, or transitioning between phases of life (entering adulthood, parenting, retirement). Of course, end-of-life issues and living with chronic or terminal illnesses require a more holistic approach to counseling than what standard modalities offer. Existential therapy provides a comprehensive and integrative method for exploring these complicated yet universal issues. People with anxiety disorders such as posttraumatic stress disorder, agoraphobia, and panic disorder may also respond well to the existential therapist's efforts to help them explore and understand the meaning of their fears so that they can develop an acceptance of what is happening in their lives. Looking at how they have made choices and the meaning of their lives so far might enable people to live their lives more deliberately, create more meaning for themselves, and be more authentic and connected in their relationships.

Researchers have found that existential therapy works well for various populations, including older people who are facing end-of-life issues and experiencing existential anxiety (Barekati, Bahmani, Naghiyaaee, Afrasiabi, & Marsa, 2017), women with dependent personality disorder (Sadati, Hosseini, Hakami, & Sadati, 2017), and clients who struggle with addiction (Thompson, 2016). Existential therapy can be particularly helpful for people who have addictions because addiction can be related to isolation and a lack of personal meaning. Existential therapy can counteract addiction by helping clients live more fulfilling lives (Thompson, 2016). In addition, focusing on interpersonal relatedness and responsibility for choices and life goals can help clients who struggle with addiction. Although the scope and sample size of the aforementioned studies are insufficient to firmly establish the approach's effectiveness, research does suggest a broad application for existential therapy, especially when considered in the context of the common factors discussed in Chapter 1 that are effective across all theoretical boundaries.

Logotherapy can also help with end-of-life issues and with those who are aging because it addresses the spiritual core at the center of every human. It provides a strengths-based approach for gaining a sense of meaning and self-acceptance. Coming to terms with death, integrating this knowledge into life, and having a positive attitude toward life and death can help people to transcend suffering and fear (Xu, 2010). Logotherapy has been associated with positive outcomes, including better physical and mental well-being; enhanced self-esteem, self-acceptance, and happiness; and improved health in older adults (Homan, 2016; Ryff, 2014).

An existential approach is beneficial for individuals, couples, and groups. The existential "here-and-now" focus may be especially helpful with some clients (Correia, Cooper, Berdondini, & Correia, 2017). Existential issues are common to many therapy groups addressing both psychological and somatic illness. Topics such as alcohol abuse, midlife adjustment, and serious mental illness regularly touch on matters of an existential nature.

Existential therapy can be particularly useful in group therapy, counteracting participants' sense of meaninglessness and isolation with the opportunity to connect with others who have similar problems. Existential group therapy may help people who are experiencing physical illness, such as cancer, terminal illness, and human immunodeficiency (HIV) infection (Vos, Craig, & Cooper, 2015). Existential group therapy offers many benefits to participants. For example, group members have the chance to share their concerns about death and dying, which can help them feel more supported by others with shared experiences. Participants may also cope better with their concerns through various techniques, such as discussion, relaxation, experiential exercises, and reflection (Vos et al., 2015). Furthermore, members in groups have the opportunity to gain new perspectives, encourage each other to be authentic, and clarify meaning in their lives. Participants can find purpose in their lives, experience a reduction of depression and anxiety, and improve their self-efficacy (Vos et al., 2015). Group members are also more likely to find meaning by giving back and helping others outside the group (Garrow & Walker, 2011; Vos et al., 2015). The group dynamic offers a unique way to learn and take personal responsibility because all group members are responsible for how they behave in the group and how they interact with each other (Yalom, 1980).

Existential theory may be best suited for:

- People coping with life-threatening and chronic illnesses
- People whose lives have challenging limitations, such as those who are incarcerated, those with disabilities, and those living in poverty
- People who have suffered important losses, such as bereavement, disappointments in relationships, and failure to achieve their goals
- People who have had traumatic experiences
- People with long-standing mild-to-moderate anxiety or depression
- People at a crossroads in their lives who are looking for direction, such as those who are recently divorced, approaching midlife, retired, or graduated from college.

It quickly becomes apparent that all human beings at some point in their lives can benefit from existential therapy. Anyone experiencing "pervasive postmodern symptoms," such as excessive anxiety, apathy, alienation, nihilism, avoidance, shame, addiction, despair, or purposelessness, as well as those who are seeking meaning in life, truth, self-actualization and transcendence, can benefit from an existential approach to psychotherapy (Diamond, 2009). In other words, existential therapy seems relevant to all types of people, in all age groups. It can even be useful in working with children and adolescents.

Application to Multicultural Groups

Existential therapy is based on a universal worldview and is, by its very nature, adaptive to culturally diverse groups (Vontress, 2008a). Because existential therapy has no one specific view of reality, this approach is suitable for people from all cultural backgrounds. For almost 50 years, Vontress has been integrating existential therapy with cross-cultural counseling and is credited for his culture-centered focus for stressing the importance of being aware of culture, race, and ethnicity in the counseling setting (Moodley & Walcott, 2010). Cross-cultural counseling focuses more on cultural sensitivity rather than specific interventions for various cultures. Vontress' work has been described as connecting the existentialism of Europe and the spirituality of Africa (Moodley, 2010) and reminds us that philosophers from Asia and other non-Western areas have addressed issues of the meaning of life for many more years than Western philosophers have. In addition, people from all cultures face the inevitable issues of love, anxiety, suffering, and death. The phenomenology perspective of existential therapy is another strength for working with diverse clients because clients have subjective experiences. This approach recognizes the importance of validating the reality of all clients. Another strength of existential therapy is that it allows clients to determine how their culture is influencing them. This approach emphasizes freedom in making choices; therefore, clients are challenged to gain awareness about the responsibility they have for their lives. When clients gain awareness about their lack of freedom and how social and cultural aspects are influencing their freedom, their freedom can be increased. It is important to note that the freedom of clients may be limited by society and their family structure, which makes it challenging to separate their freedom from their family structure.

EVALUATION OF EXISTENTIAL THERAPY

The majority of the literature on the effectiveness of existential therapy relies on in-depth case studies (Bugental, 1990; May 1983; Yalom, 1980). Like all approaches to counseling and psychotherapy, existential therapy has both strengths and limitations. As with many types of therapy, additional research is necessary to empirically validate existential therapy. However, some interventions, such as paradoxical intention, have shown effectiveness.

Limitations

Existential therapy relies heavily on developing a strong client–therapist relationship and on verbal communication. It is an individualized approach in which the therapist offers little structure or direction. This approach takes a stance that responsibility, choice, and self-determination are desirable but does not offer specific steps and has few strategies for intervention. Existential therapy may be a leisurely and lengthy process. Because of these limitations, many people may be skeptical of its value, be reluctant or unable to engage in the thinking and self-exploration that it requires, and find its underlying philosophy unacceptable. Of course, therapists need to respect those reactions and select carefully the people for whom existential therapy is suited.

In addition, this approach does not seek to directly alleviate symptoms of mental disorders. Therefore, people struggling with prominent mental health symptoms (e.g., extreme mood symptoms, psychosis) are probably not good candidates for this approach.

One of the biggest limitations of this approach is that not all therapists will have the personal qualities or capacities required to apply this theory. For the approach to be effective, therapists must have a high level of maturity, life experience, and training (van Deurzen, 2002). Learning existential therapy is more than just knowing about the skills and beliefs; it is learning about yourself and being fully authentic.

Strengths and Contributions

The existential approach to counseling has many strengths. Its greatest contribution is probably not as a separate approach to psychotherapy and counseling but as a philosophy of human development that can be infused into other counseling theories. This idea was advanced by May and Yalom (1995), who stated that their primary objective was the integration of the theory's goals and concepts into all approaches to psychotherapy. They wanted all therapists to become aware of the importance of choice, meaning, self-actualization, and the therapeutic alliance. Certainly, few would argue with the premise that counseling should promote people's overall wellness, help them live fully and authentically, encourage them to take responsibility for their lives, make more positive and deliberate choices, and create meaning for themselves.

Addressing existential and spiritual needs can be an important part of a holistic approach to counseling. Particularly with an aging population, an existential approach, either alone or in combination with other approaches, can be helpful (Xu, 2010; Barekati et al., 2017). Existential therapy integrates well with other approaches, including positive psychology (Thompson, 2011; Wong, 2010; Wong, 2014; Wong, 2015), narrative therapy (Richert, 2010), brief therapy (Bugental, 2008), experiential therapy (Madison, 2014), and cognitive therapy (Barekati et al., 2017).

Time-limited existential therapy models have been developed, including both a short-term existential integrative therapy (Bugental, 2008) and a modular approach that can be administered in 12 to 15 sessions. Working within a time-sensitive framework not only offers clients a focus but also provides flexibility and allows additional support and more sessions to be added, if necessary, based on the clients' needs. Brief therapy may be especially useful because a time-limited approach accurately represents the notion that life is time limited. This approach would act as a starting point for clients to become more active in taking responsibility for their lives.

Existential therapy has made many important contributions to the fields of counseling and psychotherapy. Like person-centered counseling, it emphasizes the importance of a collaborative, respectful, and authentic client–therapist relationship. The existential therapist is viewed as traveling alongside their clients and helping them navigate through life's challenges, while still stressing the importance of clients' autonomy. As previously discussed, research has supported the connection between the therapeutic alliance and counseling outcomes.

Existential therapy has broadened the reaches of psychotherapy beyond pathology and symptoms and legitimized inclusion in the counseling process of such deep and philosophical issues as existential anxiety, isolation, fear of death, self-actualization, freedom, and the meaning of life. For example, clients begin to view death as a motivator to give life meaning and become comfortable with the concept of death. Existential therapy is a holistic and growth-promoting approach that de-emphasizes pathology and has relevance to everyone.

Logotherapy, along with other humanistic and emotionally oriented interventions, is beneficial for people who suffer from on-going feelings of meaninglessness in their lives (Frankl, 2010). Frankl emphasizes the need for a "meaning-focus" as a way to uplift people from despair to growth.

Although existential therapy was developed more than 75 years ago, it is compatible with current trends in counseling and psychotherapy. It takes a broad perspective on the meaning of spirituality and affirms its significance in people's lives. It is phenomenological and emphasizes the importance of meaning making. While espousing an emphasis on people's commonalities, existential therapy also attends to the importance of people's experience within their cultural context. It acknowledges the worth of people's thoughts and values flexibility and creativity in thinking. Existential therapy also encourages balance in people's lives, another important contemporary value.

Paradoxical intention is a technique associated with existential therapy that may be effective in addressing various client concerns (Fabry, 2010). A meta-analytic review of 15 studies on existential therapy found that specific interventions, such as paradoxical intentions, are effective for populations that have mental and physical illnesses (Vos et al., 2015). Specifically, paradoxical intention has been found to be helpful in treating anorexia nervosa, agoraphobia, anxiety, urinary retention, and insomnia. Studies on the empirical efficacy of logotherapy have found paradoxical intent to be helpful with populations as diverse as at-risk urban adolescents (White, Wagener, & Furrow, 2010) and nurses working in palliative care settings (Vachon, Fillion, Achille, Duval, & Leung, 2011). Family therapists and cognitive behavioral therapists, in particular, use this intervention in their work and find it a powerful tool for change, although one that requires careful use.

Existential therapy is a hopeful, optimistic, and timely approach, differentiated from other theories by its overarching philosophical attitude toward human existence (Vontress, 2008a). Existential therapists' holistic focus and their emphasis on universal themes of life, death, love, and responsibility are widely applicable. Existential therapists aim to connect with others on a spiritual level and across cultural, national, and racial barriers.

SKILL DEVELOPMENT: VALUES CLARIFICATION

Understanding values is relevant to existential therapy as well as to other counseling approaches. Our values are an important aspect of our identities and affect the choices we make. Our success in leading lives consistent with our values is strongly connected to the meaningfulness of our lives and our sense of fulfillment. Values can be expressed, manifested in our daily activities, and assessed through inventories. Ideally, our expressed values (i.e., what we express our values are), manifest values (i.e., how our values are reflected in how we actually live), and inventoried values (i.e., how our values are reflected in a formal assessment) will all be congruent. However, sometimes discrepancies emerge, particularly between expressed and manifest values. This can lead us to feel unfulfilled and unmotivated.

Wanda, for example, reported that she valued close interpersonal relationships, spending time in nature, and demonstrating her creativity. However, her manifest values were different. She worked long hours as a bank manager and made a high salary but had little time for friends and leisure activities. In addition, she lived in a small apartment in an urban setting. Her place of residence did not allow her to grow a garden, make space for her painting, or have much contact with the beauty of nature. Not surprisingly, Wanda reported that she was unhappy with her life and felt unmotivated at work.

Seeing the discrepancy between her expressed and manifest values prompted her to take a more honest look at her values. She realized that the security and income of her job were important values to her but that she was neglecting the interpersonal and creative values that also mattered. She was able to transfer to a bank in a more rural area and purchased a small house. These changes allowed her more time and opportunity for hiking, painting, and gardening. Although Wanda did take a cut in pay, she was able to maintain an adequate and stable income and decided that the loss in income was more than offset by her ability to realize some of her other values. Table 9.2 provides examples of questions that can be asked to ascertain a client's values. Of course, the therapist can modify these questions to ensure that they are well received by a particular client.

Inventoried values can be assessed using a variety of inventories, both standardized and nonstandardized. Inventories and assessment scales developed by existential thinkers provide other potentially useful tools for addressing clients' experiences. Some of these are:

- Reker's (2001) Life Attitude Profile–Revised (LAP-R) for assessing meaning and purpose in life
- The Sources of Meaning Profile Revised (SOMP-R; 1996), also developed by Reker, measuring how people find meaningful aspects of their lives
- Purpose in Life Test (Bauman & Waldo, 1998), which measures level of existential meaning and future time perspective.

Inventories such as these can promote discussion and awareness, helping people give meaning to their lives.

TABLE 9.2 Existential Therapy Values Questions

Expressed Values

- What do you view as the most important and meaningful parts of your life?
- What accomplishments have you had that make you particularly proud?
- If you had only 1 year to live, how would you want to use your time?
- What do you view as your three most important values?
- If you were to write a brief biography of yourself for publication in a national magazine, what information would you include?

Manifest Values

- Describe a typical day (or week or month) in your life.
- If someone who did not know you read a biography of your life, what would that individual view as your greatest accomplishments? Your greatest disappointments?
- Assume that you have 16 waking hours each day. Tell me the number of hours you typically spend in each of the following roles and what you usually do in that role:
  - Spouse/partner/friend
  - Parent
  - Career person
  - Self-care (e.g., exercise, meditation, walking in nature)
  - Life manager (e.g., shopping, cleaning, paying bills)
  - Other roles
- If you could redistribute your time among these roles, what changes would you make?
- How have your activities and the ways in which you spend your time changed during the past 5 to 10 years?
- When you awaken in the morning, what parts of your life do you look forward to and engage in as much as possible and what parts do you avoid whenever you can?
- What do you enjoy doing when you are on vacation?

TABLE 9.3 Existential Therapy Values Activity

Instructions 1: Review the following list of values. Place a check mark by all of the values that are important to you. Then review the values you have checked and list, in priority order, the three that are most important to you.

Instructions 2: Assume that you have $1000 to spend at an auction of values. Review the following list and decide how you would allocate your money. Allocating too little to any one value may mean you will lose the auction for that value, but allocating too much to a value limits how much you can allocate to other values.

List of Values	
Achievement	Learning and knowledge
Beauty	Love and romance
Career success	Nature/outdoor activities
Child rearing	Order
Creativity	Possessions and wealth
Fame	Power
Friendship	Prestige and admiration
Health and fitness	Security
Helping others	Spirituality
Independence	Variety and excitement

Sometimes paper and pencil or computerized inventories elicit more objective responses than do discussion questions such as those previously listed. Table 9.3 provides an example of an activity that can offer another perspective on what is important to a person. It may also be helpful to give clients the opportunity to add their own values that may not be on the list. Either of the two sets of instructions can be used with the accompanying list of values, depending on which seems more likely to engage a person's interest and cooperation. Discussion of the person's responses should follow completion of the inventory to clarify the information provided.

CASE APPLICATION

The following dialogue illustrates use of a Symbolic Growth Experience with Edie. As you learned earlier in this chapter, processing a Symbolic Growth Experience entails four steps:

1. People are educated about the concept of the Symbolic Growth Experience.
2. They select an important past experience and explore its importance and symbolism in their lives.
3. They are helped to understand the meaning in the experience.
4. They develop a clearer sense of meaning and can repeat their use of these strategies to understand the significance of other experiences.

Assume that Edie has already been educated about the concept of the SGE. As you read the following dialogue, observe how exploring the significance of past experiences helps her develop a greater sense of meaningfulness in her life as well as an understanding of some of her emotions and choices. Also note the existential therapist's role.

THERAPIST: Edie, I see great sadness on your face today.

EDIE: Yes, the weekend was tough. I told you that Roberto and I were planning to attend my 20th high school reunion. I bought a new dress, got my hair styled, decided on pictures of Ava to show off. I thought it would be wonderful, but it was horrible.

THERAPIST: How did something you were so looking forward to bring you so much pain?

EDIE: You remember my telling you that when I was 10 years old, I was diagnosed with cancer. No one thought I would survive, except maybe my father. I had chemotherapy and lost all my hair. And I took steroids to help with the nausea and that made me gain weight. There I was, disgusting-looking, maybe dying . . . and I was supposed to go to school, if I could drag myself there. The other children would make fun of me, laugh at me, call me baldy. I know they didn't understand, but it was so awful.

THERAPIST: It's hard for me to imagine how difficult that must have been for you, not only coping with cancer but also with the teasing. Tell me about the connection to the reunion?

EDIE: I guess I wanted to show everyone that I had survived, that I was attractive now and had a family. But when I got to the reunion, all those feelings I had when I was 10 came rushing back to me.

THERAPIST: So in your mind, the reunion was meant to be an affirming experience, but somehow it was just the opposite. What sense do you make of that?

EDIE: I don't know.

THERAPIST: Edie, you have talked quite a bit about the impact cancer had on your life and your concern that it might recur despite the doctors' reassurances. Perhaps that strong fear of death has never left you and the reminder of the reunion intensified that fear.

EDIE: That's true. You know, when I hit the tenth anniversary of my cancer diagnosis, the doctors said I was cured, but I never really believed it.

THERAPIST: And you're still living as though death is imminent.

EDIE: Yes, I am. I felt like a fake at the reunion. How could I present myself as a woman who had survived when I knew inside that I was really dying?

THERAPIST: Most of us have anxiety about death, but for you, of course, it is particularly strong. How do you think this fear affects your life now?

EDIE: I worry a lot about dying before Ava is grown. She needs me so much, and I don't want to abandon her. I try to do all I can for her while I still have time, but I never feel like I do enough. Roberto can't understand. He says I pamper her and I should stop, but she's my only child. I couldn't get pregnant again because of the cancer. It's a miracle I got pregnant with Ava. She's like a gift from God.

THERAPIST: I hear you saying so many important things. Ava's birth and your role as a mother have given meaning to your life, and you want to make the most of that. But I also hear a sense of urgency, a fear that time might run out for you before Ava is grown and that terrifies you.

EDIE: Yes, I still feel like it's just a matter of time before the cancer catches up with me again. Why can't Roberto understand that?

THERAPIST:	You feel very alone. I think one of the hardest things about being human is that no matter how much other people care about us, they can't really know what it is like to feel the way we feel. That can be very lonely.
EDIE:	That's true. I know Roberto loves me and Ava, but he never does seem to really understand me. Maybe I've been too hard on him and expected too much.
THERAPIST:	What could you choose to do differently?
EDIE:	Instead of blowing up at him, I could remind myself that he hasn't been through what I have, that there's no way he could really understand, and that's all right. I have a better awareness of myself now that I understand why I treat Ava the way I do.
THERAPIST:	How does that fit with the importance in your life of being a good mother?
EDIE:	I love Ava and do all I can for her. Roberto says it's not good for her, though—that she needs more independence and confidence in herself.
THERAPIST:	I know your anxiety pushes you to do everything possible for Ava and to be a different parent to her than your parents were to you. Could it be that your anxiety makes it hard for you to see any value in what Roberto is saying?
EDIE:	You mean that I'm scared something bad will happen to Ava if I don't keep a close watch on her? Yes, I guess I can be overprotective . . . and I know that's not really good mothering. I want her to feel confident and good about herself, not the way I felt when I was growing up.

At this point, Edie has developed a clearer idea of her own meaning of both her experiences with cancer and the recent reunion. She is more aware of the impact that her fear of death and her sense of aloneness have on her. She has gained some clarification about the primary purpose of her life—to stay alive so that she can continue to be a good parent to Ava—and has begun to increase her awareness of both her own behavior and the possible validity of Roberto's words. She is now in a better position to make choices that will help her to move toward the meaning she has created in her life, to feel more actualized, and to improve her relationships with both Ava and Roberto.

REFLECT AND RESPOND

1. Viktor Frankl said, "When we are no longer able to change a situation, we are challenged to change ourselves." Ponder this for a moment. Has there ever been a time when something occurred in your life that you could not change? How did you react? What did you do? Write about this in your journal. Over time, how did you adjust to the situation?
2. Imagine that you are home alone reading a book, when you hear an explosion outside. Within minutes you are told by the fire department that you must evacuate the building immediately because of the risk of fire. Knowing that time is precious, and that your home might be destroyed, what items do you choose to take with you? What do you leave behind? Journal about the experience.
3. Existential therapy is about finding purpose in one's life and personal growth. In your journal follow the prompts below and consider your reactions. How might a therapist use this activity with a client and how might it be beneficial for a client?
    - What do I need more of in my life? What do I need less of?
    - When did I experience joy this week?

- What does my ideal day look like?
- What do I want my legacy to be?
- What advice would I give to my future self?

4. Gratitude is the essence of feeling thankful and appreciating what you have. Sometimes, we may not have the time to notice all that we have to be grateful for. For this exercise, you will go on a "gratitude hunt" and journal about your experience. Follow the sequence below. Reflect on how this exercise may be helpful for a client.
   - Find something that you enjoy listening to.
   - Find something that you see as "beautiful."
   - Find something that you enjoy smelling.
   - Find something that is your favorite color.
   - Find something that you are thankful for.
   - Find something that brings you comfort.

Summary

Existential therapy grew out of a European society devastated by two world wars. Existential therapy seeks to help people deal with the deep and powerful issues that affect all people and are unique to the human condition. Both a philosophy and an approach to counseling, existential therapy addresses deep dimensions of the human condition, such as the inevitability of death and loss, loneliness and alienation, meaninglessness, and guilt.

One of the main developers of existential therapy was Victor Frankl, who survived imprisonment at Nazi concentration camps in Dachau and Auschwitz. Frankl's resilience allowed him to find meaning during this torturous time. From his experience, he developed logotherapy, therapy through meaning. Helping clients find meaning in their lives is one of the most important goals of logotherapy.

Existential therapy differentiates between neurotic anxiety and existential anxiety. Neurotic anxiety is pathological and disruptive, and existential anxiety is a normal part of human life caused by the fears and anxieties that all people experience. When individuals explore their existential anxiety, they are more likely to take responsibility for their own lives and make choices to be more authentic.

Humans have many strengths or capacities that help them achieve their goals. The first capacity is self-awareness, or when individuals become aware of themselves, the world, and their anxieties, such as the fear of death. Authenticity is another capacity, and this involves people taking responsibility and making choices based on who they are rather than the expectations of others. Freedom and personal responsibility is a capacity that allows humans to become aware, grow, better themselves, and take control of their lives regardless of circumstance. Cultural differences need to be taken into consideration when discussing the concepts of freedom and personal responsibility. Self-actualization is capacity that involves people reaching their full potential. People also have the capacity to make meaning in their lives by exploring their values and gaining awareness. Finally, people strive for identity and relationship to others by discovering who they really are and entering into healthy relationships with others.

Existential therapy is one of the most widely used forms of therapy, as it provides a philosophical approach that can be helpful in conceptualizing the counseling process. Therapists and their relationships with their clients are the primary instruments of change in existential therapy; establishment of a genuine, caring, supportive, and authentic client–therapist relationship is essential in this model. The counseling relationship and a focus on the present are essential to the development and therapeutic progress of clients. Existential therapy enables people to become more actualized, aware, and connected to others, which can help them make wise and responsible choices and create meaning in their lives. Other goals of existential therapy include confronting the inevitable parts of human life, such as death and isolation and being more present.

Because existential therapy is a philosophy and not focused on symptom alleviation, only a few established interventions are associated with this theory, including Symbolic Growth Experience, logotherapy, paradoxical intention, dereflection, and addressing the four dimensions of the human condition. Therapists who use this approach often focus on the counseling relationship, gaining awareness, and exploring deep fears and anxieties, rather than relying on techniques. Existential therapy is effective in treating a wide variety of different issues, such as anxiety, adjustment issues, and grief and loss and can be used in conjunction with other therapies, such as CBT, brief therapy, and group counseling.

Recommended Readings

Bugental, J. F. T. (1990). *Intimate journeys.* San Francisco, CA: Jossey-Bass.

Bugental, J. F. T. (1992). *The art of the psychotherapist: How to develop skills that take psychotherapy beyond science.* New York, NY: Norton.

Frankl, V. (2014). *Man's search for meaning.* Boston, MA: Beacon.

Hoffman, L., Yang, M., Kaklauskas, F., & Chan, A. (Eds.). (2009). *Existential psychology East–West.* Colorado Springs, CO: University of the Rockies Press.

Klingberg, H. (2001). *When life calls out to us: The love and lifework of Viktor and Elly Frankl.* New York, NY: Doubleday.

May, R. (1969). *Love and will.* New York, NY: Norton.

Moodley, R., & Walcott, R. (Eds.). (2010). *Counseling across and beyond cultures: Exploring the work of Clemmont E. Vontress in clinical practice.* Toronto, Canada: University of Toronto Press.

Van Deurzen, E., & Adams, M. (2016). *Skills in existential counselling and psychotherapy.* Thousand Oaks, CA: Sage.

Yalom, I. D. (2009). *Staring at the sun: Overcoming the terror of death.* San Francisco, CA: Jossey-Bass.

Yalom, I. D. (2017). *The gift of therapy: An open letter to a new generation of therapists.* New York, NY: Harper Collins.

MyLab Counseling

Try the Topic 4 Assignments: Existential Therapy.

CHAPTER 10

Person-Centered Therapy

Learning Outcomes

When you have finished this chapter, you should be able to:
- Understand the context and development of Person-Centered Therapy.
- Communicate the key concepts associated with Person-Centered Therapy and understand how they relate to therapeutic processes.
- Describe the therapeutic goals of Person-Centered Therapy.
- Identify the common techniques used in Person-Centered Therapy.
- Understand how Person-Centered Therapy relates to counseling diverse populations.
- Identify the limitations and strengths of Person-Centered Therapy.

CARL ROGERS (1902–1987)

Carl Rogers, the developer of person-centered therapy, led a life consistent with the theory he developed and espoused. Carl Rogers was born in 1902, in Oak Park, Illinois, a suburb of Chicago. Rogers' recollections during his early years included being socially isolated from children other than family, being teased mercilessly by his older brothers, and developing a closeness with his mother, perhaps in large part due to several illnesses he suffered in childhood.

When Rogers was 12, his father moved the family to a rural farming area where the children were raised simply with strong Midwestern and fundamentalist Christian values (Kirschenbaum, 2009). His family instilled in him the importance of hard work, humility, and a sense of responsibility, values that were reflected in his academic pursuits. He was also schooled in the scientific method because his father insisted that the farm be run scientifically (Hergenhahn & Olson, 2007).

Rogers went off to college at the University of Wisconsin, majoring in agriculture. In 1922, he was selected as one of 10 students to attend a World Christian Student Federation seminar in China. During the 6-month trip, he was exposed to alternative views on religion, philosophy, and cultures that caused him to rethink the traditional fundamentalist Christian beliefs of his family. It was during this trip that the seeds of his later phenomenological perspective of reality were planted. He started to question whether there was just one true religion and started to consider the interconnectivity of all living beings.

After graduating from the University of Wisconsin, in 1924, he married his college sweetheart, Helen Elliot. The couple moved to New York City, where they started a family and he studied for the ministry at the Union Theological Seminary. It was while he was at Union that Rogers took several courses in psychology and began to realize that he could accomplish his ultimate goal, which was to help people change, grow, develop, and live more satisfying lives, without having to do so under the umbrella of religion (Kirschenbaum, 2009). Shortly thereafter he transferred to Columbia University, where he received a PhD in psychology.

After receiving his PhD, Rogers spent a number of years working in academia, holding positions at the University of Wisconsin, the Ohio State University, and the University of Chicago. He conducted the first research ever to be done on psychotherapy sessions (Kirschenbaum, 2009). It was during this time that Rogers developed his approach to therapy, which he initially termed "nondirective therapy." This approach, which involves the therapist acting as a facilitator rather than a director of the therapy session, eventually came to be known as client-centered therapy.

In 1946, Rogers was elected president of the American Psychological Association and received their first award for scientific achievement. Rogers wrote 19 books and numerous articles outlining his humanistic theory. Among his best-known works are *Client-Centered Therapy* (1951), *On Becoming a Person* (1995b), and *A Way of Being* (1980).

Rogers spent the rest of his life in California. Carl Rogers and his wife were happily married and stayed so for 55 years until Helen's death. In 1968, at the age of 66, he and several of his colleagues formed the Center for the Studies of the Person in La Jolla, where he worked until his death in 1987.

Rogers' ideas and methods were applied not only to counseling individuals but also to families, business and administration, education, cross-cultural settings, conflict resolution, and, perhaps most important to Rogers, the promotion of world peace, with his efforts culminating in his being nominated for the Nobel Peace Prize in 1987.

INTRODUCTION/DEVELOPMENT OF PERSON-CENTERED THERAPY

Carl Rogers is one of the most influential counseling theorists, and he revolutionized both the art and science of therapy (Kirschenbaum, 2009). Some argue that no one since Freud has had a greater influence on psychotherapy than Carl Rogers (Hergenhahn & Olson, 2007). This is largely due to three factors: (1) Outcome research on the core conditions he promoted continues to verify that Rogers was correct—empathy, unconditional positive regard, and a sound therapeutic alliance have all been shown to be effective and necessary ingredients in positive therapeutic outcomes; (2) his approach has broad applications and can be integrated easily into other theoretical models; and (3) its positive and optimistic nature is appealing.

Perhaps one of Carl Rogers' greatest contributions was teaching therapists to listen with sensitivity and caring and without judgment (Cain, 2012). Rogers' optimistic view of people and his belief in people's innate striving for self-actualization changed the focus of psychotherapy from one of pathology to that of viewing clients as people who come to therapy to help themselves live more fully and function in more satisfying ways. His synthesis of humanism with the scientific method revolutionized psychology, turning it from an art form into a science.

Rogers emphasized that the attitude and personal characteristics of the therapist and the quality of the therapeutic relationship determined therapy outcomes. In fact, Carl Rogers embodied his theory and people described him as being an attentive, careful, and sensitive listener (Cain, 1987). Rogers' habits of hard work, self-discipline, organization, and concentration continued throughout his life. He enhanced these strengths with his optimism, his sense of self-actualization, and his ability to be open to experience and live in the moment. He was not afraid to express ideas that were new and innovative and he was deeply committed to improving the world. His life and his ideas are inseparable.

The evolution of Rogers' theories closely mirrored his personal development, with his ideas growing richer as his insight, personality, and compassion deepened (Kirschenbaum, 2009). When Carl Rogers published his first major work, *Counseling and Psychotherapy* (1942), the field was dominated by two theoretical approaches: psychoanalytic/psychodynamic approaches and behavioral approaches. Rogers criticized both for their assumption that therapists know best and should tell clients how they should change. Instead, he proposed what he called **nondirective counseling**, in which the primary role of the therapist is to help people express, clarify, and gain insight into their emotions through reflection and empathic listening. The emphasis of expertise was taken off the therapist and placed on the client.

Rogers' second stage of development was marked by the publication of *Client-Centered Therapy* (1951). Although Rogers maintained his emphasis on the importance of people's emotions, the book signaled several important changes in his thinking. He renamed his approach **client-centered therapy**, reflecting his realization that counseling cannot, and probably should not, be completely nondirective. Rogers now saw the therapist's role as more active and important and believed that by communicating accurate empathy, congruence, and unconditional positive regard (also known as acceptance), therapists create an environment that is conducive to helping people make positive changes. These three core facilitative conditions—empathy, congruence, and unconditional positive regard—became hallmarks of Rogers' work. In addition, Rogers emphasized the phenomenological viewpoint for understanding clients, and the actualizing tendency is what helps clients feel motivated to change.

In the 1960s, Rogers began his third developmental period, again signaled by the publication of a major work, *On Becoming a Person* (1995b). Rogers' interest in promoting people's healthy development led him to extend his reach beyond the clinical setting. For example, he promoted the idea of student-centered teaching, which applied to education. Rogers was one of the founders of the human potential movement and the creator of **encounter groups**, which were self-actualization groups designed to promote constructive insight, sensitivity to others, and personal growth. Encounter groups based on Rogers' ideas became widely used to promote positive development (Rogers, 1970). Encounter groups were popular in the 1970s and 1980s. His work during the 1960s also reflected his interest in research by testing the process and outcomes of therapy.

The last two decades of Rogers' life, the 1970s and 1980s, reflected a continued broadening of his ideas and their application, which became the fourth phase. The term client-centered was replaced with **person-centered** to reflect Rogers' concern with all of humanity, rather than just the clinical relationship.

KEY CONCEPTS

Carl Rogers' theory is informed by his years of experience working with clients. His theory is comprehensive and based on the assumption that people are basically good and have a natural tendency toward growth. According to Rogers, understanding, appreciating, and relating to others in positive ways are the ultimate goals of counseling. Rogers' ideas embody the humanistic perspective. He perceived people as strong and capable and trusted their ability to handle their difficulties, grow and develop, and realize their potential. The humanistic view includes the belief that clients have the capacity for self-awareness and self-healing.

Because all of the choices we make in our lives stem from our perceptions, we are, in effect, the focus of our universe. Rogers believed that each of us exists at the center of a constantly changing world of experience. Even when we believe we are being objective, our subjective perceptions determine the direction of our lives. Thus, person-centered therapy is phenomenological; each of us reacts to life events in a way that is consistent with our own reality. Every moment of the day, we have perceptions that evolve out of our experiences and influence all aspects of our lives. Understanding ourselves, our relationships, and our clients depends on our awareness and acceptance of these subjective perceptions.

This section discusses important person-centered therapy concepts, including human potential and actualization, conditions of worth, organismic valuing process, and the concept of the fully functioning person.

Human Potential and Actualization

Abraham Maslow contributed to the concept of self-actualization. **Self-actualization** refers to people's innate need for personal growth and discovery, and their desire to live up to their fullest potential. Maslow believed that people are always becoming and never remain static in these terms. Maslow researched people who are self-actualized and found that they tend to be self-aware, are autonomous, experience freedom, accept and care for self and others, are creative, and balance alone time with interpersonal relationships. Rogers discovered the actualizing tendency in his personal and professional life and applied it to his work. An important aspect of the human potential is people's natural inclination toward actualization, expansion, growth, and health. Actualizing is a universal tendency, although the self-actualization efforts of individuals are unique as they strive to master ongoing challenges within the context of their shifting social worlds (Adler, 2011). An analogy that Rogers (1980) returned to again and again was an outgrowth of his childhood days on the farm and his scientific interest. He spoke of the potatoes his family would store in the basement during the winter months. Even though the potatoes were kept in the cold and dark, away from the nourishing earth and heat of the sun, they would still sprout roots that would creep across his basement, extending toward the only small windows that received any sunlight; they would inherently move toward the light. Rogers believed that a tendency to self-actualize was a driving force in every living thing.

Just as plants need rich soil, adequate water, and sunlight to grow healthy and strong, Rogers believed that people also require the right conditions to evolve in optimal ways. In counseling, the therapist's role is to provide those necessary conditions. Carl Rogers believed that this innate tendency toward self-actualization is a process that occurs across the lifespan, manifesting itself as movement toward self-awareness and self-realization, autonomy, and self-regulation.

Conditions of Worth

According to person-centered theory, children's self-concepts are shaped through interactions with important people in their lives and the messages they receive from those people (Rogers, 1995b). If children experience **conditions of worth**, which are judgmental and critical messages that they are only worthwhile and lovable if they think, feel, and act in ways that meet the needs of others, their self-images and growth may be impaired. This happens because they may act in certain ways that are incongruent with who they really are in order to receive other people's love, acceptance, and positive regard. Environments that are overprotective, dominating, or intimidating exert a particularly negative influence on children's development and make it difficult for them to feel free and powerful. Children in these environments typically experience **conditional positive regard**, which involves them only receiving praise, attention, or approval from others as a result of behaving in accordance with the expectations of others.

Children in negative environments typically internalize the criticisms they receive, perceiving aspects of themselves as worthy or unworthy. They tend to devalue, shut down, and inhibit what they perceive as the unworthy aspects of themselves. This creates inner conflicts and incongruities and disrupts their natural tendency toward growth. According to Rogers, messages of conditional worth restrict authenticity so that people cannot respond with honesty in their emotions, thoughts, or behaviors. They have not learned to value the self, the total organism, and so they become fragmented. Children such as these have a high likelihood of developing into adults who are timid, inhibited, and conformist or angry and defensive.

In contrast, children who receive **unconditional positive regard**—the message that they are special and wonderful for who they are, not because of their importance to another person or the children's specific behaviors or characteristics—are far more likely to become actualizing and fully functioning adults. This does not mean that parents need to be permissive and condone children's harmful behaviors. However, they should correct undesirable behavior in such a way that affirms both the child's worth and the parents' worth.

Consider the case of Maddy, who is fearful of vaccinations and reacts to her parents' efforts to take her to the pediatrician by kicking and hitting them. Parents who apply conditions of worth to their children might say, "I don't like you when you hit me. Stop acting like such a baby over a little shot." Parents who seek to affirm the child but shape the behavior might say, "I can understand that you are scared of the shot and are angry that I am taking you to the doctor, but you hurt my leg when you kicked me. I love you and we can find ways to help you with your feelings, but I need you to stop kicking me."

Rogers acknowledged the harm that an aversive background can do to a person's development, but he remained optimistic due to his belief that people have the ability to self-understand, grow, and reach their full potential. Person-centered therapy aims to provide a climate of **acceptance**—accepting clients for who they are without judgment—that is free of conditions of worth; to counteract negative messages that people have received; to enable them to have complete freedom to be and to choose for themselves; and to realize their potential as fully functioning, self-actualizing people. Self-acceptance, agency, and the ability to rewrite one's own story are important concepts in psychotherapy and are associated with improvements in mental health (Adler, 2011; Bernard, 2013).

Organismic Valuing Process

The **organismic valuing process** is people's intuitive ability to know what they need to feel fulfilled and self-actualized. Rogers believed that people automatically evaluate their experiences and actions to ascertain whether they are actualizing and if they are not, a "nagging sense that something isn't right" results and this motivates people to make needed changes (Sheldon, Arndt, & Houser-Marko, 2003, p. 836). Rogers believed that all people have this built-in mechanism for evaluating their current situation and moving toward health.

As children abandon their own valuing system due to conditions of worth, they begin to accept the values of others rather than their own as a way to maintain their positive regard. According to Rogers, this distorts children's healthy development and derails their development of congruence as well as their self-actualizing tendencies.

When people are not being true to their own internal sense for making value judgments and instead behave in a manner they think is expected of them or will please other people, they lose touch with their organismic valuing process and are considered to be **incongruent**.

The Fully Functioning Person

Rogers (1995b) believed that a **fully functioning person** is one who is in touch with his or her deepest and innermost feelings and desires. Fully functioning individuals understand their own emotions and place a deep trust in their own instincts and urges, and they are constantly striving to live to their fullest potential. Rogers believed that one becomes a fully functioning person through an increased awareness and through experience. Fully functioning people meet their own need for positive regard rather than relying on the expectations of others. Such people have authenticity and can respond with congruence and honesty. Rogers' concept of the fully functioning person reflects his idea of emotional health. He also stated that living is a risky thing and that it takes a great deal of courage to be constantly moving toward one's potential. To help other people, Rogers believed that therapists should work toward becoming fully functioning themselves. The following personality dimensions are characteristics of the fully functioning person:

- Openness to experience
- Living with a sense of meaning and purpose
- Trust and congruence in self
- Unconditional positive self-regard and regard of others
- Internal locus of evaluation
- Being fully aware in the moment
- Living creatively.

THE THERAPEUTIC PROCESS

Person-centered therapy is primarily a way of being with clients and providing the therapeutic conditions of congruence, empathy, and unconditional positive regard that will facilitate change. When these conditions are present, actualizing forces take over, clients cease to deny or distort experience, and they become more fully functioning human organisms (Rogers, 1995b).

Carl Rogers identified the following six conditions as those that facilitate constructive personality change and are essential to the therapeutic process:

1. A relationship exists—two people are in psychological contact.
2. Clients are in a state of incongruence, which causes them to be vulnerable or anxious.
3. The therapist is congruent (genuine or authentic) in the relationship.
4. The therapist experiences unconditional positive regard for the client.
5. The therapist experiences and expresses an empathic understanding of the client's internal frame of reference.
6. The therapist's unconditional positive regard, empathic understanding, and congruence must be perceived by the client, at least to some degree.

Congruence, unconditional positive regard, and empathy form the core conditions used by the therapist to create a safe, accepting, warm, and understanding environment and relationship. The core conditions help clients drop natural defensiveness and enables them to truly work in this environment (Rogers, 1946). Each of the three core conditions will be discussed in greater depth later in this chapter.

Therapeutic Goals

Rogers was interested in bettering his understanding of the process of person-centered therapy. To do this, he spent many hours listening "as naively as possible" to recorded counseling sessions (Rogers, 1995b, p. 128). He found that, early in counseling, people were characterized by remoteness, rigidity, and a limited awareness of their inner selves. By the end of counseling, however, people were able to experience the present and trust both themselves and the therapeutic process. A central goal of person-centered therapy, then, is to facilitate people's trust and their ability to be in the present moment. This enables them to become more honest with themselves and their therapist and to fully express their emotions and thoughts, even those that are painful and viewed as unacceptable by others. Another major goal for person-centered therapy is for clients to develop congruence. Congruence is achieved by helping clients to discover how they have created a façade and by finding ways to become more authentic by identifying beliefs and desires. Additional counseling goals include promoting self-awareness, empowerment, optimism, responsibility, and autonomy. Development of these strengths, in turn, helps people build an internal locus of control, become more aware of external reality, make better use of their potential, gain the ability to manage their lives and resolve their concerns, and become more actualized. Rogers' approach does not focus on the resolution of specific presenting problems but on developing fully functioning people with deeper self-understanding who are capable of creating rewarding lives and dealing successfully with life's joys and challenges. Therapists do not impose specific goals onto their clients, but rather, clients choose their own goals. Carl Rogers' and the person-centered tradition is a positive and self-directed philosophy of life.

No matter what theoretical orientation therapists adhere to, they all express empathy, which, according to Rogers, is synonymous with the therapeutic relationship. Therapists also emphasize promoting self-awareness, congruence, and autonomy. The development of these strengths, in turn, helps people build an internal locus of control, become more integrated and genuine, and gain the ability to manage their lives and resolve their concerns. Rogers aimed to help clients accept their feelings without interpreting, giving praise, criticism, or advice. Specifically, Rogers noted that clients become stronger and more independent, begin to take positive steps, and develop a sense of courage, which allows them to be more open and honest with therapists in the counseling session and eventually in all their relationships.

Therapist's Function and Role

In person-centered therapy, the attitude of therapists, instead of their techniques and knowledge, is most important. Basically, therapists use themselves as the vehicles for client change. Therapists who use a person-centered approach are personable with their clients. When therapists are genuine, supportive, and empathic, clients are more likely to open up about their experience and explore their emotions and thoughts in a more meaningful way.

Most clients begin therapy because they are in a state of incongruence and are experiencing uncomfortable feelings, such as anxiousness or helplessness. For example, a client's career goal to be a physician may be inconsistent with her academic abilities, and thus she needs help understanding discrepancies and acquiring congruence. Clients are invited to explore their experiences, thoughts, feelings, and beliefs in therapy to become more self-aware and understanding. Because the therapeutic approach is nondirective, clients are believed to be capable of healing themselves with the help of the therapeutic relationship. This means that therapists do not give clients answers but instead invite clients to provide solutions to their problems. Clients feel heard, accepted, and understood, which can help them experience these feelings for themselves and make the changes required to become more fully functioning.

Relationship Between Therapist and Client

Rogers believed that positive and real change only occurs in a relationship (Rogers, 1967). In fact, study after study has indicated the importance of the therapeutic relationship in counseling. As discussed in Chapter 1, research suggests that the variables most related to success in counseling and outcomes are the client–therapist relationship and the personal and situational resources of the client. Not only do therapists need to establish a positive therapeutic alliance, but they also need to communicate the core therapeutic conditions.

Rogers' view of this relationship evolved over many years (Rogers, 1995b). In his early writings, he described a distant and impersonal therapeutic relationship, perhaps reflecting his early training. However, he later described himself as taking risks in the relationship by diving into the immediacy and present moment of the relationship, which happened naturally (Rogers, 1955). By the 1960s, he acknowledged that although he initially feared being trapped by a close and loving involvement with his clients, he now found a close client–therapist relationship to be something that added to the lives of both participants (Rogers, 1995b). Therapist and client are viewed as two equal and capable human beings who become collaborators in a shared journey in which both grow and are enriched by the process. The egalitarian relationship is important in influencing therapeutic outcomes. Therapists also use their own experiences and knowledge for the therapeutic relationship and continuously work on themselves; therapists themselves are their own best therapeutic tool.

The three core conditions—congruence, unconditional positive regard, and empathy—are necessary to create a climate in which individuals can grow, become self-actualizing, and ultimately strive to become fully functioning people. Rogers believed that providing such a positive climate allowed clients to be free to trust their feelings and, ultimately, allowed self-directed change to occur. He believed these conditions were necessary regardless of whether it was a therapy session or a relationship between parent and child, teacher and student, or leader and group.

THERAPEUTIC TECHNIQUES AND PROCEDURES

Other than providing the core conditions, techniques or other therapeutic tools are not used in a pure person-centered approach. Rather, person-centered therapy is primarily a way of being with clients and providing the therapeutic conditions that will facilitate change. This is because the heart of person-centered therapy is the therapeutic relationship. Therapists also rarely use elaborate diagnostic and assessment tools. They are viewed as unnecessary and as detracting from the client–therapist relationship. All interventions in person-centered therapy should promote the therapeutic relationship and enhance clients' awareness and empowerment. Strategies that promote and deepen communication and that reflect therapists' caring and interest are likely the most useful interventions in person-centered therapy. These include the use of empathic reflections, paraphrasing, and therapist self-disclosure. Research shows that clients experience relational depth when therapists are trustworthy, real, genuine, accepting, understanding, and respectful. When these qualities were absent from the therapeutic process, therapists were described as distant, powerful, and not understanding (Knox & Cooper, 2010). Furthermore, it is important for therapists to be flexible by adjusting their therapeutic relationship and style to fit the needs of individual clients (Bohart & Watson, 2011; Cain, 2010, 2012).

Facilitative Conditions

Consistent with the emphasis Rogers placed on the importance of the therapist in the therapeutic process is his belief that effective therapists have certain qualities they communicate to their clients. These qualities help create a positive client–therapist relationship and promote clients' self-awareness and ability to direct their lives in positive ways. The following sections will describe the three most important facilitative conditions: congruence, unconditional positive regard, and empathy.

CONGRUENCE Therapists' ability to be genuine and authentic, well integrated, and aware of themselves and how they are perceived by others is known as **congruence**. People who are congruent transmit messages that are clear and coherent; their inner and outer selves are consistent.

Rogers believed that therapists should be genuine, real, and not put up a professional front or façade for clients. The more the therapists could be authentic, transparent, sincere, real, and open in the therapeutic relationship, the more likely the clients would change and grow in a positive manner. Congruence is a way of being, in that particular moment, between the therapist and the clients, that brings in sync what is being experienced, what is present in the room, and what is expressed to the clients (Rogers, 1980). In fact, if therapists dislike their clients and pretend to like them, this results in insincerity and can negatively influence the therapeutic process.

Unlike therapists in classic psychoanalysis, whose self-disclosure interferes with the transference process and is thus discouraged, person-centered therapists respond spontaneously and are congruent in thoughts, mannerisms, and communication. The **genuineness**—therapists' way of being themselves with clients—and consistency of therapists promote trust and openness of clients, establish a relationship that is free of deception and hidden agendas, and provide a positive role model. For some clients, this sort of relationship is new and can help them see that such relationships are possible in other settings. In fact, modeling this congruence may help clients become more congruent and genuine themselves. Many clients come into therapy because they are incongruent, which is causing anxiety. For example, Mike and his wife, Shay, came to therapy to get help working out problems in their 10-year marriage. Shay admits that Mike is a "wonderful father, a good provider, and he never drinks in front of the children. But as soon as the children go to bed, out comes the alcohol and the nastiness begins." Mike shares that not only does he not think this is a problem, but he feels nothing is wrong in their marriage that couldn't be changed by his wife "just being nice to me." In a separate, individual session Mike reveals that he married Shay when their daughter was 3 years old and that he feels he and his wife have been incompatible from the start. He now feels trapped into staying in the marriage until his children are grown. "As soon as my son graduates high school," he said, "I'm out of here, that is, if I can wait that long. In the meantime, sure I have a drink at night. But what's wrong with that? It's the only pleasure I have in my life."

Mike is living an incongruent life. He feels the need to present himself as a good father, provider, and husband during the day, but his underlying unhappiness is still expressed, albeit indirectly, through his behavior. It is not surprising that Mike feels misunderstood. He even tries to convince the therapist he's living up to the ideal role of husband and father. However, Mike's need to perform the perfect father role during the day, while drinking at night, is confusing to his wife and has created barriers between them. Mike's "image," based on introjected values he probably developed in childhood, has set up conditions of worth, from which he evaluates his experiences, rather than from his own actualizing tendency.

In person-centered therapy, the careful and deliberate use of self-disclosure or immediacy can enhance the therapeutic alliance and advance counseling. For example, the therapist uses present-moment awareness (what psychoanalysts refer to as countertransference) to illuminate the therapy. If therapy is not being productive, the therapist finds a way to express that to the client. Rogers (1980) noted that when he trusted this gut feeling, and was able to communicate in a nonthreatening way that therapy was not productive, it was helpful in advancing the therapeutic relationship.

There are three types of therapist self-disclosure: (1) disclosing information related to the personal identity and experiences of the therapist, (2) disclosing emotional responses of the therapist to the client, and (3) disclosing professional experiences and identity of the therapist (Henretty & Levitt, 2010). Research has shown that certain amounts and types of self-disclosure by the therapist can have a positive impact on counseling by demystifying the therapy process, normalizing the client's concerns, showing the universality of the human condition, and providing a role model for positive change (Ziv-Beiman, Keinan, Livneh, Malone, & Shanar, 2017). However, inappropriate self-disclosure, too much disclosure, or poorly timed self-disclosure on the part of the therapist may cause harm (Kirschenbaum, 2009).

Self-disclosure that is in the moment responses to what clients say, that is spontaneous and focused on the client, and that is in the service of enhancing therapy can help to create a more real, intimate, and genuine client–therapist relationship. What constitutes appropriate self-disclosure is complicated, unique to the relationship, and open to therapist judgment about what, at that particular moment in time between those two specific people, would be in the best interest of the client. Certainly, an appropriate self-disclosure for one client may be completely inappropriate for another.

While therapist congruency is pertinent, some limitations exist for how open and honest therapists can be. Potential drawbacks to therapist self-disclosure include the possibility of evoking negative reactions, violating therapeutic boundaries, clients' fear of intimacy that may result from such disclosure, and the therapist being left vulnerable. Before self-disclosing, therapists should assess their reasons for disclosing, consider whether the self-disclosure will help the client, and consider whether it is well timed and if they should consult with a colleague before disclosing. If the self-disclosure is about therapists meeting their own needs, they should obviously not disclose. What constitutes appropriate and helpful self-disclosure in person-centered therapy is a question that would benefit from additional research, although such research is difficult to undertake due to the very specific nature of each self-disclosure in terms of type, timing, and the client–therapist relationship (Sue, Sue, Neville, & Smith, 2019).

After his move to La Jolla, California in the 1960s and his work with encounter groups, Carl Rogers became more comfortable sharing his own feelings and manifesting congruence in helping relationships. At one point, Carl Rogers walked out of an encounter group that appeared to be stuck in discussions of trivia (Kirschenbaum, 2009). Rogers got up, left the room, and went to bed. The following day when members of the encounter group expressed anger that he had walked out, he explained that while the group kept returning to discussions of trivia, at least he was being congruent by making his behavior match his feelings. Congruence can also relate to the behavior of therapists outside the counseling session. Especially for clients from collectivist cultures or those in which traditional healers and therapists are both part of and separate from society, how therapists interact as community members, interact as members of society, and exhibit (or do not exhibit) social responsibility can be important attributes in the client's eyes and may enhance, or reduce the effect of the therapeutic alliance (Sue, Sue, Neville, & Smith, 2019).

Therapists should be aware that clients' subjective interpretation of information may lead to misinterpretation. Therapists need to be aware of both their verbal and nonverbal messages, maintain consistency between the two, and address clients' reactions if therapists inadvertently give confusing or potentially negative messages. Recent research on the client–therapist relationship reinforces Rogers' beliefs and indicates that attention must be paid to the relationship throughout the course of counseling. It is not enough to foster an alliance early on and then assume that all is well. Therapists must notice and address any ruptures or tears in the relationship, even those that seem minor or inconsequential. Therapists who are attuned to their clients develop an intuitive sense of when and how to intervene, what to say, and, equally important, when not to say anything. The timing of interventions is also important to ensure the information is appropriate and likely to be well received.

UNCONDITIONAL POSITIVE REGARD   Rogers' writings emphasize the importance of what he called unconditional positive regard: caring about, respecting, liking, and accepting people for who they are without placing any requirements on them to act, feel, or think in certain ways to please their therapists. Rogers viewed people as inherently worthy, although he recognized that people have both positive and negative impulses and feelings (Kirschenbaum, 2004). Communication of warmth and positive regard is essential in helping people to like themselves, emphasize their positive impulses and emotions, feel powerful enough to successfully cope with their difficulties, and become more fully functioning.

Unconditional positive regard does not mean that therapists view everything people do or think as wise and appropriate, but simply that therapists see people as doing the best they can at the present time. It involves acknowledging that clients have a right to feel and think as they do. Person-centered therapists are consistent in their acceptance of and confidence in clients, although they might express concern about a particular client's choices. Rather than saying, "You seem to be an angry person," they might say, "You sounded angry when I could not change our appointment time."

This perspective is reflected in current child-rearing practices that advocate focusing feedback and evaluation on the behavior, not on the child. Parents are encouraged to comment specifically on the child's behavior, and not on the child herself. Saying, for example, "You did a great job picking up your toys," rather than, "You're such a good girl for cleaning your room." The first comment focuses specifically on the behavior ("picking up your toys"), while the second comment is too general and focuses on the child rather than the behavior.

Communication of acceptance and unconditional positive regard in a nonpossessive way helps people believe that they are worthy and can trust their own feelings and thoughts. It can counter devaluing messages they have received throughout their lives. It allows people to recognize that they can change undesirable behaviors, thoughts, and feelings while still viewing themselves as likable and worthwhile. Knowing that they will be accepted for who they are enables people to disclose to therapists aspects of themselves that cause them shame or discomfort. Rogers (1980) believed that the more therapists prize and value people for who they are, the more likely it is that they will make positive changes.

EMPATHY Rogers (1980) defined **empathy** as "temporarily living in the other's life, moving about in it delicately without making judgments; it means sensing meanings of which he or she is scarcely aware, but not trying to uncover totally unconscious feelings, since this would be too threatening. . . . It means frequently checking with the person as to the accuracy of your sensings . . ." (p. 142). In other words, empathy is the therapist's ability to see the world through the client's eyes and to communicate that understanding so that the client feels heard and validated.

Rogers viewed sensitive, accurate, and active listening—deeply grasping the subjective world of another person and transmitting understanding of that world to enhance a person's own self-awareness—as the most powerful force for change. Therapists must always remain aware that they have not walked in their clients' shoes and, therefore, cannot possibly know exactly how clients are feeling in that moment. Thus, empathy is never expressed by saying "I know exactly how you feel"; rather, empathic expressions maintain the respectful distance of the "as if" condition. The "as if" condition is when therapists communicate understanding to the clients as if they are feeling what the client is feeling, also known as accurate empathic understanding. Empathy allows clients to acknowledge their experiences, process their experiences more fully, change perspective on experiences, and promote confidence to make changes (Cain, 2010). Therapists must understand their clients both emotionally and cognitively and can ask for feedback on the accuracy of their understanding. In addition, clients must perceive and believe that their therapist is truly being empathic.

Empathy is different from sympathy. Sympathy can make people feel pitiful and can communicate a distance between the sympathizer and the other person, whereas empathy brings people closer in a shared experience. Empathy, on the one hand, opens the door for further discussion, usually at a deeper level, and is empowering. Sympathy, on the other hand, encourages people to view themselves as wounded victims and limits productive conversation. The following example illustrates the difference:

> CLIENT: I can't believe the terrible grade I got on the exam. I hope no one finds out.
>
> SYMPATHY: I'm sorry you did so poorly on the test.
>
> EMPATHY: I can hear the deep sense of shame you feel about your grade.

True empathy is transmitted to the client through genuine reflection of feeling, by closely tracking the client's words and changing felt meaning as it occurs in the moment, and through the continued expression of nonjudgmental and unconditional positive regard.

Rogers believed that the most effective approach was to attentively listen to what clients were saying in order to identify and reflect feelings they were experiencing. He used the term **validation** to refer to the therapist's empathic confirmation of the client's emotions. More will be said about empathy in the Skill Development section at the end of this chapter.

Nondirectiveness

Rogers originally called his work nondirective counseling to distinguish it from the prevailing models of the time (mainly psychoanalytic and behavioral) in which practitioners were viewed as experts whom clients looked to for advice on what they should do (Rogers, 1945). Nondirective counseling emphasizes the importance of clients taking the lead and being the focus of the counseling process. Although Rogers later changed the name of his approach to client-centered therapy and then person-centered therapy, to highlight the fact that his theory applied to all relationships, the nondirective aspects of this approach still merit attention.

Person-centered therapists do not manipulate change, but neither are they passive recipients of client input. They are busy creating the necessary conditions that are conducive to client growth. Although nondirectivity has been a part of person-centered therapy since the beginning, Rogers affirmed that complete nondirectivity is impossible. Whether through the choice of questions asked or the reflections chosen, therapists cannot help but insert themselves into the therapeutic process. However, all therapists must have a compelling reason for the interventions they choose and when and why they choose to use them. Perhaps a better course than trying to remain exclusively nondirective would be to consider how best to be directive in the service of the therapy.

APPLICATION AND CURRENT USE OF PERSON-CENTERED THERAPY

Counseling Applications

During the past 70 years, empathy, unconditional positive regard, and congruence have been essential common factors of effective psychotherapy, regardless of the theoretical approach or the population served (Duncan, Miller, Wampold, & Hubble, 2010). Astoundingly, one study of outcomes in marital counseling found that the couples' perceptions of the therapeutic alliance at the third session predicted counseling outcome (Fife, Whiting, Bradford, & Davis, 2013). Overall, clients attribute 30% of the change they experience in counseling to the *therapist–client relationship* (Duncan et al., 2010).

Person-centered approaches are effective in addressing a host of issues. A review of studies comparing client-centered or nondirective/supportive therapies to cognitive behavioral therapy (CBT) found person-centered or nondirective/supportive therapies to be as effective as CBT in the treatment of those who have anxiety, depression, marital and interpersonal problems, personality disorders, trauma, and schizophrenia (Churchill et al., 2010).

Person-centered therapy has shown effectiveness equal to that of other approaches (including eye movement desensitization and reprocessing [EMDR] and exposure-based behavioral therapies) for the treatment of those who have posttraumatic stress disorder (PTSD; Benish, Imel, & Wampold, 2008; Rose, 2010). This is an interesting finding, because exposure-based treatments had long been considered the "gold standard" for treating those who have PTSD, and person-centered therapy does not include exposure.

Other research indicates that person-centered therapies are helpful in addressing a variety of populations and presenting problems, and may work with people who have social anxiety, people who experience chronic pain, and people who have been dually diagnosed (Kress & Paylo, 2019; Lempp et al., 2017; MacLeod & Elliott, 2014). In addition, research suggests the efficacy of using person-centered therapy with people who have anxiety, including social anxiety, panic attacks, generalized anxiety, and phobias (Elliott, 2013). Person-centered therapy provides a way of being with clients who may be too disturbed to participate in therapy as a result of psychosis or because they have a severe intellectual disability. Pre-therapy treatment based on person-centered therapy accommodates the needs of clients who cannot express their feelings, by providing content reflections, such as "It's a beautiful day"; face reflections, such as "You look angry"; and body reflections, such as "Your head is down" (Rogers, 1951). Such exchanges have been found to facilitate affective content and to provide a map for more meaningful therapy with clients who have severe mental illnesses (Sommerbeck, 2011). Similarly, the use of feeling charts with children, adolescents, and others who do not have an emotion orientation can be instrumental in providing a baseline language on which therapy can be built.

Carl Rogers' vision of person-centered therapy was more than just a counseling approach. Person-centered therapy was meant to be not only a form of psychotherapy, but also a goal for society that focuses on freedom and determination of individuals (Anderson, Lunnen, & Ogles, 2010). Specifically, his theory has been applied successfully to training programs for pastoral counseling, nursing, and first responders, and across myriad environments from education to business management, human resources, and peace negotiations in many countries (Cooper, O'Hara, Schmid, & Bohart, 2013). Empathy is now being taught in some preschools and elementary schools to help children develop social/emotional intelligence and ward off later bullying and aggressive behavior in schools (Miller & Goldsmith, 2017).

Empirical support is also available for process-experiential therapies that have evolved from the Rogerian tradition. A meta-analysis of 64 studies of experiential therapies supports the effectiveness of emotion-focused therapy in general (Johnson & Wittenborn, 2012), and the benefits of EFT for addressing depression and social anxiety specifically (Herrmann, Greenberg, & Auszra, 2016; Shahar, Bar-Kalifa, & Alon, 2017). In addition, experiencing as a process in cognitive behavioral therapy has been shown to lead to positive outcomes, which means the process of experiencing may be important no matter which theoretical orientation is in use (Grosse et al., 2019).

Experiential focusing is a stand-alone theory or it can be used as a technique and integrated into other theories, such as emotion-focused therapy and Gestalt, especially in situations when a client feels stuck. It can be used with individuals or in focusing groups. Focusing has been used successfully to help people make difficult decisions, such as those related to abortion (Scharwachter, 2008), recovery from addictions (Barbieri, 2008; Lee & Rovers, 2008), cases of trauma, and people who are incarcerated (Pos et al., 2008).

Person-centered approaches may be particularly helpful for individuals who are experiencing a crisis. The use of empathic responding helps people in crisis to feel heard and acknowledged, which can help them explore and express themselves more fully. When people respond with empathy, individuals are more likely to feel calm and grounded, which can help them make better, rational decisions, especially when they are in crisis. This may also lead individuals to engage in a more action-oriented approach to solving their crisis. In addition, the positive experience of feeling validated and accepted may lead them to continue seeking help in the future.

Person-centered therapy can work well for group counseling. Therapists are called facilitators instead of leaders when they are doing group counseling because they respond with empathy and understanding rather than using specific techniques. Trust in the group members to discover their own ways of growth rather than specifically promoting change allows clients to open up more and discover their own resources (Rogers, 1970). Without the use of empathy and other person-centered approaches, group counseling may not have much success or movement.

Several experiential approaches that have grown out of person-centered theory include Person-Centered Expressive Arts Therapy, developed by Natalie Rogers; Focusing, developed by Eugene Gendlin (Gendlin, 1982); emotion-focused therapy (also known as process-experiential therapy), developed by Leslie Greenberg and colleagues (Greenberg, 2010; Greenberg & Johnson, 1988); and narrative therapy, developed by Michael White and David Epston (1990), which helps people to connect with possibilities and rewrite the stories of their lives. All of these approaches will be discussed in greater detail in upcoming chapters. Person-centered therapy is also at the core of motivational interviewing (Miller & Rollnick, 2013), which was originally developed to promote behavioral change in people with substance abuse problems. Motivational interviewing has since grown into motivational enhancement therapy, for use with a variety of client problems and populations.

Person-centered therapy can be easily integrated with other types of therapy. For example, person-centered principles are commonly combined with CBT approaches (Lempp et al., 2017). In addition, person-centered principles have been used in expressive arts therapy, career counseling, reality therapy, couples and family counseling, and group therapy (Akbas, 2015; Cooper, O'Hara, Schmid, & Bohart, 2013; Ono, 2018; Wilson & Ray, 2018; Wubbolding, Casstevens, & Fulkerson, 2017). Play therapy also draws heavily from person-centered therapy and has shown effectiveness when working with children (Lin & Bratton, 2015).

Person-centered therapy has application not just for the counseling profession but also in the government and the workplace (Henderson et al., 2007) and with children in schools (Wormington & Linnenbrink-Garcia, 2017). Person-centered therapy is particularly helpful for students because it increases their motivation, enables them to accomplish their academic goals, and improves their social and emotional well-being. Person-centered educational theory has encouraged learner-centered instruction—an application to teaching and learning that prioritizes facilitative relationships and honors the uniqueness of every learner (Cornelius-White, 2015). Rogers' concept of student-centered teaching involves prizing, accepting, trusting, and empathic attitudes of the teachers toward their students (Rogers, 1967). Student-centered teaching has spread to the fields of nursing, organizational psychology, interpersonal relationships, and education. Schools have been developed that are based on Rogers' principles.

What follows are areas in which person-centered therapy has been applied to develop unique counseling approaches.

PERSON-CENTERED EXPRESSIVE ARTS THERAPY Carl Rogers' daughter, Natalie Rogers, integrated aspects of person-centered therapy with creativity to develop expressive arts therapy, which uses various art forms, such as movement, visual art, journal writing, drawing, music, and more. Through the use of these art forms, clients are able to access their deepest feelings, gain greater awareness, and express themselves. This approach integrates mind, body, emotions, and spirit, and as clients experience the therapy, their feelings and thoughts become better connected. Expressive art therapy is founded on many different ideas, which include the following: Everyone has the ability to be creative; the art forms that people use are healing; growth results from awareness, which results from exploring emotions; the use and creation of art helps people channel their emotions; the use of art forms enable people to access unconscious material; and as people discover their connection to the outside world, their inner and outer worlds become better connected (N. Rogers, 1993). When expressive arts therapists create an environment that is supportive, nonjudgmental, and trusting, clients are more likely to open up and get the most out of their experience.

PROCESS-EXPERIENTIAL THERAPIES Process-experiential therapies focus on the role of emotion in processing through experiences (Elliott & Greenberg, 2007). Processing through emotions and experiences gives clients a sense of meaning and purpose. In fact, emotion schemes are identified, which helps clients understand how they self-organize. Clients pay close attention to, and gain deeper understanding of, their experiences and emotions to heal and grow. The first goal of all process-experiential therapies is to establish the necessary conditions of a good therapeutic relationship, as set forth by Carl Rogers (congruence, unconditional positive regard, and empathy). After a safe, genuine, and helpful environment has been created, goals can be worked on that focus on both content and process.

In content-focused goals, the client chooses an issue that is the most pressing or emotionally alive at the moment (e.g., relationship problems, career change) to work on. The therapist provides the process goals by selecting interventions that deepen the client's in the moment experiencing.

Therapists may ask clients to talk about where the tension is felt in the body, or where the body is tightening when they talk about a stressful event. Therapists may also focus on a particular feeling, with the intention of helping clients feel empathically understood, while at the same time drawing attention to the most poignant aspect of the experience. Therapists facilitate the clients' experiencing of emotion in the here and now and, through empathic attunement, focus on the moment-to-moment shifts in client experiencing and processing, in an effort to help clients better understand their experiences (Pos et al., 2008).

Emotion-focused therapy (EFT) is one type of process-experiential therapy. It is used with couples and will be discussed in greater detail later in the text, when couples and family counseling is addressed. EFT combines person-centered empathic responding, the directiveness of Gestalt therapy, and existential therapy as therapists guide clients toward certain emotion-processing activities that will result in new insights and new meaning for clients. Homework, silence, vocal tone, appropriate therapist nonverbal behavior that indicates interest, and experiential teaching all help clients to tease out their underlying feelings (Greenberg & Johnson, 1988). Clients actively participate in the change process. Put simply, EFT involves a three-step process—bonding, emotion evoking, and emotion restructuring (Greenberg & Elliott, 2002; Greenberg & Johnson, 1988). Change occurs through awareness, regulation, reflection, transformation of emotion, and acceptance of the self taking place in an empathically attuned relationship.

The experiential process may be continued through homework. For example, if the client is working on his relationship with his daughter, he might be asked to notice how he reacts to his daughter during the week. The awareness homework would not be intended to change the client, but to continue to focus attention on those experiences.

With its emphasis on the importance of the relationship, empathic responding, bodily felt experience, and emotion awareness, access, and regulation, emotion-focused therapy provides an exciting new counseling approach with many applications for specific problems (depression, relationships, trauma) and varied populations. Emotion-focused therapy for couples, which integrates process-experiential theory with attachment theory, has shown efficacy for relationship distress in couples and for relationships in which one partner has been traumatized (Johnson, 2004; Wiebe et al., 2017).

PARENT EFFECTIVENESS TRAINING Rogers' ideas formed the basis for Thomas Gordon's *Parent Effectiveness Training* (1970), a classic text that, for the past 50 years, has helped parents raise children with a focus on empathy and attachment. Parent effectiveness training (PET) has produced evidence-based outcomes for generations of parents. The use of active listening skills, empathic attunement, nonconfrontational discipline, and creative conflict resolution improves the relationship and attachment between parents and children. Parents learn a new way to interact with their children that does not trigger the children's innate instinct to resist (counterwill). In this evidence-based counseling approach, children begin to cooperate because they care about their relationship with the parent. PET training programs exist worldwide and have been proven effective for working with toddlers, children, and adolescents (Medlow, Klineberg, Jarrit, & Steinbeck, 2016).

EXPERIENTIAL FOCUSING Focusing is a stand-alone experiential therapy as well as a powerful intervention developed by Eugene Gendlin (1982). When using focusing, therapists invite clients to nonjudgmentally pay attention and notice the source of feelings or experiences in their bodies. Focusing assumes that this felt sense is a source of information relating to current issues and that if clients can tune in to this feeling in the here and now, they can access needed information (Pos et al., 2008). Focusing involves connecting with an internal knowing that is directly experienced but is not yet connected to words. Focusing can, among other things, be used to become clear on what one feels or wants, to obtain new insights about one's situation, and to stimulate change and growth. Focusing sense is an experiential process that interweaves existential and Gestalt processes into a holistic approach to psychotherapy.

For example, Sylvia arrives for her session and reports, "I don't know what to talk about. I feel stuck." The focusing therapist invites Sylvia to consider where she feels that in her body. Sylvia responds, "As I sit here, my stomach feels like it's jumping all around." Sylvia is then asked to stay focused on that feeling and to describe what she is experiencing.

In focusing, the therapist directs attention to the experiential elements of the counseling session as they occur in the here and now. Rather than telling a story or looking for insight, the focusing therapist looks at four layers of interaction between the therapist and client: the body, behavior in the moment (e.g., tapping, moving), interpersonal interaction, and symbolizing the experience in words and reflections (Day, 2008). The therapist often uses metaphors to react to the client's feelings. We continue with our example of Sylvia:

THERAPIST: So, even though you're sitting here quietly on the couch, you feel as if a flagman is inside your stomach.

SYLVIA: That's right!

THERAPIST: Can you sense what that's about?

SYLVIA: I have all this energy and so many things to do, and I need to move forward with finding a place to live and separating from my husband, but inside my stomach there's all this turmoil, like this flagman is waving these flags and making me come to a complete halt once again.

THERAPIST: Once again?

SYLVIA: Yes. Like the last time I was ready to leave my husband, and then couldn't do it at the last moment.

THERAPIST: Can you sense what's behind the flagman right now?

SYLVIA: He's warning me about the danger that lies ahead if I proceed with moving out. I feel like I'm going too fast, rushing into this, and maybe my body is telling me to slow down, and make sure I'm making the right decision.

THERAPIST: Your stomach is telling you to proceed with caution.

SYLVIA: That's right.

This somatic feeling is called the "the felt sense" (Gendlin, 1996, p. 60) or the feeling before emotion. Recognizing this felt sense enables people to access information from a deeper level than their thoughts or emotions. For many clients, this body sense is unclear and vague at first, but with practice, clients learn to focus on the felt sense with an interested, curious attention. Once attention has been focused on a felt sense, and it has been brought into awareness, it moves, changes, or unfolds, and becomes a felt shift in the body (Gendlin). Attending to this immediacy in the body heightens clients' awareness and connection to their experience, and some believe that this is necessary for meaningful change to occur (Gendlin, 1996).

Six steps are involved in the process of focusing (Gendlin, 1996):

1. *Clearing a space:* Clients take time to be still, relax, and focus inwardly on their body before asking themselves how their life is going or what the main issue is.
2. *Felt sense:* Clients choose one issue to focus on, experience what the problem feels like, and allow themselves to feel it.
3. *Handle:* The client is asked to choose a word or phrase that comes to mind to describe the felt sense. It might be a word like *heavy* or *tight,* or it might be an image like a big gray blob.
4. *Resonating:* The client is asked to go back and forth between the felt sense and the word, phrase, or image to check how they resonate with each other. The client continues going back and forth until it feels just right.
5. *Asking:* The client is asked questions such as "What is in this sense?" that illuminate the felt sense and move it forward. The client stays with the felt sense until a shift or release is felt.
6. *Receiving:* The client receives whatever comes with a shift in a friendly way.

Focusing brings insight and relief. It can also bring about new behavior. Focusing therapists discuss the "wisdom of the body" in the sense that a deeper, wiser self exists inside the body. By paying attention to a deeper sense of knowing, the body knows what it needs to become. Through just being, and focusing interest and curiosity on the felt sense, a shift is made. Focusing provides the conditions in which this change can happen.

MOTIVATIONAL INTERVIEWING Motivational interviewing is described by its creators as a client-centered, directive method that enhances people's intrinsic motivation to change by exploring, processing, and resolving ambivalence (Miller & Rollnick, 2013). Motivational interviewing is deeply rooted in Rogers' person-centered theory, and helps therapists to meet clients where they are, accept their worldview, and enhance their efforts to change (Arkowitz, Westra, Miller, & Rollnick, 2008). Originally created for treating those who have addictions, motivational interviewing has become a standard intervention used with many behavioral-related therapies and used when addressing health-related concerns (e.g., smoking cessation, weight loss; Rollnick, Miller, & Butler, 2008).

As with person-centered therapy, motivational interviewing avoids diagnosis, avoids direct attempts to persuade clients, and allows clients to control the agenda. Therapists function as a partner, not an authority figure. Therapists use reflective listening, support, change talk, and open-ended questions to help clients explore their attitudes about change. **Reflective listening**, or seeking to understand what the client is saying by confirming it back to the client, is most often used. Resistance is not confronted; rather, it is reframed as ambivalence to change (Zinbarg & Griffith, 2008). In addition, motivational interviewing operates on the beliefs that clients want to change, that they are capable of doing so through the use of their strengths and resources, and that they must take personal responsibility.

Therapists who use motivational interviewing produce the conditions in which clients can choose to change; therefore, the therapists' skills in developing a therapeutic alliance using Rogers' core conditions not only are important but also have been found to be directly linked to how much client disclosure, cooperation, and emotional expression occurs in the session (Ardito & Rabellino, 2011). Through empathy, caring concern, and unconditional positive regard, a strong therapeutic alliance is created that allows clients to access their motivations for change. The goal of motivational interviewing is to help clients work through ambivalence through the use of self-talk and an analysis of the advantages and disadvantages of making changes.

Five basic principles underlie motivational interviewing (Miller & Rollnick, 2012). First, therapists see their clients' perspective and are nonjudgmental. Instead of forcing clients to change, therapists understand that clients may have good reasons for not moving forward. Therapists use empathic responding to show their clients that they understand. The second principle is the exploration of discrepancies, reasons for change, and reasons against change. Therapists typically use change talk by reflecting reasons clients state for wanting to change. The third principle is that therapists understand and explore clients' resistance. Resistance and ambivalence are seen as normal. The fourth principle is that therapists support clients' self-efficacy by reflecting on strengths and resources. Therapists believe that their clients can change and help their clients believe in themselves as well. Finally, when clients are making progress and using more change talk, therapists use this as an opportunity to create goals and plans, which is the fifth principle.

Therapists who use motivational interviewing also keep the stages of change in mind when working with clients because the role of the therapist shifts according to which stage of change clients are in (Prochaska & Norcross, 2018). To best understand, help, and validate clients, therapists must consider the client's stage of change. Change consists of five stages that involve varying levels of readiness for change. People do not necessarily go through the stages in a linear order and may regress to an earlier stage if they experience unsuccessful attempts to solve their problem.

The associated stages are as follows: precontemplation, contemplation, preparation, action, maintenance, and termination:

- In the **precontemplation stage**, clients are not aware that a problem exists and they typically have little motivation to change any aspect of their current situation. Example: A client who self-injures may say things like "I don't have a problem . . . my parents are the ones with the problem . . . it is no one's business if I want to self-injure."
- In the **contemplation stage**, clients are able to acknowledge that a problem exists, but they are apprehensive about making changes. Clients feel as though they are at a crossroads because both pros and cons of the behaviors are evident. Example: A client who self-injures may say, "I really know I should stop self-injuring. I know it is really hurting my relationship with my parents and I hate the scarring, but it makes me feel better . . ."
- In the **preparation stage**, clients are getting ready to change. More ownership of personal responsibility is evident in their speech. Example: A client who self-injures might say, "I've really got to do something about this self-injury . . . this is serious . . . something has to change. I am sick of these scars and the kids at school think I am nuts."
- In the **action stage**, clients begin to change their behaviors. Clients believe that change is possible and they act on this belief. Example: A client who self-injures might say, "I am ready to change. This self-injury is a problem. I am going to stop. When I want to self-injure, I am going to use my distraction skills, and if those don't work, I will use my relaxation skills or call a friend." The client then follows through on using these preventative skills and is better able to control and thus prevent the behavior.
- In the **maintenance stage**, clients continue to maintain productive behavioral changes. During this stage, clients must avoid the temptation to slip back into old habits and prior ways of being. Clients in this stage need to continually remind themselves how much change has occurred, and how the change has been positive. Clients at this stage must learn and use new skills to avoid relapsing into prior behaviors. Example: A client who self-injures might say, "I have made these changes and I have the self-injury on the run. But I know I need to keep using what I learned in counseling or I might begin to self-injure again."

- The **termination (or relapse) stage** occurs when clients return to older behaviors and abandon the new changes. In these situations, clients are encouraged to pick up where they left off. Ideally, if clients relapse into old behaviors, they will be back at the preparation or action stage again, and not the precontemplation stage.

Motivational interviewing is a widely used and supported approach to helping people change. Therapists typically use the guiding style of motivational interviewing early on in therapy to help clients identify obstacles to counseling, elicit intentional statements, and set the agenda. The approach is now being used with a variety of clients (e.g., adolescents, people who are incarcerated, couples, and groups) and for a variety of situations in which resistance is a factor (e.g., eating disorders, those who self-injure). A meta-analysis of 25 years of empirical research found that therapists who use this intervention are more likely to empower reluctant clients to change (Lundahl, Kunz, Brownell, Tollefson, & Burke, 2010). Overall, motivational interviewing is another example of how Rogers' person-centered approach has evolved over the years and has been helpful to a variety of people (Arkowitz et al., 2008; Lundahl & Burke, 2009).

Application to Multicultural Groups

Person-centered multicultural counseling is an effective way to facilitate learning across age, race, ethnicity, and geographic location (Cornelius-White, 2015). The respectful and accepting nature of person-centered therapy, coupled with its phenomenological perspective, makes it appropriate for people from a wide range of ethnic, cultural, and socioeconomic backgrounds. Person-centered theory emphasizes the importance of valuing and understanding people, of viewing them from their own frame of reference, of building a positive client–therapist relationship, and of attending to the client's world through that person's perspective (Cornelius-White, 2015). People from diverse cultural backgrounds are likely to accept and respond well to person-centered therapy. In addition, many places around the world, such as European countries, South America, and Japan, have adapted aspects of person-centered therapy. Specifically, core beliefs of person-centered therapy, such as empathy, unconditional positive regard, and respect are helpful when used to understand diversity and various cultural beliefs. Through utilizing these beliefs and purposefully putting oneself in another person's shoes, people are more likely to understand the other person's worldview, even if it is different than theirs.

While person-centered approaches have widespread applicability, they also have some limitations. For example, people from some cultural groups may be hesitant to self-disclose and, therefore, might be uncomfortable with experiential therapies that focus on clients' internal emotional states (Sue, Sue, Neville, & Smith, 2019). Clients who prefer indirect communication may also feel uncomfortable when therapists self-disclose and use direct empathic responding. People from various socioeconomic groups and ethnic minorities may not particularly value insight (Sue, Sue, Neville, & Smith, 2019). Furthermore, humanistic therapies that assume self-actualization as a goal may not be affiliated with the client's frame of reference, but with the ideals and goals of the practitioner. Another limitation is that clients who come from a collectivist background may not value internal locus of control. For example, person-centered approaches focus on interdependence, freedom, and autonomy. These concepts may not be well received by people who view themselves in the context of their group or family.

Although person-centered theory does reflect American ideals of independence, self-direction, and individuality, many aspects of this approach are also relevant to a diverse and multicultural society. These include:

- The emphasis on people's rights to their own opinions and thoughts
- The importance placed on respect, genuineness, acceptance, and empathy
- The focus on people's own experience and frames of reference

- The emphasis on personal growth and self-actualization
- The interest in relationships and commonalities among people
- The attention to present-moment awareness and the immediacy of the counseling situation.

These perspectives are pertinent to all people, regardless of cultural background.

EVALUATION OF PERSON-CENTERED THERAPY

Rogers' influence in psychology and the human potential movement of the 1970s has had a far-reaching influence on today's therapists.

Limitations

Despite its enormous contributions, Rogers' theory has some limitations. Research has shown that depth of experiencing in therapy is related to outcome. The heavy emphasis on emotions may be helpful for some populations but may cause people from different cultural backgrounds to feel uncomfortable. Person-centered therapists who are culturally cognizant and adapt their therapeutic style to the client's needs are more likely to be successful.

The nondirective focus of person-centered therapy may also be unfamiliar to some clients, particularly those who view therapists as experts and are looking for someone to more directly help them solve their problems. Clients might ask, "Aren't you going to tell me what I should do?" Therapists should recognize that some clients will prefer and even require a more directive counseling approach. This is especially true when clients use therapy as a last resort and desire specific answers, advice, and guidance.

Some may view person-centered therapy as being easier to implement than more technique-heavy approaches; however, in reality, person-centered therapy demands much of the therapist. Instead of relying on techniques or manualized workbooks, therapists use themselves as tools. Therapists must be congruent, genuine, self-actualized, present in the moment, focused, nonjudgmental, patient, and, above all, empathic. This way of being with clients can be exhausting and requires a great deal of attention and focus on the part of the therapist. Without this finely tuned way of being with the client, therapy is unlikely to be as effective. Some therapists might not be comfortable working from a purely person-centered perspective without the use of homework, manuals, and other techniques commonly found in other approaches.

Strengths and Contributions

Carl Rogers was the first person to measure the effectiveness of therapy (Hergenhahn & Olson, 2007). He opened the field of psychotherapy to research investigation. Rogers was the first to record and publish complete transcripts of psychotherapy sessions. Through his extensive writings for both mental health professionals and the general population, his demonstrations, tapes, and transcripts of his sessions, his research on the process of counseling, and his emphasis on education and the widespread need for person-centered relationships, Rogers gave us an accessible and comprehensible counseling approach. In addition, Rogers established the basis for testing hypotheses and providing support for the effectiveness of counseling.

Rogers' ideal of the client–therapist relationship has infiltrated and influenced all theories of counseling and psychotherapy:

- Carl Rogers developed one of the most comprehensive theories of the self ever created.
- He believed in the dignity and worth of each individual and in people's innate movement toward actualization and growth.

- Although his theory first started to evolve in the 1940s and 1950s, it is still appropriate and relevant today—nearly 70 years later.
- Rather than a fixed theory with prescribed techniques, Rogers created a solid foundation on which future theories can build.
- The theory is optimistic, affirming, and has a positive perspective on human nature.
- Psychotherapy outcome research supports the major tenets of person-centered therapy.
- Person-centered therapy can be easily integrated into other counseling approaches. The majority of person-centered therapists integrate person-centered therapy with other compatible theories, depending on the needs of the client (Prochaska & Norcross, 2018). Almost all approaches integrate the three conditions: empathy, unconditional positive regard, and congruence.

Rogers is credited with being one of the first to introduce the concept of therapist transparency into counseling. The importance of therapist transparency—of being open, honest, genuine, and revealing any biases or limitations—later became core concepts in the development of narrative therapy and feminist therapy, which will be discussed later in this text.

Rogers also had a profound influence on the development of the field of positive psychology (Kirschenbaum, 2009). Psychologists such as Martin Seligman and Michael Csikszentmihalyi continue to search for answers to questions such as "What is psychological health?" "How do people develop resilience in the face of what life offers?" and "Why do optimistic people live longer and enjoy better health than those who are pessimistic?" The literature continues to support Rogers' underlying assumptions about the importance of the therapeutic alliance and the power of positive emotions to enhance the person's development of a strengths-based focus in life.

The work of Carl Rogers is well known internationally and is the preferred counseling approach used by many (Totton, 2010; Usakli, 2012), such as European countries, Japan, Mexico, the United Kingdom, and many more. His writings have been translated into 12 languages and his approach has been adapted or used in over 30 countries (Cooper, O'Hara, Schmid, & Bohart, 2013). Carl Rogers is viewed not only as a leader in counseling and psychology but also as a world peacemaker. Rogers was a humanitarian and an educator who traveled the world to bring peace and understanding to groups in conflict with each other. In fact, in the final decade of his life, Carl Rogers' contributions to international peace efforts resulted in his nomination for a Nobel Peace Prize, as his ideas have been helpful for resolving conflict within and between countries (Ryback, 2011). From Northern Ireland, the Soviet Union, South Africa, Central America, and other hotspots around the globe, Rogers spread his emotionally honest approach to conflict resolution, which fosters interaction in private settings with a flexible agenda and allows for intense expression of emotion. His paradigm has been credited with influencing President Carter's work on international diplomacy (Ryback, 2011) and found expression in the philosophy of "deliberative democracy" espoused by President Obama (Packer, 2008). The Center for Studies of the Person in La Jolla, California, and the World Association for Person-Centered and Experiential Psychotherapy and Counseling continue to promote and teach Rogers' ideas.

SKILL DEVELOPMENT: EMPATHIC RESPONDING

Empathy and empathic responding on the part of the therapist help to facilitate a compassionate and safe environment in which an individual can feel free to explore deeper emotions. All therapists, regardless of theoretical orientation, use empathic listening when working with a client.

Rather than a technique that therapists use, Rogers (1980) considered empathy to be a process or a way of being with another person. "This kind of sensitive, active listening is exceedingly rare in our lives. We think we listen, but very rarely do we listen with real understanding, true empathy.

Yet listening, of this very special kind, is one of the most potent forces for change that I know" (pp. 115–116).

Empathy is effective for a variety of reasons. First, it helps to normalize people's feelings—by experiencing empathy, people no longer feel that they are isolated or alone in their experiences. Empathy also promotes examination of clients' subjective experience—hearing their feelings reflected back to them invites an exploration of the nuances of those feelings. The most effective empathic responses focus on what is just below the surface of awareness. Finally, empathy helps clients create new meaning.

Yet empathy alone is not sufficient. Empathy must be experienced, reflected, and accepted by the client for it to be meaningful. Empathic responding begins with the therapist, who must first understand the client's feelings, accurately express those feelings to the client, and then the client must recognize the empathic attunement. All three steps in the process are necessary.

Even so, some people have viewed person-centered therapy as deceptively simple and seemingly easy to master, yet when therapists begin to practice empathic listening they often find it is not quite so easy. Carl Rogers began to deplore the term reflective listening because of the implication that the therapist simply mirrored back, or parroted, the other person's words.

The following skill development exercise focuses on validating a client's feelings by making accurate empathic responses. Although many different ways to rate empathy are possible, we will only focus on three types of responses:

Nonempathic response (N) = Responses in which no empathy is expressed. Either no emotion was implied in the client's statement or the therapist was completely off track in the reflection.

Interchangeable response (I) = Interchangeable responses in which the therapist captures the essence of what the client said, but nothing more was added. Such responses can be a direct repetition of the client's words or an accurate rephrasing of the client's words.

Empathic response (E) = Empathic response. This more valuable empathic response is at the outer border of the client's awareness. Sometimes empathic reflections are followed up with a question to clarify the client's internal experience.

Example:

CLIENT: I am so sick of fighting this disease. I just want to give up.

RESPONSE 1: You don't look sick to me. (No empathy.)

RESPONSE 2: You're really tired of it all and just want to stop fighting. (Interchangeable.)

RESPONSE 3: You've been battling this for a long time, and you're wondering what it would be like if you just didn't do it anymore. (Most empathic response.)

Notice how the first response lacks empathy, does not focus on the client, and rather than uniting the client and therapist in shared experiencing, the response actually inserts distance between them. The second response is an accurate and interchangeable response to what the client said. This type of response can help clients to clarify feelings, hear their own words resonate back to them, and give them time to think about their next response. The third response focuses more on the person's felt meaning. It is noticeably more poignant and more at the leading edge of what the client has implied in the statement "I just want to give up."

Review the following examples and determine which one is the nonempathic response (N), the interchangeable response (I), and the most empathic response (E).

CLIENT: I miss my husband so much since he died, sometimes I want to claw at his grave to dig him up.

RESPONSE 1: You are so desperately sad since he died, that sometimes you feel like you would do almost anything to see him again.
RESPONSE 2: You miss him so much that sometimes you want to dig him up from his grave.
RESPONSE 3: Oh, don't do that!
CLIENT: Since we've gotten married, John and I do absolutely everything together. I'm starting to feel stifled.
RESPONSE 1: You and John do everything together, and it's stifling.
RESPONSE 2: You're not thinking about divorce, are you?
RESPONSE 3: You love your husband but you're starting to wonder if it's okay to want to spend time away from each other.
CLIENT: If I fail this final, my parents will kill me!
RESPONSE 1: I'm sure everything will be fine.
RESPONSE 2: You're feeling anxious about this final exam and worry that your parents will be furious if you don't get a good grade.
RESPONSE 3: You believe your parents would be very angry if you fail.

Now, look at the following examples of client statements, and come up with empathic and interchangeable responses of your own.

1. Yesterday marked my first anniversary with AA.
2. I think my wife might be having an affair.
3. I'm so worried. My cat didn't come home last night.
4. After years of infertility, I just found out I'm pregnant!
5. My girlfriend was a half-hour late to the movie—again.
6. My husband always plays with the kids right when it's time for them to go to bed.

Carl Rogers believed empathy could be learned, although he never explained how to teach it. Later works by others have evaluated empathic attunement and the application of empathy (Greenberg, 2010; Norcross, 2011; Truax & Carkhuff, 2007).

CASE APPLICATION

The following dialogue between Edie and her therapist illustrates many hallmarks of person-centered therapy, including active listening, communicating empathy, valuing the client, modeling genuineness, congruent therapist disclosure, and focusing on the present.

Edie's responses are abbreviated to demonstrate the therapist's use of person-centered approaches. Most person-centered therapists typically talk much less than their clients do. Edie is working on her relationship with her mother and stepfather, Pete, who has been abusive to Edie in the past.

EDIE: I feel so angry at my mother! Ava and I were visiting her and in came Pete. I could smell the liquor across the room. And my mother said nothing. How could she be like that?
THERAPIST: You're feeling pretty frustrated that she doesn't assert herself.
EDIE: Yes, and to expose Ava to that.

THERAPIST: You wish she would have done something to protect Ava.

EDIE: But she never does.

THERAPIST: She never protects her?

EDIE: Nope. She's always been like that. She didn't protect me from my grandfather either.

THERAPIST: You're remembering what it was like for you when your grandfather abused you. You know, I may be off base here, but I just had a picture of you as a helpless little girl. . . .

EDIE: Yes! Exactly! I feel like a helpless child again (thinking for a moment, then angrily . . .) but I'm *not* helpless! I'm a wife and mother, I've coped with cancer, and gone back to school, and I can figure out how to protect my child.

THERAPIST: You've overcome a lot in your life, and you can figure out how to deal with this, too.

EDIE: Darn right I can. I could keep Ava from ever going over there or seeing Pete again.

THERAPIST: Part of you would like to just cut off ties with them completely.

EDIE: Yes. But then Ava wouldn't be able to see my mother, either. That seems so drastic.

THERAPIST: So, that seems to you like too big a step.

EDIE: Yes, sometimes I do feel like never seeing them again, but that seems very childish. My mother is Pete's victim just as I was. Maybe I could set some limits . . . tell my mother that if Pete is angry or drunk again around me or Ava we'll just have to leave, even if it seems rude.

THERAPIST: You're thinking that if you set a boundary around Pete's behavior, and let your mother know ahead of time what you are planning to do, that it will protect Ava and your mother will understand.

EDIE: I don't care what Pete thinks of me, but it's very important to me that my mother understands I have to protect Ava from his behavior.

THERAPIST: As long as your mother understands and Ava is safe, then it will be worth it.

EDIE: Yes, that's right. I'm starting to feel better about this. I think that I really *can* protect Ava, stand up for myself, and still have a close relationship with my mother. Wouldn't that be great?

REFLECT AND RESPOND

1. Listening is something we often take for granted, not realizing that it is an art. Plan for an hour to practice your listening skills. Use reflection of feelings to let people know you hear and understand the meaning of what they are saying. Maintain good eye contact. Monitor your verbal and nonverbal messages to be sure they are congruent and that you are genuine, caring, and accepting. Write about this experience in your journal.
2. The goal of motivational interviewing is to strengthen the client's readiness and commitment to change. Consider a behavior that you would like to change and answer the following questions in your journal.

- What change do you want to make? (Include positive statements such as "to increase," "to improve," "to begin to.")
- What are the most important reasons why you want to make this change? List the consequences of both action and inaction.
- How will you achieve this change? List specific, concrete, and small first steps that you will take. Include when, where, and how these actions will be taken.
- How can other people help you? List specific ways in which people can help you. How will you solicit this support?
- How will you know your plan is working? List the benefits that will occur as a result of this change.
- What might interfere with your plan? Anticipate what might go wrong and list situations, obstacles, or setbacks that might occur. List what you could do in each situation to continue the plan despite any problems that might interfere.

3. Develop and write in your journal an appropriate therapist self-disclosure in response to the following client statements and questions:

   CLIENT A: There must be something really wrong with me. Everybody else seems to love parties, but I hate going into a big room full of strangers.

   CLIENT B: I finally had a great weekend. I woke up early, took a walk, had brunch with a friend, and then went to that great Georgia O'Keeffe exhibit at the museum.

   CLIENT C: I feel embarrassed that my parents found out I had too much to drink last night and had to have someone drive me home. Did anything like that ever happen to you when you were younger?

   CLIENT D: My older brother hits me and pushes me whenever we are alone. Yesterday, when he pushed me, I fell down and really hurt myself. I don't know what to do. I'm afraid he'll get into trouble if I tell anyone.

   CLIENT E: It feels like once I let people know I'm a lesbian, that changes all their reactions to me and they don't see me as a person anymore. Sometimes I think that happened here too. When I told you my partner was a woman, your expression changed, and I sensed that you disapproved of me.

4. Empowerment is an essential person-centered therapy goal. When using person-centered therapy, it is important that clients feel empowered to move toward their goals. In your journal, respond to the following prompts. How can you use this activity with a client?

   - Write down 10 inspirational words that best describe you.
   - Create a mantra for each word.
   - How can you apply these mantras to your everyday life and how may they be helpful as you move toward your goals?

5. Being mindful of your emotions is foundational to emotion regulation. Using your journal, connect with and observe a recent strong emotion and respond to these questions. How might this activity be beneficial for a client? How can this activity be used with emotion-focused therapy?

   - What does it feel like and what does it look like?
   - Is it positive or negative?
   - Is it small or big?
   - Where in your body do you feel this emotion?
   - If you could give this emotion a color, what color would it be?
   - Are there any other emotions present? If so, what are they?
   - Is there an experience connected to your emotion?

Summary

Carl Rogers first developed person-centered therapy in the 1940s and 1950s, as a humanistic and phenomenological approach to counseling that values the dignity and worth of all people, as well as their potential to resolve their difficulties. The person-centered approach, which focuses on the present rather than past problems or future concerns, transformed thinking about counseling and psychotherapy and provided the first comprehensive alternative to Freudian psychoanalysis and the directiveness of the early behaviorists.

The primary source of healing in person-centered therapy is the establishment, by the therapist, of the core conditions of congruence, unconditional positive regard, and empathy. By accepting clients as they are and providing a safe environment for them to explore their feelings, counseling moves along a path of growth toward actualization of clients' potential, helping them to become more fully functioning and self-actualized. This is especially useful due to conditions of worth, which are expectations placed upon people from others like parents. When people experience conditions of worth, they feel loved if and only if they meet others' specific requirements, and this results in incongruence, which leaves clients vulnerable in regard to living authentically. The organismic valuing process, or the natural tendency for individuals to know what they need in order to grow, is another concept that was discussed.

Certain conditions are necessary to the therapeutic process and success. A relationship must exist between clients and therapists; clients, in a state of incongruence, feel anxious and vulnerable; therapists must be congruent and genuine; both parties must be completely authentic in the therapeutic relationship; and therapists must experience and show clients unconditional positive regard and empathy. When these things occur, clients feel accepted, heard, understood, and valued for who they are, and client growth can occur.

Not only did Carl Rogers establish one of the most comprehensive theories of the self, but he also revolutionized counseling by opening the field of psychotherapy to research investigation. He was the first to record and publish complete transcripts of psychotherapy sessions. Through his own experience with clients and his commitment to scientific research and writing, Rogers delineated the most important strategy for change—the establishment of a collaborative therapeutic alliance. Rogers envisioned his theory as just the beginning of a theoretical orientation on which future theorists would build. His expectations are being fulfilled in the present with modern theories such as Gendlin's focusing, Greenberg and Johnson's emotion-focused therapy, Thomas Gordon's Parent Effectiveness Training, and motivational interviewing. Furthermore, person-centered therapy can address a variety of client presenting issues. Because of its phenomenological focus, person-centered therapy has strengths for application to diverse clients, but still has some limitations. For example, some clients from certain cultural backgrounds may feel uncomfortable self-disclosing, discussing emotions, and practicing autonomy, and they may seek a more directive counseling approach.

Person-centered therapy principles related to the counseling relationship are considered necessary for creating and maintaining a sound therapeutic alliance regardless of which therapeutic orientation a therapist chooses. Rogers' work is well known internationally, as his writings have been translated into many languages and he is viewed not only as a leader in counseling and psychology but also as a leader in conflict resolution and as a peacemaker.

Recommended Readings

Arkowitz, H., Miller, W. R., & Rollnick, S. (2nd ed.). (2017). *Motivational interviewing in the treatment of psychological problems*. New York, NY: Guilford.

Cain, D. J., Keenan, K., & Rubin, S. (2nd ed.) (2016). *Humanistic psycho-therapies: Handbook of research and practice*. Washington, DC: American Psychological Association.

Cooper, M., O'Hara, M., Schmid, P. F., & Bohart, A. (2013). *The handbook of person-centered psychotherapy and counselling* (2nd ed.). New York, NY: Palgrave Macmillan.

Cooper, M., Watson, J. C., & Bolldampt, D. (Eds.). (2010). *Person-centered and experiential therapies work: A review of the research on counseling, psychotherapy, and related practices*. Ross-on-Wye, UK: PCCS Books.

Gendlin, E. T. (1998). *Focusing-oriented psychotherapy: A manual of the experiential method*. New York, NY: Guilford.

Greenberg, L. S. (2015). *Emotion-focused therapy: Coaching clients to work through their feelings* (2nd Ed.). Washington, DC: American Psychological Association.

Greenberg, L. S., & Johnson, S. M. (1988). Emotionally focused therapy for couples. New York, NY: Guilford.

Kirschenbaum, H. (2009). *The life and work of Carl Rogers*. Alexandria, VA: American Counseling Association.

Rogers, C. R. (1951). *Client-centered therapy: Its current practice, implications and theory*. Boston, MA: Houghton Mifflin.

Rogers, C. R. (1995). *A way of being*. Boston, MA: Houghton Mifflin.

Rogers, C. R., & Kramer, P. D. (1995). *On becoming a person: A therapist's view of psychotherapy*. Boston, MA: Houghton Mifflin.

MyLab Counseling

Start with the the Topic 8 Assignments: Humanistic Therapy.

Then try the Topic 15 Assignments: Person-Centered Therapy.

CHAPTER 11
Gestalt Therapy

Learning Outcomes

When you have finished this chapter, you should be able to:
- Understand the context and development of Gestalt Therapy.
- Communicate the key concepts associated with Gestalt Therapy and understand how they relate to therapeutic processes.
- Describe the therapeutic goals of Gestalt Therapy.
- Identify the common techniques used in Gestalt Therapy.
- Understand how Gestalt Therapy relates to counseling diverse populations.
- Identify the limitations and strengths of Gestalt Therapy.

FRITZ PERLS (1893–1970)

Frederick Perls, known as Fritz Perls, was born in 1893, the middle child and only son of a middle-class Jewish family living in Berlin, Germany. Although not always a motivated student, Perls succeeded in receiving a medical degree with a specialization in psychiatry (Perls, 1992b). Interested in becoming a practicing psychoanalyst, Perls moved to Vienna, home of Sigmund Freud, where he met many of the leaders in his field. Perls studied with Karen Horney and was psychoanalyzed by both Horney and Wilhelm Reich. Reich's emphasis on the use of facial, bodily, and linguistic cues to promote understanding and personal growth had a powerful influence on Perls and on the concepts and strategies of Gestalt therapy (Wulf, 1998).

Several other experiences also strongly affected Perls. During World War I, he served in the military and spent time in the trenches, where he volunteered as a medic and later an officer. After the war, he worked with soldiers who had brain injuries. He was mentored by Kurt Goldstein, who applied Gestalt psychology perspectives in his work. Both experiences led Perls to reflect on the workings of the human mind, on Gestalt psychology principles, and on better ways to help people (Simkin, 1975; Wheeler, 1991). Early in his career as a psychoanalyst, he became disenchanted with psychoanalysis as well as with behaviorism.

The versatile and extroverted Perls also worked as an actor in the 1920s. He later reported that his experiences in the military gave him an understanding of and appreciation for nonverbal communication, an essential aspect of Gestalt therapy. In 1930, Fritz Perls married Laura Posner.

When Hitler came to power, the couple left Europe, relocating first in Holland and then in South Africa, where Fritz Perls served as a captain in the South African Medical Corps. During his years in South Africa, he outlined his theory of personality integration, which later became Gestalt therapy (Simkin, 1975). In 1946, the couple immigrated to the United States, where Fritz Perls published *Gestalt Therapy: Excitement and Growth in the Human Personality* (Perls, Hefferline, & Goodman, 1951). In 1952, he established the Gestalt Institute of America.

The most important drive for the growth of Gestalt therapy was Fritz Perls' work between 1962 and 1969 at the Esalen Institute in Big Sur, California. He became best known there for his use of the "hot seat" in his workshops and soon was regarded as an innovative and charismatic advocate of the human potential movement.

Perls' personality enhanced the popularity and success of Gestalt therapy. An outspoken free spirit, unafraid to challenge and reject established traditions and procedures, both Perls and his work were in tune with the 1960s, when many people sought more fulfillment in their lives and new ways to live. Fritz Perls emphasized independence and confrontation.

Fritz Perls died in 1970, when the popularity of Gestalt therapy was at its peak. Many therapists abandoned traditional counseling approaches in favor of this exciting approach, while others incorporated elements of Gestalt therapy into already established therapy approaches.

LAURA POSNER PERLS (1905–1990)

Laura Perls was born in Germany in 1905. Laura was a concert pianist and professional dancer (Serlin, 1992). She incorporated her music and dance background into her professional work with clients. Laura attended law school and obtained a doctoral degree in Gestalt psychology. She also studied existentialism with Martin Buber and Paul Tillich and drew on this background as she became involved in developing Gestalt therapy. She then began work as a psychoanalyst but became more interested in Gestalt therapy. When she met Fritz, they began working together to develop Gestalt therapy. In her career, she advocated for support, contact, and connections. Laura made many contributions to Gestalt therapy and coauthored the book *Gestalt Therapy: Excitement and Growth in the Human Personality* (Perls, Hefferline, & Goodman, 1951). After her husband's death, Laura Perls continued to develop Gestalt therapy until her death in 1990.

INTRODUCTION/DEVELOPMENT OF GESTALT THERAPY

Like many other counseling theories, Gestalt therapy has its roots in Europe. A group of Gestalt psychologists in Berlin, including Max Wertheimer, Kurt Koffka, and Wolfgang Köhler, laid the groundwork for Gestalt therapy with their studies of perception and integration of parts into perceptual wholes. The word *Gestalt* is of German origin and it means a whole or completion, or a form that cannot be separated into parts without losing its essence. Gestalt therapists believe that the whole is greater than the sum of the parts (Wulf, 1998). Since Gestalt therapists are interested in the whole person, they place no particular value on certain aspects of the person and instead focus on multiple human experiences (e.g., thoughts, feelings, behaviors, memories, dreams).

Although Gestalt psychologists provided the name and a basic premise for Gestalt therapy, Fritz Perls drew on many sources of knowledge in developing his approach, including Kurt Lewin's field theory, existentialism, and Eastern thought (Sapriel, 2012). In addition, Jacob Moreno's **psychodrama**, along with Perls' own experiences as an actor, are reflected in the development of Gestalt therapy. Psychodrama encourages people to work out personal difficulties by creating dramatizations of problematic situations such as a family fight. With the help of a therapist, members of the audience assume family and other roles and give the protagonist an opportunity to relive and change painful experiences. Feedback from observers both enhances the impact of the process and provides observers with vicarious benefits. Perls' techniques, including the empty chair, role plays, group feedback, and perhaps even the hot seat, were influenced by Moreno's ideas, as was Perls' emphasis on spontaneity, creativity, and enactment (Wulf, 1998).

During Perls' lifetime, the highly charged techniques associated with his approach received attention because of their use at the Esalen Institute, their powerful impact, and their application to encounter groups, widely used during the 1960s and early 1970s. Gestalt theory also draws heavily on mindfulness meditation and Buddhist thought. Fritz and Laura Perls first became familiar with Zen Buddhism through a friend (Clarkson & Mackewn, 1993) who was also training in Gestalt theory with Fritz Perls. The friend introduced Perls to Eastern ideas, which Perls wholeheartedly incorporated into his work. Buddhist theories such as the paradoxical notion of change, the polarity of life, and present-moment awareness are important in Gestalt therapy. Clinging and aversion, Buddhist concepts that are considered hindrances to mindfulness meditation, correspond to Gestalt concepts, as do self-acceptance and maintaining a nonjudgmental approach to life, free of "shoulds" and "oughts" (Kim, 2011). Perls believed his exercises offered a Zen-like experience for Westerners. He later studied Zen Buddhism in Kyoto, Japan.

Some consider Fritz Perls as a flamboyant and controversial figure. In his autobiography he wrote, "I believe that I am the best therapist for any type of neurosis in the States, maybe in the world. How is that for megalomania?" (Perls, 1969b, p. 228). Writers sometimes comment on "Perlisms"—habits unique to Perls—in reference to his confrontive, showy demonstrations, which he enjoyed doing in public forums (Parlett & Hemming, 1996).

Gestalt therapy continues to be developed and refined. Modern approaches to Gestalt therapy are less confrontive and more relation focused than Perls' approach. Particularly important were the contributions of Laura Perls and Erving and Miriam Polster. The Polsters served for many years as codirectors of the Gestalt Training Center in San Diego, expanded on Perls' ideas, and emphasized the importance of theory to increase the credibility of this counseling approach (Polster & Polster, 1973). Others, including Yontef (1993, 2012), Evans and Gilbert (2005), and Lichtenberg (2012), have also contributed to the maturation of Gestalt therapy in more recent years (Finlay & Evans, 2009).

Some (e.g., Miller, 1989) argue that most therapists are familiar with but know relatively little about Gestalt therapy. Despite this assessment, most major U.S. cities have a Gestalt institute, where people continue to learn about and promote Gestalt therapy concepts. Gestalt therapy is also popular in Europe. In more recent years, emotion-focused therapy (a couples counseling approach that will be discussed in the family systems chapter; Greenberg & Johnson, 1988) has grown in popularity and blends Gestalt and person-centered concepts.

KEY CONCEPTS

Although Perls often used distinctive terminology, his key concepts are in many ways consistent with person-centered and existential approaches. Gestalt therapy is existential and humanistic in that it emphasizes individual choice, stresses personal responsibility, and holds that people are growth oriented. Gestalt therapy is also **phenomenological** because it recognizes that people's perceptions of a situation can vary widely; that even within a person, perceptions can change; and that perceptions greatly influence thoughts, emotions, and behaviors. However, Perls and his colleagues did add their own ideas, which distinguish Gestalt therapy from other approaches. In addition, the interventions used in Gestalt therapy, discussed later in the chapter, represent a considerable departure from existential and person-centered approaches, which make minimal use of specific intervention strategies.

Like other humanists, Perls placed great importance on self-actualization, or reaching one's fullest potential (Perls, 1992a). Perls believed that people were basically self-directed, and had the capacity to cope with their lives successfully, although he recognized that they sometimes needed help. According to Perls, healthy people engage productively in the tasks of survival and maintenance and intuitively move toward self-preservation and growth. In the following section, two key Gestalt therapy concepts will be discussed: wholeness, integration, and balance; and awareness. This chapter serves as a starting place for understanding these concepts, as many of them are complex, abstract, and difficult to fully comprehend.

Wholeness, Integration, and Balance

As its name implies, Gestalt therapy is a holistic approach that emphasizes the importance of integration and balance in people's lives. People cannot be separated from their environment, nor can they be divided into parts (such as body and mind, or thoughts and feelings; Murdock, 2009). In discussing the human experience, Perls (1992a) said, "We *have* not a liver or a heart. We *are* liver and heart and brain and yet, even this is wrong—we are *not* a summation of parts but a *coordination* of the whole. We do not have a body, we *are* a body, we *are* somebody" (p. 6).

FIELD THEORY: INTEGRATING FIGURE AND GROUND Kurt Lewin's field theory is foundational to Gestalt therapy. **Field theory** states that people must be seen in context with their environment, and as part of the constantly changing field or environment (Perls et al., 1951). More simply put, Gestalt therapists focus not just on what is in clients' immediate awareness, but what is just outside their awareness. Therapists focus on the **figure and ground**, and they are interested in what occurs at the boundary between the individual and the environment. Therapists may draw clients' attention to the **figure** (aspects of clients' experience that are most important in that moment; aspects of which they are aware) or the **ground** (aspects of clients' experience that are outside of their awareness). In Figure 11.1,

FIGURE 11.1 Figure and Ground Illustration.

a classic illustration of this concept of figure and ground is provided. At first glance, one might see only one figure. However, closer inspection and a closer look at the ground may reveal a different picture. The figure and ground taken together reveals the whole, which is something entirely different from the parts.

To help clients increase their awareness, therapists pay attention to and point out clients' physical gestures, tone of voice, and any other nonverbal content, as these can give clues to the ground experiences that are outside clients' awareness. Therapists direct clients' attention to how these different parts and experiences fit together, and how clients are making contact with their environment, with an eye to integrating these different experiences.

Clients connect their figure and ground experiences in a way and at a pace that feels comfortable for them. Therapists simply facilitate this awareness, and over time, connections become more apparent to both therapists and clients. By allowing what is outside of clients' awareness to become figural (i.e., a figure, or in their awareness), clients can create new meanings about their experiences. They are able to develop a deeper awareness of themselves. Not changing or integrating figure and ground experiences results in stagnation and a sense of being "stuck."

This process of shifting back and forth between figure and ground is the crux of Gestalt therapy. According to Perls, the Gestalt approach has as its basis the paradoxical situation that people have a two-part existence: both the awareness of what is happening in the present moment and the relationship that the present moment contrasts with. In Perls' view, recognizing these splits and activating both is the goal of therapy. Through increased awareness, boundaries become fluid, disappear, and then reappear.

Therapists can use their observations of the field as a tool in therapy. Through the use of Gestalt techniques such as the empty chair and the two-chair technique, therapists help clients become aware of the figure and ground, recognize dualities, and connect that things are not "either/or," but, rather, are "both/and." This both/and way of thinking results in a paradigm shift for the client that encourages being nonjudgmental, increases compassion, and eventually brings about change (Neff, Kirkpatrick, & Rude, 2007).

More significant figure/ground shifts lead to sudden and often important changes in our understanding of events and experiences. For example, after dating for 10 months, Kristen arrived about 45 minutes late to pick up her boyfriend, Luke, for a party at a friend's house. Before she could explain that an accident had caused her delay, Luke became enraged and hit Kristen in the face. He had become angry with her before and had come close to hitting her, but Kristen had overlooked those signs of Luke's violent behavior. She had grown up in an environment in which anger and shouting were acceptable and even desirable expressions of feeling. However, when Luke actually hit her, she saw those early warning signs in a new light, integrating figure and ground. She recognized that Luke presented a danger to her, that they did not have a healthy relationship, and that she needed to move on.

INTEGRATING POLARITIES People's need for balance and homeostasis can lead them to view themselves and their world in terms of **polarities**, or extremes. As an example, the world may seem easier to understand if people categorize others as either good or bad and place them in boxes. Other examples of polarities include life and death, passive and aggressive, and connection and separation (Levitsky & Perls, 1970). People experience both ends of polarities; however, sometimes people, for varied reasons, do not want to accept one end of the polarity and so they reject the opposite end of the continuum (Levitsky & Perls, 1970). To truly achieve wholeness, people must become aware of and integrate their polarities. Unless they accomplish this, the neglected or rejected side of the polarity is likely to build barriers against efforts toward growth. For instance, people who believe they must always be independent may deny the part of themselves that craves connection and intimacy; people who believe that their intellect is their greatest gift may cut themselves off from their emotions and sensations; and people who are passive in their romantic relationships may be disconnected from their assertiveness and lose themselves within relationships.

Polarization and denial of parts of the self stem from a drive toward homeostasis, or a drive to keep things familiar. People have difficulty dealing with ambiguity, not knowing, or disequilibrium, and they tend to prefer stability and the familiar. This drive for a state of comfort, even when not ideal, may lead some people to become stuck. For example, they may stay "stuck" in an unsatisfying marriage because they fear the alternative, or they may exclude from awareness the parts of themselves that seem incongruent or cause discomfort, in a misguided effort to force balance and equilibrium.

GROWTH DISORDERS AND RESISTANCE TO CONTACT Although Perls sometimes used the term *neuroses* to describe emotional problems, he believed that these difficulties should more accurately be referred to as "growth disorders" (Perls, 1992a, p. 30). People who do not adapt to life's changes develop growth disorders. This term is also used in connection with people who deny or reject aspects of themselves and their environment, are not living in the present, are not making fulfilling contact with others, lack awareness, and are not becoming actualized. Rather than changing or growing, they have become stuck. Behaviors and attitudes done out of habit, without thinking, get in the way of change. Change is an inevitable part of life, and those who do not change become stagnant.

Perls thought of resistance as a deeply rooted fear of contact caused by an unhealthy blockage used to avoid some form of pain, whether it be real or imagined. With this reframe, Gestalt therapists came to see resistance as a problem to be worked through. Commonly addressed resistances to contact include introjection, projection, retroflection, confluence, deflection, and desensitization. Table 11.1 provides an overview and description of these types of resistances.

TABLE 11.1 Gestalt Therapy: Common Resistances

Type of Common Resistance	Description	Example
Introjection	Involves experiencing something "whole" or fully without looking for evidence or questioning the facts; adopting the beliefs of others just because they said these beliefs are true. Characterized by naïvetés and gullibility.	The belief that boys should not show emotion.
Projection	Placing unwanted or uncomfortable feelings, thoughts, and characteristics of oneself onto others. Expecting people to act a certain way, or accusing them of acting a certain way, related to one's own fears.	Someone who has thoughts of infidelity may accuse the partner of cheating.
Retroflection	Doing to yourself what you want to do to others or what you want others to do to you; turning one's energy inward.	Suppressing anger to avoid conflict and forcing yourself to relax when afraid.
Confluence	Agreeing with others and denying one's own beliefs and feelings to avoid conflict and feel accepted.	Agreeing with another person's opinion to avoid an argument.
Deflection	Avoiding an uncomfortable experience or direct contact by changing the subject. This can manifest as using humor, ignoring a compliment, or talking about something completely different when feeling uncomfortable.	A friend confronts you for arriving late to a dinner party, you feel uncomfortable, and you change the subject to talking about your day at work.
Desensitization	Avoiding direct contact physically, emotionally, or mentally. Feeling nothing or feeling numb to avoid painful or difficult issues.	Being apathetic after a divorce to avoid pain.

Avoidance and resistance to contact and awareness keep people trapped in an unhealthy state. In this state, they avoid dealing with uncomfortable feelings, remain unaware, and circumscribe their lives to minimize flux or change. They make extensive use of ego defenses, such as **projection** of disowned aspects of themselves onto others, distraction, failure to set boundaries between themselves and others, and withdrawal from their surroundings. Individuals may also experience **introjection**, which is the tendency to uncritically accept other people's beliefs and standards without assimilating them to make them congruent with who they are. In addition, when individuals who are going through difficult times do not seek the proper methods of releasing their negative energy into the environment, they may direct the negative energy inward, which is known as **retroflection**. An example of this would be someone in a toxic relationship who, instead of communicating with his partner (environment) about the situation, blames himself and only focuses on what he has done wrong to create the bad relationship; that is, he retroflects. Wholeness, integrity, freedom of choice, and actualization are sacrificed for the illusion of safety and homeostasis. Such people do not allow themselves to be aware of, anticipate, and cope successfully and flexibly with the changes in their lives. Rather, they persist in unsuccessful ego defenses to avoid change. Paradoxically, as Perls observed, even stagnation indicates that movement has occurred and hope is alive. Ironically, turmoil and discomfort can result significant growth for many people.

People who are not developing in healthy ways often have a great deal of **unfinished business**, which is unexpressed feelings from the past that occur in the present and interfere with psychological functioning. According to Perls (1992a), "Our life is basically practically nothing but an infinite number of unfinished situations—incomplete Gestalts. No sooner have we finished one situation than another comes up" (p. 15). Healthy people may be confused by the constant unfinished business in their lives but learn to use their resources to deal with it effectively. However, some people become alienated from many aspects of their environments and themselves, which leads to not dealing effectively with the demands of their lives, so they accumulate more and more unfinished business. Their energy is sapped by their unproductive efforts to cope, leaving them depleted of the resources they need to live their lives successfully. People who are overwhelmed by unfinished business typically feel stuck or blocked and may experience physical symptoms. Their current issues tend to mirror unresolved past issues and are never finished because they are not addressed in the here and now. Because of this, a major goal of Gestalt therapy is to help people become aware of their backlog of unfinished business and bring it to closure so that they are able to live more fully in the present.

CONTACT DISTURBANCE When our awareness is disrupted, problems are seen at the ego boundary (sometimes referred to as contact boundaries). **Ego boundaries** are the boundaries that distinguish one individual, an object, another individual, or another aspect of the self. This boundary is where contact with others takes place; in other words, this is where relationships are formed. When contact with others happens in a healthy manner, the ego boundary is flexible, which means that we are capable of distinguishing me from you, while also forming a we. A number of conflicts of interest arise in any relationship, and we often experience conflict between our needs and the demands of others. In healthy ego boundary situations, we are capable of understanding that others are not there to meet our needs and wishes, and that both people in the relationship are complete and autonomous individuals. Another threat to healthy ego boundaries is that out of a sense of obligation, we often behave in ways we think we should behave in relationships, not how we want to behave. In the long run, this rigidity can become worse and form an obstacle to communicating and authentically connecting with others.

The identification and alienation phenomena constitute additional important aspects of the ego boundary. Gestalt therapy proposes that people often identify with only small parts of their own true selves. This affects the way people see what is in themselves and what is in others. People generally make assumptions that certain characteristics of themselves belong to others, a process known as **identification**.

People may also consider some qualities as belonging only to others when in reality they are also parts of their own selves; this phenomenon is known as **alienation**. For example, a person who believes she is always open minded and does not recognize the times she can be rigid and closed minded may criticize others for being closed minded. Again, awareness of these phenomena and integration of various aspects of the self lead to psychological health.

Ideally, people have an awareness of all aspects of themselves—the good, the bad, and the ugly—and they understand and they monitor to ensure they keep their interpersonal wants and needs in check. Healthy individuals also understand that others are separate from them; and healthy individuals monitor to keep their wants, needs, and expectations of others appropriate. In other words, people's awareness of where they end and others begin helps them to establish healthy ego boundaries and thus healthy relationships.

HOMEOSTASIS VERSUS FLUX Perls used many terms, including figure/ground, ego boundary, and polarities, to refer to the constant state of flux that people experience. These constructs all pose threats to homeostasis. **Homeostasis**, or balance and equilibrium, relates to people's need to complete or resolve unfinished situations (Perls & Philippson, 2012). Although people strive for homeostasis, their lives and the world are always in flux, always changing. People constantly experience disequilibrium and then naturally try to restore balance. They are hungry, so they eat. They are tired, so they nap. They shift priorities based on the nature and importance of the rising needs that must be met. Clearly, people cannot achieve a state of fixed homeostasis and then freeze; lives are always changing. However, through awareness of and identification with all aspects of themselves, they can deal successfully with flux and still have a sense of integration and wholeness.

As an example, if you are reading this chapter and you are very hungry, it will be difficult for you to focus on reading. When you become hungry enough, your hunger becomes figural and you move ahead with figuring out how to get that need met. Once you eat, you have completed the gestalt, the need disappears out of your perception, the need is said to be destroyed, and you reach closure (Frew, 2012). Soon though, another incomplete Gestalt emerges; thus, whatever need is most urgent to you at any given time becomes the figure. Gestalt therapists believe that awareness of these shifting needs is the aim of therapy.

Awareness

For Gestalt therapists, **awareness** is an essential element of emotional health and can be curative. Awareness is the knowledge and observation of what is happening in the present and is seen as the most essential aspect of change. Once an individual gains awareness, decisions become more natural and the individual is better able to self-regulate. Awareness is both a hallmark of the healthy person and a goal of counseling.

Several possible causes have been identified for limited awareness. Preoccupation is one of the foremost. We may be so caught up with our pasts, our fantasies, and our perceived flaws or strengths that we lose sight of the whole picture and become unaware. Another reason for lack of awareness is low self-esteem: "The less confident we are in ourselves, the less we are in touch with ourselves and the world, the more we want to control" (Perls, 1992a, p. 21). In other words, low self-esteem makes it difficult for us to trust ourselves, to allow our natural health and strength to propel us toward growth and self-actualization. Rather, those of us with low self-esteem typically set out to control ourselves and others in an effort to realize an idealized self-image rather than to truly become actualized. The result is often exactly the opposite of what is intended.

Gestalt therapy facilitates awareness by the use of experiments, a here-and-now focus, and process statements. Because it is not enough for clients to merely talk about their feelings—talking leads to intellectualization—Gestalt therapists do not practice reflective listening. Rather, they focus on their clients' nonverbal language—the way they sit, their tone of voice, or a tapping finger. By attending to these and other body movements, the therapist requires clients to go deeper, to re-experience their emotions in the here-and-now environment of the therapy session, and to understand the physical as well as verbal meaning of what they are projecting.

ENVIRONMENTAL CONTACT TO PROMOTE GROWTH People engage in many efforts to achieve awareness, and contact with the environment is one of the most important. We make **contact** through seven functions: looking, listening, touching, talking, moving, smelling, and tasting (Polster & Polster, 1973). Contact is necessary for growth; when we make contact with other people or aspects of our world, we must react and change. The experience of contact teaches us about ourselves and our environment and helps us to feel as though we are a part of our world, while defining more clearly who we are. When we avoid closeness with others and live isolated lives, we may believe that we are protecting ourselves, but, in reality, we are preventing our growth and actualization. An unclear connection between ourselves and others is referred to as confluence. **Confluence** involves blurring the differentiation between ourselves and others. Confluence often occurs because of the natural desire to blend in and get along with others. As we strive for harmony, we are often less authentic, and a disconnect occurs between our internal experiences of others and what is taking place in reality. Confluence can manifest as slowness to become angry or irritated with others, an absence of interpersonal conflicts, and a belief that everyone experiences the same feelings and thoughts. Those of us who have a strong desire to be liked or accepted have higher degrees of confluence, and this makes genuine connection difficult. Therapists can challenge clients to become more aware of what they want and how they feel to help minimize confluence.

Perls (1992a) identified five levels or stages of contact and growth:

1. *The phony layer.* Refers to the fake or inauthentic way that people act with other people. At this point, clients pretend to be something they are not. This can often be seen in the games that people play day to day and the way people make small talk to avoid delving into anything too deep. At this level, people mindlessly assume roles, react in stereotyped and inauthentic ways, and are insincere.
2. *The phobic layer.* Clients show a fear of revealing their real identity, and thus they deny its existence. At this layer people resist seeing their true selves, especially aspects of themselves that might cause emotional disturbance or pain. As a result, aspects of the real self are denied, and self-acceptance is forfeited. People hide their real selves to prevent rejection, as well as feeling vulnerable and helpless.
3. *The impasse layer.* At this point, clients will appear stuck and unable to meet their counseling goals. People at this layer frequently experience feelings of emptiness or nothingness. They often feel stuck, and they avoid. Perls thought this was an important layer, and saw it as the source of many problems for people.
4. *The implosive layer.* This layer involves clients allowing themselves to come into contact with feelings they might have pushed away previously because they felt vulnerable. This layer happens as a result of pushing through the previous layers, and desiring to seek completion and integration of different aspects of themselves. People become aware that they have limited

themselves and begin to experiment with change, to deal with unfinished business, to lower defenses, and to move toward greater integration. People connect with their possibilities and shed old layers. This implosion, or turning inward, turns into an explosion in the fifth layer.

5. ***The explosive layer.*** When all the previous layers have been worked through, clients enter the explosive layer. People at this layer react authentically and strongly express their emotions and feelings. People here often experience catharsis, and this involves strong emotions and feelings. People experience reintegration and wholeness, become their authentic selves, gain access to great energy, feel and express emotions, and become better actualized. The energy that was used on maintaining a phony existence is released and used in more productive ways.

Counseling often involves helping people progress through the layers, peeling away each one like the skin of an onion to expose the next, healthier layer of the adult personality. In this way, people truly become their authentic, actualized selves, capable of full contact with the environment, other people, and themselves.

ENERGY AND BLOCKS TO ENERGY Gestalt therapy pays attention to how clients cope with energy, where it is located, and how they block the energy. Energy is an important concept because it involves awareness or lack thereof. When clients block energy, they are engaging in a defense mechanism. Some ways energy may be blocked is by not breathing deeply, by keeping the body tense, by avoiding eye contact, and by avoiding feelings. Therapists using Gestalt therapy aim to help clients understand where their energy is located and how they are blocking their energy, especially in their body. Finding healthier alternatives instead of blocking energy helps increase awareness.

HERE AND NOW Another way to increase awareness is to live in and be conscious of the present moment rather than remaining tied to the past or trying to control the future. According to Perls (1992a), "Nothing exists except the here and now. . . . The past is no more. The future is not yet. . . . You should live in the here and now" (p. 44). When we are centered in the present, we are more likely to be congruent—to have our minds, our bodies, and our emotions integrated. When we are not fully in the present, we may be fragmented. Our emotions may be stuck in past hurts and our thoughts may wander to future anticipations while we talk with people in the present. When we are not centered in the present, we give confusing messages to others, have a poorly integrated sense of ourselves, and have difficulty making contact because we are not fully present.

Gestalt therapy takes place in the here and now. The therapist reacts in a genuine, empathic, and transparent way to the client's material. This transparency may include disclosures from the therapist, but any disclosure must be made in the best interest of the client. The use of the here and now is not a technique to be selected for use with the client, but a way of being that reflects the I-Thou relationship found in all humanistic therapies (Buber, 1970; Finlay & Evans, 2009; Yontef, 1993). More will be said about the I-Thou relationship in the discussion of the therapeutic alliance.

RESPONSIBILITY Like the other humanistic theorists, Gestalt therapists place importance on accepting responsibility for our own lives rather than giving that power away or blaming and resenting others for our disappointments. Gestalt therapists believe that we must make our own choices rather than allowing others to choose for us.

In keeping with the climate of the 1960s, Perls focused on the individual; but contemporary Gestalt therapists have modified the concept of responsibility. Now it refers not only to taking care of ourselves but also to recognizing that from birth we rely on the presence of interdependent relationships. To maintain a healthy balance between interconnectedness and independence, we must have awareness and self-acceptance, which lies at the core of the healthy person.

THE THERAPEUTIC PROCESS

The process of Gestalt therapy is experiential. Rather than focusing on what is being said, Gestalt therapists focus on what is happening, or what is being experienced, in that particular moment. This is especially helpful in enhancing awareness, which is the ultimate purpose of Gestalt therapy. Gestalt therapy is helpful for people who want to gain awareness and make changes, not for people who simply seek relief from discomfort.

It is important to assess clients' willingness to engage in the work of Gestalt therapy, agree to the frequency of sessions, and develop the connection between the therapist and the client. Gestalt therapy also focuses on direct engagement, or contact, between the therapist and the client. Authenticity and honesty are important in the therapeutic relationship to promote growth and progress.

Perls had two main goals when conducting Gestalt therapy. First, he aimed to help clients recognize that the resources they need for positive growth and change are within, rather than outside, themselves (e.g., in a partner, title, career, or therapist). To help clients develop this self-sufficiency, he challenged them to develop their awareness, their sense of inner strength, and their self-sufficiency. The second goal was to reintegrate the denied parts of the clients' personality and experience.

Unlike person-centered and existential therapy, Gestalt therapy includes a rich array of directive strategies that facilitate therapy. These strategies have been developed to further what Perls et al. (1951) identified as the four major emphases in Gestalt work:

1. To pay attention to experience and become aware of and concentrate on the actual present situation
2. To maintain and promote the integrity and interrelationships of social, cultural, historical, physical, emotional, and other important factors
3. To experiment
4. To encourage creativity.

Perls pushed clients to be self-sufficient, and he strongly believed that clients need to take responsibility for their own lives and that they have control over themselves. This belief that people have control over themselves and their experiences contributed to Perls' direct, challenging, confrontational manner in the therapeutic setting. While Perls' style could be abrasive to some, it was founded in the idea that through awareness, people could grow and enhance their sense of control over their experiences.

Therapeutic Goals

While Gestalt therapy is not necessarily goal oriented, Gestalt therapists do keep in mind important objectives. Many of these objectives are similar to those of person-centered and existential therapy.

Gestalt therapists do not analyze; they integrate (Perls, 1992a). In other words, the ultimate aim of Gestalt therapy is to help people integrate different aspects of themselves through awareness, thus promoting clients' growth and enabling them to live fully actualized lives. By accessing denied parts of the self and fully experiencing the present moment, clients can feel whole and unified. Gestalt therapists do not simply solve problems or promote adaptation to situations—they help clients feel more fulfilled and whole.

Gestalt therapists believe that awareness is the primary vehicle of change. If people can gain awareness of their unfinished business (the areas in which they are blocked and alienated) and their own strengths and resources, they can grow and become more actualized. Particularly important is awareness gained through the body, since, according to Gestalt theory, most people overemphasize intellectual awareness and ignore messages from the body and the senses. Once people gain awareness, they have more choices and have the tools for change. When people are aware, they understand themselves and their environment, accept themselves, and are able to make contact. Awareness is constantly changing because people are constantly changing; therefore, people must continuously learn about themselves. Awareness can be developed through a genuine therapeutic relationship.

The most important goals of Gestalt therapy are as follows:

- Promoting attention, clarity, and *awareness*
- Helping people live in the *here and now*
- Improving people's sense of *wholeness, integration*, and *balance.*

Additional goals of significance in this approach include:

- Enabling people to bring *closure* to their unfinished business
- Increasing people's appreciation of and *access to their own considerable resources*
- Promoting responsibility, appropriate choices, and *self-sufficiency*
- Promoting self-esteem, self-acceptance, and *actualization*
- Facilitating people's efforts to have *meaningful contact* with all aspects of themselves, other people, and their environment
- Developing the skills people need to *manage their lives successfully* without harming others.

Therapist's Function and Role

Gestalt therapists strive to be genuine and aware of their own feelings, experiences, and perceptions. They build relationships with clients in which both client and therapist are free from judgment, narcissism, or expectations; are respectful and accepting of the other; are open; and are fully present in the here and now (Buber, 1970; Finlay & Evans, 2009). Gestalt therapists serve as facilitators of growth; they do not urge or persuade people to change or tell people how they should be. Rather, they establish a climate that promotes trust, awareness, and a willingness to experiment with new ways of thinking, feeling, and acting. Therapists and clients enter into a partnership in which both are committed to and active in the therapy process. However, clients take responsibility for their own development and decide for themselves how they will use the information that emerges in their sessions. In this way, therapists create an environment for growth, but clients are responsible for the work they do in therapy.

Gestalt therapists believe that true change occurs when people become aware of who they are, not when they try to become what they are not (Beisser, 1970). This heightened awareness is often referred to as the **paradoxical theory of change**. Only through ownership and integration of previously denied aspects of the self can change become truly possible. According to this concept, the more people try to be something they are not, the more they will stay right where they are. When therapists observe that clients' attention is wandering, that conflicts are emerging, or that the clients seem fragmented or out of contact, the therapists call attention to these phenomena in the "here and now" of the session. The therapists make this observation without interpretation or judgment, but simply to provide information that is likely to refocus attention, create awareness of blocks, and help people maintain contact with their present activities and experiences. Instead of trying to figure out their clients, Gestalt therapists focus on listening and helping clients find their own way. Because Gestalt therapists view clients as experts on their own lives, they encourage self-discovery and trust that clients can discover ways to increase their awareness and fully integrate disowned aspects of themselves.

Therapists are also aware of and manage a form of client resistance called deflection. **Deflection** involves avoiding direct contact by breaking the mood, shifting attention, or changing the subject.

Examples of deflection include making a joke or being sarcastic to defuse an emotionally laden situation, or, say, ignoring or refusing a compliment because it creates discomfort. Clients who avoid experiencing true emotions, certain scenarios, or particular environments may be engaging in deflection. Deflection is a form of resistance, but also a psychological defense, and clients may only be able to discuss pieces of their story so that they do not have to be fully exposed to a flood of emotions all at once. In using deflection, clients avoid experiencing the full effect of the encounter and thus they deal only with what they are able to digest at that given moment.

Therapists are also responsible for paying attention to clients' body language. Body language says a lot about what clients may be experiencing, and therapists must point out incongruities. For example, clients may smile while saying they are sad. Bringing awareness to incongruities is essential to promote growth. Therapists may even ask their clients to give voice to their body language to further increase awareness. In addition, therapists pay attention to the language clients use and nonjudgmentally point it out. Therapists encourage clients to change their language in order to stay in the present moment and promote growth. For example, therapists point out to clients when they use language that denies power, such as "maybe," "I guess," and "sort of." As another tactic, therapists encourage clients to replace the words "I can't" with "I won't" to help them accept responsibility. Furthermore, therapists can learn more about their client by listening to metaphors they use and paying close attention to what they are saying in order to uncover a story about their struggles.

Experience in the here and now is the process used to increase awareness. Awareness occurs in the present experiential moment, so even though clients may be addressing a past experience, the focus in therapy is on the "present moment where the past is embedded and therefore alive and obvious" (Melnick & Nevis, 2005, p. 105). It is only through this web of relational interconnections that clients know themselves (Finlay & Evans, 2009).

Relationship Between Therapist and Client

As two people relate together they can either treat each other as objects, thus creating an I-it relationship, or they can have a real person-to-person relationship in the form of an I-Thou (You) relationship (Buber, 1970). *Thou* refers to the presence of uniqueness and wholeness in people that is the outcome of genuine listening and responding. The *I-Thou* relationship involves both individuals entering into a conversation with their unique whole being. Like the existential therapists discussed in the previous chapter, Gestalt therapists seek to create an I-Thou relationship in contrast to the I-it relationship. The I-it relationship is the type of everyday relationship that moves individuals forward throughout the day but does not involve a deep meaningful connection. Although I-it ways of relating are not to be shunned (because they make up the bulk of communications), they miss the depth of people's humanity (Crocker, 2005).

The I-Thou relationship is a willingness to truly know the other person as that person is, as well as the willingness to be transparent and to be fully known. Not only do therapists aim to truly understand their clients for who they are, they also show genuineness and ensure that they are being themselves. Therapists may even be influenced by their clients and are honest with their perceptions to stay in the present moment. Because of the here-and-now emphasis, therapists and clients form an alliance based on self-responsibility and an agreement to be present with each other during their time together.

Because therapists are such important instruments in Gestalt therapy, it is vital for them to understand themselves and be self-aware. When they use themselves as tools, they are more likely to facilitate trust and be authentic. Therapists and clients influence each other, and they must be in tune with each other. Therapists are responsible for reflecting on their attitudes and being fully aware.

Using Gestalt therapy requires a willingness to truly connect with an individual when possible; an I-it relationship may create a therapeutic bond, but to bring about true change, the relationship must be developed and grounded in a deeper level of vulnerability. Overall, the therapeutic relationship in Gestalt therapy is authentic, respectful, and accepting.

THERAPEUTIC TECHNIQUES AND PROCEDURES

Gestalt therapists pull on a diversity of creative, often spontaneous counseling techniques. More than person-centered or existential therapies, Gestalt therapy is known for its use of such techniques.

Exercises, Experiments, and Enactments

Gestalt therapy is practiced in the form of exercises and experiments. Exercises are established practices in gestalt therapy, designed to arouse client action or emotion. **Exercises** are techniques used to accomplish a purpose relevant to the client, and they are usually planned beforehand. The therapist and client examine the result of the exercise to increase awareness and help the client understand the "here and now" of the experience.

In contrast to exercises, **experiments**—or learning experiences for clients—arise throughout the development of the therapeutic process and therapeutic relationship. These are individually tailored to clients to promote awareness and bring problems and unfinished business into the present, where they can be resolved. They are a core component of Gestalt therapy and allow clients to understand different aspects of a conflict, experience, or mental health issue. Typically, experiments are experiential, in the moment, and emerge from the dialogue between therapists and clients. Experiments might take the form of role plays, homework, or activities for clients to accomplish between sessions (Polster & Polster, 1973). These experiments should not be threatening or negative; instead, they should be positive and growth promoting. Presentation of suggested experiments should always be respectful, inviting, and carefully timed. Although confrontation may be used to encourage involvement, clients are never demeaned and can always choose whether or not to involve themselves in the experiments.

Enactments, a technique that involves the client putting feelings or thoughts into action, is also frequently used in counseling. As an example of an enactment, a Gestalt therapist might suggest to a withdrawn and guarded woman who wants to have closer relationships with people that she tell a friend something about herself that would surprise and please the friend. Spending time thinking about what she would tell the friend might promote the woman's self-awareness, and the eventual sharing might increase the closeness between the woman and her friend.

Use of Language

Language plays an important part in Gestalt therapy. By choosing their words carefully and encouraging clients to use specific language, therapists create an environment that fosters change.

EMPHASIS ON STATEMENTS Although questions are part of Gestalt therapy, therapists typically prefer statements. They are more likely to say, "I am experiencing a loss of contact between us," than "Where has your attention gone?" The **immediacy** (present moment) and direct person-to-person contact of a statement promotes a collaborative client–therapist relationship. Questions, in contrast, are reminiscent of a teacher–student relationship in which the power differential may undermine the process. Talking *with* someone rather than *at* someone is critical in building a connection.

"WHAT" AND "HOW" QUESTIONS When Gestalt therapists do ask questions, they usually begin them with "what," "how," or sometimes "where," but rarely with "why." Questions such as "What are you experiencing when you stamp your foot?" and "How does it feel when you stamp your foot?" are more likely to keep the client in the present moment and promote integration than are questions such as "Why are you stamping your foot?" "Why" questions typically lead to a focus on past experiences, encourage the intellectualization of experiences, and increase manifestations of resistance.

"I" STATEMENTS Gestalt therapists encourage people to own and focus on their own feelings and experiences rather than talk about other people (they) or events (it). Statements beginning with "I," such as "I feel angry" and "In the dream, I am lost," encourage ownership and responsibility as well as integration. Statements such as "My mother made me angry" and "My dream was about being lost" take the focus off the clients and the present moment and promote fragmentation and externalizing of responsibility.

ENCOURAGING RESPONSIBILITY Gestalt therapists encourage people to take responsibility for themselves, their words, their emotions, their thoughts, and their behaviors to facilitate integration. Language can help further that goal. For example, the therapist might suggest that people temporarily begin all their sentences with the phrase "I take responsibility for . . ." to help them recognize and accept their feelings. To facilitate awareness of their projections, they might also apply to themselves statements they have made about others. The woman who says, "My sister only thinks of herself," might be asked to say, "I think only of myself," and then talk about what feelings this brings up for her.

Another way to encourage people to take responsibility for themselves is for therapists to help them make the implicit explicit. For example, a woman assured her husband that she would be happy to accompany him to church as he requested. However, each Sunday she told him that she had work to do so she could not go to church. Her therapist encouraged her to make her feelings explicit by stating, "I really don't want to go to church with you; I feel uncomfortable and out of place there because it is not the religion I was brought up to believe."

THE PRESENT TENSE Even when clients talk about past events, Gestalt therapists encourage them to focus on their present experience of the events—to bring events into the room and into the moment. For example, rather than focusing on a client's perceptions of how his father abandoned him when he was a child, the therapist might suggest that the client describe how that early abandonment affects his feelings and behaviors in the therapy session. A tactic such as this fosters awareness as well as a true connection with the clients' experience of the events.

Dreams

Dreams play an important role in Gestalt therapy. Perls viewed dreams as the royal road to integration rather than the royal road to the unconscious, as Freud had viewed them. Perls believed that the parts of a dream represent projections or aspects of the dreamer. Awareness comes from assuming the various roles or parts of the dream and enacting the dream as though it is happening in the present. When working with dreams, it is best for clients to list details of the dream and remember the people, feelings, and events in the dream. Clients can then act out each part of the dream and act as each person in the dream, creating dialogue. Clients will then gain awareness about their opposing feelings and sides because this would be represented in the dream. By gaining awareness, clients can integrate their opposing selves and personalities.

For example, a man had a dream about a rabbit, which was being chased across a field by a fox, escaping into a burrow. On the one hand, Freud, of course, would focus on the unconscious meaning of the conflict between the fox and the rabbit and the possibly sexual significance of the burrow. Perls, on the other hand, would encourage the man to assume the roles of each of the salient parts of the dream. One at a time, the client would enact the roles of the frightened rabbit, the menacing fox, the open field, and the protective burrow, speaking the thoughts and feelings that arose for him in each role. For example, he might say, "I am that rabbit, running scared, afraid that I will be swallowed up. I am always running for cover, safe just in the nick of time, but knowing that I might not make it the next time."

This approach to understanding dreams puts clients in charge of the process. It also allows people to take responsibility for their dreams, see their dreams as part of themselves, increase integration, and become aware of thoughts and emotions reflected in the dream that they might otherwise disown. Many concise examples of dreamwork can be found in Perls' book *Gestalt Therapy Verbatim* (1992a).

Fantasy

Fantasies, like dreams, can help people become more self-aware and in contact with their feelings. Therapists might use guided imagery to take people on a journey into their imaginations. Clients might be encouraged to imagine themselves walking through a beautiful meadow with a ramshackle house, looking around to see who is with them, and deciding what to do in that situation. Therapists might make the fantasy more productive by asking questions to promote exploration and suggesting actions the person might take in the fantasy.

As with dreams, Gestalt therapists assume that the parts of a fantasy represent projections or aspects of people. When the fantasy is completed, therapists encourage people to process the experience by becoming the parts of the fantasy, speaking as though they are each part.

Fantasies also can be used to bring closure to unfinished business. For example, a woman who had undergone surgery was left with some angry feelings about her surgeon and the need to have her surgery redone. When she called to express her feelings to the physician, he failed to return her telephone calls. To help her reach closure, her therapist led her on a guided fantasy in which she expressed her feelings to the physician and affirmed her ability to take care of herself and have the unsatisfactory surgery corrected.

Role Play Using Empty Chair Methods

Role play, in various forms, is an essential tool of Gestalt therapists. Although Perls was influenced by Moreno's psychodrama, Gestalt therapy rarely uses other people to play roles, in part because that might encourage fragmentation. Rather, an empty chair is more often used to represent a role, with the clients playing out the role as opposed to others.

THE TWO-CHAIR METHOD FOR ADDRESSING AN INNER CONFLICT This common type of role play is intended to help people become aware of and resolve inner conflicts, develop clarity, and gain insight into all aspects of a problem (Strumpfel & Goldman, 2002). It can also help people become aware of their self-judgments, see how they respond to their self-judgments, and enable them to develop compassion for themselves (Barnard & Curry, 2011). Two chairs are used, representing two parts of the person that are in conflict, perhaps the intellect and the body or love and anger. Resolving conflicts involving anger, accompanied by emotions such as shame, grief, and sadness, seems especially therapeutic. The client spends time sitting in each chair and talking from the perspective represented by that chair.

Underlying this exercise is the Gestalt concept of the top dog and the underdog. Perls believed that "we constantly harass ourselves with . . . the top dog/underdog game where part of ourselves attempts to lecture, urge, and threaten the other part into 'good behavior'" (Fagan & Shepherd, 1970, p. 4). The top dog, a sort of superego or conscience, makes judgments and tells the underdog how it should feel, think, or act. The underdog tends to be meek and apologetic but does not really try to change. Although the top dog may seem more powerful, the underdog really has control by refusing to change or cooperate despite feelings of guilt. In addition to having both a top dog and an underdog within them, people may cast another person into the role of top dog while they assume the role of the guilty but ineffectual underdog. Some clients seek such a relationship with their therapists, creating a hierarchical and nonproductive relationship.

When the two-chair method is used to address an inner conflict or split, the dialogue generally begins with the top dog or dominant part of the person expressing strong criticism of the other part, which is likely to become defensive and vulnerable. As the dialogue continues, the therapist encourages the critic to become even harsher while prompting the underdog to express its pain and sadness. Recollections, misunderstandings, and previously unspoken and unacknowledged feelings may surface at this point. This, in turn, creates what Perls has described as an "ah-ha" experience: the shock of recognition in which the client gains new emotional awareness and understanding. The goal of this exercise is to avoid an impasse and enable the two parts to achieve resolution; the critic becomes more tolerant and accepting, while the underdog gains self-confidence and a direct means of self-expression. The client becomes more able to own and integrate both parts of the self.

The polarity of the top dog versus the underdog is one of the most well known of the Gestalt polarities. As the name suggests, the top dog polarity is the underlying need to be right, to be in charge, and to "one up" other people. At the opposite pole, the underdog is the inclination to be the victim, to act lazy, stupid, or passive, to avoid the responsibility of being the top dog. Although people swing between these two polarities, healthy individuals find balance, whereas unhealthy individuals cling to one of the polar extremes in an effort to avoid emotional pain. This is true with all of the polarities, whether connection/separation, strength/vulnerability, or others (Prochaska & Norcross, 2018). If people stay in the either/or mode of the polarities and fail to accept that they are also the opposite of what they pretend to be, they will not experience the entirety of life, the full Gestalt. The full Gestalt takes a both/and approach to life.

THE EMPTY CHAIR METHOD FOR ADDRESSING UNFINISHED BUSINESS Gestalt therapists believe that significant unmet needs do not fully recede from awareness, and they manifest as unfinished business (Polster & Polster, 1973). Using empty chair work, clients can encounter unfinished situations in their imagination, thus moving toward resolution of the unfinished business. The **empty chair** dialogue is a way of addressing and resolving those unclosed Gestalts. The empty chair might represent another person, a troubling and confusing part of clients' dreams or fantasies, or a physical symptom clients are experiencing, such as a headache.

Typically, clients visualize a person with whom they have unfinished business in the empty chair; however, they may also visualize a symptom or a part of a dream. They then express their thoughts and feelings to that person, in an effort to complete a process that had been interrupted. The goal of this experience is a resolution in which clients develop greater understanding and acceptance of the other person or issue, as well as growth in their own self-confidence.

Empty chair work assists in addressing past issues of neglect, abandonment, abuse, and/or trauma. Neglect or abandonment unfinished business often emerges in the context of current relationships and often symbolically relates to past unfinished business. The representation of the other in the chair serves an important function and helps clients to resolve their unfinished experience.

As an example, consider Sujata, a woman born in India, who had unfinished business with her father. Constantly trying to earn his approval, she proudly called him with each professional and academic achievement. His usual response was to ignore her information or ask when she was going to produce another grandchild for him. When she finally earned her doctorate after many years of hard work and received the same reply from her father, she became discouraged and devalued her accomplishments. Through an empty chair dialogue with her father, she came to understand the influence of his cultural background and the messages he had received from his parents. This led her to become more tolerant and accepting of his values while maintaining pride in her own accomplishments.

The Body as a Vehicle of Communication

Gestalt therapy seeks to give people a sense of wholeness, enabling them to access and be aware of their thoughts, emotions, and physical sensations. Many people have fairly good awareness of their thoughts and emotions. However, they ignore or cut themselves off from their bodily sensations. Consequently, Gestalt therapists pay particular attention to the messages of the body.

The following strategies are especially useful in focusing attention on the body:

- *Identification:* Therapists remain alert to bodily messages. If they notice that a part of a person's body is in a reactive state, such as fingers tapping on a table or a leg strenuously swinging, they call attention to the movements and ask about their message. A therapist might say, "I notice that your leg began swinging when we started to talk about your relationship with your sister. What is your leg saying?" or "Become your leg and give your leg a voice. What is your leg feeling?"
- *Locating emotions in the body:* Another strategy is helping people locate their emotions in the body so that they can more fully experience their feelings. A therapist might say, "You have told me that you feel rage toward your sister. Show me where you are experiencing this rage." Once the client locates the rage, perhaps in her stomach, the therapist can explore the client's physical sensations, enabling her to more fully connect with and express her feelings.
- *Repetition and exaggeration:* When they observe body movements or symptoms, therapists often encourage clients to repeat and exaggerate them. For example, a therapist might say, "I notice you are tapping your foot. I would like you to exaggerate the tapping, do it as hard as you can, and then talk about what feelings come up." The techniques of exaggeration or repetition also can be applied to a tone of voice or a meaningful phrase that the person uses. This intervention focuses attention on where energy is located and can succeed in releasing blocked awareness and energy.

Group Gestalt Therapy

Initially, Gestalt therapy usually took the form of individual therapy practiced in a group. Today, individual therapy is the primary mode of therapy, but use of this approach in a group setting offers many benefits. Gestalt therapy groups focus on both interpersonal dynamics and the dynamics of the group system. Feedback and support from both the therapist and the group members can accelerate the process of awareness and empowerment. Members also can learn vicariously from each other. Gestalt group therapists are very active and directive, and this directiveness can contribute to the intensity and power of the group experience for the participants. Gestalt groups heavily emphasize experience within the group with an eye toward interpersonal relations and group processes. Gestalt group work can also be applied in clinical group supervision (Gaffney, 2008). The use of Gestalt therapy in a group setting has led to the development of several useful techniques, such as the hot seat and making the rounds.

THE HOT SEAT Fritz Perls' work in Big Sur at the Esalen Institute emphasized the use of the **hot seat** in a group setting. This powerful technique brought him considerable attention, and it was widely adopted by encounter groups during the 1960s and 1970s. The hot seat is a chair placed in the middle of the group. Group members volunteer, one at a time, to spend 5 to 10 minutes in the hot seat, becoming the center of the group's attention. When people occupy the hot seat, they are encouraged to express and stay with their feelings, and if done right, this activity can invoke strong emotions. Feedback from the group on their body language and verbal messages promotes their awareness of themselves and their feelings.

MAKING THE ROUNDS When making the rounds, people in the hot seat speak to each member of the group, perhaps identifying something they want from each member of the group or something about a particular person that reminds them of themselves. Alternatively, group members might take turns giving people in the hot seat feedback, perhaps on their strengths, in an effort to empower them. Like many of the other experiments used in Gestalt therapy, this is a powerful technique likely to have an enduring impact on people.

APPLICATION AND CURRENT USE OF GESTALT THERAPY

Gestalt therapy is actively evolving through the work of many practitioners and at more than 60 Gestalt therapy institutes around the world. Current trends in Gestalt therapy integrate relational themes, a focus on emotion, attachment theory, and the use of experiments in a relational therapy. Clients might process topics of identity, trauma, childhood abuse, and other developmental bruises that may have shaped their early years (Finlay & Evans, 2009). The past two decades have witnessed a resurgence of interest in Gestalt therapy (Bowman, 2012). This may be attributed to the fact that Gestalt therapists have an increased awareness of the importance of the client–therapist relationship and have striven to establish a collaborative relationship with a focus on caring confrontations, rather than adopting the charismatic and powerful role modeled by Fritz Perls (Bowman).

Gestalt therapists help clients to understand the subjective interconnectedness of everything, while also encouraging them to take responsibility for their own feelings and actions. Any variety of topics, including ruptures in the therapeutic alliance, may initiate discussion that is beneficial to clients in the here and now of the therapy session. For example, the therapist and client might discuss the client's feelings of shame and guilt that resulted from her parent's overly strict socialization process, how that shame is erupting in her current relationship with her husband, what triggers it, and how it impacts the therapeutic relationship and therapy progress.

Gestalt therapy is flexible enough to be easily integrated with a broad range of other counseling approaches. The empty chair and two-chair dialogues of Gestalt therapy, as well as other strategies, have also been integrated into newer process-experiential therapies. For example, in two studies utilizing Gestalt therapy integrated with emotion-focused therapy, the two therapies were found to be effective when combined (Berdondini, Elliot, & Shearer, 2012; Muntigl, Chubak, & Angus, 2017). Furthermore, studies have examined the efficacy of Gestalt therapy combined with other entities for working with couples. This research has shown that Gestalt is effective, whether it would be used in resolving relationship trauma, used in combination with well-known trauma techniques (e.g., eye movement desensitization and reprocessing; Capps, 2006), or used simply to provide clients with opportunities for overall growth (Kennedy & Gordon, 2017). In addition, the Gestalt approach to dreamwork, as well as the use of role plays, continues to play a prominent role in Gestalt therapy.

Counseling Applications

Gestalt therapy's present orientation, as well as its use of powerful exercises, can quickly bring all aspects of an issue into awareness and encourage closure as well as growth. Used skillfully, and adapted to the needs of a particular client or group, the range of this approach is almost unlimited.

Gestalt therapy has been effectively used with women transitioning through divorce (Saadati & Lashani, 2013). Gestalt group therapy has also been helpful for people in the prison system (Doric, 2017). Because of its emphasis on living life to its fullest in the present, this therapy is likely to help people who are dealing with issues of loss, grief, and/or death and dying (Roubal, 2016). In addition, Gestalt therapy has benefited people with both chronic pain and depression (Ellegaard & Pedersen, 2012), with this population experiencing an increase in their ability to take responsibility for themselves, a reduction in stress and muscle tension, and a gain in self-worth.

Case studies in the literature show Gestalt therapy being adapted for use with a wide range of problems that impact emotion regulation, including sexual trauma, narcissistic self-hatred, shame, and aggression (Bloom & Brownell, 2011). Case studies have also shown Gestalt therapy to be helpful in supporting those who have bipolar disorder (Dominitz, 2017) or other mental disorders such as anorexia nervosa (Munro, Randell, & Lawrie, 2016), bulimia nervosa (Angermann, 1998), substance use disorders (Dominitz, 2017), and schizophrenia (Arnfred, 2012), and it may show benefit for people who channel emotional concerns into their bodies (Munro, Randell, & Lawrie, 2016). Several meta-analytical analyses of Gestalt effectiveness studies found evidence supporting the use of Gestalt therapy in the treatment of affective disorders, personality disorders, and substance use disorders (Dominitz, 2017; van Rijn & Wild, 2013). In addition, recent research suggests that techniques derived from Gestalt therapy are an essential component in effective trauma treatments and that eliciting emotion can cause lasting change (Lenz & Lancaster, 2017).

In addition, therapists who work with children and adolescents may find Gestalt play therapy to be helpful (see Oaklander, 1994, 1997). This play therapy provides a highly experiential, existential "here-and-now" philosophy that can work well with children (Blom, 2006). Gestalt therapy has also been used with young children who are vulnerable from a preverbal trauma (Ferreira, Eloff, Kukard, & Kriegler, 2014) and with couples struggling with relationship satisfaction and intimacy (Kennedy & Gordon, 2017).

Application to Multicultural Groups

Because Gestalt therapists view people holistically, it is by definition an approach that can be useful with diverse populations. Gestalt therapists believe that people cannot be understood in isolation, but only within the broader perspective of their historical and social backgrounds. Thus, Gestalt therapy innately attends to cultural differences and sociocultural and historical contexts. In addition, experiencing beyond words is suitable for cultures in which nonverbal communication has great meaning.

Gestalt therapy may also be suitable for those who feel disempowered and are struggling to find their voice. Some people from various cultural groups who have experienced discrimination and oppression may benefit from Gestalt therapy. In the same vein, Gestalt therapy and a few of its respected techniques (e.g., two-chair technique) might help individuals dealing with gender-related issues and the subsequent issues that follow, such as a lack of self-compassion, feelings of powerlessness, and complicated emotions (Barnard & Curry, 2011). Dealing with disempowerment and a lack of self-compassion may work with Gestalt therapy because the roots of this approach lie in truly understanding who people are as individuals and in helping them develop better relationships with others as well as with themselves.

When working with people from a variety of cultures, therapists must take care to select culturally appropriate interventions that respect non–Western European communication styles. Traditional Asian or Native American clients may view direct and confrontational forms of therapy such as Gestalt to be lacking in respect and sensitivity (Sue, Sue, Neville, & Smith, 2019). Similarly, clients from cultures that value restraint of strong emotions, unassertiveness, or filial piety (i.e., a virtue of respect for one's parents, elders, and ancestors), as do many Asian cultures, may feel uncomfortable or intimidated if therapists use role plays, behavioral rehearsal, or the Gestalt empty chair technique (Sue et al.). Rather than taking a universal perspective or a one-size-fits-all approach, therapists should show respect for clients' cultural background and adapt their techniques, interventions, energy level, and tone of voice to match those of the clients (Sue et al.). Recognizing when Gestalt techniques such as the empty chair or the hot seat should not be used is as important as knowing when to use them.

For example, when working with Asian American clients, using the empty chair technique can be appropriate if the client is struggling to have a conversation with parents about moving out of the family home to be independent and suppressing one's own desires and wishes as an expression of respect and sensitivity to older authoritative figures. In comparison, the empty chair technique may not be suitable for the same client with a higher level of psychological distress when exploring and confronting feelings arising from a traumatic incident such as a history of childhood sexual trauma, causing a strong emotional reaction that is unproductive and harmful.

EVALUATION OF GESTALT THERAPY

Like other counseling approaches, Gestalt therapy has both strengths and limitations. Because of its powerful nature, therapists need to be particularly aware of its limitations and appropriate use.

Limitations

Gestalt techniques are not for everybody. Gestalt therapy techniques that are confrontive may have limited applicability with people who have severe cognitive disorders or impulse control disorders—acting out, delinquency, and explosive disorders—or with people who have sociopathic or psychotic symptoms (Kress & Paylo, 2019). Gestalt techniques may even cause harm if not used carefully (Wagner-Moore, 2004). Other criticisms of the therapy are that it focuses too much on felt bodily sensations and not enough on cognitions, and that getting in touch with internal polarities to relieve emotional problems sounds too much like blaming the victim. Due to its emphasis on self-regulation, people who come from collectivist cultural backgrounds and those who are uncomfortable putting themselves first may have difficulty with the "I-ness" instead of "we-ness" of Gestalt therapy (Prochaska & Norcross, 2018, p. 197).

Gestalt therapy may oversimplify people's problems and neglect important past concerns. A focus on immediacy to the exclusion of the past may contribute to clients feeling unheard (Kasper, Hill, & Kivlighan, 2008). Gestalt therapy also runs the risk of overemphasizing emotions and ignoring cognitions, which most therapists now view as important determinants of emotions and vehicles for modifying feelings.

Just as this approach has the power to do good, it also has the power to do harm. Gestalt therapy tends to evoke strong emotional reactions, and for some clients, these reactions may be unwanted. Its strategies are appealing and may seem deceptively simple, but in reality they require a skilled and experienced therapist who can determine their appropriate use, guide people through the therapy process, and protect them. This is more likely to happen if therapists do not take on the powerful role embodied by Fritz Perls but, instead, temper that role with support, education, exploration of cognitions, and recognition of the importance of culture and background (Stoehr, 2009). In addition, combining Gestalt strategies with those from other approaches, including process-experiential and cognitive behavioral therapy, reduces the risk of overemphasizing emotions and creates a more supportive therapy environment.

Strengths and Contributions

Despite these limitations, Gestalt therapy has many strengths. Studies on the impact of the empty chair and two-chair experiences have been particularly positive. In one study, when compared to empathic responses, the two-chair technique resulted in greater depth of experience and greater awareness than the use of empathic techniques (Pugh, 2016). The two-chair technique has also been empirically validated for reducing marital conflict, indecision, conflict splits, and other interpersonal difficulties (Strumpfel & Martin, 2004; Wagner-Moore, 2004). Gestalt therapy in general has also shown effectiveness for a wide variety of populations.

The flexibility of Gestalt therapy is one of its strengths, making it naturally integrative. It has been successfully combined with other approaches, including cognitive behavioral therapy, person-centered therapy, mindfulness meditation, and brief therapy.

Gestalt therapy is a philosophy of life, growth, and change and also provides specific ways to help the individual realize that growth. It respects the individual and adapts counseling to the needs of each person. Its emphasis on process and the client–therapist relationship is consistent with current understandings of how counseling effects change. Gestalt therapy is a compassionate approach that can empower people and enable them to have more joy and fulfillment in their lives.

Gestalt therapy has made many contributions to counseling and an understanding of the therapeutic change process. The concepts of field theory, and of immediacy and wholeness, and the importance of mind–body integration are particularly important and have been assimilated into other theoretical systems (Woldt & Toman, 2005). Similarly, many innovative strategies, including the empty chair, the emphasis on nonverbal messages, Perls' approach to processing dreams, and "I" statements, have achieved wide acceptance. Chair work has been so well accepted that many forget its Gestalt origins. The Gestalt approach to dreamwork has become an often-used and powerful alternative to psychoanalytic dream interpretation. In addition, the work of Gestalt therapists, along with that of the person-centered and existential theorists, established the importance of phenomenological, experiential, and humanistic approaches to counseling as well as the realization that the therapeutic alliance is probably the most important element in successful therapy.

This Gestalt philosophy transcends cultural boundaries and understands the contextualization of human experience (Polster, 2012). Perls' ideas are consistent with modern ways of thinking about cultural, political, and religious absolutes in that the relative nature of realty is taken into consideration.

SKILL DEVELOPMENT: GESTALT CHAIR WORK

Gestalt therapy uses various experiential exercises to help clients re-experience (rather than retell) emotionally charged incidents in the here and now of the therapy session. The most effective experiments are those that arise spontaneously in the therapy session as a result of clients' needs in that given moment. Chair work is one of the most effective and frequently used experiments or techniques in Gestalt therapy, developed by Fritz Perls to help people overcome blockages in awareness and work through unfinished business. Rather than intellectualizing or talking about their problems, in Gestalt therapy, clients are asked to re-experience the feelings in the here and now of the therapy session.

Clients easily learn the steps in this exercise, and are supported in their emotions and encouraged by their therapists. Two-chair work includes the following steps (Houston, 2003):

1. Ask if the client wants to participate in chair work.
2. Repeat the names of the two polarities that will be the focus of the work.
3. Ask which polarity is more present in the chair where the client is seated.
4. Encourage the client to make statements from the vantage point of one polarity to the other chair.
5. When the client is ready, suggest that the client move to the second chair and assume that polarity.
6. Remind the client of the statements made from the other seat. Ask for feelings and a response.
7. Continue to suggest that the client move back and forth between the two seats, as appropriate.

8. If the dialogue seems stuck, ask the client what is needed from the other polarity. Consider whether there is movement toward change.
9. If not, consider that for the moment, the client has decided to retain the same feelings.
10. If change does occur, continue the two-chair dialogue until the client has integrated the new insight and feelings.

Example

A 37-year-old woman has come to counseling because she is having difficulty accepting responsibility for her failed marriage. She has been experiencing some anger and begins to recognize that she might have some unfinished business left over from childhood.

CLIENT: I think I'm angry at my mother. It's silly because my mother died before my marriage fell apart, so what could I be mad at her for?

THERAPIST: Would you like to explore that using the empty chair?

CLIENT: Sure, I guess so.

THERAPIST: So, you will be exploring the anger that you never expressed to your mother before she died. Which position feels more real for you where you are seated?

CLIENT: Me. Me and my anger.

THERAPIST: Okay. Now, imagine that your mother is sitting in the other chair. What would you like to tell her?

CLIENT: Mom, I am so mad at you for the way you always coddled Mark [her older brother]. You always yelled at me. I always got in trouble. Even when he did something wrong, you punished *me* for his bad behavior. It was so unfair.

THERAPIST: Okay. Stay with that feeling. . . .

CLIENT: (raising her voice) I just can't get past how unfair it was. Now that he's an adult he has this sense of entitlement. He doesn't work, and Dad has to support him. It just really makes me mad. You did both of us a disservice. It's not fair. Now that my husband is gone, I need support, too. And where are you? Where is any help for me?

THERAPIST: Would you like to change chairs and respond from your mother's perspective? Your daughter is very angry at you.

CLIENT (CHANGES CHAIRS): I know. Honey, I'm sorry you're hurt and upset, but your brother was always so needy. It took him longer to do things, and you know how socially inept he was. I don't believe that I ever punished you for your brother's bad behavior. . . .

THERAPIST: Switch chairs. Do you have a response to your mother?

CLIENT: I sure do! Of course you knew! You made me hold his hand and walk around the yard smiling as if we were best friends! I was so embarrassed when the neighbors saw us. What were you thinking?

THERAPIST: Can you keep going with that?

CLIENT: (CHANGES CHAIRS; THINKS FOR A MOMENT FROM HER MOTHER'S PERSPECTIVE, THEN RESPONDS THOUGHTFULLY): Maybe I hoped you would be a good influence on him; you were always so friendly and active. You were the cheerleader, the good student, the good daughter. I never had any problems with you. I hoped you would somehow influence your brother in a positive way.

CLIENT (CHANGES BACK TO HER OWN CHAIR):
Oh, I never thought of that before. I never looked at it from my mother's perspective.

THERAPIST: Stay in the role.

CLIENT (BEGINS TO CRY SOFTLY):
I never realized how difficult it was for you, Mom. You had to raise us and Dad was always working, then it seems as soon as I went to college you got sick, and I never had a chance to know you as an adult. We never had time to have these conversations.

THERAPIST (GENTLY):
It sounds like you're feeling very sad.

CLIENT: It never occurred to me that my mother was frustrated, too.

THERAPIST: What's it like for you to see your mother's frustration?

CLIENT: It's like she's human. She had her issues, too, and as a mother I think she tried to do the best that she could. I just wish she hadn't died so young. I would really like to talk to her.

This example illustrates how the two-chair technique can quickly stir up emotionally laden content. Therapists should remember to use caution with this technique and to avoid using the two-chair technique with populations for which it is not recommended.

CASE APPLICATION

The following dialogue illustrates use of the two-chair technique with Roberto to address a split within him. This is one of the most powerful and widely used of the Gestalt strategies.

THERAPIST: Roberto, you have talked about feeling like there is a split within you between your tough side and your caring side and how hard it is for you to express that caring side. I have set up two chairs here, one to represent your tough side and one to represent your caring side. I would like you to role-play each side of you while sitting in the chair that represents that side.

ROBERTO: All right. I'll start out with the tough side. That's the easy one. I was the biggest bully on the block.

THERAPIST: Would you talk in the present?

ROBERTO: Okay. I am the biggest bully on the block. No one messes with me. I have quite a reputation. My father is proud that I can take care of myself. I protect the younger kids.

THERAPIST: Now change seats.

ROBERTO: Well, here I am, in the caring seat. I'm not sure what to say. I do care deeply about my family, Edie and Ava. I make sure they are safe, that we have enough money, that Ava goes to a good school. But they say that's not enough. I feel invisible. No one seems to see me and all that I do.

THERAPIST: What do you look like?

ROBERTO: I am small and weak.

THERAPIST: Continue to be the caring side and talk to the tough side in the empty chair.

ROBERTO: I feel overshadowed by you. I try to let people know I'm here, but you're all they notice. I feel powerless and helpless.

THERAPIST: Now change chairs and have the tough side talk to the caring side.

ROBERTO: I know you're there, but I want to keep you hidden. What will it do to my reputation if people see you? They won't think I'm the tough guy anymore. You're not worth much to me.

THERAPIST: Change chairs and continue the conversation.

ROBERTO: Yes, I know your tough reputation is important to you. But I'm important, too. Without me, you don't get along very well with people. Edie gets mad at you, and Ava goes off and cries. You need me even if you don't know it. I don't want to be as big as you, but maybe you could let me grow a little bigger.

THERAPIST: How could the caring side grow?

ROBERTO: It . . . I could exercise. That's how the tough side got so big. Practice. If I could just keep the tough guy from sitting on me every time I try to show my face. . . .

THERAPIST: Can you tell him that?

ROBERTO: Yeah. Hey, tough guy, how about giving me a little space? I won't take over your turf. You don't have to be afraid of me ruining your reputation. I have respect for you. You worked hard to get where you are. Can you give a little guy a chance?

THERAPIST: Change chairs again and respond.

ROBERTO: Yeah, I guess I could do that. As long as we agree that I run the show, I'm in charge . . . at least for now.

Roberto has a top dog and an underdog as well as a split within himself. His tough side has served him well, and he identifies strongly with that aspect of his personality; but he has nearly cut himself off from his caring side. This dialogue increased his awareness of these two sides of himself and the negative impact the neglect of his caring side has on his life. Although Roberto is still apprehensive about revealing his caring side, he has moved toward integrating the two sides and allowing them to coexist. He also has begun to recognize that he does not need to choose between the two.

REFLECT AND RESPOND

The individual exercises in this chapter are especially challenging. If you want to engage in these exercises but have difficulty doing so, you might seek help from your professor, a therapist, or someone else you trust.

1. Spend a day observing your own body language, your eye contact, the way you sit, the way you use your hands, and any other body movements you display. What messages do they seem to give? What can you learn about yourself from your body language? What incongruities

did you notice between your verbal and your nonverbal messages? Think about whether your body language reflects any internal splits or disowned parts of yourself. Write about this in your journal.
2. Conduct an experiment with yourself using the top dog/underdog technique. Sit quietly in a room with two empty chairs and think for a moment about a situation in the past week in which you struggled with yourself. Perhaps you procrastinated on a homework assignment, or were rude to your friend. Voice the dialogue of the top dog as he justifies his actions. Now, move to the second chair and respond from the underdog position. Pay attention to how you talk to your "two selves." Notice any judgments in how you talk to yourself. Instead of being judgmental, try to compassionately defend yourself. Write down in your journal what you noticed, how it felt to be superior and "right," on the one hand, and what it felt like to be judged, on the other hand. What price do you pay for listening to the judgmental self? Write some ideas about how you can be less critical and more compassionate in your self-talk. What did you learn about yourself from this exercise?
3. Think about a criticism you recently made of someone else. Turn the statement around so that you apply it to yourself. For example, instead of saying, "My friend is an irresponsible person," say "I am an irresponsible person." Think about whether the new statement has any truth to it. Write about this in your journal.

Summary

Fritz Perls and Laura Perls, developed Gestalt therapy in the 1950s. Gestalt therapy is a humanistic and phenomenological approach that pays particular attention to in-the-moment emotions and sensations. The concept of Gestalt implies that patterns and wholes are important to people, opposed to the collection of parts. To achieve wholeness and integration, it is essential for clients to understand and integrate their polarities. Gestalt therapists believe that people have a natural drive toward integration, homeostasis, and self-actualization. However, people sometimes deny or become alienated from parts of themselves and/or their experience within the world. A lack of awareness and integration of disowned aspects of the self can lead to fragmentation, an overload of unfinished business (i.e., matters that need to be addressed, integrated, and resolved), and what Perls termed growth stagnation.

Gestalt therapy is an active approach that emphasizes the importance of a trusting, collaborative relationship between clients and therapists. The security of the therapeutic relationship enables people to engage in growth-promoting experiments developed by the therapist to meet the individual needs of clients. Techniques such as dreamwork, the hot seat, the empty chair, the two-chair technique, the fantasy trip, the use of "I" statements, a focus on "what" and "how," and attention to nonverbal communication all help people achieve the goals of Gestalt therapy, which include awareness, integration, and actualization. Gestalt therapy emphasizes the here and now, which helps individuals live in the present and become integrated with themselves and the emotions that are attached to the past. One key element of Gestalt therapy is avoiding the intellectual analysis of clients' situations; instead, experiential, in-the-moment awareness is what is important. Experiential awareness helps clients to develop a sense of responsibility for themselves, their experiences, and their actions.

Gestalt therapy is highly individualized, and its applications will differ with every client. As such, it is flexible and useful with a wide variety of clients and settings. Gestalt therapy is an active approach in that it empowers individuals to increase their awareness and take responsibility for their experiences and it consistently provides opportunities to promote change within counseling sessions.

Recommended Readings

Buber, M. (1970). *I and thou*. New York, NY: Scribner.

Harris, T. A. (1969). *I'm OK—You're OK*. New York, NY: HarperCollins.

Levine, T. B. (2012). *Gestalt therapy: Advances in theory and practice*. New York, NY: Routledge.

Oaklander, V. (2018). *Hidden treasure: A map to the child's inner self*. New York, NY: Routledge.

Parlett, M., & Hemming, J. (1996). Developments in gestalt therapy. In W. Dryden (Ed.)., *Developments in psychotherapy: Historical perspectives* (pp. 91–110). Thousand Oaks, CA: Sage.

Perls, F. (1992a). *Gestalt therapy verbatim*. Gouldsboro, ME: The Gestalt Journal Press.

Perls, F. (1992b). *In and out of the garbage pail*. Gouldsboro, ME: The Gestalt Journal Press.

Philippson, P. (2009). *The emergent self: An existential-Gestalt approach*. London, UK: Karnac Books.

Polster, E., & Polster, M. (1993). Fritz Perls: Legacy and invitation. *Gestalt Journal, 16*(2), 23–25.

Woldt, A. L., & Toman, S. M. (Eds.). (2005). *Gestalt therapy: History, theory, and practice*. Thousand Oaks, CA: Sage.

MyLab Counseling

Try the Topic 7 Assignments: Gestalt Therapy.

CHAPTER

12 Feminist Therapy

With Jessica A. Headley and Katherine A. Feather

Learning Outcomes

When you have finished this chapter, you should be able to:
- Understand the context and development of Feminist Therapy.
- Communicate the key concepts associated with Feminist Therapy and understand how they relate to therapeutic processes.
- Describe the therapeutic goals of Feminist Therapy.
- Identify the common techniques used in Feminist Therapy.
- Understand how Feminist Therapy relates to counseling diverse populations.
- Identify the limitations and strengths of Feminist Therapy.

Without doubt, our culture and the environment in which we live greatly impact the human experience. The fourth force in counseling and psychotherapy theories places an emphasis on context, culture, and the idea that all of reality is constructed in the contexts and environments in which we live; these factors are believed to be the most important in influencing clients' experiences, and the solutions to clients' problems are believed to lie in changes in these arenas.

The theories discussed in this section include feminist therapy, postmodern theories with a focus on solution-focused brief therapy and narrative therapy, and family therapies. A number of additional theories have been associated with the fourth force, including transpersonal psychology (i.e., theories that focus on spirituality as this is related to culture) and multicultural theories (i.e., theories that focus on the role that culture plays in helping others).

INTRODUCTION TO THE FOURTH FORCE IN COUNSELING AND PSYCHOTHERAPY: CULTURE, CONTEXT, AND CONSTRUCTIVISM

As with the previously discussed forces, the fourth force in psychotherapy was greatly influenced by the social and cultural influences of the day. During the postmodern era, which began around the second half of the 20th century, the importance of the social and moral contexts of people was growing in popularity (Peteet, 2018). People became increasingly more concerned with seeing others as whole people with many different contextual factors (e.g., ethnicity, spirituality, gender) and stories that contribute to their well-being. Because of this emphasis on context, scientific inquiries and evidence-based treatments became less important, and an understanding of clients' culture, context, and unique perspectives on their experiences became more important. People also became less focused on psychopathology and more concerned with promoting overall well-being and a focus on personal growth (Peteet, 2018).

The postmodern era also greatly contributed to the development of the fourth force in psychotherapy. Postmodern thinking has permeated all aspects of culture from philosophy to art (Grenz, 1996). The postmodern era emphasized how knowing is constructed; the significance of culture, environmental, and social influences on the human experience; and the importance of realities as being socially constructed, or the idea that there is no reality and all things are relative to people's contextual experiences. Postmodern concepts such as a focus on social connections and relationships as constructing reality and the emphasis on unique experiences of reality are cornerstones of postmodern thinking (Gergen, 1991). The postmodernism movement also believes that language influences knowledge through social construction, which is when individuals give their own meaning to experiences.

The development of the fourth force in psychotherapy can also be seen as a result of poststructuralism (Grenz, 1996). This is a philosophical movement that holds the belief that there is no objective experience when reading literature and no inherent meaning in texts; instead, people give their own meaning to what they read. The language in the text is particularly relevant for influencing people's meaning of what they read.

In summary, the fourth force was rooted in a value of relativism over absolute truth; the social construction of experience; and a focus on social, cultural, and political influences. All of these factors influenced the development of the three theories discussed in this section of the text: feminist therapy, postmodern therapies, and family systems therapies.

LAURA S. BROWN (b. 1952)

Laura Brown is one of the founders of the Feminist Therapy Institute, an organization committed to the advancement of feminist therapy practice and standards, and she is regarded as one of the innovative forces in the development of feminist therapy. She has contributed over 150 scholarly writings, with the bulk of her work in the field of feminist therapy where she writes about the fundamentals of this approach. Her book *Subversive Dialogues: Theory in Feminist Practice* (1994, 2005) describes helpful approaches and techniques that can be used by feminist therapists and is considered by many to be the foundational book that addresses the actual practice of feminist therapy. Brown continues to be a visionary in feminist therapy, especially relating to feminist therapy interventions and clinical strategies. Brown has also done work on the application of feminist therapy to trauma survivors and forensic feminist psychology.

JEAN BAKER MILLER (1927–2006)

Jean Baker Miller worked as a clinical professor of psychiatry at Boston University School of Medicine, and the director of the Jean Baker Miller Training Institute at the Stone Center, Wellesley College. She maintained that at the hands of men, psychoanalytic theory had gone off course. Through her work, she illuminated the power dynamics between males and females and questioned how power relations were used within psychoanalysis. Miller collaborated with colleagues and scholars in the development of relational-cultural theory, an approach that challenged prevailing psychoanalytic ideas, and instead focused on mental health, growth, and wellness. Her innovative book *Toward a New Psychology of Women* (Miller, 1976, 1986) sketched the relationship between women's mental health and sociopolitical factors. Other popular books by Miller included *The Healing Connection: How Women Form Relationships in Therapy and in Life* (Miller & Stiver, 1997) and *Women's Growth in Connection* (Jordan, Kaplan, Miller, Stiver, & Surrey, 1991). In the 1970s, her ground-breaking ideas awakened women's involvement in the feminist movement and reframed women's abilities. Miller raised consciousness about how being members of the dominant and subordinate groups impacts personality development. She also promoted the idea that women's capacity to nurture does not make them inferior; instead, this can be an asset and necessary for the psychological growth of self and others. She explored new applications to multifaceted issues such as diversity, **social action**, human health, and cultural well-being.

CAROLYN ZERBE ENNS (b. 1951)

Carolyn Zerbe Enns, a psychology professor at Cornell College in Iowa, focuses on viewing clinical practice through a feminist lens, with an eye to the therapeutic relationship and therapeutic goals. In her major contribution to the field, *Feminist Theories and Feminist Psychotherapies*, Enns (1997, 2004) systematically united feminist philosophy and feminist therapy and offered a classification of types of **feminism** that have helped to illuminate ways of approaching feminist therapy. Enns also concentrates on multicultural feminist therapy and the application of feminist therapy across the world. She is an advocate of self-analysis of feminism.

Cornell College, Emerita Professor of Psychology

INTRODUCTION/DEVELOPMENT OF FEMINIST THERAPY

Feminist therapy is a multicultural counseling approach that has historically centered on the ways in which gender roles, gender socialization, and lack of power and privilege due to minority status in a patriarchal society impact the psychological well-being and wellness of women in their everyday lives. Today, feminist therapy attends to the constantly evolving role of sociopolitical and cultural contexts as a contributor to experienced distress not only among women but also other social groups without power in society (e.g., persons of color, children), as well as populations that have power in society (e.g., men). In the therapeutic context, feminist therapists, who include both diverse women and men, mutually collaborate with clients to examine clients' experiences of disempowerment in relationships with themselves, others, and/or the broader society. Feminist therapists use individualized, strength-based strategies to promote clients' sense of personal **empowerment**. Within the community, feminist therapists serve in various leadership roles as researchers, program directors, volunteers, and movement organizers to address injustices using a feminist lens, such as intimate partner violence, human trafficking, poverty, rape, and child abuse and neglect. Across all contexts, feminist therapists aim to create a more just world wherein all individuals across the globe can equally benefit from, and take responsibility for, shared **power**.

Feminist therapy, initially rooted in the humanistic therapies, strongly emerged as a separate form of psychotherapy during the 1960s women's movement (Brown, 2010). Feminist therapists' involvement in, and response to, **consciousness-raising** groups of the time (i.e., leaderless groups wherein women gave voice to their everyday experiences) created a context to (1) raise awareness of the biases in the helping professions that contributed to unsupportive contexts for women and, in many instances, psychological harm and (2) take steps to transform mental health practice to promote women's psychological health and well-being. Brown (2010) identified three foundational works that highlighted the ways women were negatively perceived and harmed through "scientific" psychological research:

- The book *Women and Madness* by Phyllis Chesler (1972) included descriptive examples of sexism in psychotherapy and proposed radical changes within the mental health system to address patriarchal practices such as the pathologizing of women for nonconformity to prescribed gender-role stereotypes and the therapist as expert role.
- The essay "Kinder, Küche, Kirche as Scientific Law: Psychology Constructs the Female," by Naomi Weisstein (1968), served as a critique of the role of psychological science in drawing conclusions about women's lives that were not rooted in their real experiences due to excluding them as a data source. The beginning phrase of the essay exemplified Nazi ideology rooted in bias about women's roles in society – that they should be restricted to three areas of life: children ("Kinder"), kitchen ("Küche"), and church ("Kirche").
- The journal article "Sex Role Stereotypes and Clinical Judgement of Mental Health," by Broverman, Broverman, Clarkson, Rosenkrantz, and Vobel (1970), empirically demonstrated that mental health professionals held biases toward women, viewing them as having less desirable attributes in comparison to men that were synonymous with being less adult-like.

Taken together, these scholarly works were influenced by feminist thinking that contributed to early "waves" of feminism in U.S. culture, and, in turn, these works contributed to the evolution of subsequent waves. An understanding of these phases is an essential aspect of becoming and developing as a feminist therapist, and a brief overview of these feminist waves will be discussed here. The waves of feminism capture how the philosophy and priorities of the feminist movement have shifted over time. It is important to note that not every period has a distinct time frame and that a great deal of overlap and even debate exists regarding the underpinning values, categories, and ideas that shape the second, third, and fourth waves of feminism.

It is difficult to determine an exact moment when the feminist movement began, but feminist scholars pinpoint women's suffrage throughout the United States and Europe during the 19th and early 20th centuries as the start of the first wave of feminism. The movement emerged from an environment of urban industrialism and liberal, socialist politics. Feminists focused on achieving political equality for women, such as the right to vote, equal opportunities to education and employment, the right to own property, and reproductive freedoms (Dicker, 2008). After passage of the 19th Amendment granting women the right to vote, the movement as a whole began to dissolve, as women no longer had a unified goal. Women of color were a part of the first wave and were dedicated to women's suffrage, as well as universal suffrage (Kroløkke & Sørenson, 2006). However, the movement revolved around White, middle class, cisgender women, and after the parliamentary achievement of the 19th Amendment, it remained difficult for women of color to vote, specifically in the South. Noteworthy legislation during the first wave of feminism included:

- The Married Women's Property Act of 1839 allowed married women the right to own, but not control, property in their name.
- In 1886, all but six states in the United States permitted divorce on the grounds of cruelty.
- Almost all states in the United States had passed some form of sole trader laws, property laws, and earning laws (1895), granting married women the legal right to trade without their husbands' permission, own their own property, and govern their own money, respectively.

The second wave of feminism emerged during the early 1960s and continued into the late 1980s. The cultural momentum at that time centered on the anti-war and civil rights movements. The voices of the second wave of feminism focused on issues such as reproductive rights, social equality regardless of gender, equal pay for women and men, raising awareness of intimate partner and sexual violence, and differentiating between sex and gender (Gray & Boddy, 2010). Further, feminists critiqued **patriarchy**, capitalism, and the rigid ascription of gender roles to women (i.e., wife, mother) and actually named the systemic oppression ingrained in society that women were facing: sexism. During this phase, feminists formed consciousness-raising spaces, established women-only organizations (e.g., National Organization for Women), and coined the phrase *the personal is political* (Kroløkke & Sørenson, 2006). The second wave sought sisterhood and solidarity, pulling in women of color and women from developing nations with the goals of increasing Western feminists' awareness of the oppression experienced by Third World women and of organizing global action. However, many women of color found themselves alienated from the mainstream women's movement and wanted to combat other forms of oppression. Notable legal and social victories during the second wave included:

- The Equal Pay Act of 1963 abolished wage discrepancies based on gender.
- The Civil Rights Act of 1964 banned discrimination based on race, color, religion, gender, or national origin.
- The Washington D.C. Rape Crisis Center forms in 1972 and serves as the first model for future centers.
- The *Roe v. Wade* case of 1973 protected, under the 14th Amendment, women's constitutional right to a safe and legal abortion.

Not much consensus exists on what constitutes the third wave, but most cite it as beginning in the early 1990s and continuing into the fourth wave. The third wave was informed by postmodern thinking—that is, it questioned and redefined what it meant to be a feminist. The term **intersectionality**, the recognition of multiple and interlocking layers of oppression, emerged during this phase (Carastathis, 2016). The third wave focused on abolishing gender norms and stereotypes, challenging the rape culture that has persisted, reclaiming derogatory words, and addressing workplace concerns (e.g., glass ceiling, maternity leave policies; Kroløkke & Sørenson, 2006). Significant events during the third wave included:

- In the "Year of Women" (1992), four female senators were elected, joining two women already holding seats to the U.S. Senate.
- The Violence Against Women Act of 1994 provided $1.6 billion toward investigating intimate partner violence (e.g., domestic violence, dating violence, sexual assault, and stalking) and prosecuting violent crimes against women.
- Nancy Pelosi becomes the first woman Speaker of the House in the U.S. Congress in 2007.

The cultural momentum of hashtag activism (e.g., #MeToo) and the Time's Up movement, the Women's March on Washington, and the record number of women running for office signify the shift from the third to the fourth wave of feminism (Cochrane, 2013). The fourth wave places a greater emphasis on the digitally driven role of social media in advocacy (Munro, 2013). This phase also supports the "call out" culture, which allows for oppressed individuals to use social media as a means to raise awareness about injustice in broader audiences. Social media has made it easier than ever to criticize the systems of power that feminist therapists believe traditionally marginalize groups of people. The agenda of the fourth wave includes a more expansive understanding of intersectionality and equality, body image positivity, challenging "isms" (e.g., sexism, racism, ageism, heterosexism, and ableism), and social justice. The wave is the most inclusive to date, focusing on diversity and including *all* individuals. Movements and initiatives that have evolved and grown during the fourth wave include:

- The White House Task Force to Protect Students from Sexual Assault, formed in 2014, increased awareness of sexual assault on college campuses and strengthened compliance and resources to respond to campus rape and sexual assault.
- #MeToo, starting in 2017, was a movement on social media that attempted to reveal the widespread pervasiveness of sexual harassment and sexual assault
- The Women's March, on January 21, 2017, was the largest worldwide, single-day demonstration in U.S. history, which challenged what the participants perceived to be an anti-woman position taken by the incoming president.

Through the waves of feminism, numerous branches of feminist thought have emerged. Each shade of feminism established its own goals, strategies, and affiliations. Some feminist ideologies overlap, and feminists may identify with more than one type. Table 12.1 presents the main positions of feminism and brief descriptions of each.

TABLE 12.1 Different Positions Within Feminism

Ideology	Brief Description
Liberal/reformist feminism	Seeks to equalize power (i.e., rights, treatment, and opportunities) between women and men and promotes freedom of personal and political autonomy. Focuses on eliminating political, legal, and other forms of discrimination against women to allow them opportunities similar to those men have. Lobbies women-friendly legislation through affirmative action and antidiscrimination campaigns.
Cultural feminism	Recognizes that women's values and attributes are superior, but undervalued, in society and seeks to reclaim, as well as celebrate, women's roles. Emphasizes the distinctive gender differences and highlights that the *essence* of women or attributes of women (e.g., being caring, kind, cooperative, egalitarian) could restore societal decay. Cultural feminists debate, among themselves, the essential nature of women as either biological (nature) or persistently ingrained by culture.
Radical feminism	Views society as being deeply patriarchal, one in which men dominate and oppress women. Promotes uprooting and reconstructing the male-dominated capitalist hierarchy within society and believes women can be themselves once they have eliminated the inherently oppressive and controlled patriarchal systems. Further, they believe society cannot be reformed if male-based authority and power structures are in place.
Socialist feminism	Focuses on the intersection of patriarchy and institutionalized oppression, especially within economic injustices, gender roles, and cultural contexts (i.e., within the workplace and domestic spheres). For example, women are exploited in a patriarchal system that devalues women and the substantial work they may do (e.g., child care).
Postmodern feminism	Moves away from absolute assertions of what a feminist "should be" and instead focuses on the lived experiences of all: the multiple truths, multiple realities, and multiples roles one embraces. Rejects the notion that identity and gender are a product of biology (nature) but instead are fluid and unstable.
Women of color (womanists) feminism	Emerged as a reaction to the early feminist movement which was predominantly about a White, middle-class, cisgender discourse; early leaders rarely included women of color. The early movement also did not emphasize oppression such as racism and classism. Womanists focus on intersectionality, diversity among women, the social construction of gender, and structures of domination.
Lesbian feminism	Believes heterosexuality encompasses more than sexual desire, familial structure, and traditional gendered roles—it is actually a form of supporting male supremacy and domination over women. Examines conventional sexual identities and gender roles as social institutions grounded in patriarchy and capitalism. Uses lesbian identity as a platform for community building and collective activism.
Postcolonial feminism	Addresses unique and complex experiences of non-White, non-Western women. Centers on racism, ethnic issues, and the long-lasting economic, political, and cultural impact of colonialism (i.e., the policy or practice of acquiring full or partial political control over another country, occupying it with settlers, and exploiting it economically). Recognizes parallels between decolonized nations and the state of men within patriarchy—the relationship of the marginalized group to the dominant culture.

The various positions within feminism have contributed to societal shifts that impact the lives of individuals, couples, and families within a patriarchal cultural context. Some notable feminist scholars and therapists who have been part of the progress, and part of overcoming setbacks and challenges across the waves of feminism, include:

- Laura S. Brown
- Jean Baker Miller
- Carolyn Zerbe Enns
- Carol Gilligan
- Nancy Chodorow
- Lillian Comas-Diaz
- Olivia Espîn
- Frederick Douglass
- John Stuart Mill
- bell hooks.

Contributions from these women and men, alongside others not mentioned, have provided a strong foundation for contemporary approaches to feminist therapy.

KEY CONCEPTS

Feminist therapy focuses on individual and social change and attends to five key concepts. These concepts include the following: the personal is political, women's experiences are honored, reframing mental health and disorders, the primacy of the egalitarian relationship, and the role of social locations and **multiple identities**. Brief descriptions of these key concepts and the underlying assumptions applied to the therapeutic process are presented below.

The Personal Is Political

At the heart of feminist therapy is the belief that the personal is political; that is, no lasting individual change can take place without social change. Clients are grounded by their personal, relational, and sociopolitical realities; therefore, psychological change will not occur unless the sources of the clients' problems within these domains are addressed. The personal is political stance recognizes all types of oppression, including:

- Collective disenfranchisement—Clients with less or no power live at the margins of society, experiencing a lack of resources and a lack of access to power that contribute to deprivation of equal rights. Those with more power have greater resources and privileges to shape society, and thus a more powerful voice.
- Institutionalized "isms"—Clients experience "isms" (i.e., forms of oppression based on dominant ideologies), such as sexism, heterosexism, racism, classism, ableism, anti-Semitism, and ageism. The experience of these "isms," which often go hand in hand, represents how people experience inequitable treatment in society.
- Gender-role stereotyping—Clients' lives are shaped by dominant views of how women and men "are" or "should be" based on their assigned gender. For example, adherence to female gendered norms (e.g., empathy, cooperation, nurturance, interdependence, and intuition) results in a constant double bind for women: They are reinforced for being "appropriately" female and, at the same time, are undervalued for being that way (Worell & Remer, 2003). Additionally, male gendered norms (e.g., emotional control, winning, dominance, self-reliance, pursuit of status, power over women) can also become a double jeopardy in male help seeking;

males struggle between asking for help and battling dominant expectations that they should be independent and self-reliant (Addis & Mahalik, 2003).

Feminist therapists recognize the above types of oppression and continue to examine their impact on clients' mental health and wellness throughout the therapeutic process. Furthermore, they attend to the ways in which these forms of oppression intersect with one another within the culture in which clients' realities are experienced.

Women's Experiences Are Honored

Feminist therapists believe that society and traditional psychotherapies operate on patriarchal (i.e., male-dominated), young, Protestant, able-bodied, heterosexist norms rooted in White, middle-class values that define "reality." Therefore, they aim to shift the focus away from women's experiences being minimized and ignored to, instead, appreciating their perspectives and value systems. In other words, feminist therapists want women to own and determine their own reality and what their good life should be. Feminist therapists believe that women need to reject male-dominated definitions of womanhood; learn to value their female characteristics; and endorse their own, women-centered views of the world (Worell & Remer, 2003). Feminist therapists focus on women's experiences, but this does not mean men's experiences are devalued (Evans, Kincade, & Seem, 2011). When using feminist therapy, both women and men's realities should be considered and valued equally; thus, feminist therapy supports the diverse lived experiences of *all* individuals and can be used with males (Evans et al.).

Reframing Mental Health and Disorders

In conceptualizing client distress, feminist therapists attend to the ways in which societal factors contribute to clients' distress. Feminist therapists never view clients as "pathological" because diagnostic labels perpetuate power over women and vulnerable populations and ignore contextual influences. Instead, feminist therapists prefer to use phrases such as "problems with" or "problems of living" and reframe pathology as coping with an oppressive society (Enns, 2004). Thus, the problem is not within the clients but, rather, lies within the larger society. Feminist therapists recognize that nothing is fundamentally wrong with clients and that their reactions are natural, given environmental influences.

The feminist therapy assessment process is collaborative, and therapists aim to discover and understand their clients' experience of distress using an interpersonal, developmental, strength-based, and holistic growth lens (Evans & Miller, 2016). The holistic growth focus is wellness based and assesses interconnected domains such as physical, vocational, emotional, and spiritual health, as well as cultural, societal, and environmental factors.

Feminist therapists have challenged the historical and contemporary practice of clinical diagnosis (Eriksen & Kress, 2005, 2008). Traditionally, diagnostic labeling has focused exclusively on clustering psychological symptoms and not on social and political factors that contribute to intrapsychic conflicts. Some argue that the *Diagnostic Statistical Manual of Mental Disorders* (5th ed., *DSM-5*; American Psychiatric Association, 2013) is a sexist diagnostic classification system, in that distress caused by external factors (e.g., abuse, trauma) is labeled as disordered and suggested to be a problem that resides within the individual (Conlin, 2017; Worell & Remer, 2003). The *DSM-5* evaluates human behavior through the norms, values, and expectations of a masculine paradigm (Kahn, 2011). While some feminist therapists avoid the use of the *DSM* for diagnosis altogether, others use the manual with caution, typically out of necessity (Eriksen & Kress, 2006). When this does occur, feminist therapists are transparent about the entire assessment process and discuss the consequences and implications of mental health diagnoses so that clients can make informed decisions regarding their rights to receive or not receive a diagnosis (Kress, Hoffman, Adamson, & Eriksen, 2013).

The Primacy of the Egalitarian Relationship

Feminist therapists embrace a therapeutic relationship model focused on the idea that power should be balanced between clients and therapists, thereby avoiding acceptance of the therapist-as-expert model that is inherent in many traditional counseling theories. In recognition that the therapist-as-expert model contributes to unequal power dynamics and oppressive experiences among women and other marginalized and oppressed groups, feminist therapists acknowledge their power and take responsibility for managing the inherent power differential that exists within the therapeutic context. By managing the power base, feminist therapists are less likely to impose their values and reproduce power imbalances that hinder clients' growth and development. Clients are viewed as being the expert of their own lived experiences, whereas therapists contribute their expertise of the therapeutic process with clients. The mutual sharing of expertise, rooted in mutuality and equality, fosters healthy relational exchanges that establish and maintain the **egalitarian** therapeutic relationship.

The Role of Social Locations and Multidimensional Identities

In addition to focusing on the role of gender, feminist therapists attend to other social locations or identities that shape clients' experiences of empowerment and disempowerment in their everyday lives. To facilitate therapists' understanding and examination of clients' social locations and diverse identities, as well as their own through self-reflective practice, Hays (2001) proposed the "ADDRESSING" framework (which was mentioned in Chapter 1). The letters of the acronym stand for the following: **A**ge and generational influences, **D**evelopmental disability, **D**isability (acquired), **R**eligion or spiritual orientation, **E**thnicity, **S**ocioeconomic status, **S**exual orientation, **I**ndigenous heritage, **N**ational origin, and **G**ender. Each of these social locations intersect with one another in complex ways and evolve into multiple identities held by clients. More so, each of these social locations and identities is associated with holding more or less power within society (see Figures 12.1 and 12.2 here for a representation of how social locations and multidimensional identities relate to power within the culture of the United States).

Other social locations beyond those identified in the ADDRESSING framework might also be considered (Brown, 2010). These can include being (or not being) a veteran, being (or not being) a parent, and being (or not being) partnered. In addition, it is important to understand the histories of cultures and societies that create the context for clients' experiences of social locations and multidimensional identities (e.g., an African American woman who identifies as a lesbian with a disability).

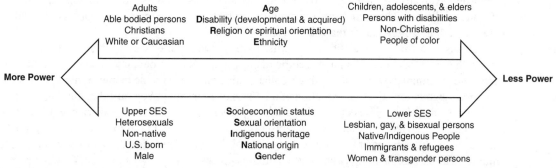

FIGURE 12.1 Social Locations and Identities

THE THERAPEUTIC PROCESS

The process of feminist therapy is collaborative and strongly rooted in the notion that the client–counselor relationship serves as a vehicle for clients' increased sense of empowerment in their everyday life. Clients are treated as experts of their own experiences and play an active role in the therapeutic process related to the conceptualization and treatment of their presenting issue(s). Feminist therapy is not bound by predetermined therapeutic stages, transitions, time limits, or outcomes. Rather, the course of therapy evolves through a process of negotiation and re-negotiation between clients and therapists.

In establishing a groundwork for positive change, the onset of feminist therapy involves the initiation and nurturance of an egalitarian relationship between clients and counselors. In a safe and affirmative context, clients are invited to examine their experienced distress through a feminist lens. This entails (1) centralizing the role of gender; (2) examining the impact of society in the development of distress; (3) investigating the impact of power dynamics in relationships; and (4) considering the client's context. Overall, the voices of clients are valued and their diverse lived experiences are honored throughout the therapeutic process.

As clients experience increased consciousness, the therapeutic process shifts to include the integration of feminist therapy interventions (e.g., gender-role analysis, power analysis, reframing and relabeling, assertiveness training, and social action) and the development of therapeutic goals. Clients work with feminist therapists to discover ways to promote empowerment in their lives through identifying strategies that are specific to their unique needs along a spectrum ranging from individual to relational to societal/political change processes.

As clients make progress in achieving their goals, they experience an increased sense of empowerment. Clients learn to better navigate oppressive forces within their environment through the integration of new, empowering ways of thinking, feeling, and behaving. This sense of strength allows clients to become active agents on their own behalf and even on the behalf of others. As the therapeutic relationship comes to an end, the therapist encourages a therapeutic ending by collaboratively discussing the healing, meaning, and transformation that unfolded throughout the counseling process. Ideally, the therapeutic relationship continues to serve as a healthy model for relationships as the client transitions out of counseling with a sense of accomplishment and pride.

Therapeutic Goals

Feminist therapy differs from other theories with regard to how they think about therapy goals. Therapists who ascribe to traditional models of therapy tend to focus solely on the reduction and elimination of symptoms of particular mental health disorders as indicative of therapeutic progress and recovery, thereby representing a medical model approach to treatment. As previously mentioned, feminist therapists are critical of the medical model approach and the *DSM-5* diagnostic system (American Psychiatric Association, 2013). Feminist therapists often use the term "distress" rather than "mental illness." The term distress acknowledges that clients are reacting to oppressions within society, and thus society, rather than clients, should change.

Consistent with honoring clients' expertise of their own experiences and change processes, the feminist therapy model does not have specific therapy goals. Rather, outcomes and effectiveness of therapy are determined by the client using a collaborative process with the therapist that involves the discussion, negotiation, and re-negotiation of the focus of counseling. Feminist therapists are careful not to impose their own biases during this process, particularly when clients experience difficulties in knowing their goals. The focus for therapists is to aid clients in an on-going discovery process aimed at individual empowerment throughout therapy. Clients determine the focus of counseling; feminist therapists are facilitators and partners in this process.

In the absence of specific therapy goals, feminist therapists follow two general guidelines that ground the direction of their therapeutic work with clients. These guidelines follow:

1. Clients and feminist therapists examine (1) the lived experiences of clients' distress and (2) the role of strengths in the context of clients' personal, relational, and/or social (political) life.
2. Clients and feminist therapists identify personal, relational, and/or social (political) strategies that can be used to (1) navigate disempowerment experienced by clients and (2) promote clients' sense of empowerment.

Feminist therapists recognize the external and contextual variables that contribute to clients' distress (disempowerment) and strive for transformational change, not adjustment (symptom removal). Therapeutic techniques and procedures that align with change goals are gender-role analysis, power analysis, assertiveness training, reframing and relabeling, therapy-demystifying strategies, consciousness-raising, and social activism (these will be discussed later in the chapter). Client satisfaction and self-report are the primary tools for assessing therapeutic progress and counseling outcomes.

Therapist's Function and Role

Feminist therapists recognize that society impacts client distress. More so, they commit to a proactive stance and aim to reduce the influence of oppressive societal forces and to promote client empowerment and a more just world. Within their practices—spanning various roles such as counselor, educator, researcher, and advocate—feminist therapists adhere to shared principles that are reflected in The Feminist Therapy Code of Ethics (Feminist Therapy Institute, 1999). These ethics are aspirational in nature and meant to be additive to other ethical codes set forth by professional associations to which feminist therapists belong. Table 12.2 presents the five areas of the Feminist Therapy Institute Code of Ethics and brief descriptions of each.

In addition to the Feminist Therapy Code of Ethics (FTI, 1999), feminist therapists use another set of general guidelines in their work specifically with girls and women. The Guidelines for Psychological Practice with Girls and Women, adopted by the American Psychological Association (APA) in 2007, address the unique counseling needs of diverse girls and women in a rapidly changing society wherein stressors, discrimination, and oppression persist in various life areas, including health, education, personal relationships, and career. The 11 guidelines, organized into three sections, are presented in Table 12.3. In the original document, each guideline is accompanied by a rationale for its inclusion, as well as recommendations for therapeutic application.

Relationship Between Therapist and Client

Feminist therapists believe that therapists operating under traditional theoretical orientations run the risk of using their power (i.e., expert-therapist model) to encourage and even coerce clients to adapt to an unhealthy environment (Worell & Remer, 2003). As such, feminist therapists aim to avoid the "expert" role by recognizing their power, acknowledging the power differential, and accepting responsibility for that power (FTI, 1999). By equalizing power relations, therapists are less likely to impose their values and reproduce power imbalances. Feminist therapists do not embrace the expert role and, instead, become a collaborative partner, where clients are the expert.

Feminist therapists use several strategies to minimize the power differential inherent in the therapeutic relationship. One is for therapists to share their values so as to minimize imposing them onto clients. Since therapy is a value-laden process, it is critical for therapists to share their theoretical approach to demystify therapy so clients have an informed choice (Worell & Remer, 2003).

TABLE 12.2 The Feminist Therapy Institute Code of Ethics

Area	Brief Description
I. Cultural Diversities and Oppressions	Feminist therapists take responsibility for serving diverse clients. They engage in on-going reflection of how their own identities and experiences influence their practices in therapy and other contexts, and seek ways to address biases and promote their cultural competencies.
II. Power Differentials	Feminist therapists are aware of the role of power in their relationships with clients. They continuously seek ways to model and encourage effective uses of power throughout the therapy process (e.g., educating clients about power in relationships, reaching mutual agreements for client-therapist contracts, using self-disclosure only when appropriate).
III. Overlapping Relationships	Feminist therapists take accountability for maintaining healthy dynamics in their relationships within therapeutic, institutional, and community settings (e.g., clearly communicating obligations, roles, responsibilities, and allegiances). They are aware of power dynamics in overlapping relationships with clients and are responsible for preventing abuse and harm. Feminist therapists do not engage in sexual relationships, or sexualizing behaviors, with current or former clients.
IV. Therapist Accountability	Feminist therapists are accountable to their clients, as well as colleagues and themselves. They seek ways to maintain and improve their competencies (e.g., self-evaluation, consultation, continuing education) and their well-being (e.g., self-care activities, personal counseling) on an on-going basis.
V. Social Change	Feminist therapists embrace the "personal is political" stance in an ever-changing society. They engage in social change efforts (e.g., public education, lobbying) across various contexts (e.g., therapy, community, criminal justice system) to address oppressive practices that are harmful to clients, therapists, and the broader community.

Source: Based on Feminist Therapy Institute. (1990). *Feminist Therapy Institute Code of Ethics.* Denver, CO: Author.

Another important strategy for minimizing the power gap is to offer appropriate self-disclosure during sessions and to share here-and-now emotional reactions with clients. When therapists share emotional responses, clients receive immediate feedback on how they are impacting another individual. In addition, by sharing their feelings, therapists allow their own vulnerability to be revealed (Worell & Remer, 2003). Self-disclosure and here-and-now reactions are used only when they are relevant to clients' concerns, when they are meant to foster psychological growth, and when clients can manage these interactions (Worell & Remer, 2003).

The feminist therapist also interprets transference differently than do many theorists from other theoretical orientations. Historically, transference has been understood as a psychological phenomenon in which the client unconsciously projects unresolved feelings and conflicts onto the therapist. By interpreting transference through this lens, the client must resolve these unconscious distortions and re-experience unresolved conflicts through the therapeutic relationship. The therapist analyzes and interprets the interactions in session to make the unconscious material conscious. From this perspective, the therapist holds all the power in the therapeutic relationship. Feminist therapists believe "transference" issues are legitimate here-and-now reactions to the attributes and behaviors of the therapist and are accepted as valid (Worell & Remer, 2003). The client–therapist relationship is explored, and the therapist is open to the client's feedback (Worell & Remer, 2003). What follows

TABLE 12.3 APA Guidelines for Psychological Practice with Girls and Women

Sections	Guidelines
Diversity, Social Context, and Power	1. Therapists strive to be aware of the effects of socialization, stereotyping, and unique life events on the development of girls and women across diverse cultural groups.
	2. Therapists are encouraged to recognize and utilize information about oppression, privilege, and identity development as they may affect girls and women.
	3. Therapists strive to understand the impact of bias and discrimination on the physical and mental health of those with whom they work.
Professional Responsibility	4. Therapists strive to use gender sensitive and culturally sensitive, affirming practices in providing services to girls and women.
	5. Therapists are encouraged to recognize how their socialization, attitudes, and knowledge about gender may affect their practice with girls and women.
Practice Applications	6. Therapists are encouraged to use interventions and approaches that have been found to be effective in the treatment of issues of concern to girls and women.
	7. Therapists strive to foster therapeutic relationships and practices that promote initiative, empowerment, and expanded alternatives and choices for girls and women.
	8. Therapists strive to provide appropriate, unbiased assessments and diagnoses in their work with women and girls.
	9. Therapists strive to consider the problems of girls and women in their sociopolitical context.
	10. Therapists strive to acquaint themselves with and utilize relevant mental health, education, and community resources for girls and women.
	11. Therapists are encouraged to understand and work to change institutional and systemic bias that may impact girls and women.

Source: Based on American Psychological Association. (2007). *Guidelines for Psychological Practice with Girls and Women.* Washington, DC: Author.

is an example of a counselor–client interaction that involves an exploration of here-and-now reactions of the therapist:

JANE: I don't know if I can trust you anymore . . .

THERAPIST: I'm sorry to hear that this space is not feeling safe for you. I want to do everything I can to gain your trust back. I want to acknowledge that I appreciate you feeling empowered to disclose your reservations with me. Can I ask you a question?

[Therapist labels the client's personal power and uses an open-ended question, giving more power to the client.]

JANE: Yeah, I guess.

THERAPIST: I noticed you clenched your fists and your shoulders were pretty tight when I was offering examples of when you have used different styles of communication. If your fists and shoulders had a voice, what would they say?

[Therapist shares here-and-now nonverbals and empowers the client to express her reactions.]

JANE: They would say, "why are you using my own behaviors against me?" You continue to use examples from my past of when I used aggressive and even passive communication. It's like you're looking for mistakes I have made in the past and putting a spotlight on them . . . Just like my father.

THERAPIST: Jane, thank you for sharing this with me. I sense your anger, frustration, and you may even be feeling judged by me?

[Therapist uses reflection of feelings and poses them as a question, giving the client power to agree or disagree with reflection.]

JANE: That's exactly how I feel!

THERAPIST: All those feelings are exactly the opposite of how I want you to feel in therapy. Moving forward, I will be mindful of the examples I use so you do not feel what you have disclosed in here is used "against you." Is this a solution you feel comfortable with?

[Therapist acknowledges how his behavior (not labeling it as transference) mirrors the client's father. Therapist also uses the client's words and a check-out to make sure the client is in agreement with the solution.]

JANE: Yeah, I guess . . . It's a start.

THERAPIST: I'd love to hear if you have any other feedback regarding our relationship and the degree to which you feel heard, understood, and respected.

At this point, the therapist is actively trying to repair the therapeutic alliance by empowering the client to use her voice, honoring the client's here-and-now reactions, as well as soliciting further feedback on the therapeutic relationship.

THERAPEUTIC TECHNIQUES AND PROCEDURES

In their work with clients, feminist therapists draw from a wide range of techniques that often span multiple therapeutic modalities. Worell and Remer (2003) asserted that *all* techniques used by feminist therapists must first undergo an evaluation to determine their compatibility with feminist principles. In instances when feminist therapists determine that a technique is incompatible, they can discard the technique or modify it as appropriate. Therapeutic interventions are tailored to clients' strengths with the goal of fostering their personal power and increasing their critical consciousness.

Two primary techniques considered distinctive to feminist therapy, and often used in combination, are gender-role analysis and power analysis. Additional feminist therapy strategies include assertiveness training, reframing and relabeling, therapy-demystifying strategies, consciousness-raising, and social activism. The sections below briefly describe each of these techniques.

Gender-Role Analysis

Gender-role analysis is used in feminist therapy to increase clients' awareness of gender socialization and how prescribed gender-role expectations impact their psychological well-being (Evans et al., 2011; Evans & Miller, 2016; Worell & Remer, 2003). The content of gender-role messages can vary across different cultural contexts (Worell & Remer, 2003). Therefore, feminist therapists working with minority clients should tend to both internalized gender expectations from the dominant culture, as well as gendered expectations from the culture(s) in which clients belong (Worell & Remer). Gender-role analysis is meant to provide clients with insights about their social identities and how social expectations impact their experience of personal power. The six sequential steps of gender-role analysis are as follows (Worell & Remer, pp. 77–78):

Step 1: The client identifies experienced gender-role messages. During this initial step, clients are prompted by the therapist to list direct and indirect gender-role messages that they experienced across their lifespan (e.g., as a child, adolescent, adult, older adult). These can come in the form of verbal messages, nonverbal messages, and even modeling. Clients are encouraged to consider verbal messages (e.g., "girls should _____"; boys should _____"), nonverbal messages (e.g., a disapproving or approving facial expression from a parent for breaking a gender stereotype), and the impact of modeling (e.g., ways in which they have witnessed role models "do their gender").

Step 2: The client identifies the consequences of received gender-role messages. This second step involves clients' exploration of both positive and negative consequences of received gender-role messages from step 1. Clients are encouraged to consider these consequences through a personal and societal lens. In working through this step, for example, a female client may share that being accommodating and emotional in relationships with others promotes a sense of connection and fulfillment (positive consequences); yet, the societal pressure to meet these stereotypical expectations for women contributes to discomfort in using assertive communication to express her needs in relationships (negative consequences). A male client may share that demonstrating self-confidence and aggression has helped him negotiate higher salaries in the workforce (positive consequences); yet, the pressure to meet these stereotypical expectations for men contributes to his discomfort in expressing vulnerability with co-workers and asking for help (negative consequences).

Step 3: The client identifies external gender-role messages that have been internalized. During the third step, clients become more aware of how gender-role messages have influenced self-talk, that is, the self-generated dialogue that consciously and unconsciously takes place in their minds. For a male client, an identified stereotypical self-talk statement about physical appearance might be "I have to be tall and muscular," whereas for a female client it might be "I have to be thin and graceful."

Step 4: The client selects internalized messages that she or he would like to change. This fourth step is deeply rooted in clients' subjective experience of the impact of internalized messages and the privileging of their choice process. A prompt that may be useful in aiding clients during this process may be "Is this internalized message empowering or disempowering?" When clients' internalized messages are disempowering and they have chosen not to change them, the therapist's role is to recognize that some messages are strongly held, and rather than pushing clients toward changing them, work should focus on the message or messages that clients are willing to change (Evans et al., 2011).

Step 5: The client develops a plan for implementing the desired change to an internalized message. For the fifth step, a plan for implementing changes is collaboratively developed. This process is similar to cognitive restructuring (Worell & Remer, 2003), in which the therapist assists clients in identifying and challenging maladaptive thoughts. Feminist therapists may want to ask, "What steps would you like to take to implement these changes?" "You talked about _____, do you see _____ as part of your plan?" or "What thoughts continue to be a barrier for you implementing this change?"

Step 6: The client implements the change. The last step is executing the change and preparing clients to possibly manage negative reactions to the changes. Feminist therapists may prompt, "Can you think of any situations that may involve a negative reaction to your perspective from others?"

Power Analysis

The aim of utilizing a **power analysis** in therapy is to help clients understand the ways in which unequal access to power and resources can impact personal realities. The term power can simply be understood as the capacity or right to have influence on the self and/or others. Those who have less power typically belong to marginalized groups within a particular culture. In the context of the United States, for example, groups that have been relegated to the margins and often have limited power include women; persons of color; persons with disabilities; and persons belonging to lower socioeconomic classes. Conversely, those with power in this context tend to be White, androcentric, young, Protestant, able-bodied, heterosexual, middle-class men.

Power analysis is a feminist therapy technique that can be used with individuals from subordinate and dominant groups. In using this technique, feminist therapists aim to (1) raise clients' awareness about differentials of power that exist between different social groups in a particular culture, and (2) invite and empower clients to use power in effective, non-oppressing ways within their lives (Worell & Remer, 2003). Prior to the implementation of power analyses with clients, feminist therapists must have a thorough understanding of power and how it connects with clients' lived experiences. Table 12.4 describes the six steps of conducting a power analysis (Worell & Remer, 2003).

Four categories of power are often recognized, and each of these categories encompasses specific indications of power, many of which are identified below (Brown, 2010):

- Somatic power—Clients feel a sense of power over their bodies; they experience their bodies as safe places and their physical needs are met (e.g., hunger, comfort).
- Intrapersonal/intrapsychic power—Clients feel a sense of power over their thinking and feeling states and demonstrate the ability to stay in the present moment. They also feel confident in their intuition and thought processes and they perceive themselves as having the ability to self-soothe in healthy, adaptive ways.
- Interpersonal/social-contextual power—Clients perceive they have power in their relationships and social context. They believe in their ability to have desired impacts on others, and they accept personal limitations related to power and control. Clients form healthy relationships and engage in interpersonal self-protection strategies as needed.
- Spiritual/existential power—Clients feel a sense of power over their lives and their spirituality. They are able to respond to existential life challenges, create meaning in their lives, and experience satisfaction with their overall well-being. Clients are aware of how heritage, culture, and social context influence their use of spiritual/existential power in their lives.

TABLE 12.4 Six Steps of Power Analysis

Step 1	Clients review different definitions of power and choose the one that best fits their experience (see four categories of power above).
Step 2	Clients are provided information about the various kinds of power.
Step 3	Clients learn about the differential access that dominant and subordinate groups have to various kinds of power (discussed in Step 2).
Step 4	Clients review the strategies individuals use to exert power.
Step 5	Clients identify how societal messages and environmental barriers impact their use of power.
Step 6	Clients conduct a cost-benefit analysis of the different power strategies and decide which strategies to retain and discard.

Source: Based on Worell, J., & Remer, P. (2003). *Feminist perspectives in therapy: Empowering diverse women* (2nd ed.). Hoboken, NJ: John Wiley & Sons.

Assertiveness Training

Feminist therapists stress the importance of women and those from groups that have less power asserting themselves by standing up for their rights and expressing their opinions freely. Women are often constrained by traditional gender-role expectations and socialization (Linehan & Egan, 1979). When women adhere to these expectations and norms surrounding gender, they may act in a nonassertive, passive manner, which, in turn, can (1) prevent them from being treated equally and (2) contribute to distress that results from a loss of power in their lives. Assertiveness training does not aim for women and low-power groups to learn ways to dominate others; rather, it aims to honor the rights of all parties in communication so that no one is left powerless.

Assertiveness training, a traditional behavior therapy technique discussed earlier in this text, provides a vehicle for clients to engage with others in ways that meet their wants and needs, yet respects the rights of others. In applying assertiveness training, clients are able to transcend gender stereotypes (e.g., women should be passive, men should be aggressive) rather than adapt to cultural expectations and gender roles that others consider appropriate (Enns, 2004). Assertiveness training incorporates four basic procedures:

1. Helping clients identify and accept their own personal rights and needs, and the rights and needs of others
2. Teaching clients the differences between assertive, aggressive, and passive communication styles
3. Reducing blocks to acting assertively, such as irrational thinking, anxiety, guilt, and anger
4. Developing assertive skills through active practice methods.

Before using assertiveness training, it is important for clients to understand how it can be helpful to them. The following is a list of beliefs regarding how assertiveness training can be valuable, and these ideas can be shared with clients to help them connect with the value of assertive communication:

- By standing up for myself and letting myself be known to others, I gain self-respect and respect from other people.
- Even though I may strive not to hurt another person, there are times when the other person may feel hurt. I cannot control someone else's feelings.
- When I directly stand up for myself and express my feelings and thoughts, everyone usually benefits in the long run.
- Personal relationships become more authentic and satisfying when we share our honest reactions with other people and do not block others from sharing their reactions with us.
- By being assertive and sharing with other people how their behavior affects me, I am offering them an opportunity to change their behavior, and I am showing respect for their right to know where they stand with me.

Assertiveness training is also about reviewing clients' rights and helping them learn how to validate their own needs, opinions, and boundaries with others. Clients' awareness of their rights promotes personal responsibility for actions. Some basic rights include: (1) the right to make choices; (2) the right to be treated with respect; (3) the right to make mistakes; (4) the right to set limits; (5) the right to change their mind; (6) the right to ask for what they want, need, and prefer; (7) the right to say "no" and not feel guilty; and (8) the right to feel that an explanation is not required for their thoughts and actions. Feminist therapists support clients in developing a belief system that supports their interpersonal rights to assert their thoughts, feelings, and needs.

Feminist therapists may also offer psychoeducation to clients on the difference between the three primary communication patterns: passive, assertive, and aggressive. (Figure 12.2 offers a visual depiction of the styles of communication.)

	Passive	Assertive	Aggressive
	Statement: "I forgot to tell you, I changed your appointment time from Tuesday to Wednesday. I hope you don't mind . . . "		
Message Delivery Example	"Oh, no big deal." [*Soft spoken, quiet, looks down and away.*]	"Next time, please let me know in advance so I can coordinate my schedule. I feel a bit frustrated I have to restructure my day on Wednesday. In the future, I would appreciate communicating changes in a timely manner." [*Confident tone, direct eye contact**]	"What is the matter with you?! Because of YOU, I now have to reschedule my entire day. Thanks a lot!" [*Loud, overbearing, domineering.*]
Definition	Avoiding conflict by not expressing needs, thoughts, and feelings	The ability to express needs, thoughts, and feelings in a clear, direct, and respectful way	Expressing needs, thoughts, and feelings that do not reflect taking into account the welfare of others
Impact	Giving up one's rights and granting others the right to disregard your needs	Standing up for one's rights while honoring the rights of others	Demanding one's rights while simultaneously violating the rights of others

Note: *Direct eye contact: Looking directly into another person's eyes is considered a sign of disrespect in some cultures. Clients can focus on other components of assertive communication if direct eye contact is disrespectful.

FIGURE 12.2 The Continuum of the Styles of Communication

Assessing and identifying clients' usual communication patterns can be a helpful first step in assertiveness training. Clients can explore why it is difficult for them to act assertively (e.g., guilt, anger, anxiety, irrational thinking). Clients can practice using assertive behavior in a variety of everyday interactions within their family, work, and other social contexts. Assertive behavior can increase when therapists coach, model, and encourage clients to practice assertive communication responses (Enns, 2004). The use of role play, repetition, and collaborative problem solving with clients has been recommended to increase their self-efficacy (Enns).

Reframing and Relabeling

Reframing is a technique that involves giving a new or different explanation so that clients come to think about something in a new way. In feminist therapy, this often involves helping individuals to understand how social and political pressures can affect their perceptions of their problems and solutions (Worell & Remer, 2003). To facilitate this shift, feminist therapists aid clients in the exploration of societal contributions to their distress. For example, in working with a female college student who shares that she has been feeling depressed after a sexual assault on campus due to self-blame, the therapist can help her (1) examine societal messages, as well as campus practices and policies, that serve to reinforce sexual violence against college women; and (2) conceptualize depression as a normative response to trauma and oppression.

Relabeling is another technique used by feminist therapists to facilitate a client's shift in focus (Worell & Remer, 2003). Feminist therapists relabel a client's experiences and thus change how a client thinks about those experiences. For example, when counseling a woman who is a victim of interpersonal partner violence, a feminist therapist might use the term "abuse" to describe how her partner approaches her. The client may not have considered her partner's behavior to be abuse; thus, the feminist therapist facilitates a shift in the client's thinking. As a result of the therapist's use of reframing from the previous college student example, the student may come to recognize that she was a victim of rape. The student may have experienced a sense of empowerment and changed her presenting identity in therapy as a "victim" to embrace her newfound identity as a "survivor." The importance of this shift is not in the change of labels per se, but the meaning that is ascribed to these labels.

Therapy-Demystifying Strategies

Feminist therapists strive to demystify the therapy process; they want clients to feel in control and understand how all aspects of counseling work so that they can feel empowered and in control of their counseling experience. This is done by (1) the development of an egalitarian relationship and (2) the promotion of clients' sense of empowerment in making decisions related to their therapy process (Evans et al., 2011; FTI, 1999; Worell & Remer, 2003). At the onset of therapy sessions with clients, feminist therapists carefully attend to issues related to informed consent by providing information about topics, which include:

- Feminist theory and the process of feminist therapy
- Their theoretical orientation(s) and strategies
- Relevant personal and professional values that they hold
- General expectations for themselves and the client
- Terms and conditions of counseling (e.g., fees, session time, length of services)
- Rights that the client has as a consumer of counseling.

In a collaborative approach, clients are supported as being the final decision makers about their therapy experiences. Clients and therapists work together to conceptualize the presenting issue(s), establish therapeutic goals, and agree to the use of therapeutic interventions that will help clients achieve their goals (Worell & Remer, 2003). Two additional demystifying strategies that feminist therapists may use throughout the therapy process include psychoeducation and self-disclosure.

Consciousness-Raising

Founded on the feminist notion that "the personal is political," consciousness-raising groups were established during the women's movement as a grassroots effort for women to share their personal life experiences in safe, supportive, and leaderless spaces (Israeli & Santor, 2000). The overarching goal of consciousness-raising groups was societal transformation rather than individual modification (Evans, Kincade, Marbley, & Seem, 2005). Among the social gender-role–related topics discussed by women were motherhood, marriage, sexual harassment, workplace inequalities, and women's mental health. Through these discussions, commonalities across narratives were identified; women recognized they were not the single cause of their distress and they began to examine the ways in which social/external forces contributed to their personal distress. To address the shared consciousness of oppression that developed, women imparted information, provided support for one another, and discussed solutions for creating personal and social change.

Consciousness-raising in present-day feminist practice is a core therapeutic mechanism used by therapists that benefits the lives of women. Feminist therapists facilitate contexts for women to openly share their experiences, develop a sense of community with other women, end self-blame for structural problems, and experience empowerment for change (Israeli & Santor, 2000). Among the ways that feminist therapists promote consciousness-raising are (1) providing education in therapy about feminist issues; (2) using prompts and open-ended questions to invite clients to explore how society impacts their personal distress; (3) inviting clients to consume educational information (e.g., published works, blogs, documentaries) outside of session to expand their understandings of feminist points of view; and (4) connecting clients with organizations that provide feminist-based resources, such as educational programming, support groups, and legal services (e.g., rape crisis centers; lesbian, gay, bisexual, transgender [LGBT] centers). It is important to note that each of these strategies is intentionally selected to promote the process of women becoming stronger and more confident in managing their lives and their personal rights.

Social Activism

Engagement in social activism entails the use of direct and often confrontational action(s) aimed at supporting or opposing a particular cause or causes. Social activism is a component of feminist therapy that is not advocated for by all feminist therapists due to controversy surrounding its use (Israeli & Santor, 2000). While most feminist therapists and scholars contend that activism is vital to improve the mental health and well-being of women and members of minority groups and their communities, debate has centered on whether integrating social activism into counseling has direct therapeutic benefits for clients. In recognition of concerns related to client choice (i.e., whether social activism is congruent with clients' values) and ethical boundary violations (e.g., therapist value imposition), feminist therapists introduce social activism as a treatment intervention only when therapeutically and ethically appropriate (FTI, 1999). In these instances, clients and therapists should work together to integrate social activism into counseling in ways that are congruent with clients' goals in counseling.

Within the context of feminist therapy, social activism can take many forms and may involve participation by both the therapist and the client (Evans et al., 2005; Israeli & Santor, 2000). Examples of social activism include:

- Letter writing to newspapers or politicians
- Engaging in organized marches and rallies
- Speaking out on social media platforms
- Using visual and performing arts to create social justice projects
- Serving in volunteer and leadership positions within organizations that serve women and underserved populations (e.g., rape crisis centers, domestic violence and child advocacy centers).

Feminist therapists may also engage in, and support, social activism as a broad-scale intervention in their personal and professional pursuit to treat the ills of society that contribute to oppression and disempowerment.

APPLICATION AND CURRENT USE OF FEMINIST THERAPY

Counseling Applications

Feminist therapy practice is diverse and encompasses various feminist theoretical orientations, which has contributed to scholars and therapists aptly referring to "feminist therapy" as "feminist therapies." Among the diverse range of therapists—both women and men—who use feminist therapies are professional counselors, psychologists, psychiatrists, and social workers. Despite differences in practice, common to feminist therapists are the following two principles: The personal is political, and the therapist–client relationship should be egalitarian. Another commonality among feminist therapists is the use of some form of interventions unique to feminist therapy, namely, gender-role analysis and power analysis, in their work with diverse populations.

Feminist therapy has been used for over four decades to address the personal struggles that women face, as well as commonalities related to these struggles. Broad topics that have received considerable attention in feminist therapy include mental health concerns (e.g., eating disorders, depression, nonsuicidal self-injury), body image and sexual objectification, intimate partner violence, childhood sexual abuse, and sexual assault. Demonstrating feminist therapy's inherent multicultural and global focuses, feminist therapists have started important conversations to address the unique needs of persons of color, as well as refugees, immigrants, and persons who have experienced human rights violations. Feminist therapy has also been used with men, children and adolescents, couples, families, and groups across a variety of settings (e.g., mental health agencies, hospitals, private practices, and prisons). Applications of basic feminist therapy principles with diverse populations have been the focus of numerous works (see the following resources for more information on this topic: Brown & Root, 1990; Enns, 2004; Enns & Williams, 2013; Evans et al., 2011; Maas, 2002; Worell & Remer, 2003).

Many feminist therapists integrate feminist therapy principles with other forms of therapy. In doing so, they ensure biases rooted in sexism and oppression related to assessment, diagnosis, and treatment are addressed. Feminist therapy has been integrated with humanistic and existential therapies (e.g., Brown, 1994, 2007; Enns, 2004), narrative therapy (e.g., Lee, 1997), Gestalt therapy (e.g., Enns, 1997, 2004), Adlerian therapy (e.g., McLean, La Guardia, Nelson, & Watts, 2016), solution-focused therapy (e.g., Dermer, Hemesath, & Russell, 1998; Seponski, 2016), art therapy (e.g., Hogan, 1997), psychodrama (e.g., Worell & Remer, 2003), psychodynamic therapy (e.g., Daugherty & Lees, 1988), cognitive and cognitive behavioral therapy (e.g., Srebnik, 1994; Worell & Remer, 2003), family systems therapies (e.g., Silverstein & Goodrich, 2003), and eye movement desensitization therapy (e.g., Brown, 2002).

Group therapy is another important counseling application of feminist therapy that can be traced back to the formation of consciousness-raising groups in the 1960s. These groups were safe, leaderless forums that involved the examination of how social and political factors influenced women's health and well-being, as well as how these factors could be changed to promote women's empowerment via social activism. Among the topics of contemporary feminist-orientated groups are women's experiences with life stages; mental health issues (e.g., eating disorders, depression, substance use issues, posttraumatic stress disorder); relationship issues (e.g., intimate partner violence, divorce, infidelity, competitiveness among women); and role strain in the contexts of motherhood, work, and daily life. While some groups focus on commonalities among all women, others focus on the unique experiences of subgroups of women, such as women of color, women with disabilities, college students, and adolescents.

Within feminist-oriented groups, members are treated as experts in their own lives; an effort is made to reduce the power differential between group members and leaders; and interpersonal interactions are marked by mutuality, respect, and authenticity. The factors, in turn, contribute to shared benefits among women, such as (1) ending experienced isolation and increasing interaction between women; (2) emphasizing the role of social and political factors, rather than a sole concentration on personal factors, in regard to personal problems and common concerns; (3) developing a support network; and (4) skill development and empowerment. In addition to a growing body of scholarly articles on feminist-oriented groups, Maas (2002) published a noteworthy book that provides in-depth case studies and transcripts for a variety of women's groups to demonstrate the process and utility of feminist group therapy.

Moving beyond direct counseling applications, feminist theory can be used to inform clinical supervision. Feminist supervisors work with supervisees and establish a collaborative relationship that involves questioning and examining hierarchical factors in the supervision relationship. Focusing on the use of feminist therapy within the supervisee's relationships with clients, supervisors and supervisees utilize a feminist approach to case conceptualization that entails the examination of clients' sociocultural context and the role of multiple, intersecting identities. To centralize the importance of empowering clients and decreasing the power differential within the therapeutic context, self-examination and reflective practices are integrated within the feminist supervision process. Additionally, this process centers on using a spectrum of therapeutic interventions geared toward addressing sociopolitical and psychological issues that are adversely affecting clients' lives.

Application to Multicultural Groups

While feminist therapy was initially developed to improve the lives of women, male clients are among the many unique populations that have benefited from its broadened scope. Central to therapeutic work with men is an understanding of the effects of normative masculinity and male privilege (Addis & Mahalik, 2003; Kahn, 2011). Feminist therapists work with diverse male clients to explore, and better understand, how pursuing power over others and maintaining masculine ideals serve as sources of oppression in relationships with self, others, and the broader society (Kahn, 2011). The strains associated with internalizing the masculine ideal can lead to physical and psychological concerns, particularly for populations such as gay and bisexual men, veterans, professional athletes, and male survivors of childhood sexual abuse (Enns, 2004). A few specific applications include practical guidance for working with traditional men in therapy (Silver, Levant, & Gonzalez, 2018), group treatment for men who abuse their partners (Lawson et al., 2001), and recommendations for working with men who have anorexia nervosa (Soban, 2006) and men who have trauma histories (Crete & Singh, 2015).

In addition to men, feminist therapists have addressed the unique issues that affect persons of color. Central to therapeutic work with these populations is the facilitation of awareness, understanding, and change through (1) the valuing of their diverse and multifaceted experiences and (2) engagement in dialogues around intersectionality factors, oppression, and power. For example, it may be helpful to discuss the harmful effects of racism and sexism, process feelings imposed by society on their status as ethnic minorities, and explore the presentation of opportunities to recognize themselves as agents of change in achieving solutions to their concerns (Worell & Remer, 2003). Among the distinct populations that have been the focus of feminist therapy literature are African American women and men (Carr & West, 2013; Greene & Sanchez-Hucles, 1997), Asian American women (Kawahara & Espín, 2007), and Latina women (Kawahara & Espín, 2013).

Feminist therapy is also an ideal approach in addressing the concerns of lesbian, gay, bisexual, transgender, and queer (LGBTQ) persons who may experience distress as a result of living in cultures that are deeply rooted in heterosexism, homophobia, and transphobia. LGBTQ persons may confront concerns such as rejection by families and even communities, as well as minority stress (Addison & Coolhart, 2015). In working with this population, feminist therapists examine political, legal, religious, and psychological sources of oppression; validate clients' experiences of discrimination; and work with clients to navigate and challenge normative gender-role expectations and societal values. Feminist therapy has been applied to specific populations within the LGBTQ community, such as lesbian women (Worell & Remer, 2003); transgender persons (Mallory, Brown, Conner, & Henry, 2017); and lesbian, bisexual, and queer women (Hagen, Arczynski, Morrow, & Hawxhurst, 2011).

Couples and families can benefit from a feminist therapy approach. Feminist therapists take a broad view of the family system, acknowledging diverse forms of structures to include blended families, stepfamilies, and nuclear families. A few distinct applications of feminist therapy with families include working with lesbian and gay families (Negy & McKinney, 2006), working with single mothers and fathers (Maier & McGeorge, 2014), and addressing injustices (gender oppression, family scapegoating) in family therapy with adolescents (Bowling, Kearney, Lumadue, & St. Germain, 2002). Similar to how feminist therapists conceptualize the family unit, they also embrace a broad understanding of the term couple (e.g., same-sex, cohabitating, married). In regard to couples and feminist therapy, some applications include feminist-informed internal family systems therapy with couples (Prouty & Protinsky, 2002); addressing gender roles and the emotionally focused couples therapy (Vatcher & Bogo, 2001); mixed-orientation marriages (Schwartz, 2012); and same-sex, queer couples (Addison & Coolhart, 2015).

As with couples and family therapy, using a feminist therapy approach is ideal when working with children and adolescents. By fostering a social perspective, youth are able to reclaim their voices, express their lived experiences (i.e., their subjective reality), and identify personal strengths. Feminist therapy has been used with this population to promote resilience among children in a school setting who have experienced bullying and harassment (Markey, 2015) and in children who have experienced intimate partner violence (Callaghan, Fellin, & Alexander, 2018). Additional areas of focus have been the integration of feminist therapy and expressive arts in work with adolescents (Otting & Prosek, 2016), relational-cultural group therapy with female adolescents (Cannon, Hammer, Reicherzer, & Gilliam, 2012), and queer affirmative therapy with youth and families (Tanner & Lyness, 2004).

In working with persons with disabilities, feminist therapists recognize and use information about privilege, oppression (e.g., ableism), and identity development. Further, they examine the impact of biases and discriminatory practices within health systems, education, the workplace, religious institutions, communities, and the legal system. Much of the feminist counseling scholarship to date has focused on women's experiences with disabilities, both visible and invisible (Banks, 2010; Banks & Kaschak, 2013; Prilleltensky, 1996).

Feminist therapists recognize the importance of integrating and honoring indigenous communities and ethnic worldviews throughout the therapeutic process. Indigenous feminists argue the experiences and ideals of Western culture and colonization inhibit treatment. Therefore, feminist therapists seek ways to explore the harmful effects of colonization and oppression, as well as dismantle oppressive power structures that result from settler colonization. Additionally, feminist therapists decolonize the therapeutic process, and infuse cultural and indigenous-based healing practices and concepts into therapy. Some feminist therapy applications include raising critical consciousness among Native communities (Ramirez, 2007), promoting healing practices with Asian immigrant women (Wang & Iwamasa, 2018), and addressing the unique needs of Latina immigrant women (Díaz-Lázaro, Verdinelli, & Cohen, 2012).

FEMINIST THERAPY SPOTLIGHT

Relational-cultural therapy is an important therapy that was developed during the feminist movement and shares principles and beliefs of feminist therapy. Textbox 12.1 will briefly describe relational-cultural therapy and its application to counseling.

Textbox 12.1: Feminist Therapy Spotlight: The Relational-Cultural Model of Development

Relational-cultural theory (RCT), and by extension relational-cultural therapy, was developed alongside the feminist movement in the 1970s. During this time, Jean Baker Miller published a ground-breaking book, *Toward a New Psychology of Women* (1976), wherein she proposed a relational model of development that challenged Western psychotherapy approaches being used to conceptualize and treat women's psychological distress. Based on her therapeutic observations, Miller contended that autonomy and independence were not markers of women's psychological healing and growth (as emphasized by traditional theories), but rather the development of deep, meaningful connection in relationships with the self and others was central to a client's development. Since the inception of her model, Miller has collaborated with other influential scholars, such as Irene Stiver, Judith V. Jordan, Janet Surrey (known as the Stone Center Theory Group and then the Founding Scholars), and others affiliated with the Stone Center's Jean Baker Miller Training Institute (for a collection of writings, see Jordan, Walker, and Hartling, 2004), to expand RCT and its application to marginalized groups across the lifespan.

According to RCT, the source of psychological suffering is chronic disconnection in relationships at the individual or societal level (Jordan, 2010). Chronic disconnections extend beyond misunderstandings and rejections in relationships (i.e., acute disconnections) and entail repeated exposure to profound nonempathic responses and unequal power dynamics that contribute to marginalization and oppression in relational patterns (e.g., abuse) and the broader sociocultural context (e.g., sexism, racism; Jordan, 2010). Clients who experience chronic disconnection develop negative relational images that contribute to feelings of isolation and negative expectations for relationships with others, which in turn create barriers for them to enter into and experience growth-fostering relationships. Working through the central relational paradox—clients' desire for connection, yet their use of strategies of disconnection as a form of self-protection—is central to therapists' work with clients (Jordan, 2010).

The relationship between clients and therapists, which is a core focus of RCT, is bi-directional in nature, meaning both parties influence each other. Central to the dynamics of these relationships is the openness and willingness on the part of clients and counselors to be influenced by one another (i.e., mutual empathy), as well as a sense of aliveness to foster a context for greater possibility and agency (i.e., mutual empowerment; Jordan, 2010). As healthy connection is nurtured in the therapeutic relationship, the aim of therapists is to assist clients in developing **relational resilience** (i.e., the movement toward growth-fostering relationships despite experienced disconnections) and **relational competence** (i.e., the ability to be empathic in relationships with self and others). According to Miller (1986, pp. 2–3), growth-fostering relationships are characterized by "five good things," or essential attributes, including:

- Sense of zest or energy
- Productivity
- Relational clarity
- Increased sense of worth
- Desire for more connection.

Two additional aspects of *good* relationships that were added to the list include (Jordan, 2010) mutual empathy and empowerment. As clients connect with and build upon these aspects of their relationships, they are able to foster deeper connections that contribute to psychological healing and growth.

The applicability of RCT as a framework for working with specialized populations has been a focus of the counseling literature, particularly beginning in the 2000s. Among the specialized populations that have received attention are clients who have traumatic stress disorders (Kress, Haiyasoso, Zoldan, Headley, & Trepal, 2018); lesbian, gay, bisexual, transgender, queer, and questioning (LGBTQQ) clients who experience heterosexism (Singh & Moss, 2016); clients who have eating disorders (Trepal, Boie, & Kress, 2012); and men (Duffey & Haberstroh, 2014). Additionally, scholars have demonstrated the utility of integrating RCT with other counseling approaches, such as cognitive behavioral therapy (e.g., Crumb & Haskins, 2017) and creativity in mental health (e.g., Headley, Kautzman-East, Pusateri, & Kress, 2015; Headley & Sangganjanavanich, 2014) to foster relational development in the therapeutic relationship, as well as serving as a framework for bridging relational, multicultural, and social justice counseling competencies (Comstock et al., 2008). Within the American Counseling Association, RCT serves as an organized forum for feminist scholars and practitioners in the *Journal of Creativity in Mental Health*, the flagship journal for the Association for Creativity in Counseling (Division 19). Works within and outside the scope of this journal demonstrate the ways in which RCT continues to evolve to serve the needs of multicultural populations who have experienced oppression and marginalization in a patriarchal society.

EVALUATION OF FEMINIST THERAPY

Limitations

Feminist therapy, like other theories, is met with a range of criticisms that are important to consider. One of the major criticisms relates to the foundation of feminist therapy, which is based on the political feminism of White, heterosexual, middle-class women. Historically, there has been a lack of attention to the experiences of women of color, as well as other sociocultural factors other than gender (Evans et al., 2005). However, a growing body of scholarship has focused on diversity and complexity in feminist therapy, particularly within the past two decades. It is essential that feminist therapists keep abreast of this scholarship so that they are knowledgeable about the most current, inclusive conceptualizations of mental health and well-being among diverse populations.

Another major criticism of feminist therapy is that feminist therapists do not take a neutral stance, which may contribute to imposing their own values on clients. In addition, their approach of examining the impact of traditional perspectives and oppressive practices in society on psychological functioning can contribute to anxiety and discomfort on the part of the client. Clients who hold anti-feminist beliefs, in particular, may experience feminist therapy as incompatible with their needs and goals related to growth and development. Feminist therapists are transparent about their values and approach, which is a unique aspect of feminist therapy that sets it apart from some of the other major counseling theories.

The lack of research on the efficacy and effectiveness of feminist therapy is another important criticism, with some critics arguing that feminist therapy is not as clearly defined as other major counseling theories. Other critics have taken the stance that it is not a theory at all due to the incorporation of politics into the psychological understanding of distress. Research, however, has shown that feminist therapy is a specific intervention and that it is both effective, and distinctive, from other counseling theories (see Brown, 2010, for a discussion).

Critics of feminist therapy have also pointed to the focus on the impact of societal factors in contributing to client distress as potentially problematic, contending that this focus may neglect the exploration of a client's intrapsychic world. Some have argued that a "victim mentality" is created when clients place too much blame on external factors for their distress, and that having this mentality might contribute to clients' motivation to abandon their personal responsibility for experienced issues.

A final noteworthy limitation, rooted in societal misunderstanding and misconception rather than criticism, is that feminist therapy is conducted only by women therapists with women clients. The stigma of the term "feminist" may serve to discourage individuals, particularly men, who are experiencing distress from seeking counseling services that are rooted in a feminist approach.

The continued response from feminist therapists and allies to address misguided concerns about this term is essential in broadening effective services to diverse populations and creating meaningful change in society.

Strengths and Contributions

Feminist counseling scholars and practitioners have made numerous contributions to research, clinical practice, and societal progress since the development of feminist therapy in the 1970s. A notable strength of feminist therapy is its attention to the sociopolitical context—a focus that is not central to other major counseling theories, many of which overlook the impact of societal influences due to overemphasizing individual causes for client distress. By reframing suffering as adaptive responses to oppression, clients can cultivate an active change agent role in challenging inequalities and fostering resilience. Feminist therapists work with clients to separate dysfunctional environmental pressures from internal factors of distress. A benefit of this focus is that feminist therapists must keep abreast of how the sociopolitical context shapes mental health and well-being. Feminist therapy, therefore, is not static. Rather, it continues to evolve to promote the growth and development of diverse individuals.

Attention to diversity is central to the foundation of feminist therapy. Unique to feminist therapy is the centralization of gender and how it relates to experiences of oppression and interacts with other identity variables (e.g., race, age, disability). Feminist therapists attend to the multifaceted experiences of women, men, children, and other diverse populations by examining and addressing environmental factors (i.e., biases, stereotyping, oppression, discrimination, and other factors) that limit empowerment and well-being within personal, relational, social (political), and spiritual realms. The emphasis on an individualized and intersectional approach in counseling broadens feminist therapists' understanding of client distress and allows for the identification and implementation of a spectrum of strategies aimed to achieve mutually agreed-upon goals in counseling.

The ground-breaking work of feminist theorists, as well as multicultural, social justice, and advocacy theorists, has created a new way of thinking about client distress and how it should be approached. To confront environmental challenges and social injustices, these paradigms incorporate common threads to include empowerment, validating the range of injustices that impact clients' lives rather than the disease model (Crethar, Rivera, & Nash, 2008). By embracing the overarching commonalities among these approaches, therapists will be positioned to cultivate empowerment and psychological liberation in ways that help build a more equitable society (Crethar et al., 2008).

Finally, the availability of training opportunities is noteworthy. Feminist therapists can find educational groups, workshops, lectures, and information about advocacy events through engagement with two well-known feminist counseling organizations. The first organization, the Women's Therapy Centre Institute (WTCI; http://www.wtci-nyc.org) focuses on the integration of the feminist relational model with social justice. The second organization, the Jean Baker Miller Training Institute (JBMTI; https://www.wcwonline.org/Active-Projects/jean-baker-miller-training-institute), is well known for its theoretical works and trainings in relational-cultural theory. Both institutes were founded in 1981 and have continued to shape the practice of future generations of feminist therapists.

SKILL DEVELOPMENT: SELF-DISCLOSURE

Self-disclosure is a communication skill used by feminist therapists, often in tandem with others such as empathy, congruence, and genuineness. Many feminist therapists use self-disclosure to demystify the therapy process and promote an egalitarian relationship. Being open and clear with clients about relevant values that impact the therapeutic process is one way that feminist therapists acknowledge and respect clients' rights to make informed decisions about their participation in, and the nature of, the therapeutic process. Additionally, feminist therapists may also seek to minimize power differences in the therapeutic relationship by self-disclosing about their own personal struggles. This form of self-disclosure provides therapists with an opportunity to (1) serve as a role model for coping with distress, rather than being viewed as an all-powerful expert; and (2) challenge potentially held notions by clients that they are alone or deficient in resolving personal difficulties (Enns, 2004). Other content areas of self-disclosures include feelings about clients and the counseling process, social identities (e.g., sexual orientation, class, gender), and lifestyle (Enns, 2004).

Feminist counselors use self-disclosure only for the purposes of benefiting the client. Careful consideration related to the nature, timing, length, and frequency of self-disclosures is essential to their therapeutic effectiveness. As generally agreed upon by feminist therapists, self-disclosures should follow these three guidelines:

- *Self-disclosures should be appropriate.* Feminist therapists use self-disclosures to address the needs of the client, rather than their own needs as a therapist. The appropriateness of self-disclosures falls on a continuum from most appropriate (e.g., self-disclosure about professional training and background) to least appropriate (e.g., self-disclosure about current struggles in an intimate relationship).
- *Self-disclosures should be well timed.* Feminist therapists use self-disclosures in ways that support healthy relationship dynamics, intentionally avoiding self-disclosures that would cause disruption in the natural flow of the session. Self-disclosures are used when clients demonstrate a readiness to hear and apply the shared information from the therapist in ways that promote their growth and development.
- *Self-disclosures should be brief and infrequent.* Feminist therapists use self-disclosures in ways that maintain the focus on clients. When self-disclosures are lengthy and frequent, clients may feel invalidated and unsupported as the therapeutic focus becomes less about their experiences and needs. This dynamic, in turn, can contribute to disengagement and disconnection from the therapeutic relationship.

Below is an example of appropriate self-disclosure:

JANE: This is my first semester back at college and I'm really struggling. I am working part-time, taking classes, and have tennis practices and matches every week! If I quit something, I won't feel so overwhelmed. However, all of these activities are so important to me . . . I don't know what to do.

THERAPIST: I remember having a difficult time with balancing multiple responsibilities as a college student, too, while working.

[Self-disclosure is brief, is well timed, and is intended to normalize the client's experience.]

JANE: I can't imagine you struggling. You seem to have it all together, all the time. You are probably a pro at time management!

THERAPIST: Therapists are people, too, who deal with struggles in their own lives. You make a good point about time management. What advice related to time management would you have given me back when I was a college student?

[Therapist uses self-disclosure to invite the client to explore ways to think about and respond to her distress.]

JANE: First thing I would tell you to do is schedule your activities and prioritize. I have a college planner for that, but I haven't even used it! My anxiety got in the way and I couldn't focus. Thank you for sharing about your experience. It helps me put things into perspective.

[Client response to the therapist's self-disclosure suggests it was beneficial in addressing her distress and maintaining the egalitarian relationship.]

CASE APPLICATION

The following dialogue demonstrates the utility of assertiveness training with Edie. Based on the specific concerns raised in therapy, the therapist engaged in a dialogue with Edie about empowering and disempowering power dynamics within personal, relational, and social contexts in her life. Additionally, the therapist provided psychoeducation on assertive communication and invited Edie to explore ways that this technique can be used in her relationship with her mother and stepfather to promote more equal power dynamics. The therapist and Edie mutually agreed to incorporate assertiveness training into therapy and identified the following three goals:

1. Recognize the right to express thoughts, feelings, and needs to others respectfully.
2. Practice communications in a direct, honest, and open style without undue anxiety or fear.
3. Cultivate empowerment and personal pride.

For this next section, assume Edie has received assertiveness training in counseling. As you read the following dialogue, observe how the therapist fosters an egalitarian relationship, addresses Edie's blocks of acting assertively, and infuses the concept that the personal is political.

THERAPIST: Edie, we have discussed your feelings of distress around your mother and stepfather, which has led you to feel disempowered within these relationships. As we have explored, there are lingering feelings of anger toward your mother for not protecting you from the physical and emotional abuse you endured at the hands of your stepfather. I also hear that you feel empowered to have an honest conversation with your stepfather regarding your thoughts and feelings about your mistreatment in your childhood and how it impacts you to this day. After discussing assertive communication as an option to promote empowerment, I invite you to pick one relationship you would like to focus on today. Which one would you choose?

[Therapist allows the Edie to choose what concern she would like to address first, which promotes an egalitarian relationship.]

EDIE: Hmm, I think the one I'd like to start with today is my relationship with my mother. I keep thinking about that little girl . . . me. I was too afraid to share my feelings about my stepfather, her husband, out of fear of punishment.

THERAPIST: That is a definitely a place we can start. How have you communicated your thoughts and feelings so far?

EDIE: Well, that's the problem . . . I find myself trying to build up the courage to have an honest conversation with her . . . Bring up the past and how it is affecting me now . . . But again, I become that little girl . . . Too afraid to share how I really feel. So, I avoid it completely, just like I did with my stepfather. I prefer to dodge the conversation altogether.

THERAPIST:	[Shares information about communication styles]: Based on this information, how would you label your communication style with your mother?
EDIE:	I believe that it is passive communication . . . When talking to my mother, it is hard for me to express how I feel, my thoughts, and what I really want.
THERAPIST:	That's what I am hearing too. Usually when one uses passive communication, feelings of disempowerment build and sometimes the real issue is never addressed. For example, you reported feeling "afraid" as you get closer to sharing your thoughts and feelings with your mother about the abuse and how it is currently impacting you. As we discussed, practicing assertive behavior is key to minimizing this feeling. Women often experience difficulties doing so because there is an expectation to behave in nonassertive ways. *[Therapist uses a keyword from Edie's narrative instead of labeling the feelings as anxiety and offers psychoeducation on stereotypical gender roles (i.e., the personal is political).]*
EDIE:	Yeah! I have always struggled with finding my voice. I don't want to feel like this any longer, this feeling of powerlessness. I can't protect my mother anymore from truly understanding the pain I endured as a child and how this abuse has followed me into the present. I have a voice and I want to start using it.
THERAPIST:	You have a voice . . . Edie, that's your personal power! Let's role-play ways that you can state your needs, thoughts, and feelings to your mother in a clear, appropriate, and respectful way by using assertive communication. Remember to use "I" statements, be aware of your vocal tone and body language, and foster your power.

At this point, Edie has recognized the different communication styles and will continue to develop her assertive communication skills. She is more aware of the power that she holds and how assertiveness can guide her in her interpersonal functioning, while also meeting her needs and achieving her personal goals.

REFLECT AND RESPOND

1. Using your journal, respond to the following reflection questions:
   - As we started the chapter and you heard the word "feminist" what thoughts or images came to mind? How do these thoughts and/or images influence your attitudes about feminism and feminist therapy?
   - Do you identify as a feminist? Why or why not?
   - Is it necessary for those who practice feminist therapy to identify as feminists?
   - Is feminist therapy still needed today? Why or why not?
2. Draw a picture or write a poem in your journal that represents your understanding of the egalitarian relationship in feminist counseling. Following this creative exercise, write three to five sentences about the meaning(s) that you are trying to convey through your work.
3. Conduct the following self-assessment in your journal to explore the significance of gender norms (i.e., informal rules and socially based expectations for behavior related to gender) in your life. In the space next to each category, identify at least one gender norm that you follow.

   Personality Trait _____

   Domestic Behavior _____

Occupation/Career _____

Physical Appearance _____

Explore your responses and answer the following questions: In what ways do these norms empower and/or disempower you? What are your thoughts and feelings about challenging these norms? And, how does this exercise relate to feminist therapy?

4. Body image issues can impact anyone of any gender or age. Imagine that you are working with an adolescent girl, Amanda, who does not have positive thoughts and feelings about her body image. Identify one feminist therapy technique that you plan to use in the next session with her. In your journal, describe how you would introduce and implement your chosen technique.

Summary

Feminist therapy is rooted in the feminist movement and grew out of concerns that other theoretical orientations informing therapeutic work were not addressing the needs of women. Feminist therapy seeks to help *all* individuals examine their distress and focuses on the role of strengths and strategies that can be used in the context of clients' personal, relational, and/or social (political) lives to promote a sense of personal power, particularly in women and girls. Feminist therapists consider environmental variables and assume they contribute to client distress (disempowerment); therapists strive for transformational change rather than adjustment.

Feminist therapy focuses on individual and social change and attends to five key principles. One of the overarching principles is that no lasting change can occur without social change—the personal is political. Another concept is that the lived experiences of all individuals should be considered and valued throughout the therapeutic process. Feminist therapists also reframe pathology as coping and maintain that the distress of clients is understandable due to oppressive systems and society. The egalitarian relationship between therapists and clients is key to avoid unequal power dynamics that mirror oppressive experiences outside the counseling room. Finally, social location and multidimensional identities are considered, as feminist therapists believe they shape clients' experiences of empowerment and disempowerment.

Feminist therapy is collaborative and rooted in the client–therapist relationship. In a safe and affirmative context, clients are invited to examine their experienced distress using a feminist lens. Feminist therapy is not bound by predetermined therapeutic stages, transitions, time limits, or outcomes but, instead, evolves through a process of negotiation between the client and therapist. Clients are seen as the experts of their own realities and play an active role in the therapeutic process. In their work with clients, feminist therapists draw from a wide range of techniques that often span multiple therapeutic orientations. Therapeutic interventions are tailored to clients' strengths with the goal of fostering empowerment and increasing critical consciousness. Two primary techniques considered distinctive to feminist therapy, and often used in combination, are gender-role analysis and power analysis. Additional feminist therapy strategies include assertiveness training, reframing and relabeling, therapy-demystifying strategies, consciousness-raising, and social activism.

Feminist therapy has been used for over four decades to address the personal struggles that women face, as well as those who live at the margins of society. This therapeutic approach has focused considerable attention on specific mental health concerns, such as eating disorders, depression, nonsuicidal self-injury, body image and sexual objectification, intimate partner violence, childhood sexual abuse, and sexual assault. Many feminist therapists combine feminist therapy principles with other forms of therapy. Specific integrations of feminist therapy include humanistic and existential therapies, narrative therapy, Gestalt therapy, Adlerian therapy, solution-focused therapy, art therapy, psychodrama, psychodynamic therapy, cognitive and cognitive behavioral therapy, family systems therapies, and eye movement desensitization therapy.

Recommended Readings

American Psychological Association. (2007). *Guidelines or psychological practice with girls and women*. Washington, DC: Author.

Brown, L. S. (2010). *Feminist therapy*. Washington, DC: American Psychological Association.

Evans, K. M., Kincade, E. A., & Seem, S. R. (2011). *Introduction to feminist therapy: Strategies for social and individual change*. Thousand Oaks, CA: Sage.

Jordan, J. V. (2010). *Relational-cultural therapy*. Washington, DC: American Psychological Association.

Journal of Creativity in Mental Health—all issues.

Journal of Feminist Family Therapy—all issues.

Women & Therapy—all issues.

MyLab Counseling

Try the Topic 6 Assignments: Feminist Therapy.

CHAPTER

13 Postmodern Therapy

Learning Outcomes

When you have finished this chapter, you should be able to:
- Understand the context and development of Postmodern Therapies.
- Communicate the key concepts associated with Postmodern Therapies and understand how they relate to therapeutic processes.
- Describe the therapeutic goals of Postmodern Therapies.
- Identify the common techniques used in Postmodern Therapies.
- Understand how Postmodern Therapies relates to counseling diverse populations.
- Identify the limitations and strengths of Postmodern Therapies.

DEVELOPMENT OF POSTMODERN THEORIES

During much of the 20th century, when most of the theories discussed in this book were being developed, scientific observation—a modernist philosophical approach—was considered the best way to learn the "truth." Modernism takes a rationalist approach and is rooted in and emphasizes scientific truth and discovery. Modernists believe that true knowledge of phenomena can be discovered through objective observation (Gergen, 2009), and it arises from the concept that observers can separate themselves from whatever is being observed (Hansen, 2006). Each of the theories discussed in this book thus far is founded on the idea that there is one correct way of thinking about and explaining human behavior and how we can help people change. However, is it not possible that many competing "truths" can exist at once? Is it possible that there are no right or wrong ways to live or make sense of one's world?

By the end of the 20th century, critiques of modernist ways of thinking contributed to the development of postmodernism, a new philosophy and way of considering the world. Unlike modernism, which assumes one reality can be known, postmodernism assumes that people create their own realities (Scholl & Hansen, 2018). "Reality" then, is a human construction, and not something that can be objectively uncovered or discovered. Postmodernists believe that theories do not reflect what is "real" or "accurate" in an objective way; instead, postmodern therapists focus on the reality that clients construct, meeting clients within those realities, and helping clients connect with and move towards new, more satisfying realities. Postmodern epistemology, thus, maintains that reality is never objectively discovered; rather, it is always constructed by the observer.

Postmodern ways of thinking hold that concepts of truth, honesty, and authenticity are subjective and based on individual perceptions of the world. Instead of one fixed, agreed-upon reality, reality is co-created, constructed by individuals and based on what they perceive and experience.

Dogs, for example, might be considered cherished members of a family; a source of food; a source of danger; or, in Ancient Egypt, spiritual creatures who guided the dead into the afterlife (Hansen, 2006). As such, what can be determined about the nature of dogs? A postmodernist believes that the reality of dogs' nature is in the mindset or the context of the observer; no inherent, observable, measurable essence about dogs can be discovered (Hansen, 2006). To use a counseling example, consider a client who lost his brother a year earlier and perceives he has been grieving too long and seeks out counseling. How grief is handled is highly dependent upon culture and individual experience, thus how long individuals "should" grieve is a subjective matter. What counts in this case is that the client perceives he wants to address the issue. Meeting the client in his reality and helping him create a new story and a way forward is what is important.

Constructivism—the belief that individuals create their own views, constructs of events, and relationships in their own lives based on their own perceptions and experiences—relates to a postmodern philosophy. In other words, constructivism is the belief that individuals create or construct their ideas about their experiences. **Constructivists** pay attention to meanings that their clients give to their experiences and problems, and how clients make sense of and relate to their experience of their problems. While several constructivist theory schools of thought have been developed, this text addresses social constructivism. **Social constructivism**, the theory upon which the constructivist therapies discussed in this chapter are founded, holds that people's individual sense of reality and the meaning they find in their experiences are constructed and created in social situations and interactions with others, rather than discovered. In this way, clients' realities of their problems are valued, and whether these realities are right, wrong, or otherwise distorted is irrelevant; clients' perceptions are what matters. Social constructivists emphasize that what people "know" is constructed rather than discovered, and this knowledge is constructed within, and therefore affected by, its social context. This means that knowledge cannot be separated from its contexts, and this includes ethnicity, social class, gender, or a time in history.

While a modernist might ask, "What are the facts?" social constructivists ask, "What are the person's assumptions?" While the modernist might ask, "What are the answers?" social constructivists ask, "What are the questions and how were these questions constructed?" Therefore, according to social constructivists there is not one objective reality, but rather multiple ways of viewing the world, and these are based on social constructs and context. In this way, people experience multiple culturally defined selves, and possibilities and new ways of perceiving and experiencing are always close at hand (Gergen, 1991).

Postmodern theorists believe that clients are the experts about their situations. Therapists do not focus on assessing clients' problems and intervening. Instead, they partner with clients to explore clients' experiences of their problems and they co-create new realities with their clients.

Many approaches to therapy have emerged from the postmodern, social constructivist perspective, including narrative therapy (White & Epston, 1990), solution-focused brief therapy (SFBT; de Shazer, 1988), the positive psychology movement, and other strengths-based practices. All of these theories are phenomenological, experiential, and focus on people's perceptions of themselves and their worlds. These approaches adopt the postmodern assumption that there is no such thing as universal, objective knowledge and that people's perceptions reflect the language, values, and beliefs of their particular community or social system. These theories are holistic and seek to understand people fully and from many perspectives. Postmodern theories also assume that all people create meaning in deeply personal, unique, and individualized ways.

In all postmodern theories, the therapeutic alliance is collaborative and nonauthoritarian. Clients are the experts on their own lives and therapists are guides on the side. Therapists do not direct the process or seek to persuade, analyze, or instruct. Rather, they use empathy, encouragement, affirmation, reflection, elaboration, stories, and metaphors to advance counseling. They provide clients a safe place, focus on clients' strengths and abilities, and are caring and compassionate. Therapists help people construct more coherent and comprehensive self-theories or, as coauthors, assist clients in the identification and revision of central themes in their personal narratives; however, the clients are the primary change agents (Neimeyer, 1993).

Postmodern theorists view people in positive and optimistic terms, seeing them as proactive, goal directed, and always moving forward (Neimeyer, 1993). People operate according to the knowledge they possess, reflecting their construction of their experiences and actions. Knowledge evolves and changes with new experiences and perceptions. A central goal of constructivist counseling is helping clients connect with possibilities and recognize that all experiences have alternative meanings and interpretations. Clients' knowledge can then be assessed and either changed or validated, leading to knowledge that allows more satisfying ways of being.

Counseling initially begins with a focus on current problems and distress, then shifts to an exploration of patterns or recurrent difficulties, and finally moves to an understanding of underlying processes or constructions that perpetuate patterns. This approach can enable people to develop more rewarding ways of being and of navigating life.

Postmodern therapies have some therapeutic strategies in common. Language is an important focus because people create meaning through language. Language and how language is used is of central importance to all postmodern therapists. Language is the foundation of stories, and the stories people tell themselves and others reflect their experience of their situation. In fact, language not only labels human experience but also forms it. It is also through language that new, more helpful realities can be co-constructed. Through interactions with friends, family, culture, and society, people constantly create new stories that are more or less helpful and satisfying. Therapists work with clients to deconstruct their language or discourse, and construct—through language—more satisfying, hopeful, empowering stories.

Deconstructing or breaking down constructs is another frequently used strategy, as are co-creating new constructs, promoting empowerment, exploring themes and metaphors, expanding people's behavioral options, externalizing problems, and helping people create supportive networks (Richert, 2010). Behavioral strategies and the development of skills are also important aspects of these approaches, and many postmodern therapists integrate skill development into therapy as needed (Mahoney, 2003).

Postmodern theories highlight the importance of the individual in society, diversity, and the client–therapist collaboration. They are holistic, integrative, and flexible. They are respectful and optimistic, viewing people's efforts to cope as sources of knowledge that can promote positive change.

Postmodern and constructivist themes run through all areas of contemporary society, including education, government, science, and human resources (Mahoney, 2003). The expressions of these concepts will likely continue to grow in importance and influence the helping professions and the larger society. Now we look more deeply at two popular postmodern constructivist approaches: narrative therapy and solution-focused brief therapy.

NARRATIVE THERAPY

MICHAEL WHITE (1948–2008)

Michael White, one of the founders of narrative therapy, was born and raised in Australia. White's journey in counseling first began as a probation and welfare worker. After majoring in social work as an undergraduate, he worked at Adelaide Children's Hospital as a psychiatric social worker. He founded and became codirector of the Dulwich Centre in Adelaide in 1983. He also began a private practice, where he worked as a family therapist. In 2008, White founded the Adelaide Narrative Therapy Centre, where counseling services and training workshops are provided. Narrative therapy has been used with children, families, and communities around the world.

White also worked and applied narrative therapy to work with Indigenous Aboriginal communities. White authored several books, including *Narrative Means to Therapeutic Ends* (White & Epston, 1990), *Reauthoring Lives: Interviews and Essays* (1995), *Narrative of Therapists' Lives* (1997), and *Maps of Narrative Practice* (2007). White died in 2008 while conducting a workshop in San Diego, California.

DAVID EPSTON (b. 1944)

David Epston, one of the founders of narrative therapy, was born and raised in Canada but later moved to New Zealand in 1964. Epston attended Auckland University, where he earned a BA in sociology and anthropology. Two years later, in 1971, he earned a degree in community development from Edinburgh University. He then attended graduate school at Warwick University in the United Kingdom, where he earned an MA in applied social studies. Epston worked at a hospital in Auckland as a senior social worker. He then worked at the Leslie Centre as a family therapist from 1981 to 1987. He is currently the codirector of the Family Therapy Centre located in Auckland, New Zealand. He is also a visiting professor at John F. Kennedy University and an affiliate faculty member at North Dakota State University in the couple and family therapy doctorate program. Epston has presented lectures and led workshops throughout the world. He is coauthor of the seminal work on narrative therapy, *Narrative Means to Therapeutic Ends* (White & Epston, 1990); and has also co-authored *Playful Approaches to Serious Problems: Narrative Therapy with Children and Their Families* (Freeman, Epston, & Lobovits, 1997) and *Biting the Hand That Starves You* (Maisel, Epston, & Borden, 2004).

© Paola Arias Fotografia

INTRODUCTION/DEVELOPMENT OF NARRATIVE THERAPY

According to narrative therapy, people are interpretive beings who make meaning of themselves and their world through the language of stories that have become part of themselves, as well as their understanding of those stories. People make sense of their worlds and experiences as they create adaptive or maladaptive stories through language and their interactions with others (Gergen, 2009). Narrative theorists believe that through exploration, deconstruction, and revision of problematic stories, people can shift their perceptions and create alternative scripts, leading to greater empowerment and the ability to more successfully manage their lives.

Narrative therapy is based on the idea that identity or perceptions of problems are shaped by the stories that people tell themselves and others. Narrative therapists encourage clients to share these stories. They believe that by sharing these stories, clients can examine their stories in a new light. The word *narrative* refers to the emphasis placed upon the stories of people's lives and the differences that can be made through particular tellings and retellings of these stories (Morgan, 2000). In essence, an essential aspect of narrative therapy is the idea that clients reauthor their stories, or they create new stories that are more adaptive in thinking about their experiences and problems (Morgan).

Narrative therapy takes the phenomenological emphasis of humanistic counseling theories one step further. Not only do narrative therapists believe that people's perceptions determine their realities, but they also believe that loosening and changing people's perceptions are the best routes to facilitating their positive development. Rather than looking at clients as having pathological disorders or being somehow problematic or flawed, narrative therapists consider people who consult them to be under the influence of problem-saturated stories (Malinen, Cooper, & Thomas, 2011). With narrative tools such as mapping, externalization, and other strategies that will be discussed later, narrative therapists collaborate with clients to deconstruct their stories and then create new ones so that clients essentially reauthor their lives.

Narrative therapy's roots lie in Australia in the work of Michael White and David Epston (1990). However, therapists and researchers worldwide have shown interest in its application and study. Important influences on narrative therapy include the ideas of Gregory Bateson, George Kelly, and French philosopher Michel Foucault. Other important influences on White's philosophy and thinking include family systems theory, cybernetics, and Vygotsky's social development theory. White was able to combine his interest in philosophy, particularly the poststructuralist philosophy of French philosopher Michel Foucault, with his desire to help people. He had special interest in helping those who had become disenfranchised or marginalized by society. Michael Foucault's writing on the interrelationship of knowledge and power led White to address the damaging effects of encouraging people to adjust and comply with stereotyped standards of behavior. He believed that this could undermine their efforts to lead a life of their own design (White & Epston, 1990).

In several important ways, narrative therapy represents a departure from conventional counseling and psychotherapy. White referred to himself as a consultant, and in many ways he was an anthropologist in that he did not seek to heal or fix people, but to learn about them, understand them, and help them identify a new path forward.

Narrative therapists believe that people's lives are created and interpreted through stories: the ones they hear, the ones they create in their own minds, and the ones they tell and retell (Lee, 1997). No essential truths exist on their own; realities are constructed and maintained through language, social interactions, and stories (Mascher, 2002).

Consider the following example. Suki, a young Asian woman, sought counseling because of her difficulty trusting others, her inability to form close relationships, and what she termed her "self-hatred" that led her to cut herself repeatedly. Suki's mother had told her the following story many times since Suki was a young child: "When I became pregnant with you, I was living with your father. He was a terrible man. He beat me, he stayed with other women, and he took all the money I had. I wanted so badly to leave him. When I found out I was pregnant, I was devastated. I thought I would never be able to escape. So I went to a wise woman in the village and asked her to help me abort you. I did everything she told me, but it didn't work. I went back to her, and she told me other things to do. I did everything again, but it still didn't work. Then I decided that this baby was meant to be. I packed up everything I could carry and ran away. I found my way to the home of my aunt, who took me in and helped me until you were born."

Hearing this story again and again led Suki to adopt a negative view of herself and her world. She perceived herself as unwanted by both her father and her mother. She saw herself as a burden to her mother and viewed men as abusive and untrustworthy. She believed that she could only survive if she avoided closeness and intimacy with others. At the same time, she viewed herself as unworthy of survival and thought that everyone would have been happier if the abortion had been successful. Her self-injurious behavior and her inability to trust reflected views of herself and the world that grew out of the story her mother had told her. Although Suki's mother later married an American man who brought Suki and her mother to the United States and was a loving father to Suki, the story continued to have an impact. Stories give messages and can become the road maps of our lives. Narrative therapy helped Suki to deconstruct those stories, consider alternative stories, choose a preferred path, and improve her life.

KEY CONCEPTS

Narrative therapy uses a different framework from that of many other traditional theories. Establishing a collaborative relationship with clients and viewing clients as experts on their own lives are essential. Therapists aim to listen to their clients' stories and pay attention to the various resources and skills clients possess. Narrative therapy is also different from most other therapies because therapists tend to not pathologize, diagnose, or otherwise put clients in a box. Therapists help their clients create alternative stories by asking questions to initiate exploration and separating clients from their problem-saturated, dominant stories (Freedman & Combs, 1996). Many of the key concepts and therapeutic processes that will be discussed in these sections are modified from those of various authors, including Winslade and Monk (2007); Monk (1997); Winslade, Crocket, and Monk (1997); and Freedman and Combs (1996).

Stories

People have a large repertoire of stories they carry with them. All stories are accepted as legitimate and important in narrative therapy. However, stories tend to fall into several categories. People often have a single **dominant story** that shapes who they are. A dominant story typically acts as a sort of tyrant that censors and changes a person's other stories and can send those stories into oblivion. White (1986) posed the idea of **specifications of personhood**, which is the information in the stories that tells people how to behave as individuals or family members. Specifications of personhood act as restraints and keep people stuck in and limited by their dominant stories.

Lost, untold, or marginalized stories also need to be told and may serve people better than their dominant stories, particularly if the lost stories portray a life in which problems are either solved or absent. These stories are known as **alternative stories**. By focusing on the strengths, positive aspects, and good outcomes of the story rather than a problem outcome, people are more likely to create a new, preferred story. For example, Suki's stepfather told her stories about how she used to make up poems when she was a child and how much he enjoyed reading her poems. However, as long as her single dominant story was in control, Suki paid little attention to her stepfather's stories, which reflected appreciation for her intelligence and creativity. Accessing those untold stories helped Suki value herself and use her intelligence and creativity to relate to others more successfully.

People are constantly trying to make sense of life's events. The narratives they tell themselves determine their self-identity. Different types of stories result in unhappiness or dysfunction (Richert, 2010). Some narratives are too constricting but have become accepted by the dominant culture and internalized by clients. People who do not have all options available to them become labeled or otherwise constrained, which leads to personal frustration and dissatisfaction. Unhelpful narratives around themes of gender, race, or psychological illness are examples of these types of stories. When people's stories are fragmented, disorganized, and/or lack cohesiveness, client distress can also occur. When this happens, people's realities become fragmented and difficult to cope with, leading to stress, anxiety, depression, and, ultimately, an inability to conduct goal-oriented behavior (Richert, 2010).

In all cases, narrative therapists believe the solution is to help people open up new pathways and possibilities for living so they can find greater satisfaction in their lives. In narrative therapy, the work begins by eliciting stories.

Narrative therapists believe that stories have a cultural and interpersonal basis and that their meanings are generated through social interactions (Richert, 2003). Consequently, therapists maintain awareness of people's social and cultural contexts and incorporate them into counseling. Stories may be passed from one person to another, shaped along the way, and given to people as a legacy from their families. Clients are encouraged to recognize the family origins of some of their stories and to find people in their social and family networks who have similar experiences and problems. Drawing on those relationships and learning about ways in which other people have addressed similar problems can provide support, resources, and education about problem solving.

Because of the importance of social systems in creating and forming people's stories, narrative therapists also use social systems to promote and solidify people's revisioned stories. Clients may be encouraged to tell their new stories to significant members of their social system who are chosen to hear and witness the new self-narrative (Carr, 1998). This public declaration helps solidify changes and puts others on notice to expect people to reauthor their lives.

Listening with an Open Mind

Therapists strive to listen to their clients with a nonjudgmental and nonblaming attitude. It is essential that therapists affirm, value, and respect their clients. In fact, therapists even go against normalizing judgment, which is any kind of judgment that assesses intelligence, mental health, and normal behavior based on a normal curve. Therapists who use this framework believe that listening without personal judgment includes listening without normalizing judgment, as well. Therapists even invite clients to reflect on how normal judgments have impacted them and how they feel about themselves. Specifically, what is "normal" for someone might be completely different for someone else. Clients have the opportunity to value their own experiences and feel validated that their reality is what matters.

Narrative therapists aim to help clients change their painful beliefs and interpretations without imposing their own values on the clients. Therapists guide clients in creating their own meaning and possibilities and reinforce the clients' own beliefs and stories. Narrative therapists also listen to their clients' problem-filled stories with an effort to bring optimism, talents, and competencies of clients to light (Winslade & Monk, 2007). Therapists have the responsibility of showing their clients that they believe in them.

THE THERAPEUTIC PROCESS

Stages of Narrative Therapy

The three stages of narrative therapy include eliciting stories, deconstruction of stories, and revisioning and reauthoring, each of which will be discussed below. The following list provides an overview of the structure of narrative therapy, but it is important to consider that narrative therapy is not a linear process and is best described as circular:

- Form a collaborative dialogue with clients and agree upon a name for their problem. Understand the negative effects the problem has on clients and personify/externalize the problem.
- Initiate new perspectives of clients' stories by creating new meanings for the story.
- Bring to light exceptions to the problem by focusing on moments of resilience in the story. To illustrate competencies, discover evidence of ways clients have protected themselves from the oppressive effects of the problem. (This begins the start of rewriting the story.)
- Invite clients to think about their less problem-saturated future by seeing themselves as strong and competent.
- Encourage clients to live their new story outside of the therapy room and include the social environment to create lasting effects.

ELICITING STORIES Narrative therapists begin counseling by listening to clients' stories, also known as the eliciting stories stage of counseling. Therapists concentrate on the effects rather than the cause of clients' problems. Most people produce stories spontaneously and typically enjoy telling stories. However, those stories that support the dominant theme are usually closest to the surface and most accessible. Narrative therapists use various strategies to encourage people to tell a wider variety of stories, and some of these follow (Carr, 1998):

- Therapists may ask clients to tell alternative stories about a single event or emotion.
- Therapists may suggest that clients create a story about themselves and their lives as if they were another individual or ask them to assume a different perspective.
- Therapists may suggest that clients extend their stories into the future.
- Therapists may ask about neglected aspects of the stories clients tell.
- Therapists may ask clients to tell stories in which they are more powerful than their problems.

DECONSTRUCTION OF STORIES Before stories can be changed, they must be taken apart, analyzed, and understood, which is referred to as **story deconstruction**. Narrative therapists use several strategies to accomplish this, such as mapping and externalizing. The main goals in this stage are to identify **themes** and metaphors that are prominent in the stories, enable clients to recognize the influence the stories have had on them, and help clients see that they did not totally create their stories themselves. In addition, identifying **positive narratives**, or things that are going well in clients' stories, is essential to deconstructing and understanding stories.

Clients' stories contain both landscapes of consciousness and landscapes of action (Bruner, 2002). **Landscapes of consciousness** are the backdrops of values, feelings, motives, beliefs, and attitudes that recur in clients' stories. **Landscapes of action** are the sequences of behaviors related to events in clients' lives that similarly pervade and recur in their stories. Questions help people identify, reflect on, determine the meaning of, and perhaps change these landscapes. In Suki's stories, the landscapes of consciousness generally reflected hopelessness, sorrow, and pain. People in her stories usually experienced rejection and loss. In the landscape of action, Suki was usually withdrawn and ineffectual.

REVISIONING AND REAUTHORING Once stories have been told and deconstruction has begun, the stories can be modified or revisioned. Only the clients have the right to make and accept changes to their stories, although therapists often suggest alternative viewpoints and elicit stories of power and resourcefulness.

Revisioning entails both changing the story and changing people's visions of their lives. The two are inseparable; as people come to see the rules and meanings that govern the old stories more clearly, their vision changes, a new interpretation of their lives emerges, and the stories can be revisioned. As revisioning proceeds, it provides opportunities for further deconstruction, which in turn allows for more story revisioning. Gradually, alternative stories that offer exceptions to the dominant story emerge, and other perspectives become available for incorporation into the stories (White, 1989).

Once clients begin to revision their stories, **reauthoring** can take place. Possibilities for new thoughts, actions, and emotions are expanded as therapists and clients create new descriptions of old stories (Gottlieb & Gottlieb, 1996). As they reauthor stories, clients come to understand their meaning constructions and can move toward a more productive version of their self-narratives in terms of their feelings about themselves and their relationships with others (Lee, 1997). Through revisioning and reauthoring, clients are empowered to develop alternative and preferred self-narratives extending into the future, in which the self is viewed as more powerful than the problem (Carr, 1998; White, 1995). At this point, clients are ready to solidify their gains and share them with others.

Therapeutic Goals

Narrative therapy does not seek to change clients. Instead, it aims to transform the effects of clients' perceived problems. Narrative therapists aim to make space between a person and their struggle, and to help them create more satisfying relationships with their perceived problems. Through new language, clients come to experience their struggles in new ways, develop new stories that better serve their interests, and find new meaning (Freedman & Combs, 1996). Another goal of narrative therapy is to help clients gain new insights into how the dominant culture has impacted their lives. Along with this, gaining a broader perspective and enhancing the options clients have to create new stories are essential.

Therapist's Function and Role

In narrative therapy, the therapists are consultants, collaborators, and facilitators. Clients are the experts on themselves and their stories, whereas therapists are the experts on narrative therapy. In other words, therapists adopt a stance of not knowing (Carr, 1998). Therapists and clients are coauthors and collaborators, sharing the responsibility for shaping the counseling process. In fact, both parties bring a great deal to the conversation (Brown, 2007). In addition, throughout counseling, therapists are consulting with clients to understand the issue based on clients' own personal definitions. Therapists understand that the personal definitions clients have for their stories are unique to them, which creates a more personal and inviting relationship between therapists and clients. The collaborating and consulting technique gives clients more authority and control in hopes that they will move forward with achieving their goals. Narrative therapists have referred to themselves as "collaborationists" and state that they are creating a shift in clients' consciousness rather than solving problems (Malinen et al., 2011).

Narrative therapists strongly emphasize being respectful and encouraging of clients' strengths and resources. Although therapists do share their own perceptions and stories, including those about the clients, they assume a tentative stance, never prescribing or judging. This allows clients to know the therapeutic environment is a safe and comfortable place. Concepts such as resistance, denial, and mental pathology, which may give therapists the upper hand, are not a part of narrative therapy. In fact, resistance is viewed as the clients' attempt to make the pace of counseling more comfortable for them.

Relationship Between Therapist and Client

Narrative therapists are curious, optimistic, respectful, and persistent; they value the client's knowledge and perceptions, and they are collaborative and egalitarian. Narrative therapists focus on encouraging and facilitating rather than changing people. They are inquiring rather than knowing, asking questions about the content and context of clients' stories, as well as the meaning of their stories. They are active in suggesting exercises, offering new viewpoints, and soliciting feedback (Winslade & Monk, 2007). They help their clients appreciate themselves and enable them to play an important part in their counseling. Therapists use careful listening, empathy, summarization, and paraphrasing to give people ownership over their right to create themselves and to listen to themselves in new ways that engender courage, hope, and resourcefulness.

Typical of the approaches discussed in this chapter, narrative therapists remain aware of the part they play in clients' development and often discuss this with them. Narrative therapists are authentic and reflect themselves honestly through all interactions with clients. Narrative therapists are active, asking questions designed to help people deconstruct old stories and identify new possibilities that can lead to fresh outcomes (Richert, 2010). This collaborative process between clients and therapist, called co-construction or coauthoring of stories, is an essential part of the therapeutic process. Narrative therapy emphasizes the resurrection of clients' suppressed voice (Brown, 2007) to create open knowledge that has once been disqualified. Therapists and clients work together to share meanings and identify expectations inherent in the culture, gender, race, or other relevant frameworks, to view them in context and therefore decrease their power or effect on clients.

Similarly, every effort is made to elevate the client and decrease the therapist's position of power. In narrative therapy, the client is encouraged to ask questions about the reasoning behind the therapist's questions, and therapist self-disclosure is considered helpful because it reduces the power differential in the relationship (Richert, 2010).

Narrative therapists avoid judgments and categorizations, and help clients look for exceptions and times in the past in which the problem did not occur. Planning for setbacks is frequently done ahead of time by asking clients what they would do if their problem reappeared. Positive affirmations such as celebrations and certificates that recognize accomplishments are methods frequently used by narrative therapists to encourage, acknowledge, and document progress (White & Epston, 1990). At the conclusion of therapy, many narrative therapists give their clients thoughtful letters delineating their progress. Such letters are a means of helping clients maintain the changes they have made, as well as carrying on the connection between therapists and the clients.

THERAPEUTIC TECHNIQUES AND PROCEDURES

Mapping

Clients' presenting problems are identified and linked to their stories, illustrating how their problems emerged and are handled in the stories through **mapping**. Similarly, clients are encouraged to look at how their positive interpersonal experiences mesh with and potentially change their dominant stories and landscapes.

Clients find it difficult to make changes. As such, clients need encouragement in bridging the gap between familiar actions and new possibilities. Narrative therapists use language and conversation to help guide clients toward these new possibilities. Mapping is discussed further in the Skill Development section at the end of this chapter.

Externalizing

The process of separating clients from their problems is called **externalizing**. The therapist uses externalizing language to reinforce that the problem is having an effect on clients and that the problems do not exist *within* clients (Payne, 2006). For example, a therapist might say "Anger has power over you" or "Anxiety robbed you of your peace" to help clients separate their identities from the problems. Externalization is facilitated by helping people identify the threads connecting many stories and the assumptions the stories suggest about the self and the world. Once externalization occurs, access points for changing the story can be identified. Careful and deliberate use of language by the therapist facilitates externalization and can empower clients.

This process of externalization seems to conflict with the emphasis of Gestalt therapists on helping people own and take responsibility for their difficulties. However, narrative therapists believe that externalizing and objectifying problems reduces feelings of failure and guilt, decreases unproductive discussions about fault and blame, provides people with new perspectives on their difficulties, reduces blocks to action and change, and opens the way for clients to reclaim their lives from their problems. Instead of believing they are the problem, clients can mobilize their resources to combat the problem, which is now separate from who they are. They can establish new views of their problems and themselves, seeing themselves as competent and powerful people who have some problems that need attention rather than people who are problem ridden and flawed. Three main strategies enhance the externalization process, including naming the problem, letter writing, and drawing the problem.

NAMING THE PROBLEM Narrative therapists believe that their job is to facilitate a safe, exploratory therapeutic environment where diverse, nonpathological, and alternative perspectives and stories can be entertained, which is markedly different from approaches in which therapists function as experts by providing clients with authoritative, complete, or definitive responses. Narrative therapists often encourage clients to use metaphors to turn the problem into an object.

In naming the problem, clients are asked to label the negative influence or the problem. Clients select a name for the influence that seems appropriate and adequately describes the problem's influence. Having clients select their own individual names ensures that the names are meaningful to clients while also giving the therapist a sense of how the problem is experienced by clients. For example, clients who self-injure may be encouraged to develop a title (e.g., The Red Razor) to metaphorically represent the now objectified problem. As the problem is discussed in counseling, the externalized name is used. Using client-generated names further contributes to the clients' sense of meaning and connection to the externalized problem.

THE USE OF LETTER WRITING Narrative therapy pulls on the use of letter writing as an important part of the therapeutic process (White & Epston, 1990). Within the narrative therapy framework, letter writing can allow a physical way for the problem to be externalized, named, and then confronted. In addition, because clients for the most part direct the content of such letters, they determine pacing, as well as what, when, and whether to disclose. Thus, letter writing proves beneficial because it provides a means for people to trace their stories through time at a self-guided pace, thereby embodying changes and avenues for potential change for which clients are searching (White & Epston, 1990).

The intent of the letter writing is to assist clients in reauthoring unique aspects of their lives, aspects that may have been restrained by their problems. To empower clients to take charge of their problem, they are encouraged to write letters directly to the problem (e.g., Dear Red Razor). Therapeutic letters can be re-read and the story can be reconsidered both during the session and after the session has ended (White & Epston, 1990). These therapeutic letters then provide clients with a supportive resource to which they can refer back for encouragement or reminders.

DRAWING THE PROBLEM The purpose of drawing the problem is to further enhance the externalization process. Once clients have successfully identified and named the problem, they can be invited to further boost the externalization process by creating a new reality of the problem through drawing the externalized object.

To effectively stimulate creativity, clients should be allowed access to a variety of art mediums, such as markers, paints, crayons, and colored pencils. Therapists then encourage clients to draw a visual representation that is meaningful to the externalization of their problem. Clients may be given the following directions:

> "Please draw your visual perceptions of the named influence. What does the influence look like? Consider your internal perceptions and visualizations of what the influence looks like."

After sharing the meanings of their drawing, clients are asked to add to the drawing or revise it in a way that indicates how they will visualize themselves confronting the influence. Therapists then ask clients to do the following:

> "Consider what the influence will look like as you continue to confront it and remove it from your life. Draw a picture of "what the influence looks like as you continue to push its influence away."

This activity provides a visual and concrete technique that clients can use to externalize the problem and enhance their sense of efficacy in controlling the problem influence.

Therapeutic Documents

Materials, usually prepared by therapists in collaboration with clients, that reinforce and provide evidence of accomplishments are **therapeutic documents**. The documents help to reinforce and punctuate successes and new stories. Both clients and therapists decide on the form for the documents, how they should be prepared, when and how they should be consulted, and with whom they should be shared (Crocket, 2012). The documents may take the form of literary productions such as personal letters, lists, reports, certificates and awards, news releases, personal declarations, letters of reference, or manifestos that articulate clients' problems, contradict the dominant plots of their lives, and suggest ways for them to deal with these problems (White & Epston, 1990).

An exchange of letters between clients and therapists is another form of documentation; these letters may be used to promote clients' reflection and to put their ideas and alternatives into a concrete form that can be kept as a resource. Therapeutic documents have shown power and effectiveness, with some research suggesting that one therapeutic letter is worth 4.5 sessions of good therapy in terms of its impact (Crocket, 2012).

APPLICATION AND CURRENT USE OF NARRATIVE THERAPY

Until recently, not much research was available on the effectiveness of narrative therapy; however, in the past decade, there have been a number of investigations into the construct of narrative identity, spanning almost every theoretical orientation in psychology, including personality and lifespan development, cultural and clinical psychology, existential and end-of-life issues, and cognitive therapy (Adler, 2012). In addition, a longitudinal study of narrative identity development and mental health seems to suggest that increased agency brought about by creating new stories may lead to symptom relief and improved mental health among people exposed to narrative therapy. One recent empirical study even found narrative therapy to be as effective as cognitive behavioral therapy in treating depression (Lopes et al., 2014). However, much support for the effectiveness of narrative therapy is based on case study research. Clearly, more research is necessary before conclusions about its effectiveness can be made. Still to be determined is which comes first, feeling better or telling a new story? (Adler, 2012).

Narrative therapy may be helpful when counseling people who abuse alcohol (Sanders, 2007; Winslade & Smith, 1997). Narrative therapists take a unique approach that contradicts the traditional Alcoholics Anonymous stance, which encourages people to internalize their problem ("I am an alcoholic"). Instead, narrative therapists help clients to externalize the problem and give it a name (e.g., "Al"). In this way, people separate themselves from a close identification with alcohol and are, according to narrative therapists, in a better position to combat its influence. In addition, rather than assuming the role of expert and teaching people skills to change their behaviors, therapists help clients discover and use the knowledge they already have to deal with the problems alcohol has brought into their lives. Rather than pathologizing clients, this therapy empowers them to develop agency through the reauthoring of their stories. Through the acceptance that comes from being heard as they attest to their stories, clients begin to reflect on their choices, develop hope for the future, and start to create alternative identities (Sanders, 2007).

Counseling Applications

Because the approach does not focus on diagnosis of pathology and is deeply respectful of people's ownership of their own lives, it can be useful with a broad range of clients and concerns. Narrative therapy seems particularly helpful for treating people who have been victimized and disenfranchised by others, such as women, older adults, and those from certain ethnic and cultural groups. Specifically, this approach can be useful for women who have been abused because it challenges sociopolitical views, focuses on advocacy, and supports the reauthoring of people's life stories (Drauker, 1998). Similarly, when used with older adults, narrative therapy can be positive and life affirming, transforming stories that are based on loss and worthlessness into those that reflect a rich and full life. Narrative therapy can also provide a respectful way to understand people from diverse cultural backgrounds and those who are oppressed, giving them the opportunity to tell the stories of their lives and revise those stories in ways that give them greater power and control and also are consistent with the values and beliefs of their cultures. For example, narrative therapy has been effectively used with clients who are transgender (Mallory, Brown, Conner, & Henry, 2017), as it provides them with an opportunity to deconstruct and reconstruct their current views of gender as related to themselves.

Narrative therapy has also been used with couples who are experiencing conflict, survivors of suicide, women with eating disorders, and men who have perpetrated violence (White, 2011). In addition, narrative therapy has found success in helping people cope with trauma (Erbes, Stillman, Wieling, Bera, & Leskela, 2014); in helping children with social phobia (Looyeh, Kamali, Ghasemi, & Tonawanik, 2014); and in helping people with substance abuse issues (Szabo, Toth, & Pakai, 2014). The focus on affirmative life stories and emphasizing the positives rather than the negatives is particularly helpful for people who experience depression (Seo, Kang, Lee, & Chae, 2015). Narrative therapy can also work well for clients with learning disabilities because it empowers them and enables them to find resources and strengths (McParland, 2015).

Narrative therapy also benefits children and adolescents who are experiencing grief (Hedtke, 2014). Therapists help their clients find hope and healing through their pain. Meaning-making, the subjectivity of stories, and forming a resilient story are all emphasized, which helps clients see their story from different perspectives that promote adaptation and healing. Children with emotional and social skill deficits may also benefit from narrative therapy, especially when using techniques like externalization and reauthoring (Beaudoin, Moersch, & Evare, 2016). Specifically, children are likely to gain self-awareness, make better decisions, and problem solve more effectively. In addition, their interpersonal relationships may improve.

This approach has also been used with clients who experienced sexual abuse. Narrative therapy provides a safe and protected relationship for clients to relive and reprocess their trauma (van der Kolk, 2014). They may use expressive practices, such as sand trays; genograms; visualization during the restoration of their trauma; and **narradrama**, which is the combining of drama therapy and narrative therapy in which clients can act out their story. Narrative therapy allows clients to view themselves and their story in a more positive light by focusing on strengths, resilience, and courage.

Incorporating people's stories and their revisions into counseling seems to be a beneficial strategy; therefore, narrative techniques are frequently integrated into other theoretical approaches. For example, psychiatrists are discovering the value of using a narrative approach in medicine to create empathic and meaningful connections with clients (Lewis, 2011). In addition, narrative therapy has been combined with emotion-focused therapy and can be beneficial in group settings (Seo et al., 2015; Szabo et al., 2014).

Application to Family Interventions and Involvement

Despite the fact that narrative therapy is not a family systems theory and does not consider psychological symptoms to be related to family conflict—nor does it view some problems as interactional—White and Epston's narrative approach to individual therapy has broad applications for work in child, adolescent, couples, and family therapy. In a family setting, the goal is to promote the exploration of solutions among common family problems. This can include child behavior management, parent-adolescent conflict, school problems, couple relationship difficulties, and other forms of family conflict (Madigan, 2011). Overall, the goal is to create positive interactions within the family and transform negative communication or responses into more accepting, nonjudgmental, and meaningful exchanges. This form of therapy helps families reconnect their relationships and create ways toward a healthier future. Narrative therapy for children and families has helped children with attention-deficit/hyperactivity disorder (Looyeh, Kamali, & Shafieian, 2012), eating disorders (Freeman, Epston, & Lebovitz, 1997), attachment issues (Dallos, 2006), and trauma (White & Morgan, 2006) and has assisted parents in putting an end to negative multigenerational patterns such as alcohol abuse and abusive anger. It has also been used in play therapy with children, with adolescents individually, and with their families.

Application to Multicultural Groups

Narrative therapy is particularly relevant for working with diverse clients because it is grounded in a belief that clients' sociocultural context is very important. Clients' problems do not exist within the individual, but rather within social, cultural, and political contexts. Various aspects of culture, such as race, sexual orientation, and spirituality and religion are considered important and are often addressed in therapy. Narrative therapy allows clients to reauthor their stories to determine their own identity rather than living their lives based on social constructions. Clients have the opportunity to recognize how society has been oppressive and gain awareness to create their own preferred story.

Narrative therapists recognize the importance of clients' worldviews and believe that all people construct their own reality. Therapists using narrative therapy make an effort to learn about the experiences of their clients and are respectful of their clients' beliefs and worldviews. The perspective that many realities exist lends itself well to working with diverse clients.

EVALUATION OF NARRATIVE THERAPY

Limitations

Narrative therapy may not be suitable for people who cannot engage in a coherent conversation because of their poor contact with reality, for those who seek a quick solution to a specific problem, for those who are in crisis, and for those who anticipate little benefit from counseling. The strategies used in this therapy are much more extensive than people typically think. Therapists must be highly trained and skilled in a variety of techniques. In addition, some therapists may view the ideas of narrative therapy in a mechanistic fashion. Relying too much on only a few of the techniques associated with the theory also presents a danger.

Strengths and Contributions

Narrative therapy offers a new perspective on counseling as well as considerable promise. Its effectiveness has been shown with a wide variety of populations, such as people who have experienced trauma, people with substance abuse issues, and people who are experiencing grief. The central theme of using questions as a technique is essential for assessing people's thoughts, feelings, behaviors, attitudes, and perceptions. Questions can also be used effectively to help clients gain new insights, a different perspective, and a new story. The approach is optimistic, relies on the client as the expert, and pays much attention to the therapeutic relationship.

SOLUTION-FOCUSED BRIEF THERAPY

STEVE DE SHAZER (1940–2005)

Steve de Shazer, one of the founders of solution-focused brief therapy, was born in Milwaukee, Wisconsin. De Shazer attended the University of Wisconsin–Milwaukee, where he earned a BA in fine arts and trained as a classical musician, specializing as a professional jazz saxophonist. He then earned a master's of science degree in social work from the University of Wisconsin–Milwaukee. In the 1970s and early 1980s, he worked with his wife, Insoo Kim Berg, Milton Ericksen, and others at the Mental Research Institute in Palo Alto, California (Presbury, Echterling, & McKee, 2008). He and Berg founded the Brief Family Therapy Center in 1978, located in Milwaukee, Wisconsin. He provided many workshops, trainings, and teachings throughout the world. Some of his major books include *Keys to Solutions in Brief Therapy* (1985), *Clues: Investigating Solutions in Brief Therapy* (1988), *Putting Differences to Work* (1991), and *Words Were Originally Magic* (1994). He wrote six well-known books that were translated into 14 different languages. De Shazer died in 2005 in Europe while on a teaching tour.

INSOO KIM BERG (1934–2007)

Insoo Kim Berg, one of the founders of solution-focused brief therapy, was born in Korea. She was a pharmacy major at Ewha Womans University and then moved to the United States in 1957 to continue her pharmacy degree at the University of Wisconsin–Milwaukee, where she earned a BS and an MS. She worked in the medical field and conducted research on stomach cancer. Her interest then changed to social work and psychotherapy, and after obtaining a graduate degree in social work, she moved to Palo Alto to train at the Mental Research Center. Berg first met Steve de Shazer at the Mental Research Center and they later married. In 1978, they cofounded the nonprofit Brief Family Therapy Center in Milwaukee, Wisconsin, where Berg served as director. Berg consulted and shared solution-focused brief therapy principles in a wide variety of settings and populations, including drug and alcohol abuse treatment facilities, foster homes, shelters for homeless people, schools, and corrections departments. Berg led workshops across the world and wrote a total of 10 books. Several of her most well-known books include *Family Based Services: A Solution-Focused Approach* (1994), *Working with the Problem Drinker: A Solution-Focused Approach* (Berg & Miller, 1992), and *Interviewing for Solutions* (De Jong & Berg, 2013). She made many contributions to the field of consulting, supervision, psychotherapy, and coaching, using a resource-orientation and brief therapy approach. Berg died in September 2007, not long after her husband passed away.

INTRODUCTION/DEVELOPMENT OF SOLUTION-FOCUSED BRIEF THERAPY

In the 1980s and 1990s, Steve de Shazer (1985, 1988) and Insoo Kim Berg (De Jong & Berg, 2013) developed a therapy approach they called *solution-focused brief therapy* (SFBT). Solution-focused brief therapy (SFBT) has become a popular and well-known counseling theory in recent years. This approach seeks solutions, rather than focusing on underlying problems. Counseling is usually brief; initially, counseling was generally limited to 10 sessions. However, progress is measured by results, not by the number of sessions. Typical interventions encouraged people to reverse or alter what they were doing, not just do more of the same behavior (de Shazer & Dolan, 2012).

De Shazer, Berg, and their colleagues used a decision tree to determine which interventions to use with a client. They generally began counseling with a standard task, such as suggesting that clients observe and describe what was happening in their lives that they wanted to continue to happen. If clients completed such a straightforward task, counseling continued in a fairly traditional way. However, if people failed to complete suggested tasks, indirect counseling strategies were implemented, such as the use of metaphors or paradoxical interventions. These counselors were known for creative use of clues or suggested tasks to help people find solutions to their problems.

De Shazer and Berg contributed tremendously to brief therapy, and their legacy continues to evolve and gain in importance, especially in light of considerable pressure from managed care.

Schools, agencies, clients, and therapists themselves must be accountable and demonstrate results. Brief counseling, which builds on natural, spontaneous, and ongoing changes in people, can be very powerful. Effective interventions can begin in the first moment of contact with a client. Change can happen quickly, usually in less than six sessions (Winbolt, 2011).

KEY CONCEPTS

Solution-focused therapists assume that people's complaints involve behavior that stems from their view of the world and negative cognitions. These behaviors are maintained when people do more of the same in the belief that only one behavior is right and logical. Therefore, using different ways of viewing and coping with problems by focusing on solutions is one of the main goals of SFBT.

In SFBT, clients take on the role of expert, and thus clients take the lead on defining goals and deciding how to achieve them. Problems receive less focus, and solutions receive more. The focus on solutions instead of problems is so strong that therapists avoid using clinical terms, such as depression, as they believe these terms add to problem-saturated stories and make change harder. Because of this, those who work from this theory spend little time helping people figure out why they have been unable to resolve their problems, and they avoid giving people the message that they have been deficient in their efforts to help themselves. Instead, the approach assumes that people are doing the best they can at any given time. In other words, SFBT moves the clients away from what is "wrong" and pushes clients toward what is "right." This approach utilizes resources and skills clients already have. Clients take responsibility, set their own goals, and reach their goals through encouragement from the therapist to increase the frequency of current useful behaviors. The thrust of counseling is to increase people's hope and optimism by creating expectancy for change, no matter how big or small. In this way, people become more aware of what is working rather than what is not. This optimistic approach believes that small changes lead to greater changes because the pattern of their previous behavior has been broken. To help with this process, therapists ask their clients about times when the problem seems less important, when the problem was not there, how they have already made changes, and past successful ways of coping with the problem. As clients become cognizant of the possibility of positive change, their empowerment and motivation increase correspondingly, creating a beneficial circle. That is, positive change fuels people's belief that change can happen, which enhances their motivation and efforts to change, which in turn leads to more positive changes.

Solution-focused therapists believe that change is constant, and that things cannot *not* change. Often, all that is needed to help people is to enable them to notice and build on positive changes that are already happening. To accomplish this, therapists help co-construct solutions to problems, foster independence rather than dependence, and strive to make themselves unnecessary as soon as possible (Winbolt, 2011). Finally, therapists practicing SFBT believe that solutions may not directly relate to the problems, and this creative way of finding solutions is necessary. Table 13.1 provides an overview of the assumptions of an SFBT model.

A Future-Oriented Focus

Solution-focused brief therapy lacks many of the features associated with a well-developed counseling approach. SFBT does not offer a detailed understanding of human development, does not address the impact of past experiences on present difficulties, and does not elaborate on the causes of problems in living. These omissions might be interpreted to mean that SFBT is an emerging approach rather than a full-fledged counseling theory. However, these omissions are consistent with the nature of the approach, which pays little attention to the origins of people's difficulties and

TABLE 13.1 Assumptions of the SFBT Model

- Change is constant and always occurring; change is inevitable.
- Counseling should focus on what is changeable and possible.
- Clients want to change, are capable of changing, and are doing their best to change.
- Clients are the experts in therapy and they must develop their own goals.
- Clients already have the resources and strengths they need to solve their own problems; there is no right way to change, as it depends on each individual client.
- Every problem has exceptions, and developing awareness of these exceptions provides clues for finding solutions.
- Therapy should be brief and short term.
- Therapy should focus on the future; a client's past is not a focus of therapy.

touches lightly, if at all, on their histories. In fact, therapists believe they usually only need limited information about a complaint to resolve it and do not seek to discover the cause or purpose of a complaint. Adopting an idea suggested by Albert Einstein, this counseling theory maintains that a problem cannot be solved at the same level it was created. Therefore, SFBT focuses on the present and the future rather than on the past. Because little attention is paid to understanding where problems come from, the focus is on finding solutions, which may look different for individual clients. In addition, behavior change is seen as the most effective approach for growth and improvement. SFBT also emphasizes even small glimmers of health and positive change rather than past pathology (de Shazer, 1985).

Strength-Based Orientation

Solution-focused brief therapy relies on the belief that people are healthy, are competent, and have the ability to provide their own solutions to grow and change. Therapists view their clients as already having resources and skills within them to make changes. People may not have much awareness about their skills or are not putting them into action, so therapists help clients gain awareness and begin to activate their strengths to make progress and accomplish their goals. This approach is optimistic, provides hope, and is nonpathologizing. As with **positive psychology**, it focuses on strengths rather than weaknesses, skills rather than deficits, and what is right rather than what is wrong. Clients are typically in a problem-oriented state, so therapists encourage them to view their lives more positively, find solutions, and create possibilities. This approach is empowering because clients resolve their own problems and accomplish their goals.

A Focus on Solutions

Finding solutions or clues to resolve complaints is an essential component of SFBT. Therapists put considerable thought into identifying strategies that are likely to succeed and avoiding those that are discouraging or likely to fail. One of the main ways solutions are identified is by looking for what is already working. SFBT assumes that exceptions to the problem (i.e., times when the problem is absent) give clues to effective solutions. Identifying these exceptions and building on the ingredients that created them provide further opportunities for change. By becoming more aware of exceptions to problems, clients can apply this knowledge to continue making progress. When clients find out what is working, they are encouraged to continue what they are doing; when clients are doing something that is not working, they are encouraged to try something new. Table 13.2 provides guidelines counselors can use in identifying effective and empowering solutions.

TABLE 13.2 Guidelines for Identifying Solutions

- View clients as experts on their complaints as well as on what solutions will work.
- Reinforce evidence of clients' strengths, resources, positive qualities, and their competence in solving their own problems.
- Focus on natural and spontaneous changes that are already in progress.
- Pinpoint the behaviors clients are already engaging in that are helpful and effective and find new ways to facilitate problem-solving through these behaviors.
- Interrupt and change repetitive and nonproductive sequences of behavior.
- Provide a rationale to explain how tasks can be helpful to increase clients' motivation to perform the tasks. If people are skeptical, tasks might be presented as an experiment that they can stop at any point.
- Make interventions congruent with people's worldviews.
- Learn from past solutions when formulating future solutions. For example, if people respond to direct suggestions, keep providing them. If they do the opposite of what is suggested, create paradoxical interventions in which doing the opposite is desirable.
- Embed compliments in suggestions to promote optimism and encourage follow-through on tasks.
- Encourage new behaviors rather than simply cessation of old and ineffective ones.
- Create an expectancy for change and a context in which people can think and behave differently.
- Ask questions rather than try to "sell" clients on answers.
- Make solutions practical and specific and develop action plans that work for clients.

Source: Based on de Shazer, S. (1982). *Patterns of brief family therapy: An ecosystem approach.* New York, NY: Guilford Press.

THE THERAPEUTIC PROCESS

As its name suggests, most SFBT relationships are relatively short, and clients are aware from the beginning that counseling is likely to be brief. Because SFBT emphasizes present-oriented efficient counseling that seeks solutions to specific concerns, counseling usually requires fewer than 10 sessions, with an average counseling length of between 3 and 5 sessions (Prochaska & Norcross, 2018). However, duration is not determined by an artificial conception of how long therapy is supposed to be; rather, counseling is as long as it needs to be to help people meet their goals and resolve their complaints. Therapists do not hesitate to extend counseling as long as positive change and forward movement are evident.

Solution-focused therapists tend to be flexible in scheduling appointments. Breaks within sessions allow therapists the opportunity to develop clues, sometimes in consultation with a **reflecting team**, which is a small group of therapists (say, two to seven) who observe a therapy session and then have a conversation regarding what they noticed about the session while the therapist and client observe. Therapists might plan counseling session intervals of one or more months to give clients time to implement suggested strategies and allow changes to evolve. Therapists may also use extended follow-up if people need continued reinforcement over a longer period of time. Adapting counseling to individuals is essential.

Stages of SFBT typically proceed in seven steps (de Shazer, 1985):

1. *Identifying a solvable complaint* is an essential first step in counseling. Not only does it facilitate development of goals and interventions, but it also promotes change. The client and therapist collaborate to determine complaints that are solvable and provide realistic solutions. For example, a client may state her counseling goal is to "make my spouse stop being mean to me." Such a goal is out of the client's control and it is not a readily solvable complaint. A better goal would be "asserting myself and expressing my frustrations and needs when my spouse says mean things to me." Such a goal is within the client's control.

Therapists use change language and phrase questions to their clients that communicate optimism and expectancy for change. For example, a therapist might assume change will occur by asking, "When you have reached your goal what will you notice will be different for you?" Therapists also aim to empower and encourage their clients. People's difficulties are viewed as normal and changeable. Therapists might ask, "What led you to make an appointment *now?*" rather than "What problems are bothering you?" or they might ask, "What do you want to change?" rather than "How can I help you?"

Therapists use empathy, summarization, paraphrasing, open-ended questions, and other active listening skills to understand the client's situation in clear and specific terms. They might ask, "How do you express your anxiety?" "What would help me to really understand this situation?" and "How does this create a problem for you?"

2. *Establishing goals* continues the counseling process. Therapists collaborate with clients to determine goals that are specific, observable, measurable, and concrete. Goals typically take one of three forms: *changing the doing* of the problematic situation; *changing the viewing* of the situation or the frame of reference; and *accessing resources,* solutions, and strengths (O'Hanlon & Weiner-Davis, 2003). Again, questions assume success: "What will be the first sign of change?" "How will you know when counseling has been helpful to you?" "How will I be able to tell that you have met your goals?" Discussing positive change is helpful for obtaining a clear view of what solutions look like to the client. To establish goals, therapists typically use the miracle question and questions about exceptions to the problem. These strategies will be discussed later in the chapter.

3. When *designing an intervention,* therapists draw on both their understanding of their clients and their creative use of counseling strategies to encourage change, no matter how small. Typical questions during this stage include "What changes have already occurred?" "What worked in the past when you dealt with similar situations?" "How did you make that happen?" and "What would you need to do to have that happen again?" **Mindmaps**, which are outlines of sessions that therapists use to focus on organizing goals and solutions, are often incorporated into this stage, as well.

4. *Strategic tasks,* also known as solution prescriptions, are then used to promote change. These are generally written down so that clients can understand and agree to them. Tasks are carefully and collaboratively planned to maximize client cooperation and success. People are praised for their efforts and successes and for the strengths they draw on in completing tasks. Careful assessment of the client is essential in determining an appropriate task. Therapists can determine the level of client motivation, which is known as **assessing motivation**, and decide on appropriate tasks based on the three main types of therapeutic relationships, which will be discussed later in the chapter.

5. *Positive new behaviors and changes are identified and emphasized* when clients return after they have been given a task. Questions focus on change, progress, and possibilities and might include "How did you make that happen?" "Who noticed the changes?" and "How did things go differently when you did that?" The problem is viewed as "it" or "that" and as external to the client. This helps people view their concerns as amenable to change, not as an integral part of themselves. Particularly during this stage of counseling, solution-focused therapists serve as a cheering squad for their clients. They provide compliments and highlight areas of strength and competence.

6. *Stabilization* is essential in helping people consolidate their gains and gradually shift their perspectives in more effective and hopeful directions. During this stage, therapists might actually restrain progress and predict some backsliding. This gives people time to adjust to their changes, promotes further success, and prevents them from becoming discouraged if change does not happen as rapidly as anticipated.

7. Finally, *termination* of counseling occurs, often initiated by the clients who have now accomplished their goals. Because SFBT focuses on presenting complaints rather than resolution of childhood issues or significant personality change, it recognizes that people may return for additional counseling and clients are reminded of that option. At the same time, SFBT is not just seeking to help people resolve immediate concerns. Through the process of developing confidence, feeling heard and praised rather than blamed, and finding their strengths and resources, people can become more self-reliant and capable of resolving future difficulties on their own.

Therapeutic Goals

Goals play an important role in SFBT. Therapists who use a SFBT approach believe that clients have the capacity to define their own counseling goals and that they have the resources required for success in achieving these goals. Clients are encouraged to express what they would like to get out of counseling, and this then becomes the focus of counseling. The job of therapists is to create a climate that encourages possibilities and change.

It is important for therapists to ensure that their clients feel heard and validated before jumping in too quickly to establish goals. Clients must be given the opportunity to express their concerns fully. Once they feel understood, they are more likely to develop meaningful goals. Therapists must also not get lost in the mechanics of finding solutions. If therapists do not pay enough attention to interpersonal aspects, they may inadvertently disrupt the therapeutic alliance.

Clients are encouraged to establish their own goals, which should be clear, concrete, and well defined. Goals are also best when they are stated in a positive manner in the client's language, are process or action oriented, and are focused on the present moment. Because small changes are believed to lead to larger changes, realistic and rapidly attainable goals are encouraged. Clients are often asked during each session to scale how they perceive their progress toward reaching different goals (e.g., "on a scale of 1 to 10 rate your progress toward reaching your goal"). Clients are asked goal-directed and future-oriented questions such as "What did you do differently since our last session?" "What has changed since our last meeting?" or "What did you notice improved since we last met?" In addition, clients are encouraged to use change and solution talk rather than problem talk. When clients use change and solution language, they are more likely to produce successful results.

Therapist's Function and Role

In SFBT, therapists adopt a not-knowing position that allows clients to be the experts on their own lives. Clients choose what they want to work on and determine the direction and purpose of their counseling. This is much different than traditional therapies that view therapists as experts in assessment and treatment. When clients have more responsibility and are believed to be the experts, they are more likely to participate fully in therapy. While clients are experts on what they want changed, therapists are experts on the change process. Clients take the lead in the conversation while therapists are actively listening and providing guidance. Therapists create an environment conducive to change by their tone of voice, metaphorical stories, and suggestions embedded in discussions. This enables people to become more open to new possibilities and interpretations, more creative, more amenable to changing the ways they have always behaved, and more able to assess neglected or overlooked alternatives.

An important task of therapists is to help clients imagine their desired lives and what steps they must take to make those changes. Therapists ask questions, gather information, and then ask more questions to give clients the opportunity to brainstorm desired changes and discover skills they have within themselves to make those changes. Therapists can ask questions like "What do you hope to get out of therapy?" and "What steps can you start taking to accomplish your goals?" Therapists also ask clients what progress they have made with questions like "What strengths or resources did you use to make the improvement?" To effectively help clients achieve their goals, therapists can use the acronym **EARS**, which stands for **E**licit exceptions, **A**mplify exceptions, **R**einforce clients' successes, and **S**tart again. Eliciting exceptions is used to acknowledge clients' efforts and successes; amplify exceptions is used to gain more details about what clients are doing to positively contribute to their goals; reinforcing clients' successes helps them gain more awareness and continue doing what they are doing; and start again is used to start the process over again.

Relationship Between Therapist and Client

The client–therapist relationship is an important element in SFBT, and as with narrative therapy, SFBT therapists develop a collaborative and egalitarian therapeutic alliance. Trust is an essential ingredient in the therapeutic relationship. When clients trust their therapists, they are more likely to follow through with homework assignments and actively engage in session. Therapists aim to maximize client involvement to empower people and enhance their commitment to change (Presbury et al., 2008). Building on clients' strengths is an especially useful way to encourage a positive therapeutic relationship. Although therapists have primary responsibility for creating and suggesting solutions and presenting them in ways that promote action, they view the relationship as a reciprocal process in which clients can help therapists as the therapists help clients in the counseling process.

Active listening, empathy, open questions, explanation, reassurance, and suggestion are all important, while interpretation and confrontation are rarely used. Therapists actively engage with their clients, communicating acceptance, promoting cooperation, serving as role models, and suggesting actions to effect change. Because therapists recognize the importance of people's social systems, they may use resources in the environment and involve clients' significant other in the therapeutic process to further the goals of counseling. Therapists also provide positive feedback and affirmation to their clients through summarization, which shows empathy and understanding, and compliments, which point out strengths. Therapists maintain a positive, respectful, and health-oriented focus and assume that every session is important, that change is inevitable, and that problems will have a solution.

Three types of therapeutic relationships can develop between clients and therapists (de Shazer, 1988). Therapists can determine tasks and suggestions that are most appropriate for their clients based on their relationship and the level of client motivation. However, therapists must not rigidly assign any of the roles listed below to their clients, as roles are constantly changing. Instead, it is best to use these roles as a starting point.

- If people are *visitors or window shoppers* who have not presented clear complaints or expectations of change, therapists should only give compliments. Suggesting tasks prematurely is likely to lead to failure that can jeopardize the counseling process.
- If people are *complainants* who have concerns and expect change, but generally in others rather than in themselves, therapists should suggest observation tasks. This helps people become more aware of themselves and their situations and are more able to describe their wants. The therapist might suggest, "Between now and our next appointment, I would like you to notice things that are happening in your life that you want to continue." Observation tasks require little effort or motivation from the client and, once suggested, are usually done almost automatically.
- Finally, if clients are *customers* who want to take steps to find solutions to their concerns, therapists can suggest action tasks with the expectation that they will be completed. Tasks

should both empower clients and effect a change in their complaints. For example, Neva had many fears, including learning to drive a car and initiating conversations. Her therapist suggested she ask at least two people to tell her how they learned to drive. Neva found that people enjoyed talking about this topic. She not only gained useful information on driving but also initiated several conversations.

THERAPEUTIC TECHNIQUES AND PROCEDURES

SFBT uses a broad range of counseling techniques. Some are particular to SFBT and some integrate cognitive and behavioral techniques into the process. Following are interventions often used in SFBT (de Shazer & Dolan, 2012).

Pre-Therapy Changes

In the first therapy session, many SFBT therapists search for **pre-therapy changes** by asking clients what changes they have already made to help their problem since they scheduled their first appointment. Making an appointment is a positive first step, so this is recognized and discussed. It is assumed that change is always occurring, and these positive changes are to be highlighted and amplified. In addition, by highlighting changes that have already occurred and so did not involve the therapeutic process, therapists help clients see that they have resources within themselves to accomplish their goals.

Formula First Session Tasks

Formula First Session Tasks (FFST) are used between the first and second sessions as homework assignments. For example, therapists may ask clients to observe and reflect on what is currently going well in their family dynamic. During the second session, therapists may ask clients to reflect on their experience and talk about what other changes they would like to see. This technique illustrates that change is inevitable; it is not a matter of *if* change will occur, but *when* it will occur. This technique is used to instill hope and optimism. In addition, it is important to use this technique after clients share their story, typically near the end of the first session. That way, clients can receive validation before they are asked to make changes.

Miracle Question

One of the most useful ways for solution-focused therapists to establish counseling goals is to use the **miracle question** (de Shazer, 1991): "Suppose that one night there is a miracle and while you were sleeping the problem that brought you to therapy is solved. How would you know? What would be different? What will you notice different the next morning that will tell you that there has been a miracle? What will your spouse notice?" (p. 113). This question enables people to imagine that their problems are solved, instills hope, and facilitates discussion on how to make the miracle a reality. The miracle question can also be used to assess clients' perceptions of their problems and solutions.

The delivery of the miracle question is important to its success. Therapists typically speak slowly and use an almost hypnotic tone of voice when presenting this question. This engages the client and evokes openness and responsiveness. Therapists can adapt the miracle question to be compatible with the client's concept of the divine. The miracle might be presented as a magic pill, divine intervention, a silver bullet, or a magic wand, depending on the client's beliefs (Berg & Miller, 1992).

Solution-focused therapists accept and use whatever clients present. For example, when asked the miracle question, one woman replied, "The first thing I will notice is that my husband has brushed his teeth before returning to bed for some romance." She had tried to tell her husband that his morning breath bothered her, but increasing nagging yielded no results. After determining that the woman and her husband were playful, the therapist suggested that the woman hide a toothbrush and toothpaste under her pillow and whip it out to brush her husband's teeth the next morning. She felt empowered by having something to do other than complain and tried this suggestion. This conveyed her message to her husband and also introduced humor into their interaction. Table 13.3 presents variations of the miracle question that may prove useful with clients.

Therapists will have to adapt the exact phrasing of questions to accommodate the clients' age, developmental level, personality, needs, and/or interests. For example, a young child may not clearly understand what a miracle is.

Exception Questions

Therapists use **exception-seeking questions** to identify exceptions to the problem clients are experiencing and to note successful ways they are coping. Although people commonly enter into counseling with a desire to vent and process their difficulties, solution-focused therapists believe that a negative focus stabilizes the system and makes change difficult and that a positive focus is far more likely to lead to beneficial transformations. As a result, solution-focused therapists encourage people to examine times when their difficulties were absent. These times are used as sources of information about ways to effect desired change. Very few problems are present all the time. Often the problem is not happening at all or is happening to a lesser degree. Helping clients to notice these times can reduce the feeling of being overwhelmed by the problem or challenge and can assist in identifying things they or others are already doing to solve the problem.

For example, Fredda, in her first job as a teacher, sought help with anxiety that she experienced nearly every morning before beginning to teach. Rather than focusing on her unpleasant feelings, the therapist asked whether she could remember a morning when she did not experience anxiety. Fredda described one morning when she got to school early, organized her materials for the day, and then had tea with another teacher who gave Fredda some good ideas about managing a difficult student.

TABLE 13.3 Miracle Question Variations

- Imagine that you discover you have a unique superpower—with the mere snap of your fingers, you are able to make your problem vanish. Tell me about the first time you would use your superpower. Describe the situation leading up to the snap, and tell me all about what changes would occur after you snap your fingers.
- Suppose you find a magic wand, and whenever you wave your wand, this problem would no longer exist. When would you wave your magic wand? How would you know the magic was working?
- Let's think about this same time next year. Imagine we run into each other at your favorite place. It's a beautiful day and you are excited to tell me all about the positive changes that have brought about happiness in your life. Describe what would have changed? What does that happiness feel like? What are you doing differently?
- What if you wanted to surprise your family by doing something super special for them . . . something to show how well you are doing. What would you have to do to not only surprise them, but also convince them that promising changes are taking place?

Source: Based on de Shazer, S., & Dolan, Y. (2012). *More than miracles: The state of the art of Solution-Focused Brief Therapy.* New York, NY: Routledge.

This exception suggested several routes to alleviating Fredda's symptoms: arriving early, being well prepared, relaxing before class, and seeking advice from more experienced teachers. By building these behaviors into her routine, Fredda gained control over her anxiety.

If clients cannot readily recall exceptions to their difficulties, therapists can take an active role in promoting exceptions. They might suggest a strategic change in behavior. They might predict an exception if one seems likely to occur. They also might encourage clients to search for exceptions, a strategy likely to be fruitful if exceptions seem to go unnoticed. The following are examples of questions therapists may ask clients to search for exceptions. Remember to ask for detail: *"What else?"* and *"Tell me more."*

- *"What is different about the time when the difficulty does not happen?"*
- *"When is the problem less severe?"*
- *"How does your day go differently without the problem?"*
- *"How is that different from the way you handled the situation the last time it occurred?"*
- *"How did you resolve this concern before?"*
- *"What would you need to do to have that happen again?"*
- *"Tell me about times when the problem is less troubling or when it is not happening."*
- *"Tell me about times when you cope better with the problem."*
- *"What is different about the times when the problem is better?"*
- *"When things are tough, how do you cope?"*
- *"Tell me what has worked in the past even if only for a short time."*

Scaling Questions

Like other behavior-oriented therapists, solution-focused therapists often use **scaling questions** to establish a baseline and facilitate identification of possibilities and progress. The therapist might ask, "Let's say 1 stands for how bad you felt when you first came to see me with this concern and 10 stands for how your life will be when you don't need to see me anymore. On a scale between 1 and 10, where would you put yourself today?" (Berg & Miller, 1992, p. 362). This scale also can be used to assess specific areas of focus, including symptoms and relationships. Scaling questions are especially helpful when clients are struggling to identify goals or exceptions to their problem. Examples of scaling questions include:

- *"Imagine a scale from 0 to 10, 10 represents how you want things to be when the problem is solved and 0 is the opposite."*
- *"What number are you on the scale right now?"*
- *"What number were you when the problem was at its worst?"*
- *"What will you notice if you moved up one or two numbers toward your goal?"*

When clients describe themselves at a very low number, therapists can ask questions that include:

- *"How do you cope when things are so difficult?"*
- *"Who is helping you to cope?"*
- *"What is stopping you from moving down one number?"*
- *"Describe the different changes you will notice as you move up each number on the scale."*

Questions like these encourage clients to imagine change and to focus on their strengths and coping skills. With younger clients, therapists can use more playful and imaginative scales involving pictures. Therapists can be as imaginative as they would like with the scales and adapt them according to the age, interests, and characteristics of individual clients.

Solution Talk

Solution talk, also known as problem-free talk, is an important tool in SFBT. Therapists choose their words carefully so that they increase clients' hope and optimism, their sense of control, and their openness to possibilities and change. Solution talk also helps therapists and clients identify solutions by exploring times when the problem or challenge was not impacting clients' lives. Therapists concentrate on solutions, strengths, and successes, not problems. Some examples of how language can enhance counseling are listed below:

- Emphasize *open questions*.
- Use *presuppositional language* that assumes that problems are temporary and positive change will occur. For example, therapists speak of *when,* not *if,* the problem is solved: "When this problem is solved, what will you be doing?"
- *Normalize people's problems* to provide reassurance and reduce feelings of inadequacy. A therapist might say to a parent who is coping with a child's drug use, "Your son seems to be engaging in some risky behaviors and it makes sense that you are worried."
- *Focus on coping behavior* using **coping questions**, such as "What has kept you from harming yourself?" and "How do you manage to keep going?"
- *Reinforce and notice strengths and successes*. Congratulate and compliment people for their improvements and efforts; avoid emphasizing problems and failures.
- *Create hypothetical solutions* such as "If you weren't feeling afraid, what might you be feeling and doing instead?" This expands possibilities and encourages change.
- *Concentrate on describing and changing behaviors* rather than thoughts or emotions.
- *Use rituals, metaphors, stories, and symbols* to convey indirect messages that can promote change. For example, Mary envisioned a formidable brick wall standing between her and the sort of life she wanted. Her therapist suggested that she remove one brick, leaving it up to Mary to determine how she would complete this task. She responded by changing several behavioral patterns and reported that she had made a hole in the wall big enough for her to crawl through.
- Make frequent use of words such as *change, different, possibility, what,* and *how* that suggest change.
- Use *inclusive language such as "and"* that allows potentially incompatible outcomes to coexist. Rather than saying, "You might feel like you can't do it, but you can do it," the therapist might say, "You might feel like you can't do it, *and* you can do it."
- *Use reframing and relabeling* to offer different perspectives. For example, an event might be viewed as an opportunity for learning rather than a disappointment, and an individual might be depicted as "taking the time to sort out options" rather than "stuck" or "paralyzed by fear."
- *Match clients' vocabulary or style of talking* to promote a collaborative therapeutic alliance. Then change the language to encourage change in clients' perspectives.

Preferred Future

Helping clients to identify clear goals or a clear description of their preferred future without the problem can be very valuable. This involves **questions about the future** that concentrate on what life will be like without the problem or challenge. It is best for therapists to always ask for detail and remember to ask *"what else,"* to ensure that clients and therapists understand and explore the whole picture.

Examples of future questions include:

- *"What will you notice when the problem is better?"*
- *"How will things be different when the problem is better?"*

- *"What will you be doing differently when things are better?"*
- *"What will you be doing instead?"*
- *"How will your parents/friends tell that things are going better?"*
- *"How will others tell when the problem is better? Tell me more about that."*

Well-described goals will be as follows:

- Positive
- What is wanted rather than what is not wanted
- Broken down into small, achievable steps
- Specific and observable
- Realistic.

It is preferable to use language that implies a positive outcome:

- *"How* will you do that," rather than *"Why* will you do that?"
- *"When* this happens," rather than *"If* this happens ..."
- "What *will* you be doing," rather than "What *would* you be doing?"
- "What *will* be happening," rather than "What *won't* be happening?"

Therapist Feedback to Client

Toward the end of the therapy session, therapists typically take a quick break to review the session and develop a summary of the session. Therapists then provide feedback to their clients that includes compliments, a bridge, and suggesting a task. Compliments are genuine affirmations about what clients are already doing well. A bridge is what links the compliments and the suggested task; it provides a rationale for why the suggestion was chosen. A task, typically a homework assignment, is something that clients are instructed to do outside of session to enhance the therapeutic process. Feedback is typically used to help clients engage in new ways of behaving so they can reach their goals.

Solution Prescriptions

Solution prescriptions, a common form of suggestion in SFBT, are tasks designed to help people discover ways to resolve their concerns. These may be designed to fit a particular person or situation or may be a standard prescription in the therapist's repertoire. Commonly used prescriptions include "Do one thing different," "Continue doing something that has been successful," and "Notice times when the problem is slightly less of a problem and what you did to bring that about" (Sklare, 2000, p. 442). When it comes to solutions prescriptions and other forms of suggestions, it is important to recognize that indirectness and implied suggestions are sometimes more powerful than direct suggestions and advice.

APPLICATION AND CURRENT USE OF SOLUTION-FOCUSED BRIEF THERAPY

Because SFBT encourages thoughtful use of interventions and homework tasks, it lends itself well to integration with other counseling approaches, particularly those that take a phenomenological perspective and focus on behavior change. SFBT can also be integrated with cognitive behavioral therapy, rational emotive behavior therapy, Adlerian, and reality therapies (Scholl & Hansen, 2018).

SFBT emerged from a social constructivist, family systems perspective and is very useful with couples and families. SFBT is generally well received by clients, is encouraging and empowering, and offers new ways of thinking about helping people. It addresses immediate problems while enabling people to make better use of their strengths and resources in addressing future difficulties.

Counseling Applications

The nature of SFBT lends itself well to work with a wide variety of populations. For example, SFBT is helpful for people with depression and anxiety (Bond, Woods, Humphrey, Symes, & Green, 2013). The scope of SFBT has expanded beyond treating people with mild or moderately severe problems to successfully treating people in crisis, people who have experienced trauma, and people with behavioral issues and impulse control issues (Scholl & Hansen, 2018). Some of the concepts and strategies associated with SFBT—notably, attention to motivation, emphasis on small successes, and efforts to find exceptions—are likely to enhance counseling for people with a variety of presenting issues. SFBT is particularly useful when counseling those who have substance use disorders because the strengths-based approach leads to increased positivity, inspiration, and focus, which helps clients move forward (Suitt, Geraldo, Estay, & Franklin, 2019; Lewis, 2014). SFBT has also been effectively used with clients who have long-term physical health conditions (Carr, Smith, & Simm, 2014) and people who have intellectual disabilities (Carrick & Randle-Phillips, 2018). In addition, using solution-focused language versus problem-focused language, particularly in intake sessions, has been shown to modify the information that clients provide and even initiate pre-treatment change due to the positive and strengths-based focus (Richmond, Jordan, Bischof, & Sauer, 2014). SFBT has shown efficacy with children and adolescents as well as with adults, although it should be modified when used with children (Kress, Paylo, & Stargell, 2019).

Increasingly, SFBT is being used in crisis situations, to reduce suicidal risk, and to help those who have been victims of domestic violence or trauma. SFBT's focus on resilience and coping skills seems particularly beneficial to people seeking to move past a traumatic situation and rebuild a future. SFBT is particularly useful for adolescent survivors of sexual abuse because strengths, resources, and capabilities of the individual are emphasized (Scholl & Hansen, 2018). This approach can assist individuals in gaining more control by redefining the traumatic experience, creating meaning around the experience, and preventing revictimization. Through this, clients are more likely to gain self-esteem, suffer less self-blame, and experience less symptomology.

SFBT can also be effective in a broad range of settings, including work environments, employee assistance programs, schools and colleges, corrections and medical settings, inpatient psychiatric units, chemical dependency centers, homeless shelters, and child protective services (Kim & Franklin, 2009; Zhang, Franklin, Currin-McCulloch, Park, & Kim, 2018). Therapists can also use this approach when working with groups in both school and mental health settings (Metcalf, 1998).

Application to Multicultural Groups

Solution-focused brief therapy is a culturally respectful approach to working with clients of diverse backgrounds because it focuses on clients' personal frames of reference (Erford, Eaves, Bryant, & Young, 2010). Because clients are seen as experts on their own lives, SFBT inherently values the cultural backgrounds and resources of all clients. This approach has been given multicultural relevance because of its flexibility and its emphasis on health, resources, strengths, client dignity, collaboration, empowerment, and self-determination (De Jong & Berg, 2013). In addition, SFBT's respect for people's views of the world, its recognition of the importance of people's connections with their environment and with others, and its brief and nonintrusive nature make it suitable for a broad range of people. Solution-focused therapists recognize the importance of client motivation, and efforts to promote clients' involvement in counseling make SFBT a good fit for people who are hesitant or wary about counseling. SFBT can also be easily individualized to best fit the needs of clients.

EVALUATION OF SOLUTION-FOCUSED BRIEF THERAPY

Although most of the literature on solution-focused counseling consists of case studies and descriptions of counseling strategies, additional empirical research is expected to enhance the reputation of this powerful approach.

Limitations

SFBT has limitations, which many of its practitioners seem to recognize and troubleshoot. Unless clients and therapists carefully co-create problem definitions, the approach can cause therapists to focus prematurely on a presenting problem and thereby miss an issue of greater importance. SFBT is not usually appropriate as the primary or only approach for severe or urgent emotional difficulties or when clients do not have the skills or internal resources to cope with their problems. In addition, its implementation appears easier than it is. In reality, this approach requires well-trained therapists who are skilled and experienced in assessment, goal setting, and effective use of a range of creative and powerful interventions.

Another drawback of SFBT is the misconception among some therapists and clients, as well as some managed care organizations, that brief counseling is all that is ever needed to help clients. This is, of course, a dangerous overgeneralization, with the result that people may fail to receive the intensive therapy they need. Therapists should exercise caution when using SFBT to be sure that this approach is adequate to meet their clients' needs.

Strengths and Contributions

SFBT is widely used, has made an impact on counseling and psychology, and is internally coherent and consistent. This approach moved the focus of counseling from problems to solutions. SFBT has also provided therapists with powerful interventions. Its use of the miracle question, its emphasis on exceptions and possibilities, its use of presuppositional and other solution-focused language, and its concentration on small behavioral changes are innovative concepts that are modifying the way many therapists think about and provide counseling. The miracle question, in particular, has gained widespread acceptance as a useful tool for information gathering and goal setting.

SKILL DEVELOPMENT: MAPPING

A narrative approach assumes that people live their lives based on the stories they tell themselves and the stories they are told. This constructivist approach proposes that these stories shape people's reality. By deconstructing the stories, narrative practitioners help people see the parts of their stories they have overlooked in their focus on problem-laden narratives. This overlooked material may contain stories of resilience, hope, and courage—certain lived experiences that are more desirable than others. Unpacking the influence of the problem on clients' lives and helping them to recognize the restrictive cultural assumptions that might lie beneath the stories are the goals of narrative mapping. After clients have externalized their problems and the effects of the stories have been mapped and deconstructed, clients are ready to create new, alternative stories that empower them to move forward with life.

Four categories of inquiry help the therapist (White, 2007):

1. Developing an experience-near position of the problem
2. Mapping the influence of the problem in the person's life
3. Evaluating the problem's effects
4. Justifying the problem.

Each category of inquiry includes a certain line of questioning by the therapist to help clients tell their stories.

Developing an experience-near position of the problem. In the first stage of mapping, the therapist seeks clarification of the presenting problem as it is experienced from clients' unique perspectives. Clients, especially those who are children, may believe that they are the problem and become resigned to the fact that nothing can be done to solve the problem. Through therapist questioning about the problem, a distinct shape of the problem emerges. Clients are then able to talk about the problem in a very real, experience-near, manner.

Mapping the influence of the problem in the person's life. After the problem has been externalized, outlined, given a name, or discussed as an object rather than viewed as part of the person, it becomes less personalized and easier to discuss. For example, Antika came for counseling to help her overcome her shyness at school. She was embarrassed to sit with others at lunchtime and her shame prevented her from discussing her problem with anyone. After a few sessions, she labeled her problem as a big caped man who spreads his shadow over her whenever she is around people. As it became visible and developed its own outline, the problem became less personal and Antika was able to recognize the control this shadowman had on her life and to take action in a more positive direction.

By asking questions that probe the size (length, breadth, and depth) of the problem, the therapist begins to get a picture of the extent of the problem's influence on every aspect of the individual's life, including home, school, work, relationships, motivation, dreams, aspirations, and even the future. Talking to Antika about times when the shadowman came around, where she was at the time, how far the shadow extended, how long it lasted, and its impact on her relationships with classmates and family helped her to see the problem as separate from herself. This provided hope that it could be changed. Questions for Antika might include any of the following:

- What has the shadowman persuaded you to think about yourself?
- What has it convinced others to say about you?
- How does it convince them of these things?
- What decisions does the shadowman make for you?
- Are there any benefits of having the shadowman around at times?
- What are the shadowman's intentions for your future?

Mapping the influence and control clients have over the lives of their problem is another line of questioning that begins to pave a road to recovery. By looking for **unique outcomes**, or times when the problem hasn't been a problem, the therapist uncovers powerful messages that can be used to form an alternative story. Not surprisingly, Antika said the shadowman only came into her home when strangers were present, such as when her father invited colleagues home for a gathering. During those times, she was able to overcome her shyness because she told herself her father would protect her. This led to a discussion of exceptions, such as:

- Have there been other times when you've overcome or ignored the shadowman?
- How did you feel when this happened?
- How might you stand up to it in the future?
- By ignoring the hold this shadowman has over you, do you think you are becoming less vulnerable? Stronger?
- What will the future be like without this dominating your life?
- How is this future different from the one the shadowman would have planned for you?

Evaluating the problem's effects. Once the therapist has a handle on the extent of the problem for clients, it is helpful to question the larger effect it has on their lives. Beginning with summaries, or editorials (White, 2007), therapists make a brief statement about the problem and its accompanying consequences. The summary with Antika is as follows:

THERAPIST: Antika, I understand that apart from the shadowman, people tend to treat you differently as a result. Students stay away from you, no one calls you to go to the movies, and you said you spend a lot of time alone.

ANTIKA: Yes, that's right.

THERAPIST: What is that like for you?

ANTIKA: Lonely. I don't like it.

THERAPIST: You don't like it. What other words might you use to explain this?

ANTIKA: Sad. I hate being alone. I feel left out of everything and my parents think I'm a loser.

THERAPIST: And you don't want to be a loser?

ANTIKA: No! I want to be like everyone else!

Justifying the problem. In the fourth stage of mapping, therapists may ask "why" questions such as these: "Why is this situation not okay with you? Why do you want this to stop? Why do you feel the way you do?" (White, 2007) Such questions are not asked in a judgmental way, or in a manner that elicits defensiveness, but more out of curiosity in an effort to discover the values and assumptions that underlie a person's narrative. "Why" questions can lead into reauthoring conversations and revelations about what the client had intended life to be like. In addition, these questions replace problem definitions with aspirations and goals for the future. In Antika's case, the question of why she wanted the shadowman to go away elicited a wealth of information about her goals for the future. She reported that she wanted friends, relationships, and one day to have a career. "Don't I deserve to be happy?" she asked. "I want to overcome this, to get this shadowman behind me and just be like everyone else."

Externalizing conversations and mapping are powerful interventions used by narrative therapists to help people rewrite their stories. Mapping can also be documented through the use of a chart (White, 2007).

CASE APPLICATION

The following dialogue illustrates a conversation between Edie and her therapist, using SFBT techniques.

THERAPIST: Edie, what's been going well this week?

EDIE: Things have been getting a little better with Roberto and I'm happy about that. I've also been trying to focus more on myself lately.

THERAPIST: That's great! You're noticing positive changes in your relationship with Roberto and are doing more things for yourself. What have you done to encourage these changes?

EDIE: I don't know. I guess I have been spending less time on my phone and on Facebook. That has opened up a lot more of my time. I'm feeling more present with my family.

THERAPIST: So spending less time on social media has helped your relationship and helped you to focus more on your needs. It is hard to limit your social media use, and you did it! How were you able to keep yourself off social media this week?

EDIE: Hmmmm, I just think about how unsatisfying it is, and how time with my family is more meaningful to me.

THERAPIST: So you tell yourself that the social media use won't be satisfying and talking to yourself in this way helps you stay off. Talk to me about what strategies you have used to keep yourself off social media.

EDIE: Well, I only let myself go on social media during certain times of the day.

THERAPIST: What is one other strategy you have tried that has helped you to limit your social media use?

EDIE: Hmmmm . . . I am not sure, but I would like to take the Facebook app off my phone so it isn't so tempting to look at it. I want to try that this week and see how it goes. It's just that I want to feel connected with my friends, but social media doesn't feel like a meaningful connection.

THERAPIST: That sounds like a great plan, to take the app off your phone! I will check back in with you next week to see if that strategy was helpful. There was something else, though, I just heard you say—you want to have more meaningful connections with your friends.

EDIE: Right. Well I've really missed my friends lately. I don't feel like I have seen them in a while. I've just been so busy and overwhelmed with my life and family. I haven't really made them a priority, but I think I need more friend time. I feel really disconnected from them.

THERAPIST: So it sounds like you have been feeling withdrawn from your friends. You have been busy and it has been hard to connect with them. On a scale of 1 to 10, with 10 being you feel totally satisfied with your relationship with your friends, and 1 being you are totally unsatisfied with your friend connections, where are you at right now?

EDIE: I'd say about a 3. My friends help to keep me sane. I know more time with them would really make my life better.

THERAPIST: When you move to a 4 on the scale, what will you be doing that is different?

EDIE: I don't know. I mean I've just been so overwhelmed worrying about Ava and Roberto. I don't initiate plans and when I do make plans, I often back out.

THERAPIST: You have been overwhelmed with caring for your family and so it's been hard to make and keep plans. So tell me about the 4 on the scale. What is one thing you will be doing that is different when you are at a 4 on that scale?

EDIE: Well, I would make plans in advance. I know the further in advance I plan to do things with my friends, the more likely I am to follow through. Maybe I would even have a night with the girls, say, once or twice a month. Knowing that I had something scheduled would give me something to look forward to and help me actually get out of the house!

THERAPIST: Great. Let's talk about these plans and what all of this might look like.

REFLECT AND RESPOND

1. Externalization is an important technique in narrative therapy. By placing the problem outside themselves, people can be empowered to do something about the problem. Think about a problem you have had over the years. Imagine what it looks like. What color is it? Give it a name. Draw or paint an image of the problem. Write a letter to the problem. Have the problem write a letter back to you.
2. Identify a problem or concern you are currently experiencing. Then find at least one exception to the problem or a time when you handled a similar problem successfully. Plan a small change based on this information. Write about this in your journal.
3. Storytelling is an important part of narrative therapy. This activity can help you outline important aspects of your life story and gain a broader perspective. First, identify a title for the book of your life. The title can be simple or can reflect themes in your life. Then come up with at least seven chapter titles that represent significant events or stages in your life. Write a sentence or two to describe each chapter. Then reflect on your last chapter, which is meant to be a description of your life in the future. Consider what you want to do, where you want to go, and who you will be. Finally, reflect more on your chapters and add to them to create additional clarity and understanding of your life story.
4. Apply the miracle question to a problem you are experiencing and write about your experience. Answer the following question in your journal. "Suppose that one night there is a miracle and while you were sleeping the problem you are experiencing is solved. What would be different?" Through this question, determine a goal that you would like to work on. Ensure that your goal is clear, concrete, and well defined. Goals are also best when they are process or action oriented, and focused on the present moment. Write about your experience and determine a plan to accomplish your goal.

Summary

This chapter provided information on two postmodern constructivist therapy approaches, narrative therapy and solution-focused brief therapy. Narrative therapy holds that people's conceptions of themselves and their lives come from the stories they have constructed and made a part of themselves. Narrative therapy consists of three main stages, which include understanding the effects of the problem, understanding and finding meanings in stories, and then exploring alternatives to the problem-saturated story so that preferred stories can be created. Narrative therapists are consultants and collaborators who see their clients as experts on their own lives. Therapists use a variety of strategies, such as eliciting stories, deconstructing stories, and revisioning and reauthoring. Therapists often rely on externalization, a process that allows clients to view their problem as separate from themselves, thus enhancing their sense of control over the problem. Externalization is facilitated by having clients name the problem, write letters to the problem, and draw the problem.

While research on narrative therapy is lacking, there is some support for this therapy as an effective counseling approach. Narrative therapy is particularly helpful for people who have been victimized or disenfranchised by others, as they have the opportunity to create positive, life-affirming, and transformative stories. Possibilities for new thoughts, actions, and emotions are explored through new descriptions of old stories. Essentially, clients create their own meaning and stories. By helping people to explore, understand, and modify their stories, therapists can enable them to revision and reauthor their lives in healthier, more uplifting, and positive ways.

SFBT focuses on helping clients to create solutions, rather than focusing on problems. One of the main goals of SFBT is to use different ways of viewing and coping with problems by centering on solutions and exceptions to the problem. SFBT places a heavy emphasis on what is going right instead of what is going wrong, and this approach offers a strong belief that clients inherently have the strengths and resources required to provide solutions and overcome their problems. Therapists help clients expect and celebrate change, no matter how big or small. SFBT consists of seven main stages, which include identifying a solvable complaint, establishing goals (mainly through the use of the miracle question), designing an intervention, eliciting strategic tasks, identification of positive new behaviors and changes, stabilization, and termination. The main role therapists play is creating an environment conductive to change. The therapeutic relationship is collaborative and affirming. The main strategies therapists use are identifying exceptions to problems, using solution talk, exploring the preferred future, and making suggestions. SFBT has shown effectiveness when counseling a wide variety of clients, including people with mild-to-severe problems, people who are in crisis, people who are court mandated, and people who have addictions.

SFBT can best be summed up as "If it isn't broke, don't fix it. If it works, do more of it. If it's not working, do something different" (de Shazer & Dolan, 2012, p. 2). SFBT also holds that small steps can lead to big changes; solutions are not necessarily directly related to problems; change talk and solution-focused language are more important than problem talk; exceptions to problems are always occurring; and exceptions that can be pulled upon to create change are always available.

Recommended Readings

Constructivist

Journal of Constructivist Psychology—all issues.

Narrative

White, M. (2007). *Maps of narrative practice*. New York, NY: Norton and Company.

White, M. (2011). *Narrative practice: Continuing the conversation*. New York, NY: Norton.

Solution-focused Brief Psychotherapy

De Jong, P., & Berg, I. K. (2013). *Interviewing for solutions* (4th ed.). Belmont, CA: Brooks/Cole.

de Shazer, S. (1988). *Clues: Investigating solutions in brief therapy*. New York, NY: Norton.

de Shazer, S. (1991). *Putting difference to work*. New York, NY: Norton.

de Shazer, S., & Dolan, Y. (2012). *More than miracles: The state of the art of solution-focused brief therapy*. Binghamton, NY: Haworth Press.

MyLab Counseling

Start with the Topic 13 Assignments: Narrative Therapy.

Try the Topic 19 Assignments: Solution-Focused Therapy.

CHAPTER 14

Family Systems Therapies

Learning Outcomes

When you have finished this chapter, you should be able to:
- Understand the context and development of Family Systems Therapies.
- Communicate the key concepts associated with Family Systems Therapies and understand how they relate to therapeutic processes.
- Describe the therapeutic goals of Family Systems Therapies.
- Identify the common techniques used in Family Systems Therapies.
- Understand how Family Systems Therapies relates to counseling diverse populations.
- Identify the limitations and strengths of Family Systems Therapies.

Family. The word itself conjures up all types of memories, feelings, and thoughts. We are influenced tremendously by our families of origin and by the families we create. From the time we are born, we begin to develop attachments with our primary caregivers. Throughout our lives, the need for connection and attachment to others continues, and we eventually create a new family system. Our families shape us, influence our development, and model appropriate or inappropriate behavior. Only within the context of our larger family system can we be fully understood.

Family systems therapy is a branch of psychotherapy that involves working with families and couples to encourage change and development. Family systems therapists believe change should occur at the system level, around interactions between family members. Family therapists also believe that family dynamics play an important role in psychological health.

Family therapy's history and development, general family therapy principles, and specific types of family therapies will be addressed in this chapter. Readers should keep in mind that the goal of this chapter is to provide an overview of the important family and couples counseling approaches. An in-depth discussion of the topic would require at least several semesters of course work, and even an entire program of study. Family systems therapy is its own discipline and profession in and of itself. In fact, many people earn degrees in family therapy and focus only on systems change processes. It is impossible to do this topic justice in one book chapter. Therefore, readers are encouraged to seek out additional resources and training, should they have an interest in family systems theories.

INTRODUCTION/DEVELOPMENT OF FAMILY THERAPY

In the previous chapters in this text, theories that conceptualized people from an individual level of analysis were discussed. The primary vehicle of change—from those perspectives—is at the individual level; individual change is not incumbent upon others changing. In contrast, the approaches of family systems therapy (hereafter referred to simply as family therapy or couples therapy) focus on the interactions and patterns of interactions between family members (Goldenberg, Goldenberg, & Stanton, 2017). Family therapists contend that people's problems originate and are maintained within the context of a family system. It is within the family system that meaningful change occurs (Minuchin & Fishman, 1981). In family therapy, all members of the family unit reflect upon themselves and make changes that support the well-being of all other members of the family.

General systems theory, a foundation of family therapy, was first proposed by Ludwig von Bertalanffy, a biologist, in the 1920s, and later adopted by family therapists. Bertalanffy created a theory that provided a system for understanding living organisms and social groups (von Bertalanffy, 1968/1976). Within this framework, he found that general system laws apply to any type of system, that each organism is an open system that experiences continuous input and output, and that a system can be defined by the interrelationships among the subunits. Each participating unit not only contributes to the whole but also has an effect on the other participating units. Thus, understanding how a system works first requires an understanding of the interactional process that takes place between each of its subunits.

In 1929, the Marriage Consultation Center was opened in New York City, and in 1941, the American Association of Marriage Counselors (AAMC) was formed. AAMC eventually changed its name to the American Association of Marriage and Family Therapists (AAMFT), in recognition of the growth of family therapy.

Conjoint family therapy, therapy in which two or more people are counseled together, first occurred after World War II as a result of the increased need for family therapy. Much of the early research and development took place in the area of helping families who had a member with severe mental illness, such as schizophrenia (Lebow, 2008). From 1950 to 1970, most of the major theoretical orientations in psychology developed family-focused applications (these will be touched on later in the chapter). During this time, **cybernetics**, the study of processes that occur in systems, also became popular. Through the pioneering work of Murray Bowen, Jay Haley, Virginia Satir, Carl Whitaker, Salvador Minuchin, and others, each of these early family theories incorporated general systems theory as well as **first-order cybernetics** principles, or looking at the communication patterns and feedback loops within the family system from an outside perspective. It was believed that observers of a system were immune to the system's influence and therapists were considered to be experts.

In more recent decades, newer types of family therapies have emerged that postmodern thinking has strongly influenced. The impact of postmodern thought can be seen in the development of constructivist and narrative approaches; cultural, sexual orientation, and gender-sensitive family therapy theories; and eclectic and integrated approaches to family therapy. **Second-order cybernetics** also emerged, and this way of thinking highlights the idea that therapists influence the family system and are non-experts. Instead, their role is to co-construct meanings and solutions with the family.

Family systems approaches became increasingly popular in the 1970s and 1980s, and some have suggested that family systems theories are central to, or at least part of, the fourth force in counseling (L'Abate, 2013). Unlike individual-level counseling theories, family systems therapies provided a postmodern understanding of humans in that they focus on family members' unique experiences in their own social context, experiences that are co-created and shared with others. By the end of the 20th century, family systems therapy had become mainstream, developing its own professional identity, journals, societies, educational training standards, and even its own state licensure. At present, family therapy foundations play an important role in youth counseling, especially when working with young people who have behavior problems (Henggeler & Schaeffer, 2017).

The basic premise of family therapy is that people's behavior is rooted in important interactions within the family. Family therapists contend that the ways people interact with members of their family repeats, and if repeated enough, these interactions and ways of being within the family become a predictable pattern and are difficult to change. The idea that problems are rooted in family or systemic interactions stands in contrast to the idea that problems in living are due to medical model explanations (e.g., mental disorders) or problems, struggles, deficiencies, or other maladaptive conditions within an individual person. Individual-level therapy puts the person in the forefront, while the influence of the family recedes into the background. In the family systems perspective, the family is in the forefront and individuals are seen as subunits, or parts of the whole. The only time family therapists focus on individual-level considerations is when they are impacting the dynamics within the family system. Family therapy differs from individual therapy in several important ways in that it:

- Involves meeting with all members of the family together
- Focuses not just on the child (who is generally the person identified as having a problem; i.e., the "identified patient") but also on all family members who relate to or influence the client's problem
- Focuses on the needs of all members of the family
- Focuses on how the family members' ways of interacting affect all members of the family and on how these ways impact the rest of the family's behavior.

Most families seeking therapy need help in finding a solution to a problem the family is experiencing. Single-parent, blended, multigenerational, and multinuclear families present many unique issues that family therapists can address. Most family therapy and couple's therapy, regardless of structure or theoretical orientation, is:

- Brief
- Solution focused
- Action oriented
- Focused on here-and-now interactions among family members
- Focused on how the family creates, contributes to, and maintains the problem.

Family therapists hold to the Aristotelian view that the *whole is greater than the sum of its parts.* In other words, each system has unique dynamics. For example, a married couple may have a conflictual relationship full of strife and contempt. Yet, they may have a pattern of healthy, nonconflictual relationships with others in their lives. As such, it is not enough to say these two individuals are aggressive, conflict-oriented people. To understand them and help them change, we must understand their relationship in the system in which they function. We will first begin with an overview of family therapy concepts and interventions before looking more closely at some of the prominent schools of family therapy.

KEY CONCEPTS

Family is defined as a group of people who intimately share their lives with one another, and family can include any combination of parents (biological, step, and/or adoptive), siblings (biological, step, and/or adoptive), extended family (aunts, uncles, cousins, grandparents), and even friends or neighbors. It is common for parents to bring children to counseling eager for a therapist to "fix" the child; they do not typically seek out family therapy per se. The person in the family perceived to have the problem is often referred to as the identified client or the **identified patient** (i.e., the "IP"; Becvar & Becvar, 2013). Regardless of the problem a child presents (e.g., behavior difficulties, attention-deficit hyperactivity disorder [ADHD]), family therapists believe that the root of the problem lies within the family system dynamics, and what may look like a child's problem is generally a manifestation of unhealthy family interactional patterns (Van Ryzin & Fosco, 2016). Altering relationships and changing patterns that are causing or supporting a child's struggles become the aim of family therapy (Haley, 1963). An important difference between family therapy and many other theoretical approaches is that the IP, the person presented as having a problem, is not viewed as more or less pathological or disturbed than the rest of the family members. Family therapists view the family system as the mechanism of change rather than working to change any one person within the family system. This section of the chapter discusses several key concepts common to many family therapy approaches.

Behavioral Functions Within Family Systems

Family therapists tend to consider the functions that behaviors serve within a system. Functions can be assessed by determining the flexibility of family members' subsystems and boundaries, or the structure of the family. **Subsystems** within a family are smaller groupings of individuals who have unique ways of relating and interacting with one another (Bertalanffy, 1968; Bowen, 1978). Subsystems are any subunit of a family having its own autonomous function as well as a role within the larger system (e.g., siblings, parents, children). For instance, in our example family of Roberto, Edie, and Ava, Edie is a wife and partner to Roberto, a mother to Ava, and a daughter to her mother and stepfather. We can consider Edie to be a member of four independent and functioning subsystems. She is a participant in the partner subsystem, the parent subsystem, the child subsystem, and even the subsystem of women in the family. Each of these subsystems functions autonomously (as when Edie and Roberto, working from the parental subsystem, establish and enforce bedtime rules for their daughter, Ava), and yet is also a part of the overall interactional system.

As an example of the importance of family system dynamics and functioning, consider a girl who is acting out and getting in trouble in school. The girl's parents have been experiencing marital discord and have been fighting regularly. The girl is worried, as she has heard her parents speak of a possible divorce. She finds that when she acts up, her parents come together to discipline her. The girl's behavior is serving the function of bringing her parents closer together.

As will be discussed in this chapter, family functioning has many different aspects. Boundaries are one commonly addressed aspect. **Boundaries**, or the emotional or physical barriers between two or more individuals in a family, can be healthy, enmeshed, or disengaged (Minuchin, 1974). Healthy boundaries are achieved when individuals within the system are sufficiently attached to one another and can reach out to one another for support and guidance (Bowen, 1978). Individuals with healthy boundaries are also able to separate themselves from their family members to gain a sense of independence and autonomy when appropriate. One technique that therapists can use is **boundary marking**, which is meant to alter interactions among individual family members. Boundaries can also be flexible or "permeable" among individual family members, allowing connections and adaptation to be made; this quality is called **boundary permeability**. More will be said about boundaries in the Bowenian Family Therapy and Structural Family Therapy sections later in the chapter.

Reciprocal Influence

Systems thinking contends that families have a **reciprocal influence** process by which one person or aspect of a family affects all other parts of the family, and vice versa. However, the mechanism through which one person affects another within a family is complex and synergistic. In its simplest form, the action of one individual leads another individual to respond. This is known as **linear causality** because the effect pattern is in a straight, one-way line (Shapiro, 2015; See Figure 14.1). However, family therapists do not generally focus on linear causality. It is too simplistic, and this type of logic typically misses the bigger picture. People's thoughts, feelings, and behaviors develop across time as an intricate, underlying pattern of interactions that have fostered and maintained their problems in living.

FIGURE 14.1 Linear Causality.

A $\longrightarrow$ B

In contrast to linear causality, Bertalanffy's theory of **circular causality** is believed to better explain most family system dynamics (Bertalanffy, 1968; see Figure 14.2). Circular causality goes beyond linear causality to identify a long-standing, complex spiral of interactions that includes all family dynamics and can become problematic across time. Often, circular causality is a subtle, long-term process in which one person says or does (or fails to do) something, and another family member interprets this behavior (correctly or incorrectly), then acts upon it. Then, other family members interpret these behaviors and act upon them. With circular causality, a therapist can understand that another family member's behaviors come as the result of multiple family interactions, which must be addressed slowly and systematically. More importantly, family systems theorists are able to understand how a family member's behaviors are sustained by the family system, and how family members' behaviors are influenced and affected by other family members.

The **dynamics**, or interactional patterns of a family, include the ways in which members' rules, beliefs, values, and experiences are expressed within the household and within the larger society as a whole (Walsh, 2012). Each family member plays a distinct role in the family, and the family member's thoughts, feelings, and behaviors are typically consistent across situations. The family system is relatively stable, and its patterns have been built over time (Bertalanffy, 1968). Family members respond and behave in predictable ways that have an identifiable purpose or function within the family system. For example, one child might serve as the clown in a family to create distractions and relieve tension between his parents. A pattern such as this might show up across settings and transfer into school or social situations.

Enhancing Communication

Many families have difficulties managing boundaries (i.e., the separation of self and others) and in maintaining clear parental roles. In addition, many parents engage in inconsistent parenting, which creates confusion and misunderstanding. Healthy family communication is essential in building family unity and consistency, and in aiding the ability of families to navigate the challenges of everyday life (McBride, 2008; Murdock, 2009). Therefore, the development of communication skills may be helpful in family therapy, and many family therapy approaches address the need to improve or develop healthy family communication.

Furthermore, since one of the major assumptions of family therapy is that emotional and behavioral difficulties primarily result from disturbed family communication and interaction patterns,

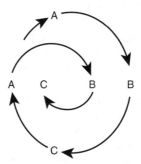

FIGURE 14.2 Circular Causality.

focusing on communication within the family tends to be the first course of action within most family therapy approaches. **Family communication** is the verbal and nonverbal exchange of information (e.g., thoughts, feelings, values, beliefs) between family members, which involves not only talking but also listening to others. Communication is the means by which family members express their wants, desires, dreams, and concerns; by communicating, they attempt to express differences and admiration, and even to resolve unavoidable conflict.

Conversely, poor or dysfunctional communication can lead to an increase in conflict, to a lack of bonding and intimacy, and to the use of ineffective problem-solving skills (Murdock, 2009). For example, a parent may lecture a young child on the value of sharing, and do so in a manner the child cannot comprehend. Similarly, in other situations, yelling, blaming, name calling, passive-aggressive statements (e.g., appearing angry yet denying being angry), labeling a person as bad, using terms like "always" or "never," and engaging in the silent treatment can all lead to dysfunctional communication patterns. In addition, conflict exacerbates and even complicates already present difficulties in communicating.

One of the most essential rules of communication is to be directive, explicit, and clear. Family therapists teach and model clear and explicit communication, which allows clients to respond to the therapists and to each other more accurately. Therapists can emphasize communicating thoughts, views, feelings, and needs.

Ultimately, therapists need to inquire and facilitate discussions that pull out every family member's perspective on the presenting situations, family structure, and boundaries within the family. While many family members will not know how other members think and/or feel about any one issue or topic, this new level of awareness can often promote curiosity, thus leading to an increased desire to communicate and engage other family members (Shapiro, 2015). Therapists can improve family communication by helping the family to increase the frequency with which they have positive interactions, increase their clear and direct communication, pay closer attention to both verbal and nonverbal communication, enhance their ability to be active listeners, and develop positive attitudes toward all family members (Goldenberg et al., 2017). Communication is important in many family therapies; however, communication is particularly important for Satir's experiential family therapy, which will be further discussed later in the chapter. Table 14.1 provides examples of creative family therapy interventions that promote communication.

TABLE 14.1 Examples of Creative Family Therapy Interventions That Promote Positive Communications

Goal	Intervention
To improve parent–child relationships	Give each family member a piece of paper. Have each individual write his or her name at the top and pass the paper to the right. Direct each family member to write one nice thing about the individual whose name is at the top and continue passing until each family member receives his or her own paper. Process how the individuals feel to learn the positive things their family members wrote about them. Ask them how they can use their specific talents to continue building positive relationships with other family members.
To increase understanding of expectations in the home	Work with parents and youth to create a succinct list of concrete, positively worded rules to encompass the main behaviors that should be exemplified in the home. Make sure no rules overlap and create only as many as needed to cover all basic requirements. For example, a list might include: (1) complete chores on a daily basis; (2) attend to parental requests the first time they are made; (3) keep hands, feet, and objects to yourself; (4) speak in a calm tone at all times.

TABLE 14.1 (Continued)

Goal	Intervention
To improve disciplinary practices in the home	Create a list of succinct, positively worded family rules. Ask youth to brainstorm a list of reinforcements that parents could offer to motivate desired behaviors. Ensure that praise and thanks are included in the list. Also, ensure that small rewards that don't cost much and don't involve food (e.g., trinkets and tokens) are included. Ask youth to create a list of punishments that can be used when rules are broken (not including corporal punishment). Encourage parents to provide plenty of reinforcements, especially praise, when youth behave as desired. Provide tokens on a 1:1 schedule at first and gradually reduce the frequency to a variable rate. Exchange a set number of tokens for some larger reinforcers. Use punishment only as a last resort.
To improve communication between family members	Fill a jar or box with sentence stems and ask each family member to take turns pulling a sentence stem and completing it aloud. Process each sentence, see if any family members agree or disagree, and identify ways the answers could be shifted for healthier communication habits. Some sentence stems might include "I feel most sad when __." or "I know mom is mad when __."
To enhance relationships between family members	Challenge each family member to compliment every other family member at least once per day.
To enhance a natural support system for the family	Ask family members to list the family, friends, neighbors, and other community members with whom they commonly associate. Identify one inexpensive way the family can show gratitude toward each of these people (e.g., telling them "thank you" or making them cookies).

BOWENIAN (MULTIGENERATIONAL) FAMILY THERAPY

"It is factual that dysfunctioning and overfunctioning exist together." –Murray Bowen

MURRAY BOWEN (1913–1990)

Murray Bowen is credited with the development of Bowenian family therapy, arguably one of the most important schools of family therapy. The oldest of five children, he was born in 1913 and raised in Tennessee. After medical school, he became a psychiatrist specializing in childhood schizophrenia and began applying Freudian principles to the treatment of severe mental illness. Bowen worked at the Menninger Clinic and later at the National Institute of Mental Health, where he conducted research on his theory of treating family members together rather than individually. In the 1940s, Murray Bowen was among the first to combine psychoanalysis with systems theory and is credited with creating the first comprehensive theory of family development.

The Bowen Center for the Study of the Family

In 1959, he moved to Georgetown University, and after years of clinical experience and research, Bowen established the Georgetown University Family Center, where he taught his multigenerational theory for 30 years. Bowen worked there until his death in 1990 and is credited as the first founder and first president of the American Family Therapy Association.

INTRODUCTION/DEVELOPMENT OF BOWENIAN FAMILY THERAPY

Murray Bowen conceptualized the family as a network of interlocking, emotional relationships that is best understood when considered within a multigenerational or historical framework (Goldenberg et al., 2017). Bowen's approach provided a bridge between psychodynamic approaches that focused on the individual and the development of family systems theory with its emphasis on the family unit as a whole. His theory includes new language to explain complex family interactions (e.g., emotional cutoff, multigenerational transmission process, differentiation of self), as well as a deliberate and systematic method of counseling.

KEY CONCEPTS

Theory and practice in Bowenian family therapy are intertwined. Bowen believed that theory provided the frame for working with families and children, and was confident that if the theory was strong enough, it could be used without the need for techniques.

Bowen highlighted the importance of subsystems, which include the dyad and triad (Bowen, 1978). A **dyad** consists of two family members who interact in a unique way, and a **triad** is a close relationship between three family members. These basic components interact with one another in regular, predictable patterns to create subsystems within the larger family system.

Bowen developed eight key concepts to explain the emotional relationship system within the family. Each concept is described briefly below. For a more detailed discussion, see Bowen's *Family Therapy in Clinical Practice* (1978).

Differentiation of Self

Differentiation of self is conceptualized as people's ability to separate their own intellectual and emotional functioning from that of their family members (Bowen, 1978). This development of the self was not confined to the individual but emerged more fully within the context of family. Therapy is less about uncovering family communication patterns and more about differentiating the self from other family members (Bowen, 1978). The balance between appropriate connectedness to others and autonomous functioning is the key to psychological health. Separating emotions from reason results in differentiation, or people's ability to work through their own emotional and rational processes to make decisions. The more differentiated people are, the higher their level of functioning. Differentiated people are also more likely to resist participation in dysfunctional family patterns. Fully differentiated people are able to use both thoughts and emotions in determining their own best course of action. Differentiated individuals can concurrently hold defined beliefs, values, and convictions while also recognizing their own need and dependence on other members of the family (Bowen, 1978). The opposite of differentiation is **fusion**, in which emotions tend to rule decision making. People are experiencing a lack of individuation or appropriate interpersonal boundaries. Less differentiated individuals (those in fusion) attempt to gain the approval of others within the family, thus maintaining a pseudo or pretend sense of self. At times, when family members are not differentiated, this may result in a **symbiotic relationship**, which is an intense relationship between two people in which the boundaries are blurred and they respond as one (often occurs between mother and child). Stated simplistically, these individuals struggle to differentiate between their own thoughts and feelings and those thoughts and feelings of others within their family system. In contrast, **diffusion** results when boundaries develop and individual family members can think in terms of "I" rather than "we." Therefore, the goal of family therapy—from this family perspective—is to increase differentiation of all family members.

Triangulation

Triangulation results when two family members are experiencing conflict or uncontrolled anxiety and they bring in another family member to dilute the tension. When the triangulated person is undifferentiated, this may result in two people uniting and blaming the third person for the family dysfunction. This **alignment**—when family members join or oppose each other in handling situations—with another person may relieve individual anxiety, but the resulting triangulation ultimately causes problems in the family system. However, when the person who is being triangulated is differentiated, that person is less likely to take sides and may even help to solve the problem.

Nuclear Family Emotional System

Bowen believed that the nuclear family emotional system was a multigenerational phenomenon, with recurrent patterns over the years. It included both the nuclear family that physically lived together and the effects of the extended family, regardless of where family members resided or even if they were living or dead. In Bowenian theory, the only way to resolve current family problems is to differentiate from the family of origin and change interactional patterns. The greater the emotional stress, the more likely the family is to experience fusion in order to seek security. Dysfunction and pathology result when individuals are unable to differentiate themselves from their family (Bowen, 1976, 1978).

Family Projection Process

The **family projection process** is a means of projecting or transmitting parental conflict onto one or more children. Within the mother–father–child triangle, parents have a tendency to select the most vulnerable child, the one who has the least differentiation of self, to project their own problems onto. For example, a child may respond to her mother's anxiety and become anxious herself. The mother, being the primary caregiver, responds to the child's anxiety and the father becomes supportive of the mother in efforts to deal with the child. The child then becomes identified as having the problem and the family projection process has been created.

Emotional Cutoff

One or more of the children in a family, especially those least involved in the family projection process, are likely to escape from the family dysfunction by putting geographic or emotional distance between themselves and their families. Bowen noted that such a cutoff is an attempt to deny attachments and unresolved conflicts that exist. An **emotional cutoff** reflects a problem (unresolved fusion), solves a problem (reduces anxiety by limiting contact), and creates a problem (isolates family members; Kerr, 1981). Cutoffs tend to occur in families in which a high level of anxiety and dependence is present (Bowen, 1978).

Multigenerational Transmission Process

Newly formed nuclear families unconsciously repeat the behavior patterns of their parents. In Bowen's multigenerational model, basic patterns are passed down from generation to generation through modeled behavior, and family assumptions about gender roles, finances, family responsibility, work ethics, coping skills, and ways of dealing with stress are maintained. In this way, family systems become models of expectations and form replicas of past generations. People either try to copy their family of origin or do the opposite—even choosing a partner who is similar to, or decidedly different from, their opposite sex parent. Through awareness of this **multigenerational transmission process**, therapists could truly understand the family system and the individual. The way families cope with stress and anxiety is a key consideration. If the stress level is high, several patterns are likely to reoccur based on how previous generations handled stress.

Sibling Position

Like Adler, Bowen believed birth order shaped people's future relationships. Specifically, children develop certain traits based on their relationship within the family. For example, a woman who was the oldest child would be more suited to marry a man who had an older sister. Sibling positions come with certain assumptions and interactive patterns that are learned in the family of origin.

Societal Regression

The concept of societal regression was added later to Bowen's theory; thus, the concept is less well developed and integrated. **Societal regression** means that problems of differentiation and individuation are reflected in society as a whole. Under conditions of chronic stress (e.g., economic, societal), society as a whole reacts the same way that individual families would—experiencing more anxiety, regression, and less differentiation between the intellect and emotion.

RELATIONSHIP BETWEEN THERAPIST AND CLIENT

In Bowenian systems theory, the therapist remains objective and takes a neutral stance. The therapist does not join with the family but, rather, remains differentiated and curious about patterns, beliefs, and assumptions that led the family to its particular problem or dysfunction. The therapist serves as a catalyst to help the family gain insight into the impact of multigenerational influences.

Before therapists can help families differentiate, they must first address their own family dynamics and emotional ties. Such work is necessary so that the therapist's own family issues do not seep into the therapist's work with a family. Therefore, training in this method involves extensive personal work to ensure the therapist becomes fully differentiated (Lebow, 2008). Within sessions, therapists avoid becoming triangulated with the families and model calm impartiality instead.

THE THERAPEUTIC PROCESS

The goals in Bowenian family therapy are to reduce family members' anxiety, increase individuals' differentiation of the self while remaining connected to other family members, and establish healthy emotional boundaries between family members. These results can only occur through an understanding of how the family system has influenced the current family dynamics by going back through several generations. To accomplish these goals, Bowenian therapy is a process that looks at patterns, especially as they relate to emotion, structure, and triangulation. Counseling assessment interventions serve dual functions of promoting exploration and insight within the family unit and providing further information for ongoing conceptualization. New information and understandings will unfold across time, and therapists are likely to find that some of their preconceived notions are inaccurate. Bowenian family therapy does not necessarily involve children in the therapy process because parents are believed to be responsible for their children's problems. Instead, change can be initiated by working with parents on their own self-differentiation with the hope that those efforts would trickle down into increased insight and reduced anxiety in the family as a whole (Becvar & Becvar, 2013). It is important to work with parents conjointly and help them accept the premise that the basic problem in the family was between the two of them. The next step is to help the couple improve their insight on self-differentiation and detriangulation—with therapists always taking care, of course, not to be drawn into the triangle.

Through therapist coaching, couples gradually become diffused. Their new interactional patterns have positive effects on other family members until a new equilibrium is reached. This might require as few as 5 to 10 sessions for some families and as many as 20 to 40 sessions for others (Goldenberg et al., 2017). Sometimes only one member of the couple, usually the most differentiated, would be seen in therapy for a period of time. Therapy would occur until the person was sufficiently differentiated for the couple to be able to work together as a team to address dysfunction in the family and begin to function more cognitively and less emotionally.

THERAPEUTIC TECHNIQUES AND PROCEDURES

The main interventions used in Bowenian family therapy are asking assessment questions, using genograms to gather information and increase insight, and detriangulation. Table 14.2 provides examples of questions a family therapist might ask to obtain additional information about a family's functioning and patterns.

Genograms

During the assessment stage of counseling, a **genogram** of at least three generations of a client's family tree is constructed. Genograms are a way to chart the family's relationship system as well as family interactional patterns within the family, including **intergenerational family patterns**, or patterns of interacting that are shared and transmitted throughout generations of a family (Haley, 1963; Minuchin & Fishman, 1981). Altering these patterns can help to prevent them from affecting the next generation (McGoldrick et al., 2008). The genogram also delineates structural relationships (marriages, births, deaths) and emotional relationships (fusion, cutoffs, triangulation) in conjunction with the family, as well as other patterns such as substance abuse, depression, and physical or emotional abuse. The genogram serves as a **tracking** tool, which is a therapeutic tactic in which the therapist attends to the language, style, tone, and values of the family and uses this information to influence the family's patterns of interaction. **Family structure** can also be identified, which involves the rules that have been developed in the course of family life to determine who interacts with each other and how they interact (McGoldrick et al., 2008). Table 14.3 shows the steps involved in creating and implementing a genogram. Genograms are discussed in greater detail in the Skill Development section at the end of this chapter.

TABLE 14.2 Informal Family Assessment Questions

- Who is the most warm-hearted person in the family?
- Who is the toughest person in the family?
- Who in the family is most emotional?
- Who usually gets angry first?
- How does each member of the family show anger?
- How does each member of the family show sadness?
- How does each member of the family show happiness?
- Describe a typical Tuesday night in your house.
- Describe a typical Sunday morning in your house.
- Whom do each of you turn to for support?
- What is the best part of being a member of this family?
- What is the toughest part of being a member of this family?

Source: Based on Kress, V. E., Paylo, M. J., & Stargell, N. A. (2019). *Counseling children and adolescents.* Upper Saddle River, NJ: Pearson.

TABLE 14.3 Implementing a Genogram in Family Therapy

Step One: Determine the purpose for making the genogram. It might serve as a general exploration of the family system. It could include just the immediate family or a larger extension of the family. The genogram could focus on a family history of mental health disorders, communication patterns, or boundary issues. This depends on the purpose.

Step Two: Explain the purpose of the genogram to the family. Explain that the therapist and family will first map out all the family members. Then, specific themes will be applied (if relevant).

Step Three: Determine the symbols that will be used to indicate various factors and dynamics. Some common genogram symbols include:

- ☐ = Male
- ○ = Female
- ------ = Relationship
- _____ = Marriage
- _____ = Divorce
- \/ = Death (inside the circle or square)
- △ = Family

- Every genogram has its own key with its unique symbols.
- The birth date/year is typically written above each individual's symbol.
- Names can be added to genograms when space is available.
- Additional symbols should be created to support the specific purpose of the genogram. For example, "Dx" might be written above any person who had a mental health disorder, or a wavy line might be used to indicate a stressed relationship.

Materials: Large writing surface (e.g., poster board, white board), appropriate writing utensil.

Directions:
The therapist begins by explaining the process and purpose of the activity to the family. Then, the family works together to draw the immediate family. Next, extended family members are drawn in as necessary to accomplish the goal of the genogram. Finally, special symbols and details are added to the genogram.

Process Questions:
What is it like to see your family drawn like this?
What patterns do you notice in the genogram?
What can you learn from this exercise?
How was it to do this activity with each other?
What would you like to do with this genogram?

Detriangulation

Detriangulation involves separating parts of the triangle. Typically, therapists choose to work with the healthiest member (the most differentiated) of the triangle individually. Once this member of the triangle gains insight and makes changes, the rest of the triangle is more likely to separate. Finding healthy ways to manage stress and anxiety is a key component to successfully separating the triangle.

APPLICATION AND CURRENT USE OF BOWENIAN FAMILY THERAPY

Bowenian theory has implications for working with couples and adults in individual counseling who want to better understand their family dynamics and children (Piercy, 2010). The theory is culturally inclusive due to its focus on family of origin patterns, which are deeply related to culture. This theory may also be particularly helpful for cultures that emphasize interdependence.

As with other psychoanalytic theories, Bowenian therapy can be lengthy, time consuming, and costly, and may not be practical. It shows a cultural gender bias by valuing reason and rationality—a commonly accepted male trait—over emotion, a traditionally female trait. In Bowenian theory, mothers are frequently viewed as overly involved, while fathers are often absent. In addition, families in crisis may have more immediate needs that must be attended to before delving into past patterns of behavior.

EXPERIENTIAL AND HUMANISTIC FAMILY THERAPY

"Communication is to relationships what breath is to life." –Virginia Satir

"There are no individuals in the world, only fragments of families." –Carl Whitaker

VIRGINIA SATIR (1916–1988)

Virginia Satir is regarded as one of the early pioneers in experiential family therapy. Born on a farm in Wisconsin in 1916, she first became a schoolteacher before obtaining an advanced degree in psychiatric social work from the University of Chicago. After nearly a decade as an agency therapist, she opened a private practice in Chicago. Satir was an international lecturer, trainer, and family therapist, and helped to establish the Mental Research Institute (MRI) in Palo Alto, California, where she was known to frequently begin training workshops with a meditation (Banmen & Banmen, 1991). Satir's work with clients was unique. She believed in the power of congruence and helped family members communicate more honestly. She focused more on the therapeutic relationship to help clients become more themselves, become in touch with what was important within, and to be one's best self. In 1964, she first published *Conjoint Family Therapy* (1975), a ground-breaking work that is considered a classic in family therapy literature. She wrote many other well-known books, including *Peoplemaking* (1972) and *The New Peoplemaking* (1988). Over her lifetime, Satir worked with more than 5000 families, sometimes providing group family therapy to multiple families at a time. She founded the Virginia Satir Global Network in 1977, was appointed to the Steering Committee of the International Family Therapy Association, and was a member of the Advisory Board for the National Council for Self-Esteem. She received many awards, including honorary doctorates and gold medal of "Outstanding and Consistent Service to Mankind" by the University of Chicago. Until her death in 1988, Satir remained at the forefront of the family therapy movement. Her work continues through the Virginia Satir Global Network.

CARL WHITAKER (1912–1995)

Carl Whitaker is also known for his contributions to experiential family therapy. Whitaker and his colleagues began including children and spouses in their treatment of schizophrenia. He believed that fear of loss, either real or imagined, is the primary driving force in families (Keith, Connell, &

Whitaker, 1992). Whitaker was humanistic in that he emphasized humanness over pathology and believed families had a built-in drive to solve their own problems. The therapist's role was to activate this potential. Whitaker was often creative with his interventions; he thought that creativity could foster new outlooks and perspectives.

INTRODUCTION/DEVELOPMENT OF EXPERIENTIAL AND HUMANISTIC FAMILY THERAPY

Virginia Satir was instrumental in establishing the importance of congruent communication patterns in family relationships. She believed that good communication encouraged healthy emotional expression. Satir noted that people speak with their entire bodies. More than just an expression of words, communication includes body language, tone, posture, facial expressions, and other subtle indications of affect. Frequently, words and body language are in conflict when people say one thing while their facial expressions and body language reveal something completely different. Such incongruence sends out mixed messages. Her model, Transformational Systemic Therapy, is a strengths-based, change-directed approach to family therapy (Andreas, 2012; Banmen, 2008). Her model is sometimes referred to as the human validation process model.

KEY CONCEPTS

Several important concepts underscore both Whitaker's and Satir's experiential humanistic family therapy approaches.

Humanistic

The experiential therapies are considered humanistic and place an emphasis on building self-esteem and self-worth in all individuals, as well as self-actualization. Carl Rogers' core conditions of empathy, unconditional positive regard, and congruence are implemented. This approach is rooted in the belief that people have the answers within themselves and that after they learn effective communication skills, they are able to create solutions to their own problems.

Process/Experiential

After establishing trust in the therapeutic relationship, development of awareness through the experiential process is necessary for change to occur. In other words, it is not enough for the therapist to point out how the client is acting; the client must experience it within the session. The term **reconstruction** is used to help families re-enact and clarify their dysfunctional communications.

Communication

Healthy families are more emotionally open and expressive in their feelings, and their affect tends to be congruent with their communications. Unless raised in a healthy environment, however, children do not usually learn how to express their feelings. In fact, children are often told to suppress their feelings, or deny them, when parents give them messages such as "Always be polite," "Don't let them see you cry," and "Put on your game face." Such statements give children a mixed message, or double bind, which often confuses them and prevents effective communication.

All relationships are built on trust, and Virginia Satir believed that when that trust is threatened, stress results. Under stress, people retreat into survival mode and will communicate from one of five survival strategies: placating, blaming, super-reasonable, irrelevant, or congruent (Satir, 1975).

Placators agree with others at the expense of their own true opinion; blamers tend to think only of themselves and communicate with anger and emotion; super-reasonable people focus only on cognition and logic and ignore feelings; irrelevant people respond with communication that is unrelated in an effort to distract or avoid; and congruent people respond honestly with what they are thinking and feeling.

Of these five communication stances, only the congruent stance is healthy and leads to improved communication and connections between people. One technique used by Satir in family therapy was to ask family members to exaggerate their own communication stance. In doing so, the blaming father might point his finger and furrow his brow in an expression of anger, the irrelevant son might look out the window and hum a silly song, and the placating mother might implore everyone to just get along.

Satir stressed that all communication stances are learned behaviors and can be changed. Symptoms signal that something is wrong in the family's communication patterns or that family rules are interfering with a family member's growth. The problem is never the problem—it is how people cope that becomes the problem. Under stress, people will fall back on their survival communication stance as their best attempt to cope with a situation. By improving communication skills, helping family members to be more congruent in their interactions, and focusing on the process, not the problem, family members become more aware of themselves and others in the family, become more congruent and authentic, and increase their self-esteem.

RELATIONSHIP BETWEEN THERAPIST AND CLIENT

Satir and Whitaker had similar styles when working with clients. Satir was reported to be a warm, humorous therapist who did not believe a cognitive approach was sufficient. She was also an active and directive therapist who believed in equality among family members. She was known to stand a child on a chair so that the child could communicate at the same level as other members of the family. She believed in bringing the therapy hour to life, and she frequently used metaphors to help make a point (Springer & Wheeler, 2012). Rather than relying on techniques or intellectualization, she believed change occurs only through experiential moments. The therapist is responsible for creating a safe environment in which family members can risk looking at themselves, their interactions, and their own wisdom. Establishing trust with every member of the group is essential for change to take place. All family members take part in the process, a family history that includes a chronology of family events is explored, and flexibility in time and place of therapy is practiced.

Whitaker believed that the therapeutic alliance was sacred (Connell, 1996) and was based on a mutually caring relationship (Whitaker & Napier, 1977). In other words, therapists and clients connect with each other and see fragments of themselves in each other. In general, therapists should be nondirective and let families work out their own solutions to problems. However, therapists should be very directive within the session and become an authority figure to the family, which allows the family to act out its dysfunctional communication patterns. Early in therapy, even with the first phone call, Whitaker began to tip the balance of power and assert his authority. Within sessions, his humor, spontaneity, and even absurdity were reflected in interventions that helped the family members to recognize and express feelings that had previously been outside their awareness (Whitaker, Warkentin, & Malone, 2011). Whitaker stressed the need for playfulness and family humor in fostering family resilience, but avoided humor that was sarcastic, cruel, or had the potential to be destructive (Walsh, 1998). Whitaker believed loyalty, commitment, and accountability are necessary foundations for relational permanence and a sense of wholeness and will help families weather the inevitable stress storms that arise.

Because Whitaker's style was so personal, spontaneous, and intuitive, it did not lend itself to structured training. Students of his theory were required to conduct internships with him as a condition of training. Whitaker's work with families did not lend itself to research either, so little empirical research exists on the effectiveness of his methods.

THE THERAPEUTIC PROCESS

The goal of Satir Transformational Systemic Therapy is to help family members to experience and communicate their emotions and to recognize the communications they leave out. Once clients gain awareness, their understanding increases and they are more likely to realize that multiple options and choices for change are available. The goal of family therapy is not to heal people but, rather, for the therapist to serve as a change agent and facilitator (Satir, 1975). As people become more aware of their dysfunctional communication styles, they learn to express themselves on a deeper emotional level. For example, rather than expressing anger that her husband went out with his friends after work without her, a wife might convey her underlying feeling of how hurt she felt. Expressions of primary emotions such as hurt or sadness are more likely than defensive and angry ones to elicit empathy and understanding in the other partner and result in supportive and caring communicative overtures.

Therapy has five phases. The first phase involves establishing trust with the family. An assessment and a treatment plan are formulated earlier in therapy to help clients feel more confident. In the second phase, therapists help all family members gain awareness about the role they are playing in their family, which is done through experiential methods. After that, therapists use various techniques to help clients gain new understandings. Once clients accomplish this, therapists ask them to explicitly state their understandings to the rest of the family. In the last phase, family members are requested to use their new behaviors and insights in real life.

The main goal of Whitaker's experiential family therapy is to help clients reduce defensiveness and experience more deeply by decreasing impulsivity. Another main goal is to help families live more authentically and fully in the present moment. Whitaker did this by focusing on the process during the family session rather than on the presenting problem. Whitaker's experiential family therapy was less structured than Satir's approach. Whitaker was spontaneous and unstructured, and therapeutic sessions were often unpredictable. Whitaker used himself as the primary agent for change and often incorporated experiential techniques to create deeper experiencing and intensify the here and now. He encouraged creativity and connection with clients' own unhelpful beliefs.

Whitaker also believed that all family members should attend counseling sessions, including grandparents and even ex-spouses. Multigenerational support was necessary, he believed, to the effectiveness of counseling. As do other experiential therapists, Whitaker emphasized increasing affect in the family, modeling good communication skills, and focusing on what is happening in the moment rather than on past or future concerns. He concentrated on humanness instead of pathology and believed families had a built-in drive to solve their own problems. The therapist's role was to activate this potential (Connell, 1996).

Whitaker was convinced that more than insight was necessary. For change to occur, insight had to be accompanied by meaningful experience. In particular, two types of experiences seemed to be most effective—when a family risks being more disconnected or more angry than usual and when a family risks being more intimate.

THERAPEUTIC TECHNIQUES AND PROCEDURES

This type of therapy includes a blend of Gestalt, psychodrama, role plays, modeling, family sculpting, videos, or other exercises or games to re-enact old wounds and help family members develop new awareness, change misperceptions, and foster empathy for each other. Satir often used family sculpting and choreography.

Family Sculpting

Family sculpting is a technique in which family members are physically molded and directed to take a role that represents how the family views its relationships. Family members are asked to use various bodily positions and gestures to represent how close they are to other family members and to show communication patterns. This technique is used to increase awareness about family rules and misconceptions.

Choreography

With this technique, family members are asked to act out an event or pattern in relation to another family member. For example, a family member may enact a scene of what a typical day is like at dinnertime. Choreography helps family members gain new perspectives.

While Whitaker primarily used himself as the main agent for change, several of his techniques include:

- Reframing symptoms as ways for achieving growth
- Encouraging clients to engage in fantasies to deal with stress
- Understanding the difference between interpersonal stress and intrapersonal stress
- Helping family members understand other family members better by intensifying their feelings
- Promoting affective confrontation.

APPLICATION AND CURRENT USE OF EXPERIENTIAL AND HUMANISTIC FAMILY THERAPY

As an early pioneer, Satir had an incredible influence on the development of family systems therapy. The insistence on open and direct communication, the recognition of the importance of language, and the belief in family resilience were vital contributions in the early years of family therapy's development and have been instrumental in the development of dynamic, nonlinear systems of therapy. The Satir model remains a popular way to work with families and is being taught worldwide (Li & Vivien, 2010). Satir's influence continues to be seen in the development of holistic, experiential, systemic theories such as Susan Johnson's work on emotionally focused couples therapy and in the work of the Satir Institute of the Pacific (http://www.Satirpacific.org), which provides worldwide training in Virginia Satir's growth model and publishes the *Satir Journal.*

STRUCTURAL FAMILY THERAPY

> "In all cultures, the family imprints its members with selfhood. Human experience of identity has two elements; a sense of belonging and a sense of being separate. The laboratory in which these ingredients are mixed and dispensed is the family, the matrix of identity." – Salvador Minuchin

INTRODUCTION/DEVELOPMENT OF STRUCTURAL FAMILY THERAPY

Structural family therapy, developed by Salvador Minuchin, was the dominant form of family therapy in the 1970s (Becvar & Becvar, 2013). Born and raised in Argentina, Salvador Minuchin began his career as a family therapist in the early 1960s. In his classic text, *Families and Family Therapy* (1974), Minuchin identified family subsystems with boundaries that were often invisible to family members. Minuchin specified two patterns common to troubled families: Some become enmeshed, chaotic, and tightly interconnected, whereas others remain disengaged, isolated, and seemingly unrelated. Organizational structures, rules, communication, and behavior among family members are the focus of clinical attention.

KEY CONCEPTS

Every family consists of multiple subsystems. By recognizing and identifying how the family is organized, the therapist becomes familiar with how the family functions as a whole. The therapist delineates boundaries between the family subsystems and sometimes draws diagrams or family maps to illustrate the family structure. The main concepts of structural family therapy as described by Minuchin are discussed next.

Subsystems

Three subsystems are of particular interest to structural family therapists: parental (those who are responsible for the children), spousal (may be different than parental), and sibling (all related children). Generally, the spousal subsystem is the first to develop. It comprises the original partners. The way these two people support each other impacts how the family is structured and how well it will function. Once children come along, a parental subsystem develops based on those responsible for the care and raising of the children. A healthy and cohesive parental subsystem is necessary for the development of a functioning family system, yet the parental subsystem must be flexible enough to change as the children's needs change. Membership in one subsystem should not interfere with membership in another. For example, the intimacy of a husband and wife should not interfere with their ability to parent their children. As a team, parents define appropriate boundaries that distinguish among subsystems.

Boundaries Between Systems

In families, **boundaries**—how family members distinguish self from others—are the established ways family members, subsystems (e.g., parental, siblings), and individuals interact and get their individual and collective needs met (Minuchin & Fishman, 1981). Boundaries, in a sense, can be considered on a continuum of closeness and autonomy, with the ideal balance being in the middle of the continuum, attempting to have the needs for both closeness and autonomy met. Frequently, therapists will see the extreme ends of this continuum: enmeshed and disengaged families (See Figure 14.3).

Rigid boundaries result in **disengagement**, or the disconnection between family members. Individuals with **disengaged** boundaries are not able to make meaningful connections with their family members, and therefore lack the guidance and support that all people require. Too much emotional distance exists between family members. These rigid boundaries may also lead to **scapegoating**, which is when a member of the family, likely to be the identified patient, is the object of criticism, blame, or scorn. In contrast, individuals with **enmeshed** boundaries are overly invested in one another and have difficulty making decisions for themselves, taking responsibility for their own actions, holding others accountable, and maintaining individual autonomy (Minuchin, 1974). For example, in a disengaged family, a parent may not even make his child dinner or be concerned if the child does not eat, while in an enmeshed family, a parent may be upset and take it personally if a child does not finish her dinner (Minuchin, 1974). Healthy boundaries, or balanced boundaries, are achieved when individuals within the system are connected to one another, can reach out to one another for support and guidance, and experience a sense of independence and autonomy when appropriate.

[---Enmeshed --------------------------Balanced -------------------------- Disengaged ---]

FIGURE 14.3 Family Boundaries Continuum.

Enmeshed families are often characterized by (Kress, Paylo, & Stargell, 2019):

- Guilt used to control or motivate behaviors
- Family members that do not share family matters with others outside of the family
- A lack of separation between members on thoughts, feeling, and ideas (children may remain enmeshed with their parents into adulthood)
- Indoctrination of children on what they *should* think and feel
- Members speaking for each other
- A fear that if one becomes too different, one will run the risk of being cut off from the family.

Conversely, disengaged families are often characterized by (Kress, Paylo, & Stargell, 2019):

- A lack of consistent engagement or experiences with some or all family members
- A pervasive sense that unrequested permission to do as one pleases is always available
- A tendency to seek guidance and support from those outside of the family
- Family members who seek isolation and privacy more than being available for other members
- A fear of intimacy rooted in rejection, discomfort with closeness, fear of losing oneself within relationships, and fear of ridicule
- Rarely sharing opinions, feelings, and thoughts, especially by parents with their children.

When working with enmeshed families, therapists can aim to enhance insight and awareness around family members' discomfort with separation. When working with disengaged families, therapists can aid family members in exploring what feels threatening about closeness and reliance on other members of the family. In both enmeshed and disengaged families, the goal is to create open discussion and conscious thought so that families will gravitate toward the middle of the continuum and achieve balance (Shapiro, 2015).

Therapists can highlight the way of being in the family that has been overemphasized, while deciphering and encouraging the ideal that has been underemphasized. Ultimately, therapists must strike a balance with family members' need to feel autonomy and their need to belong and feel connected. Therapists will also need to aid family members in realizing that moving back and forth between connectedness and autonomy can actually enhance both aspects of this continuum for the individual and the family (e.g., togetherness and independence), ultimately providing family members with the security and strength required to venture out into the external world.

Healthy families are able to adapt to change and encourage and support the positive development of individual family members (Minuchin, 1974). If family members are able to support one another and effectively adapt to change, difficult events such as a death or illness of a family member can actually promote healthy relationships and family development. It is especially important for family members to foster healthy boundaries in youth who are experiencing pivotal developmental milestones (Kress, Paylo, & Stargell, 2019). Family boundaries change over time, depending on environment, culture, developmental stages, and relationship styles (Rigazio-DiGilio & McDowell, 2008).

Family Hierarchy

Each family has a hierarchy that determines power and control within the family. Questions of how decisions are made, what role each family member plays, and where authority and status reside all contribute to the family hierarchy. Different hierarchies exist in different families; as long as it is fulfilling the needs of all family members and is clearly delineated, the family's hierarchy can work well. Problems arise, however, when a family develops **coalitions**, or alliances between family members against another family member. For example, two siblings who exclude their 4-year-old brother are forming a coalition. This may result in the left-out child beginning to expect the mother to provide more time for activity and comfort. This may, in turn, put more stress on the mother, who is already busy taking care of a newborn baby. The result is disruption and a negative impact on the functioning of the entire family system.

Another example of a coalition may be that between a parent and a child, which can result in a **parentified child**—one who is given responsibilities within the family that are inconsistent with the child's role or age (Minuchin, 1974). Coalitions that form across generations can be especially problematic. Structural family therapists identify coalitions and triangulation in families and work toward creating functional **alliances**. Unlike coalitions, which form when family members team up against another family member, alliances occur when family members connect with and support one another (e.g., mother and father supporting each other). Alliances are best when they are flexible and allow for a range of interactions within the family. One example of a healthy, functional alliance is when several family members come together to help a son with a substance use problem.

THE THERAPEUTIC PROCESS

The goal of structural family therapy is to restructure the family transactional system so that more effective and healthy interactions are established among family members, and the family as a whole copes better with stress. In counseling, the family's hierarchy is established, appropriate boundaries between subsystems are discovered, and new rules are developed. For structural family therapists, the easiest way to improve dysfunctional family behavior and decrease symptoms is to eliminate or change the family's transactional patterns that maintain the dysfunctional behaviors (Goldenberg et al., 2017).

The process of change consists of three phases (Minuchin, 1974). In the first phase, the therapist joins with the family and assumes a leadership position. In the second phase, the therapist determines the family's structure, and in the third phase, the therapist works to change that structure. Toward that end, the structural family therapist uses multiple techniques, alone or sequentially, either to form a therapeutic system (as in joining) or to disrupt the current system and facilitate change. Following is a brief discussion of some of these interventions.

THERAPEUTIC TECHNIQUES AND PROCEDURES

Joining

Joining happens when the therapist becomes part of a family system in order to understand and ultimately improve aspects of the system. Minuchin (1974) describes how he sometimes became like a distant uncle, and joined with the family system by accommodating to the family's style, using their language and terminology, respectfully sharing in their myths and stories, and adopting their affective style. For example, if they are expressive, he becomes expressive, too; if detached, he remains aloof. Through the joining process, the hierarchy, boundaries, coalitions, and structure of the family system is revealed to the therapist.

Reframing

When family members become entrenched in negatively viewing certain events or other family members' behaviors, actions, and/or intentions, **reframing** can place the original event or situation into a different context. Therapists should consider reframing when existing interpretations of family members' behaviors are inaccurate, incomplete, maladaptive, or unfairly blaming of another family member. The goal is to relabel the event to give it a more positive, adaptive slant (Watzlawick, Weakland, & Fisch, 1974). Reframing can change family perceptions and, as a result, provide more options and explanations based on a new way of looking at the situation (Minuchin & Fishman, 1981).

Enactment

Enactment is a technique in which the therapist may have the client act out a previous experience or a characteristic in session. This process brings an issue of family conflict into the here and now of the therapy session so that hierarchies and family dynamics can be mapped and alternative transactional patterns can be introduced. By re-enacting a problem, a family member learns that the problem is not the fault of the individual, but of the entire family system that continues to contribute to the same behaviors.

Family Maps

Structural family therapists use family mapping as a tool to illustrate the family relationships listed above. **Family maps**, similar to genograms, visually represent family subsystems, boundaries, hierarchies, and alliances. Therapists can also use maps to set goals and assess the progress of counseling.

APPLICATION AND CURRENT USE OF STRUCTURAL FAMILY THERAPY

Structural family therapy has proved helpful in a variety of settings and with different family problems. Minuchin applied structural family therapy in his work with families dealing with anorexia, diabetes, asthma, and other chronic disorders (Minuchin, Rosman, & Baker, 1978). Structural family therapy is also effective for people who have depression and for child behavioral problems, and it has even been used in the school setting (Weaver et al., 2013; Yasar, 2017).

Structural family therapy is open to family structures that differ from the traditional model. Minuchin recognized that a family does not always consist of the traditional two parents and their biological children. Holding all families up to this model is harmful. Families may be one-parent families, stepparent and blended families, or three-generation families. Families, regardless of their makeup, go through change. The therapist's role should be to help families through the inevitable transitions and stressors that come along with that change.

STRATEGIC FAMILY THERAPY

"Change will lead to insight far more often than insight will lead to change." –Milton Erickson

INTRODUCTION/DEVELOPMENT OF STRATEGIC FAMILY THERAPY

Strategic family therapy had its beginnings in the 1950s in Palo Alto, California, in conjunction with the development of the Mental Research Institute (MRI). It was there that Gregory Bateson, Jay Haley, John Weakland, Paul Watzlawick, Don Jackson, and others influenced by Milton Erickson and his work with hypnotherapy became interested in applying paradoxical techniques in their work with families. Strategic therapy evolved through the work of Jay Haley after he left the Palo Alto group to join Salvador Minuchin at the Philadelphia Child Guidance Clinic. In 1976, Haley and Cloe Madanes, a therapist and former MRI colleague, moved to Washington, DC, where they developed the Family Therapy Institute.

Haley was a student of Milton Erickson, whose hypnotic techniques required the therapist to assume full charge of counseling and to set directives and goals to help clients change. Haley became interested in issues of power and control in interpersonal relationships. His classic text *Strategies of Psychotherapy* (1963) underscores his view that symptoms can be seen as a pathological control strategy. Although Haley's work became popular in the 1980s, many seasoned therapists expressed concern about his unconventional techniques. For example, in working with a family to solve a child's bed-wetting problem, parents were instructed to tell their child to wet the bed on certain nights, with increasingly longer periods of time in between (Haley & Richeport-Haley, 2007).

Strategic therapy focuses on family member communication patterns. Specifically, Haley noted that the functionality of a family system could be determined by the manner in which individuals within the family communicate with one another and the alliances they form with other family members. In strategic therapy, neither insight nor multigenerational information is important. Instead, the therapist focuses on the present and is responsible for setting behavior-oriented goals for the family. Change occurs through the process of the family carrying out the therapist's directives (Goldenberg et al., 2017). Haley strategized closely with families to develop unique interventions that would work for their particular problems.

KEY CONCEPTS

Problem-Centered

Strategic family therapy is a problem-centered approach concerned with the immediate presenting problem. Symptoms result from misguided attempts at changing the existing issue. Attempted solutions and symptoms are embedded in **feedback loops**. A **negative feedback loop** occurs when families correct a deviation in family functioning, thereby returning to a state of **homeostasis**. A **positive feedback loop** arises as families attempt to add new information into the system.

Nature of Symptoms

Rather than thinking of symptoms as uncontrollable, strategic family therapy looks behind the symptoms to explore any secondary gain that might be reinforcing the symptoms. Haley (1963) described symptoms as strategies that were adaptive for a particular situation and also served the purpose of controlling or manipulating the behavior of others. For example, a husband who always works late at the office and complains that he has no control over the situation may actually be benefiting from the underlying "payoff" of not having to help with the household responsibilities when he gets home late.

RELATIONSHIP BETWEEN THERAPIST AND CLIENT

Strategic counseling is directive and concrete. The therapist acts as educator and director, providing homework, setting up assignments, teaching new skills, and offering advice. The therapist focuses on the here and now of control struggles and communication patterns within the family. The role of the therapist is to use specific techniques and skills to promote change (Haley & Richeport-Haley, 2007).

THE THERAPEUTIC PROCESS

The goals of strategic family therapy are simply to change the behavior and resolve the presenting concern. This is done by breaking the pattern of incongruence and promoting change using feedback loops to promote overall change in the family system. Therapy begins by identifying ways in which the system maintains the problem, identifying the rules and family communication patterns that contribute to the problem, and then changing the rules. After the problem has been identified, the strategic family therapist explores the family's history of trying to solve the problem, efforts the therapist believes might actually be contributing to the family dysfunction and to continuation of the pattern.

Solutions that perpetuate problems tend to fall into three categories: (1) denial that a problem exists, and therefore nothing is done to solve it; (2) a family focus on solving a different, unrelated problem, resulting in action being taken when it is not needed; and (3) hierarchical problems (action is taken but at the wrong level). After surveying the family's unsuccessful efforts, the therapist develops interventions specific to the family's problems and convinces the family to implement the interventions, thereby interrupting the problem-perpetuating pattern.

THERAPEUTIC TECHNIQUES AND PROCEDURES

Strategic family therapy interventions take the form of directives prescribed by the therapist. These directives often run counter to common sense and are considered the most basic and important tool of the approach. These powerful interventions encourage the family to change, unite the family (even if it becomes united against the therapist), and promote feedback the therapist can use to help solve the family's problems.

Ordeals

Ordeals are not intended to cause harm but may sometimes seem to be punishing or even absurd. Ordeals are of two main types. The first type comprises **straightforward ordeals**, which take place when clients are asked to perform an unpleasant event after the problem behavior has occurred. For example, a man who has repetitive nights of insomnia is given a directive to get up and clean the house every time he cannot sleep. Another directive that Haley once made involved a contract with a married couple with alcohol use problems. Under the terms of the contract, the first person who had a drink and broke the contract agreed to walk around the house naked the following day. The "ordeal" is generally more unpleasant than the symptom. The other main type of ordeal comprises **paradoxical ordeals**, which are directives that demand the performance of the symptom on purpose. However, for these ordeals to be effective, the client must have a willingness to solve the problem and a commitment to following the therapist's directives, no matter how ridiculous or punitive such actions might seem.

Paradoxical Interventions

A commonly used directive within strategic family therapy is the paradoxical intervention. **Paradoxical interventions** are directives in which therapists prescribe an action to clients that the therapists want resisted. Change occurs when clients defy the directive (Haley, 1963, 1996). These interventions initially appear to be opposed to the goals of counseling. Therapists, for instance, can assign a specific time to be angry (e.g., Tuesday from 8 to 9 p.m.) or schedule family conflict for a specific time and place (e.g., Friday at 6 p.m. in the kitchen). The intention is not to re-enact the problem, but the directive has been prescribed for a certain time to disrupt individuals' attempted solutions. In addition, if clients do not comply with these interventions, then the problem can often be resolved because the prescribed behavior did not occur. Paradoxical interventions often include the following: asking family members to interact or argue in a new place (e.g., move arguments to the bathroom if all fighting occurs within the kitchen); interacting in a different way (e.g., move away from *you* statements to *I* statements); change something about the process (e.g., stop fighting and change into formal clothing to argue); or change the physical environment in some way (e.g., play jazz music in the background; Becvar & Becvar, 2013).

Directives in strategic family therapy are generally paradoxical and create a **double bind**, which occurs when an individual receives an important message with two different meanings and is unable to respond to it; thus, the individual is in an impossible situation, or "bind." For example, a teenage daughter whose behavior of staying out all night is causing problems in the family might be directed by the therapist to stay out every night and only come home once a week. This sets up a double bind for the daughter, who now feels she is being told she can't stay in her own house. If she complies, she is letting the therapist control her; if she doesn't comply with the directive, she is changing her behavior in the direction her parents want. Such double binds are intended to overcome any resistance to change (Nichols, 2009). Haley believed the real issue in families was often one of power and control. Paradoxical interventions can be implemented either within sessions or outside of sessions (Dattilio, 2010).

Examples of other types of paradoxical interventions used in strategic family therapy include:

- **Relabeling:** Defining the problem, behavior, or event differently by using language that positions it in a more favorable light to elicit more positive responses
- **Restraining:** Directing clients not to change too quickly or not to change at all
- **Declaring hopelessness:** Agreeing with clients that their situation is hopeless and that nothing can be done.

Circular Questioning

The therapist can use circular questions to expose interaction and communication patterns within the family (Patterson, Williams, Edwards, Chamow, & Grauf-Grounds, 2009). **Circular questioning** is an interviewing technique used within family therapy to gather more information and to introduce new information and awareness into the family system. This technique has since been adopted and adapted by many other models of family therapy (Patterson et al., 2009). By asking all family members about their perception of their relationships and differences between family members, circular questioning enhances the development of a more explicit family structure, and an increased awareness of the nature of each relationship within the family can be revealed (Patterson et al., 2009). As an example, if an adolescent is chronically truant from school, circular questions a counselor could ask family members might be as follows: Who is usually the first to find out about Billy skipping school? What happens within the family after Billy is caught skipping school? How does Billy act when he does not skip school? What is happening in the family before Billy decides to skip school? Can anyone predict when Billy might skip school? These types of questions may lead to the realization that Billy skips school more frequently after his mother and stepfather fight. Circular questions can increase family members' awareness of how family interactions and behaviors can maintain or exacerbate the initial issues presented in counseling (Kress, Paylo, & Stargell, 2019). Circular questions can increase family members' awareness of not only the process of the presenting issue but also of how family interactions and behaviors can maintain, exacerbate, or even hinder the presenting issue.

APPLICATION AND CURRENT USE OF STRATEGIC FAMILY THERAPY

Overall, strategic family therapy provides a brief, directive, problem-focused approach that addresses the family's presenting problem. Several concepts, particularly the idea that the family is contributing to the problem through its unsuccessful attempts at solutions, and the idea that many symptoms are reinforced by secondary gains (e.g., controlling others' actions, avoidance of responsibility), were first suggested by Milton Erickson and became an important part of strategic family therapy. Interventions such as paradoxical interventions, guaranteeing therapeutic success, and the use of absurd directives represent several of the unconventional techniques to come out of strategic family therapy. These "experiments" helped the family overcome resistance and created experiential moments that facilitated change. However, many of the paradoxical interventions are viewed by some as punitive or even manipulative. It was this manipulative aspect of the theory that eventually encouraged many family therapists to disagree with strategic family therapy (Nichols, 2009). Contemporary strategic family therapists have moved toward developing a more positive, collaborative, and congruent relationship with clients.

Brief strategic therapy has been successfully used with people with behavior problems (Horigian et al., 2015) and substance abuse issues (Horigian et al., 2015). More research is needed on strategic family therapy with other types of clients and different problems. Some critics of the strategic approach question whether focusing on change without psychological assessment or a full history of the presenting problem could be harmful or, at best, only result in **first-order change**. This is a change in behavior on the part of one person in a family unit that does not result in change to the overall organization of the system, and it is considered superficial. The ultimate goal is **second-order change**, or a lasting change in the fundamental organization of a family system.

EMOTIONALLY FOCUSED COUPLE THERAPY

> "Being the 'best you can be' is really only possible when you are deeply connected to another. Splendid isolation is for planets, not people." – Susan M. Johnson

SUSAN M. JOHNSON (b. 1947)

Susan M. Johnson is a clinical psychologist who was born in England in the middle of the last century. She later moved to Canada and worked with children in a therapeutic treatment center. Johnson is currently a professor of clinical psychology and psychiatry at the University of Ottawa, director of the Ottawa Couple and Family Institute, and director of the International Centre for Excellence in Emotionally Focused Therapy. She conducts international training and certification programs on emotionally focused couple therapy; has authored numerous articles and chapters on this approach; and has written several books, including *The Practice of Emotionally Focused Couple Therapy* (2004) and *Hold Me Tight* (2008), that concentrate on the importance of emotional connection to the success of committed relationships.

INTRODUCTION/DEVELOPMENT OF EMOTIONALLY FOCUSED COUPLE THERAPY

Emotionally focused therapy, a couples therapy approach, was developed in the 1980s by Susan M. Johnson and Leslie Greenberg (1985, 1987). It was named emotionally focused therapy (EFT) because it combines attachment theory with process-experiential theory to draw attention to the importance of emotion as a powerful agent of change.

EFT primarily combines person-centered therapy and Gestalt therapy and applies these principles to working with couples. EFT draws from Gestalt therapy by focusing on accessing and heightening emotional experience. For this to be effective, the person-centered approach of providing a safe environment and strong therapeutic relationship is necessary. EFT also has roots in experiential and existential therapies. For example, this approach draws from experiential therapy by emphasizing the interaction between emotion and symbolism for creating meaning. In addition, the deepening of experience and emotion is important. Johnson also used a cognitive and emotion theory perspective to view her approach. Emotion theory views emotions as fundamentally adaptive in nature. Thus, EFT explores emotion to help people process complex information automatically and thereby increase well-being. EFT has become one of the most researched and validated approaches to addressing distress in couples and has also been expanded for use with a wide variety of populations and presenting problems (Johnson & Woolley, 2009).

KEY CONCEPTS

Emotionally focused therapy is a systemic theory that synchronizes a humanistic-experiential approach with theories of adult attachment, using emotion as the language of change. These four important concepts are outlined as follows.

Systemic

Emotionally focused therapy is a systems theory founded on von Bertalanffy's early works and based more specifically on Minuchin's structural approach (Johnson & Woolley, 2009). EFT holds that individual behavior can only be considered as part of the whole. The focus is on patterns of behavior. Change must occur not only in the individual's behavior (a level one change) but also in the pattern of the couple as a whole (level two change).

Humanistic-Experiential

Emotionally focused therapy follows in the humanistic tradition of belief in the basic goodness of people, their innate desire to self-actualize, and the importance of unconditional positive regard, congruence, and empathy. The creation of a positive therapeutic alliance is a necessary condition for change to take place. As in all experiential therapies, EFT therapists believe that new behavior and new insight come through as a result of reprocessing emotions in the here and now of the therapy session.

Attachment

Emotionally focused therapy is also grounded in attachment theory, which holds that having a safe emotional connection to loved ones is a basic survival need, developed through evolution (Johnson & Greenman, 2006). Securely attached couples are emotionally accessible and responsive to each other. They reach for and find that safe connection in their partner, or effective dependency (Johnson, 2007). However, when partners experience disconnection, a predictable process begins to unfold. Initial anxiety results in protest and anger, which is followed by clinging and seeking behavior. If the attachment figure does not respond, depression and despair set in. Attachment theory offers marriage and family therapists a map to the key moves that shape a love relationship.

Emotion

Emotionally focused therapy centers on emotion as the prime mover in couples therapy. Emotion is accessed and unpacked in the therapy session. It is not enough to develop insight; emotions must be re-enacted in the presence of the partner. The partner will then experience empathy, or a softening of feelings. Only then can a "new corrective emotional experience of engagement with the partner" occur. The accessing and unpacking of emotion viewed by the other partner is the main agent of change (Johnson, 2004). EFT therapists concentrate on the core emotions and use their listening skills and reflective interventions to enhance and reduce expressed emotion (Johnson & Greenman, 2006).

RELATIONSHIP BETWEEN THERAPIST AND CLIENT

The therapist provides a safe, warm environment in which partners can explore emotions, both positive and negative. To do so, the therapist must establish and maintain a positive therapeutic alliance with both partners. As in other humanistic theories, the therapist takes on a collaborative role, is respectful of both partners, and focuses on the moment-by-moment processes. Rather than a coach, diagnostician, or teacher, the EFT therapist is a process consultant, a choreographer, and a collaborator.

THE THERAPEUTIC PROCESS

In EFT, the emotional connection between partners is always the central focus. The goal of EFT is to reprocess through emotions in order to experience feelings naturally, act in healthy ways, and create a deeper connection between partners (Johnson, 2004). After the couple is more securely attached, they are able to work out their problems with less resentment and free from attachment insecurity.

In emotionally focused couple therapy, the change process has been divided into nine steps designed to be used in 8 to 20 sessions (Johnson, 2004). These nine steps take place in three distinct phases: de-escalation, change in interactional positions, and consolidation and integration of gains and progress made. What follows is a brief description of the three phases of counseling in which these steps would unfold:

1. *Phase 1: **De-escalation*** (steps 1–4). The first four steps involve assessment, understanding of problematic cycles, and the emotional states that go along with them. In this phase of counseling, the couple is encouraged to express their emotions. Negative cycles are identified and couples are helped to recognize the primary feelings (e.g., sadness, anger, hurt) underlying their reactive secondary emotions (e.g., resentment, withdrawal). At the end of phase 1, couples begin to detach from their negative patterns and the relationship becomes more stable. At this stage of counseling, the presenting problem is no longer the problem; rather, the negative cycle and lack of connection between the couple become the problem.
2. *Phase 2: **Change in interactional positions*** (steps 5–7). The couple recognizes and unites to overcome the negative interactional cycle that has developed between them. The second phase of counseling is when the bulk of therapy work unfolds. Here each partner is encouraged to express, first individually and later together, the deeper emotions behind their feelings. The therapist choreographs emotional re-enactments. Partners are no longer overwhelmed by their emotions, but are able to hear and accept their partner's needs and integrate their own needs into new interactional behavior. Withdrawn partners become more emotionally involved, and more hostile partners begin to express their fears and take new risks.
3. *Phase 3: **Consolidation and integration*** (steps 8 and 9). By now, couples have developed a new, secure attachment to each other. The old distress has been relieved, they can communicate effectively about problem areas, and they become capable of solving ongoing problems in the relationship. In the final phase of counseling, the couple's gains are solidified; they are reminded of their old negative interactional cycle and encouraged to maintain the positive interactions they have developed so that both members of the couple continue to communicate effectively and get their emotional needs met.

THERAPEUTIC TECHNIQUES AND PROCEDURES

Emotionally focused therapy is a simple yet revolutionary method of couples counseling. Couples are not taught how to communicate more effectively. Techniques such as genograms, behavioral exercises, and homework are not prescribed. Instead, the EFT therapist uses empathy and Rogerian reflective listening skills to track emotion and uses those emotions to produce alternative feelings in the partner through enactments during the session. When one partner hears the other's pain, that partner is more likely to "soften" or empathize with the partner, thus reducing negative, angry, or resentful feelings. The EFT therapist can help both partners express the pain they have kept to themselves and experience catharsis. This is the underlying cause of change in EFT.

EFT therapists use both interactive and structural techniques, such as enactments, to help couples access and express their emotions. As negative feelings are reduced, the couples are more likely to rebuild their connection based on expressed emotion, empathy, and a secure attachment bond.

Specific interventions used by emotionally focused therapists include:

- Asking evocative questions
- Reflecting emotional responses
- Reframing patterns in terms of attachment and negative cycles
- Tracking and replaying key moments
- Creating enactments in which the partners make their patterns explicit
- Slowly encouraging new ways of connecting
- Validating and normalizing responses.

APPLICATION AND CURRENT USE OF EMOTIONALLY FOCUSED COUPLE THERAPY

The EFT model is increasingly being used throughout the world and growing in popularity. It appeals to people from a variety of cultures and backgrounds because it focuses on issues that are universal—attachment and connection—and uses interventions that are respectful and collaborative (Greenman, Young, & Johnson, 2009). Perhaps because of its solid grounding in attachment theory, a lack of pathologizing, and a focus on the healing powers of emotion, EFT is suitable for all types of couples, including older couples; gay and lesbian couples; couples struggling with chronic illnesses, such as cancer or depression; and military couples (Rheem, Woolley, & Weissman, 2012). EFT has even shown effectiveness with inexpressive partners; with traditionally avoidant male partners; and with issues that are difficult to address, such as infidelity, sexual disorders, and sexual abuse trauma (Johnson & Woolley, 2009; MacIntosh & Johnson, 2008). EFT has been found to work particularly well for couples in which one member has experienced severe trauma or posttraumatic stress disorder (PTSD; Greenman & Johnson, 2012). It provides a structured, experiential, attachment-intervention model for helping couples communicate on a deeper level. However, EFT is not appropriate for working with couples who have different agendas, such as a separating couple or a couple in which one person seeks to maintain an affair, or in abusive and/or violent relationships.

EFT has entered the mainstream for couples therapy, in large part due to its empirically validated support and its focus on love and connection. This is the first relational theory of adult love to be synchronistic with other research on the nature of emotion and attachment and to provide a road map for therapists. EFT is also consistent with new developments in the field of neuroscience that relate to health and emotion, stress, and bonding. Clearly, emotionally focused therapy has much to offer therapists who work with couples. Newer research concentrates on its effectiveness in working with families, as well.

INDIVIDUAL THERAPY THEORIES APPLIED TO FAMILY THERAPY

Psychoanalysis

In psychoanalytic family therapy, concepts like drive and ego theory are combined with a confrontive and active therapeutic style (Ackerman, 1958). Therapists who practice psychoanalytic family therapy rely heavily on object relations theory. It is important for therapists to point out when family members are being supportive and caring, and providing warm and safe environments to work through problems. Therapists also pay attention to attachment and separation patterns. Psychoanalytic family therapists consider past relationships and experiences to be important. For example, the way clients interact in counseling (e.g., any forms of resistance) may be related to past relational experiences, so it is vital to explore and understand this connection.

Adlerian Therapy

Alfred Alder, the creator of Adlerian therapy, was the first psychoanalyst to adopt a holistic view that considered the importance of family relationships in the creation of the individual. Adler even involved the entire family in the counseling process. Many of Adler's concepts, such as birth order, sibling rivalry, inferiority, and social interest, can be understood in relation to the individual, as well as the whole, making it applicable to family therapy. Family members are taught how to solve conflict by understanding the problem, respecting each other, and deciding on how to solve the problem together.

Adlerian therapy can be applied to children, especially for classroom use by school counselors and Adlerian play therapy. Adlerian therapy can also be applied to parenting, with programs such as Active Parenting and Systematic Training for Effective Parenting (STEP). Adlerian family therapy is a positive, empowering, strengths-based approach for working with families.

Behavior Therapy

The underlying assumption of behavioral family therapies is that when problematic behavior is changed, the overall functioning of the family is changed and can improve. The focus of behavioral family therapy approaches involves changing problematic behavior using behavioral interventions, such as role playing, modeling, and teaching parents new ways of managing their children's behavior. Therapists who use behavioral approaches are active, are collaborative, and act as experts.

Using foundational behavior therapy principles, Gerald Patterson created a variety of interventions that can be used by parents to improve children's behavior and reduce family stress and dysfunction. This is known as behavioral parent training. By using operant conditioning interventions such as contingency contracting, token economies, modeling, and time-out, parents learned to improve their children's positive behaviors and extinguish the negative behaviors.

Rather than working with the entire family, behaviorists are more likely to work with one family member (most often a parent) individually. Through didactic instruction and the use of written materials, the therapist teaches the parent specific skills to manage the child's problem behavior. The therapist may also use interventions such as role playing, rehearsal, modeling, and prompting to improve the parent's interactions with the child. Regardless of which methods are used, progress is charted over the course of counseling and success is rewarded with positive reinforcement.

Behaviorists do not see the problem as embedded in the family system. However, as social learning theorists, behaviorists believe that the child's behavior, although disruptive to the family, has actually been learned and reinforced by parental actions. To change behavior, parents learn to change the consequences.

Cognitive Behavioral Therapy

Cognitive behavioral therapy (CBT) used in family therapy involves changing thinking patterns of family members and incorporating psychoeducation. Therapists analyze cognitive distortions and schemas among family members. For example, a family member may think, "My brother hates me because he never wants to spend time with me." The therapist may use the A-B-C–D-E-F approach from rational emotive behavior therapy (REBT) or other cognitive interventions to invite the family member to change her thinking into something more accurate. For example, a family member may instead think, "Just because my brother isn't spending as much time with me as I'd like, that doesn't mean he hates me. Maybe he is busy." The therapist may then introduce behavioral interventions such as assertiveness training by inviting the client to express her feelings to her brother. Thoughts are changed from hurtful and blaming to more positive ways of thinking. Therapists especially challenge cognitive distortions such as mind reading and "should" and "must" statements, which are common in family relationships. Therapists using CBT family therapy encourage all family members to assume responsibility for themselves and their interactions. Therapists are active and take on a teacher role. They implement a variety of cognitive and behavioral techniques that can help them manage any issues and prevent problems from arising. Cognitive behavioral approaches to family therapy are frequently integrated with other counseling theories or used as an adjunct to other family therapy approaches (Dattilio, 2005).

Behavior and cognitive behavioral family therapies provide the most diversity in terms of type and scope of counseling options. Following are just a few of the different family therapy modalities that reside under the cognitive behavioral and behavioral umbrella of counseling approaches:

- Functional family therapy
- Cognitive behavioral family therapy
- Behavior modification
- Behavioral parent training and parent skills training
- Behavioral treatment of sexual dysfunctions
- Cognitive behavioral couples therapy
- Family-focused therapy
- Behavioral family systems therapy
- Dialectical behavior therapy for children and adolescents
- Rational emotive behavior therapy for childhood behavior problems.

A discussion of each of these counseling approaches is beyond the scope of this chapter.

Reality Therapy

Reality therapists who practice family therapy evaluate how family members make choices and how they interact with each other. Therapists pay attention to the feelings, wants, values, and needs of family members. Attention is paid to activities and needs both for each family member and for the family as a whole. Reality therapists believe that family members benefit from doing activities together and separately, as individual growth is just as important. By assessing individuals' wants and activities, therapists can understand whether or not the family is meeting their needs and suggest activities that can promote connection if necessary.

Existential Therapy

Existential family therapy focuses on helping family members gain awareness of themselves, their relationships, and other family members. One way to gain awareness of another family member, especially in couples counseling, is for one partner to observe the other partner's session and to take notes and reflect on the experience. Clients may also be asked to keep track of their therapy using a journal. This helps clients gain awareness of both themselves and their partners. In addition, finding meaning in the interactions between family members and living more authentically individually and in relationships are key elements in existential family therapy.

Person-Centered Therapy

Therapists who use person-centered therapy with couples and families demonstrate the core conditions, which include empathy, unconditional positive regard, and congruence. Therapists aim to deeply understand the conflict between family members and show empathy for all family members. Showing empathy toward all family members may help all individuals feel heard, accepted, and equal. Therapists may even show empathy for a family member who is absent. For example, the therapist may say, "I am sensing that you are frustrated with Susan because she is parenting differently than you, but I wonder how she would feel if she were here and what her reasons are for making those parenting decisions." The goal of this tactic is to help clients gain empathy for, and understanding of, their family members as well, which may lead to being more open and connected with each other. Therapists' demonstration of empathy may help individual family members learn how to become more empathic with their family.

Gestalt Therapy

Gestalt family therapists pay attention to boundaries and patterns between family members. Therapists are active, focus on the present moment, and use many Gestalt therapy techniques. One of the main goals is to increase overall awareness of family members, especially awareness of their own needs and those of other family members. Gestalt therapists pay attention to the interactions and relationships between family members and may even discuss the therapist's relationship with the family. Experiential techniques are often used with family members and couples to increase present-moment awareness and promote change.

Feminist Therapy

Therapists who use feminist therapy with families and couples explore how social and political factors affect individuals and family relationships. Therapists do not place blame on anyone; instead, they punctuate how gender and power issues impact their clients. Cultural identity and racial identity play a huge role in clients' lives, and therapists take this into consideration when conceptualizing and working with clients and families. Therapists may also incorporate psychoeducation about various topics like gender roles, language, and societal expectations.

Postmodern Therapy

Postmodern therapists especially emphasize social context and the social systems within which people live, and they believe that all of individual reality is socially situated. In other words, people only understand or "know" the context in which they reside, and this reality is continually shifting and phenomenological. As such, postmodern approaches to family therapy highlight the relativity associated with what all people think they know. There are few clear-cut answers, a lot of ambiguity, and a variety of choices that could lead to change.

Narrative therapy and solution-focused brief therapy are two of the more prominent postmodern theories used today. Both theories have their origins in family therapy. Because of their prominence, and because of their frequent use in individual therapy as well as family therapy, they have been assigned their own chapter.

GENERAL ASSESSMENT OF FAMILY THERAPY

APPLICATION AND CURRENT USE OF FAMILY THERAPY

Counseling Applications

To date, the research literature has not identified one single approach to family therapy that is more effective than the others. Certainly, some family therapies have shown greater efficacy for specific populations or in treating certain disorders, but no theoretical orientation has been found to be the most effective overall. Most family therapists today use an integrated or eclectic counseling approach (Prochaska & Norcross, 2018).

Bountiful research supports the use of family therapy in the treatment of addictions, eating disorders, adolescent mood and anxiety disorders, ADHD, childhood conduct disorder, and autism spectrum disorders (Kaslow, Broth, Smith, & Collins, 2012). Psychoeducation for families in which a family member has schizophrenia is also effective and has been shown to reduce the incidence of rehospitalization (Lieberman & Murray, 2012).

Family therapy has found success with children and adolescents in particular. Children with internalizing disorders, such as depressive disorders and eating disorders, may benefit from therapy (Retzlaff, Sydow, Beher, Haun, & Schweitzer, 2013). Externalizing disorders, such as ADHD, conduct disorders, and substance use disorders, are also helped by family therapy (Sydow, Retzlaff, Beher, Huan, & Schweitzer, 2013). In work with adolescents and their parents, family therapy can boost family unity, improve positive interactions, and decrease depressive symptoms (Guo & Slesnick, 2013). In addition, children and adolescents who experience delinquency, rearrests, and substance use can also benefit from this approach (Dakof et al., 2015). Furthermore, family therapy has been shown to work well for the following concerns: child maltreatment, grief, self-harm, somatic problems, and first episode psychosis (Carr, 2014a).

Adults can also benefit from family therapy. Recent research has provided empirical support for family therapy in addressing the following concerns: relationship distress, psychosexual problems, intimate partner violence, anxiety disorders, mood disorders, substance use issues, and schizophrenia (Carr, 2014b). In addition, family therapy can help improve overall well-being, self-worth, self-acceptance, connection between family members, and relationship independence (Hunger, Bornhäuser, Link, Schweitzer, & Weinhold, 2014).

Application to Multicultural Groups

Families are becoming increasingly diverse in terms of ethnicity, family structure, and family roles and expectations (Walsh, 2012). Today's families are **multinuclear** (two separate families who live in the same house), multiracial, multigenerational, and have diverse economic and spiritual needs.

Along with the changing family structures comes the need for culturally competent therapists and those who can adopt a strengths-based perspective. All therapists should be culturally competent and sensitive to race, gender roles, ethnicity, socioeconomic status, and sexual orientation. They should be capable of developing a sound therapeutic alliance with people whose cultural backgrounds differ from their own. When family therapists do not understand or value cultural diversity or the importance of specific traditions or beliefs in a particular family, they are likely to misunderstand, stereotype, or even pathologize the family (Gladding, 2019).

Remarried, blended, multinuclear, or multigenerational families share many of the same problems that most families face but also present with concerns specific to their unique situation. For example, in a multigenerational model for working with African American families, intergenerational kinship is a source of support and care for relatives and nonbiological family members alike (Waites, 2009). This support often continues across the lifespan. The intergenerational solidarity model provides an Afrocentric worldview that helps therapists to build on the family's strengths and incorporate culturally relevant issues, questions, and empowerment-oriented strategies.

Healthy adjustment for remarried or blended families often involves solidifying the bond between the couple while simultaneously adjusting to the differing developmental needs of the children. Stepfamilies often come to counseling in crisis or after problems have strained the relationship. Experiential and structural family therapy can be particularly helpful in working with these families. Virginia Satir's family sculpting techniques can help blended family members become more aware of interpersonal connections. Similarly, Susan Johnson's emotionally focused therapy can help them become more emotionally connected. Minuchin's structural family therapy, with its goal of establishing a clearly defined hierarchy, can help families to form new boundaries after the blended family is created. Developing a multigenerational genogram can also help families to recognize patterns of behavior in their families of origin and to avoid the mistakes of prior generations (Gladding, 2019).

It is important for marriage and family therapists who work with gay and lesbian couples to be able to address issues of cultural discrimination and homophobia related to being gay; understand intergenerational dynamics that may contribute stress to the family; and be familiar with community resources, state and local laws, and the diversity of gay and lesbian lifestyles. Issues of social support and levels of satisfaction in the relationship are common presenting problems (van Eeden-Moorefield, Few-Demo, Benson, Bible, & Lummer, 2018).

EVALUATION OF FAMILY THERAPY

Limitations

In the beginnings of family therapy, some people focused too heavily on the language of the system. For example, too many dichotomies—such as "functional" or "dysfunctional," "positive" or "negative," and "enmeshed" or "disengaged"—were in use. This type of language may have resulted in overlooking individual functioning and well-being and focusing too heavily on the overall functioning of the system. In addition, some techniques may have been considered manipulative, like paradoxical interventions and enactments, with clients possibly not having awareness that these interventions were being done to them.

Currently, one criticism of family therapy is that it is sometimes viewed as its own field, with a separate language of its own. Other criticisms include administrative issues such as the difficulty of scheduling appointments with multiple people, increased record keeping, and concerns about confidentiality. In addition, it can be challenging to involve all family members in the change process. Family therapists must have awareness of, and willingness to work on, their own family issues. It is essential for therapists to receive adequate training and supervision for assessing and treating families and couples.

Strengths and Contributions

The systemic perspective offers a new way of viewing families in that all members are contributing to the problem. In this way, not one particular family member is blamed for the problem. Therefore, all members of the system assume responsibility, and no one person is seen as the "bad" or "problem" person. This perspective could improve collaboration and willingness to participate in therapy. By working with the entire family or viewing the individual from a systemic perspective, a greater understanding of dysfunctional patterns comes about.

Family approaches tend to be empowering, strengths based, and easily integrated together. Family members may feel empowered from undergoing family therapy due to the exploration of patterns within the family. Family members can work together to find solutions, which can be an uplifting experience for improving family unity. In addition, family therapy views external factors as important influencers for family dysfunction. For example, gender roles, culture, and societal expectations are taken into consideration, providing a more holistic framework. Overall, family therapy approaches have shown value in helping a wide variety of people and in addressing diverse presenting concerns.

SKILL DEVELOPMENT: GENOGRAMS

Therapists who work with families use many different techniques to gather and organize family information. Murray Bowen was the first to develop genograms—graphic depictions of several generations of a family—as an information-gathering and assessment tool in therapy. Genograms are a concise and practical tool for maintaining a great deal of information about the family, its interrelationships, and patterns.

Typically, genograms are created in the first session, with additional information added as it becomes known. Most genograms include at least three generations. Family patterns are often transmitted from generation to generation, and the genogram provides a graphic illustration through which such patterns can be identified. Repetitive patterns in behavior, relationships, and family structure can be seen both horizontally and vertically across generations.

Gathering Information

When eliciting information for a genogram, the therapist either works with one family member individually or with the family as a whole. Gathering a family's history should always be done respectfully, and as with all other session documents, confidentiality of information should be maintained (McGoldrick & Hardy, 2008).

Drawing a Genogram

There is no right or wrong way to develop a genogram, and information can be presented in many different ways. Ultimately what most matters is that it helps the client and therapist. Most genograms begin with the index person (IP) at the bottom of the page. The index person is designated by a double box. The IP's parents are documented on the row above, and the top row illustrates grandparents. Births, deaths, marriages, divorces, siblings, parents, and grandparents are documented. Adoptions, foster children, abortions, and miscarriages can also be included. When known, dates of birth, marriage, and death are listed.

After the initial family has been drawn, the genogram can be expanded to identify the relationships between people. Closeness, enmeshment, disengagement, and family cutoffs are indicated by the appropriate type of line (see Figure 14.4). Physical and sexual abuse is designated by a zigzag line attached to an arrow to indicate who was abused.

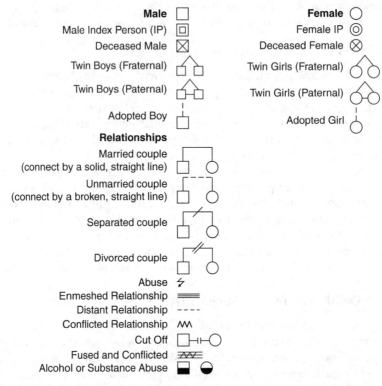

FIGURE 14.4 Symbols for Constructing a Family Genogram.

Disorders such as substance abuse, depression, or severe mental illness can also be shown on the genogram by shading in a portion of the circle or square. Addictions are indicated by shading in the bottom half of the symbol. Serious mental or physical illnesses are shown by filling in the left half of the circle or square. The type of disorder should be written near the symbol.

Additional genograms can be created to portray different types of information. The basic genogram may indicate the family's structure and demographics, while another may be used to show patterns of relationships between family members. Additional biographical information such as occupations, incomes, level of education, cause of death, or any other information the therapist would like to track can also be added.

Every genogram will contain some missing items (McGoldrick et al., 2008). This is to be expected and may actually be the source of important information for therapists, such as when clients do not have information about their immediate family members, or when former spouses or stepchildren have become cut off from the family.

Genograms can also be used to display a variety of interpersonal issues, such as family members who are extremely close, those who are helpful, and types of relationship difficulties. Even the power dynamics within the family, such as who is intimidated by others, who has more power, or who has no power, can be shown. Genograms can illustrate culture, race, religion, socioeconomic status, and so on. Because of the wealth of information that can be collected, it often becomes necessary to create a separate genogram for these types of questions.

Sample Genogram

Figure 14.5 represents a genogram of the Diaz family. The genogram provides a quick illustration of the demographic information we have about Roberto and Edie. Roberto comes from a large Puerto Rican–American family and was married twice before he met Edie. Edie's background is quite different. She grew up as one of two sisters in a Jewish–American family. Her parents are divorced and her mother remarried. The genogram also shows Edie's history of abuse. Roberto and Edie have been married for 14 years, and their 10-year-old daughter, Ava, is the index person in this genogram.

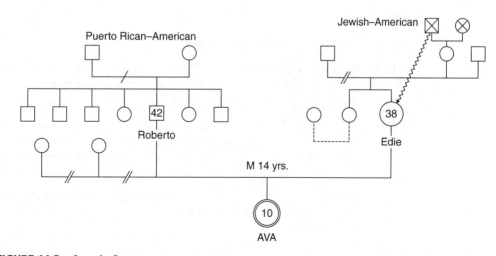

FIGURE 14.5   Sample Genogram.

CASE APPLICATION

Edie and Roberto mentioned to the family's therapist that Roberto had recently changed jobs. This had resulted in his frequent absences from home to attend weeklong business trips in another state. During Roberto's absence, Edie reported that their 10-year-old daughter, Ava, seemed withdrawn and had been shutting herself in her room. When Roberto returned home for the weekend, Ava continued to ignore her parents and refused to do what she was told.

The therapist had previously met with Ava in several individual sessions and together with her family. She remembered the girl's openness, and encouraged Edie and Roberto to bring Ava to their next session, during which the therapist used family sculpting techniques to help Ava and her parents understand the child's underlying feelings:

THERAPIST: Ava, I'm so glad that you are with us today. I've noticed you've been very quiet during our session. Is there anything you'd like to talk about?

AVA: Not really.

THERAPIST: Okay. Well, I have an idea of something you might enjoy doing that doesn't involve talking. Would you like to try it?

AVA: Okay. What do I have to do?

THERAPIST: First, let's have everybody stand up. Roberto, Edie . . . now, Ava, I'd like for you to take a minute to think about this past week and what it was like at home. When you're ready, I'd like you to position your parents and yourself as if you are all statues frozen in place. As you do this, try to represent for me what it was like at home this week.

For a few minutes Ava thought about how she would like to position each of her parents. Then she took her father's hand and walked with him toward the door. She turned him to face the door, with his back to the people in the room. Then Ava moved her mother into the center of the room, turning her to face her husband's back. Ava took her mother's right hand and positioned the hand up to her ear as if her mother were talking on the telephone. Appearing satisfied with her mother's pose, Ava moved behind and away from her, so that her mother could not see her, as she slowly curled up on the couch and stared off into space.

The therapist invites Ava to tell her about her sculpture.

AVA: Well, I put Daddy by the door because he was working all week so he was never home, not even at night for dinner. It's like he wasn't even there.

THERAPIST: That must have been very difficult for you.

AVA: I missed him. He always comes home from work at night and makes me laugh. We goof around doing silly things until dinner's ready. But Daddy doesn't come home from work anymore and I just sit in my room with nothing to do.

THERAPIST: I see you positioned yourself on the couch.

AVA: That's because you don't have a bed in here. But at home, I just go to my bed and wrap up in my favorite blanket. I wish Daddy was there. I wish I had something to do.

THERAPIST: But what about your mother? Explain to me what your mother is doing.

AVA: She's always on the phone whenever Daddy isn't home. She just talks, talks, talks, blah, blah, blah. She calls Grandma, my aunt, her friends, anybody she

	can find to talk to and just ignores me. She even calls and orders pizza over the phone and then calls someone else while she's waiting for the pizza to come. She never talks to me! When Daddy's not around, it's as if I don't exist. Like I'm in the way or something. She'd be better off without me so that she could just go and have fun with her friends.
EDIE:	I never knew she felt that way! I miss Roberto terribly while he's gone and I guess I do spend a lot of time trying to keep myself busy by calling friends. And with Roberto not around, there's no reason to make a big dinner. But I didn't realize Ava felt that way, too! Is that why you go in your room? Because there's nothing to do?
ROBERTO:	I can't believe how much has changed in our family in just a few short weeks. I don't like going away either, but I have to travel for my new job. I guess both of my girls are feeling lost without me. It's nice to be missed, but this has got to change.
THERAPIST:	What do you think you could do differently?
EDIE:	Well, Ava and I can do something together. Maybe we can start making dinner together when Daddy's not home. Would you like to do that?
AVA:	Can we make spaghetti?

REFLECT AND RESPOND

1. Using the symbols and genogram example illustrated in the Skill Development section, construct a three-generation genogram of your family. Begin at the bottom. Use the appropriate symbols for yourself and your siblings in chronological birth order. Move up to the previous generation and include your parents and their siblings if space allows. Complete the genogram with your grandparents at the top of the page. Add as much information as possible, including birth dates, dates of marriages and divorces, and dates of deaths. Use appropriate lines to connect relationships. Include themes and family patterns (drug/alcohol abuse, violence, any mental illnesses). Also indicate strengths (education, cultural ties, professional success). Put ages inside the symbols and write names and birth dates on the side. You might want to consult with your parents or grandparents for specific details and dates, but that is not necessary. Every person's genogram looks different. In your journal, write about your experience in completing your genogram. Were there any challenges or difficulties? How might the use of genograms impact your effectiveness as a therapist?

2. Write a family snapshot. In 100 words or fewer, capture a poignant moment in the life of your family. Describe a memorable event or a time that was particularly important to your family. The snapshot may be of an event, a celebration, or a spontaneous occurrence in the daily life of your family. The purpose of the exercise is to capture a poignant moment, describe it in an engaging way, and color in the emotions, thoughts, and feelings. Record this family snapshot in your weekly journal.

3. Think for a few minutes about what constitutes a family. In your family, what roles, if any, are traditionally assigned to the men? To the women? Now think about your cultural and religious or spiritual background. How does your background influence your own attitudes? Will your attitudes make it hard for you to be objective in working with families? What types of issues, populations, or families would be difficult for you to work with? Write about this in your journal.

4. Using your journal, create a family mission statement. First write a "mission statement" of your family. This can be a summary of your family's values and roles that make up your family. Then follow the prompts below:

- We have the most fun together when . . .
- We have the most conflict when . . .
- As a family, we can help each other more by . . .
- What values do we want our family to be based on?
- What changes do we need to make as a family?
- What needs does each of us have going into the future?

Process the mission statement and think about how this can be helpful to your future clients in session.

Summary

Family therapy involves working collaboratively with all members of the family unit. It focuses on understanding and changing the pattern of interactions and relationships that occur on an ongoing basis between all members of the family system.

In this chapter, the concepts that cut across all of family therapy were discussed. More specifically, the reciprocal influences family members have within the family system were discussed. Family boundaries and the importance of healthy boundaries were also reviewed. When healthy familial boundaries are demonstrated, members of the family can retain a unique sense of identity and independence while still leaning into each other for support. Healthy families are flexible, and family members support one another in achieving their goals. Unhealthy family boundaries may involve enmeshment, in which certain members of the system are highly dependent upon one another, or disengagement, in which family members do not turn toward each other as a resource.

The assessment process begins at the first meeting and continues throughout the family therapy relationship. Assessment may include the use of formal and informal assessments, the creation of genograms, and the exploration of family feedback loops. The therapist may join with the family in an attempt to better understand the family dynamics. Some family members might be hesitant to participate in counseling for a variety of reasons. Perhaps they fear the discomfort that may come with counseling.

Alternatively, some family members might not believe in the effectiveness of family therapy and might think their time, energy, and resources will be wasted in the counseling process. To overcome resistance to family therapy, therapists should take plenty of time to explain how family therapy works, and therapists should be open and transparent about the ultimate goal of shifting the communication and interactional patterns of the family system as a whole. Therapists can also work to overcome any resistance within the family by pulling on clients' strengths and highlighting their desire to help and support the "identified patient" (Satir, 1975).

Therapists should explain that family therapy requires hard work and dedication from all members of the family system, yet therapists should also communicate to family members a sense of hope and excitement. Therapists should take time to explain the number, length, general content, and structure of counseling sessions. At first, therapists will work to help family members gain insight into their own behaviors, needs, desires, values, and communication styles. Additionally, each member of the system will be encouraged to explore the ways in which other members of the family system affect their own experiences and interactional patterns. Finally, clients will be encouraged to explore and understand ways in which their behaviors affect other members of the family system in an ongoing, cyclical pattern. After therapists have fostered this insight, clients can be encouraged to enact quantitative changes in their behaviors, which will effectively shift the dynamic of the system.

Therapists also help family members increase their communication. The primary goals of family therapy include facilitating helpful and supportive verbal and nonverbal communication patterns between all members of the family, promoting system-wide insight, and addressing any unhealthy boundaries within the family system. Family therapists are generally directive, and they actively strive to form a therapeutic relationship with each member of the family. Table 14.4 provides an overview of each of the leading family therapies.

TABLE 14.4 Overview of Prominent Family Therapy Approaches

	Multigenerational Theory (Bowen)	**Experiential Humanistic Approaches (Satir, Whitaker)**	**Emotionally Focused Couple Therapy (Johnson)**
Basic philosophies	All behaviors are influenced by past experiences. To facilitate change, emotional reactivity and anxiety in relationships need to be reduced. The key to helping family members change is helping them to manage emotional reactions within the system and to change family patterns.	Family members must identify their suppressed feelings and needs, communicate these, and have them validated so that they can move toward growth within the family. When everyone's needs are expressed and met, the family can be fully functioning.	When couples express and reprocess their emotions with each other, they experience empathy and change is likely to occur. Emotion being accessed and unpacked in the therapy session leads to a stronger connection with the couple.
Key concepts	The differentiation of self from others, as well as the ability to separate thoughts from emotional reactions, is key. Too much togetherness can lead to fusion; differentiation is ideal. Intergenerational transmission of interaction patterns is important, and these patterns must be recognized and changed.	This theory encourages personal growth, choice, and self-awareness. Symptoms arise when the needs relating to self-esteem of the individual family members are not mutually met. Individual family members must overcome their personal blockages and move toward growth.	Systemic, humanistic-experiential, attachment, and emotion are the main key concepts. The main issue in relational conflict is the security of the emotional bond between partners. Emotion underlies all attachment behavior and is the prime mover behind interpersonal change.
Goals of counseling	Differentiation of the self is assessed with the goal of increasing each family member's differentiation from others. Decrease emotional reactivity rooted in a lack of differentiation that is unhealthy. End generation-to-generation transmission of problems by resolving emotional entanglement.	Facilitate a sense of togetherness yet a healthy separation from others in the family. Genuineness within the family; healthier individual self-esteem; a sense of well-being among family members; decreased negativity in interactions; a movement toward personal growth.	The goal of EFT is to reprocess through emotions in order to experience feelings naturally, act in healthy ways, and create a deeper connection between partners.

(Continued)

TABLE 14.4 (*Continued*)

	Multigenerational Theory (Bowen)	**Experiential Humanistic Approaches (Satir, Whitaker)**	**Emotionally Focused Couple Therapy (Johnson)**
Therapeutic relationship	The therapist is an educator and coach. The therapist pays attention to the family patterns of emotion and relationship dynamics and points these out. Though objective, this approach emphasizes a strong therapeutic relationship.	The therapist is an active facilitator who encourages sharing and honesty, and creates a space where family members can dig deep, realize, and express their feelings, thoughts, and needs.	The therapist provides a safe, warm environment in which emotions, both positive and negative, can be explored. The therapist must establish and maintain a positive therapeutic alliance with both partners. The therapist takes on a collaborative role, is respectful of each person, and focuses on the moment-by-moment processes.
Counseling techniques/ interventions	Learning new skills and communication patterns within the family. Genograms, role playing, and assessing patterns in the family of origin are important techniques. Questions that emphasize personal choice in how one feels, thinks, and responds are also important.	Confrontation that promotes individual family members' self-discovery and awareness; any techniques that uncover hidden struggles or conflicts, such as role plays, family sculpting, or reconstruction of events.	EFT therapists use empathy and reflection to track emotions and use those emotions to produce alternative feelings in the partner through enactments during the session. Other techniques include asking evocative questions, reframing patterns in terms of attachment and negative cycles, tracking and replaying key moments, creating enactments in which the couple make their patterns explicit, slowly encouraging new ways of connecting, and validating and normalizing responses.
Multicultural counseling	Family tradition and beliefs are central to this theory. Family of origin patterns, which are deeply related to culture, are assessed and addressed. Theory has a strong emphasis on individuation, and this idea of independence can conflict with the idea of interdependence that is central to many cultures. However, in collectivist cultures, this theory may not be as applicable.	Individuals in the context of their family are emphasized, and this focus on individual needs, self-awareness, and self-esteem may not be consistent with all cultures' values.	EFT appeals to people from a variety of cultures and backgrounds because it focuses on issues that are universal—attachment and connection—and uses interventions that are respectful and collaborative. However, EFT may not be appropriate to use with people from cultures that value restraint of emotions.

TABLE 14.4 (*Continued*)

	Multigenerational Theory (Bowen)	**Experiential Humanistic Approaches (Satir, Whitaker)**	**Emotionally Focused Couple Therapy (Johnson)**
Limitations	Bowenian therapy can be lengthy, time consuming, and costly, and may not be practical. It shows a cultural gender bias by valuing reason and rationality—a commonly accepted male trait—over emotion, a traditionally female trait. Mothers are frequently viewed as overly involved, while fathers are often absent. Families in crisis may have more immediate needs that must be attended to before delving into past patterns of behavior.	Whitaker's style was very personal; it did not lend itself to structured trainings or research, so little empirical research exists on the effectiveness of his methods.	EFT is not appropriate for working with couples who have different agendas, such as a separating couple or a couple in which one person seeks to maintain an affair, or in clearly abusive relationships. EFT may also be uncomfortable for clients who tend to suppress or hide their emotions.
Strengths and contributions	The assessment process and multigenerational view allows for an in-depth information-gathering process to facilitate change. The theory is also culturally inclusive due to its focus on family of origin patterns, which are deeply related to culture. This theory may also be particularly helpful for cultures who place an emphasis on interdependence.	Satir's insistence on open and direct communication, the recognition of the importance of language, and the belief in family resilience were vital contributions in the early years of family therapy's development and have been instrumental in the creation of dynamic, nonlinear systems of therapy.	EFT is both theoretically sound and shown to be effective for a wide variety of presenting concerns and relationship issues. Its focus on love and connection makes it appealing to many people. It provides a structured, experiential, attachment-intervention model for helping couples communicate on a deeper level. This is the first relational theory of adult love to be synchronistic with other research on the nature of emotion and attachment and to provide a road map for therapists. EFT is also consistent with new developments in the field of neuroscience that relate to health and emotion, stress, and bonding.

Recommended Readings

Contemporary Family Therapy Journal. (2002). Special Issue on Virginia Satir, *24*.

Goldenberg, I., Goldenberg, H., & Stanton, M. (2017). *Family therapy: An overview* (9th ed.). Boston, MA: Cengage Learning.

Johnson, S. M. (2004). *The practice of emotionally focused couple therapy: Creating connection.* New York, NY: Brunner-Routledge.

Journal of Individual Psychology. (2007, Fall). Special Issue on Couples Therapy, Relationship Education, and Individual Psychology, *63*(3).

McGoldrick, M., Gerson, R., & Petry, S. (2008). *Genograms: Assessment and intervention* (3rd ed.). New York, NY: W. W. Norton.

Walsh, F. (Ed.). (2012). *Normal family processes: Growing diversity and complexity* (4th ed.). New York, NY: Guilford.

MyLab Counseling

Try the Topic 5 Assignments: Family Therapy.

CHAPTER 15

Developing Your Theoretical Orientation

Learning Outcomes

When you have finished this chapter, you should be able to:
- Identify your preferred theoretical orientation.
- Identify the benefits and challenges associated with eclectic and integrated therapies.
- Describe the nature and characteristics associated with eclectic and integrated therapies.
- Describe the various types of theoretical eclecticism.
- Identify examples of integrative therapies and give descriptions of each.
- Identify the factors that should be considered in selecting and developing a theoretical orientation.
- Identify the current trends that are likely to impact the future of counseling and psychotherapy.
- Compare and contrast the counseling theories discussed in this text.

Finally! You have reached the concluding chapter in this book and probably the end of your course. Your mind is swimming with all things theories. While you may be eager to apply what you have learned, you may also feel overwhelmed by all this information; that is a normal reaction. This chapter will discuss how you might proceed in developing your approach to counseling.

Because most practitioners identify as integrative/eclectic (Prochaska & Norcross, 2018), this chapter will begin with a discussion of theory integration, along with several examples of integrative therapies so that you might develop an understanding of what such theories can look like. Also provided is a brief review of common factors found in counseling theories. Next, the chapter focuses on the factors you should consider in selecting and developing your theoretical orientation. An overview of all the theories discussed in this text will also be presented in an organized, table format. Anticipating changes in the field can help you meet your professional goals, provide effective counseling, and contribute to your profession. As such, a section on future directions in counseling and psychotherapy brings this chapter and this book to a close.

INTEGRATIVE THERAPIES

Many mental health professionals prefer an integrated or eclectic approach to counseling. In fact, nearly 34% of counseling psychologists, 26% of social workers, and 23% of counselors describe their *primary* theoretical orientation as eclectic or integrative, with most others indicating they pull on at least several approaches (Prochaska & Norcross, 2018). These percentages have increased over the years, and the integration trend seems likely to continue. Even therapists who adhere to one theoretical orientation commonly incorporate interventions from other counseling approaches. However, it should be stressed that before therapists can integrate approaches, they must first be grounded in and able to apply at least one theory.

Most therapists would probably benefit from having a framework or theory to guide them in organizing and applying a diverse array of counseling strategies, so that they can successfully address a broad range of clients and concerns. Not only is this desirable from a therapeutic point of view, but also a systematic approach to eclecticism may facilitate therapists' efforts to demonstrate accountability to third parties.

Knowledge of an array of theoretical approaches is necessary so that therapists can determine which approach is best for each of their clients; this also affords therapists a range of useful interventions. Most therapists draw on a variety of theories and interventions in developing a counseling plan that seems likely to help a given person.

The Growth of Eclectic and Integrated Approaches

Many factors account for the trend toward integrative and eclectic approaches to counseling. Most importantly is the fact that no single theory has yet been found that can clearly capture the entire range of human experiences across the lifespan. In light of the diversity of people seeking counseling—who vary according to many dimensions, including culture, ethnicity, gender, sexual orientation, intelligence, abilities, interpersonal skills, life experiences, self-awareness, support systems, and symptoms—strictly adhering to one specific model of counseling or psychotherapy may greatly reduce therapeutic options. At the same time, evidence increasingly indicates that matching clients who have a preferred counseling approach or type of therapist with that preference reduces the dropout rate and is more likely to result in improvements in therapeutic outcomes (Swift, Callahan, & Vollmer, 2011).

As therapists' years of experience increase, they are less likely to strictly follow just one theoretical approach (Miller, Duncan, & Hubble, 2002). Perhaps this happens because finding and combining the best research-based practices that match specific client needs has been shown to require therapeutic expertise (APA Presidential Task Force on Evidence-Based Practice, 2006).

In addition, no one theoretical model has proven itself superior to the rest despite efforts to identify such a theory. According to Hansen (2002), " . . . meta-analysis of counseling outcome studies clearly shows that no one approach has emerged as the correct or most helpful . . . it seems that all well-established approaches promote healing" (p. 315).

At the same time, research has demonstrated that some approaches are more effective than others with particular client problems, when addressing different mental illnesses with which clients struggle, and when working with different types of people. For example, cognitive therapy and interpersonal psychotherapy are especially powerful when working with those who have major depressive disorder (Nathan & Gorman, 2002), whereas reality therapy has been widely used when working with youth who have conduct disorder. In addition, research suggests that counseling is an essential ingredient when counseling those who struggle with various mental disorders, and medication alone is not enough (Kress & Paylo, 2019).

The following factors have combined during the past 30 years to move therapists in the direction of preferring integrative and eclectic approaches over adherence to one specific theory (Prochaska & Norcross, 2018):

1. The large and growing number of approaches to counseling, with more than 500 counseling theories having been identified
2. The increasing diversity and complexity of clients and their concerns
3. The inability of any one approach to successfully address all clients' needs and all problems

4. The growing importance of solution-focused brief approaches that encourage therapists to draw on and combine interventions from various systems of therapy to find the most effective and efficient strategy for each situation
5. The availability of training opportunities, as well as case studies and other informative literature, that give therapists the opportunity to study, observe, and gain experience in a wide variety of approaches
6. The requirement of most state and national credentialing bodies that therapists obtain postgraduate continuing education units, which encourages continued professional growth and development of new skills and ideas
7. Increasing pressure from managed care organizations, governmental agencies, consumers, and others for therapists to determine the most effective and efficient approach for each client, to plan and document their work, and to maintain accountability
8. The growing body of compelling research demonstrating which approaches are most likely to be successful in helping particular people, those with certain disorders or problems (Kress & Paylo, 2019)
9. The increasing availability of manuals, providing detailed and empirically validated treatment plans for use in helping people who have specific mental disorders or presenting problems (e.g., anger management difficulties).
10. The development of organizations such as the Society for the Exploration of Psychotherapy Integration that focus on studying and promoting theoretical integration
11. The emergence of models providing blueprints or guidelines for logical and therapeutically sound integration of approaches
12. Therapists' increasing awareness that common factors among counseling approaches, such as the nature of the therapeutic alliance, are at least as important in determining counseling success as are specific strategies.

This array of factors nudges many therapists toward an eclectic or integrative model as their preferred orientation toward counseling.

The Challenges of Eclectic and Integrated Approaches

Choosing to adopt an eclectic or integrated theoretical orientation is challenging and probably demands more of therapists than does adherence to one specific theory. If therapists decide, for example, to specialize in cognitive therapy, they should develop expertise in that approach and know when it is and is not likely to be helpful so that they can refer out those clients unlikely to benefit from cognitive therapy. Because they have limited the scope of their work, these therapists do not have to develop expertise in other approaches, although they should be familiar with them.

However, therapists who view their primary theoretical orientation as eclectic or integrated need expertise in a range of counseling approaches so they can draw on them in creating effective counseling experiences. Of course, therapists who have an eclectic or integrated orientation also set limits on the scope of their practice; no therapist could have sufficient knowledge and expertise in the entire range of therapeutic approaches required to address all clients and all problems. Therapists should define the scope of their practice according to the nature of their clientele, the client problems they address, and the strategies they employ. Nevertheless, therapists who prefer eclectic or integrated approaches still have a more comprehensive and challenging professional role than that of therapists with a specific theoretical orientation.

In addition, therapists advocating for an eclectic or integrated approach must carefully consider their approach to working with each client to ensure that the disparate parts of counseling constitute a seamless whole in which each intervention is chosen deliberately to accomplish a purpose.

Counseling must not just be an amalgam of "tricks of the trade" but, rather, should reflect coherence, relevance, and planning and be solidly grounded in both theory and empirical research. "The danger of creating a 'hodge-podge' of apples and oranges can be avoided if the theories are compatible, carefully integrated, and if they reflect the basic characteristics of mental health counseling" (Schwartz & Waldo, 2003; pp. 101–102).

The Benefits of Eclectic and Integrated Approaches

Integrated and eclectic theoretical approaches have benefits as well as challenges. They bring flexibility to the counseling process, enabling therapists to tailor their work to specific clients and concerns in an effort to find a good fit between the counseling approach and clients.

This is especially important when therapists work with people from diverse cultural backgrounds who may respond better to modified or integrated approaches than to standardized ones. For example, some people from Asian backgrounds may respond best to approaches that are structured in nature but that also recognize the importance of the family and society. Therapists can demonstrate multicultural competence by creating an integrated approach to counseling that reflect sensitivity to clients' culture and context.

Because they have greater flexibility in their work, therapists espousing an integrated or eclectic approach probably can work with a broader range of people and problems than those who affiliate themselves with a single counseling theory. Of course, all therapists must practice within their areas of expertise or obtain supervision or training to expand their skills.

In addition, integrated and eclectic approaches allow therapists to adapt standard counseling approaches to their own beliefs about human growth and development as well as to their natural style and personality.

Finally, integrated and eclectic approaches facilitate therapists' efforts to assume a scientist-practitioner role and to combine theoretical information, empirical research, and practical experience. Basing their work on counseling approaches that have demonstrated their value through research, therapists can expand on that foundation by incorporating into their work ideas that have face validity as well as strategies they have used successfully with other clients.

The Nature of Eclectic and Integrated Approaches

When therapists first began to describe their theoretical orientations as *eclectic*, the term lacked a clear meaning; it simply suggested that therapists drew on more than one approach to counseling. Although some therapists who characterized their work as eclectic were gifted therapists and astute theoreticians with a clear rationale for combining interventions in their work, others lacked a thoughtful and systematic approach to therapy. Eysenck (1970) denounced what he referred to as "lazy eclecticism" (p. 140), the use of a grab bag of interventions combined without an overriding logic. Without a logic or structure, eclecticism can lead to counseling that is haphazard and inconsistent, lacking in direction and coherence. Such an approach reflects a lack of knowledge and professionalism and is incompatible with current emphases on accountability in counseling and psychotherapy.

Examples of Eclectic and Integrated Approaches

Different strategies can be used to practice from an integrated or eclectic perspective. Four types of eclecticism are commonly identified:

1. **Atheoretical eclecticism** is characterized by combining interventions without an overriding theory of change or development. Unless an intuitive or underlying logic prevails, therapists

whose work reflects atheoretical eclecticism run the risk of syncretism—providing counseling that is without direction, including elements that are disparate and perhaps incompatible. Such an approach probably will be confusing to clients, may lead them to question the therapist's competence (as well as their own), can interfere with client cooperation and motivation, and may well lead to counseling failure.

2. **Common factors eclecticism** hypothesizes that certain elements of counseling, notably a therapeutic alliance that communicates support, empathy, and unconditional positive regard, are primarily responsible for promoting client growth and change (Norcross & Wampold, 2011). Specific interventions are linked to these common factors rather than to a specific theory. In Chapter 1 you learned about commonalities in successful counseling.

3. **Technical eclecticism** provides a framework for combining interventions from different approaches without necessarily subscribing to the theories or philosophies associated with those interventions. In general, therapists who practice technical eclecticism seek out the most effective techniques available for their clients' specific problems. Technical eclecticism can be thought of as an organized collection of interventions, rather than an integration of ideas. The selection of interventions should have an empirical basis, reflecting research on the effectiveness of various interventions in successfully addressing clients' concerns. However, technical eclecticism lacks a coherent model for human development and growth. Lazarus' multimodal therapy exemplifies this type of eclecticism.

4. **Theoretical integration** offers conceptual guidelines for combining two or more counseling approaches to provide a clearer understanding of clients and more effective ways to help them. A theoretical integration usually provides therapists with a framework for understanding how people grow and change and guidelines for developing counseling plans that reflect that understanding. Integrated counseling approaches often include a multistage, systematic approach to therapy as well as information on assessing client strengths and difficulties and matching theories to clients. Therapists have guidelines to help them answer the seminal question "*What* treatment, by *whom*, is the most effective for *this* individual with *that* specific problem, and under what set of circumstances?" (Paul, 1967, p. 109). In a true theoretical integration, the whole is greater than the sum of its parts. The combination of approaches blends well and forms a new theory or approach that builds on and improves each of the individual approaches to form a better product. Counseling is theory focused rather than technique driven.

Characteristics of Sound Eclectic and Integrated Approaches

Certain hallmarks distinguish conceptually sound integrated and eclectic approaches from eclecticism that is haphazard and ill conceived. Sound eclecticism has the following characteristics:

- Evidence of building on the strengths of existing theories
- A coherent combination of theories that creates a unified whole
- An underlying theory of human behavior and development
- A philosophy or theory of change
- Logic, guidelines, and procedures for adapting the approach to a particular person or problem
- Strategies and interventions, related to the underlying theories, that facilitate change
- Inclusion of the commonalities of effective counseling, such as support, positive regard, empathy, and client–therapist collaboration.

Formulating an Integrative Theory

When therapists formulate an integrative counseling theory, they must address many questions, including the following:

1. What model of human development underlies the theory?
2. How does this theory suggest that change is best facilitated?
3. What information should be obtained in an intake interview?
4. What conception does this approach have of the influence of the past on the present, and how should past experiences and difficulties be addressed in counseling?
5. How important is insight in promoting change, and how much attention should be paid in counseling to improving insight?
6. How important is exploration of emotions in promoting change, and how much attention should be paid to helping people identify, express, and modify their emotions?
7. How important is identification and modification of dysfunctional cognitions in promoting change, and how much attention should be paid in counseling to helping people alter their cognitions?
8. How important is identification and modification of self-destructive and unhelpful behaviors in promoting change, and how much attention should be paid in counseling to helping people alter their behaviors?
9. What sorts of people and problems are likely to respond well to this approach?
10. In what counseling settings and contexts is this approach likely to succeed?
11. How well does this approach address issues of diversity, and what is the appropriate use of this approach with people from multicultural backgrounds?
12. What is the place of diagnosis and treatment planning in this approach?
13. What are the overall goals of counseling?
14. What types of therapeutic alliances and client–therapist interactions are most likely to be productive?
15. What counseling skills are especially important for those who adopt this approach?
16. What interventions and strategies are compatible with this theory?
17. How should this approach be adapted for use with individuals? Families? Groups?
18. How long is counseling likely to last?
19. How is effectiveness measured, and what determines when counseling is finished?
20. Has this theory been adequately substantiated by empirical research? If not, what information is needed to support the value of this approach?

The therapist can overcome some of the shortcomings of eclectic and integrated approaches by adopting a sound and systematic rationale for how counseling is focused. Procedures should not be selected haphazardly; instead, their selection should depend on a logical decisional process that takes into account the client, the setting, the problem, and the nature of the therapist's skills (Lazarus & Beutler, 1993).

Examples of Integrative Theories

Although most therapists do not adhere to a systematic approach to theoretical integration, they probably have formulated their own logic for combining compatible theories. The most common combinations of theories, in descending order of frequency, include (1) cognitive and behavioral approaches, (2) humanistic and cognitive approaches, and (3) psychoanalytic and cognitive approaches (Prochaska & Norcross, 2018). The presence of cognitive therapy in all three combinations is noteworthy, suggesting the flexibility of that approach and its importance in counseling. A brief overview of three integrative therapies will be provided in this section.

CYCLICAL PSYCHODYNAMIC THERAPY The first person to truly integrate two separate theoretical orientations was Paul Wachtel (1977), who combined psychodynamic therapy with behavior therapy to create **cyclical psychodynamic–behavior therapy**. As its name implies, this approach integrates the insight achieved through psychodynamic therapy with applied behavioral interventions, with the goal of providing a more powerful intervention than with either modality alone.

Wachtel's groundbreaking work is considered an example of technical eclecticism (Sharf, 2016). It broadened the field by providing a primary and secondary approach to therapy while also emphasizing the need to adapt counseling to the client's worldview, to consider both social and psychological dimensions, and to empower the client (Wachtel, 2008; Wachtel, Kruk, & McKinney, 2005).

Wachtel's theory has been called "the most comprehensive and influential integrative theory of personality" (Stricker & Gold, 2011, p. 343). Wachtel and others found much support for the theory of a cyclical nature of personality dynamics. The term "vicious cycles" comes to mind, in which people continue to repeat patterns of behavior, or even make reality consistent with their expectations of what will happen. Research has shown that people induce in others the behavior they expect from them (Gilbert & Jones, 1986). Such self-fulfilling prophesies, also known as fundamental attribution errors or expectancy biases, can keep people stuck in a continuing pattern despite their greatest efforts to overcome that pattern.

Wachtel suggests that early experiences trigger cycles or patterns of behavior that are maintained by present attitudes or inclinations. He believes that an integration of psychodynamic and behavioral approaches provides a dynamic approach in which insight leads to behavioral change and behavioral change leads to insight into a cyclical pattern.

The opposite is also true. For example, individuals who lean toward depression may actually elicit and contribute to relationships that maintain that negativity. Even while protesting that they want to change, these individuals may actually surround themselves with people who reinforce negative behaviors and increase the sense of victimization. A similar dynamic occurs when individuals solicit an opinion from a friend or colleague—they are seeking out the person who will give them the answer they want to hear. Alternatively, they avoid people who do not act in accordance with their needs (Wachtel, 1997). Cyclical psychodynamic–behavior therapy emphasizes the contextual nature of psychological processes and circular causation—how people mutually shape each other's experience (Stricker & Gold, 2011).

When assessing clients, therapists who use cyclical psychodynamic–behavior therapy look at areas such as conflict, character, resistance, and object representations. After initial assessments, ongoing evaluations and adjustments occur throughout the counseling process to integrate behavioral or psychodynamic interventions, as the need arises.

For example, Mark, a 35-year old government employee, came for therapy because he had an affair. He noted in the first session that he did not know why he did it, but recalled "doing stupid things" when he was a teenager and thinks that might somehow be related to his current behavior. During the session he reveals that sometimes he also participates in self-defeating behaviors (smokes pot, drinks alcohol), but he doesn't know why he does this either. He recognizes the potential risks involved (job loss, relationship loss, arrest) but also is feeling "stuck" in his job and he has a sense of insecurity that he is not good enough for promotion.

Using Wachtel's cyclical dynamics and an interpersonal perspective, the therapist first focused on Mark's externalization of his feelings, to help him become aware of, and recognize, the anger and resentment that he suppressed and then tried to avoid by reaching for drugs, alcohol, or sex. Encouraging both insight and action gradually exposes people to their frightening images and fantasies so that they can learn to cope with them more effectively. Mark was able to identify a pattern of behavior that had been with him since childhood, of not wanting to recognize or express difficult feelings that made him uncomfortable. Over the years, Mark had externalized his feelings, and would turn to drugs or sex to make himself feel better and reaffirm his self-worth. He recognized the cyclical nature of the pattern, and the fact that it was self-defeating, but he felt helpless to do anything about it. Consider the following excerpt from a therapy session with Mark:

THERAPIST: So, you said a woman approached you in a bar, made overtures, and you went home with her, but you don't know why.

MARK: Yes, exactly. She came on to me. She was beautiful.

THERAPIST: How did you feel about that?

MARK: I feel stupid now. I told my girlfriend about it and she wants to break up with me.

THERAPIST: But what did you feel back in the bar, when this was happening?

MARK: I guess I thought here's this great opportunity that doesn't come around very often.

THERAPIST: Mmmm. How do you feel right now, talking to me about this?

MARK: What do you mean?

THERAPIST: What do you feel here, telling me this? What are your feelings?

MARK: I don't know. It was difficult to come here today.

THERAPIST: Okay, so you don't know how you are feeling . . . you are struggling to identify your feelings.

MARK: Right.

THERAPIST: What would you like to do about that?

MARK: About what?

THERAPIST: About struggling to recognize your feelings.

MARK: Ummm. That's why I'm here. I don't seem to know what I'm feeling or even that I'm feeling something, I just want to go off and do something else, and . . .

THERAPIST: And avoid the uncomfortable feelings?

MARK: Exactly. I just want to put the feelings out of my mind and go have fun. Why do I do that?

THERAPIST: Mark, I'd like to help you, and part of that is getting to know you better, staying connected and being honest, and exploring in the session how this feels—how this interaction between us feels to you as you try to explore your feelings more deeply.

MARK: Does it matter?

THERAPIST: It matters a great deal. If you are willing to do that, to be more open with me and to try to express what you're going through as feelings come up, I will understand you better, and feel more connected to you.

MARK: But it's hard for me. I get frustrated when I can't put it in words.

THERAPIST: Let's see if we can slow it down a bit. I wonder if this is similar to what happens in your relationships. You feel something, and those feelings quickly

	become overwhelming and all jumbled together, and then you become frustrated or angry and start to feel overwhelmed and . . .
MARK:	Exactly! And then I just want to DO something to make those feelings go away. Can you help me?
THERAPIST:	I think you've taken a good first step. You said that you have problems recognizing feelings, and why you act on them. I'm here to help you figure that out. I think if you can slow down, try to explain what you feel in the moment, and when you get overwhelmed or frustrated just sit with those feelings for a moment. There's no need to escape or act on the feelings. You can also start trying to do this with other relationships in your life. With your girlfriend. You can try to feel what you feel, and ask her to help out. That's how we connect with each other, right? Do you think you can try that this week?
MARK:	This isn't something I usually do so it will be weird, but I'll try.

In a departure from the traditional stance of psychoanalytic therapy, the therapist is active and affirming, working from a relational psychodynamic perspective. The therapist helped Mark to identify that his feelings become overwhelming and he acts out to escape from the discomfort. By providing an opportunity in the session for Mark to try to express his feelings, the therapist is helping Mark to recognize the pattern of disengagement that seems to be causing him problems in relationships, and to substitute another, more effective behavior of attempting to express himself to others. Practicing this new type of behavior will raise more feelings, and at times Mark may feel overwhelmed and be tempted to disengage. Prior to this session the therapist had helped Mark to identify alternative, healthy behaviors he enjoys, such as exercise, playing music, and reading, which he can substitute for the self-defeating behaviors (substance use, sex) when he starts to feel overwhelmed.

As we can see from this short vignette, the cyclical psychodynamic–behavior therapist is supportive and directive and provides a safe environment within the session for Mark to explore his feelings and attempt to change his interactional patterns. With continued practice, Mark's goal will be to recognize his feelings and share them in the moment, reduce his anxiety, and eliminate the behaviors that continue to cause problems in his life.

Integrative therapies that are client centered or interpersonal tend to focus on empathy, unconditional positive regard, and re-creating the client's problems in the therapy session with the therapist. The relationship becomes the "vehicle of change" (Stricker & Gold, 2011, p. 442). Most cognitive behavioral therapy (CBT)–focused integrative therapies do not dismiss the importance of the therapeutic alliance but view the alliance as only one of many factors in the change process.

Wachtel's cyclical psychodynamic therapy is just one of many forms of integrative therapy that provide a dynamic source of behavioral change. Now, we turn to a discussion of multimodal therapy.

MULTIMODAL THERAPY **Multimodal therapy** is one of the best known of the technical eclectic approaches (Harwood, Beutler, & Charvat, 2010). Multimodal therapy was developed by Arnold Lazarus, a pioneer in technical eclecticism. Lazarus was trained in behavior therapy, although he soon recognized the limitations of that approach and began to incorporate cognitive and other strategies into his work. Suggesting that therapists take a broad view of people and ways to help, Lazarus advocates technical eclecticism, which draws on many theories and strategies to match an approach to a client and problem.

Multimodal therapy is firmly grounded in behavior therapy, emphasizes outcomes, and draws from social learning and cognitive theories, while pulling on interventions from a number of theories. In addition, multimodal therapy has a humanistic component and values the uniqueness and self-determination of each individual. This approach also pays attention to context, looking at the individual as well as the individual's culture, society, politics, and environment (Lazarus, 1996).

Multimodal therapists look at the client holistically; consequently, counseling needs to be flexible and versatile, drawing on a variety of approaches. For Lazarus, technical eclecticism, in which therapists select procedures from different modalities based on what works best for the client's needs, but without necessarily subscribing to the overall theories, is the ideal way to plan such an approach (Lazarus, 1989). The ability to address client concerns from multiple vantage points simultaneously gives multimodal therapists considerable power and leverage, and results in more effective outcomes.

Counseling that reflects technical eclecticism, as described by Lazarus, has the following characteristics. It is:

1. Grounded in a theory of the therapist's choice
2. Enhanced by interventions associated with compatible approaches to counseling
3. Focused on interventions that have had their value substantiated by research.

Selection of specific counseling strategies is guided by a systematic framework for matching intervention to client, problem, and situation (Lazarus, 2006).

In multimodal therapy, a careful assessment of clients and their concerns is an essential precursor to planning counseling. One of Lazarus' most important contributions to the growing movement toward integrative counseling was the development of an assessment model that delineates seven basic categories of client functioning, represented by the acronym BASIC I.D.:

1. *Behavior:* observable actions, responses, and habits
2. *Affect:* moods and emotions
3. *Sensations:* physical concerns, sensory experiences (touch, taste, smell, sight, hearing)
4. *Images:* fantasies, dreams, memories, mental pictures, and people's views of themselves, their lives, and their futures
5. *Cognitions:* thoughts, beliefs, philosophies, values, plans, opinions, insights, self-talk
6. *Interpersonal relations:* friendships and intimate relationships, interactions with others
7. *Drugs, biology:* broadly defined as biological functioning, including overall health, nutrition, exercise, self-care.

Therapy via multimodal therapy typically begins with a comprehensive assessment of these seven areas, using questions and scales to identify both strengths and problem areas. This helps therapists identify interventions that might be helpful in the specific area of concern. For example, let's create a BASIC I.D. for Edie. Imagine that Edie came in for the first session. Our initial goal is to assess her functioning in each area of the BASIC I.D. During the intake interview, we elicit information from Edie about her history, her family life, and her relationships with Roberto and with her daughter Ava. Based on Edie's responses, we develop the following chart:

B: *Behavior:*		Edie is arguing with Roberto more than usual. She is having trouble sleeping, and her relationship with her daughter is tense.
A: *Affect:*		She feels taken for granted and angry.

S: *Sensations:* She is starting to get headaches.

I: *Images:* Edie imagines that all of the stress she is under is causing her cancer to come back. She visualizes the cancer cells growing inside her.

C: *Cognitions:* Normally very compassionate with herself, she has started to criticize herself and engage in negative self-talk that she is a poor wife and mother.

I: *Interpersonal relations:* Edie has distanced herself from her friends and from her mother.

D: *Drugs:* Edie denies any problems with substance abuse.

Now that we have elicited this information from Edie, the question becomes one of where to begin and how to use the information to create an effective approach to counseling that takes the client's needs into account. Lazarus (2006) found that each person favors some BASIC I.D. modalities over others. For example, a person might be characterized as a sensory reactor, an affective reactor, or an imagery reactor, depending on which modality is preferred.

The *Structural Profile Inventory* helps identify a person's preferred modalities. This form asks people to indicate on a scale of 1 to 7 how important each of the seven areas of functioning is in their lives. Listing the seven areas in descending order of a person's ratings yields a structural profile for that person. Constructing a diagram or bar graph of the relative strengths of a person's seven areas of functioning is useful in clarifying patterns (Lazarus, 1976).

As an example, we asked Edie to rank order the list of seven modalities. Following are her results:

- Interpersonal relations: 7
- Affect: 6
- Cognitions: 5
- Behavior: 4
- Sensations: 3
- Images: 2
- Drugs, biology: 1.

Completing this profile helped Edie realize that she sometimes lets her strong emotions and need for approval and closeness cloud her judgment so that her feelings control her decisions. Changes she saw as desirable included moderating these two areas and improving her self-care and health habits.

Another way to use the BASIC I.D. is to look at a person's modality firing order. Lazarus suggests that each person has a characteristic sequence of reactions to stressors and that this sequence usually mirrors that person's structural profile. For example, when Edie was under stress, she usually first felt rejected and unloved (interpersonal relations), while becoming angry and scared (affect). Then she began a dialogue with herself, focused on how unlovable she felt and how many mistakes she had made in her relationships. This often caused her difficulty because she would erroneously accuse others of not caring about her, would overreact with anger and fear, and would then blame herself for the conflict. None of these reactions afforded her a way to discuss and dispel conflict with others. Consciously making some changes—in particular, moderating her emotions, considering new cognitions, and developing behaviors that promoted dialogue and resolution—helped Edie handle stress more effectively.

An individual seems to respond best to interventions that target preferred modalities. For example, a person who emphasizes imagery is likely to benefit from visualization, whereas a person who focuses on thinking and analyzing probably will respond well to interventions that help identify and modify cognitive distortions. The resulting chart can then be discussed with the client, along with recommended counseling approaches that have shown effectiveness for the client's specific problems.

THE TRANSTHEORETICAL MODEL OF CHANGE The **transtheoretical model of change**, developed by Prochaska and others (Prochaska & DiClemente, 1986; Prochaska & Norcross, 2018), provides a theory of behavior change that incorporates elements from many different theoretical perspectives (hence the name, *transtheoretical*). Inherent in the theory is recognition of the uniqueness and diversity of other models, as well as their commonalities. Also known as the stages-of-change model, the transtheoretical model reflects the scientist-practitioner approach to developing theories and is based on both empirical research and practice.

The transtheoretical model can be applied to mental health and behavioral health problems and has been used successfully to reduce smoking, stress, violence, and bullying behaviors. It is a stage model that links interventions (*processes of change*) and the target of change efforts (*levels of change*) to the person's *stage of change*. Assessment and matching are essential ingredients in this approach, as they are in many eclectic and integrated theories.

The transtheoretical model provides an organized and methodical approach to planning and integrating counseling strategies based on the following:

- **Five stages of change:** Clients go through predictable stages as they engage in counseling, and that theory must be matched to clients' level of readiness for change. Although progression through these phases may be direct and linear, it is more likely to reflect a spiral, with relapses and other factors causing people to cycle back through previous phases in the change process. The five stages include (Petrocelli, 2002):

    1. **Precontemplation:** People in this stage see no need to change. They may be involuntary clients, seeking help because of a court order or family pressure.
    2. **Contemplation:** People in this stage recognize that they have difficulties but have not made a commitment to take action needed for change.
    3. **Preparation:** At this stage, people have decided to change and have even taken some small steps toward change.
    4. **Action:** Now people are motivated and committed to making changes. They exert effort over time to accomplish those changes.
    5. **Maintenance:** People act in ways that are likely to maintain and continue their positive changes and avoid relapse.

- **Ten processes of change:** Determining a person's stage of change is used to identify strategies and interventions likely to be successful and to help that person progress to the next stage of change. The developers of the model identified 10 change processes that demonstrated their value in both research and practice: consciousness raising, catharsis/dramatic relief, self-reevaluation, environmental reevaluation, self-liberation, social liberation, counterconditioning, stimulus control, contingency management, and helping relationships (Prochaska & Norcross, 2018). Strategies that promote awareness, such as consciousness raising and evaluation of self and environment, are particularly helpful and well received during the early precontemplation and contemplation stages, whereas action-oriented interventions, such as contingency management and conditioning, are more useful in the later action and maintenance stages.

- **Five levels of change:** The transtheoretical model considers a hierarchical organization of five levels of psychological problems that are likely to be addressed in psychotherapy (Prochaska & Norcross, 2018). The five levels include:

  1. Symptom/situational problems
  2. Maladaptive cognitions
  3. Current interpersonal conflicts
  4. Family/systems conflicts
  5. Intrapersonal conflicts.

The transtheoretical model recognizes the importance of the therapeutic alliance, which is viewed as the most robust common factor in therapy. They also see the value of a healing setting and a confiding relationship. The therapist is viewed as an expert on change who has the task of tailoring the therapeutic relationship, as well as tailoring counseling, to each client's stage of change.

The transtheoretical model shows considerable promise. It provides a conceptual scheme to explain how people change and how to facilitate that change. It generalizes to a broad range of problems, it encourages innovation, and advocates both empirical research and experience to determine the value of this approach. Overall, 25 years of controlled research on the transtheoretical model indicate that the model is an evidence-based self-help approach for addressing addictions and habits that need to be changed and shows promise as a psychotherapy for depression and other disorders, but more research is needed (Prochaska & Norcross, 2018). Even so, behavioral health programs that have tailored interventions to match the client's stage of change and the processes of change have shown greater efficacy. Specific programs have increased abstinence rates for smokers, improved stress management in an at-risk population, and reduced bullying and violence among high school and middle school students at 25 selected schools in the United States (Prochaska & Norcross, 2018). These aforementioned programs and the transtheoretical model program for stress reduction, have both achieved evidence-based status from the Substance Abuse and Mental Health Services Administration. Additional controlled research trials are on-going.

Opposition, rejection of therapists' suggestions, and not following through on counseling interventions are all typical of highly resistant clients. When clients are more resistant, therapists might consider less directive counseling approaches, at least until trust is established. Conversely, clients who are highly motivated are more likely to do well with approaches that require a higher level of involvement (e.g., cognitive behavioral therapy), as these approaches require clients to complete homework assignments and practice identified behaviors (Norcross & Beutler, 2019).

Motivational interviewing (discussed in the person-centered therapy chapter) and the transtheoretical model are often linked and connected in the literature (Miller & Rollnick, 2013). However, motivational interviewing is not based on the transtheoretical model (Miller & Rollnick, 2013). Miller and Rollnick describe motivational interviewing and the transtheoretical model as 'kissing cousins who never married' (2013, p. 35). The transtheoretical model, on the one hand, provides an understanding of what initiates behavior change and how change may occur (Prochaska & DiClemente, 2002). Motivational interviewing, on the other hand, is a specific counseling approach that encourages, promotes, and optimizes the client's drive for change. The transtheoretical model is often used in motivational interviewing to help assess clients' current level of readiness for behavior change. The main focus in motivational interviewing is, however, on helping people through conversations that support and initiate behavior change (Miller & Rollnick, 2013).

Not all theories are strategically integrated, nor do they all fit into a specific theories category. Textbox 15.1 and Textbox 15.2 describe two examples of such theories.

> ### Textbox 15.1 Interpersonal Psychotherapy
>
> Interpersonal psychotherapy is based on a psychobiological approach to mental illness and informed by the interpersonal work of the ego psychologist Harry Stack Sullivan (1953, 1970). While it has a focus on interpersonal relationships, it is not really a psychodynamic approach, nor is it a humanistic approach. Some would argue that its lack of underlying theory of personality and development indicates that it is not a full-fledged approach at all. But without doubt, this time-limited approach is effective and growing in popularity worldwide, especially in places where it offers an alternative to costly medication when working with people who have psychological disorders.
>
> Interpersonal psychotherapy was initially developed by Gerald Klerman and colleagues in the 1970s in New Haven, Connecticut, as part of a collaborative research program on depression (Verdeli & Weissman, 2011). Interpersonal psychotherapy emphasizes social and interpersonal experiences. It recognizes the importance of the unconscious and of early childhood interactions but gives more attention to current relationships and patterns, social roles, and coping skills.
>
> According to interpersonal psychotherapy, the loss of a parent, or any other disruption in the relationship between a child and the child's primary caregiver, can increase vulnerability to depression as an adult. Once the vulnerability to depression has been established, stressful interpersonal experiences in adulthood can lead to the onset or recurrence of depression. Interpersonal psychotherapy postulates that strong social bonds reduce the likelihood of depression.
>
> Interpersonal psychotherapy is a focused, time-limited approach in which client and therapist typically meet for 14 to 18 weekly sessions. Therapy is focused on (1) interpersonal deficits (social roles and interactions among people), (2) role expectations and disputes, and (3) role transitions, or (4) grief (Weissman, Markowitz, & Klerman, 2007). Therapy seeks to identify a focal concern, alleviate symptoms, and improve interpersonal functions.
>
> Counseling via IPT includes three phases:
>
> 1. **Initial sessions.** Counseling objectives of phase 1 include assessment of symptoms and identification of one or two focal concerns linked to the symptoms, such as grief, interpersonal conflicts, role transitions, or interpersonal deficits. In addition, therapists explain IPT and help clients recognize that their symptoms represent a disorder that can be ameliorated through counseling.
> 2. **Intermediate phase.** This phase focuses on the problem or interpersonal difficulty identified in phase 1. Goals are established, and strategies are used to achieve those goals. IPT encourages use of a variety of strategies, including support, questions to elicit emotion and content, interpretation, identification of patterns, advice giving, education, clarification, feedback on communication, teaching of decision-making skills, behavior change techniques, role playing, and use of the therapeutic relationship. Although therapists play an active role, clients are encouraged to take as much responsibility as possible for their therapy.
> 3. **Termination phase.** Termination is planned and carefully processed, beginning at least two to four sessions before the conclusion of therapy. Clients' feelings of anger, sadness, loss, and grief are accepted and discussed. Therapists give clients the message that they are now capable of handling these feelings and moving ahead in their lives.
>
> Research has given considerable support to IPT, which was originally designed to address depression but has since found value in addressing a number of other conditions, including bipolar disorder in conjunction with medication management (Frank, 2005), specific types of depression (peripartum, in conjunction with medical illnesses, with older adults, in the Hispanic population), bulimia and other eating disorders, posttraumatic stress disorder (PTSD), social anxiety disorder, and conflicts in interpersonal relationships (Kriston, Wolff, Westphal, Holzel, & Harter, 2014; Mann, McGrath, & Roose, 2013; Markowitz & Weissman, 2012; Mufson, Dorta, Moreau, & Weissman, 2011; Rafaeli & Markowitz, 2011).

Interpersonal psychotherapy provides a time-limited, manualized counseling approach for working with people of all ages, from adolescents to older adults, and in a variety of settings (Weissman et al., 2007). Many professionals appreciate this approach because it recognizes the role of relationships in people's lives and provides a prescribed course of therapy that is concise and easy to follow.

Textbox 15.2 Eye Movement Desensitization Reprocesssing (EMDR)

Eye movement desensitization and reprocessing (EMDR) includes elements of behavior therapy (e.g., exposure therapy), CBT (e.g., a focus on changing cognitions), and neuroscience (i.e., bilateral stimulation facilitated by eye movements, alternating sounds, and/or tapping). EMDR was discovered in 1987 by Francine Shapiro (2018), a senior research fellow at the Mental Research Institute in Palo Alto, California. EMDR requires the client to visualize an important memory followed by the physical sensations it invites. The client follows the therapist's finger as it moves rapidly back and forth; this is repeated again and again until the client's anxiety is reduced. The client then moves to reprocessing other memories that come up after previous memories are reprocessed. Essentially, the EMDR approach involves integrating a behavioral assessment, exposure such as imaginal flooding (i.e., evoking the memory of a traumatic event), cognition (i.e., recognizing and replacing negative thoughts), relaxation (i.e., intentional breathing exercises), and guided eye movements to help the individual learn to access, process, and resolve traumatic memories.

EMDR has eight phases. The first phase involves taking a client history to assess the client's readiness for undergoing EMDR. The second phase is psychoeducational, in which the therapist teaches the client about what EMDR is and what reactions may occur from the process. The third phase occurs when the therapist gathers baseline data from the client. In this phase, the client selects a memory and uses subjective units of distress (SUDS) to label the distress level. These first three phases are the introduction to behavioral assessment phases. The fourth phase is the desensitization phase, which is the longest phase. The client focuses on the memory that was selected and experiences the emotions that arise as the therapist conducts the bilateral stimulation. This could include moving the hand back and forth 12 inches from the client's face, using hand taps, or repeating verbal cues. After the bilateral set, which usually consists of 15 to 30 eye movements, the client takes a deep breath and reflects on what the experience was like, including thoughts, feelings, and sensations. The fifth phase is the installation phase, which involves linking the positive thought to the original memory through the use of eye movements. During the sixth phase, the client does a body scan to gain awareness of any tension, which would then be decreased through eye movements. The seventh and eighth phases are the emotional equilibrium phases. The client is also asked to keep a journal containing distressing thoughts, dreams, and images throughout the week. The client is taught to use relaxation techniques to reduce the distressing thoughts. EMDR typically takes four to six sessions that are 1.5 to 2 hours long.

Eye movement desensitization and reprocessing originally focused on people who had suffered trauma, including rape, molestation, and war experiences, by helping them to reduce negative images and emotions related to those images and modify self-destructive cognitions. EMDR is particularly helpful for treating clients who have experienced trauma (Chen et al., 2012). It also shows promise for anxiety, depression, eating disorders, and obsessive-compulsive disorder (OCD; Balbo, Zaccagnino, Cussino, & Civilotti, 2017; Chen et al., 2012; Marsden, Lovell, Blore, Ali, & Delgadillo, 2018). In a meta-analysis, trauma-focused CBT and EMDR were shown to be more effective in addressing PTSD as compared to other therapies (Bisson et al., 2007). Some argue that its effectiveness lies in the exposure therapy aspects of the approach, which overlap with the

(Continued)

previously mentioned interventions (Schubert & Lee, 2009). Nevertheless, given the prevalence of EMDR as an approach for addressing PTSD, it is important for therapists to understand this approach and its value in helping those who have PTSD.

Eye movement desensitization and reprocessing with children has not yet proved as effective as EMDR with adults. Existing studies have so far suggested that positive results of EMDR with children are due to the cognitive component of this approach rather than the eye movements or bilateral stimulation (Greyber, Dulmus, & Cristalli, 2012).

FINDING YOUR COUNSELING THEORY

Readers who are relatively new to counseling and psychotherapy may view it as presumptuous or unrealistic to consider which counseling theory is best for them. However, choosing and emulating a style is a good way to learn almost any skill. Even Picasso, generally regarded as one of the most creative and innovative artists of the 20th century, began his career as a representational artist, painting in the traditional styles of the masters and only moving on to seek his own style after he had developed skill in established approaches to painting.

On the one hand, having studied many counseling theories, you may already have a preferred approach in mind. On the other hand, you may feel overwhelmed by the vast array of appealing choices.

Personal experiences can inform and influence the theories you value. Responding to the following questions can help you consider how your past experiences may impact your theory selection:

- What theoretical approaches have been emphasized in your training and modeled by your professors? What are your reactions to these theories? What do you value and not value about these models?
- If you have been employed as a therapist, what counseling approaches were advocated at your place(s) of employment? Which ones seemed most effective and compatible with your personal style?
- If you received counseling or psychotherapy yourself, what approaches did your therapist emphasize? How successful were those approaches in helping you? What elements of your therapist's approach did you value and not value?

Chapter 1 discussed common factors. Because of the importance of common factors in understanding what helps clients change in counseling, it is worth reviewing their importance as you find your preferred counseling approach. Research and experience increasingly confirm the existence of **common factors** in counseling and psychotherapy, overriding characteristics associated with successful counseling, regardless of a therapist's theoretical orientation. Therapists have clues indicating what kind of therapeutic contexts, relationships, and processes are most likely to lead to positive therapy outcomes, and these cut across all counseling theories. Now that you know about a broad range of counseling theories, you probably have realized that beneficial commonalities in counseling approaches also play an important part in determining counseling outcome. In fact, as much as 70% of the outcome variance between different types of therapy can be attributed to common factors shared by all successful therapies (Wampold, 2010). The factors most commonly found across all therapeutic types and orientations are as follows:

- A positive therapeutic alliance that is collaborative
- A credible approach that addresses the client's problems
- Factors related to the client, such as self-efficacy, problem solving, motivation for change, and hopefulness that therapy will work (Norcross & Lambert, 2011).

> The research on common factors accounting for client improvement can be divided into three broad categories (Lambert, 1992; Lambert & Bergin, 1994):
>
> 1. **Support factors**, including a positive, reassuring, and trusting therapeutic alliance and a therapist who communicates warmth, respect, empathy, genuineness, and acceptance
> 2. **Learning factors**, including changes in clients' thinking and perceptions, receiving advice, acquisition of insight, corrective emotional experiences, and increased self-acceptance and expectations for personal effectiveness
> 3. **Action factors**, including an expectation for positive change, improved behavioral regulation, reality testing, modeling, practicing, completing homework tasks, receiving suggestions, confronting fears and problems, processing, working through, and having success experiences.
>
> Does this mean that your theoretical orientation is not important? Absolutely not! Counseling factors account for between 8% and 15% of the variance. However, this research does suggest that whatever theory you select, counseling is likely to be effective, and this is reassuring. Counseling needs to be tailored to the needs of the specific client, and regardless of which modality is used, therapists must also attend to the relationship between client and therapist (Norcross & Lambert, 2011).

Clients' diagnoses—if applicable—are one example of an important variable to consider when selecting and applying a theory (Norcross & Beutler, 2019). For better or worse, the *Diagnostic and Statistical Manual of Mental Disorders*, Fifth Edition (American Psychiatric Association, 2013), is the classification system on which all U.S. mental health professionals rely when diagnosing. Diagnoses can help suggest what theories or approaches may be most useful with clients. For example, if a client is experiencing severe, debilitating depression, the research suggests the client might benefit from behavior activation therapy. Therefore, clients' diagnoses might impact what theory or interventions are used in counseling. Therapists are increasingly called upon to be dynamic in their understanding and application of various counseling approaches (Kress & Paylo, 2019).

Many suggest that it may be most helpful for new therapists to become competent in applying one theory. Once newer therapists have a solid understanding of a theory's strengths, limitations, and applications, they are better able to integrate other theories. In counseling and psychotherapy, acquiring expertise in counseling theories that have established their value can provide a solid foundation for eventually developing a personal eclectic or integrated approach or deciding to specialize in one or two established theories.

Determinants of Theoretical Orientation

Many determinants, including the factors that follow, contribute to therapists' choice of theoretical orientation:

1. Therapists who are encouraged, through course work and professional experiences, to adopt a particular approach to counseling are more likely to embrace a specific theory than an integrated or eclectic approach (Robertson, 1979). This is especially true if they are exposed to a charismatic proponent of that theory.
2. Beginning therapists are more likely to embrace one, specific theoretical approach. They have not yet determined which theory best fits them and their clients, nor have most beginning therapists acquired enough understanding of the entire spectrum of counseling approaches to allow thoughtful integration of a variety of approaches. In addition, adherence to a single theory can provide new therapists with reassuring structure and guidelines.
3. Similarly, length of therapy experience bears a positive relationship to the likelihood that therapists will have adopted an integrated or eclectic orientation (Prochaska & Norcross, 2018).

Exposure to a diverse and complex array of clients and concerns, as well as to therapists who practice a range of counseling approaches, leads many therapists and psychologists to conclude that any one theory is too limited to meet their needs. Even theories that seem comprehensive and well supported in the literature may have gaps and shortcomings in practice.

4. Therapists' perceptions of their work are another relevant factor. Therapists who view their work as a reflection of their philosophy of life are more likely to assume an integrated or eclectic stance than are therapists who view their work in practical terms, seeing it primarily as a way to earn a living (Robertson, 1979).
5. Therapists' personalities and worldviews are other important factors. Finding a theoretical approach that is compatible with who they are and how they conceive of the process of helping people seems likely to enhance therapists' effectiveness as well as their enjoyment of their work.

For many therapists, their early years in the profession give them the opportunity to experiment with many approaches; determine what is and is not successful for them; and find a counseling system that is compatible with their professional roles, their self-images, their personalities, and their worldviews. For example, among counseling students, several factors contributed to their counseling theory choice (Petko, Kendrick, & Young, 2016). Personal values play a role in how therapists select their counseling theory. When people's values match with the counseling theory, people are more likely to use that theory. Other contributors to theory selection include the theory making sense logically and the techniques being well liked. Most therapists find that their professional interests and ideas evolve with experience, enabling them to refine their counseling approaches as they hone their skills. Later in their careers, therapists who are self-employed and who are able to practice a theoretical orientation that is congruent with their personalities report greater job satisfaction (Topolinski & Hertel, 2007).

Counseling Theory and Therapist Personality

Whether or not you have honed in on your current theory of choice, be sure to pay attention to the influence your personality has on the theories you are drawn to. Therapists tend to prefer approaches that are compatible with their personality styles. For example, therapists' preferred theoretical orientations and their personality types as reflected on the Myers-Briggs Type Indicator (MBTI) may predict what theories therapists are most interested in (Ciorbea & Nedelcea, 2012). Thinking types (Ts) may be more likely to choose predominantly cognitive and behavioral techniques (e.g., behavioral, rational emotive, and reality therapy). Specifically, ENTJs (i.e., those who are **E**xtraverted, i**N**tuitive, **T**hinking, **J**udging) may be more likely to choose cognitive and behavioral therapies. Feeling types (Fs) may be more likely to choose predominantly humanistic and experiential therapies. Specifically, ESFJs (i.e., those who are **E**xtraverted, **S**ensing, **F**eeling, **J**udging) and ISFPs (i.e., those who are **I**ntroverted, **S**ensing, **F**eeling, **J**udging) may be more likely to choose humanistic and experiential therapies. Those who score higher on the perceiving preference on the MBTI are more likely to choose a humanistic or existential theoretical orientation, and those who score higher on the judging type are more likely to choose a cognitive or behavior therapy.

Using your self-knowledge, feedback you have received from others, and the results of the MBTI or any personality inventories you might have taken, think about your personality and the counseling theories that seem most compatible with who you are and what you value. Again, further reading about and exposure to those approaches might help you choose a theoretical approach that is best for you at this point in your career. Keep in mind that you are not making an irrevocable commitment, but merely choosing a starting point that will help you continue the development of your counseling skills in a comfortable and focused way. With experience, you will become increasingly clear about the best approach for you and your clients, and you will find your theoretical approach changing, evolving, and improving.

Theoretical Orientation Reflection Questions

It is important to remember that your theoretical orientation will evolve as you begin to work with clients. The theory you apply will also be influenced by the setting in which you work and the populations you work with. It is also unlikely that your theory will be black and white; you will likely draw on many aspects of various theoretical orientations as you determine what theories best fit the needs of individual clients. It is also necessary to tailor your therapeutic approach to meet the needs of all your clients, and you must consider their culture, as this inevitably impacts the therapeutic relationship and progress. While most therapists assimilate techniques and methods from diverse theoretical perspectives, it takes many years of practice and experience to cultivate the ability to integrate; both art and science are required for integrating approaches, and the development of such skills can truly be learned only in the trenches, with experience. Remember, the therapeutic relationship is at the core of each theoretical orientation no matter what approach you choose. It is important to keep an open mind as you grow in your theoretical orientation(s) and understand that the best way to develop your theoretical orientation is through your real-life experiences as a therapist. The following questions can help you reflect on what theoretical orientation you may be drawn to:

- What is the core of human nature? Are human beings good, neutral, bad, or a mix?
- Do you think that only one reality exists, or do you think that multiple realities can exist?
- What causes human behavior (i.e., biology, learning, social relationships/influence of others)? In other words, what do you believe motivates human behavior?
- When working with a client, would you consider the target to be the whole person or a specific aspect of the person/problem?
- What are the principal concepts that explain human experience?
- What are your beliefs about the development of problems in living? Is it necessary to understand the current problem or do you need to focus only on the current behavior?
- What foundations or ingredients make up a healthy person? What approach fits best with your ideas around what a healthy person is (i.e., someone who has rational thoughts, someone who reaches self-actualization, someone who has a healthy family)?
- What do you believe should be the target of therapy (e.g., clients' thoughts, behavior, or feelings)? What do you believe most facilitates clients' change processes?
- What is the impact of social relationships on people's mental health? How important are social relationships in influencing and supporting mental health?
- What style do you think is most effective in encouraging clients' change processes (i.e., active, directive, laid back, problem solving)? Who has the most responsibility for change (i.e., the client, the therapist, both)?

OVERVIEW OF COUNSELING THEORIES

In this section of the chapter, an overview of the theories discussed in this text will be provided. I hope that in reviewing the theories in a cohesive way, you will be able to more clearly identify the theory or theories that most resonate with you.

Basic Philosophy/Key Concepts

Each counseling theory has basic theoretical foundations that are critical in guiding therapist practice. That said, there should be room in therapists' practice to thoughtfully select interventions associated with other theories, as needed. For example, consider a client who is struggling with supervisor problems at work. Using a feminist therapy theory, a therapist will aim to empower the client to assert herself and ask to have her needs met. Yet the client may not have the skills to know how to do this secondary to a lifetime of subverting her voice because of societal expectations of women. As such, a feminist theorist might integrate behavior therapy interventions to help teach her the skills she requires to be successful in meeting her goals. In this situation, the therapist did not lose sight of the overarching philosophy of feminist therapy (e.g., client empowerment, breaking down limiting societal barriers that hold women/girls down) when selecting this intervention commonly associated with a different theoretical approach. What is important is that therapists are faithful to their underlying philosophies yet have the capacity to be technically integrative. As another example, it would not make sense for a therapist to tell a client she worked from a person-centered and cognitive behavioral perspective. The underlying philosophies of these two approaches are very different: CBT holds that learning cognitive and behavioral skills is the key to change, while a person-centered perspective is founded on the idea that the counseling relationship and enhanced awareness are foundational to change. At times a CBT therapist might pull on techniques associated with a person-centered approach, and vice versa, but the basic philosophy and theory should guide therapists' thinking and approach. Table 15.1 provides an overview of basic philosophies that guide major theories and Table 15.2 provides an overview of key concepts that guide the major theories discussed in this text.

TABLE 15.1 Basic Philosophies of Counseling Theories

Classic Psychoanalysis	Humans are motivated by psychic energy and early experiences. The interplay between the unconscious and conscious aspects of personality and the successful resolution of these stages of development are required for people to develop a healthy personality; when this does not occur, psychological and behavioral problems arise. Early childhood relationships and clients' experiences within these relationships are central to understanding and helping clients.
Adlerian therapy	Humans are social beings who are motivated to become better versions of themselves. Humans have an inherent drive to contribute positively to society, and people use self-comparison with peers to assess their competence in life. Personal difficulties, especially physical setbacks and overbearing/underattentive parents, can lead to an inferiority complex. Individuals adopt different lifestyles—patterns in living—to achieve their short-term and long-term goals. Factors that contribute to individual lifestyle include biology, birth order, family structure, life experiences, and social relationships. Clients' positive capacities are encouraged to help them reach their full potential for benefiting society.
Post- and Neo-Freudian therapies	Childhood experiences, especially early relationships with family and caretakers, has a significant impact on functioning. When those experiences are explored and brought to the conscious, overall well-being improves. The role of the unconscious is explored along with relationship dynamics, which is where early childhood experiences and important psychological experiences play out. Promotion of awareness and insight is essential.
Behavior therapy	Humans are both the product and the producer of the environment. All behaviors are either adaptive or maladaptive, and they are learned, and thus they can be unlearned. All maladaptive behaviors can be modified and relearned, and behaviors that clients need to be successful can be learned. The key to helping people change is teaching them new skills or helping them to unlearn and replace targeted, problematic behaviors or reactions.
Cognitive behavioral therapy	Cognitions, or how people think, is foundational to how they feel and behave. Clients experience change when they alter how and what they think and how they behave. Psychoeducation around thinking patterns and ways these can be changed, and an increased understanding of one's thoughts and engaging in adaptive behaviors, can create a new, more adaptive perspective that helps clients feel and function better.

TABLE 15.1 (Continued)

Reality therapy	This approach is based on choice theory and is classified as a type of cognitive behavioral therapy. People require quality relationships with others, which help fulfill their basic needs of survival, love and belonging, power, freedom, and fun. Problems arise when those basic needs are not being effectively met, and people go about trying to meet these needs in unproductive ways. Problems also arise when we resist control by others and when we attempt to control others. Reality therapy, a CBT approach, focuses on helping clients to change their thoughts and actions so they can make healthy decisions, engage in healthy behaviors, and live their best lives.
Contemporary CBT therapies	These therapies encourage mindfulness of internal experiences and emphasize acceptance instead of controlling negative internal sensations and thoughts. Understanding the underlying processes associated with the interactions between thoughts, feelings, and behaviors is more important than understanding the content of thoughts and attempting to change or otherwise control these thoughts. Goal oriented, these approaches rely on behavioral strategies to target more metacognitive processes. When clients gain awareness, alter their perspective of their experiences, and engage in healthy behaviors, change will occur; understanding thought/feeling/behavior cycles and how they function can be helpful, but it is equally important to engage in behaviors that promote and encourage behavior change.
Existential therapy	All people experience existential anxiety and search for meaning in their lives. When clients become aware and accept the ultimate concerns of the human condition (i.e., death, isolation, meaninglessness, freedom), they will experience less anxiety, live in the present moment, and reach their full potential. Clients are provided with a safe, respectful environment within the therapeutic relationship to express themselves, gain awareness, take responsibility for their choices, create meaning, and thus learn how to live their best lives.
Person-centered therapy	Positive, optimistic view of people and human nature. People have an innate capacity to resolve their own problems, to grow, and to reach self-actualization within a safe, warm, empathic environment. Through the therapeutic relationship, clients experience feelings that were previously denied. Clients are experts on their own lives and are believed to have internal resources that can be discovered with the help of the therapist. The therapist's unconditional positive regard supports clients' empowerment, and allows clients to flourish, self-actualize, and grow into being their best selves.
Gestalt therapy	An experiential therapy approach based on the idea that people strive for wholeness and integration of their thinking, feeling, and behaving. Contact with the self and others, ego/contact boundaries, and awareness are central concepts. Through awareness and integration of different aspects of the self and interactions with the environment, as well as being present and aware in the here and now, change is likely to occur. This approach emphasizes personal responsibility and holds that people have a capacity for growth and aim to strive to move toward integration of the different parts of themselves.
Feminist therapy	Feminist therapy places an emphasis on the ways in which gender roles, power, socialization, and marginalized identities affect how people make meaning of their lives and the psychological distress they experience. Feminists often question traditional theories based on their gender-biased concepts. Clients work with feminist therapists to identify ways to promote empowerment in their lives through the identification of strategies that are specific to their unique needs along a spectrum ranging from individual to relational to societal (political) change processes. This approach is a systems approach that pays attention to how cultural, social, and political factors impact the individual.

(Continued)

TABLE 15.1 (*Continued*)

Postmodern therapies	Client-perceived problems are rooted in clients' problem-saturated perceptions, and creating new, more positive realities can result in more satisfying perceptions. Clients are experts on their problems and have the resources they need to be successful. Therapists facilitate the co-creation of new, more adaptive, realities through language and through the co-construction of more satisfying stories.
Family systems therapies	The family is viewed as an interactive, living system that maintains its own system of balance. Dysfunction within this system is balanced by other parts of the system. Family therapists believe a disruption to the homeostasis of one part of the system will institute a change in the whole system. Thus, family dynamic/system changes, as opposed to individual-level change, is the focus of counseling.

TABLE 15.2 Key Concepts of Counseling Theories

Classic Psychoanalysis	Clients' personality development requires the successful navigation of early stages of development, and these stages vary depending on the specific psychoanalytic theory. Ego defense mechanisms serve to protect the ego from anxiety-producing memories or events. When clients do not successfully resolve a developmental stage, they become stuck and will manifest problematic psychological and behavioral concerns. The unconscious leads to current behavior.
Adlerian therapy	All perspectives are subjective and unique to individuals, and multiple factors are involved in the creation of a unique lifestyle. Consistently encouraging clients and aiding them to move in a prosocial direction are key. Clients are inherently motivated to develop a sense of direction and achieve socially useful life goals. Clients have an innate need for social connection, which creates meaning and fulfillment.
Post- and Neo-Freudian therapies	The various Neo-Freudian approaches have diverse key concepts. For example, analytical therapy focuses on the components of the personality, separation and individuation from others, the importance of spirituality, and balance and polarities. Key concepts of ego psychology include self-realization and awareness and strengthening of the ego. Self psychology is developmental and focuses on the self and the development of self-esteem. Object relations relies heavily on attachment theory. All of the theories emphasize early life experiences and their impacts on current relationship dynamics, and they all focus on helping clients develop, through the counseling relationship, more satisfying ways of connecting with others.
Behavior therapy	Identification and classifications of problematic or needed behaviors lead to the identification of behaviors that need to be changed, altered, or learned. Counseling addresses the development of measurable counseling goals focused on changing specific behaviors and replacing them with more adaptive behaviors.
Cognitive behavioral therapy	New, more adaptive thoughts and behaviors can be learned. Distorted thinking reinforces pre-existing thoughts, which then influence feelings and behaviors. A person's beliefs and thoughts are the main cause of distress and struggle. Change occurs when faulty beliefs are replaced with effective beliefs, and when maladaptive behaviors are replaced with adaptive behaviors. Over time, these new ways of thinking will be less forced, and they will become automatic ways of thinking.
Reality therapy	This therapy focuses on what clients are behaviorally doing and helping them to evaluate if what they are doing is effectively working for them. Humans make decisions based on their basic needs. This approach places the responsibility of choices firmly on clients and whether they are currently making choices that are working effectively or not.

TABLE 15.2 *(Continued)*

Contemporary CBT therapies	Third-wave approaches use cognitive, behavioral, and emotional principles to facilitate change, with an eye to mindfulness concepts. Third-wave approaches are holistic, optimistic, contextual, and process based. Overall well-being is the focus rather than specific issues only (e.g., presenting problems). Acceptance of distressing emotions, situations, and cognitions and present moment awareness is particularly important.
Existential therapy	The ultimate concerns of all humans are the inevitability of death, isolation, meaninglessness, and the freedom to choose their experiences and actions. People can achieve wellness when they enhance their awareness, authenticity, and self-actualization; when they create meaning; and when they deepen their sense of identity. Counseling focuses on the present and the clients' process of becoming, and is experiential, or based on clients' unique experiences and reactions.
Person-centered therapy	Discomfort and struggle result from incongruence between who people want to be and how they are currently living. When clients are congruent with the ideal self and the real self, they are mentally healthy. The person-centered approach seeks to empower clients within the context of a warm, empathic, and nonjudgmental environment to recognize this incongruence and manifest self-actualization toward being their own genuine self. Therapy revolves around experiencing emotions and being in the present moment. The client has the potential to become aware of problems and is capable of resolving them.
Gestalt therapy	Gestalt therapy is optimistic in that it holds people are capable of self-actualization, and this is done by integrating all aspects of themselves. Emphasis is on the here and now and the what and the how, not on the past or the future or interpretations. The main key concepts include wholeness, integration and balancing different aspects of the self, and awareness (of the self, the environment, and unfinished business).
Feminist therapy	Feminist therapists focus on promoting empowering individual, relational, and social (political) changes in the lives of their clients. Attention is paid to the following five key concepts: the personal is political, women's experiences are honored, reframing mental health and disorders, the importance of the egalitarian relationship, and the role of social locations and multiple identities.
Postmodern therapies	The focus is on solutions and the creation of new stories rather than problems. A premium is placed on clients' resources, capacities, and skills, and these are tapped into to help them identify solutions and create a new, more satisfying reality. Therapy is often brief and focuses on the present and the future.
Family systems therapies	Counseling is done within the family context and/or with the entire family unit, as individual family members' struggles are believed to be a manifestation of larger familial dynamics. Generational transmission of issues is common and manifests itself in the actions and thoughts of the family. Most often the focus is on present functioning and working on communication patterns, both verbal and nonverbal, within the family unit.

Therapy Goals

In Table 15.3 an overview of the counseling goals associated with each theory is provided. As can be seen, counseling goals in particular have tremendous diversity. In many ways, this dimension—the goals of counseling—is what most readily distinguishes one theory from another. All of the theories hold the relationship as important to some extent, but when you begin to consider the focus and goals of counseling, the theories begin to stand apart. For example, existential theory has as its goal finding

TABLE 15.3 Goals of Counseling

Classic Psychoanalysis	The goal is to help clients make the unconscious conscious and work through repressed conflicts. The personality is reconstructed by working through and resolving previously unachieved developmental states. Awareness in clients is increased, specifically emotional and intellectual awareness. When counseling young clients, it is best to head off developmental issues before they arise by pre-emptively reinforcing the ego.
Adlerian therapy	People sometimes use unhelpful behaviors to have their interpersonal needs met, and the primary goal of counseling is to provide encouragement for clients to accomplish goals in healthy ways. Therapists help clients uncover unconscious reasoning and reframe it in more socially useful ways. Positive social relationships and movement toward broader social involvement should be encouraged. Therapists help clients build self-understanding and insight; build new levels of self-confidence and courage; and promote social interest, social connectedness, and belonging.
Post- and Neo-Freudian therapies	The goal of these approaches is to increase awareness and insight by exploring early experiences and the unconscious. Other goals include self-actualization, overall wellness, the development of healthy coping skills, an integrated sense of self, the formation of healthy relationships, and resolving presenting concerns.
Behavior therapy	Learning theories are used to help clients unlearn maladaptive behaviors and replace them with new, more adaptive behaviors. The main goal is for clients to take the skills and strategies learned in counseling and apply them in real-world settings to change their behaviors and accomplish pre-identified and operationalized goals.
Cognitive behavioral therapy	Clients identify distorted, faulty, or irrational beliefs and automatic thoughts, and replace these with new ways of thinking. Once identified, those thoughts and beliefs are challenged with contradictory evidence. CBT therapists also focus on behavioral change and emphasize the importance of engaging in new behaviors as well as new thinking patterns.
Reality therapy	Clients learn how their choices affect their quality world and the reality in which they live. Counselors promote self-responsibility, healthy choices, and the development of relationships that fulfill clients' needs in adaptive ways.
Contemporary CBT therapies	The goals of third-wave approaches include increasing awareness, acceptance, and present-moment experiencing, or mindfulness. Other goals include increased emotion regulation, improved relationships, and commitment to making positive changes. These approaches provide skills and tools to help clients cope in a healthy way and handle stressors. Instead of just reducing symptoms, the goal is to help clients become more whole and create a peaceful existence in which they can effectively handle the problems life presents with equanimity (i.e., mental calmness even in stressful situations).
Existential therapy	The fundamental goal of existential therapy is to help people find value, meaning, and purpose in their lives. Other goals include helping clients become aware of the freedom they do have, recognizing their options, and making choices that help them become more actualized and able to lead a life that reflects their values and priorities. Not only does therapy aim to help clients live more authentically, it also strives to help clients be fully present in their daily lives.
Person-centered therapy	This therapy aims to encourage and assist clients in self-exploration; to uncover blocks to growth and ways to overcome them; to increase openness of self; to find meaning in life; to experience life fully; and to promote self-directed growth, greater trust in self, and increased spontaneity and aliveness. This is done in the context of a safe, empathic counseling relationship.

TABLE 15.3 (*Continued*)

Gestalt therapy	The main goal is to integrate aspects of the self to achieve wholeness and unity. Through awareness, wholeness is possible. Once clients become aware, they can make choices and take responsibility for their current experience and choices. Awareness is the main agent of change. Other important goals include being in the here and now, reaching self-actualization, and promoting meaningful contact with the self and others.
Feminist therapy	The feminist therapy model does not hold that therapists should determine specific therapy goals, rather clients are the experts regarding their own lived experiences and the change process. Feminist therapists subscribe to two universal guidelines that ground the direction of their therapeutic work with clients: (1) examine the lived experiences of client distress and assess the role of personal, relational, and/or social (political) strengths; and (2) identify personal, relational, and social (political) strategies that can be used to navigate disempowerment and promote a sense of empowerment.
Postmodern therapies	Therapists following this approach co-create, through change talk and language, a new reality that assumes clients have what they need to solve their problems and move forward. Therapists help clients connect with their competence and resourcefulness so they can resolve present/future concerns. The aim is to help clients view their lives more positively, rather than focusing on problems.
Family systems therapies	The goal is to increase awareness of dysfunctional family interactions and patterns. Therapists focus on altering the current dysfunctional patterns that may be found within a family and aid family members in developing new patterns of interaction. They also help family members disrupt any dysfunctional maladaptive homeostasis, which may be preventing the family unit from optimal functioning.

meaning in one's life, while person-centered theory has as its focus becoming more self-actualized. Even though these theories both value the therapeutic relationship and have humanistic foundations, they have different goals.

The theories also differ in terms of how specific they are; some theories' goals are easier to pin down and drill in on (e.g., CBT, behavior therapy), while others are less well defined (e.g., person-centered or postmodern approaches). Along these lines, these same theories' goals can be more short term focused (e.g., traditional CBT approaches), while others are more focused on a person's long-term growth and development (e.g., contemporary CBT approaches).

Relationship Between Therapist and Client

Boiled down to its essence, therapy is founded on the idea that a human connection is valuable. As such, all of the theories discussed in this text consider the therapeutic relationship to be important, with some (e.g., person-centered, Gestalt, existential theories) believing it is more important than others (e.g., CBT, behavior therapy). Because therapists bring their personal characteristics to the counseling relationship, it is vital for them to be self-aware of their personality, values, cultural experiences and cultural limitations, and expectations of themselves and their clients, along with many other factors. Personal therapy is a great way for therapists to enhance their self-awareness so that they can be prepared to promote and encourage healthy relationships with their clients. On a related note, it is important that therapists have an awareness of the types of clients with whom they may struggle to develop a therapeutic relationship. For example, some counselors may have a difficult time building a relationship with certain populations (e.g., sex offenders, clients who abuse substances, children). An awareness of limitations is important, and addressing these issues will help deter problems from developing in the long run. Table 15.4 presents an overview of the therapeutic relationship in each theory.

TABLE 15.4 The Therapeutic Relationship

Classic Psychoanalysis	In classic psychoanalysis, therapists are anonymous and aloof so that clients can develop projections that can be used to help them overcome the developmental struggles they need to resolve. Clients may project onto therapists the role of a surrogate parent, and the role therapists choose is largely dependent on the age, needs, and developmental stage of clients.
Adlerian therapy	The therapeutic relationship, from an Adlerian perspective, is one of equality. Both therapist and client should take equal responsibility. The therapist should provide encouragement to the client, while sensitively uncovering mistaken goals and assumptions within the client's lifestyle. The therapist and the youth are equals on the path toward achieving socially useful short-term and long-term goals. The therapist fosters mutual trust and respect.
Post- and Neo-Freudian therapies	The therapeutic relationship is an important vehicle for change. Providing support, safety, and predictability within the therapeutic relationship is essential. Clients and therapists often influence each other. Therapists themselves provide healing and healthy modeling for relationships. Countertransference and transference are important aspects of the therapeutic relationship. Many of the approaches focus on the here-and-now experiences to promote insight and change.
Behavior therapy	Though it is an objective, systematic, scientific, directive, instructional counseling approach, this therapy emphasizes a strong therapeutic relationship, as this is important in engaging the client in the development and implementation of skills and the new behaviors needed to achieve behavioral change. Therapists are active and directive and may take on a teacher role.
Cognitive behavioral therapy	CBT approaches emphasize the importance of a warm therapeutic connection. In some CBT modalities, therapists act as a teacher and behave in an active, directive manner, while in others therapists works collaboratively via a Socratic dialogue to aid clients toward recognizing and changing their cognitions.
Reality therapy	Reality therapy is a didactic and directive approach, yet a strong relationship is important; if clients are not engaged with the therapist, they may not be open to sharing what they want and to revealing how effective they are in getting their needs met. Therapists should provide support and advocacy during the formation of new choices and relationships.
Contemporary CBT therapies	The therapeutic relationship is collaborative and reciprocal. Clients must trust their therapists to actively participate in therapy. Therapists are warm, compassionate, and empathic. Therapists are also open and appreciative of cultural differences. Therapists using these approaches pay particular attention to staying in the present moment with their clients. Therapists are active and take on the role of a coach, using psychoeducation and providing skills training to help their clients cope more effectively.
Existential therapy	Existential therapists aim for I-Thou relationships, which involve therapists sharing a journey with their clients and empowering them through a strong relationship and connection. The relationship includes empathy, positive regard, intimacy, openness, and real human exchange. Therapists are companions and co-explorers, share their own values, and use humor. Both therapists and clients are changed by the relationship. The immediacy and here-and-now aspects of the therapeutic relationship are essential.
Person-centered therapy	The therapeutic relationship is the single most important factor in this approach, as this is the vehicle for clients' change process. This relationship is typified by warmth, genuineness, empathy, respect, and unconditional positive regard. Therapists must remain congruent (genuine) throughout the relationship. Ensuring that clients perceive that the therapist has these attitudes is essential. Through this relationship, clients connect with the experiences they require to have more satisfying relationships outside of therapy.

TABLE 15.4 *(Continued)*

Gestalt therapy	The therapeutic relationship in Gestalt therapy is focused on a deep, meaningful, authentic connection. Rather than focusing on techniques, Gestalt therapists view their presence and attitude as most important. Therapists assist with change, but clients are responsible for the work they do in therapy. Therapists are open and honest in their interactions, at times utilizing self-disclosure, and they frequently use immediacy. Therapists do not make interpretations but instead look to clients to develop their own interpretations of their experiences.
Feminist therapy	Feminist therapists do not support the expert-therapist model and, instead, create a collaborative partnership with clients throughout the therapeutic process. In doing so, the therapist aims to minimize value imposition and the power differential in therapy. The relationship is egalitarian and empowering.
Postmodern therapies	Counseling is a collaborative partnership between therapists and clients. Clients are viewed as the experts in their own lives. Therapists help guide and support clients through the process, and facilitate the development of a new story in which the clients/families are successful and forward moving.
Family systems therapies	In most family therapy approaches, therapists work with the family unit as a whole and may act as coaches, experts, or teachers. At times the relationship is personal and in-depth, and at other times it is more distant. Some approaches will seek to intensify the maladaptive behaviors in session to highlight any dysfunctions. Regardless of the specific family therapy approach, family therapists consider the primary relationship to be with the entire family unit as a whole and maintain strong therapeutic alliances with all family members.

Counseling Techniques and Applications

Clients have unique counseling needs, and not all clients will respond to certain techniques in the same way. It would be short sighted and potentially harmful to clients if the same techniques were used with everyone. As previously discussed, clients' personal characteristics (e.g., motivation to make changes) and their presenting problems/diagnoses (e.g., anxiety) are just some of the considerations that may impact the counseling techniques used. Ideally, the counseling techniques chosen will be the ones most beneficial to the client. Knowing when clients need what techniques, though, is complicated. As a start, it is helpful for therapists to be well versed in a variety of techniques; in other words, good therapists have many tools in their toolbox.

In Chapter 1, the setting in which a therapist works was discussed as important when considering what counseling theory or techniques to use. **Level of care** was also examined as a major consideration that will significantly determine a therapist's methods. The setting and the level of care, then, will influence which counseling theories a therapist uses. As an example, a school counselor who is helping a student with a peer conflict may use counseling techniques that differ from those used by a mental health therapist working with a psychotic patient on a psychiatric ward who is experiencing a conflict with another patient.

When selecting counseling techniques, therapists should consider evidence-based practices. However, they must also take into account the approaches they are trained to use, clients' counseling preferences, the confines of the setting in which they work, and a myriad of additional considerations (Kress & Paylo, 2019). The use of evidence-based approaches is more or less important, depending on the clients' needs. To use an extreme example, if the therapist is counseling a 5-year-old who has endured significant trauma secondary to child sex trafficking, it would be irresponsible and unethical to not pull on the wide array of research that points to counseling approaches that may help the child resolve trauma and thus its long-term effects. At the other extreme, if a therapist is counseling a college student dealing with roommate conflicts, the therapist will have more freedom and flexibility in terms of the interventions used, as the stakes are not as high and the client is likely not as complex.

Therapists should consider what is already known in the research literature (e.g., peer-reviewed journals and federal registries) with regard to effective counseling techniques. Some helpful guidelines that may assist therapists in evaluating whether a theory, approach, or intervention should be deemed evidenced based and used in practice are (SAMHSA, 2009):

- **Guideline 1:** Approaches and interventions need to be based on some documented, clear conceptual model of change.
- **Guideline 2:** Approaches and interventions must be similar to, or found in, federal registries and/or the peer-reviewed literature.
- **Guideline 3:** The approaches and interventions should be supported by the documentation of multiple scientific inquiries that seem credible, and rigorous, and by evidence consistent with positive effects.
- **Guideline 4:** The approaches and interventions should have been reviewed and deemed credible by informed experts in the identified area.

Additionally, when determining what interventions and techniques to use and when and how to use them, the following might also apply:

- Therapists should ensure that they have developed a strong therapeutic alliance with the client.
- Therapists should consider the client's issue or concern and what the client wants to get out of counseling.
- Therapists should consider how the client's preferences may intersect with the techniques being selected.
- Therapists should consider their history with using the techniques and ensure that they have the competency to use such techniques.

Adhering to these considerations enables therapists to select interventions that are consistent with clients' preferences and that adhere to therapists' individual competencies. Table 15.5 provides an overview of the techniques associated with different theories, and Table 15.6 presents an overview of the populations that each theory works well with.

TABLE 15.5 Counseling Techniques

Classic Psychoanalysis	Free association through play observation (with children) and interpretation of representational objects, dream and daydream analysis, interpretation of transference, countertransference, and analysis of resistance are just some of the techniques in a therapist's toolbox. The associations and interpretations a therapist recognizes arise during counseling.
Adlerian therapy	Therapists work to understand clients' unique lifestyles and identify healthier behaviors that can help clients achieve their short-term and long-term goals, which are socially motivated. The therapist may collect information regarding life history, early recollections, family constellation, and social history. The role of encouragement in supporting clients during counseling is critical to growth and socially useful functioning. Therapists may also share interpretations and assist clients in finding new possibilities.
Post- and Neo-Freudian therapies	These approaches do not rely heavily on techniques. Common techniques include free association, analysis of dreams, countertransference and transference, interpretation, and projective identification. Brief psychodynamic therapy in particular uses both expressive and supportive techniques.

TABLE 15.5 *(Continued)*

Behavior therapy	Behavior therapy is a technique-heavy approach that involves a multitude of different techniques, which all focus on changing behaviors and learning new, more adaptive behaviors. A premium is placed on learning new skills. These skills may include reinforcement (positive or negative), role playing, functional behavioral assessments, or behavior contracts. Other techniques include relaxation techniques, flooding, systematic desensitization, modeling, assertiveness training, and social skills training.
Cognitive behavioral therapy	CBT approaches involve a wide variety of techniques that focus on helping clients to alter their thinking and behaviors. Techniques from behavioral theory are sometimes used along with perspective and thought-changing techniques. These include the A-B-C–D-E-F model from REBT, Socratic questioning and dialogue, as well as mindfulness-based techniques. Other techniques include self-monitoring, learning new coping skills, imagery, and changing one's language.
Reality therapy	Counselors find out what clients want, invite them to evaluate their present choices and behaviors, help them to make plans for behavioral changes moving forward, and help them to commit to these changes. The WDEP (wants, direction, evaluation, and planning) system functions as a primary method of therapeutic work with clients. The WDEP system aids clients in defining their quality world and understanding how their choices and relationships impact their lives.
Contemporary CBT therapies	Common techniques in third-wave approaches include the use of mindfulness training and acceptance. Techniques focus on behavioral, cognitive, and emotional change. Techniques are applied based on individual clients and what best fits their needs. Therapists help clients develop their own toolbox to use as they face life's challenges, with a focus on global well-being across situations and over time. DBT uses techniques such as emotional regulation, mindfulness, distress tolerance, and interpersonal effectiveness. ACT relies heavily on acceptance and awareness. MBCT uses conscious thought processing, mindfulness, and decentering. Schema therapy uses empathic confrontation and schema flash cards.
Existential therapy	This approach is not technique heavy, as the focus is on awareness and the idea that change will follow once awareness comes. Diagnosis, assessment, and testing are not of value in this approach. Therapists may borrow techniques from other approaches. Existential therapists address isolation, freedom to choose, the creation of meaning and struggles with meaninglessness, personal responsibility, life and death struggles, and relationships. The therapeutic relationship is also used as a vehicle for change.
Person-centered therapy	Techniques that center on promoting the therapeutic relationship are the focus of this theory. Therapists' attitude and their "way of being" with clients is their best tool. Key techniques from person-centered theory include active listening, accurate reflections, and accurate empathic understanding. This approach does not involve diagnosing, formal testing, or interpretation.
Gestalt therapy	Techniques used in Gestalt therapy are meant to intensify experiencing and increase awareness. Some techniques include experiments, use of language, and working with clients' dreams and fantasies. One of the most widely used techniques is role play using the empty chair method to resolve inner conflicts and unfinished business. Formal diagnosis and assessment are not a focus of this approach.

(Continued)

TABLE 15.5 (*Continued*)

Feminist therapy	Feminist therapists draw from a wide variety of techniques that span multiple theoretical orientations. Techniques are tailored to clients' strengths, with the goal of cultivating their personal power and critical consciousness. Two primary techniques considered unique to feminist therapy are gender-role analysis and power analysis. Additional strategies that may be used include assertiveness training, reframing and relabeling, therapy demystifying strategies, consciousness-raising, and social activism.
Postmodern therapies	These approaches rely heavily on questions to create dialogue, understand stories, and generate experiences. Change talk, which assumes clients are forward moving and have their own resources, is a common technique. In solution-focused brief therapy (SFBT), miracle questions and scaling questions assist the client in developing alternative solutions. Exception-seeking questions are also used to discover times when the problem was not a problem or was less of a problem. Narrative therapy techniques focus on listening to clients' problem-saturated stories and helping them find a new, more fulfilling story. Narrative therapy also emphasizes letter-writing techniques that focus on their progress and help them find supports that will encourage new stories. Other techniques include externalization and pointing out competencies.
Family systems therapies	Short-term techniques are generally preferred over long-term therapy, but family therapists may draw upon a variety of techniques, depending on the specific family approach they take. Therapists may use family mapping or genograms, joining with the family as a pseudo-member, or use direct psychoeducation. Other techniques may include reframing, restructuring, enactments, and setting boundaries.

TABLE 15.6 Counseling Applications

Classic Psychoanalysis	This approach is not as widely applied today due to the lengthy time requirements for proper analysis. It has been influential in establishing many play therapy approaches. Brief approaches have been developed and have become more popular than traditional psychoanalysis in recent years. Generally, this therapy uses a one-on-one therapy approach, but it has had successful application in group settings, family counseling, and parent–child counseling.
Adlerian therapy	Due to its emphasis on encouraging a client's growth toward more prosocial behaviors and attitudes, Adlerian theory is extremely applicable to a diverse range of professional fields, which include personal counseling, school counseling, parent education, teacher education, and social advocacy. It is best for prevention purposes and alleviating growth-related concerns.
Post- and Neo-Freudian therapies	The Post- and Neo-Freudian theories are applicable to a wide variety of populations and presenting concerns. These approaches have helped inform an understanding of the etiology and treatment of those who have personality disorders or who have experienced traumatic early life experiences. Brief psychodynamic therapy is a sound theoretical approach for use in settings where a limited number of counseling sessions are available.
Behavior therapy	Behavioral techniques are rooted in the scientific method and lend themselves well to assessment, evaluation, and verification. As such, these techniques have a strong evidence base for use with a variety of issues. This approach is effective in addressing a number of issues, such as problematic school and home behaviors, stuttering, enuresis, phobias, and depressive and anxiety disorders. Behavior therapy can be used with individuals, groups, couples, and families.
Cognitive behavioral therapy	CBT is one of the most widely used theoretical perspectives due to its multitude of techniques and its evidence base as being helpful with many specific problems clients present in counseling. It is also a helpful approach with clients who require more active, directive, concrete approaches to counseling.

TABLE 15.6 *(Continued)*

Reality therapy	This therapy is applicable in individual, school, group counseling, and other diverse settings. Clients benefit from the focus on responsibility, choice, and positive relationships. The approach provides a logical structure for progress, which clients can readily understand and implement during and post counseling.
Contemporary CBT therapies	Mindfulness and acceptance have received much recent support as being effective in addressing a wide array of issues clients present, and these approaches are frequently used to deal with specific presenting problems. DBT and schema therapy are particularly helpful for individuals with personality disorders, specifically BPD; ACT is particularly helpful in addressing anxiety; and MBCT is particularly helpful in addressing depression. These approaches have wide applicability for a variety of mental health and physical health concerns.
Existential therapy	Existential therapy is particularly useful for people who are managing life transitions or developmental crises; those who are coping with life and death matters, such as grief and loss, terminal illness, or transition between phases of life; or those seeking to live their best lives. It can be useful with individuals, couples, and groups, and in crisis intervention or work with those experiencing traumatic events.
Person-centered therapy	This approach is applicable to nearly all counseling situations, whether they be family interventions and improving relationships, individual or group counseling, community initiatives, or working with culturally diverse populations. The core values of empathy, unconditional positive regard, and genuineness are applied to some extent in almost all other counseling theoretical orientations. The strong research base, which indicates that relationship factors are critical to successful counseling outcomes, suggests this approach is foundational and widely applicable in all helping relationships.
Gestalt therapy	Gestalt therapy can be used effectively with both individuals and groups. The associated techniques are powerful and can help clients connect with their feelings and experiences.
Feminist therapy	Feminist therapy is useful in addressing specific mental health concerns (e.g., eating disorders, body image, sexual objectification, intimate partner violence, childhood sexual abuse, or sexual assault). Feminist therapy can be used with all genders to encourage empowerment.
Postmodern therapies	SFBT and narrative therapy are particularly helpful for people experiencing adjustment issues, or anyone who can benefit from creating a new story. Postmodern approaches can be used in individual, group, couples, family, and school counseling. These approaches can be used with children, adolescents, and adults. Their strength-based focus has wide appeal.
Family systems therapies	Family systems approaches are highly applicable to situations involving conflict within the family, divorce, or relationship dysfunctions. When working with youth with disruptive behaviors, these approaches are helpful. In-home family therapy is useful for youth who have multiple needs and require a greater level of care than outpatient counseling can provide. Couples counseling is helpful when treating those experiencing relationship problems.

Multicultural Counseling

Therapists must be sensitive to cultural issues if they are to best meet clients' needs. Every theory presented in this text is founded on assumptions that are more or less compatible with different cultures' ways of being. Therapists are all challenged to consider the cultural strengths and limitations of each theory and how that theory can be modified for use with those from diverse backgrounds. Some theories are easier to modify than others, depending on the population. In Chapter 1, culture and diversity considerations related to theories were discussed, and this topic was reviewed in each subsequent chapter. In Tables 15.7 and 15.8, multicultural strengths and limitations of the theories are presented.

TABLE 15.7 Multicultural Strengths

Classic Psychoanalysis	Emphasis on family and family dynamics is relevant cross-culturally. Some clients may be more comfortable with a therapist who is more or less distant professionally.
Adlerian therapy	Adlerian theory is considered broadly applicable to individuals from diverse cultures. Its focus on the individual experience and the promotion of prosocial interests and social ties meshes well with many culture-based values from both collectivist and individualistic cultures. The holistic approach, the emphasis on cooperation versus competition, and the acknowledgement of the subjective experiences of clients also lend themselves to working with clients from diverse cultures. The importance of family, goals, and belonging is also applicable to diverse cultures.
Post- and Neo-Freudian therapies	Jung's concepts offer an alternative to conventional therapy that may be compatible with the spiritual and cultural beliefs and behaviors of many diverse clients. Horney's emphasis on unpacking cultural and interpersonal factors and the development of nonlinear systemic connections that are inconsistent with the unconscious assumptions of mainstream Western scientific thought are consistent with today's postmodern belief in the fluidity of subjective and objective reality, and may fit with those from some cultural backgrounds.
Behavior therapy	Behavior therapy models are largely applicable cross-culturally due to their focus on behavioral change, a focus many seeking help desire. Behavior therapy can be particularly applicable for people from cultures who view the expression of emotions as uncomfortable or shameful. The techniques can be modified to fit cultural constraints without jeopardizing the validity of the interventions.
Cognitive behavioral therapy	Collaborative and educational in nature, CBT focuses on how thoughts influence feelings and behaviors, which is an idea generally well received across diverse populations. As a large portion of CBT involves psychoeducation, it is readily tailored to those of different cultural or social backgrounds. CBT is generally brief, with an emphasis on goal completion, and this brevity appeals to those from many cultures.
Reality therapy	This therapy focuses on personal choice influencing clients' lives and its insistence on clients' self-evaluation. Clients can choose to behave based on their cultural beliefs. They can benefit from the focus on personal responsibility that embodies choice theory and the formation of positive relationships.
Contemporary CBT therapies	Therapists who use third-wave CBT approaches respect individual differences, take culture into consideration, honor diversity, and are open to spirituality. The emphasis on mindfulness is consistent with some cultural and religious orientations.
Existential therapy	Existential therapy is based on a universal worldview and is, by its very nature, adaptive to culturally diverse groups. It is founded in matters that relate to the human condition and thus affect all people. Existential therapy is suitable for people from all cultural backgrounds, especially because of its emphasis on finding meaning in life, which is common to all people. The focus on personal responsibility may lead to the empowerment of people who are being oppressed by society.
Person-centered therapy	This approach is widely applicable to diverse populations due to the core values of genuineness, respect, unconditional positive regard, nonjudgmental attitude, openness to differences, and empathy, which are nearly universal across cultures. This approach respects and honors all people and their experiences and perspectives, with a phenomenological focus on clients' experience of their cultural experiences.

TABLE 15.7 (*Continued*)

Gestalt therapy	Gestalt therapists view clients holistically, which makes the approach useful for working with diverse populations. Gestalt therapists take into consideration the impacts of historical and social backgrounds and pay attention to cultural differences. Experiencing beyond words is appropriate for those from cultures in which nonverbal communication is valued or cultures in which emotions are somaticized (i.e., expressed through physical symptoms, such as a stomachache). The associated techniques may be powerful for clients from cultures in which feelings are not typically discussed.
Feminist therapy	Demonstrating feminist therapy's inherent multicultural and social justice roots, feminist therapists tailor the counseling process to attend to the unique needs of persons of color, as well as refugees, immigrants, and individuals who have experienced human rights violations. Other populations include men, LGBTQ (lesbian, gay, bisexual, transgender, queer and/or questioning) persons, couples and families, children and adolescents, persons with disabilities, and indigenous and ethnic communities with an eye to intersectionality.
Postmodern therapies	This approach holds that multiple realities exist and individuals determine their own perceived truth. Clients have the opportunity to explore their beliefs and provide their own meanings. Problems are not within clients but, rather, are social, cultural, relational, and political. Clients' cultural issues are an important part of their reality and clients pull these factors in as they want. Therapists learn from their clients and accept their worldviews, stories, and beliefs.
Family systems therapies	Many cultures focus on and value the family, with extended family sometimes being seen as important members of the family. Family therapy appeals to many from diverse cultural backgrounds, as the family is often considered the primary unit greater than the individual members, and solutions to problems are often believed to exist within the family.

TABLE 15.8 Multicultural Limitations

Classic Psychoanalysis	The emphasis on insight and self-exploration may be alien to some, especially those who are living in poverty or a circumstance where they are in transition or in crisis; many clients desire quick changes, and the length associated with these approaches may be prohibitive. Clients with limited cognitive abilities might have difficulty gaining insight and self-awareness. Some clients do not have the personal characteristics, disposition, or interest that may be required when applying an insight-oriented approach.
Adlerian therapy	The egalitarian nature of the therapeutic alliance may not mesh well with cultures that defer to the expertise of elders and professionals. Western ideas of family structure and growth toward autonomy may conflict with some cultures that do not emphasize the individual experience. Clients who desire a brief, solution-focused counseling experience might lose patience when building insight into early memories and social experiences. Clients with limited cognitive abilities might have difficulty gaining insight into their behavioral motivations. Clients from cultures in which family matters are not shared may feel uncomfortable with this theory's emphasis on childhood experience.
Post- and Neo-Freudian therapies	Techniques such as exploration of childhood experiences, probing, confrontation of maladaptive patterns, and interpretation may be uncomfortable for people from some cultures. A full understanding of an individual's culture may not be congruent with the time-sensitive nature of brief psychodynamic therapy.

(*Continued*)

TABLE 15.8 (*Continued*)

Behavior therapy	Western ideas of empiricism and the linear progression of behavior are not a universal cultural value; many cultures prefer a more holistic form of counseling that examines and cherishes the wholeness of experience. The behaviors associated with behavior therapy (i.e., assertiveness) may not mesh well with some cultures, so an understanding of culture-specific behaviors is essential.
Cognitive behavioral therapy	It is impossible to keep culture out of discussions about what is and is not dysfunctional thinking; cultural appropriateness should always be factored into discussions about cognitions. Collectivist cultures emphasize social harmony, deference to experts, and respect toward elders, which will influence thoughts. Symptomology differs cross-culturally, with some demonstrating physical symptoms more than psychological or emotional ones, and this should be considered in applying this model.
Reality therapy	Counselors should avoid confusing their personal vision of a quality with a client's vision. Western-centric ideals of individualism, as well as the active, directive, sometimes challenging approach and use of direct questions, may be inappropriate in some collectivist cultures.
Contemporary CBT therapies	Concern has been raised over the spiritual aspects of mindfulness-based approaches, as this concept may not resonate with all clients. Some believe that separating mindfulness concepts from the original religious orthodoxy and teachings associated with Eastern religions is culturally disrespectful.
Existential therapy	Opportunities to integrate traditional healing into psychotherapy are challenging because they are comprehensive and concerned with illness prevention as well as cure. In addition, the concept of choice may vary for different cultures, such as those that are collectivist or experience oppression. Oppression can severely limit choices and options. Therapists must tailor their approach when working with diverse clients in general and especially regarding concepts of choice, responsibility, and freedom.
Person-centered therapy	The minimal structuring of this approach may not be appropriate for people from cultures that prize direction and action-oriented interventions from an expert. Collectivist cultures do not share common Western themes of autonomy, individual preference, and self-actualization that are emphasized in person-centered therapy and may not fit with those from all cultural backgrounds. Individuals from cultures that focus on concealing emotions may also feel uncomfortable with the heavy reliance on emotions.
Gestalt therapy	Clients from cultures that value restraint of strong emotions, unassertiveness, or filial piety (i.e., the virtue of respect for one's parents, elders, and ancestors), as do many Asian cultures, may feel uncomfortable or intimidated if therapists use role plays, behavioral rehearsal, or the empty chair technique. Therapists must tailor their approach to respect the needs of clients and their cultural background. The active, directive approach may not be appropriate with people from all cultures, and some may not understand how being aware of experiences and feelings will help them resolve their presenting problems.
Feminist therapy	A major criticism of feminist therapy is that feminist therapists do not take a neutral stance, which may contribute to imposing their own values onto clients. Clients who hold anti-feminist beliefs are not likely to benefit from feminist therapy.

TABLE 15.8 (*Continued*)

Postmodern therapies	Although social and cultural context is assessed during intervention, the focus is on the present and future. The past is not a consideration during the development of solutions, and this may be inconsistent with some cultures. In addition, the not knowing stance of the therapist may make some people from certain cultures lack confidence in the therapist. To correct this issue, it is important for the therapist to explain that clients are the experts in their lives and the therapist is an expert in the therapy process.
Family systems therapies	Concepts related to family boundaries and structure are culturally dependent, and navigating these can be difficult for therapists who are from a different culture than their clients. Concepts such as independence and self-expression may not be consistent with some clients' cultural values. In some cultures, it may be shameful to admit problems at all, and/or it may not be acceptable to discuss family struggles with an outsider.

Closely related to cultural considerations are spirituality and religious considerations in counseling. Spirituality is a part of clients' worldview and culture; thus, therapists must assess the role clients' religion and spirituality might play—or not play—when selecting and applying various theories and techniques. Therapists should never ignore clients' religion or spirituality, and they should always make sure to assess the role this plays in their clients' lives, if any. Spirituality and religious considerations are very important to many clients, and, in fact, for many clients they may be the most important factor influencing their existence, with it defining their beliefs about themselves and their world (Cashwell & Young, 2011). Since many clients' religious and spiritual beliefs provide their foundation, these beliefs can be harnessed, supported, and mobilized to help clients reach their goals. For many clients, their religion or spirituality can offer a great source of comfort during difficult times; it can guide clients when they do not know which direction to head; and it can help clients identify their life's meaning and purpose. It is important for therapists to understand their own thoughts, values, and attitudes concerning spirituality and religion so they can better understand how they might influence or respond to clients who have different ideas (Cashwell & Young, 2011).

Strengths and Limitations of Theories

Every theory has strengths and limitations; there is no theory that is a best theory for all therapists or all clients. Tables 15.9 and 15.10 present the limitations and the contributions of each theory.

One important consideration related to theory selection is the amount of time required to effect change (Hoyt, 2017; Norcross, Hogan, & Koocher, 2008). Therapists, school counselors/psychologists, and all who work with those seeking mental health services are increasingly required to help their clients as quickly as possible. Pressure to be brief comes not only from third-party payers and employers (e.g., schools) but also from clients, as most clients want their problems resolved in as little time as possible. Brief therapy methods can be applied to all of the theories discussed in this text, some more readily than others, of course (Hoyt, 2017).

Providers are also increasingly called upon to demonstrate effectiveness of their methods. Again, some of the theories discussed in this text lend themselves to measurement and evaluation, whereas the effectiveness of some other theories may be more difficult to determine. For example, behavior therapy has as its focus behavioral change that can readily be measured, whereas postmodern approaches have as their focus subjective client perceptions of change. Both outcomes are meaningful; it is just that one outcome is easier to objectively determine than the other.

TABLE 15.9 Limitations of the Theory

Classic Psychoanalysis	Psychoanalysis is a time-intensive and costly process. The approach is not designed to help people experiencing immediate, pressing concerns, and it may not pay adequate attention to multicultural dimensions. The slowly paced nature of the process; the relatively passive role of the client and therapist; and the emphasis on sexuality, early childhood, and the unconscious make the approach a poor choice for some clients. Freud's psychosexual stages theory has been criticized and may not resonate with some. Freud also advanced some erroneous and harmful ideas about women.
Adlerian therapy	Adlerian therapy is dynamic and has many facets, which makes it hard to empirically validate. Many of the concepts are not well defined and attempts to operationalize the concepts can lead to losing the content and oversimplification. Adlerian therapy may oversimplify complex human experiences.
Post- and Neo-Freudian therapies	Because the concepts are complicated and sometimes abstract, they are hard to measure, making it difficult to assess their efficacy. These theories are involved, and they can be difficult to understand and apply, as the language is complex and abstract.
Behavior therapy	Some believe that behavior therapy may be overly focused on behaviors and not focused enough on insight, emotional experiences, and other dimensions that may be important to some clients. Symptom substitution may result from treating symptoms rather than addressing underlying causes of behavior. Behavior therapists may be perceived as being too active and even controlling by some clients.
Cognitive behavioral therapy	CBT does not focus on gaining insight, unless it is around individuals' cognitive processes or behaviors per se. CBT may also concentrate too little on emotions or clients' background experiences. In addition, CBT may be too structured and active for some clients, and its expectation that clients engage in between-session work may not fit for all clients.
Reality therapy	Reality therapy does not attend to a client's past, unconscious, or early childhood experiences. Exploring a client's history can add value to the therapeutic process, and this approach only focuses on the present. The approach centers primarily on simple problems and pays little attention to more complex ones. It relies heavily on problem solving and negates the value of exploring deeper issues and understanding of emotional experiences.
Contemporary CBT therapies	These approaches are not for everyone, as clients must be active participants in the counseling process, and actively engage in therapy and take ownership of their change process. Clients are expected to practice skills outside of therapy and apply what they have learned. Therapists must also have extensive training to use these approaches effectively, as they are complex and involved.
Existential therapy	Many of the key concepts are not defined well and are abstract, making the theory difficult to understand and apply in a real-life setting. This approach does not meet the needs of clients who are nonverbal and those in crisis. The techniques cannot be used in a planned or methodical way.
Person-centered therapy	Therapists do not offer clear direction, which may cause some clients to feel uncomfortable. Some clients may require a more directive approach, active techniques, and more structure than this approach offers. Clients may need concrete guidance, especially those in crisis.
Gestalt therapy	Associated techniques can be powerful, and if strong feelings are not explored, debriefed, and integrated cognitively, clients may be left feeling unsettled and not integrated. The focus on bodily sensations may oversimplify and neglect cognitions. Some clients may feel uncomfortable with experiential approaches. Some clients may not have the capacity for creativity and imagination that is required to benefit form Gestalt experiments.

TABLE 15.9 *(Continued)*

Feminist therapy	Therapists need to be careful not to impose feminist values onto clients, such as equality or equal power in relationships, or social change values. Clients are the experts on their own lives, and it is essential to explore and validate clients' own values. The imposing of therapists' personal values or beliefs onto clients can be harmful and reduce multicultural competence.
Postmodern therapies	Implementations of postmodern therapies seem easy; however, therapists must be highly experienced to artfully apply these approaches. Concepts may be too simplistic and overgeneralized for some, and some clients may seek a more directive approach, wanting therapists to provide more guidance or teach them skills.
Family systems therapies	Family therapy is sometimes viewed as its own field, with a separate language of its own. Administrative issues may arise, such as the difficulty of scheduling appointments with multiple people, increased record keeping, and concerns about confidentiality. It can be challenging to involve all family members in the change process. Family therapists must have awareness of and willingness to work on their own family issues.

TABLE 15.10 Contributions of the Theory

Classic Psychoanalysis	Freud's personality development concepts are acknowledged today. Most of us acknowledge the importance of childhood experiences, understand the major role that sexuality plays in development, recognize the powerful influence of parent figures in our lives, and assume that dreams and slips are often meaningful. We also recognize the healing power of the therapeutic relationship, believe that talk therapy can be a powerful vehicle for promoting positive change, and are optimistic that counseling can help most people to lead more productive and rewarding lives.
Adlerian therapy	Adler's concepts have greatly influenced many theories of psychotherapy and can easily be integrated into other theories. This theory is dynamic, in that it addresses individual- and social-level factors, and it is holistic, comprehensive, and goal directed. Our growing awareness of the enduring harm that can result from childhood trauma has focused attention on the significance to adults of their early childhood experiences and memories. Adler's call for social equality of women, respect for cultural and religious diversity, and an end to marginalization of minority groups is important. Probably of greatest importance is Adler's emphasis on respect for individual differences and the importance of each of us becoming a contributing part of a larger social system.
Post- and Neo-Freudian therapies	These theories address the important role of early life experiences in shaping future experiences and relationships. These theories have wide applicability to understanding those who have personality disorders. Compared to traditional psychoanalysis, these approaches de-emphasize the importance of sexuality, which is attractive to many. In addition, these theories were the first to introduce child analysis and to address how to help children.
Behavior therapy	Behavior therapy has emphasized the importance of research on counseling effectiveness. Behavior therapy has also provided a foundation for the development of numerous other approaches. Behavior therapy is specific and concrete, which helps clients move from unclear goals toward plans and action. Therapists explore the historical roots and antecedents of people's concerns, are sensitive to individual differences, develop positive and collaborative therapeutic alliances, and seek to know and understand their clients as individuals. The positive outcomes of behavior therapy tend to be enduring.

(Continued)

TABLE 15.10 (*Continued*)

Cognitive behavioral therapy	CBT is associated with many cognitive, behavioral, and emotive techniques, and evidence suggests its effectiveness with many diverse presenting issues and in treating people who have a variety of mental disorders. CBT is also easily integrated with other approaches. CBT is present focused, time efficient, and teaches clients how to be their own therapists.
Reality therapy	Reality therapy is positive, action oriented, short term, and direct. The concepts are well defined and easy to understand. This approach can be applied to a wide variety of concerns and settings. Many helping professionals, such as teachers, educators, counselors, and nurses, can use this approach. Reality therapy can be applied to diverse populations, and many appreciate its focus on action.
Contemporary CBT therapies	The focus on experiencing and accepting emotions and thoughts may fit well with people who are struggling to let go of something. Mindfulness has become an increasingly popular and effective skill that clients can access at any time, and it has a strong research base. The focus of exploring ingrained approaches to the world and providing necessary tools to improve wellness and overall functioning is also important. These approaches are also culturally sensitive and focus on context. The changes that clients make are demonstrated to be long lasting. These approaches are also manualized, have a collaborative nature, are easily integrated with other approaches, and are applicable to a wide range of people and problems.
Existential therapy	The phenomenological and holistic view of this approach is particularly meaningful. Its philosophical standpoint makes a positive contribution to what it means to be a human. Concepts such as anxiety, freedom, death, and isolation provide a beneficial perspective to common life experiences, and they are experiences all people navigate.
Person-centered therapy	Clients assume responsibility and take control of their session. This approach has been empirically supported by research. It is the foundation for all therapeutic relationships, and the conditions are used in all theoretical orientations. It has contributed greatly to the positive psychology movement and has influenced and informed many other theorists/theories.
Gestalt therapy	The concentration on experiencing thoughts, emotions, and behaviors, as opposed to talking *about* feelings, thoughts, and actions, may be helpful to many clients. The associated techniques are easily adapted to fit with other theoretical approaches. The focus on awareness can be powerful; it can help clients be more present and enhance their overall growth and development, not just address the issues that are initially presented in counseling.
Feminist therapy	This approach can be used to empower women to voice their concerns about gender stereotypes and the way gender is used to gain power in relationships. Therapists using this approach are sensitive to gender and to those who have experienced discrimination. The feminist movement has raised awareness about topics such as child abuse, rape, incest, and domestic violence. Feminist therapy is easily integrated with other approaches, and the principles can be used as a framework for almost any interaction with clients.
Postmodern therapies	These approaches are easily integrated into other types of therapies. Views are more optimistic and uplifting, with greater emphasis placed on solutions, hope, and strengths. Clients are seen as the expert, which may suit the needs of many clients.
Family systems therapies	The systemic perspective offers a new way of viewing families in that all members are contributing to the problem. Family approaches tend to be empowering, strengths based, and easily integrated. Family therapy approaches have shown effectiveness for a wide variety of people and presenting concerns.

FUTURE DIRECTIONS IN COUNSELING AND PSYCHOTHERAPY

The following trends and issues are likely to impact the direction of systems and strategies of counseling and psychotherapy in the 21st century (Kress & Paylo, 2019; Prochaska & Norcross, 2018):

- Cultural competence will become the norm as therapists attend to their own, as well as their clients', worldviews. Background, culture, religion and philosophy, ability, age, and gender are important aspects of people's social location and must be integrated into any efforts to tailor therapy to meet the needs of individuals.
- As research methods evolve, providers will develop a better sense of what theories or interventions may be most effective in addressing different presenting issues. In other words, counselors will get better at answering the critical question: "*What* treatment, by *whom*, is most effective for *this* individual with *that* specific problem under *which* set of circumstances?" (Paul, 1967, p. 111).
- Attention to the contributions of biology and neurophysiology to emotional health and development will increase. Assessments such as magnetic resonance imaging (MRI) and functional MRI (fMRI) will find more frequent application in diagnosis. Researchers may better identify when and how psychotropic medications may be useful.
- The use of telemental health counseling will continue to develop and expand. Legal and ethical guidelines will evolve to regulate the use of technology in the counseling profession. Therapists who use online counseling, Skype, virtual reality, e-mail, text messaging, and social media will need to stay current with federal, state, and local laws regarding insurance reimbursement, confidentiality, and privacy requirements.
- Recognition of childhood antecedents to adult mental disorders will lead to the development of earlier prevention programs. Counselors all play a role in the advocacy of such programs, as they prevent the development of future problems.
- Managed care will continue to focus on accountability. Many federal, state, and military funding agencies already require the use of empirically supported treatments as a prerequisite of reimbursement for services. For better or worse, the medical model will continue, and therapists will be expected to use evidence-based practices if they want to be eligible for third-party reimbursement.
- In the future, an increasing number of therapists will elect not to participate in insurance plans, as managed care systems continue to exert influence over therapeutic decision making, require manualized care, set therapy guidelines, and track therapist effectiveness.
- Research will continue to focus on and clarify the common elements across counseling approaches that are linked to counseling success.
- Not only will a positive and collaborative therapeutic alliance continue to be one of the most important elements of successful therapy, but also research into the specific factors that foster an effective and collaborative alliance will increase.
- New models of psychotherapy will be proposed, theoretical integration will expand, and many existing theories will be further refined.
- With increasing recognition of the negative lifelong effects of childhood trauma, neglect, and abuse, attachment-related and trauma-based therapies will grow in importance and use.
- Postmodern and other nonlinear approaches will continue to influence conceptions of counseling and psychotherapy and are increasingly likely to be integrated into other counseling approaches.
- Spirituality and religion will be integrated into the assessment, conceptualization, and practice of all different types of counseling, as clients seek to find holistic therapies that focus on mind, body, and spirit.

- Eastern-influenced philosophies and the tools of mindfulness meditation, acceptance, and compassion (loving kindness) will be integrated into counseling approaches as a way to reduce stress and provide a holistic approach to counseling.
- Collaborations between school counselors and mental health therapists will increase in an effort to address problems of school violence, suicide, and crisis management.
- Counseling and psychotherapy will continue to be important in helping people cope with problems and emotional difficulties, in part because the value of mental health counseling has been so well established and in part because research and holistic thinking will extend the breadth of its reach.

REFLECT AND RESPOND

1. By now, you probably have learned a great deal about yourself as a therapist. In your journal, list three counseling strengths that you believe you have. List three areas in which you think you need to improve your counseling skills. List three topics in this book that you would like to study further. Identify the first steps you could take in improving your skills and continuing your learning.
2. Identify the exercise or learning experience in this book that has been most interesting or enlightening for you. Write briefly in your journal about what made that experience so meaningful.
3. After reading this book, you have a good idea about different theories, how to apply those theories, and which style fits you the best. In the beginning of the book, you were asked to write a letter to your future self as a therapist. Using that as a guide and knowing what you know now after reading the chapters, did anything change? Write a reflection on this and follow the questions below:
   - Did anything in your letter change?
   - How do you see yourself fitting with specific theories?
   - Did your vision of your future therapist self change after reading this book?
4. Self-care is very important to practice. It is vital to be aware of signs of stress and burnout. These signs might include cognitive, behavioral, and emotional red flags. By creating a personalized action plan, you can become more self-aware of your needs, along with how they can be handled. Develop a self-care plan, taking into account the following:
   1. Signs I am becoming burned out:
   2. Emotions during times of stress:
   3. Contact list for people I depend on for support:
   4. Sources of professional support (e.g., professors, peers):
   5. Places I go to calm myself down:
   6. Activities I enjoy:
5. Some therapists care for others but neglect themselves. It is important that you are intentional in engaging in self-care to prevent burnout. To increase intentionality, therapists may benefit from "depositing" at least one self-care strategy daily into the bank to build a savings for "wellness." Decorate a container to use as a piggy bank. Prior to beginning the activity and starting to put "funds" into the piggy bank, brainstorm and create a list of potential self-care strategies in which you engage in each day. At the end of each day, reflect on what self-care strategy you engaged in and write it on a piece of paper and place it in the "bank." At the

end of each week, review the self-care strategies placed in the "bank" and reflect on the most helpful strategies as well as additional strategies that could be included. The goal is to create a ritual that allows for the intentional daily engagement in self-care strategies and reflection on the strategies.

Summary

This chapter addressed integration of theories and provided several examples of integrated theories. A majority of therapists report that their primary theoretical orientation is an integrative or eclectic approach. Integrated approaches are grounded in theory and seek to combine and blend multiple counseling strategies into a unique whole that is more than the sum of its parts. Eclecticism, in contrast, lacks a unifying theory but is practical, providing a prototype or structure for selecting and applying interventions drawn from many approaches to counseling and psychotherapy. An increase in research on the common factors that exist in therapies across all theoretical orientations has provided additional support for the development of systems that allow therapists to create tailored experiences for clients that address the seminal question of what works best for whom, in the here and now of the therapy session.

As Lazarus predicted decades ago, technical integration of different modes of therapy is becoming the new worldview in psychotherapy. We expect to see the development of even newer integrated approaches in the areas of religion and spirituality, multicultural psychotherapy, and common factors approaches to counseling in the not too distant future.

In this chapter, information about a broad range of approaches to counseling and psychotherapy was also synthesized and summarized. The questions posed in this chapter can help therapists identify their preferred approaches to counseling, as can the exercises designed to facilitate professional growth. This chapter also reviewed trends expected to have an impact on counseling and psychotherapy in the future.

Counseling is an exciting profession. Helping others can be quite rewarding and fulfilling. As a therapist, you are never finished growing—there are perpetual opportunities to grow and learn more. I hope that this text has helped you to learn more about the important counseling theories, skills, and strategies you can use to help others. However, like any book on counseling theories, it can give you only an introduction to these approaches. The counseling field is constantly changing, and I strongly encourage you to continue to study and practice these counseling approaches through additional reading, continuing education, supervised experience, peer feedback, and research on your own practice.

Therapists do very important work, work that can make a great difference in the lives of individuals, groups, families, and even societies. I hope you will treasure and honor the trust that people put in you and will do your best to use your skills to do good for others. I also hope this book will help you to keep the energy and spirit of the mental health professions alive in your work.

Recommended Readings

Hill, C. E. (2014). *Helping skills: Facilitating exploration, insight, and action* (4th ed.). Washington, DC: American Psychological Association.

Lazarus, A. A. (2006). *Brief but comprehensive psychotherapy: The multimodal way.* New York, NY: Springer.

Lazarus, A. A. (2008). Technical eclecticism and multimodal therapy. In J. L. Lebow (Ed.), *Twenty-first century psychotherapies: Contemporary approaches to theory and practice* (pp. 424–452). Hoboken, NJ: John Wiley & Sons.

Schneider, K. (2008). *Existential-integrative psychotherapy: Guideposts to the core of practice*. New York, NY: Routledge.

Teyber, E., & McClure, F. H. (2011). *Interpersonal process in therapy: An integrative model* (6th ed.). Belmont, CA: Thomson/Brooks Cole.

Wachtel, P. L. (2011). *Inside the session: What really happens in psychotherapy*. Washington, DC: American Psychological Association.

Also recommended is the *Journal of Psychotherapy Integration*.

MyLab Counseling

Start with the Topic 9 Assignments: Integrative.

Then try the Topic 12 Assignments: Multimodal Therapy.

Finish with the Topic 20 Assignments: Transtheoretical.

GLOSSARY

A-B-C Model (REBT) The original model for the current A-B-C-D-E-F model that has evolved to include new components. The A-B-C model originally included activating events, consequences, and beliefs. Therapists used these three components for psychoeducational purposes and to conceptualize and identify clients' problems.

A-B-C-D-E-F model (REBT) A structured, psychoeducational model for identifying, assessing, disputing, and modifying beliefs which includes: Activating events; Beliefs; Consequences of having these beliefs; Disputing these beliefs; Effect of having new rational beliefs; and, Feeling a new, improved way.

Abreaction (Psychoanalysis) The release or purge of previously repressed emotions through relived experiences.

Acceptance (Contemporary CBT) A willingness to experience psychological events (i.e., thoughts, feelings, memories) without having to avoid them or let them unduly influence behavior.

Acceptance (Person-Centered) Accepting clients for who they are without judgment.

Acting as if (Adlerian Therapy) Having the client enact the best possible outcome to create a new experience or outlook.

Acting out (Psychoanalysis) A defense mechanism that operates by exhibiting negative behaviors rather than using thoughts or emotions to deal with a situation.

Affiliation (Psychoanalysis) A healthy defense mechanism that involves turning to others for help and support, but retaining responsibility for one's own difficulties.

Aha response (Adlerian Therapy) When the client "catches oneself," the client may have an "aha" moment by developing sudden insight into a solution.

Alienation (Gestalt) One polarity of the ego boundary; when people believe that some characteristics only belong to others and not themselves.

Alignment (Family Therapy) Family members join or oppose each other when handling situations.

Alliance (Family Therapy) Connection and support with another person in the family subsystem.

All-or-nothing thinking (Cognitive Therapy) A cognitive distortion that involves thinking in extremes, rather than on a continuum, or attending to "black and white" thinking, such as all good or all bad.

Alternative stories (Narrative Therapy) Focusing on the strengths, positive aspects, and helpful outcomes of the story rather than a problem outcome, thus creating a new, preferred story. These are lost, untold, or marginalized stories that may serve people better than their dominant stories, particularly if the lost stories portray a life in which problems are either solved or absent.

Altruism (Psychoanalysis) A healthy defense mechanism in which people derive satisfaction from investing heavily in helping others.

Anal stage (Psychoanalysis) The second stage in personality development, which is focused on the anus, whereby the child obtains pleasure from elimination. Fixation at this stage can lead to personalities such as *anal retentive* (i.e., one who hates mess, is obsessively tidy, punctual, and respectful of authority) or *anal explosive* (i.e., one who is messy, disorganized, and rebellious).

Anima (Neoanalytic/Post-Freud) In Jung's theory, the archetype representing the feminine component of the male personality.

Animus (Neoanalytic/Post-Freud) In Jung's theory, the archetype representing the masculine component of the female personality.

Antecedent-Behavior-Consequence (ABC) Model (Behavior Therapy) A descriptive assessment that is conducted as an initial part of a complete functional behavior assessment. The goal of this analysis is to develop a hypothesis regarding the function that a problem behavior serves for an individual.

Anticathexes (Psychoanalysis) The control of the ego over the id to keep id impulses out of consciousness.

Anticipation (Psychoanalysis) A healthy defense mechanism used to reduce anxiety by considering the probable consequences of future events and finding ways to address them effectively.

Anxiety hierarchy (Behavior Therapy) Listing fears in ascending order from the mildest fear to the most frightening, using a subjective units of distress scale.

Applied Behavior Analysis (ABA; Behavior Therapy) A therapy technique that involves applying techniques based upon the principles of learning to change behavior.

Appropriate emotions (REBT) Emotions that are transient, manageable, in proportion to the stimulus, and enhancing of self-acceptance.

Archetypes (Neoanalytic/Post-Freud) In Jung's theory, these are universal images or symbols that are pathways from the collective unconscious to the conscious.

Assent (Ethics) Typically used when counseling children who are too young to give legal informed consent, assent refers to a minor's willingness to participate in counseling after being versed on the possible benefits/risks, and the activities expected of them as subjects.

Assertiveness training (Behavior Therapy) A technique used to teach clients to empower themselves and to effectively express positive and negative feelings to others.

Assessing motivation (Solution-Focused Brief Therapy) Therapists pay attention to the degree of client motivation to make changes. Assessing motivation can be done effectively through the use of scaling questions.

Assets (Adlerian Therapy) The strengths of an individual's lifestyle.

Attachment theory (Neoanalytic/Post-Freud) A set of concepts that explain the emergence of an emotional bond between an infant and primary caregiver and the way in which this bond affects the child's behavioral and emotional development into adulthood.

Attitudes (Neoanalytic/Post-Freud) In Jung's theory, these are the way the psyche interacts with the world; includes extraversion and introversion.

Authenticity (Existential) Being genuine, real, and aware of one's being. Those who are authentic consider and navigate the meaning of life, moral choices, and their innate humanness.

Automatic thoughts (Cognitive Therapy) "Pop up" thoughts that come to mind without conscious thought, usually in response to a trigger or activating event.

Aversive stimulus (Behavior Therapy) A frightening or unpleasant stimulus used to decrease the strength of a fear response or decrease the likelihood of an undesirable behavior happening in the future.

Avoidance (Psychoanalysis) A defense mechanism that involves refusing to deal with negative situations or experiences that provoke anxiety.

Avoiding the tar baby (Adlerian Therapy) Not falling into the trap of the client's faulty assumptions or not getting stuck in clients' perception of the problem.

Awareness (Gestalt) Knowledge and observation of what is happening in the present.

Basic mistakes (Adlerian Therapy) Self-defeating aspects of individuals' lifestyle that may affect their later behavior. Such mistakes often include avoidance of others, seeking power, a desperate need for security, or faulty values.

Behavioral activation (Contemporary CBT) Technique used in behavior activation therapy that involves increasing pleasurable activities on a daily basis; typically used to help break the cycle of isolation and depression.

Behavioral rehearsal (Behavior Therapy) Practicing a behavior clients wish to develop which gives them an opportunity to practice new behaviors they have perhaps witnessed or want to engage in.

Behaviorism (Behavior Therapy) The theory that behavior can be explained by conditioning, without emphasis on thoughts or feelings, and that psychological disorders are best treated by changing behavior.

Bibliotherapy (Behavior Therapy) The use of books in therapy to supplement therapists' efforts to teach new skills to clients, such as assertiveness, time management, and parenting.

Biofeedback (Behavior Therapy) Involves the use of instruments that monitor bodily functions such as heart rate, sweat gland activity, skin temperature, and pulse rate and give people feedback on those functions via a tone or light.

Birth order (Adlerian Therapy) The idea that order of birth—first born, second born, third, and so on—can potentially have an impact on one's later personality and relationship functioning.

Blank-screen approach (Psychoanalysis) An anonymous stance to facilitate transference, which allows clients to project feelings for another person onto the therapist, thereby helping them to work through unresolved feelings.

Boundaries (Family Therapy) Emotional or physical barriers between people.

Boundary marking (Family Therapy) A technique to alter interactions among individual family members.

Boundary permeability (Family Therapy) Boundaries can be flexible or "permeable" among individual family members, allowing connections and adaptation to be made.

CARE acronym (Adlerian Therapy) An acronym that stands for catch, assess, respond, and execute, that can be used by therapists to help parents interact with youth from an Adlerian perspective.

Castration anxiety (Psychoanalysis) The fear of losing one's penis or having one's penis damaged.

Catastrophizing (Cognitive Therapy) Exaggerating the consequences of an event, therefore becoming fearful of the worst possible outcome.

Catching oneself (Adlerian Therapy) Having the client "catch oneself" in the client's own irrational experiences.

Catharsis (Psychoanalysis) Previously repressed feelings that are expressed.

Challenging absolutes (Cognitive Therapy) Statements that are usually exaggerations (i.e., never, no one) that therapists make clients become aware of.

Choice theory (Reality Therapy) The view that humans are internally motivated and behave to control the world around them according to some purpose within them. We are basically self-determining and create our own destiny.

Circular causality (Family Therapy) A type of reciprocal influence that goes beyond linear causality to identify a long-standing, complex spiral of interactions that includes all family dynamics and can become problematic across time.

Circular questioning (Family Therapy) An interviewing technique used to draw out different perceptions and views about events or relationships from each family member.

Classical conditioning (Behavior Therapy) A type of learning in which a neutral stimulus is presented repeatedly with one that elicits a specific response so the neutral stimulus eventually elicits the response by itself.

Client-Centered Therapy (Person-Centered) Newer term for person-centered therapy that reflected Rogers' realization that counseling cannot, and probably should not, be completely nondirective. Rogers' ideas evolved in that he saw the therapist's role as more active and important and believed that by communicating accurate empathy, congruence, and unconditional positive regard, therapists create an environment that is conducive to helping people make positive changes.

Coalition (Family Therapy) Alliances between family members against another family member.

Cognitive distortions (CBT) Ways that our mind convince us that something is true when it is not, which reinforce negative thinking, emotions, and behavior. Evaluating and modifying thoughts, if necessary, can lead to healthier emotions and behaviors.

Cognitive model (Cognitive Therapy) Beck's cognitive therapy is based on the cognitive model which holds that the way individuals perceive a situation is more closely connected to their reaction than the situation itself.

Cognitive rehearsal (Cognitive Therapy) A technique in which people mentally rehearse a new behavior and then create a cognitive model of themselves successfully performing that behavior; practicing ways to handle a situation or problem.

Cognitive restructuring (CBT) Modifying cognitions by finding words to express their new cognitions accurately, realistically, and in ways that are compatible with their emotions.

Cognitive schema (Cognitive Therapy) Patterns of thoughts and behaviors that coincide with a set of core beliefs and assumptions about society.

Cognitive triad (Cognitive Therapy) The negative views that individuals have about themselves, their world, and their future.

Collective unconscious (Neoanalytic/Post-Freud) In Jung's theory, this is the part of the unconscious that contains memories and images that are universal to the human species.

Commitment (Reality Therapy) The act of sticking to a realistic plan aimed at change.

Committed action (Contemporary CBT) Setting goals according to values and carrying them out in a responsible way.

Common factors (Effective Counseling) All counseling approaches share common factors which that explain the effectiveness and importance of counseling.

Community feeling (Adlerian Therapy) A sense that one belongs to and is connected to all of humanity and committed to making the world a better place.

Competence (Effective Counseling) Possessing the knowledge, skills, and diligence required to effectively function and meet professional expectations and standards.

Complexes (Neoanalytic/Post-Freud) In Jung's theory, this is a group of associated feelings, thoughts, and memories that have intense emotional content, which may be a part of the personal unconscious and collective unconscious.

Concentration technique (Psychoanalysis) Patients lay down with their eyes closed while Freud placed his hand on their foreheads and urged them to say whatever thoughts arose (now called free association).

Conditional positive regard (Person-Centered) Receiving praise, attention, or approval from others as a result of behaving in accordance with others' expectations.

Conditioned stimulus (Behavior Therapy) In classical conditioning, a previously neutral stimulus that eventually triggers a conditioned response after being paired with the conditioned stimulus.

Conditions of worth (Person-Centered) Judgmental and critical messages that give children the message that they are only worthwhile and lovable if they think, feel, and act in ways that meet the needs of others; children may act in certain ways that are incongruent with who they really are in order to receive other people's love, acceptance, and positive regard.

Confluence (Gestalt) Blurring the differentiation between one's self and others; as people try to blend in and get along with others, this may manifest as slowness to anger, an absence of interpersonal conflicts, and a belief that everyone experiences the same feelings and thoughts.

Confrontation (Adlerian Therapy and Reality Therapy) Facing the conflict head on.

Congruence (Person-Centered) Genuineness with a client that contributes to the establishment of a positive therapeutic relationship; one of the three core conditions.

Conjoint therapy (Family Therapy) Therapy in which two or more people are treated together.

Conscious (Psychoanalysis) Significant material we are fully aware of.

Conscious suppression (Psychoanalysis) A healthy defense mechanism that involves intentionally avoiding paying attention to nonproductive and troubling issues, experiences, and emotions.

Consciousness-raising (Feminist Therapy) A form of activism, often occurring in a group setting, that involves people becoming more aware of experienced oppression due to cultural norms, rather than their individual deficits.

Constructivism (Postmodern approaches) The belief that individuals create their own views, constructs of events, and relationships in their own lives based on their own perceptions and experiences.

Constructivists (Postmodern approaches) Therapists who pay attention to meanings that their clients give to their experiences and problems, and how clients make sense of and relate to their experience of their problems.

Contact (Gestalt) The relationship between oneself and others in the world; involves seeing, hearing, smelling, touching, and moving, and healthy contact involves interacting with our environment and others without losing one's sense of individuality.

Contingency contract (Behavior Therapy) A behavior contract such as a written agreement between the therapist and the client that specifies the target behavior and the consequence that will follow.

Contingency management (Behavior Therapy) Based on the behavioral principle that if a behavior is reinforced or rewarded, it is more likely to occur in the future. The systematic delivery of reinforcing or punishing consequences contingent on the occurrence of a target response, and the withholding of those consequences in the absence of a target response (e.g., a client receiving methadone treatment for a heroin addiction is provided with take-home methadone privileges for maintaining a long period of abstinence).

Control theory (Reality Therapy) The early and no longer used term for choice theory. The theory that individuals try to control the world and themselves and others as a part of that world to satisfy their psychological needs.

Coping questions (Narrative Therapy) Coping questions focus on the successful experiences that clients have had when handling an issue.

Core belief (Cognitive Therapy) Central ideas about ourselves and the world that underlie many of our automatic thoughts and usually are reflected in our intermediate beliefs.

Cost-benefit analysis (Cognitive Therapy) This technique gives clients the opportunity to gain awareness about the advantages and disadvantages of a decision or a behavior in order to have a better understanding of which direction to take.

Counterconditioning (Behavior Therapy) Pairing the behavior with a strong, incompatible response to the same cue to change the behavior and reverse the habit.

Countertransference (Psychoanalysis) When the therapist transfers feelings onto the client.

Covert behaviors (Behavior Therapy) Behaviors that others cannot directly perceive or see.

Covert modeling (Behavior Therapy) A behavioral technique in which a client mentally rehearses or pictures a person behaving a certain way, imagines themselves behaving in this way, and then imagines the favorable consequences of the behavior.

Cybernetics (Family Therapy) The study of processes that occur in systems.

Cyclical psychodynamic–behavior therapy (Integrative) A theoretical integration approach to psychotherapy, developed by Paul Wachtel, that is based on the idea that psychological problems create problems in behavior, and problems in behavior create psychological conflicts or problems.

Dasein (being-in-the-world; Existential) Refers to an awareness and examination of oneself, others; a sense of oneself as distinct and autonomous. A strong sense of being is important for the development of a healthy personality.

DEAR MAN GIVE FAST (Contemporary CBT) An acronym DBT therapists use with clients to teach a variety of nuanced social skills that encourage interpersonal effectiveness.

Decatastrophizing (Cognitive Therapy) A technique in which clients are asked about a "what if" scenario such as, "what if ____ happened, what would you do?" to identify the most negative possible outcome or interpretation of a cognition and then assess its likelihood, probable impact, and possible solutions.

Decentering (Contemporary CBT) Also known as diffusion in ACT, this is the process of maintaining a degree of separation from inner experiences, such as thoughts, feelings, or perceptions, and recognizing such experiences as mental processes rather than facts or truth.

Defense mechanisms (Psychoanalysis) Ways we behave or think to protect ourselves from conflict or anxiety; ways the ego fights off instinctual outbursts of the id or warnings that come from the superego.

Deflection (Gestalt) A form of resistance that involves avoiding direct contact by breaking the mood, shifting attention, or changing the subject.

Defusion (Contemporary CBT) The ability to "step back" and separate from thoughts and language.

Denial (Psychoanalysis) A defense mechanism that involves ignoring an aspect of reality, which is evident to others.

Depressive position (Neoanalytic/Post-Freud) In object relations theory, this position reflects people's concern that images of and connections with the internalized objects are threatened by internal conflicts; the depressive position is characterized by the defense of regression; people in this position focus on emotions such as love, understanding, empathy, and reparation of the internalized object.

Dereflection (Existential) A therapeutic technique in which clients focus away from their problems instead of on them in an attempt to reduce anxiety.

Detriangulation (Family Therapy) A technique used in Bowenian therapy to separate parts of the triangle by working with clients directly.

Development (Effective Counseling) A growth process that involves cognitive, physical, social, personal, and emotional maturity.

Dialectics (Contemporary CBT) A DBT concept which involves accepting that two simultaneous yet opposing truths can be true at the same time.

Diaphragmatic breathing (Behavior Therapy) A relaxation technique that involves taking slow, deep breaths and focusing on the breath. People breathe in through the nose, expanding the diaphragm, and then expel the air through the mouth.

Differentiation of self (Family Therapy) A balance between emotions and cognitions that leaves one with healthy boundaries that are not too rigid and not too permeable. A person who is differentiated will resist participation in dysfunctional family patterns.

Diffusion (Family Therapy) Boundaries are established and individual family members can think in terms of "I" rather than "we." Similar to differentiation and is the opposite of fusion.

Disengaged (Family Therapy) Family members are not able to make meaningful connections with their family members, and therefore lack the guidance and support that all people require.

Disengagement (Family Therapy) The process, found in rigid family systems, in which one or more members withdraw and feel unconnected from the day-to-day family transactions.

Displacement (Psychoanalysis) A defense mechanism that involves transferring strong feelings from the situation in which they originated to a less threatening situation.

Dissociation (Psychoanalysis) A defense mechanism that involves temporarily disconnecting from a situation and experiencing memory loss or loss of awareness.

Distress tolerance (Contemporary CBT) A DBT skill which involves clients learning how to accept and tolerate distress. Categorized into two primary domains: self-soothing skills, which are intended to combat intense emotions and physiological sensations and assist clients with letting go of distress; and distraction skills clients use when they are unable to practice radical acceptance or when letting go of intense emotions does not seem possible.

Dominant story (Narrative Therapy) Unhelpful, problem-saturated stories that people tell themselves and that keep them stuck and unsatisfied.

Double bind (Family Therapy) When an individual receives an important message with two different meanings and is unable to respond to it, the individual is in an impossible situation or a "bind."

Dream analysis (Psychoanalysis) When clients recount the latent and manifest content of a dream and therapists interpret the dream.

Drive (Psychoanalysis) A physiological state of tension, such as hunger, sex, or elimination, that motivates an individual.

Dyad (Family Therapy) A two-person relationship; consists of two family members who interact in a unique way.

Dynamics (Family Therapy) Interactional patterns of a family, which include the ways in which members' rules, beliefs, values, and experiences are expressed within the household and within the larger society as a whole.

Dysfunctional thought record (Cognitive Therapy) A self-monitoring log that facilitates identification and modification of thoughts, feelings, and behaviors.

Early maladaptive schemas (Contemporary CBT) In schema therapy, these are unhelpful schemas that individuals assume to be true about themselves and their world.

Early recollections (Adlerian Therapy) Memories of actual incidents that clients recall from their childhood.

EARS (Solution-Focused Brief Therapy) A mnemonic device that stands for **E**licit exceptions, **A**mplify exceptions, **R**einforce client's successes, and **S**tart again and that therapists use to help clients achieve their goals.

Egalitarian (Feminist Therapy) A psychotherapy relationship model based on the belief that power should be balanced between the client and counselor.

Ego (or contact) boundaries (Gestalt) People establish a relationship with their surrounding environment, and this relationship defines a boundary. This boundary is what allows a distinction to be made between self and non-self, but it is also the area where contact takes place. Relationships with other people are made at this boundary. The boundaries distinguish one individual, an object, another individual, or another aspect of oneself.

Ego (Psychoanalysis) The part of the personality structure that seeks to please the id's drive in a realistic way and serves as a "mediator" between the id and the superego.

Ego anxiety (REBT) When individuals' sense of self-worth is threatened and they feel they must perform well.

Eigenwelt (Existential) Refers to being aware of oneself and how we relate to ourselves. How we relate to our own subjective world.

Electra complex (Psychoanalysis) A term used to describe a young girl's sense of competition with her mother for the affections of her father, thus leading to her adopting the sex characteristics of her mother.

Emotional cutoff (Family Therapy) The establishment of rigid boundaries that disconnect or cut off contact from problematic family members.

Empathy (Effective Counseling) The therapist's ability to see the world through the client's eyes and to communicate that understanding so that the client feels heard and validated.

Empathy (Person-Centered) Therapist's ability to see the world through the client's eyes and to communicate that understanding so that the client feels heard and validated.

Empowerment (Feminist Therapy) A personal and/or social change process involving individuals who have experienced greater decision-making ability and power within their lives, communities, and/or society that was previously lesser or denied.

Empty chair (Gestalt) A technique in which clients engage in a role-played interaction with an imagined person. Clients sit facing an empty chair, and imagine that a person or some aspect of themselves is sitting there and they engage in a discussion with that imagined person/aspect of themselves.

Enactment (Family Therapy) A technique in which the therapist may have the client act out a previous experience or a characteristic in session.

Enactment (Gestalt) A technique that involves the client putting feelings or thoughts into action.

Encounter groups (Person-Centered) A group designed to promote constructive insight, sensitivity to others, and personal growth among its members. These were popular in the 1970s and 1980s.

Encouragement (Adlerian Therapy) Building a relationship with clients by supporting their beliefs and behaviors to foster client change.

Enmeshed (Family Therapy) A family system in which members are overly concerned or involved in each others' lives, thus preventing individual autonomy.

Eros (Psychoanalysis) Competing with thanatos, this "life" drives purpose is to functions to preserve human species and life.

Evidence-based practices (Effective Counseling) Therapies that have been tested and proven to be effective through procedures and research.

Exception-seeking questions (Solution-Focused Brief Therapy) One of the main techniques therapists use to find solutions by identifying exceptions to the problem clients are experiencing and how clients are already coping.

Exercises (Gestalt) Counseling techniques/interventions, generally preplanned, that are used to increase client awareness within counseling sessions.

Existential anxiety (Existential) Occurs as a result of being confronted with the four givens of existence: death, freedom, existential isolation, and meaning. All people experience this and they have apprehension caused by a threat to a value deemed critical to one's well-being. Death is a fact of life, and as such, all humans experience some anxiety.

Existential guilt (Existential) Guilt that results from the impossibility of fulfilling all of our innate potentials.

Existential vacuum (Existential) The inability to find or create meaning in life, leading to feelings of emptiness, alienation, futility, and aimlessness.

Existentialism (Existential) A philosophy that emphasizes an awareness of matters related to one's existence, including personal responsibility for one's psychological existence. Existential themes include death and dying, freedom, personal responsibility to self and others, meaning in one's life, and authenticity.

Experience near (Neoanalytic/Post-Freud) In self psychology, this reflects the belief that although past experiences have a profound impact on our development, it is the present or here-and-now experiences that lead to their resolution.

Experiential avoidance (Contemporary CBT) In ACT, this is the cause of suffering and maladjustment, as avoidance of unpleasant stimuli allows clients' current sources of distress to continue as barriers.

Experiments (Gestalt) An intervention/technique that facilitates the collaborative exploration of clients' experience; this technique gives clients a chance to "do" and it heightens awareness and provides clients with an opportunity to explore and experience their world.

Exposure (Behavior Therapy) Exposure therapy involves exposing the client to the anxiety source or its context while the client is in a safe space. Doing so helps clients overcome their anxiety or distress associated with the feared stimulus.

Exposure and response prevention (ERP; Behavior Therapy) A form of treatment used primarily with obsessive-compulsive disorders, in which clients are confronted by their fears for an hour or more at a time, then asked to avoid participating in the rituals.

Externalizing (Narrative Therapy) The process of separating individuals from their problems to demonstrate that the problem has an external effect on individuals instead of being intrinsic.

Extinction (Behavior Therapy) The process of no longer presenting reinforcement in order to decrease or eliminate certain behaviors in operant conditioning; the conditioned response decreases over time after the presentation of the conditioned stimulus is removed in classical conditioning.

Extinguishing (Behavior Therapy) Gradually decreasing conditioned responses such as undesirable behaviors, using operant conditioning, or a response of fear to a phobia, using systematic desensitization.

Extraversion (Neoanalytic/Post-Freud) In Jung's theory, this describes people who direct their energy toward and become energized by the outside world; they tend to be outgoing and adapt easily to external change.

Eye Movement Desensitization and Reprocessing (EMDR; Integrative) Initially designed to treat post-traumatic stress, EMDR involves the client visualizing a memory of choice and noticing accompanying physical sensations. The client repeats negative self-statements associated with the scene. The client follows the therapist's finger as it moves rapidly back and forth (other forms of bilateral stimulation can be used). After completing the eye movements, the client stops thinking about the scene. The procedure is repeated again and again, with the client connecting to other selected memories until the client's anxiety is reduced and the client feels better with regard to the concerning experiences.

Family (Family Therapy) A group of people who intimately share their lives with one another. Family can include any combination of parents (biological, step, and/or adoptive), siblings (biological, step, and/or adoptive), extended family (aunts, uncles, cousins, grandparents), and even friends or neighbors.

Family communication (Family Therapy) The verbal and nonverbal exchange of information (e.g., thoughts, feelings, values, beliefs) between family members, which involves not only talking but also listening to others.

Family constellation (Adlerian Therapy) Family dynamics and how they have an impact on the family relationship; includes the composition of the family, each person's roles, and the reciprocal transactions that a person has, during the early formative years, with siblings and parents.

Family maps (Family Therapy) A technique used in structural family therapy to identify the structural outline of the family, including boundaries and subsystems; maps can also be used to set goals and to assess the progress of counseling.

Family projection process (Family Therapy) A means of projecting or transmitting a parental conflict onto one or more children.

Family sculpting (Family Therapy) A technique used by therapists in which family members are physically molded and directed to take a role that represents a view of family relationships.

Family structure (Family Therapy) The rules that have been developed in the course of family life to determine who and how members interact with each other.

Family systems therapy (Family Therapy) An approach to counseling that seeks to improve interactions among family members as changing these interactions creates system and individual level change.

Feedback loops (Family Therapy) Information about how a system is functioning is fed back into the system to correct or govern the system's functioning.

Felt minus (Adlerian Therapy) The key human struggle of feeling inadequate, unappreciated, incompetent, or generally less acceptable than others.

Feminism (Feminist Therapy) A range of beliefs and social/political movements that seek to achieve the goal of equality between women and men in social, political, and economic spheres.

Fictional final goal (Adlerian Therapy) Future-oriented striving toward an ideal goal of significance, superiority, success, or completion; inferiority, for which one aims to compensate, leads to the creation of a fictional final goal that subjectively promises relief from feelings of inferiority and promises future security and success.

Fictional finalism (Adlerian Therapy) An image, usually unconscious, of what life will be like when the goals individuals have that involve achievement of significance, superiority, competence, and mastery are reached.

Field theory (Gestalt) The interaction patterns between individual people and the field (i.e., the environment).

Figure (Gestalt) That part of a field (i.e., the environment) that stands out from the background.

Figure and ground (Gestalt) The ability to separate the figure (i.e., something that stands out in a situation) from the background (e.g., a person sees words on a printed paper as the "figure" and the white sheet as the "ground" or the "background"). Gestalt therapists not only attend to what is figural for the client at the present moment but also attend to what is in the ground of the client's experience (i.e., what is out of the client's awareness).

First-order change (Family Therapy) A change in behavior on the part of one person in a family unit that does not result in change to the overall organization of the system. Considered to be superficial change.

First-order cybernetics (Family Therapy) Looking at the communication patterns and feedback loops within the family system from an outside perspective; the observer does not influence the system.

Fixation (Psychoanalysis) When an individual is "stuck" in any stage of psychosocial development.

Flooding (Behavior Therapy) Intense exposure to a stimulus that evokes high levels of anxiety, with no ability to avoid or escape the stimuli in hopes of desensitizing the individual to the feared stimulus.

Formula first session tasks (Solution-Focused Brief Therapy) Homework assignments that are used between the first and second sessions to instill hope and show that change is inevitable.

Fortune telling (Cognitive Therapy) The cognition that something bad is going to happen despite no evidence to support this belief.

Forward Motion and Creativity (Adlerian Therapy) The path that all humans are inherently on, as a result of the felt minus, to create a life that is progressively more similar to the perceived plus by being creative and responsible, which leads to their healthiest and happiest capabilities.

Free association (Psychoanalysis) Freely sharing thoughts, random words, emotions, and experiences regardless of how appropriate they are.

Freudian slip (Psychoanalysis) An unintentional verbal error due to subconscious feelings.

Friendly involvement (Reality Therapy) The process of building a relationship with a client, thus providing the foundation for effective reality therapy.

Fully functioning person (Person-Centered) A person who meets his or her own need for positive regard rather than relying on the expectations of others.

Functional behavior assessment (Behavior Therapy) FBA is a process of identifying a specific target behavior, the purpose of the behavior, and what factors maintain the behavior.

Functions (Neoanalytic/Post-Freud) In Jung's theory, it is believed that people respond to the world in these four ways- thinking, feeling, sensing, and intuiting.

Fusion (Family Therapy) A family that lacks individuation or appropriate interpersonal boundaries. See also *enmeshed*.

General systems theory (Family Therapy) A theory that provided one holistic organizational system for understanding living organisms and social groups; general system laws apply to any type of system; each organism is an open system that experiences continuous input and output, and a system can be defined by the interrelationships among the subunits. Each participating unit not only contributes to the whole but also has an effect on the other participating units.

Generalization (Behavior Therapy) Using skills and behaviors learned in therapy and applying them to real life to promote their establishment and continue making positive changes.

Genital stage (Psychoanalysis) The fifth and final stage in personality development, during which puberty takes place and the sexual instinct is directed to heterosexual pleasure.

Genogram (Family Therapy) A technique therapists may use in session to help clients chart the family's relationship system as well as patterns within the family.

Genuineness (Person-Centered) Therapists' way of being themselves with clients that promotes trust and openness of clients, establishes a relationship that is free of deception and hidden agendas, and provides a positive role model.

Graded task assignments (Cognitive Therapy) Activities that clients complete between sessions. Starting with easy assignments that guarantee success, therapists gradually increase the difficulty of the tasks, so that people continue to learn from them and feel a sense of mastery and accomplishment.

Graduated exposure (Behavior Therapy) The person confronts his or her fear for a short period, and the length of exposure is gradually increased with each session.

Ground (Gestalt) The background that contrasts with the figure in one's perceptual field.

Guided discovery (Cognitive Therapy) Also known as Socratic dialogue, this is a series of questions which help the client arrive at logical answers.

Homeostasis (Family Therapy) Balance, equilibrium, or status quo in a system that families have an inherent pull toward.

Homeostasis (Gestalt) Balance and equilibrium; can be explained by people's need to complete and wrap up unfinished situations.

Hot seat (Gestalt) A technique used in group therapy in which individuals work one at a time with the therapist and the audience observes.

Humor (Psychoanalysis) A healthy defense mechanism that involves focusing attention on the amusing aspects of situations.

Id (Psychoanalysis) Part of the personality structure that contains the human basic, instinctual drives, particularly sexual and aggression, which includes our bodily needs, wants, desires, and impulses.

Idealization (Psychoanalysis) A defense mechanism that involves amplifying the positive and avoiding the negative aspects of an individual or situation.

Identification (Gestalt) One polarity of the ego boundary; when people assume that certain characteristics of themselves belong to others.

Identification (Psychoanalysis) A defense mechanism that involves modeling oneself after another individual to gain approval.

Identified patient (Family Therapy) The individual whom other family members identify as having the problem and for whom treatment is needed.

Immediacy (Gestalt and Adlerian Therapy) Using the "here and now," which involves asking the client to think about what is happening in the present moment.

Implosion (Behavior Therapy) A type of prolonged, intense exposure therapy in which the client imagines anxiety-producing situations or events in order to develop a more appropriate response for the future.

IMPROVE (Contemporary CBT) An acronym DBT therapists can use to provide clients with a foundation of distress tolerance skills that can be practiced and developed over the course of counseling.

In vivo (Behavior Therapy) Therapeutic procedures that take place in the client's natural environment.

Incongruent/Incongruence (Person-Centered) The clash when there is a disagreement between individuals' experience and their view of themselves.

Individual Psychology (Adlerian Therapy) Adler's theory of human development that holds that people strive for superiority and power, partly in compensation for their feelings of inferiority. Every individual is unique, and one's personality structure—including goals and ways of striving for goals—finds expression in one's style of life.

Individuation (Neoanalytic/Post-Freud) In Jung's theory, this is the process of integrating opposing elements of personality to become one with the self.

Inferior function (Neoanalytic/Post-Freud) In Jung's theory, this is the function (i.e., thinking, feeling, sensing, intuiting) that is the least well developed in an individual.

Inferiority (Adlerian Therapy) Feelings of inadequacy and incompetence, which develop during infancy and serve as the basis for striving for superiority to overcome feelings of inferiority.

Inferiority complex (Adlerian Therapy) A strong and pervasive belief that one is not as good as other people.

Informed consent (Ethics) (Effective Counseling) Permission granted by a client to receive services after an explanation of the possible risks and benefits is provided.

Instinct (Psychoanalysis) Basic drives such as hunger, thirst, sex, and aggression that must be fulfilled to maintain physical or psychological equilibrium.

Intellectualization (Psychoanalysis) A defense mechanism that involves blocking emotions and confrontations by focusing on thoughts and abstractions.

Intentionality (Existential) The ability of people to have a conscious and unconscious sense of purpose and to behave with purpose.

Intergenerational (or multigenerational) family patterns (Family Therapy) Patterns of interacting that are shared and transmitted throughout generations of a family.

Intermediate beliefs (Cognitive Therapy) Underlying attitudes, perspectives, assumptions, standards, or rules for living that guide behavior and influence automatic thinking and appraisal processes; connect core beliefs to automatic thoughts; and often reflect extreme and absolute rules and attitudes.

Internal objects (Neoanalytic/Post-Freud) In object relations theory, internal objects are the most important, which are the psychological structures people internalize from their interactions with others; they include an image of the self, an image of the other person, and associated emotions.

Interoceptive exposure (Behavior Therapy) A structured treatment approach that encourages people to experience feared bodily sensations (such as shortness of breath or heart flutters) in the safe environment of a therapy session without engaging in avoidance or escape strategies.

Interpersonal effectiveness (Contemporary CBT) Skills that help clients appropriately make requests or convey their wants to others, manage and resolve conflicts, establish and maintain positive relationships with others, and maintain and enhance self-respect when interacting with others.

Interpretation (Adlerian Therapy) When therapists share perceived insights with clients relative to their behavior.

Interpretation (Psychoanalysis) The process of elucidating the unconscious meaning of the symbols in material that clients present and of linking those new insights to their present concerns and struggles.

Intersectionality (Feminist Therapy) The interconnected nature of social categorizations such as race, class, and gender as they apply to a given individual or group, regarded as creating overlapping and interdependent systems of discrimination or disadvantage.

Intersubjectivity (Neoanalytic/Post-Freud) The process through which the analyst and client influence each other in therapy.

Intrapsychic processes (Psychoanalysis) Impulses, ideas, conflicts, or other psychological phenomena that occur within the mind.

Introjection (Gestalt) The tendency to uncritically accept others' beliefs and standards without assimilating them to make them congruent with who we are.

Introjection (Neoanalytic/Post-Freud) A defense mechanism which involves the individual internalizing attitudes, behaviors, emotions, and perceptions of others, usually influential or authoritative people in one's life, such as parents.

Introversion (Neoanalytic/Post-Freud) In Jung's theory, this describes people who channel their energy inward. Although they may have good social skills, they tend to be introspective and replenish their energy by being alone.

Intuition (Neoanalytic/Post-Freud) In Jung's theory, this relates to having a hunch or guess about something.

Irrational belief (REBT) Absurd views or feelings that produce emotional and behavioral problems; thoughts with no rationality.

I-Thou relationship (Existential) The ideal therapeutic relationship in existential therapy; refers to moments when people come together in an authentic and meaningful way, thus enriching each others' lives.

Joining (Family Therapy) A therapeutic tactic in which the therapist becomes part of a family system in order to understand and ultimately improve aspects of the system.

Labeling (Cognitive Therapy) Categorizing the cognitive distortion into one of the types of cognitive distortions, which helps people see more clearly the nature of their unrealistic thinking, reminds them that other people have had similar distorted cognition, and gives them a tool for assessing subsequent thoughts.

Labeling and mislabeling (Cognitive Therapy) A cognitive distortion that involves creating a negative view of oneself or someone else based on errors or mistakes made in the past; attaching an extreme, broad, and unjustified label to oneself or someone else.

Landscapes of action (Narrative Therapy) Sequences of behaviors related to events in people's lives that similarly pervade and recur in people's stories; the major themes of actions that frequently occur in people's stories.

Landscapes of consciousness (Narrative Therapy) Backdrops of values, feelings, motives, beliefs, and attitudes that recur in a person's stories; the major underlying themes of feelings that frequently occur in a person's stories.

Latency stage (Psychoanalysis) The fourth stage in personality development, in which development is "latent" or "dormant." The child's energy is channeled into developing new skills and acquiring new knowledge, and play becomes largely confined to other children of the same gender.

Level of Care (Effective Counseling) The setting and intensity of services that clients require to be safe and successful in meeting their counseling goals.

Libido (Psychoanalysis) Component of the life instinct, including the sexual drive; its meaning has been broadened over the years to refer to energy and vitality, a zest for life.

Lifestyle (Adlerian Therapy) People's way of being that is fundamentally informed by their fictive final goals.

Limited reparenting (Contemporary CBT) A schema therapy concept that involves the use of the power of the therapeutic alliance as an intervention; takes a variety of forms, depending on the clients' needs, and may involve connection, warmth, and nurturance. This process encourages a temporary and healthy dependency on therapists with the result of an increased ability to tolerate and regulate negative emotions.

Linear causality (Family Therapy) A type of reciprocal influence in which the action of one individual leads another individual to respond; the effect pattern is a straight, one-way line.

Logical consequences (Behavior Therapy) Consequences that caregivers impose in response to children's actions to help them learn from their behavior and choices.

Logotherapy (Existential) A school of existential therapy that focuses on challenging clients to search for and create meaning in their lives. Associated techniques include: paradoxical intention, attitude modulation, dereflection, and socratic Socratic dialogue.

Love object (Neoanalytic/Post-Freud) An object in which the individual relates to in a loving way; a sense of security in the love object leads to healthy functioning.

Low frustration tolerance (REBT) Difficulty with tolerating events or situations that are unpleasant and do not go as planned.

Magnification (Cognitive Therapy) A cognitive distortion in which we exaggerate the negative or "blow it out of proportion."

Mapping (Narrative Therapy) An approach that helps individuals reflect on their stories by understanding links of stories and illustrating how problems have emerged and how they present.

Mind reading (Cognitive Therapy) A cognitive distortion that one knows the thoughts in another person's mind.

Mindfulness (Contemporary CBT) Observing one's inner and outer experiences and remaining in the present moment without judgment.

Mindmaps (Solution-Focused Brief Therapy) Diagrams and outlines of clients' ideas that therapists use to focus on organizing goals and solutions.

Minimization (Cognitive Therapy) A cognitive distortion in which one minimizes the importance of something, especially the positive aspects.

Miracle question (Solution-Focused Brief Therapy) A method of questioning used to help the client envision what the future will look like without the problem present.

Mirroring (Neoanalytic/Post-Freud) In Kohut's theory, this involves the parent showing the child that he or she is happy with the child, therefore, the child's grandiose self is supported.

Mitwelt (Existential) Refers to being-in-the-world with other people, to relationships, interactions, and concepts we introject about society, race, gender, and religion.

Modeling (Behavior Therapy) A behavioral technique in which a client observes the behavior of another person and then mimics that observation.

Motivation (Effective Counseling) Client's readiness for treatment and ability to engage productively in the counseling process.

Multigenerational transmission process (Family Therapy) Basic patterns are passed down from generation to generation through modeled behavior, and family assumptions about gender roles, finances, family responsibility, work ethics, coping skills, and ways of dealing with stress are maintained.

Multimodal therapy (Integrative) Developed by Arnold Lazarus, this approach uses multiple modalities to identify and treat a mental disorder or presenting problem.

Multinuclear family (Family Therapy) Two separate families who live in the same house. The number of multinuclear families has been increasing largely as a result of financial constraints.

Multiple identities (Feminist Therapy) Many forces affect the way that gender is experienced; these include ethnicity, social class, gender orientation, disabilities, and other characteristics.

Musterbation (REBT) A phrase that explains the behavior of clients who are inflexible and absolutist in their thinking and who set absolute and unrealistic demands on themselves.

Narradrama (Narrative Therapy) Combining drama therapy and narrative therapy in such a way that clients can act out their story.

Needs (Reality Therapy) Psychological needs include desires for belonging, power, freedom, and fun.

Negative feedback loop (Family Therapy) Method of communicating and interacting within the family that creates a pattern of moving away from homeostasis, and then quickly returning to homeostasis; limits change.

Negative punishment (Behavior Therapy) Type of punishment in which the removal of a favorable stimulus decreases the likelihood that the behavior will be performed again.

Negative reinforcement (Behavior Therapy) Type of reinforcement in which the response or behavior is increased by removing or stopping an unfavorable outcome.

Neurofeedback (Behavior Therapy) A subset of biofeedback that allows people to monitor and regulate brain wave patterns and change behavior as a result.

Neuroses (Psychoanalysis) Disorders of thoughts, emotions, and behaviors that interfere with people's capacity for healthy functioning that may include anxiety, fear, or depression; less severe than psychosis.

Neurotic anxiety (Existential) Anxiety that is out of proportion to a particular event. It is often an indication that an individual is not living authentically and is not making choices and assuming responsibility.

Nondirective counseling (Person-Centered) Original name of Rogers' theory used to distinguish it from the prevailing models of the time (mainly psychoanalytic and behavioral) in which practitioners were viewed as experts whom clients looked to for advice on what they should do; emphasizes the importance of the client taking the lead and being the focus of the counseling process.

Object (Neoanalytic/Post-Freud) In object relations theory, defined not as another person but as the internal mental structure that the infant forms of that person through introjection.

Object cathexis (Psychoanalysis) The investment of psychic energy or libido in objects outside the self.

Observational learning (Behavior Therapy) A type of learning in which people are influenced by observing the behaviors of another.

Oedipus complex (Psychoanalysis) The conflict between erotic attraction, resentment, rivalry, jealousy, and fear in boys, whereby the child adopts the characteristics of the same-sex parent.

Operant conditioning (Behavior Therapy) A type of learning in which behavior is increased or decreased by systematically changing its consequences.

Optimal frustration (Neoanalytic/Post-Freud) In object relations theory, this refers to mild disruptions in empathy that push people to take steps to form a cohesive self.

Optimal responsiveness (Neoanalytic/Post-Freud) In self psychology, this describes the response from the therapist that is most relevant for the client that allows clients to change their internalizations.

Oral stage (Psychoanalysis) The first stage of personality development, which is centered on the mouth, whereby the child gets stimulation from putting all sorts of things in his or her mouth. Oral fixation can lead to oral personalities, and these people may become smokers, nail-biters, finger-chewers, and thumb suckers.

Organismic valuing process (Person-Centered) People's intuitive ability to know what they need to feel fulfilled and self-actualized.

Overgeneralization (Cognitive Therapy) Distorted thinking that occurs when individuals draw conclusions based on a few negative events and apply those conclusions broadly.

Paining behaviors (Reality Therapy) Choosing misery by developing symptoms (e.g., headaching, depressing, and anxietying) because these seem like the best behaviors available to one at the time.

Paradoxical intention (Existential) A technique in which therapists encourage clients to do or wish for the very thing they fear the most.

Paradoxical interventions (Family Therapy) A therapeutic technique in which therapists prescribe an action to the client that they want resisted. Change occurs when the client defies the directive.

Paradoxical ordeals (Family Therapy) Directives that demand the performance of the symptom on purpose.

Paradoxical theory of change (Gestalt) The idea that people change by becoming more fully themselves, not by trying to make themselves be something or someone they are not. People cannot truly change until they accept who they are, and the more people try to be something they are not, the more they will stay right where they are.

Paranoid-schizoid position (Neoanalytic/Post-Freud) In object relations theory, this position stems from infants' natural fearfulness or paranoia; in an attempt to ward off danger, infants separate good objects and feelings from bad objects and feelings.

Parentified child (Family Therapy) A child who is given responsibilities within the family that are inconsistent with the child's role or age.

Passive aggression (Psychoanalysis) A defense mechanism that involves expressing anger and hostility in indirect ways.

Patriarchy (Feminist Therapy) A concept, central to many feminist theories, that describes unjust power structures within social systems wherein men have more power than women.

Penis envy (Psychoanalysis) The experience of anxiety and jealousy in girls when they realize they do not have a penis.

Perceived plus (Adlerian Therapy) The subjective perception that the individual has achieved an area of mastery above peers.

Persona (Neoanalytic/Post-Freud) In Jung's theory, these are the roles that people play in response to social demands of others; a disguise that individuals assume when causally interacting with their environment.

Personal unconscious (Neoanalytic/Post-Freud) In Jung's theory, this is the thoughts, feelings, and perceptions that are stored that's not accepted by the ego; unique to each individual and forms over the person's lifetime.

Personalization (Cognitive Therapy) A cognitive distortion in which individuals take on responsibility for an event by relating the event to themselves.

Person-centered (Person-Centered) Term that replaced client-centered to reflect Rogers' concern with all of humanity, rather than just the clinical relationship; final name for Carl Rogers' theory.

Phallic stage (Psychoanalysis) The third stage in personality development, which is centered on genitals and masturbation, which become the new source of pleasure.

Phenomenology/Phenomenological (Person-Centered) The psychological study of subjective experience that is based on phenomena as they appear, apart from any scientific theories and without reduction of a phenomenon to its parts.

Picture album (Reality Therapy) The quality world picture album is an accumulation of specific mental images of people, events, life circumstances, and possessions that represent our very own personal utopia, or most preferred life experience; subjective perceptions of one's ideal reality.

Pleasure principle (Psychoanalysis) The tendency to avoid pain and seek pleasure; operated by the id.

Polarities (Gestalt) Two extremes or opposites; generally reflect internal or interpersonal conflicts. To truly achieve wholeness, people must become aware of and integrate their polarities, especially the polarities of mind and body.

Positive addictions (reality) Behaviors that are used to cope that provide mental strength and alertness, creativity, energy, confidence, and focus, but do not dominate or control people's lives in unhelpful ways (e.g., running, meditating).

Positive feedback loop (Family Therapy) The communication pattern between two or more family members that results in movement further and further away from homeostasis, promotes change, and causes a loss of stability.

Positive narratives (Narrative Therapy) Parts of client's stories that are going well.

Positive psychology (Person-Centered and Solution-Focused Brief Therapy) Positive psychology is a scientific approach to studying human thoughts, feelings, and behavior with a focus on strengths instead of weakness, building on the good in life instead of repairing the bad, and helping people to live optimally.

Positive punishment (Behavior Therapy) Type of punishment in which the addition of an unfavorable stimulus decreases the likelihood that the behavior will be performed again.

Positive reinforcement (Behavior Therapy) Type of reinforcement in which the addition of a reward increases the likelihood that the behavior will be performed again.

Power (Feminist Therapy) The capacity or right to have influence on self and/or others.

Power analysis (Feminist Therapy) A technique used to enhance clients' awareness of the power structure in society and the differences in power between men and women.

Preconscious (Psychoanalysis) Holds information that may not be part of current awareness but that can be readily accessed.

Prescribing the symptom (Adlerian Therapy) The therapist asks clients to increase the frequency of the unwanted behavior or feeling to, ironically, help them achieve distance from the struggle.

Pre-therapy changes (Solution-Focused Brief Therapy) Changes that take place before the client arrives to therapy that therapists typically ask about in the first session.

Private logic (Adlerian Therapy) Our beliefs about ourselves and our place in the world, which is subjective and based on lifestyle; the individual's own evaluation of the self, others, and the world.

Projection (Psychoanalysis and Gestalt) A defense mechanism that involves applying one's own unacceptable thoughts, emotions, or actions to another.

Projective identification (Neoanalytic/Post-Freud) In object relations theory, this describes the split-off parts of the self that are projected onto another person with whom the self can then identify.

Psyche (Neoanalytic/Post-Freud) In Jung's theory, this is the personality structure which includes the conscious and unconscious thoughts, feelings, and behaviors.

Psychic energy (Neoanalytic/Post-Freud) In Jung's theory, this is the energy of the psyche which is developed from desire, motivation, thinking, and looking.

Psychoanalysis (Psychoanalysis) Based on Freud's work, this therapy includes free association, dream analysis, and working through transference issues. Based on the assumption that problems derive from the unconscious mind.

Psychodrama (Gestalt) Psychodrama is an active and creative therapeutic approach that uses guided drama and role playing to work through problems.

Psychoses (Psychoanalysis) A loss of contact from reality; a significant disturbance in an individual's ability to accurately perceive and interpret both internal and external experiences.

Psychosexual stages of development (Psychoanalysis) Freud's five stages of development, in which the components of personality (i.e., id, ego, and superego) form and through which they progress.

Punishment (Behavior Therapy) Punishment is a term used in operant conditioning to refer to any change that occurs after a behavior that reduces the likelihood that that behavior will occur again in the future. While positive and negative reinforcement are used to increase behaviors, punishment is focused on reducing or eliminating unwanted behaviors.

Pushing the button (Adlerian Therapy) A reframing technique whereby clients are encouraged to think of a pleasant moment they have experienced, become aware of feelings connected to it, and then switch to an unpleasant image and those feelings.

Quality world (Reality Therapy) The perceptions and images we have of how we can fulfill our basic psychological needs; another phrase for picture album.

Questions about the future (Narrative Therapy) Questions used by therapists that may help clients look into the future and develop positive, new stories and understand their preferred future.

Radical acceptance (Contemporary CBT) Complete and total acceptance of something or some situation; a term used in DBT.

Rational emotive imagery (REBT) An emotive technique used to help clients change their self-defeating emotions into more adaptive emotions.

Rationality (REBT) Thinking, feeling, and acting in ways that will help individuals attain their goals.

Rationalization (Psychoanalysis) A defense mechanism that involves attempting to explain and justify one's own choices and behaviors in self-serving but invalid ways through the use of logical reasons.

Reaction formation (Psychoanalysis) A defense mechanism that involves replacing unacceptable thoughts and emotions with the contrary to overcompensate for them.

Reality principle (Psychoanalysis) An action of the ego that allows gratification so that environmental demands can be met.

Reality therapy (Reality Therapy) Reality therapy is a therapeutic approach that focuses on problem-solving and making better choices to achieve specific goals.

Reattribution (Cognitive Therapy) Helping clients distribute responsibility for an event.

Reauthoring (Narrative Therapy) Possibilities for new thoughts, actions, and emotions are expanded as therapists and clients share new descriptions of old stories to create alternative stories.

Reciprocal influence (Family Therapy) A process by which one person or aspect of a family affects all other parts of the family, and vice versa.

Reciprocal inhibition (Behavior Therapy) Eliciting a novel response brings about a decrease in the strength of a concurrent habitual response.

Reconstruction (Family Therapy) Helping families re-enact and clarify their dysfunctional communications.

Reflecting team (Solution-Focused Brief Therapy) A small group of therapists (say, two to seven) who observe a therapy session and then have a conversation regarding what they noticed about the session while the therapist and client observe; conversations are always positive, strength based, and often include the use of stories or metaphors.

Reflective listening (Person-Centered) Seeking to understand what the client is saying by confirming it back to the client.

Reframing (Family Therapy) Aiding family members in their re-interpretation of events and/or others' actions and/or intentions, especially when existing interpretations of family members' behaviors are inaccurate, incomplete, maladaptive, or unfairly blaming of another family member.

Reframing (Feminist Therapy) Giving a new or different explanation for an event so that constructive change can occur. In feminist therapy, reframing helps individuals understand how social pressures can affect their problems.

Regression (Psychoanalysis) A defense mechanism that involves returning to an earlier developmental level in terms of one's thoughts, emotions, and behavior.

Relabeling (Family Therapy) Verbally redefining an event to elicit more positive responses.

Relabeling (Feminist Therapy) Attaching a new name to a problem to help clients gain clarity and feel empowered. For example, saying that a client is overwhelmed by an issue rather than "depressed" may allow the client to feel less like the problem is him or her and thus feel more empowered.

Relational competence (Feminist Therapy) This refers to being able to have empathy toward self and others. It also includes the ability to participate in and build a sense of strength in a community.

Relational frame theory (Contemporary CBT) A behavioral theory of human language and cognition used in ACT that helps people recognize how they become entangled in thoughts and words and how those entanglements result in internal struggles against themselves.

Relational resilience (Feminist Therapy) Refers to growing a relationship and being able to move forward despite setbacks. Resilience also concerns recognizing when relationships are not mutual and moving on from them.

Relationship factors (Effective Counseling) Characteristics of the therapeutic interaction between the client and the therapist, such as, open listening, unconditional acceptance, or the insight and awareness of the current issues.

Relationship filter (Reality Therapy) Part of our perceptual system that labels functions and connections among perceived units of incoming information.

Reorientation (Adlerian Therapy) Clients change their lifestyles by altering rules of interaction, process, and motivation through awareness.

Repression (Psychoanalysis) A defense mechanism that involves dismissing disturbing thoughts and feelings to the unconscious rather than dealing with them appropriately.

Resistance (Psychoanalysis) Deterrence of memories or insights to diffuse anxiety; blocking of counseling progress that involves the client ceasing to discuss, address, think about, or accept an interpretation from a therapist.

Responsibility (Reality Therapy) The process of satisfying one's own needs without interfering with others' fulfillment of their personal needs.

Restricted (Existential) The lack of awareness of oneself and one's problems.

Retroflection (Gestalt) Turning back onto ourselves what we would like to do to someone else, or doing to ourselves what we would like someone else to do to us.

Role induction (Effective Counseling) The process of orienting clients to counseling so they are more likely to become successful clients who understand and can make good use of the therapeutic process.

SAMI^{2}C^3 (Reality Therapy) An acronym pertaining to the essence of a good action plan: simple, attainable, measurable, immediate, involved, controlled by the planner, committed to, and continuously done.

Scaling (Cognitive Therapy) A technique used to challenge the "all-or-none" thinking, such as turning a dichotomy into a continuum.

Scaling questions (Solution-Focused Brief Therapy) Questions used by therapists to establish a baseline and facilitate identification of possibilities and progress, often used on a 1 to 10 scale.

Scapegoating (Family Therapy) Occurs when a member of the family, likely to be the identified patient, who is the object of criticism, blame, or scorn.

Schemas (Cognitive Therapy) Patterns of thoughts and behaviors that coincide with a set of core beliefs and assumptions about society.

Second-order change (Family Therapy) A lasting change in the fundamental organization of a family system.

Second-order cybernetics (Family Therapy) A philosophy that views therapists as influencing the family system and being non-experts.

Secular humanism (REBT) Emphasizes the best and most practical aspects of the scientific method, human choice, and meaningfulness; views people as unique individuals who usually value and choose to live in interdependent social groups; views people as neither good nor bad but as simply human; only people's behaviors and actions are evaluated.

Selective abstraction (Cognitive Therapy) Selecting one idea or fact from an event while ignoring others.

Self object (Neoanalytic/Post-Freud) In self psychology, a generic term for our intrapsychic experiences of others, our mental representations of them experienced as part of the self or in service of the self.

Self-actualization (Person-Centered and Existential) The innate tendency all people have toward reaching their full potential; occurs across the lifespan, manifesting itself as movement toward self-awareness, autonomy, and self-regulation.

Self-destructive emotions (REBT) Emotions that are enduring, immobilizing, and nonproductive; reflect overreactions to stimuli; and lead to negative self-images and actions.

Self-efficacy (Behavior Therapy) Belief in one's ability to accomplish something.

Self-evaluation (Reality Therapy) Clients' assessment of current behavior to decide whether it is working and if what they are doing is meeting their needs; the cornerstone of reality therapy procedures.

Self-instructional training (CBT) A program designed to help people respond with positive self-talk in the face of stressors or negative thinking.

Self-monitoring (CBT) A method therapists use to assess clients' thoughts, emotions, or behaviors outside therapy, in which clients are asked to keep records of events, feelings, and/or thoughts.

Self-realization (Neoanalytic/Post-Freud) According to Horney, this involves developing one's innate capacities, emotions, and interests; people who achieve self-realization are self-aware, responsible, and able to make sound judgments.

Self-Transcendence (Existential) Going beyond one's immediate situation to understand one's being and taking responsibility for this being. Going beyond one's own needs to take responsibility for others.

Sensation (Neoanalytic/Post-Freud) In Jung's theory, sensation involves receiving and identifying physical stimuli through the senses and relaying them to consciousness. People who have sensation as their dominant function look at the facts and the substance of a stimulus, seeking concrete evidence of its meaning and value.

Shadow (Neoanalytic/Post-Freud) In Jung's theory, the archetype represents unacceptable sexual, animalistic, or aggressive impulses, usually the opposite of the way we see ourselves.

Shame-attacking exercises (REBT) A technique used to empower clients to face their fears by doing whatever they are afraid of.

Shaping (Behavior Therapy) A process of gradually reinforcing particular target behaviors to approximate the desired behavior.

Signal anxiety (Psychoanalysis) An early warning for the ego anticipating danger; the anxiety that results from a conflict between internal wishes or drives and constraints that come from either internalized prohibitions or external reality.

Social action (Feminist Therapy) An important goal in feminist therapy; to work toward changing gender-role stereotyping, and addressing and changing societal sexism and discrimination.

Social beings (Adlerian Therapy) The idea that humans have an inherent human need for connections with others and a desire to contribute to society in positive ways.

Social constructivism (Postmodern approaches) A theory that proposes people's individual sense of reality and the meaning they find in their experiences are constructed and created, rather than discovered; thus there is no truth, only a socially constructed, evolving reality.

Social interest (Adlerian Therapy) The caring and concern for the welfare of others that can serve to guide people's behavior; being as concerned about others as one is about oneself.

Social learning theory (Behavior Therapy) A theory that emphasizes how individuals learn by observing and modeling others; includes an additional focus on one's worldview, beliefs, perspectives, and other cognitive processes, as internal appraisals or interpretations of events are assumed to significantly influence one's behavior.

Societal regression (Family Therapy) Problems of differentiation and individuation are reflected in society as a whole.

Socratic questioning (Cognitive Therapy) Dialogue between individuals (i.e., therapist and counselor), based on asking and answering questions to stimulate and challenge ideas and thoughts.

Solution prescriptions (Solution-Focused Brief Therapy) A form of suggestion that uses tasks designed to help people discover ways to resolve their concerns.

Solution talk (Solution-Focused Brief Therapy) The language that therapists use to increase clients' hope and optimism, their sense of control, and their openness to possibilities and change by focusing on solutions, strengths, and successes instead of problems.

Somatization (Psychoanalysis) A defense mechanism that involves channeling conflicts/psychological distress into physical symptoms.

Specifications of personhood (Narrative Therapy) The information in stories that tells people how to behave as individuals or family members; specifications of personhood act as restraints and keep people stuck in and limited by their dominant stories.

Spitting in the client's soup (Adlerian Therapy) Therapists identify the underlying motivations behind clients' self-defeating behaviors and then spoil their imagined payoff by making it unappealing.

Splitting (Neoanalytic/Post-Freud) In object relations theory, splitting is an unconscious way of dealing with unwanted parts of the self or threatening parts of others; this defense serves to keep incompatible feelings separate from each other.

Splitting (Psychoanalysis) Perceiving the self and others as either all good or all bad and vacillating from idealization to devaluation of self and others.

Stimulus discrimination (Behavior Therapy) To perceive and respond differently to stimuli based on different cues or antecedent events; the ability to distinguish among similar cues.

Stimulus generalization (Behavior Therapy) Responding the same way to similar stimuli.

Stimulus-response (Behavior Therapy) The more frequently a stimulus and a response coincide, with the response being rewarded, the stronger is the tendency to emit the response when that stimulus occurs, leading to the development of a habit or habitual response.

Story deconstruction (Narrative Therapy) The process of taking apart, analyzing, and understanding the meaning and themes of stories in order to move forward with creating new alternative stories.

Straightforward ordeals (Family Therapy) Directives not intended to harm but may sometimes seem to be punishing or even absurd, such as performing an unpleasant event after the problem behavior has occurred.

Strengths-based approach (Effective Counseling) An approach that focuses on the inherent strengths of individuals and families. These strengths are used to aid in recovery and empowerment.

Stress inoculation training (CBT) An approach to reduce stress; assumes that if people can successfully cope with relatively mild stressors, they will be able to tolerate and successfully cope with more severe ones.

Stress-vulnerability model (Cognitive Therapy) As more stress occurs, the more the person's automatic thoughts are at the mercy of underlying dysfunctional beliefs and schemas. Because the processing of thoughts is already biased, distorted cognitions result.

Style of life (Adlerian Therapy) A way of seeking to fulfill particular goals that individuals set in their lives, which include their own patterns of beliefs, cognitive styles, and behaviors that express their style of life.

Subjective units of distress scale (SUDS; CBT) System for clients to rate their stressors in hierarchical order; helps track clients' progress in coping with their stressors.

Sublimation (Psychoanalysis) A healthy defense mechanism that involves translating harmful emotions or impulses into something more socially acceptable.

Subsystem (Family Therapy) Smaller groupings of individuals within a family who have unique ways of relating and interacting with one another; any subunit of a family having its own autonomous functions as well as a role within the larger family system (e.g., siblings, parents, children).

Superego (Psychoanalysis) Part of the personality structure that aims for perfection and seeks morally rigid and culturally correct rules.

Superior function (Neoanalytic/Post-Freud) In Jung's theory, the superior function (i.e., thinking, feeling, sensing, intuiting) is the function that is the most developed.

Superiority (Adlerian Therapy) The drive to become superior that allows individuals to become skilled, competent, and creative.

Superiority complex (Adlerian Therapy) A means of masking feelings of inferiority by displaying self-centered, boastful, or arrogant superiority to overcome feelings of inferiority; inflating one's superiority at the expense of others.

Symbiotic relationship (Family Therapy) An intense relationship between two people in which the boundaries are blurred and they respond as one (often occurs between mother and child).

Symbolic Growth Experience (Existential) Intentional interpretation of an immediate experience to discover the symbolism and meaning behind it, in order to develop awareness, personal worth, and meaning.

Symbols (Neoanalytic/Post-Freud) In Jung's theory, symbols represent the content, representations, and expression of archetypes.

Synchronicity (Neoanalytic/Post-Freud) In Jung's theory, synchronicity relates to the idea that nothing happens without having meaning and purpose, thus there are no random coincidences.

Systematic desensitization (Behavior Therapy) A powerful technique that pairs relaxation with controlled exposure to a feared stimulus; typically used to treat phobias.

Target behavior (Behavior Therapy) A particular part of the client's problem that has been selected to change and can be clearly defined and easily assessed.

Task assignments (Adlerian Therapy) A way to help the client break down an activity into smaller, more manageable steps.

Technical eclecticism (Integrative) An approach in which one personality theory is selected and techniques may be used from any theory, but are used in a way that is consistent with the personality theory selected.

Thanatos (Psychoanalysis) Competing with eros, this "death" drive is focused on risk, negativity, and destruction.

The Self (Neoanalytic/Post-Freud) In Jung's theory, an archetype is the center of personality that provides organization and integration of the personality through a process of individuation.

The Wise Mind ACCEPTS (Contemporary CBT) An acronym DBT therapists teach clients to use as a script to help them work through distressing situations.

Themes (Narrative Therapy) The meanings that clients have for their story that allow them to recognize the influence stories have had on them and how other influences have created the story.

Theoretical integration (Integrative) An approach that combines the personality theory concepts and techniques of two or more theories.

Therapeutic documents (Narrative Therapy) Materials prepared by both the therapist and the client to reinforce and provide evidence of accomplishments.

Therapeutic relationship (Effective Counseling) The connection and collaboration between the therapist and client, characterized by trust, respect, genuineness, positive emotional feelings, and a holistic understanding.

Thought sampling (Cognitive Therapy) To collect a sample of one's own thoughts using a journal or notebook outside of session.

Token economies (Behavior Therapy) A system of contingency management based on the systematic reinforcement of target behavior by providing symbols or tokens after behaving in desired ways that can be exchanged for tangible reinforcements.

Total behavior (Reality Therapy) People's overall functioning involves *total behavior,* which is composed of four inseparable components: doing, thinking, feeling, and physiology.

Total knowledge filter (Reality Therapy) Our perceptual system that represents everything we have known or experienced.

Tracking (Family Therapy) A therapeutic tactic in which therapists attend to the language, style, tone, and values of the family, which is used to influence the family's patterns of interaction.

Transference (Psychoanalysis) When the client transfers feelings onto the therapist.

Transpersonal therapy (Person-Centered) An aspect of a person that is beyond the physical realm; a type of therapy that does not focus on a person's body and mind, but on the health of a person's spirit. This type of therapy puts an emphasis on people's spiritual paths or spiritual enlightenment during their lives.

Transtheoretical model of change (Integrative) An integrative theory of therapy that assesses an individual's readiness to act on new, healthier behaviors and provides strategies, or processes of change, to guide the individual.

Triad (Family Therapy) A close relationship between three family members.

Triangle of conflict (Neoanalytic/Post-Freud) Includes the defense mechanisms people use to protect themselves from feeling anxious or uncomfortable in regards to the three types of relationships (past relationships, current relationships, relationship with therapist); the triangle of conflict is typically related to the client's presenting problem and it is the therapist's responsibility to understand and point out any connections.

Triangle of insights (Neoanalytic/Post-Freud) Involes interpretations from the therapist that connect emotional past relationships, emotional current relationships, and the relationship with the therapist; the purpose of the triangle of insight is for clients to gain awareness of how they are using the same defense mechanisms currently that they developed in childhood.

Triangulation (Family Therapy) An interactional pattern in which a third person becomes involved in conflict between two individuals to reduce the tension between the original two people.

Tyranny of should (Neoanalytic/Post-Freud) The expectations that people put on themselves.

Uberwelt (Existential) Religious or spiritual beliefs about the ideal world; the way a person wants the world to be.

Umwelt (Existential) Relating to the environment, the objects and living beings within it; a tending to the biological and physical aspects of the world.

Unconditional other acceptance (REBT) Acknowledging and accepting individuals as they are without placing any judgment on them.

Unconditional other acceptance-multicultural (REBT) Therapists accept people from other cultures "as they exist," without placing any conditions on them.

Unconditional positive regard (Effective Counseling) Conveyed emotional warmth, appropriate reassurance, the interest in the client, and the use of therapeutic interventions that empower the client.

Unconditional positive regard (Person-Centered) The basic acceptance and support of a person regardless of what the person says or does.

Unconditioned stimulus (Behavior Therapy) In classical conditioning, a stimulus that naturally and automatically triggers a response; no learning is needed.

Unconscious (Psychoanalysis) The significant and disturbing material, which may include socially unacceptable ideas, wishes and desires, traumatic memories, and painful emotions, that we keep out of our awareness due to how threatening it is to acknowledge.

Unfinished business (Gestalt) Unexpressed feelings from the past that occur in the present and interfere with psychological functioning.

Unique outcomes (Narrative Therapy) Moments that stand in contrast to a client's otherwise problem-saturated narratives.

Validation (Person-Centered) The therapist's empathic confirmation of the client's emotions.

Valuing filter (Reality Therapy) When people decide perceived information is meaningful, it passes through their value filter, and in doing so people place one of three values on it: a positive value, a negative value, or—if it neither helps nor hinders people in meeting their needs—a neutral value.

Vicarious introspection (Neoanalytic/Post-Freud) In self psychology, this is also known as empathy; therapists should take a nurturing role; emphasize active and open listening; and provide acceptance, understanding, and explanations or interpretations to facilitate the unfolding of the client's subjective world.

Virtual reality therapy (Behavior Therapy) A form of treatment that can be used for exposure that takes place in a computer-generated environment where the client can interact with the environment by using a joystick, a head-band, a glove with physiological sensors, or a similar device.

WDEP system (Reality Therapy) The key procedures applied to the practice of reality therapy. The strategies help clients identify their wants, determine the direction their behavior is taking them, make self-evaluations, and design plans for change.

Will (Existential) Our conscious capacity to move toward our self-selected goals.

Wise mind (Contemporary CBT) A DBT technique that integrates philosophical foundations of dialectics, CBT, and mindfulness through three different mind states (emotional mind, rational mind, wise mind) that are used to explain behavior based on cognitive, affective, and balanced ways of responding to distress.

Word association tests (Neonanalytic/Post-Freud) Therapists read single words, one at a time, to the client, who replies with the first word that comes into mind thus providing clues to unconscious material.

Working through (Psychoanalysis) Exploration of the unconscious and of defense mechanisms with the purpose of transforming the ego; repetitive interpretations and exploring resistance enhance the working-through process.

REFERENCES

Abbass, A., Rabung, S., Leichsenring, F., Refseth, J., & Midgley, N. (2013). Psychodynamic psychotherapy for children and adolescents: A meta-analysis of short-term psychodynamic models, *Journal of the American Academy of Child and Adolescent Psychiatry, 52*(2), 863–875.

Ackerman, N. W. (1958). *The psychodynamics of family life*. New York, NY: Basic Books.

Active Parenting. (2016). 30 years of helping families find their way. Retrieved from http://www.activeparenting.com/

Addis, M. E., & Mahalik, J. R. (2003). Men, masculinity, and contexts for help seeking. *American Psychologist, 58*, 5–14.

Addison, S. M., & Collhart, D. (2015). Expanding the therapy paradigm with queer couples: A relational intersectional lens. *Family Process, 54*(3), 435–453.

Adibah, S. M., & Zakaria, M. (2015). The efficacy of expressive arts therapy in the creation of catharsis in counselling. *Mediterranean Journal of Social Sciences, 6*(6), 298–306.

Adler, A. (1931). *What life should mean to you*. Boston, MA: Little, Brown.

Adler, A. (1938). *Social interest: A challenge to mankind* (J. Linton & R. Vaughan, Trans.). London, UK: Faber and Faber.

Adler, A. (1956). Understanding life. In H. L. Ansbacher & R. R. Ansbacher (Eds.), *The individual psychology of Alfred Adler: A systematic presentation in selections from His writings*. New York, NY: Harper Torch Books.

Adler, A. (1963a). *The practice and theory of individual psychology*. Paterson, NJ: Littlefield, Adams.

Adler, A. (1963b). *The problem child*. New York, NY: Putnam.

Adler, A. (1998). *Social interest: Adler's key to the meaning of life*. Boston, MA: One World Publications.

Adler, J. (2011). Epistemological tension in the future of personality disorder diagnosis. *American Journal of Psychiatry, 168*, 1221–1222.

Adler, J. (2012). Living into the story: Agency and coherence in a longitudinal study of narrative identity development and mental health over the course of psychotherapy, *Journal of Personality and Social Psychology, 102*, 367–389.

Ainsworth, B., Eddershaw, R., Meron, D., Baldwin, D. S., & Garner, M. (2013). The effect of focused attention and open monitoring meditation on attention network function in healthy volunteers. *Psychiatry Research, 210*(3), 1226–1231. doi: 10.1016/j.psychres.2013.09.002

Ainsworth, M. D. S., & Bell, S. M. (1970). Attachment, exploration, and separation: Illustrated by the behavior of one-year-olds in a strange situation. *Child Development, 41*, 49–67.

Ainsworth, M. D. S., Blehar, M. C., Waters, E., & Walls, S. (1978). *Patterns of attachment: A psychological study of the strange situation*. Hillsdale, NJ: Erlbaum.

Akbas, A. (2015). Application of humanistic approach in family counseling. *European Journal of Research on Education, 3*(1), 80–88.

Alexander, F., & French, T. M. (1946). *Psychoanalytic therapy: Principles and application*. New York, NY: Ronald Press.

ALGBTIC LGBQQIA Competencies Taskforce. Harper, A., Finerty, P., Martinez, M., Brace, A., Crethar, H. C., Loos, B., Harper, B., Graham, S., Singh, A., Kocet, M., Travis, L., Travis, L., Lambert, S., Burnes, T., Dickey, L. M., & Hammer, T. (2013). Association for Lesbian, Gay, Bisexual, and Transgender Issues in Counseling Competencies for Counseling with Lesbian, Gay, Bisexual, Queer, Questioning, Intersex, and Ally Individuals. *Journal of LGBT Issues in Counseling, 7*(1), 2–43.

Al-Krenawi, A. (1999). An overview of rituals in Western therapies and intervention: Argument for their use in cross-cultural therapy. *International Journal for the Advancement of Counseling, 21*, 3–17.

Almagor, M. (2011). *The functional dialectic system approach for therapy with individuals, couples, and families*. Minneapolis, MN: University of Minnesota Press.

American Art Therapy Association. (2013). *Ethical principles for art therapists*. Alexandria, VA: Author.

American Association for Marriage and Family Therapy. (2012). *Code of ethics*. Alexandria, VA: Author.

American Association of Christian Counselors. (2014). *AACC code of ethics*. Forest, VA: Author.

American Counseling Association. (2014). *Code of ethics*. Alexandria, VA: Author.

American Counseling Association. (2015). *Multicultural and social justice counseling competencies*. Retrieved from https://www.counseling.org/docs/default-source/competencies/multicultural-and-social-justice-counseling-competencies.pdf?sfvrsn=8573422c_20

American Mental Health Counselors Association. (2015). *AMHCA Code of Ethics*. Alexandria, VA: Author.

American Psychiatric Association. (2004). *Practice guideline for the treatment of patients with acute stress disorder and posttraumatic stress disorder*. Arlington, VA: Author.

American Psychiatric Association. (2013). *The diagnostic and statistical manual of mental disorders* (5th ed.). Arlington, VA: Author.

American Psychological Association. (2006). Special issue: The relevance of Sigmund Freud for the 21st century. *Psychoanalytic Psychology, 23*(2).

American Psychological Association. (2017). *APA code of ethics*. Alexandria, VA: Author.

American School Counselors Association. (2010). *Ethical standards for school counselors*. Alexandria, VA: Author.

Anderson, T., Lunnen, K. M., & Ogles, B. M. (2010). Putting models and techniques in context. In B. L. Duncan, S. D. Miller, B. E. Wampold, & M. A. Hubble (Eds.), *Heart and soul of change in psychotherapy* (2nd ed., pp. 143–166). Washington, DC: American Psychological Association.

Andreas, S. (2012). The true genius of Virginia Satir. *The Satir Journal: Transformational Systemic Therapy, 5*, 1.

Angermann, D. (1998). Gestalt therapy for eating disorders: An illustration. *Gestalt Journal, 21*, 19–47.

Ansbacher, H. L., & Ansbacher, R. R. (Eds.). (1956). *The individual psychology of Alfred Adler: A systematic presentation in selections from his writings*. New York, NY: Basic Books.

Antony, M. M., & Roemer, L. (2011). *Behavior therapy*. Washington, DC: American Psychological Association.

APA Presidential Task Force on Evidence-Based Practice. (2006). Evidence-based practice in psychology. *American Psychologist, 61*, 271–285.

Ardito, R. B., & Rabellino, D. (2011). Therapeutic alliance and outcome of psychotherapy: Historical excursus, measurements, and prospects for research. *Frontiers in Psychology, 2*, 1–11. doi: 10.3389/fpsyg.2011.00270

Arkowitz, H., Westra, H. A., Miller, W. R., & Rollnick, S. (Eds.). (2008). *Motivational interviewing in the treatment of psychological problems*. New York, NY: Guilford Press.

Arnfred, S. M. H. (2012). Gestalt therapy for patients with schizophrenia: A brief review. *Gestalt Review, 16*(1), 53–68.

Arntz, A., van Genderen, H., & Drost, J. (2009). *Schema therapy for borderline personality disorder*. Malden, MA: Wiley.

Aronson-Fontes, L. (2005). *Child abuse and culture: Working with diverse families*. New York, NY: Guilford.

Austad, C. (2009). *Counseling and psychotherapy today*. New York, NY: McGraw Hill.

Avdagic, E., Morrissey, S. A., & Boschen, M. J. (2014). A randomised controlled trial of acceptance and commitment therapy and cognitive-behaviour therapy for generalized anxiety disorder. *Behaviour Change, 31*(2), 110–130. doi: 10.1017/bec.2014.5

Baer, R. A., Smith, G. T., Hopkins, J., Krietemeyer, J., & Toney, L. (2006). Using self-report assessment methods to explore facets of mindfulness. *Assessment, 13*(1), 27–45. doi: 10.1177/1073191105283504

Balbo, M., Zaccagnino, M., Cussino, M., & Civilotti, C. (2017, October). Eye movement desensitization and reprocessing (EMDR) and eating disorders: A systematic review. *Clinical Neuropsychiatry, 14*(5), 321–329.

Bandura, A. (1969). *Principles of behavior modification*. New York, NY: Holt, Rinehart, & Winston.

Bandura, A. (1973). *Aggression: A social learning analysis*. Upper Saddle River, NJ: Prentice Hall.

Bandura, A. (1977). *Social learning theory*. Upper Saddle River, NJ: Prentice Hall.

Bandura, A. (1986). *Social foundations of thought and action: A social cognitive theory*. Upper Saddle River, NJ: Prentice Hall.

Bandura, A. (2006). Toward a psychology of human agency. *Perspectives on Psychological Science, 1*, 164–180.

Banks, M. E. (2010). 2009 Division 35 presidential address: Feminist psychology and women with disabilities: An emerging alliance. *Psychology of Women Quarterly, 34*, 431–442.

Banks, M. E., & Kaschak, E. (2013). *Women with visible and invisible disabilities: Multiple intersections, multiple issues, and multiple theories*. New York, NY: Routledge.

Banmen, A., & Banmen, E. (Eds.). (1991). *Meditations of Virginia Satir: Peace between, peace within, peace among.* Palo Alto, CA: Science and Behavior Books.

Banmen, E. (Ed.). (2008). *In her own words . . . Virginia Satir: Selected papers 1963–1983.* Phoenix, AZ: Zeig, Tucker, and Theisen.

Barber, C. (2008). *Comfortably numb: How psychiatry is medicating a nation.* New York, NY: Pantheon.

Barbieri, J. L. (2008). The URGES approach: Urge reduction by growing ego strength (URGES) for trauma/addiction treatment using alternate bilateral stimulation, hypnotherapy, ego state therapy and energy psychology. *Sexual Addiction & Compulsivity: The Journal of Treatment & Prevention, 15,* 116–138.

Barekati, S., Bahmani, B., Naghiyaaee, M., Afrasiabi, M., & Marsa, R. (2017). The effectiveness of cognitive-existential group therapy on reducing existential anxiety in the elderly. *Middle East Journal of Family Medicine, 15*(8), 75–83.

Barlow, D. H., Conklin, L. R., & Bentley, K. H. (2015). Psychological treatments for panic disorders, phobias, and social and generalized anxiety disorders. In P. E. Nathan & J. M. Gorman (Eds.), *A guide to treatments that work* (p. 409–461). New York, NY: Oxford University Press.

Barnard, L. K., & Curry, J. F. (2011). Self-compassion: Conceptualizations, correlates, & interventions. *Review of General Psychology, 15,* 289–303.

Bartholomew, K., & Horowitz, L. M. (1991). Attachment styles among young adults: A test of a four-category model. *Journal of Personality and Social Psychology, 6,* 226–244.

Barton, A. (1992). Humanistic contributions to the field of psychotherapy: Appreciating the human and liberating the therapist. *Humanist Psychologist, 20,* 332–348.

Bateman, A., & Fonagy, P. (2012). *Handbook of mentalizing in mental health practice.* Washington, DC: American Psychiatric Publishing.

Battagliese, G., Caccetta, M., Luppino, O. I., Baglioni, C., Cardi, V., Mancini, F., . . . Buonanno, C. (2015). Cognitive-behavioral therapy for externalizing disorders: A meta-analysis of treatment effectiveness. *Behaviour Research and Therapy, 75,* 60–71.

Bauman, S., & Waldo, M. (1998). Existential theory and mental health counseling: If it were a snake, it would have bitten! *Journal of Mental Health Counseling, 20,* 13–27.

Beal, D., Kopec, A. M., & DiGiuseppe, R. (1996). Disputing clients' irrational beliefs. *Journal of Rational-Emotive & Cognitive–Behavior Therapy, 14*(4), 215–229.

Beaudoin, M., Moersch, M., & Evare, B. S. (2016). The effectiveness of narrative therapy with children's social and emotional skill development: An empirical study of 813 problem-solving stories. *Journal of Systemic Therapy, 35*(3), 42–59.

Beck, A. T. (1976). *Cognitive therapy and the emotional disorders.* Madison, CT: International Universities Press.

Beck, A. T., Davis, D. D., & Freeman, A. (2015). *Cognitive therapy of personality disorders* (3rd ed.). New York, NY: Guilford.

Beck, A. T., & Emery, G. (with Greenberg, R. L.). (2005). *Anxiety disorders and phobias: A cognitive perspective* (15th anniversary ed.). New York, NY: Basic Books.

Beck, A. T., & Greenberg, R. L. (1995). *Coping with depression.* Bala Cynwyd, PA: The Beck Institute.

Beck, A. T., Rector, N. A., Stolar, N., & Grant, P. (2008). *Schizophrenia: Cognitive theory, research, and therapy.* New York, NY: Guilford Press.

Beck, A. T., Rush, A. J., Shaw, B. F., & Emery, G. (1979). *Cognitive therapy of depression.* New York, NY: Guilford Press.

Beck, J. S. (2005). *Cognitive therapy for challenging problems: What to do when the basics don't work.* New York, NY: Guilford Press.

Beck, J. S. (2011). *Cognitive behavioral therapy: Basics and beyond* (2nd ed.). New York, NY: Guilford Press.

Becvar, D. S., & Becvar, R. J. (2013). *Family therapy: A systemic integration* (8th ed.). Upper Saddle River, NJ: Pearson.

Bedics, J. D., Korslund, K. E., Sayrs, J. R., & McFarr, L. M. (2013). The observation of essential clinical strategies during an individual session of dialectical behavior therapy. *Psychotherapy, 50*(3), 454–457.

Beidel, D. C., Alfano, C. A., Kofler, M. J., Rao, P. A., Scharfstein, L., & Sarver, N. W. (2014). The impact of social skills training for social anxiety disorder: A randomized controlled trial. *Journal of Anxiety Disorders, 28,* 908–918.

Beisser, A. (1970). The paradoxical theory of change. In J. Fagan & I. Sheperd (Eds.), *Gestalt therapy now* (pp. 77–80). Palo Alto, CA: Science and Behavior Books.

Benard, B. (2004). *Resiliency: What do we know?* San Francisco, CA: WestEd.

Benish, S., Imel, Z. E., & Wampold, B. E. (2008). The relative efficacy of bona fide psychotherapies of post-traumatic stress disorder: A meta-analysis of direct comparisons. *Clinical Psychology Review, 28,* 746–758.

Berdondini, L., Elliott, R., & Shearer, J. (2012). Collaboration in experiential therapy. *Journal of Clinical Psychology, 68*(2), 159–167. doi: 10.1002/jclp.21830

Berg, I. K., & Miller, S. D. (1992). Working with Asian American clients one person at a time. *Families in Society: The Journal of Contemporary Human Services, 73*, 356–363.

Bernard, M. E. (2011). *Rationality and the pursuit of happiness: The legacy of Albert Ellis*. New York, NY: Wiley.

Bernard, M. E. (2013). *The strength of self-acceptance: Theory, practice and research*. New York, NY: Springer.

Bernard, M. E., Froh, J. J., DiGiuseppe, R., Joyce, M. R., & Dryden, W. (2010). Albert Ellis: Unsung hero of positive psychology. *The Journal of Positive Psychology, 5*, 302–310.

Bertalanffy, L. V. (1968). *General systems theory: Foundation, development, applications*. New York, NY: Braziller.

Bertolino, B. (2010). *Strengths-based engagement and practice: Creating effective helping relationships*. New York, NY: Pearson.

Binder, J. L. (2004). *Key competencies in brief dynamic psychotherapy: Clinical practice beyond the manual*. New York, NY: Guilford Press.

Binswanger, L. (1963). *Being-in-the-world: Selected papers of Ludwig Binswanger*. London, UK: Condor Books.

Bioler, L., Haverman, M., Westerholf, G. J., Riper, H., Smit, F., & Bohlmeijer, E. (2013). Positive psychology interventions: A meta-analysis of randomized controlled studies. *BMC Public Health, 13*(119), 1–20. doi: 10.1186/1471-2458-13-119

Bisson, J., & Andrew, M. (2007). Psychological treatment of post-traumatic stress disorder (PTSD). *Cochrane Database of Systematic Reviews*, 2007(3). doi: 10.1002/14651858.CD003388.pub3

Bisson, J., Ehlers, A., Matthews, R., Pilling, S., Richards, D., & Turner, S. (2007). Psychological treatments for chronic post-traumatic stress disorder. Systematic review and meta-analysis. *British Journal of Psychiatry, 190*, 97–104.

Bitter, J. R. (2011). *Contributions to Adlerian psychology*. Bloomington, IN: Xlibris.

Bleske-Rechek, A., & Kelley, J. A. (2014). Birth order and personality: A within-family test using independent self-reports from both firstborn and laterborn siblings. *Personality and Individual Differences, 56*, 15–18. doi: 10.1016/j.paid.2013.08.011

Blom, R. (2006). *Handbook of Gestalt play therapy*. Philadelphia, PA: Jessica Kingsley.

Bloom, D., & Brownell, P. (2011). *Gestalt therapy now*. Newcastle upon Tyne, UK: Cambridge Scholastic.

Bluett, E. J., Homan, K. J., Morrison, K. L., Levin, M. E., & Twohig, M. P. (2014). Acceptance and commitment therapy or anxiety and OCD spectrum disorders: An empirical review. *Journal of Anxiety Disorders, 28*, 612–624. doi: 10.1016/j.janxdis.2014.06.008

Bohart, A. C., & Tallman, K. (2010). Clients: The neglected common factor in psychotherapy. In B. L. Duncan, S. D. Miller, B. E. Wampold, & M. A. Hubble (Eds.), *Heart and soul of change in psychotherapy* (2nd ed., pp. 83–111). Washington, DC: American Psychological Association.

Bohart, A. C., & Watson, J. C. (2011). Person-centered psychotherapy and related experiential approaches. In S. B. Messer & A. S. Gurman, (Eds.), *Essential psychotherapies: Theory and practice* (3rd ed., pp. 223–260). New York, NY: Guilford.

Bond, C., Woods, K., Humphrey, N., Symes, W., & Green, L. (2013). Practitioner review: The effectiveness of solution focused brief therapy with children and families: A systematic and critical evaluation of the literature from 1990–2010. *Journal of Child Psychology & Psychiatry, 54*(7), 707–723. doi: 10.1111/jcpp.12058

Boss, M. (1963). *Psychoanalysis and Daseinsanalysis*. New York, NY: Basic Books.

Boutot, E., & Hume, K. (2012). Beyond time out and table time: Today's applied behavior analysis for students with autism. *Education and Training in Autism and Developmental Disabilities, 47*, 23–38.

Bowen, M. C. (1976). Principles and techniques of multifamily therapy. In M. P. H. Guerin, Jr. (Ed.), *Family therapy: Theory and practice* (pp. 388–404). New York, NY: Gardner Press.

Bowen, M. C. (1978). *Family therapy in clinical practice*. New York, NY: Aronson.

Bowlby, J. (1978). Attachment theory and its therapeutic implications. *Adolescent Psychiatry, 6*, 5–33.

Bowlby, J. (1988). *A secure base: Parent–child attachment and healthy human development*. New York, NY: Basic Books.

Bowling, S. W., Kearney, L. K., Lumadue, C. A., & St. Germain, N. R. (2002). Considering justice: An exploratory study of family therapy with adolescents. *Journal of Marital and Family Therapy, 28*(2), 213–223.

Bowman, C. E. (2012). Reconsidering holism in Gestalt therapy: A bridge too far. In T. B. Levine (Ed.), *Gestalt therapy: Advances in theory and practice* (pp. 27–38). New York, NY: Routledge.

Bradley, H. (2007). *Gender*. Hoboken, NJ: Wiley.

Brady, V. P., & Whitman, S. M. (2012). Acceptance and mindfulness-based approach to social phobia: A case study. *Journal of College Counseling, 15*, 81–96.

Bratter, T. E. (2010). Rejection of psychotropic medicine and DSM-IV nomenclature produce positive outcomes for gifted, alienated, and dually diagnosed John Dewey Academy students who were self-destructive: Part I. *Journal of Ethical Human Psychology and Psychiatry, 11*, 16–28.

Bratter, T. E., Esparat, D., Kaufman, A., & Sinsheimer, L. (2008). Confrontational psychotherapy: A compassionate and potent therapeutic orientation for gifted adolescents who are self-destructive and engage in dangerous behavior. *International Journal of Reality Therapy, 27*, 13–25.

Broderick, P. C., & Blewitt, P. (2015). *The life span: Human development for helping professionals* (4th ed.). Upper Saddle River, NJ: Pearson.

Broverman, I. K., Broverman, D. M., Clarkson, F., Rosenkrantz, P., & Vogel, S. (1970). Sex role stereotyping and clinical judgments of mental health. *Journal of Consulting and Clinical Psychology, 45*, 250–256.

Brown, C. (2007). Situating knowledge and power in the therapeutic alliance. In C. Brown and T. Augusta-Scott (Eds.), *Narrative therapy: Making meaning, making lives* (pp. 3–22). Thousand Oaks, CA: Sage.

Brown, C., & Augusta-Scott, T. (Eds.). (2007). *Narrative therapy: Making meaning, making lives*. Thousand Oaks, CA: Sage.

Brown, L. S. (1994). *Subversive dialogue: Theory in feminist therapy*. New York, NY: Basic Books.

Brown, L. S. (2002). Feminist therapy and EMDR: A theory meets a practice. In F. Shapiro (Ed.), *EMDR as an integrative psychotherapy approach: Experts of diverse orientations explore the paradigm prism* (pp. 263–287). Washington, DC: American Psychological Association.

Brown, L. S. (2007). Empathy, genuineness and the dynamics of power: A feminist responds to Rogers. *Psychotherapy: Theory, Research, Practice, Training, 44*(3), 257–259.

Brown, L. S. (2008). *Cultural competence in trauma therapy: Beyond the flashback*. Washington, DC: American Psychological Association.

Brown, L. S. (2010). *Feminist therapy*. Washington, DC: American Psychological Association.

Brown, L. S., & Root, M. P. P. (Eds.). (1990). *Diversity and complexity in feminist therapy*. New York, NY: Harrington Park Press.

Bruner, J. (2002). *Making stories*. New York, NY: Farrar, Strauss, and Giroux.

Bryant, R. A., Moulds, M. L., Guthrie, R. M., Dang, S. T., Mastrodomenico, J., Nixon, R. D., . . . Creamer, M. (2008). A randomized controlled trial of exposure therapy and cognitive restructuring for posttraumatic stress disorder. *Journal of Consulting and Clinical Psychology, 76*(4), 695–703. doi: 10.1037/a0012616

Buber, M. (1970). *I and thou*. New York, NY: Scribner.

Bucci, S., Seymour-Hyde, A., Harris, A., & Berry, K. (2016). Client and therapist attachment styles and working alliance. *Clinical Psychology and Psychotherapy, 23*, 156–165. doi: 10.1002/cpp.1944

Bugental, J. F. T. (1965). *The search for authenticity: An existential-analytic approach to psychotherapy*. New York, NY: Holt, Reinhart, & Winston.

Bugental, J. F. T. (1978). *Psychotherapy and process: The fundamentals of an existential humanistic approach*. Reading, MA: Addison-Wesley.

Bugental, J. F. T. (1990). *Intimate journeys*. San Francisco, CA: Jossey-Bass.

Bugental, J. F. T. (1997). There is a fundamental division in how psychotherapy is conceived. In J. K. Zeig (Ed.), *The evolution of psychotherapy: The third conference* (pp. 185–196). New York, NY: Brunner/Mazel.

Bugental, J. F. T. (2008). Preliminary sketches for a short-term existential-humanistic therapy. In K. Schneider (Ed.), *Existential integrative therapy* (pp. 165–167). New York, NY: Routledge.

Burdenski, T. K., & Wubbolding, R. E. (2011). Extending reality therapy with focusing: A humanistic road for the choice theory total behavior car. *International Journal of Reality Therapy, 31*, 14–30.

Burns, D. D. (1999). *The feeling good handbook*. San Francisco, CA: HarperCollins.

Busse, R. T., & Downey, J. (2011). Selective mutism: A three-tiered approach to prevention and intervention. *Contemporary School Psychology, 15*, 53–63.

Butler, A. C., Chapman, J. E., Forman, E. M., & Beck, A. T. (2006). The empirical status of cognitive–behavioral therapy: A review of meta-analyses. *Clinical Psychology Review*, *26*, 17–31.

Butler, G., Fennell, M., & Hackmann, A. (2008). *Cognitive–behavioral therapy for anxiety disorders: Mastering clinical challenges*. New York, NY: Guilford Press.

Butler, J., & Ciarrochi, J. V. (2007). Psychological acceptance and quality of life in the elderly. *Quality of Life Research*, *16*(4), 607–615.

Cain, D. J. (1987). Carl R. Rogers: The man, his vision, his impact. *Person-Centered Review*, *2*, 283–288.

Cain, D. J. (1987). Our international family. *Person-Centered Review*, *2*(2), 139–149.

Cain, D. J. (2010). *Person-centered psychotherapies*. Washington, DC: American Psychological Association.

Cain, D. J. (2012). Person-centered therapy. In J. Frew & M. D. Spiegler (Eds.), *Contemporary psychotherapies for a diverse world* (pp. 177–227). Boston, MA: Taylor & Francis.

Callaghan, J. E. M., Fellin, L. C., & Alexander, J. H. (2018). Promoting resilience and agency in children and young people who have experienced domestic violence and abuse: The "MPOWER" intervention. *Journal of Family Violence*, *34*(6), 521–537.

Cambray, J. (2009). *Synchronicity: Nature and psyche in an interconnected universe*. College Station: Texas A&M University Press.

Cannon, K. B., Hammer, T. R., Reicherzer, S., & Gilliam, B. J. (2012). Relational-cultural theory: A framework for relational competencies and movement in group work with female adolescents. *Journal of Creativity in Mental Health*, *7*(1), 2–16.

Caplan, E. (1998). Popularizing American psychotherapy: The Emmanuel Movement, 1906–1910. *History of Psychology*, *1*, 289–314.

Capps, F. (2006). Combining eye movement desensitization and reprocessing with gestalt techniques in couples counseling. *The Family Journal*, *14*(1), 49–58. doi: 10.1177/1066480705282055

Carastathis, A. (2016). *Intersectionality: Origins, contestations, horizons*. Lincoln, NE: University of Nebraska Press.

Carlson, J., & Englar-Carlson, M. (2017). *Adlerian psychotherapy*. Washington, DC: American Psychological Association.

Carlson, J., & Maniacci, M. P. (2011). *Alfred Adler revisited*. New York, NY: Routledge.

Carlson, J., Watts, R. E., & Maniacci, M. (2006). *Adlerian therapy: Theory and practice*. Washington, DC: American Psychological Association.

Carlson, J. D., & Englar-Carlson, M. (2012). Adlerian therapy. In J. Frew & M. D. Spiegler (Eds.), *Contemporary psychotherapies for a diverse world* (pp. 93–140). Boston, MA: Taylor & Francis.

Carlson, J. D., & Robey, P. A. (2011). An integrative Adlerian approach to family counseling. *The Journal of Individual Psychology*, *67*(3), 232–244.

Carlson, J. D., Watts, R. E., & Maniacci, M. (2006). *Adlerian therapy: Theory and practice*. Washington DC: American Psychological Association.

Carr, A. (1998). Michael White's narrative therapy. *Contemporary Family Therapy*, *20*, 485–503.

Carr, A. (2014a). The evidence-base for family therapy and systemic interventions for child focused problems. *Journal of Family Therapy*, *36*, 107–157.

Carr, A. (2014b). The evidence-base for couple therapy, family therapy and systemic interventions for adult-focused problems. *Journal of Family Therapy*, *36*, 158–194.

Carr, E. R., & West, L. M. (2013). Inside the therapy room: A case study for treating African American men from a multicultural/feminist perspective. *Journal of Psychotherapy Integration*, *23*(2), 120–133.

Carr, S. M., Smith, I. C., & Simm, R. (2014). Solution-focused brief therapy from the perspective of clients with long-term physical health conditions. *Psychology, Health & Medicine*, *19*(4), 384–391. doi: 10.1080/13548506.2013.824594

Carrick, H., & Randle-Phillips, C. (2018). Solution-focused approaches in the context of people with intellectual disabilities: A critical review. *Journal of Mental Health Research in Intellectual Disabilities*, *11*(1), 30–53.

Carter, J. D., Luty, S. E., McKenzie, J. M., Mulder, R. T., Frampton, C. M., & Joyce, P. R. (2011). Patient predictors of response to cognitive behaviour therapy and interpersonal psychotherapy in a randomized clinical trial for depression. *Journal of Affective Disorders*, *128*, 252–261.

Cashdan, S. (1988). *Object relations therapy: Using the relationship*. New York, NY: W. W. Norton.

Cashwell, C. S., & Young, J. S. (Eds.). (2011). *Integrating spirituality and religion into counseling: A guide to competent practice* (2nd ed.). Alexandria, VA: American Counseling Association.

Chen, Y. R., Hung, K. W., Tsai, J. C., Chu, H., Chung, M. H., Chen, S. R., . . . Chou, K. R. (2012). Efficacy of eye-movement desensitization and reprocessing for patients with posttraumatic stress disorder: A meta-analysis of randomized controlled trials. *PLoS ONE, 9*(8), 1–17.

Chesler, P. (1972). *Women and madness*. Garden City, NY: Doubleday.

Churchill, R., Philippa, D., Caldwell, D., Moore, T. H. M., Jones, H., Lewis, G., & . . . Hunot, V. (2010). Humanistic therapies versus other psychological therapies for depression. *Cochrane Database System Review, 9*, 1–23.

Ciorbea, I., & Nedelcea, C. (2012). The theoretical orientation shapes the personality of the psychotherapist? *Social and Behavioral Sciences, 46*, 495–503.

Claessens, M. (2009). Mindfulness and existential therapy. *Existential Analysis, 20*, 109–119.

Clark, D., & Beck, A. T. (2011). *Cognitive therapy of anxiety disorders: Science and practice*. New York, NY: Guilford Press.

Clarkson, P., & Mackewn, J. (1993). *Fritz Perls*. London, UK: Sage.

Clement, P. (2013). Practice-based evidence: 45 years of psychotherapy's effectiveness in a private practice. *American Journal of Psychotherapy, 67*(1), 23–46.

Cochrane, K. (2013). *All the rebel women: The rise of the fourth wave of feminism*. London: Guardian Shorts.

Cocks, G. (Ed.). (1994). *The curve of life: Correspondence of Heinz Kohut*. Chicago, IL: University of Chicago Press.

Coelho, H. F., Canter, P. H., & Ernst, E. (2007). Mindfulness-based cognitive therapy: Evaluating current evidence and informing future research. *Journal of Consulting and Clinical Psychology, 75*, 1000–1005.

Cohen, J. A., Mannarino, A. P., & Deblinger, E. (2006). *Treating trauma and traumatic grief in children and adolescents*. New York, NY: Guilford.

Coles, R. (1992). *Anna Freud: The dream of psychoanalysis*. New York, NY: Addison-Wesley.

Colman, W. (2011). Synchronicity and the meaning-making psyche. *Journal of Analytical Psychology, 56*, 471–491.

Comstock, D., Hammer, T., Strentzsch, J., Cannon, K., Parsons, J., & Salazar, G. (2008). Relational-cultural theory: A framework for bridging relational, multicultural, and social justice competencies. *Journal of Counseling & Development, 86*, 279–287.

Conlin, S. E. (2017). Feminist therapy: A brief integrative review of theory, empirical support, and call for new directions. *Women's Studies International Forum, 62*, 78–82.

Connell, G. M. (1996). Carl Whitaker: In memoriam. *Journal of Marital and Family Therapy, 22*, 3–8.

Conradi, H. J., & de Jonge, P. (2009). Recurrent depression and the role of adult attachment: A prospective and a retrospective study. *Journal of Affective Disorders, 116*, 93–99.

Cooper, M. (2008). Existential psychotherapy. In J. L. LeBow (Ed.), *Twenty-first century psychotherapies: Contemporary approaches to theory and practice*. New York, NY: Wiley.

Cooper, M., O'Hara, M., Schmid, P. F., & Bohart, A. (2013). *The handbook of person-centered psychotherapy and counselling* (2nd ed.). New York, NY: Palgrave Macmillan.

Cooper, M., Watson, J. C., & Bolldampt, D. (Eds.). (2010). *Person-centered and experiential therapies work: A review of the research on counseling, psychotherapy, and related practices*. Ross-on-Wye, UK: PCCS Books.

Corey, G., Corey, M., Corey, C, & Callanan, P. (2015). *Issues and ethics in the helping professions* (9th ed.). Belmont, CA: Brooks/Cole.

Cornelius-White, J. H. D. (2015). *Person-centered approaches for counselors (theories for counselors)*. Thousand Oaks, CA: Sage.

Correia, E. A., Cooper, M., Berdondini, L., & Correia, K. (2017). Characteristic practices of existential psychotherapy: A worldwide survey of practitioners' perspectives. *The Humanistic Psychologist, 45*(3), 217–237.

Craig, M., Vos, J., Cooper, M., & Correia, E. A. (2015). Existential psychotherapies. In D. J. Cain, K. Keenan, & S. Rubin (Eds.), *Humanistic psychotherapies: Handbook of research and practice* (2nd ed.; pp. 283–317). Washington, DC: American Psychological Association.

Cramer, P. (2006). *Protecting the self: Defense mechanisms in action*. New York, NY: Guilford Press.

Crane, R. (2012). *Mindfulness-based cognitive therapy: Distinctive features*. New York, NY: Routledge.

Crane, R. S., Kuyken, W., Hastings, R. P., Rothwell, N., & Williams, M. G. (2010). Training teachers to deliver mindfulness-based interventions: Learning from the UK experience. *Mindfulness, 1*, 74–86.

Craske, M. G., & Barlow, D. H. (2014). Panic and agoraphobia. In D. H. Barlow (Ed.), *Clinical handbook of psychological disorders: A step-by-step treatment manual* (5th ed., pp. 1–61). New York, NY: Guilford.

Crete, G. K., & Singh, A. (2015). Counseling men with trauma histories: Developing foundational knowledge. In M. Englar-Carlson, M. P. Evans, & T. Duffey (Eds.). *A counselor's guide to working with men* (pp. 285–204). Alexandria, VA: American Counseling Association.

Crethar, H., Rivera, E. T., & Nash, S. (2008). In search of common threads: Linking multicultural, feminist, and social justice counseling paradigms. *Journal of Counseling & Development, 86*, 269–278.

Crocker, S. F. (2005). Phenomenology, existentialism, and Eastern thought in Gestalt therapy. In A. L. Woldt & S. M. Toman (Eds.), *Gestalt therapy: History, theory, and practice* (pp. 65–80). Thousand Oaks, CA: Sage.

Crocket, K. (2012). Narrative therapy. In J. Frew & M. D. Spiegler (Eds.), *Contemporary psychotherapy for a diverse world* (pp. 489–533). Boston, MA: Houghton Mifflin.

Crowther-Heyck, H. (1999). George A. Miller, language, and the computer metaphor of mind. *History of Psychology, 2*, 37–64.

Crumb, L., & Haskins, L. (2017). An integrative approach: Relational cultural theory and cognitive behavior therapy in college counseling. *Journal of College Counseling, 20*(3), 263–277.

Curran, J., Ekers, D., McMillan, D., & Houghton, S. (2012). Behavioural activation. In W. Dryden (Ed.), *Cognitive behaviour therapies* (pp. 236–260). Thousand Oaks, CA: Sage.

Dakof, G. A., Henderson, C. E., Rowe, C. L., Boustani, M., Greenbaum, P. E., Wang, W., . . . Liddle, H. A. (2015). A randomized clinical trial of family therapy in juvenile drug court. *Journal of Family Psychology, 29*(2), 232–241.

Dallos, R. (2006). *Attachment narrative therapy: Integrating systemic, narrative and attachment approaches.* Maidenhead, Berkshire, UK: Open University Press.

Danielian, J. (2010). Meta-realization in Horney and the teaching of psychoanalysis. *American Journal of Psychoanalysis, 70*, 10–22.

Danziger, P. R., & Welfel, E. R. (2001). The impact of managed care on mental health counselors: A survey of perceptions, practices, and compliance with ethical standards. *Journal of Mental Health Counseling, 23*(2), 137–150.

Dattilio, F. M. (2005). Restructuring family schemas: A cognitive–behavioral perspective. *Journal of Marital and Family Therapy, 31*, 15–30.

Dattilio, F. M. (2010). *Cognitive-behavioral therapy with couples and families: A comprehensive guide for clinicians.* New York, NY: Guilford.

Daugherty, C., & Lees, M. (1988). Feminist psychodynamic therapies. In M. A. Dutton-Douglas & L. E. Walker (Eds.). *Feminist psychotherapies: Integration of therapeutic and feminist systems* (pp. 68–90). Norwood, NJ: Ablex Publishing Corporation.

Davanloo, H. (1979). Techniques of short-term psychotherapy. *Psychiatric Clinics of North America, 2*, 11–22.

Davanloo, H. (1980). A method of short-term dynamic psychotherapy. In H. Davanloo (Ed.), *Short-term dynamic psychotherapy.* Northvale, NJ: Aronson.

Day, S. X. (2008). *Theory and design in counseling and psychotherapy* (2nd ed.). Boston, MA: Houghton Mifflin.

Deckersbach, T., Hölzel, B., Eisner, L., Lazar, S. W., & Nierenberg, A. A. (2014). *Bipolar disorder and mindfulness: Mindfulness-based cognitive therapy for bipolar disorder.* New York, NY: Guilford.

Dehing, J. (1992). The therapist's interventions in Jungian analysis. *Journal of Analytical Psychology, 37*, 29–47.

De Jong, P., & Berg, I. K. (2013). *Interviewing for solutions* (4th ed.). Pacific Grove, CA: Brooks/Cole.

Demos, V. C., & Prout, M. F. (1993). A comparison of seven approaches to brief psychotherapy. *International Journal of Short-Term Psychotherapy, 8*, 3–22.

Dermer, S. B., Hemesath, C. W., & Russell, C. S. (1998). A feminist critique of solution-focused therapy. *American Journal of Family Therapy, 26*(3), 239–250.

De Saeger, H., Bartak, A., Eder, E. E., & Kamphuis, J. H. (2016). Memorable experiences in therapeutic assessment: Inviting the patient's perspective following a pretreatment randomized controlled trial. *Journal of Personality Assessment, 98*(5), 472–479. doi: 10.1080/00223891.2015.1136314

de Shazer, S. (1982). *Patterns of brief family therapy: An ecosystem approach.* New York, NY: Guilford Press.

de Shazer, S. (1985). *Keys to solutions in brief therapy.* New York, NY: W. W. Norton.

de Shazer, S. (1988). *Clues: Investigating solutions in brief therapy.* New York, NY: W. W. Norton.

de Shazer, S. (1991). *Putting difference to work.* New York, NY: W. W. Norton.

de Shazer, S., & Dolan, Y. (2007). *More than miracles: The state of the art of solution-focused brief therapy.* New York, NY: Routledge.

Diamond, S. A. (2009). What is existential psychotherapy? In D. A. Leeming, K. Madden, & S. Marlan (Eds.), *Encyclopedia of psychology and religion* (pp. 304–305). New York, NY: Springer Verlag.

Dîaz-Lázaro, C. M., Verdinelli, S., & Cohen, B. B. (2012). Empowerment feminist therapy with Latina immigrants: Honoring the complexity and socio-cultural contexts of clients' lives. *Women & Therapy, 35*(1-2), 80–92.

Dicker, R. C. (2008). *A history of U.S. feminisms.* Berkeley, CA: Seal Press.

DiGiuseppe, R. (1996). The nature of irrational and rational beliefs: Progress in rational emotive behavior therapy. *Journal of Rational-Emotive & Cognitive–Behavior Therapy, 14*(1), 5–28.

Dinkmeyer, D. C., & McKay, K. (1997). *Systematic training for effective parenting.* Circle Pines, MN: American Guidance Services.

Dobson, K. S. (Ed.). (2010). *Handbook of cognitive behavioral therapies.* New York, NY: Guilford Press.

Dobson, K. S., & Dozois, D. J. A. (2010). Historical and philosophical bases of the cognitive–behavioral therapies. In K. S. Dobson (Ed.), *Handbook of cognitive behavioral therapies* (p. 38). New York, NY: Guilford Press.

Dominitz, V. A. (2017). Gestalt therapy applied: A case study with an inpatient diagnosed with substance use and bipolar disorders. *Clinical Psychology & Psychotherapy, 24*(1), 36–47. doi: 10.1002/cpp.2016

Doric, J. Z. (2017). Co-creating gestalt therapy research on rehabilitation of high security offenders. *Gestalt Journal of Australia and New Zealand, 13*(2), 45–55.

Dourley, J. P. (2008). *Paul Tillich, Carl Jung, and the recovery of religion.* New York, NY: Routledge.

Drauker, C. B. (1998). Narrative therapy for women who have lived with violence. *Archives of Psychiatric Nursing, 7,* 162–168.

Dreikurs, R. (1973). Private logic. In H. H. Mosak (Ed.), *Alfred Adler: His influence on psychology today* (pp. 19–32). Park Ridge, NJ: Noyes.

Dreikurs, R., Cassel, P., & Ferguson, E. D. (2004). *Discipline without tears* (rev. ed.). Toronto, Canada: Wiley.

Dreikurs, R., & Soltz, V. (1991). *Children: The challenge.* New York, NY: Plume Books.

Dryden, W. (2011). *Dealing with emotional problems using rational emotive cognitive behavior therapy.* New York, NY: Routledge.

Dryden, W., & Branch, R. (2008). *The fundamentals of rational emotive behavior therapy: A training handbook* (2nd ed.). Chichester, UK: Wiley.

Dryden, W., DiGiuseppe, R., & Neenan, M. (2010). *A primer of rational emotive behavior therapy* (3rd ed.). Champaign, IL: Research Press.

Dryden, W., & Ellis, A. (2001). Rational emotive behavior therapy. In K. S. Dobson (Ed.), *Handbook of -cognitive–behavioral therapy* (pp. 295–348). New York, NY: Guilford Press.

Duffey, T., & Haberstroh (2014). Developmental relational counseling: Applications for counseling men. *Journal of Counseling & Development, 92,* 104–113.

Duncan, B. L. (2010). Prologue: Saul Rosenzweig: The founder of the common factors. In: B. L. Duncan, S. D. Miller, B. E. Wampold, & M. A. Hubble (Eds.), *Heart and soul of change in psychotherapy* (2nd ed., pp. 3–22). Washington, DC: American Psychological Association.

Duncan, B. L., Miller, S. D., Wampold, B. E., & Hubble, M. A. (Eds.). (2010). *Heart and soul of change in psychotherapy* (2nd ed.). Washington, DC: American Psychological Association.

Dunn, T. W., Vittengl, J. R., Clark, L. A., Carmody, T., Thase, M. E., & Jarrett, R. B. (2012). Change in psychosocial functioning and depressive symptoms during acute-phase cognitive therapy for depression. *Psychological Medicine, 42,* 317–326.

Eckardt, M. H. (2005). Karen Horney: A portrait. The 120th anniversary, Karen Horney, September 16, 1885. *American Journal of Psychoanalysis, 65,* 95–101.

Edwards, D., & Arntz, A. (2012). Schema therapy in historical perspective. In M. van Vreeswijk, J. Broersen, & M. Nadort (Eds.), *The Wiley-Blackwell handbook of schema therapy: Theory, research, and practice.* Malden, MA: Wiley.

Eger, E. E. (2017). *The chose: Embrace the impossible.* New York, NY: Simon & Schuster.

Elkins, D. N. (2009). Why humanistic psychology lost its power and influence in American psychology: Implications for advancing humanistic psychology. *Journal of Humanistic Psychology, 49,* 267–291.

Ellegaard, H., & Pedersen, B. D. (2012). Stress is dominant in patients with depression and chronic low back pain. A qualitative study of psychotherapeutic interventions for patients with non-specific low back pain of 3–12 months' duration. *BMC Musculoskeletal Disorders, 13.* 166. doi: 10.1186/1471-2474-13-166

Elliott, A. (2015). *Psychoanalytic theory: An introduction* (3rd ed.). New York, NY: Palgrave.

Elliott, R. (2013). Person-centered/experiential psychotherapy for anxiety difficulties: Theory, research and practice. *Person-Centered & Experiential Psychotherapies, 12*(1), 16–32.

Elliott, R., Bohart, A. C., Watson, J. C., & Greenberg, L. S. (2011). Empathy. In J. C. Norcross (Ed.), *Psychotherapy relationships that work: Evidence-based responsiveness* (2nd ed., pp. 132–152). New York, NY: Oxford.

Elliott, R., & Greenberg, L. (2007). The essence of process-experiential/emotion-focused therapy. *American Journal of Psychotherapy, 61*, 241–254. doi: 10.1176/appi.psychotherapy.2007.61.3.241

Ellis, A. (1957). *How to live with a neurotic*. Oxford, UK: Crown Publishers.

Ellis, A. (2007). *Overcoming resistance: A rational emotive behavior therapy integrative approach* (2nd ed.). New York, NY: Springer.

Ellis, A. (2009). *All out! An autobiography*. New York, NY: Prometheus Books.

Ellis, A., & Dryden, W. (2007). *The practice of rational emotive behavior therapy* (2nd ed.). New York, NY: Springer.

Ellis, A., & Ellis, D. J. (2011). *Rational emotive behavior therapy*. Washington, DC: American Psychological Association.

Ellis, A., & MacLaren, C. (2005). *Rational emotive behavior therapy: A therapist's guide* (2nd ed.). Atascadero, CA: Impact Publishers.

Ellis, A., & Velten, E. (1998). *Optimal aging: Getting over getting older*. Chicago, IL: Open Court Books.

Ellis, A. E. (1984). Foreword. In W. Dryden, *Rational-emotive therapy: Fundamentals and innovations* (pp. i–xv). London, UK: Croom Helm.

Ellis, A. E. (1986). An emotional control card for inappropriate and appropriate emotions using rational-emotive imagery. *Journal of Counseling and Development, 65*, 205–206.

Ellis, A. E. (1988). *How to stubbornly refuse to make yourself miserable about anything—Yes, anything!* Secaucus, NJ: Lyle Stuart.

Ellis, A. E. (1992). Secular humanism and rational-emotive therapy. *Humanistic Psychologist, 20*(2/3), 349–358.

Ellis, A. E. (1995). Changing rational-emotive therapy (RET) to rational emotive behavior therapy (REBT). *Journal of Rational-Emotive & Cognitive–Behavior Therapy, 13*(2), 85–89.

Ellis, A. E. (1996). The treatment of morbid jealousy: A rational emotive behavior approach. *Journal of Cognitive Psychotherapy, 10*(1), 23–33.

Ellis, A. E. (1997). Using rational emotive behavior therapy techniques to cope with disability. *Professional Psychology: Research and Practice, 28*, 17–22.

Ellis, A. E. (2001). *Overcoming destructive beliefs, feelings, and behaviors: New directions for rational emotive behavior therapy*. New York, NY: Brunner/Mazel.

Ellsworth, L. (2007). *Choosing to heal: Using reality therapy in treatment with sexually abused children*. New York, NY: Routledge.

Ellwood, R. (1999). *The politics of myth: A study of C. G. Jung, Mircea Eliade, and Joseph Campbell*. New York: State University of New York Press.

Emmelkamp, P. M. G., Ehring, T., & Powers, M. B. (2010). Philosophy, psychology, cases, and treatments of mental disorders. In N. Kazantzis, M. A. Reinecke, & A. Freeman. *Cognitive and behavioral theories in clinical practice* (pp. 1–27). New York, NY: Guilford Press.

Enns, C. Z. (1987). Gestalt therapy and feminist therapy: A proposed integration. *Journal of Counseling & Development, 66*(2), 93–95.

Enns, C. Z. (1993). Twenty years of feminist counseling and psychotherapy: From naming biases to implementing multifaceted practice. *The Counseling Psychologist, 21*, 3–87.

Enns, C. Z. (2004). *Feminist theories and feminist psychotherapies: Origins, themes, and diversity* (2nd ed.). Binghamton, NY: Haworth Press.

Enns, C. Z., & Williams, E. N. (Eds.). (2013). *The Oxford handbook of feminist multicultural counseling psychology*. New York, NY: Oxford University Press.

Epp, L. R. (1998). The courage to be an existential counselor: An interview of Clemmont E. Vontress. *Journal of Mental Health Counseling, 20*, 1–12.

Erbes, C. R., Stillman, J. R., Wieling, E., Bera, W., & Leskela, J. (2014). A pilot examination of the use of narrative therapy with individuals diagnosed with PTSD. *Journal of Traumatic Stress, 27*(4), 730–733.

Erford, B. T., Eaves, S. H., Bryant, E. M., & Young, K. A. (2010). *35 techniques every counselor should know*. Upper Saddle River, NJ: Pearson.

Eriksen, K., & Kress, V. E. (2005). *Beyond the DSM story: Ethical quandaries, challenges, and best practices*. Thousand Oaks, CA: Sage.

Eriksen, K., & Kress, V. E. (2006). The DSM and professional counseling identity: Bridging the gap. *Journal of Mental Health Counseling, 28*(3), 202–217.

Eriksen, K., & Kress, V. E. (2008). Gender and diagnosis: Struggles and suggestions for counselors. *Journal of Counseling & Development, 86*(2), 152–162.

Erikson, E. H. (1982). *The life cycle completed*. New York, NY: W. W. Norton.

Evans, D. B. (1982). What are you doing? An interview with William Glasser. *Personnel and Guidance Journal, 60*(8), 460–466.

Evans, K., & Gilbert, M. C. (2005). *An introduction to integration psychotherapy*. London, UK: Palgrave.

Evans, K. M., Kincade, E. A., Marbley, A. F., & Seem, S. R. (2005). Feminism and feminist therapy: Lessons from the past and hopes for the future. *Journal of Counseling & Development, 83*, 269–277.

Evans, K. M., Kincade, E. A., & Seem, S. R. (2011). *Introduction to feminist therapy: Strategies for social and individual change*. Thousand Oaks, CA: Sage.

Evans, K. M., & Miller, M. (2016). Feminist therapy. In I. Marini & M. A. Stebnicki (Eds.), *The professional counselor's desk reference* (2nd ed., pp. 247–251). New York, NY: Springer.

Ewen, R. B. (1993). *An introduction to theories of personality* (4th ed.). Hillsdale, NJ: Erlbaum.

Eysenck, H. J. (1970). A mish-mash of theories. *International Journal of Psychiatry, 9*, 140–146.

Fabry, D. (2010). Evidence base for paradoxical intention: Reviewing clinical outcome studies. *International Forum for Logotherapy, 33*, 21–29.

Fagan, J., & Shepherd, I. L. (1970). *Gestalt therapy now*. Palo Alto, CA: Science and Behavior Books.

Fairburn, C. G., Bailey-Straebler, S., Basden, S., Doll, H. A., Jones, R., Murphy, R., . . . Cooper, Z. (2015). A transdiagnostic comparison of enhanced cognitive behaviour therapy (CBT-E) and interpersonal psychotherapy in the treatment of eating disorders. *Behaviour Research and Therapy, 70*, 64–71.

Farber, B. A., & Metzger, J. A. (2009). Attachment theory. In J. H. Obegi & E. Berant (Eds.), *Attachment theory and research in clinical work with adults* (pp. 46–70). New York, NY: Guilford Press.

Farrell, J. M., Shaw, I. A., & Webber, M. A. (2009). A schema-focused approach to group psychotherapy for outpatients with borderline personality disorder: A randomized controlled trial. *Journal of Behavior Therapy and Experimental Psychiatry, 40*, 317–328.

Feminist Therapy Institute. (2000). *Feminist therapy institute code of ethics*. Denver, CO: Author.

Ferreira, R., Eloff, I., Kukard, C., & Kriegler, S. (2014). Using sandplay therapy to bridge a language barrier in emotionally supporting a young vulnerable child. *The Arts in Psychotherapy, 41*(1), 107–114.

Fife, S. T., Whiting, J., Bradford, K. P., & Davis, S. D. (2013). The therapeutic pyramid: A common factors synthesis of techniques, alliance, and way of being. *Journal of Marital and Family Therapy, 40*(1), 20–33.

Finlay, L., & Evans, K. (2009). *Relational-centered research for psychotherapists*. Malden, MA: Wiley-Blackwell.

Finlay, S. W. (2000). Influence of Carl Jung and William James on the origin of Alcoholics Anonymous. *Review of General Psychology, 4*, 3–12.

Flynn, S. D., & Lo, Y. (2016). Teacher implementation of trail-based functional analysis and differential reinforcement of alternative behavior for students with challenging behavior. *Journal of Behavior Education, 25*(1), 1–31. doi: 10.1007/s10864-015-9231-2

Foa, E. B., Keane, T. M., & Friedman, M. J. (2009). *Effective treatments of PTSD: Guidelines from the International Society for Traumatic Stress Studies*. New York, NY: Guilford Press.

Foa, E. B., & Yadin, E. (2011). Assessment and diagnosis of posttraumatic stress disorder: An overview of measures. *Psychiatric Times, 28*, 1–8.

Fonagy, P. (2015). The effectiveness of psychodynamic psychotherapies: An update. *World Psychiatry, 14*(2), 137–150.

Fonagy, P., & Luyten, P. (2009). A developmental, mentalization-based approach to the understanding and treatment of borderline personality disorder. *Developmental Psychopathology, 21*, 1355–1381.

Fonagy, P., & Target, M. (2009). Theoretical models of psychodynamic psychotherapy. In G. O. Gabbard, Ed., *Textbook of psychotherapeutic treatments* (pp. 3–42). Washington, DC: American Psychiatric Publishing.

Forcehimes, A. A. (2004). *De profundis*: Spiritual transformations in Alcoholics Anonymous. *Journal of Clinical Psychology, 60*, 503–517.

Forsyth, J. P., Fuse, T., & Acheson, D. T. (2009). Interoceptive exposure for panic disorder. In W. T. O. Donohue & J. E. Fisher (Eds.), *Cognitive behavioral therapy: Applying empirically supported techniques in your practice* (pp. 296–308). New York, NY: John Wiley & Sons.

Francis, L., & Allan, S. (2014). Cognitive behavioural therapy for anorexia nervosa: A systematic review. *Clinical Psychology Review, 34*(1), 54–72. doi: 10.1016/j.cpr.2013.11.001

Frank, E. (2005). *Treating bipolar disorder: A clinician's guide to interpersonal and social rhythm therapy.* New York, NY: Guilford Press.

Frank, M. L. B. (2007). Existential theory. In D. Capuzzi & D. Gross (Eds.), *Counseling and psychotherapy: Theories and interventions* (4th ed., pp. 164–188). Upper Saddle River, NJ: Pearson/Prentice Hall.

Frankl, V. (1965). *The doctor and the soul.* New York, NY: Bantan Books.

Frankl, V. E. (1963). *Man's search for meaning.* Boston, MA: Beacon.

Frankl, V. E. (1969). *The will to meaning: Foundations and applications of logotherapy.* New York, NY: Penguin Books.

Frankl, V. E. (1978). *The unheard cry for meaning.* New York, NY: Simon & Schuster.

Frankl, V. E. (1987). On the meaning of love. *International Forum for Logotherapy, 10*, 5–8.

Frankl, V. E. (1992). Meaning in industrial society. *International Forum for Logotherapy, 15*, 66–70.

Frankl, V. E. (2000). *Man's search for ultimate meaning.* New York, NY: Perseus.

Frankl, V. E. (2010). *The feeling of meaninglessness: A challenge to psychotherapy and philosophy.* Milwaukee, WI: Marquette University Press.

Freedman, J., & Combs, G. (1996). *Narrative therapy: The social construction of preferred realities.* New York, NY: Norton.

Freeman, J., Epston, D., & Lebovitz, D. (1997). *Playful approaches to serious problems: Narrative therapy with children and their families.* New York, NY: W. W. Norton.

Freud, A. (1946). *The ego and the mechanisms of defense.* New York, NY: International Universities Press.

Freud, A. (1965). *Normality and pathology in childhood.* New York, NY: International Universities Press.

Freud, A., & Burlingham, D. T. (1943). *War and children.* New York, NY: Medical War Books, International Universities Press.

Freud, A., & Burlingham, D. T. (1944). *Infants without families: The case for and against residential nurseries.* New York, NY: Medical War Books, International Universities Press.

Freud, S. (1915). The unconscious. *Standard edition* (Vol. 14, pp. 159–216). London, UK: Hogarth Press.

Freud, S. (1938). *The basic writings of Sigmund Freud* (A. A. Brill, Trans.). New York, NY: Modern Library.

Freud, S. (1957). Mourning and melancholia. In J. Strachey (Ed.), *The standard edition of the complete psychological works of Sigmund Freud, Volume XIV (1914–1916): On the history of the psycho-analytic movement, papers on metapsychology and other works* (pp. 237–258). London, UK: Hogarth Press and Institute of Psycho-Analysis.

Frew, J. (2012). Gestalt therapy. In J. Frew & M. D. Spiegler (Eds.), *Contemporary psychotherapies for a diverse world* (pp. 215–258). New York, NY: Taylor & Francis.

Frick, W. B. (1987). The symbolic growth experience and creation of meaning. *International Forum for Logotherapy, 10*, 35–41.

Fruzzetti, A. E., & Erikson, K. R. (2010). Mindfulness and acceptance interventions in cognitive–behavioral therapy. In K. S. Dobson (Ed.), *Handbook of cognitive behavioral therapies* (3rd ed., pp. 340–372). New York, NY: Guilford Press.

Gabbard, G. O. (2005). *Psychodynamic psychiatry in clinical practice* (4th ed.). Washington, DC: American Psychiatric Publishing.

Gaffney, S. (2008). Gestalt group supervision in a divided society. Theory, practice, perspective, and reflections. *British Gestalt Journal, 17*, 27–40.

Gallagher-Thompson, D., Steffen, A. M., & Thompson, L. W. (Eds.). (2008). *Handbook of behavioral and cognitive therapies with other adults.* New York, NY: Springer.

Galsworthy-Francis, L., & Allan, S. (2014). Cognitive behavioural therapy for anorexia nervosa: A systematic review. *Clinical Psychology Review, 34*(1), 54–72. doi: 10.1016/j.cpr.2013.11.001

Garrow, S., & Walker, J. A. (2001). Existential group therapy and death anxiety. *Adultspan Journal, 3*, 77–87.

Gendlin, E. T. (1982). *Focusing* (2nd ed.). New York, NY: Bantam.

Gendlin, E. T. (1996). *Focusing-oriented psychotherapy: A manual of the experiential method.* New York, NY: Guilford Press.

George, C., Kaplan, N., & Main, M. (1996). *Adult attachment interview.* Berkeley: University of California–Berkeley.

Gergen, K. J. (2009). *An invitation to social construction* (2nd ed). Thousand Oaks, CA: Sage.

Gergen, K. J. (1991). *The saturated self: Dilemmas of identity in contemporary life.* New York, NY: Basic Books.

Gershoff, E. T., & Grogan-Kaylor, A. (2016). Spanking and child outcomes: Old controversies and new meta-analyses. *Journal of Family Psychology, 30*(4), 453–469.

Gharebaghy, S., Rassafiani, M., & Cameron, D. (2015). Effect of cognitive intervention on children with ADHD. *Physical & Occupational Therapy in Pediatrics, 35*(1), 13–23.

Giesen-Bloo, J., van Dyck, R., Spinhoven, P., van Tilburg, W., Dirksen, C., van Asselt, T., . . . Arntz, A. (2006). Outpatient psychotherapy for borderline personality disorder: A randomized trial of schema-focused therapy versus transference-focused therapy. *Archives of General Psychiatry, 63,* 649–658.

Gifford, S. (1997). *The Emmanuel Movement: The origins of group treatment and the assault on lay psychotherapy.* Boston, MA: Countway Library of Medicine.

Gilbert, D. T., & Jones, E. E. (1986). Perceiver-induced constraint: Interpretations of self-generated reality. *Journal of Personality and Social Psychology, 50,* 269–280.

Gilbert, P. (2010). *Compassion focused therapy: The CBT distinctive features series.* New York, NY: Routledge.

Gilman, S. L. (2001). Karen Horney, M.D., 1885–1952. *American Journal of Psychiatry, 158,* 1205.

Gladding, S. T. (2019). *Family therapy: History, theory, and practice* (7th ed.). Upper Saddle River, NJ: Pearson/Prentice Hall.

Glasser, W. (1975). *Reality therapy: A new approach to psychiatry.* New York, NY: Harper & Row.

Glasser, W. (1976). *Positive addiction.* New York, NY: Harper & Row.

Glasser, W. (1984). *Control theory.* New York, NY: Harper & Row.

Glasser, W. (1985). *Control theory: A new explanation of how we control our lives.* New York, NY: Harper & Row.

Glasser, W. (1986). *Control theory in the classroom.* New York, NY: Harper & Row.

Glasser, W. (1992). *The quality school: Managing students without coercion.* New York, NY: HarperCollins.

Glasser, W. (1998a). *Choice theory.* New York, NY: HarperCollins.

Glasser, W. (1998b). *The quality school.* New York, NY: HarperCollins.

Glasser, W. (2000). *Counseling with choice theory.* New York, NY: HarperCollins.

Glasser, W. (2001). *Fibromyalgia: Hope from a completely new perspective.* Chatsworth, CA: William Glasser, Inc.

Glasser, W. (2003). *Warning: Psychiatry can be hazardous to your mental health.* New York, NY: HarperCollins.

Glasser, W. (2005). *Defining mental health as a public health problem.* Chatsworth, CA: William Glasser, Inc.

Goldenberg, I., Goldenberg, H., & Stanton, M. (2017). *Family therapy: An overview* (9th ed.). Boston, MA: Cengage Learning.

Goldfried, M. R. (2004). Integrating integratively-oriented brief psychotherapy. *Journal of Psychotherapy Integration, 14,* 93–100.

Goldstein, E. G. (2001). *Self-psychology and object relations theory in social work practice.* New York, NY: Free Press.

Goldstein, J., Freud, A., & Solnit, A. J. (1979). *Before the best interests of the child.* New York, NY: Free Press.

Goldstein, T. R., Podrat-Fersch, R. K., Rivera, M., Axelson, D. A., Merranko, J., Haifeng, Y., . . . Birmaher, B. (2015). Dialectical behavior therapy for adolescents with bipolar disorder: Results from a pilot randomized trial. *Journal of Child and Adolescent Psychopharmacology, 25*(2), 140–149.

Goldstone, D. (2017). Cognitive-behavioural therapy versus psychodynamic psychotherapy for the treatment of depression: A critical review of evidence and current issues. *South African Journal of Psychology, 4*(1), 84–96.

Goodman, G. (2010). *Therapeutic attachment relationships: Interaction structures and the processes of therapeutic change.* Lanham, MD: Jason Aronson.

Goodwin, G. (2009). Evidence-based guidelines for treating bipolar disorder: Revised second edition—recommendations from the British Association for Psychopharmacology. *Journal of Psychopharmacology, 23*, 346–388. doi: 10.1177/0269881109102919

Gotink, R. A., Chu, P., Busschbach, J. J., Benson, H., Fricchione, G. L., & Hunink, M. G. (2015). Standardized mindfulness-based interventions in healthcare: An overview of systematic reviews and meta-analysis of RCTs. *PLoS ONE, 10*(4), 1–17. doi: 10.1371/journal.pone.0124344

Gottlieb, D. T., & Gottlieb, C. D. (1996). The narrative/collaborative process in couples therapy: A postmodern perspective. *Women and Therapy, 19*, 37–47.

Gray, M., & Boddy, J. (2010). Making sense of the waves: Wipeout or still riding high? *Journal of Women and Social Work, 25*(4), 368–389.

Green, J. G., McLaughlin, K. A., Berglund, P. A., Gruber, M. J., Sampson, N. A., Zaslavsky, A. M., & Kessler, R. C. (2010). Childhood adversities and adult psychiatric disorders in the national comorbidity survey replication I: Associations with first onset of DSM-IV disorders. *Archives of General Psychiatry, 67*, 113–123.

Greenberg, J. R., & Mitchell, S. A. (1983). *Object relations in psychoanalytic therapy*. Cambridge, MA: Harvard University Press.

Greenberg, L. S. (2010). *Emotion-focused therapy*. Washington, DC: American Psychological Association.

Greenberg, L. S., & Elliott, R. (2002). Emotion-focused therapy. In F. W. Kaslow (Ed.), *Comprehensive handbook of psychotherapy: Integrative/eclectic* (pp. 213–240). New York, NY: John Wiley & Sons.

Greenberg, L. S., & Goldman, R. N. (2008). *Emotion-focused couples therapy: The dynamics of emotion, love, and power*. Washington, DC: American Psychological Association Press.

Greenberg, L. S., & Johnson, S. (1988). Emotion in systemic therapies. *Journal of Systemic Therapies, 17*, 1–17.

Greenberg, L. S., & Johnson, S. M. (1988). *Emotionally focused therapy for couples*. New York, NY: Guilford.

Greenberg, L. S., & Safran, J. D. (1987). *Emotion in psychotherapy*. London, UK: Guilford Press.

Greene, B., & Sanchez-Hucles, J. (1997). Diversity: Advancing an inclusive feminist psychology. In J. Worell & N. G. Johnson (Eds.), *Shaping the future of feminist psychology: Education, research, and practice* (pp. 173–202). Washington, DC: American Psychological Association.

Greenman, P., Young, M., & Johnson, S. M. (2009). Emotionally focused therapy with intercultural couples. In M. Rastogi & V. Thomas (Eds.), *Multicultural Couple Therapy* (pp. 143–166). Thousand Oaks, CA: Sage.

Greenman, P. S., & Johnson, S. M. (2012). United we stand: Emotionally focused therapy in the treatment of couples with posttraumatic stress disorder. *Journal of Clinical Psychology, 68*, 561–569.

Gregory, B., & Peters, L. (2017). Changes in self during cognitive behavioural therapy for social anxiety disorder: A systematic review. *Clinical Psychology Review, 52*, 1–18. doi: 10.1016/j.cpr.2016.11.008

Grenz, S. J. (1996). *A primer on postmodernism*. Grand Rapids, MI: William B. Eerdmans.

Grey, L. (1998). *Alfred Adler, forgotten prophet: A vision for the 21st century*. Westport, CT: Praeger.

Greyber, L. R., Dulmus, C. N., & Cristalli, M. E. (2012). Eye movement desensitization reprocessing, posttraumatic stress disorder, and trauma: A review of randomized controlled trials with children and adolescents. *Child & Adolescent Social Work Journal, 29*(5), 409–425. doi: 10.1007/s10560-012-0266-0

Grosse, H. M., Krieger, T., Zimmermann, J., Altenstein-Yamanaka, D., Dorig, N., Meisch, L., . . . Hayes, A. M. (2019). A randomized-controlled trial of cognitive-behavioral therapy for depression with integrated techniques from emotion-focused and exposure therapies. *Psychotherapy Research, 29*(1), 30–44.

Guo, X., & Slesnick, N. (2013). Family versus individual therapy: Impact on discrepancies between parents' and adolescents' perceptions over time. *Journal of Marital and Family Therapy, 39*, 182–194.

Hagen, W. B., Arczynski, A. V., Morrow, S. L., & Hawxhurt, D. M. (2011). Lesbian, bisexual, and queer women's spirituality in feminist multicultural counseling. *Journal of LGBT Issues in Counseling, 5*(3-4), 220–236.

Haley, J. (1963). *Strategies in psychotherapy*. New York, NY: Grune-Stratton.

Haley, J. (1996). *Learning and teaching therapy*. New York, NY: Guilford.

Haley, J., & Richeport-Haley, M. (2007). *Directive family therapy*. Binghamton, NY: Haworth Press.

Hansen, J. T. (2002). Postmodern implications for theoretical integration of counseling approaches. *Journal of Counseling and Development, 80*(3), 315–321.

Hansen, J. T. (2006). Counseling theories within a postmodern epistemology: New roles for theories in counseling practice. *Journal of Counseling and Development, 84*, 291–297.

Harrington, N., & Pickles, C. (2009). Mindfulness and cognitive behavioral therapy: Are they compatible concepts? *Journal of Cognitive Psychotherapy: An International Quarterly, 23*, pp. 315–323.

Harvey, M. T., Luiselli, J. K., & Wong, S. E. (2009). Application of applied behavior analysis to mental health issues. *Psychological Services, 6*(3), 212–222. doi: 10.1037/a0016495

Harwood, T. M., Beutler, L. E., & Charvat, M. (2010). Cognitive–behavioral therapy and psychotherapy integration. In K. S. Dobson (Ed.), *Handbook of cognitive–behavioral therapies* (3rd ed., pp. 94–130). New York, NY: Guilford.

Haule, J. R. (2010). *Jung in the 21st century, Vol. II: Synchronicity and science*. New York, NY: Routledge.

Hawes, E. C. (1993). Marriage counseling and enrichment. In O. C. Christensen (Ed.), *Adlerian family counseling* (Rev. ed., pp. 125–163). Minneapolis, MN: Educational Media Corporation.

Hay, P. (2013). A systematic review of evidence for psychological treatments in eating disorders: 2005–2012. *International Journal of Eating Disorders, 46*, 462–469.

Hayes, S. C. (2004). Acceptance and commitment therapy, relational frame theory, and the third wave of behavior therapy. *Behavior Therapy, 35*, 639–665.

Hayes, S. C., & Levin, M. E. (2012). *Mindfulness and acceptance for addictive behaviors: Applying contextual CBT to substance use and behavioral addictions*. Oakland, CA: New Harbinger.

Hayes, S. C., & Lillis, J. (2012). *Acceptance and commitment therapy: Theories of psychotherapy series*. Washington, DC: American Psychological Association.

Hayes, S. C., Luoma, J. B., Bond, F. W., Masuda, A., & Lillis, J. (2006). Acceptance and commitment therapy: Models, processes and outcomes. *Behaviour Research and Therapy, 44*, 1–25.

Hayes, S. C., Strosahl, K. D., & Wilson, K. G. (1999). *Acceptance and commitment therapy: An experiential approach to behavior change*. New York, NY: Guilford.

Hayes, S. C., Strosahl, K. D., & Wilson, K. G. (2012). *Acceptance and commitment therapy: The process and practice of mindful change* (2nd ed.). New York, NY: Guilford.

Hays, P. A. (2001). *Addressing cultural complexities in practice: A framework for clinicians and counselors*. Washington, DC: American Psychological Association.

Hays, P. A. (2008). *Addressing cultural complexities in practice: Assessment, diagnosis, and therapy* (2nd ed.). Washington, DC: American Psychological Association.

Hays, P. A. (2009). Integrating evidence-based practice, cognitive–behavior therapy, and multicultural therapy: Ten steps for culturally competent practice. *Professional Psychology: Research and Practice, 40*, 354–360.

Hazan, C., & Shaver, P. (1987). Romantic love conceptualized as an attachment process. *Journal of Personality and Social Psychology, 52*, 511–524.

Headley, J. A., Kautzman-East, M., Pusateri, C. G., & Kress, V. E. (2015). Making the intangible tangible: Using expressive art during termination to co-construct meaning. *Journal of Creativity in Mental Health, 10*(1), 89–99.

Headley, J. A., & Sangganjanavanich, V. F. (2014). A recipe for change: Promoting connection through relational-cultural theory. *Journal of Creativity in Mental Health, 9*(2), 245–261.

Hedtke, L. (2014). Creating stories of hope: A narrative approach to illness, death and grief. *Australian and New Zealand Journal of Family Therapy, 35*, 4–19.

Heidegger, M. (1962). *Being and time*. New York, NY: Harper & Row.

Henderson, V. L., O'Hara, M., Barfield, G. L., & Rogers, N. (2007). Applications beyond the therapeutic context. In M. Cooper, M. O'Hara, P. F. Schmid, & G. Wyatt (Eds.), *The handbook of person-centered psychotherapy* (pp. 306–324). New York, NY: Palgrave Macmillan.

Henggeler, S. W., & Schaeffer, C. M. (2017). Treating serious antisocial behavior using multisystemic therapy. In J. R. Weisz & A. E. Kazdin (Eds.), *Evidence-based psychotherapies for children and adolescents* (3rd ed., pp. 197–214). New York, NY: Guilford.

Henretty, J., & Levitt, H. (2010). The role of therapist self-disclosure in psychotherapy: A qualitative review. *Clinical Psychology Review, 30*(1), 63–77. doi: 10.1016/J.CPR.2009.09.004

Herbert, J. D., & Forman, E. M. (2011). *Acceptance and mindfulness in cognitive behavior therapy: Understanding and applying the new therapies*. Hoboken, NJ: Wiley.

Hergenhahn, B. R. (2009). *An introduction to the history of psychology* (6th ed.). Belmont, CA: Wadsworth.

Hergenhahn, B. R., & Olson, M. H. (2007). *An introduction to the theories of personality* (7th ed.). Upper Saddle River, NJ: Pearson Prentice Hall.

Herlihy, B., & Corey, G. (2015). *ACA ethical standards casebook* (7th ed.). Alexandria, VA: American Counseling Association.

Hermmann, I. R., Greenberg, L. S., & Auszra, L. (2016). Emotion categories and patterns of change in experiential therapy for depression. *Psychotherapy Research, 26*(2), 178–195.

Hertenstein, E., Rose, N., Voderholzer, U., Heidenreich, T., Nissen, C., Thiel, N., . . . Kulz, A. (2012). Mindfulness-based cognitive therapy in obsessive-compulsive disorder—A qualitative study on patients' experiences. *BMC Psychiatry, 12*, 185–194.

Higdon, J. (2012). *Psychodynamic theory for therapeutic practice* (2nd ed.). New York, NY: Palgrave Macmillan.

Hill, C., Schottenbauer, M., Lui, J., Spangler, P., & Sim, W. (2008). Working with dreams in psychotherapy. What do psychoanalytic therapists report that they do? *Psychoanalytic Psychology, 25*, 565–573.

Hill, C. E. (2009). *Helping skills: Facilitating exploration, insight, and action* (3rd ed.). Washington, DC: American Psychological Association.

Hill, M., & Jeong, J. Y. (2008). Putting it all together: Theory. In M. Ballou, M. Hill, & C. West (Eds.), *Feminist therapy: Theory and practice* (pp. 135–151). New York, NY: Springer.

Hinrichsen, G. A., & Clougherty, K. F. (2006). *Interpersonal psychotherapy for depressed older adults*. Washington, DC: American Psychological Association.

Hinton, D. E., Rivera, E. I., Hofmann, S. G., Barlow, D. H., & Otto, M. W. (2012). Adapting CBT for traumatized refugees and ethnic minority patients: Examples from culturally adapted CBT (CA-CBT). *Transcultural Psychiatry, 49*, 340–365.

Hoch, A. L. (2009). Trauma-focused cognitive behavioral therapy for children. In A. Rubin & D. W. Springer (Eds.), *Treatment of traumatized adults and children: Clinician's guide to evidence-based practice* (pp. 179–253). Hoboken, NJ: John Wiley & Sons.

Hoffman, L. (2009). Introduction to existential psychology in a cross-cultural context: East-West dialogue. In L. Hoffman, M. Yang, F. Kaklauskas, & A. Chan (Eds.), *Existential psychology East-West* (pp. 1–67). Colorado Springs, CO: University of the Rockies Press.

Hoffman, L., Yang, M., Kaklauskas, F., & Chan, A. (Eds.). (2009). *Existential psychology East-West* (pp. 1–67). Colorado Springs, CO: University of the Rockies Press.

Hofmann, S. G. (2012). *An introduction to modern CBT: Psychological solutions to mental health problems*. Malden, MA: Wiley-Blackwell.

Hofmann, S. G., Asnaani, A., Vonk, I. J., Sawyer, A., & Fang, A. (2012). The efficacy of cognitive behavioral therapy: A review of meta-analyses. *Cognitive Therapy and Research, 36*, 427–440.

Hofmann, S. G., Sawyer, A. T., & Fang, A. (2010). The empirical status of the "new wave" of cognitive behavioral therapy. *Psychiatric Clinics of North America, 33*, 701–710.

Hogan, S. (Ed.). (1997). *Feminist approaches to art therapy*. New York, NY: Routledge.

Hoglend, P., Daul, H., Hersoug, A., Lorentzen, S., & Perry, J. (2011). Long-term effects of transference interpretation in dynamic psychotherapy of personality disorders. *European Psychiatry, 26*(7), 419–424.

Hollon, S. D., Stewart, M. O., & Strunk, D. (2006). Enduring effects for cognitive behavioral therapy in the treatment of depression and anxiety. *Annual Review of Psychology, 57*, 285–315.

Holzel, B. K., Lazar, S. W., Gard, T., Schuman-Olivier, Z., Vago, D. R., & Ott, U. (2011). How does mindfulness meditation work? Proposing mechanisms of action from a conceptual and neural perspective, *Perspectives on Psychological Science, 6*, 537–559.

Homan, K. J. (2016). Self-compassion and psychological well-being in older adults. *Journal of Adult Development, 23*, 111–119.

Horigian, V., Feaster, D., Brincks, A., Robbins, M., Perez, M., & Szapocznik, J. (2015). The effects of Brief Strategic Family Therapy (BSFT) on parent substance use and the association between parent and adolescent substance use. *Addictive Behaviors, 42*, 44–50.

Horigian, V. E., Feaster, D. J., Robbins, M. S., Brincks, A. M., Ucha, J., Rohrbaugh, M. J., . . . Szapocznik, J. (2015). A cross-sectional assessment of the long term effects of brief strategic family therapy for adolescent substance use. *American Journal on Addictions, 24*(7), 637–645.

Horney, K. (1937). *The neurotic personality of our time*. New York, NY: W. W. Norton.

Horney, K. (1939). *New ways in psychoanalysis*. New York, NY: W. W. Norton.

Horney, K. (1945). *Our inner conflicts.* New York, NY: W. W. Norton.

Horney, K. (1950). *Neurosis and human growth: The struggle toward self-realization.* New York, NY: W. W. Norton.

Horowitz, M., Marmar, C., Krupnick, J., Wilner, N., Kaltreider, N., & Wallerstein, R. (2001). *Personality styles and brief psychotherapy.* New York, NY: Basic Books.

Hotz, J. V., & Pantano, J. (2015). Strategic parenting, birth order, and school performance. *Journal of Population Economics, 28*(4), 911–936. doi: 10.1007/s00148-015-0542-3

Houston, G. (2003). *Brief Gestalt therapy.* Thousand Oaks, CA: Sage.

Hoyt, M. F. (2017). *Brief therapy and beyond: Stories, language, love, hope, and time.* New York, NY: Routledge.

Hubble, M. A., Duncan, B. L., Miller, S. D., & Wampold, B. E. (2010). Introduction. In B. L. Duncan, S. D. Miller, B. E. Wampold, & M. A. Hubble (Eds.), *The heart and soul of change* (2nd ed., pp. 23–46). Washington, DC: American Psychological Association.

Hung, S., Spencer, M. S., & Dronamraju, R. (2012). Selective mutism: Practice and intervention strategies for children. *Children & Schools, 34*(4), 222–230. doi: 10.1093/cs/cds006

Hunger, C., Bornhäuser, A., Link, L., Schweitzer, J., & Weinhold, J. (2014). Improving experience in personal social systems through family constellation seminars: Results of a randomized controlled trial. *Family Process, 53,* 288–306.

Iftene, F., Predescu, E., Stefan, S., & David, D. (2015). Rational-emotive and cognitive-behavior therapy (REBT/CBT) versus pharmacotherapy versus REBT/CBT plus pharmacotherapy in the treatment of major depressive disorder in youth; A randomized clinical trial. *Psychiatry Research, 225*(3), 687–694.

Israeli, A. L., & Santor, D. A. (2000). Reviewing effective components of feminist therapy. *Counselling Psychology Quarterly, 13,* 233–248.

Jacobson, E. (1938). *Progressive relaxation.* Chicago, IL: University of Chicago Press.

James, W. (1890). *The principles of psychology.* New York, NY: Holt. (Reprinted 1950, Dover Publications)

Jeffrin Margreat, J., & Rohini, N. S. (2014). Management of hopelessness and coping among breast cancer patients. *Indian Journal of Health & Wellbeing, 5*(8), 961–964.

Johnson, S. M. (2004). *The practice of emotionally focused couple therapy: Creating connection.* New York, NY: Brunner-Routledge.

Johnson, S. M. (2007). A new era for couple therapy: Theory, research, and practice in concert. *Journal of Systemic Therapies, 26,* 5–16.

Johnson, S. M. (2008). *Hold me tight: Seven conversations for a lifetime of love.* New York, NY: Little, Brown and Company.

Johnson, S. M., Bradley, B., Furrow, J., Lee, A., Palmer, G., Tilley, D., & Woolley, S. (2005). *Becoming an emotionally focused couple therapist: The workbook.* New York, NY: Routledge.

Johnson, S. M., & Greenman, P. S. (2006). The path to a secure bond: Emotionally focused couple therapy. *Journal of Clinical Psychology, 62,* 597–609.

Johnson, S. M., & Whiffen, V. E. (Eds.). (2005). *Attachment processes in couple and family therapy.* New York, NY: Guilford Press.

Johnson, S. M., & Wittenborn, A. K. (2012). New research findings on emotionally focused therapy: Introduction to special section, *Journal of Marital and Family Therapy, 38*(1), 18–22.

Johnson, S. M., & Woolley, S. (2009). Emotionally focused couples therapy: An attachment based theory. *Psychotherapeutic Treatments,* 121–142.

Jones, E. (1953). *The life and work of Sigmund Freud* (Vol. 1). New York, NY: Basic Books.

Jones, E. (1955). *The life and work of Sigmund Freud: Years of maturity, 1901–1919* (Vol. 2). New York, NY: Basic Books.

Jones, E. (1957). *The life and work of Sigmund Freud: The last phase, 1919–1939* (Vol. 3). New York, NY: Basic Books.

Jongsma, A. E., Peterson, L. M., & Bruce, T. J. (2014). *The complete adult psychotherapy treatment planner* (5th ed.). New York, NY: Wiley.

Jordan, J. V. (2010). *Relational-cultural therapy.* Washington, DC: American Psychological Association.

Jordan, J. V., Handel, M., Alvarez, M., & Cook-Nobles, R. (2004). Application of the relational model to time-limited therapy. In J. V. Jordan, M. Walker, & L. M. Hartling (Eds.), *The complexity of connection.* New York, NY: Guilford Press.

Jordan, J. V., Kaplan, A. G., Miller, J. B., Stiver, I. P., & Surrey, J. L. (1991). *Women's growth in connection.* New York, NY: Guilford.

Jordan, J. V., Walker, M., & Hartling, L. M. (Eds.). (2004). *The complexities of connection: Writings from the Stone Center's Jean Baker Miller Training Institute*. New York, NY: Guilford.

Jung, C. G. (1907/1960). The psychology of dementia praecox. In *The collected works of C. G. Jung* (Vol. 4). Princeton, NJ: Princeton University Press.

Jung, C. G. (1912/1956). Symbols of transformation. In *The collected works of C. G. Jung* (Vol. 5). Princeton, NJ: Princeton University Press.

Jung, C. G. (1921/1971). Psychological types. In *The collected works of C. G. Jung* (Vol. 6). Princeton, NJ: Princeton University Press.

Jung, C. G. (1953). Two essays on analytical psychology. In *The collected works of C. G. Jung* (Vol. 7). Princeton, NJ: Princeton University Press.

Jung, C. G. (1960). *Collected works 8: The structure and dynamics of the psyche*. New York, NY: Pantheon.

Jung, C. G. (1963). *Memories, dreams, reflections*. New York, NY: Pantheon.

Jung, C. G. (1964). *Man and his symbols*. Garden City, NY: Doubleday.

Kabat-Zinn, J. (1990). *Full catastrophe living: Using the wisdom of your body and mind to face stress, pain, and illness*. New York, NY: Delacorte.

Kahn, J. S. (2011). Feminist therapy for men: Challenging assumptions and moving forward. *Women & Therapy, 34*, 59–76.

Kakar, S. (2006). Culture and psychoanalysis. *Social Analysis, 50*, 25–44.

Kandel, E. R. (2008). *In search of memory: The emergence of a new science of mind*. New York, NY: W. W. Norton.

Kaner, A., & Prelinger, E. (2005). *The craft of psychodynamic psychotherapy*. Lanham, MD: Rowman and Littlefield.

Kanter, J., Busch, A., & Rusch, L. (2009). *Behavioural activation*. London, UK: Routledge.

Kaslow, N. J., Broth, M. R., Smith, C. O., & Collins, M. H. (2012). Family-based interventions for child and adolescent disorders. *Journal of Marital and Family Therapy, 38*, 82–100.

Kasper, L. B., Hill, C. E., & Kivlighan, D. M. (2008). Therapist immediacy in brief psychotherapy: Case study I. *Psychotherapy: Theory, Research, Practice, Training, 45*(3), 281–297. doi: 10.1037/a0013305

Kaufman, M. (2007, July 25). Albert Ellis, provoker of change in psychotherapy is dead at 93. *New York Times*.

Kawahara, D. M., & Espîn, O. M. (Eds.) (2007). *Feminist reflection on growth and transformation: Asian American women in therapy*. New York: NY: Haworth.

Kawahara, D. M., & Espîn, O. M. (2013). *Feminist therapy with Latina women*. New York, NY: Routledge.

Kaysen, D., Schumm, J., Pedersen, E., Seim, R., Bedard-Gilligan, M., & Chard, K. (2014). Cognitive processing therapy for veterans with comorbid PTSD and alcohol use disorders. *Addictive Behaviors, 39*(2), 420–427.

Kegerreis, S., & Midgley, N. (2014). Psychodynamic approaches to counselling children and young people. In *The handbook for counselling children and young people* (pp. 35–48). Thousand Oaks, CA: Sage.

Keith, D. V., Connell, G., & Whitaker, C. A. (1992). Group supervision in symbolic experiential family therapy. *Journal of Family Psychotherapy, 3*, 93–102.

Kellogg, S. H., & Young, J. E. (2006). Schema therapy for borderline personality disorder. *Journal of Clinical Psychology, 62*(4), 445–458. doi: 10.1002/jclp.20240

Kellogg, S. H., & Young, J. E. (2008). Cognitive therapy. In J. L. Lebow (Ed.), *Twenty-first century psychotherapies: Contemporary approaches to theory and practice* (pp. 43–79). Hoboken, NJ: John Wiley & Sons.

Kelly, D. F., & Lee, D. (2007). Adlerian approaches to counseling with children and adolescents. In H. T. Prout & D. T. Brown (Eds.), *Counseling and psychotherapy with children and adolescents: Theory and practice for school and clinical settings* (4th ed., pp. 131–179). Hoboken, NJ: Wiley.

Kelly, G. (1955). *The psychology of personal constructs*. New York, NY: W. W. Norton.

Kelly, W. L. (1990). *Psychology of the unconscious: Mesmer, Janet, Freud, Jung, and current issues*. New York, NY: Prometheus.

Kennedy, S. C., & Gordon, K. (2017). Effects of integrated play therapy on relationship satisfaction and intimacy within couples counseling. *The Family Journal, 25*(4), 313–321. doi: 10.1177/1066480717732169

Kern, R. M., Wheeler, M. S., & Curlette, W. L. (1997). *BASIS-A interpretive manual*. Coral Springs, FL: CMTI Press.

Kernberg, P. F., Ritvo, R., & Keable, H. (2012). Practice parameters for psychodynamic psycho-therapy with children; American Academy of Child & Adolescent Psychiatry (AACAP) Committee on Quality Issues (CQI). *Journal of the American Academy of Child & Adolescent Psychiatry, 51*(5), 541–557. doi: 10.1016/j.jaac.2012.02.015

Kerr, M. E. (1981). Family systems theory and therapy. In A. S. Gurman & D. P. Kniskern (Eds.), *Handbook of family therapy* (pp. 226–264). New York, NY: Brunner/Mazel.

Key, B. L., Rowa, K., Bieling, P., McCabe, R., & Pawluk, E. J. (2017). Mindfulness-based cognitive therapy as an augmentation treatment for obsessive-compulsive disorder. *Clinical Psychology and Psychotherapy, 24*(5), 1–12. doi: 10.1002/cpp.2076

Kierkegaard, S. (1941). *Concluding unscientific postscript.* Princeton, NJ: Princeton University Press.

Kierkegaard, S. (1944). *The concept of dread.* Princeton, NJ: Princeton University Press.

Kim, B. H. (2002). Church as a self-object environment: A self-psychological psychoanalytic exploration of male members of two Korean immigrant congregations. *Dissertation Abstracts International, 62* (10-A) (UMI No. 3438).

Kim, J. (2007). A reality therapy group counseling program as an Internet addiction recovery method for college students in Korea. *International Journal of Reality Therapy, 26,* 3–9.

Kim, J. (2011). Structuring background by letting go of clinging and avoidance. *Korean Journal of Gestalt Therapy, 1*(1), 1–11.

Kim, J. S., & Franklin, C. (2009). Solution-focused brief therapy in schools: A review of the out-come literature. *Children and Youth Services Review, 31,* 464–470.

Kim, M., Chen, J., Kools, S., & Weiss, S. (2016). Mental health problems among Korean american adolescents, *Scientific Research Publishing, 7,* 1872–1882.

Kirk, U., Downar, J., & Montague, P. R. (2011). Interoception drives increased rational decision-making in meditators playing the ultimatum game, *Frontiers in Decision Neuroscience, 5,* 49. doi: 10.3389/fnins.2011.00049

Kirschenbaum, H. (2004). Carl Rogers's life and work: An assessment on the 100th anniversary of his birth. *Journal of Counseling and Development, 82,* 116–124.

Kirschenbaum, H. (2009). *The life and work of Carl Rogers.* Alexandria, VA: American Counseling Association.

Klingberg, H. (2001). *When life calls out to us: The love and lifework of Viktor and Elly Frankl.* New York, NY: Doubleday.

Klinger, E., Bouchard, S., Legeron, P., Roy, S., Lauer, F., Chemin, I., & Nugues, P. (2005). Virtual reality therapy versus cognitive behavior therapy for social phobia: A preliminary controlled study, *CyberPsychology & Behavior, 8,* 76–88.

Knox, R., & Cooper, M. (2010). Relationship qualities that are associated with moments of relational depth: The client's perspective. *Person-Centered and Experiential Psychotherapy, 9,* 236–256.

Koemer, N., Vorstenbosch, V., & Antony, M. M. (2012). Panic disorder. In P. Sturmey & M. Hersen (Eds.), *Handbook of evidence-based practice in clinical psychology volume 2: Adult disorders* (pp. 285–312). Hoboken, NJ: John Wiley & Sons.

Kohut, H. (1982). Introspection, empathy, and the semicircle of mental health. *International Journal of Psychoanalysis, 63,* 395–407.

Kohut, H., & Wolf, E. S. (1978). The disorders of the self and their treatment: An outline. *The International Journal of Psychoanalysis, 59*(4), 413–425.

Kondratyuk, N., & Perakyla A. (2011). Therapeutic work with the present moment: A comparative conversation analysis of existential and cognitive therapies. *Psychotherapy Research, 21*(3), 316–330.

Kress, V. E., Dixon, A., & Shannonhouse L. (2018). Multicultural diagnosis and conceptualization. In D. G. Hays & B. T. Erford (Eds.), *Handbook of developing multicultural competency: A systems approach* (3rd ed., pp. 558–590). Columbus, OH: Pearson.

Kress, V. E., Haiyasoso, M., Zoldan, C. A., Headley, J. A., & Trepal, H. (2018). The use of relational-cultural theory in counseling clients who have traumatic stress disorders. *Journal of Counseling & Development, 96,* 106–114.

Kress, V. E., Hoffman, R., Adamson, N., & Eriksen, K. (2013). Informed consent, confidentiality, and diagnosing: Ethical guidelines for counselor practice. *Journal of Mental Health Counseling, 35,* 15–28.

Kress, V. E., & Paylo, M. (2019). *Treating those with mental disorders: A comprehensive approach to case conceptualization and treatment* (2nd ed.). Upper Saddle River, NJ: Pearson.

Kress, V. E., Paylo, M., & Stargell, N. A. (2019). *Counseling children and adolescents.* Upper Saddle River, NJ: Pearson.

Kriston, L., Wolff, A. V., Westphal, A., Hölzel, L. P., & Härter, M. (2014). Efficacy and accept ability of acute treatments for persistent depressive disorder: A network meta-analysis. *Depression and Anxiety, 31*(8), 621–630.

Kroløkke, C., & Sørenson, A. S. (2006). Three waves of feminism: From suffragettes to grrls. In C. Kroløkke & A. S. Sørenson (Eds.), *Gender communication theories and analyses: From silence to performance* (pp. 1–23). Thousand Oaks, CA: Sage.

Kuusisto, K., & Artkoski, T. (2013). The female therapist and the client's gender. *Clinical Nursing Studies, 1*(3), 39–56. doi: 10.5430/cns.v1n3p39

L'Abate L. (2013). *Beyond the systems paradigm: Emerging constructs in family and personality psychology.* New York, NY: Springer.

Lacewing, M. (2014). Psychodynamic psychotherapy, insight, and therapeutic action. *Clinical Psychology Science and Practice, 21*(2), 154–171. doi: 10.1111/cpsp.12065

Lachmann, F. M., & Beebe, B. (1995). Self psychology: Today. *Psychoanalysis Dialogues, 5*, 375–384.

Lam, R. W., Kennedy, S. H., McIntyre, R. S., & Khullar, A. (2014). Cognitive dysfunction in major depressive disorder: Effects on psychosocial functioning and implications for treatment. *Canadian Journal of Psychiatry, 59*, 649–654.

Lambert, M. J. (1992). Psychotherapy outcome research: Implications for integrative and eclectic therapists. In J. C. Norcross & M. R. Goldfried (Eds.), *Handbook of psychotherapy integration* (pp. 94–129). New York, NY: Basic Books.

Lambert, M. J. (2016). Does client-therapist gender matching influence therapy course or outcome in psychotherapy? *Evidence Based Medicine and Practice, 2*(2), 1–8. doi: 10.4172/2471-9919.1000108

Lambert, M. J., & Bergin, A. E. (1994). The effectiveness of psychotherapy. In A. E. Bergin & S. L. Garfield (Eds.), *Handbook of psychotherapy and behavior change* (4th ed., pp. 143–189). New York, NY: John Wiley & Sons.

Landes, S. J., Burton, J. R., King, K. M., & Sullivan, B. F. (2013). Women's preference of therapist based on sex of therapist and presenting problem: An analogue study. *Counseling Psychology Quarterly, 26*(3-4), 330–342. doi: 10.1080/09515070.2013.819795

Lane, R. C. (1997). Dream controversies. *Psychotherapy in Private Practice, 16*(1), 39–68. doi: 10.1300/J294v16n0104

Lanfredi, M., Deste, G., Ferrari, C., Barlati, S., Magni, L. R., Rossi, R., . . . Vita, A. (2017). Effects of cognitive remediation therapy on neurocognition and negative symptoms in schizophrenia: An Italian naturalistic study. *Cognitive Neuropsychiatry, 22*(1), 53–68.

Lantz, J. (2000). Phenomenological reflection and time in Viktor Frankl's existential psychotherapy. *Journal of Phenomenological Psychology, 3*, 220–228.

Lantz, J., & Gregoire, T. (2000). Existential psychotherapy with couples facing breast cancer: A twenty-year report. *Contemporary Family Therapy, 29*, 315–327.

Lanza, M. L., Anderson, J., Boisvert, C. M., LeBlanc, A., Fardy, M., & Steel, B. S. (2002). Assaultive behavior intervention in the Veterans Administration: Psychodynamic group psychotherapy compared to cognitive behavior therapy. *Perspectives in Psychiatric Care, 38*, 89–97.

Lawson, D. M., Dawson, T. E., Kieffer, K. M., Perez, L. M., Burke, J., & Kier, F. J. (2001). An integrated feminist/cognitive-behavioral and psychodynamic group treatment model for men who abuse their partners. *Psychology of Men & Masculinity, 2*(2), 86–99.

Lazar, S. G. (Ed.). (2010). *Psychotherapy, is it worth it? A comprehensive review of its cost-effectiveness.* Arlington, VA: American Psychiatric Publishing.

Lazarus, A. A. (1976). *Multimodal behavior therapy.* New York, NY: Springer.

Lazarus, A. A. (Ed.). (1985). *Casebook of multimodal therapy.* New York, NY: Guilford.

Lazarus, A. A. (1989). *The practice of multimodal therapy (update).* Baltimore, MD: Johns Hopkins University Press.

Lazarus, A. A. (1996). Some reflections after 40 years of trying to be an effective psychotherapist. *Psychotherapy: Theory, Research, Practice, Training, 33*, 142–145.

Lazarus, A. A. (2006). *Brief but comprehensive psychotherapy: The multimodal way.* New York, NY: Springer.

Lazarus, A. A. (2008). Technical eclecticism and multimodal therapy. In J. L. Lebow (Ed.), *Twenty-first century psychotherapies: Contemporary approaches to theory and practice* (pp. 424–452). Hoboken, NJ: John Wiley & Sons.

Lazarus, A. A., & Beutler, L. E. (1993). On technical eclecticism. *Journal of Counseling and Development, 71*(4), 381–385.

Leaf, J. B., Leaf, R., McEachin, J., Taubman, M., Ala'i-Rosales, S., Ross, R. K., . . . Weiss, M. J. (2016). Applied behavior analysis is a science and, therefore, progressive. *Journal of Autism and Developmental Disorders, 46*(2), 720–731. doi: 10.1007/s10803-015-2591-6

Leahy, R. L., Tirch, D., & Napolitano, L. A. (2011). *Emotion regulation in psychotherapy: A practitioner's guide.* New York, NY: Guilford Press.

Lebow, J. (2008). *Twenty-First Century Psychotherapies.* Hoboken, NJ: John Wiley & Sons.

Lebow, J. L. (2008). Couples and family therapy. In J. L. Lebow (Ed.), *Twenty-first century psychotherapies: Contemporary approaches to theory and practice* (pp. 307–346). Hoboken, NJ: John Wiley & Sons.

Lee, B. K., & Rovers, M. (2008). Bringing torn lives together again: Effects of the first congruence couple therapy training application to clients in pathological gambling. *International Gambling Studies, 8*, 113–129.

Lee, C. C. (2007). *Counseling for social justice* (2nd ed.). Alexandria, VA: American Counseling Association.

Lee, C. C. (2013). *Multicultural issues in counseling new approaches to diversity* (4th ed.). Alexandria, VA: American Counseling Association.

Lee, C. W., Ree, M. J., & Wong, M. Y. (2018). Effective insomnia treatments: Investigation of processes in mindfulness and cognitive therapy. *Behaviour Change, 35*(2), 71–90.

Lee, J. (1997). Women re-authoring their lives through feminist narrative therapy. *Women & Therapy, 20*(3), 1–22.

Leibert, T. W., & Dunne-Bryant, A. (2015). Do common factors account for counseling outcome? *Journal of Counseling and Development, 93*, 225–235. doi: 10.1002/j.1556-6676.2015.00198.x

Leichsenring, F. (2009). Psychodynamic psychotherapy: A review of efficacy and effectiveness studies. In K. N. Levy and J. S. Ablon (Eds.), *Handbook of evidence-based psychodynamic psychotherapy: Bridging the gap between science and practice, Part I* (pp. 3–28). New York, NY: Humana Press.

Lempp, H., Wearn, E., Duffort, P., Ibrahim, F., Osumili, B., Romeo, R., . . . Cope, A. (2017). Efficacy of brief person-centered cognitive behavioral therapy to facilitate self-management for patients with rheumatoid arthritis: A mixed methods case series feasibility study. *Behavioral Psychology, 25*, 331–347.

Lennon, B. (2003). Review: "Warning: Psychiatry can be hazardous to your mental health." *International Journal of Reality Therapy, 23*(1), 15–17.

Lenz, A. S., & Lancaster, C. (2017). A mixed-methods evaluation of intensive trauma-focused programming. *Journal of Counseling & Development, 95*(1), 24–34. doi: 10.1002/jcad.12114

Lerner, H. D. (2008). Psychodynamic perspectives. In M. Hersen & A. M. Gross (Eds.), *Handbook of clinical psychology* (Vol. 1, pp. 127–160). Hoboken, NJ: John Wiley & Sons.

Levenson, H. (2003). Time-limited dynamic psychotherapy: An integrationist perspective. *Journal of Psychotherapy Integration, 13*, 300–333.

Levenson, H. (2010). *Brief dynamic therapy*. Washington, DC: American Psychological Association.

Levin, J., & Levine, T. B. (2012). Gestalt in the new age. In T. B. Levine (Ed.), *Gestalt therapy: Advances in theory and practice* (pp. 1–12). New York, NY: Routledge.

Levitsky, A., & Perls, F. (1970). The rules and games of Gestalt therapy. In J. Fagen & I. L. Shepherd (Eds.), *Gestalt therapy now*. Palo Alto, CA: Science and Behavior Books.

Levy, K. N., Ellison, W. D., Scott, L. N., & Bernecker, S. L. (2011). Attachment style. In J. C. Norcross (Ed.), *Psychotherapy relationships that work: Evidence-based responsiveness* (2nd ed.). New York, NY: Oxford University Press.

Levy, R. A., Ablon, J. S., & Kachele, H. (Eds.). (2012). *Psychodynamic psychotherapy research*. New York, NY: Humana Press.

Levy, R. A., Wasserman, R. H., Scott, L., & Yeomans, F. E. (Eds.). (2012). Empirical evidence for transference-focused psychotherapy and other psychodynamic psychotherapies for borderline personality disorder. In R. A. Levy, J. S. Ablon, and H. Kachele (Eds.), *Psychodynamic psychotherapy research* (pp. 93–120). New York, NY: Humana Press.

Lewis, B. (2011). Narrative and psychiatry. *Current Options in Psychiatry, 24*, 489–494.

Lewis, T. F. (2014). *Substance abuse and addiction treatment: Practical application of counseling theory*. Columbus, OH: Pearson.

Li, C. (1998). Impact of acculturation on Chinese-Americans' life and its implications for helping professionals. *International Journal of Reality Therapy, 17*(2), 7–11.

Li, Y., & Vivien, W. (2010). Applying the Satir Model of counseling in mainland China: Illustrated with case studies. *The Satir Journal: Transformational Systemic Therapy, 4*(1).

Lichtenberg, P. (2012). In gratitude. In T. B. Levine (Ed.), *Gestalt therapy: Advances in theory and practice* (pp. 116–122). New York, NY: Routledge.

Lieberman, J. A., & Murray, R. M. (2012). *Comprehensive care of schizophrenia: A textbook of clinical management*. New York, NY: Oxford University Press.

Lin, Y., & Bratton, S. C. (2015). A meta-analytic review of child-centered play therapy approaches. *Journal of Counseling & Development, 93*(1), 45–58.

Linehan, M. (1993). *Cognitive–behavioral treatment of borderline personality disorder*. New York, NY: Guilford Press.

Linehan, M. (2015). *DBT skills training manual* (2nd ed.). New York, NY: Guilford.

Linehan, M. M., Comtois, K. A., Murray, A. M., Brown, M. Z., Gallop, R. J., Heard, H. L., . . . Lindenboim,

N. (2006). Two-year randomized controlled trial and follow-up of dialectical behavior therapy vs. therapy by experts for suicidal behaviors and borderline personality disorder. *Archives of General Psychiatry, 63*, 757–766. doi: 10.1001/archpsyc.63.7.757

Linehan, M. M., & Egan, K. J. (1979). Assertion training for women. In A. S. Bellack & M. Hersen (Eds.), *Research and practice in social skills training* (pp. 237–231). Boston, MA: Springer.

Linehan, M. M., & Kehrer, C. A. (1993). Borderline personality disorder. In D. A. Barlow (Ed.), *Clinical handbook of psychological disorders* (2nd ed., pp. 396–441). New York, NY: Guilford Press.

Linehan, M. M., McDavid, J., Brown, M. Z., Sayrs, J. H. R., & Gallop, R. J. (2008). Olanzapine plus dialectical behavior therapy for women with high irritability who meet criteria for borderline personality disorder: A double blind, placebo-controlled pilot study. *Journal of Clinical Psychiatry, 69*, 999–1005.

Looyeh, M. Y., Kamali, K., Ghasemi, A., & Tonawanik, P. (2014). Treating social phobia in children through group narrative therapy. *The Arts in Psychotherapy, 41*, 16–20.

Looyeh, M. Y., Kamali, K., & Shafieian, R. (2012). An exploratory study of the effectiveness of group narrative therapy on the school behavior of girls with attention-deficit/hyperactivity disorder symptoms. *Archives of Psychiatric Nursing, 26*, 404–410.

Lopata, C. (2003). Progressive muscle relaxation and aggression among elementary students with emotional or behavioral disorders. *Behavioral Disorders, 28*(2), 162–172.

Lopes, R. T., Goncalves, M., Machado, P., Sinai, D., Bento, T., & Salgado, J. (2014). Narrative therapy vs. cognitive-behavioral therapy for moderate depression: Empirical evidence from a controlled clinical trial. *Psychotherapy Research, 24*(6), 662–674.

Lubbe, T. (2011). *Object relations in depression: A return to theory*. New York, NY: Routledge.

Luborsky, E. B., O'Reilly-Landry, M., & Arlow, J. A. (2008). Psychoanalysis. In R. J. Corsini & D. Wedding (Eds.), *Current psychotherapies* (8th ed., pp. 15–62). Belmont, CA: Brooks/Cole.

Luborsky, L. (1984). *Principles of psychoanalytic psychotherapy: A manual for supportive-expressive treatment*. New York, NY: Basic Books.

Luborsky, L., & Mark, D. (1991). Short term supportive-expressive psychoanalytic psychotherapy. In P. Crits-Cristoph & J. P. Barber (Eds.), *Handbook of short-term dynamic psychotherapy* (pp. 110–136). New York, NY: Basic Books.

Luborsky, L., Singer, B., & Luborsky, L. (1975). Comparative studies of psychotherapies. *Archives of General Psychiatry, 32*, 995–1008.

Lundahl, B., & Burke, B. I. (2009). The effectiveness and applicability of motivational interviewing: A practice friendly review of four meta-analyses. *Journal of Clinical Psychology: In Session, 11*, 1232–1245.

Lundahl, B., Kunz, C., Brownell, C., Tollefson, D., & Burke, B. I. (2010). A meta-analysis of motivational interviewing: Twenty-five years of empirical studies. *Research on Social Work Practice, 22*, 137–160.

Ma, S. H., & Teasdle, J. D. (2004). Mindfulness based cognitive therapy for depression: Replication and exploration of differential relapse prevention effects. *Journal of Consulting and Clinical Psychology, 72*, 31–40.

Maas, V. S. (2002). *Women's group therapy: Creative challenges and options*. New York, NY: Springer.

MacIntosh, H. B., & Johnson, S. (2008). Emotionally focused therapy for couples and childhood sexual abuse survivors. *Journal of Marital and Family Therapy, 34*, 298–315.

MacLeod, R., & Elliott, R. (2014). Nondirective person-centered therapy for social anxiety: A hermeneutic single-case efficacy design study of a good outcome case. *Person-Centered & Experiential Psychotherapies, 13*(4), 294–311.

Madigan, S. (2011). *Instructor's Manual for Narrative Family Therapy*. Retrieved from http://www.psychotherapy.net/data/uploads/5113d78866002.pdf

Madison, G. (2014). The palpable in existential counselling psychology. *Counselling Psychology Review, 29*(2), 25–33.

Mahalik, J. R., Good, G. E., & Englar-Carlson, M. (2003). Masculinity scripts, presenting concerns, and help seeking: Implications for practice and training. *Professional Psychology: Research and Practice, 34*, 123–131.

Mahler, M. S., Pine, F., & Bergman, A. (1975). *The psychological birth of the human infant: Symbiosis and individuation*. New York, NY: Basic Books.

Mahoney, M. J. (2003). *Constructive psychotherapy*. New York, NY: Guilford Press.

Maier, C. A., & McGeorge, C. R. (2014). Positive attributes of never-married single mothers and fathers: Why gender matters and applications for family therapists.

Journal of Feminist Family Therapy, 26(3), 163–190. doi: 10.1080/08952833.2014.944060

Maisel, R. L., Epston, D., & Borden, A. (2004). *Biting the hand that starves you: Inspiring resistance to anorexia/bulimia*. New York, NY: W. W. Norton.

Makari, G. (2008). *Revolution in mind: The creation of psychoanalysis*. New York: Harper.

Malinen, T., Cooper, S. J., & Thomas, F. N. (2011). *Masters of narrative and collaborative therapies: The voices of Anderson, Anderson, and White*. New York, NY: Routledge.

Mallory, A., Brown, J., Conner, S., & Henry, U. (2017). Finding what works: New clinicians' use of standards of care with transgender clients. *The American Journal of Family Therapy*, 45(1), 27–36.

Maltzman, S. (2016). *The oxford handbook of treatment processes and outcomes in psychology: A multidisciplinary, biopsychosocial approach*. New York, NY: Oxford.

Manaster, G. J. (2009). Private logic and the logic of social living. *Journal of Individual Psychology*, 65, 4–12.

Mann, J. J., McGrath, P. J., & Roose, S. P. (2013). *Clinical handbook for the management of mood disorders*. New York, NY: Cambridge.

Markey, C. (2015). Exploring feminist narrative practice and ethics in a school setting. *The International Journal of Narrative Therapy and Community Work*, 4, 1–10.

Markowitz, J. C., & Weissman, M. M. (2012). *Casebook of interpersonal psychotherapy*. New York, NY: Oxford University Press.

Maroda, K. J. (2010). *Psychodynamic techniques: Working with emotion in the therapeutic relationship*. New York, NY: Guilford.

Marra, T. (2005). *Dialectical behavior therapy in private practice: A comprehensive and practical guide*. Oakland, CA: New Harbinger.

Marsden, Z., Lovell, K., Blore, D., Ali, S., & Delgadillo, J. (2018). A randomized controlled trial comparing EMDR and CBT for obsessive–compulsive disorder. *Clinical Psychology & Psychotherapy*, 25(1), e10–e18.

Martin, G., & Pear, J. (2007). *Behavior modification: What it is and how to do it* (8th ed.). Upper Saddle River, NJ: Pearson/Prentice Hall.

Mascher, J. (2002). Narrative therapy: Inviting the use of sport as metaphor. *Women and Therapy*, 25, 57–74.

Maslow, A. (1954). *Motivation and personality*. New York, NY: Harper & Row.

Maslow, A. (1968). *Toward a psychology of being* (2nd ed.). New York, NY: Van Nostrand.

Matlin, M. (1996). *The psychology of women*. Orlando, FL: Harcourt Brace.

Matson, F. W. (1964). *The broken image*. New York, NY: Braziller.

Matson, J. L., Turygin, N. C., Beighley, J., Rieske, R., Tureck, K., & Matson, M. L. (2012). Applied behavior analysis in autism spectrum disorders: Recent developments, strengths, and pitfalls. *Research in Autism Spectrum Disorders*, 6, 144–150.

May, R. (1950). *The meaning of anxiety*. New York, NY: Dell.

May, R. (1960). *Symbolism in religion and literature*. New York, NY: George Braziller.

May, R. (Ed.). (1969a). *Existential psychology* (2nd ed.). New York, NY: Random House.

May, R. (1969b). *Love and will*. New York, NY: W. W. Norton.

May, R. (1975). *The courage to create*. New York, NY: W. W. Norton.

May, R. (1981). *Freedom and destiny*. New York, NY: W. W. Norton.

May, R. (1983). *The discovery of being: Writings in existential psychology*. New York, NY: W. W. Norton.

May, R. (1990a). On the phenomenological bases of therapy. *Review of Existential Psychology and Psychiatry*, 20, 49–61.

May, R. (1990b). Will, decision and responsibility. *Review of Existential Psychology and Psychiatry*, 20, 269–278.

May, R. (1996). *Psychology and the human dilemma*. New York, NY: W. W. Norton.

May, R., Angel, E., & Ellenberger, H. F. (Eds.). (1958). *Existence: A new dimension in psychiatry and psychology*. New York, NY: Simon & Schuster.

May, R., & Yalom, I. (1995). Existential psychotherapy. In R. J. Corsini & D. Wedding (Eds.), *Current psychotherapies* (5th ed., pp. 262–292). Itasca, IL: Peacock.

Mayes, L. C., & Cohen, D. J. (1996). Anna Freud and developmental psychoanalytic psychology. *Psychoanalytic Study of the Child*, 51, 117–141.

McBride, J. (2008). *Quick steps: Information to help your stepfamily thrive*. Hyattsville, MD: US Department of Health & Human Services.

McGoldrick, M., Gerson, R., & Petry, S. (2008). *Genograms: Assessment and intervention* (3rd ed.). New York, NY: W. W. Norton.

McGoldrick, M., & Hardy, K. V. (2008). *Re-visioning family therapy: Race, culture, and gender in clinical practice* (2nd ed.). New York, NY: Guilford Press.

McGuire, J. F., Piacentini, J., Brennan, E. A., Lewin, A. B., Murphy T. K., Small B. J., & Storch, E. A. (2014). A meta-analysis of behavior therapy for Tourette syndrome. *Journal of Psychiatric Research, 50,* 106–112. doi: 10.1016/j.jpsychires.2013.12.009

McGuire, J. F., Piacentini, J., Lewin, A. B., Brennan, E. A., Murphy, T. K., & Storch, E. A. (2015). A meta-analysis of cognitive behaviour therapy and medication for child obsessive-compulsive disorder: Moderators of treatment efficacy, response, and remission. *Depression and Anxiety, 32,* 580–593. doi: 10.1002/da.22389

McKay, D., Sookman, D., Neziroglu F., Willhelm, S., Stein, D. J., Kyrios, M., . . . Veale, D. (2015). Efficacy of cognitive-behavioral therapy for obsessive-compulsive disorder. *Psychiatry Research, 227,* 104–113. doi: 10.1016/j.psychres.2015.02.004

McLean, L. L., La Guardia, A. C., Nelson, J. A., & Watts, R. E. (2016). Incorporating Adlerian and feminist theory to address self-objectification in couples therapy. *The Family Journal: Counseling and Therapy for Couples and Families, 24*(4), 420–427.

McMain, S. F., Links, P. S., Gnam, W. H., Gruimond, T., Cardish, R. J., Korman, L., & Steiner, D. L. (2009). A randomized trial of dialectical behavior therapy versus general psychiatric management for borderline personality disorder. *American Journal of Psychiatry, 166,* 1365–1374.

McParland, J. (2015). Narrative therapy in a learning disability context: A review. *Tizard Learning Disability Review, 20*(3), 121–129.

Meany-Walen, K. K., Kottman, T., Bullis, Q., & Taylor, D. D. (2015). Effects of Adlerian play therapy on children's externalizing behavior. *Journal of Counseling & Development, 93*(4), 418–428.

Mearns, D., & Thorne, B. (1999). *Person-centered counseling in action* (3rd ed.). Thousand Oaks, CA: Sage.

Medlow, S., Klineberg, E., Jarrett, C., & Steinbeck, K. (2016). A systematic review of community-based parenting interventions for adolescents with challenging behaviours. *Journal of Adolescence, 52,* 60–71.

Meichenbaum, D. (1969). The effects of instruction and reinforcement on thinking and language behaviors of schizophrenics. *Behaviour Research and Therapy, 7,* 101–114.

Meichenbaum, D. (1985). *Stress inoculation training.* Elmsford, NY: Pergamon.

Meichenbaum, D. (1993). Changing conceptions of cognitive–behavior modification: Retrospect and prospect. *Journal of Consulting and Clinical Psychology, 61*(2), 202–204.

Meichenbaum, D. (1994). *A clinical handbook/practical therapist manual: For assessing and treating adults with post-traumatic stress disorder.* Waterloo, Canada: Institute Press.

Melnick, J., & Nevis, S. M. (2005). Gestalt therapy methodology. In A. L. Woldt & S. M. Toman (Eds.), *Gestalt therapy: History, theory, and practice* (pp. 101–115). Thousand Oaks, CA: Sage.

Menassa, B. M. (2009). Theoretical orientation and play therapy: Examining therapist role, session structure, and therapeutic objectives. *Journal of Professional Counseling, Practice, Theory, & Research, 37,* 13–26.

Messer, S. B., & Warren, C. S. (1995). *Models of brief psychodynamic therapy: A comparative approach.* New York, NY: Guilford Press.

Metcalf, L. (1998). *Solution-focused group therapy: Ideas for groups in private practice, schools, agencies, and treatment programs.* New York, NY: Free Press.

Miklowitz, D. J. (2010). A pilot study of mindfulness-based cognitive therapy for bipolar disorder. *International Journal of Cognitive Therapy, 2,* 373–382.

Miller, J. B. (1976). *Toward a new psychology of women.* Boston, MA: Beacon Press.

Miller, J. B. (1986). *What do we mean by relationships?* (Work in Progress, No. 22). Wellesley, MA: Stone Center Working Paper Series.

Miller, J. B., & Stiver, I. P. (1997). *The healing connection: How women form relationships in therapy and in life.* Boston, MA: Beacon.

Miller, M. M., & Goldsmith, H. H. (2017). Profiles of social-emotional readiness for 4-year-old kindergarten. *Frontiers in Psychology, 8*(132), 1–9.

Miller, M. V. (1989). Introduction to Gestalt therapy verbatim. *The Gestalt Journal, 12,* 5–24.

Miller, N., Haas, S., Waschbusch, D., Willoughby, M., Helseth, S., Crum, K., . . . Pelham, W. (2014). Behavior therapy and callous-unemotional traits: Effects of a pilot study examining modified behavioral contingencies on child behavior. *Behavior Therapy, 45*(5), 606–618.

Miller, S. D., Duncan, B. L., & Hubble, M. (1997). *Escape from Babel: Toward a unifying language for psychotherapy practice*. New York, NY: W. W. Norton.

Miller, S. D., Duncan, B. L., & Hubble, M. A. (2002). Client-directed, outcome-informed clinical work. In F. W. Kaslow & J. Lebow (Eds.), *Comprehensive handbook of psychotherapy, Vol. 4: Integrative/eclectic* (pp. 185–212). New York, NY: Wiley.

Miller, S. D., Hubble, M. A., Duncan, B. L., & Wampold, B. E. (2010). Delivering what works. In B. L. Duncan, S. D. Miller, B. E. Wampold, & M. A. Hubble (Eds.), *Heart and soul of change in psychotherapy* (2nd ed., pp. 421–430). Washington, DC: American Psychological Association.

Miller, W., & Rollnick R. S. (2012). *Motivational interviewing: Preparing people for change*. (3rd ed). New York, NY: Guilford.

Miller, W. R., & Rollnick, S. (2013). *Motivational interviewing: Helping people change*. New York, NY: Guilford.

Miltenberger, R. G. (2012). *Behavior modification: Principles and procedures*. Belmont, CA: Cengage.

Minuchin, S. (1974). *Families and family therapy*. Cambridge, MA: Harvard University Press.

Minuchin, S., & Fishman, H. C. (1981). *Family therapy techniques*. Cambridge, MA: Harvard University Press.

Minuchin, S., Rosman, B. L., & Baker, L. (1978). *Psychosomatic families: Anorexia nervosa in context*. Cambridge, MA: Harvard University Press.

Miranda, J., Chung, J. Y., Green, B. L., Krupnick, J., Siddique, J., Revicki, D. A., & Belin, T. (2003). Treating depression in predominantly low-income young minority women: A randomized controlled trial. *Journal of the American Medical Association*, *290*, 57–65.

Mitchell, S. A. (1988). *Relational concepts in psychoanalysis: An integration*. Cambridge, MA: Harvard University Press.

Mitchell, S. A., & Black, M. J. (1995). *Freud and beyond: A history of modern psychoanalytic thought*. New York, NY: Basic Books.

Monk, G. (1997). How narrative therapy works. In G. Monk, J. Winslade, K. Crocket, & D. Epston (Eds.), *Narrative therapy in practice: The archaeology of hope* (pp. 3–31). San Francisco, CA: Jossey-Bass.

Moodley, R. (2010). In the therapist's chair is Clemmont E. Vontress: A wounded healer in cross-cultural counseling. *Journal of Multicultural Counseling and Development*, *38*, 2–15.

Moodley, R., & Walcott, R. (Eds.). (2010). *Counseling across and beyond cultures: Exploring the work of Clemmont E. Vontress in clinical practice*. Toronto, Canada: University of Toronto Press.

Moore, H. L. (2007). *The subject of anthropology: Gender, symbolism, and psychoanalysis*. Boston, MA: Polity.

Morgan, A. (2000). *What is narrative therapy? An easy read introduction*. Adelaide, SA: Dulwich Centre Publications.

Morris, E., & Oliver, J. E. (2012). Acceptance and commitment therapy. In W. Dryden (Ed.), *Cognitive behavior therapies* (pp. 70–92). Thousand Oaks, CA: Sage.

Morrison, M. O. (2009). Adlerian psychotherapy with a traumatized boy. *Journal of Individual Psychology*, *65*, 57–68.

Mosak, H. H. (2013). Adlerian psychotherapy. In R. J. Corsini & D. Wedding (Eds.), *Current psychotherapies* (10th ed., pp. 55–91). Belmont, CA: Brooks/Cole.

Mufson, L., Dorta, K. P., Moreau, D., & Weissman, M. M. (2011). *Interpersonal psychotherapy for depressed adolescents* (2nd ed.). New York, NY: Guilford Press.

Munro, C., Randell, L., & Lawrie, S. M. (2016). An integrative bio-psycho-social theory of anorexia nervosa. *Clinical Psychology & Psychotherapy*, *24*(1), 1–21. doi: 10.1002/cpp.2047

Munro, E. (2013). Feminism: A fourth wave? *Political Insight*, *4*(2), 22–25.

Muntigl, P., Chubak, L., & Angus, L. (2017). Entering chair work in psychotherapy: An interactional structure for getting emotion-focused talk underway. *Journal of Pragmatics*, *117*, 168–189. doi: 10.1016/j.pragma.2017.06.016

Murdock, N. L. (2009). *Theories of counseling and psychotherapy: A case approach* (2nd ed.). Upper Saddle River, NJ: Pearson/Merrill.

Myers, J. E., & Sweeney, T. J. (Eds.). (2005). *Counseling for wellness: Theory, research, and practice*. Alexandria, VA: American Counseling Association.

Myers, J. E., & Young, J. S. (2012). Brain wave biofeedback: Benefits of integrating neurofeedback into counseling. *Journal of Counseling and Development*, *90*, 20–29.

Nadort, M., Arntz, A., Smit, J. H., Giesen-Bloo, J., Eikelenboom, M., Spinhoven, P., . . . van Dyck, R. (2009). Implementation of outpatient schema therapy for borderline personality disorder with versus without crisis support by the therapist outside office hours: A randomized trial. *Behavior Research and Therapy, 47*, 961–973.

Najavits, L. M., & Strupp, H. H. (1994). Differences in the effectiveness of psychodynamic therapists: A process-outcome study. *Psychotherapy, 31*(1), 114–123.

Nathan, P. E., & Gorman, J. M. (Eds.). (2002). *A guide to treatments that work* (2nd ed.). London, UK: Oxford University Press.

National Association of Social Workers. (2008). NASW Code of Ethics (Guide to the Everyday Professional Conduct of Social Workers). Washington, DC: NASW.

National Autism Center. (2009). *National standards report* (phase 1). Retrieved from http://www.nationalautismcenter.org/reports/

National Board of Certified Counselors. (2012). NBCC code of ethics. Greensboro, NC: Author.

Neenan, M., & Dryden, W. (2011). *Rational emotive behavior therapy in a nutshell* (2nd ed.). London, UK: Sage.

Neff, K., Kirkpatrick, K., & Rude, S. (2007). Self-compassion and adaptive psychological functioning. *Journal of Research in Personality, 41*, 139–154.

Negy, C., & McKinney, C. (2006). Application of feminist therapy: Promoting resiliency among lesbian and gay families. *Journal of Feminist Family Therapy, 18*(1/2), 67–83.

Neimeyer, R. A. (1993). An appraisal of constructivist psychotherapies. *Journal of Consulting and Clinical Psychology, 61*, 221–234.

Nichols, M. P. (2009). *The essentials of family therapy* (4th ed.). Boston, MA: Pearson Education.

Nicoll, W. G. (2007). Resilience-focused brief family therapy: An Adlerian approach. *Journal of Individual Psychology, 67*, 206.

Nielsen, S. L., & Ellis, A. E. (1994). A discussion with Albert Ellis: Reason, emotion and religion. *Journal of Psychology and Christianity, 13*, 327–341.

Nolte, T., Guiney, J., Fonagy, P., Mayes, L. C., & Luyten, P. (2011). Interpersonal stress regulation and the development of anxiety disorders: An attachment-based developmental framework. *Frontiers in Behavioral Neuroscience, 5*, 1–21.

Norcross, J. C. (2010). The therapeutic relationship. In B. L. Duncan, S. D. Miller, B. E. Wampold, & M. A. Hubble (Eds.), *Heart and soul of change in psychotherapy* (2nd ed., pp. 113–141). Washington, DC: American Psychological Association.

Norcross, J. C. (Ed.). (2011). *Psychotherapy relationships that work: Evidence-based responsiveness* (2nd ed.). New York, NY: Oxford University Press.

Norcross, J. C., & Beutler, L. E. (2019). Integrative psychotherapies. In D. Wedding & R. J. Corsini (Eds.), *Current psychotherapies* (11th ed., pp. 527–560). Belmont, CA: Brooks/Cole.

Norcross, J. C., Hogan, T. P., & Koocher, G. P. (2008). *Clinician's guide to evidence-based practices*. New York, NY: Oxford University Press.

Norcross, J. C., & Karpiak, C. P. (2012). Clinical psychologists in the 2010s: Fifty years of the APA Division of Clinical Psychology. *Clinical Psychology: Science and Practice, 19*, 1–12.

Norcross, J. C., & Lambert, M. J. (2011). Evidence-based therapy relationships. In J. C. Norcross (Ed.), *Psychotherapy relationships that work: Evidence-based responsiveness* (2nd ed., pp. 3–21). New York, NY: Oxford.

Norcross, J. C., & Rogan, J. D. (2013). Psychologists conducting psychotherapy in 2012: Current practices and historical trends among Division 29 members. *Psychotherapy, 50*(4), 490–495. doi: 10.1037/a0033512

Norcross, J. C., & Wampold, B. E. (2011). Evidence-based therapy relationships: Research conclusions and clinical practices. *Psychotherapy, 48*, 98–102.

Norcross, J. C., & Wampold, B. E. (2011). Research conclusions and clinical practices. In J. C. Norcross (Ed.), *Psychotherapy relationships that work: Evidence-based responsiveness* (2nd ed., pp. 423–430). New York, NY: Oxford.

Noronha, K. J. (2014). Dream work in grief therapy. *Indian Journal of Psychological Medicine, 36*(3), 321–323.

Oaklander, V. (1994). Gestalt play therapy. In K. J. O'Connor & C. E. Schaefer (Eds.), *Handbook of play therapy* (Vol. 2, pp. 143–156). New York, NY: Wiley Interscience.

Oaklander, V. (1997). The therapeutic process with children and adolescents. *Gestalt Review, 1*, 292–317.

Obiageli, J. (2015). Management of negative self-image using rational emotive and behavioural therapy and assertiveness training. *ASEAN Journal of Psychiatry, 16*(1), 42–53.

Ohanian, V., & Rashed, R. (2012). Schema therapy. In W. Dryden (Ed.), *Cognitive behavior therapies* (pp. 166–188). Thousand Oaks, CA: Sage.

O'Hanlon, W. H., & Weiner-Davis, M. (2003). *In search of solutions: A new direction in psychotherapy* (Rev. ed.). New York, NY: Norton.

Olatunji, B. O., Davis, M. L., Powers, M. B., & Smits, J. A. (2013). Cognitive-behavioral therapy for obsessive-compulsive disorder: A meta-analysis of treatment outcome and moderators. *Journal of Psychiatric Research, 47*, 33–41.

Olatunji, B. O., & Feldman, G. (2008). Cognitive–behavioral therapy. In M. Hersen & A. M. Gross (Eds.), *Handbook of clinical psychology* (Vol. 1, pp. 551–584). New York, NY: John Wiley & Sons.

Oliver, A. C., Pratt, L. A., & Normand, M. P. (2015). A survey of functional behavior assessment methods used by behavior analysts in practice. *Journal of Applied Behavior Analysis, 48*(4), 817–829. doi: 10.1002/jaba.256

Ono, K. (2018). Psychological growth through person-centered expressive arts therapy training in Japan. *Person-Centered & Experiential Psychotherapies, 17*(2), 91–110.

Ost, L. G. (2008). Efficacy of the third wave of behavioral therapies: A systematic review and meta-analysis. *Behaviour Research and Therapy, 46*, 296–321.

Otting, T. L., & Prosek, E. A. (2016). Integrating feminist therapy and expressive arts with adolescent clients. *Journal of Creativity in Mental Health, 11*(1), 78–89.

Ouimet, A. J., Covin, R., & Dozois, D. J. (2012). Generalized anxiety disorder. In P. Sturmey & M. Hersen (Eds.), *Handbook of evidence-based practice in clinical psychology, Vol. 2: Adult disorders* (pp. 651–680). Hoboken, NJ: John Wiley & Sons.

Owens, G. P., Held, P., Hamrick, L., & Keller, E. (2018). The indirect effects of emotion regulation on the association between attachment style, depression, and meaning made among undergraduates who experienced stressful events. *Motivation and Emotion, 42*(3), 429–437.

Packer, G. (2008, January 28). The choice. *New Yorker*.

Paige, M., DeVore, J., Chang, C. Y., & Whisenhunt, J. (2017). The trauma-competent clinician: A qualitative model of knowledge, skills, and attitudes supporting adlerian-based trauma psychotherapy. *Journal of Individual Psychology, 73*(1), 8–37.

Panfile, T. M., & Laible, D. J. (2012). Attachment security and child's empathy: The mediating role of emotion regulation. *Merrill-Palmer Quarterly, 58*(1), 1–21.

Pantalone, D. W., Iwamasa, G. W., & Martell, C. R. (2010). Cognitive behavioral therapy with diverse populations. In K. S. Dobson (Ed.), *Handbook of cognitive behavioral therapies* (3rd ed., pp. 445–464). New York, NY: Guilford Press.

Paris, B. J. (1994). *Karen Horney: A psychoanalyst's search for self understanding.* New Haven, CT: Yale University Press.

Parker, G., Roy, K., & Eyers, K. (2003). Cognitive behavior therapy for depression? Choose horses for courses. *American Journal of Psychiatry, 160*, 825–834.

Parlett, M., & Hemming, J. (1996). Developments in gestalt therapy. In W. Dryden (Ed.)., *Developments in psychotherapy: Historical perspectives* (pp. 91–110). Thousand Oaks, CA: Sage.

Patterson, C. L., Anderson, T., & Wei, C. (2014). Clients' pretreatment role expectations, the therapeutic alliance, and clinical outcomes in outpatient therapy. *Journal of Clinical Psychology, 70*(7), 673–680. doi: 10.1002/jclp.22054

Patterson, J., Williams, L., Edwards, T. M., Chamow, L., & Grauf-Grounds, C. (2009). *Essential skills in family therapy* (2nd ed.). New York, NY: Guilford.

Paul, G. L. (1967). Strategy of outcome research in psychotherapy. *Journal of Consulting Psychology, 31*, 109–118.

Pavlov, I. P. (1927). *Conditioned reflexes* (G. V. Anrep, Trans.). London, UK: Oxford University Press.

Payne, M. (2006). *Narrative therapy: An introduction for counselors* (2nd ed.). Thousand Oaks, CA: Sage.

Peck, K. R., Coffey, S. F., McGuire, A. P., Voluse, A. C., & Connolly, K. M. (2018). A cognitive processing therapy-based treatment program for veterans diagnosed with co-occurring posttraumatic stress disorder and substance use disorder: The relationship between trauma-related cognitions and outcomes of a 6-week treatment program. *Journal of Anxiety Disorders, 59*, 34–41.

Penn, P. E., Brooke, D., Brooks, A. J., Gallagher, S. M., & Barnard, A. D. (2016). Co-occurring conditions clients and counselors compare 12-step and smart recovery mutual help. *Journal of Groups in Addiction & Recovery, 11*(2), 76–92.

Perls, F. (1992a). *Gestalt therapy verbatim.* Gouldsboro, ME: The Gestalt Journal Press.

Perls, F. (1992b). *In and out of the garbage pail*. Gouldsboro, ME: The Gestalt Journal Press.

Perls, F., Hefferline, R. F., & Goodman, P. (1951). *Gestalt therapy: Excitement and growth in the human personality*. New York, NY: Julian.

Perls, F., & Philippson, P. (2012). *From planned psychology to Gestalt therapy*. Gouldsboro, ME: The Gestalt Journal Press.

Persons, J. B. (1989). *Cognitive therapy in practice*. New York: W. W. Norton.

Peteet, J. R. (2018). A fourth wave of psychotherapies: Moving beyond recovery toward well-being. *Harvard Review of Psychiatry, 26*(2), 90–95.

Petko, J. T., Kendrick, E., & Young, M. E. (2016). Selecting a theory of counseling: What influences a counseling student to choose? *Universal Journal of Psychology, 4*(6), 285–291.

Petrocelli, J. V. (2002). Processes and stages of change: Counseling with the transtheoretical model of change. *Journal of Counseling and Development, 80*(1), 22–30.

Piercy, K. W. (2010). *Working with aging families: therapeutic solutions for caregivers*. New York, NY: W. W. Norton.

Polster, E. (2012). Flexibility in theory formation: Point and counterpoint. In T. B. Levine (Ed.), *Gestalt therapy: Advances in theory and practice* (pp. 15–25). NewYork, NY: Routledge.

Polster, E., & Polster, M. (1973). *Gestalt therapy integrated*. New York, NY: Brunner/Mazel.

Pos, A. E., Greenberg, L., & Elliott, R. (2008). Experiential therapy. In J. L. Lebow (Ed.), *Twenty-first century psychotherapies: Contemporary approaches to theory and practice* (pp. 80–122). Hoboken, NJ: John Wiley & Sons.

Powers, M. B., & Emmelkamp, P. M. G. (2008). Virtual reality exposure therapy for anxiety disorders: A meta-analysis. *Journal of Anxiety Disorders, 22*, 561–569.

Powers, M. B., Zum Vorde Sive Vording, M. B., & Emmelkamp, P. M. G. (2009). Acceptance and commitment therapy: A meta-analytic review. *Psychotherapy and Psychosomatics, 78*, 73–80.

Powers, R. L., & Griffith, J. (1987). *Understanding life-style: The psycho-clarity process*. Chicago, IL: American Institute of Adlerian Studies.

Powers, R. L., & Griffith, J. (2012). *IPCW the individual psychology client workbook with supplements*. Port Townsend, WA: Adlerian Psychology Associates.

Powers, W. T. (1973). *Behavior: The control of perception*. Chicago, IL: Aldine.

Presbury, J. H., Echterling, L. G., & McKee, J. E. (2008). *Beyond brief counseling and therapy: An integrative approach* (2nd ed.). Upper Saddle River, NJ: Pearson Education.

Prilleltensky, O. (1996). Women with disabilities and feminist therapy. *Women and Therapy, 18*(1), 87–97.

Prochaska, J. O., & DiClemente, C. C. (1986). The transtheoretical approach. In J. C. Norcross (Ed.), *Handbook of eclectic psychotherapy* (pp. 163–200). New York, NY: Brunner/Mazel.

Prochaska, J. O., & DiClemente, C. C. (2002). Transtheoretical therapy. In F. W. Kaslow & J. Lebow (Eds.), *Comprehensive handbook of psychotherapy, Vol. 4: Integrative/eclectic* (pp. 165–183). New York, NY: Wiley.

Prochaska, J. O., & Norcross, J. C. (2018). *Systems of psychotherapy: A transtheoretical analysis* (9th ed.). Pacific Grove, CA: Oxford Univeristy Press.

Prouty, A. M., & Protinsky, H. O. (2002). Feminist-informed internal family systems therapy with couples. *Journal of Couple & Relationship Therapy, 1*(3), 21–36.

Pugh, M. (2016). Chairwork in cognitive behavioural therapy: A narrative review. *Cognitive Therapy and Research, 41*(1), 16–30. doi: 10.1007/s10608-016-9805-x

Rafaeli, A. K., & Markowitz, J. C. (2011). Interpersonal psychotherapy for PTSD: A case study. *American Journal of Psychotherapy, 65*, 205–223.

Rafaeli, E., Bernstein, D. P., & Young, J. (2011). *Schema therapy: The CBT distinctive features series*. New York, NY: Routledge.

Ramirez, R. K. (2007). Race, tribal nation, and gender: A Native feminist approach to belonging. *Meridians Feminism Race Transnationalism, 7*(2), 22–40.

Ratts, M. J., Singh, A. A., Nassar-McMillan, S., Butler, S. K., & Rafferty McCullough, J. (2016). Multicultural and social justice counseling competencies: Guidelines for the counseling profession. *Journal of Multicultural Counseling and Development, 44*, 28–48. doi: 10.1002/jmcd.12035

Reker, G. T. (2001). *The life attitude profile—revised: (LAP-R)*. Peterborough, ON: Student Psychologists Press.

Remley, T. P., & Herlihy, B. (2016). *Ethical, legal, and professional issues in counseling* (5th ed.). Upper Saddle River, NJ: Pearson.

Retzlaff, R., Sydow, K. V, Beher, S., Haun, M. W., & Schweitzer, J. (2013). The efficacy of systemic therapy for internalizing and other disorders of childhood and adolescence: A systematic review of 38 randomized trials. *Family Process, 52*(4), 619–652.

Reyes-Rodriguez, M., Bulik, C., Hamer, R., & Baucom, D. (2013). Promoviendo una Alimentacion Saludable (PAS) design and methods: Engaging Latino families in eating disorder treatment. *Contemporary Clinical Trials, 35*(1), 52–61.

Rheem, K. D., Woolley, S. R., & Weissman, N. (2012). Using emotion focused therapy with military couples. In B. A. Moore (Ed.), *Handbook for counseling military couples* (pp. 89–112). New York, NY: Routledge.

Richert, A. J. (2003). Living stories, telling stories, changing stories: Experiential use of the relationship in narrative therapy. *Journal of Psychotherapy Integration, 13*, 188–210.

Richert, A. J. (2010). *Integrating existential and narrative therapy: A theoretical base for eclectic practice*. Pittsburgh, PA: Duquesne University Press.

Richmond, C. J., Jordan, S. S., Bischof, G. H., & Sauer, E. M. (2014). Effects of solution-focused versus problem-focused intake questions on pre-treatment change. *Journal of Systemic Therapies, 33*(1), 33–47.

Rigazio-DiGilio, S. A., & McDowell, T. (2008). Systemic family therapy theories. In J. Frew and M. Spiegler (Eds.), *Contemporary psychotherapies for a diverse world* (pp. 442–488). New York, NY: Lahaska Press/Houghton Mifflin.

Rijn, B. V., & Wild, C. (2013). Humanistic and integrative therapies for anxiety and depression. *Transactional Analysis Journal, 43*(2), 150–163. doi: 10.1177/0362153713499545

Ritvo, L. B. (1990). *Darwin's influence on Freud: A tale of two sciences*. New Haven, CT: Yale University Press.

Robertson, M. (1979). Some observations from an eclectic therapy. *Psychotherapy, 16*, 18–21.

Robey, P. (Ed.). (2011a). *Contemporary issues in couples counseling: A choice theory and reality therapy approach*. Portland, OR: Book News.

Robey, P. (2011b). Reality therapy and choice theory: An interview with Robert Wubbolding. *Family Journal, 19*, 231–237.

Robey, P., Burdenski, T. K., Britzman, M., & Crowell, J. (2011). Systematic application of choice theory and reality therapy: An interview with Glasser scholars. *Family Journal, 19*, 421–433.

Rogers, C. R. (1945). The nondirective method as a technique for social research. *American Journal of Sociology, 50*(4), 279–283.

Rogers, C. R. (1946). Significant aspects of client-centered therapy. *American Psychologist, 1*, 415–422.

Rogers, C. R. (1967). The conditions of change from a client-centered viewpoint. In B. Berenson & R. Carkhuff (Eds.), *Sources of gain in counseling and psychotherapy*. New York, NY: Holt, Rinehart, & Winston.

Rogers, C. R. (1970). *Carl Rogers on encounter groups*. New York, NY: Harper & Row.

Rogers, C. R. (1980). *A way of being*. Boston, MA: Houghton Mifflin.

Rogers, C. R. (1995a). What understanding and acceptance mean to me. *Journal of Humanistic Psychology, 35*(4), 7–22.

Rogers, C. R. (1995b). *On becoming a person: A therapists view on psychotherapy* (2nd ed.). Willmington, MA: Mariner Books.

Rogers, N. (1993). *The creative connection: Expressive arts as healing*. Palo Alto, CA: Science & Behavior Books.

Roghanchi, M., Mohamad, A., Mey, S., Momeni, K., & Golmohamadian, M. (2013). The effect of integrating rational emotive behavior therapy and art therapy on self-esteem and resilience. *The Arts in Psychotherapy, 40*(2), 179–184.

Rohrer, J. M., Egloff, B., & Schmukle, S. C. (2015). Examining the effects of birth order on personality. *Proceedings of the National Academy of Sciences of the United States of America, 112*(46), 14224–14229. doi: 10.1073/pnas.1506451112

Rollnick, S., Miller, W. R., & Butler, C. C. (2008). *Motivational interviewing in health care: Helping patients change behavior*. New York, NY: Guilford Press.

Rose, J. (2010). An example of client-centered therapy for post-traumatic stress disorder. *The Person-Centered Journal, 17*(1-2), 52–78.

Rossano, F. (1996). Psychoanalysis and psychiatric institutions: Theoretical and clinical spaces of the Horney approach. *American Journal of Psychoanalysis, 56*, 203–212.

Rothbaum, B. O. (2005). Commentary on Riva, G., Virtual reality in psychotherapy: Review. *Cyber Psychology & Behavior, 8*, 239–240.

Roubal, J. (2016). *Towards a research tradition in gestalt therapy*. Newcastle upon Tyne, UK: Cambridge Scholars Publishing.

Rule, M. L., & Bishop, W. R. (Eds.). (2005). *Adlerian lifestyle counseling: Practice and research*. New York, NY: Routledge.

Ryback, D. (2011). Humanistic psychology's impact and accomplishments. *Journal of Humanistic Psychology, 51*, 413–418.

Ryff, C. D. (2014). Psychological well-being revisited: Advances in science and practice of eudaimonia. *Psychotherapy and Psychosomatics, 83*(1), 10–28.

Saadati, H., & Lashani, L. (2013). Effectiveness of gestalt therapy on self-efficacy of divorced women. *Social and Behavioral Sciences, 84*, 1171–1174.

Sadati, N. S., Hosseini, B., Hakami, M., & Sadati, N. S. (2017). The effectiveness of existential group therapy on social and emotional adjustment in women with dependent personality disorder. *International Journal of Existential Psychology & Psychotherapy, 7*(1), 1–11.

Salande, J. D., & Perkins, G. R. (2011). An object relations approach to cult membership. *American Journal of Psychotherapy, 66*, 381–391.

Samai, S., & Almagor, A. (2011). *The dialectical approach as a tool for changing perception and level of anxiety symptoms*. Unpublished manuscript, University of Haifa, Israel.

Sanchez, W., & Garriga, O. (1996). Control theory, reality therapy and cultural fatalism: Toward an integration. *Journal of Reality Therapy, 15*(2), 30–38.

Sanders, C. J. (2007). A poetics of resistance: Compassionate practice in substance misuse therapy. In C. Brown & T. Augusta-Scott (Eds.), *Narrative therapy: Making meaning, making lives* (pp. 59–76). Thousand Oaks, CA: Sage.

Sandler, A. (1996). The psychoanalytic legacy of Anna Freud. *Psychoanalytic Study of the Child, 51*, 270–284.

Sandler, J., & Freud, A. (1985). *The analysis of defense: The ego and the mechanisms of defense revisited*. New York, NY: International Universities Press.

Sapp, M. (2006). The strength-based model for counseling at-risk youths. *The Counseling Psychologist, 34*, 108–117.

Sapriel, L. (2012). Creating an embodied, authentic self: Integrating mindfulness with psychotherapy when working with trauma. In T. B. Levine (Ed.), *Gestalt therapy: Advances in theory and practice* (pp. 107–122). New York, NY: Routledge.

Saroglou, V. (2012). Are we born to be religious? *Scientific American Mind, 23*, 52–57.

Sarter, M., Bernston, G. G., & Cacioppo, J. T. (1996). Brain imaging and cognitive neuroscience. *American Psychologist, 51*, 13–21.

Sartre, J. P. (1956). *Being and nothingness*. New York, NY: Philosophical Library.

Satir, V. (1975). *Conjoint family therapy*. Palo Alto, CA: Science and Behavior Books.

Sayers, J. (1991). *Mothers of psychoanalysis: Helene Deutsch, Karen Horney, Anna Freud, Melanie Klein*. New York, NY: W. W. Norton.

Scharff, J. S., & Scharff, D. E. (2005). *The primer of object relations* (2nd ed.). Northvale, NJ: Aronson.

Scharwachter, P. (2008). Abortion decision making by focusing. *European Journal of Contraception & Reproductive Health Care, 13*, 191–197.

Schneider, K. (2008). *Existential-integrative psychotherapy: Guideposts to the core of practice*. New York, NY: Routledge.

Schneider, K. J., & Krug, O. T. (2010). *Existential-humanistic therapy*. Washington, DC: American Psychological Association.

Schnyder, U. (2009). Future perspectives in psychotherapy, *European Archives of Psychiatry and Clinical Neuroscience, 259*, Suppl. 2, S123–S128.

Schoen, D. E. (2009). *The war of the gods in addiction: C. G. Jung, Alcoholics Anonymous, and archetypal evil*. New Orleans, LA: Spring Journal.

Scholl, B., Ray, D. C., & Brady-Amoon, P. (2014). Humanistic counseling process, outcomes, and research. *Journal of Humanistic Counseling, 53*, 218–239. doi: 10.1002/j.2161-1939.2014.00058.x

Scholl, M. B., & Hansen, J. T. (2018). *Postmodern perspectives on contemporary counseling issues*. New York, NY: Oxford University Press.

Schoo, A. (2008). Motivational interviewing in the prevention and management of chronic disease: Improving physical activity and exercise in line with choice theory. *International Journal of Reality Therapy, 27*, 26–29.

Schottenbauer, M. A., Glass, C. R., & Arnkoff, D. B. (2007). Decision making and psychotherapy integration: Theoretical considerations, preliminary data, and implications for future research. *Journal of Psychotherapy Integration, 17*, 225–250.

Schubert, S., & Lee, C. W. (2009). Adult PTSD and its treatment with EMDR: A review of controversies, evidence, and theoretical knowledge. *Journal of EMDR Practice & Research, 3*(3), 117–132. doi: 10.1891/1933-3196.3.3.117

Schulenberg, S. E., Schnetzer, L. W., Winters, M. R., & Hutzell, R. R. (2010). Meaning-centered couples therapy: Logotherapy and intimate relationships. *Journal of Contemporary Psychotherapy, 40*, 95–102.

Schultz, D. P., & Schultz, S. E. (2013). *Theories of personality* (11th ed). Boston, MA: Cengage.

Schultz, D. P., & Schultz, S. E. (2011). *A history of modern psychology*. Belmont, CA: Cengage.

Schwartz, A. M. (1995). School reform and restructuring through the use of "quality school" philosophy. *Journal of Reality Therapy, 14*(2), 23–28.

Schwartz, J. P., & Waldo, M. (2003). Interpersonal manifestations of lifestyle: Individual psychology integrated with interpersonal theory. *Journal of Mental Health Counseling, 25*(2), 101–108.

Schwartz, L. B. (2012). Mixed-orientation marriages: Coming out, staying together. *Journal of GLBT Family Studies, 8*(1), 121–136.

Scott, J., & Freeman, A. (2010). Beck's cognitive therapy. In N. Kazantzis, M. A. Reinecke, & A. Freeman (Eds.), *Cognitive and behavioral theories in clinical practice* (pp. 28–75). New York, NY: Guilford Press.

Sedgwick, D. (2001). *Introduction to Jungian therapy*. New York, NY: Brunner-Routledge.

Segal, Z. V., Anderson, A. K., Gulamani, T., Dinh Williams, L., Desormeau, P., Ferguson, A., Walsh, K., & Farb, N. A. S. (2019). Practice of therapy acquired regulatory skills and depressive relapse/recurrence prophylaxis following cognitive therapy or mindfulness based cognitive therapy. *Journal of Consulting and Clinical Psychology, 87*(2), 161–170.

Segal Z. V., Williams J. M. G., & Teasdale J. D. (2002). *Mindfulness-based cognitive therapy for depression: A new approach to preventing relapse*. New York, NY: Guilford.

Seiler, L. (2008). *Cool connections with cognitive behavioral therapy: Encouraging self-esteem, resilience and well-being in children and young people using CBT approaches*. London, UK: Jessica Kingsley.

Seligman, M. E. P. (1995). The effectiveness of psychotherapy. *American Psychologist, 50*(12), 965–974.

Seligman, M. E. P. (2012). *Flourish: A visionary new understanding of happiness and well-being*. New York, NY: Simon and Schuster.

Seo, M., Kang, H. S., Lee, Y. L., Chae, S. M. (2015). Narrative therapy with an emotional approach for people with depression: Improved symptom and cognitive-emotional outcomes. *Journal of Psychiatric and Mental Health Nursing, 22*(6), 379–389.

Seponski, D. M. (2016). A feminist-informed integration of emotionally focused and solution focused therapies. *Journal of Family and Psychotherapy, 27*(4), 221–242.

Serlin, I. (1992). Tribute to Laura Perls. *Journal of Humanistic Psychology, 32*, 57–66.

Shahar, B., Bar-Kalifa, E., & Alon, E. (2017). Emotion-focused therapy for social anxiety disorder: Results from a multiple-baseline study. *Journal of Consulting and Clinical Psychology, 85*(3), 238–249.

Shamdasani, S. (Ed.). (2009). *Liber novus: The "red book" of C. G. Jung* (Philemon Series). New York, NY: W. W. Norton.

Shapiro, F. (2018). *Eye movement desensitization and reprocessing: Basic principles, protocols, and procedures* (3rd ed.). New York, NY: Guilford.

Shapiro, J. L. (2015). *Pragmatic existential counseling and psychotherapy: Intimacy, intuition, and the search for meaning (1st ed.)*. Thousand Oaks, CA: Sage.

Shapiro, J. P. (2015). *Child and adolescent therapy: Science and art* (2nd ed.). Hoboken, NJ: John Wiley & Sons.

Sharf, R. S. (2016). *Theories of psychotherapy & counseling: Concepts and cases* (6th ed.). Boston, MA: Cengage.

Sharp, J. G., & Bugental, J. F. T. (2001). Existential-humanistic psychotherapy. In R. J. Corsini (Ed.), *Handbook of innovative therapies* (2nd ed., pp. 206–217). New York, NY: Wiley.

Shaw, S. L., & Murray, K. W. (2014). Monitoring alliance and outcome with client feedback measures. *Journal of Mental Health Counseling, 36*(1), 43–57.

Shea, M., Cachelin, F., Uribe, L., Striegel, R., Thompson, D., & Wilson, T. (2012). Cultural adaptation of a cognitive behavior therapy guided self-help program for Mexican American women with binge eating disorders. *Journal of Counseling & Development, 90,* 308–318.

Shedler, J. (2010). The efficacy of psychodynamic psychotherapy. *American Psychologist, 65,* 98–109.

Shedler, J. (2012). The efficacy of psychodynamic psychotherapy. In R. A. Levy, J. S. Ablon, & H. Kachele (Eds.), *Psychodynamic psychotherapy research* (pp. 9–26). New York, NY: Humana Press.

Sheffield, A. Waller, G., Emanuelli, F., Murray, J., & Meyer, C. (2006). Links between parenting and core beliefs: Preliminary psychometric validation of the Young Parenting Inventory. *Cognitive Therapy and Research, 29*(6), 787–802. doi: 10.1007/s10608-005-4291-6

Sheldon, K. M., Arndt, J., & Houser-Marko, L. (2003). In search of the organismic valuing process: The human tendency to move towards beneficial goal choices. *Journal of Personality, 71,* 835–869.

Sherman, R., & Dinkmeyer, D. (1987). *Systems of family therapy: An Adlerian integration.* Philadelphia, PA: Brunner/Mazel.

Sherman, R., & Nwaorgu, A. (2002). Adlerian therapy: A century of tradition and research. In F. W. Kaslow (Ed.), *Comprehensive handbook of psychotherapy: Interpersonal/humanistic/existential.* New York, NY: John Wiley & Sons.

Shifron, R. (2010). Adler's need to belong as the key to mental health. *Journal of Individual Psychotherapy, 66,* 10–29.

Shriver, M. D., Anderson, C. M., & Proctor, B. (2001). Evaluating the validity of functional behavior assessment. *School Psychology Review, 30*(2), 180–192.

Shulman, B. H., & Mosak, H. H. (2015). *Manual for life style assessment.* New York, NY: Routledge.

Sifneos, P. E. (1979a). *Short-term dynamic psychotherapy: Evaluation and technique.* New York, NY: Plenum.

Sifneos, P. E. (1979b). *Short-term psychotherapy and emotional crisis.* Cambridge, MA: Harvard University Press.

Sifneos, P. E. (1984). The current status of individual short-term dynamic psychotherapy and its future: An overview. *American Journal of Psychotherapy, 38*(4), 472–483.

Silver, K. E., Levant, R. F., & Gonzalez, A. (2018). What does the psychology of men and masculinities offer the practitioner? Practical guidance for the feminist, culturally sensitive treatment of traditional men. *Practice Innovations, 32*(2), 94–106.

Silverstein, L. B., & Goodrich, T. J. (Eds.). (2003). *Feminist family therapy: Empowerment in social context.* Washington, DC: American Psychological Association.

Simkin, J. S. (1975). An introduction to Gestalt therapy. In F. C. Stephenson (Ed.), *Gestalt therapy primer: Introductory readings in Gestalt therapy* (pp. 3–12). Springfield, IL: Charles C Thomas.

Simpson, J. A., & Rholes, W. S. (2017). Adult attachment, stress, and romantic relationships. *Current Opinion in Psychology, 13,* 19–24.

Singh, A. A., & Moss, L. (2016). Using relational-cultural theory in LGBTQQ counseling: Addressing heterosexism and enhancing relational competencies. *Journal of Counseling & Development, 94*(4), 398–404.

Skinner, B. F. (1948/2005). *Walden II.* Indianapolis, IN: Hackett.

Sklare, G. (2000). Solution-focused brief counseling strategies. In J. Carlson & L. Sperry (Eds.), *Brief therapy with individuals and couples* (pp. 437–468). Phoenix, AZ: Zeig, Tucker & Theisen.

Slikboer, R., Nedeljkovic, M., Bowe, S. J., & Moulding, R. (2015). A systematic review and meta-analysis of behaviourally based psychological interventions and pharmacological interventions for trichotillomania. *Clinical Psychologist, 21*(1), 20–32. doi: 10.1111/cp.12074

Smith, E. J. (2006). The strength-based counselling model. *The Counselling Psychologist, 4,* 13–79. doi: 10.1177/0011000005277018

Smout, M. F., Hayes, L., Atkins, P. W. B., Klausen, J., & Duguid, J. E. (2012). The empirically supported status of acceptance and commitment therapy: An update. *Clinical Psychologist, 16,* 97–109. doi: 10.1111/j.1742-9552.2012.00051.x

Soban, C. (2006). What about the boys?: Addressing issues of masculinity within male anorexia nervosa in a feminist therapeutic environment. *International Journal of Men's Health, 5*(3), 251–267.

Sommerbeck, L. (2011). An introduction to pre-therapy. *Psychosis, 3,* 235–241.

Sperry, L. (2010). *Core competences in counseling and psychotherapy: Becoming a highly content and effective therapist.* New York, NY: Routledge.

Spiegler, M. D., & Guevremont, D. C. (2016). *Contemporary behavior therapy* (6th ed.). Boston, MA: Cengage.

Springer, P. R., & Wheeler, M. A. (2012). The relational self-esteem pot. A Satir intervention in family therapy. *The Satir Journal: Transformational Systemic Therapy, 5*(1).

Srebnik, D. S. (1994). Feminist cognitive-behavioral therapy for negative body image. *Women & Therapy, 15*(2), 117–133.

Stein, B. C., Jaycox, L. H., Kataoka, S. H., Wong, M., Tu, W., Elliott, M. N., & Fink, A. (2003). A mental health intervention for school children exposed to violence. *Journal of the American Medical Association, 290,* 603–611.

Stein, M. (Ed.). (2010). *Jungian psychoanalysis: Working the spirit of C. G. Jung.* Chicago, IL: Carus.

Steinert, C., Munder, T., Rabung, S, Hoyer, J., & Leichsenring, F. (2017). Psychodynamic therapy: As efficacious as other empirically supported treatments? A meta-analysis testing equivalence of outcomes. *The American Journal of Psychiatry, 174*(10), 943–953.

Steketee, G., Frost, R. O., Tolin, D. F., Rasmussen, J., & Brown, T. A. (2010). Waitlist-controlled trial of cognitive behavior therapy for hoarding disorder. *Depression and Anxiety, 27,* 476–484.

Stoehr, T. (2009). Perls, Hefferline, and Goodman: Gestalt therapy—An afterword. *Gestalt Review, 13,* 82–95.

Stone, D. A., Conteh, J. A., & Francis, J. D. (2017). Therapeutic factors and psychological concepts in alcoholics anonymous. *Journal of Counselor Practice, 8*(2), 120–135.

Stoykova, Z. (2013). Social interest and motivation. *Trakia Journal of Sciences, 11*(3), 286–290.

Stratton, S. P. (2015). Mindfulness and contemplation: Secular and religious traditions in western context. *Counseling and Values, 60*(1), 100–118.

Stricker, G., & Gold, J. (2011). Integrative approaches to psychotherapy. In S. Messer & A. Gurman (Eds.), *Essential psychotherapies* (3rd ed., pp. 425–459). New York, NY: Guilford Press.

Strozier, C. B. (2001). *Heinz Kohut: The making of a psychoanalyst.* New York, NY: Farrar, Strauss and Giroux.

Strumpfel, U., & Goldman, R. (2002). Contacting Gestalt therapy. In D. J. Cain & J. Seeman (Eds.), *Humanistic psychotherapies: Handbook of research and practice* (pp. 189–219). Washington, DC: American Psychological Association.

Strumpfel, U., & Martin, C. (2004). Research on Gestalt therapy. *International Gestalt Journal, 27,* 9–54.

Strupp, H. H. (1992). The future of psychodynamic psychotherapy. *Psychotherapy, 29*(1), 21–27.

Stutey, D., & Wubbolding, R. (2018). Reality play therapy: A case example. *International Journal of Play Therapy, 27,*(1), 1–13. doi: 10.1037/pla0000061

Substance Abuse and Mental Health Services Administration (SAMHSA). (2009). *Integrated treatment for co-occurring disorders: The evidence.* (DHHS Publication No. SMA-08-4366). Rockville, MD: Center for Mental Health Services, Substance Abuse and Mental Health Services Administration, U.S. Department of Health and Human Services.

Sue, D. W., Sue, D., Neville, H. A., & Smith, L. (2019). *Counseling the culturally diverse: Theory and practice* (8th ed.). Hoboken, NJ: Wiley.

Suitt, G. K., Geraldo, P., Estay, M., & Franklin, C. G. S. (2019). Solution-Focused Brief Therapy for individuals with alcohol use disorders in Chile. *Research on Social Work Practice, 29*(1), 19–35. doi: 10.1177/1049731517740958

Sullivan, H. S. (1953). *The interpersonal theory of psychiatry.* New York, NY: W. W. Norton.

Sullivan, H. S. (1970). *The psychiatric interview.* New York, NY: W. W. Norton.

Summers, R. F., & Barber, J. P. (2009). *Psychodynamic therapy: A guide to evidence-based practice.* New York, NY: Guilford Press.

Sundquist, J., Lilja, A., Palmer, K., Memon, A. A., Wang, X., Johansson, L. M., . . . Sundquist, K. (2015). Mindfulness group therapy in primary care patients with depression, anxiety and stress and adjustment disorders: Randomised controlled trial. *The British Journal of Psychiatry, 206*(2), 128–135. doi: 10.1192/bjp.bp.114.150243

Surcinelli, P., Rossi, N., Montebarocci, O., & Baldaro, B. (2010). Adult attachment styles and psychological disease: Examining the mediating role of personality traits. *Journal of Psychology Interpersonal and Applied, 144,* 523–534.

Surrey, J. L. (1991). The "self-in-relation": A new theory of women's development. In J. V. Jordon, A. G. Kaplan, J. B. Miller, I. P. Stiver, & J. L. Surrey (Eds.), *Women's growth in connection: Writings from the Stone Center.* New York, NY: Guilford Press.

Sweeney, T. J. (2009). *Adlerian counseling and psychotherapy: A practitioner's approach* (5th ed.). New York, NY: Routledge.

Sweet, A. D. (2010). Paranoia and psychotic process: Some clinical applications of projective identification in psychoanalytic psychotherapy. *American Journal of Psychotherapy, 64*, 339–358.

Swift, J. K., Callahan, J. L., & Vollmer, B. M. (2011). Preferences. In J. C. Norcross (Ed.), *Psychotherapy relationships that work: Evidence-based responsiveness*. New York, NY: Oxford University Press.

Sydow, V. K., Retzlaff, R., Beher, S., Haun, M. W., & Schweitzer, J. (2013). The efficacy of systemic therapy for childhood and adolescent externalizing disorders: A systematic review of 47 RCT. *Family Process, 52*(4), 576–618.

Szabo, J., Toth, S., & Pakai, A. K. (2014). Narrative group therapy for alcohol dependent patients. *International Journal of Mental Health & Addiction, 12*, 470–476.

Tacey, D. (2009). *Edge of the sacred: Jung, psyche, and earth*. Einsiedein, Switzerland: Daimon Verlag.

Tanner, L. R., & Lyness, K. P. (2004). Out of the closet, still in the home: Providing queer affirmative therapy for youth and families. *Journal of Feminist Family Therapy, 15*(1), 21–35.

Teasdale, J., Williams, J., Soulsby, J. M., Segal, Z. V., Ridgeway, V. A., & Lau, M. A. (2000). Prevention of relapse/recurrence in major depression by mindfulness-based cognitive therapy. *Journal of Consulting and Clinical Psychology, 68*, 623–625.

Thompson, G. (2011). A meaning-centered therapy for addictions. *International Journal of Mental Health and Addiction, 10*(3), 9367–9411.

Thompson, G. R. (2016). Meaning therapy for addictions: A case study. *Journal for Humanistic Psychology, 56*(5), 457–482.

Tillich, P. (1952). *The courage to be*. New Haven, CT: Yale University Press.

Tindall, L., Mikocka, W. A., McMillan, D., Wright, B., Hewitt, C., & Gascoyne, S. (2017). Is behavioural activation effective in the treatment of depression in young people? A systematic review and meta-analysis. *Psychology & Psychotherapy: Theory, Research, and Practice, 90*(4), 770–796.

Topolinski, S., & Hertel, G. (2007). The role of personality in psychotherapists' careers: Relationships between personality traits, therapeutic schools, and job satisfaction. *Psychotherapy Research, 17*, 378–390.

Totton, N. (2010). *The problem with the humanistic therapies*. London, UK: Karnac Books.

Town, J. M., & Driessen, E. (2013). Emerging evidence for intensive short-term dynamic psychotherapy with personality disorders and somatic disorders. *Psychiatric Annals, 43*(11), 502–507.

Trepal, H., Boie, I., & Kress, V. (2012). A relational cultural approach to working with clients with eating disorders. *Journal of Counseling & Development, 90*, 346–356.

Truax, C., & Carkhuff, R. (2007). *Toward effective counseling and psychotherapy*. Chicago, IL: Transaction Publishers.

Tuckey, M. R., & Brewer, N. (2003). The influence of schemas, stimulus ambiguity, and interview schedule on eyewitness memory over time. *Journal of Experimental Psychology: Applied, 9*, 101–118.

Tummala-Narra, P. (2009). The relevance of a psychoanalytic perspective in exploring religious and spiritual identity in psychotherapy. *Psychoanalytic Psychology, 26*, 83–95.

Turner, M., & Marker, J. B. (2013). Examining the efficacy of rational-emotive behavior therapy (REBT) on irrational beliefs and anxiety in elite youth cricketers. *Journal of Applied Sport Psychology, 25*(1), 131–147.

Uhlmann, E., Pizarro, D., & Bloom, P. (2008). Varieties of social cognition. *Journal for the Theory of Social Behavior, 38*, 293–322.

Underwood, L. A., & Dailey, F. L. (2017). *Counseling adolescents competently*. Thousand Oaks, CA: Sage.

Usakli, H. (2012). Turkish university students' preference from Rogers, Perls, Ellis and their therapeutic styles. *Social and Behavioral Sciences, 69*, 967–976.

Vachon, M., Fillion, L., Achille, M., Duval, S., & Leung, D. (2011). An awakening experience: An interpretative phenomenological analysis of the effects of a meaning-centered intervention shared among palliative care nurses. *Qualitative Research in Psychology, 8*, 39–54.

Vallejo, Z., & Amaro, H. (2009). Adaptation of mindfulness-based stress reduction program for addiction relapse prevention. *The Humanistic Psychologist, 37*, 192–206.

van der Kolk, B. A. (2014). *The body keeps the score: Brain, body, and mind in the healing of trauma*. New York, NY: Viking.

van Deurzen, E. (2002). *Existential counseling and psychotherapy in practice* (2nd ed.). London, UK: Sage.

van Deurzen, E. (2010). *Everyday mysteries: A handbook of existential psychotherapy* (2nd ed.). New York, NY: Routledge.

van Deurzen, E., & Adams, M. (2011). *Skills in existential counseling and psychotherapy*. Thousand Oaks, CA: Sage.

van Deurzen, E., & Adams, M. (2016). *Skills in existential counselling & psychotherapy (skills in counselling & psychotherapy series)* (2nd ed.). Thousand Oaks, CA: Sage.

Van Dijk, S., Jeffrey, J., & Katz, M. R. (2013). A randomized, controlled, pilot study of dialectical behavior therapy skills in a psychoeducational group for individuals with bipolar disorder. *Journal of Affective Disorders*, *145*(3), 386–393. doi: 10.1016/j.jad.2012.05.054

van Eeden-Moorefield, B., Few-Demo, A. L., Benson, K., Bible, J., & Lummer, S. (2018). A content analysis of LGBT research in top family journals 2000–2015. *Journal of Family Issues*, *39*(5), 1374–1395.

Van Ryzin, M. J., & Fosco, G. M. (2016). Family-based approached to prevention. In M. J. Van Ryzin, K. L. Kumpfer, G. M. Fosco, & M. T. Greenberg (Eds.), *Family-based prevention programs for children and adolescents: Theory, research, and large-scale dissemination* (pp. 1–20). New York, NY: Taylor & Francis.

Vatcher, C., & Bogo, M. (2001). The feminist/emotionally focused therapy practice model: An integrated approach for couple therapy. *Journal of Marital and Family Therapy*, *27*(1), 69–83.

Verdeli, H., & Weissman, M. M. (2011). Interpersonal therapy. In R. J. Corsini & D. Wedding (Eds.), *Current psychotherapies* (9th ed., pp. 383–416). Belmont, CA: Brooks/Cole.

Vereen, L. G., Hill, N. R., Sosa, G. A., & Kress, V. E. (2014). The synonymic nature of professional counseling and humanism: Presuppositions that guide our identities. *Journal of Humanistic Counseling*, *53*(3), 191–201. doi: 10.1002/j.2161-1939.2014.00056.x

von Bertalanffy, L. (1968/1976). *General system theory: Foundations, development, application*. New York, NY: George Braziller.

Vontress, C. E. (2008). Preface. In P. B. Pedersen, J. G. Draguns, W. J. Lonner, & J. E. Trimble (Eds.), *Counseling across cultures* (6th ed., pp. ix–xii). Alexandria, VA: American Counseling Association.

Vos, J., Craig, M., & Cooper, M. (2015). Existential therapies: A meta-analysis of their effects on psychological outcomes. *Journal of Consulting and Clinical Psychology*, *83*(1), 115–128.

Vygotsky, L. (1967). Play and its role in the mental development of the child. *Journal of Russian and East European Psychology*, *5*, 6–18.

Wachtel, P. L. (1977). *Psychoanalysis and behavior therapy: Toward an integration*. New York, NY: Basic Books.

Wachtel, P. L. (1997). *Psychoanalysis, behavior therapy, and the relational world*. Washington, DC: American Psychological Association.

Wachtel, P. L. (2008). *Relational psychotherapy*. New York, NY: Guilford Press.

Wachtel, P. L., Kruk, J., & McKinney, M. K. (2005). Cyclical psychodynamics and integrative relational therapy. In J. C. Norcross & M. R. Goldfried (Eds.), *Handbook of psychotherapy integration* (2nd ed., pp. 172–195). New York, NY: Oxford University Press.

Wagner, W. G. (2008). *Counseling, psychology, and children* (2nd ed.). Upper Saddle River, NJ: Pearson.

Wagner-Moore, L. E. (2004). Gestalt therapy: Past, present, and future research. *Psychotherapy: Theory, Research, Practice, Training*, *41*, 180–189.

Waites, C. (2009). Building on strengths: Intergenerational practice with African American families. *Social Work*, *54*, 278–287.

Walen, S. R., DiGiuseppe, R., & Dryden, W. (1992). *A practitioner's guide to rational-emotive therapy*. New York, NY: Oxford University Press.

Wallach, H. S., Safir, M. P., & Bar-Zvi, M. (2009). Virtual reality cognitive behavior therapy for public speaking anxiety: A randomized clinical trial. *Behavior Modification*, *33*, 314–338.

Walsh, F. (1998). *Strengthening family resilience*. New York, NY: Guilford Press.

Walsh, F. (Ed.). (2012). *Normal family processes: Growing diversity and complexity* (4th ed.). New York, NY: Guilford Press.

Wampold, B. E. (2010). *The basics of psychotherapy: An introduction to theory and practice*. Washington, DC: American Psychological Association.

Wampold, B. E. (2010). The research evidence for the common factors models: A historically situated perspective. In B. L. Duncan, S. D. Miller, B. E. Wampold, & M. A. Hubble. (Eds.), *Heart and soul of change in psychotherapy* (2nd ed., pp. 49–81). Washington, DC: American Psychological Association.

Wampold, B. E. (2015). How important are the common factors in psychotherapy? An update. *World Psychiatry*, *14*(3), 270–277. doi: 10.1002/wps.20238

Wang, S. C., & Iwamasa, G. Y. (2018). Indigenous healing practices and Asian immigrant women. *Women & Therapy*, *41*(1-2), 149–164.

Waska, R. (2010). Moments of uncertainty in psychoanalytic practice: Interpreting within the matrix of projective identification, counter-transference, and enactment. New York, NY: Columbia University Press.

Watson, J. B. (1925). *Behaviorism*. New York, NY: W. W. Norton.

Watts, R. E. (2000). Entering the new millennium: Is individual psychology still relevant? *Journal of Individual Psychology*, *56*, 21–30.

Watts, R. E. (Ed.). (2003). *Adlerian, cognitive, and constructivist therapies: An integrative dialogue*. New York, NY: Springer.

Watts, R. E. (2012). On the origin of striving for superiority and of social interest. In J. Carlson & M. P. Maniacci (Eds.), *Alfred Adler revisited* (pp. 41–47). New York, NY: Routledge.

Watts, R. E. (2013). Adlerian counseling. In B. J. Irby, G. Brown, R. Lara-Alecio, S. Jackson, B. J. Irby, G. Brown, & S. Jackson (Eds.), *The handbook of educational theories* (pp. 459–472). Charlotte, NC: IAP.

Watzlawick, P., Weakland, J., & Fisch, R. (1974). *Change: Principles of problem formation and problem resolution*. New York, NY: Norton.

Weakland, J., Fisch, R., Watzlawick, P., & Bodin, A. (1974). Brief therapy: Focused problem resolution. *Family Process*, *13*, 141–168.

Weaver, A., Greeno, C. G., Marcus, S. C., Fusco, R. A., Zimmerman, T., & Anderson, C. (2013). Effects of structural family therapy on child and maternal mental health symptomatology. *Research on Social Work Practice*, *23*(3), 294–303.

Weinbrecht, A., Schulze, L., Boettcher, J., & Renneberg, B. (2016). Avoidant personality disorder: A current review. *Current Psychiatry Reports*, *18*(3), 29–45. doi: 10.1007/s11920-016-0665-6

Weishaar, M. E. (1993). *Aaron T. Beck*. London, UK: Sage.

Weissman, M. M., Markowitz, J., & Klerman, G. L. (2007). *Clinician's quick guide to interpersonal therapy*. New York, NY: Oxford University Press.

Weisstein, N. (1968). *Kinder, küche, kirche as scientific law: Psychology constructs the female*. Boston, MA: New England Free Press.

Welfel, E. (2015). *Ethics in counseling and psychotherapy* (6th ed.). Boston, MA: Cengage.

Wells, A. (2009). *Metacognitive therapy for anxiety and depression*. New York, NY: Guilford.

Wheeler, G. (1991). *Gestalt reconsidered: A new approach to contact and resistances*. New York, NY: Gardner.

Whitaker, C., Warkentin, J., & Malone, T. (2011). The involvement of the professional therapist. In C. Whitaker, J. Warkentin, T. Malone, & A. Burton (Eds.), *Case studies in counseling and psychotherapy* (pp. 218–256). Englewood Cliffs, NJ: Prentice Hall.

Whitaker, C. A., & Napier, A. Y. (1977). Process techniques of family therapy. *Interaction*, *1*, 4–19.

White, J., Campbell, L., & Steward, A. (1995). Associations of scores on the White-Campbell Psychological Birth Order Inventory and the Kern Lifestyle Scale. *Psychological Reports*, *77*, 1187–1196.

White, K. J., Wagener, L. M., & Furrow, J. L. (2010). What am I here for? A qualitative examination on the expression, development and integration of purpose in at-risk and thriving male adolescents. *International Journal of Existential Psychology and Psychotherapy*, *3*, 1–16.

White, M. (1986). Negative explanation, restraint, and double description: A template for family. *Family Process*, *25*, 169–184.

White, M. (1988–1989, Summer). The externalization of the problem and the re-authoring of lives and relationships. *Dulwich Centre Newsletter*, pp. 3–20.

White, M. (1989). *Selected papers*. Adelaide, Australia: Dulwich Centre.

White, M. (1995). *Re-authoring lives*. Adelaide, Australia: Dulwich Centre.

White, M. (2007). *Maps of narrative practice*. New York, NY: W. W. Norton.

White, M. (2011). *Narrative practice: Continuing the conversation*. New York, NY: W. W. Norton.

White, M., & Epston, D. (1989). *Literate means to therapeutic ends*. Adelaide, Australia: Dulwich Centre.

White, M., & Epston, D. (1990). *Narrative means to therapeutic ends*. New York, NY: W. W. Norton.

White, M., & Morgan, A. (2006). *Narrative therapy with children and their families*. Adelaide, Australia: Dulwich Centre.

Whitmarsh, L., & Mullette, J. (2009) An integrated model for counseling adolescents. *Journal of Humanistic Counselling, 48*, 144–159.

Wiebe, S. A., Johnson, S. M., Lafontaine, M. F., Moser, M. B., Dalgleish, T. L., & Tasca, G. A. (2017). Two-year follow-up outcomes in emotionally focused couple therapy: An investigation of relationship satisfaction and attachment trajectories. *Journal of Marital and Family Therapy, 43*(2), 227–244.

Williams, J. M. G., Alatiq, Y., Crane, C., Barnhofer, T., Fennell, M. J. V., Duggan, D. S., . . . Goodwin, G. M. (2008). Mindfulness-based cognitive therapy (MBCT) in bipolar disorder: Preliminary evaluation of immediate effects on between-episode functioning. *Journal of Affective Disorders, 107*(1–3), 275–279. doi: 10.1016/j.jad.2007.08.022

Williams, M. (2010). Mindfulness and psychological process, *Emotion, 10*, 1–7.

Williams, M., Alato, Y., Crane, C., Bernhofer, T., Fennell, M. J. V., Duggan, D. S., . . . Goodwin, G. M. (2008). Mindfulness-based cognitive therapy (MBCT) in bipolar disorder: Preliminary evaluation of immediate effects on between-episode functioning. *Journal of Affective Disorders, 107*, 275–279.

Williams, T. I., Salkovskis, P. M., Forrester, L., Turner, S., White, H., & Allsopp, M. A. (2010). A randomised controlled trial of cognitive behavioural treatment for obsessive compulsive disorder in children and adolescents. *European Child and Adolescent Psychiatry, 19*, 449–456.

Wilson, B. J., & Ray, D. (2018). Child-centered play therapy: Aggression, empathy, and self-regulation. *Journal of Counseling & Development, 96*(4), 399–409.

Wilson, H. N. M., Weatherhead, S., & Davies, J. S. (2015). Clinical psychologists' experiences of accessing personal therapy during training: A narrative analysis. *International Journal of Practice-based Learning in Health and Social Care, 3*(2), 32–47. doi: 10.18552/ijpblhsc.v3i2.238

Winbolt, B. (2011). *Solution focused therapy for the helping professions*. Philadelphia, PA: Jessica Kingsley.

Winslade, J., Crocket, K., & Monk, G. (1997). The therapeutic relationship. In G. Monk, J. Winslade, K. Crocket, & D. Epston (Eds.), *Narrative therapy in practice: The archaeology of home (pp. 53–81)*. San Franciso, CA: Jossey-Bass.

Winslade, J., & Smith, L. (1997). Countering alcoholic narratives. In G. Monk, J. Winslade, K. Crocket, & D. Epston (Eds.), *Narrative therapy in practice: The archaeology of hope* (pp. 158–193). San Francisco, CA: Jossey-Bass.

Winslade, J. M., & Monk, G. D. (2007). *Narrative counseling in schools*. Thousand Oaks, CA: Sage.

Woldt, A. L., & Toman, S. M. (2005). *Gestalt therapy: History, theory, and practice*. Thousand Oaks, CA: Sage.

Wolf, E. S. (1994). Varieties of disorders of the self. *British Journal of Psychotherapy, 11*, 198–208.

Wolitzky, D. L. (2011). Psychoanalytic theories of psychotherapy. In J. C. Norcross, G. R. VandenBos, & D. K. Freedheim (Eds.), *History of psychotherapy: Continuity and change* (pp. 65–100). Washington, DC: American Psychological Association.

Wolpe, J. (1969). *The practice of behavior therapy*. New York, NY: Pergamon.

Wong, P. (2010). Meaning therapy: An integrative and positive existential psychology. *Journal of Contemporary Psychology, 40*, 85–93.

Wong, P. T. P. (2014). Viktor Frankl's meaning seeking model and positive psychology. In A. Batthyany & P. Russo-Netzer (Eds.), *Meaning in existential and positive psychology* (pp. 149–184). New York, NY: Springer.

Wong, P. T. P. (2015). Meaning therapy: Assessments and interventions. *Existential Analysis, 26*(1), 154–167.

Wong, Y. J. (2015). The psychology of encouragement: Theory, research, and applications. *The Counseling Psychologist, 42*(2), 178–216. doi: 10.1177/0011000014545091

Woon, L., Kanapathy, A., Zakaria. H., & Alfonso, C. (2017). An integrative approach to treatment-resistant obsessive-compulsive disorder. *Psychodynamic Psychiatry, 45*(2), 237–257.

Worell, J., & Remer, P. (2003*). Feminist perspectives in therapy: Empowering diverse women* (2nd ed.). Hoboken, NJ: John Wiley & Sons.

Wormington, S., & Linnenbrink-Garcia, L. (2017). A new look at multiple goal pursuit: The promise of a person-centered approach. *Educational Psychology Review, 29*(3), 407–445. doi: 10.1007/s10648-016-9358-2

Wright, J. H., Basco, M. R., & Thase, M. E. (2006). *Learning cognitive-behavior therapy: An illustrated guide.* Arlington, VA: American Psychiatric Publishing.

Wubbolding, R. (2011). *Reality therapy: Theories of psychotherapy series.* Washington, DC: American Psychological Association.

Wubbolding, R. (2018). Contemporary controversial issues and how to use reality therapy in an ethical and mainstreamed manner: Thoughts to ponder. *International Journal of Choice Theory and Reality Therapy, 38*(1), 58–62.

Wubbolding, R., Casstevens, W., & Fulkerson, M. (2017). Using the WDEP system of reality therapy to support person-centered treatment planning. *Journal of Counseling and Development, 95*(4), 472–477.

Wubbolding, R. E. (1988). *Using reality therapy.* New York, NY: Perennial.

Wubbolding, R. E. (1991). *Understanding reality therapy.* New York, NY: HarperCollins.

Wubbolding, R. E. (1995). Integrating theory and practice: Expanding the theory and use of the higher level of perception. *Journal of Reality Therapy, 15*(1), 91–94.

Wubbolding, R. E. (2000). *Reality therapy for the 21st century.* New York, NY: Taylor & Francis.

Wubbolding, R. E. (2007a). Glasser quality school. *Group Dynamics: Theory, Research and Practice, 11,* 253–261.

Wubbolding, R. E. (2007b). Reality therapy theory. In D. Capuzzi & D. Gross (Eds.), *Counseling and psychotherapy: Theories and interventions* (4th ed., pp. 289–312). Upper Saddle River, NJ: Pearson/Prentice Hall.

Wubbolding, R. E. (2011). *Reality therapy: Theories of counseling series.* Washington, DC: American Psychological Association.

Wubbolding, R. E. (2016). Reality therapy/choice theory. In D. Capuzzi & D. Gross (Eds.), *Counseling and psychotherapy: Theories and interventions* (6th ed., pp. 311–338). Alexandria, VA: American Counseling Association.

Wubbolding, R. E., & Brickell, J. (2008). Frequently asked questions and not so brief answers: Part II. *International Journal of Reality Therapy, 27,* 46–49.

Wulf, R. (1998). The historical roots of Gestalt therapy theory. *Gestalt Journal, 21,* 81–92.

Xu, J. (2010). Logotherapy: A balm of Gilead for aging? *Journal of Religion, Spirituality & Aging, 22,* 180–195.

Yalom, I. (1998). *The Yalom reader: Selections from the work of a master therapist and master storyteller.* New York, NY: Basic Books.

Yalom, I., & Leszcz, M. (2005). *Theory and practice of group psychotherapy* (5th ed.). New York, NY: Basic Books.

Yalom, I. D. (1980). *Existential psychotherapy.* New York, NY: Basic Books.

Yalom, I. D. (1989). *Love's executioner and other tales of psychotherapy.* New York, NY: Basic Books.

Yalom, I. D. (2008). *Staring at the sun: Overcoming the terror of death.* San Francisco, CA: Jossey-Bass.

Yasar, M. (2017). Adaptation of general system theory and structural family therapy approach to classroom management in early childhood education. *Cukurova University Faculty of Education Journal, 46*(2), 655–969. doi: 10.14812/cuefd.300993

Yontef, G. (1993). *Awareness, dialogue, and process: Essays on Gestalt therapy.* Highland, NY: The Gestalt Journal Press.

Yontef, G. M. (2012). The four relationships of Gestalt therapy couples work. In T. B. Levine (Ed.), *Gestalt therapy: Advances in theory and practice* (pp. 123–137). New York, NY: Routledge.

Young, J. E. (1990/1999). *Cognitive therapy for personality disorders: A schema-focused approach.* Sarasota, FL: Professional Resource Exchange.

Young, J. E. (2003a). *Young Compensation Inventory.* New York, NY: Schema Therapy Institute.

Young, J. E. (2003b). *Young Parenting Inventory.* New York, NY: Cognitive Therapy Center of New York.

Young, J. E. (2005). *Young Schema Questionnaire.* New York, NY: Schema Therapy Institute.

Young, J. E., Arntz, A., Atkinson, T., Lobbastael, J., Weishear, M. E., vanVoleeswijk, M. F., & Klokman, J. (2007). *The Schema Mode Inventory.* New York, NY: Schema Therapy Institute.

Young, J. E., Klosko, J. S., & Weishaar, M. E. (2003). *Schema therapy: A practitioner's guide.* New York, NY: Guilford Press.

Young, K. S., Craske, M. G., Roepstorff, A., Parsons, C. E., van der Velden, A. M., Pallesen, K. J., & Fjorback, L. (2018). The impact of mindfulness-based interventions on brain activity: A systematic review of functional magnetic resonance imaging studies. *Neuroscience &*

Biobehavioral Reviews, 84, 424–433. doi: 10.1016/j.neubiorev.2017.08.003

Young, S. (2010). Responding to bullying in primary schools. In T. S. Nelson (Ed.), *Doing something different: Solution focused brief therapy practices* (pp. 99–101). New York, NY: Routledge.

Young-Bruehl, E. (2008). *Anna Freud: A biography*. New Haven, CT: Yale University Press.

Zakszeski, B. N., & DuPaul, G. J. (2017). Reinforce, shape, expose, and fade: A review of treatments for selective mutism (2005–2015). *School Mental Health, 9*, 1–15. doi: 10.1007/s12310-016-9198-8

Zarbo, C., Tasca, G. A., Cattafi, F., & Compare, A. (2015). Integrative psychotherapy works. *Frontiers in Psychology, 6*, 1–3. doi: 10.3389/fpsyg.2015.02021

Zhang, A., Franklin, C., Currin-McCulloch, J., Park, S., & Kim, J. (2018). The effectiveness of strength-based, solution-focused brief therapy in medical settings: A systematic review and meta-analysis of randomized controlled trials. *Journal of Behavioral Medicine, 41*(2), 139–151. doi: 10.1007/s10865-017-9888-1

Zilberstein, K. (2014). The use and limitations of attachment theory in child psychotherapy. *Psychotherapy, 51*(1), 93–103. doi: 10.1037/a0030930

Zinbarg, R. E., & Griffith, J. W. (2008). Behavior therapy. In J. L. Lebow (Ed.), *Twenty-first century psychotherapies: Contemporary approaches to theory and practice* (pp. 8–42). Hoboken, NJ: John Wiley & Sons.

Ziv-Beiman, S., Keinan, G., Livneh, E., Malone, P. S., & Shahar, G. (2017). Immediate therapist self-disclosure bolsters the effect of brief integrative psychotherapy on psychiatric symptoms and the perceptions of therapists: A randomized clinical trial. *Journal of Psychotherapy Research, 27*(5), 558–570.

NAME INDEX

A
Abbass, A., 142
Ablon, J. S., 5, 69
Abraham, K., 118
Acheson, D. T., 170
Achille, M., 300
Ackerman, N. W., 452
Adams, M., 285
Adamson, N., 368
Addis, M. E., 368, 382
Addison, D., 382
Addison, S. M., 383
Adibah, S. M., 285
Adler, A., 78, 80, 81, 82, 84, 86, 88, 90, 92, 93, 94
Adler, J., 310, 311, 403
Afrasiabi, M., 297
Ainsworth, B., 261
Ainsworth, M. D. S., 125, 126
Akbas, A., 320
Alexander, F., 134, 135
Alexander, J. H., 383
Alfonso, C., 141
Algamor, A., 270
Ali, S., 481
Al-Krenawi, A., 116, 142
Allen, S., 212
Almagor, M., 248
Alon, E., 319
Amaro, H., 263
American Psychiatric Association, 368, 370, 483
American Psychological Association (APA), 18, 33, 71, 371, 373, 468
Anderson, T., 7, 8, 140, 319
Andreas, S., 438
Angel, E., 282
Angermann, D., 353
Angus, L., 352
Ansbacher, H. L., 79, 80
Ansbacher, R. R., 79, 80
Antony, M. M., 154, 155, 158, 210
Arczynski, A. V., 383
Ardito, R. B., 5, 323
Arkowitz, H., 323, 325
Arlow, J. A., 63
Arndt, J., 311
Arnfred, S. M. H., 353

Arntz, A., 268, 269
Aronson-Fontes, L., 165
Artkoski, T., 10
Asnaani, A., 210
Atkins, P. W. B., 258
Austad, C., 63
Auszra, L., 319
Avdagic, E., 258

B
Baer, R. A., 259
Bahmani, B., 297
Baker, L., 445
Balbo, M., 481
Baldaro, B., 126
Baldwin, D. S., 261
Bandura, A., 169, 172
Banks, M. E., 383
Banmen, E., 438
Barber, C., 242
Barber, J. P., 135
Barbieri, J. L., 319
Barekati, S., 297, 299
Bar-Kalifa, E., 319
Barlow, D. H., 210
Barnard, A. D., 210
Barnard, L. K., 349, 353
Bartak, A., 280
Bartholomew, K., 126
Barton, A., 287
Bar-Zvi, M., 169
Basco, M. R., 199
Bateman, A., 130
Bateson, G., 396
Battagliese, G., 213
Baucam, D., 214
Bauman, S., 283, 288, 296, 301
Beal, D., 192
Beaudoin, M., 404
Beck, A., 181, 182, 196, 197, 198, 201, 203, 206, 209, 210, 212, 268
Beck, A. T., 196, 210
Becvar, D. S., 427, 434, 441, 447
Becvar, R. J., 427, 434, 441, 447
Bedard-Gilligan, M., 211
Bedics, J. D., 270
Beebe, B., 132, 141
Beher, S., 456
Beidel, D. C., 173

Bell, S. M., 126
Benard, B., 21
Benish, S., 318
Benson, K., 457
Bera, W., 404
Berdondini, L., 297, 325
Berg, I. K., 406, 413, 414, 418
Bergin, A. E., 483
Bergman, A., 127
Bernard, M. E., 183, 188, 190, 311
Bernecker, S. L., 130
Bernstein, D. P., 267
Bernston, G. G., 150
Berry, K., 9
Bertalanffy, L. V., 428, 429
Bertolino, B., 142
Beutler, L. E., 471, 475, 479, 483
Bible, J., 457
Bieling, P., 263
Binder, J. L., 140
Bischof, G. H., 418
Bishop, W. R., 103
Bisson, J., 481
Bitter, J. R., 103
Black, M. J., 70
Blehar, M. C., 125, 126
Bleske-Rechek, A., 86
Blewitt, P., 13
Blom, R., 353
Bloom, D., 353
Bloom, P., 268
Blore, D., 481
Bluett, E. J., 258
Boddy, J., 364
Bogo, M., 383
Bohart, A. C., 7, 9, 314, 319, 320, 327
Boie, I., 385
Bond, C., 418
Bond, F. W., 258
Borden, A., 395
Bornhäuser, A., 456
Boschen, M. J., 258
Boss, M., 290
Boutot, E., 166
Bowe, S. J., 173
Bowen, M. C., 428
Bowlby, J., 125, 127, 128, 130, 141
Bowling, S. W., 383

Bowman, C. E., 352
Bradford, K. P., 318
Bradley, H., 70
Brady, V. P., 258
Brady-Amoon, P., 8
Branch, R., 190, 191
Bratter, T. E., 234, 241
Bratton, S. C., 320
Brewer, N., 198
Brickell, J., 230
Broderick, P. C., 13
Brooke, D., 210
Broth, M. R., 456
Broverman, D. M., 364
Broverman, I. K., 364
Brown, J., 383, 404
Brown, L. S., 18, 363, 364, 369, 376, 381, 385, 400
Brown, M. Z., 248
Brown, T. A., 217
Brownell, C., 325
Brownell, P., 353
Bruce, T. J., 4
Bruner, J., 399
Bryant, E. M., 418
Bryant, R. A., 171
Buber, M., 294, 342, 345, 346
Bucci, S., 9
Bugental, J. F. T., 284, 290, 293, 294, 298, 299
Bulik, C., 214
Bullis, Q., 98
Burdenski, T. K., 242
Burke, B. I., 325
Burlingham, D. T., 124
Burns, D. D., 206
Burton, J. R., 10
Busch, A., 271
Busse, R. T., 173
Butler, A. C., 196
Butler, C. C., 323
Butler, J., 259
Butler, S. K., 16

C

Cacioppo, J. T., 150
Cain, D. J., 280, 308, 314, 317
Callaghan, J. E. M., 383
Callahan, J. L., 468
Cambray, J., 117
Cameron, D., 213
Campbell, L., 86
Cannon, K. B., 383
Canter, P. H., 263

Caplan, E., 52
Capps, F., 352
Carastathis, A., 365
Carkhuff, R., 329
Carlson, J., 85, 86, 90, 102
Carlson, J. D., 89, 100
Carlson, J. E., 98, 101
Carr, A., 398, 399, 400, 456
Carr, E. R., 382
Carr, S. M., 418
Carrick, H., 418
Carter, J. D., 210
Cashdan, S., 125, 127
Cassell, P., 101
Casstevens, W., 233, 320
Cattafi, F., 2
Chae, S. M., 404
Chamow, L., 448
Chan, A., 296
Chang, C. Y., 98
Chapman, J. E., 196
Chard, K., 211
Charvat, M., 475
Chen, J., 142
Chen, Y. R., 481
Chesler, P., 364
Chubak, L., 352
Churchill, R., 318
Ciarrochi, J. V., 259
Ciorbea, I., 483
Civilotti, C., 481
Claessens, M., 296
Clark, D., 196, 210
Clarkson, F., 364
Clarkson, P., 336
Clougherty, K. F., 142
Cochrane, K., 365
Cocks, G., 131, 132
Coelho, H. F., 263
Coffey, S. F., 211
Cohen, B. B., 383
Cohen, D. J., 123, 124
Cohen, J. A., 211
Coles, R., 122, 123
Collhart, D., 382
Collins, M. H., 456
Colman, W., 115, 116
Combs, G., 397, 400
Compare, A., 2
Comstock, D., 385
Conlin, S. E., 368
Connell, G. M., 437–438, 439, 440
Conner, S., 383, 404
Connolly, K. M., 211

Conradi, H. J., 126
Contech, J. A., 98
Cooper, M., 284, 285, 297, 314, 319, 320, 327
Cooper, S. J., 396
Corey, G., 31, 35, 36
Cornelius-White, J. H. D., 320, 325
Correia, E. A., 285, 297
Correia, K., 297
Covin, R., 210
Craig, M., 285, 297
Cramer, P., 68
Crane, R. S., 258, 259, 260, 261
Craske, M. G., 210
Crete, G. K., 382
Crethar, H., 386
Cristalli, M. E., 482
Crocker, S. F., 346
Crocket, K., 397, 402, 403
Crowther-Heyck, H., 150
Crumb, L., 385
Curlette, W. L., 92
Curran, J., 271
Currin-McCulloch, J., 418
Curry, J. F., 349, 353
Cussino, M., 481

D

Dailey, F. L., 211
Dakof, G. A., 456
Dallos, R., 404
Danielian, J., 119, 142
Danziger, P. R., 32
Dattilio, F. M., 448, 454
Daugherty, C., 381
Daul, H., 140
Davanloo, H., 135
David, D., 210
Davies, J. S., 11
Davis, D. D., 182, 197, 198
Davis, M. L., 173, 210
Davis, S. D., 318
Day, S. X., 89, 98, 119, 322
Deckersbach, T., 263
Dehing, J., 114
De Jong, P., 126, 406, 418
Delgadillo, J., 481
Demos, V. C., 135
Dermer, S. B., 381
De Saeger, H., 280
de Shazer, S., 393, 406, 408, 409, 412, 413
DeVore, J., 98
Diamond, S. A., 298

Díaz-Lázaro, C. M., 383
Dicker, R. C., 364
DiClemente, C. C., 478, 479
DiGiuseppe, R., 185, 188, 190, 192
Dinkmeyer, D. C., 80, 99
Dixon, A., 17
Dobson, K. S., 210, 212
Dolan, Y., 406, 413
Dominitz, V. A., 353
Dorta, K. P., 480
Dourley, J. P., 117
Downar, J., 263
Downey, J., 173
Dozois, D. J., 210
Drauker, C. B., 403
Dreikurs, R., 84, 88, 101
Driessen, E., 141
Dryden, W., 183, 185, 188, 189, 190, 191, 192
Duffey, T., 385
Duguid, J. E., 258
Dulmus, C. N., 482
Duncan, B. L., 6, 7, 9, 318, 468
Dunn, T. W., 210
Dunne-Bryant, A., 7
DuPaul, G. J., 173
Duval, S., 300

E
Eaves, S. H., 418
Echterling, L. G., 135
Eckardt, M. H., 118
Eddershaw, R., 261
Eder, E. E., 280
Edwards, D., 269
Edwards, T. M., 448
Egan, K. J., 377
Egloff, B., 86
Ehring, T., 214
Eisner, L., 263
Ekers, D., 271
Elkins, D. N., 279
Ellegaard, H., 353
Ellenberger, H. F., 282
Elliott, A., 68
Elliott, R., 9, 280, 318, 320, 321, 352
Ellis, A. E., 183, 184, 189, 191, 192, 213, 214
Ellis, D. J., 183, 186, 189, 191
Ellison, W. D., 130
Ellsworth, L., 239
Ellwood, R., 117
Eloff, I., 353

Emery, G., 196, 210
Emmelkamp, P. M. G., 169, 214, 216, 258
Englar-Carlson, M., 85, 86, 102
Enns, C. Z., 70, 368, 377, 378, 381, 382, 387
Epp, L. R., 289
Epston, D., 393, 395, 396, 401, 402, 403, 404
Erbes, C. R., 404
Erford, B. T., 208, 418
Eriksen, K., 15, 17, 32, 368
Erikson, E., 118
Erikson, K. R., 270
Ernst, E., 263
Esparat, D., 234
Espín, O. M., 382
Estay, M., 418
Evans, D. B., 226
Evans, K. M., 336, 342, 345, 346, 352, 368, 374, 375, 379, 380, 381, 385
Evare, B. S., 404
Ewen, R. B., 109, 114
Eysenck, H. J., 470

F
Fabry, D., 300
Fagan, J., 349
Fairburn, C. G., 212
Fang, A., 210
Farber, B. A., 141, 263
Farrell, J. M., 269
Feminist Therapy Institute (FTI), 379, 380
Ferguson, E. D., 101
Ferreira, R., 353
Few-Demo, A. L., 457
Fife, S. T., 318
Fillion, L., 300
Finlay, L., 336, 342, 345, 346, 352
Finlay, S. W., 117
Fisch, R., 444
Fishman, H. C., 426, 435, 442, 445
Flynn, S. D., 161
Foa, E. B., 171
Fonagy, P., 53, 71, 126, 130, 140, 141
Forcehimes, A. A., 117
Forman, E. M., 196
Forsyth, J. P., 170
Fosco, G. M., 428
Foucault, Michel, 396
Francis, J. D., 98

Frank, E., 480
Frank, M. L. B., 290
Franklin, C. G. S., 418
Freedman, J., 397, 400
Freeman, A., 182, 197, 198, 201
Freeman, J., 395, 404
French, T. M., 134, 135
Freud, A., 63, 67, 122, 123, 124
Freud, S., 56, 65, 67
Frew, J., 341
Frick, Willard, 294
Froh, J. J., 190
Frost, R. O., 217
Fruzzetti, A. E., 270
Fulkerson, M., 233, 320
Furrow, J. L., 300
Fuse, T., 170

G
Gabbard, G. O., 131
Gaffney, S., 350
Gallagher, S. M., 210
Gallagher-Thompson, D., 213
Gallop, R. J., 248
Galsworthy-Francis, L., 212
Garner, M., 261
Garriga, O., 240
Garrow, S., 297
Gendlin, E. T., 280, 322, 323
George, C., 126, 130
Geraldo, P., 418
Gergen, K. J., 362, 392, 393, 395
Gershoff, E. T., 165
Gharebaghy, S., 213
Ghasemi, A., 404
Giesen-Bloo, J., 269
Gifford, S., 52
Gilbert, D. T., 473
Gilbert, M. C., 336
Gilliam, B. J., 383
Gilman, S. L., 119
Gladding, S. T., 456
Glasser, W., 233, 235, 236, 237, 239, 241
Gold, J., 473
Goldenberg, H., 426
Goldenberg, I., 426, 430, 435, 444, 446
Goldman, R. N., 130, 349
Goldsmith, H. H., 319
Goldstein, E. G., 131, 132
Goldstein, J., 124
Goldstein, T. R., 254
Goldstone, D., 141

Golmohamadian, M., 210
Gonzalez, A., 382
Goodman, G., 115, 141
Goodman, P., 335
Goodrich, T. J., 381
Goodwin, G., 32
Gordon, K., 352, 353
Gorman, J. M., 468
Gotink, R. A., 263
Gottlieb, C. D., 399
Gottlieb, D. T., 399
Grant, P., 196
Grauf-Grounds, C., 448
Gray, M., 364
Green, J. G., 130
Green, L., 418
Greenberg, L. S., 9, 125, 129, 130, 280, 319, 320, 321, 329, 336
Greene B., 382
Greenman, P. S., 450, 452
Gregory, B., 210
Grenz, S. J., 362
Grey, L., 79, 82
Greyber, L. R., 482
Griffith, J. W., 92, 323
Grogan-Kaylor, A., 165
Grosse, H. M., 319
Guevremont, D. C., 158, 160
Guiney, J., 130
Guo, X., 456

H

Haberstroh, 385
Hagen, W. B., 383
Haiyasoso, M., 384
Hakami, M., 297
Haley, J., 428, 435, 446, 447
Hamer, R., 214
Hammer, T. R., 383
Hamrick, L., 130
Hansen, J. T., 392, 393, 417, 418, 468
Hardy, K. V., 458
Harrington, N., 263
Harris, A., 9
Härter, M., 480
Hartling, L. M., 384
Harvey, M. T., 167
Harwood, T. M., 475
Haskins, L., 385
Haule, J. R., 117
Haun, M. W., 456
Hawes, E. C., 100
Hawxhurst, D. M., 383
Hay, P., 212

Hayes, L., 258
Hayes, S. C., 152, 256, 258, 259, 271
Hays, P. A., 17, 18, 369
Hazan, C., 126
Headley, J. A., 384, 385
Hedtke, L., 404
Hefferline, R. F., 335
Held, P., 130
Hemesath, C. W., 381
Hemming, J., 336
Henderson, V. L., 320
Henggeler, S. W., 426
Henretty, J., 315
Henry, U., 383, 404
Hergenhahn, B. R., 108, 111, 120, 121, 196, 290, 293, 307, 308, 326
Herlihy, B., 30, 31, 35, 36, 37
Herrmann, I. R., 319
Hersoug, A., 140
Hertel, G., 483
Hertenstein, E., 263
Hill, C. E., 9, 116, 354
Hill, N. R., 13
Hinrichsen, G. A., 142
Hinton, D. E., 213
Hoch, A. L., 213
Hoffman, L., 296
Hoffman, R., 368
Hofmann, S. G., 173, 210, 212, 261, 269
Hogan, S., 381
Hogan, T. P., 34
Hoglend, P., 140
Hölzel, B., 260, 263
Hölzel, L. P., 480
Homan, K. J., 297
Hopkins, J., 259
Horigian, V. E., 449
Horney, K., 70, 119, 120, 121, 142
Horowitz, L. M., 126
Horowitz, M., 140
Hosseini, B., 297
Hotz, J. V., 86
Houghton, S., 271
Houser-Marko, L., 311
Houston, G., 355
Hubble, M. A., 6, 9, 318, 468
Hume, K., 166
Humphrey, N., 418
Hung, S., 173
Hunger, C., 456
Hutzell, R. R., 295

I

Iftene, F., 210
Imel, Z. E., 318
Israeli, A. L., 379, 380
Iwamasa, G. Y., 383

J

Jacobson, E., 170
James, W., 150
Jarrett, C., 321
Jeffrey, J., 254
Jeffrin Margreat, J., 210
Johnson, S. M., 130, 319, 321, 336, 449, 450, 452
Jones, E. E., 54, 55, 57, 109, 473
Jongsma, A. E., 4
Jordan, J. V., 384
Jordan, S. S., 418
Joyce, M. R., 190
Jung, C. G., 109, 110, 112, 113, 115

K

Kabat-Zinn, Jon, 258–263
Kachele, H., 5, 69
Kahn, J. S., 368, 382
Kakar, S., 69, 142
Kaklauskas, F., 296
Kamali, K., 404
Kamphuis, J. H., 280
Kanapathy, A., 141
Kandel, E. R., 242
Kaner, A., 129
Kang, H. S., 404
Kanter, J., 271
Kaplan, A. G., 363
Kaplan, N., 130
Karpiak, C. P., 68
Kaschak, E., 383
Kaslow, N. J., 456
Kasper, L. B., 354
Katz, M. R., 254
Kaufman, A., 234
Kaufman, M., 183
Kautzman-East, M., 385
Kawahara, D. M., 382
Kaysen, D., 211
Kearney, L. K., 383
Kegerreis, S., 53, 69
Kehrer, C. A., 254
Keinan, G., 315
Keith, D. V., 437–438
Keller, E., 130
Kelley, J. A., 86

Name Index

Kellogg, S. H., 264, 268
Kelly, D. F., 82
Kelly, George, 396
Kelly, W. L., 109, 113
Kendrick, E., 483
Kennedy, S. C., 352, 353
Kennedy, S. H., 210
Kern, R. M., 92
Kernberg, P. F., 66
Kerr, M. E., 433
Key, B. L., 263
Khuller, A., 210
Kim, J. S., 239, 336, 418
Kim, M., 142
Kincade, E. A., 368, 379
King, K. M., 10
Kirk, U., 263
Kirkpatrick, K., 338
Kirschenbaum, H., 307, 308, 309, 315, 316, 327
Kivlinghan, D. M., 354
Klerman, G. L., 480
Klineberg, E., 321
Klinger, E., 169
Klosko, J. S., 264, 269
Klusen, J., 258
Knox, R., 314
Koemer, N., 210
Kohut, H., 131, 132
Koocher, G. P., 34
Kools, S., 142
Kopec, A. M., 192
Korslund, K. E., 270
Kottman, R., 98
Kreitemeyer, J., 259
Kress, V. E., 4, 8, 13, 14, 15, 17, 20, 22, 27, 29, 32, 33, 34, 35, 141, 162, 168, 173, 210, 212, 238, 318, 354, 368, 384, 385, 418, 435, 443, 448, 468, 469, 483, 493, 505
Kriegler, S., 353
Kriston, L., 480
Kroløkke, C., 364, 365
Krug, O. T., 293
Kruk, J., 473
Kukard, C., 353
Kunz, C., 325
Kuusito, K., 10

L

L'Abate, L., 426
Lacewing, M., 67
Lachmann, F. M., 132, 141

La Guardia, A. C., 381
Laible, D. J., 130
Lam, R. W., 210
Lambert, M. J., 5, 10, 11, 482, 483
Lancaster, C., 353
Landes, S. J., 10
Lane, R. C., 67
Lanfredi, M., 212
Lantz, J., 295
Lanza, M. L., 173
Lashani, L., 353
Lawrie, S. M., 353
Lawson, D. M., 382
Lazar, S. G., 140
Lazar, S. W., 263
Lazarus, A. A., 471
Leaf, J. B., 161
Leahy, R. L., 199
Lebovitz, D., 395, 404
Lebow, J., 426, 434
Lee, B. K., 319
Lee, C. C., 16
Lee, C. W., 212, 482
Lee, D., 82
Lee, J., 381, 396, 399
Lee, Y. L., 404
Lees, M., 381
Leibert, T. W., 7
Leichsenring, F., 5, 136, 142
Lempp, H., 318, 320
Lennon, B., 241
Lenz, A. S., 353
Lerner, H. D., 124, 132, 133
Leskele, J., 404
Leszcz, M., 282
Leung, D., 300
Levant, R. F., 382
Levenson, H., 135, 138, 139, 140
Levitsky, A., 338
Levitt, H., 315
Levy, K. N., 130, 141
Levy, R. A., 5, 69
Lewis, B., 404
Lewis, T. F., 418
Li, Y., 441
Lichtenberg, P., 336
Lieberman, J. A., 456
Lillis, J., 258
Lin, Y., 320
Linehan, M. M., 248, 254, 377
Link, L., 456
Linnenbrink-Garcia, L., 320
Livneh, E., 315
Lo, Y., 161

Looyeh, M. Y., 404
Lopata, C., 170
Lopes, R. T., 403
Lorentzen, S., 140
Lovell, K., 481
Lubbe, T., 128
Luborsky, E. B., 63
Luborsky, L., 135, 142
Lui, J., 116
Luiselli, J. K., 167
Lumadue, C. A., 383
Lummer, S., 457
Lundahl, B., 325
Lunnen, K. M., 319
Luoma, J. B., 258
Luyten, P., 130
Lyness, K. P., 383

M

Ma, S. H., 263
Maas, V. S., 381
MacIntosh, H. B., 452
Mackewn, J., 336
MacLaren, C., 184
MacLeod, R., 318
Madigan, S., 404
Madison, G., 299
Mahalik, J. R., 368, 382
Mahler, M. S., 127
Mahoney, M. J., 394
Maier, C. A., 383
Main, M., 130
Maisel, R. L., 395
Makari, G., 52
Malan, D., 135
Malinen, T., 396, 400
Mallory, A., 383, 404
Malone, P. S., 315
Malone, T., 439
Maltzman, S., 5
Manaster, G. J., 88
Maniacci, M., 89, 100
Mann, J. J., 135, 480
Marbley, A. F., 379
Mark, D., 142
Marker, J. B., 210
Markey, C., 383
Markowitz, J. C., 480
Maroda, K. J., 139
Marra, T., 248, 249, 254
Marsa, R., 297
Marsden, Z., 481
Martin, C., 355
Martin, G., 154

Mascher, J., 396
Masuda, A., 258
Matlin, M., 70
Matson, F. W., 150
Matson, J. L., 166
May, R., 282
Mayes, L. C., 123, 124, 130
McBride, J., 429
McCabe, R., 263
McDavid, J., 248
McDowell, T., 443
McFarr, L. M., 270
McGeorge, C. R., 383
McGoldrick, M., 435, 458
McGrath, P. J., 480
McGuire, A. P., 211
McGuire, J. F., 173, 210
McIntyre, R. S., 210
McKay, D., 210
McKay, K., 99
McKee, J. E., 135
McKinney, C., 383
McKinney, M. K., 473
McLean, L. L., 381
McMain, S. F., 254
McMillan, D., 271
McParland, J., 404
Meany-Walen, K. K., 98
Medlow, S., 321
Melnick, J., 346
Meron, D., 261
Messer, S. B., 135, 136
Metcalf, L., 418
Metzger, J. A., 141, 263
Mey, S., 210
Midgley, N., 53, 69, 142
Miklowitz, D. J., 263
Miller, J. B., 336, 363, 384
Miller, M., 368, 374
Miller, M. M., 319
Miller, N., 173
Miller, S. D., 6, 9, 318, 413, 414, 468
Miller, W., 7, 320, 323, 324, 479
Miller, W. R., 323
Miltenberger, R. G., 160, 162
Minuchin, S., 426, 428, 435, 442, 445
Mirand, J., 214
Mitchell, S. A., 70, 125, 129
Moersch, M., 404
Mohamad, A., 210
Momeni, K., 210
Monk, G. D., 397, 398, 400

Montague, P. R., 263
Montebarocci, O., 126
Moodley, R., 289, 298
Moore, H. L., 70
Moreau, D., 480
Morgan, A., 395, 404
Morris, E., 256, 258
Morrison, M. O., 98
Morrissey, S. A., 258
Morrow, S. L., 383
Mosak, H. H., 83, 92, 93
Moss, L., 385
Moulding, R., 173
Mufson, L., 480
Mullette, J., 14
Munro, C., 353
Munro, E., 365
Muntigl, P., 352
Murdock, N. L., 337, 429, 430
Murray, K. W., 7, 8
Murray, R. M., 456
Myers, J. E., 20, 172

N

Naghiyaaee, M., 297
Najavits, L. M., 137
Napier, A. Y., 439
Napolitano, L. A., 199
Nardort, M., 269
Nash, S., 386
Nassar-McMillan, S., 16
Nathan, P. E., 468
Nedelcea, C., 483
Nedeljkovic, M., 173
Neenan, M., 185, 189
Neff, K., 338
Negy, C., 383
Neimeyer, R. A., 394
Nelson, J. A., 381
Neville, H. A., 174, 316, 325, 353
Nevis, S. M., 346
Nichols, M. P., 448, 449
Nicoll, W. G., 98
Nielsen, S. L., 214
Nierenberg, A. A., 263
Nolte, T., 130
Norcross, J. C., 5, 8, 9, 11, 34, 68, 69, 140, 324, 327, 329, 350, 354, 455, 467, 468, 471, 478, 479, 482, 483, 505
Normand, M. P., 161
Noronha, K. J., 98
Nwaorgu, A., 78

O

Oaklander, V., 353
Obiageli, J., 210
Ogles, B. M., 319
Ohanian, V., 267, 268
O'Hara, M., 319, 320, 327
Olantunju, B. O., 173, 210
Oliver, A. C., 161
Oliver, J. E., 256, 258
Olson, M. H., 120, 121, 196, 293, 307, 308, 326
Ono, K., 320
O'Reily-Landry, M., 63
Otting, T. L., 383
Ouimet, A. J., 210
Owens, G. P., 130

P

Packer, G., 327
Paige, M., 98
Pakai, A. K., 404
Panfile, T. M., 130
Pantalone, D. W., 213
Pantano, J., 86
Paris, B. J., 119, 120
Park, S., 418
Parlett, M., 336
Patterson, C. L., 7, 8, 140
Patterson, J., 448
Paul, G. L., 471, 505
Pawluk, E. J., 263
Paylo, M., 4, 8, 15, 20, 22, 27, 29, 33, 34, 141, 168, 173, 210, 318, 354, 418, 435, 443, 448, 468, 469, 483, 493, 505
Payne, M., 401
Pear, J., 154
Peck, K. R., 211
Pedersen, B. D., 353
Pederson, E., 211
Penn, P. E., 210
Perkins, G. R., 130
Perls, F., 335, 338, 341
Perry, J., 140
Persons, J. B., 202
Peteet, J. R., 361, 362
Peters, L., 210
Peterson, L. M., 4
Petko, J. T., 483
Petrocelli, J. V., 478
Philippson, P., 341
Pickles, C., 263
Pine, F., 127
Pizarro, D., 268

Polster, E., 342, 347, 350, 355
Polster, M., 342, 347, 350
Pos, A. E., 280, 319, 321, 322
Powers, M. B., 169, 173, 210, 214, 258
Powers, R. L., 92
Pratt, L. A., 161
Predescu, E., 210
Prelinger, E., 129
Presbury, J. H., 135, 138, 412
Prilleltensky, O., 383
Prochaska, J. O., 324, 327, 350, 354, 455, 467, 468, 471, 478, 479, 483, 505
Prosek, E. A., 383
Protinsky, H. O., 383
Prout, M. F., 135
Prouty, A. M., 383
Pugh, M., 355
Pusater, C. G., 385

R
Rabellino, D., 5, 323
Rabung, S., 142
Rafaeli, A. K., 480
Rafaeli, E., 267, 268, 269
Rafferty McCullough, J., 16
Ramirez, R. K., 383
Randell, L., 353
Randle-Phillips, C., 418
Rashed, R., 267, 268
Rasmussen, J., 217
Rassafiani, M., 213
Ratts, M. J., 16
Ray, D. C., 8, 320
Rector, N. A., 196
Ree, M. J., 212
Refseth, J., 142
Reicherzer, S., 383
Reker, G. T., 301
Remer, P., 368, 371, 372, 374, 375, 376, 378, 379, 381, 382, 383
Remley, T. P., 30, 31, 35, 36, 37
Retzlaff, R., 456
Reyes-Rodriguez, M., 214
Rheem, K. D., 452
Rholes, W. S., 130
Richeport-Haley, M., 446
Richert, A. J., 293, 299, 394, 397, 400, 401
Richmond, C. J., 418
Rigazio-DiGilio, S. A., 443
Ritvo, L. B., 52

Rivera, E. T., 386
Robertson, M., 483
Robey, P. A., 98, 101
Roemer, L., 154, 155, 158
Rogan, J. D., 69
Roghanchi, M., 210
Rohini, N. S., 210
Rohrer, J. M., 86
Rollnick, R. S., 7, 320, 323, 324, 479
Rollnick, S., 323
Roose, S. P., 480
Root, M. P. P., 381
Rose, J., 318
Rosenkrantz, P., 364
Rosman, B. L., 445
Rossano, F., 121
Rossi, N., 126
Rothbaum, B. O., 169
Roubal, J., 353
Rovers, M., 319
Rowa, K., 263
Rude, S., 338
Rule, M. L., 103
Rusch, L., 271
Rush, A. J., 196
Russell, C. S., 381
Ryback, D., 327
Ryff, C. D., 297

S
Saadati, H., 353
Sadati, N. S., 297
Safir, M. P., 169
Salande, J. D., 130
Samai, S., 270
SAMHSA, 494
Sanchez, W., 240
Sanders, C. J., 403
Sandler, A., 123
Sandler, J., 123
Sangganjanavanich, V. F., 385
Santor, D. A., 379, 380
Sapp, M., 98
Sapriel, L., 336
Saroglou, V., 117
Sarter, M., 150
Sauer, E. M., 418
Sawyer, A., 210
Sayers, J., 122, 124
Sayrs, J. H. R., 248
Sayrs, J. R., 270
Schaeffer, C. M., 426
Scharff, D. E., 128, 129

Scharff, J. S., 128, 129
Scharwachter, P., 319
Schmid, P. F., 319, 320, 327
Schmukle, S. C., 86
Schneider, K. J., 290, 293
Schnetzer, L. W., 295
Schnyder, U., 15
Schoen, D. E., 117
Scholl, B., 8
Scholl, M. B., 392, 417, 418
Schoo, A., 239
Schubert, S., 482
Schulenberg, S. E., 295
Schultz, D. P., 51, 81, 82, 91, 149–150
Schultz, S. E., 51, 81, 82, 91, 149–150
Schumm, J., 211
Schwartz, A. M., 112, 114
Schwartz, J. P., 470
Schwartz, L. B., 383
Schweitzer, J., 456
Scott, J., 197, 201
Scott, L. N., 69, 130
Sedgewick, D., 111, 112, 115, 116
Seem, S. R., 368, 379
Segal, Z. V., 210, 258
Seiler, L., 213
Seim, R., 211
Seligman, M. E. P., 21
Seo, M., 404
Seponski, D. M., 381
Seymour-Hyde, A., 9
Shafieian, R., 404
Shahar, B., 319
Shamdasani, S., 117
Shanar, G., 315
Shannonhouse, L., 17
Shapiro, F., 481
Shapiro, J. L., 65, 285, 428, 430, 443
Sharf, R. S., 103, 109, 473
Sharp, J. G., 284
Shaver, P., 126
Shaw, B. F., 196
Shaw, I. A., 269
Shaw, S. L., 7, 8
Shearer, J., 352
Shedler, J., 69, 71, 140
Sheffield, A., 268
Sheldon, K. M., 311
Shepherd, I. L., 349
Sherman, R., 78, 80
Shifron, R., 100
Shottenbauer, M., 116
Shriver, M. D., 162
Shulman, B. H., 92

Sifneos, P. E., 135, 137
Silver, K. E., 382
Silverstein, L. B., 381
Sim, W., 116
Simkin, J. S., 334, 335
Simm, R., 418
Simpson, J. A., 130
Singh, A. A., 16, 382, 385
Sinsheimer, L., 234
Sklare, G., 417
Slexnick, N., 456
Slikboer, R., 173
Smith, C. O., 456
Smith, E. J., 21
Smith, G. T., 259
Smith, I. C., 418
Smith, L., 174, 316, 325, 353, 403
Smits, J. A., 173, 210
Smout, M. F., 258
Soban, C., 382
Solnit, A. J., 124
Sørenson, A. S., 364, 365
Sosa, G. A., 13
Spangler, P., 116
Sperry, L., 10
Spiegler, M. D., 158, 160
Springer, P. R., 439
Srebnik, D. S., 381
Stanton, M., 426
Stargell, N. A., 15, 22, 29, 168, 173, 418, 435, 443, 448
Stefan, S., 210
Steffen, A. M., 213
Stein, M., 117
Steinbeck, K., 321
Steketee, G., 217, 218, 219
Steward, A., 86
St. Germain, N. R., 383
Stillman, J. R., 404
Stiver, I. P., 363
Stoehr, T., 354
Stolar, N., 196
Stone, D. A., 98
Storzier, C. B., 131
Stoykova, Z., 103
Stratton, S. P., 285, 296
Stricker, G., 473
Strosahl, K. D., 271
Strumpfel, U., 349, 355
Strupp, H., 135
Strupp, H. H., 134, 137, 138
Stutey, D., 242
Sue, D. W., 16, 17, 174, 316, 325, 353, 354

Suitt, G. K., 418
Sullivan, B. F., 10
Sullivan, H.S., 480
Summers, R. F., 135
Sundquist, J., 263
Surcinelli, P., 126, 130
Surrey, J. L., 363, 384
Sweeney, T. J., 20, 81, 83, 90, 91, 97, 100
Sweet, A. D., 128, 129
Swift, J. K., 468
Sydow, K. V., 456
Symes, W., 418
Szabo, J., 404

T
Tacey, D., 117
Tallman, K., 7
Tanner, L. R., 383
Target, M., 53, 71, 126
Tasca, G. A., 2
Taylor, D. D., 98
Teasdale, J. D., 258, 263
Thase, M. E., 199
Thomas, F. N., 396
Thompson, G. R., 297, 299
Thompson, L. W., 213
Tillich, P., 284
Tindall, L., 271
Tirch, D., 199
Tolin, D. F., 217
Tollefson, D., 325
Toman, S. M., 355
Tonawanik, P., 404
Toney, L., 259
Topolinski, S., 483
Toth, S., 404
Totton, N., 327
Town, J. M., 141
Trepal, H., 384, 385
Truax, C., 329
Tuckey, M. R., 198
Tummala-Narra, P., 69
Turner, M., 210

U
Uhlmann, E., 268
Underwood, L. A., 211
Usakli, H., 327

V
Vachon, M., 300
Vallejo, Z., 263
van der Kolk, B. A., 404

van Deurzen, E., 285, 289, 299
Van Dijk, S., 254
van Eeden-Moorefield, B., 457
Van Ryzin, M. J., 428
Vatcher, C., 383
Verdeli, H., 480
Verdinelli, S., 383
Vereen, L. G., 13
Vivien, W., 441
Vogel, S., 364
Vollmer, B. M., 468
Voluse, A. C., 211
von Bertalanffy, L., 426
Vonk, I. J., 210
Vontress, C. E., 291, 296, 298, 300
Vorstenbosch, V., 210
Vos, J., 285, 297, 300
Vygotsky, L., 180, 396

W
Wachtel, P. L., 473
Wagener, L. M., 300
Wagner, W. G., 68, 69, 160
Wagner-Moore, L. E., 354, 355
Waites, C., 456
Walcott, R., 298
Waldo, M., 283, 288, 296, 301, 470
Walen, S. R., 188
Walker, J. A., 297
Walker, M., 384
Wallach, H. S., 169
Walls, S., 125, 126
Walsh, F., 429, 439, 456
Wampold, B. E., 5, 6, 9, 11, 318, 471, 482
Wang, S. C., 383
Warkentin, J., 439
Warren, C. S., 135, 136
Waska, R., 128
Wasserman, R. H., 69
Waters, E., 125, 126
Watson, J. C., 9, 314
Watts, R. E., 78, 82, 89, 94, 100, 103, 381
Watzlawick, P., 444
Weakland, J., 444
Weatherhead, S., 11
Weaver, A., 445
Webber, M. A., 269
Wei, C., 7, 8, 140
Weinbrecht, A., 269
Weinhold, J., 456
Weishaar, M. E., 195, 196, 264, 269

Weissman, M. M., 480, 481
Weissman, N., 452
Weisstein, N., 364
Welfel, E., 31, 32, 35
West, L. M., 382
Westphal, A., 480
Westra, H. A., 323
Wheeler, G., 334
Wheeler, M. A., 439
Wheeler, M. S., 92
Whisenhunt, J., 98
Whitaker, C. A., 437–438, 439
White, K. J., 300
White, M., 86, 393, 396, 397, 399, 401, 402, 403, 404, 419, 421
Whiting, J., 318
Whitman, S. M., 258
Whitmarsh, L., 14
Wiebe, S. A., 321
Wieling, E., 404
Wiess, S., 142
Wiffen, V. E., 130
Williams, E. N., 381
Williams, J. M. G., 258
Williams, L., 448
Williams, M., 263
Williams, T. I., 210

Willson, B. J., 320
Wilson, H. N. M., 11
Wilson, K. G., 271
Winboldt, B., 407
Winslade, J. M., 397, 398, 400, 403
Winters, M. R., 295
Wittenborn, A. K., 319
Woldt, A. L., 355
Wolf, E. S., 131, 132
Wolff, A. V., 480
Wong, M. Y., 212
Wong, P. T. P., 5, 299
Wong, S. E., 167
Woods, K., 418
Woolley, S., 449, 450, 452
Woolley, S. R., 452
Woon, L., 141
Worell, J., 368, 371, 372, 374, 375, 376, 378, 379, 381, 382, 383
Wormington, S., 320
Wright, J. H., 199
Wubbolding, R. E., 227, 228, 229, 230, 232, 233, 234, 235, 236, 237, 238, 240, 242, 320
Wulf, R., 334, 335, 336

X
Xu, J., 289, 296, 297, 299

Y
Yadin, E., 171
Yalom, I., 282
Yang, M., 296
Yasar, M., 445
Yeomans, F. E., 69
Yontef, G., 336, 342
Young, J., 267
Young, J. E., 264, 268, 269
Young, J. S., 172
Young, K. A., 418
Young, K. S., 263
Young, M., 452, 483
Young-Bruehl, E., 122

Z
Zaccagnino, M., 481
Zakaria, M., 285
Zakszeski, B. N., 173
Zarbo, C., 2
Zarkaria, H., 141
Zhang, A., 418
Zilberstein, K., 13
Zinbarg, R. E., 323
Ziv-Beiman, S., 315
Zoldan, C. A., 384
Zum Vorde Sive Vording, M. B., 258

SUBJECT INDEX

A
ABCDEF approach, 186–188, 191–192, 219–221, 235, 453–454, 509
A-B-C Model, 162, 186–187, 509
Abraham, Karl, 118
Abreaction, 67, 509
Absolutes, challenging of, 190
Acceptance, 259, 509
   mindfulness-based cognitive therapy, 258–259, 261–262
   person-centered therapy and, 311
Acceptance and commitment therapy (ACT)
   application and current use, 258
   awareness and acceptance, 257
   development of, 255
   experiential avoidance, 255
   hexaflex model, 257
   limitations and strengths, 270–271
   relational frame theory, 256
   therapeutic process, 256–257
Access to care, 32, 34, 140–141
Acculturation, 16
Achievement, need for, 228
Acting "as if", 96, 99, 317–318, 509
Acting out, 62
Action factors, 483
Action stage, 324, 478–479
Activating event, 187, 192
Active Parenting, 99, 453
Addiction
   acceptance and commitment therapy, 258
   Adlerian therapy, 98
   existential therapy, 297
   family therapy, 456
   Gestalt therapy, 353
   mindfulness-based cognitive therapy, 263
   narrative therapy, 403, 404
   schema therapy, 269
   solution-focused brief therapy, 418
ADDRESSING acronym, 17–18, 369
Adjustment disorder, 263
Adler, Alfred, 51, 56, 77–78, 108, 281, 282, 453
Adlerian therapy
   applications and current use of, 98–102, 496

basic mistakes, 83–84
basic philosophy of, 486
Case Application, 105–106
development of, 78–79
encouraging insight and understanding, 93–97
family constellation and birth order, 84–86, 92, 453
goals of counseling, 490
key concepts, 79–87, 488
lifestyle, 82–83, 90–93
limitations of, 102–103, 502
multicultural groups, 101–102, 498, 499
personality, patterns of, 80–84
phases of, 89–98
Skill Development, analyzing earliest recollections, 104–106
social interest and community feeling, 86–87
strengths and contributions, 103–104, 503
techniques of, 94–97, 494
therapeutic goals, 87
therapeutic relationship, 88–90, 492
therapist function and role, 87–88
Adolescents
   Adlerian therapy, 99, 101
   behavioral therapies, 163, 172, 173, 176, 248, 271
   cognitive behavioral therapy, 203, 208, 210, 211, 213
   developmental needs, 14, 58
   existential therapy, 298, 300
   family therapy, 448, 454, 455–456
   feminist therapy, 369, 375, 381, 383
   Gestalt therapy, 353
   informed consent and assent, 31
   interpersonal psychotherapy, 481
   narrative therapy, 404
   person-centered therapy, 319, 321, 325
   psychoanalytic therapy, 118, 122, 124, 142
   psychosexual stages of development, 60–61
   reality therapy, 224, 225, 238, 239, 241
   solution-focused brief therapy, 418

Adult Attachment Interview, 130
Affiliation, 62, 509
Affirmations, 208
Agoraphobia, 297
Aha response, 96, 509
Ainsworth, Mary, 125, 126
Alcoholics Anonymous (AA), 117, 210
Alexander, Franz, 134
Alienation, 341, 509
Alignment, 433, 509
Alliances, 444, 509
All-or-nothing thinking, 206, 509
Aloneness. *See* Existential therapy
Alternative story, 397–398, 509
Altruism, 62, 509
American Art Therapy Association, 28
American Association for Marriage and Family Therapy, 28, 426
American Association of Christian Counselors, 28
American Association of Marriage Counselors, 426
American Counseling Association (ACA), 28
   Code of Ethics, 13, 32
   Multicultural Counseling Competencies, 15
American Mental Health Counselors Association (AMHCA), 34
American Psychiatric Association, 368, 370, 483
American Psychological Association (APA), 18, 28, 33, 71, 371, 373, 468
American School Counselor Association, 28
Anal stage, 59–60, 61, 509
Analysis, psychoanalysis, 66–67
   Skill Development, 72–74
Analytical psychology. *See* Jungian analytical psychology
Anima and animus, Jung archetypes, 110, 112, 115, 509
Anna Freud Centre, 122
Anticathexes, 58, 509
Anticipation, 62, 509
Anxiety, 254
   acceptance and commitment therapy, 258
   Beck Anxiety Inventory (BAI), 202

Subject Index

behavior therapy, 173–174
cognitive behavioral therapy
    applications, 209–214
compassion-focused therapy
    (CFT), 273
existential anxiety, 287–288
existential therapy, 284, 297
exposure-based interventions,
    169–170
eye movement desensitization
    and reprocessing (EMDR),
    481–482
family therapy, 455–456
Horney, ego psychology,
    119–120
metacognitive therapy, 273
mindfulness-based cognitive
    therapy, 263, 273–274
neurotic anxiety, 287–288
object relations theory, 130
person-centered therapy, 318
prolonged exposure therapy, 170
relaxation techniques, 169–170
schema therapy, 269
Skill Development, exposure-
    based CBT for hoarding,
    216–219
social anxiety, behavior therapy,
    165–166
solution-focused brief therapy, 418
Anxiety hierarchy, 158, 509
Applied behavior analysis (ABA),
    166–168, 509
Appropriate emotions, 186, 510
Arbitrary inferences, 206
Archetypes, 110, 111–112, 117, 510
Aristotle, 283
Arts therapy, 320
Asian culture, 16
Assent, 30–31, 36, 510
Assertiveness training, 172–173,
    376–377, 510
Assessing motivation, 410, 510
Assessment
    Adlerian therapy, 90–92
    BASIC I.D., 476–478
    behavior therapy, 161–162
    cognitive behavioral therapy, 182
    cognitive therapy, 202–203
    developmental, Anna Freud,
        123–124
    ethical and legal issues, 31–33
    intake interview and assessment,
        42–48
    rational emotive behavior
        therapy, 189

Assets, Adlerian therapy, 510
Assets, personal, 89
Atheoretical eclecticism, 470–471
At-risk youth, 98
Attachment, 14
    anxious/avoidant, 126–127, 130
    anxious/resistant, 126–127
    disorganized/disoriented,
        126–127
    ego psychology, 54
    emotionally focused couple
        therapy, 450
    narrative therapy, 404
    object relations theory,
        125–131
    psychodynamic theory, 52, 57
    secure, 126–127
    self psychology, 131–132
Attachment theory, 126–127, 510
Attention, mindfulness practices,
    261–262
Attention deficit hyperactivity
    disorder (ADHD), 172, 173,
    213
Adlerian therapy, 98
family therapy, 455–456
mindfulness-based cognitive
    therapy, 263
narrative therapy, 404
reality therapy, 241
Attitudes, 111, 510
Authenticity, 290, 510
Autism spectrum disorders, 162,
    166–168, 455–456
Automatic thoughts, 197–198, 510
Autonomy, client, 21–22
Autonomy, moral principle, 35
Aversive stimulus, 158, 510
Avoidance, 62, 97, 271–272,
    339–340, 510
Avoidant attachment, 126, 130
Avoidant personality
    disorder, 269
Avoiding lifestyle, 82–83
Avoiding the tar baby, 510
Awareness
    acceptance, 257
    behavior change, 478–479
    existential therapy, 290, 293
    field theory, 337–338
    Gestalt therapy, 341–343, 510

B

Balance, 110, 111, 113, 114–115,
    116, 117, 120
Bandura, Albert, 153–154, 155, 157

Bare attention, 261–262
BASIC I.D., 476–478
Basic mistakes, 83–84, 510
BASIS-A Interpretive Manual
    (1997), 92
Bateson, Gregory, 396, 445
Beck, Aaron, 2, 179
    biography, 195–196
    development of cognitive
        therapy, 196–199
Beck, Judith, 196, 197
Beck Anxiety Inventory (BAI), 202
Beck Depression Inventory
    (BDI), 202
Beck Hopelessness Inventory, 202
Beck Scale for Suicidal Ideation, 202
Behavioral activation, defined, 510
Behavioral activation therapy
    (BAT), 271–272
Behavioral rehearsal, 172–173
Behavior change, 151
    brief psychodynamic therapy,
        136–138
    client characteristics for success,
        7–8
    commitment to change, 232
    factors of, 6
    five levels of change, 479
    motivational interviewing,
        323–325
    psychoanalytic theory, 53
    stages of, 324–325
    ten processes of change, 478–479
    transtheoretical model of change,
        478–479
    See also Behavior therapy;
        Family systems therapy
Behaviorism, 2, 3, 151–153,
    154–155, 156, 510
    See also Behavior therapy
Behavior rehearsal, 510
Behavior therapy, 2
    application and current use, 496
    applied behavior analysis (ABA),
        166–168
    assessment, 161–162
    Bandura, Albert, 153–154
    basic philosophy of, 486
    Case Application, 158, 176–177
    classical conditioning, 156,
        169–172
    contingency management, 166
    counseling applications, 173–174
    cyclical psychodynamic-behavior
        therapy, 473–475
    development of, 154–155

Behavior therapy (*Continued*)
  exposure-based intervention, 169–170
  family therapy, 453
  key concepts, 155, 488
  limitations and strengths, 174–175, 502, 503
  measurement, evaluation, and research, 151
  multicultural applications, 174, 498, 500
  multimodal therapy, 475–476
  operant conditioning techniques, 162–168
  relaxation techniques, 171–172
  Skill Development, muscle relaxation, 175–176
  skills training, 172–173
  Skinner, B. F., 154
  social learning theory, 157–158
  therapeutic goals, 159–160
  therapeutic process, 158–159, 495
  therapeutic relationship, 492
  therapist function and role, 160
  three waves of, 151–153
  token economies, 166
  See also Cognitive behavioral therapy (CBT)
Belief, rational emotive behavior therapy, 187, 192
Belonging, 228
Beneficence, 35
Berg, Insoo Kim, 406
Bernays, Martha, 55
Bias, of therapist, 16, 35–36
Bibliotherapy, 172–173, 208–209, 510
Binswanger, Ludwig, 284, 288
Biofeedback, 172, 510
Bipolar disorder
  behavior therapy, 173
  cognitive behavioral therapy, 212, 254, 263
  Gestalt therapy, 353
  interpersonal psychotherapy, 480–481
  mindfulness-based cognitive therapy, 263
  possible causes of, 229
  reality therapy, 239
Birth order, 81, 84–86, 92, 99–101, 434, 453, 510
"Blank-screen" approach, 64, 510
Bobo doll experiment, 153, 157
Body language. *See* Nonverbal communication

Body scan, 274
Borderline personality disorder, 212, 258
  See also Dialectical behavior therapy (DBT); Schema therapy
Boss, Medard, 284, 290
Boszormenyi-Nagy, Ivan, 125
Boundaries, 428, 442–443, 510
Boundary marking, 428
Boundary permeability, 428, 510
Bowen, Murray, 426, 428, 431–437
Bowenian family therapy, 463
  application and current use, 437
  detriangulation, 436
  development of, 431–432
  differentiation of self, 432
  dyads and triads, 432
  emotional cutoff, 433
  family projection process, 433
  genograms, 435–436
  multigenerational transmission process, 433
  nuclear family emotional system, 433
  sibling position, 434
  Skill Development, genograms, 457–459
  societal regression, 434
  therapeutic process, 434–435
  therapeutic relationship, 434
  triangulation and alignment, 432–433
Bowlby, John, 54, 108, 125, 126, 127, 128, 130, 141
Brain. *See* Neurobiology
Breathing techniques, 171–172
Breuer, Josef, 55–56
Brief psychodynamic therapy (BPT)
  application and current use, 140–141
  development of, 134–135
  differences from classical therapy, 135
  ego strengthening, 135–136
  limitations and strengths, 142–143
  multicultural groups, 141–142
  Skill Development, identifying focal concern, 142–143
  therapeutic process, 136–138
  therapeutic techniques, 138–140
  triads, 136
Buber, Martin, 284, 294, 335, 342, 345, 346
Buddhism, 336
Bulimia nervosa. *See* Eating disorders

C
Campbell, Joseph, 117
Camus, Albert, 284
CARE acronym, 100, 510
Case Application
  A-B-C-D-E-F model, use of, 219–221
  Adlerian therapy application, 105–106
  basic behavior therapy concepts, 158
  family systems therapy, 460–461
  feminist therapy, 388–389
  functional behavior assessment, 176–177
  Gestalt therapy, 357–358
  interpretation, 72–74, 144–145
  multimodal therapy, 476–478
  person-centered therapy, 329–330
  questioning and interviewing, 39–48
  reality therapy, 243–244
  solution-focused brief therapy, 421–423
  Symbolic Growth Experience, 302–304
  Wise Mind ACCEPTS technique, 274–276
Case formulation, 202
Castration anxiety, 60, 510
Catastrophize, 188, 207, 510
Catching oneself, 94, 510
Catharsis, 63, 114, 478–479, 511
Chaining, 163
Challenge absolutes, 190, 511
Charcot, Jean-Martin, 56
Child development, 513
  Adler, families and birth order, 84–86, 92
  Adler, Individual Psychology, 78–79, 80
  Adler, personality development, 80–82
  Anna Freud, ego psychology, 122–124
  defined, 13
  developmental needs, 14
  female development and culture, 121
  Freud, personality structure, 57–58
  Freud, psychoanalytic theory, 54, 57, 59–61
  interpersonal psychotherapy, 480–481
  Jung, individuation, 112–113
  neuroplasticity, 241–242
  object relations theory, 125–127
  psychosocial development, 118

Subject Index

reality therapy, 227
See also Schema therapy; Self psychology
Children
  Adlerian therapy, childhood recollections, 92–93
  Adlerian therapy applications, 99–101
  earliest recollections, 104–106
  informed consent and assent, 31
  psychoanalysis, 123–124
  Skill Development, muscle relaxation, 175–176
  See also Adolescents; Family therapy; Object relations theory
Choice theory, 226, 227, 231, 511
Choreography, 441
Circular causality, 429, 511
Circular questioning, 448, 511
Classical conditioning, 156, 158, 169, 511
  exposure-based interventions, 169–170
  prolonged exposure therapy, 170
  relaxation techniques, 171–172
Client-centered therapy, 309, 511
  See also Person-centered therapy
Clients
  common factors, 6–7
  developmental needs, 13–15
  engagement, 8
  expectations, 7–8
  informed consent and assent, 30–31
  intake interview and assessment, 42–48
  motivation, expectations, and engagement, 7–8
  progress monitoring, 12
  role induction, 8
  strengths and resiliencies, 21–26
  worldview of, 16–17
  See also Therapeutic relationship
Clinical psychologists, theoretical orientation of, 3–7
  See also Theoretical orientation
Closed questions, 40–41
Coalitions, 443–444, 511
Coauthoring, 400
Co-construction, 400
Code of Ethics. *See* Ethics
Cognitive behavioral therapy (CBT)
  application and current use, 209–214, 496
  basic philosophy of, 486
  behavioral activation therapy (BAT), 271–272

Case Application, 219–221
cognitive therapy, 195–209
compassion-focused therapy (CFT), 273
contemporary therapies, overview of, 487, 489, 490, 492, 495, 497, 498, 500, 502, 504
cyclical psychodynamic-behavior therapy, 473–475
development of, 152–153, 179–181, 195–197
eye movement desensitization and reprocessing (EMDR), 481–482
family therapy, 453–454
goals of counseling, 490
key concepts, 181–182, 488
limitations and strengths, 214–216, 502, 504
metacognitive therapy, 273
multicultural applications, 213–214, 498, 500
multimodal therapy, 475–476
rational emotive behavior therapy (REBT), 183–195
Skill Development, mindfulness, 273–274
therapeutic process, 495
therapeutic relationship, 492
third generation of therapies, 246–247, 270–273
See also Acceptance and commitment therapy (ACT); Behavior therapy; Dialectical behavior therapy; Reality therapy; Schema therapy
Cognitive development, 15
Cognitive distortions, 202–203, 511
Cognitive model, 197, 511
Cognitive rehearsal, 207–208, 511
Cognitive restructuring, 197–199, 511
Cognitive schemas, 198, 511
Cognitive theory, 2, 3, 150
Cognitive therapy, 2, 138
  application and current use, 209–214
  assessment, 202–203
  Case Application, 219–221
  case formulation, 202
  cognitive model, 197
  cognitive restructuring, 197–199
  development of, 196–197
  dysfunctional thought record, 203–204
  labeling distortions, 206–207
  limitations and strengths, 214–216
  modifying cognitions, strategies for, 207–209

multicultural applications, 213–214
Skill Development, exposure-based CBT for hoarding, 216–219
termination and relapse prevention, 209
therapeutic process, 199–201
therapeutic techniques, 201–209
therapist function and role, 200–201
validity of cognitions, 204–205
Cognitive triad, 202–203, 511
Collective disenfranchisement, 367
Collective unconscious, 110, 111–112, 114, 117, 511
Commitment to change, 232, 511
Committed action, 256, 511
Common factors, 5, 6–7, 482–483, 511
Common factors eclecticism, 471
Communication
  ethical decision making and, 36
  family systems therapy, 429–431, 438
  nonverbal, 342, 346, 438
  professional qualities for, 11–13
  survival strategies and, 438–439
  See also Language
Community feeling, Adler, 86–87, 511
Comorbidity, 214
Compassion-focused therapy (CFT), 273
Competence, 31, 511
Complexes, 110, 112, 511
Concentration technique, 56, 511
Conditional positive regard, 310–311, 511
Conditioned stimulus, 158, 511
Conditions of worth, 310–311, 511
Conduct disorder
  behavior therapy, 173
  cognitive behavioral therapy, 213
  family therapy, 456
  reality therapy, 214, 468
Confidentiality, 31, 32
Conflict, 53, 56–57
Confluence, 339, 342–343, 512
Confrontation, 512
  Adlerian therapy, 93–97
  Gestalt therapy, 344–347, 353–354
  reality therapy, 234–235
  reality therapy, Skill Development, 242–243
  schema therapy, 268–269
Congruence, 9–10, 312–316, 512
Conjoint family therapy, 426, 512

Connecting the smell, mindfulness activity, 262
Conscious, 61, 512
Consciousness
  Jung, psyche and, 110–112
  levels of, psychoanalytic theory, 61
  ten processes of change, 478–479
Consciousness-raising, feminist therapy, 379–380, 512
Consciousness-raising groups, 363
Conscious suppression, 62
Conscious thought processing, 260–261
Consequences
  rational emotive behavior therapy, 187, 192
  reality therapy, 238
Constructive narrative, 181
Constructivism, 393, 512
  See also Narrative therapy
Constructivists, 393, 512
Constructivist theory, 3, 361–362, 392–394
  See also Acceptance and commitment therapy (ACT)
Contact, 342–343, 512
Contemplation stage, 324, 478–479
Contextual/Systemic therapy, 2
  See also Adlerian therapy
Contingency contract, 160, 512
Contingency management, 166, 173–174, 478–479, 512
Control theory (control system theory), 227, 512
Co-occurring disorders, 33–34
Coping questions, 416, 512
Core beliefs, 198, 512
Core conflict relationship theme (CCRT), 142–143
Corporal punishment, 165
Correctional institution, 174, 239–241
Cost-benefit analysis, 193, 208, 512
Counseling
  common factors, 6–7
  developmental considerations, 13–15
  effectiveness of, 5–6
  future directions in, 505–506
  identifying client strengths and resiliencies, 21–26
  interview questions for cultural context, 18–20
  theories, use of, 2–7 (*See also* specific theory names)
  theories and setting, 21, 27–28, 29
  use of term, 4–5

Counseling plan, 11–12
Counseling psychologists, theoretical orientation of, 3–7
Counselor, use of term, 5
  See also Therapist
Counterconditioning, 157, 158, 478–479, 512
Countertransference, 64–65, 72–74, 121, 512
  brief psychodynamic therapy, 138, 139–140
  object relations theory, 129, 130
  person-centered therapy, 315
Couples counseling
  Adlerian therapy, 100–101
  cognitive behavioral therapy, 213
  emotionally focused couple therapy, 449–455
  Gestalt therapy, 336
  mindfulness, 263
  See also Family systems therapy
Court-mandated treatment, 151
Covert behaviors, 181, 512
Covert modeling, 158, 512
Creativity
  Adlerian therapy, 82
  arts therapy, 320
  existential therapy, 291, 296, 300, 302
  Gestalt therapy, 320
  Jung, unconscious mind, 111–112, 114
  narrative therapy, 397, 402
  reality therapy, 234, 236, 237
  relational-cultural model of development, 385
Credentials, professional, 31
Csikszentmihalyi, Michael, 327
Cultural feminism, 366
Cultural Formulation Interview (CFI), 18
Culture
  ADDRESSING acronym, 17–18
  Adlerian therapy, 101–102
  behavior therapy, 174
  cognitive behavioral therapy, 213–214
  cultural competence skills, 15–20, 36
  defined, 15
  existential therapy, 298
  family therapy, 456–457
  female development, 121
  feminist theory, 361–362
  future directions in counseling, 505–506
  gender role analysis, 374–375

Gestalt therapy, 353–354
  interview questions for cultural context, 18–20
  narrative therapy, 403–404, 405
  person-centered therapy, 325–326
  post- and neo-Freudian therapies, 141–142
  reality therapy, 240–241
  solution-focused brief therapy, 418
  summary table of therapies, 497–501
  See also Contextual/Systemic therapy; Feminist therapy
Cybernetics, 426, 512
Cyclical psychodynamic-behavior therapy, 473–475, 512

D

Darwin, Charles, 52
Dasein, 284, 512
Daseinanalysis, 284
DEAR MAN GIVE FAST acronym, 254, 512
Death, existential therapy, 286, 296, 297–298, 300
Death instinct, 59, 128
Decatastrophizing, 193, 513
Decentering, 261–262, 513
Decision making, ethics, 35–37
Declaring hopelessness, 448
Deconstruction, 394
Defense mechanisms, 52–53, 61–63, 513
  brief psychodynamic therapy, 136
  depressive position, 128
  ego defense mechanisms, 123
  introjection, 125
  paranoid-schizoid position, 128
  triangle of conflict, 136
  triangle of insights, 136
Deflection, 339, 345–346, 513
Defusion, 256, 257, 513
Delusions, 109
Denial, 62, 513
Depression, 254
  acceptance and commitment therapy, 258
  behavioral activation therapy (BAT), 271–272
  behavior therapy, 173–174
  cognitive behavioral therapy, 209–214, 468
  cognitive therapy, 196–197
  compassion-focused therapy (CFT), 273
  existential therapy, 288, 297

Subject Index **581**

eye movement desensitization and reprocessing (EMDR), 481–482
family therapy, 455–456
feminist therapy, 381
Gestalt therapy, 353
interpersonal psychotherapy, 480–481
metacognitive therapy, 273
mindfulness-based cognitive therapy, 259, 263
narrative therapy, 403
schema therapy, 269
solution-focused brief therapy, 418
See also Dialectical behavior therapy (DBT)
Depressive position, 128, 130, 513
Dereflection, 295, 513
Desensitization, 339
de Shazer, Steve, 393, 405–406, 408, 409, 412, 413
Detriangulation, 436, 513
Deutsch, Helene, 118
Development. *See* Child development
Developmental needs, clients, 13–15
Diagnosis, ethical and legal issues, 31–33
Diagnostic and Statistical Manual of Mental Disorders (DSM-5), 18, 32
Diagnostic or Metapsychological Profile, 123
Dialectical behavior therapy (DBT), 247
  application and current use, 254
  development of, 247–258
  dialectics, 248
  distress tolerance, 252–253
  emotional regulation, 248–249
  emotion regulation, Skill Development, 250–251
  interpersonal effectiveness, 253–254
  limitations and strengths, 270–271
  mindfulness, 251–252
  therapeutic process, 249–250
Dialectics, defined, 248, 513
Diaphragmatic breathing, 171–172, 513
Diaz family. *See* Case Application
Didactic style, 192–193
Differentiation of self, 432, 513

Difficult topics, addressing of, 12
Diffusion, 261–262, 432, 513
Direction and doing, reality therapy, 232
Disabilities,
  ADDRESSING framework, 369
  Adlerian therapy, 81, 92, 101, 102
  behavior therapy, 162, 173
  existential therapy, 298
  feminist therapy, 376, 381, 383, 386
  functional behavior assessments, 162
  narrative therapy, 404
  person-centered therapy, 319
  solution-focused brief therapy, 418
Discrepancies, 65
Discrete trial training (DTT), 167
Disengaged, defined, 513
Disengagement, 442–443, 513
Disorganized/disoriented attachment, 126, 130
Displacement, 62, 513
Dispute (debate), 187–188, 192
Disputing styles, 192–193
Disqualifying the positive, 206
Dissociation, 62, 513
Distancing, 208, 261
Distortions, labeling of, 206–207
Distractions, 208, 252–253
Distress, 370–371
Distress tolerance, 252–253, 513
Diversions, 208
Diversity. *See* Multicultural approaches
Documentation, ethics and, 35
Dollard, John, 157
Dominant lifestyle, 82–83
Dominant story, 397–398, 513
Double bind, 447–448, 513
Dramatic relief, 478–479
Drawing the problem, 402
Dreams and dream analysis, 67, 513
  Adlerian therapy, 92
  ego psychology, 121
  Gestalt therapy, 348–349
  Jung, unconscious mind, 110, 111–112
  Jungian analytical psychology, 115, 116
  psychoanalytic theory, 56
Drives, 59–61, 119–120, 513
Dual (Multiple) relationships, 34
Dyad, 432, 513
Dynamics, family systems, 429, 513
Dysfunctional thought record, 203–204, 514

E
Early maladaptive schemas, 264, 514
Early recollections, 104–106, 514
EARS acronymn, 412, 514
Eating disorders, 34
  behavior therapy, 173, 254
  cognitive behavior therapy, 212, 213
  compassion-focused therapy (CFT), 273
  eye movement desensitization and reprocessing (EMDR), 481–482
  family therapy, 455–456
  feminist therapy, 381, 384
  Gestalt therapy, 353
  interpersonal psychotherapy, 480–481
  motivational interviewing, 7, 325
  narrative therapy, 404
  psychoanalysis, 128
  schema therapy, 269
Eclectic theory, 3
  See also Integrative and eclectic therapies
Education, Jungian psychology, 114
Education, reality therapy, 225
Educational development, 14
Effective new thinking, 188, 192
Egalitarian, 514
Eger, Edith Eva, 289
Ego, 118, 514
  brief psychodynamic therapy, 135–136
  self psychology, 131
Ego anxiety, 193, 514
Ego boundaries, 340–341, 514
Ego psychology, 54, 58, 108
  application and current use, 124–125, 141
  child development, 122–123
  child psychoanalysis, 123–124
  development of, 117–118
  female development and culture, 121
  Freud, Anna, 122–125
  Horney, Karen, 118–121
  Jung, psyche, 110–112
  limitations and strengths, 142–143
  multicultural groups, 141–142
  neurosis and basic anxiety, 119–120
  self-realization, 119
  selves and self-image, 120
  therapeutic process, 121, 123
  therapeutic techniques, 121, 123–124

Eigenwelt, 285, 288–289, 514
Electra complex, 60, 112, 514
Ellis, Albert, 2, 179, 181, 183–186, 196
Elucidation, 114
Emmanuel Movement, 52
Emotional cleansing, 114
Emotional cutoff, 433, 514
Emotional development, 14
  ego psychology, 121
  Jung, unconscious mind, 111–112
  object relations theory, 125, 128
  psychoanalytic theory, 60–61
  self psychology, 132
Emotional health
  Adler on, 86–87
  fully functioning person, 311–312
  reality therapy on, 229
Emotionally focused couple therapy, 449–455, 463–465
Emotional mind, 251
Emotional reasoning, 207
Emotional regulation
  dialectical behavior therapy, 248–251
  Gestalt therapy, 353
  mindfulness, 260
  skill development, 250–251
  See also Dialectical behavior therapy (DBT)
Emotion-focused therapy, 138, 319, 321, 322–323
Emotions
  abreaction, 67
  cultural differences, 174
  Gestalt therapy, body messages, 351
  nuclear family emotional system, 433
  process-experiential therapies, 320–321
  rational emotive behavior therapy, 186
Empathic confrontation, 268–269
Empathy, 9, 121, 514
  brief psychodynamic therapy, 139
  empathic responding, Skill Development, 327–329
  person-centered therapy, 317–318
  self psychology, 132, 133
  teaching of, 319
Empirical disputes, 192
Empowerment, 363, 514
Empty chair technique, 338, 349–351, 355–358, 514
Enactments
  family systems therapy, 445, 514
  Gestalt therapy, 347, 514

Encounter groups, 279, 309, 336, 351–352, 514
Encouragement, Adlerian therapy, 514
Encouragement, of clients, 89–90
End-of-life issues, existential therapy and, 297
Energy, Gestalt therapy, 343
Enjoyment, 228
Enmeshed, defined, 514
Enmeshed boundaries, 442–443
Environment, responsive, 132
Environmental contact, Gestalt therapy, 342–343
Erickson, Milton, 445, 448
Erikson, Erik, 51, 53, 118
Eros, 59, 514
Ethics
  assessment and diagnosis, 31–33
  codes of, 13, 28, 34
  competence, 31
  decision making, practical suggestions, 35–37
  evidence-based practices (EBPs), 33–34
  feminist therapy, 371, 372
  informed consent and assent, 30–31
  medical records, 35
  moral principles, 35
  multiple (dual) relationships, 34
  overview of, 28, 30
Evidence-based approaches, 12, 514
  Active Parenting Today, 99
  psychoanalysis, applications of, 69
  trauma-focused cognitive behavioral therapy, 211–212
Evidence-based practices (EBPs), 33–34
Evolutionary theory, 52
Exception-seeking questions, 414–415, 514
Excesses, 66
Exercises, 347, 514
Existential anxiety, 514
Existential guilt, 287–288, 514
Existential-humanistic psychotherapy, 2
Existentialism, 283, 284, 515
Existential power, 376
Existential theory, 3
  Frankl, Viktor, 281
  Jung and, 116
  May, Rollo, 281–282
  overview of, 278–281
  Yalom, Irvin, 282–283
  See also Gestalt therapy

Existential therapy
  anxiety, existential and neurotic, 287–288
  application and current use, 296–298, 497
  authenticity, 290
  awareness, 290
  basic philosophy of, 487
  Case Application, Symbolic Growth Experience, 302–304
  Dasein, 284, 288–289
  dereflection, 295
  development of, 283–286
  family therapy, 454
  freedom and responsibility, 290–291
  goals of counseling, 490
  I-Thou (You) relationships, 294
  key concepts, 286–292, 489
  limitations and strengths, 298–300, 502, 504
  logotherapy, 295, 297, 300
  making meaning, 291
  multicultural groups, 298, 498, 500
  paradoxical intention, 295, 298, 300
  potentials, human condition, 289–292
  relationships to others, 291–292
  restricted existence, 293
  self-actualization, 291
  self-transcendence, 295
  Skill Development, values clarification, 300–302
  striving for identity, 291–292
  Symbolic Growth Experience, 294
  therapeutic process, 292–294, 495
  therapeutic relationship, 492
  ultimate concerns, human condition, 286–287, 296
Existential vacuum, 287, 515
Expectancy bias, 473
Experience near, 133, 515
Experiential avoidance, 255, 515
Experiential awareness, 281
Experiential focusing, 322–323
Experiential therapy, 3
  emotionally focused couple therapy, 449–455
  family therapy, 437–441, 463–465
Experiments, 347, 515
Explanation of client problems, 11

Exposure and response prevention, 515
Exposure-based interventions, 169–170, 515
  applications and current use, 173–174
  eye movement desensitization and reprocessing (EMDR), 481–482
  prolonged exposure therapy, 170
  Skill Development, hoarding, 216–219
Expressive arts therapy, 320
Expressive techniques, 138–139
Externalizing, 401–402, 515
External locus of control, 240
External objects, 127
Extinction, 156, 157, 163, 165, 515
Extinguishing, 158, 515
Extratherapeutic factors, 6
Extraversion, 110–112, 114, 515
Eye Movement Desensitization and Reprocessing (EMDR), 481–482, 515
Eysenck, Hans, 155, 470

F
Failure identity, 225
Family, defined, 515
Family communication, 429–431, 515
Family constellation, 84–86, 92, 99–101, 515
Family hierarchy, 443–444
Family maps, 445, 515
Family projection process, 433, 515
Family sculpting, 441, 515
Family structure, genograms, 435–436, 515
Family systems therapy, 516
  Adlerian therapy and, 99, 101, 453
  application and current use, 455–457, 497
  basic philosophy of, 488
  behavioral functions within families, 428
  boundaries, 428
  Bowenian (multigenerational) therapy, 431–437
  Case Application, 460–461
  cognitive behavioral therapy and, 453–454
  communication, enhancing of, 429–431

development of, 425–428
emotionally focused couple therapy, 449–455
existential therapy, 454
experiential and humanistic therapy, 437–441
feminist therapy and, 455
Gestalt therapy and, 455
goals of counseling, 491
key concepts, 427–431, 489
limitations and strengths, 457, 503, 504
multicultural groups, 456–457, 499, 501
narrative therapy and, 404
postmodern therapy and, 455
psychoanalytic family therapy, 452
reality therapy, 454
reciprocal influence, 428–429
Skill Development, genograms, 457–459
strategic family therapy, 445–449
structural family therapy, Minuchin, 441–445
summary table of, 463–465
therapeutic process, 496
therapeutic relationship, 493
See also Adlerian therapy; Contextual/Systemic therapy
Fantasy, 349
Fatalism, 240
Feedback loops, 446, 516
Feeling function, 113
Feeling in new ways, 188, 192
Felt minus, 81, 516
Feminism, defined, 516
Feminism, positions in, 365–367
Feminist theory, 108
  culture, context, and constructivism, 361–362
  female development and culture, 121
  Karen Horney and, 118–121
  See also Acceptance and commitment therapy (ACT); Contextual/Systemic therapy
Feminist therapy
  application and current use, 380–383, 497
  assertiveness training, 376–377
  basic philosophy of, 487
  Case Application, 388–389
  consciousness-raising, 379–380
  development of, 363–367
  egalitarian relationship, 369
  family therapy and, 455

gender-role analysis, 374–375
goals of counseling, 491
honoring women's experiences, 368
key concepts, 367–369, 489
limitations and strengths of, 385–386, 503, 504
mental health disorder, reframing of, 368
multicultural groups, 382–383, 499, 500
multiple identities, 367
personal is political, 367–368
power analysis, 376
reframing and relabeling, 378–379
relational-cultural theory (RCT), 384–385
Skill Development, self-disclosure, 386–388
social activism, 380
social locations and identities, 369
therapeutic process, 370–374, 496
therapeutic relationship, 493
therapy-demystifying strategies, 379
Feminist Therapy Code of Ethics, 371, 372
Feminist Therapy Institute (FTI), 362, 371, 372, 379, 380
Ferenczi, Sándor, 134
Fictional final goal, 82, 516
Fictional finalism, 82–83, 516
Fidelity, 35
Fiduciary-therapeutic relationship, 34
Field theory, 337–338, 516
Figure, defined, 516
Figure and ground, 337–338, 516
First force, 51–54
First-order change, defined, 516
First-order cybernetics, 426, 516
Five levels of change, 479
Fixation, 59–60, 516
Flexibility, of therapist, 12
Flooding, 169–170, 516
Focused attention, 261–262
Focusing, experiential, 322–323
Forceful self-statements and dialogue, 194
Formula first session tasks (FFST), 413, 516
Fortune telling, 206, 516
Forward motion and creativity, 82
Foucault, Michel, 396
Frankl, Viktor, 2, 281, 284, 287, 294, 295
Free association, 65–66, 121, 516
Freedom, 286, 287, 290–291, 293, 296

Freud, Anna, 53, 54, 63, 67, 108, 118, 122, 123, 124, 134
   biography, 122
   ego psychology, 122–125
Freud, Sigmund, 1, 56, 65, 67, 285
   abreaction, 67
   Alfred Adler and, 78, 79
   attachment and development, 57
   biography, 54–55
   consciousness, levels of, 61
   defense mechanisms, 61–63
   development of psychoanalysis, 55–57
   dream analysis, 67
   evaluation of psychoanalysis, 70–71
   first force, 51–54
   free association, 65–66
   influence of, 108, 109
   life and death instincts, 59
   personality structure, 57–58
   stages of development, 59–61
   strengths and contributions of, 71
   therapeutic process, 63–65
Freudian slip, 61, 516
Frick, Willard, 294
Friendly involvement, 236, 516
Fully functioning person, 311–312, 516
Fun, need for, 228
Functional behavior assessments (FBAs), 161–162, 176–177, 516
Functional disputing strategies, 192
Functionalism, 150
Functions, defined, 516
Fundamental attribution errors, 473
Fusion, 432, 516

G

Gender
   birth order and, 85–86
   client-therapist relationship and, 10
   female development and culture, 121
   Karen Horney on Freud, 118–119
   male privilege, 382
   psychoanalytic theory and, 60, 70–71
   See also Contextual/Systemic therapy; Feminist therapy
Gender role analysis, 374–375, 379–380
Gender-role stereotyping, 367–368
Gendlin, Eugene, 280, 319, 322, 323

Generalization, 166, 516–517
General systems theory, 426, 516
Genetic factors, 14–15, 80
Genital stage, 60–61, 517
Genograms, 435–436, 517
   Skill Development, Genograms, 457–459
Genuineness, 315, 517
Gestalt, 3, 116, 175, 319, 335
Gestalt therapy, 279
   application and current use, 352–354, 497
   awareness, 341–343
   basic philosophy of, 487
   body, messages of, 351
   Case Application, 357–358
   contact disturbance, 340–341
   deflection, 345–346
   development of, 334–336
   dreams and fantasy, 348–349
   emotionally focused couple therapy and, 449–455
   empty chair technique, 349–351, 355–358
   energy and energy blocks, 343
   environmental contact and growth, 342–343
   exercises, experiments, and enactments, 347
   family therapy and, 455
   field theory, 337–338
   figure, 337–338
   goals of counseling, 491
   ground, 337–338
   group therapy, 351–352
   growth disorders and resistance, 339–340
   here and now, 343
   homeostasis *versus* flux, 341
   hot seat, 351–352
   integrating polarities, 338–339
   I-Thou (You) relationship, 346
   key concepts, 336–343, 489
   language, use of, 347–348
   limitations and strengths, 354–355, 502, 504
   making the rounds, 352
   multicultural groups, 353–354, 499, 500
   paradoxical theory of change, 345
   psychodrama, 336
   responsibility, 343
   role playing, empty chair methods, 349–351
   Skill Development, chair work, 355–357
   therapeutic process, 344–347, 495

therapeutic relationship, 493
wholeness, integration, and balance, 337–341
Getting lifestyle, 82–83
Gilbert, Paul Raymond, 273
Glasser, William, 2, 224–231, 233, 235, 236, 237, 239, 241
Goal setting
   Adlerian theory, 79, 87
   behavior therapy, 151, 159–160
   cognitive behavioral therapy, 182
   cognitive therapy, 199–200
   feminist therapy, 370–371
   fictional final goal, Adler, 82
   hexaflex model, 257
   lifestyle, Adler, 82–83
   rational emotive behavior therapy, 189–190
   reality therapy, 233, 234–235
   solution-focused brief therapy, 407, 410, 411
Goldstein, Kurt, 334
Graded task assignments, 209, 517
Graduated exposure, 169–170, 517
Greenberg, Leslie, 319, 449–455
Grief and loss
   Adlerian therapy, 98
   brief psychodynamic therapy, 137
   cognitive behavioral therapy, 209, 216
   existential therapy, 297
   experiences of, 393
   family therapy, 456
   Gestalt therapy, 349, 353
   interpersonal psychotherapy, 480
   narrative therapy, 404, 405
   psychoanalytic therapy, 141
Ground, 337–338, 517
Group counseling
   Adlerian therapy, 99
   cognitive behavioral therapy, 212–213
   existential therapy, 297–298
   feminist therapy, 381
   Gestalt therapy, 351–352
   person-centered therapy, 319
Growth-fostering relationships, 384–385
Guided discovery, 200–201, 517

H

Haley, Jay, 426, 428, 435, 445–446, 447
Hallucinations, 109
Hampstead Psychoanalytic Index, 123

Health care costs, 34, 140–141
  future directions in counseling, 505
Health insurance
  brief psychodynamic therapy, 140–141
  cost of care, 34
  diagnosis and reimbursement, 32, 505
Heidegger, Martin, 284
Here and now, 343
Hexaflex model, 257
Hoarding, 216–219
Homeostasis, 341, 446, 517
Hope, 7–8, 12
Horney, Karen, 51, 54, 70, 108, 118–121, 124, 142, 183, 184, 334
Hot seat, 351–352, 517
Human condition,
  potentials, 289–292
  ultimate concerns, 286–287, 296
Humanistic theory, 3, 278–281, 285
  emotionally focused couple therapy, 449–455
  family therapy, 437–441, 463–465
  Jung and, 116
  multimodal therapy, 475–476
  See also Adlerian therapy; Existential therapy; Gestalt therapy; Person-centered therapy
Human validation process model, 438
Humor, 62, 517
Humorous style, 193
Husserl, Edmund, 283, 284
Hyper-reflection, 295
Hypnosis, 52, 56

I

Iceberg theory, 51
Id, 58, 63–64, 118, 132, 517
Idealization, 62, 120, 517
Identification, 62, 341, 351, 517
Identified patient, 517
Identity
  existential therapy, 291–292
  feminist therapy, 369
  narrative therapy, 397
Immediacy
  Adlerian technique, 95, 517
  Gestalt therapy, 347, 517
Implosion, 169, 517
IMPROVE, acronym, 253, 517
Impulse control disorders, 254, 418
  See also Attention deficit hyperactivity disorder (ADHD); Obsessive-compulsive disorder (OCD)
Incongruent, 311, 517
Individual Psychology, 78–80, 517
  applications and current use, 98–102
  basic mistakes, 83–84
  community feeling, 86–87
  family constellation and birth order, 84–86
  lifestyle, 82–83
  limitations and strengths, 102–104
  patterns of personality, 80–84
  social interest, 86–87
  therapeutic process, 87–89
  See also Adlerian therapy
Individuation, 112–113, 517
Inferior function, 110, 111, 517
Inferiority, 80–82, 88, 101–102, 517
Inferiority complex, 81, 517
Information processing, 181
Informed consent, 30–31, 36, 517
Insight, rational emotive behavior therapy, 186
Insomnia, 212
Instincts, 59, 128, 518
Institutionalized "isms", 367
Insurance
  brief psychodynamic therapy, 140–141
  cost of care, 34
  diagnosis and coverage, 32
  future directions in counseling, 505
  liability, professional, 37
Intake interview, 42–48
Integrative and eclectic therapies
  benefits of, 470
  challenges of, 469–470
  characteristics of sound approaches, 471
  cyclical psychodynamic-behavior therapy, 473–475
  examples of, 470–471, 472–482
  eye movement desensitization and reprocessing (EMDR), 481–482
  formulating an integrative theory, 472
  growth of, 468–469
  identifying a counseling theory, 482–485
  interpersonal psychotherapy, 480–481
  multimodal therapy, 475–478
  as theoretical orientation, 467–468
  transtheoretical model of change, 478–479
Integrative theory, 3
Intellectual disabilities, 162, 418
Intellectualization, 62, 518
Intentionality, 287, 518
Intergenerational family patterns, 435–436, 518
Intermediate beliefs, 198, 518
Internal locus of control, 313
Internal objects, 127, 518
Internet addiction, 239
Interoceptive exposure, 170, 518
Interpersonal effectiveness, 253–254, 518
Interpersonal psychotherapy, 480–481
Interpersonal skills, 11
Interpersonal theory, 3
Interpretation, 518
  Adlerian therapy, 93–97
  brief psychodynamic therapy, 139
  Case Application, 72–74, 144–145
  defined, 66
  object relations theory, 129
  psychoanalysis, 66–67
  self psychology, 133
  Skill Development, 72–74
Intersectionality, 365, 518
Intersubjectivity, 133, 518
Interviews
  Adult Attachment Interview, 130
  for cultural context, 18–20
  identifying client strengths and resiliencies, 21–26
  intake interview, 42–48
  Lifestyle Interview, 90–92
  motivational interviewing, 323–325, 479
  Skill Development, 39–48
Intrapersonal power, 376
Intrapsychic power, 376
Intrapsychic processes, 58, 518
Introjection, 125, 339, 340, 518
Introspection, vicarious, 133
Introversion, Jung, 110–112, 114, 518
Intuition, defined, 518
Intuition function, 110, 111, 113
Inventories
  Beck Anxiety Inventory (BAI), 202
  Beck Depression Inventory (BDI), 202
  Beck Hopelessness Inventory, 202
  Structural Profile Inventory, 477
  values clarification, 301

Subject Index

In vivo contexts, 170, 517
Irrational beliefs, 184–185, 518
Isolation, existential therapy, 286, 296
I-Thou (You) relationships, 294, 346, 518

J
Jackson, Don, 445
James, William, 150, 284
John Dewey Academy, 241
Johnson, Susan, 441, 449–455, 456
Joining, 444, 518
Jumping to conclusions, 206
Jung, Carl, 51, 56, 108, 109–117
   analytical psychology, development of, 110
   biography, 109
Jungian analytical psychology, 108
   anima and animus, 112, 115
   application and current use, 116–117, 141
   archetypes, 111–112
   balance and polarities, 113
   collective unconscious, 111, 114
   complexes, 112
   conscious mind, 111
   development of, 110
   dream interpretation, 115, 116
   individuation, 112–113
   limitations and strengths, 142–143
   multicultural groups, 141–142
   persona, 111, 113
   personality, functions and attitudes, 113–114
   personal unconscious, 112, 114
   psyche, components of, 110–112
   rituals, 116
   Self, 112, 113
   shadow, 112, 113, 115
   symbols, use of, 115
   therapeutic process, 114–115
   unconscious mind, 111–112
   word association tests, 116
Justice, 35

K
Kabat-Zinn, Jon, 258–263
Kafka, Franz, 284
Kelly, George, 196, 396
Kernberg, Otto, 125
Kierkegaard, Søren, 283, 284
Klein, Melanie, 54, 108, 125, 128
Klerman, Gerald, 480
Koffka Kurt, 335

Köhler, Wolfgang, 335
Kohut, Heinz, 54, 108, 131–134

L
Labeling, defined, 518
Labeling distortions, 206–207
Landscapes of action, 399, 518
Landscapes of consciousness, 399, 519
Language
   use in Gestalt therapy, 347–348
   use in narrative therapy, 401–402
   use in postmodern therapy, 394
   use in solution-focused brief therapy, 409–410, 416
Latency stage, 60, 519
Latent content, 67
Lazarus, Arnold, 155, 475–476, 477
Learning factors, 483
Learning teams, 239
Legal issues
   assessment and diagnosis, 31–33
   competence, 31
   informed consent and assent, 30–31
   overview of, 28, 30
   professional development, 37
Lesbian feminism, 366
Letter writing, 208, 401, 402–403
Level of care, 27–28, 29, 493, 519
Levenson, Hanna, 135
Lewin, Kurt, 335, 337–338
LGBT (lesbian, gay, bisexual, transgendered)
   cultural competency skills, 15
   feminist therapy and, 382–383
Liability insurance, 37
Liberal feminism, 366
Libido, 59, 113, 114, 519
Licensure, 28, 31
Life instinct, 59, 128
Lifestyle, 82–83, 88, 90, 519
   family constellation and birth order, 84–86
   reorientation, 97–98
Lifestyle Interview, 90–92
Limited reparenting, 268–269, 519
Linear causality, 428–429, 519
Linehan, Marsha M., 247–254, 377
Logical consequences, 100, 519
Logical disputes, 192
Logotherapy, 281, 284–285, 295, 297, 300, 519
Loss. *See* Grief and loss
Love object, 127, 519
Low frustration tolerance, 185, 519

M
Madanes, Cloe, 445
Magnification, 206, 519
Mahler, Margaret, 125
Maintenance stage, 324, 478–479
Making the rounds, 352
Mandated reporting, 31
Manifest content, dreams, 67
Mapping, family systems therapy, 445
Mapping, narrative therapy, 401, 419–421, 519
Maslow, Abraham, 291, 294, 310
May, Rollo, 281–282, 284, 287, 291, 293, 294, 298, 299
Meaning
   existential therapy and, 291
   Frankl on, 281
   postmodern therapy and, 394
   post-structuralism, 362
   Yalom on, 282–283
   See also Existential therapy; Narrative therapy
Meaninglessness, 286–287, 296, 300
Medical records, ethics and, 35
Medication, use of, 241
Meichenbaum, Donald, 2, 179–181, 197
Memory, Jung and unconcious mind, 110, 111–112
Mental filter, 206
Mental health
   definition of, Horney, 121
   existential theory on, 289
   feminist therapy, 368
Mental illness
   early treatments for, 51–52
   feminist therapy, 368
   neuroses, 69
   psychoses, 69
Mesmerism, 52
Metacognitive therapy, 273
Metacommunication, 139
Metaphorical style, 193
Metaphors, reality therapy, 236
#MeToo movement, 365
Miller, Jean Baker, 336, 362–363, 384
Miller, Neal, 157
Mindfulness, 247, 251–252, 519
   distress tolerance skills, 252–253
   practice of, 261–262
   Skill Development, 273–274
   See also Acceptance and commitment therapy (ACT)

Mindfulness-based cognitive therapy (MBCT)
  acceptance, 258–259
  application and current use, 262
  being mode, 259
  conscious thought processing, 260–261
  decentering, 261–262
  development of, 258
  limitations and strengths, 270–271
  tenets of mindfulness, 259–260
  therapeutic process, 260
Mindmaps, 410, 519
Mind reading, 206, 519
Minimization, 206, 519
Minuchin, Salvador, 426, 428, 435, 441–445, 456
Miracle question, 413–414, 519
Mirroring, 131–132, 133, 519
Mislabeling, 207, 518
Mitwelt, 285, 288–289, 519
Modeling, 157, 158, 167, 519
  skills training, 172–173
Modernism, defined, 392
Moral development, 14
Moreno, Jacob, 336
Motivation, 7, 271–272, 410, 519
Motivational interviewing, 7–8, 138, 323–325, 479
Multicultural approaches
  Adlerian therapy, 101–102
  behavior therapy, 174
  cognitive behavioral therapy, 213–214
  cultural competence skills, 15–20, 36
  culture, defined, 15
  existential therapy, 291, 298
  family therapy, 456–457
  future directions in counseling, 505–506
  gender role analysis, 374–375
  Gestalt therapy, 353–354
  narrative therapy, 405
  person-centered therapy, 325–326
  post- and neo-Freudian therapies, 141–142
  psychoanalysis, application of, 69–70
  reality therapy, 240–241
  solution-focused brief therapy, 418
  summary table of therapies, 497–501
  See also Contextual/Systemic therapy; Feminist therapy

Multicultural Counseling Competencies, ACA, 15
Multicultural theory, 3
Multidimensional identities, 369
Multigenerational family therapy, 463
  See also Bowenian family therapy
Multigenerational transmission process, 433, 519
Multimodal therapy, 475–478, 519
Multinuclear family, 520
Multiple identities, 367, 520
Multiple (Dual) relationships, 34
Musterbation, 185, 520
"Must" statements, 207
My colorful emotions, 262
Myers-Briggs Type Indicator, 117, 484–485
My five senses, 262

N

Naming the problem, 401–402
Narcissism, 54, 120, 132, 133, 134
Narradrama, 404, 520
Narrative therapy, 138, 393
  applications and current use, 403–405
  development of, 394–396
  externalizing, 401–402
  family interventions and involvement, 404
  key concepts, 397–398
  limitations and strengths, 405
  listening with an open mind, 398
  mapping, 401
  Skill Development, mapping, 419–421
  specifications of personhood, 397–398
  stories, 397–399
  therapeutic documents, 402–403
  therapeutic goals, 399–400
  therapeutic process, 398–401
  unique outcomes, 420
  See also Acceptance and commitment therapy (ACT)
National Association of Social Workers, 28
National Board of Certified Counselors, 28
Naturalistic teaching strategies, 168
Needs, reality therapy, 228, 230–231, 520
Needs, schema therapy, 268
Negative feedback loop, 446, 520
Negative punishment, 163, 164–165, 520

Negative reinforcement, 157, 163, 164, 520
Neo-Freudian therapy
  application and current use, 496
  basic philosophy of, 486
  goals of counseling, 490
  limitations and strengths, 502, 503
  multicultural counseling, 498, 499
  theoretical concepts, 488
  therapeutic process, 494
  therapeutic relationship, 492
  See also Brief psychodynamic therapy (BPT); Ego psychology; Jungian analytical psychology; Object relations theory; Self psychology
Neurobiology, 212
  eye movement desensitization and reprocessing (EMDR), 481–482
  future directions in counseling, 505
  meditation, effect on brain, 263
  neuroplasticity, 241–242
  schema therapy, 268
Neurofeedback, 172, 520
Neurohypnology, 52
Neuroses, 69, 520
  Gestalt therapy, 339–340
  Horney, ego psychology, 119–120, 121
Neurotic anxiety, 287–288, 520
Nietzsche, Friedrich, 283, 284
Nondirective counseling, 309, 318, 520
Nonmaleficence, 35
Nonverbal communication
  Family systems therapy, 438
  Gestalt therapy, 342, 346

O

Object, defined, 520
Object cathexis, 58, 520
Object relations theory, 108
  application and current use, 129–131, 141
  attachment theory, 126–127
  development of, 125–126
  fundamental positions, 128
  limitations and strengths, 142–143
  multicultural groups, 141–142
  separation-individuation theory, 127
  therapeutic process, 128
  therapeutic techniques, 128–129

Objects
  defined, 125
  internal and external, 127
  love object, 127
  self object, 131–132, 133
Observational learning, 172–173, 520
Obsessive-compulsive disorder (OCD), 210
  acceptance and commitment therapy, 258
  eye movement desensitization and reprocessing (EMDR), 481–482
  metacognitive therapy, 273
  mindfulness-based cognitive therapy, 263
Oedipus complex, 60, 70, 112, 520
Omissions, 65–66
Open questions, 40–41
Operant conditioning, 150, 156–157, 158, 520
  techniques for, 162–168
Oppositional defiant disorder, 98, 173–174, 213
Oppression, 291
  narrative therapy, 403–404
  reframing mental health and disorder, 368
  relational-cultural theory (RCT), 384–385
  See also Feminist therapy
Optimal frustration, 132, 520
Optimal responsiveness, 133, 520
Optimism, 7–8, 12
Oral stage, 59, 61, 520
Ordeals, 447
Organismic valuing process, 311, 520
Overgeneralization, 206, 520

P
Paining behaviors, 238, 520
Pain management, 212
  acceptance and commitment therapy, 258
  Gestalt therapy, 353
  mindfulness, 274
  person-centered therapy, 318
  schema therapy, 269
Panic disorder, 210
  acceptance and commitment therapy, 258
  existential therapy, 297
  mindfulness-based cognitive therapy, 263
  person-centered therapy, 318

Paradoxical intention, 95, 295, 298, 300, 520
Paradoxical interventions, 238, 447–448, 520
Paradoxical ordeals, 447, 520
Paradoxical theory of change, 345, 520–521
Paranoid-schizoid position, 128, 521
Parent Effectiveness Training (PET), 321
Parentified child, 444, 521
Parents
  Adler, personality development, 81
  behavior therapy strategies, 174
  children and informed consent, 31
  family therapy, 99–101
  psychodynamic theory, 52–53
  Systematic Training for Effective Parenting (STEP), 30, 99, 453
  See also Object relations theory
Passive aggressive, 62, 521
Patriarchy, 364, 521
Patterson, Gerald, 453
Pavlov, Ivan, 155, 156
Payment for services, 32, 34, 505
Peer training, 168
Penis envy, 60, 121, 521
Perceived plus, 81, 521
Perls, Fritz (Frederick), 2, 334–355
Perls, Laura Posner, 335, 336
Persona, 111, 113, 521
Personal is political, 367–368
Personality
  Adler, Individual Psychology, 80–84
  Jung, functions and attitudes, 113–114
  psychoanalytic theory, 57–58
Personality styles, 484–485
Personalization, 207, 521
Personal unconcious, 110, 112, 114, 521
Person-centered, use of term, 309, 521
Person-centered theory, 3
  Case Application, 329–330
  facilitative conditions, 314–318
  Skill Development, empathic responding, 327–329
  See also Gestalt therapy
Person-centered therapy, 8–9, 175
  acceptance, 311
  application and current use, 318–326, 497
  basic philosophy of, 487

conditions of worth, 310–311
congruence, 312–313, 314–316
development of, 307–309
emotionally focused couples therapy, 449–455
empathy, 317–318
experiential focusing, 322–323
expressive arts therapy, 320
family therapy, 454–455
fully functioning person, 311–312
goals of counseling, 490
human potential and actualization, 310
limitations and strengths, 325–327, 502, 504
motivational interviewing, 323–325
multicultural groups, 325–326, 498, 500
nondirective counseling, 318
organismic valuing process, 311
Parent Effectiveness Training, 321
process-experiential therapies, 320–321
theoretical concepts, 489
therapeutic process, 312–314, 495
therapeutic relationship, 492
unconditional positive regard, 316–317
validation, 317–318
Phallic stage, 60, 61, 521
Phenomenological, defined, 80, 521
  See also Adlerian therapy
Phenomenological approach, 232, 280–281, 284, 285, 309
  See also Gestalt therapy; Narrative therapy; Person-centered therapy
Phenomenology, defined, 278, 279, 521
Philosophy-based theories, 51
Phi phenomenon, 279
Phobias
  acceptance and commitment therapy, 258
  behavioral therapy, 154, 155, 156, 158, 159, 169, 170, 173
  cognitive behavioral therapy, 181, 210, 216
  existential therapy, 297, 300
  feminist therapy, 382
  narrative therapy, 404
  person-centered therapy, 318
Physical development, 14–15
  See also Child development
Picture album, 230–231, 521

Subject Index

Planning, 233
Play therapy, 98, 101, 118
Pleasure principle, 58, 521
Polarities, Gestalt therapy, 338–339, 349–350, 521
Polarities, Jung, 113
Polarized thinking, 206
Positive addictions, 237, 521
Positive feedback loop, 446, 521
Positive narratives, 399, 521
Positive potentials, 132
Positive psychology, 279, 393, 521
Positive punishment, 163, 164–165, 521
Positive reinforcement, 157, 158, 163, 164, 521
Postcolonial feminism, 366
Post-Freudian therapy
    application and current use, 496
    basic philosophy of, 486
    goals of counseling, 490
    limitations and strengths, 502, 503
    multicultural counseling, 498, 499
    theoretical concepts, 488
    therapeutic process, 494
    therapeutic relationship, 492
    See also Brief psychodynamic therapy (BPT); Ego psychology; Jungian analytical psychology; Object relations theory; Self psychology
Postmodern feminism, 366
Postmodern therapy, 361–362
    application and current use, 497
    basic philosophy of, 488
    development of, 392–394
    family therapy, 455
    goals of counseling, 491
    key concepts, 397–398, 407–408, 489
    limitations and strengths, 503, 504
    multicultural counseling, 499, 501
    therapeutic process, 496
    therapeutic relationship, 493
    See also Contextual/Systemic therapy; Family systems therapy; Feminist theory; Narrative therapy; Solution-focused brief therapy (SFBT)
Post-structuralism, 362
Posttraumatic stress disorder (PTSD)
    acceptance and commitment therapy, 258
    cognitive behavioral therapy, 211–212
    evidence-based practices, 33
    existential therapy, 297
    eye movement desensitization and reprocessing (EMDR), 481–482
    feminist therapy, 381
    Gestalt therapy, 353
    interpersonal psychotherapy, 480–481
    metacognitive therapy, 273
    person-centered therapy, 318
    prolonged exposure therapy, 170
    solution-focused brief therapy, 418
Power, 521
    See also Feminist therapy
Power, need for, 228
Power analysis, 376, 521
PRACTICE acronym, 211–212
Preconscious, 61, 521
Precontemplation stage, 324, 478–479
Preparation stage, 324, 478–479
Prescribing the symptom, 95, 522
Pre-therapy changes, 413, 522
Privacy, 31, 32
Private logic, 88, 522
Problem-centered family therapy, 446
Problem-free talk, 416
Problem solving skills, 21–22
Process-experiential therapies, 320–321
Professional credentials, 31
Professional development, 36–37
Professional liability, 37
Progressive muscle relaxation, 169–170, 175–176
Progress monitoring, 12
Projection, 62, 339, 340, 522
Projective identification, 125, 129, 522
Prolonged exposure therapy, 170
Prompting, 163
Psyche, 110–112, 522
Psychic energy, 111, 522
Psychoanalysis, 522
    abreaction, 67
    analysis and interpretation, 66–67
    application and current use of, 68–70, 496
    basic philosophy of, 486
    classic psychoanalysis, Sigmund Freud, 54–55
    defined, 54, 66
    dream analysis, 67
    family therapy, 452
    free association, 65–66
    goals of counseling, 490
    key concepts, 57–63, 488
    limitations and strengths, 70–71, 502
    multicultural counseling, 498, 499
    resistance, 68
    Skill Development, interpretation, 72–74
    strengths and contributions, 71, 503
    therapeutic process, 63–65, 494
    therapeutic relationship, 492
Psychoanalytic theory, 3
    attachment and development, 57
    basic assumptions of, 53–54
    defense mechanisms, 61–63
    development of, 55–57
    individuation, 112–113
    levels of consciousness, 61
    life and death instincts, 59
    personality structure, 57–58
Psychobiological approaches, 480–481
Psychodrama, 336, 522
Psychodynamic theory, 3, 52–54
Psychodynamic therapy, 175
    cyclical psychodynamic-behavior therapy, 473–475
Psychologists, theoretical orientation of, 3–7
Psychopathology, early treatments for, 51–52
Psychoses, 69, 522
Psychosexual stages of development, 59–61, 522
Psychosocial development, Erikson, 118
Psychotherapy
    first force, 51–54
    second force, 149–153
    third force, 278–281
    fourth force, 361–362
    development of, 2
    future directions in counseling, 505–506
Punishment, 157, 163, 164–165, 522
Purpose, sense of, 21–22
Purposeful questions, 40
Purpose in Life Test, 301
Pushing the button, 94, 522

Q

Quality school model, 239
Quality worlds, 230–231, 522

Questioning skills
  Adlerian therapy techniques, 94–97
  circular questioning, 448
  intake interview and assessment, 42–48
  open and closed questions, 40–41
  pacing, 41
  phrasing, 41
  purposeful questions, 40
  Skill Development, 39–48
  solution-focused brief therapy, 413–417
  subject matter of questions, 41
Questions, Gestalt therapy, 347–348
Questions about the future, 416–417, 522

R

Race. *See* Contextual/Systemic therapy; Multicultural approaches
Radical acceptance, 252, 522
Radical feminism, 366
Randomized controlled trials (RCTs), 33
Rational alternative beliefs, 192
Rational emotive behavior therapy (REBT), 152, 153, 181, 453–454
  A-B-C-D-E-F Model, 186–188, 191–192
  A-B-C Model, 186–187
  behavioral strategies, 193–195
  cognitive and questioning strategies, 192–195
  development of, 183–184
  emotive strategies, 194–195
  irrational beliefs as cause of struggle, 184–185
  limitations and strengths, 214–216
  therapeutic goals, 189–190
  therapeutic process, 188–189
  therapeutic techniques, 191–195
  therapist function and role, 190–191
Rational emotive imagery (REI), 194, 522
Rationality, 189–190, 522
Rationalization, 63, 522
Rational mind, 251
Reaction formation, 63, 522
Reality principle, 58, 522
Reality therapy, 522
  application and current use, 239–241, 497
  basic philosophy of, 487

Case Application, 243–244
defined, 226
development of, 224–227
evaluation, 232–233
family therapy, 454
five basic human needs, 228
goals of counseling, 490
key concepts, 227–233, 488
limitations and strengths, 241–242, 502, 504
metaphors, 236
multicultural groups, 240–241, 498, 500
paining behaviors, 238
positive addictions, 237
quality worlds, 230–231
questions, use of, 237
reasonable consequences, 238
relationships, 236–237
SAMI^{2}C^3, 233, 237
skill building, 238
Skill Development, caring confrontation, 242–243
therapeutic goals, 234
therapeutic process, 495
therapeutic techniques, 236–238
therapist function and role, 234–235, 492
WDEP system, 231–233
Reattribution, 207, 522
Reauthoring, 399, 522
Reciprocal influence, 428–429, 522
Reciprocal inhibition, 156, 158, 522
Reconstruction, 438, 522
Reflecting "as if", 96
Reflecting team, 409, 523
Reflective listening, 323, 523
Reformist feminism, 366
Reframing, 378–379, 444–445, 523
Regression, 63, 114, 523
Reich, Wilhelm, 334
Reimbursement for services, 32, 34, 505
Reinforcement, 157, 158, 163, 164
Reker's Life Attitude Profile-Revised (LAP-R), 301
Relabeling, 378–379, 448, 523
Relapse stage, 325
Relational competence, defined, 523
Relational-cultural theory (RCT), 384–385
Relational frame theory, 256, 523
Relational resilience, 523
Relational theory, 130–131
Relationship factors, 11, 523
Relationship filter, 232, 523
Relationships

existential therapy, 291–292
psychoanalytic theory, 53
See also Object relations theory; Reality therapy
Relaxation techniques, 171–172
  Skill Development, progressive muscle relaxation, 175–176
Reliability, evidence-based practices, 33
Religion
  future directions in counseling, 505–506
  views of mental illness, 51–52
  See also Spirituality
Reorientation, 97–98, 523
Repression, 63, 67, 523
Resilience, 21–26
Resistance, 63, 68, 129, 523
Resistant attachment, 126, 130
Response cost, 163, 164–165
Responsibility, existential therapy, 290–291
Responsibility, Gestalt therapy, 343, 348
Responsibility, reality therapy, 225, 523
Responsive environment, 132
Restraining, 448
Restricted, defined, 523
Restricted existence, 293
Retroflection, 339, 340, 523
Revisioning, 399
Rituals, 116
Rogerian theory, 3
Rogers, Carl, 2, 8–9, 184, 279, 285, 291, 307–329
  biography of, 307–308
Rogers, Natalie, 319, 320
Role induction, 8, 523
Role playing, 193–194, 208, 349–351
Rumination, 259, 263

S

Sachs, Hans, 118
SAMHSA, 494
SAMI^{2}C^3, 233, 237, 523
Sartre, Jean-Paul, 284
Satir, Virginia, 426, 437–441, 456
Satir Tranformational Systemic Therapy, 440–441
Scaling, 205, 523
Scaling questions, 415, 523
Scapegoating, 442–443, 523
Schedules, applied behavior analysis, 168
Schemas, 198, 523

Schema therapy
    application and current use, 269
    cognitive interventions, 269
    common maladaptive schemas, 265–267
    development of, 263–264
    early maladaptive schemas, 264
    limitations and strengths, 270–271
    limited reparenting, 268–269
    schema domains, 264–268
    schema flash cards, 269
    therapeutic process, 268
Schizophrenia
    cognitive behavioral therapy, 180, 196, 212
    family therapy, 426, 456
    Gestalt therapy, 353
    person-centered therapy, 318
    reality therapy, 229
School counseling
    Adlerian therapy, 98–99
    person-centered therapy, 320
    reality therapy applications, 239–241
    transtheoretical model of change, 479
Second-order change, defined, 523
Second-order cybernetics, 426, 524
Secular humanism, defined, 524
Secure attachment, 126, 130
Segal, Zindel, 258
Selective abstraction, 206, 524
Self, differentiation of, 432
Self, Jung archetypes, 110, 112, 113, 526
Self, sense of
    Adlerian therapy, 78–79
    Horney, ego psychology, 120
    separation-individuation theory, 127
Self-acceptance, 190
Self-actualization, 280, 524
    encounter groups, 309
    existential therapy, 291
    Gestalt therapy, 337
    person-centered therapy, 310
Self-awareness, therapists, 12, 35–36
Self-care, professionals, 37
Self-compassion, 262
Self-destructive emotions, 186, 524
Self-detachment, 295
Self-determination. *See* Reality therapy
Self-disclosure, Skill Development, 386–388
Self-efficacy, 157, 227, 524
Self-efficacy theory, 157
Self-esteem
    Adlerian therapy, 98, 101–102
    Gestalt therapy, 341–342
    multiculturalism and, 101–102
Self-evaluation, 226, 478–479, 524
Self-fulfilling prophesies, 473
Self-harm, 95, 128, 250, 456
    See also Dialectical behavior therapy (DBT)
Self-instructional training, 180, 524
Self-liberation, 478–479
Self-management, applied behavior analysis, 168
Self-monitoring, 201, 203–204, 524
Self object, 131–132, 133, 524
Self-preservation, human needs, 228
Self psychology, 54, 108
    application and current use, 134, 141
    development of, 131
    limitations and strengths, 142–143
    multicultural groups, 141–142
    positive potentials, 132
    responsive environment, 132
    therapeutic process, 132–133
    therapeutic techniques, 133
Self-realization, 119, 524
Self-regulation, 14, 113, 260
Self-talk, 208
Self-transcendence, 295, 524
Seligman, Martin, 327
Sensation function, Jung, 110, 111, 113, 524
Sensitivity training groups, 279
Separation-individuation theory, 127
Setting, 21, 27–28, 29
Sexual abuse
    emotionally focused couple therapy, 452
    family therapy, 458
    feminist therapy, 381, 382
    narrative therapy, 404
    reality therapy, 239
    solution-focused brief therapy, 418
Sexual disorders, 212
Sexuality
    psychoanalytic theory, 54, 56, 60–61
    psychodynamic theories, 52
Sexual orientation
    cultural competency skills, 15
    feminist therapy, 382–383
    Freud on, 57
    See also Contextual/Systemic therapy
Shadow, Jung archetypes, 110, 112, 113, 115, 524
Shame-attacking exercises, 193, 524
Shaping, 163, 165–166, 524
Shapiro, Francine, 481
Shell shock, 56
"Should" statements, 207
Signal anxiety, 61–62, 524
Skill Development, 1
    analyzing earliest recollections, 104–106
    caring confrontation, 242–243
    empathic responding, 327–329
    exposure-based CBT for hoarding, 216–219
    focal concern, identification of, 142–143
    genograms, 457–459
    Gestalt chair work, 355–357
    interpretation, 72–74
    mapping, 419–421
    questioning and interviewing, 39–48
    self-disclosure, 386–388
    values clarification, 300–302
Skills training, 172–173
Skinner, B. F., 2, 154, 155
SMART Recovery, 210
Social action, 363, 380
Social anxiety, 165–166, 173–174, 210, 524
    acceptance and commitment therapy, 258
    interpersonal psychotherapy, 480–481
    person-centered therapy, 318
Social beings, 81, 524
Social competence, 21–22
Social constructivism, 393, 524
Social contexts
    for children, 124
    narrative therapy and, 397–398
    See also Adlerian therapy
Social-contextual power, 376
Social development, 14
Social factors. *See* Feminist therapy
Social interest, Adler, 86–87, 102, 524
Socialist feminism, 366
Social learning, 158, 475–476
Social learning theory, 157–158, 524
Social liberation, 478–479
Social locations, 369
Socially useful lifestyle, 82–83
Social media, feminism, 365
Social position, worldview, 17

Social supports, for children, 124
Societal regression, 434, 524
Socioeconomic status, worldview and, 17
Socrates, 283
Socratic questioning (method), 193, 204–205, 524
Solution-focused brief therapy (SFBT), 393
  acting "as if", 317–318
  application and current use, 417–418
  Case Application, 421–423
  development of, 405–407
  EARS, 412
  exception-seeking questions, 414–415
  formula first session tasks (FFST), 413
  future-oriented focus, 407–408
  identification of solutions, guidelines for, 408–409
  limitations and strengths, 419
  mindmaps, 410
  miracle question, 413–414
  multicultural groups, 418
  positive psychology, 408
  pre-therapy changes, 413
  questions about the future, 416–417
  reflecting team, 409
  scaling questions, 415
  solution prescriptions, 417
  solution talk, 416
  therapeutic process, 409–413
  therapist feedback, 417
Solution prescriptions, 417, 525
Solution talk, 416, 525
Somatic power, 376
Somatization, 63, 322–323, 342, 344–345, 351, 525
Sources of Meaning Profile Revised (SOMP-R), 301
Spangler, P., 116
Specifications of personhood, 397–398, 525
Spirituality
  existential therapy and, 296, 297
  future directions in counseling, 505–506
  humanistic approaches, 279–280
  Jung, unconcious mind, 111–112, 117
  Uberwelt, 289
Spiritual power, 376
Spitting in the client's soup, 95, 525
Splitting, 62, 63, 128

Splitting, defined, 525
Stages-of-change model, 478–479
Star Wars, 117
Stigma, 32
Stimulus control, 478–479
Stimulus discrimination, 156, 158, 525
Stimulus generalization, 156, 158, 525
Stimulus-response conditioning, 156, 157, 158, 525
Stiver, I. P., 363
Stoehr, T., 354
Stolar, N., 196
Stone, D. A., 98
Stories, 397, 398–399
Story-based interventions, 168
Story deconstruction, defined, 525
Straightforward ordeals, 447, 525
Strategic family therapy, 445–449
Strategic tasks, solution-focused brief therapy, 410
Strengths-based approach, 20–26, 393, 525
Stress, mindfulness-based cognitive therapy, 263
Stress inoculation training (SIT), 180–181, 525
Stress-vulnerability model, 197, 525
Structural family therapy, 441–445
Structural Profile Inventory, 477
Strupp, Hans, 134, 135
Style of life, 525
Subjective units of distress scale (SUDS), 180, 481–482, 525
Subjectivity, 150
Sublimation, 62, 525
Substance abuse, 210, 254
  acceptance and commitment therapy, 258
  Adlerian therapy, 98
  existential therapy, 297
  family therapy, 456
  Gestalt therapy, 353
  mindfulness-based cognitive therapy, 263
  motivational interviewing, 7
  narrative therapy, 403, 404
  reality therapy, 226, 239–241
  schema therapy, 269
  solution-focused brief therapy, 418
Substance Abuse and Mental Health Services Administration (SAMHSA), 99
Subsystems, 428, 442, 525
Success identity, 225

Successive approximations, 165–166
Suicidal ideation, 212
  mindfulness-based cognitive therapy, 263
  solution-focused brief therapy, 418
  See also Dialectical behavior therapy (DBT)
Sullivan, Harry Stack, 54, 108, 118, 124, 131, 134, 135, 480
Superego, 58, 63–64, 118, 132, 525
Superior function, Jung, 110, 111, 525
Superiority, 80–82, 88, 101–102, 525
Superiority complex, 81, 525
Support factors, 483
Supportive techniques, 138
Survival, human needs, 228
Symbiotic relationship, 432, 525
Symbolic Growth Experience, 294, 525
Symbols, 115, 117, 526
Sympathy, 317–318
Synchronicity, 116, 117, 526
Systematic assessment of alternatives, 208
Systematic desensitization, 156, 158, 170, 526
Systematic Training for Effective Parenting (STEP), 30, 99, 453
Systemic approaches. *See* Contextual/Systemic therapy
Systems theory, 3, 426
  See also Family systems therapy

T

Tar-baby, 97, 510
Target behaviors, 158–159, 526
Task assignment, 96, 526
Technical eclecticism, 471, 526
Technology, future directions in counseling, 505
Ten processes of change, 478–479
Termination stage, 325
T (training) groups, 279
Thanatos, 59, 526
Theme, narrative therapy, 399, 526
Theoretical eclecticism, 471
Theoretical integration, defined, 526
Theoretical orientation
  basic philosophy and key concepts of theories, 485–489
  counseling techniques and uses, summary table, 493–497
  determinants of, 483–484

future directions in counseling, 505–506
identifying a counseling theory, 482–485
limitations and strengths, summary table, 501–504
multicultural counseling, summary table, 497–501
personality styles and, 484–485
reflection questions, 485
therapeutic relationship, summary table, 491–493
therapy goals, summary table, 489–491
See also Integrative and eclectic therapies
Therapeutic documents, 402–403, 526
Therapeutic-fiduciary relationship, 34
Therapeutic relationship, 6, 8–10, 526
acceptance and commitment therapy, 256–257
Adlerian therapy, 88–90
behavior therapy, 160–161
brief psychodynamic therapy, 137–140
characteristics of, 8–13
child psychoanalysis, 123–124
cognitive therapy, 199–201
cyclical psychodynamic-behavior therapy, 475
dialectical behavior therapy, 249–250
ego psychology, 121
emotionally focused couple therapy, 450
existential therapy, 285, 292–294, 299
family systems therapy, Bowen, 434–435
family systems therapy, Satir and Whitaker, 439–440
feminist therapy, 369, 370–374, 379, 384–385
Gestalt therapy, 344–347
humanistic approaches, 279, 280
importance of, 318
Jungian analytical psychology, 115
mindfulness-based cognitive therapy, 260
multiple (dual) relationships, 34
narrative therapy, 397, 398–401
nondirective counseling, 309
object relations theory, 127, 128, 129, 130
person-centered therapy, 308–309, 312–318, 326–327

postmodern therapy, 393–394
psychoanalysis, 64–65
psychoanalytic theory, 53
rational emotive behavior therapy, 189–191
reality therapy, 225, 226, 234–236, 242–243
resistance, 68
role induction, 8
schema therapy, 268–269
self psychology, 133–134
setting, 21, 27–28, 29
solution-focused brief therapy, 407, 411–413
strategic family therapy, 446
summary table of therapy types, 492–493
therapist self-disclosure, 315–316
transtheoretical model of change, 479
See also Skill Development
Therapist
Adlerian therapy, role in, 87–88
behavior therapy, role in, 160
bias of, 16, 35–36
characteristics of, 8–13
credentials, 31
cultural competence skills, 15–20
future directions in counseling, 505–506
personality styles, 484–485
professional support system, 37
self-awareness, 12
self-disclosure, Skill Development, 386–388
self-disclosure by, 315–316, 372
setting, 21, 27–28, 29
therapeutic-fiduciary relationship, 34
use of term, 5
See also Ethics; Legal issues; Skill Development; Theoretical orientation
Therapy, use of term, 4–5
Thinking function, Jung, 113
Third party relationships, 34
Thought sampling, 203–204, 526
Threats, response to, 259
Tillich, Paul, 284, 291, 335
Time-limited dynamic psychotherapy, 134–135
Token economies, 166, 526
Total behavior, 229–230, 526
Total knowledge filter, 232, 526
Tracking, defined, 526
Tracking, genograms, 435–436
Tragic man, 132, 134

Transference, 64–65, 121, 129, 130, 133, 134, 138, 526
Transformation, Jungian psychology, 114
Transformational Systemic Therapy, 438
Transpersonal therapy, 279
Transtheoretical model of change, 478–479, 526
Trauma, 254
Adlerian therapy, 98
Anna Freud on, 122, 124–125
cognitive behavioral therapy, 211–212
eye movement desensitization and reprocessing (EMDR), 481–482
future directions in counseling, 505
Gestalt therapy, 352–353
narrative therapy, 404
solution-focused brief therapy, 418
See also Dialectical behavior therapy (DBT); Posttraumatic stress disorder (PTSD)
Traumatic neurosis, 56
Treatment plans, 11–12
Triad, 432, 526
Triangle of conflict, 136, 526
Triangle of insights, 136, 526
Triangulation, 432–433, 436, 526
Trichotillomania, 173
Tunnel vision, 207
Twinship, 131–132, 133
Two-chair technique, 338, 349–350
Tyranny of the shoulds, 118, 120, 526

U

Uberwelt, 289, 527
Ultimate concerns, human condition, 286–287, 296
Umwelt, 285, 288–289, 527
Unconditional other acceptance (UOA), 214, 527
Unconditional other acceptance-multicultural (UOA-M), 213–214, 527
Unconditional positive regard, 9, 311, 316–317, 527
Unconditioned stimulus, 158, 527
Unconscious mind, 61, 63–64, 527
brief psychodynamic therapy, 138–139
existential theory on, 289
first force and, 51–54
Jung, psyche and, 110–112
psychoanalytic theory, 53–54, 71
resistance, 68

Unfinished business, 340, 350–351, 527
Unique outcomes, 420, 527

V
Validation, defined, 527
Validation of emotions, 317–318
Validity, evidence-based practices, 33
Values, 291, 295
  Skill Development, values clarification, 300–302
Valuing filter, 232, 527
Veracity, 35
Vicarious introspection, 133, 527
Vienna Psycho-Analytical Society (1910), 56, 78, 79
Virtual reality therapy, 169, 527

W
Wachtel, Paul, 473–474
Wants, reality therapy, 231–232
Watson, John, 156
WDEP system, 225, 231–233, 527
Weakland, John, 445
Wells, Adrian, 273
Wertheimer, Max, 279, 335
Whitaker, Carl, 426, 437–441
White, Michael, 394–395
White-Campbell Psychological Birth Order Inventory, 86
Will, 287, 527
Wilson, Bill, 117
Wise mind, 251, 274–276, 527
Wise Mind ACCEPTS, 252–253, 274–276, 526
Wolpe, Joseph, 155, 156
Women
  female development and culture, 121
  feminist perspectives, 118
  Karen Horney on Freud, 118–119
  psychoanalytic theory, limitations of, 70–71
  See also Feminist theory
Women of color (womanists) feminism, 366
Word association tests, 116, 527
Working alliance, 11
Working through, 63–64, 129, 527
Worldview, 16–17, 36, 82–83

Y
Yalom, Irvin, 282–283, 285, 288, 291, 293, 295, 298, 299
Young-Bruehl, E., 122